AMHARIC-ENGLISH
ENGLISH-AMHARIC
DICTIONARY

Compiled and Revised by
A. Zekaria

Zekaria, A.
AMHARIC-ENGLISH
ENGLISH-AMHARIC DICTIONARY

© 2006 Languages of the World Publications

Published by:
LANGUAGES OF THE WORLD PUBLICATIONS
P.O. Box 7188, New Delhi-110002 (India)

U.S. & Canada Distributors:
Hippocrene Books, Inc
171 Madison Avenue,
New York, NY 10016
www.hippocrenebooks.com

ISBN 0-7818-0115-X

Printed at Lahooti Fine Art, Press, Delhi.

FROM THE PUBLISHERS :

We have planned to bring out a series of dictionaries compiled by prominent scholars in different languages of the world.

THIS DICTIONARY is one in that series, and we hope readers will find it useful.

This is our contribution in bringing various languages of the world together, and closer to English.

AMHARIC-ENGLISH

ሀ

ሀሁ	hahu n. alphabet, "abc"
ሀብት	habt n. wealth
ምጣኔ—	mǝṭṭane— n. economy
ሀብታም	habtam adj. wealthy, rich
ሀብታምነት	habtamǝnnät n. wealthiness
ባለሀብት	balä habt adj. rich, wealthy; owner
የተፈጥሮ ሀብት	yätäfäṭro habt n. natural resources
ሀይ ሀይ አለ	hai hai alä v.t. conciliated, calmed down conflict, cooled down
ሀይ ሀይ ባይ	hai hai bai n. one who conciliates, calms down conflict, cools down
ሀገር	hagär n. country (also አገር)
ሁለት	hulätt adj. two
ሁሉ	hullu adj. all, every, everybody
ሁለመና	hullämäna adv. all over (the body)
ሁሉም	hullumm all of them
— ቦታ	-bota adv. everywhere
ሁልቀን	hulǝqän adv. daily
ሁልጊዜ	also ሁሌ hulgize, hulle adv. always, all the time
ሰው ሁሉ	säw hullu everybody, everyone
ሁከት	hukät n. disturbance, unrest, trouble, violence
ሁከተኛ	hukätäñña adj. trouble maker, disturber
አዋኪ	awwaki adj. trouble maker, disturber, nuisance
ያች	hačč in እዚያያች ǝzziya hačč adv. there, over there
ሀቻምና	haččamna adv. the year before
ሃያ	haya adj. twenty
ሃያኛ	hayañña adj. twentieth
ሂስ	his n. criticism
ሂስና ግለሂስ	hisnna gǝllähis criticism and self-criticism

ሃይማኖት	haimanot n. religion
ሃይማኖተኛ	haimanotäñña adj. religious
ሃይማኖታዊ	haimanotawi adj. religious
ሄደ	hedä v. went
ሂያጅ	hiyag̱ n. one who goes; riotous liver; profligate; libertine
ሂደት	hidät n. process
ሀላዌ	hǝllawe n. existence
ሀልውና	hǝllǝwna n. existence
ሀንድ	hand n. India
ሀንዳዊ	handawi adj. Indian
ሀዋእ	hǝwa'ǝ n. space
ሆሣዕና	hossa'ǝna n. Palm Sunday
ሆመጠጠ	homäṭṭäṭä v. was acid, turned sour
ሆምጣጣ	homṭṭaṭa adj. sour, acid, tart
ሆምጣጤ ኮምጣጤ	homṭaṭe/ komṭaṭe n. vinegar
ሆነ	honä v.i. became, happened
ሁነኛ	hunäñña n. trust-worthy person
ሁኔታ	huneta n. condition, situation
ሆነለት	honällät he succeeded, he made it
ሆን ብሎ	hon bǝlo adv. intentionally, deliberately
ሆኖም	honomm adv. nevertheless, at any rate
ለማሆኑ መሆን	lämähonu by the way mähon inf. to be, become
ምንም ቢሆን	mǝnǝmm bihon whatever happens, by any means
በዚሀም ሆነ በዚያ	bäzzihǝmm honä bäzziya one way or the other, at any rate
ቢሆን ቢሆን ባይሆን አኩሁዋን	bihon bihon at least bayhon at least akku" ahu" an n. situation, manner, condition

5

እንደሆን	əndähon in የመጣ yämaṭṭa — if he comes, in case he comes	ጃንሆይ	ǧanhoy Your Majesty! His Majesty!
የሆነ ቢሆንም	yähonä bihonəmm in any event; whatever happens	ሆታ	hota n. cheering, acclaim, shout
		ሆቴል	hotel n. hotel, restaurant
የሆነ ያልሆነ	yähonä yalhonä all sorts of things, irrelevent things	ሆድ	hod n. stomach, belly abdomen
የሆነውን ያህል	yähonäwən yahəl as much as possible	— ቁርጠት	—qurṭät n. stomachache, colic
የማይሆን	yämmayhon adj. inappropriate, impossible	— ድርቀት	—dərqät n. constipation
ያልሆነ	yalhonä adj. inappropriate, improper	ሆደ ሰፊ	hodä säffi adj. phlegmatic, not susceptible, patient
ያም ሆነ ይህ	yamm honä yəh in any case	— ባሻ	hodä bašša adj. excitable, susceptible, easily hurt
ይሆናል	yəhonal it is possible, it is probable	ሆዳም	hodam adj. greedy, gluttonous, big eater
ሆይ	hoy interj. oh!	ሆድቃ	hodəqa n. guts (innards), entrails
ለዑል ሆይ	—lə'ul hoy Oh! Prince!	ሆጛ	hoǧǧa n. title deed (Harar)
ከቡር ሆይ	kəbur hoy Your Excellency!		

ለ

ለ	lä prep. for, to	ለምላሚ	lämlami adj. green, verdant
ለምን	lämən why?	ልምላሜ	ləmlame n. greenness, verdure
ለሱ ንገረው	lässu nəgäräw tell him	ተለመለመ	tälämällämä v.i. was stripped, for tree, etc.
ለሀጭ	lähač n. dribble	አለመለመ	alämällämä v.t. became green
ለሀጫም	lähučam adj. dribbling	አለግለም	alämaläm n. turning green
ለሐቴ	lähote n. whetstone		
ለመለመ	lämällämä v.i, v.t. became green (of landscape of vegetation); stripped leaves (from a tree)	ለመሰሰ	lämässäsä v.t. smoothed (hair); trampled or flattened (grass, etc.)
		ተለመሰሰ	tälämässäsä v. i. was smoothed; was trampled or flattened
ለምላም	lämläm adj. green; soft	ለመነ	lämmänä v.t. asked, beseeched, begged
ለምላም ጆሮ	lämläm ǧoro n. lobe	ለማኝ	lämmañ adj. beggar
ለምለምነት	lämlämnənät n. greenness, verdure	ለማኝነት	lämmaññənnät n. beggary

ልማኅ	*ləmmāna* n. begging, imploring	ተለማመደ	*tālāmammādā* v. i. practiced, trained himself
ተለመነ	*tālāmmānā* v. i. was begged	ተለማማኺ	*tālāmamaǧ* n. trainee
ተለማኝ	*tālāmmañ* adj. (person) entreated	መለማመኺ	*māllāmamāǧā* n. means of training
ተለማመነ	*tālāmammānā* v. i. pleaded with	ተላመደ	*tālammādā* v. i. got gradually accustomed to
ተለማማኝ	*tālāmamañ* adj. pleading, pleader	ተላማኺ	*tālamaǧ* n. trainee
አለማመነ	*allāmammānā* v.t. supported a plea, helped in begging	አለመደ	*alāmmādā* v.t. trained
አላመነ	*allammānā* v.t. supported a plea, helped in begging	አልማኺ	*almaǧ* adj. trainer (animals, persons)
አላማኝ	*allamañ* n. helper in begging	አለማመደ	*alāmammadā* v.t. trained or tamed to some extent
አስለመነ	*aslāmmānā* v.t. caused or allowed to beg	አላማመደ	*allāmammādā* v.t. caused to become aquainted with each other
ለማዘገ	*lāmāzzāgā* v. pinched very hard		
ተለመዘገ	*tālāmāzzāgā* v. t. was pinched very hard	አላመደ	*allamādā* v.t. caused to get used to each other
ለመደ	*lāmmādā* v.t became accustomed to, got used to	አስለመደ	*aslāmmādā* v.t. caused or allowed to become accustomed, taught
ለግዳ	*lāmmada* adj. tame, domestic (animals)	አስለማኺ	*aslāmmaǧ* n. trainer instructor
ለግዳነት	*lāmmadannāt* n. tameness	ለመጠ	*lāmmāṭā* v.t./v.i. bent; stroke
ለማኺ	*lāmaǧ* adj. n. beginner, trainee, learner	ለማጠ	*lāmmaṭṭa* adj. flattering; insincere
ለማድ	*ləmad* n. custom, habit	ለምጥ	*ləmmaṭṭ* adj. curved
ለማዳኛ	*ləmadāñña* adj. habitual, customary	ለመጥ አለ	*lāmmāṭ alā* v.i. bent a little
ለምድ	*ləmd* n. custom, habit	ለምጥ አለ	*ləmmaṭṭ alā* v.i bent forcefully
መለመኝ	*mālmāǧa* n. exercise, drill	ተለመጠ	*tālāmmāṭā* became warped, was bent
ለማመደ	*lāmammādā* v. t started to be accustomed, began to learn	ተለማጭ	*tālāmmaǧ* adj. bendable, flexible
ለምምድ	*ləməmmad* n. experience, training; exercise (military, sport)	ተለማመጠ	*tālāmammāṭā* v.t. curried favour, cajoled
		ተለማማጭ	*tālāmamaǧ* n. one who curries favour
ተለመደ	*tālāmmādā* v. i. used, became used	አለመጠ	*alāmmāṭā* v.t. made fun of, mocked
		አልማጭ	*almaǧ* n. mocker
ተለማኺ	*tālāmmaǧ* adj. habitual or customary	ለመጠጠ	*lāmāṭṭāṭā* v.t. burned; stung with whip

7

ተለመጠጠ	*tälämäṭṭäṭä* v.i. was _burned; was strung (with whip)	
ለማ	*lämma* v.i. was developed; blazed up (*fire*)	
ላሚ	*lāmi* adj. developing	
ላም	*läm* adj. fertile, rich (soil, farmed land)	
ለምነት	*lämǝnnät* n. fertility (*land*); the state of being developed	
ልማት	*lǝmat* n. development	
አለማ	*alämma* v.t. developed; made fertile	
አልሚ	*almi* adj.n. developing, developer	
—ምግብ	—*mǝgǝb* nutritious food	
አስለማ	*aslämma* v.t. caused to become developed or fertile	
ለምቦጭ	*lämboč* n. thick lip	
ለምቦጫም	*lämbočam* adj. thick-lipped	
ለምን	see ምን	
ለምድ	*lämd* n. sheepskin (*used as cloak for shepherds etc.*)	
ለምጽ	*lämṣ* n. discoloured skin, *also* ለምጥ	
ለምጻም	*lämṣam* adj/n. one who has a discoloured skin, *also* ለምጣም	
ለሰለሰ	*läsälläsä* v. i was or became tender,smooth	
ለስላሳ	*läslassa* adj. smooth, tender, soft	
ለስላሳነት	*läslassannät* n. tenderness	
ልስላሴ	*lǝsǝllasse* adj. smooth, soft	
ልስልስ	*lǝslǝs* adj. smooth,soft	
ተለሳለሰ	*täläsalläsä* v.i. was tender; became idle	
አለሰለሰ	*aläsälläsä* v.t. smoothed, made tender, softened	
አለሳለሰ	*alläsaläs* n. smoothness, tenderness	
ለሰሰ	*lässäsä* v.i. became lukewarm	

ለስ አለ	*läss alä* v. became a little warm (*for water*)	
ለስታ ቅቤ	*lästa qǝbe* n. fresh butter	
ለሰነ	*lässänä* v. plastered	
ለሳኝ	*lässañ* n. plasterer	
ልስን	*lǝssǝn* adj. plastered	
ተለሰነ	*tälässänä* v.i. was plastered; kept silent	
አላሰነ	*allassänä* v.t. helped to plaster	
አስለሰነ	*aslässänä* v.t. caused to be plastered	
ለሸለሸ	*läšälläšä* v.t. flattened (*crops, grass* etc.)	
ለቀለቀ	*läqälläqä* v.t. daubed; smeared	
ልቅላቂ	*lǝqǝllaqi* n. dishwater	
ልቅልቅ	*lǝqlǝq* n. something daubed	
ለቅለቅ አደረገ	*läqläqq adärrägä* v.t. daubed or rinsed a little	
ተለቀለቀ	*täläqälläqä* v.i. was smeared, was daubed	
ተለቃለቀ	*täläqalläqä* v.i. rinsed slightly; smeared each other	
መለቃለቂያ	*mälläqaläqiya* n. washing water, rinsing water	
አለቀለቀ	*aläqälläqä* v.t. rinsed	
አለቃለቀ	*aläqalläqä* v.t. rinsed slightly	
አስለቀለቀ	*asläqälläqä* v.t. caused to be smeared	
ለቀመ	*läqqämä* v.t./v.i. picked, picked up; reaped, gathered	
ለቀማ	*läqäma* n. picking, gathering	
ለቃሚ	*läqami* adj. picker, gatherer	
ልቃሚ	*lǝqqami* n. leavings or rubbish	
ልቅም	*lǝqqǝm* adj. free from impurities (grain etc.); polite	

8

ለቀም አደረገ   *lāqämm adärrägä* v.t. grabbed

ለቀቀመ   *lāqaqqämä* v.t. picked, gathered a little here and there; picked out

ለቃቃሚ   *lāqaqami* n. scavenger

ልቅም አደረገ   *ləqqəmm adärrägä* v.t. removed all impurities (*grain etc.*)

ተለቀመ   *täläqqämä* v.i. was picked (*e.g. crops*)

አለቀመ   *aläqqämä* v.t. grazed, took to pasture (*specially in a dry season*)

አላቀመ   *allaqqämä* v.t. helped to pick, helped to gather

አስለቀመ   *asläqqämä* v.t. made (*s/o*) pick

*ለቀስ   *see* አለቀስ

ለቀቀ   *lāqqäqä* v.t./v.i. let go; released; abandoned; gathered; threaded on to distaff

ለቃቂ   *ləqqaqi* n. distaff

ለቃቂት   *ləqqaqit* n. distaff

ለቅ   *ləqq* n/adj. loose liver; abandoned (*moral*)

ለቅነት   *ləqqənnät* · n. abandon, loose living

ለቅ አደረገ   *lāqäqq adärrägä,* v.t. relaxed one's hold on s/o

ልቅቅ አደረገ   *ləqəqq addärrägä* v.t. let go, set free

ተለቀቀ   *täläqqäqä* v.i. was set free, released

ተላቀቀ   *tälaqqäqä* v.i. became separated; got free from

አላቀቀ   *allaqqäqä* v.t. made free from, caused to be free from

አስለቀቀ   *asläqqäqä* v.t. caused to be free from, separated

ለበለበ   *lābälläbä* v.t. scorched, burnt slightly, singed

ለብላቢ   *lāblabi* adj. scorching

ልብለብ   *ləbləb* adj. scorched

ተለበለበ   *tälābällābä* vi. burnt, scorched

አለብላቢት   *aläblabit* n. nettle

አስለበለበ   *asläbälläbä* v.t. caused to be burnt

ለበሰ   *läbässä* v.t. dressed, put on clothes, wore

ልባስ   *ləbas* n. cloth; covering

ልባሽ   *ləbbaš* adj. worn out (*clothes*)

ልብስ   *ləbs* clothes, garment

ልብስ   *ləbbəs* adj. worn out (*clothes*)

ለባበሰ   *läbabbäsä* v.t. put on clothes

ተለባበሰ   *täläbabbäsä* v.i. was kept secret, hidden

አለበሰ   *aläbbäsä* v.t. dressed (*s/o*)

አልባሽ   *albaš* n. dresser, valet

አለባበሰ   *aläbabbäsä* v.t. caused to be dressed, covered; kept hidden (*secret*)

አላበሰ   *allabbäsä* v.t. helped in dressing

አስለበሰ   *asläbäsä* v.t. made (*s/o*) get dressed

ለበቀ   *läbbäqä* v.t./v.i. bended; :

ለበቅ   *läbäq* n lath

ለባቃ   *läbbaqqa* adj. bent, flexible; cowardly

ልብቅ   *ləbbəq* adj. flexible

ተለበቀ   *täläbbäqä* v.i. was bent

ተለባቂ   *täläbbaqi* adj. flexible

ለበበ   *läbbäbä* v.t. put a halter or head-stall on

ልባብ   *ləbab* n. halter, head-stall

ተለበበ   *täläbbäbä* v.i. was harnessed

አስለበበ   *asläbbäbä* v.i. caused to be harnessed

ለበደ	*läbbädä* v.t. covered with leather etc. (e.g. *scabbard*)	ሰወጠ	*läwwäṭä* v.t. changed, exchanged, shifted, altered; cashed *(a check)*
ልብዳት	*ləbbədat* n. leather covering etc.	ሰውጥ	*läwṭ* n. change; exchange
ለብድ	*ləbbəd* adj. covered with leather etc.	ልውጥ	*ləwwaç* n. things given in return
ተለበደ	*täläbbädä* v.i. was covered with leather etc.	ልውውጥ	*ləwəwwəṭ* n exchange
አስለበደ	*asläbbädä* v.t. caused to be covered with leather, etc.	ተለወጠ	*täläwwäṭä* vi. was changed, changed
ለበጠ	*läbbäṭä* v.t. covered with cloth *(e.g. cushions)*	ተለዋጭ	*täläwwaç* n. substitute
ለብጥ	*ləbbəṭ* adj. covered with cloth	አባል	—*abal* n. alternate member
ተለበጠ	*täläbbäṭä* v.i. was covered with cloth	ተለዋወጠ	*täläwawwäṭä* v.i. exchanged *(mutually)*, interchanged
አስለበጠ	*asläbbäṭä* v.t. caused to be covered with cloth	ተለዋዋጭ	*täläwawaç* adj. changeable, inconsistent, variable
ለብ አለ	*läbb alä* v. became luke-warm	መጠባበቂያ	in የማኪና መለዋወጫ *yämäkina mäläwawäça* n. spare parts *(car)*
ለብታ	*läbbəta* slight drunkenness		
ለብ አለው	*läbb aläw* v.i. was slightly drunk	መለዋወጫ	in የዘመን መለዋወጫ *yäzämän mälläwäça* n. New Year
ለተመ	*lättämä* v.t hit; crashed into	ሰውዝ	*läwz* n. peanut, ground nut
ተለተመ	*tälättämä* v.i. was hit; crashed into	ለዘበ	*lazzäbä* v.i. was tender; was gentle
ለካ	*läkka* (particle indicating surprise, remorse, sorrow, discovery etc.)	ለዘብተኛ	*läzzäbtäñña* adj moderate *(pols.)*
		ልዝብ	*ləzzəb* adj. gentle, smooth, soft
ለካ	*läkka* v.t. measured	አለዘበ	*aläzzäbä* v.t. smoothed; rehearsed, *(music, song)*
ልክ	*ləkk* n. measurement		
ልክ ልኩን ነገረው	*ləkk ləkkun näggäräw* he told him off, scolded him	ለዛ	*läzza* n. charisma *(in speaking)*
ለኩሰ	*läku^wäsä* v.t. set fire to, lit; *(cigarette etc.)*	—ቢስ	—*bis* adj. unattractive *(in speech etc.)*
ለኩፈ	*läkku^wäfä* v,i. stroked gently, tapped	—የለሽ	—*yälläš* adj. *(same as above)*
ለወሰ	*läwässä* v.t. kneaded *(flour for bread)*, mixed powder and liquid; crippled *(disease)*	ለየ	*läyyä* v.t. separated divided; distinguished, differentiated; recognized, identified.
ለዋሳ ተላወሰ	— *läwwassa* adj. crippled *tälawwäsä* v.i. moved to and fro, started moving	ልዩ	*ləyyu* adj. special, different; private; extraordinary
		— ልዩ	—*ləyyu* adj. various

10

---መልእክተኛ	—mälə'ktäñña n, envoy extraordinary	እላጋ	allagga v.t. dashed (against s/t. boat etc)
— ጸሐፊ.	—ṣähafi n. private secretary	ሰ?ም	läggämä v.i. worked with ill will and badly
ልዩነት	ləyyunnät n. difference, distinction; division, variation	ልግሙኛ	ləgmäñña n. resentful worker
የዘር—	yäzär - n discrimination (race)	ለገሰ	läggäsä v.i. was charitable, was generous
ለያየ	läyayyä v.t. classified; separated; dismantled	ለጋስ	läggas adj. generous
ተለየ	täläyyä differed, was different; parted from	ለጋስነት	läggasənnät n. generosity
መለዮ	mälläyyc n. badge, insignia; uniform	ልግስና	ləggəsənna n. charity, generosity
በተለይ	bätäläyy adv. especially, in particular	*ለጋጠ	*läggäṭä
ተለያየ	täläyayyä v.i. differed (in opinion), was different; branched off	አላጋጠ	allaggäṭä vt. made fun of, mocked, derided
		ልግጭ	ləgča n. mocking, mockery, derision
የተለያየ	yätäläyayyä adj. different, varied	አላጋጭ	allagač n. mocker
አለያየ	alläyayyä v.t. detached, took apart; created enmity among people	ለግላጋ	läglagga adj. young and well-built; sturdy (of person)
ላይ	lay prep./adv. on, upon, above	ለጐመ	lägguʷ ämä v.t. fitted with bridle; kept quiet
—ላዩን	-layun adv. superficially, externally	ልጓም	ləguʷam n. bridle
ላይኛ	layəñña adj. upper, top	ልጕም	ləggum adj. fitted with bridle
በ...ላይ	bä...lay on, on top of ...e.g በጠረጴዛው ላይ on the table	ተለጐመ	täläguʷ ämä v.i. was bridled
		አለጐመ	alägguʷ ämä v.i. criticized others (while being lazy oneself)
	በዚህም ላይ on top of this		
እንድላይ	andlay adv. together	አልጓሚ	alguʷ ami adj./n hypocritical; sarcastic
እዚህ ላይ	əzzih lay adv. at this point	አልጕም	algum adj. critical; sarcastic
ከመጠን በላይ	kämäṭän bälay adv. unusually, too much	አስለጐመ	aslägguʷ ämä v.t. made (s/o) fit a bridle; had (an animal) bridled
ከዚህ ላይ	käzzih lay at this point		
ከዚህ በላይ	käzzih bälay adv.moreover, furthermore	ለጐደ	lägguʷ ädä v.t. covered, stained with mud
ወደላይ	wädälay adv. upwards	ለጠለጠ	läṭälläṭä v.t. compressed oil seed
ለጋ	läga adj. fresh, e.g. ለጋ ቅቤ fresh butter	ልጥልጥ	läṭləṭ n. lump of compressed oil seed
ለጋ	lägga v.t. hit (the ball), served (tennis etc.)	ተለጠለጠ	täläṭälläṭä v.i. was compressed, squeezed (oil seed)

አለጠለጠ alāṭāllātā v.i. grew to be in fine physical condition ·(i.e. with round strong face)

ለጠቀ läṭṭäqä v.t. went behind (s/o i.e. in moving line)

ለጣቂ läṭṭaqi adj./n. one who follows, goes behind s/o

ለጠጠ läṭṭäṭä v.t. expanded stretched (elastic, spring, arms etc.)

ለጣጥ ləṭṭäṭ adj. stretched, expanded; proud; boastful

ለጣጭ ləṭṭäč n. peel, rind

ተለጠጠ täläṭṭäṭä v.i. was stretched; was proud, boastful

ተለጣጭ täläṭṭäč adj. stretchable, elastic

አስለጠጠ aslaṭṭäṭä v.t. had s/t stretched, expanded,

ለጣፈ läṭṭäfä v.t. stuck (s/t) on to (s/t), stuck (s/t) together; threw against a wall (to make stick); accused falsely

ለጣፈት ləṭṭäfat n. pad (e.g. wound dressing) poultice

ለጣፍ ləṭṭäf adj. padded, patched

መለጣፊያ mäläṭṭäfiya n. s/t used for jointing, sticking; glue; jointing piece; sticking plaster

ተለጣፈ täläṭṭäfä v.i. was stuck, joined together; was hidden to eavesdrop, eavesdropped

ተለጣጣፈ täläṭaṭṭäfä v. was glued up, stuck together

አስለጣፈ aslaṭṭäfä v.t. made (s/o) stick (s/t) together, had (s/t) stuck

ለጥ አለ läṭṭ alä v.i. lay flat ; was submissive (e.g. to a superior power after a battle)

ለጥ ያለ läṭṭ yalä adj. lying flat; submissive, subdued

—ሜዳ —meda n. wide plain

ለፈለፈ läfälläfä v. i. talked too much; chattered

ለፍላፊ läflafi adj. overtalkative, chatterbox

ለፍላፋ ləfläfa n. rambling conversation, prattle

ተለፋለፈ täläfulläfä v. chattered together, held idle conversation

ተለፋላፊ täläfalafi adj. chattering

አስለፋለፈ asläfälläfä v.t. interrogated, made (s/o) talk

ለፈፈ läffäfä v.t. announced, spread the news, heralded

ለፋፊ läfäfi n. public announcer, herald, spreader of tidings

ለፈፋ ləffäfa n. public announcement, proclamation

ተለፈፈ täläffäfä v.i. was announced, was proclaimed publicly

አስለፈፈ asläffäfä v.t. had (s/t) announced

ለፋ läffa v. worked very hard, toiled

ለፊ läfi adj. n. hard worker

ለፍያ ləffyia n. romping

ለፋት ləfat n. weariness, extreme tiredness

ተላፋ tälaffa v.t. horsed around, pretended to fight with each other

ተላፊ tälafi adj. / n. one who plays around (physically)

አላፋ aläffa v.t. fatigued, made (s/o) tired, tired (s/o) out; tanned (leather, skins)

አስላፋ asläffa v.t. had (s/t) tanned (leather, skins)

ሉህ luh n. legal size paper

ሉል lul n. pearl; regal orb; globe

12

ሉ-ካንዳ lukanda n. butcher's shop
ሉ-ማ lučča n. smooth hair
ሊቅ liq n. learned, wise,
ሊቅ መንበር liqä mänbär n. chairman, president (of a meeting)
ሊቅነት liqənnät n. learning, scholarliness
ሊትር litər n. litre
ሊጋባ ligaba n. chief usher, senior official (for ceremonies etc.)
ሊጥ liṭ n. dough mixture (for preparing ənğära), dough
ሊጦን liṭon n. litany
ላላ lalla v.i. was loose, relaxed, was supple (physically); not geminated (of consonants)
ልል ləl adj. soft, loose, relaxed; easy going, not hard in manner
አላላ alalla v.t. made soft, loose, relaxed s/t (one's grip,hold);eased off (e.g, belt, harness law, restriction)
ለመ lamä v.i. became powdered, fineley ground
ልም ləm adj. powdery, finely ground
አላመ alamä v.t. ground finely, reduced to powder
አላላም allalam n. powdery quality, fineness
አስላመ aslamä v.t. had (s/t) ground finely
ላመል lamäl adv. lightly, slightly, barely, only, see also አመል
ላም lam n. cow
ላምባ lambba n. kerosene, lamp (oil or paraffin)
ላምፋ lamfa n. husk, also ላንፋ
ላሰ lasä v.t. licked
ላሽ laš n. ring worm, tinea

መላስ mälas n. tongue; inf. to lick
ምላስ məlas n. tongue
ምላሰኛ məlasäñña adj. talkative
ምላሰኛነት məlasäññənnät n. talkativeness
ምላሳም məlasam adj. talkative
ተላሰ tälasä v.i. was licked
አላሰ alasä v.t. sweetened (ṭäğğ with honey) have s/o lick s/t (e.g. from fingers)
ግላሽ malaša n. honey (used to sweeten ṭäğğ)
አስላሰ aslasä v.t. had s/o lick s/t
ላሸ laššä v.t. became weak, tender, very soft
አላሸ alaššä v.t. made (s/t) weak, tender, soft
ላሸቀ laššäqä v.i. become churned up (e.g. mud); kneaded forcefully
አላሸቀ alaššäqä v.t. churned up, made muddy
ላቀ laqä v.t. was superior, excelled
ሊቅ liq adj. learned, scholarly
ሊቅነት liqənnät n. learning, scholarliness
ላቂያ laqqiya n. superiority
ላቋ in ከሁሉም ላቋ kähullumm ləqo more than any thing
ይልቅ yəlq conj. than (rather than)
ከሁሉም— kähullumm-above all, more than this, more than that
ከኔ ይልቅ käne yələq more than I.
ላቅ አለ laqq alä v.i. was slightly better than, excelled (a little than)
አላቀ alaqä v.t. made (s o) better; preferred
ላቀጠ läqqu° äṭä v.i. became churned up, muddy, was kneaded

አላቴጠ	*alaqqu*ʷ*äṭä* v.t. made muddy, churned up; kneaded
ላባ	*laba* n. feather
ላባም	*labam* adj. feathered, covered with feathers
ላጵ	*lab* n. sweat, perspiration
ላቦት	*labot* n. sweat, perspiration
አላበ	*alabä* v.i. made to sweat
ላቦራቲር	*laboratu*ʷ*ar* n. laboratory *(Amh. also* ቤተ ሙከራ*)*
ላቲን	*ḷatin* n. Latin
ላት	*lat* n. fat *(on sheep's tail only)*
ላታም	*latam* adj. fat-tailed *(sheep only)*
ላንቃ	*lanqa* n. soft palate
ላከ	*lakä* v.t. sent *(message, letter etc.)*
ላኪ	*laki* n. sender
መላክት	*mälakt* n. message
መላክተኛ	*mälaktäñña* n. messenger
መልእክት	*mälə'əkt* n. message *also* መልክት
መልእክተኛ	*mälə'ktäñña* n. messenger *also* መልክት
ተላከ	*tälakä* v.i. was sent
ተላኪ	*tälaki* adj n. *(one who)* is sent, messenger
ተላላከ	*tälalakä* v.i. acted as a messenger; corresponded
ተላላኪ	*tälalaki* n. runner, messenger
ተላላኪነት	*tälalakinnät* n. the job of being a messenger
አላላከ	*ullalakä* v.t. made enquiries
አስላከ	*aslakä* v.t. had *(s/t)* sent
ላከከ	*lakkäkä* v.t. put the blame on *(s/o)*; stuck onto
ተላከከ	*tälakkäkä* v.i. was stuck to, stuck onto
ላዕላይ	*la'lay* adj. upper

—መዋቅር	—*mäwaqər* n. superstructure
ላይ	*lay* adv. on, above
ላይኛ	*layəñña* adj. top, upper
በ+noun+ ላይ ፤ በ+ infinitive +ላይ ነው· e.g. የምርምሩን ጥናት በመጨ ረስ ላይ ነው ፤ በዚህ ላይ ፤ እንዲ ላይ ፤ እዚህ ላይ ፤	e.g. በጠረጴዛው ላይ on the table. He is in the process of completing his research in addition to this together there, at this point *(also* ከዚህ ላይ*)*
ከመጠን በላይ	unusually, beyond measure, too much
ከዚህም በላይ	furthermore, besides, moreover
የበላይነት	*yäbälayənnät* n. superiority
ላይዳ	*layda* n. winnowing fan *(made of* wood*)*
ላገ	*lagä* v.t. planed *(wood etc. in carpentry)*
ተላገ	*tälagä* v.i. was planed
አስላገ	*aslagä* v.t. had *(s/t)* planed, made smooth
መላጊያ	*mälagiya* plane
ላጠ	*laṭä* v.t. peeled *(fruit, etc.)*; unsheathed
ልጣጭ	*ləṭṭač* n. peel, outer skin
ልጥ	*ləṭ* n. bark *(of plant, tree)*
መላጣ	*mälaṭa* adj. bald-headed
መላጫ	*mälača* n. peeling knife, peeler; shaving instrument
ላላጠ	*lalaṭä* y.t. cut shavings from
መላላጫ	*mälalača* n. chicken leg, drumstick *(chicken)*
ተላጠ	*tälaṭä* v.i. was peeled
ተላጭ	*tälač* adj. capable of being peeled

14

ተላላጠ	*tälalaţä* v.i. was peeled off *(skin)*	ሌጥነት	*leţannät* n. the single state, bachelorhood, spinsterhood
አስላጠ	*aslaţä* v.t. had *(s/t)* peeled	ሌጦ	*leţo* n. hide *(sheep or goat only)*
ላጨ	*laččä* v.t. shaved, shaved off: fooled *(s/o)*	ለ	*lə*, with imperfect in orde: that, so that
ላጭ	*lač* adj. n one who shaves		*with imperfect+* ነው is about
መላጪ	*mälaĉa* n. shaving instrument		*with imperfect+* ነበር was about to
ምላጭ	*məlaĉ* n. razor, blade; adj. cunning	ለሙጥ	*ləmuţţ* adj. plain, undecorated
ጢም ላጭ	*ţim laĉ* n. barber		
ተላጨ	*tälaĉĉä* v.i. was shaved, was shaved off	ለሙጥነት	*ləmuţţnät* n. plainness
አስላጨ	*aslaĉĉä* v.t. had *(s/o)* shaved	ለማጭ	*ləmmaĉĉ* n. lath, thin whippy stick
ላጲስ	*lappis* n. eraser	ለሳን	*ləssan* n. tongue;
ላፈ	*lafä* v.t. burned off, singed; guzzled		language; organ (pols.
ተላፈ	*tälafä* v.i. was burned off, singed; was guzzled	ለሻን, ሊሻን	*ləšan, lišan,* ፈሻን *niša*n n. decoration *(medal)*
ላፒስ	*lappis* n. eraser; indelible pencil	ለዛዝ	*ləbab* harness
ሌሊት	*lelit* n. night, nighttime	ለቡና	*ləbbuna* n. conscience
ሌላ	*lela* adj. other, extra. additional, another	ለቅሶ	*ləqso* n. crying, mourning, lamentation
— ሌላውን	--*lelawən* something else	ለብ	*ləbb* n heart; courage, mental acuteness
— ጋ	—*ga* elsewhere, *also* ሌላ ስንደ	ለብ ሰፊ	*ləbbä säffi* adj. tolerant; long-suffering
ከዚህ —	*käzzih*— besides this	— ቅን	—*qən* adj. kindhearted, well-disposed
ከዚያም	*käzziamm*— besides, moreover	— ቁራጥ	—*qu^w ärraţ* adj. courageous ; decisive in manner
ሌማት	*lemat* n. basket tray *(for serving ənğära bread)*	— ቢስ	—*bis* adj. forgetful,
ለባ	*leba* n. thief	— ተራራ	--*tärara* adj. indomitable, unyielding
ሌባሻ	*lebaša* n. thief catcher	— ደንዳና	—*dändanna* adj. stout-hearted
ሌባ ጣት	*leba ţat* n. index finger	— ደፋር	--*däffar* adj. daring. courageous
ሌብነት	*lebənnät* n. thieving, skill in thieving	ለባም	*ləbbam* adj. conscientious, mindful *(of details)*
ሌጋሲዮን	*legasion* n. legation	ለባዊ	*ləbbawi* adj. cordial; warm
ለጣ	*leţa* adj. not pregnant; *(single , unmarried*	ለዑል	*lə'ul* n. prince
—ሴት	*leţaset* n. spinster. unmarried woman	ሉዓላዊ	*lu'alawi* adj. raised, *(dais/or platform)*, sovereign
		ለዕልት	*lə'əlt* n. princess

15

ልዕልና	lə'lənna n. prince-liness. nobility; great-ness ; supremacy
ልደት	lədät n. birthday; Christmas
ልደታ	lədäta n. first day of the month see ወለዲ
ልጅ	ləǧ n. child; esq. *(general title for aristocracy)*
ልጃገረድ	ləgagäräd n. young girl; virgin
ልጃገረድነት	ləgagärädənnät n. youth *(for girls)* ; virginity
ልጅነት	ləǧənnät n. childhood
የልጅ ልጅ	yäləǧ ləǧ n. grand-child
ልጥ	see ላጠ
ልጫኛ	ləččäñña adj. polite, courteous

ልፋጭ	ləffač n. gristle, sinew; tough, inedible meat
ልፍስፍስ	see ተልፈሰፈሰ
ሎሌ	lole n. old retainer
ሎሌነት	lolennät n. long ser-vice *(as a domestic)*
ሎሚ	lomi n. lime *(fruit)*
ባህረ —	bahrä—n. grape fruit
ሎሚታ	lomita n. metal orna-ment *(at point of scabbard)*
ሎሚናት	lominat n. lemonade
ሎተሪ	lotäri n. lottery
ሎቲ	lotti n. ear pendant
ሎጋ	loga n. slim, tall and young
ሎጣዊ	loṭawi n. homosexual *(male)*, sodomite
ሎፊሳ	lofisa n. leather saddle cloth

ሐ

ሐሙስ	hamus n. Thursday
ጸሎተ—	ṣälota — n. Maundy Thursday
ሐማል	hammal n. coolie *(Harar)*
ሐማልነት	hammalənnät n. coolie work
ሐሜት	hammet n. backbit-ing, malicious gossip
ሐሜተኛ	hametäñña n. backbiter, gossip see አማ
ሐምሌ	hamle n. tenth Ethiopian month *(July)*
ሐምራዊ	hamrawi n. purple
ሐሞት	hamot n. bile
ሐሞቱ ቢስ	hamotä bis adj. lack-ing initiative; dull
ሐረርጌ	harärge n. one of the Administrative Re-gions, Eastern Ethiopia *(Hararge)*
ሐረር	harär n. the city

	of Harar
ሐረግ	haräg n. shoot of a creeping plant; decor-ation *(in printed book)*
ሐረግ ወይን	harägä wäyn n. vine shoot
ሐሩር	harur n. heat-wave; spell of hot weather
ሐራ ጥቃ	haraṭəqa n. heretic
ሐራጅ	harraǧ n. auction
ሐር	harr n. silk
የሐር ትል	yäharr təl n. silkworm
ሐሰት	hassät n. lie, falsehood
ሐሰተኛ	hassätäñña n. liar
ሐሳዌ መሲሕ	hassawe mäsih n. false prophet
ሐሳብ	see አሰበ
ሐቅ	haqq n. truth
ሐቀኛ	haqqäñña adj. truthful
ሐቀኛነት	haqqäññannät n. truthfulness
ሐበሻ	habäša adj/n. Abyssinian; Abyssinia

16

ሐብል	habl n. necklet
ሐብሐብ	habhab n. watermelon
ሐተታ	hatäta n. investigation (scientific, academic); discursiveness
ሐተተኛ	hatätäñña adj. discursive, digressive
አታች	attač adj. discursive digressive
ሐች	hačč adv. yonder, over there
ሐኪም	hakim n. physician, doctor
—ቤት	—bet n. hospital
ሕክምና	həkkəmənna n. medical profession, medical treatment,
ሐኬት	haket n. laziness
ሐካይ	hakkay adj. lazy
ሐኬተኛ	haketäñña adj. lazy
ሐኬተኝነት	haketäññənnät n. laziness
ሐዋላ	hawwala n. money transfer (through bank)
ሐዋርያ	hawarəya n. appostle
ሐዋርያነት	hawarəyannät n. apostleship
ሐዋርያዊ	hawarəyawi adj. apostolic
ሐውልት	hawəlt n. statue
ሐዘን	see አዘነ
ሐይቅ	hayq n. lake
ሐዲስ ኪዳን	haddis kidan n. New Testament
ሐዲድ	hadid n. railway line (metal), track
(የ)ባቡር—	(yä)babur—n. railway line, track
ሐጂ	haği n. one who has made the pilgrimage to Mecca (title)
ሐፍረት	hafrät n. shame
ሐፍረተ ሥጋ	hafrätä səga n. sexual organ (male or female), see አፈረ
ሑር ወጣ	hurr wätta v.i. was set free
ሑርነት	hurrənnät n. freedom (e.g. as given to slave)
ሑዳዴ	hudade n. lent
ሒሳብ	hisab n. calculation, mathematics; account, bill see አሰበ

ሔዋን	hewan n. Eve
ሕልም	həlm n. dream, see አለመ
ሕመም	həmäm n. sickness, disease
ሕመምተኛ	həmämtäñña n. sick person, patient
ሕማም	həmam n. pain
ሕማማት	həmamat n. Holy Week, see አመመ
ሕቅ አለ	həqq alä v.i. hiccoughed, hiccupped
ሕቅታ	həqqəta n. hiccough, hiccup
ሕንፃ	hənşa n. building (usually of stone) see አነጠ and አነፀ
ሕዋስ	həwas n. sense e.g. hearing, sight etc.) cell (pols)
ተሐዋስያን	tähawasəyan n. small crawling insects (general term)
ሕዝብ	həzb n. people, population
ሕዝባዊ	həzbawi adj. popular, public, social (of the people)
ሠራዊት	—särawit n. militia
ተራ ሕዝብ	tära həzb n. crowd, masses
አሕዛብ	ahəzab infidels, gentiles
የሕዝብ ካፒታሊዝም	yähəzb kappitalism, people's capitalism
ሕይወት	həywät n. life
ሕይወቱን ሳተ	lost consciousness
—አሳለፈ	gave one's life
በሕይወት ዋረ	or ቆየ kept alive
—አለ	be alive
የሕይወት ታረክ	biography, memoires autobiography
— ዋስትና	life insurance
ዘለዓለማዊ ሕይወት	eternal life
ሕያው	həyaw animate; vivid
ሕያውነት	həyawənnät n. immortality
ሕግ	həgg n. law, rule, regulation; virginity matrimony pl. ሕግጋት or ሕጋጋት
ሕግ ወጥ	həggä wätt adj. illegal, lawless

ሕጋዊ	həggawi adj. lawful, legitimate, legal, juridical	—እውጪ	—awči legislator lawgiver, lawmaker,
—ወራሽ	—wäraš n. legal heir	— የለሽ	—yälläš lawless
ሕጋዊነት	həgguwinnät n. legality	ሕግ መንግ ሥት	həggä mängəst constitution
የሕግ መወሰኛ ምክር ቤት	yähəgg mäwässäña məkər bet n. parliament	— ወጥ	wäṭṭ outlaw, illegal; irregular
— ሚስት	— mist n. legal wife	የሕግ ረቂቅ	yähəgg räqiq draft (of law), bill
ሕግ ተላለፈ	həgg tälaläffä v.t. broke the law	ጠቅላይ ዐቃ ቤ ሕግ	ṭäqlay aqqabe nəgg Procurator General
—አስከባሪ	—askäbbari n. public prosecutor	ሕግ ጣሽ	həgg ṭaš n. ʾlaw breaker
—አወጣ	—awäṭṭa v.t. legislated, drew up rules.	ሕፃን	həṣan n. child, baby pl. ሕፃናት
		ሕፃንነት	həṣannənnät n. babyhood, early childhood

መ

መሀል	mähal n. centre		and slim; attractively built (person)
—ሠፋሪ	— säfari n. vacillator (pols) neutral, (pols.)	መላላ	mälala adj. tall
		ሰላላ—	sälala— adj; tall and slim
—ከተማ	— kätäma n. city-centre	መለል አለ	mäläll alä v.i. grew fairly tall and slim
መሀንዲስ	mähandis n. engineer, civil engineer, architect		
		መለመለ	mälämmälä v. t. stripped off leaves; made a selection (of people), recruited; pruned
መሀንዲስነት	mähandisənnät n. the work of an engineer		
መሀከል	mähakkäl n. middle, centre	መልማይ	mälmay adj. n. (one who) strips; selects; prunes
መሀከለኛ	mähakkäläñña adj. central, middle, medium		
		ምልመላ	məlmäla n. the action of stripping; pruning; selecting; recruiting
መሃይምን	mähayyəmn n. illiterate person: layman		
መሃይምነት	mähayyəmənnät n. illiteracy; status of layman	ምልምል	məlməl n. selected person, chosen candidate; young paramour for rich widow; gigolo
መለለ	mällälä v. t. became attenuated, grew thin and long		
		ተመለመለ	tämälämmälä v. i. was pruned, stripped, was selected, recruited
መለሎ	mälälo adj. tall		

18

መለሰ	*mälläsä* v.t. answered; returned; put back; gave back; translated	
መላሽ	*mällaš* adj./n. *(one)* who answers, returns; gives back, etc.	
መልስ	*mäls* n. answer; return invitation *(esp. after marriage)*	
መልሶ ማቋቋም	*mälləso maquʷaquʷam* n. rehabilitation	
ምላሽ	*məllaš* n. answer; change *(from pur-chase)*	
ምልስ	*mälləs* adj. pliant, complaisant	
ተመለሰ	*tämälläsä* v.i. returned, came back	
ተመላሽ	*tämällaš* adj./n. *(one)* who returns, comes back	
ተመላለሰ	*tämälalläsä* v.i. went to and fro	
ተመላላሽ	*tämälalaš* adj/n. *(one)* who goes to and fro	
አመላለሰ	*ammälalläsä* v.t. transported, carried from place to place	
አመላላሽ	*ammälalaš* adj/n *(one)* who transports, carries from *(place to place)*	
ማመላለሻ	*mammälaläša* n. means of transportation	
አስመለሰ	*asmälläsä* v.t. had *(s/t)* brought back; vomited	
°መለከት	see አመለከተ / ተመለከተ	
መለከት	*mäläkät* n. long, single-note trumpet, ceremonial trumpet	
°መለከ	see አመለከ	
መለኩት	*mäläkuʷät* n. Divinity	
መለኩታዊ	*mäläkuʷätawi* adj. Divine	
መለኩትነት	*mäläkuʷätənnät* n. Divine power	
መለዮ	*mälläyyo* see ለየ	
መለጠ	*mällätä* v.t. removed all the hair from	
መላጣ	*mälata* adj. bald; bare; barren *(for land)*	
መላጣነት	*mälatannät* n. baldness	
ምልጥ	*mält* adj. skinless, hairless	
ተመለጠ	*tämällätä* v.i. was made bald; wa. peeled	
ተመላለጠ	*tämälallätä* v.i. became, was made completely bald; was completely stripped of skin	
አመለጠ	*amällätä* v.t. slipped from the hands; escaped *(from custody, danger etc.)*	
አመለጠው	*amällätaw* v.t. broke wind	
አስመለጠ	*asmällätä* v.t. caused *(s/o)* to escape; caused *(s/t)* to fall from the hands	
መላ	*mäla* n. idea for solving a problem, scheme	
—መታ	—*mätta* v.t. predicted, foresaw, made a guess	
—ምት	—*mət* n. hypothesis, guess	
—ቢስ	—*bis* adj. without hope *(person);* unsolvable	
—ቅጡን አጣ	—*qətun atta* v.i. was thrown into utter confusion, was at a loss	
—ተናገረ	—*tänaggärä* v.t. made a helpful suggestion	
—የሌለው	—*yälellaw* adj. without hope; unsolvable	
መላ	*mälla* adj. whole, entire	
መልሕቅ	*mälhəq* n. anchor	
መልቲ	*mälti* adj. mischievous, roguish	
መልቲነት	*mältinnät* n. roguishness, mischievousness	
መልአክ	*mäl'ak* n. angel	
መልአክ ሞት	*mäl'akä mot* n. the Angel of Death	

19

መልአክ ዑ.ቃቢ	mäl'akä uqabi n. guardian angel
መልከኛ	mälkäñña n. landlord
መልካም	mälkam adj. good, nice, well
መልክ	mälk n. face; appearance
መልክ መልካም	mälkä mälkäm adj. beautiful, handsome
— ቀና	—qänna adj. attractive, good - looking
— ጥፉ	—ṭəfu adj. ugly,
መሐለቅ	mähälläq n. coin
መሐላ	mähalla n. oath, see ግለ
መሐረም(ብ)	mäharäm(b) n. handkerchief
መምህር	mämhər n. professor, high-level teacher
መምህርነት	mämhərənnät n. teaching profession
ምሁር	məhur n. scholar
ምሁራዊ	məhurawi adj. scholarly
መሠረተ	mäsärrätä v.t. established, founded
መሠረት	mäsärät n. foundation; reason
መሠረታዊ	mäsärätawi adj. basic, fundamental
መሥራች	mäsrač n. founder
ተመሠረተ	tämäsärrätä v.i. was founded, established
አመሠራረት	ammäsärarät n. manner of establishing
አስመሠረተ	asmäsärrätä v.t. had (s/t) established
መሠሪ	mäsärri n. malicious, uncharitable, vicious
መሠሪነት	mäsärrinnät n. maliciousness, uncharitableness
መስመር	mäsmär n. line, circuit \ see also ሡመረ
መረመረ	märämmärä v.t. investigated, examined; scrutinised, checked
መርማሪ	märmari n. investigator
ምርመራ	mərmära n. investigation
ምርምር	mərmmər n. investigation; research

ተመረመረ	tämärämmärä v.i. was investigated, checked
ተመርማሪ	tämärmari n. person under investigation
ተመራመረ	tämärammärä v.t. researched into (s/t), studied (s/t) deeply
ተመራማሪ	tämäramari adj/n. (one) who researches, studies; a researcher
አመራመረ	ammärammärä v.t. tried to get the truth; pursued an investigation
አመራመር	ammäramär n. method of investigation
አመራማሪ	ammäramari n. informer's fee also የአመራማሪ ገንዘብ
አስመረመረ	asmärämmärä v.t. had (s/t) investigated, checked
መረረ	märrärä v.i. was bitter, (to the taste)
መረረው	märräräw v.i. was bitter about it
መራሪ	märari adj. bitter-tasting
መራራ	märara adj. bitter-tasting
መራራነት	märarannät n. bitterness
መርር	märrar adj. bitter (fig. e.g. sorrow)
መርርነት	märrarənnät n. bitterness
ምሬት ምረት	mərret; mərrät n. bitter taste
ምር	mərr n. serious-mindedness
የምር	yämərr adv. seriously
የምሩን ነው	yämərrun näw he is very serious
ምርር አለ	mərarr älä v.i. became very bitter; was very sad
ተመረረ	tämärrärä v.t. was irritated by; was impatient with; was embittered
ተማረረ	tämarrärä v.i. took to heart; became serious about (e.g.

20

እመረረ	fighting, reciprocal) amärrärä v.t. became serious about (s/t); took too much to heart; became offended (e.g. if it goes too far); made up one's mind (finally, surprisingly)
አምራሪ	amrari adj. n. (one who takes (s/t) too seriously
አማረረ	ammarrärä v. i. complained, grumbled; caused others to quarrel
አማራሪ	ammarari adj/n. (one) who grumbles
አስመረረ	asmärrärä v.t. made (s/o) embittered
መረቀ	märräqä v.t. wished (s/o) well; blessed, gave benediction to; made an outright gift; inaugurated
ምሩቅ	mərruq n. graduate; one who completes a course of instruction successfully
መራቂ	märraqi adj. n. (one) who blesses; wishes (s/o) well; makes a gift to; inaugurator
ምረቃ	märräqa n. graduation
ድህረ —	dəhərä — n. graduate studies, post graduate studies
ምርቃት	mərraqat n. blessing; good wishes; outright gift
ምርቃን	mərraqan n. blessing; good wishes; outright gift
ተመረቀ	tämärräqä v.i. was blessed; was given graduating certificate
ተመራቂ	tämärraqi adj./n. (one) who is blessed: graduate
አስመረቀ	asmärräqä v.t. had (s/o) blessed; treated one's friends (after buying a new car, suit, etc.)

መረቅ	märäq n. broth, bouillon
መረቀዘ	märäqqäzä v.i. suppurated (after seeming to be healed); turned sour (of a relationship)
አመረቀዘ	amäräqqäzä v.i. suppurated; turned sour. broke out afresh (wounds, hatred)
መረባ	märäbba adj. square(for measurement - as 'square metre'- arch.)
መረብ/መርበብ	märäb/märbäb n. net for fishing, tennis etc.)
— ጣለ	—ṭalä v.t. netted (fish)
— ጣይ	—ṭay n. fisherman
መረተ	märrätä v.i. yielded; was cleaned and threshed (grain)
ምርት	mərt n. production; yield, crop
ስልተ ምርት	səltä mərt mode of productoin
አመረተ	amärrätä v.t. threshed crop, harvested; produced
አምራች	amrač n. producer
መረነ	märränä v.t. tied with a thong (joined ploughshare to handle)
ምራን	məran n. leather thong
መረን	märän adj/n. loose-living, libertine
መረዋ	märäwwa n. bell (large, e.g. of church)
መረዘ	märräzä v.t. poisoned: hated strongly
መራዥ	märraž adj/n. (one) who poisons; (one) who hates strongly
መርዘኛ	märzäñña adj. poisonous
መርዘም	märzam adj. full of poison
መርዝ	märz n. poison
ተመረዘ	tämärräzä v.i. was poisoned
ተማረዘ	tämarräzä v.i. hated each other (very strongly)
አማረዘ	ammarräzä v.t. caused

	(people) to hate each other
አስመረዘ	*asmärräzä* v.t. had *(s/o)* poisoned; caused *(s/o)* to be hated
መረጻ	see አረጻ
መረገ	*märrägä* v.t. daubed *(cement)*, plastered
መምረጊያ	*mämrägiya* n. tool, method used in plastering, daubing
መራጊ	*märagi* adj./n. *(one)* who plasters, daubs
ምርጊት	*mərgitt* n. plaster *(usually mud or dung)*
ምርግ	*mərg* adj. plastered, daubed with mud *(wall, etc.)*
ተመረገ	*tämärrägä* v.i. was plastered, daubed
አግረገ	*ammarrägä* v.t. helped *(s/o)* to plaster, daub
አስመረገ	*asmärrägä* v.t. had *(s/t)* plastered
መረግድ	*märägd* n. emerald
መረጠ	*märräṭä* v.t. chose, selected, voted for, preferred
መረጣ	*märäṭa* n. choice, election
መራጭ	*märač* adj/n. *(one)* who chooses, votes
መራጭነት	*märačənnät* n. process of voting, choosing
መምረጫ	*mämräča* n. polling booth; place where choice is made
ምራጭ	*mərrač* n. second best, what is left over after choice is made
ምርጥ	*mərṭ* adj/n. *(that)* which is chosen; best
ምርጫ	*mərča* n. choice; election
ተመረጠ	*tämärräṭä* v.i. was chosen, selected
ተመራጭ	*tämärrač* n. candidate for selection; preference
ተመራጭነት	*tämärraçənnät* n. candidature
አግረጠ	*ammarräṭä* v.t. helped in choosing; decided between the best

አግራጭ	*ammaraç* adj/n. *(one)* who selects the very best; alternative
አስመራጠ	*asmärräṭä* v.t had *(s/o, s/t)* chosen
መራ	*märra* v.t. led; led in singing, chanting; distributed land
መሪ	*märi* n. leader
መሪነት	*märinnät* n. leadership
መሪጌታ	*märigeta* n. choir leader, chant leader *(in church)*
መርህ	*märh* n. principle
መምሪያ	in የመምሪያ ኃላፊ *yämämriya halefi* department head *(in a ministry etc.)*
ምሪት	*mərrit* n. the assigning of plots of land, lodging
ተመራ	*tämärra* v.i. was led; was assigned *(plot of land)*
ተመሪ	*tämäri* adj/n *(one)* who is led; assigned *(plot of land)*
መመሪያ	*mämmäriya* n. policy, guideline
ተግራ	*tämarra* v.t. led each other *(e.g. two blind people)*
አመራ	*amärra* v.t. took one's course, went one's way; headed for; went towards
አመራር	*ammärar* n. way of guiding, leading; leadership
አስመራ	*asmärra* v.t. had *(s/o)* guided, led
መሬት	*märet* n. land, earth, ground, soil
— ነው	—*näw* he is patient
ባለመሬት	*balä märet* n. land-owner
የመሬት	*yämäret yəzota* n. land tenure
—ይዞታ	
— ከበርቴ	—*käbbärte* n landlord
ከመሬት ተነስ ሥቶ	*kämäret tänästo* without any reason, provocation
ድንግል መሬት	*dəngəl märet* virgin land

22

መር አለ *märr alä* v.i. jumped, leaped

መርበብ *märbäb* n. net *(for fishing)* also *መረብ*

— ጣለ —*ṭalä* v.t. cast net

— ጣይ —*ṭay* n. fisherman

መርከብ *märkäb* n. ship, large boat, large vessel

መርከበኛ *märkäbäñña* n. sailor

መርፅ *see አረዳ*

መርፌ *märfe* n. needle *(sewing, hypodermic)*; injection

— ቀዳዳ —*qädada* n. eye of a needle

— ቁልፍ —*qulf* n. safety pin

— ወጋ —*wägga* v.t. gave an injection

መር *märo* n. chisel

መሰለ *mässälä* v.t. resembled; pretended to be; made a model of; spoke in parables

መሳይ *mäsay* adj/n. *(one)* who resembles, pretends

ምሳሌ *məssale* n. example; parable

ምስለኔ *məsläne* n. district officer *(in earlier days lowest Govt. rank in Ethiopia)*

ምስል *məsəl* n. statue; model; graven image

ተመሰለ *tämassälä* v.t. took the form, shape of *(s/t)*

ተማሰለ *tämassälä* v.t. was stirred, mixed, homoge_ nised; resembled each other

እማሰለ *ammassälä* v.t. stirred, broth etc; assessed points of similarity

ማማሰያ *mammasäya* n. stirring stick, stirrer

አመሳሰል *ammäsasäl* n. point or resemblance

አስመሰለ *asmässälä* v.t. spoke convincingly; pretended

አስመሳይ *asmässay* adj/n. *(one)* who pretends, speaks convincingly; pretender, impostor

መሰላል *mäsälal* n. ladder

* መስቃቀለ *see አመስቃቀለ*

መሰነ *mässänä* v.i. became barren *(for animals)*

መሲና *mäsina* adj./n. fat and sterile *(cow)*

መሰንቆ *mäsänqo* n. *also* ማሲንቆ *masinqo* n. single-string violin *(Ethiopian)*

— መጭ —*mäči* adj./n. *(one)* who plays a *mäsänqo*

መስከረ *mäsäkkärrä* v.i. testified, acted as witness

መስካሪ *mäskari* adj/n. *(one)* who testifies, acts as witness

መስካሪነት *mäskarinnät* n. act of testifying

ምስክር *məsəkkər* n. witness *(in court)*

ምስክራ *məskära* n. testimony

ተመሰከረ *tämäsäkkärä* v.i. was certified by witnesses

ተመሳከረ *tämäsakkärä* v.t. produced witnesses against each other

አመሳከረ *ammäsakkärä* v.t. made *(both parties)* testify; compared *(two things of the same kind)*

አመሳካሪ *ammäsakari* adj/n. *(one)* who compares; *(one)* who makes *(both parties)* testify

አስመሰከረ *asmäsäkkärä* v.t. had *(s/o)* testify; had *(s/o)* testify by proxy

አስመስካሪ *asmäskari* adj.*(one)* who has *(s/o)* testify on his behalf

መስከነ *mäsäkkänä* v.i. became very poor

ምስኪን *məskin* adj. very poor; pathetic

ምስኪንነት *məskinənnät* n. extreme poverty

23

መሰገ mässägä v.t. packed into (animals into stable), put in a fold .
ምስግ məssəg n. fold
*መስገነ see አመስገነ
መሰጠ mässäṭä v.t. took (one's) attention, absorbed (one's thought, plan etc.)

መሳጭ mässač adj. absorbing
ተመሰጠ tämässäṭä v.t. was absorbed (in thought)
*መሰጠረ see ተመሰጠረ and ምስጢር

መሲሕ masih n. Messiah
መሲሓዊ mäsihawi adj, Messianic

መሳ mässa adj. half (e.g. "the tea was half water")
— ለመሳ —lämässa adj. half and half

መስቀል see ሰቀለ
መስቃ mäsqa n. unjustified reproach
መስተአምር mästä'ammər n. article (gram.)
መስተዋድድ mästäwadəd n. preposition
መስተጋብር mästägabər n. interaction
መስተጻምር mästäṣamər n. conjunction (gram.)
መስተዋት mästäwat n. mirror; glass; window glass
መስቲካ mästika n. chewing-gum
መስኖ mäsno n. irrigation
መስከረም mäskäräm n. first Ethiopian month (Sept. / Oct.)
መስክ mäsk n. field, meadow (pasture)
— አልፋ —alfa adj. idle, loafer
መስኮብ mäskob n. Russia
መስኮባዊ mäskobawi adj. Russian
መስኮብኛ mäskobəñña n. Russian (language)
መስኮት mäskot n. window
መስጊድ mäsgid n. mosque
መስፍ mäsf n. anvil
መስፍን mäsfən n. nobleman (used as title, equivalent to "Duke")

መሳፍንት mäsafənt n. the nobility
መሶብ mäsob n. food-table (made of basketwork, peculiar to Ethiopia)
መሰበወርቅ mäsobäwärq n. small food-table (highly decorated)
መሸ mäššä v.i. night fell, became evening, got dark
ምሽት məššət n. evening, dusk
አመሸ amäššä v.i. spent the evening, was late in the evening
እንዴት አመሸህ əndət amäššäh good evening
አምሾቶ መጣ amšəto maṭṭa he came late in the evening
አማሸ ammaššä v.t. kept (s/o) company (for the evening)
አማሺ ammaši adj/n. one who keeps (s/o) company (for the evening)
አስመሸ asmäššä v.t. made (s/o) late (in the evening)
መሸተ mäššätä v.t. prepared drink for sale (beer or ṭäg)
መሸተኛ mäšätäñña adj/n. (one) who frequents drinking houses
መሸታ mäšäta n. a drink in a public house; a drinking spree
መሸታ ቤት mäšäta bet n. public house; bar
መሸገ mäššägä v.t. built a fortification; manned a barricade
ምሽግ məššəg n. barricade, fortification
አስመሸገ asmäššägä v.t. had (a place) fortified
መቀመቅ mäqämäq n. abyss
መቀስ mäqäs n. scissors
መቀነት see ቀነተ

መታ — *mäqa* n. reed
— ብዕር — *b'ər* n. reed pen
መቅሠፍት — see ቀሠፈ
መቅረዝ — *mäqräz* n. candle stick, lampholder
መቅን — *mäqn* n. bone marrow
መቅኛ ቢስ — *mäqno bis* adj. short-lived; lacking support; having no hope of success; in a desperate situation
መቋሚያ — *mäquʷamiya* n. staff (e.g. priest staff), see ቆመ
መበለት — *mäbällät* n. nun (in Ethiopia, usually a widow who has vowed the remainder of her life to the Church)
መበ — *mäba* n. holy vow; small offering given to the Church
መባቻ — *mäbaća* n. first day of any month
መብረቅ — *mäbräq* n. lightning; thunderbolt
መብት — *mäbt* n. right (as in "the rights of the citizen")
ባለ — *balä* — adj/n. (one) who is within his rights
መተረ — *mättärä* v.t. chopped (meat, etc.)
መታሪ — *mätari* adj/n. (one) who chops (meat, etc)
ምትር — *mətər* adj. chopped up
መታተረ — *mätattärä* v.t. chopped (a certain amount of)
ተመተረ — *tämättärä* v.i. was chopped up
አስመተረ — *asmättärä* v.t. had (s/t) chopped up
መተት — *mätät* n. magic, spell
መታ — *mätta* v.i. hit, struck; put (animals) together for breeding
ምታት — *mətat*, also ምትሐት *məthat* n. conjuring trick, optical illusion
ራስ ምታት — *ras mətat* n. headache
ምት — *mət* n. way of hitting; beat

ምች — *məčč* n. attack of fever
መታታ — *mätatta* v.t. tapped gently
ተመታ — *tämätta* v.i. was hit, struck
ተማታ — *tämatta* v.t. hit each other; hit, struck; was confused
ተማች — *tämač* adj/n. (òne) who tends to use his fists, violent person, bully
አማታ — *ammatta* v.t. made s/o hit s/o; confused (s/o) in order to deceive
አማች — *ammač* adj/n (one) who makes others hit each other; (one) who confuses in order to deceive
አምታታ — *amtatta* v.t. deceived, beguiled
አምታች — *amtač* n. deceiver
አስመታ — *asmätta* v.t. had (s/o) hit
መትረየስ — *mäträyyäs* n. machine gun
መቶ — *mäto* adj./n. hundred
መቶኛ — *mätoñña* adj. hundredth
መቶ በመቶ — fully, wholly; hundred per cent
— አለቃ — lieutenant
— ዓመት — century
በመቶ or ከመቶ — percent, percentage
መቶኛ ዓመት — centennial, centenary
መች — see ተመች
መጭ — *mäče* መች *mäč* adv/ conj. when
መጭም — *mäččem* interj. well of course, after all, any way
መጭ አጣሁት — *mäče aṭṭahut* I know it well
— ጠፋኝ — *ṭäffañ* I know it well.
መጭውንም — *mäččewənəm* adv. all the time
ከመጭ ጀምሮ — *kämäčče ğämməro* since when?

ከመጨወም	kämäččewəmm more than ever before	
መነመነ	mänämmänä v.i. got thin; became emaciated	
ምንምን	mənmən adj. thin; emaciated	
መንማና	mänmanna adj. very thin, emaciated	
አመነመነ	amänämmänä v.t. made thin	
መነቀረ	mänäqqärä v.t. gouged out; churned up (ground)	
መንቃራ	mänqarra adj./n. (one) who walks clumsily, ungraceful in walking	
መነቃቀረ	mänäqaqqärä v.t. disarranged, messed up; gouged; churned up completely	
መነተፈ	mänättäfä also **ሞነተፈ**. monättäfä v.t. snatched, grabbed (for thief)	
መንታፊ	mäntafi adj/n. (one) who snatches, thief	
ተመነተፈ	tämänättäfä v.i. was snatched, grabbed, was stolen	
መነቻከ	mänäččäkä also **ቻከ** **አለ** čəkk alä v.t. importuned, annoyed by asking; would not come clean (laundry, etc.)	
መንቻካ	mänčaᴋka adj/n. (one) who is stubborn, importunate	
አመነቻከ	amänäččäkä v.t. made (s/t) too dirty for washing, cleaning	
መነነ	männänä v.i. became a hermit; forsook the world	
መናኝ	männañ n. hermit	
ምነና	männäna n. the action of retiring from the world	
ምናኔ	männane n. the action of retiring from the world	
መመነኛ	mämännäña n. place of retirement from	the world; hermitage
አስመነነ	asmännänä n. caused (s/o) to become a hermit	
መነኮሰ	mänäkkʷäsä v.t. became a monk	
መነኩሴ	mänäkwəse n. monk	
መንኩሽ	mänkuʷaš n. religious novice (male or female)	
ምንኩስና	mənkʷəsənna n. state of being a monk, monkhood	
የምንኩስና ኑሮ	yämənkʷəsənna nuro monastic life	
አመነኮሰ	amänäkkʷäsä v.t. made (s/o) a monk	
አስመነኮሰ	asmänäkkʷäsä v.t. had (s/o) made a monk	
መነዘረ	mänäzzärä v.t. gave change (money), changed (money)	
መንዛሪ	mänzari adj/n. money changer	
ምንዛሬ	mənzar adj/n. fornication, adultery; follower (of a chief) e.g. **አለቃና ምንዛሬ** a leader and his followers	
መነዛዘረ	mänäzazzärä v.t. changed completely (i.e. break down total amount into small change)	
ተመነዛዘረ	tämänäzzärä v.i. was changed (money)	
መመንዛዘሪያ	mämänzäriya n. place where money is changed	
አመነዘረ	amänäzzärä v.i. committed adultery, fornicated	
አስመነዘረ	asmänʸzzärä v.t. had (money) changed	
መነገገ	mänäggägä. v.t. forced (s/o's) mouth wide open	
መንጋጋ	mängaga n. lower jaw, mandibles	
መነጠረ	mänäṭṭärä v.t. cleared, uprooted completely (to clear land for	

ploughing)

ምንጣሪ mənəṭṭari n. s/t. which is uprooted

ምንጥር mənṭər adj. uprooted (plants, tree stumps etc.)

ምንጠራ mənṭāra n. the action of uprooting. clearing (of land)

መነጣጠረ mänäṭaṭṭärä v.t. uprooted completely, cleared completely (land)

ተመነጠረ tämänäṭṭärä v.i. was uprooted

አስመነጠረ asmänäṭṭärä v.t. had (s/t) uprooted, cleared (e.g. field)

መነጠቀ mänäṭṭäqä see also ነጠቀ näṭṭäqä v.t. snatched, grabbed (took rudely, forcibly)

መንጠቆ mänṭäqqo n. fish-hook

ተመነጠቀ tämänäṭṭäqä v.i. was snatched, grabbed (rudely); walked off (angrily, abruptly)

መነጥር mänäṭṭər n. eyeglasses, spectacles also መነፅር

መነጨ mänäč̣č̣ä v.i. sprang out (for water); sprang from the mind (idea, suggestion)

ምንጭ mənč̣ n. spring, source

መነጨረ mänäč̣č̣ärä v.t. clawed at

መንጫራ mänč̣arra adj. ungainly, clumsy

መነጨቀ mänäč̣č̣äqä v.t. snatched, grabbed

መንጫቃ mänč̣aqqa adj. irritable, ill-tempered

አመነጫጨቀ ammänäč̣ač̣č̣äqä v.t denigrated

አመናጨቀ ammänäč̣äqä v.t. denigrated

መነጽር mänäṣṣər n. eyeglasses, spectacles

መና mäna adj. useless, unsuccessful

— ቀረ —qärrä was without hope, was irredeemable

መና männa (in the Bible, food provided by God for the Israelites)

መናኛ mänaňňa adj. commonplace, of the lowest grade

መናፍቅ mänafəq adj/n. heretic, heretical

መንሺ mänš n. pitchfork, fork (farm tool)

መንበር mänbär n. throne

መንታ mänta adj/n. twin
— መንገድ —mängäd n. fork (in road)

መንካ mäŋka or ማንካ manka n. spoon

መንኮራኩር mänkorakur n. wheel; rocket

ሰው ሥራሽ säw särraš - n space satellite

መንዳሪን mändärin n. tangerine (orange)

መንደር mändär n. village

መንደራኛ mändäräňňa n. villager, one who lives in a village

መንደርተኛ mändärtäňňa adj/n fellow-villager

መንገድ mängäd n. road, way; method, system

መንገደኛ mängädäňňa n. traveller, passerby

እግረ መንገዴን əgrä mängäden on my way

አቋራጭ መንገድ aqu"arač̣ mängäd crosscut

የአየር መንገድ yä'ayyär mängäd airlines

የእግር መንገድ yä'əgər mängäd footpath, path, track

መንጋ mänga n. flock (of sheep, goats, etc.) swarm (of locusts, birds etc.)

— ፈሪ —färi n. bunch of cowards

መንጋጋ mängaga n. lower jaw mandible see መንጋጋ

መንገሡት see ነገሠ

መንጠቀ see ነጠቀ

መንጦ mänṭo or መንጦ menṭo n. hook

27

መንጯረር *mänçorär* n. duct

መንፈሳዊ *mänfäsawi* adj. spiritual, religious; theological

መንፈሳዊነት *mänfäsawinnät* n. spirituality, *see also* ነፈስ

መንፈቅ *mänfäq* n. period of six months

መንፈቀ ሌሊት *mänfäqä lelit* n. midnight

መኖ *männo* n. fodder, animal food

መከረ *mäkkärä* v.t. advised, counselled

መካሪ *mäkari* adj/n. *(one)* who advices, advisoɪ

ምክር *mǝkǝr* n. advice

— ቤት *—bet* n. parliament

የምክር ቤት አባል *yämǝkǝr bet abal* n. member of parliament

መካከረ *mäkakkärä* v.t. gave a certain amount of advice to

ተመከረ *tämäkkärä* v.i. was advised

ተማከረ *tämakkärä* v.i. gathered together *(e.g. to study a problem)*, held a seminar; asked advice from s/o; took counsel together, consulted each other

ተመካከረ *tämäkakkärä* v.t. discussed *(a problem)* together, took counsel, sought advice, consulted

አማከረ *ammakkärä* v.t. asked advice ; gave advice, consulted with s/o

አማካሪ *ammakari* adj/n. *(one)* who asks, gives, advice; counsellor, member of parliament

የሕግ — *yähǝgg* – legal advisor

አስመከረ *asmäkkärä* v.t. had *(s/t)* discussed

መከራ *mäkära* n. trouble, distress, hardship, misfortune, tribulation

መካረኛ *mäkäräñña* adj. mischievous, trouble-making; *(one)* who is prone to trouble

መከር *mäkär* n. harvest-time; autumn also መኸር *mähär*

መከተ *mäkkätä* v.t. defended oneself *(from a blow etc.)*

መካች *mäkkač* adj/n.*(one)* who defends himself

መከታ *mäkäta* n. structure of a wall, lath; screen *(against cold air, draughts)*; barɪicade

ተመከተ *tämäkkätä* n. was defended

መከነ *mäkkänä* v.i. became sterile,barren*(women)*

መከን *mäkkan* adj/ n. *(one)* who is sterile, barren

መካንነት *mäkkänǝnnät* n. sterility, barrenness

አመከነ *amäkkänä* v.t. made *(s/o)* sterile, barɪen

መከዳ *mäkkädda* n. pillow, cushion

*መከኝ *see* አመከኝ

መኪና *mäḳina* n. machine, mechanical device; motor car

— ነጅ *—näǧi* n. driver, chauffeur

በመኪና ጻፈ *bämäkina ṣafä* v.t. typed *also* ተየሰ

የመኪና መሪ *yämäkina märi* n. steering wheel

የጭነት መኪ ና *yäčǝnät mäkina* n. lorry, truck

የጽሕፈት መኪና *yäṣǝhǝfät mäkina* n. typewriteɪ

መካከል *mäkakkäl* adj. central, middle, medium; n. centre, middle

መካከለኛ *mäkakkäläñña* adj. medium, average

መካከለኛው ምሥራቅ Middle East

መክረጅ *mäkräǧ* n. tea kettle

መክሰስ *mäksäs* n. snack; quick meal *(not at set mealtime)*

መኩዓንን *mäku^wännən* n. officer (army)

ዕጩ — *əččʼu–* n. cadet

መውጅ *mäwǧ* n. sea wave, storm wave

መዐልት *mä'alt* n. daytime

መዓት *mä'at* n. horror; wrath of God; huge number *(for crowd of people)*; calamity

— አውሪ *–awri* n. doom sayer

መዐተኛ *mä'atäňňa* adj. shocking, horrifying

መዓዛ *mä'aza* n. fragrance, odour

መዘመዘ *mäzämmäzä* v.t. sucked; drew out *(molten gold, silver)*

ምዝምዝ *məzməz* adj. drawn out *(molten gold, silver)*

ተመዘመዘ *tämäzänmäzä* v.i. was sucked; was drawn out *(gold, silver)*

መዘበረ *mäzäbbärä* v.t. looted, pillaged, exploited

መዝባሪ *mäzbari* adj/n. *(one)* who loots, pillages

ምዝበራ *məzbära* n. looting pillaging; exploitation

ተመዘበረ *tämäzäbbärä* v.i. was looted, pillaged, was exploited

መዘነ *mäzzänä* v.t. weighed, balanced

መዛኝ *mäzzaňň* adj/n. *(one)* who weighs; *(one)* who has good judgement

ሚዛን *mizan* n. scale; balance; weight

የሌባ ሚዛን *yäleba mizan* n. false scale

መመዘኛ *mämäzzäňa* n. instrument, place for weighing; criterion

ተመዘነ *tämäzzänä* v.i. was weighed

ተመዛዘነ *tämäzazzänä* v.t. was comparable *(with)*, was in equilibrium, balanced one another

ተመዛዛኝ *tämäzazaňň* adj/n. *(one)* who is comparable *(with)*, comparable, equivalent, symmetrical

አመዘነ *amäzzänä* v.t. gave weight to; was heavier than, surpassed

አመዛዘነ *ammäzazzänä* v.t. compared; balanced; had good judgement, evaluated; took into account

አመዛዛኝ *ammäzazaňň* adj/n. *(one)* who compares, *(one)* who balances; *(one)* who has good judgement; judicious *(person)*

አስመዘነ *asmäzzänä* v.t. had *(s/t)* weighed

መዘዘ *mäzzäzä* v.t. drew out *(e.g. thread from cloth, sword from sheath)*

መዘዝ *mäzäz* n. bad behaviour, fault

መዘዘኛ *mäzäzäňňa* adj. troublesome

ተመዘዘ *tämäzzäzä* v.i. was drawn out

ዱላ ተመዘዘ *dulla tämäzzäzä* took up cudgels *(to start fighting)*

—አማዘዘ *—ammäzzäzä* v.t. caused *(s/o)* to start fighting *(took up cudgels)*

አስመዘዘ *asmäzzäzä* v.t. had *(s/t)* drawn out

መዘገበ *mäzäggäbä* v.t. registered, kept a record, had on file; enrolled; catalogued

መዝጋቢ *mäzgäbi* n. registrar

መዝገብ ቃላት *mäzgäbä qalat* n. dictionary, lexicon

መዝገብ ቤት *mäzgäb bet* n. archives, record office

—ያዘ *—yazä* v.t. kept records

የሒሳብ መዝገብ *yähisab mäzgäb* n. accounts

መዥገር	mäžgär n. crab lice, tick
መዥገራም	mäžgäram adj. ticky
መዳመደ	mädämmädä v.t. made level *(by cutting)*
መደበ	mäddäbä v.t. allotted, shared out, apportioned; put in the kitty *(gambling)*
ምደባ	* məddäba n. allotment, share ; money put in bank or kitty *(gambling)*
መደብ	mäddäb n. allotment apportion; class *(political)*
የሚመደብ ትግል	yämädäb təgəl n. class-struggle
የሠራተኛው—	yäsärratäññaw – the working class
የገዢው—	yägäžəw– the ruling class
ተመደበ	tämäddäbä v.i. was allotted; was put aside was stationed, put into position
አስመደበ	asmäadäbä v.t. had *(s/t, s/o)* allotted, positioned
መደብር	mädäbbər n. department store, large shop; warehouse
መደደ	mäddädä v.i. acted foolishly
መደ	mädäda n. row, series; position in line, *(often irrespective of rank)*
መደ	mädäde n. beginner, novice
መዲና	mädina n. metropolis
መዳብ	mädab n. copper
መዳፍ	mädaf n. palm *(of the hand)*
መድረክ	mädräk n. threshold; stage, platform, tribune, rostrum; forum
መደን	in የመደን ድርጅት yämädən dərəǧǧət n. insurance company see also ዳኝ
መድፍ	mädf n. cannon, artillery
መድፈኛ	mädfäñña n. artilleryman
መዶሻ	mädoša n. hammer
መጆመሪያ	see ጆመረ
መጅ	mäǧ n. upper millstone, upper grindstone; callus
መጋለ	mäggälä v.t. gave out pus *(for a wound)*
መጋላም	mäglam adj. full of pus
መጋል	mägəl n. pus
አመጋለ	amäggälä v.t. squeezed out pus
መጋመገ	mägämmägä v.t. drank greedily, with relish *(making sucking noise with lips)*
መጋበ	mäggäbä v.t. fed, gave food to
መጋቢ	mäggabi adj/n. *(one)* who feeds; catering manager ; quartermaster, administrator of a church, monastery
—መንገድ	—mängäd n. feeder-road
ምግብ	məgəb n. food, meal, nourishment, aliment
—ቤት	—bet n. restaurant, dining—room
የምግብ አዳራሽ	yäməgəb addaraš n. dining—hall
–ሽቀጣሽቀጥ መደብር	– šäqäṭašäqäṭ mädäbbər n. grocery store
—ዝርዝር	—zərzər n. menu
—ዘይት	—zäyət n. edible oil
ዋና ምግብ	ʷanna məgəb n. staple food
ተመጋበ	tämäggäbä v.t. ate, was given food
ተመጋቢ	tämäggabi adj/n. *(one)* who is fed; lodger, *(one)* supported by a household; *(one)* who eats at a hotel, restaurant
አመጋገብ	ammägagäb n. diet *(general sense)*

አስመገበ	asmäggäbä v.t. had (s/o) fed; made (s/o) eat	
መጋላ	mägäla n. market place (mainly Harar)	
መጋዝን	mägazän n. store-room, ware house	
መጋዝ	mägaz n. saw (tool for cut ing wood)	
መጋቢት	mäggabit n. March	
መጋዣ	mägaža n. pack horse	
መግላሊት	mäglalit n. clay pot lid	
መግነጢስ	mägnäṭis n. magnet also ማግኔት	
መጠመጠ	mäṭämmäṭä v.t. sucked (lemons etc.), suckled	
መጠቀ	mäṭṭäqä v.i. soared	
ምጥቀት	məṭqät n. the action of soaring	
አመጠቀ	amäṭṭäqä v.t. launched, caused to soar up	
መጠነ	mäṭṭänä v.t. judged accurately (amount), measured out the right amount	
መጠነኛ	mäṭänänña adj/n average, of medium size, medium sized, moderate, proportionate	
መጠን	mäṭän n. size, amount, measure, proportion, magnitude	
—የሌለው	—yällelläw adj. inordinate, enormous	
በተቻለ—	bätäčalä– as much as possible	
ከመጠን በላይ	kämäṭän bälay too much, unusually, beyond measure	
መጣኝ	mäṭṭänñ adj/n. (one) who judges (amounts) accurately	
ምጣኔ	mäṭṭane n. accurate judgement (of quantity)	
—ሀብት	—hcbt economy	
ምጥን	mäṭṭən n. pea, bean powder (highly	

	spiced)	
ተመጠነ	täm̈ṭṭänä v.p. was judged accurately	
ተመጣጠነ	tämäṭaṭṭänä v.i. was equal in quantity, standard; was proportionate, was comparable	
ተመጣጣኝ	tämäṭaṭañ adj/n (s/t, s/o) equal in quantity, standard, (s/t) correspondingly sufficient	
—ምግብ	—məgəb balanced diet, also የተመጣጠነ ምግብ	
አመጣጠነ	ammäṭaṭṭänä v.t. made correspondingly equal (e.g. wages equal to work)	
መጠወተ	mäṭäwwätä also መጸወተ mäṣäwwätä v.t. gave (alms to the poor)	
መጥዋች	mäṭwač adj/n. (one) who gives alms	
ምጥዋት	mäṭwat n. alms	
ምጥዋተኛ	mäṭwatänña adj/n. (one) who takes alms	
ተመጠወተ	tämäṭäwwätä v.i. was given alms	
ተመጥዋች	tämäṭwač adj/n. (one) who is given alms	
አስመጠወተ	asmäṭäwwätä v.t. caused (s/o) to receive alms	
መጠጊያ	see ተጠጋ	
መጣጣ	mäṭṭätä v.t. sucked	
መጣጭ	mäṭač adj/n. (one) who sucks	
መጣጣ	mäṭaṭa n. vinegar adj. emaciated	
ምጣጭ	mäṭṭač n. remains of sucked lemon, orange, etc.	
ተመጠጠ	tämäṭṭäṭä v.t. was sucked	
አመጠጠ	amäṭṭäṭä v.i. dried out a little (e.g. wet clothes)	
አስመጠጠ	asmäṭṭäṭä v.t. gave (s/o, s/t) to suck	

ግምጣዉ	mămṭăča n. blotting paper; wiping up cloth
መጣጥ	see ጠጣ
መጢቃ	mățiqa adj/n. crossbred, crossbred (animals, particularly sheep)
መጣ	mățța v. came
ሞጢ	mățțe adj. recent arrival
መጥ	in አዲስ መጥ addis mățț newcomer
ምጣት	məțat n. Day of Judgement
የመጣዉ ቢመጣ	yämățțaw bimăța whatever may be
—ይምጣ	—yəmța come what may!
የሚመጣዉ ሳምንት/ ዓመት	next week/ year
አመጣ	amățța v.t. brought, brought about
አማጣ	ammațța v.t. helped to bring (s/t)
አማጭ	ammač n. go-between (in marriage negotiations)
አስመጣ	asmățța v.t. had (s/t, s/o) brought
አስመጪ	asmațči adj/n. (one) who has s/o, s/t brought, importer (of goods)
አስመጪና ላኪ	asmățčinna laki n. import- export businessman
መጥፎ	see ጠፋ
መጣጢስ	mățațis n. sweet potato also በጣጢስ
መጨመጨ	măčămmăčă v.t. kissed closely
መጸወተ	măṣăwwătä v.t. gave alms to the poor also መጠወተ
መጽሐፍ	see ጸፈ
መጸዉ	măṣăw n. season after the summer rains, autumn
መገጉ'ዐ	măṣagwu'ə adj/n. cripple, handicapped, person; stunted
መፍትሔ	măftəhe n. solution (of a problem) sec ፈታ
ሙሀቻ	muhačča n. storage vessel (for the liquid dough used in making ənğăra)
ሙላ	mula n. hip-joint
ሙልሙል	mulmul adj. oblong
ሙሬ	mure or ሙሪ muri n. brush (for cleaning ground grain)
ሙርጥ	murț n. penis
ሙሴ	muse n. head of a self help fraternity (ማኅበር)
ሙሾ	mušo n. dirge, funeral chant
—አዉራጅ	—awrağ n. funeral chant leader
ሙቀጫ	muqăčča n. mortar (for grinding coffee, grain etc.), see ወቀጠ
ሙዋለጠ	muwăllățä or ጓለጠ muʷallăță v.i. became slippery; was worn smooth
ሙልጥ	mulț adj. slippery; worn smooth
ሙልጭ	mulč adj. slippery worn smooth; poverty-stricken
ሙዋላጠ	muʷalața adj. slippery
ሙዋሙዋ	muwammuwa or ጓሟ muʷammʷa v.i. dissolved, melted
ሙዋሚ	muwami adj/n. (s/t) which can be easily dissolved, melted
ሙዋርት	muwart n. pessimism
ሙዋርተኛ	muwartäñña adj pessimistic; (one) who is a prophet of doom; ill-wisher
አጓረተ	amuʷarrätä v.t foretold disaster
አጓራች	amuʷarač n. one who predicts disaster
ሙዋሸሸ	muwaššäsä or ጓሸሸ muʷaššäsä v.i. shrank, softened; became shrunken and soft

መ-ዋጠጠ	*muwaṭṭäṭä* or **ሟጠጠ** *muʷaṭṭäṭä* v.t. ate up everything *(impolite in Ethiopia)*; took every thing away	መ-ዳይ	*muday* n. small woven basket *(decorative, for buttons etc.)*
መ-ጣጭ	*muṭṭač* n. crumb, scraps cf. **ፍርፋሪ**	መ-ዳየ ምጽዋት	*mudayä məṣwat* n. alms box
ተሟጠጠ	*tämʷaṭṭäṭä* v.t. was eaten up, was removed completely	መ-ኛ	*muǧǧa* n. tall weed grass
ለዛው የተሟ ጠጠ	*läzzaw yätämuʷ-aṭṭäṭä* adj. graceless, uncouth	መ-ኛም	*muǧǧamma* adj. covered with weed grass
መ-ዋጨ	*muwaččä* or **ሟጨ** *mʷaččä* v.t. cleaned one's teeth *(especially with the small stick used in Ethiopia)*	መ-ገሰ	*see* **ሟገሰ**
		መ-ጢ	*muṭi* adj. talkative
		መ-ጢአፍ	*muṭi'af* adj. talkative *also*
መመ-ዋጫ	*mämuwača* n. s/t used to clean the teeth		**መ-ጢያፍ**
መ-ዋጨረ	*muwaččärä* or **ሟጨረ** *mʷaččärä* v.t. scratched *(with the fingernails)*; scribbled	መ-ጠኘ	*muṭṭäññ* n. protection *(e.g. aegis of a stronger person)*
		መ-ጠኘ አለ	*muṭäññ alä* v.t. sought protection; clung to *(s/o, s/t)*
መ-ጭራት መ-ጭርጭ	*muččərat* n. a scratch *mučərčər* adj/n. *(s/t)* which is scratched, scribbled		
		መ-ጫ	*muččä* n. gum, resin *(of tree)*
ሞጫጨረ	*močaččärä* v.t. scratched slightly, scribbled	ሚሊዮን	*milliyon* or **መልዮን** *mälyon* adj/ n. million
ተሟጨረ	*tämuʷaččärä* v.t. was scratched, was scribbled	ሚስት ባለና— ባለና—ቁልፍ	*mist* n. wife *balənna*—couple *balənna*—*qulf* n. press-stud
ተሞጫጨረ	*tämočaččärä* v.i. was scratched all over; was scribbled all over	ሚኒስትር ሚኒስቴር	*ministr* n. minister *minister* n. ministry
		ሚዜ	*mize* n. best man
አስሟጨረ	*asmuʷaččärä* v.t. had s/o scratched by s/t	ሚና	*mina* n. role
		ሚዳቈ	*midaqqʷa* n. bush duiker
መ-ዚቃ —ተጫወተ	*muziqa* n. music —*täčawwätä* v.t. played music	ሚዶ	*mido* n. comb
		ሚጥሚጣ	*miṭmiṭṭa* n. chilli *(pepper)*
መ-ዚቀኛ	*muziqäñña* n. musician	ማ ?	*ma* inter. pron. who?
		ማህደር	*mahədär* n. leather book case, folder, *see also* **አደራ**
መ-ዝ	*muz* n. banana		
መ-ያሌ	*muyyale* n. jigger, chigoe	ማለ ማላ	*malä* v.t. swore *(an oath)* *malla* or **መሐላ** *mähalla* n. oath
መ-ዳ	*mudda* n. hunk of meat	ማለለ ማለደ	*mallälä* v.t. implored *mallädä* v.i. went out *(early in the morning)*; was early *(in doing things)*; interceded
		ማለዳ	*maläda* n. early in the morning
		ምልጃ	*məlga* n. intercession

ተማለደ	*tāmallādā* v.i. was approachable *(as a source of help)*
መማለጃ	*mämmalağa* n. gift *(to smooth the way for intercession)*
አማለደ	*ammallādā* v.t. interceded for s/o
አማላኟ	*ammalağ* adj/n. *(one)* who makes intercession; job of being a go-between
አማላኟነት	*ammalagϵnnät* n. intercession ; job of being a go-between
መማለጃ	*mämmalağa* n. gift *(to smooth the way for intercession)*
ማለገ	*mallāgä* v.i. became sticky, viscous
ማለጋ	*malaga* adj . sticky *(e.g. dough mixture),* viscous
ማለጋነት	*malagannät* n. stickiness, gluey consistency, viscosity
ማሕሌት	*mahϵlet* n. ecclesiastical song of praise
ማሕሌተኛ	*mahϵletäñña* n. one who sings hymns of praise in church, cantor
ማሕሌታይ	*mahϵletay* n. cantor
ማጎሌተ ጋምቦ	*mahϵletä gämbo* n. priests' song in praise of founder of a feast
ቅኔ ማሕሌት	*qϵne mahϵlet* n. middle section of Ethiopian church i.e. between the Holy of Holies, corresponds to chantry of European church
ማሕፀን	*mahϵṣän* n. womb, uterus
ማሚቱ	*mammite* n. term of address for small girl
ማሚቶ	*mammito* n. echo

የጋደል—	*yägädäl*—n. echo
ማሞ	*mammo* n. form of address for small boy
ማረ	*marä* v.i. forgave, was merciful; cancelled a debt
መሐሪ	*mähari* adj. merciful
ምሕረት	*mϵhrät* n. mercy, forgiveness ; compassion
ዓመተ—	*amätä*— n. Year of Grace, Anno Domini *(A.D.)*
ያለ —	*yalä* - adv. ruthlessly
ተማረ	*tämarä* v.i.was forgiven
ተማማረ	*tämamarä* v.i. forgave each other
አስማረ	*asmarä* v.t. had *(s/o)* forgiven
ማረረ	*marrärä* v.t. gleaned, picked up
ማራሪ	*marari* adj/n. gleaner
ማረከ	*marräkä* v.t. took captive; took the attention of
ማራኪ	*maraki* adj/n. *(one)* who takes s/o captive; who is attentive, takes the attraction of
ምርኮ	*mϵrko* adj/n. *(one)* who is taken captive, booty
ምርኮኛ	*mϵrkoñña* adj /n*(one)* who is taken captive
ተማረከ	*tämarräkä* v.t. was taken captive
ተማራኪ	*tämaraki* adj/n. *(one)* who is taken captive
ማረዲያ	see ዐረዲ
ማራገቢያ	*marragäbiya* n. fan see also ረገበ
ማር	*mar* n. honey
ማርመላታ	*marmälata* n. jam, marmalade
ማርሽ	*marš* n. gear *(of car)*
ማርክ	*mark* n. grade *(in exam.)*
ማርያም	*maryam* n. Mary
ምርኩዝ	see ተመረኮዘ
ማርዳ	*marda* n. glass ring *(used as neck charm)*

34

ግሰ masā v.i. dug a hole
ግላ masa n. tilled land, farm
ግሰር masāro n. pot, pitcher (usually of earthen-ware)
ግሲንቀ masinqo or መስንቀ māsānqo n. Ethiopian single-stringed violin
ግላሰቢያ see አሰበ
ግሸላ mašəlla n. white sorghum
የባሕር— yābahər- n. maize, also ባርግሸላ
ግሸንk mašənk adj. spiteful, vicious
ግቀቀ maqqāqā v.i. languished (in prison)
ግቅ maq n. coarse woollen cloth
ግተብ matāb n. neck-band (worn under the shirt, sign of Christianity); religion (Christian)
ግቲ mati n. crowd of small children
ግታ mata evening
የግታ— yāmata—at last, at the end
ግቲግቲk matematik n. mathematics
ግት mat also መዐት mā'at n. wrath of God; multitude, crowd of people
ግቶት matot n. coffee-pot stand
ግኅበር mahəbār n. association; self-help group; company see አበረ
ግኅበር (ረ) ተኛ mahəbār(ä)täñña n. member of a society, association, self-help group;
ግኅበራዊ mahəbārawi adj. social; pertaining to society or group;
ኅብረት həbrāt n. unity; union
ኅብረተሰብ həbrātā sāb n. society
ግኅተም mahətām n. seal, rubber stamp, see አተመ
ግን man inter. adj. who

ግንም manəmm pron. nobody, not anyone, not anything; anybody, anyone, everyone
ግንኛውም mannəññawəm pron. whoever
ግን አለብኝ ባይ man allābbəññ bay n. despot
ግንዘራሽ manzārraš n. riff-raff, street-boy, person of no family
እነግን ənnāmann pron. pl. who?
ግንቀርቀርያ see አንቀረቀረ
ግንቀርት manqurt n. Adam's apple
ግንቀርታም manqurtam n. person who has a large Adam's apple
ግንካ manka also መንኪ፣ግንኪያ n. spoon
ግክሰኛ see ግግሰኛ
ግዐረግ ma'ərāg n. rank, title
ግዐረግ ቢስ ma'ərāgā bis n. one who acts below his station, in an un-dignified way
ግዐረገኛ ma'ərāgāñña or ግረ ገኛ marāgāñña n. a pretentious person, one who gives himself airs
ግዐቀብ ma'əqāb n. sanction
ግዐበል ma'əbāl n. storm (at sea)
ግዐከል ma'əkāl n. centre
ግዐከላዊ ma'əkālawi adj. central
—መንግሥት —māngəst n. central government
ግዐዘን ma'əzān n. corner, angle
ግዐዘን ዓለም ma'əzānā alām n. cardinal points of the compass
ግዐድ ma'ədd n. the meal-table also ግድ madd
—ቤት —bet also ግድቤት madbet n. kitchen
ግዐድን ma'əddən n. mine; minerals
ግድቤት see ግዐድ
ግየ ዐይግ mayā ayh n. Noah's flood (lit. water of destruction)

35

<table>
<tr><td>

ግይል — *mayl* n. mile (*English distance measure*)

ግይክሮስኮፕ — *mavkroskopp* n. microscope

ግደያ — see እደለ

ግድያት — *madiyat* n. blemish

ግድያታም — *madyatäm* n. blemished

ግድጋ — *madəgga* n. large water pot (*earthenware*)

ግዶ — *mado* adv. opposite; yonder

ባሕር— — *bahər* — n. abroad

ግጆት — *mağät* n. larder

ግጆራት — *mağərät* n. nape of the neck

—መቺ — *—mäči* n. gangster

ግጎ — *magä* v.t. drunk

እግጎ — *amagä* v.t. sipped loudly, sucked up (*to wash down food which is difficult to swallow*)

ግግጊያ — *mamagiya* n. a drink to wash down food

ግገረ — *maggärä* v.t. fitted reinforcing beams (*in house walls*)

ግገር — *magär* n. wall reinforcing beam

ተግገረ — *tämaggärä* v. i. was fitted with reinforcing beams

እግገረ — *ammaggärä* v.t. helped (*s/o*) to reinforce a wall

እስግገረ — *asmaggärä* v.t. had (*a wall*) fitted with reinforcing beams

ግገዶ — *maggädä* v.t. stoked up, fuelled (*e.g a wood burning oven*)

ግገዶ — *magädo* n. firewood

ተግገዶ — *tämaggädä* v.i. was stoked up, fuelled

ግገጠ — *maggäṭä* v.i. became idle, lax in, lazy in his work

ግጋግ — *magaṭa* adj. idle, slack, lazy

</td><td>

ግጋጣነት — *magaṭannät* n. idleness

ግጋጭ — *magač* adj. idle, slack, lazy

ግጋጭነት — *magačännät* n. idleness

እግገጠ — *amaggäṭä* v.t. influenced (*s/o*) to be lazy, idle, spoiled (*a child*)

እግጋጭ — *amagač* adj/n. (*one*) who influences (*s/o*) to be idle, lazy; (*s/t*) that spoils (*a child*)

ግግ — *mag* n. weft (*in cloth weaving*), woof

ግግሥት — *magəst* n. the morrow, the next day

በግግሥቱ — *bämagəstu* the following morning, the following day

ግግሰኞ — *magsäñño* also ግከሰኞ *maksäñño* n. Tuesday

ግጠ — *maṭ* n. swampy place, bog

ግጣም — *maṭam* adj. swampy, boggy

ግዐይድ — *mačäd* n. sickle see እጨደ

ሜትር / መተረ — *metər* n. metre / *mättärä* v.t. measured (*with a metre*)

ሜንጦ — *menṭo* n. hook

ሜካኒክ — *mekanik* n. mechanic

ሜዳ — *meda* n. field, grassy plain

የጦር— — *yaṭor* —n. battlefield

ሜዳግ — *medamma* n. level plain, level ground

ሜዳ ፍየል — *meda fəyyäl* n. gazelle

ሜዳይ — *meday* n. medal

ሜጀር ጀኔራል — *meğär general* n. major-general

—ም — *—m* suffix. also, too and

ምሁር — *məhur* n. intellectual, learned, scholar

ምህዋር — *məhwar* n. orbit see ሰወ

</td></tr>
</table>

ምስራች massaračč n. good tidings, good news

ምሥራቅ masraq n. East

መካከለኛው— mäkakkälänñaw— the Middle-East

ምሥራቃዊ masraqawi n Eastern

ምስጢር mastir n. secret: private affairs

ምስጢረኛ mastirähña n. confidant

ምስጢራዊ mastirawi adj. confidential, secret

በምስጢር bämastir adv. confidentially

ምራቅ maraq n. saliva

ምራቁን የዋጠ maraqun yäwata adj. well-experienced (in life): serious - minded

ምራት marat n. daughter-in-law, sister-in -law

ምር marr n. in የምር yämarr adj. serious e.g. የም ራን ነው I am serious

ምርቅ marq n. beard (of grain).

ምሰሶ masässo n. central-pillar (of traditional Ethiopian house)

ምሳ masa n. lunch

ምሳር massar n. axe

ምስ mass ñ. personal preference, thing one likes most (zar etc.)

ምስማር masmar or ሚስማር mismar n. nail (carpentry etc.)

ምስሪት massarit n. lens

ምስጥ mast n. termite

ምሽት mašt see also ሚስት mist n. wife

ምሽት maššat n. evening see መሽ

ምቀኛ maqqañña adj. envious, spiteful

ምቀኝነት maqqäññannät n. envy, spite

ምኑ manu inter adj. pron. which ?

ምናልባት manalbat adv. perhaps

ምናምን manaman pron. something; anything; nothing

ምናምንቴ manamante adj. degraded, worthless (of people)

ምን! man int. adj. pron. what ?

ምንም manamm pron. nothing

ምንኛ manañña conj. phrase however...., whatever

ምን ቆርጦኝ man qortoñ I wouldn't dare do such a thing (except that... this phrase introduces an excuse)

— አለበት – alläbät what does it matter? what is wrong with it ?

—አልባት –albat also ምናል ባት manalbat adv. perhaps, possibly

ምንድን manddan n. interj. adj. what !

ምንኛ manañña excl. how.!

ምን ገዶኝ man gäddoñ excl. phr. what do I care

ለምን läman what for ?

ስለምን saläman why?

በምን ጊዜ bäman gize when ?

ምንቻት mančät n. clay amphora (medium sized, for making talla)

ምንዳኛ mandäñña n. hired shepherd

ምንዳ manda n. wages (for hired shepherd), wage

ምንጅላት managallat n. great-great grand-mother, great- great grandfather

ምንጭር mančar n. lower lip

ምንጣፍ see * ነጠፈ

ምኞት mañňot n. wish, desire, aspiration, ambition, see ተመኝ

ምኩራብ makurab n. synagogue

ምዕራብ ma'arab n. west

ምዕራባዊ	*mə'rabawi* western
—በስተ **ምዕራብ**	*bästä mə'rab* towards the West
ምዕራፍ	*mə'əraf* n. chapter, see also ዐረፈ
ምድር	*mədər* n. earth, country, land
የምድር ወገብ	*yämədər wägäb* n. equator, *also* የምድ ስቅ
—**ዋልታ**	*walta* n. pole
ምድረ በዳ	*mədrä bäda* n. wilderness, desert
ምድራዊ	*mədrawi* adj. earthly, óf the earth
ምድጃ	*mədəǧǧa* n. oven, fireplace
ምግባር	*məgbar* n. virtue
ምጣድ	*see* ጣደ
ምጥ	*məṭ* n. labour (pains of childbirth)
አጣ	*amaṭa* v.t was in labour
ምጥግጥ	*see* ሽለምጥግጥ
ምጸት	*məṣṣät* n. irony
ምጽአት	*məṣ'at also* ምጣት *məṭat* n. the second Advent, Judgement Day, the second coming of Christ *see* መጣ
ሞለለ	*mollälä* v. was oval, egg-shaped; was sausage-shaped
ሙሰል አለ	*muləll alä* v. was slightly oval, egg-shaped
ሞላላ	*molala* adj. oval, egg-shaped; sausage-shaped
ሞላላነት	*molallannät* n. oval shape; sausage shape
ሞለሞለ	*molämmolä* v. was oval, egg-shaped, sausage-shaped
ሙልሙል	*mulmul* adj. oval egg-shaped, sausage-shaped
ሞልጓላ	*molmʷalla* adj. sausage shaped
ሞለቀቅ	*moläqäq* adj. spoiled (child), *also* ሞላቃቃ
ሞለጨ	*molläčä* v.t. cropped

	close *(hair, grass etc)*
ሙልለጭ	*mulllač* n. last scrap *(soap, etc.)*
ሙልጭን ወጣ	*muluč̣un wäṭṭa* v.t. went broke, was bankrupt
ሙልጭ	*mulč̣* adj. destitute, having lost everything
ሞላጫ	*mollač̣č̣a* n. swindler, dishonest, cheater
ተሞለጨ	*tämolläč̣ä* v.t. was robbed completely, was fleeced
አሞለጨ	*amolläč̣ä* v.i. slipped (e.g wet soap from grasp)
አጓላጭ	*amuʷalač̣* adj. slippery
ሞለፈጠ	*moläffäṭä* v.i. laughed inanely, laughed for nothing cf. ገለፈጠ
ሞልፈጣ	*molfaṭṭa* adj. given to inane laughter
ተሞለፈጠ	*tämolaffäṭä* v.i laughed inanely, pointlessly
ሞላ	*molla also* መላ *mälla* v.i. v.t was full, became full; filled out, filled up; was plentiful; overflew; charged (battery); wound (a watch)
ሙሉ	*mulu* adj. full, whole complete
—**ልብስ**	*ləbs* n. suit
—**ቁጥር**	*quṭər* n. even number
—**በሙሉ**	*bämulu* adv. entirely, fully, completely, wholly
በሙሉ/ በሞላ	*bämulu/ bämolla* adv. entirely, fully, in full, all over
—**ልብ**	*ləbb* adv. wholeheartedly
ከሞላ ጎደል	*kämolla goddäl* by and large, roughly, approximately, more or less
አሞላ	*amolla* v.i. was fattened

38

ሙላት   *mulat* n. extent to which s/t. is filled; overflow; abundance

የወሃ—   *yäwəha*—n. flood

መሙያ   *māmuya* n. device for, means of filling; noun in apposition

ሞላላ   *molalla* v.t poured out (e.g. from glass to glass)

ተሞላ   *tämolla* v.p. was filled

ተጓላ   *täm"alla* v.i. was successful (in an enterprise, undertaking, etc.;) was complete, was done completely

የተጓላ   *yätämu"alla* adj. full, exhaustive, complete, perfect

ያልተጓላ   *yaltämu"alla* adj. incomplete, imperfect, inadequate

አጓላ   *amm"alla* v.t. made up (a sum of money) to the required amount; completed, met the need

ማጓያ   *mamm"aya* n. means of making up to required amount; complement (gram.)

አሞላላ   *ammolalla* v.t. filled up (one vessel, container, from several partially full)

አስሞላ   *asmolla* v.t. has s/o fill

ሞረሞረ   *morämmorä* v.i. was extremely hungry, felt the pangs of extreme hunger

ሞረደ   *morrädä* v.t. filed s/t (i.e. with a metal file)

መረዳ   *murräda* n. action of filing

ሞረድ   *morād* n. file (metal)

ተሞረደ   *tämorrädä* v.i. was filed

አስሞረደ   *asmorrädä* v.t. had (s/t) filed

ሞራ   *mora* n. abdominal fat

ሞራል   *moral* n. morale, morals

ሞርሳ   *morsa* n. mandrel, clamp (It.)

ሞሻለቀ   *mošälläqä* v.t. burned scalded (e.g. with boiling water)

ሞሻላቃ   *mošlaqqa* adj. n. utterly dishonest, without scruple; persistently and deliberately untruthful

ተሞሻለቀ   *tämošälläqä* v.t. was scalded, badly burned; was robbed completely

ሞሻረ   *moššärä* v.t. accommodated and entertained newly wed couple

መሻረት   *mušərrit* n. bride

መሻሬ   *muššərra* n. bride groom

ተሞሻሬ   *tämoššärä* v. spent (one's honeymoon)

ሞቀ   *moqä* v.i. got hot, became warm (weather),

ሞቀኝ   *moqäññ* I feel hot

ሞቀው   *moqäw* felt warm; got slightly drunk

እሳት ሞቀ   *əsat moqä* warmed oneself by the fire

ፀሐይ—   *şähai*—warmed oneself in the sun

መቅ   *muq* adj. hot, warm; n. thick broth (made mainly of flour and butter)

መቀት   *muqāt* n. heat, temperature, warmth

ሞቃት   *moqqat* adj. warm, hot

አሞቀ   *amoqä* v.t. warmed s/t.), made s/t warm, heated up, kept warm

ማሞቂያ   *mamoqiya* n. heater, device for heating

ተጓጓቀ   *täm"am"aqä* v.t. gave warmth to each other, reached a climax (party, ceremony, song etc.)

የተጓጓቀ   *yätämu"amu"aqä* adj. animated, full of cheer

አጓጓቀ ** amm^wam^waqä** v.t. caused *(s t)* to reach its climax: made *(the party)* go, gave life, enlivened up *(a party etc.)*

አጓጓቂ **amm^wam^waqi** n. one who makes a party lively, gets things going

አስሞቀ **asmoqä** v.t. had *(s t)* warmed

ሞቀሞቀ **moqämmoqä** v.i. became morbid, infected *(of wound)* ; became rotten *(fruit etc.)*

ሙቅሙቅ **muqmuq** adj. swollen, morbid, full of pus *(wound)*; rotten *(fruit etc.)*

ሞቅጓቀ **moqm^waqqa** adj. swollen, full of pus *(wound)*; rotten *(fruit etc.)*

ሞቅጓቀ ዐይን **moqm^waqqa ayn** n. adj. rheumy-eyed *(person)*

አሞቀሞቀ **amoqämmoqä** v.i. became morbid, infected *(of wound; became rotten (fruit etc.)*

ሞተ **motä** v.i. died

ሙት **mut** adj. dead; adv. Truly! Certainly! *(col.)*

አባተ ይሙት **abbate yəmut** I give you my word of honour

የሙት ልጅ **yämut ləǧ** n. orphan

የሞት ቅጣት **yämot qəṭat** death penalty

—ፍርድ **—fərd** death sentence

ይሙት **yəmut** ——

በቃ ፍርድ **bäqqa fərd** capital punishment

ሙትያ **mutəčča** adj. inactive, lazy, lacking initiative

ሞት **mot** n. death

ሞኖፖል **monopol** n. monopoly

ሞኝ **mofiñ** adj. fool, silly, foolish

ሞከረ **mokkärä** v.t. tried, tested, attempted

ሞካሪ **mokkari** n/adj. *(one)* who tries, tests

ሙከራ **mukkära** n. trial, test

ተሞከረ **tämokkärä** v.t. made a trial, test *(often of strength, skill etc.)* between one another

ተጓከረ **täm^wakkärä** v.t. tried each other out, had a test of strength

ተሞካከረ **tämokakkärä** v.i. tried each other out, put each other to the test

አሞካከረ **ammokakkärä** v.t. caused *(s o), (s t)* to be tested, tried out

አጓከረ **amm^wakkärä** v.t. caused *(people)* to have a mutual test *(strength etc.)*

አስሞከረ **asmokkärä** v.t. had *t/s* tried out

ሞከተ **mokkätä** v.t. fattened up *(sheep, goat)*

ሞካች **mokkač** n. adj. *(one)* who fattens up *(sheep goat)*

ሙከት **mukkət** n. animal which is fattened up *(sheep, goat)*

ተሞከተ **tämokkätä** v.t. was fattened up *(sheep, goat)*

አስሞከተ **asmokkätä** v.t. had *(sheep, goat)* fattened up

ሞከከ **mokkäkä** also ጓከከ **m^wakkäkä** v.i. was overcooked, overripe, overfed *(flabby)*

ሙከክ አለ **mukəkk alä** v.i. be extremely overcooked, overripe, overfed *(flabby)*

ሞክሼ **mokše** n. namesake

ሞዘዘ **mozzäzä** v.i. became unbearably boring, oppressive *(speech behaviour)*; became importunate

ሞዛዛ **mozaza** adj. importunate, boring, oppressive *(speech, behaviour)*

40

ምዛዛነት mozazannät n. tire-
someness, importunity,
quality of being
boring, dullness

ሙዝዝ አለ muzəzz alä v.i. became boring, tiresome

ሞያ moya or ሙያ muya n.
special, ability, craft,
profession

ሞያተኛ moyatäñña n. daily
labourer

ባለሞያ balämoya adj. n.
(one) who is skilled
well-trained, who has
wide experience, expert

ሞዴል model n. design, model

ሞጸረ moǧǧärä v.t. overfilled,
filled to excess

ሙጸር mugǧarr adärrägä
አደረገ v.t. overfilled hastily,
pour in more than
one wanted to (by
mistake)

ተሞጸረ tämoǧǧärä v.t.
poured in too great
a quantity

*ሞገሰ *moggäsä

ሞገስ mogäs n. appreci-
ation, liking

ግርማ ሞገስ gərma mogäs n. dignity, high esteem

አሞገሰ amoggäsä v.t. spoke
well (of s/o)

አሞጋሽ amoggaš n/adj. (one)
who speaks well of
another

አሞጋገሰ amogaggäsä v.t. spoke
well of s/o often, fre-
quently

ተሞገሰ tämoggäsä v.t. was
spoken of, praised

ተሞጋሽ tämoggaš n. adj. (one)
who is praised,
honoured

ተሞጋገሰ tämogaggäsä v.t.
praised, spoke well of
each other

ሞገተ moggätä v.t. made
a case against s/o
(in court); disputed,
argued

ሞጋች moggač n/ adj. (one)

who makes a case
against s/o (in court):
(one) who disputes
argues

ሙግት muggət n. argument,
dispute (e.g. before
a judge)

ተሞገተ täm*äggätä v.t. made
a case against s/o;
disputed, argued

ተሞጋች täm*agač n. s/o
who represents an-
other in court (not
necessarily a lawyer);
one skilled in pre-
senting legal cases

አሟገተ amm*aggätä v.t. arbitrated

አሟጋች amm*agač n. arbi-
traior (legal)

አስሞገተ asmoggätä v.t. caused
s/o to be accused
before the court

ሞገደ moggädä v.t. made
trouble; caused a
storm; made diffi-
culties

ሞገደኛ mogädäñña n. trouble
maker

ሞገድ mogäd n. wave, tide

ሞገገ moggägä v.i. became
emaciated, wasted
away

ሞጋጋ mogaga adj. em-
aciated, thin cheecked,
thin faced

ሙገግ ያለ mugəgg yalä v.i. very
thin faced, extremely
emaciated, ugly

ሞግዚት mogzit n. nurse (for
children); guardian,
trustee

*ሞጠሞጠ *moțämmoțä

ሞጠሞጥ moțämoț adj. agres-
sive in speech and
facial expression

ሞጥማጣ moțm*ațța adj. agressive in speech, having
a tendency to thrust
the fact at one's op-
ponent in argument

ሙጢ አፍ muți af adj. agressive
in speech and facial
expression

41

አፕጠፕጠ	amoṭämmoṭä v.t. had protruding lips; was insulting, attacked s/o with words
ፕዉለፈ	močälläfä v.t. grabbed, snatched by force, rav shed (with the extra meaning of, «grabbed and ran off»)
ፕቍላፈ	močlafi n. thief
ሙፕለፈ	mučläfa n. robbery
ተፕዉለፈ	tämočälläfä v.i. was robbed, stolen, snatched
አስፕዉለፈ	asmočälläfä v.t. had s/t stolen
ፕዉፕዉ	močämmočä also መዉ መዉ mäčämmäčä v.i. streamed, were runny (of the eyes only)

ፕቝጎግ	mocmʷaččä or መቝ ግግ mäčmaččä adj./ n. (one) who is rheumy-eyed
ፕፈC	mofär n. beam of plough ፕፈC ዘመት አርሻ mofär zämmät ärša cultivated land far away from the farmer's house
ጎለጠ	muʷalläṭä v.i. slipped from the hand, was slippery, also አጎለጠ
ጎጎ	muʷammuʷa v.i. was dissolved in water
ጎጠጠ	muʷaṭṭäṭä v. t. scraped
ጎዉፈ	muʷaččärä v.t. scratched

ሠ

ሠለሰ	sälläsä v.t. did (s/t) on alternate days; made sauce thinner by adding water
ሣልስ	saləs n. the third order of the Amharic vowel system
ሡሉስ	səllus adj. threefold, triple
ሡላሴ	səllase n. the Holv Trinity
ሠለስት	säläst or saləst ሣለ ስት n. third day after funeral (in Ethiopia obligatory day to visit bereaved)
ሦስት	sost adj. three
አሠለሰ	asälläsä v.t. did s/t on alternate days
ሠለጠ	sälläṭä v.t. meddled in everyone's affairs; had a finger in every pie
ሠላጠ	sällaṭṭe n. bay
ሡሉጥ	səlluṭ adj. meddlesome, interfering, nosey
ሠለጠነ	säläṭṭänä v.i. became

	skilled, was well trained; acquired power; became civilised
ሡልጣን	sulṭan n. Sultan
ሡልጡን	səlṭun adj. well trained; highly competent
ሡልጣን ሰጠ	səlṭan säṭṭä v.t. authorized, gave power
ባለሡልጣን	bäläsəlṭan n. authority) official
ባለሡልጣኖች	bäläsəlṭanočč n. authorities
ባለሙሉ ሡልጣን	balä mulu səlṭan plenipotentiary
ሡልጣኔ	sälläṭṭane n. civilisation
አሠለጠነ	asäläṭṭänä v.t. trained (s/o), coached (for sport); made (s/o) civilised
አሠልጣኝ	asälṭaññ n. trainer, coach
ሠለዳ	säleda n. wooden board
የመኪና—	yämäkina–n. car plate

የማስታ	yămastawăqīya — n. notice board, bulletin board		
ወቂያ—			
ጊዜ—	gize — n. multiplication table		
ጥቁር—	ʃǝqur — n. blackboard		
ሠመረ	sämmärä v.i. reached successful conclusion (work, scheme, plan etc.)		
አሠመረ	asämmärä v.t. ruled (e.g. line, margin)		
ማስመሪያ	masmäriya n. rule, ruler		
መሥመር	mäsmär line,		
—መከፈቻ	—mäkfäča n. area code number (telephone)		
—ኛኛ	—daňňa n. linesman		
አሠግመረ	asämammärä v.t. ruled a line ; put things in order		
ተሠመረ	täsämmärä v.i. was ruled (line)		
ሠረሠረ	särässärä v.t. bored (a hole)		
ሠርሣሪ	särsari n. burglar		
መሠርሠሪያ	mäsärsäriya n. borer (tool)		
ተሠረሠረ	täsärässärä v.i. was bored		
ሠረገ	särrägä v.i. sank, went down; penetrated infiltrated; permeated		
ሠርጎ ገባ	särgo gäbba v.i. infiltrated		
—ገባ	—gäbb n. infiltrator		
ሠረገ	särrägä v.t. prepared a wedding		
ሠራጊ	särragi n. / adj. s/o who prepares a wedding		
ሠርግ	särg n. wedding		
ተሠረገ	täsärrägä v.i. were bride and bridegroom		
ሠራ	särra v.t. made, worked, did, manufactured, operated; built; have an effect (medicine)		

ሠሪ	säri n. one who does s/t, e.g ቤት ሠሪ one who builds a house
ሠራተኛ	särratäňňa n. worker, labourer, employee
የመንግሥት—	yämängǝst—n. civil servant
መሥሪያ ቤት	mäsriya bet n. office, department (of government)
ሥራ	sǝra n. work, job occupation, labour, task, act, deed; action, employment
—በዛበት	—bäzzabbät was too busy
—ያዘ	—yazä v.i. was busy was employed
—ገባ	—gäbba got work, was employed
—ፈታ	—fätta was out of work
—ፈት	—fätt adj. unemployed, jobless
በሥራ ላይ አዋለ	put into practice, used
የሥራ ቀን	yäsǝra qän n. weekday
—ጓደኛ	—guʷaddäňňa n. colleague
የቤት ሥራ	yäbet sǝra n. home work, house work
የእጅ—	yä'ǝǧǧ—n. handicraft
ሠርግ	särg n. wedding
ሠቀሠቀ	säqässäqä v.i. levered up; lifted (e.g. bread, eggs from cooking plate with slice)
መሠቅሠቂያ	mäsäqsäqiya n. lever; cooking slice etc. (anything used to lift off, lever s/t up)
ተሠቀሠቀ	täsäqässäqä v. i. was levered up
ተንሠቀሠቀ	tänsäqässäqä v.i, cried ones heart out, sobbed bitterly

ሠቀቀ	säqqäqä v.t. horrified shocked s/o *(i.e. a cruel, abhorent act or sight)*	ሠየመ	säyyämä v.t. named, gave *(s/o)* a name
ሠቀቀን	säqäqän n. deep sadness, desolation, melancholy	ሠያሚ	säyyami n. adj. one who gives names
ሠቀቀናም	säqäqänam adj. pessimistic, melancholic *(of person)*	ሥያሜ	säyyame, n. nomenclature, terminology
ሥቅቅ አለ	səqəqq alä v.i. was shocked, was horrified	·ተሠየመ	täsäyyämä v.t. was given a name, was assigned to a particular court *(for judges)*
ሠቀጠጠ	säqäṭäṭä v.t. grated, squeaked, screeched *(e.g. of harsh noise such as chalk on blackboard, of rusty hinges)*	አሠየመ	assäyyämä v.t. had s/o given a name
		ሠዶቃ	sdädqa n. basketwork table, ənğära stand; muslim commemoration of the dead
ሠወረ	säwwärä v.t. concealed kept out of sight, hid	ሠገረ	säggärä v.t. trotted *(of mules only)*
ሠዋሪ	säwwarra n/adj. hidden out of sight *(place etc.)*	ሠጋር	säggar adj. trotting, which can trot
ሥውር	səwwər adj. hidden, out of sight, concealed	ሠጋሪ	sägari n/adj. trotting
ዐይነ—	aynä— adj/n: blind, sightless	አሠገረ	assäggärä v.t. made *(a mule)* to trot
ሠወርዋራ	säwärwarra adj. very hidden, inaccessible *(place, road etc.)*	አሠጋሪ	asgari n adj. *(one)* who makes a mule trot
ዕፀ መሠውር	əṣä mäsäẉwər n. magical plant said to be used to make objects disappear	ዓሣ—አሠጋገር	asa- n. a fisherman assägagär n. style of trotting *(for mule)*
ተሠወረ	täsäwwärä v.t. was concealed, hidden, kept out of sight	ሠጋ	sägga v.t. was, became anxious, uneasy in mind
ተሠዋሪ	täsäwwari adj. liable to disappear	ሥጉ	səgu n/adj. anxious
ሠዋ	säwwa v.t. sacrificed	ሥጋት	səgat n. anxiety, apprehension, fear, worry
ሠዊ	säwwi n./adj one who sacrifices	አሠጋ	asägga v.t. made anxious, caused fear, caused apprehension,
መሥዋዕት	mäswa'ət n. sacrifice		
መሥዋዕትነት	mäswa'ətənnät n. act of sacrificing, of being sacrificed, sacrifice	አሥጊ	asgi n/adj. worrying; causing fear, critical, serious, alarming, dangerous
መሠዊያ	mäsäwwiya n. place of sacrifice; an altar	አሠጋ	assägga v.t. worried *(s/o,)* made *(s/o)* anxious
ተሠዋ	täsäwwa v.i. was sacrificed, was offered as a sacrifice	ሢሶ—አራሽ	siso adj. one third araš a tenant that pays one third of his farm yield to the land owner
አሠዋ	assäwwa v.t. had s/o sacrificed	ሣለ	salä v.t. drew, painted *(pictures)*

44

<table>
<tr><td>ሠዓሊ</td><td>sä'ali n/adj. one who draws pictures, artist</td><td>—እልባ</td><td>—alba n. anarchist</td></tr>
</table>

ሠዓሊ   *sä'ali* n/adj. one who draws pictures, artist

ሠዓሊነት   *sä'alinnät* n. art (the state of being artist)

ሥዕል   *sə'əl* n. picture, drawing

መሣያ   *mäsaya* n. brush, pencil (any painting or drawing instrument)

ተሣለ   *täsalä* v.t. was drawn (picture)

አሣለ   *assalä* v.t. had (a picture) drawn, painted

ሣሣ   *sassa* v.i. grew thin; became greedy

ሣሡ   *səssu* n/adj. greedy

ሣስ   *səs* adj. thin; fine (cloth etc.)

ሥሥነት   *səsənnät* n. thinness

ሥሥት   *səssət* n. greed, cupidity

አሣሣ   *asassa* v.. made thin, thinned out (plants); had sentimental value for (s/o)

ሣር   *sar* n. grass

ሣርማ   *sarəmma* adj. grassy

ሣር ቅጠል   *sar qəṭäl* (pron.) everyone

ሣጥን   *saṭən* n. box, chest

ቁም—   *qum — n.* cupboard; wardrobe

ሥራ   *səra* n. work; duty; job; profession

ሥር   *sər* n. root: source

ቀይ—   *qäyy—n.* beet root

ሥራሥር   *sərasər* n. various roots

ሥርቻ   *səračča* n. nook along the wall

ሥርዓት   *sər'at* n. order; etiquette, procedure, formality, discipline, system, regulation

---

—እልባ   —*alba* n. anarchist

ሥርዓተ አልባነት   *sər'atä albannät* n anarchism

-ትምህርት   *-təmhərt* n. curriculum

ነጥብ   —*nətəb* n. punctuation

ሥርዓት   —*sər'at valellä* adj. unmannerly, disorganized

ሥርወ ቃል   *sərwä qal* n. stem of a word)

ሥን   *sən* n. (G.) beauty

ሥነ ልቡና   *sänä ləbbuna* n. psychology

— ሕይወት   —*həywät* biology

ምግባር   *mägbar* n. ethical behaviour, virtue, good deeds

— ምግብ   —*məgəb* n. nutrition (the science of food value)

— ሥርዓት   —*sər'at* n. ceremony, protocol; order, procedure

— ጥበብ   —*ṭəbäb* n. fine arts

— ጽሑፍ   —*ṣəhuf* n. literature, belles lettres

— ፈለክ   —*fäläk* n. astronomy

— ፍጥረት   —*fəṭrät* n. nature, natural sciences

ሥጋ   *säga* n. meat

—ሻጭ   *səga šač* n. butcher

—በል   —*bäll* adj. carnivorous

ሥጋዊ   *səgawi* adj. carnal

ሥጋ ዘመድ   *səga zämäd* n. blood relative

—አምላክ   —*amlak* n. Host; Holy Communion

—ደዌ   —*däwe* n. leprosy

—ወይሙ   —*wädämu* n. Host; Holy Communion

ኅፍረተ—   *hafrätä* – n. genitals

ጥሬ—   *ṭare* – n. raw meat

ሦስት   *sost* adj. three

ሦስተኛ   *sostäñña* adj. third

ረ

ረመጠ	rämmäṭä v. t. baked (by putting into hot ashes of fire)
ረመጥ	rämäṭ n. hot ashes
ርምጦ	rəmmiṭo n. bread (baked in hot ashes)
ርምጥምጥ	rəmaṭmaṭ n. slattern (person who is never really clean)
ተርመጠመጠ	tärmäṭämmäṭä v. i. was always engaged in dirty work; was always too busy in the kitchen
አርመጠመጠ	armäṭämmaṭä v.t. did (s/t) in a slovenly way
ረሞጭ	rämoča adj. hot, burning (of ashes)
ረሰረሰ	räsärräsä v.t. mowed down (grass, men in war etc.)
ርስርስ	rəsrəs adj. mown flat
ርሰራሽ	rəsərraš n/adj. s/t lying flat
ረሳ	rässa v.i. forgot, left s/t, s/o behind
ሞት የረሳው	mot yärässaw n. a very old man
ረሺ	räši n/adj. forgetful (person)
ተረሳ	tärässa v.i. was forgotten, left behind
ተረሳሳ	täräsassa v.i. became forgotten (due to the passage of time), forgot each other
አረሳሳ	arräsassa v.t. distracted; took (s/o's) attention from (s/t)
አስረሳ	asrässa v.t. made (s/o) forget
ረሳን	rässänä v.t. executed by shooting, gunned down
ረሽ	räš n. shot gun
ረቀቀ	räqqäqä v.i. grew thin; was drafted (letter, agreement etc.)
ረቂቅ	räqiq adj. thin; fine, delicate (of fabrics;) draft (of letter etc.)
ረቂቅነት	räqiqənnät n. thinness, fineness
ርቀት	rəqqät n. fineness; depth (of thinking), subtlety
አረቀቀ	aräqqäqä v.t. drafted (piece of writing)
ተረቀቀ	täraqqäqä v. . was subtle, deep (in thought); was casuistic, casuistical
ተረቃቂ	täraqaqi adj/n. (one who is) subtle, deep; casuistic
አስረቀቀ	asräqqäqä v.t. caused (letter etc.) to be drafted
ረበረበ	räbärräbä v.t. stacked, corded (wood); laid, set (fire, ready for lighting)
ርብራብ	rəbrab n. lattice, framework; scaffold
ርብርብ	rəbrəb or ርብራብ rəbrab adj./n. piled, corded (wood)
ተረበረበ	täräbärräbä v.i. was stacked, laid (of wood)
ተረባረበ	täräbarräbä v.i. piled on each other (of children playing); rushed in
አስረበረበ	asräbärräbä v.t. had (s/t) piled up, stacked
ረበሸ	räbbäšä v.t. disturbed, annoyed
ረብሻ	räbša n. riot, brawl
ረብሻኛ	räbšäñña n. rioter, riotous
ረበበ	räbbäbä v.i. hovered
ረባቢ	räbabi adj. hovering
ረቡዕ	räbu'ə or ሮብ rob n. Wednesday
ረባ	räbba v. i. multiplied (of animals etc.); be profitable; be useful, be fertile (cattle)

ረብ	*räb* n. gain profit, usefulness		*disease e.g.)*
(እ)ርባታ	*(ə)rbata* n. animal husbandry; conjugation *(gram.)*	ረኃብ	*see* ራብ
		ረከሰ	*räkkäsä* v.i. was cheap; was impure, was defiled
እርባና	*ərbana* n. usefulness		
ርቢ.	*rəbbi* n. animal husbandry; cattle breeding	ርኩስ	*rəkus also* እርኩስ *ərkus* adj. impure unclean; vicious
መርቢያ	*märbiya* n. breeding ground	ርካሽ	*räkkaš* adj. cheap, inexpensive; of low quality
አረባ	*aräbba* v. t. bred, caused to breed, multiply; engaged ın animal husbandry	አረከሰ	*aräkkäsä* v.t. profaned, defiled, debased; devaluated
ገሥ—	*gəss*—v.t. conjugated a verb	* ረከበ	**räkkäbä*
		ተረከበ	*täräkkäbä* v.t. took over, received
የግሥ እርባታ	*yägəss ərbata* n. conjugation of a verb	አስረከበ	*asräkkäbä* v. t. delivered, handed over
አርቢ.	*arbi usually preceeded by* ከብት *käbt* n. cattle breeder, animal breeder, cattleman	*ረከፈከፈ	**see* እርከፈከፈ.
		ረካ	*räkka* v.i. was satisfied,
		አረካ	*aräkka* v.t. satisfied, made contented; gave *(s/o)* his fill *(e.g. food, drink)*
አይረ ባም	*ayräbam* he is good for nothing, he is useless	ረኸጥ	*rähäṭ* adj. lazy, dull bovine, stupid, slovenly *(usually of a women)*
የማይረባ ነገር	*yämmayräba nägär* nonsense, trifle	ረኸጥነት	*rähäṭənnät* n. laziness, slovenliness, stupidity
ተረባ	*täräbba* v. multiplied, increased *(of animals)*	ረዘመ	*räzzämä* v.i. lengthened out, became extended
መራቢያ	*märrabiya* n. breeding ground	ረዠም	*räžžəm or räggəm* adj. long, tall
አራባ	*arraba* v.t. crossed, cross bred	እርዝማኔ	*ərzamane* n. length
ማራቢያ	*märrabiya* n. place where breeding is carried on	እርዝመት	*ərzmät or* ርዝመት *räzmät* n. length
		አረዘመ	*aräzzämä* v.t. prolonged, made longer
ረባዳ	*räbbadda* adj/n. low lying *(land)*	ረዘረዘ	*räzärräzä* v.i. dripped out; flowed slowly *(e.g. oil)*
ረታ	*rätta* v. t. won *(argument, court case, wager* etc.)	ርዝራዥ	*räzərraž* n. leftovers, remains *(food, drink* etc.)
ረቺ	*räči* n. winner *(of argument* etc.)	ረዘቀ	*räzzäqä* v.t. donated
(እ)ርታታ	*(ə)rtata* n. victory *(in argument* etc.)	ርዝቅ	*rəzq* n. bounty, abundance *(God given)*
ተረታ	*tärätta* v. t. lost *(case, bet, argument)* ; lost hope *(of: recovery from*	ረዳ	*rädda* v.t. helped, assisted
		ረጂ	*räǧi* n. assistant, helper
		ረዳት	*räddat* n. helper,

47

ረድእ	räd'ə n. assistant, pupil	
ተረዳ	tärädda v.i. was helped, got help	
ተረዳዳ	tärädadda v.i. gave mutual help; helped each other, cooperated	
*ረዳ	rädda	
መርዶ	märdo n. announcement of death (of relative or close friend)	
ተረዳ	tärädda v.t. understood, realized, was convin..d, was aware; was ..ormed of the deat.. of a near relativ.. or a close friend	
ተረጂ	tärä..i n. one who get help	
መረጃ	m..räǧa n. inforn..ion department c public security	
ተረዳዳ	t ädadda v.i. helped, ded each other	
መረዳዳኛ ማህበር	tärrädaǧa mahəbär i. mutual help association	
አረዳ	arädda v.t. broke the news of someone's death (relative, close friend)	
አስረዳ	asrädda v.t. explained, informed, persuaded, convinced, proved	
ማስረጃ	masräǧǧa n. proof, evidence, example	
ረድእ	rad.. n. assistant, see also ረድ	
ረድፍ	radf n. row, line (of peoples, queue	
ረገመ	räggämä v.t. cursed	
ረጋሚ	rägami n. adj. cursing rogum or አርጉም argum adj. cursed, wicked	
እርግማን	argaman n. curse, cursing	
ተረገመ	täräggämä v.i. was cursed	
ተረገመ	täraggämä v.i. cursed, wished evil on	

ተራጋሚ	täragami n/adj. (one who) curses, or rails	
አስረገመ	asräggämä v.t. made s/o be cursed	
ረገበ	räggäbä v.i. went slack; became rumpled (rope, sheet, etc.), sagged	
ረገብ አለ	rägäbb alä v.i. became a little slack, rumpled, sagged	
ርግበት	ragbät n. sagging	
አረገበ	aräggäbä v.t. caused to become slack, rumpled	
አረገበ ማረገቢያ	arraggäbä v.t. fanned marragäbiya n. fan, anything used to fan fire, chaff etc.	
*ረገረገ	see አረገረገ	
*ረገበገበ (እ)ርብግብ	*rägäbäggäbä (ə)rgəbgəb adj. kind hearted; motherly; compassionate	
(እ)ርጉብ ግቢት	argəbgəbit n. propeller; fontanel adj. kind-hearted, motherly, compassionate (fem.)	
ተርገበገበ	tärgäbäggäbä v.i. switched, quavered (eye lids;) vibrated (string instrument;) fluttered (birds wings, flag, curtain etc.); was kind-hearted, motherly, compassionate	
ተርገብጋቢ	tärgäbgabi adj. switching, quivering (eye lids); vibrating; fluttering	
አርገበገበ	argäbäggäbä v.t. waved (hand, piece of cloth etc.); blocked (eyes); fluttered (wings, piece of cloth etc.); vibrated (string instrument)	
አርገብጋቢ	argäbgabi adj/n. one (who waves hands piece of cloth etc.)	

ረጋድ rägäd n. aspect, point of view, manner (way)

ረጋጠ räggäṭä v.t. trod; kicked; inked a rubber stamp by a blow; adjudicated land dispute (by treading bounds); went over s/o's head (complaint); practised foot drill (mil.)

ርጋጭ rəggač n. trampled earth; footprint; adj. down trodden

እርጋጫ ərgäčča n. kick

መርጋጫ märgäča n. treadle, foot pedal; inking pad

ረጋገጠ rägaggäṭä v.t. trampled on

ተረጋገጠ täräggäṭä v.i. was trodden on; was kicked

መረጋገጫ märrägäča n. foothold

ተረጋጠ täraggäṭä v.t., v.i. kicked out (horse etc.), kicked each other (children fighting); recoiled (firearm)

ተረጋጭ täragač n. animal which kicks; boy who plays too much

መረጋጫ märragäča n. playground, play area

ተረጋገጠ tärägaggäṭä v.i. was trampled on; was certain, was confirmed

መረጋገጫ märrägagäča n. foothold

አረጋገጠ arrägaggäṭä v.i. became sure of, ascertained

አስረጋጠ asräggäṭä v.t. had s/o kicked, beaten; drilled (soldiers); assured s/o

ረጋፈ räggäfä v.i. fell, dropped (fruit etc. when tree is shaken); cleared up (smallpox eruptions, rashes on body); died (person)

ረጋፊ rägafi adj. likely to drop, fall; mortal

ርጋፊ rəggafi n. dus shaken

from s/t; detritus; riff-raff, low people, leftovers, scraps of food from table

አረጋገፈ aräggäfä v.t. caused fruit, leaves, etc. to drop from tree

አረ.ጋገፈ ərrägaggäfä v.t. shook out (clothes, bedsheets, etc.)

ተረጋገፈ täraggäfä v.i. was unloaded; was shaken out

አራገፈ arraggäfä v.t. shook out; unloaded

አራጋፊ arragafi n. one who unloads; shakes out

አስረጋፈ asräggäfä v.t. made s/o drop s/t (from his hand)

ረጋ rägga v.i. became calm, quiet; became coagulated; became peaceful

እርጎ ərgo n. yoghourt

እርጋታ ərgata n. calmness, quiet; peacefulness

አረጋ arägga v.t. curdled, made yoghourt

ተረጋጋ tärägagga v.i. became quiet, peaceful, settled (of country / or state, or disturbed person)

አረጋጋ arrägagga v.t. quietened down, made peaceful, soothed, pacified

ረግረግ rägräg n. marshland, marshy, swamp

ረጠበ räṭṭäbä v.i. contributed money to a needy man (due to sudden misfortune etc.)

ረጣቢ räṭabi adj. n. contributor (money)

እርጣባን arṭaban n. money given as contribution (to a needy man)

ረጠበ räṭṭäbä v.i. got wet, was moist, was wet

አረጠበ aräṭṭäbä v.t. wetted, moistened, dampened

እርጥብ arṭab adj. wet, moist,

49

እርጥበት	damp *arṭabät or* ርጥበት *raṭbät* n. moisture, dampness
ረጨ	*räčä* v.t. sprinkled
ረጪ	*räči* n. one who sprinkles
ተረጨ	*täräččä* v.i. was sprinkled; widespread (news)
ተረጨ	*täraččä* v. t. splashed (water) about
ተረጫጨ	*täräčaččä* v.t. splashed one another
አስረጨ	*asräččä* v.t. had s/o sprinkle (e.g. holy water)
ረፋረፈ	*räfärräfä* n.t. littered
ረፈደ	*räffädä* v. got late (in the morning time)
ረፋድ	*räffad* n. late morning, half a day
የረፋድ ምንገድ	*yäräffad mängäd* n. half day's journey
አረፈደ	*aräffädä* v.i. got late in the morning (person)
ግርፈጃ	*marfäǧa* n. morning's business, affairs
አረፋፈደ	*aräfaffädä* v.i. became a little late in the morning (person)
አስረፈደ	*asräffädä* v. t. delayed (s/o) in the morning
ሩማን	*ruman or* ሮማን *roman* n. pomegranate
ሩር	*rur* n. wooden, skin ball (e.g. for the "gänna" game or polo)
ሩስያ	*rusaya* a. Russia
ሩስኛ	*rusäñña* n. Russian (language) also መስኮብኛ *mäskobäñña*
ሩስያዊ	*rusyawi* n. Russian
ሩብ	*rub* adj. a quarter
—ጉዳይ	*-gudday* quarter to
ከሩብ	*kärub* quarter past
ሩካቤ	*rukabe* n. (G.) n. sexual intercourse
ሩካቤ ሥጋ	*rukabe saga* n. sexual intercourse
ሩዝ	*ruz* n. rice
ሩጫ	*ručča* see ሮጠ

ሪሕ	*rih* n. rheumatoid arthritis
ሪቅ	*riq* n. thatched grain store, (usually of wood)
ሪዝ	*riz* n. moustache, sideburns
ራራ	*rarra* v.i. was compassionate merciful, kind
ርኅሩህ	*rahruh also* ሩሩ *rurru* adj. compassionate merciful, kind
ርኅራኄ	*rahrahe* n. kindness, compassion
—የሌለው	*-yälelläw* adj. cruel, savage
አራራ	*ararra* v. made s/o kind, compassionate
ራሰ	*rasä* v.i. got wet, soaked
አራሰ	*arasä* v. t. made s/t wet; soaked s/t, drenched, moistened
ራስ	*ras* n. head; self; title (e.g. duke, lord)
ራሰ በራ	*rasä bära* adj. bald, hairless
ራሱ ዞረ	*rasu zorä* v.i. was dizzy, was perplexed
ራሱን ሳተ	*rasun satä* v.t. fainted, lost consciousness
—ቻለ	*-čalä* v. t. was independent, was self-supporting
—ዐወቀ	*-awwäqä* v.t. recovered consciousness
—ገታ	*-gätta* v.t. controlled oneself
ራስም	*rasam* adj. having a large head
ራስ ምታት	*ras matat* n. headache
—ቅል	*-qal* n. skull
—ወዳድ	*-wäddad* adj. selfish
ራስጌ	*rasge* n. in the direction of the head; head of bed
ርእስ	*ra'as* n. title (subject)
ርእሰ ብሔር	*ra'sä bäher* n. head of state
—አንቀጽ	*-anqäṣ* n. editorial (news paper)
የራስ ንብረት	*yäras nabrät* n. one's own property
ራቀ	*raqä* v.i. got far away;

50

ሩቅ	went away *ruq* adj. far
ርቀት	*rəqät* n. distance
አራቀ	*'araqä* v.t. removed; took far away; dis- liked (s/o)
ተራራቀ	*täraraqä* v.i. became, got separated; split up
አራራቀ	*arraraqä* v.t. put at a distance (two or more persons, things)
አስራቀ	*asraqä* v.t. put at a distance; got rid of
*ራቁተ	*raqquʷätä*
(እ)ራቁት	(ə)*raqut* adj. naked
እርቃን	*ərqan* n. nakedness, nudity
እርቃነ ሥጋ	*ərqanä səga* n. nakedness, nudity
ተራቁተ	*täraquʷätä* v.i. be- came naked, nude;be- came barren; be- came very poor
አራቁተ	*arraquʷätä* v.t. denuded; laid bare; made poor
ራበ	*rabä* v.i. was hungry (no person indicated)
ራብ	*rab* or ረኃብ *rähab* n. hunger
ዘመነ ረኃብ	*zämänä rähab* n. famine (particular occasion)
ራብተኛ	*rabtäñña* or ረኃብተኛ *rähabtäñña* n. hungry person
ተራበ	*täräbä* v.i. was hungry
አስራበ	*asrabä* v.t made (s/o) hungry
ራብዕ	*rab'ə* n. fourth form in the Amharic vowel system
ራት	*rat* or እራት *ərat* n. supper, dinner (evening meal)
የሳት እራት	*yäsat rat* n. moth
ራኬት	*raket* n. racket
ራዕይ	*ra'əy* n. vision, appari- tion, (revelation as in Bible)
ራደ	*radä* v.i. trembled, shook
አራደ	*aradä* v.t. caused to tremble, shake; frightened
ራድዮ	*radyo* or ሬድዮ *redyo* or ራዲዮን *radyon* n. radio, wireless, radio set
ሬሳ	*resa* n. corpse, dead body
የሬሳ ሳጥን	*yäresa saṭan* n. coffin
ሬስቶራንት	*restorant* n. restaurant
ሬብ	*reb* or እራብ *əreb* n buttocks, bottom (coll).
ሬት/ እሬት	*ret/ əret* n. aloes; bitter
እንደ ሬት የመረረ	*əndä ret yämärrärä* bitter as aloes
እሬት እሬት አለ	*əret əret alä* was bitter; was harmful
ሬንጅ	*renǧ* n. asphalt cf. ቅጥራን
ሬኮማንደ	*rekumande* n. regis- tered letter
ሬፑብሊክ	*republik* n. republic
ሬፑብሊካዊ	*republikawi* adj. repu- blican
ርሳስ	*rəsas* also እርሳስ *ərsas* n. lead; pencil
* ርስ	in የርስ በርስ *yärs bärs* adj. mutual
ርስት	*rəst* n. property (land) see ወረሰ
ርቀት	see ራቀ
ርቱዕ	in ርቱዕ and እርቱዕ ተሳቢ *rətu', iratu'* *täsabi* n. direct and indirect object
ርችት	*rəččət* n. fireworks,
ርጉሩግ	see ራራ
ርእስ	see ራስ
ርእዮተ ዓለም	*rə'əyotä aläm* n. idiology
ርካብ	*rəkab* n. stirrup also እርካብ
ርኮት	*rəkot* or እርኮት *ərkot* n. water skin, wineskin
ርዝራዥ	*rəzərraž* n. remnant, fall out, leftovers
ርግብ	*rəgb* or እርግብ *ərgəb* n. pigeon, turtle-dove; adj. kind-hearted
ዐይነ ርግብ	*aynä rəgb* n. veil
ርጭ አለ	*rəčč alä* v.i. was calm,

ርግ still (surroundings)
roma n. Rome, Italy
ሮማዊ romawi n. Roman, Italian (person)
ሮማውያን romawəyan n. pl. Romans, Italians
ሮማይስጥ romayəst n. Latin
roman. or ሮማን rəman n. pomegranate
ርሮ rorro n. remorse
—አሰግ —assammu v.t. made s/o feel remorseful; rebuked
ርብ rob n. Wednesday, also ረቡዕ
ጣ roța v.i. ran

ሮጥ አለ roțț alä v.i. jogged along
ሩጫ ručča n. running
?ሩጫ väručča wədäddər n. race
ው-ድድር
ሯጭ rwač n. runner
መሮጫ märoča n. track, running field
አሮጠ aroța v.t. chased, made s/o run
ተዳረጠ tärwarwațä v.i. chased each other, ran about
አዳረጠ arrwarwa'ö v.t. chased, hurried
አስሮጠ asroța v.t. made s/o run

ሰሀ säha n. fault, error, mistake
ሰለለ sällälä v.f. acted as a spy, spied
ሰላይ sällay n. spy, secret agent
ስለላ səlläla n. espionage, spying
ተሰለለ täsällälä v.i. was spied upon
አሰለለ assällälä v.t. had someone spied upon
አሰላይ assällay n. one who employs spies
ሰለለ sällälä v.i. became paralized, lame; was thin
ሰላላ sälala adj. paralised, crippled, lame
—ማላ —mälala thin and long
—ድምጽ —dəmş thin voice
ሰለመ sällämä v.t. greeted
ሰላም sälam interj. "peace", "greetings" "Hallo!"
—ነሳ —nässa v.t. disturbed, agitated (disturbed)
የሰላም ጓድ yäsälm guʷadd n. Peace Corps
ሰላማዊ sälamawi adj. peaceful
ሰላፍ —sälf n. demon-

—ውቅ ያኖ stration (political)
—woqyanos n. Pacific Ocean
ሰላማዊነት sälamawinnät n. peacefulness
ሰላምታ sälamta n. greeting.
—ሰጠ —säțțä v.t. greeted saluted
—ነሳ —nässa v.i. ignored (to greet s/o)
—አቀረብ —aqärräbä v.t. greeted, saluted
መስለም mäsläm inf. to become Muslim
አሰለመ asällämä v.t. converted s/o to Islam
እስላም əslam n. Islam
እስልምና əsləmənna n. Islamic religion
ተሳለመ täsällämä v.t. acknowledged by bowing
ቤተክርስቲያን betäkrəstian— went to the church
ቲያን—
—ተሳላሚ —täsalami n. churchgoer
መሳለሚያ mässalämiya n. church porch

ሰለሰለ   *sälässälä* v.i. lost weight, became thin

አሰለሰለ   *asälässälä* v.t. caused s/o to become thin

*ሰለሰለ   *sälässälä

አሰሳሰለ   *assälassälä* v.i. contemplated, pondered

ሰለቀ   *sälläqä* v.t. ground fine *(as with millstone)*; beat s/o soundly

ስልቅ   *səlləq* adj. fine ground

መሰለቂያ   *mäsälläqyia* n. fine-grinding millstone

ተሰለቀ   *täsälläqä* v.i. was ground fine

ሰለቀ   *sälläqä

ተሳለቀ   *täsalläqä* v.i. ridiculed, laughed at

መሳለቂያ   *mässaläqiya* n. laughing stock

ሰለቀጠ   *säläqqäṭä* v.t. swallowed whole

ሰለበ   *sälläbä* v.t. cut off s/o's genitals; cheated *(in weighing produce etc.)* ;plundered in war

ሰላቢ   *saläbi* n. one who cheats in the measure, etc.

ሰለባ   *sälaba* n. spoils of war, plunder

ስልብ   *səlb* n. eunach

ተሰለበ   *täsälläbä* v. i. was castrated

አሰለበ   *assälläbä* v. t. had s/o castrated

ሰለተ   *sällätä* v. t. put in order: arranged according to category

ሰላች   *sällač* n. diagonal cut

ስልት   *səlt* n. way, manner, style, mode

ስልተ ምርት   *səltä mərt* n. mode of production

የጦር ስልት   *yäṭor səlt* n. strategy, tactics *(mil.)*

ላች   *sälačča* v.i. became bored

ሰላቺ   *sälči* n. one who easily gets bored

ስላቺ   *sälču* n. one who is easily bored

ኣሰሳች   *asäläčča* v.t. bored

s/o; nagged s/o

አሰላቺ   *asälči* n. bore; shrew: nagger; adj. boring, wearisome, nagging

የሚያሰላች   *yämmiyasäläčč* adj. irksome, boring, wearisome

ተሰለች   *täsäläčča* v.i. got bored with

ተሰላቺ   *täsälči* n. boring person, thing

ተሰላች   *täsäläčča* v.i. got bored with each other, tired of each other

ተሰላቻች   *täsäläčaččä* v.i. got bored with each other

ሰሊጥ   *säliṭ* n. sesame *(grain)*

ሰላ   *sälla* v. i. turned out well; was sharpened *(knives, etc.)*; improved in speech. became eloquent

ስል   *səl* adj. sharp

ስለት   *sälät* n. sharpness; cutting edge, blade; vow

ሰላ   see ስሉት

ሰላጣ   *sälaṭa* n. salad, lettuce

ሰሌን   *sälen* n. straw mat

ሰልካካ   *sälkakka* adj. clean cut *(feature)*

ሰልፍ   *sälf* n. demonstration, parade; procession line *(row of persons)*, queue

ሰልፈኛ   *sälfaññä* n. demonstrator

ሰላማዊ ሰልፍ   *sälamawi sälf* n.demonstration *(political)*

ሰመመ   *sämmämä* v.i. day dreamed, got lost in thought

ሰመመን   *sämämän* n. day dreaming, a brown study

ሰመጠ   *sämmäṭä* or ሰጠመ *säṭṭämä* v.i. got drowned, sank

ስምጠት   *səmṭät* or ስጥመት *säṭmät* n. depth *(liquids)*

ስምጥ   *səmṭ* n. depression *(geographical)*

—ሸለቆ   -*šäläqo* n. rift-valley

ሰማ   *sämma* v.t. heard, listened; understood

ለይስሙላ	*(a language)*; became hot enough *(oven)* *läyəsmulla* only ` for show
የሰሚ ሰሚ	*yäsämi sämi* n. hearsay
ስሜት	*səmmet* n. feeling, feelings
ስሞታ	*səmota* n. complaint
መስሚያ	*mäsmiya* n. hearing aid; headphones, etc.
አሰማ	*asämma* v.t. made hot enough *(oven, pan etc.)*
አሰማ	*assämma* v.t. announced, voiced, uttered made oneself heard; urged a plea
ተሰማ	*täsämma* v.i.was heard
ተሰሚ	*täsämi* adj. influential; authoritative
ተሰማማ	*täsämamma* v.t. paid attention to each other
ተሰማማ	*täsmamma* v. i. agreed with each other, reached an agreement; bargained; got along; corresponded *(agreed)*; was consonant with
አሰማማ	*asmamma* v.t. reconciled, harmonized
ሰማዕት	*säma'ət* n. martyr
ሰማዕትነት	*säma'ətənnät* n. martyrdom pl. ሰማዕታት
ሰማኒያ	*sämanya* adj/n. eighty: legal marriage document
ሰማይ	*sämay* n. sky, heaven
ሰማያዊ	*sämayawi* adj. of the heavens, heavenly; light blue
ሰሜን	*sämen* n/adj. north
ሰሜናዊ	*sämenawi* adj.northern
—ዋልታ	—*walta* n. North Pole
ሰም	*säm* n. beeswax
ሰምና ወርቅ	*sämənna wärq* metaphor
ሰምበሉት	*sämbälet* n. grass, straw for thatching; long grass
ሰምበር	*sämbär* or ሰንበር *sänbär* n.stripe *(from a whip*
—አወጣ	*stroke)*, bruise —*awätta* v.t. bruised
ሰሞን	*sämon* n. . week
ሰሞነኛ	*sämonäñña* n. deacon during week of duty
ሰረረ	*särrärä* v.t. had sexual intercourse *(of animals)*, mated
ሰራሪ	*särari* n. animal who has sexual intercourse
ሰርያ	*sərrya* n. sexual intercourse *(animals)*, mating
ተሰረረ	*täsärrärä* v.i. was served, mated *(animal)*
ተሳረረ	*täsarrärä* v.i. had intercourse *(animals)*
አሳረረ	*assarrärä* v.t. caused *(animals)* to breed; overbid, competed in bidding
አሳራሪ	*assarari* n. one who bids competitively
አሰረረ	*assärrärä* v.i caused *(animals.)* to breed
ሰረሰረ	*särässärä* v.t. bored a whole
ሰርሳሪ	*särsari* n. burglar
መሰርሰሪያ	*mäsärsäriya* n. drill *(tool)*, auger
ተሰረሰረ	*täsärässärä* v.i. was bored
ሰረቀ	*särräqä* v.t. stole
ሰራቂ	*säraqi* n. one who steals
ሰርቀታ	*sərrəqta* n. hiccup, hicough
ሰርቆሽ	*sərqoš* n. stealing
—በር	—*bärr* n. secret door
ሰርቆት	*sərqot* n. stealing
ተሰረቀ	*täsärräqä* v.i. was stolen
ተሰርቆ ሄዳ	*täsärqo hedä* left secretly
ተሳረቀ	*täsarräqä* v.i. stole from each other
ተሰራረቀ	*täsärarräqä* v.t. stole repeatedly from each other
አሰረቀ	*assärräqä* v. had s/o robbed, caused s/o to be robbed
ሰረዘ	*särräzä* v.t. cancelled

54

ሰረዝ	säräz n. (punct. mark) dash, hyphen
ነጠላ—	näṭäla—n. comma(፣)
ድርብ—	därräb — n. semicolon (፤)
ሰረዣ	särräza n. cancellation
ሰርዝ	särräz adj. cancelled
—ድልዝ	—dälläz adj. full of cancellation (manuscript), deletion
ሰራረዘ	särarräzä v. crossed out heavily
ተሰረዘ	täsärräzä v.i. was cancelled
አሰረዘ	assärräzä v.i. had s/o crossed off a list
ሰረገ	see ሠረገ
ሰረገላ	särägälla n. chariot, wagon, coach, carriage
ሰረጎደ	säräggʷädä v.t. poked a hole in, made an indentation in, indented
ስርጎዳት	särgudat adj. hole, depression, indentation
ተሰረጎደ	täsäräggʷädä v.i. was pushed in
⁺ሰረጨ	see ተሰራጨ
ሰርን	särn n. nostrils
ሰርክ	särk adv. always, often, frequently
ሰርጣን	särṭan n. crab
ሰሰነ	ïssänä or ሴሰነ sessänä v.t. lusted (sexual); had sexual desire for s/o
ሴሰኛ	sesäñña adj. lustful
ሴሰኝነት	sesäññannät or ሴስ ኝነት sesäññannät n. lustfulness
ሰስ	säs n. klipspringer
ሰቀለ	säqqälä v.t. hanged s/t; crucified s/o
ሰቃይ	säqay adj/n. hangman
ሰቀላ	säqäla n. cottage (of rectangular shape)
ስቅለት	säqlät n. crucifixion
ስቅላት	säqqälat n. hanging (punishment)
መስቀያ	mäsqäya n. hanger scaffold
ልብስ —	läbs—n. clotheshanger
መስቀል	mäsqäl inf. to hang; n. cross
መስቀልኛ ጥያቄ	mäsqäläñña ṭäyyaqe n. cross examination
መስቀለያ መንገድ	mäsqäläyya mängäd n. cross-roads
ተሰቀለ	täsäqqälä v. i. was hanged, was crucified
ተሰቃይ	täsäqqay adj/n s/o who is to be hanged
አሳቀለ	assaqqälä v.t. helped s/o hang s/o or s/t
አሰቀለ	assäqqälä v. t. had s/t hanged, had s/o crucified
ተመሳቀለ	tämäsaqqälä v.i. became interwoven, intermingled, confused
ተመሰቃቀለ	tämäsäqaqqälä v.i. was confused, lost order
ምስቅልቅል	mäsqälqäl n. confusion, disorder, haphazardness
አመሳቀለ	ammäsaqqälä v.t. crossed one's hands; threw into disorder, confusion
አመሰቃቀለ	ammäsäqaqqälä v.t. threw into constant disorder, confusion
ሰቀቀ	säqqäqä v.i. felt uneasy, on edge
ሰቀቀኝ	säqqäqäññ v.i. made me uneasy
ሰቃቂ	säqaqi n. s/t which causes uneasiness
ተሳቀቀ	täsaqqäqä v. i. was greatly disappointed
አሰቀቀ	assäqqäqä v.i. made s/o greatly disappointed
አሰቃቂ	assäqqaqi adj. horrible, horrifying
አሳቀቀ	assaqqäqä v.t. disappointed s/o greatly
ስቅቅ አለ	säqäqq alä v.t. was grieved very deeply indeed
ስቅቅ ብሎ አለቀሰ	säqäqq bälo aläqqäsä v.i. grieved deeply and wept bitterly
ሰቀቀን	säqäqän n. great disappointment, deep sadness

55

ሰተተናም	*säqäqänam* adj. deeply unhappy; greatly disappointed
ሰቀዘ	*säqqäzä* v.t. gripped, seized with sharp pain
*ሰቀየ	*säqäyyä*
ስቃይ	*səqay* n. torment, agony, torture, plague
አሰቃየ	*assäqayyä* v.t. tortured, plagued
ተሰቃየ	*täsäqayyä* v. i. was tortured, was plagued
ሰቅ	*säqq* n. girdle, belt
ሰበረ	*säbbärä* v.t. broke, broke in
ዜማ	*zema*--- sang false notes
ሰብሮ ከፈተ	*säbro käffätä* v.t. broke open
-ገባ	---*gäbba* v. t. broke into a house
ሰባሪ	*säbari* adj/n person or thing which breaks s/t
ሰባራ	*säbara* adj. broken, broken down
ሰባሪ	*səbbari* n. broken piece
ስብርባሪ	*səbərbari* n. fragments, broken pieces, fractions
ስብራት	*səbbərat* n. fracture
ሰባበረ	*säbabbärä* v.t. broke into pieces
ተሰበረ	*täsäbbärä* v.i. was broken
ተሰባሪ	*täsäbbari* adj fragile, breakable
ተሰባበረ	*täsäbabbärä* v.i. was broken into pieces
አሳበረ	*assabbärä* v. t. found a short cut, shorter way *(on journey);* raised the bid *(at auction)*
አሳባሪ መንገድ	*assabari mängäd* n. short cut
አሰበረ	*assäbbärä* v.t. had s/t broken
ሰበሰበ	*säbässäbä* v.t. gathered, accumulated, assembled; harvested
አፉን-	*afun*---v.t kept quiet

	(through fear)
ልብሱን---	*ləbsun*---v.t. gathered up one's clothes
ሰብሳቢ	*säbsabi* adj/n. gatherer accumulator; chairman
ስብስብ	*səbsəb* n. a set, a group, collection
ስብሰባ	*səbsäba* n. gathering, meeting, assembly, session, conference, congress, convention
— አደረገ	---*adärrägä* v.t. held a conference
ሰባሰበ	*säbassäbä* v.t. heaped up; gathered randomly
ሰበሰበ አለ	*səbsəbb alä* v.i. gathered together; contracted
ተሰበሰበ	*täsäbässäbä* v.i. was gathered, accumulated, assembled
ተሰብሳቢ	*täsäbsabi* n. participating member
መሰብሰቢያ	*mässäbsäbiya* n. meeting place
አሰባሰበ	*assäbassäbä* v.t. helped in gathering s/t; organized *(people)*
ሰበቀ	*säbbäqä* v.t. beat up *(eggs etc.);* rubbed fire-stick; kindled
ሰባቂ	*säbaqi* n. backbiter, tale-bearer
ሰብቅ	*säbq* n. backbiting, sneaking
ስብቀት	*səbqät* n. backbiting, tale-bearing, sneaking
አሳበቀ	*assabbäqä* v.t. passed on gossip, told tales on s/o
አሳባቂ	*assabaqi* n. sneak, tale-bearer, one who makes malicious reports on others
ሰበብ	*säbäb* n. pretext, trumped up excuse
ሰበበኛ	*säbäbäñña* n. malingerer, one who makes occasion of an injury, who takes ad-

አሳበበ vantage of a pretext
assabbäbu v. found a pretext. made a pretext of

ተሳበበ *täsabbäbä* v. i. was used as a pretext

ሰበከ *säbbäkä* v.t. preached; flattered

ሰባኪ *säbaki* adj/n. preacher; flatterer

ሰበካ *säbäka* n. parish

ስብከት *säbkät* n. preaching

ተሰበከ *täsäbbäkä* v.i. was preached; flattered

ተሰባኪ *täsäbaki* adj/n. s/o who is easily convinced, easily flattered

አሰበከ *assäbbäkä* v.t. had s/o preach

ሰባ *säbba* v.i. became fat (animals)

ስባት *säbat* n. fatness

ስብ *säb* n. fat

አሰባ *usäbba* v.t. fattened

አሰቢ *asbi* adj/n. one who fattens (cattle) to sell

ሰባ *säba* adj/ n. seventy

ሰባኛ *säbaññä* adj. seventieth

ሰባት *säbatt* adj/n. seven

—እጅ *ǝǧǧ* adj/adv. sevenfold

ሰባተኛ *säbattäñña* adj. seventh

ሱባኤ *suba'e* n. retreat (religious,) time allocated to prayer and fasting

ሰብእ *säb'ǝ* n. (G.) man, human being

ኅብረተሰብ *häbrätä säb* n. society, the public

ቤተሰብ *betä säb* n. family

ሰብአዊ *säb'awi* n. humanist, philanthropist

—መብት *-mäbt* n. human rights

ኅብረተሰብአዊ *häbrätä säb'awi* adj. socialist

ሰብል *säbl* n. harvest, crop

ሰበዝ *säbäz* n. raffia grass

ሰበጠረ *see* አሰበጠረ

ሰተረ *sättärä* v. t. put in

ሰታራ *sättara* adj/n. reserved

ስትር *sǝttǝr* adj./n. orderly, neat

ተስተረ *täsättärä* v. i. was put in order

ሰተት አለ *sätätt alä* v.i. passed through freely

* ሰተፉ *see* ተሳተፉ

ሰታቴ *sätate* n. large earthware stewpot

ሰነቀ *sännäqä* v.i. prepared provisions for travel

ስንቅ *sǝnq* n. provisions, food for journey

ተሰነቀ *täsännäqä* v. i. was prepared (provisions)

አሰነቀ *assännäqä* v.t. had provisions prepared

ሰነቀረ *sänäqqärä* v. t. forced into (a tight place)

ተሰነቀረ *täsänäqqärä* v.i. was forced into

ሰነበተ *sänäbbätä* v.i passed the week; lived quite long

ሰንበት *sänbät* n. Sabbath; Sunday

መሰንበቻ *mäsänbäča* n. week

አሰነበተ *asänäbbätä* v.t. delayed for one week, delayed for sometime

ተሰናበተ *täsänabbätä* v.i. came to say goodbye, bade farewell; resigned (from job)

ተሰናባበተ *täsänäbabbätä* v.t. bade farewell to each other

አሰናበተ *assänabbätä* v.t. released (s/o) from duty; sacked (an employee)

ሰነበጠ *sänäbbätä* v.t. slit, nick (as with razor blade)

ስንባጭ *sǝnäbbäč* peel, rind (e.g. citrus fruits), quarters (of citrus fruit)

ሰነኘ *sänäññä* v.i. rhymed

ሰነኝ — *sənaññ* n. rhyme

ሰነከለ — *sänäkkälä* v. t. hobbled *(horse, donkey etc.);* crippled *(with a blow on the leg)*

ሰንካላ — *sänkalla* n/adj. limping, one who limps

ሰንኩል — *sənkul* n/adj. cripple; handicapped person

አካለ-- — *akalä* — adj. cripple

መሰናክል — *mäsänakəl* n. hindrance, stumbling block

ተሰነከለ — *täsänäkkälä.* v.i. was hobbled, was crippled

ተሰናከለ — *täsänakkälä* v.i. was hindered

አሰናከለ — *assänakkälä* v.t. hindered

አሰናካይ — *assänakay* n. one who hinders s/o

አሰነካከለ — *assänäkakkälä* v.t. threw everything into confusion

ሰነዘረ — *sänäzzärä* v.t. directed at *(accusation etc.),* reached out, stretched out one's arm; measured a span *(with the hand)*

ሰንዘር — *sənzər* n. a span, a hand's span

ተሰናዘረ — *täsänazzärä* v.i. was stretched out; was directed at

መሰናዘሪያ — *mässänazäriya* n. elbow-room, space to relax

ሰነድ — *sänäd* n. document

*ሰነዳ — see አሰናዳ

ሰነገ — *sännägä* v. t. ringed the nose *(of a bull esp.);* pierced beak *(of broody hen)* with feather

ሰነግ — *sənnäg* adj/n. having nose ringed *(esp. bull);* having beak pierced with feather *(broody hen)*

ተሰነገ — *täsännägä* v.i. was ringed; had feather poked up nose

ሰነጋ — *sänäggä* v. t. stuffed *(green pepper with* tomato and onions etc.)

ሰነጠረ — *sänäṭṭärä* v.t. split *(wood)* finely *(e. g. to make split, tooth pick etc.)*

ሰንጣሪ — *sənnäṭṭari* n. fine splinter

ሰንጥር — *sənṭər* n. fine splinter, tooth pick

ሰነጣጠረ — *sänäṭaṭṭärä* v.t. split into many pieces

ተሰነጠረ — *täsänäṭṭärä* v.t. was split finely

ሰነጠቀ — *sänäṭṭäqä* v.t. split *(wood etc.;)* splintered; cracked, cleaved

ሰንጣቂ — *sənäṭṭaqi* n. chip of wood, splinter, split-off piece

ሰንጥቅ — *sənṭəq* n. a split, crack rift, fissure

መሰንጠቂያ — *mäsänṭäqyia* n. saw, axe etc.

እንጨት— ሰነጣጠቀ — *ənčät* — saw mill *sänäṭaṭṭäqä* v. t. split into many pieces

ተሰነጣጠቀ — *täsänäṭṭäqä* v.j. was split, cracked

አሰነጠቀ — *assänäṭṭäqä* v.t. had s/t split, cracked

ሰነፈ — *sännäfä* v.i. became lazy

ሰናፍ — *sänäf* adj. lazy, idle; feeble, indolent

--ምርት — *—mərt* n. threshed crop *(still not winnowed*

ሰንፍና — *sənfənna* n. laziness, idleness, inaction, indolence

አሰነፈ — *asännäfä* v. t. encouraged s/o to be lazy

አሳነፈ — *assannäfä* v.t. caused s/o to be lazy

ሰነፈጠ — *sänäffäṭä* v.t. tickled the nose *(of mustard)*

ሰናድር — *sänadər* n. Schneider *(type of firearm)*

ሰናፍጭ — *sänafəčč* n. mustard see ሰነፈጠ

ሰኔ — *säne* n. June

ሰንሰለት — *sänsälät* n. chain

ሰንከሎ — *sänkällo* n. bucket, also ሸንከሎ *šänkällo*

ሰንኮፍ	šänkof or ሽንኮፍ šänkof n. scab; flesh around of burst boil
ሰንደል	sändäl n. joss-stick
—ጫማ	—čamma n. sandals
ሰንደቅ ዓላማ	sändäq alama n. flag
ሰንዱቅ	sänduq n. chest, box
ሰንጋ	sänga n. steer, bull fattened for slaughter
ሰንጠረዥ	sänṭäräž n, chess; table (mathematical)
ሰንጢ	sänṭi n. jack-knife
*ሰኘ	*säññä
አሰኘው	assäññäw he feels like, he feels up to
ሰኞ	säñño n. Monday
—ግከሰኘ	–maksäñño n. hopscotch
ሰኔና ሰኞ	sänennä säñño unexpected coincidence
ሰከረ	säkkärä v. i. became drunk, intoxicated
ሰካራም	säkkaram n/adj. drunkard, drunken
ስካር	səkar n. drunkeness
አሰከረ	asäkkärä v.t. made s/o drunk, intoxicated
አስካሪ	askari adj. alcholic
—መጠጥ	—mäṭäṭṭ alcholic drink
ማስከሪያ	maskäriya intoxicant, herb (bərbirra) used for stunning fish for catching
ተሳከረ	täsakkärä v. i. got drunk together; got confused
አሳከረ	assakkärä v.t. made drunk; confused
ሰካሰከ	säkässäkä v.t. crammed, stuffed
ሰከነ	säkkänä v.t. settled (coffee grounds); became mature (person)
አሰከነ	asäkkänä v.t. caused to settle (coffee grounds)
ሰከ	säkka v.t. impaled, stick in, thrusted in
ሰክ ሳህን	säk sahən n. triple canteen (food container)
መሰከያ	mäsäkkiya n. plug,

	(usually with የኮረንቲ)
ተሰካ	täsäkka v.i. was forced into, was pushed in
ተሳካ	täsakka v.i. succeeded (scheme, plan etc.)
አሳካ	assakka v. t. made s/t succeed
አሰካ	assäkka v.t. had something pushed in, forced
ሰኮና	säkona or ሽኮና šäkona n. hoof
ሰወጥ አለ	säwäṭṭ alä v.t. lost the thread (of speech, argument, brain of thought etc.) for a brief moment
ሰዋሰው	säwasəw n. gramm_ar
ሰዋስዋዊ	säwasəwawi adj. grammatical
ሰው	säw n. man, human being
—ሥራሽ	—särraš adj. manmade, artificial
የሰው	yäsäw adj. human; belonging to s/o else e.g. የሰው ቤት someone's house
—አገር	—agär n. foreign country
ተራ—	tära— n. layman, ordinary person
ሰውዩ	säwəyye interj. you Mr. !
ሰውየው	säwəyyäw the man, this, that man
ሰውነት	säwənnät n. body, personality; constitution (of a person)
የሰው ልጅ	yäsäw ləğ n. human being; person of free condition (not a slave)
ሰዓት	sä'at n. time, hour
—ቆጣሪ	—qoṭari n. hour hand
—እላፊ	—əllafi n. overtime: curfew
ከሰዓት በኋላ	käsä'at bähu^wala in the afternoon
—በፊት	—bäfit before noon
በሰዓቱ	bäsä'atu on time, just at the right moment
በየሰዓቱ	bäyyäsä'atu adv.

59

	hourly from time to time	በሰዓት	bäsä'at at noon
ያለ ሰዓት	yalä sä'at adj. late		
ዐቃቤ ሰዓ፞	aqqabe sä'at n. minister of protocol (palace official)		
ሰየመ	säyyämä see ሠየመ		
ሰየፈ	säyyäfä v.t. beheaded		
ሰያፊ	säyyafi n. executioner (for beheading)		
ሰያፍ	säyyaf adj. diagonal		
ሰይፍ	säyf n. sword		
ሰይፈኛ	säyfäñña n. swordsman		
ተሰየፈ	täsäyyäfä v.i. was beheaded		
አሰየፈ	assäyyäfä v. t. had s/o beheaded		
ሰይጣን	säytan n. Satan, devil		
ሰይጣናም	säytanam adj. violent-tempered, hot-tempered		
ሰይጣኑ መጣ	säytanu mätta he was very angry		
ሰዳቃ	sädäqa n. table (arch.)		
ሰደበ	säddäbä v.t. insulted, called by insulting names		
ሰድብ	sädäb n. insult,		
ተሰደበ	täsäddäbä v.i. was insulted, called bad names		
ተሳደበ	täsaddäbä v.t. insulted, called bad names		
ተሳዳቢ	täsadabi n. slanderer, one who insults, s/o who calls bad names		
ተሰዳደበ	täsädaddäbä v.i. slandered, insulted each other, called each other bad names		
አሰደበ	assäddäbä v.t. incited to call s/o bad names		
ሰደደ	säddädä y.t. sent, let go		
ሥር—	sär— v.t. took root, was firmly established; became chronic		
ሰድ	sädd adj. lawless, impolite, discourteous		
ሰደተኛ	säddätäñña n. refugee		
ሰደት	säddät n. exile		

የሰደድ እሳት	yäsädäd əsat n. wild fire		
ተሰደደ	täsäddädä v.i. was exiled		
መሰደጃ	mässädäǧa n. place of exile; refuge		
ተሳደደ	täsaddädä v.i. was chased away, ran away from, was persecuted		
አሳደደ	assaddädä v.t. chased away, followed in pursuit, persecuted		
አሳዳጅ	assadaǧ n. persecutor		
ሰዳፍ	sädäf n. butt (of gun)		
ሰገለ	sägäle n/adj. selfish, greedy (person)		
ሰገራ	in ሰገራ ቤት sägära bet n. latrine, w.c.		
ሰገሰገ	sägässägä v.t. stuffed in (e.g. straw into sack); ate too much, forced together (loose threads of hem to prevent fraying)		
ሰገሰገ	segsäg adj. stuffed in		
ሰገሰገ አለ	səgsägg alä v.t. was overcrowded; were squeezed up together (crowd of people tucked in (blankets of bed)		
ተሰገሰገ	täsägässägä v.i. was stuffed, pushed in; squeezed up together, tucked in		
*ሰገበገበ	sägäbäggäbä		
ሰግብግብ	səgbgəb adj. greedy stingy, ravenous		
ተሰገበገበ	täsgäbäggäbä v.i. was greedy, stingy, avid		
ሰገባ	sägäba n. sheath		
ሰገነት	sägännät n. balcony, grandstand		
ሰገደ	säggädä v.i. bowed, prostrated, genuflected, worshipped		
ሰጋጅ	sägaǧ n. one who bows, prostrates himself		
ሰጋጃ	sagaǧǧa n. carpet, rug		
ስግደት	səgdät n. adoration		
መስጊድ	mäsgid n. mosque		

60

መስገጃ *mäsgäǧǧa* n. prayer mat, prayer rug

አሰገደ *assäggädä* v.t. made s/o bow, prostrate himself; made s/o submissive

ሰገገ *säggägä* v.t. stretched the neck out *(attacking, threatening posture)*

አሰገገ *asäggägä* v.t. ran full tilt *(at s/o)* charged *(e.g. rhinoceros)*

ሰጉን *sägon* n. ostrich

ሰጐደ *säggʷädä* v.t. depressed *(formed a depression)*, made an imprint of concavity

ሰጓዳ *säg"adda* adj. depressed

ሰጉደት *sägudät* n. depression

ሰጐዳት *sägguddat* n. dimple

ሰጠ *säṭṭä* v.t. gave

አሳልፎ— *asalləfo*—v.t. betrayed

እጁን— *əǧǧun*— v.t. surrendered

ድምፅ— *dəmṣ*— v.t. voted, elected

አብሮ ይስጠን *abro yesṭänn* don't mention it!

እግዚአብሔር/ እግዘርይስጠልኝ *əgziabher/əgzer yäsṭ-əläññ* thank you!

የሰጠ *yäsäṭṭä* adj. ideal, comfortable

ጤና ይስጥልኝ *ṭena yəsṭälläññ* good morning, evening! etc., goodbye, hello!

ሰጪ *säči* adj. giver, bestower

ስጦታ *säṭota* n. gift, reward, endowment

ተሰጠ *täsäṭṭä* v.i. was given

ተሰጥዎ/ ተሰጥኦ *täsäṭwo/täsäṭ'o* n. gift, talent

አሰጠ *assäṭṭä* v.t. had s/t given to s/o

አሳጣ *assaṭṭa* v.t. exposed *(s/o)*

ሰጠመ *saṭṭämä see also* ሰመጠ *sämmäṭä* v.i. sank

ስጠጥ አለ *säṭäṭṭ alä or* ሲጠጥ አለ *siṭiṭṭ alä* v.i. squeaked

ሰጥ አለ *säṭṭ alä* v.i. was com-

---

pletely subdued

ሰጥ ለጥ አለ *säṭṭ läṭṭ alä* v.i. was utterly overcome and pacified

ሰፈረ *säffärä* v.i. camped; measured *(grain etc.)*

ሰፈረተኛ *säfärätäñña or* ሰፈርተኛ *säfärtäñña* n. district neighbour

ሰፈር *säfär* n. district, area *(of town)*

ሰፋሪ *säfari* n. settler; one who measures grain, etc.

ስፍራ *səfra* n. place

ስፍር *səfər* adj. measured out *(grain, etc.)*

—ቁጥር የሌለው *—quṭər yällelläw* adj. innumerable

መስፈሪያ *mäsfäriya* n. camping place; measuring aid *(e.g. bushel)*

እልቆ መሳፍርት *əlqo mäsafərt* adj. innumerable, immeasurable

ተሰፈረ *täsäffärä* v.i. got on board

ተሳፋሪ *täsafari* n. passenger, s/o on board

መሳፈሪያ 7ንዘብ *mässafäriya gänzäb* n. fare

አሰፈረ *asäffärä* v.t. settled people in a given area; put on *(in writing)*

ማስፈሪያ *masfäriya* n. area of settlement

አሰፈረ *assäffärä* v.t. had grain etc. measured

አሳፈረ *assaffärä* v.t. put s/o on board, arranged s/o's departure

አሳፋሪ *assafari* n. one who accompanies s/o getting on board

ሰፈነ *säffänä* v.t. ruled over

መስፈን *mäsfən* n. ruler, aristocrat

መሳፍንት *mäsafənt* n. pl. aristocratic ruling class

ዘመነ— *zämänä* — n. time of the aristocratic rulers, barons (18th century)

ምስፍና *məsfənna* n. reign,

61

	rule
ሰፈፈ	säffäfä v.i. floated
ሰፋፊ	säfafi adj. floating
ሰፋፍ	säfäf n. unpurified bee wax *(as it floats in fermentation)*
ሰፋፊ	saffafi adj. buoyant
አሰፈፈ	asäffäfä v.t. made s/t float
ሰፋ	säffa v.i. became wide, broad
ሰፊ	säffi adj. wide, broad, large, extensive
ሰፊው ሕዝብ	säffiw həzb the broad masses
በሰፊው	bäsäffiw adv. abundantly, extensively, widely
ሰፋ አለ	säfa alä v.i. became rather wide, broad
ሰፋት	səfat n. width, breadth, area, size *(of room etc.)*
ተሰፋፋ	täsfaffa v.i. thrived, flourished, expanded, was wide, spread, developed
አሰፋ	asäffa v.t. widened, broadened, increased in magnitude,
አሰፋፋ	asfaffa v.t. widened or broadened gradually, increased gradually in magnitude; developed, expanded; promoted
ሰፋ	säffa v.t. served, sewed up; stitched
ልብስ ሰፊ	ləbs säfi n. tailor
ጫማ—	čamma— n. shoemaker
ሰፈድ	säfed n. basketwork disc *(for winnowing grain)*
ሰፈት	səfet n. sewing, stitching
ሰፍ	səf adj. sewn
ወስፈ	wäsfe n. plaiting bodkin
ወሳፈቻ/ መሳፍቻ	wässafəčča also mässafəčča n. leather work bodkin, awl
አሰፋ	assäffa v.t. had tailored

ልብስ ማሰ ፊያ ገንዘብ	ləbs massäfiya gänzäb n. tailor's fee
ሰፍሳፋ	säfsəffa adj. ravenous, over-eager *see also* አሰፈሰፈ
ሰፍነግ	säfnäg n. sponge
ሱማሌ	sumale n. Somalia, Somali
ሱረት	surrät n. snuff
ሱሪ	surri n. trousers
ሱስ	sus n. addiction
ሱሰኛ	susäñña adj/n. addicted, addict
ሱቅ	suq n. shop
—በደራቴ	—bädäräte n. peddler
ባለሱቅ	baläsuq n. shopkeeper
ሱባኤ	suba'e n. retreat *(religious)*
ሱቲ	suti n. richly coloured cloth, hangings *(for church use)*
ሱክር	sukkar n. sugar
—በሽታ	—bäššəta n. diabetes
—በሽተኛ	—bässətäñña n. diabetic
—ድንች	—dannəčč n. sweet potato
ሱዳን	Sudän n. the Sudan; Sudanese, *also* ሱዳናዊ
ሱፋጭ	suffač n. obsidian, cutting stone
ሱፍ	suf n. wool; sunflower seed
—ልብስ	—ləbs n. woollen dress
ሲል አለ	sill alä v.i. choked to death
ሲሚንቶ	siminto n. cement, mortar, concrete
ሲር	sir n. shoe-lace
ሲሳይ	sisay n. daily bread; fortune *(money, possessions etc.)*
ሲቃ	siqa n. sob
ሲባጎ	sibago n. string
ሲኒ	sini or ሰኒ səni n. cup
ሲኒማ	sinima n. cinema, movie
ሲናር	sinar n. tare, weed
ሲኖዶስ	sinodos n. synod
ሲኦል	si'ol n. hell
ሲዳሞ	sidamo n. one of the Administrative Re-

62

ሲጋራ sigăra also ሲጃራ sigara
n. cigarettes

ሲጥ አለ siṭṭ alä v.i. squeaked
(door, mouse etc.)

ሳ— sa—imperfect verb pre-
fix, without e.g.
ሳያስብ ተናገረ sayassəb
tänaggärä he spoke
without thinking

ሳ·- —ssa ሳ pro-phrase
indicating a question
e.g. ከበደ ሄደ እኔሳ
Käbbädä hedä ənessa
Kebede has gone;
what about me? cf. ስ

ሳለ sala v.t. coughed
ሳላም salam adj n. (one)
who coughs fre-
quently

ሳለ salä v.t. sharpened
ሰለት səlät n. blade of a
knife cutting edge
መሳል mäsal inf. to sharpen
n. whetstone,
sharpening stone
መሳያ mäsaya n. whetstone
strop, file
ተሳለ täsalä v.i. was sharpened; made a vow
አሳለ assalä v.t. had s/o
sharpen blade etc.

ሳላ sala n. oryx
ሳሌ salle n. crock
ሳሎን salon n. salon
ሳሕን sahən n. dish, plate
ጎድጓዳ— godgu"adda-
bowl, basin

ሳመ samä v.t. kissed
ቤተክርስቲያን betäkrəstian sami n.
ሳሚ church goer
ተሳመ täsamä v. i. was
kissed
ተሳሳመ täsasamä v. i. kissed
each other
አሳሳመ assasamä v.t. made
kiss each other
አሳመ assamä v.i. made
s/o kiss s/o s.t, (e.g.
priest's cross)
ሳሙና samuna n. soap; adj.
deceitful (coll.)
ሳማ samma n. stinging

nettle
ሳምባ see ሳንባ

ሳምንት sammənt n. week
ሳምንታዊ samməntawi adj.
weekly
ባለሳምንት balä sammənt n.
one on duty for a
given week

ሳቀ saqä v.i. laughed
ሳቂታ saqqitta adj. jocund
ሳቅ saq n. laughter
ሳቅ አለ saqq alä v.i.
chuckled, smiled
አሳቀ assaqä v.t. amused
(caused to laugh),
evoked a laughter
አሳሳቀ assasaqä v.t. flirted
with
አስቂኝ assəqiññ adj. funny,
humorous, laughable,
amusing, comic
የሚያስቅ yämmiyassəq adj.
ridiculous

ሳበ sabä v.t. pulled, at-
tracted, lead (a horse
etc.)
ሳቢ sabi adj. /n (one)
who pulls
ሳቢ ዛር sabi zär n. noun of
manner (gram.)
ሰበት səbät n. gravity,
gravitation
ሳቢያ sabbiya n. reason
ተሳበ täsabä v.i. was
pulled; crawled,
creeped
ተሳቢ täsabi n. trailer;
object (gram.)
ተሰቦ täsəbo n. epidemic
ተሳሳበ täsasabä v.t. pulled
each other, attracted
each other
አሳሳበ assasabä v.t. had
(people) pull each
other
አሳበ assabä v.t. had
s/o or s/t pulled
ሳቢሳ sabisa n. gull, seagull;
pelican
ሳብዕ sab'ə adj. seventh order
of Amh. vowel system
ሳተ satä v.i. erred; missed
ስተት or ስሕተት səhtät
n. mistake, fault

63

ስተተኛ	sətätäñña adj./n. faulty, wrong-doer
ተሳተ	täsatä v.i. was missed (target)
ተሳሳተ	täsasatä v.i. erred, made mistake
አሳሳተ	assasatä v.t. caused s/o make a mistake, misled
አሳሳች	assasač adj./n. misleading, one who misleads
አሳተ	assatä v.t misled
አሳቻ	assačča adj. mis- • leading, deceptive (person, road etc.)
አሳች	assač adj. misleading
ሳንቃ	sanqa n. board (wood)
ሳንባ	sanba also ሳምባ samba n. lung
ሳንባማ	sanbamma adj. buff-coloured
ሴንቲሜትC	sentimetər n. centimetre
ሳንቲም	santim n. cent
ሳንጃ	sanǧa n. bayonet
ሳይንስ	sayəns n. science
ሳይንሰኛ	sayənsäñña n. scientist
ሳይንሳዊ	sayənsawi adj. scientific
ሳዱላ	sadulla n. young girl
ሳድስ	sadəs n. adj. sixth order of Amh. vowel system
ሳገ	sagä v. t. forced in, packed in tightly
ሳጋ	saga n. roofing slats, sticks (to support thatch)
ሳጣራ	satara n. rush matting, wicker fencing
ሳጥን	satən n. chest, box
ሳጥናኤል	satna'el n. Satan
*ሳፈፈ	*safäffä
ተንሳፈፈ	tänsaffäfä v.i. floated; drifted (of logs in the river)
አንሳፈፈ	ansaffäfä v.t. floated, got afloat
ሳፋ	safa n. tub
ሴም	sem n. shem (Bibl.)
ሴማዊ	semawi adj. Semitic
ሴራ	sera n. plot, con-

	spiracy
ሴረኛ	seräñña n. plotter, conspirator
አሴረ	aserä v.t. plotted, conspired
ሴሰነ	sessänä see ሰሰነ
ሴት	set n. woman
ሴተኛ አዳሪ	setäñña adari n. prostitute
ሴታሴት	setaset adj. womanish, effemina e
ሴቴ	sete adj. female (of species)
ሴት ልጅ	set ləǧ n. daughter
የሴት ልጅ	yäset ləǧ adj. rude, unmannerly child
ሴትነት	setənnät n. femininty, womanly quality
ሴኮንድ	second n. second time, also ሰኮንድ
ስ—	sə—ver bal pref. denoting time e.g. ስመጣ səmaţa when I come
—ስ	—s nominal suff., What about? as for e.g.
እኔስ	əness What about me?
ስለሱስ ግድየለኝም	səlässus gəddelläññəm as for him, I have nothing to worry
ስለ—	səlä—conj. because, due to the fact that etc.
ስለምን	sälämən int. adv. why? because of what?
ስለዚህ	səläzzih because (of this)
ስለዚያ	səläzziya because (of that)
ስሌት	səllet n. calculation
ስልም አለ	səlləmm alä v.i. lost consciousness
ስልምልም አለ	sələmləmm alä v.i. lost consciousness completely
ስልሳ	səlsa adj. sixty
ስልባቦት	səlbabot n. cream; skim on boiled milk
ስልት	səlt n. manner, mode; knack
ስልተ ምርት	səltä mərt n. mode of production
ስልቻ	səlläčča n. leather pouch, sack

ኅልክ	*səlk* n. telephone, telephone wire
ስልከኛ	*səlkäñña* n. telephone operator
ስልክ ቤት	*səlk bet* n. telegraph office
ስልጆ	*səlǧo* n. dip *(bean flour, oil, mustard and spices)*
ሥሕተት	*see* ሳተ
ሰሙኒ	*səmuni* n. quarter *(of a birr)*
ስማ በለው	*səma bäläw* interj. oyez! oyez!
ስም	*səm* n. name
ስመኛ	*səmäñña* n. one who blames others for his own faults
ስም አወጣ	*səm awäṭṭa* v.t. named *(a child)*
—አጠፋ	—*aṭäffa* v.t. blackened ones's name, ruined one's reputation .
—አጥፊ	—*aṭfi* adj. slanderous
—ማጥፋት ወንጀል	—*maṭfat wänǧäl* n. defamation crime
—ጠራ	—*ṭärra* v.t. called the roll
ስመ ጥሩ/ጥር	*səmä ṭäru/ṭər* adj. reputable, prestigious, celebrity, famous
የሐሰት ስም	*yähassät səm* n. alias
የነገር—	*yänägär*— n. abstract noun *(gram.)*
የተጸውዖ	*yätäṣäwwə'o*— n. proper noun *(gram.)*
የቁሳቁስ—	*yäqusaqus*— n. material noun *(gram.)*
የወል—	*yäwäl*— n. common noun *(gram.)*
የክርስትና—	*yäkərəstənna*— n. Christian name
የጥቅል—	*yäṭəqəll*— n. collective noun *(gram.)*
ተውላጠ—	*täwlaṭä*— n. pronoun
ስያሜ	*səyyame* n. nomenclature, naming
ስያሜ ቃላት	*səyyame qalat* n. coinage *(of terms)*
ስምም	*səməmm* n. agreement
ስምምነት	*səməmənnät* n. agreement, accord, con-

sent, treaty, *see also* ሰጣ

ስምንት	*səmmənt* adj./n. eight
ስምንተኛ	*səmäntäñña* adj. eighth
ስሞታ	*səmota* n. complaint, grumble
ስሞተኛ	*səmotäñña* adj./n. complaining
ስርቅታ	*sərrəqta* n. hiccup
ስርቅ አለ	*sərrəq alä* v.i. hiccupped
ስርየት	*səryät* n. absolution
ስርጥ መንገድ	*sərṭ mängäd* n. narrow path
ስቅጥጥ አለ	*səqṭäṭṭ älä* v.i. be horrified, cringed with horror
ስብሐት	*səbhat* n. praise
ስንት	*sənt* int. adv. how much? how many
—ጊዜ	—*gize* how often? how long?
በስንት ሰዓት	*bäsənt sä'at* when? at what time?
ከስንት አንዴ	*käsənt ände* once in a blue moon
ስንተኛ	*səntäñña* intr. adv. in what order? which number?
ባለስንት	*balä sənt* intr. adv. at which price?
ስንኝ	*sənəññ* rhyme
ስንኳ	*sənk*a or እንኳ *ənkwa* adv. even, not even, ''no!''
ስንዳዶ	*səndädo* n. thick plaiting reed
ስንዴ	*sənde* n. wheat
ስንድድ	*səndəd* n. bracelet *(of glass beads)*
ስዊድን	*swidən* n. Sweden, Swedish
ስድሳ	*sədsa* or *səlsa* ስልሳ adj. sixty
ስድሳኛ	*sədsañña* or ስልሳኛ *səlsañña* sixtieth
ስድስት	*səddəst* adj./n. six
ስድስተኛ አንድ—	*səddəstäñña* adj. sixth *and*—adj. one sixth
ስፖርት	*sport* n. sport
ሶላግ ውሻ	*solag wəšša* n. pointer *(kind of dog)*
ሶመሶመ	*somässomä* v. cantered
ሶምሶማ	*somsoma* n. canter

ሶማሌ   *somale* n. somali

ሶማልያ   *somalya* n. Somalia

ሶረን   *sorän* type of partridge

ሶሻሊዝም   *sošalizm* n. socialism

ሶሻሊስታዊ   *sošialistawi* n. socialist

ሸ

ሸለለ   *šällälä* v.t. chanted
war-chant; v.i. was
very smartly dressed;
boasted

ሸላይ   *šallay* n. chanter of
war chant; smartly
dressed person;
boaster

ሸለላ   *šəlläla* n. war chant;
boast

አሸለለ   *aššällälä* v.t. had
s/o give war-chant;
got s/o smartly dressed

ሸለመ   *šällämä* v.t. decorated;
gave present to

ሸላሚ   *šällami* n. decorator;
one who gives present

ሸለማት   *šälləmat* n. present,
prize

ሸለም   *šälləm* adj. decorated

ሸላለመ   *šälallämä* v.t. decorated over-elaborately

ተሸለመ   *täšällämä* v.i. was
given a present,
prize; was decorated

ተሸላሚ   *täšällami* n. prize
winner, one who
receives a present

ተሸላለመ   *täšälallämä* v.i. ex-
changed presents

አሸለመ   *aššällämä* v.t. had s/o
given a present, prize

ሸለምለም   *šäləmləm* adj. black
and white stripped;
zebra stripped

ሸለምጥማጥ   *šälämətmat* n. genet
(geneta abyssinica)

ሸለሸለ   *šäläššälä* v.t. weeded
young crops (with
plough between rows)

ሸልሻሉ   *šəlšalo* n. weeding
of young crops (with
plough between rows)

ሸለቀቀ   *šäläqqäqä* v.t de-
husked (maize)

ሸልቅቅ   *šəlqəq* adj. de-husked
(maize)

ሸልቃቃ   *šəlqaqa* n. action
of de-husking

ተሸለቀቀ   *täšäläqqäqä* v.t. was
maize

አሸለቀቀ   *aššäläqqäqä* v.t. had
maize de-husked

ሸለቆ   *šäläqo* n. valley

ሸለብ አደረገን   *šälläbb adärrägä* v.i.
dozed off

ሸለብታ   *šäläbta* n. doze

አሸለበ   *ašälläbä* v.i. dozed,
took a nap

ሸለተ   *šällätä* v.t. sheared

ሸላች   *šällač* n. shearer

ሸልት   *šəllət* adj. sheared

መሸለቻ   *mäšälläča* n. shear-
ing aid, shears

ተሸለተ   *täšällätä* v.i. was
sheared

አሸለተ   *aššällätä* v.t. had (a
sheep etc.) sheared

ሸለገ   *šällägä* v.t. drew in
one's stomach

ሸልግ   *šälləg* adj. drawn in

ሸለፈት   *šäläfät* n. foreskin

ሸመቀ   *šämmäqä* v.i. had
grudge, ill will, re-
sentment; plotted

ሸማቂ   *šämmaqi* adj./n.
grudging; plotting,
ill willed

ሸመቃ   *šəmmäqa* n. grudging, ill will, resent-
ment; plotting

ሸመቀቀ   *šämäqqäqä* v.t. drew
tight (belt, noose etc)

ሸምቃቅ   *šəmqaq* n. drawstring

ሸምቃቃ   *šəmqaqqa* n. jumpy,
nervous (person)

ሸምቀቆ   *šämqäqqo* n. noose,
lasso

ተሸመቀቀ   *täšämäqqäqä* v.i. was
drawn tight

ተሸጣቀቀ	tāšämaqqāqā v.i. was jumpy, nervous; cringed
ሸመተ	šämmätä v.t. bought commodities (especially grain)
ሸማች	šämmäč n. consumer
ሸመታ	šämmäta n. market price of grain
ተሸመተ	tāšämmätä v.i. was bought (grain)
አሸመተ	aššämmätä v.t. had bought (grain)
ሸመደደ	šämäddädä v.t. crammed (commit facts to memory)
ሸመድማዳ	šämädmaddu adj./n. (one) who walks awkwardly (usually through bad injury)
ሽምድምድ	šəmədməd adj. walking awkwardly, crippled
ተሸመደመደ	tāšmädämmädä v.i. walked awkwardly
ሸመገለ	šämäggälä v.i. grew old; acted as mediator
ሽምጋይ	šämgay adj. peacemaker, reconciler
ሽምግና	šəmgələnna n. old age; act of mediation
ሽማግሌ	šämagəlle n. old man; a peace-maker, reconciler, mediator
አሸመገለ	ašämäggälä v.t. made s/o old. (work etc.)
ሸመጠጠ	šämäṭṭäṭä v.i. galloped furiously; stripped leaves from branch; told complete lies
ሽምጥ	šəmäṭṭ n. bunch of stripped twigs
ሽምጠጣ	šəmṭäṭa n. furious gallop, run
አሸመጠጠ	aššämäṭṭäṭä v. had (twig) stripped
ሸሚዝ	šämiz n. shirt
*ሸማ	see ተሸማ and ሻማ
ሸማ	šämma n. tunic
ሸማኔ	šänmane n. weaver
የሸማኔ እቃ	yäšämmane əqa n. loom
ሸምበቆ	šämbäqqo n. cane

	(material)
ሸረሞጠ	šärämmöṭä v.i. prostituted
ሸርሙጣ	šärmuṭa n. harlot, prostitute; promiscuous person (male)
ሸርሙጥና	šərmuṭənna n. prostitution
አሸረሞጠ	ašärämmöṭä v.t. pandered, pimped
ሸራሪት	šärärit n. spider
የሸራሪት ድር	yäšärärit dər n. spider web
ሸረሸረ	šäräššärä v.t. eroded (with water)
ሸርሸር	šəršər adj. eroded
ተሸረሸረ	tāšäräššärä v.i. was eroded
*ሸረሸረ	see ተንሸረሸረ
*ሸረተተ	see ተንሸራተተ
ሸረኛ	šärräñña adj. wicked, mischievous
ሸር	šärr n. wickedness, mischief
ሸረኝነት	šärräññənnät n. wickedness, mischievousness
ሸረከተ	šäräkkätä v.t. ripped, tore apart; ground coarsely
ሸርከት	šərkət adj. ripped, torn apart; coarsely grounded
ሸረካከተ	šäräkakkätä v. gashed, tore to shreds
ተሸረከተ	tāšäräkkätä v.t. was ripped, torn; was ground coarsely
ተሸረካከተ	tāšäräkakkätä v.i. was torn to pieces
ሸረደደ	šäräddädä v.t. derided, talked behind s/o's back, mocked
ሸርዳጅ	šärdaǧ n. backbiter, mocker
ሸርዳዳ	šərdada n. backbiting, gossipping (behind s/o's back)
ሸረፈ	šärräfä v.t. broke off (a piece of s/t), pulled out (milk tooth), lost (tooth); changed (into small money)

67

ሽራፋ	*šarafa* n/adj. *(one)* who has lost some teeth
ሽራፊ	*šərrafi* n. segment, piece *(broken off)*
ሽርፋት	*šərrəfat* n. main part *(after piece is broken off)*
ሽራረፈ	*šärarräfä* v.t. broke off *(several pieces)*
ተሽረፈ	*täšärräfä* v.i. was broken off; pulled out; changed *(money)*
ተሽራፊ	*täšärrafi* adj. likely to break off
ተሽራረፈ	*täšärarräfä* v.i. be chipped, broken in several places
አሽረፈ	*aššärräfä* v. i. caused *(s/t)* to be chipped, broken off
ሽራ	*šära* n. canvas
ሸሸ	*šäššä* v.i. ran away
ሸሺ	*šäši* n. fugitive
ሽሽት	*šəššət* n. running away
መሸሸ	*mäšaša* n. place of refuge
አሸሸ	*ašäššä* v.t. took into safety, harboured
አሸሸ	*aššäššä* v.t. helped *(s/o)* run away
ሸሸገ	*šäššägä* v.t. hid *(s/t)*
ሸሻጊ	*šäššagi* n. one who hides
ሽሹግ	*šəššəg* adj. hidden
መሸሸጊያ	*mäšäššägiya* n. hiding place *(for s/t or s/o)*
ተሸሸገ	*täšäššägä* v. i. was hidden
መሸሸጊያ	*mäššäšägyia* n. hiding · place *(for oneself)*
አሸሸገ	*aššäššägä* v. t. help s/o hide himself
ሸቀለ	*šäqqälä* v. i. worked, toiled *(manual work, occasionally)*
ሸቃይ	*šäqqay* n. occasional worker, toiler
ሸቀላ	*šəqqäla* n. working, toiling
አሸቀለ	*aššäqqälä* v. t. had s/o work, toil

ሸቀሸቀ	*šäqäššäqä* v. t. poked repeatedly *(e.g. with stick)*
መሸቅሸቂያ	*mäšäqšäqiyä* n. stick, etc. *(used to poke s/t)*
ሸቀበ	*šäqqäbä* v. i. predicted bad luck; rigged a balance *(to give short measure)*
ሸቃቢ	*šäqqabi* n. pessimist; one who falsifies balance *(to give short measure)*
ሽቀባ	*šəqqäba* n. predicting bad luck; rigging a balance
ተሸቀበ	*täšäqqäbä* v.i. was rigged *(scales, balance)*; was wished bad luck
*ሸቀበ	*see* አሸቀበ
ሸቀን	*šäqän* n. filth
ሸቀናም	*šäqänam* adj filthy
ሸቀጠ	*šäqqätä* v.t. retailed
ሸቀጣ ሸቀጥ	*šäqäta šäqät* n. retail· goods
ሸቃጭ መሸቀጪ ገንዘብ	*šäqqač* n. retailer *mäšäqqäča gänzäb* n. retailer's capital
ሸበለለ	*šäbällälä* v. t. rolled up *(carpet, etc.)*
ሽብለል	*šəblal* adj. rolled up
*ሸበለበለ	*šäbäläbbälä*
ተሸበለበለ	*täšbäläbbälä* v. i. curled
ሸበላ	*šäbäla* adj. tall and handsome
*ሸበረ	*see* ተሸበረ
ሸበረቀ	*šäbärräqä*
ሸብራቃ	*šäbraqqa* adj. elaborately decorated *(e.g. cloth embroidery)*
አሸበረቀ	*ašäbärräqä* v.t./v.i. adorned, decorated; sparkled *(with decorations)*; was elegant
አሸብራቂ	*ašäbraqi* adj/n. *(one)* who is elaborately dressed, *(place)* which is elaborately decorated
ሸበሸበ	*šäbäššäbä* v.t. ruched,

68

pleated, *(tailoring)*; wrinkled *(forehead)*

ሸብሸብ *šəbšəb* adj. pleated *(cloth)*

ሸብሸቦ *šəbšəbo* n. pleated dress

አሸበሸበ *ašäbäššäbä* v. swayed gracefully *(dancing)*

ሸበበ *šäbbäbä* v.t. haltered; muzzled

መሸበቢያ *mäšäbbäbiya* n. halter; muzzle ·

ተሸበበ *täšäbbäbä* v.i. was haltered; muzzled

አሸበበ *äššäbbäbä* v.i. had *(an animal)* haltered, muzzled

ሸበተ *šäbbätä* v.i. got grey *(hair)*

ሸበት *šəbät* n. grey hair

ሸበታም *šəbätam* adj. very grey *(hair)*

ሸበቶ *šäbbäto* adj. grey haired

አሸበተ *ašäbbätä* v.t. caused s/o to go grey

ሸብ አደረገ *šäbb adärrägä* v.t. hitched, tied loosely

ሸተ *šätä* or አሸተ *ašätä* v.t. became partly ripe *(peas, beans, maize etc. soft enough to eat)*

እሸት *əšät* n/adj. (s/t) just ripe enough to eat *(peas etc.)*

እሸትነት *əšätətnnät* n. part-ripeness *(soft, edible stage)*

ሸተተ *šättätä* v.t. smelt bad, stank

ሸታ *šətta* p. smell

መጥፎ— *mäṭfo*—unpleasant odour

ሸቶ *šätto* or ሸቱ *šättu* n. perfume

አሸተተ *ašättätä* v.t. smelt

አሸተተ *aššättätä* v.t. got s/o to smell s/t

ሸተት አደረገ *šätätt adärrägä* v.t. slid along

ሸተትየ *šätätəyya* n. slide *(smooth slope)*

ሸታታ *šätata* adj. sloping

—መሬት *—märet* n. slopy ground

ሸነሸነ *šänäššänä* v.t. divided up *(land)*; cut into equal slices, parts; pleated *(cloth)*

ሸንሸና *šənsäna* n. division cutting up

ሸንሸን *šənšən* adj. divided, cut up; pleated

ተሸነሸነ *täšänäššänä* v.i. was divided up *(land)*, was cut into equal pieces; was pleated, ruched

አሸነሸነ *aššänäššänä* v.t. had s/o divide up, cut up, pleat

ሸነቀረ *šännäqqärä* v.ṭ. forced in, jammed in

ሸነቈረ *šänäqqʷärä* v.t. bored *(hole)*

ሸንቈር *šänqʷər* n. small bored hole

ሸነቀጠ *šänäqqäṭä* v.i. kept fit

ሸንቃጣ *šənqaṭṭa* adj. fit *(in good athletic condition)*

ሸነቈጠ *šänäqqʷäṭä* v.t. whipped, lashed

ሸነተረ *šänättärä* v.ṭ. made rows *(in earth for cultivation)*; made grooves*(water erosion)*

ሸንትር *šəntər* n. groove

ሸንትራት *šəntərat* n. row *(of earth for cultivation)*

ሸነታተረ *šänätattärä* v.t. made many rows; severely eroded

ተሸነተረ *täšänättärä* v.i. was cultivated in rows; was eroded

ሸንከፈ *šänäkkäfä* v.t. hobbled

ሸንካፋ *šänkaffa* adj. hobbled

ሸነደረ *šänäddärä* v.i. was cross-eyed

ሸንዳራ *šändarra* adj. cross-eyed

ሸነገለ *šänäggälä* v.t. comforted *(e.g. child with promises of gifts etc.)*

ሸንጋይ *šängay* n./adj. *(one)* who gives false re-

ሸንገላ šəngäla n. giving false reassurance; cajolery

ሸነጠ šännäṭä or ነሸጠ näššäṭä v.t. inspired, aroused great enthusiasm, made excited

ሸና šänna v.t. urinated
ሸንት šənt n. urine
—ቤት —bet n. lavatory
ሸንታም šəntam adj./n. incontinent, cowardly (person)
መሸኒያ mäšniya n. chamber pot, container for passing urine
አሸና aššänna v.t. had s/o urinate (chiid, a sick person)
ሸንበቆ šänbäqqo also ሸምበቆ šämbäqqo n. cane (plant)
ሸንተረር šäntärär n. ridge; escarpment
ሸንተረርማ šäntärärəmma adj. ridge like
ሸንከሉ šänkällo n. bucket
ሸንኮር አገዳ šänkor agäda n. sugar cane
ሸንዳ šända also አሸንዳ ašända n. water container; gutter (spout of roof)
ሸንጎ šängo n. assembly, meeting (e.g. of village elders); parliament
ሸንጎበት šängobät n. side of the face
ሸኘ šäññä v.t. showed out, saw s/o on his way
ሸኚ šäññi n. one who shows out, sees s/o on his way
መሸኛ mäšäñña adj. covering (letter)
የመሸኛ ግብዣ yämäšäñña gəbža n. farewell party
ተሸኘ täšäññä v.i. was shown out, seen on one's way
አሸኘ aššäññä v.t. had s/o shown out
አሸኛኘት aššäñañät n. fare-

well ceremony
* ሸከመ see ተሸከመ
* ሸክረከረ *šäkäräkkärä
ሸክርክሪት šäkrkərit n. hoop, wheel, see also ተሸ ክርክር ፣ አሸክርክረ
ሸከሸከ šäkäššäkä v.t. de-husked (grain etc. in a mortar); crushed (e.g. hops, in a mortar)
ተሸከሸከ täšäkäššäkä v. i. was de-husked, crushed (in a mortar)
አሸከሸከ aššäkaššäkä v. t.helped another to de-husk, crush (in a mortar, a two-man operation)
ሸከፈ šäkkäfä v.t. arranged neatly, put in order
ሸካፉ šäkkaffa n. orderly, methodical person
ሸክፍ šəkkəf adj. orderly, methodical (e.g. good housewife)
* ሸካካ see አሸካካ
ሸክላ šäkla n. clay
—ሠሪ —särri n. potter
—ቀለም —qäläm adj. light brown
የሸክላ እቃ yäšäkla əqa n. earthenware
ሸክሌ šäkle n. mule of light brown colour
ሸክም šäkəm n. load
*ሸክረመመ see ተሸክረመመ
ሸኩት šäkkʷätä v. t. scuffed, grazed; (made hand movement for "stone," "scissors" and "paper" game)
ተሸኩን täšakkʷätä v. i. played "stone, "scissors" and "paper" hand game
ሸኮና šäkona n. hoof
*ሸወረረ *šäwärrärä
ሸውራራ säwrarra adj. cross-eyed
መንሸዋረር mänšäwarär inf. to go cross-eyed
ሸዋ šäwa n. Shewa (name of one of the fourteen Administrative Regions of Ethiopia)

70

ሻይ or ሻይ
ሻየኛ   *šäyäññä* n. Shewan dialect

ሻዉሻዋ   *šäwšawwa* n. adj. (one) who has shallow affections

ሻጋሻገ   see አሸጋሸገ

ሻጐረ   *šägg^wärä* v.t. bolted (e.g. door), locked up (animals in byre, stable)

ሻጐር   *šəggur* adj. bolted; locked in

መሻጐሪያ   *mäšägg^wäriya* n. bolt

ተሻጐረ   *täšägg^wärä* v.i. was bolted; was locked up

ሻጐጠ   *šägg^wäṭä* v.t. holstered, tucked into (belt or armpit as gun or knife)

ሻጐጥ   *šəgguṭ* n. revolver, pistol

ሻጐጥ አለ   *šəgguṭṭ alä* v.t. hid o/s in a confined space

—አደረገ   —*adärrägä* v.t. hid (s/o, s/t in a confined space)

ተሻጐጠ   *täšägg^wäṭä* v.t. hid o/s

ሻጠ   *šäṭä* v.t. sold

ሻጠኝ   *šäṭäññ* he fooled me

ሻጭ   *šač* n. seller, vendor

ሻያጭ   *šəyyač* n. sale

መሻጫ   *mäšača* n. selling place

ሻሻጠ   *šašaṭä* v.t. sold out, sold quickly

ተሻጠ   *täšäṭä* v.i. was sold

አሻሻጠ   *aššašaṭä* v.t. helped in selling, acted as a broker

አሻሻጭ   *aššašač* n. broker; salesclerk, salesman

አሻጠ   *aššäṭä* v.t. had s/t sold

ሻፈተ   *šäffätä* v.i. rebelled

ሻፍች   *šäffač* adj/n. rebellious, one who rebels

ሻፍታ   *šəfta* n. a rebel

ሻፍትነት   *šəftənnät* n. rebellion

መሻፈቻ   *mäšäffäčä* sanctuary, hideout (for escaped rebels)

አሻፈተ   *aššäffätä* v.t. had s/o rebel

ሻፈነ   *šäffänä* v.t. covered,

concealed; veiled (of fog)

ዓይን—   *ayn—* v.ṭ. blindfolded

ሻፈን   *šäfan* n. cover (of book etc.); cover (pretence); wrapper, casing

የዓይን—   *yä'ayn—* n. eyelid

ሻፍን   *šäffən* adj. covered

ሻፍንፍን   *šäfənfən* adj. covered, concealed

መሻፈኛ   *mäšäffäña* n. cover, lid

ሻፈፈነ   *šäfaffänä* v.t. put cover on; tried to conceal, tried to evade the issue

ተሻፈነ   *täšäffänä* v.i. was covered

ተሻፈፈነ   *täšäfaffänä* v.t. wrapped oneself, covered oneself (with cloak) etc.; was concealed

አሻፈነ   *aššäffänä* v.t. had s/t covered, wrapped

ሻፈጠ   *šäffäṭä* v.ṭ. denied falsely, deceived; broke out afresh (wound)

ሻፋጭ   *šäffač* adj. dishonest

ሻፍጥ   *šäfṭ* n. false denial, deception

ሻፍጠኛ   *šäfṭäñña* n. perfidious

ሻፈፈ   *šäffäfä* v.i. had splay-feet

ሻፈፉ   *šäfafa* adj. splay-footed

መንሻፈፍ   *mänšafäf* inf. to be splay-footed, to warp

አንሻፈፈ   *anšaffäfä* v.t. turned one's feet out

ተንሻፈፈ   *tänšaffäfä* v.i. was splay-footed

ሹልዳ or ሹልዳ   *šuludä* or *šulädä* n. thigh-muscle

ሹሩባ   *šurrubba* n. hair style (tightly plaited)

ሹሩቤ   *šurrubbe* n. ṭäg flask (bərälle)

ሹራብ   *šurrab* n. sweater

የግር—   *yägər—* n. socks, stockings

የጅ—   *yäǧǧ—* n. gloves

ሹሮ   *šuro* n. thickening (powdered bean or chick pea, used in wäṭ)

ሹሮፕ   *šurop* n. syrup

ሹካ	šukka n. fork
ሹክ አለ	šukk alä v.ṭ. whispered (in s/o 's ear)
ሹክክ አለ	šukǝkk alä v.i. acted stealthily, was furtive (manner)
ሾካካ	šokaka n. tell-tale, tale-bearer
አንሿከከ	anšʷakkäkä v. t. gossiped; bore bad report about s/o
አንሿካኪ	anšʷakaki adj/n.(one) who gossips; tells tales
አንሾካሾከ	anšokäšokkä v.t. gossiped
ሹዋ አለ	šwa alä v.i. whooshed (e.g. grain poured from container)
ሹጥ	šuṭ n. tapeworm (a detached piece)
ሹጣም	šuṭam adj. n. one who has tapeworm (insult)
ሺ	ši or ሺሁ ših adj thousand
ሺህኛ	šihǝñña adj. thousandth
ሻለቃ	šaläqa or ሻቃ šaqa n. major (title)
—ጦር	—ṭor n. battalion
ሻምበል	šambäll n. captain
—ጦር	—ṭor n. company
ሺል	šil n. embryo
ሻ	ša v.t. wanted, wished
ምን ትሻለህ?	mǝn tǝšalläh what do you want?
ምንም አልሻ	mǝnǝmm alša I want nothing
ሻለቃ	šaläqa see ሺ.
*ሻለ	*šalä
ተሻለ	täšälä v.i. improved, was better, was preferable, was advisable
ተሻለው	täšaläw felt better; preferred
ተሻሻለ	täšašala v.i. improved ameliorated
አሻለ	aššälä v.t. improvd; ameliorated
አሻሻለ	aššäšälä v.t. improved, ameliorated; amended, reformed
ማሻሻያ	in የማሻሻያ ሐሳብ yämaššašaya hassab

	amendment
ሻማ	šama n. candle,
ሻሞ	šamo struggle (to abtain s/t desirable)
ሻምበል	see ሺ.
ሻምላ	šamla n. rapier
ሻረ	šarä v.t dismissed (from office); reversed (a decision) impeached; cured (wound)
ከሹመት—	käšumät— v.t impeached; dismissed from office
በዓል—	bä'al—v.i worked on a holiday
ሹምሽር	šumšǝr n. re-shuffle, shake up (government, administration)
ሽረት	šǝrät n. cure
አሻረ	ašarä v.t cured; cured of tapeworm
ተሻረ	täšarä v.i was impeached
የማይሻር የማይለወጥ	yämmayǝššar yämmayǝlläwwäṭ hard and fast (rule)
አሻረ	aššarä v.t. had s/o impeached
ሻሽ	šaš n. head scarf (usually of fine gauze), gauze
ሻሽ	šašc adj. white in colour (e.g. cow, horse, clothes)
ሻቀለ	šaqqälä v.i. worried, tormented with anxieties, bothered
ሻንቅላ	šanqǝlla n. negro
ሻንቆ	šanqo n. nickname for a very dark person
ሻንጣ	šanṭa n. suitcase
ሻኛ	šañña n. hump
ሻከረ	šakkärä v.i. got coarse rough (in texture,) rough, harsh (sound)
ሻከር አለ	šakärr alä v.i. got rather coarse (in texture)
ሻካራ	šakara adj. coarse (in texture)
አሻከረ	ašakkärä v.t. made coarse, rough
ሆድ—	hod — v.t. disappointed, antagonised,

	caused *(s/o)* to bear a grudge	ሽቦ	*šabo* n. wire
ሽኵራ	*šakʷǝra* n. censer decoration *(usually small bells)*	ሽንብራ	*šǝnbra* or ሽምብራ *šǝmbǝra* n. chick-pea
ሻይ	*šay* n. tea	ሽንት	*šant* n. urine see ሽና
—ቤት	—*bet* n. tea house	ሽንኩርት	*šǝnkurt* n. onion
*ሻገረ	see ተሻገረ	ቀይ—	*qäyy*— n. onion
ሻገታ	*šaggätä* v.i. went mouldy	ነጭ—	*näčč*— n. garlic
ሻጋታ	*šagata* n. mould; caries	ሽንጥ	*šanṭ* n. waist-line
አሻገተ	*ašaggätä* v.t. caused *s/t* to go mouldy	ሽንጣም	*šanṭam* adj. long-waisted
ሻግያ	*šagǝyya* adj. extremely dark *(person, insult)*	ሽንፈላ	*šǝnfǝlla* n. rumen *(second stomach of ruminating animals)*
ሻጠ	*šaṭä* v.t. forced in *(bayonet etc.)*	ሽክና	*šakkǝnna* n. drinking gourd
ተሻጠ	*täšaṭä* v.i. was forced in	ሽክ አለ	*šǝkk alä* v.i. was smartly dressed *(chic)*
ሻፈደ	*šaffädä* v.i. felt aroused *(sexually)*	ሽኮኮ	*šǝkokko* n. rock hyrax
ሻፋዳ	*šafada* adj. highly aroused *(sexually)*	ሽው አለ	*šaww alä* v.i. whispered *(light breeze, wind)*
አሻፈደ	*ašaffädä* v.t. aroused *(sexually)*	ሽውታ	*šawwǝta* n. sudden attack of sickness
ሼክ	*šek* n. sheik	ሽፋል	*šafal* n. eye-brow
ሽህር	*šǝhǝr* n. heifer	ሽፍ አለ	*šǝff alä* v.i. came out in a rash
ሽል	*šǝl* also ሺል *šil* n. embryo	ሽፍታ	*šǝffǝta* n. rash
ሽለጦ	*šǝllǝṭo* n. black bread	ሾለ	*šolä* v.i. tapered, grew to a point
ሽመላ	*šǝmäla* n. stork	ሹል	*šul* adj. pointed
ሽማል	*šǝmäl* n. bat *(stick)*; bamboo, cane	ሹልአፍ	*šul'af* adj. talkative
ሽምብራ	*šǝmbǝrra* or ሽንብራ *šǝnbǝra* n. chick-pea	አሾለ	*äšolä* v.t. sharpened, made tapered
—ዱቤ	*dubbe* n. chick-pea *(large)*	ሾለከ	*šolläkkä* v.t. passed through; found one's way out
ሽር አለ	*šǝrr alä* was smartly dressed	ሾላከ	*šollaka* n. adj. in-quisitive *(person)*: nosey-parker
ሽሩ	*šǝrǝru* or ሹሩሩ *šururu* or እሹሩሩ *ǝššǝruru* n. lullaby	መሿለኪያ	*mäšuʷaläkiya* n. opening
		አሾለከ	*ašolläkä* v.i. helped *s/o* squeeze out *(through narrow opening)*; smuggled *s/t* out
ሽርሽር	*šǝrräšǝrr* n. walk *(for pleasure)*; pleasure trip		
ሽርጥ	*šǝrrǝṭ* n. apron	መሿለኪያ	*mäšuläkiya* n. bolt-hole; escape hole
አሸረጠ	*äšärräṭä* v.t. put on, wore *(apron)*	አሾለከ	*ašolläkä* v.t. smuggled *(s/t.)* helped *(s/o)* out
ሽርካ	*šǝrka* n. partner, associate, also ሽርክ	ተሿለከለከ	*täšuläkälläkä* v.t. wriggled out, through
ሽባ	*šǝba* adj. lame	ሾላ	*šola* n. fig tree, fig *(fucus sycomorus)*
ሽብልቅ	*šǝbǝlläq* n. wedge *(used in splitting logs)*	ሾመ	*šomä* v.t. promoted, gave rank
ሽብር	*šǝbbǝr* n. terror		

ሿ˙ᜒ *ʼami* n. one who promotes

ሹⵄ *šumät* n. promotion, rank

ሹ˙ም *šum* n. superior, official

ሹምሽር *šumšər* n. re-shuffle, shake-up

ተሿᜒ *täšoma* v.i. was appointed, was given rank

ተሿᜒᜒ *täšʷami* adj./ n candidate for rank, promotion

ተሿᜒᜒ *täšʷašʷamä* v. t. honoured each other, promoted

each other

አሿᜒ *aššoma* v.t. had (s/o) appointed, promoted

ሿርባ *šorba* n. soup, bouillon

ሿቀ *see* አሿቀ

ሿተል *šotäl* n. sword

ሿከከ *šokkäkä* v.i. acted stealthily cf. ሿከከ አለ

ሿካካ *šokaka* adj. tell-tale, tale-bearer

ሿጠጠ *šoṭṭäṭä* v.i. was wedge-shaped, tapered

ሿጣጣ *šoṭaṭa* adj. wedge-shaped

ሿጥ አደረገ *šoṭṭ adärrägä* v.t. whipped, struck sharply

*ሿᜒ *see* አሿᜒ

— ቀ —

ቀለን *ʼaläh* n. cartridge (spent)

ቀለለ *ʼällälä* v.i. became light, lost weight; acted disrespectfully

ተለል አለ *qäläll alä* v.i. became rather light

ቀላል *qällal or* ቀሊል *qälil* adj. light; disrespectful

ቑᜒት *qəllet* n. disrespect, scandal

ቑሌታም *qälletam or* ቅሌተኛ *qäletäñña* adj. disrespectful, scandalous

አቀለለ *aqällälä* v.t. made lighter, simplified

ተቃለለ *täqallälä* v.i. was made lighter, was simplified; became notorious

አቃለለ *aqqällälä* v.t. oversimplified, made completely light

ቐለᜒ *qällämä* v.i. became coloured, tinted

ቀለም *qäläm* n. colour, tint; ink

ጎብረ— *häbrä—* n. colour harmony

የቀለም አባት *yäqäläm abbat* n.

teache. Master

ቀለም ነከረ *qäläm näkkärä* v.t. dyed

—ቀባ *—qäbba* v.t. painted

—አገባ *—agäbba* v.t. dyed

አቀለᜒ *aqällämä* v.t. coloured dyed, tinted

ማቀለᜒያ *maqlämiya* n. dye, tint

ቀለሰ *qälläsä* v.t. stooped, bent down

ቤት— *bet—* v.t. built a small house

ቅልስልስ *qəlsləs* adj. bashful

ቀላለሰ *qälalläsä* v.t. erected a small house in haste

ተቀለሰ *täqälläsä* v.i. was erected (a house) hastily

አስቀለሰ *asqälläsä* v.t. had a small house erected in haste

የለበ *qälläbä* v.t. fed (people), provided board

ቀለበተኛ *qälläbtäñña* n. boarder

ቀለብ *qälläb* n. board, full-board; provisions (for journey)

ቀላቢ *qällabi* n. landlady; housekeeper

ቅልብ *qälləb* adj. fattened up (animals)

74

ቀሰሰ *qässäsä* be ordained priest, become a priest
[See ቄስ, ቀሲስ, ቅስና]

'ለበ *qälläbä* catch in midair (ball or a falling object)

ኦለበ *qälläbä* (B) feed (oxen), provide support, nourish
ቀለብ *qälläb* food supplies, rations, stipend
የቤት ፡ ቀለብ supplies (of food)
የቤት ፡ ቀላቢት *yäbet qällabit* housekeeper

ኦልብ *qälb* mind, intelligence, power of reasoning
ቀልበ ፡ ቢስ scatterbrain
ቀልባም *qälbam* prudent

ቃሊብ *qalib* mold (casting)

ቀለበሰ *qäläbbäsä* turn down (the collar)

ቀለበት *qäläbät* ring (finger ring), loop
የቀለበት ፡ ጣት ring finger

ቃልቻ *qalläčča* magician

ቆለኛ, see ቄላ

ቀላዋጭ *qälawač* one who goes from house to house to get food, parasite

ቀለደ *qällädä* (B) joke, have fun, play a joke on, make fun of, trifle, kid, tease
ተቃለደ *täqallädä* joke with each other, joke with people
ቀልድ, see below

ቀላድ *qälad* rope serving to measure land, land that is measured

ቀልድ *qäld* joke, fun, jest, mockery, farce, wit, humor (see ቀለደ)
ቀልደኛ *qäldäñña* joker, witty, jocular
ቀልደኛ ፡ ነህ no kidding, are you kidding?
ቀልደኛነት *qäldäññannät* sense of humor

ኦለጠ *qällätä* melt, vi. (of butter, of metal), liquefy, vi. (of butter), be animated (applause), to be in quantity (of an item)
አቀለጠ *aqällätä* liquefy, vt. (butter), smelt (ore), melt (vt.), thaw (the ice), cause to resound
የቀለጠ *yäqällätä* molten (metal)
የቀለጠ ፡ ሀብታም very rich
ማቅለጫ *maqläča* melting pot
መቅለጫ *mäqläča*, in የብረት ፡ መቅ
ለጫ foundry

ቅልጥም *qältəm* marrow, shin, shinbone, shank

ቀለጠፈ *qälättäfä* hasten (vi.), hurry (vi.), make haste, be quick in doing something
አቀለጠፈ *aqälättäfä* make to hasten, hasten (vt.)
ቀልጣፋ *qältaffa* quick, rapid, fast, swift, supple, deft, nimble (acrobat), agile, dexterous, handy, skillful, efficient, expeditious, facile (writer)
ቅልጥፍና, see below
አቀላጠፎ *aqqälatfo* fluently
የቀለጠፈ *yäqälättäfä* limber (piano player)

ቅልጥፍና *qəltafənna* dispatch (promptness), dexterity, efficiency, skill (facility); see ቀለጠፈ
ቅልጥፍና ፡ ጉደለው be clumsy
በቅልጥፍና skillfully

ቁልጭ ፡ ቁልጭ ፡ አለ *qulləčč qulləčč alä* light up (of eyes); see *ቄለጨለጨ

*ቄለጨለጨ, ተቀለጨለጨ *täqʷläčälläčä* blink repeatedly (of eyes); see ቁልጭ

*ቀላፋ, እንቀላፋ *anqälaffa* doze, fall asleep
እንቅልፍ *ənqəlf* sleep (n.)

ቁልፍ *qulf* key, button, snap (of dress); see ቄለፈ
ቁልፍ ፡ ሠራተኛ locksmith
ቁልፍ ፡ ያዥ custodian, guard (see ያዘ)

የቁልፍ ፡ ቀዳዳ keyhole
የቁልፍ ፡ እናት lock
የቁልፍ ፡ ጋን lock
መርፌ ፡ ቁልፍ safety pin
የእጅጌ ፡ ቁልፍ cuff link

ቄለፈ qʷälläfä (B) lock (vt.), close with a key, buckle, button, hook (a dress), fasten
ተቄለፈ täqʷälläfä, passive of the preceding; lock (vi.)
ተቄላለፈ täqʷälalläfä be locked together (bumpers)
አቄላለፈ aqqʷälalläfä interlace (vt.), couple together (two cars)
ቁልፍ, see above
መቄለፊያ ፡ ጋን mäqʷälläfiya gan lock

ቀማ qämma (B) rob, take by force, carry away by force, snatch from the hand
†ቀማኛ qämmañña brigand, robber

*ቀማ, አቅማማ aqmamma falter (hesitate), play with the idea of doing something

ቁም qum, see ቆመ
ቁም ፡ ለቁም lengthwise
ቁም ፡ ሣጥን cupboard, cabinet, wardrobe (closet)
(ባለመሳቢያ ፡ ቁም ፡ ሣጥን chest of drawers)
ቁም ፡ ነገር worthwhile thing, important matter, significance, serious matter, basic thing, essential thing
ቁም ፡ ነገር ፡ አለው carry weight
ቁም ፡ ነገረኛ trustworthy (person), dutiful (person)
ቁም ፡ ጸሐፊ scribe, calligrapher
(የ)ቁም ፡ ጽሕፈት calligraphy
በቁሙ in his lifetime
በቁሙ ፡ ቀረ be unchanging, be constant

ቂም qim resentment, grudge, rancor, ill feeling, revenge (see *ቀየመ)
ቂም ፡ በቀል vengeance, feud
ቂም ፡ ያዘ nurse a grudge

ቂመኛ qimäñña vindictive, person who holds a grudge

ቃመ qamä swallow without chewing, eat powdery things (roasted grain, sugar) from the hand

ቆመ qomä stop (vi.), be erected, stand, stand up, halt (vi.), come to a halt, cease, land (of a ship), be under way (of market)
(ቆማ ፡ ቀረች she is an old maid)
አቆመ aqomä stand something up, erect (a monument), raise, bring to rest, arrest (stop), put an end to, stop (vt.), bring to a stop, halt (vt.), park (a car), settle (an argument)
ተቃወመ täqawwämä be against, oppose, be opposed to, hinder, protest, resist, object, raise an objection, contradict, dissent, disapprove, take issue with, defy (the authority)
ተቋቋመ täqʷaqʷamä be established, be founded, be set up, be constituted, come into being, withstand (oppose), defy, resist, fight against, counter, cope with, come to grips with (a problem)
አቋቋመ aqqʷaqʷamä establish, set up (a business), situate, build (a factory), found (a bank), organize (a committee)
ቆም ፡ አለ qomm alä pause (v.)
ቁም, see above
ቋሚ qʷami permanent, steady (work), salaried (employee), skeleton (of building)
(ቋሚ ፡ ሥራ career)
(ቋሚ ፡ ንብረት immovable property
ቋመት, see below
አቋም aqʷam stand (position), standpoint, approach (attitude), structure (of human body, of organization), makeup, framework, bearing (manner)
ተቃዋሚ täqawami opponent, dissident
ተቃውሞ täqawmo opposition, ob-

76

jection, protest, resistance, disapproval (expression against)
(ካላንዳች ፡ ተቃውሞ unopposed; see አንዳች)
መቃወም mäqqawäm opposition
(በመቃወም against, in opposition)
መቋቋም mäqqʷaqʷam, in የመቋቋም ፡ ኃይል resistance (power of resisting)
መቋሚያ mäqʷamiya prayer stick
መቆሚያ, see above

ቀመለ qämmälä be filled with lice; (B) remove lice
ቅማል qəmal louse

ቀመመ qämmämä (B) add condiments, add spices, season (v.)
ቀማሚ qämmami, in መድኃኒት ፡ ቀማሚ druggist, pharmacist
ቅመም, see below

ቅመም qəmäm spice, condiment, seasoning (see ቀመመ)
ቅመማ ፡ ቅመም qəmäma qəmäm all kinds of spices, ingredients, seasoning
ቅመም ፡ የሌለው bland (food)
ቅመም ፡ የበዛበት —yäbäzzabbät spicy

ቀመረ qämmärä reckon (time)

ቁማር qumar gambling, game of chance
ቁማር ፡ ተጫወተ gamble (v.); see *ጫወተ
ቁማርተኛ qumartäñña gambler

ቀመሰ qämmäsä taste, take a taste, eat a little
(ኑር ፡ ቀመስ experience life)
አቀመሰ aqämmäsä give someone something to taste

ቀሚስ qämis gown, dress (of woman)
ጉርድ ፡ ቀሚስ skirt

ቀመቀመ qämäqqämä hem (v.)
ቅምቅማት qəmqəmat hem (n.)

ቀምበር, see ቀንበር

ቁመት qumät size (of a person), height (of man), stature (see ቆመ)

ቀማኛ qämmaňña robber, brigand (see ቀማ)
ቀማኝነት qämmaňňannät robbery
ቁመኛ, see ቂም

*ቀመጠ, ተቀመጠ täqämmäṭä (B) sit, sit down, seat oneself, settle (vi.), sojourn, mount (a horse, mule), ascend (the throne), be put away (set apart), be set aside
አስቀመጠ asqämmäṭä place, seat, make to sit, lay, set apart, set aside, save, put aside, keep (reserve), store, deposit, purge (of medicine)
የቅምጥ yäqəmməṭ sitting, seated
መቀመጫ mäqqämäča seat
ማስቀመጫ masqämmäča container, depository, repository, saucer
ተቀምጥ, see below
ተቀማጭ täqämmač resident, reserve (saved money), savings deposit
አቀማመጥ aqqämamäṭ manner of sitting, seating, location, placement, situation (position), layout
የሚያስቀምጥ ፡ መድኃኒት yämmiyasqämmäṭ mädhanit purgative

ቁምጣ qumṭa shorts, short trousers

ቆማጥ qomäṭ cudgel

ቆማጣ qomaṭa, ቁማጣ qʷämaṭa leper, leperous, maimed by leprosy
ቁምጣና qumṭənna leprosy

ቀረ qärrä be left, remain, be missing, be absent, absent oneself, stay away, be cancelled (meeting), be omitted, be no longer in existence, go out of use, die out (of custom), be called off
(ኋላ ፡ ቀረ stay behind)
(ወደ ፡ ኋላ ፡ ቀረ be slow (of watch), be backward, lag)
(እንደወጣ ፡ ቀረ he never returned, he is still missing)

77

አስቀረ *asqärrä* make remain, leave, leave out, abolish, exclude, cancel, omit (details), deprive, prevent (keep from happening), keep out (vt.), keep aside (vt.), hold back (vt.), put an end to, waive
(ወደ ፡ ኋላ ፡ አስቀረ cause to lag behind)
ቀርቶ *qärto* let alone, leaving aside
(ሌላው ፡ ቀርቶ to say nothing of others)
ቢቀረው *biqäräw*, in አንድ ፡ ቀን ፡ ቢቀ ረው one day before
ቢቀር *biqär*, in ሌላው ፡ ቢቀር let alone
ሳይቀር *sayqär*, in አንድም ፡ ሳይቀር without exception
ቀሪ *qäri* balance, remainder, residual
ቀሪ ፡ ገንዘብ balance
ቅሪት, see below
የቀረ *yäqärrä* absent (adj.), extinct, rest (remaining), remnant
የቀረው ፡ ቢቀር at least, at worst
የማይቀር *yämmayəqär* unavoidable
ል + imperfect + ምንም ፡ አልቀረውም come to the point of doing something, almost, nearly
ስ + negative imperfect + አይቀርም be liable to, most probably (as in ሳይመጣ ፡ አይቀርም he will most probably come, he may come)
[See also በቀር, በተቀር, በስተቀር, ይቅር, ይቅርታ]

*ቀራ, see ቀራራ

ቄራ *qura* crow, raven

ቁር *qur*, in የራስ ፡ ቁር helmet

ቃር *qar* heartburn

ቄራ *qera* slaughterhouse

ቅር ፡ አለ(ው) *qərr alä(w)* be discontented, be disappointed, be sore (vexed), feel amiss, have misgivings, have ill will
ቅር ፡ አሰኘ *qərr assäňňä* disappoint, be disappointing, dissatisfy, hurt one's feelings, irk, make gloomy,

slight, chagrin, depress, make resentful
ቅር ፡ ተሰኘ *qərr täsäňňä* be dissatisfied, be disenchanted, feel aggrieved, be chagrined, be resentful
ቅሬታ, see below

ቃረም *qarrämä* glean, pick up (information)

*ቀራራ, አቅራራ *aqrarra* sing a battle song
ቀረርቶ *qärärto* war cry, battle song

ቄርስ, see ቄረስ

ቅርስ *qərs* heritage, heirloom, legacy, relic

ቈረሰ *qʷärräsä* tear off a portion (of bread and other things), cut bread
ቁርስ *qurs* breakfast
ቁራሽ *qurraš* piece (of bread)

*ቀረሸ, አቀረሸ *aqäräššä* regurgitate

ቄራሽ, see ቄረስ

ቅርሸም ፡ አለ *qəršämm alä* crack, vi. (of branch)

ቀረቀረ *qäräqqärä* bolt (the gate), bar (the gate)
ተቀረቀረ *täqäräqqärä* be wedged, be lodged (be caught), get stuck (get caught), be jammed

ቈረቈረ *qʷäräqqʷärä* found (a city), establish (a city)

ቈረቈረ *qʷäräqqʷärä* cause discomfort (e.g. lumpy bed)

*ቈረቈረ, ተንቈረቈረ *tänqʷäräqqʷärä* exude, pour down (of sweat)
አንቈረቈረ *anqʷäräqqʷärä* pour water in a thin stream, decant
ማንቈርቈሪያ *manqʷärqʷäriya* pitcher

ቆርቆሮ *qorqorro* tin, tin can, corrugated iron
ቆርቆሮ ፡ መክፈቻ can opener
ቆርቆሮ ፡ ቤት house with tin roof

78

በቆርቆር ፡ አሸገ can (food)
የቆርቆር ፡ ምግብ canned food

ኮረቀበ qäräqqäbä join two packs into a single load before putting them on the pack animal, tie up a load
ቅርቃብ qərqab load, pack

ቅራቅንቦ qəraqənbo odds and ends

ቈረቈዘ q^wäräqq^wäzä fail to grow (of grain), be dwarfed, be stunted
አቈረቈዘ əq^wäräqq^wäzä dwarf, vt. (of diet), stunt

ቀረበ qärräbä approach, come close, come near, be near, appear (stand before an authority), come forward, be presented to, be served (food), be submitted (bill, resolution)
አቀረበ aqärräbä present, offer, bring near, put forward, serve (dinner), convey (greetings), introduce (a bill), submit (a proposal), bring to the attention of (see also ሐሳብ)
ተቃረበ täqarräbä near (vi.), come near, approach, approximate
አቃረበ aqqarräbä bring together
ተቀራረበ täqärarräbä be in close vicinity, be about the same
አቀራረበ aqqärarräbä bring together, cause to come to a rapprochement
ቀርብ qərb near (adj.), shallow
መቀራረብ mäqqäraräb affinity
ማቅረቢያ maqräbiya tray, serving tray
አቀራረብ aqqärarräb presentation
አቅራቢያ, see below

ቅርብ qərb near (adj.), shallow (see ቀረበ)
በቅርብ recently, close by, closely
በቅርቡ before long, recently, lately, shortly, soon, closely
በቅርብ ፡ ጊዜ recently, shortly, soon
ከቅርብ ፡ ጊዜ ፡ ወዲህ lately, recently
የቅርብ recent, close (friend), intimate (friend)
(የ)ቅርብ ፡ ዘመድ close relative
የቅርብ ፡ ጊዜ recent
ቅርብነት qərbənnät neighborhood (nearness), vicinity

ቈረበ q^wärräbä receive holy communion
አቈረበ aq^wärräbä administer the communion
ቁርባን, see below

ቁርበት qurbät tanned hide used as a sleeping mat

ቁርባን qurban holy communion, eucharist (see ቈረበ)
የቁርባን ፡ ሥነ ፡ ሥርዓት sacrament of communion

ቅርብነት, see ቅርብ

ቅሪት qərrit remainder (see ቀረ)
ቅሪት ፡ አካል fossil

ቅሬታ qərreta discontent, resentment, displeasure, disappointment, chagrin, grievance, breach (in friendship); see ቅር ፡ አለ
የቅሬታ reproachful

*ቀረነ, ተቃረነ täqarränä go against, clash (of stories), be irreconcilable, contradict, conflict with
ተቃራኒ täqarani opponent, opposite, contrary (term), conflicting, converse, inverse, reverse, counterpart, antipode, antithesis
ተቃራኒነት täqaraninnät contradiction, opposition, discrepancy (between two accounts)
መቃረን mäqqarän contradiction

ቅርንጫፍ qərənčaf bough, branch (of tree, of a company), subsidiary (of a company), chapter (of an association)

ቅርንፉድ qərənfud clove
የቅርንፉድ ፡ ምስማር screw

ቈረኘ q^wäräňňä bind, attach, shackle
አቈረኘ aqq^wäräňňä tie (prisoner to guard), bind (to a job)
ተቈረኘ täq^wäräňňä be tied (prisoner to guard)
(በካቴና ፡ ተቈረኘ be shackled)
(ከአልጋ ፡ ተቈረኘ be bedridden)

ቄራኛ *quraňňa*, in በዓይን ፥ ቄራኛ ፥
ተመለከተ keep an eye on
በዓይን ፥ ቄራኛ ፥ ጠበቀ keep under
surveillance
የመጽሐፍ ፥ ቄራኛ bookworm
የአልጋ ፥ ቄራኛ bedridden

ቀርከሃ *qärkäha* wicker cane (plant)

ቃሬዛ *qareza* stretcher, litter (stretcher)

ቃሪያ *qariya* green pepper, immature
(person)

ቀረጠ *qärräṭä* tax (v.), make pay custom duties
ቀረጥ, see below

ቀረጠ, see ቀረጸ

ቀረጥ *qäräṭ* tax, taxation, tariff, custom
duties (see ቀረጠ)
ቃረጥ ፥ ጣለ tax (v.)
ቀረጥ ፥ ተቀባይ tax collector

ቁርጥ *qurṭ* cut, definite, decided, expli-
cit, just like (see ቄረጠ)
ቁርጥ ፥ ሐሳብ resolution, determination, decision
ቁርጡን ፥ ቃል ፥ ልንገርህ let me tell
you once and for all
ቁርጠኛ *qurṭäňňa* definite, resolute

ቁርጥ ፥ ቁርጥ ፥ አለ *qurrəṭṭ qurrəṭṭ alä*
come in gasps (breath), be abrupt
(speech, words); see ቄረጠ
ቁርጥ ፥ ያለ *qurrəṭṭ yalä* decisive,
downright (answer), firm (price),
terse, positive, categorical

ቄረጠ *qʷärräṭä* cut, cut down, chop
(wood), chop off, hew (logs), cut
loose, clip, amputate, disconnect,
slice (bread, onions), rupture, determine, decide, fix, make a resolution,
make up one's mind, be determined
(ሆዱን ፥ ቄረጠ gripe (of unripe fruit)
(ሐሳቡን ፥ ቄረጠ set one's mind,
decide on, resolve)
(ተስፋ ፥ ቄረጠ despair, give up hope,
be discouraged, be disheartened)

(ቲኬት ፥ ቄረጠ sell tickets)
(ቄርጦ ፥ ተነሣ *qʷärṭo tänässa* set
oneself to, have one's mind set on)
(በፍሱ ፥ ቄረጠ at the risk of his
life)
አስቄረጠ *asqʷärräṭä*, causative of the
preceding
(ተስፋ ፥ አስቄረጠ discourage, deject,
dishearten)
(ቲኬት ፥ አስቄረጠ buy a ticket)
ተቄረጠ *täqʷärräṭä* discontinue (vi.),
be interrupted, cease (vi.), go dead
(of telephone)
አቄረጠ *aqqʷärräṭä* cut off, break
off (relations), cut short (interrupt),
discontinue, cease, sever (relations),
terminate, cross (a street, border),
take a short cut, cut across (a field),
traverse
ቄራረጠ *qʷärarräṭä* mutilate
ቁርጥ, see above
ቄረጥ *qʷärraṭ* resolute, strongminded, determined (person), firm (attitude)
(ሐሳብ ፥ ቄረጥ determined, resolute)
ቄራጥነት, see below
ቁርጠት, see below
ቄራጭ *qʷäraç* one who cuts
(ቲኬት ፥ ቄራጭ ticket seller)
ቁራጭ *qurraç* piece, slice, slab, stub
(of pencil), slip (of paper), clipping,
butt
ማቄረጥ *maqqʷäraṭ* interruption
(ያለማቄረጥ *yalämaqqʷäraṭ* perpetually, continuously, regularly, on
and on)
መቀረጫ *mäqʷräča* clippers
ማቄረጫ *maqqʷäräča* crossing
ማቄረጫ ፥ ስፍራ crosswalk
ተቄራጭ *täqʷaraç*, in ሥራ ፥ ተቄራጭ
contractor
አቄራጭ *aqqʷaraç* cutoff, short cut
የማይቄረጥ *yämmayaqqʷärraṭ* constant (ceaseless), continual, perpetual
(clatter), persistent
ሳይቄረጥ *sayəqqʷärraṭ* constantly,
steadily, regularly, without interruption

80

ተቀነባበረ	nation, coherence *täqänähabbärä* v.i. was accumulated, compiled, was synthesised *(ideas)*; was coordinated, was organized
አቀናበረ	*aqqänabbärä* v.t. accumulated, synthesized, compiled; coordinated; organized *(work)*
አቀነባበረ	*aqqänäbabbärä* v.t. accumulated, synthesized, compiled; coordinated; reorganized
አቀነባባሪ	*aqqänäbabari* n. compiler; coordinator, organizer
ቀነተ	*qännätä* v.t. girded up
ቅናት	*qənat* n. girdle
መቀነጀ	*mäqännäča* n girth band *(animals)*
መቀነት	*mäqännät* n. cloth waist-band
ቀነዘረ	*qänäzzärä* v.t. committed fornication, adultery
ቅንዝረኛ	*qənzəräñña* n. fornicator, adulterer
ቅንዝር	*qənzər* n. fornication, * adultery
ቀነደበ	*qänäddäbä* v.t. beat, struck *(with stick)*; drank off, drank down
ቀነጠሰ	*qänäṭṭäsä* v.t. broke off *(e.g. twig)*
ቅንጠሳ	*qənṭäsa* n. breaking off *(e.g. twig)*
ቅንጣሽ	*qənəṭṭaš* n. piece broken off
ተቀነጠሰ	*täqänäṭṭäsä* v.i. was broken off
አስቀነጠሰ	*asqänäṭṭäsä* v.t. had *(s/t)* broken off
ቀነጠበ	*qänäṭṭäbä* v.t. cut off *(small piece, e.g. meat)* ;brought *(meat)* in small quantities
ቅንጣቢ	*qənəṭṭabi* n. small piece *(which is cut off)*
ቅንጥብጣቢ	*qənṭəbṭabi* n. pl. small pieces of meat *(cut*

	off)
ቀነጣጠበ	*qänäṭaṭṭäbä* v.t. cut off several small pieces
ተቀነጠበ	*täqänäṭṭäbä* v.i. was cut off
*ቀነጠ	*qänäṭṭä
ቅንጡ	*qənṭu* n./adj. *(one who is)* abandoned, free living, without principle; spendthrift
ቅንጦት	*qənṭot* n. free living, luxury
የቅንጦት ዕቃ	*yäqənṭot əqqa* n. luxury item
ተቀናጣ	*täqänaṭṭa* v.i. felt free *(to do as one pleased)*
ቀነጨረ	*qänäččärä* v.i. was stunted *(in growth or development*
ቀንጨረ	*qänčära* adj. stunted
ቀነጨበ	*qänäččäbä* v.t, got a story wrong; passed on only part of piece of gossip, information
ቀነፈ	*qännäfä* v.t. put between brackets, in parentheses
ቅንፍ	*qənnəf* n. brackets, parentheses
ተቀነፈ	*täqännäfä* v.i. was put in parentheses, brackets
ቀና	*qänna* v.i. straightened up
ቀና	*qänna* adj. cooperative, agreeable, good, honest
መልከ—	*mälkä—* adj. handsome, good looking
ቀና አለ	*qäna alä* v.i. straightened up a little
ቅን	*qən* adj. straightforwa d; good-hearted good-willed
ቀኝ	*qäññ* n. colony
—ግዛት	*—gəzat* n. colony
ቅንነት	*qənənnät* n. straightforwardness, good-heartedness
ይቅናህ	*yəqnah* good luck
ቀና አለ	*qäna alä* v.i. straight

81

—አደረገ	ened up, looked up —adärrägä v.t. held up (the head); held erect
ተቀና	täqänna v.i. was sold (grain etc.)'
ተቃና	täqanna v.i. was made straight; was successful
እድሉ—	əddəlu—v.t. was lucky
ተቀናና	täqänanna v.i. envied each other
አቀና	aqänna v.t. straightened; raised (the head); colonized
እህል—	əhəl—v.t. sold (grain)
አገር አቀና	agär aqänna v.t. settled and developed a country
አቅኚ	aqñi n. settler, developer
አገር—	agär— colonizer (a country), settler
አቃና	aqqana v.t. rectified, straightened
ቀና	qänna v.i. became jealous, was envious
ቅናት	qənat n. jealousy
ቀናተኛ	qännatäñña adj. jealous, envious
ቀናኢ	qäna'i adj. jealous
ተቀናና	täqännana v.i. envied each other
አስቀና	asqänna v.t. made (s/o) jealous
ቀን	qän n. day, time
የቀን መቁጠሪያ	yäqän mäqutäriya n. calendar
ሁል ቀን	hull qän adv. daily
በቀን	bäqän during the day
ቀን አስፈበት	qän alläfäbbät was out of date
—ወጣለት	—wäṭṭallät it has seen its days
ባለቀን	baläqän n. one having his "day" (time of "success, power)
ቀን በቀን	qän bäqän n. in broad day light, every day, daily
በዓል ቀን	bä'äl qän n. holiday
ከቀን ቀን	käqän qän day after

	day
ከቀን ወደ ቀን	käqän wädä qän from day to day
ከፉ ቀን	kəfu qän n.bad time; time of famine
አዘቦት ቀን	azäbot qän n. working day
በየቀኑ	bäyyäqänu n. every day
እኩለ ቀን	əkkulä qän n. mid-day
ቀንበር	qänbär n. yoke; burden
ቀንበጥ	qänbäṭ or ቀምበጥ qämbäṭ n. tendril, shoot
ቀንዲል	qändil n. candle stick; annointing of the sick (unction)
ቀንድ	qänd n. horn (animal)
ቀንደኛ	qändäñña n. ring leader
ቀንድ አውጣ	qänd awṭa n. snail
ቀንዳም	qändam n/adj. (one) having large horns
የቀለም ቀንድ	yäqäläm qänd n. inkstand; intellectual
የቀንድ ከብት	yäqänd käbt n. horned cattle, cattle
ቀንጃ	qänga n. harness mate (plough oxen)
ቀኖና	qännona n. canon (church), repentance
ቀኝ	qäññ n. right (direction)
—እጅ	— əǧǧ n. right hand; collaborator
ቀኛዝማች	qäññazmač n. leader of the right flank
*ቀወለለ	see ተንቀዋለለ
*ቀወሰ	see ተቃወሰ
ቀዘቀዘ	qäzäqqäzä v.i. got cool, cooled down; dropped off (business), was lifeless (town)
ቀዘቀዘው	qäzäqqäzäw felt cold
ቀዝቃዛ	qäzqazza adj. cold, cool
ቅዝቃዜ	qəzəqqaze n. coolness
አቀዘቀዘ	aqäzäqqäzä v.t. cooled, cooled down
ማቀዝቀዣ	maqäzqäža n. refrigerator
ተቀዛቀዘ	täqäzaqqäzä v.i. was cool, was chilly
አቀዛቀዝ	aqqäzaqäz n. coolness

ቀዘነ   *qäzzänä* v.t. produced stool, faeces, diarrhea *(small child);* had loose bowel movement *(adults);* was extremely cowardly

ቅዘን   *qəzän* n. loose faeces, loose stool

ቅዘናም   *qəzänam* adj./n. *(one)* who is very cowardly

መቅዘኛ   *mäqzäña* n. chamber pot

አስቀዘነ   *asqäzzänä* v.t. encouraged *(e.g. child)* to defecate; frightened *(s/o)* extremely

ቀዘዘ   *qäzzäzä* v.i. was low-spirited

ቅዝዝ አለ   *qəzəzz alä* v.i. felt depressed, uneasy, melancholic

ቀዘፈ   *qäzzäfä* v. t. rowed *(a boat)*

ቀዛፊ   *qäzafi* adj./n. rower, oarsman

መቅዘፊያ   *mäqzäfiya* n. oar

ተቀዘፈ   *täqäzzäfä* v.i. was rowed

አስቀዘፈ   *asqäzzäfä* v.t. had *(a boat)* rowed

*ቀየመ   see **ተቀየመ**

ቀየሠ   *qäyyäsä* v.t. surveyed *(land);* planned, put up a scheme

ቀያሽ   *qäyyaš* n. surveyor

ቅየሣ   *qəyyäsa* n. surveying *(land)*

መቀየሻ   *mäqäyyäša* n. surveyor's measure

ተቀየሠ   *täqäyyäsä* v.i. surveyed, planned

አስቀየሠ   *asqäyyäsä* v.t. had *(land)* surveyed; had *(s/t)* planned

ቀየረ   *qäyyärä* v.t. changed; relieved *(changed)*

ቅያሪ   *qəyyari* adj. change

—ልብስ   *—ləbs* n. change of clothes

ቀያየረ   *qäyayyärä* v.t. changed *(one's clothes, suits)*

ተቀያየረ   *täqäyyärä* v.i. was relieved *(by a sub-*

stitute); was transferred *(of post)*

አቀያየረ   *aqqäyayyärä* v.t. interchanged

ቀየደ   *qäyyädä* v.t. hobbled *(an animal)*

ቅይድ   *qəyyəd* adj. hobbled

ተቀየደ   *täqäyyädä* v.i. was hobbled

አቀያየደ   *aqqäyayyädä* v.t. hobbled *(two animals or more together)*

አስቀየደ   *asqäyyädä* v.t. had *(an animal)* hobbled

ቀየጠ   *qäyyäṭä* v.t. mixed; adulterated

ቅይጥ   *qəyyəṭ* adj./n. mixed, adulterated

ቀያየጠ   *qäyayyäṭä* v.t. mixed in small quantity; adulterated slightly

ተቀየጠ   *täqäyyäṭä* v.i. was mixed; adulterated

አቀያየጠ   *aqqäyayyäṭä* v.t. mixed, adulterated *(completely)*

አስቀየጠ   *asqäyyäṭä* v.t. had *(s/t)* mixed, adulterated

ቀይ   *qäyy* adj. red; *see also* **ቀላ**

ቀደመ   *qäddämä* v.t. overtook, passed s/o in a course of action

ቀደም ሲል   *qädämm sil* adv. previously, prior, before

—በሎ   *—bəlo* adv. earlier, previously, prior

ቀደምትነት   *qäddämtənnät* n. priority

ቀዳሚ   *qädami* adj./n. foremost; overtaker, first *(in rank)*

ቀዳሚነት   *qädaminnät* n. priority

ቀዳማዊ   *qädamawi* or **ቀዳማይ** *qädamay* adj. first *(m.)*

ቀዳሚት   *qädamawit* adj. first *(f.)*

ቅዳሜ   *qədame* n. Saturday

ቀድሞ   *qädmo* adv/n. earlier; formerly, in olden times

በቀድም ዘመን ቅደም ተከተል	bāqādəmo zamān in former days qədām täkättäl priority, one after the other
በቅደም ተከተል	bāqədām täkättäl in sequence, one after the other
ቅድሚያ —መንገድ	qədmiya n. priority —mängäd right of way
በቅድሚያ ቅድም ቅደም ታሪክ	bāqədmiya in advance qəddəm adv. earlier qədmä tarik n. pre-history
—አያት	—ayat n. great grand mother/father
—ዓለም	—aläm n. before the creation of the world
መቅድም በቀደም	māqdəm n. preface bāqāddäm the other day
ተቀደመ	tāqāddāmä v.t. was overtaken; was passed in a course of action
ተቀዳሚ	tāqāddami adj./n first, prior
ተቀዳደመ	tāqādaddāmä v.t. competed in running
ተሸቀዳደመ	tāšqādaddāmä v.t. competed in running
ተሸቀዳዳሚ	tāšqādadarni n. competitor (in running)
አሸቀዳደመ	ašqādaddāmä v.t. had (s/å) compete in running
እሽቅድድም	əšqədəddəm or እሽቅድ ምድም ešqədəmdəm n. running competition
አስቀደመ	asqāddāmä v. t. gave priority to
አስቀድም	asqāddəmo adv. in advance, previously; already; beforehand
ከሁሉ— ቀደስ	kähullu— first of all qāddāsä v.t. sanctified, blessed; said the mass (liturgy)
ቀዳሽ	qāddaš adj./n. officiating priest, deacon
ቅዱስ —ዮሐንስ	qəddus adj. holy, saint —yohannəs New year (St. John's Day)

መንፈስ—	mänfäs— n. Holy Ghost, Spirit
መጽሐፍ— ቅዱስንነት	mäs'haf— Bible qəddusənnät n. holiness, sanctity
ቅዳሴ	qəddase n. liturgy, Mass
ቅድስት ቅድስተ ቅዱሳን ቅድስት ሥላሴ	qəddəst adj. holy (f.) qəddəstä qəddusan n. the Holy of Holies qəddəst səllase n. Holy Trinity
ንዋየ ቅድሳት	nəwayä qəddəsat n. church furniture
ቅድስና	qəddəsənna n. holiness, righteousness, piety
መቅደስ	mäqdäs n. sanctuary (of church)
ቤተ መቅደስ	betä mäqdäs n. temple
ተቀደሰ	täqāddäsä v.i. was sanctified, blessed
የተቀደሰ	yätäqāddäsä adj. sacred, venerable, blessed
አስቀደሰ	asqāddäsä v.t. had (s/o) say the mass; attended the mass
አስቀዳሽ	asqāddaš adj./n. church goers
ቀደደ	qāddädä v.t. tore; cut out (tailor); ripped (clothes)
ጎህ ሲቀድ ቀዳጅ ሐኪም	goh siqädd at dawn qädağ hakim n. surgeon
ቀዳዳ	qādada n. hole, opening
ቀዶ ጥገና	qāddo ţäggäna n. operation, surgery
ቅድ	qədd adj. cut, torn; style of cut (clothes)
ቅዳጅ ተቀደደ	qəddağ n. rent tāqāddädä v.i. was torn; told lies
ተቀዳደደ	tāqādaddädä v.i. was torn up
አስቀደደ	asqāddädä v.t. had (s/t) torn; had (a dress, suit) cut off
ቀዳ	qādda v.t. hauled (water); drew water copied from

84

ቀጂ	qäǧi adj./n. one who hauls water; one who copies; imitates
ቅጅ	qəǧǧ adj./n. copy; imitation
ተቀዳ	täqädda v.i. was hauled (water:) was copied
አስቀዳ	asqädda v.t. had (s'o) haul water;had (s,o) copy from
ቀጠለ	qäṭṭälä v.t. continued; joined interconnecting parts together; came next in a series
ቀጣይ	qäṭṭay adj./n. continuing; next in a series
ቅጣይ	qəṭṭay n. extension, part connected to, annexed to
ቅጥል	qəṭṭəl n. extension, part connected to, annexed to
ቅጥልጥል	qəṭəlṭəl adj. articulated, made up of connecting parts (e.g. chain, train)
ቀጣጠለ	qäṭaṭṭälä v.t. joined several parts together
ተቀጠለ	täqäṭṭälä v.i. was joined together (main part to a subsidiary part e.g. extension to cord or wire)
ተቀጣይ	täqäṭṭay n. extension piece
ተቀጣጠለ	täqäṭaṭṭälä v.i. were joined to each other; caught fire (spreading from one place to another)
አስቀጠለ	asqäṭṭälä v.t. had (s/t) joined on, connected
ቀጠረ	qäṭṭärä v.t. employed (in a job), gave appointment (to meet)
ቀጣሪ	qäṭari adj./n. employer
ቀጠሮ	qäṭäro n. appointment (for meeting)
ቅጥረኛ	qəṭräñña n. employee
ቅጥር	qəṭər n. employee
ተቀጠረ	täqäṭṭärä v.i. was employed; was given appointment (meeting)
ተቀጣሪ	täqäṭṭari n. employee
ተቀጣረ	täqäṭṭärä v.t. made an appointment to meet)
መቃጠሪያ	mäqqaṭäriya n. rendezvous (place)
ተቀጣጠረ	täqäṭaṭṭärä v.t. made an appointment to meet)
አቃጠረ	aqqaṭṭärä v.t. acted as a pimp
አቃጣሪ	aqqaṭari n. pimp
አቀጣጠረ	aqqäṭaṭṭärä v.t. have (s/o) made a rendezvous, appoint ment (with s/o)
አስቀጠረ	asqäṭṭärä v.t. had (s'o) employed
አስቀጣሪ	asqäṭṭari n. job broker
ቀጠቀጠ	qäṭäqqäṭä v.t. hammered: bruised, struck repeatedly
ቀጥቀጣ	qäṭqaṭṭa adj. shivering (with fear; coward
ቀጥቃጭ	qäṭqač adj./n. blacksmith (derogatory)
ቅጥቅጥ	qəṭqəṭ adj. bruised;
ቅጥቀጣ	qəṭqäṭa n. hammering, bruising repeated striking
ተቀጠቀጠ	täqäṭäqqäṭä v.t. was hammered, bruised struck repeatedly
አስቀጠቀጠ	asqäṭäqqäṭä v.t. had iron etc.) forged; had s,o) beaten repeatedly
ቀጠነ	qäṭṭänä v.i. became thin; was diluted
ቀጠና	qäṭäna n. famine
ቀጠና	qäṭana n. zone. region.
ቀጭን	qäččən adj. thin slender
ቅጥነት	qəṭnät n. thinness
አቀጠነ	aqäṭṭänä v.t. made thin; diluted

አቀጣጠን aqqāṭaṭän n. thinness
ቀጣፊ qäṭṭäfä v.i. told lies
ቀጣፊ. qäṭafi n./adj. (one) who tells lies
ቀጣፊኔት qäṭafinnät n. lying. perfidy
ቅጥፊት qəṭfät n. lying, perfidy
ቀጣፊ. qäṭṭäfä v.t. plucked (e.g. fruit, flowers)
ተቀጣፊ. täqäṭṭäfä v.i. was plucked
አቃጣፊ. aqqaṭṭäfä v.t. helped (s/o) to pluck
አስቀጣፊ. asqäṭṭäfä v.t. had (s/t) plucked
ቀጣ qäṭṭa v.t. punished, chastised, took disciplinary action
ቅጣት qəṭat n. punishment, chastisement, disciplinary action, fine, penalty
ተቀጣ täqäṭṭa v.i. was punished, chastised had disciplinary action taken against
ተቀጪ. täqäči n. s/o against whom disciplinary action is taken
መቀጫ mäqqäča n. fine. penality
መቀጮ mäqqäčo n. fine, penalty
መቀጣጫ mäqqäṭača n. exemplary punishment
አስቀጣ asqäṭṭa v.t. had (s/o) punished
*ቀጨለ ጨለ see ተቀጨለ ጨለ
ቀጨመ qäččämä v.t. grimaced; qəčam n. louse eggs, nits
ቅጫምም qəčamam adj. n.(one) infested with nits
አቀጨመ aqäččämä v.t. made (face) grimace
ቀጩም qäččämo n. tree (Myrsina Africana) fruit of which is a cure for tape-worm
ቀጨቀጨ qäčäqqäčä v.t. crunched (with teeth), chewed noisily
ቀጨጨ qäččäčä v.t. wasted away, became very

thin
ቀጫጫ qäčača adj. skinny (insult)
አቀጨጨ aqäččäčä v.t. made (s/o) very thin, caused (s/o) to waste away
ቀጭኔ qäččəne n. giraf
*ቀጸበ qäṣṣäbä
ቅጽበት qəṣbät n. instant
ከመ— kämä—adv. instantly
ቀፈረረ qäfärrärä v.i. disarranged (hair)
ቀፍ ራራ qäfrarra adj. disarranged (hair)
ቅፍር qəfərr adj. disarranged (hair)
ቅፍርር አለ qəfrərr alä v.i. became dishevelled, disarranged (hair)
ተቀፈረረ täqäfärrärä v.i. was rumpled, ruffled (hair)
ቀፈቀፈ qäfäqqäfä v.t. hatched
ተቀፈቀፈ. täqäfäqqäfä v.i was hatched
አስቀፈቀፈ. asqäfäqqäfä v.t. had a hen hatch eggs; had too many children (irony)
ቀፈት qäfät n. belly
ቀፈታም qäfätam adj. big bellied (insult)
ቀፈ ዳዳ qäfäddädä v.t. tied very tightly
ተቀፈዳዳ täqäfäddädä v.i. was tied very tightly
አስቀፈ ዳዳ. asqäfäddädä v.t. had (s/o) tied; bound very tightly; caused (s/o) to be imprisoned
ቀፈፈ. qäffäfä v.t. aroused (people's) suspicion; projected an atmosphere of fear or distaste
ቀፋፊ. qäfafi adj. causing fear, suspicion, distate in others
ቀፈፈ. qäffäfä v.t. scraped (as in preparing leather); went collecting scraps (begging)
ቀፈፋ. qäfäfa n. begging (from house to

86

መቅፈፈያ	*house for scraps)* māqfäfiya n. scrapping instrument *(e.g. for skins, leather)*
ተቀፈፈ	täqäffäfä v.i. was scrapped *(leather)*
ቀፎ	qäfo n. bee-hive
ቁልቋል	qulquʷal n. euphorbia
ቁልፍ	see ቁለፈ
ቁማር	qumar n. gambling
ቁማርተኛ	qumartäñña n. gambler
ቁምጣ	qumţa n. shorts *(usually* ቁምጣ ሱሪ *qumţa surri)*
ቁራ	qura n. crow
ቁር	qurr n. helmet
ቁር	qurr n. frost
ቁርበት	qurbät n. skin, hide
ቁርበተ አሊም	qurbätä alim n. umber
ቁርንጯጭ	qurančuč n./adj. kink; kinky
ቁርጥማት	see ቁረጠመ
ቁቅ አደረገ	quqq adärrägä v.i. farted, popped off
ቁባት	qubat n. concubine, mistress
ቁና	qunna n. grain measure *(straw, holding about 10 kilos)*
- -ተነፈሰ	- -tänäffäsä v. panted
ቁንዶ በርበሬ	qundo bärbärre n. black pepper
ቁንጣን	qunţän n. over-eating pains
ቁንጣናም	qunţanam adj./n.*(one)* who is sick from overeating
ቁጢጥ አለ	quţiţţ alä v.i. squated
*ቁጣ	see ተቆጣ
ቁጫጭ	qučač n. black ant *(small, house variety)*
ቁጭ አለ	quČč alä v.i. sat down
ቂል	qil adj. fool
ቂላቂል	qilaqil adj. foolish
ቂም	qim n. grudge
ቂመኛ	qimäñña n./adj. *(one)* who holds a grudge
ቂም በቀል	qim bäqäl n. vengeance
ቂም ያዘ	qim yazä v.t. held a grudge 'against
አቂመ	aqemä v.t. held a

	grudge against
ቁንድ	qind n. seed pod, bed *(as in maize core)*
ቁንጥር	qinţər n. clitoris
ቂጣ	qiţţa n. pan cake, unleavened bread
ቂጥ	qiţ n. buttock, bottom
ቂጥኝ	qiţţəññ n. syphilis
ቃል	qal n. word
ቃለ ጉባዔ	qalä guba'e, n. minutes *(of a meeting)*
—አጋኖ	—agganno n. interjection
ቃል ሰጠ	qal säţţä v.i. made solemn declaration, made an affidavit; promised
— ገባ	—gäbba v.t. gave promise
ቃሉ ተዘጋ	qalu täzzägga v.i. lost o/s voice
ቃሊብ	qalib n. mold *(casting)*
ቃልቻ	qallačča n. soothsayer *(Moslem)*
ቃመ	qamä v.t. tossed into the mouth; chewed čat
አቃመ	aqamä v.t. gave s/o mouthful
ቃረመ	qarrämä v. t. gleaned
ቃራሚ	qarami n. gleaner
ቃርሚያ	qarmiya n. gleanings
ቀራረመ	qärarrämä v.t. gleaned; gathered here and there
ተቃረመ	täqarrämä v.i was gleaned
አቃረመ	aqqarrämä v.t. helped *(s/o)* to glean
አስቃረመ	asqarrämä v.t. had *(s/o)* glean
ቃረነ	see ተቃረነ
ቃሪያ	qariya n. green pepper
ቃሬ	qarre n. crest *(of hair, traditional for small boys)*
ቃሬዛ	qareza n. stretcher
ቃር	qar n. heart burn
*ቃሰተ	see አቃሰተ
ቃበዘ	abbäzä v.t. searched about, looked here and there, got lost, lost o/s way
ቃባዥ	qabaž n./adj. *(one)*

87

	who gets lost
ቃብድ	qabd n. down payment, deposit, *also* ቃብዱ qäbdu
ቃተተ	qattätä v.t tried in vain
ቃታ	qata n. chamber *(gun)*
ቃና	qana n. taste, flavour *(beverage)*, aroma
—ቢስ	— *bis* n. flavourless, non-aromatic
ቃኘ	qcññä v.t. tuned up; looked around; surveyed
ቅኝት	qəññət b. tuning up; surveying
ተቃኘ	täqaññä v.i. was tuned up; was surveyed
ቃጀ	qažžä v.t. had a nightmare
ቅጀት	qəžät n. nightmare
ቅጀታም	qəžätam n./adj. *(one)* who has nightmares; *(one)* who talks nonsense
አቃጀ	aqažžä v.t. was given nightmares; had nightmares
ቃዲ	qadi n. a Muslim judge *(for religious affairs)*
*ቃጠለ	*see* ተቃጠለ
ቃጣ	qatta v.t. pretended, threatened to hit *(s/o)*; made as if to do *(s/t)*
ቃጫ	qačča n. sisal
ቃጭል	qačəl n. small bell *(e.g. mass bell in church)*
ቃፊር	qafir n. scout *(military)*
ቄራ	qera. h. abattoir, slaughter house
ቄስ	qes n. priest
ቄስ ገበዝ	qesä gäbäz n. church administrator
ቅስና	qəssənna n. ministry *(of priest)*, priesthood
ቄብ	qeb n. pullet
ቄንጥ	qenṭ n. style, fashion, savoir faire *(be-— haviour)*
— አወጣ	—awäṭṭa v.t. mocked *(by imitating)*, mimicked
ቄንጠኛ	qenṭäñña n./adj.

	stylish *(person)*
ቄጠማ	qeṭäma or ቃጤማ qäṭema n. sedge
ቅሉ	qəlu *in* ቢሆንም ቅሉ bihonəmm qəlu adv. nevertheless
ቅሌት	qəllet n. scandal; loss of face *(dignity)*,
ቅሌተኛ	qəlletäñña adj. /n. *(one)* who loses face *(dignity)*
ቅሌታም	qəlletam adj./n *(one)* who loses face *(dignity)*, scandalous
ቅል	qəl n. gourd
የራስ ቅል	yäras — n. skull
ቅልሽልሽ አለ አቅለሽለሽ	qələšləšš alä v.i. felt sick aqläšälläšä v.t. caused *(s/o)* to feel sick
ቅልብቑ አለ	qəlbəčč alä v.i. was easy to hold, use, was handy
ቅልጥም	qəlṭəm n. shin; marrow *(of bone)*
ቅመም	*see* ቀመመ
ቅማያት	qəmäyat or ቅድማያት qədmayat n. greatgrandfather, greatgrandmother
ቅምምጦሽ	qəməmməṭoš n. pick-a back, piggy-back
ቅምቡርስ	qəmburs n. blow-fly larva, rootworm
ቅምብጭ	qəmbəčča n. wicker potta storage pot
—ሆድ	—hod n. small pot belly
ቅምጫና	qəmčana n. gourd *(dried for use as container)*
ቅርሳ	qərilla n. processed hide; adj. shabby *(person)*
ቅርስ	qərs n. heritage, legasy, relic, antiquity
ቅር አለ	qərr alä v.i. became discontented
—አሰኘ	— asäñña v.t. disappointed, hurted *(s/o's)* feeling
ቅሬታ	qərreta n. discontent
ቅርንጫፍ	qərənčaf n. branch
ቅርንፉድ	qərənfud n. clove
ቅርጫት	qərčat n. basket
ቅርፈት	*see* ቀረፈ

88

ቀስም qəsm n. spirit, vigour
ቀስሙ· ተሰበረ qəsmu täsäbbärä
v.i. broke (s/o's)
spirit
ቀስና see ቀሰሰ
ቀበኑግ qəbanug n. noug oil
ቀቤ see ቀብ
ቅብጥ qəbṭ adj. Coptic (lang.)
ልሳነ ቅብጢ. ləssanä qəbṭi n. the
Coptic language
ቀኔ qəne n. poetry
·ተቀኘ täqäññä v.t. com-
posed (poetry)
ባለቀኔ balä qəne n. poet
ቀን qən adj. good-hearted,
straight-forward,
good-natured, see also
ቀና
ቅንቅን qənqən n. moth
ቅንቅናም qənqənam adj.
moth-eaten; stingy,
mean
ቅንዲላ qəndilla n. loop
ቅንድብ qəndəb n. eyebrow,
eyelashes
ቅንጣት qənṭat n. grain (ear of
corn, grain of sand etc.)
ቀነፋ see ቀነፋ
ቅዝዝ አለ qəzzəz älä v. felt low,
melancholic
ቅዝዝታ qəzəzta n. depres-
sion, lethargy
ቀዳሜ qədame n. Saturday
ቅድሚያ see ቀደመ
ቅጠል qəṭäl n. leaf
ቀጠልያ qəṭäləyya adj.
greenish
ቅጥ qəṭ n. manner, method,
system
—የለሽ —yälläš adj. un-
systemic
መላ— mäla— n. usually
followed by a nega-
tive verb e. g.
መላ ቅጥ mäla qəṭ yälelläw
የሌለው haphazard
ውጥንቅጥ wəṭənqəṭ n. hodge-
podge
ቅጣቢስ qəṭäbis n. mishmash
ቅጥራን qəṭran n. tar cf. ሬንጅ
ቅጥር qəṭər n. enclosure,
encircle
—ግቢ. —gəbbi n. campus
ቀጽ qəṣ n. volume

ቀጽበት qəṣbät n. wink
ቀጽል qəṣṣəl n. adjective
ቆለለ qollälä v.t. heaped
ቁለለ qulläla n. heaping up
ተቆለለ täqollälä n. was
heaped; pounced on
አስቆለለ asqollälä v.t. had
(s/o) heaped up
ቆለመም qolämmämä v.t. bent
round
ቆልማማ qolmamma adj. bent-
round
ቆላ qolla n. lowland
ቆለኛ qolläñña n. low-
lander
ቆላ qolla v.t. roasted (coffee
etc.)
ጅራቱን— ǧəratun— v.t. wag-
ged the tail
ቁሌት qullet n. degree of
roasting
መቁዓሊያ mäqʷaliya n. pan
(for ensuring coffee
etc. roasts evenly)
ተቆላ täqolla v.i. was roasted
ተቁላ täqʷalla v. t. shot
at each other
አስቆላ asqolla v.t. had (s/t)
roasted, (coffee etc.)
አቁላላ aqulalla v.t. stirred
up (onion, fat for wäṭ)
ማቁላያ maqulaya n. ingredi-
ents (onions, fat,
spices)
ቆሌ qolle n. guardian spirit
—ቢስ —bis adj. un-
dignified
—የራቀው —yäraqäw adj. un-
dignified
ቆሎ qolo n. roasted grain
(e.g. peas, beans,
barley, wheat etc.)
ቆመ qomä v.i. stood up;
stopped; halted,
came to a halt; ceased,
was under way (of
market)
ቆማ የቀረች qoma yäqärräč an
old maid
ቋሚ qʷami n. usher
(banquet etc.:) adj.
permanent, steady
(work); skeleton (of
building)

—ተጠሪ —*tätäri* n. permanent secretary

ንብረት —*nəbrät* n. immovable property

ቁም *qum* adj. standing; stopping; head *(of cattle)*

ቁምሳጥን *qum saṭən* n. cupboard, wardrobe, locker

ቁምስቅል አሳጣ *qum səqəl asaṭṭa* v.t. got *(s/o)* mixed up, confused

ቁም ነገር —*qum nägär* n. serious matter

—ነገረኛ —*nägärräñña* n. a serious person

ቁመት *qumät* n. stature, height

ቁመታም *qumätam* adj. tall

ቆም አለ *qomm alä* v.i. paused

መቁሚያ *mäqumamiya* n. staff *(support, prayer stick)*

አቆመ *aqomä* v.t. erected; stopped *(s/t;)* brought to rest; put an end to, halted; parked *(a car)*

ማቆሚያ *mäqomiya* n. parking place

አቋም *aqʷam* n. standing, status, condition; standpoint; approach *(attitude)*

ተቋቋመ *täqʷaqʷämä* v.t. was established, well-established; resisted *(enemy etc.)*

መቋቋሚያ *mäqqʷaqʷamiya* n. means of resistance

ተቃወመ *täqawwämä* v.i. opposed, objected, protested, resisted, disapproved

ተቃዋሚ *täqawami* n. opponent, dissident

ተቃውሞ *täqawəmo* n. opposition, objection, protest; resistance, disapproval

አቋቋመ *aqqʷaqʷamä* v.t. established, set up *(a business)*, founded *(an organization)*

አስቆመ *asqomä* v.t. had *(s/o)* stand up; stopped *(s/o)*; interrupted

ቆመጠ *qommäṭä* v.t. amputated, cut off

ቁምጣ *qumṭa* adj./n. cut off

ሱሪ —*surri* n. shorts

ቁምጥና *qumṭənna* n. leprosy

ቁምጥ አለ *qumməṭ alä* v.i. fell off; became detached

ቆመጥ *qomäṭ* b. baton, truncheon, stick, cudgel

ቁማጭ *qumaṭ̌* n. cut-off piece, clip *(cigarette)*, butt

ቁምጥምጥ *qumaṭmaṭ* adj. cut into many pieces

ቆማጣ *qomaṭa* interj. leper *(gross insult)*

ቆሞስ *qomos* n. elder priest; vicar

ቆረጠ *see* ቆረጠ

ቆረጠመ *qoräṭämä* v.t. crunched

—ቁርጥማት —*qurṭəmat* n. rheumatism

ቆሪ *qori* n. wooden mixing bowl

ቆርቆሮ *qorqorro* n. tin; corrugated iron, tin can

ቆርኪ *qorke* n. bottle top *(crown type)*

ቆርኪ *qorke* n. tora harte-beest

ቆሸሸ *qoššäšä* v.i. was dirty

ቆሻሻ *qošaša or* ቁሻሻ *qušaša* n./adj. dirt, rubbish filth, waste matter, litter, dirty, filthy, unclean, impure

አቆሸሸ *aqoššäšä* v.t. made dirty, filthy, littered

አንቋሸሸ *anqʷaššäšä* v.t. belittled, disdained, scorned

ቆሽማዳ *qošmadda* adj. weak; having a small appetite

ቆሽት *qošt* n. rectum

ቆሽታም *qoštam* n./adj. *(one)* who has a small appetite

ቆቅ *qoq* n. partridge

ቆብ *qob* n. skull cap; cap

—ቻነ —*čanä* v.i. became

90

ጣለ	a monk —ṭalä v.i. re- nounced (o s) habit (monk)
ቆነጀ	qonäğğä v.i. became beautiful
ቆንጆ	qonğo adj. beautiful
ቄንጅና	qunğɔnna n. beauty
አቆነጀ	aqonäğğä v.t. beautified, adorned
ቆነጠረ	qonäṭṭärä v.t. took a pinch of
ቆንጥር	qonṭɔr n. bur(r,
ቄንጣሪ	qunäṭṭari n. pinch, small amount of
ቆነጣጠረ	qonaṭṭaṭṭärä v.t. took several pinches of
ተቆነጣጠረ	täqonäṭṭärä v.t. was pinched, had small pinch taken from
ተቆናጠረ	täqonaṭṭärä v.i. was in ill humor, was grouchy
አስቆነጠረ	asqonäṭṭärä v.t. had (s o) take a pinch (of (s/t)
ቆንሲል	qonsil n. consul
ቆንስላ	qonsɔla n. consulate
ቆየ	qoyyä v.i. waited, awaited, lingered, remained, was late; lasted; lived long
ቆይታ	qoyyɔta n. prolonged appointment, engage- ment
መቆያ	mäqoyya n. snack
ቆይቶ	in ቆይቶ መጣ qoyɔto mäṭṭa he came late
የቆየ	yäqoyyä adj. old (food); long stand- ing, ancient
አቆየ	aqoyyä v.t retarded; delayed; kept (s/t) back (for s/o), kept waiting, detained (kept in); spared (put aside); pre- served
አስቆየ	asqoyyä v.t. had s/o delayed; kept s/o (waiting)
ቆዳ	qoda n. leather, hide
የቆዳ በሽታ	yäqoda bäššɔta n. dermatosis, skin

	disease
ቆዳው ቂል	qodaw qil adj./n. apparently naive (person); (one) clever than he seems
ደንዳና	—dändanna adj. brave, unassailable (person)
ቆጠቆጠ	qoṭäqqoṭä v.i. smarted, burned
ቆጥቋጣ	qoṭqʷaṭṭa adj. mean, stingy, tight-fisted
*ቆጠቆጠ	*qoṭäqqoṭä
ቁጥቋጦ	quʷṭqʷäṭo n. bush
አቆጠቆጠ	aqoṭäqoṭṭä v.t. sprouted new leaves, sent out fresh shoots
ቆጠበ	qoṭṭäbä v.t. saved (money) economised, was thrifty
ቆጣቢ	qoṭṭabi n. one who saves; thrifty
ቁጥብ	quṭṭɔb adj. reserved, shy
ቁጠባ	quṭṭäba n. savings
ተቆጠበ	täqoṭṭäbä v.t. was saved (e.g. money); refrained
ተቆጣቢ	täqoṭṭabi adj. re- fraihing
ቆጥ	qoṭ n. roost, nesting box
ቆፈረ	qoffärä v.t. dug
ቆፋሪ	qoffari adj./n. (one) who digs
ቁፍር	quffɔr adj. dug-out (place)
ቁፋራ	quffära n. digging
ቁፋሮ	quffaro n. digging
ቁፋሪ	quffari n. excavated earth
መቆፈሪያ	mäqoffäriya n. digging aid (e.g. spade)
ቆፋፈረ	qofaffärä v.t. dug here and there
ተቆፋፈረ	täqoffärä v.i. was dug
አቋፈረ	aqqʷaffärä v.t. helped in digging
አስቆፈረ	asqoffärä v.t. had (s/t) dug; had (s/o) dig
ቆፈነነ	qofännänä v.t. became stiff with cold

ቆፈን	qofän n. stiffness due to cold
ቆፈናም	qofänam n. one who is stiff with cold; frozen stiff
ቄለmመ	q"älämmämä v.t. bent over
ቁልmም	qulmäma n. twisting, wringing
ቁልም	quləmni adj. bent over, round
ተቄለmመ	täq"älämmämä v.t. was twisted, wrung
አስቄለmም	asq"älämmämä v. t. had s/t bent round
ቄለቄለ	q"äläqq"älä v. i. went down
ቁልቁል	qulqul adj. sloping down; adv. downward
ቁልቁለት	q"ulq"əlät adj. sloping; n. slope
ቄልቋላ	q"älq"alla adj. inclined, down-ward sloping
አቄለቄለ	aq"äläqq"älä v. i. went downwards,
ቄለፈ	q"älläfä v.t. closed, locked; buttoned up
ቄላፈ	q"ällaffa adj. hook-shaped
ቄላፍ	q"ällaf adj. uncircumcised (arch.)
ቁልፍ	q"uləf n. botton; key; padlock
ባልና ሚስት-	balənna mist —n. press-stud
—ያዥ	—yaž n, guard, custodian
የቁልፍ ቀዳዳ	yäq"ulf qädada n. keyhole
መርፈ ቁልፍ	märfe q"ulf n. safety pin
ቁልፍ	q"ulləf adj. locked up
ቁልፍ አደረገ	q"ulləff adärrägä v.t. locked (s/t) up
ቄላለፈ	q"älalläfä v.t. locked up (all round house etc.)
ተቄለፈ	täq"älläfä v.i. was locked up, bottoned
ተቋለፈ	täq"allafä v.i. became interlocked
አቋለፈ	aqq"alläfä v.t. interlocked, intertwined
አቄላለፈ	aqqu"älalläfä v.t. intertwined (in a complex way)
አስቄለፈ	asq"älläfä v.t. had (s/t) locked
ቄረመዳ	q"ärämmädä v.i. shrivelled up
ቁርመዳ	q"ärmadda adj. shrivelled up
ቁርምድምድ	q"urmədmɔd adj. extremely shrivelled up
አቄረመዳ	aqq"ärammädä v.t. caused (s/t) to shrivel up
ተቄረመዳ	täq"ärammädä v.i. was caused to shrivel up, was stricken
ቄረሰ	q"ärräsä v.t. broke off (bread); took breakfast
ቁራሽ	q"ərraš n. morsel of bread
ቁርስ	qurs n. breakfast
ቁርስራሽ	qurəsraš n. left-overs (food)
ቆራረሰ	qorarräsä v.t. broke into pieces (bread etc.)
ተቆረሰ	täqorräsä v.i. was broken into pieces
ተቆራረሰ	täqorarräsä v. i. was crumbled, broken into many small pieces
አስቆረሰ	asqorräsä v.t. had (s/t) broken into pieces
ቄረቄረ	q"äräqq"ärä v.t. hammered; knocked on; tapped; sprang to mind (s/t bad); established (a town etc.)
መቄርቄሪያ	mäq"ärq"äriya n. hammer, (s/t) used as a hammer
ተቄረቄረ	täq"äräqq"ärä v. t. was disturbed (about maltreatment of one-self or others); was founded (town etc.)
ተቄርቋሪ	täq"ärq"ari n. sympathiser
አስቄረቄረ	asq"äräqq"ärä v.t. had

92

ቄረቄስ (a town etc.) founded q^{w}äräqq^{w}äsä v.t. bullied off (hockey, polo, gännä.)

ቄረቋሽ q^{w}ärq^{w}aš n. first striker of ball

ተቄራቄሰ täq^{w}äraqq^{w}äsä v. t. striked simultaneously (in ball games)

ቄርቄዘ q^{w}äräqq^{w}äzä v. i. become feeble, emaciated (through ill health), wasted away

ቄርቋዛ q^{w}ärq^{w}azzä adj. feeble, emaciated

አቄረቄዘ aq^{w}äräqq^{w}äzä v. t. cause (s/o) to become feeble, emaciated;

አቄርቋዥ aq^{w}ärq^{w}až n. exploiter

ቄረበ q^{w}ärräbä v. i. took Holy Communion

ቆራቢ qorabi n. communicant

የቆራቢ ራት yäq^{w}ärabi rat n. food (in payment for saying of special Mass)

ቀርባን q^{w}ərban n. Holy Communion

አቄረበ aqwärräbä v.t. made (s/o) take the Holy Communion

አስቄረበ asq^{w}ärräbä v.t. had (s/o) ∗take Holy Communion

∗ቄረኘ see አቄራኘ

ቄረጠ q^{w}ärräṭä v.t. cut, amputated

ሐሳቡን— hassabun— set ones mind, decided on, resolved

ተስፋ— täsfa— lost hope, gave up hope; was discouraged, was disheartened

ቲኬት— ticket— sold ticket

—አስቄረጠ —asq^{w}ärräṭä bought ticket

ቄርጦ ተነሳ qu^{w}ärṭo tänässa had one's mind set on

በነፍሱ ቄርጦ bänäfsu qu^{w}ärṭo at the risk of his life

ቄራጭ q^{w}äraç adj. n. one who cuts

እንጨት— ənçät— n. s/o who fetches wood

ቄራጣ q^{w}äraṭa adj. amputated

ቀርጥ q^{w}uərṭ n. cut off piece; row meat (dish); adj. definite

ቀርጣት q^{w}ərṭät n. stomach-ache

ቀራጭ qurraç n. piece, slice, stub, slab

ቄራጥ q^{w}ärraṭ adj. decisive, daring, resolute, strongminded, determined

ቄረጣ q^{w}äräṭa n. cutting (action)

መቄረጫት mäquraçit n. scissors

ቀርጣት qu^{w}rṭät n. stomach ache

መቄረጫ mäquräça n. cutting aid

ቄራረጠ q^{w}ärarräṭä v.t. cut into pieces, chopped down

ቀርጥ ቀርጥ አለ qu^{w}ərraṭ qu^{w}ərreṭ alä was v.i. abrupt (speech), came in gasps (breath)

ተቄረጠ täq^{w}ärräṭä v.i. was cut; was decided

ተቄራጭ täq^{w}ärraç n. maintenance money (for family while absent taken from salary)

ተጿረጠ täq^{w}arräṭä v.i. was discontinued, was interrupted

ተጿራጭ täq^{w}arraç n. contractor usually with ሥራ—

ተቄራረጠ täq^{w}ärarräṭä v.t. was cut into pieces; was broken off (relationship)

አጿረጠ aqq^{w}arräṭä v.t. interrupted, discontinued used a short cut (road)

አጿራጭ aqq^{w}araç n. short cut (road)

አቄራረጠ aqq^{w}ärarräṭä v.t. in-

93

duced *(s/o)* to break off *(relationship)*

አስቈረጠ asqwärräṭä v.t. had *(s/t)* cut, decided

ቄረጠመ qʷäräṭṭämä v.t. crunched

ቍርጥማት qʷərṭəmat n. rheumatism

ቍርጥምጥም አደረገ qʷərṭəmṭəmm adärrägä v.t. chewed to pulp

ቄረጣጠመ qʷäräṭaṭṭämä v. t. chewed, ground *(teeth)*

ተቈረጠመ täqʷäräṭṭämä v. i. was chewed, was, ground

ቄረፈደ qʷäräffädä v.t. became covered with goose pimples; was chapped

ቍርፉዳ qʷärfadda adj. covered with goose pimples

አቄረፈደ aqʷäräffädä v.t. caused *(skin)* to become goose-pimply

ቄሪ qʷäri n. wooden bowl

ቄራ qʷärra v.t. made a cut *(wound on skin)*, made a groove

ቍር qur n. cut *(wound)*

ተቄራ täqʷärra v.i. was cut *(wound)*

አስቄራ asqʷärra v.t. had *(s/o)* cut *(e.g. for tribal markings)*

ቄሰለ qʷässälä v.i. was wounded

ቍስል qʷəsəl n. wound

ቍስል ሥጋ qʷəsllä səga n. body sores

የቄላ ቍስል yäqolla qʷəsəl n. running sore; infected wound; ulcer *(external)*

ቍስለኛ qʷəsläñña adj. /n. *(one)* who's wounded

አቄሰለ aqʷässälä v.t. wounded

ልብ አቄሰል ləbb aqusəl adj. incorrigible, pestering

አቄሳሰለ aqʷäsassälä v.t. wounded a little

ቄሰቄሰ qʷäsäqqʷäsä v.i. poked *(the fire)*; started trouble

ቄስቋሽ qʷäsqʷaš adj./n. trouble-maker

ነገር— nägär— n. trouble-maker; agitator

መቄስቄሻ mäqʷäsqʷäša n. poker *(for the fire)*

ተቄሰቄሰ täqʷäsäqqʷäsä v.i. was poked *(fire)*

ቄነሰ qʷännäsä v.i. stank

ቍናስ qʷənas n. stink

ቍናሳም qʷənasam adj. stinking

አቄነሰ aqʷännäsä v.t. caused to stink

*ቄነቄነ qʷänäqqʷänä

ቄንቋና qʷänqʷanna adj./n miser*(ly)*

ቄነነ qʷännänä v.t. allocated *(rations)*

መቄነን mäqʷənän n. ration *(soldiers, monks etc.)*

ተቄነነ täqʷännänä v.i. was rationed; looked extremely proud, haughty

ተቄናኝ täqʷännaññ adj./n. *(one)* who receives ration; *(one)* who is exteremly proud, haughty

ቄነደደ qʷänäddädä v.t. struck

ተቄነደደ täqʷänäddädä v.i. was struck

ቄነጐለ qʷonäggʷälä v.i. sprouted

ቍንጐል quʷəngʷəl n. sprouting beans *(food)*

አቄነጐለ aquʷänäguʷälä v.t. sprouted

ቄነጠለ see ቆነጸለ

ቄነጠጠ qʷänäṭṭä v.t. pinched *(with fingers)*; punished *(children)*

ቍንጢጥ qʷənṭiṭ n. pinching

ቍንጠጣ qʷənṭäṭa n. pinching

መቄንጠጫ mäqʷänṭäča n. pincers, tongs

ተቄነጠጠ täqʷänäṭṭäṭä v.i. was pinched; was punished

ተቄናጠጠ täqʷänaṭṭäṭä v.t. pinched; had a steady job

አስቄነጠጠ asqʷänäṭṭäṭä v.t. had s/o pinched

ቁነጸለ	quʷänäṣṣälä v.t. tore, ripped (paper etc.)
ተንጸል	quʷənṣəl adj. torn up
ቈጠረ	qʷäṭṭärä v.t. counted, (number)
ቈጣሪ	qʷäṭari adj./n. (one) whc counts; (water eletric-gasmetre) etc.
ቈጠራ	qoʷäṭära n. counting, calculation
ሕዝብ—	həzb— n. census
ቍጥር	qʷəṭər adj./n. number; knot (e.g. in string
መደበኛ—	.nädäbäñña— n. cardinal number
ቁጥር አለ	quṭərr alä v.i. huddled together
ቁጥርትር	quṭərṭər n. tangle
ቁጥጥር	quṭaṭṭər n. supervision
ቈጣጠረ	qʷäṭaṭṭärä v.t. counted (not accurately), made a rough calculation
ተቈጠረ	täqʷäṭṭärä v.i. was counted
ተቈጣሪ	täqʷäṭṭari adj. countable
መቍጠሪያ	mäqqʷəṭärya n. rosary, prayer beads
ተቈጣጠረ	täqʷäṭaṭṭärä v.i. supervised; superintended; was entangled (rope, string)
ተቈጣጣሪ	täqʷäṭaṭari n. supervisor, superintendant
አቈጣጠረ	aqqʷäṭaṭṭärä v.t. interlocked
አስቈጠረ	asqʷäṭṭärä v.t. had (s/t) counted; scored (made points in game)
ቈጨ	qʷäččä v.i. regretted, had feeling of remorse
ቍጭት	qʷəččət n. regret, remorse
ተቈጨ	täqʷäččä v.i. had regret, remorse
አስቈጨ	asqʷäččä v.t. caused s/o to feel remorse
ቍለ	qʷəla n. penis; clapper (of bell)
ቍልጭ አለ	quʷälläčç alä v.i. was visible, clear lighted up (eyes)
ቈልቋል	qʷəlqʷal n. euphorbia, cactus
ቈረንጮ	qʷəränčo n. untanned hide, worn out leather
ቈርንጫጭ	qʷərančač n. kink adj. kinky
ቈርጭምጭሚት	qʷərčəmčəmit n. ankle
ቈባት	qʷəbat n. concubine, also እቈባት
ቈንጣን	qʷənṭan n. stomach-ache (through over eating)
ቈንጫ	qʷənəčça n. flea
ቈንጮ	qʷənčo n. pinnacle, summit
ቈሊማ	qʷalima n. sausage
ቈመጠ	qʷammäṭä v.i. was tantilized; had fervent desire
ቈማጭ	qʷamač adj. tantalized, full of fervent desire
አቈመጠ	aqʷammäṭä v.t. tantalized
ቈ አለ	qʷa alä v.i. made sudden noise, went "crash"
ቈቅ አለ	qʷaqq alä v.t. felt sick; felt nausea
ቈቅታ	qʷaqqəqtta n. vomit
ቈቀቻ	qʷaqəčča n. impetigo
ቈቄተ	qʷaqʷate n. knuckle-cracking
ቈቄቲያም	qʷaqʷäteam adj./n. bony "bag of bones", (thin person)
ቈት	qʷat n. flour bin (in grinding mill)
ቈንቈ	qʷanqʷa n. language
ቈንጃ	qʷanǧa n. achilles tendon
ቈንጣ	qʷanṭa n. dried meat; thin person
ቈያ	qʷayya n. bush fire, forest fire
ቈድ	qʷad n. plaited necklet (cloth, leather for pendent cross etc.)
ቈጠረ	qʷaṭṭärä v.t. made a knot, stowed away (in pocket etc.); swelled with pus, liquid; blistered
ቈጥኝ	qʷaṭṭəññ n. rock
ቈጨ	qʷaččä v.t. plaited, twisted (fringe of šämma)

በ—	*bä*—pro. prefix in, at, on, etc. adv. prefix.+ simple imperfect, when, if; + perfect + ጊዜ when
በሃ ደንጋይ	*bäha dänigay* n. limestone
በለስ	*bäläs* n. euphorbia, cactus
ባለቀጠ	*bäläqqäţä* v.t. prised open, prised apart *(eyelids)*
በልቀጣ	*bälqaţţa* adj./n. *(insult)* legs akimbo; immodest *(in posture way of sitting)*
ብልቅጥቅጥ	*bəlqəţqəţ* adj.¹ legs spread apart, immodest in posture
ተበላቀጠ	*täbäläqqäţä* v.i. was prised open
ተበላቀጠ	*täbälaqqäţä* v.i. sat legs akimbo *(immodesty)*
*በለበለ	see ተንበለበለ
በለተ	*bällätä* v.t. cut up *(animal)*
ብልት	*bəllət* n. portion of meat; genitals *(polite)*
— አውጪ.	—*awči* n. meat cutter; skilled butcher
በለዘ	*bälläzä* v.i. tarnished
ብልዝ	*bəlz* n. tarnish
ብልዝ አለ	*bəlləzz alä* v.i. was tarnished
አበለዘ	*abälläzä* v.t. caused *(s/t)* to become tarnished
በለገ	*bällägä* v.i. rained *(small rains)*
ብላጊ	*bəllagi* n. little rains
በልግ	*bälg* n. little rains *(April-May);* small rainy season
በለጠ	*bälläţä* v.t. exceeded; surpassed
ፅላጥ አለ	*bäläţţ alä* v.t. exceeded, surpassed *(somehow)*
በላጭ	*bälač* adj./n. ex-

ቢ.በልጥ	
ብልጥ	ceeding, surpassing *bibälţ* at the most *bälţ* adj. cunning, shrewd, smart, astute, crafty
ብልጣ—	*bälţa* — adj. cunning, crafty ,smart aleck
ብልጣት	*bälţät* n. cunning, subtlety
ብልጫ	*bälča* n. excess; superiority
የበለጠ	*yäbälläţä* adj. adv. best
ከሁሉ—	*kähullu*— more than
ተበለጠ	*täbälläţä* v.i. was fooled
ተበላለጠ	*täbälalläţä* v.i. competed with each other; surpassed one other; was unequal in status; varied; was not of the same height or age
ተበላላጭ	*täbälalač* adj. surpassing one another
ተብለጠለጠ	*täbläţälläţä* v.i. acted cunningly; tried to fool others
ተብለጥላጭ	*täbläţlač* n. slick, smart, cunning *(person)*
አበለጠ	*abälläţä* v.i. caused excess, increased; preferred
አበለጠ	*abballäţä* v.t. measured *(s/t)* against (s/t) else
አብልጦ	*ablţo* adv. best, more
ከሁሉ—	*kähulu*— adv. more than
አበላለጠ	*abbälalläţä* v.t. compared *(two things with other);* made great difference between, favoured
አስበለጠ	*asbälläţä* v.t. preferred
በለጠገ	*bäläţţägä* or በለፀገ
	bäläşşägä v.i. became rich
ባለጠጋ	*baläţägga* or ባለፀጋ

ብልጣግና balä̱ɣ̌ägga adj./n. rich; a rich man bɔlṭəggənna or ብል ዕግና bɔlɣ̌əgənna n. richness, riches

አበለጠገ abälätṭägä v.t. made rich

በለጠጠ bälätṭäṭä v.t. prised open cf. በለቀጠ

በልጣጣ bälṭaṭṭa adj. staring open, open-eyed; shameless

ብልጥጥ bɔlṭɔṭ opened wide, staring

ተበለጠጠ täbälätṭäṭä v.t. was prised open

*በለጫለጫ *bäläč̣älläč̣ä

ተብለጫለጫ täbläč̣älläč̣ä v.i. sparkled, glittered

ብልጭልጭ bɔläč̣lɔč̣ adj flashy, showy, flamboyant

በሉጥ bälluṭ n. oak

በላ bälla v.t. ate; consumed; won (gambling)

ብል bɔl n. cloth eating vermin

በል bäl in ሥጋ በል sɔga bäll adj. carnivorous, carnivore

በሊታ bällitta n. big eater አደራ በሊታ adära bällitta embezzler

ተበላ täbälla v.i. was eaten; wore away

መበያ mäbbäya n. an item of food that complements another (e.g. ənğära and wäṭ, bread and cheese etc.)

መብል mäbəl n. food

አብላላ ablalla v.t. digested (took into the mind)

ይብላኝ yɔblañ interj. "I'm sorry for!"

በላተኛ bällatäñña n. regular customer (hotel or restaurant)

ብሉት bɔllot n. non-fasting day

ብልት አደረገ bɔllɔtt adärrägä v.t. ate up (everything)

ተበላ täbälla v.i. was eaten up; was corroded

መበላት mäbbälat inf. to be eaten; n. corrosion

ተበዪ täbäyi adj.n. edible; loser (gambling)

መበያ mäbbäya n. that which accompanies a dish (sauce etc.), appetizer

አበላ abälla v.t. fed

ተበላላ täbälalla v.i. backbited against each other

ተብላላ täblalla v.i. was fermented; was digested (idea)

ተባላ täballa v.i. backbited against each other

ተባይ täbay n. insect

አባላ abbälla v.t. accompanied at table

አስበላ asbälla v.t. had s/o eat

አብላላ ablalla v.t. pondered, digested (idea, plan etc.)

በራሐ bäräha n. desert, wilderness

በረኸኛ bärähäñña n. desert traveller

በራሐም bärähamma adj. desert

በረረ bärrärä v.i. flew; piloted

በራሪ bärari adj./n. flying; that which flies; express (bus)

በረራ bärära n. flight (of bird, plane)

አበረረ abärrärä v.t. piloted, navigated (air craft)

አብራሪ abrari n. pilot (aircraft)

ተባረረ täbarrärä v.i. was chased away, driven away

ተባራሪ täbarari n. fugitive

—ወሬ —wäre n. gossip

—ጣይት —ṭäyyəṭ n.

97

	stray bullet
አባረረ	abbarrärä v.t. chased away, drove away; dismissed, fired
አባራሪ	abbarari adj./n. (one) who chases s/o
በረሮ	bäräro n. cockroach
በረቀ	bärräqä v.i. struck (lightning) see also ባረቀ
ብራቅ	bəraq n, lightning
ብርቅ	bərq n. rare pleasure adj. rare, precious, unique
ተብረቀረቀ	täbräqärräqä v.i. glittered, shimmered
አብረቀረቀ	abräqärräqä v.i. sparkled
አብረቅራቂ	abräqraqi adj. sparkling
ገረተሰ	bäräqqäsä v.i. forced in (usually s/t which is ·tender); broke (virginity, maidenhead)
ብርቅስ	bərqəs n. gash, tear
ብርቅስቅስ አደረገ	bərqəsqqəss adärrägä v.t. forced into violently
በረቃቀሰ	bäräqaqqäsä v.t. pushed into; forced a way into (virginity, maidenhead)
ተበረቀሰ	täbäräqqäsä v.t. was forced into
ተበረቃቀሰ	täbäräqaqqäsä v.i. was forced into (by s/t)
አስበረቀሰ	asbäräqqäsä v.t. had s/o force a way into s/t
ገረበረ	bäräbbärä v.t. searched around; went through o/s pockets, etc.
በርባሪ	bärbari n. thief, one who searches around
ብርባራ	bərbära n. searching
ተበረበረ	täbäräbbärä v.i. was searched; had o/s pockets etc. gone through
አስበረበረ	asbäräbbärä v.t. had s/o searched; had s/o's pockets gone through

በረታ	bärätta v.i. became strong; was in good shape (person); succeeded through difficulties
ብርቱ	bərtu adj. strong; in good shape (person)
ብርታት	bərtat n. strength, success
አበረታ	abärätta v.t. strengthened, encouraged
በረት	bärät n. byre, barn
በረንዳ	bärända n. verandah
በረከተ	bäräkkätä v.i. was plentiful; became abundant
በርካች	bärkač adj. abundant, plentiful, surplus
በርካታ	bärkatta adj. plentiful, surplus
ብርክቴ	bərəkkate n. abundance, plenty, surplus
በረከት	bäräkät n. abundance, plenty; prosperity; blessing
ገጸ—	gäṣṣä— n. present
አበረከተ	abäräkkätä v.t.gave present, offered a gift for s/o who is higher in rank
ተበራከተ	täbäräkkätä v. i. was more than sufficient; was abundant, multiplied
አበራከተ	abbäräkkätä v. t. caused to be plentiful; managed supply efficiently (e.g. housewife)
*በረከከ	see ተንበረከከ
በረዘ	bärräzä v.t. mixed with water; infiltrated (political)
በራዥ	bärraž n. infiltrator (political)
ብርዝ	bərz n. a drink which is a mixtuʒ of honey and water, unfermented mead
በራረዘ	bärarräzä v.t. mixec with some water
ተበረዘ	täbärräzä v.i. was

98

ሀ

አስበረዘ	mixed with water asbärräzä v.t. had (s/t) mixed with water		በራ	caused (s/t), (s/o) to shy, bolt; frightened bära adj. bald-headed; n. bald-head
በረደ	bärrädä v.t. became cold, cool, chilly		በራ ብራ	bärra v.i. lit (light only) bərra n. sunny day, clear weather, bright weather
በረደኝ	bärrädäññ I feel cold			
ብርድ	bərd n. cold		ብርሃን	bərhan n. light
—ልብስ	bərd ləbs n. blanket		መብራት	mäbrat inf.to be-
ብርዳም	bərdam adj. cold			come light n. light,
ብርዳማ	bərdamma adj. cold (month)			electric light; lamp
በራድ	bärrad adj. chilly; n. tea pot (metal, oriental type)		አበራ	abärra v.t. lit, put on light
			ማብሪያ	mabriya n. light switch
በረዶ	bärädo n. hail		ተብራራ	täbrarra v.i. was clari-
አበረደ	abärrädä v.t. cooled; cooled down, ap- peased (anger), calmed down			fied, was made clear (idea etc.); was eluci- dated, elaborated
			አብራራ	abrarra v.t. clarified,
ማብረጃ	mabräǧa n. serving jug			made clear, eluci- dated, explained, elaborated
ተበረደ	täbarrädä v.i. was cold		አስበራ	asbärra v.t. had light
አስበረደ	asbärrädä v.t. had (s/t) cooled, made (s/o) feel cold			put on
			በራፍ	bärraf n. doorway
			በሬ	bäre n. ox; adj. stupid
በረገደ	bäräggädä v.t. opened by force, burst open (door etc.)		በር	bärr n. gate, door
			በረኛ	bärräñña n. porter, gate-keeper
ብርግድ አለ	bərgədd alä v.t. made burst open		በርሚል	bärmil or በርሜል bär- mel n. barrel (for liquids), drum
—አደረገ	—adärrägä v.t. burst open			
በረጋገደ	bärägaggädä v.t. threw (everytning) open (e.g. all doors etc.)		በርበሬ	bärbärre n. red pepper, chilli
			በርኖስ	bärnos n. burnous, woollen cloak
ተበረጋገደ	täbärägaggädä v.i. was burst, thrown open		በርጩማ	bärčumma n. stool
			በሰለ	bässälä v.i. was cooked
አስበረገደ	asbärägagädä v.t. had (s/t) burst, thrown open			enough, was ripe; aged (wine); reached maturity; was mature
			በሳይ	bäsay adj. easy to cook
በረጋ	bäräggägä v.t. shied, bolted (e.g. horse, with fright)		በሳል	bässal adj. easy to cook
በርጋጊ	bärgagi adj./n. bolt- ing, extremely emotional, fearful		ብስል	bəsəl adj. mature (youngster); well- cooked
ብርጋጋ	bərgäga n. bolting			
አበረጋገ	abäräggägä v.t. caused (s/o), (s/t) to bolt		አበሰለ	abässälä v.t. cooked enough
			አብሳይ	absay n.-cook
አስበረጋ	asbäräggägä v.t.		ማብሰያ	mabsäya n. cooking

99

ተብሰለሰለ	pot, cooking utensil
	täbsälässälä v.t. was too pre-occupied (with s/t); was obsessed
አብሰለሰለ	*absälässälä* v.t. was obsessed
አስበሰለ	*asbässälä* v.t. had s/t cooked enough
*በሰረ	see አበሰረ
በሰበሰ	*bäsäbbäsä* v.i. rotted, was rotten
በሰባሽ	*bäsbaš* adj. liable to rot
በሰባሳ	*bäsbasa* adj. rotten; filthy; ill-mannered
አበሰበሰ	*abäsäbbäsä* v.t. let (s/t) to get rotten; get rotten, get completely soaked (clothes etc.); mixed flour with water
ተበሰበሰ	*täbäsabbäsä* v.i. became completely dirty; overdid (s/t); became a nuisance
በሳ	*bässa* v.t. made a hole drilled; bored
በሺ	*bäši* adj. borer, drill
ብስ	*bas* n. hole (drilled)
መብሻ	*mäbša* n. s/t used to drill, bore, drill
ተበሳ	*täbässa* v.i. was bored, drilled
ተበሳሳ	*täbäsassa* v.i. was drilled, riddled (with many holes)
አስበሳ	*asbässa* v.t. had s/t riddled with holes
*በሳጡ	see ተበሳጡ
በስተ—	*bästä*—prefix; towards
በስቲያ	*bästya* adv. suffix; after
ተነገ—	*tängä*—n. the day after tomorrow
በሶ	*bässo* n. food from roasted barley flour
—ብላ	*bəla* n. sacred basil
በሻቀ	*bäššäqä* v.i. was very angry
ብሻቅ	*bəšq* adj. very angry putrified; deterio-

	rated in character (person)
አበሻቀ	*abäššäqä* v.t. made very angry, annoyed seriously
አብሻቂ	*abšaqi* adj./n. annoying
ተባሻቀ	*täbaššäqä* v.t. annoyed each other (seriously)
በሻቀጠ	*bäšäqqäṭä* v.i. putrefied; got soaked (with mud)
በሽቃጠ	*bäšqaṭṭa* adj. putrefied; muddied; ill-mannered, grumbling
ብሽቅጥቅጥ	*bəšqəṭqəṭ* adj. hopelessly jumbled, mixed up
አበሻቀጠ	*abbäšäqqäṭä* v.t. soaked; soaked with mud
ተበሻቀጠ	*täbäšaqqäṭä* v.i. behaved badly; was over demanding, over critical
አበሻቀጠ	*abbäšaqqäṭä* v.t. treated (s/o) badly
በሽታ	*bäššəta* n. disease, illness
ተላላፊ—	*tälulafi*—epidemic, contagious disease
የሚጥል—	*yämmiṭəl*—also የበ ርያ በሽታ epilepsy
በሽተኛ	*—bäššətäñña* n. patient, sick person
የእንቅልፍ በሽታ	*yä`ənqəlf bäššəta* sleeping sickness
በቀለ	*bäqqälä* v.i. grew, sprouted
ቂም በቀል	*qim bäqäl* n. vengeance, revenge
ብቅል	*bəqəl* n. malt
በቅልት	*bäqqʷält* n. germinating seeds,
ቡቃያ	*buqayya* n. fresh green shoots, sprouting grain
በቀል	*bäqqäl* adj. growing
አበቀለ	*abäqqälä* v.t. grew, raised (crops); grew (hair)
ተበቀለ	*täbäqqälä* v.t. re-

100

	venged
ተበቃይ	täbaqqay adj. avenger
በቀተ	bäqqätä v.i. went into exile took refuge
በቀት	bäqat n. flight, refuge
በቃ	bäqqa v.i. was sufficient sufficed, was enough; was qualified, was competent; was righteous; interj. enough !stop!
የሚበቃ	yämmibäqa adj. sufficient, adequate
የማይበቃ	yämmaybäqa adj. insufficient, inadequate
በቂ	bäqi adj. sufficient adequate enough, satisfactory
በቃኝ	bäqqaññ I have enough
የበቁ የነቁ	yäbäqqa yänäqqa adj. holy, righteous
ብቁት	bəqat n. holiness, righteousness;
ብቁ	bəqu adj. efficient,
ብቁነት	bəqqunnät n. efficiency, competency
ተበቃ	täbäqqa v.i. got a small portion (each one)
አበቃ	abäqqa v.t. finished, completed, terminated, brought to an end, was adjourned
የሱ ነገር	yässu nagar it is all over with him, he is hopeless
አበቃ	abäqqa v.t. distributed evenly and sufficiently
አበቃቀ	abbäqaqqa v.t. distributed evenly and sufficiently
አብቃቃ	abqaqqa v.t. distributed evenly and sufficiently, used economically
በቅሎ	bäqlo n. mule
በቅበቁ	baqbäqqa n. parrot, parakeet

በቆሎ	bäqqollo n. also የበሕር ማሽላ yäbahər mašəla n. maize
ፈኪ.-	fäki-- n. popcorn
በተለይ	bätäläyy adv. especially, specially, chiefly
በተረፈ	bätärräfä adv. besides, apart from
በተነ	bättänä v.t. scattered, dispersed; broke up (a meeting), cast about (by handfuls);
ብተን	bəttən adj. scattered, dispersed; cast (in handfuls);
—ወረቀት	—wäräqät n. loose paper
—ጨርቅ	—čärq n. material (cloth)
—በርበሬ	--bärbäre n. ground red pepper
ብትንትን	bətəntən n. s t that is scattered all over, dispersed
በታተነ	bätattänä v.i. scattered all over, dispersed all over
ተበተነ	täbättänä v.i. was scattered, dispersed, cast about; was adjourned, broke up (meeting)
ተበታተነ	täbätattänä v.i. was scattered, dispersed all over
አበታተነ	abbätattänä v.t dispersed
አሰበተነ	asbättänä v.t. had scattered, dispersed all over
በተሀ	bätäha n. unfermented (e.g. mead,)
—ጠጅ	ṭäǧǧ unfermented "ṭäǧǧ" (mead)
በትሪያርክ	bäträyark n. patriarch
በትሪያርክ	bätrayarka n. patriarchate
በትር	bättər n. bat, stick
በትረ መንግሥት	bäträ mängəst n. mace, sceptre
በነነ	bännänä or ቦነነ bonnänä v.i raised (dust) in the air
ብናኝ	bənnaññ adj. raised

101

(in the air, dust); n. particle of dust

አበነነ   abonnänä v.t. made *(dust, smoke)* fill the air

በከለ   bäkkälä v.t. stained; implicated *(s/o in a crime)*; contaminated

በካይ   bäkkay adj./n. one who stains; one who puts the blame on another

ብከለት   bəklät n. contamination

ብከል አደረገ   bəkkəll adärrägä v.t. stained heavily

ተበከለ   täbäkkälä v.i. was implicated *(in a crime)*

ተበካከለ   täbäkakkälä v.i. stained each other; implicated each other *(in a crime)*

አስበከለ   asbäkkälä v.t. had *(s/o)* stained; had *(s/c)* implicated

በከተ   bäkkätä v.i. died from natural causes *(animal therefore not edible)*; became completely dirty

ብክት አለ   bəkkət alä v.i. became very dirty; filthy

ዘክት   bäkt adj. dirty *(insult)*, filthy

ብካች   bəkkač adj. dirty, filthy

አበከተ   abäkkätä v.t. made completely dirty, filthy

በኩል   bäkkul adv. in the direction of; towards

በኩር   bäkʷər or ቡሁር bähər n. first born

ሀስራት በኩራት   asrat bäkʷərat n. tithe

ብኩርና   bäkʷəranna n. status of being heir; birthright

በወዘ   bäwwazä v.t. shuffled *(cards)*

በዐል   bä'al n. festival

በዘበዘ   bäzäbbäzä v.t. plundered; exploited

በዝባዥ   bazbaž n. plunderer; exploiter

ብዝበዛ   bəzbäza adj. plundering; exploiting

ተበዘበዘ   täbäzäbbäzä v.i. was exploited

ተበዝባዥ   täbäzbaž adj. plundered; exploited

አስበዘበዘ   asbäzäbbäzä v.t. had *(s/o)* plundered; had *(s/o)* exploited

በዚህ   bäzzih adv. here; in this place; this way

በዚያ   bäzziya adv. there; over there; that way

በዛ   bäzza v.i. multiplied; exceeded; was too much

ብዙ   bazu adj. many, much

—ጊዜ   —gize adv. often, many times

ብዛት   bazat n. quantity, excess; abundance

በብዛት   bäbazat in large quantities; adv. frequently

በጊዜ ብዛት   bägize bazat in the course of time

እምብዛም   ambazamm adv. not so much; not that much

አበዛ   abäzza v.t. multiplied; made to exceed; was numerous, abundant; increased; was much

አብዛኛው   abzaññaw adj. most, the majority

ተባዛ   täbazza v.i. was multiplied *(math.)*

ተባዢ   täbaži n. multiplicand *(math.)*

አባዛ   abbazza v.t. multiplied *(math.)*

አባዥ   abbaž n. multiplier *(math.)*

በየነ   bäyyänä v.t. passed judgement

በያኝ   bäyyäññ n. one who judges

ብይን   bəyyən n. judgement

ብያኔ   bəyyane n. judgement

ተበየነ   täbäyyänä v.t. was given *(verdict)*

አስበየነ   asbäyyänä v.t. had

	(a judgement) passed, given
በየደ	*bäyyädä* v.t. welded *(metal etc.)*
በየጅ	*bäyyağ* n. welder
ብየዳ	*bəyyädda* n. welding
ብይድ	*bəyyəd* adj. welded
መበየጃ	*mäbäyyäga* n. welding tool
ተበየደ	*täbäyyädä* v.t. was welded
ተበየጅ	*täbäyyağ* n. *(s/t)* to be welded
አስበየደ	*asbäyyädä* v.t. had *s/t* welded
በደለ	*bäddälä* v.t. did *(s/o)* wrong; mistreated, treated ill
በዳይ	*bädday* n. *(one)* who does wrong to s/o
በደል	*bäddäl* n. hurt, wrong
በደለኛ	*bädäläñña* n/adj. one who does wrong to *(s/o)*
ተበደለ	*täbäddälä* v.i. was done wrong to
ተበዳይ	*täbädday* n. one who is wronged
አስበደለ	*asbäddälä* v.t. had wrong done *to (s/o)*
* በደረ	*see* ተበደረ
በደው	*bädäw* n. Bedouin
በደዊ	*bädäwwi* adj. Bedouin
በዳ	*bäda* adj. desolate
ምድረ—	*mədrä*— n. desert
በዳ	*bädda* v.t. copulated *(human beings, impolite)*
በጊ	*bägi* n/adj. *(one)* who copulates
ብድ	*bəd* n. copulation
ብዳታም	*bədatam* adj. n. *(one who)* is excessive in sexual intercourse *(woman)*
ተበዳ	*täbädda* v.i. had sexual intercourse
አባዳ	*abbada* v.t. had *(s/o)* have sexual intercourse
አስበዳ	*asbädda* v.t. had s/o fucked *(woman)*
አስበጂ	*asbäggi* n. pimp
በድረጃን	*bädrağan* n. egg-plant

በድን	*bädən* n. dead body
—ሆነ	—*honä* v.i. became or went numb
በጀ	*bäggä* v.t. was of benefit to; interj. all right! *(yes! go on!)*
አበጀ	*abäğğä* v.t. mended, repaired; adv. well done
አበጃጀ	*abägağğä* v.t. repaired somehow, fixed up roughly; ridiculed, made fun of (irony)
ተበጀ	*täbäğğä* v.i. was repaired, mended; ransomed, saved
ተበጃጀ	*täbägağğä* v.i. was repaired, mended; adorned oneself
በጅሮንድ	*bäğərond* or በኽሮንድ *bäžərond* n. government treasurer
በገነ	*bäggänä* v.i. burned with rage; was enraged
አበገነ	*abäggänä* v.t. enraged; burned with rage
በገና	*bägäna* n. harp *(Ethiopian, large variety)*
—ደረደረ	—*däräddärä* v.t. played the harp
በጋ	*bäga* n. summer
በግ	*bäg* n. sheep
የበግ ጠቦት	*yäbäg ṭäbbot* n. lamb
—ጠጉር	—*ṭägur* n. wool
ሴት በግ	*set bäg* n. ewe
በጎ	*bäggo* adv. well; in a good way
—ሆነ	—*honnä* v.i. became well *(after sickness)*
—አድራጊ	—*adragi* adj.charitable, benevolent
—አድራጎት	—*adragot* n. charitable deeds; welfare; foundation *(for the needy)*
—ሥራ	—*səra* n. charitable work
በጎነት	*bäggonnät* n. well-being
በጠረ	*see* አበጠረ

በጠሰ   *bäṭṭäsä* v.t. **snapped** *(rope)*, tore off *(button)*

ብጥስ አለ   *bäṭṭäs alä* v.i. was torn off *(by itself)*, snapped *(by itself)*

ብጣሽ   *bäṭṭaš* n. adj. torn-off piece

ብጣሻም   *bäṭṭašam* adj./n. arrogant; (s/o) with superiority complex *(insult)*

ብጥስጥስ   *bäṭäsṭäs* adj. ragged; arrogant; snobbish

በጣጠሰ   *bäṭaṭṭäsä* v.t· snapped; tore into pieces

ተበጠሰ   *täbäṭṭäsä* v·i. was snapped; was torn off *(button)*

ተበጣጠሰ   *täbäṭaṭṭäsä* v.i. was snapped, torn to pieces; acted arrogantly

ተበጣጣሽ   *täbäṭaṭaš* adj. snobbish, arrogant

አስበጠሰ   *asbäṭṭäsä* v.t. had *(s/t)* torn off, snapped

በጠበጠ   *bäṭäbbäṭä* v.t. mixed together; beat up *(cooking)*; caused disturbance, confusion

በጥባጭ   *bäṭbač* adj./n. trouble-maker, mischievous

ብጥበጥ   *bäṭbäṭ* n. disturbance, confusion

ብጥብጥ   *bäṭbäṭ* n. disturbance, uproar, confusion, rebellion, crises, violence

መበጥበጫ   *mäbäṭbäča* n. mixing-bowl, anything used for mixing

ተበጠበጠ   *täbäṭäbbäṭä* v.i. was mixed together; was disturbed

ተበጠበጠ   *täbäṭäbbäṭä* v.i. quarrelled with each other; to be disturbed

ተበጣባጭ   *täbäṭabač* adj. quarrelling

አበጣበጠ   *abbäṭabbäṭä* v.t. incited quarrel, commotion, uproar

አበጣባጭ   *abbäṭabač* n. one who incites quarrel, commotion, uproar, trouble-maker

አስበጠበጠ   *asbäṭäbbäṭä* v.t. had *(s/t)* mixed together

በጢጎ   *bäṭṭih* n. water melon, also ክርቡሽ

በጣ   *bäṭṭa* v.t. made an incision, cut *(in skin, e.g. for tribal markings)*

ብጥ   *bäṭ* n. incision

ብጣት   *bäṭat* n. incision

ተበጣ   *täbäṭṭa* v.i. was incised

አስበጣ   *asbäṭṭa* v.i. had s/o or s/t incised

በጣም   *bäṭam* adv. very, much greatly, considerably; too *(much, very)*

በጣጢስ or መጣጢስ   *bäṭaṭis* or *mäṭaṭis* n. sweet potato

ቡሀቃ   *buhaqa* n. dough pot

ቡዬ   *buhe* n. festival of transfiguration of Christ

ቡሆ   *buho* n. dough *(fermented)* see also በከ

ቡላ   *bulla* adj. grey

ቡልቅ አለ   *bullaqq alä* v.i. puffed: out *(smoke)*

—አደረገ   —*adärrägä* v.t. puffed out *(smoke)*

ቡልቅታ   *bullaqta* n. jet. *(of water)* puff *(of smoke)*

ቡሎን   *bulon* n. nut *(of metal)*

ቡራቡራ   *burraburre* adj. coloured, spotted *(in black and white or black and red, only for animal)*

ቡራ   *burre* adj. piebald *(black and white)*

ቡሬማ   *burremma* adj. particoloured

ቡሽ   *buš* n. cork

104

ባርኔጣ	*barneṭa* n. pith helmet	ተቧጨረ	*täbʷ̱aččärä* v.i. was scratched
ቡቀ	*buqa* n. appendicitis	ተቦጫጨረ	*täboč̣ač̣č̣ärä* v.i. was scratched all over
ቡቀያ	*buqayya* n. shoots *(of crops)*	ቡጭርጭር	*buč̣ərč̣ər* adj. scratched; n. scribbling, scribble
ቡችላ	*buččəlla* n. puppy, whelp		
የወርቅ	*yäwärq* n. gold-bar, bullion	አስቧጨረ	*asbʷ̱aččärä* v. t. had *(s/o)* scratched
ቡና	*bunna or* ቡን *bun* n. coffee	ቡዳ	*buda* adj./n. evil eye,
ቁርስ	—*qurs* n. any snack taken while drinking coffee	ቡዳነት *or* ቡድነት	*budannät or budənnät* n. evil influence, having the evil eye
ቤት	—*bet* n. bar, coffee bar	ቡድን	*budən* n. team
ቡናማ	*bunnamma* adj. brown	ተቧደነ	*täbʷ̱addänä* v.t. formed a team
ቡንኝ	*bunnəññ* n. short seasoned crop *(especially ṭef)*	አቧደነ	*abbʷ̱addänä* v.t. had a team formed
ቡን አለ	*bunn alä* v.i. filled the air, was blown by the wind into the air cf ቦነነ	ቡግ አለ *or* ቡግ አለ *bogg alä* v.i. flared up; glared *(light)*
ቡካን	*bukän* adj. extremely cowardly	ቡጢ	*buṭṭi* n. fist; boxing
ቡጢ	*buṭṭi* fist, punch	ቡጭ ቡጭ አለ *or* ቡጭ ቡጭ አለ	*buč̣č̣ buč̣č̣ alä or boč̣č̣ boč̣č̣ alä* v.i. slopped around *(liquids)*
በበጢ. መታ	*bäbuṭṭi mätta* v.t. punched, boxed	ሆዴ—	*hode*— I am moved *(affected with pity)*
ቧምቧ.	*bʷambʷa or* ቧንቧ *bʷanbʷa* n. pipe *(water etc.)*	በቧቡጫ	*boč̣bʷač̣č̣a* adj. slopping; cowardly
ቧገተ	*bʷaggätä* v. i. begged shamelessly	ቡፍ አለ	*buff alä* ,v.i. stiffened with rage; was swollen *(dough etc.)*
ቧጋች	*bʷagač̣* n. low beggar	ቢላዋ	*billawa or* ቢላዎ *billawo* n. knife
ቧጠጠ	*bʷaṭṭäṭä* v.t. clawed *(animals)*	ቢልቢላ	*bilbilla* n. propeller
መቧጠጫ	*mäbʷ̱aṭäč̣a* n. claw, rake *(tool)*	ቢል ቢል አለ	*bill bill alä* v.i. propelled
ተቧጠጠ	*täbʷ̱aṭṭäṭä* v.i. was clawed	ቢልቃት	*bilqaṭ or* ብልቃጥ *bəlqaṭ* n. ink pot, tube; small bottle
አስቧጠጠ	*asbʷ̱aṭṭäṭä* v.t. had *(s/t)* clawed; had throat scraped *(for tonsilitis)*	ቢራ	*bira* n. beer
		ቢራቢሮ	*birrabirro* n. butterfly
ቧጨረ	*bʷaččärä* v. scratched	ቢሮ	*biro* n. office
ቧጪሪ	*bʷač̣ari* n. scratching, liable to scrach	ቢስ	*bis* prefix/suffix adj. bad;—less
በጫጨረ	*boč̣ač̣č̣ärä* v.t. scratched all over	—ገላ	—*gäla* n. leprosy
		ጥላ—	*ṭala*— adj./n. *(one)* who is undignified
		መቅኗ—	*mäqno*— adj/n not durable, not long-lasting
		ገዳ—	*gäddä*— adj./n.

105

በቅሙ *(one who is) ill-starred, born unlucky*

ቢስክሌት *aqmä n. weakling*

ቢጣ *bisklet n. bicycle*

bite or ቢጣ. bife n. double (one who bears close resemblance), of the same kind

የኔ ቢጣ *väne bife n. beggar (polite)*

ባህል *bahəl n. custom, tradition*

ያገር *yagär— n. national custom*

ባለ *balä pref. possessing, owner of*

ባለጓል *balänʷal n. confidant, courtier*

ባለሞያ *balamoya adj/n. skilled, qualified in a certain skill; expert*

ባላልጋ *balalga n. of the royal line; rightful monarch*

ባለቤት *baläbet n. owner; husband, wife*

ባለኩል *baläkkul n. one who shares with s/o, a fifty per cent share holder*

ባለ ነገር *balä nägär n. plaintiff; one who brings legal action*

ባለዕዳ *balä'əda or ባለዳ baläda n. borrower, debtor*

ባለእጅ *balä'əǧǧ or ባለጅ baläǧǧ n. blacksmith*

ባለጠጋ *balä ṭägga adj. rich, wealthy, also ባለፀጋ*

ባላጋራ *balagara adj. enemy, foe*

ባለቤት *see ባለ*

ባለገ *ballägä v.t. behaved badly; lacked breeding, politeness*

ባለጌ *baläge adj. rude, impolite*

ባለጌነት *balägennät n. rudeness; impoliteness*

ብልግና *bəlgənna n. rude-*

ተበላገ አለ *ness; impoliteness ballägg alä v.i. became very rude, impolite*

አባለገ *aballägä v.t. made rude, impolite (usually for children by parents)*

ባላ *balla n. forked stick, "Y" shaped stick*

ባላምባራስ *balambaras Ethiopian title*

ባላባት *balabbat n. aristocrat, landlord*

ባላባትነት *balabbatənnät n. aristocracy*

ባላንጣ *balanṭa n. foe ባላንጣነት balanṭannät n. enmity, hostility*

ባላገር *balagär n. rural person, country fellow, peasant; adj. rough*

ባላገሬ *balagäre adj. rural; rustic*

ባሌ *bale n. one of the Administrative Regions, Southern Ethiopia (Bale)*

ባሌስትራ *balestra n. spring (of a truck)*

ባል *bal n. husband; festival*

ባልና ሚስት *balənnu mist qulf*

ቀልፍ *n. press stud*

ባለባል *baläbal adj. n. married; married woman*

ባለቤት *baläbet n. owner; husband, wife*

ባልቦላ *balbola n. fuse [It.]*

ባልትና *baltənna n. household management; home economics*

ባልቴት *baltet n. elderly lady*

ባለንጀራ *balanğära n. friend; regular companion*

ባለንጀርነት *balanğärənnät n. friendship*

ባልደረባ *baldäräba n. companion; courtier entrusted by a king with responsibility for another's case*

ባልደራስ *baldäras n. commander*

	of cavalry
ባልዲ	baldi n. bucket
ባልጩት	balčutt n. flint (stone), crystal
ባሐ	bäha adj/b. bald; limestone
—ራስ	—ras adj· bald-headed
ባሕር	bahər n. sea; lake
—ማሽላ	—mašəlla or ባርማ ሽላ bar mašəlla n. maize cf. በቆሎ
—ማዶ	—mado n. abroad
—ሽሽ	—šäšš n. regression of the sea
—ዐረብ	—aräb n. piece of coloured goatskin
—ነጋሽ	—nägaš n. ruler of the sea coast (ancient Ethiopian title)
—ዛፍ	—zaf n. eucalyptus
—ዳር	—dar n. sea-shore; lake shore
—ሰላጤ	—sällaṭṭe n. bay
—ኃይል	—hail n. navy
—ወሽመጥ	—wäšmäṭ n. channel
ባሕርይ	bahrəy n. nature character
የሥጋ —	yäsəga—n. animal instinct
የነፍስ —	yänäfs—n. spiritual nature
ባሕታዊ	bahətawi n. ascetic
ብሕትውና	bəhtəwənna n. asceticism
ተባሕትዎ	täbahtəwo n. asceticism
ባረቀ	barräqä n. went-off by itself (fire arms); flashed (lightning)
ብራቅ	bəraq n. lightning
መብረቅ	mäbräq n. thunder-bolt
አባረቀ	abarräqä v. t. fired unintentionally (firearms)
ባረከ	barräkä v.t. blessed, sanctified
ባራኪ	baraki adj./n. one who blesses, sanctifier
ቡራኬ	burrake n. blessing, sanctification

ቡሩክ	buruk adj. blessed, sanctified
ተባረከ	täbarräkä v.i. was blessed, sanctified
አስባረከ	asbarräkä v.t. had s/o blessed, sanctified
ባሩድ	barud n. gun-powder
ባር	bar n. bar (drinking house)
ባርባር አለ	bar bär alä v.t. felt unsettled, uneasy
ባርኔጣ	barneṭa n. hat
ባሪያ	barya n. slave
ባርነት	barənnät n. slavery
ባሪያ ፈንጋይ	bärya fängay n. slave trader
የባሪያ በሽታ	yäbariya bäššəta n. epilepsy
ባርዳ	barda n. tare (weight)
ባሰ	basä v.i. was aggravated, worsened, deteriorated
ሆዱ ባሻ	hodä baššä adj./n. touchy, over-sensitive
የባሰ	yäbasä adj. worst, worse
የባሰበት	yäbasäbbät adj./n. even worse (person)
ብሶት	bəsot n. grievance
አባሰ	abasä v.t. aggravated
አብሶ	abəso adj. especially
ተባባሰ	täbabasä v.i. went from bad to worse; was very much aggravated; reached point of no return (dispute)
አባባሰ	abbabasä v.t. caused (situation) to aggravate
ባሻ	baššä n. Pasha, Ethiopian title
ባቄላ	baqela n. horse bean
ባቡር	babur n. train; mill
—መንገድ	—mängäd n. street, avenue, boulevard (only those used by vehicles)
የባቡር ሐዲድ	yäbabur hadid n. rail-road
የምድር ባቡር	yämdər babur n. train
የሰማይ —	yäsämay— n. air-plane (arch.)

በባ	*babba* v.i. felt anxious *(for s/o's safety)*
ቡቡ	*bubbu* or ብቡ *bəbbu* adj. anxious *(about s/o)*
አባባ	*ababba* v.t. caused s/o to be anxious *(about s/o)*
በጠ	*batä* v.i. started, began *(of month)*
በእታ	*bä'ata* n. 3rd day of the month
መባቻ	*mäbača* n. first day of the month
አበታ	*abatä* v.t. moved into the month of...
በተለ	*batäle* adj. busy, industrious
—ሆነ	—*honä* v.i. became busy, industrious
በት	*bat* n. calf *(of leg)*
በታም	*batam* adj. n. having chubby calves *(legs)*
በትሪ	*batri* n. battery; flashlight
በነነ	*bannänä* v.i. woke up suddenly
አባነነ	*abannänä* v.t. awakened suddenly
በና	*bana* n. coarse woolen blanket
በኞ	*bañño* n. bath-tub
በንክ	*bank* n. bank *(institution)*
በንኮኒ	*bànkoni* n. counter *(in a café)*
በንዲራ	*bandira* n. flag
በንድነት	*bandənnät* adv. together, in a body, see አንድ
በከነ	*bakkänä* v.i. was wasted; was very busy
ብኩን	*bəkun* adj. wasteful
ብኩንነት	*bəkunənnät* n. wastefulness
አባከነ	*abakkänä* v.t. wasted *(money etc.)*
አባካኝ	*abakañň* adj. wasteful
. አበካከነ	*abäkakkänä* v.t. wasted here and there *(money)*
በውዛ	*bàwza* n. search light
በዕድ	*ba'əd* adj. /n. stranger, foreigner; unrelated *(family)*
—መነሻ	—*männäša* n. prefix *(gram.)*
—መድረሻ	—*mädräša* n. suffix *(gram.)*
በዝተ	*bazzätä* v.t. made cotton wool
በዝቶ	*bazäto* n. cotton wool
በዝቀ	*bazzäqä* v.i. laboured in vain; searched in vain; wasted *(o/s)* journey
በዜቃ	*bazeqa* n. mercury
በዝራ	*bazra* n. mare
በዳ	*bada* adj. unrelated *(family)*
በዶ	*bado* adj. empty, vacant; unoccupied *(house, seat, land)*; blank *(sheet of paper, space, bullet)*
—ለባዶ	—*labädo* nil nil *(o–o)*
—ባዶውን አስቀረ	—*badowən asqärrä* v.t. denuded
ባዶ እጁ	*bado əǧǧ* adj. penniless, empty-handed
—እግር	—*əgər* adj. barefooted
—ኪስ	—*kis* adj. broke
በጀት	*bağät* or በጀት *bäğät* n. budget
የበጀት ወር	*yäbäğät wär* n. fiscal month
—ዓመት	—*amät* n. fiscal year
በጥ	*baṭ* n. king-post
ቤሳ	*besa* n. coin
ቤት	*bet* n. house
ቤተልሐም	*betä ləhem* n. Bethlehem ; sacristy
ቤተመቅደስ	*betä mäqdäs* n. temple
ቤተክርስ ቲያን	*betäkrəstiyan* n. church
ቤተካህነት	*betäkəhnät* n. clergy; church *(administration)*
ቤተመን ግሥት	*betä mängəst* n. palace
ቤተ መዛግ ብት	*betä məzagəbt* or መዝገብ ቤት *mäzgäb bet* n. archives
ቤተ መጻሕ ፍት	*betä mäṣahəft* n. library
ቤተሰብ	*betä səb* n. family,

108

	house-hold
ቤተኛ	betäñña n. friend of the family
ቤተዘመድ	beta zämäd* n. family, relations, kin
ቤተ እግዚአ ብሔር	beta əgziabəher n. church, temple
ቤት ለቤት	bet läbet around the house
—ማታ	—mätta v.t. rhymed
የቤት ሥራ	yäbet səra n. house work; home-work
እመቤት	əmmäbet n. lady
የቤት እቃ	yäbet əqa n. furniture
—ጫማ	čamma n. slippers
ቡና ቤት	bunna bet n. bar, pub
ከቤት ቤት	käbet bet from door to door, from house to house
ጠጅ ቤት	ṭäǧǧ bet n. tǎg house
ብ—	bə— with simple imperfect, if, when
ቤንዚን	benzin n. petrol, gasoline
ቤዛ	beza n. ransom
የጣት—	yäṭat— n. thimble
ብሆር	bəhor n. reedbuck
ብሉይ ኪዳን	bəluy kidan n. Old Testament
ብሉያት	bəluyat n. books of the Old Testament
ብላሽ	bəlaš adj. useless, valueless
በብላሽ	bäbəlaš n. gratis, free of charge
ብልሹ	bələššu adj. corrupt, see also ተበላሸ
ብላታ	bəlatta n. title (Ethiopian)
ብላቴና	bəlattena n. boy (arch.)
ብላቴን ጌታ	bəlatten geta n. title (Ethiopian)
ብሌን	bəlen n. iris (of eye)
ብል	see በላ
ብልህ	bələh adj. prudent, intelligent

ብልሃት	bəlhat n. prudence, intelligence, know-how
ብልሃተኛ	bəlhatäñña adj. prudent, intelligent, wise
ብልኮ	balləkko n. heavy cotton blanket
ብልጭታ	bəlləčta n. flash, dazzling
ብልጭ አለ	bəlləčč alä v.i. dazzled, glittered, see *በለጨለጨ
ብሔር	bəher n. country, nation
ብሔረሰብ	bəheräsäb n. nationality
ብሔራዊ	bəherawi n. national
—ስሜት	—səmmet n. nationalism
—ሸንጎ	—šängo n. parliament
—በዓል	—bä'al n. national holiday
ጠባብ	ṭäbbab bəherätäñña n. tribalist
ብሔረተኛ	
—ብሔረ ተኛነት	—bəherätäññannät n. tribalism
እግዚአብሔር	əgzi'abəher n. God
የፍትሕ	yäfətha bəher həgg n. Civil Code, Civil Law
ብሔር ሕግ	
ብረት	bərät n. iron, steel, metal
ብረታ ብረት	bəräta bərät n. metals
ብረት ሠሪ	bərät säri n. smith
—ለበስ	—läbbäs adj. armoured
—ድስት	—dəst or ብረድስት bəräddəst n. saucepan
እግር ብረት	əgər bərät n. fetters
ዐረብ—	aräb— n. steel
ብሩሽ	see ቦረሽ
ብራቢሮ	bərrabirro or ቢራቢሮ birrabirro n. butterfly
ብራና	bəranna n. parchment
—ፋቂ	—faqi n. parchment-maker
ብራኪ	bərakkʷa n. shoulder-blade
ብር	bər n. reed (once used as pen); stalk

ብር   bərr n. silver; dollar

ባለብር   balä bərr adj. wealthy, rich

ብርሃን   bərhan n. light, illumination, see also በራ

ብርሌ   bərəlle n. ṭāg̃ flask (for drinking)

ብርቅ   bərq adj. rare, scant, precious

ብርቱካን   bərtukan n. orange

—ቀለም   —qäläm n. orange (colour)

ብርት   bərt n. hand-washing basin

ብርንዶ   bərəndo n. raw meat (not fat)

ብርኩማ   bərkumma n. head-rest (usually of wood); hand crutch (for legless cripple)

ብርጭቆ   bərčaqqo n. glass (drinking)

—ወረቀት   —wäräqāt n. sand-paper

ብስ   see በሳ

ብስና   bəsna n. eructation (of person)

ብስናት   bəsnat n. eructation (of person)

ብስናታም   bəsnatam n. s/o who habitually eructates (insult)

ብሶል   bəsol n. compass

ብቅ አለ   bəqq alä v.i. popped out, suddenly appeared

ብቅ ጥልቅ አለ   bəqq ṭəlləqq alä n. popped up and down

ብብት   bəbbət n. arm-pit

ብትት   bətətto n. tattered clothes

ብትቷም   bətəttʷam adj. ragged

ብቻ   bəčča adv./adj. only; but; however; alone

ቆይ—   qoy— just wait, I will show you

ለብቻ   läbbəčča adv. separately, in private; adj. secluded

—ለብቻ   —läbəčča adv. separately

ለየብቻ   läyyäbəčča adv. separately, apart

ብቻኛ   bəččäñña adj.

lonely, lone, lonesome, solitary

ብቸኛነት   bəččäññənnät n. loneliness

ብው አለ   bəww alä v.i. was set ablaze; raged

ብው ብሉ ሰከረ .   was extremely intoxicated

ብይ   bəyy n. marbles (toy)

ብዞ   በዛ see

ብድግ አለ   bədəgg alä v.i. stood up (suddenly)

—አደረገ   —adärrägä v.t. lifted

ብጉር   bəgur n. pimple

ብጉራም   bəguram adj. pimply

ብጉንጭ   bəgunğ n. boil

ብጣሪ   see አበጠረ

ብጫ   bəča or biča adj. yellow

ብጫ ወባ   bəča wäba n. yellow fever

ብጭጭ አለ   bəčačč alä v.i. was very light (complexion)

ብፁዕ   bəṣu' adj. beatitude

በላሌ   in በላሌ ሱሪ bolale surri n. wide trousers (i.e. not jodhpurs)

በሎቄ   bolloqe n. haricot bean

በራቀ   borräqä v.i. gambolled

በራቂ   borraqi n. gambolling

ቡራቃ   burräqä n. gambolling

በረበረ   boräbbora v.t. bored (hole); channeled its way (river); eroded (soil)

በርባሪ   borbʷari n. borer

መበርበሪያ   mäborboriya n. boring machine

ተበረበረ   täboräbbora v.i. was bored; was eroded (soil)

ቦራ   bora n. white starred horse

በርሳ   borsa n. purse; hand-bag

በርጭ   borğ n. large belly

በርጫም   borğam adj. big-bellied

በቃ   boqa adj. red-polled (animal)

በቃጣ   boqamma adj. red-polled

በተረፈ   botärräfä v.t. bit lump

ቡትርኝ አደረገን ተቦተረፈ	out of *(as hyena)* *butr yñ adärrägä* v.i. bit lump out of *täbotärräfä* v.i. had lump bitten out of	በዘነ	less, imbecile *bozzänä* v.i. became idle
በታ	*bota* n. place, space, area, spot, site; position, status; role	በዘንተኛ በዘኔ	*bozäntäñña* n. idle *bozäne* n. lumpen proletariat
--ያዘ	--*yazä* v.t. occu- pied *(a place;)* re- served a place	አበዘነ	*abozzänä* v.t. made idle
--ያዙ	--*bota yazu* they were seated	በይ በደሰ	*boy* n. canal, waiter *boddäsä* v.t. cut a chunk off
በት/ቡት	*in* በት ጫማ *bot* *čamma* n. high boat	ቡድስ	*buddos* n. lump, chunk which is cut off; place from
በነነ	*bonnänä or* በነነ *bännäna* v.i. rose up into the air *(dust etc.)*		which lump, chunk is cut off
ቡነናሻ	*bunnaññä* n. dust mote	ተበደሰ	*täboddäsä* v.t. was cut off *(lump)*
ቡ አለ	*bunn alä* v.i. rose up suddenly *(dust cloud)*	*በገበገ ተንበገበገ	*bogäbbogä tänbogäbbogä* v.i flamed, burned
በና	*bona* n. dry season	አንበገበገ	*anbogäbbogä* v.t. made s/t flame
በንዳ	*bonda* n. hoop *(band of wood or metal)*	በግ አለ	*bogg alä* v.i. flamed, flared up suddenly
በከበከ	*bokäbbokä* v.i. got *(soft, mushy e.g. (overripe fruit)*	--አደረገ	--*adärrägä* v.t. ignited, lit up
ቡክቡክ	*bukbuk* adj. soft, mushy	በግታ በጨቀ	*boggata* n. flame *boččäqä* v.t. ripped, clawed, seized *(as prey)*
በክዋካ	*bokbʷakka* adj. soft, mushy	ቡጫቂ	*buččaqi* n. ripped off, clawed off piece
በካ	*bokka* v.i. became fer- mented *(dough)*	በጨቀ አደረገ	*boččäq adärrägä* v.t. ripped, clawed a little
ቡኮ	*buko* n. dough, *also* ቡሁ	በጫጨቀ	*boča ̌čäqä* v.t. clawed, ripped all over; torn up *(paper etc.)*
አበካ	*abokka* v.t. kneaded		
አቡኪ	*abuki* n. one who kneads	ተበጨቀ	*täboččäqä* v.i. was clawed, ripped all over; torn up *(paper)*
ማቡኪያ	*mabukiya* n. kneading trough, pan; batch mixer	ተቢጨቀ	*täbʷaččäqä* v.t. scrambled over *(meat, etc. e.g. dogs, vultures)*
ተበካ	*täbokka* v.i. was kneaded	ተበጫጨቀ	*täboča ̌čäqä* v.i. was torn up *(paper)*
ቡኻቀ	*buhaqä* n. dough pan		
በዘ	*bozä* v.i. became life- less, imbecilic	በጭ በጭ አለ/ ተንበጫበጨ	*boč ̌ boč ̌ alä/ tänboč ̌äbboč ̌ä* v.i. slopped about *(liquids)*
በዝ አንቀጽ	*boz änqäs* n. gerund, *(gram.)*		
አበዘ	*abozä* v.t. caused *(s/o)* to become life-	ቢልት	*bʷalt* n. jokes

111

ተ

ተለመ   *tällämä* v.t. ploughed (*furrow*)

ትልም   *təlm* n. furrow

ተለቀ   *tälläqä* v.i. became big, great

ትልቅ   *təlləq* adj. big, great,

ተለቃለቀ   *täläqalläqä* v.t. rinsed off (*o/s*); smeared (*o/s*)

አለቃለቀ   *alläqalläqä* v.t. had (*s/o*) rinse off; hand (*s/o*) smear (*himself*)

ተለተለ   *tälättälä* v.t. cut into stripes (*longitudinally*)

ትልትል   *təltəl* adj. cut in strips

ተተለተለ   *tätälättälä* v.i. was cut in strips

አስተለተለ   *astälättälä* v.t. had (*s/t*) cut in strips

ተላ   *tälla* v.i. became full of maggots (*meat*)

ትል   *təl* n. maggot, worm

የሐር—   *yäharr*— n. silk-worm

አተላ   *atälla* v.t. caused (*s/t*) to get maggot ridden

ተላለፈ   *tälalläfä* v.t. passed each other; was postponed; broke the law, see አለፈ

ተላላፊ   *tälallafi* adj. contageous; n. passers-by

—በሽታ   *bäššəta* n. contageous disease

መተላለፊያ   *mättälaläfiya* n. passage, way through

ተላጋ   see ለጋ

ተልባ   *tälba* n. linseed

የተልባ እግር   *yätälba əgər* linen

ተልከሰከሰ   *tälkäsäkkäsä* v.t. sniffed around (*e.g. dog*); went around unsavoury places

ልከስከስ   *ləkäskəs* adj. frequenting unsavoury places; dirty, filthy

አልከሰከሰ   *alkäsäkkäsä* v.t. treated lightly (*serious matter*)

ተልከፈከፈ   *tälkäfäkkäfä* v.t. sniffed around (*dog*)

ተልካሳ   *tälkassa* adj. lazy, sluggish; n, lazy bones

ተልፈሰፈሰ   *tälfäsäffäsä* v.i. tired (*e.g. of burden*), weakened

ልፍስፍስ   *ləfəsfəs* adj.n. weakening, tiring; weakling, one lacking stamina

አልፈሰፈሰ   *alfäsäffäsä* v.t. worked feebly, half heartedly

ተሐዋስያን   *tähawasəyan* n. insects

ተመለሰ   see መለሰ

ተመለከተ   *tämäläkkätä* v. t. looked at, observed, see *መለከተ

ተመልካች   *tämälkač* n. observer, watcher, spectator

አመለከተ   *amäläkkätä* v.t. applied (*for job*); turned one's attention to

አመልካች   *amälkač* n. applicant

ማመልካቻ   *mamälkäča* n. application (*for job*)

አስመለከተ   *asmäläkkätä* v.t. felt the inclination (*to do s/t*)

ተመላለሰ   see መለሰ

ተመመ   *tämmämä* v. walked in step (*quietly*)

ተመሠጠ   *tämmässätä* v.i. was absorbed (*attention*)

ተመሥጦ   *tâmässəto* n. absorption (*attention*)

ተመሰጠረ   *tämäsattärä* v.t. shared secrets see ምስጢር

ተመረረ   *tämärrärä* v.i. was bitter about; resented bitterly *see*

	also መሪሪ
አማሪሪ	ammarrärä v.i. complained (bitterly, resentfully)
ተመረከዘ	tämäräkk"äzä v.t. bent on, supported (o's with a stick); have evidence
ምርኩዝ	märk"əz n. staff (stick)
ተመሳቀለ	tämäsaqqälä v.i. was confused, mixed up see also ሰቀለ
ተመሰቃቀለ	tämäsäqaqqälä v.i. was thrown into great confusion
አመሰቃቀለ	ammäsäqaqqälä v.t. was made very confused
ተመተመ	tämättämä v.t. patted down, tamped down
ትምትም	təmtəm adj. well tamped down
ትምትም አደረገ	təmtəm adärrägä v.t patted, tamped down firmly
ተተመተመ	tätämättämä v.t. had (s/t) tamped down firmly
አስተመተመ	astämättämä v.i. was tamped down firmly
ተመቸ	tämäččä v.i. was comfortable
ምቹ	məčču adj./n. comfortable; saddle cushion
ምቾት	məččot adj. comfort
ተመቻቸ	tämäčaččä v.i. kept comfortable; sat comfortably
ተመነ	tämmänä v.t. set a price, evaluated
ተመን	tämän n. price
ተተመነ	tätämmänä v.i. was evaluated and a price put on
አስተመነ	astämämänä v.t. had (s/t) evaluated, had (s/o) set a price on
ተመኘ	tämäññä v.i. wished (for)
ምኞት	məññot n. wish
አስመኘ	asmäññä v.t. wished

	(for)
ተመካ	tämäkka v.i. was proud of, relied on
ትምክህት	təmkəhət n. bragging boast, arrogance
ትምክህተኛ	təmkhətäñña adj. boastful, braggard
ተመፃደቀ	tämäsaddäqä v.i.boasted put o/s forward see also ፃደቀ
ተመፃዳቂ	tämäsadaqi n. boaster
አመፃደቀ	ammäsaddäqä v.t. encouraged (s/o) to boast
ተማረ	tämarä v.i. studied, learned
ተማሪ	tämari n. student, pupil, learner
ተማሪ ቤት	tämari bet n. school cf. ትምህርት ቤት
የተማረ	yätämarä adj. educated, learned
ትምህርት	təmhərt n. study; subject; lesson
—ሚኒስቴር	—minister n. Ministry of Education
ገብረ—	häbrä— social studies
ትምህርታዊ	təmhərtawi adj. educational; scholastic
ትምህርት ቤት	təmhərt bet n. school cf. ተማሪ ቤት
ሁለተኛ ደረጃ—	hulätäñña däräǧa— n. secondary school
መሠረተ ትምህርት	mäsärätä təmhərt n. literacy
—ትምህርት ዘመቻ	—təmhərt zämäča n. literacy campaign
መምህር	mämhər n. teacher
ምሁር	məhur adj. learned, scholarly, intellectual
አስተማረ	astämmarä v.t. taught, instructed
አስተማሪ	astämari n. teacher, instructor
ተማረ	tämarä v.i. was pardoned, forgiven see also ማረ

113

ምህረት	məhrät n. pardon, forgiveness	
ተማማረ	tämamarä v.i. forgave each other; taught each other	
አስማረ	asmarä v.t. had (s/o) forgiven, pardoned	
ተማሰለ	tämassälä v.i. resembled each other; was stirred (food)	
ማማሰያ	mammasäya n. stick used to stir food	
ተምር	tämər n. date (fruit)	
ተምታታ	tämtatta v.i. was confused see also መታ	
አምታታ	amtatta v.t. confused, put in disorder; deceived (by confusing)	
ተምች	tämč n. hairy caterpillar	
ተምነሽነሽ	tämnäšännäšä v i. dressed showily	
አምነሽነሽ	amnäšännäšä v.t. adorned s/o; dressed (s/o) in finery	
ተምዘገዘገ	tämzägäzzägä v.i./t. ran full tilt; hurled forcefully	
አምዘገዘገ	amzägäzzägä v.t. threw (e.g. stick) forcefully	
ተሟላቀቀ	tämolaqqäqä v.i. became spoiled (child); be over-demanding	
ሟልቃቃ	molqaqqa adj. spoiled; over demanding	
አሟላቀቀ	ammolaqqäqä v.t. spoiled (child)	
*ተረመሰ	see አተራመሰ	
ተረተ	tärrätä v.t. told tales (to entertain)	
ተራች	tärrač n. story-teller	
ተረት	tärät n. story, tales	
መተረቻ	mätärräča n. subject of gossip; butt (person)	
ተረተረ	tärättärä v.t. uncoiled; slit open; unzipped	
ትርትር	tərtər adj. slit open; uncoiled	
ተተረተረ	tätärättärä v.i. was uncoiled; was slit open; was unzipped	
አተራተረ	attärattärä v.i. helped to uncoil or slit open	
አስተራተረ	astärattärä v.t. had (s/t) uncoiled, slit open	
ተራተር	tärätär n. eroded (uneven) ground	
ተረከ	tärräkä v.t. narrated (history)	
ተራኪ	tärraki n. historian, narrator	
ታሪክ	tarik n. history	
ታሪከኛ	tarikäñña adj. marvellous	
ታሪክ ነገሥት	tarikä nägäst n. chronicles of the kings	
ታሪካዊ	tarikawi adj. historical, historic	
መተረኪያ	mätärräkiya n. butt of gossip	
ተተረከ	tätärräkä v.i. was related (history)	
ተረከበ	täräkkäbä v.i. was handed over, received, took over	
ተረካቢ	täräkkabi adj./n. (one) who takes over, recipient	
ርካከብ	rəkəkkəb n. handing over (formality)	
ተረካከበ	täräkakkäbä v.t. handed-over	
አረካከበ	arräkakkäbä v.t. supervised handing over	
አረካኪ	arräkakabi n. supervisor of handingover	
አስረከበ	asräkkäbä v.t. handed over; turned over (s/t in one's possession;) surrendered (arms)	
ተረከከ	täräkkäkä v.i. split (s/o's) skull	
ትርክክ አደረገ	tərkəkk adärrägä v.t. split open (s/o's) skull	
ተተረከከ	tätäräkkäkä v.i. was split open (skull)	
ተረከዝ	täräkäz n. ankle	
ባለተረከዝ ጫማ	balä täräkäz čamma n. high-heeled shoe	

114

ተረኩሰ *täräkkʷäsä* v.t. stubbed out *(e.g. cigarette)*

ትርኳሽ *tərəkkʷaš* n. ember, extinguished brand

መተርኩሻ *mätärkʷäša* n. *in* የሲጋራ— *yäsigara* -- n. ash-tray

ተተረኩሰ *tätäräkkʷäsä* v.i. was stubbed out, extinguished

ተረገረገ *tärägärrägä* v.t. walked with rolling gait, challenged vehemently

ተረግራጊ *tärägragi* n. one who walks with rolling gait

አረገረገ *arägärrägä* v.i. was springy *(bed)*

አረግራጊ *arägragi* adj. springy *(bed etc.)*

ተረጉመ *tärägɡʷämä* v.t. translated, interpreted

ተርጓሚ *tärgʷami* adj./n. translator, interpreter

ትርጉም *tərgʷum* n. translation, interpretation

ትርጓሜ *tərgʷame* n. commentary

—መጽሐፍት —*mäṣahəft* n. commentary of the Bible

ተርጁማን *tərǧuman* n. interpreter *also* ትርጉማን

ተተረጉመ *tätärägɡʷämä* v.i. was translated, interpreted

አስተረጉመ *astärägɡʷämä* v.t. had *(a book)* translated; used an interpreter

ተረፈ *tärräfä* v.i. escaped danger; was saved; remained; was surplus, was in excess ከዳጋ— *kadäga* — v.t. was out of danger

ተራፊ *tärafi* adj. *(that)* which remains, rest remainder

ትራፊ *tərrafi* n. left over *(food)*

ትርፍ *tərf* n. gain, profit
—እንጀት —*angät* n. appendix *(medicine)*
—ጊዜ —*gize* n. free time, leisure

በተረፈ *bätärräfä* adv. moreover, apart from, what else

አተረፈ *atärräfä* v.t. saved *(s/o)* from danger; made a profit

አትራፊ *atrafi* adj./n. *(one)* who makes profit; profit maker, merchant

አተራረፈ *atärarräfä* v.t. made small profit

ተትረፈረፈ *täträfärräfä* v.t. was superfluous, was abundant; was copious, overflew

ተራ *tära* adj./n. ordinary, common, mediocre quality; turn *(order)*
—ሕዝብ —*həzb* n. mass, crowd
—ሰው —*säw* n. ordinary person, insignificant person
—ቁጥር —*quṭər* n. cardinal number
—ወታደር —*wättäddär* n. private *(soldier)*
—ጠበቀ —*ṭäbbäqä* v.t. waited one's turn

ከተራ የተወለደ *kätära yätäwällädä* adj. of humble birth

ተረኛ *täräňňä* adj./n. *(one)* who is on duty; one whose turn it is

ባለተራ *balätära* n. one whose turn it is

በተራ *bätära* adv. by turn
ተራ በተራ *tära bätära* adv. turn by turn

በየተራ *bäyyätära* adv. turn by turn

ተራመደ *tärämmädä* v.i. stepped forward, walked; progressed.

ተራማጅ *täramaǧ* adj. progressive

እርምጃ ǝrmäǧǧa n. steps (walking); progress

ተረማመደ tärämammädä v.t. stepped over; walked over

መረማመጃ märrämamaǧa n. spring-board (abstract); stepping stone

አረመደ arrammädä v.t. made (s/o) step over, made (s/o, s t) progress; advocated

ተራራ tärara n. mountain
የተራራ ሰንሰለት yätärara sänsälät n. mountain-chain
ተራራማ täraramma adj. mountainous

ተራቢ tärrabi n. clown
ተራኩተ tärakkʷätä v.t. struck each other vehemently

ተራዳ tärada n. tent-pole, centre-pole (of bell tent)

ተራዳ see ረዳ
ተርመሰመሰ tärmäsämmäsä v.i. wriggled about, crawled about

ትርምስ tärämmäs n. disturbance, disorder (crowd of people)

ተተራመሰ tätärammäsä v.t. jostled, became mixed up (crowd of people)

ተተረጋመሰ tätärämammäsä v.i. jostled, became mixed up (crowd of people)

ተራመሰ attärammäsä v.t. caused (ople) to mingle, jostle about; disturbed (people)

አተረጋመሰ attärämammäsä v.t. mixed up (everything); threw into confusion

ተርመጠመጠ tärmäṭämmäṭä v.i. got cluttered up, got dirtied; got very busy (e.g. in kitchen)

እርምጥምጥ ǝrmäṭmäṭ adj. cluttered, dirty

አርመጠመጠ armäṭämmäṭä v.t. worked in a slovenly way

ተርበተበተ tärbätäbbätä v.i. shiv-

ered, trembled with fear, was terrorized

እርብትብት ǝrbätbät adj. shivering (with fear)

አርበተበተ arbätäbbätä v.t. made s/o shiver, tremble with fear, terrorized

ተርበደበደ tärbädäbbädä v.i. jumped nervously (in answer to question)

እርብድብድ ǝrbädbäd adj. jumpy, nervous

ተርበድባጅ tärbädbaǧ adj. n. (one) who is nervous, jumpy

አርበደበደ arbädäbbädä v.t. caused (s o) to jump, nervously

ተርብ tärb n. wasp
ተርታ tärta n. row (line)
በተርታ bätärta adv. in a row
ተርታውን tärtawǝn adv. in a row, continuously

ተርገበገበ tärgäbäggäbä v.i. waved about (e.g. in wind); was troubled about (s/o); fluttered (eyelids), flapped

እርግብግቢት ǝrgäbgäbit n. propeller (child's toy); fontanelle (of child)

እርግብግብ ǝrgäbgäb adj. extremely hospitable; kindhearted, humane

ተርገብጋቢ tärgäbgabi adj. flapping, waving (in wind)

አርገበገበ argäbäggäbä v.t. waved (hand)

ተሰለፈ täsälläfä v.i. went in file; got prepared; got straight, in order (to begin some action)

ተሰላፊ täsälafi n. one who goes in file; gets prepared (for task)

ሰልፍ sälf n. parade, procession

ሰላማዊ— sälamawi—n. peaceful demonstration

አሰለፈ assälläfä v.t. had s/o parade; supervised procession, marching

116

እሰላፊ	*assällafi* n. supervisor of parade; drill, marching supervisor	
—መኩንን	*—mäkonnən* n. officer in charge of parade, procession	
ተሰማ	*täsämma* v.i. was heard; was obeyed, venerated, see also ሰማ	
ተሰሚ	*täsämi* adj. respectful	
ተሰሚነት	*täsäminnät* n. respect, veneration	
ተሰረነቀ	*täsärännäqä* v.t. stick in *(o/s)* throat	
ተሰራጨ	*täsäraččä* v.i. was broadcast; was circulated	
ስርጭት	*sərəččət* n. distribution, circulation	
ተሰራጨ	*täsäräčaččä* v.i. was circulated all over *(also of blood)*	
እሰራጨ	*assäraččä* v.t. circulated *(news)*, propagated *(news)*	
እሰራጨ	*assäräčaččä* v.t. caused to be broadcast; circulated	
ተሰቀቀ	*täsäqqäqä* or ተሳቀቀ *täsaqqäqä* v.i. winced, shied away from *(s/t unpleasant); was embarrassed (e.g. to receive)*	
ሰቅቅ እለ	*səqq alä* v.i. was actually embarrassed; shied away from; was set on edge *(e.g. by grating sound)*	
እሰቀቀ	*assäqqäqä* v.t. caused s/o to be actually embarrassed; horrified *(s/o)*	
እሰቃቂ	*assäqqaqi* adj. horrifying abhorrent	
ተሰወጠ	*täsäwwäṭä* v.t. slipped from *(o/s)* mind	
ተሳተፈ	*täsattäfä* v.t. participated; partook, had a share of	
ተሳታፊ	*täsatafi* adj./n. *(one)* who participates,	

partakes, *(one)* who has a share of

እሳተፈ	*assattäfä* v.t. caused to participate, partake	
ተሳነ	*täsanä* v.t. failed, was unable to	
ተሳካ	*täsakka* v.i. was successful, was accomplished; was interlocked *see also* ሰካ	
እሳካ	*assukka* v.t. made *(s/t)* successful, accomplished; interlocked	
ተስለመለመ	*täslämällämä* v.i. felt faint, dizzy, overcome *(by heat fumes etc.)*	
ስልምልም	*sələmləmm alä* v.i.	
እለ	felt faint, dizzy	
ተስለከተከ	*täsläkälläkä* v.i. wriggled, slithered *(e.g. snakes)*	
ተስቦ	*täsəbo* n. contagious disease, epidemic *see also* ሳበ	
ተስፋ	*täsfa* n. hope, promise	
—ሰጠ	*—säṭä* v.t. gave hope; promised	
—ቆረጠ	*—qorräṭä* v.t. despaired, lost hope. was discouraged	
—እስቆረጠ	*—asqorräṭä* v.t. discouraged, disheartened	
—እደረገ	*—adärrägä* v.i. made hope, hoped	
—እጣ	*—aṭṭa* v.t. despaired	
ተሸቀዳደመ	*see* ቀደመ	
ተሸበረ	*täšäbbärä* v.i. was panic-stricken, was alarmed, was terrorized	
ሽብር	*šəbbər* n. terror, panic, commotion	
እሸበረ	*aššäbbärä* v.t. filled with panic, terrorized, alarmed, reduced to chaos	
ተሸከመ	*täšäkkämä* v.t. carried	
ተሸካሚ	*täšäkkami* adj./n. *(one)* who carries, bearer	
ሽክም	*šäkəm* n. load	
ተሸካከመ	*täšäkakkämä* v.i. ca	

117

አሽከመ	ried each other aššäkkämä v.t. had (s/o) carry; helped (s/o) to carry
ተሸጋሸገ	täšägaššägä v.t, moved up, closed up space (e.g. in file)
መሸጋሸጊያ	mäššägašögiya n. gap (in file)
አሽጋሸገ	aššägaššägä v.t. had a space closed up (e.g. in file, row etc.)
ተሻለ	täšalä v.t. felt better, recovered; became better
የተሻለ	yätäšalä adj. better, best; preferable
ምን ይሻላል	mən yəššalal what should be done?
ተሻሻለ	täšašalä v.i. was improved, got better, became a little better
አሻለ	aššalä v.t. made to feel better, made to recover a little
አሻሻለ	aššašalä v.t. improved, ameliorated
ግሻሻያ ሓሳብ	mašašaya hassab n. amendment
ተሻማ	täšamma v.t. scrambled for (e.g. children among themselves for thrown sweets etc.)
ሽሚያ	šämmiya n. scrambling for
አሻማ	aššamma v.t. caused (people) to scramble for
ተሻረከ	täšarräkä v.i. became partners: became close associates, friends
ሸሪከ	šärik n. partner, friend
ሸርከ	šərka or ሽርክና šərkənna n. partnership, friendship
አሻረከ	aššarräkä v.t. made partners, friends
ተሻገረ	täšaggärä v.t. crossed (a river etc.)
መሻገሪያ	mäššägäriya n. crossing place (bridge etc.)
ተሸጋገረ	täšägaggärä v.t. cros-

	sed, passed over; passed from one year to another
ተሸጋጋሪ	täšägagari adj. in-, tersecting (beam etc.)
አሻገረ	aššaggärä v.t. had (s/o) cross (a river etc.)
አሽጋገረ	aššägaggärä v.t. had (s/o) cross
ተሽቀጠቀጠ	täšqoṭäqqoṭä v.t. trembled with fear: was submissive
ተሽቀጥቋጭ	täšqoṭq"aç adj./n. (one) who is submissive
ሽቁጥቁጥ	šəquṭquṭ adj. submissive
አሽቀጠቀጠ	ašqoṭäqqoṭä v.t. caused (s/o) to be servile, to make (s/o) shake in his shoes
ተሽከረከረ	täškäräkkärä v.i. rolled over (e.g. wheel)
ተሽከርካሪ	täškärkari n. motor vehicle
ሽከርካሪት	skärkərit n. wheel, hoop
አሽከረከረ	uškäräkkärä v.t. rolled; drove (a car)
አሽከርካሪ	aškärkari adj./n. (one) who drives, a driver
ተሽኮረመመ	täškorämmämä v.i. shrank with embarassment (e.g. young girl)
ተሽኮርማሚ	täškormami n. shy, retiring (woman or girl
አሽኮረመመ	aškorämmämä v.t. flirted
ተቀመጠ	täqämmaṭä v.t. sat down; sat in a meeting
ተቀማጭ	täqämmaç adj./n. (one) who sits; one who is alive; saving (money)
ተቅማጥ	täqmaṭ n. diarrhoea
ቅምጥ	qəmmaṭ n. concubine (polite)
መቀመጫ	mäqqämäča n. sitting place; stool;

	bottom *(part of body)*
አቀማመጥ	aqqämamäṭ n. sitting position
አስቀመጠ	asqämmäṭä v.t. put down; put aside; kept aside; had diarrhoea
ተቀማጠለ	täqämaṭṭälä v. i. lived lavishly, luxuriously
ቅምጥል	qəmäṭṭal adj. high living *(person)*
አቀማጠለ	aqqämaṭṭälä v.t. treated *(s/o)* lavishly; spoilt *(e.g. o/s child)*
ተቀበለ	täqäbbälä v.t. received, took over; accepted
አቀበለ	aqäbbälä v.t. passed s/t over, handed over
ተቀባበለ	täqäbabbälä v.i. passed over to each other
ቅብብል	qəbäbbäl n. pass *(football, etc.)*
–ሩጫ	–ruč̣č̣a n. relay race
አቀባበለ	aqqäbabbälä v.t. passed from hand to hand; cocked *(e.g. rifle)*
አቀባባይ ከበርቴ	aqqäbabay käbbärte n. middle-man; comprador-bourgeois;
ተቀነባበረ	täqänäbabbärä v.i. was compiled, set in orderly manner
ተቀናበረ	täqänabbärä see above
አቀነባበረ	aqqänäbabbärä v.t. compiled; *(from various sources)*
አቀነባባሪ	aqqänäbabbari n. compiler
ተቀናቀነ	täqänaqqänä v.t. acted as rival competitor
ተቀናቃኝ	täqänaqäñ adj./n rival, competitor
ተቀናጣ	täqänaṭṭa v.i. felt too much at home; abused hospitality
ቅንጦት	qənṭot n. abuse of hospitality; lavish, luxurious life
ተቀየመ	täqäyyämä v.t. held a grudge, took offense
ቅያሜ	qəyyame n. rancour,

	grudge, ill-feeling
ቂም	qim n. resentment, grudge, ill-feeling, rancour,
አስቀየመ	asqäyyämä v.t. hurt one's feeling, offened
አስቀያሚ	asqäyyami adj. offensive, ugly, grotesque
ተቀዳጀ	täqädaǧǧä v.i. was crowned *(success)*
አቀዳጀ	aqqädaǧǧä v.t. had *(s/o)* crowned; invested with *(s/t)*
ተቃረነ	täqarränä v.t. went against, contradicted,
ተቃራኒ	täqarani n. opponent, conflicting, opposite
ተቃርኖ	taqarəno n. conflict, opposition
ተቃና	täqanna v.i. was successful; was straightened see also ቀና
አቃና	aqqanna v.t. straightened
ተቃወመ	täqawwämä v.t. objected, opposed, see also ቆመ
ተቃውሞ	täqawəmo n. opposition, objection
ተቃዋሚ	täqawami adj./n. *(one)* who objects, opposes
ተቃወሰ	täqawwäsä v.i. was disrupted; got out of order
ቀውስ	qäws n. disruption, disorder
የአእምሮ–	yä'a'əməro--- n. mental disorder
አቃወሰ	aqqawwäsä v.t. disrupted, made disordered
አቃዋሽ	aqqawaš adj. disrupter
ተቃጠለ	täqaṭṭälä v.i. was burnt, caught fire, was on fire
በንዴት–	bänəddet—was filled with fury
ቃጠሎ	qaṭälo n. blaze, burning
አቃጠለ	aqqaṭṭälä v.t. burnt, set on fire
ተቀጣጠለ	täqäṭaṭṭälä v.i. caught fire; was tied together

119

ተቀለሰለሰ   *see* ቀጠለ
täqläsälläsä v.i. was
submissive *(person)*

ቅልስልስ   *qaləsləs* adj. submissive ; shy

ተቀለስላሽ   *täqläslaš* n. submissive person

ተቀለበለበ   *täqläbälläbä* v.i. was too
voluble, excitable

ተቀለብላቢ   *täqläblabi* n. voluble,
excitable person

ቅልብልብ   *qaləbləb* adj. voluble, over excited

ቀለብላባ   *qäläblabba* adj.
voluble, over exicted

አቀለበለበ   *aqläbälläbä* v.t.
rushed *(s/o,)* hurried
(s/o) into forgetting
things

ተቀለጠለጠ   *täqläțälläțä* v.i. became
greasy, oily, shiny
with fat, sweat etc,
see also ቀለጠ

ተቀበዘበዘ   *täqbäzäbbäzä* v.i. run
wild despairingly

ተቀበዝባዥ   *täqbäzbäž* n. wild,
fugitive

ቀበዝባዛ   *qäbäzbazza* adj.
running away wildly,
despairingly

ቅብዝብዝ   *qəbəzbəz* adj. running away wildy,
despairingly

አቀበዘበዘ   *aqbäzäbbäzä* v.t.
caused *(s/o)* run-
away wildly

ተቀነዘነዘ   *täqnäzännäzä* v.i. became impatient

ቅንዝንዝ   *qənəznəz* adj. impatient

አቀነዘነዘ   *aqnäzännäzä* v.t.
caused *(s/o)* to be
impatient

ተቀዋም   *täqwam* n. institute

ተቀጨለጨለ   *täqčäläččälä* v.i. clinked,
jingled *(of bells)*
see also ቃጭል

ተቀረቀረ   *täqoräqqorä* v.i. was
very much concerned
(for s/o)

ተቀርቋሪ   *täqorqʷari* adj./n.
(one) who is very
much concerned *(for
s/o)*

ተቋራመጸ   *täqʷärammäḍä* v.i.
lived without hope
*(dragged out desperate
existence)*

ተቋነነ   *täqʷannänä* v.i. walked
disdainfully, proudly

ተቋናኝ   *täqʷännañ* n. disdainful,proud*(person)*

ቍንን   *qʷənnən* adj. disdainful, proud

—አለ   —*alä* v.i. was over-
bearingly disdainful

ተቆጣ   *täqoțța* v.i. was angry,
enraged; v.t. rebuked

ተቆጪ   *täqočč̣i* adj./n.
*(one)*who gets easily
angry; *(one)* who
rebukes

—የለለው   —*yälelläw* adj. un-
disciplined

ቁጡ   *quțțu* adj. bad tempered, surly

ቁጣ   *quțța* n. wrath,
anger

አስቆጣ   *asqoțța* v.t. made
angry, enraged;
stirred up trouble for
(s/o)

ተቆጣጠረ   *täqoțațțärä* v.t. con-
trolled, supervised,
superintended *see
also* ቆጠረ

ተቆጣጣሪ   *täqoțațari*
controller, supervisor,
superintendant

መቆጣጠሪያ   *mäqqoțațäriya* n.
means of controlling,
supervising

ቁጣጠር   *quțațțər* n. controlling, supervison

ተቋለጨለጨ   *täqʷəläčälläčä* v.t.
stared with surprise

ተላጭልጭ   *qʷələčləč* adj./n,
(one) who blinks,
flinches, stares with
astonishment

አቋለጨለጨ   *aqʷäläčälläčä* v.t.
blinked, flinched *(o/s
eyes)*

እንቋልልጭ   *ənqʷələləč* or
እንቋልልሞ
ənqʷələləčo n. gloat-
ing *(over possesson of
s/t)*

ተቀነጠነጠ täq"ənäṭännäṭä v.i. become restless *(to go, do s/t else)*

ቀነጥነጥ q"ənəṭnəṭ adj. restless (to go, do s/t else)

አቀነጠነጠ aq"ənäṭännäṭä v.t. caused s/o to be restless

ተቋቋመ täq"aq"amä see also ቆመ qomä v.i. was established, was well established was erected; v.t. resisted *(enemy)*

አቋቋመ aqq"aq"amä v. t. established; made well established; erected

ተበላሸ täbälaššä v.i. was spoiled, deteriorated, went wrong

አበላሸ abbälaššä v.t.damaged, spoiled, deformed,

ተበሳጨ täbäsaččä v.i. was annoyed, disturbed

ብሰጩ bəsəčču adj. annoyed, disturbed

ብሰጭት bəsəččət n. disturbance, annoyance

ብሰጭትጭት እለ bəsč̣ätčč̣ätt alä v.i. was very much annoyed, disturbed

አበሳጨ abbäsaččä v.t. annoyed, disturbed

ተበሻቀጠ täbäšaqqäṭä v.i. behaved badly; was over demanding, over-critical, *see also* በሻቀጠ

ብሸቅጥቅጥ እለ bəšqäṭqäṭṭ alä v.i. behaved very badly, was umbearably over-critical

ተበተበ täbättäbä v.t. tied up roughly; put *(s/o)* in bad terms *(with superior)*

ተብታቢ täbtabi n. *(one)* who makes trouble with o/s superior bv gossip

ተብታባ täbtabba adj. stammerer

ትብትብ təbtəb adj. trouble-making *(with superior)*

ትብትብ አደረገ təbtəbb adärrägä v.t. tied roughly *(inextricably)* but firmly, complicated matters unnecessarily

ተተበተበ tätäbättäbä v.i. was tied up roughly inextricably

ተበታተነ täbätattänä v.i. was scattered, dispersed, *see also* በተነ

ተበደረ täbäddärä v.t. borrowed, got a loan

ተበዳሪ täbäddari adj. borrower

ብድር bəddər n. loan

መበደሪያ mäbbädäria n. loan agency, security for loan; collateral

አበደረ abäddärä v.t. gave loan, lent

አበዳሪ abäddari n. lender

ተበዳደረ täbädaddärä v.i. borrowed from each other, lent each other

ተበገረ täbäggärä v.i. yielded, gave in

የማይበገር yämmayəbbäggär adj. unyielding invulnerable; obstinate, invincible

ተበጠረ täbäṭṭärä v.i. was combed

ብጥር bəṭṭər adj. combed

ብጣሪ bəṭṭari n. chaff, etc. *(left after threshing)*

አበጠረ abäṭṭärä v.t. combed: sifted grain

አበጣሪ abäṭṭari n. thresher, sifter

ማበጠሪያ mabäṭṭäriya n. comb; grain cleaning, sifting machine

አበጣጠረ abäṭaṭṭärä v.t. combed a little; cleaned *(grain)* a little

አስበጠረ asbäṭṭärä v.t. had *(s/o)* comb, clean grain

ተባ täbba v.i. became strong; was annealed, tempered

ተባረደ täbarrädä *see also* በረደ

ተባበረ	chilly *(weather)* *täbabbärä see also* አበረ v.i. unified, associated *(for a common cause)*, was coordinated
ተባባሪ	*täbabari* adj/n *(one)* · who is an associate; *(s/o)* who is implicated in a crime
ትብብር	*təbabbər* n. unification; support
አስተባበረ	*astäbabbärä* v.t. had *(people)* unified, coordinated
አስተባባሪ	*astäbabari* n. co-ordinator
ተባባሰ	*täbabasä see also* ባሰ *basä* v.i. went from bad to worse; was very much aggravated; reached a point of no return *(dispute)*
ተባት	*täbat or* ተባዕት *täba'ət* adj. male, masculine *(gram.)*
ተባታይ	*täbatay* adj. masculine *(gram.)*
ተባይ	*täbay* n. insect, vermin *(parasitic insect,)* see also በላ
ተብለጠለጠ	*täblätällätä* v.i. acted cunningly, tried to fool others, *see* በለጠ
ተብለጥላጭ	*täblätlaç* n. slick, smart, cunning
ተብረቀረቀ	*täbräqärräqä* v.i. glittered, shimmered, *see also* በረቀ
ተብረከረከ	*täbräkärräkä* v.i. wobbled *(knees;)* trembled with fear
አብረከረከ	*abräkärräkä* v.t. made *(s/o)* tremble; terrified *(s/o)*
ተብከነከነ	*täbkänäkkänä* v.i. was preoccupied, was deep in thought
ተዳደነ	*täbʷaddänä* v.t. formed a team *(sport mainly)*, see also ቡድን

ተቸ	*täččä* v.i. criticized; gave one's opinion, commented on *(s/t, s/o)*
ተቺ	*täčči* n. critic; commentator
ትችት	*təččət* n. comment, criticism
ተተቸ	*tätäččä* v.i. was criticized, commented on
አስተቸ	*astäččä* v.t. had *(s/o)* criticized, had *(s/o)* give comment on *(s/o, s/t)*
ተነሳ	*tänässa* v. i. rose up, stood up, got up *(from bed; started a journey)*
መነሻ	*männäša* n. starting point
መነሾ ትንሳኤ አነሳ	*männäšo* n. cause *tənsa'e* n. Easter *anässa* v.t. lifted; took up; withdrew *(legal charge)*
ክርስትና—	*kərəstənna* — v.t. christened
ተነሳሳ	*tänässassa* v.i. was inspired, instigated, aroused; was agitated
አነሳሳ	*annäsässa* v. t. inspired instigated, aroused; agitated
አነሳሽ	*annäsaš* adj/n *(one)* who inspires, instigates; agitator
አስነሳ	*asnässa* v.t. had *(s/t)* lifted; aroused *(from sleep)*; had *(s/o)* removed *(from position)*; agitated
ተነቃነቀ	*tänäqannäqä* v.i. was shaken, moved, see also ነቀነቀ
አነቃነቀ	*annäqannäqä* v.t. - shook, moved
ተነበየ	*tänäbbäyä* v.t. prophesied
ተንባይ	*tänbay* n. prophet; one who prophesies
ትንቢት	*tənbit* n. prophecy
ትንቢተኛ	*tənbitäñña* adj/n. *(one)* who tells

122

ነቢይ	prophecies		see also ተነጣጣሪ
	näbiyy n. prophet	ተነጻጸሪ	*tänäṣaṣari* adj./n.
ነባይ	*nabay* adj. truthful		s/t which is compared
	(opposite አባይ*, abay)*		with s t else
	adj. falseful	አነጻጸረ	*annäṣaṣṣärä* v.t. com-
ኮነተነ	*tänattänä* v.t analysed		pared
ትንተና	*təntäna* n. analysis	ተነፈሰ	*tänäffäsä* v.t. breathed;
ተነታኝ	*täntañ* adj./n. *(one)*		formed relief *(from*
	who analyses		s/t arduous) see also
ተተነተነ	*tätänattänä* v.i. was		ነፈሰ
	analysed	ጎማው—	*gommaw*— the
አስተነተነ	*astänättänä* v.t. had		tyre is flat
	(s/t) analysed	ትንፋሽ	*tənfaš* n. breath
ኮነተገ	*tänättägä* v.t. burned	ተነፈሰ አለ	*tänfäss alä* v. found
ትንታግ	*təntag* n. ember,		slight relief
	brand	አስተነፈሰ	*ästänäffäsä* v.t let
ተነነ	*tännänä* n. vapoured		air out, gave rest
ተነ	*tänn* n. vapour	ተነፈገ	*tänäffägä* v.i. gave off
ተናኝ	*tänañ* adj. n. *(that)*		noxious condensation
	which evaporates	ትንፋገን	*tənfagän* n. noxious
ተተናኮለ	*tätänakkolä* v.t. pro-		condensation
	voked	ትንፋግ	*tənfag* n. noxious con-
ተተናካይ	*tätänak"ay* adj.		densation
	provocative	ተነፋ	*tänäffa* v.i. v.i. was
ተንኮል	*tänkol* n. provo-		inflated; became
	cation		extremely proud, *see*
ተንኮለኛ	*tänkoläñña* adj. n.		*also* ነፋ
	(one) who provokes	ተነፋ	*tänaffa* v.i. boxed
ተነኮሰ	*tänäkk"äsä* v.t. prod-		each other *(coll.)*
	ded, provoked by	ተነፋፋ	*tänäfaffa* v.i. was
	prodding		extremely inflated
ተንካሽ	*tänk"aš* adj./n *(one)*	አነፋ	*anaffa* v.t. brayed
	who provokes by		*(donkey)*
	prodding	ወናፍ	*wänaf* n. bellows; liar
ተነጣጠረ	*tänäṭaṭṭärä* v.i. com-	ተነፋነፈ	*tänäfannäfä* v.i. grum-
	pared; defended *(o/s)*		bled; obeyed with bad
	in court		grace
ተነጣጣሪ	*tänäṭaṭari* n. plain-	ነፍናፋ	*näfnaffa* adj./n *(one)*
	tiff, defendant in		who obeys with bad
	lawcourt		grace
ተነጫነጨ	*tänäčannäčä* v.t. cried	ተነነቀ	*tänannäqä* v.i. v.t. grip-
	over nothing; com-		ped *(s/o)* firmly; was
	plained pointlessly		on the verge of tears
ነጭናጫ	*näčnaččä* adj/n		*see* አነቀ
	(one) who complains	ትንቅንቅ	*tənəqnəq* n. grabbing,
	pointlessly, grouchy		gripping *(firmly)*
ተነጫናጭ	*tänäčanäč* adj./n.	ተናዘዘ	*tänazzäzä* v.t. made
	(one) who complains		*(o/s)* will, confessed
	pointlessly		*(to a priest)*
አነጫነጨ	*annäčannäčä* v.t.	ተናዛዥ	*tänazaž* adj./n. *(one)*
	caused *(s/o)* to com-		who makes his will,
	plain pointlessly		*(one)* who confesses
ተነጻጸረ	*tänäṣaṣṣärä* v.i. was	ኑዛዜ	*nuzaze* n. will *(on*
	compared with s/t,		

	property) confession, testament
የኑዛዜ ቃል	yänuzaze qal n. last will
አናዘዘ	annazzäzä v.t. had(s/o) make his will
አናዛዥ	annazaž n. priest who officiates at dying man's last testament
ተናደደ	tänaddädä v.i. became furious, vexed, see also ነደደ
ተናዳጅ	tänadağ adj./n. (one) who is easily irritated, furious
ተናጠበ	tänaṭṭäbä v.i. was hindered, stopped
አናጠበ	annaṭṭäbä v. t. hindered, stopped
ተናፈጠ	tänaffäṭä v.i. blew one's nose
ንፍጥ	nəfṭ n. mucus
ንፍጡን ጠረገ	nəfṭun ṭärrägä wiped one's nose, sniffed
ተንሰቀሰቀ	tänsäqässäqä v.i. sobbed, wept bitterly
ሲቅስቅስ ብሎ አለቀሰ	səqsəqq bəlo aläqqäsä v.i. sobbed, wept bitterly
ተንሰፈሰፈ	tänsäfässäfä v.i. treated (s/o) extremely kindly; was importunate; felt very sharp pain
ተንሰፍሳፊ	tänsäfsafi adj./n. (one) who is importunate
ሰፍሰፍ አለ	səfsəff alä v.i. treated (s/o) extremely well; was importunate
አንሰፈሰፈ	ansäfässäfä v.t. gave very sharp pain (e.g. wound)
ተንሶለሰለ	tänsolässolä v.t. scrounged, cadged everywhere
ተንሸረሸረ	tänšäräššärä v.i. had a walk, a ride (for pleasure)
ሸርሸር	šärrəšärr n. walk, ride (for pleasure)
መንሸርሸሪያ	mänšäršäriya n. place for walk

ተንሸራሸረ	see ተንሸረሸረ
መንሸራሸሪያ	mänšäräšäriya n. walking place (for pleasure)
አንሸረሸረ	anšäräššärä v.t. took (s/o) for a walk, a ride
ተንሸራተተ	tänšärattätä v.i. slided glided, slipped
ተንሸዋረረ	tänšäwarrärä v.i. went cross-eyed
ሸውራራ	šäwrarra adj. cross-eyed
አንሸዋረረ	anšäwarrärä v.i. had cross-eyes
ተንቀለቀለ	tänqäläqqälä v.i. was over-hasty, over-excited
ቀልቃላ	qälqalla adj. over-hasty, over-excited
አንቀለቀለ	anqäläqqälä v.t. caused (s/o) to be over-hasty, over-excited
ተንቀረበበ	tänqäräbbäbä v.i. was slightly open, crookedly placed (e/g cover, lid)
አንቀረበበ	anqäräbbäbä v.t. put on crookedly (lid, cover)
ተንቀረፈፈ	tänqäräffäffä v.i. had slack posture; was very slow at work
ቀርፋፋ	qärfaffa adj. slack, slow at work
ቅርፍፍ አለ	qərfəff alä v.t. was very sluggish, slack
አንቀረፈፈ	anqäräffäfä v.t. handled awkwardly
ተንቀሳቀለ	see ቀለቀለ
ተንቀበቀበ	tänqäbäqqäbä v.i. was extremely mean, miserly
ቀብቃባ	qäbqabba adj. extremely mean, miserly
ተንቀበደደ	tänqäbäddädä v.i. was very pregnant, very stout; was puffed up with rage
ተንቀባደደ	tänqäbaddädä v.i. became extremely proud
ተንቀባረረ	tänqäbarrärä v.i. was

ቀብራራ spoiled *(child)*, was over-demanding *qäbrarra* adj. spoilt *(child)*; over-demanding

አንቀባረረ *anqäbarrärä* v.t. spoiled *(children)*

ተንቀዋለለ *tänqäwallälä* v.i. loitered around, walked aimlessly; grew tall *(youth)*

ቀውላላ *qäwlalla* adj. extremely tall; loitering about

አንቀዋለለ *anqäwallälä* v.t. made *(s/o)* loiter around, walk aimlessly *(through unemployment)*

ተንቀዣቀዠ *tänqäžäqqäžä* v.i. was unsettled; fussed about

ቀዠቃዠ *qäžqažža* adj. messing about, fussing around

ቅዠቅዠ አለ *qəžqəžž alä* v.i. was very unsettled; kept on fussing about

ተንቀጠቀጠ *tänqäṭäqqäṭä* v.i. trembled; shook *(with fear)*; was coward

ቀጥቃጣ *qäṭqaṭṭa* adj. shivering *(with fear)*; coward

ቅጥቃጤ *qəṭqaqqaṭe* n. tremor
አንቀጠቀጠ *anqäṭäqqäṭä* v.t. shook, made *(s/o)* tremble

እንቅጥቃጤ *ənqəṭqaqqaṭe* n. shaking, trembling

የምሬት— *yämäret*—n. earthquake

ተንቄራጠጠ *tänqʷäraṭṭäṭä* v.i. paced up and down *(nervously)*

አንቄራጠጠ *anqʷäraṭṭäṭä* v.t. caused *(s/o)* to pace up and down *(nervously)*

ተንበለበለ *tänbäläbbälä* v.i. flared up *(of fire)*

አንበለበለ *anbäläbbälä* v.i. flared up *(of fire)*; read fluently

ተንበረከከ *tänbäräkkäkä* v.i. kneeled

እንብርክ *ənbərakk* n. action of kneeling

መንበርክኪያ *mänbärkäkiya* n. kneeling place *(e/g. in a church)*

አንበረከከ *anbäräkkäkä* v.t. made *(s/o)* kneel; subdued

ተንበሸበሸ *tänbäšäbbäšä* v.i. was abundant

አንበሸበሸ *anbäšäbbäšä* v.t. offered in abundance

ተንቦለቦለ *tänboläbbolä* v.i. flowed in abundance

አንቦለቦለ *anboläbbolä* v.t. caused to flow abundantly

ተንቦረቀቀ *tänboräqqäqä* v. flowed, wore over-large *(of clothes)*

ቦርቃቃ *borqaqqä* adj. flowing, over-large *(of clothes)*

ተንቦራቀቀ *tänboraqqäqä* v.i. flowed, wore over-large *(clothes)*

አንቦራቀቀ *anboraqqäqä* v.t. caused to look baggy, ill-fitting

ተንቦገቦገ *tänbogäbbogä* v.i. blazed, flared up

አንቦገቦገ *anbogäbbogä* v.t. set ablaze

ተንቦጨቦጨ *tänbočäbboča* or ተንቦ ጫቦጨ *tänboč̣abboč̣ä* v.i. slopped about *(liquids)*

ሆዱ— *hodu* — felt pity
ቦጭቧጫ *boč̣bʷačča* n. coward; sloppy food

አንቦጨቦጨ *anboč̣äbboč̣ä* or አን ቦጫቦጨ *anboč̣abboč̣ä* v.t. caused to slop about

ተንተረከከ *täntäräkkäkä* v.i. glowed incandescently, *see* ተረከከ *tärkakka* adj. glowing incandescently

አንተረከከ *antäräkkäkä* v.t. caused to glow incandescently

ተንተራስ *täntärasä* v.t. laid one's head on a pillow

ትራስ *təras* v. pillow
አንተራስ *antärasä* v.t. slide a

ተንተባተበ täntäbattäbä v.t. stammered, see also ተበተበ

ተንተከተከ täntäkättäkä v.i. simmered

አንተከተከ antäkättäkä v.t. let (s/t) simmer

ተንቶሰቶሰ täntosättosä v.i. wandered about aimlessly; was busy to no purpose

ተንቶስቷሸ täntost"aš adj. purposely over-active

ቶስቷሳ tost"assa adj. needlessly busy

ተንቻቻ tänčaččä v.i. made hubbub (background noise of large crowd)

ቻቻታ čačata n. hubbub, noise (of crowd)

ተንከላወሰ tänkälawwäsä v.i. messed about; was busy to no purpose

ተንከረፈፈ tänkäräffäfä v.i. became shabby

ከርፋፋ kärfaffa adj. shabby

ከርፍፍ አለ kərfəff alä v.i grew extremely shabby

አንከረፈፈ ankäräffäfä v.t. carried (s/t) awkwardly

ተንከባለለ tänkäballälä v.i. rolled

ተንከባላይ tänkäbalay adj. rolling

እንክብል ənkəbəll n. tablet (aspirin, etc.)

ከብልል አለ kəbləll alä v.i rolled over (suddenly)

አንከባለለ ankäballälä v.t rolled (s/t)

ተንከተከተ tänkätäkkätä v.i cackled (laughter)

አንከተከተ ankätäkkätä v.t. caused (s/o) to burst out laughing

ተንከፈረረ tänkäfärrärä v.i. became frizzy, unkempt (hair)

ከፍራራ käfrarra aj. frizzy, unkempt (hair)

አንከፈረረ ankäfärrärä v.t caused to be unkempt (hair)

pillow under; slide one's arm under (as pillow)

ተንኮል tänkol n. mischief, trick, malice

ተንኮለኛ tänkoläñña adj. mischievous, malicious crafty

ተንኳፈፈ tänk"affäfä v.i. rose (dough)

ተንዘረጣጠ tänzäräṭṭäṭä v.i. was big-bellied.

ዘርጣጣ zärṭaṭṭa aj. big-bellied, pot bellied

አንዘረጣጠ anzäräṭṭäṭä v.t stuck out, thrust out one's belly

ተንዘረፈጠ tänzäräffäṭä or ተንዘረ ፈጠ tänzäraffäṭä v.i. sat at one's ease, flopped down

አንዘረፈጠ anzäräffaṭä v.t. sprawled one's body out

ተንዘረፈፈ tänzäräffäfä v.i. dressed untidily, carelessly; was ill-fitting (clothes etc); hung loose

ዘርፈፈ zärfaffa adj. ill-fitting; untidily dressed, droopy

አንዘረፈፈ anzäräffäfä v.t. dressed untidily, hung loose

ተንዘፈዘፈ tänzäfäzzäfä v.t. shuddered; shook oneself

አንዘፈዘፈ anzäfäzzäfä v.t. made (s/o) shudder shake, tremble

ተንዛዛ tänzazza v.i. was superfluous, excessive

አንዛዛ anzazza v.i. caused superfluity, excess

ተንዳላቀቀ tändälaqqäqä v.i lived lavishly; indulged in luxury, see also ዳለቀ

ተንጠረጋገ tänžäräggägä v.i was over-laden (e.g tree with fruit)

ጠርጋጋ zärgagga adj. over _ laden tree with fruit

ተንደረበበ tändäräbbäbä v.i was heaped full; was reserved, patient, serene (person)

126

ድርብብ   dərbäb adj. heaped full

ደርባባ   därbabba adj. serene, reserved

ተንደረከከከ   tändäräkkäkä v.i was over-laden (e.g fruit) tree; heaped up (fire)

ተንደቀደቀ   tändäqäddäqä v.i made gulping sound (liquid emptying from bottle)

አንደቀደቀ   andäqäddäqä v i sipped (from bottle)

ተንደበደበ   tändäbäddäbä or ተንደ በደበ tändäbaddäbä v.i came up in a rash (e.g skin from insect bite)

አንደበደበ   andäbäddäbä v.i caused (skin) to come up in a rash

ተንደፈደፈ   tändäfaddäfä v.i had death throes (spasms)

አንደፈደፈ   andäfaddäfä v.t caused to writhe

ተንገበገበ   tängäbäggäbä v.i was very avaricious, miserly; felt unbearable pain

ገብጋባ   gäbgabba adj. avaricious, miserly

አንገበገበ   ungäbäggäbä v.t caused unbearable pain

ተንገፈጠጠ   tängäfäṭṭäṭä v.i was inflated, swollen up (e.g in pregnancy)

አንገፈጠጠ   angäfäṭṭäṭä v.t caused to be swollen up

ተንገፈገፈ   tängäfäggäfä v.i was fed up (with s/t), was completely tired of

አንገፈገፈ   angäfäggäfä v.t caused s/o to be fed up, tired of (s/t)

ተንጋለለ   tängallälä v.t laid oneself down (on the back)

አንጋለለ   angalläkä v.t made s/o lie down (on his back)

ተንጋጋ   tängagga v.t rushed, gathered (in a disorderly crowd)

ጋጋታ   gagata n. disorderly rushing; confused noise (of crowd)

አንጋጋ   angagga v.t drove a crowd (people, cattle)

ተንጉራደደ   tängʷäraddädä v.i went to and for; paced up and down

ጉርዳዳ   gʷärdadda adj. well-knit; attractive in shape (body)

ጉርዳድ አለ   gʷärdädd alä v.i walked up and down (a little)

በዱላ አንጉ ራደደ   bädulla angʷäraddädä v.t beat into a corner; beat (about the room etc.)

ተንጠራረ   tänṭärarra v.i had a stretch, stretched up (arms); reached up; aspired (desperately)

አንጠራረ   anṭärarra v.i stretched (arms)

ተንጠራወዘ   tänṭärawwäzä v.i was debilitated, weakened (by disease, etc.)

አንጠራወዘ   anṭaräwwäzä v.t weakened (s/o), enfeebled

ተንጠፈጠፈ   tänṭäfäṭṭäfä v.i dripped off (e.g water from wet clothes)

አንጠፈጠፈ   anṭäfäṭṭäfä v.t squeezed out, squeezed dry

ላቡን—   labun — v.t sweatend

ተንጣለለ   tänṭallälä v.i spread out, spread over (e.g flood water, grain etc.)

ተንጣጣ   tänṭaṭṭa v.i made a cracking sound; chattered excessively; farted continuously

	with red-hot needles *(traditional cure for headache etc.)*		miraculous
አንጣጣ	*anṭaṭṭa* v. caused a cracking sound	ተከለ	*täkkälä* v.t planted; forced into the ground *(spear etc.)*
ተንፈራገጠ	*tänfäraggäṭä* v.i had leg convulsions *(e.g death throes)*	ተካይ	*täkay* adj/n *(one)* who plants
አንፈራገጠ	*anfäraggäṭä* v.t caused leg convulsions	ትክለኛ	*təkläñña* n. settler
		ትክል	*təkl* adj. planted
ተንፈራፈረ	*tänfäraffärä* v.i had complete bodily con- vulsions	—አለ	— *alä* v.i. was forced into the ground *(spear etc.)*
አንፈራፈረ	*anfäraffärä* v.t caused bodily convulsions	ተከከለ	*täkkakkälä* v.i. plan- ted here and there; became equal to
ተንፈቀፈቀ	*tänfäqäffäqä* v.i bubbled up; snivelled *(childern)*	ተተከለ	*tätäkkälä* v.i. was planted; was forced in; was made to settle *(at a specific place)*
አንፈቀፈቀ	*anfäqäffäqä* v.t made *(s/t)* bubble up		
ተንፉፉ	*tänfʷaffʷa* v.i made a rushing noise *(e.g waterfall)*	ተተካይ	*tätäkkay* n. settler
		መተከያ	*mättäkäya* n. settling place
ፉፉቴ	*fʷafʷate* n. waterfall	አታከለ	*attakkälä* v.t. helped to plant
ተኛ	*täñña* v.i slept		
ተኛት	*täññat* had sex- ual intercource with her	አታከልት	*atakəlt* or አትክልት *atkəlt* n. vegetables
ሆስፒታል ተኛ	hospital *täñña* he was in the hospital	ያትክልት ቦታ	*yatkəlt bota* n. garden
ጎማህ ተኛትኳል	gommah *täññətuʷal* you have a flat tyre	አትክልተኛ	*atkəltäñña* n. gardener
ተኛቶ አረፈደ	*täññəto aräffädä* he overslept	ተከላከለ	*täkälakkälä* v.i. defended see also ከለከለ
መኛታ	*mäññəta* or መተኛ *mätäñña* n. sleeping *(place)*	ተከላካይ	*täkälakay* n. defender
		መከላከያ	*mäkkälakäya* n. means of defending
—ቤት	—*bet* n. bed-room	—ሚኒስቴር	—*minister* n. Ministry of Defense
አተኛኝ	*attäñañ* or አተኛኝት *attäñañät* n. sleeping posture	አከላከለ	*akkälakkälä* v.t. hindered; stood in the way
አስተኛ	*astäñña* v.t made *(s/t)* sleep, lie down	ተከማቸ	*täkämaččä* v.i was gathered, accumulated agglomerated
የሚያስተኛ መድኃኒት	*yämmiyastäñña mäd- hanit* anesthetic	ክሙች	*kəməčču* adj. gathered, accumu- lated, agglomerated
ተአምር	*tä'ammər* or ታምር *tammər* n. miracle, pl. ተአምራት ፣ ታምራት	ክምችት	*kəməččət* n. ac- cumulation, con- centration
ተአምረኛ	*tä'amməräñña* adj.	መከማቻ	*mäkkämača* n. place of ac- cummulation

128

አከጋቸ *akkāmaččā* v.t. gathered, accummulated, agglomerated

ተከሠተ *täkässätä* v.i. was manifested, became clear in the mind, (see also ከሠተ)

ተከራየ *täkärayyä* v. t. hired (a boat etc.) rented (a house), v.i. was rented, hired (a house a boat etc.)

ተከራይ *täkäray* n. tenant

አከራየ *akkärayyä* v.t. let, rent out

አከራይ *akkäray* n. one who rents out a house etc.

ተከተለ *täkättälä* v.t followed

ተከታይ *täkättay* n. follower; that which follows, continuation

ቅደም ተከተል *qädäm täkättäl* n. sequence

ተከታተለ *täkätattälä* v.t followed each other was ordered in a sequence watched closely

ተከታታይ *täkätatay* adj. sequential; graded (books etc.), following each other

አከታተለ *akkätattälä* v.t had (s/t) followed

አስከተለ *askättälä* v.t had (s/o, s/t) follow; brought as a result of

ተከተከ *täkättäkä* v.t pecked at

ተከነ *täkkänä* v.i got overcooked; became extremely angry

አተከነ *atäkkänä* v.t caused (s/t) to get over-cooked; caused (s/o) to get very angry

ተከናነበ *täkänannäbä* v.t covered one's head (with cloth, etc.)

ክንብንብ *kanabnab* n. head-covering

መከናነቢያ *mäkkänanäbiya* n. head-covering

አከናነበ *akkänannäbä* ·v.t had (s/o) cover

his head

ተከዘ *täkkäzä* v.i was lost in thought (sadness) was melancholic; was sad, was pensive

ተካዥ *täkkaž* adj/n. melancholic (person)

ትካዜ *takkaze* n. melancholy

ትካዝ አለ *takkazz alä* v.i was deeply melancholic

መተከዣ *mätäkkäza* n. cause of melancholy, snack, nibble (nuts etc.)

አስተከዘ *astäkkäzä* v.t caused (s/o) to be sad

ተከ *täkka* v.t substituted; re- imbursed

ምትክ *matäkk* n. substitute; reimbursement; deputy

ተተከ *tätäkka* v.i was substituted; was re-imbursed

ተተኪ *tätäki* n. substitute (person or thing)

ተከለለ *täkallälä* v.t demarcated borders (see also ከለለ)

ተከላይ *täkalay* n. member of a boundary commission

አከለለ *akkällälä* v.t supervised in border demarcation

አስከለለ *askällälä* v.t had border demarcated

ተከሰሰ *täkassäsä* v. v.i accused each other, litigate each other see also ከሰሰ

ተከሳሽ *täkassaš* n. defendant

አከሰሰ *akkassäsä* v.t caused (people) to litigate against each other

አስከሰሰ *askässäsä* v.t had (s/o) accused

ተከነ *täkänä* v.i. was ordained as a priest, deacon etc. see also ካነ

ክህነት *kahnät* n. priesthood

ቤተ ክህነት *betä kahnät* n. clergy, the Church

129

ተክህኖ	tākhəno n. priestliness
ልብስ—	ləbsā — n. vestment (ecclesiastical)
አስካነ	askanā v.t had (s/o) ordained
ተካፈለ	'äkaffälä v.t shared, participated, divided (s/t) between, among see also ካፈለ
ተካፋይ	tākafay n. participant, one who shares
ተከፋፈለ	tākäfaffälä v.i divided (s/t) between, among each other; divided in opinion
አካፈለ	akkaffälä v.t shared with another, divided
አካፋይ	akkafay adj/n. (one) who divides (s/t) equally between, among people etc.
የጋራ—	yāgara— n. common denominator
አከፋፈለ	akkäfaffälä v.t distributed equal shares
አከፋፋይ	akkäfafay n. disiributor (equally)
ተከለፈለፈ	tākläfälläfä v.i meddled, interfered, was busy-body
ተከለፍላፊ	tākläflafi adj/n meddler, busy-body
ከልፍልፍ	kələfləf adj / n. meddler, busy-body
አከለፋለፈ	äkläfälläfä v. t. hustled, harried
ተከሊል	tāklil n. church marriage
ሥርዓት—	sər'atä—n. nuptial ceremony (church)
ተከበሰበሰ	tākbäsäbbäsä v.i put on airs, was pretentious
ተከበሰባሽ	tākbäsbaš adj / n pretentious (person)
ከብስብስ	kəbəsbəs adj. pretentious
ተኮማተረ	tākomattärä v.i contracted, wrinkled
ኩምትርትር አለ	kumtərtərr alä v.i. was contracted, wrinkled up
አኮማተረ	akkomattärä v.t. contracted, wrinkled
ተኮረ	see አተኮረ

ተኮረታተመ	tākorättāmā v.i. sat hunched up (e.g with sadness)
ኩርትም አለ	kurtəmm alä v.i. hunched up, curled up
ኩርትምትም አለ	kurtəmtəmm alā v.i hunched up
ተኮራመተ	tākorammātä v.t. curled up one'slimbs (thruogh illness)
ኮርማታ	kormatta adj. curled up, contorted
ኩርምት አለ	kurmətt alä v.i. was extremely contorted
ኩርምትምት አለ	kurmətmətt alä v.i was extremely contorted
አኮራመተ	akkorammātä v. t. made (s/o) curl up
ተኮሳተረ	tākosatärrä v.i frowned; looked serious see also ኮሰተረ
ኮስታራ	kostarra adj/n serious looking (person)
ተኮናተረ	tākonat'ä⁻ä v.t. made a contract with
ተኮናታሪ	tākonatari n. contractor, also ሥራ ተቋራጭ
ኮንትራት	kontrat n. contract
ተኮፈሰ	tākoffäsä v.i. dressed elegantly, impressively
ተኮፋሽ	täkoffaš adj/n (one) who is dressed impressively
ተኩስ	täkkʷäsä v.t. fired (gun); became hot; had a fever, branded (animal)
ልብስ—	ləbs— v. t. ironed (clothes)
ተኳሽ	täkkʷaš adj./n (one) who fires (a shot); who brands (animal)
ጥሩ—	ṭru—n. marksman
ተኩስ	täkkʷs n. firing
ተኳሽነት	täkuʷašǝnnät n. marksmanship
ትኩስ	tǝkkʷǝs adj. fresh (vegetables), warm (food)
ትኩሳት	täkkusat n. fever
አተኩሰ	atäkkʷäsä v.t. had fever
ተኳኩሰ	täkʷakkʷäsä v.t fired here and there

130

ተተኩስ *(gun);* ironed slightly tätäkk^wäsä v.i was fired *(gun),* was ironed; was branded *(animal)*

ተታኩስ tätäkk^wäsä v.i fired at each other *(gun),* fought each other with firearms

ተታኳሽ *tatak^waš* adj. fighting *(with arms)*

አስተኩስ astäkk^wäsä v t had *(s/o) fire (gun);* had *(animal branded);* had clothes etc. ironed

ተኩላ täk^wəla n. wolf

ተኩረፈረፈ täk^wəräfärräfä v.i purred *(cats);* shrank *(washed cloth)*

ተኩነሰነሰ täk^wənäsännäsä v.t dressed ostentatiously

ተኩነስናሽ täk^wənäsnaš adj/n. *(one)* who is ostentatiously dressed

ተወ täwä v.t left; dropped *(a case);* stopped *(doing s/t,)* gave up, left off

ተው እባክህ täw əbakkəh be quiet; is it really so; come now!

ተተወ tätäwä v.i was left; was dropped *(a case);* was stopped

አስተወ astäwä v.t had *(s/o)* leave *(s/t),* drop *(a case);* had *(s/o)* stop

ተወላመመ täwälammämä v.i bent out of shape

አወላመመ awwälammämä v.t caused to bend out of shape

ወልማማ wälmamma adj. bent out of shape

ወለምታ wäləmta n. dislocation *(limbs)*

ወለም ዘለም አለ wälänım zälämm alä v.i was unreliable; thilly-shallied; was changeable in mind

ተወላከፈ täwälakkäfä v.i stumbled; was hindered stammered, stuttered, was lost for words

ወልካፋ wälkaffa adj. twisted; dishonest in *(character)*

አወላከፈ awwälakkäfä v.t hindered, tripped *(s/o),* got in *(s/o's)* way

አወላከፊ awwäläkafi n. *(s/t)* which trips one up

ተወላገደ täwälaggädä v.i twisted, bent out of shape

ወልጋዳ wälgadda adj. twisted, bent out of shape; twisted in *(character)*

ውልግድግድ wälgädgäd adj. extremely twisted, contorted; messed up

አወላገደ awwälaggädä v.t caused s/t to be twisted, bent, messed up

ተወሐደ täwähadä or ተዋሐደ täwahadä v.i was unified

ተዋሕዶ täwahədo n. Monophysitism

አዋሐደ awwahadä v.t unified

ተወራረደ täwärarrädä v.i bet, made a wager *see also* ወረደ

ተወራራጅ täwäraraǧ n. one who bets

ውርርድ wərərrad n. bet

አወራረደ awärarrädä v.t. made *(s/o)* bet; cut meat in lumps

ተወራጨ täwäraččä v.i. tossed and turned *(in bed)*

አወራጨ awwäraččä v.t. made *(s/o)* toss and turn

ተወሰወሰ täwäsäwwäsä v.i. was sewn *(with tacking stitches);* pedalled *(sewing machine) see also* ወሰወሰ

ተወናፈለ täwänaffälä v.i. participated in communal labour *(agriculture)*

አወናፈለ awwänaffälä v.t. gave one's oxen to a communal labour

ተወዳጀ täwädaǧǧä v.t. was befriended, *see also* ወዳጀ

ተወዳደረ täwädaddärä v.t. con

ተወዳዳሪ peted
tăwădadari n. competitor

—የሌለው —yălellăw adj. matchless, incomparable, unequalled

ውድድር wədəddər n. competition

አወዳደረ awwădaddärä v.t. made to compete with each other; made comparison

ተወገደ see ወገደ
ተወጠረ tăwäṭṭärä v.i. was stretched tight (e.g. canvas); was disdainful, over-proud, see also ወጠረ

ተወጣጠረ tăwăṭaṭṭärä v.i. was disdainful, overproud; was stretched too tightly

ተወጫመደ tăwăč̣ammädä v.i. was rumpled up, wrinkled up

ወጭማዳ wăč̣madda adj. scrawny, scraggy, skinny-legged

ውጭምድምድ wəč̣mədməd adj. skinny, scrawny

ተዋሰ tăwasä v.t. borrowed (an object); was a bondage, was a guarantor

ተዋሽ tăwaš n. borrower
ውስት wəsät n. borrowing
አዋሰ awasä v.t. lent
ተዋዋሰ tăwawasä v.i. borrowed from each other
ዋስ was n. guarantor
ዋስትና wastənna n. guarantee
ተዋባ tăwabä v.i. was beautiful, v.t. beautified oneself

ተዋጋ tăwagga v.t. fought (war); engaged in combat, see also ወጋ
ተዋጊ tăwagi n. fighter (war); combatant
—ማኮንን —mäkonnən officer in charge of operations
አዋጋ awwagga v.t. made (s/o) fight, combat
ተዋጣ tăwaṭṭa v.i. was

contributed (money); succeeded (scheme), see ወጣ

መዋጮ mäwwaço n. contribution

አዋጣ awwaṭṭa v.t. contributed (money)

ተውለበለበ tăwläbälläbä v.i. waved (flag up on flag pole)

አውለበለበ awläbälläbä v.t. waved (flag or one's hand)

ተውላጠ ስም tăwlaṭä səm n. pronoun
ተውረገረገ tăwrägärrägä v.i. walked with a swaying gait (usually for tall person)

ተውረገራጊ tăwrägragi n. one who walks with a swaying gait

ተውሳክ tăwsak n. filth; parasite
ተውሳከም tăwsakam adj. filthy
ተውሳክ ግሥ tăwsakä gəss n. adverb
ተውዘገዘገ tăwzägäzägä v.i. zoomed (air craft)

ተውዘግዘጊ tăwzägzägi adj. zooming (air craft)
ተውተበተበ tăwtäbättäbä v.i was entangled (knot)
ውትብትብ wətəbtəb adj. entangled (knot)
ተዘረከተ tăzäräkkätä v.t. was cut open, laid open (e.g. entrails) see also ዘረ ከተ

ተዘረካከተ tăzäräkakkätä v.i. was cut open in many places

ተዘረፈጠ tăzäräffäṭä v.i. slumped down; plumped down, lounged about idly

ዘርፈጣ zärfaṭṭa adj. (one) who sprawls about, lounges idly

ተዘባንነ tăzăbannänä vi. was over proud see ዘበን
ተዘነጠለ tăzänäṭṭälä v.t. was wrenched off, torn off, see ዘነጠለ
ተዘንጣይ tăzänṭay adj. likely to become detached
ተዘናከተ tăzänakkätä v.i. lived comfortably, lavishly;

አዘናከተ	took ones' ease *azzänakkätä* v. t. kept *(s/o)* in great style, state
ተዘከረ	*täzäkkärä* v.t. helped *(s/o with food or money)*
ተዘካሪ	*täzäkkari* n. benefactor, alms-giver
ተዝካር	*täzkar* n. memorial feast for the dead
መዘከር	*mäzäkkər* n. museum also ቤተ መዘከር
አዘከረ	*azäkkärä* v.t. commemorated *(with feast for dead relative)*
ተዘዋወረ	*täzäwawwärä* v.i. went around from place to place *see* ዞረ
ተዘገረረ	*täzägärrärä* v.i. fell flat, *see* ዝረረ
ተዘመተ	*täzammätä*, v.i. spread gossip *see also* ዘመተ
ተዘማች	*täzamač* adj. infectious, contagious
አዘመተ	*azzammätä* v.t. caused, was the instrument of spreading *(s/t)*
አዘማች	*azzamač* adj. carrying, spreading
ተዘመደ	*täzammädä* v.i. was related to *(s/o)*, became very close to, friendly with *(s/o) see also* ዘመድ
አዘመደ	*azzammädä* v.t. brought *(people)* together, unified
አዛማጅ	*azzamaǧ* adj/n *(one)* who unifies, brings together
ተዛባ	*täzabba* v.t. went out of balance, became detached
የተዛባ ዐረፍተ ነገር	*yätäzabba aräftä nägär* ungrammatical sentences
አዛባ	*azzaba* v.t. caused *(s/t)* to get out of balance
ተዘነቀ	*täzannäqä* v.i was pressed together, was squeezed in tightly *(e.g. bus passengers)*

ተዛነፈ	*täzannäfä* v.i. was uneven, not properly placed
አዛነፈ	*azzannäfä* v.t. made *(s/t)* uneven, badly positioned
ተዛና	*täzanna* or ተዘናና *täznanna* v.i. was relaxed
ተዛወረ	*täzawwärä* v.t. changed one's job; was transferred; was moved else where, *see* ዘወረ
ተዛዋሪ	*täzawari (one)* who is due for transfer
አዛወረ	*azzawwärä* v.t. transferred *(s/o)* to another job; moved *(s/t)* elsewhere
ተዝለገለገ	*täzlägällägä* v.i. was jellified, drawn out *(e.g spittle)*
ዝልግልግ	*zəlaglag* adj. jellied, drawn out, semi-liquid
አዝለገለገ	*azlägällägä* v.t. caused to become jellified, drawn out
ተዝለፈለፈ	*täzläfälläfä* v.i. fainted, swooned, fell unconscious; was exhausted, tired out
ተዝለፍለፈ	*täzläflafi* adj./n swooning, fainting
ዝልፍልፍ	*zələflaf* adj. fainting; exhausted, tired out
ተዝረበረበ	*täzräbärräbä* v.i. dribbled *(saliva)*
አዝረበረበ	*azräbärräbä* v.t. dribbled
ተዝረከረከ	*täzräkärräkä* v.i. was messy, untidy *(esp. in work or the home)*; was unthrifty
አዝረከረከ	*azräkärräkä* v.t. cause *(s/t)* to be messy, untidy
ተዝረጠረጠ	*täzräṭärräṭä* v.i. lagged behind *(through fatigue)*; farted continuously
አዝረጠረጠ	*azräṭärräṭä* v.t. terrified *(s/o)*
ተዝረፈረፈ	*täzräfärräfä* v.t. dropped off *(e.g. pieces of s/t carried)*; dropped

	and flapped about (clothing)
ተኸገረገረ	tä̀zgoräggorä or ተዝጉ-ረ ጉ-ረ täzgu^wäräggu^wärä v.i. was patterned in black or dark brown and white (e.g. zebra, leopard)
ኸጉርጉርc	ž^əgurgur adj. patterned in black or dark brown and white
አኸጉ-ረጉ-ረ	• až̀gu^wäräggu^wärä v.ṭ. patterned (s/t) in black or dark brown and white
ተደለደለ	tädäläddälä v.i.was made level (ground); was allocated to specific job, see also ደለደለ
ተደላደለ	tädäladdälä v.i. was established firmly(e.g. job); sat comfortably; got an equal share; was in order; was pacified
አደላዳይ	addäladay n. one who allocates, distributes
ተደራጊ	tädärragi adj./n. passive (gram.) see *ደረገ
ተደረረገ	tädärarrägä v.t. had sexual intercourse (polite)
አደራረግ	addäraräg n. method, way of doing (s/t)
ተደናቀፈ	see ደነቀፈ
ተደናበረ	tädänabbärä felt one's way, felt about (through shortsightedness, bad light etc.) see ደነበረ
አደናበረ	addänabbärä v.t. caused (s/o) to feel about, feel his way
ተደናገረ	tädänaggärä v.i. was perplexed; lost the thread (of one's discourse)
ተደናገጠ	tädänaggäṭä v. . was surprised, taken aback see ደነገጠ
ተደናጋጭ	tädänagač adj. surprised, taken aback

አደናገጠ	addänaggäṭä v.t. caused (s/o) to be surprised, taken aback
ተዳረቀ	tädarräqä v.i. wasted effort, time (in teaching or debate)
ተዳረ	tädarra v.t. flirted
ተዳቀቀ	tädaqqäqä v.i. was bowed, crushed by sickness, see also ደቀቀ
አዳቀቀ	addaqqäqä v. . caused s/o to be bowed, crushed by sickness
ተዳበለ	tädabbälä v.t. shared flat, house etc.) see also ደበለ
ተዳበይ	tädabay n. flat-sharer and co-tenant
አዳበለ	addabbälä v.t. had s/o share (flat or house)
አዳበይ	addabay n. one who lets (s/o) share(house, flat)
ተገን	tägän n. shelter, protection, cover (protection)
ተዳፋ	tädaffa v.i. went down hill, see also ደፋ
ተጋ	tägga v.i. was diligent, persevered
ትጉ	t^əgu adj. diligent, vigilant, assiduous
ትጋት	t^əgat n. diligence, perseverance
ተጋለጠ	tägalläṭä v.i. was exposed (crime, wrongdoing), see also ገለጠ
አጋለጠ	aggälläṭä v.t. exposed (s/o's crime etc.)
ተጋባ	tägabba v.i. got married; was passed from one container to another, see also ገባ
ተጋፈጠ	tägaffäṭä v.t. faced danger bravely
አጋፈጠ	aggaffäṭä v.t. put (s/o) in danger, jeopardy
ተግባc	tägbar n. duty, action,

	task, occupation, function
ተገባራዊ	tägbarawi adj. functional
በተገባር	bätägbar adv. practically
ተገ እደረገ	tägg därrägä v.t. flashed (e.g. torch etc.) for a moment
ተገተረተረ	tägtärättära v.i. staggered, tried one's best
ተገተርታሪ	tägtärtari adj. staggering n. one who tries one's best
ግትርትር	gətərtər adj. staggering
ግትርትር አለ	gətərtərr alä v.i. staggered heavily
ተገፈለፈለ	tägfäläffälä v.i. bubbled up (e.g. boiling əngära and wäṭ)
ገፍልፍል	gəfəlfəl n. wäṭ with small pieces of əngära added (common for breakfast)
አገፈለፈለ	agfäläffälä v.t. boiled up (wäṭ and əngära)
ተጎናጠፈ	tägonaṭṭäfä or ተጎናፀፈ tägonaṣṣäfä v.i. wrapped šämma around (o/s shoulders)
መጎናጠፊያ	mäggonaṭäfiya n. large kind of šamma
አጎናጠፈ	aggonaṭṭäfä v.i. wrapped (s/o) in a šämma
ተጎራበተ	see ጎረበተ
ተጉለተ	tägʷällätä v.i. sat idly, see ጉለተ
ተጉመጠመጠ	tägʷmäṭämmäṭä v.t. rinsed out (o/s mouth)
መጉመጥመጫ	mägʷmäṭmäča n. rinsing water for the mouth
ተጉረበረበ	tägʷräbärräbä v.i. became uneven, bumpy came up in lumps (skin)
ጉርብርብ	gʷərəbrəb adj. uneven; bumpy: covered in bumps (skin)

ጉርብርብ አለ	gʷurəbrəbb alä v.i. became extremely uneven, bumpy; came up in many lumps (skin)
ተጓዘ	tägʷazä v.i. travelled, made a journey, see also *ጓዘ
ተጠለለ	see ጠለለ
ተጠለፈ	see ጠለፈ
ተጠበበ	täṭäbbäbä see also ጠበበ v.i became over-preoccupied
መጫነቅ መጠበብ	mäč̣č̣anäq mäṭṭäbäb extreme worry and preoccupation
ተጠናወተ	täṭänawwätä or ተጸናወተ täṣänawwätä v.i was antagonistic towards (s/o)
ተጠጋ	täṭägga v.i came near was under (s/o's) patronage, see *ጠጋ
መጠጊያ	mäṭṭägiya n. shelter, refuge
ተጠጋጋ	täṭägagga v.i came close to each other; were put close together
አጠጋጋ	aṭṭägagga v.i caused to come close to each other; put close together
አስጠጋ	asṭägga v.t sheltered (protected), harboured; brought close
ተጣረረ	täṭarrärä also ተጻረረ täṣarrärä v.i was antagonistic, see ጠC and ጸC
ተጣራሪ	täṭarari adj. antagonistic
ተጣራ	täṭarra see also ጠራ ṭarra v.t called out to (s/o); v.i. was purified, distilled
ተጣበቀ	ltäṭabbäqä v.t see also ጠበቀ ṭabbäqä stuck to
ተጣደፈ	täṭaddäfä v.i hurried see *ጠደፈ
ተጣመመ	täṭammämä v.i was crooked, twisted, see

135

ተጣፉ	ጠመመ *tāṭaffa* v.t destroyed each other, *see* ጠፋ
ተጥመለመለ	*tāṭmälämmälä* v.t writhed, shrivelled (e.g dying snake)
ጥምልምል	*ṭəməlməl* adj. writhed, shrivelled, feeble, weakling
ጥምልምል አለ	*ṭəməlməll alā* v.i withered, shrivelled (to an extreme degree)
አጥመለመለ	*aṭmälämmälä* v.t made (s/o, s/t) writh, shrivel up
ተጥመሰመሰ	*tāṭmäsämmäsä* v.t made a rustling noise
ተጨለጠ	*tāčällāṭā* v.t was drunk to the last drop *see* ጨለጠ
ተጫማ	*tāčamma* v.t put shoes on *see* ጫማ
ተፈተለከ	*tāfätälläkä* v.i dashed off, *see* *ፈተለከ
ተፉ	*tāffa* v.t spat; vomited
ትፉት	*təfat* n. vomit
ትፉታም	*təfatam* adj. prone to vomit (e.g habitual drunker)
እትፍ አለ	*əttəff alā* v.t spat
መትፊያ	*mätfiya* n. spittoon
ተታፉ	*tātaffa* v.t spat play-fully (of children)
አስተፉ	*astāffa* v.t retrieved one's possessions by force
ተፉለመ	*see* ፉለመ
ተፉለሰ	*see* ፉለሰ
ተፉቀደ	*see* ፉቀደ
ተፉተገ	*see* ፉተገ
ተፉዘዘ	*see* ፉዘዘ
ተፉጠጠ	*see* ፉጠጠ
ተፉፉመ	*see* ፉመ
ተፍ ተፍ አለ	*tāff tāff alā* v.i was busy in several places at once, was busy here and there
ተፌ	*tāffe* n. conscientious, keenworker
ተፍለቀለቀ	*tāflāqällāqā* v.i bubbled (boiling liquids) *see* ፈለቀለቀ
ተፍለከለከ	*see* *ፈለከለከ
ተፍረተረተ	*see* *ፈረተረተ

ተፍረጠረጠ	*see* *ፈረጠረጠ
ተፍገመገመ	*see* ፈገመ
ተፍካከረ	*see* ፈካከ
ቱምቢ	*tumbi* n. plumb line
ቱሪስት	*turist* n. tourist
ቱር አለ	*turr alā* v.i was chic, smartly dressed; flew off (bird)
ቱርክ	*turk* adj / n. Turkey; Turkish
ቱስ ቱስ አለ	*tuss tuss alā* v.i scut-tled along (scurried)
ቱስ አለ	*tuss alä* v.i hissed (of air in a leak)
ቱሽ አለ	*tušš alä* v.t made a farting sound; whis-pered, gossiped to (s/o)
ቱባ	*tubba* n. coil of yarn, hank
ቱቦ	*tubbo* n. pipe, tube
ቱታ	*tutta* n. overall
ቱግ አለ	*tugg alä* v.i flared up exploded with rage
ቱግ ባይ	*tugg bay* adj. easily made angry
ቱፋሕ	*tuffah* n. apple
ቲማቲም	*timatim* n. tomato
የቲማቲም ድልህ	*yätimatim dälləh* n. tomato paste
ቲአትር	*tiy'atər* or ቴአትር *te'atər* or ቲያትር *tiyatər* n theatre
ቲኬት	*tiket* n. ticket
—ቆራጭ	—*qoraç* n. ticket seller
ደርሶመልስ—	*dərso mäls*—n. roundtrip-ticket
ቲዮሪ	*tiyori* n. theory
ታላቅ	*tallaq* or ትልቅ *tälləq* adj large, big, grand *see* ተለቀ
*ታለለ	*tallälä*
ተላላ	*tälala* adj. thought-less, forgetful
ተታለለ	*tātallälä* v.i. was de-ceived, cheated
ታመመ	*tammämä* v.i. was sick, was unwell *see* ሕመም or አመመ
ታመነ	*tammänä* v.i. was be-lieved, was reliable *see* አመነ
ታምር	*tammər* or ተአምር *tä'ammər* n. miracle

ታምረኛ	tammərähña or
	ተአምረኛ tä'ammə-
	ränña adj. miraculous
ታምራታዊ	tammərutawi or ተአም
	ራታዊ tä'əmmərawi
	adj. miraculous
ታምቡር	tambur n. drum (It.)
ታረቀ	tarräqä v.i. was re-
	conciled; was corrected
	(behaviour)
ታራቂ	taraqi n. one who is
	reconciled (to s/o)
መታረቂያ	mättaräqiya n. pledge
	of re-conciliation
	(damages etc.)
እርቅ	ərq n. reconciliation
አስታረቀ	astarräqä v.t reconciled
አስታራቂ	astaraqi n. peacemaker
ታረዘ	tarräzä v.i was raggedly
	dressed
ታሪከ	see ተረከ
ታሪፍ	tarif n. tariff
ታርጋ	targa n. license plate
ታበየ	tabbäyä v.i was over-
	bearing, conceited
ትቢት	təbit or ትእቢት tə'ə-
	bit n. inordinate pride
ትቢተኛ	təbitäñña or ትእቢ.
	ተኛ tə'bitäñña adj.
	inordinately proud
ታቦት	tabot n. Ark of the
	Tabernacle
ታቦተ ጽዮን	tabotä ṣəyon n. Ark
	of Covenant
ታተረ	tattärä v.t did one's best,
	tried one's hardest
ታታሪ	tatari adj/n (one)
	who tries his best;
	energetic, ambitious
ታታ	tatta v.t intertwined,
	interlaced
ታኅሣሥ	tahəsas or ትኅሣሥ təsas n.
	December
ታኒካ	tanika n. can (for oil,
	paraffin etc.)
ታናሽ	tannaš n.young
	(brother, sister); rump
	(animals buttocks)
ታንክ	tank n. tank (military)
ታንከኛ	tankäñña n. mem-
	ber of tank corps
ታንኳ	tankʷa n. canoe (esp.
	reed pith boat of lake
	Tana)

ታከተ	takkätä v.i was over-
	worked, became
	exhausted
ትክት አለ	təkkətt alä v.ı was
	extremely exhausted
ታካች	takač n/ adj. sloth-
	ful, lazy (person)
አታከተ	atäkkätä v.t bored
	(s/o)
አታካች	atakač adj/n. bore,
	boring (person)
ታከከ	takkäkä pushed against
	see also አከከ
ታወረ	tawwärä v.i went blind
	see also ዐወር əwwər
ታክሲ	taksi n. taxi
ታዘበ	tazzäbä v.t was disap-
	pointed in (s/o),
	changed one's view of
	(s/o) for the worst;
	took critical note of
	(s/o's) work, habits,
	etc.
ታዛቢ	tazzabi n.one who is
	disappointed in (s/o's)
	work, one who takes
	critical note of (s/o's)
	work, habits etc.;
	political commen-
	tator.
ትዝብት	təzzəbt v. unfavourable
	opinion, comment,
	view (of behaviour,
	work etc.)
ተዛዘበ	täzazzäbä v.t was
	disappointed, have
	critical view of one
	another
አስተዛዘበ	astäzazzäbä v.t
	created a mutually
	unfavourable opinion
ታዘዘ	tazzäzä v.i obeyed. re-
	ceived orders, was
	ordered, see also አዘዘ
ታዛ	taza n. shelter (under
	the eaves of house),
	porch
ታደለ	taddälä v.i was well
	favoured by for-
	tune; was well en-
	dowed by birth, see
	also አደለ
ታደገ	taddägä v.i had

ታዳጊ mercy on *(s/o)*
taddagi adj./n mer-
ciful *(person);*
developing *(country)*

—አገር --*agär* n. develop-
ing country

ታዲያ *tadiya* interj. well then!

ታዲያስ *tadiyassa or* ታዲያስ

tadiyass interj. so
what next!

ታገለ *taggälä* v.i wrestled
with; struggled

ትግል *tagal* n. struggle;
wrestling

ትግያ *tagayya* n. wrestling

ታጋይ *tagay* n. wrestler;
one who takes
part in a struggle
(e.g political)

አታገለ *attaggälä* v.t had
*(people wrestle,
struggle)*

አታጋይ *attagay* n. referee
(wrestling)

ታገሠ *taggäsä* v.i was patient

ታጋሽ *taggaš* adj/n. patient
(person)

ትግሥት *tagast or* ትዕግሥት
ta'agast n. patience

ትግሥተኛ *tagastäñña or* ትዕግሥ
ተኛ *ta'agastäñña* adj/n
patient *(person)*

አስታገሠ *astaggäsä* v.i calmed
(s/o) down

አስታጋሽ *astagaš* n/adj. *(s/o,s/t)*
that calms *(s/o)* down

ግስታጋሻ *mastagäša* n . means
of calming down
(sedative), tranquilizer

ታጠቀ *taṭṭäqä* v.i belted, girded
(o's) up; was
armed

ትጥቅ *taṭq* n. equipment
(military)

ትጥቅና ስንቅ *taṭqanna sanq* n.
provisions and
supplies *(mil.)*

መታጠቂያ *mättaṭäqiya* n. girdle,
belt

አስታጠቀ *astaṭṭäqä* v.t supplied with arms
(mil.) ; helped in
fastening belt, girdle

ታጠበ *see* አጠበ

ታፈነ
ታፈገ *taffägä* v.i was crammed in *(people)*,
see also አፈገ

ታፋ *tafa* n. hip *(body)*

ቴሌስኮፕ *teleskopp* n. telescope

ቴሌግራም *telegram* n. telegram

ቴሌግራፍ *telegraf* n. telegraph

ቴምብር *tembar* n. stamp
(postage)

የቀረጥ— *yäqäräṭ*— n. rev-
enue stamp

ቴኒስ *tenis* n. tennis

ቴፕ *tepp* n. tape

ትሉግሉግ አለ *taluglugg alä* v.i bil-
lowed *(smoke)*

ትላንት *talant or* ትናንት *tan-
ant* n. yesterday

ትላንትና *talantanna or* ትናን
ትና *tanantnna* n.
yesterday

ትል *tal* n. worm, insect

የሐር— *yäharr*— n. silk-
worm

የኮሶ— *yäkoso*—n. tape-
worm

የሥጋ— *yäsaga*—n. maggot

ትልቅ *talləq* adj. big, large,
see also ተለቀ

ትልቅነት *talləqannät* n. size;
bigness; respect-
ability

ትሑት *tahut* adj. meek,
humble, modest

ትሕትና *tahatanna* n. mod-
esty, humility

ትምህርት *see* ተማሪ

ትምቡሽ አለ *tambušš alä* v.i gave,
sank in *(to the touch)*

ትምክህት *see* ተመከ

ትምባሆ *tambaho* n. tobacco

ትሩፋት *tarufat* n, charity, good
deeds *see also* ተረፈ

ትራም *taram* n. tram - car,
streetcar

ትራስ *taras* n. pillow

ትራፊክ *tarafik* n. traffic
police, traffic

ትርምስ *tarammas* n. confusion,
disarray

ትር ትር አለ *tarr tarr alä* v.i. pulsed,
beat *(heart)*

ትርታ *tarrata* n. pulse,
beat *(heart beat)*

138

ትርንጐ	tərəngo n. citron	ትዕይንት	te'əyyənt n. scene, scenery
ትርኢት	tər'it n. scene, show (e.g on television)	ትዕይንተ ሕዝብ	tə'əyəntä həzb n. demonsration (political)
ትርኪ, ምርኪ	tərki mərki n. hodge-podge, junk, nonsense, rubbish	ትዕግሥት	see ታገሠ
ትርጁማን	tərǧuman n. interpreter	ትዝ አለ	təzz alä v.i came to mind
ትሰብእት	təsbə'ət n. incarnation	ትዝታ	təzzəta n. nostalgia; memory, remembrance; recollection; memories
ትናጋ	tənnaga n. palate		
ትቢያ	təbbiya n. dust.		
ከትቢያ መነሣት	kätəbbiya männäsat to rise from obscurity	ትዮዩ	təyəyyu adj. apposite to, vis a-vis see አየ
ትንሽ	tənnəš adj. small, little, a bit, some of, a few	ትዳር	tədar n. married life, see አደረ
—ትንሽ	— tənnəš adv. just a little	ባለትዳር	balä tədar adj./n married (person)
—በትንሽ	— bätənnəš adv. gradually, bit by bit	ትጉህ	see ተጋ
ትንቢት	tənbit n. prophecy	ትግሬ	təgre adj. Tigrean
ትንታግ	təntag n. spark, shoot of flame, flash	ትግራይ	təgray n. Tigray, Administrative Region, north eastern Ethiopia
ትንኝ	tənəññ n. gnat		
የወባ—	yäwäba—n. mosquito	ትግርኛ	təgrəñña n. Tigray language
ትንኩሽት	tənkušt adj/n. aggressive (child)	ቶሎ	tolo adv. qiuckly, soon at once
ትንግርት	təngərət n. s/t strange, unusual	—ቶሎ	—tolo adv. rapidly
ትከሻ	təkäšša n. shoulder	—ባል	—bāl imp. hurry! come on!
ትከሻግ	təkäššamma adj. big-shouldered, broad-shouldered	ቶስቲሳ	tostʷassa adj/n busy-body
		አቶሰቶሰ	atosättosä v.i was a busy - body
ትከሻም	təkäššam adj/n broad-shouldered (person)	አቶስቷሽ	atostʷaš adj/n busy-body
ትኋን	təhuʷan n. bug	*ቶፈቶፈ	*tofäṭtofä
ትክትክ አለ	təkk təkk alä v.i had a dry cough	አቶፈቶፈ	atofättofä v.i curried favour (with superior by gossipping about colleagues)
ትዕቢት	tə'əbit n. conceit see ታበየ	አቶፍቷፈ	atofiʷafi adj/n (one) who curries favour through tale-bearing
		ቶፋ	tofa n. clay cooking pot

—ቸ—

ቸል አለ čäll alä v.t ignored, paid no attention to, neglected

ቸልታ čälləta n. negligence

ቸልተኛ čällätäñña adj./n negligent (person)

ቸለል አለ čäläll alä v.i was neglectful

ቸለሰ čälläsä v.t emptied over (s/o); emptied out (e.g bucket of water)

ተቸለሰ täčälläsä v.i was thrown out over s/o (e.g bucket of water)

ቸረ čärä v.i was! open-handed, generous

ቸር čär ədj. open-handed, generous

ቸርታ čərota n. gener-osity,open- hand-edness; financial assistance

ቸርነት čärənnät n. gener-osity

ቸረቸመ čäräččämä v.t chipped (esp. blade, axe etc.), dented

ቸርቻማ čärčamma adj. chip-ped, dented

ቸርችም čərčəm adj. chipped, dented

ቸረቸረ čäräččärä v.t retailed

ቸርቻሪ čärčari n. retailer

ቸርቻሮ čərčaro n. retailing

አስቸረቸረ asčäräččärä v.t had (s/t) retailed

ቸርኪዮ čärkiyo n. rim (of tyre)

ቸሰሰ čässäsä v.t sizzled

ቸስ አለ čəss alä v. sizzled

ቸበቸበ čäbäččäbä v.i sold in quantity; sold like hot cakes

ተቸበቸበ täčäbäččäbä v.i sold at a great rate

ቸብቸቦ čabčäbbo n. bob (hair style)

ቸነከረ čänäkkärä v.t nailed

ቸንካር čənkar n. cleat, large nail

ተቸነከረ täčänäkkärä v.i was nailed

አስቸነከረ asčänäkkärä v.t had (s/t) nailed

ቸነፈር čänäfär n. epidemic, plague

ቸከ čäkä v.i became boring

ቸኮ čəkko adj/n. boring (person)

ቸክ አለ čəkk alä v.i was boring

መንቻክ mänčakka adj./n. boring (person); persistent (of stains in cloth)

አቸከ ačäkä v.t rinsed perfunctorily (did not wash s/t thoroughly)

ቸከለ čäkkälä v. drove in a peg, stake

ቸካል čəkal n. stake, peg

ቸካል አለ čəkkəll alä v.i was driven n. (stake)

ተቸከለ täčäkkälä v.i was driven in (stake, peg)

አስቸከለ asčäkkälä v.t had (s/o) drive in (stake, peg)

ቸኮለ čäkkʷälä c.i hastened, was in a hurry

ቸካይ cäkkʷay adj./n.(one) who is in a hurry

ቸኩላ čəkkʷäla haste, hurry

ቸኩል čəkkul adj./n hasty

ተቻኮለ täčakkʷälä v.i was in a hurry

አቻካይ aččakʷay n. one who hurries (s/o); adj. urgent

አስቸኮለ asčäkkʷälä v.t had (s/o) hurry, hasten

አስቻካይ asčäkkʷay adj. urgent

140

ჭ7ረ   *čäggärä* v.t lacked *(s/t)* had difficulty with *(s/t)* (usually with pron. suff.) e.g ჭ7ረኝ *čagäränn* I am in difficulty, I am in need of

ჭ7ር   *čǝggǝr* n. difficulty lack, handicap: problem

ያለ-   *yalä-* adv. easily
ჭ7ረኝ   *čǝggǝränña* adj. n. needy *(person)*

ተჭ7ረ   *täčäggärä* v.i. was in need, trouble; had a problem; was needy

ነሰჭ7ረ   *asčäggärä* v.i. was nuisance, was importunate

ነチ7ር ላይ ጣለ ወደቀ   *ǝčǝggǝr lay ṭalä* got one in trouble —*wäddäqä* he is in trouble

ነሰჭ.ጋረ   *asčäggari* adj. difficult; importunate ; causing problems

ჭፈჭፈ   *čäfäččäfä* v.t cut into small pieces, chopped up

ჭፍჭፈ   *čǝfǝččafi* n. offcut, wood cuttings

መჭፍჭፈያ   *mäčäfčäfiya* n. hatchet, hand-axe

ተჭፈჭፈ   *täčäfäččäfä* v.i was chopped up; was cut into small pieces

ჭፈገ   *čäffägä* or ჭፍግ ኣለ *čǝffǝgg alä* v.i. grew thick, bushy *(forest, thicket etc.)*

ჭፍግ   *čǝffǝg* adj. bushy, thickly grown

ተჭፈገ   *täčäffägä* v.i was bushy, thickly grown

ቻለ   *čalä* v.i was able, capable
ቻይ   *čay* adj. tough, resilient, forbearing, patient

ჭሎታ   *čǝlota* n. ability, cleverness

ჭሎት   *čǝlot* n. court session
ተቻለ   *täčalä* v.i. was possible

ኣቻቻለ   *aččačalä* v.t. made do *(with what little one had)*; stretched out *(resources)*

ኣሰቻለ   *asčalä* v.t. presided over *(court);* was patient, forbearing *(with pron. suff.)* e.g. ኣሰቻለው *he was patient*

ቻቻታ   *čacata* n. noise, hum. buzz, *(of crowds)*

ቻይና   *čayna* n. China
ቻይናዊ   *čaynawi* n. Chinese
ჭ   *če* gee-up
ჭክ   *ček* n. check *(money)*
የჭክ ደብተር   *yäček däbtär* n. check-book

ჭላ ኣለ   *čǝlla alä* v.t, ignored, paid no attention *(to)* see also ჭል ኣለ

ჭላ ባይ   *čǝlla bay* adj. indifferent

ჭሎት   *čǝlot* n. session of court, tribunal, law court

ჭበ   *čǝbbo* n. torch
ჭ7ኝ   *čǝggǝñ* n. seedling, shoot

ჭፈ   *čǝfe* n. eczema *(itching skin disease)*

ჭፍ ኣለ   *čǝff alä* v.i was covered with boils, spots, had a rash; rained very lightly

ჭፍርግ   *čǝfrǝgg* n. *sida (small bush)*

ኀ

ኁለመና	hullämäna n. whole body (anatomical)
ኀላፊ	see እለፊ.
ኀሙስ	hamus n. Thursday
ኀምሳ	hamsa adj. fifty also አምሳ
የኀምሳ አለቃ	yähamsa aläqa also ያምሳ አለቃ yamsa aläqa n. sergeant
ኀምስ	hamas n. fifth order of the Amharic vowel system
ኀይል	hayl n. force, power, strength, vehemence
የባሕር—	yabähər – n. navy
የአየር—	yä'ayyär – air force
ኀይለ ቃል	haylä qal n. strong words; reproof, main point (of paragraph)
ኀያል	hayyal adj. powerful, almighty, omnipotent
ኀይለኛ	hayläñña adj. strong, powerful, mighty; violent, terrific, sharp (pain)
ኀይለኛነት	hayläññannät n. strength, potency
ኀጋይ	hagay n. little dry season (December-March)
ኀጢአት	hati'at n. sin
ኀጢአተኛ	hati'atäñña adj/n sinful (person)
ኀጢአተኛነት	hatiatäññannät n. sinfulness
ኀጥእ	hat' n. sinner
ኀፍረት	hafrät n. shame

ኀፍረተ ሥጋ	hafrätä səga n. sexual organs (polite), see also አፈረ
ኅብረት	habrät n. union, cooperation, solidarity, alliance, unity
ኅብረተሰብ	habrätä säb n. society
ኅብረተሰባዊ	hebrätä säbawi adj. socialistic
ኅብረተ ሰብአ ዊነት	habrätä säb'awinnät n. socialism
ኅብር	habr n. metaphor
ኅብረ ትርኢት	habrä tar'it n. variety show
—ቀለማት	—qälämat n. colour harmony
ማኅበር	mahabär n. society, association
ማኅበርተኛ	mahabärtäñña n. member (of society, association)
ማኅበርተኛነት	mahabärtäññannät n. membership
ማኅበራዊ	mahabärawi adj. sociable, social
—ኑር	—nuro n. social life
ኅብስት	habəst n. Host (in Eucharist); loaf (Ethiopian-bread)
ኅዳር	hədar n. November
ኅዳግ	həddag n. margin (of book)
ኅፀፅ	haşäş n. defect
ኋላ	hʷala adj. after n. behind, back (part)
ኋለኛ	hʷaläñña adj. latter
የኋላ ኋላ	yähʷala hʷala adv. later on; at the end

ነ

ነህ	näh pron. you are (sing m.)
ነሐሴ	nähase n. August
ነምር	nämər n. leopard, also ነብር
ነሣ	nässa v.t prevented; refused to give

እጅ—	əǧǧ nässa v.t greeted
—መንሻ	— mänša n. present, gift (usually to superior)
ተነሣ	tänässa v.i stood up; got up (in the morning)

መነሻ	*männäša* n. point of departure
መነሾ	*männäšo* n. source, origin *(of an incident)*
ትንሣኤ	*tənsa'e* n. Easter
ተነሣሣ	*tänäsassa* v.i was induced, stirred, motivated to do *(s/t)*
አነሣሣ	*annäsassa* v.t induced, stirred, motivated *(s/o)* to do *s/t*
አስነሣ	*asnässa* v.t woke *(s/o)*; aroused, initiated *(s/t)*, *(s/o)*; agitated *(politcal)*
አስነሺ	*asnäšši* n. agitator, arouser, incitor
ነረተ	*närrätä* v.t beat severely *(e.g with baton)*
አስነረተ	*asnärrätä* v.t had *(s/o)* beaten
ነርስ	*närs* n. nurse
ነሰረ	*nässärä* v.t bled through the nose
ነስር	*näsər* nose-bleed
አነሰረ	*anässärä* v.t had a nose-bleed
ነሰነሰ	*näsännäsä* v.t sprinkled, spread about *(e.g powder, hay etc.)*; swished *(e.g horses tail)*
ነሳነሰ	*näsannäsä* v.t sprinkled, spread here and there
አስነሰነሰ	*asnäsännäsä* v.t had *(s/t)* sprinkled, spread about
ተነሰነሰ	*tänäsännäsä* v.t was sprinkled, spread about
ነሾጠ	*näššäṭä* v.i suddenly burst out *(talking, singing etc.)*, was enthusiastic
ነሽ	*näš* pron. you are *(sing f.)*
ነቀለ	*näqqälä* v.t uprooted pulled out; dispossessed, evicted *(tenant from land)*
ነቃይ	*näqay* n. one who uproots; evicts
ንቁይ	*nəqquy* adj. uprooted
ነቀላ	*näqäla* n. action of uprooting

መንቀያ	*mänqäya* n. tool. etc. used to uproot *(s/t)*
ንቅል አለ	*nəqqəl alä* v.i was suddenly uprooted, completely uprooted
ንቅልቅል አለ	*nəqlqəll alä* v.i was completely uprooted
ተነቀለ	*tänäqqälä* v.i was uprooted; was evicted
ነቃቀለ	*näqaqqälä* v.t plucked up here and there
አናቀለ	*annaqqälä* v.t helped *(s/o)* to pluck, uproot
አስነቀለ	*asnäqqälä* v.t. had *(s/t)* uprooted; had *(s/o)* evicted
ነቀርሳ	*näqärsa* n. scrofula; chronic ulcer *(of skin)*
የሳምባ—	*yäsamba*—n. tuberculosis,
ነቀሰ	*näqqäsä* v.i was tattooed; v.t. made a discount
ነቃሽ	*näqaš* n. one who tattoos
ንቃሽ	*nəqqaš* n. discount
ንቅሳት	*nəqqəsat* n. tattoo
ንቃሳታም	*nəqqəsatam* adj. tattooed
መንቀሻ	*mänqäša* n. tattooing intrument
ተነቀሰ	*tänäqqäsä* v.i. was tattooed
አስነቀሰ	*asnäqqäsä* v.t. had *(s/o)* tattooed; had a discount made
ነቀነቀ	*näqännäqä* v.t. shook *(tree, o/s head etc.)*
ንቅናቄ	*nəqannaqe* n. uprising *(political)*; motion
ንቅነቃ	*nəqnäqa* n. agitation *(the liquids in container etc.)*
ተነቀነቀ	*tänäqännäqä* v.i was shaken, agitated
ተነቃነቀ	*tänäqannäqä* v.i was shaken up, agitated
ተነቃናቂ	*tänäqanaqi* adj. moving, having motion; mobile
አነቃነቀ	*annäqannäqä* v.t shook *(physically)*, agitated *(pols.)*

143

አነቃናቂ annäqanaqi n. agitator; one who shakes s/t

ነቀዘ näqqäzä v.i got weevilly, worm-infested *(grain)*

ነቀዝ näqäz n, weevil

ነቃዥ näqaž adj. liable to get weevils

ነቀዛም näqäzam adj. full of weevils

አነቀዘ anäqqäzä v.t caused *(s/t)* to be full of weevils

ነቃቀዘ näqaqqäzä v.i. had a few weevils in

ነቀፈ näqqäfä v.t criticized *(adversely)*, found fault, blamed

ነቃፊ näqafi n. critic, faultfinder

ነቀፋ näqäfa n. criticism *(adverse)*, faultfinding

ነቃቀፈ näqaqqäfä v.t criticised, blamed *(mildly)*

ተነቀፈ tänäqqäfä v.i was criticised, blamed

ተነቃቀፈ tänäqaqqäfä v.t criticised, blamed each other

አስነቀፈ asnäqqäfä v.i. had *(s/o)* criticised, blamed

አስነቃፊ asnäqqafi adj. liable to be criticised, improper *(deed etc.)*

ነቃ näqqa v.i got up, woke up; became lively, quick, agile; was full of cracks *(e.g wall)*

ነቁ näqu adj. wide awake, quick, agile, active

ነቃት näqat n. agility, activeness; crack *(e.g. in wall)*

ነቃት ኃሊና näqatä həllina n. consciousness

ነቃቃ näqaqqa v.i revived, came alive

ተነቃቃ tänäqaqqa v.i was made active, agile, was encouraged to be active, agile

አነቃ anäqqa v.t woke *(s/o)* up; revived *(s/o)*:

made conscious

አነቃቃ annäqaqqa v.t. made *(s/o)* active, agile; encouraged *(s/o)* to be active, agile

አነቃቂ annäqaqi n. one who encourages *(s/o)* to be active, agile

ነቈጠ näqqʷäṭä v.i was blotted, blotted *(e.g with ink)*

ነቍጥ näqʷṭ n. blot, splotch, spot

ነበልባል näbälbal n. flame, flare

ነበረ näbbärä v. was

ነባር näbär n. *(gram.)* substantive, old-timer; adj. permanent

ንብረት nəbrät n. possessions belongings

መንበር mänbär n. throne; altar

ወንበር wänbär n. chair

ነበራርት näbärart n. lynx

*ነበበረ *näbäbbärä

ንብብር nəbəbbər adj. heaped, superimposed, stratum *(layer of s/t)*

ነበበ näbbäbä v. resonated *(drum)*, see also አነበበ

ነባቢ näbabi adj. resonating

ንባብ nəbab n. reading

ምንባብ mənbab n. readingbook, reader, primer

አነበበ anäbbäbä v.t. read

አንባቢ anbabi n. reader

ተነበበ tänäbbäbä v.i was read

ተነባቢ tänäbbabi adj. legible

ተናበበ tänabbäbä v.i. compared two versions of a book etc.

ተናባቢ tannabäbi n. consonant

አናበበ annabbäbä v.t. checked *(one written version against another)*

አናባቢ annababi n. vowel

አስነበበ asnäbbäbä v.t had *(s/o)* read

*ነበነበ *näbännäbä

አነበነበ anäbännäbä v.i mumbled, gabbled; droned *(of bees)*,

ነበዘ näbbäzä v.t changed colour *(dyed cloth)*:

	look:d drawn, wasted, exhausted *(about the face)*
ንብዝ አለ	*nəbbəzz alä* v.i lost colour *(dyed cloth)*
ንብዝብዝ አለ	*nəbəzbəzz alä* v.i completely changed colour; was completely changed *(colour);* was completely drawn, pale *(about the face)*
አነበዘ	*anäbbäzä* v.t caused to lose colour; caused to look pale, drawn
ነባ	*näbba* v.i wept, cried
አነባ	*anäbba* v.i wept, cried
እንባ	*ənba* n. tears, teardrops
ነብር	*näbər* n. leopard
ነብርማ	*näbrəmma* adj. spotted *(animals)*
ነብር	*näbro* n. biceps (*meat)*
ነበጨ	*näbboǧä* v.i splattered out, exploded *(from smashed vessel)*
ነተረከ	*nätärräkä* v.i nagged, bickered, quarrelled
ነትራኪ	*nätraki* adj. nagging, bickering, quarrelling
ንትርክ	*nətərrək* n. action of nagging, bickering, quarrelling
ተነታረከ	*tänätarräkä* v.i nagged each other
ተነታራኪ	*tänätaraki* adj/n *(one)* who constantly nags
አነታረከ	*annätarräkä* v.t caused people to nag, bicker
ነተበ	*nättäbä* v.i was raged *(clothes,*
ነት	*nät* n. sleeping mat *(of decorated leather)*
ነሁ ለለ	*nähuʷällälä* v.i. grew simple - minded, imbecile
ነሁ ላለ	*nähuʷlalla* adj. imbecile
ነሁ ለል	*nähʷäläl* n/adj. imbecile
አነሁ ለለ	*anähʷällälä* v.t stupefied
	nän n. pron. we are

ነኝ	*näññ* pron. I am
ነከረ	*näkkärä* v.t soaked
ነክር	*näkər* adj. soaked
መንከሪያ	*mänkäriya* n. basin, vesssel *(for soaking)*
ተነከረ	*tänäkkärä* v.i. was soaked
አስነከረ	*asnäkkärä* v.t had *(s't)* soaked
ነከሰ	*näkkäsä* v.t bit
ነከሰ አደረገ	*näkäss adärrägä* v.t nibbled, bit a little
ንክሳት	*nəkkəsat* n. bite *(place on skin)*
ንክሻ	*nəkəša* n. bite *(place on skin)*
ነከሰ አደረገ	*näkkəs adärrägä* v.t. bit hard, severely
ነካከሰ	*näkakkäsä* v.t nibbled here and there
ተነከሰ	*tänäkkäsä* v.i was bitten
ተነካከሰ	*tänäkakkäsä* v.t bit each other; hated each other bitterly
አናከሰ	*annakkäsä* v.t set at each other *(dogs);* created animosity
ተናከሰ	*tänakkäsä* v.t bit *(dog);* had a severe grudge against each other
ተናካሽ	*tänakaš* adj. liable to bite *(dog)*
አስነከሰ	*asnäkkäsä* v.t had *(s/o)* bitten *(by a dog);* waɔ turned against one *(superior etc. through gossip)*
ነከተ	*näkkätä* v.i was broken, smashed
ነከ	*näkka* v.t touched; had sexual intercourse *(polite)*
ንክ	*nək* adj. slightly unbalanced, mentally touched
ንክኪት	*nəkəkkit* n. contamination *(by touching);* contact
ንክክ	*nəkəkk* n. contamination *(by touching);* contact

145

ነካከ	*näkakka* v.t touched lightly; felt with the hands; provoked slightly, teased	
ተነካ	*tänäkka* vi was touched; was distressed, moved *(by s/t)*	
ተነካከ	*tänäkakka* v.t contaminated s/o *(by touch)*	
አናከ	*annakka* v.i caused *(s/o)* to be contaminated; caused *(people)* to quarrel	
አናኪ	*annaki* n. trouble-stirrer, malicious gossipper	
አነካከ	*annäkakka* v.t caused s/o to be contaminated; caused *(people)* to quarrel	
አነካኪ	*annäkaki* n/adj. *(one)* who stirs up trouble between people by malicious gossip	
አስነካ	*asnäkka.* v.t had *(s/t, s/o)* touched	
ነኩት	*näkk*ʷ*ätä* v.i was broken into pieces	
ንኳች	*nakk*ʷ*ač* n. broken fragments	
እንኩቶ	*ank*ʷ*äto* n. roasted beans, peas, lentils *(etc.)* in shell; riff—raff	
አነኩት	*anäkk*ʷ*ätä* v.t roasted, *(peas, beans etc.)*	
አነኳኩት	*anäk*ʷ*akk*ʷ*ätä* v.t broke into pieces, smashed up	
ነወር አለ	*näwär alä* v.i stood up *(politely on entrance of guest etc.)*	
ነውረኛ	*näwräñña* adj/n. impolite, indecent	
ነውር	*näwar* adj/n. impolite, indecent	
አስነወረ	*asnäwwärä* v.i was shameful, indecent, impolite	
አስነዋሪ	*asnäwwari* adj. shameful, indecent	
ነው	*näw* v.t. it is	
ነው እኮ	*näw akko* excl.	

ነዘረ	indeed, it is! *näzzärä* v.i throbbed gave pain *(wound)*; tingled *(limb after cramp)*; vibrated	
ንዝራት	*nazzarat* n. throbbing, tingling vibration	
ነዘነዘ	*näzännäzä* v.t was importunate, nagged	
ነዝናዛ	*näznazza* adj. importunate, nagging	
ነዝናዥ	*näznaž* adj. importunate, nagging	
ንዝነዛ	*naznäza* n. importuning, nagging	
ተነዘነዘ	*tänäzännäzä* v.i was bothered, nagged *(by s/o)*	
ተነዛነዘ	*tänäzannäzä* v.t bothered, nagged	
ተነዛናዥ	*tänäzanaž* adj. bothersome, nagging	
ነዛ	*näzza* v.t spread *(news, gossip)*; laid out *(money)*	
ጉራውን	*gurrawan*—v.t was boastful	
ተነዛ	*tänäzza* v.i was spread *(news)*	
ነደለ	*näddälä* v.t perforated, poked a hole in	
ነዳደለ	*nädäddälä* v.t pierced here and there	
አስነደለ	*asnäddälä* v.t had s/t pierced, perforated	
ነደደ	*näddädä* v.i burned	
ነዳጅ	*nädağ* n/adj. *(petrol, diesel etc.)* inflammable	
—ማደያ ጣቢያ	—*maddäya ṭabiya* n. fueling station	
ንዴት	*naddet* n. great anger, rage, fury, vexation	
ንዴተኛ	*naddetäñña* adj. touchy, easily angered	
ንዴታም	*naddetam* adj. touchy, easily angered	
ንዳድ	*nadad* n. malaria; high fever	
ተናደደ	*tänaddädä* v.i became furious, vexed	

146

	got angry, mad. was indignant		drive *(cattle)*; rustled, took away *(cattle)*
ተናዳጅ	*tänadağ* ad. adj/n *(one)* who is easily irritated	ነዶ	*nädo* n. sheaf *(grass, hay etc.)*
አናደደ	*annaddädä* v.t incited fury, vexation; angered, infuriated, enraged	ነገ ነገሠ	see ነጋ *näggäsä* v.i. reigned
አናዳጅ	*annadağ* adj/n. *(s/t)* that incites fury, vexation	ነጋሢ	*nägasi* or ነጋሽ *nägaš* n. sovereign, ruler
ነደፈ	*näddäfä* v.t. stung *(e.g bee)*; bit *(snake)*; drew a sketch; carded, teased cotton	ንጉሥ አፈ ንጉሥ	*nəgus* n. king *afä nəgus* n. title *(equivalent to lord chamberlain)*
ነዳፊ	*nädafi* adj./n. biting, stinging	ንጉሠ ነገሥት	*nəgusä nägäst* n. emperor
ንድፍ	*nədəf* n. sketch, design; carded, teased cotton	ንግሥ ሥርዓት—	*nəgs* adj. reigning *sər'atä -* n. coronation
መንደፊያ	*mändäfiya* n. bow *(for teasing out cotton)*; sketching, designing instrument	ንግሥት ንግሥተ ነገሥታት	*nəgəst* n. queen *nəgəstä nägästat* n. empress
ነዳደፈ	*nädaddäfä* v.t stung in several places; drew a rough sketch	መንግሥት	*mängəst* n. government
ተነደፈ	*tänäddäfä* v.i was stung; was sketched; was teased, carded *(cotton)*	መንግሥተ ሰማያት	*mängəstä sämayat* n. Kingdom of Heaven
ተነዳደፈ	*tänädaddäfä* v.t. stung each other	በትረ መንግሥት	*bäträ mängəst* n. royal staff *(of office)*
አነደፈ	*annaddäfä* v.t. helped to sketch	መናገሻ	*männagäša* n. capital city
አስነደፈ	*asnäddäfä* v.t had *(s/o)* sketch *(s/t)*; had *(s/o)* tease out *(cotton)*	አነገሠ	*anäggäsä* v.t. made *(s/o)* king
ነዳ	*nädda* v. drove *(car, animals etc.)*	አንጋሽ ነገረ	*angaš* n.king-maker *näggärä* v.t told
ነጂ መንጃ	*näği* n. driver *mänğa* n. goad, stick for driving *(animals)*	ነጋሪ ነጋሪት	*nägari* n.teller *nägarit* n. large ceremonial drum
—ፈቃድ	*— fäqad* n. driving license	—ጋዜጣ	*—gazeţa* n.official gazette
ተነዳ አነዳድ	*tänädda* v.i was driven *annädad* v.i way, manner of driving	ነገር	*nägär* n. thing, case, word, matter, affair etc.
አናዳ	*annadda* v.t helped *(s/o)* to drive *(cattle)*	ነገረኛ	*nägäräñña* n. troublemaker, troublestirrer; party to legal case
አስነዳ	*asnädda* v.t had s/o	ቁም—	*qum —* adj. trustworthy, dutiful, responsible
		በነገረ ላይ	*bänägäre lai* by the way
		ነገር ግን	*nägär gən* adv. but

ንጋር	*nəggər also* ንግርት *nəggərı* n. sooth saying, prophecy	ነጋድራስ	*näggadras* n. great merchant *(arch.)*
ንግርተኛ	*nəggərtäñña* n. sooth sayer, prophet	ነጋገደ	*nägaggädä;* v.i traded a little *(as a sideline)*
ንግግር	*nəgəggər* n. talk, speech, dialogue, discourses etc.	ተነጋገደ	*tänägaggädä* v.t bartered, traded, with each other
ተነጋገረ	*tänägaggärä* v.i talked to each other, held a dialogue, chatted with each other	አስነገደ	*asnäggädä* v.t had *(s/o)* engage in . trade *(on o/s behalf)*
ተናገረ	*tänaggärä* v.t said, talked	ነጋ	*nägga* v.i dawned, became morning
ተናጋሪ	*tänagari* n/adj. good speaker, eloquent *(person)* orator; talkative	–ጠባ	*ṭäbba* adv. persistently, always, day in day out
		በበነጋው	*bäbänägaw* the following day, on the morrow
አነጋጋሪ	*annägagari* n. interpreter	ንጋት	*nəgat* n.dawn
አነጋገር	*annägagär* n. way, manner of talking	ነገ	*nägä* n. tomorrow
ትንግርት	*təngərt* adj. unbelievable, amazing	ለነገ የማይል	*länägä yämmayəl* adj. unsparing
አናገረ	*annaggärä* v.t talked to *(s/o);* made s/o talk; gave an audience to	ነጋጋ	*nägagga* v.i got light *(in the morning)*
		አነጋ	*anägga* v.i stayed up all night
		አነጋጋ	*anägagga* v.i stayed up all night
አናጋሪ	*annagari* n. *(person)* who leads *(s/o)* on, makes *(s/o)* talk	አስነጋ	*asnägga* v.t had s/o stay all night
ነጋገረ	*nägaggärä* v.t advised, warned	* ነጋ	*see* አናጋ
ተነጋገረ	*tänägaggärä* v.t talked to each other; held a dialogue; chatted with each other	ነጋሪት	*nägarit* n ceremonial drum, *see also* ነገረ
		ነጐረ	*näggʷärä* v.i was clarified *(butter, by boiling)*
አስነገረ	*asnäggärä* v.t had *(s/t)* told to *(s/o)*	ንጕር	*nəgʷur* n. boiled, clarified *(butter)*
* ነገተ	*see* አነገተ	አነጐረ	*anäggʷärä* v.t clarified, boiled *(butter)*
ነገደ	*näggädä* v.t traded		
ነጋዴ	*näggade* n. merchant	አስነጐረ	*asnäggʷärä* v.t had *(butter)* clarified, boiled
የነጋዴዎች ምክር ቤት	*yänäggadewočč məkər bet* chamber of commerce	ነጐደ	*nägʷädä* v.i thundered off; marched off determinedly
ነገድ	*nägd* n. trade	ነጐደ	*nägʷäde* n. any migrant bird
የንግድ ምልክት	*yänəgd mələkkət* n. trade mark	አነጐደ	*anäggʷädä* v.t hit heavily with a stick; hastened to finish work
—ፈቃድ	*—fäqad* trade-licence		
ነገዳ	*nəggäda* n. trading		

148

ነጠለ   *näṭṭälä* v.i split up a double sheet

ነጠላ   *näṭäla* adj. single; singular *(gram.);* kind of shawl-like garment made of a single layer of cloth

—ሥረዝ   —*säräz* comma ፤

—ጫማ   —*čamma* n. sandals

—ቁጥር   —*quṭər* n. singular *(gram.)*

ንጣይ   *näṭṭay* n. one taken from a pair

ንጥል   *näṭṭəl* n. one taken from a pair

ነጣጠለ   *näṭaṭṭälä* v.t split up *(group);* scattered, separated up

ተነጠለ   *tänäṭṭälä* v.i was taken *(from a pair);* stood out *(from a group, i.e. by disagreeing with majority)*

ተነጣይ   *tänäṭṭay* n. one who stands out in a group

ተነጣጠለ   *tänäṭaṭṭälä* v.i split up *(group)*

አነጣጠለ   *annäṭaṭṭälä* v.t caused to split up

አስነጠለ   *asnäṭṭälä* v.t had *(a group)* split up

ነጠረ   *näṭṭärä* v.t bounced *(ball);* refined *(by melting, e.g gold)*

ነጣሪ   *näṭari* n. bouncing

ንጥር   *näṭər* adj. refined

ጥንተ—   *ṭəntä–* n. element *(chemical)*

ንጥር ቅቤ   *näṭər qäbe* n. refined butter

—ወርቅ   —*wärq* n. refined gold

ተነጠረ   *tänäṭṭärä* v.i was refined

አነጠረ   *anäṭṭärä* v.t refined; bounced

አንጣሪ   *anṭari* n. refiner

ወርቅ-   *wärq–* n. goldsmith

አንጥረኛ   *anṭäränña* n . silversmith

ማንጠሪያ   *manṭäriya* n. refining flux

እናጠረ   *anäṭṭärä* v.i acted flamboyantly

አስነጠረ   *asnäṭṭärä* v.t had *(s/t)* refined

ነጠቀ   *näṭṭäqä* v.t snatched, took by force

ነጣቂ   *näṭaqi* n. robber

ንጥቂያ   *näṭqiya* n. robbery

መንጠቆ   *mänṭäqqo* n. angling, fishing rod

ነጣጠቀ   *näṭaṭṭäqä* v.t robbed, snatched *(s/t)* from several people

ተነጠቀ   *tänäṭṭäqä* v.i was snatched; was robbed

ተናጠቀ   *tänaṭṭäqä* v.t struggled over, fought *(over s/t)*

ተናጣቂ   *tänaṭaqi* n. one who takes things by force, robber, thief

ተነጣጠቀ   *tänäṭaṭṭäqä* v.t struggled over, fought *(over s/t)*

አናጠቀ   *annaṭṭäqä* v.t caused to quarrel over, fight over *(s/t)*

አስነጠቀ   *asnäṭṭäqä* v.t had s/o robbed

ነጠበ   *näṭṭäbä* v.i. dripped; blotted, blotched, *(e.g with ink)*

ነጥብ   *näṭəb* n. point, dot

ነጠብጣብ   *näṭäbṭab* n. dots *(...)*

አነጠበ   *anäṭṭäbä* v.t blotted, blotched

ነጠፈ   *näṭṭäfä* v.i dried up *(spring etc.);* went dry *(i.e stopped giving milk, cow)*

ነጣፊ   *näṭafi* v.t likely to be dry, go dry

አነጠፈ   *anäṭṭäfä* v.t caused *(s/t)* to dry up, go dry; spread mat, carpet, made *(bed)*

አንጣፊ   *anṭafi* n. chambermaid, room boy

አስነጠፈ	asnäṭṭäfä v.t had bed made; had (s/t) spread on floor
ምንጣፍ	mənṭaf n. carpet, rug, mat
ነጣ	näṭṭa v.i became white, pale (face). became clean
ነጭ	näčč adj. white; n. white (person)
ንጣት	nəṭat n. whiteness
ነጣጣ	näṭaṭṭa v.i became lighter, whitish
አነጣ	anäṭṭa v.t made (s/t) white, clean
አነጣጣ	anäṭaṭṭa v.t cleaned up a little, made whiter
አስነጣ	asnäṭṭa v.t had (s/t) whitenəd, cleaned
ነጥር	näṭər n. pound (measure of weight)
ነጨ	näččä v.t plucked out (hair, grass etc.) by the roots
ነጫጨ	näčaččä v.t plucked up here and there
ተነጨ	tänäččä v.i was plucked up
ተነጫጨ	tänäčaččä v.i plucked out each other's (hair etc.)
አስነጨ	asnäččä v.t had (s/t) plucked up
*ነጨነጨ	see ተነጫነጨ
ነጸብራቅ	see *ጸበረቀ and አንጸባረቀ
ነጻ	näṣṣa v.i became clean, see also ነጣ
ንጹሕ	nəṣuh adj. clean
ንጹት	nəṣat n. cleanliness
ንጹሕነት	nəṣuhənnät n. cleanliness
ንጽሕና	nəṣəhənna n. cleanliness
አነጻ	anäṣṣa v.i cleaned
ነጽነት	näṣannät n. freedom, liberty, independence
*ነጸደረ	see አነጸደረ
ነፈለለ	näfällälä adj. acted foolishly, idiotically, became imbecilic
ነፈለል	näfäläl adj. idiot-like, imbecilic, moronic
ነፍላላ	näflalla adj. idiot-like
ነፈረ	näffärä v.i was over-cooked, overboiled; boiled furiously (water)
ንፍር	nəfər adj. over-cooked, over-boiled; furiously boiling (water)
ንፍሮ	nəfro n. boiled beans, peas, chickpeas etc.
አነፈረ	anäffärä v.t over-cooked, overboiled
ነፈረቀ	näfärräqä v.i suppurated (boil, wound); sobbed bitterly (child)
ነፍራቅ	näfraqqa adj. who sobs bitterly (child)
ተነፋረቀ	tänäfarräqä v.i. cried, wept constantly; nagged (child of its parents)
ተነፋራቂ	tänäfaraqi adj. (child) who cries excessively, nags
አነፋረቀ	annäfärräqä v.t. spoiled (child)
ነፈሰ	näffäsä v.t blew, wind, breathed
ገራም-ቀኝ	gəramm-qäññ whatever may be, be that as it may
ነፈሰበት	näffäsäbbät he is out of favour
ነፋሽ	näfaš adj. breathing, blowing
ነፋሻ	näffašša n. airy place, open area
ነፋስ	näfas n. wind, air, fresh air
አውሎ —	awlo— n. whirlwind, dust-devil, tornado
ነፍስ	näfs n. spirit, soul
ነፍሳ ቢስ	näfsa bis adj. hectic (without rest)
—ገዳይ	—gäday n. assassin, murderer
ነፍሱን ሳተ	näfsun satä v.t fainted, lost con-

ነፍስ ዐወቀ — **nafs awwäqä** v.t. was mature; sciousness

ነፍሱን— **näfsun**—v.t. recovered consciousness

ነፍስ ዘራ — **näfs zärra** v.t regianed consciousness.

በነፍሱ ደረሰ — **bänäfsu därräsä** he came to his rescue *(on time)*

ነፍሰጡር — **näfsäṭur** n. pregnant woman *(polite)*

በነፍስ ወከፍ — **bänäfs wäkkäf** adv. one each, individually

ነፋሸ — **naffaš** n. chaff, dirt *(from winnowing)*

ነፍሳት — **näfsat** n. germs, insects

መንፈስ — **mänfäs** inf. to blow, breathe. n. ghost, spirit

—ቅዱስ — **—qəddus** n. Holy Spirit

መንፈሳዊ — **mänfäsawi** adj. spiritual

መንፈሳዊነት — **mänfäsawinnät** n. spirituality

ነፋፈሰ — **näfaffäsä** v.t blew, breathed *(slightly, lightly)*

ተነፈሰ — **tänäffäsä** v.t breathed; exhaled, was winnowed; rested a little; licked *(of a tyre)*

ጎማው— — **gommaw**—the tyre is flat

ትንፋሸ — **tanffaš** adj. breathing

ተነፋፈሰ — **tänäfaffäsä** v.i. breathed lightly; had a short rest; went out for fresh air

ትንፋሽ — **tanfāš** n. breath

ተናፈሰ — **tänaffäsä** v.i. went out for fresh air

መናፈሻ — **männafäšä** n. openair place, airy place

አናፈሰ — **anäffäsä** v.t winnowed, threw grain up in to the wind,

ወሬ— — **wäre**—talked gossip

ማንፈሻ — **manfäšä** n. winnowing fan, basket

አናፋፈሰ — **anäfaffäsä** v.t winnowed a little

አናፈሰ — **annaffäsä** v.t aerated, aired out, ventilated

አስናፈሰ — **asnäffäsä** v.t exposed to air *(with bad result)*

አስተነፈሰ — **astänäffäsä** v.i lost air *(tyre)*; gave *(s/o)* a break *(from work)*

ነፈነፈ — **näfännäfä** v.t enjoyed eating *(with good appetite)*

ነፍናፋ — **näfnaffa** n. one having nasal speech defect

ተነፈነፈ — **tänäfännäfä** v.i spoke nasally; grumbled *(obeyed with bad grace)*

ተነፋናፈ — **tänäfanafi** n. one who speaks nasally; one who grumbles *(orders)*

አነፈነፈ — **anäfännäfä** v.t sniffed, nosed about *(dog etc.)*

ነፈገ — **näffägä** v.i was miserly, stingy; denied

ነፋጊ — **näfagi** n. miser

ነፉግ — **nafug** adj. miserly, stingy

ንፍገት — **nafgät** n. miserliness, avarice

ተነፈገ — **tänäffägä** v.i was prevented from doing *(s/t)*, having *(s/t)*

ተነፋፈገ — **tänäfaffägä** v.i prevented each other from doing, having *(s/t)*

* ነፈጠ — see ተናፈጠ

ነፋ — **näffa** v.t blew *(s/t)*

ነፊ — **näffi** in ጥሩምባ ነፊ ṭarwmba näfi n. trumpeter

ንፍ — **naf** adj. inflated

ነፊት — **naffit** n. blowing,

151

መንፈያ	blowing up *mänfiya* n. air pump
ወንፈት	*wänfit* n. seive, strainer
ወናፍ	*wänaf* n. leather bellows
ነፋፋ	*näfaffa* v.t inflated slightly, blew a little air
ተነፋ	*tänäffa* v.i was inflated, blown; was extremely proud
ተነፋፋ	*tänäfaffa* v.i was blown-out, over inflated
ተናፋ	*tänaffa* v.t hit each other, boxed, each other *(coll.)*
አናፋ	*anaffa* v.t. brayed *(donkey)*
አስነፋ	*asnäffa* v.t. had *(s/t)* inflated
ነፍጥ	*näft* n. gun, firearm
ነፍጠኛ	*näftäñña* n. rifleman, sniper, armed retainer
ኑር	*see* ኖረ
ኑዛዜ	*nuzaze* n. will, testament
ተናዘዘ	*tänazzäzä* v.t. made *(o/s)* will
ተናዛዥ	*tänazaž* n. one who makes his will *(usually dying man)*
አናዘዘ	*anazzäzä* v.t had *(s/o)* make his will
አናዛዥ	*annazaž* n. s/o *(priest, elder)* who orders s/o to make his will
ኑግ	*nug* n. niger seed
ቅባ ኑግ	*qəba nug* n. oil-niger
ኒሻን	*nišan* or ሊሻን *lišan* n. medal
ኒኬል	*nikel* or ንኬል *nəkel* n. nickel
ና	*na* imp. come!
—ና	—*nna* or እና *ənna* suff. and
ናላ	*nala* n. brain
ናሙና	*namuna* n. sample, specimen
ናስ	*nas* n. brass, *also* ነሐስ
ናረ	*narä* v.i inflated *(raise of price)* in የዋጋ ናረት *yäwaga nərät* n.inflation(*price*)
ናቀ	*naqä* v. t looked down on; ignored, belittled
ንቀት	*nəqät* n. looking down on; despising, ignoring, belittling
ተናቀ	*tänaqä* v.i was looked down on; despised
ተናናቀ	*tänanaqä* v.t despised each other
አስናቀ	*asnaqä* v.i was outstanding, excellent, incomparable; degraded
ናኘ	*naññä* v.t scattered
ተናኘ	*tänaññä* v.i was scattered
ናቸው	*naččäw* pron. they are
ናችሁ	*naččəhu* you are *(pl.)*
ናወዘ	*nawwäzä* v.i was restless; wandered around
ናዎዥ	*nawwaž* v.i restless person
ናዘዘ	*see* ተናዘዘ
ናዝራዊ	*nazrawi* adj/n. ascetic *(person)*
ናደ	*nadä* v.t demolished, broke up, crumbled
ናዳ	*nada* n. boulder, land slip, land slide
ተናደ	*tänadä* v.i was broken up, demolished
አስናደ	*asnadä* v.t had *(s/t)* demolished
ናጠ	*naṭä* v.t churned *(to make butter)*
ናጭ	*nač* n. butter-churner
መናጫ	*mänača* n. churn
ተናጠ	*tänaṭä* v.i was churned
አስናጠ	*asnaṭä* v.t had *(butter churned)*
ናፈቀ	*naffäqä* v.t yearned

for, longed for; had nostalgia, missed

ናፋቂ *nafaqi* adj. nostalgic *(person)*

ናፍቆት *nafqot* n. yearning, longing, nostalgia

ተናፈቀ *tänaffäqä* v.i was longed for, missed

ተናፋቂ *tänafaqi* adj. longed for, yearned for, missed

ተናፋረቀ *tänäfaffäqä* v.t longed, missed each other

ተናፋፋቂ *tänäfafaqi* adj. !onging for *(each other)*

—ን —n *(gram.)* direct object marker

ንስሐ *nəssəha* n. repentance

—ገባ —*gäbba* v.t repented

የንስሐ አባት *yänəssəha abbat* n. father–confessor

ንስር *nəsər* n. eagle

ንብ *nəb* n. bee

የንብ ዕጭ *yänəb əč* n. bee larva

ንብረት *nəbrät* n. property

ባለ ንብረት *balä nəbrät* n. owner

የአየር *yä'ayyär nəbrät* n.

ንብረት climate, weather

ነዋይ *nəway* n. money *(G.)*

ንዋየ *nəwayä qəddəsat*

ቅድሳት n. church equipment

ንዑስ *nə'us* adj. small; sub- e.g ንዑስ ኮሚቴ sub- committe, ንኡስ ሐረግ subordinate clause

ንቱሥ *see* ነገሠ

ንፍር *see* ነፈረ

ኖረ *norä* v.i lived

ኗሪ *nʷari or* ነዋሪ *näwari* adj/n. alive, living, inhabitant

ኑር *nuro* n. life; way of living

መኖሪያ *mänoriya* n. dwelling place, domicile

ተኖረ *tänorä* v.i was lived *(a life)*

ተኗኗረ *tänʷanʷarä* v.i co-existed; accomodated, bore with *(each other)*

አኖረ *anorä* v.t. placed *(s/t)*, set *(s/t,)* down; put *(s/o)* up

ማኖሪያ *manoriya* n. place for storing, putting things

ኖር አለ *nor alä, or* ነዋር አለ *näwär alä* v.i. stood up *(politely on entrance of a guest etc.)*

አ

ኣሁን *ahun* adv. now, right now presently, at persent, soon

—ለታ —*läta* some days ago

አሁንም *ahunəmm* adv. yet, even now, still

—ይማራል —*yəmmaral* he is still learning

አሁን ባሁን *ahun bahun* adv. how quickly! here and now, at this very

moment

አሁንም አሁንም *ahunəmm ahunəmm*

አሁንም adv. constantly, repeatedly

—ሆነ ኋላ —*honä huʷala* sooner or later

አሁንስ *ahunəss* but now

አሁኑኑ *ahununu* adv. right away, at once, inmediately

አሁን ካሁን *ahun kahun* at any moment

153

—ገና	—gäna just now, just this moment
ላሁን	lahun just this once; for the time being
ባሁን ጊዜ	bahun gize adv. now a days, currently
እስካሁን	əskahun up to now, thus far; still
ካሁን ጀምሮ	kahun ğämməro from now on
ገና አሁን	gäna ahun just now
አይ	ahe or አሂሂ ahehe excl. oh, no! (disapproval of, e.g. course of action)
አህያ	ahəyya n. donkey, ass
የሜዳ--	yämeda-n. zebra, wild ass
አለ	alä v.t said, spoke
ይበል	imperfect ይል · ይላል jussive ይበል imp. በል
ይላል	yəlal he says;
ግር ግር	mar mar yəlall it is
ይላል	sweet (it has the taste of honey)
በል	bal say; come on, well then
በለው	bäläw let him have it, hit him
ለ... ብሎ	lä...bəlo for the sake of
ለ...ሲል	la...sil for the benefit of
ሲል ሲል	sil sil gradually, little by little
እንበል	ənbäl let us suppose
ማን ልበል	man ləbäl may I ask what your name is? whom shall I say? who is speaking?
ባይ	bay adj. (one) who speaks, says (s/t)
አለባለ	aləbbale adj.ordinary, unremarkable
ማለት	maldə inf. to say, speak; to mean; that is to say
አሉታ	aluta negative (gram.)
አሉባልታ	alubalta n. gossip
ተባለ	täbala v.i was said, spoken
ተባባለ	täbabalä v.t said to each other; hit each other; agreed together (on a price)
አባባለ	abbabalä v.t brought (parties) to an agreement
አባባል	abbabal n. way of explaining, saying (s/t), expression
አለ	allä v.i there is
አለሁ አለሁ ባይ	allähu allahu bay adj. pretentious, boastful
አለበት	alläbbät he must e.g· መናገር-männagär—he has to speak
ማን አለብኝ ባይ	mann alläbbəñ bay despot
ምን አለብኝ	mən alläbbəñ how much money do I owe you
በሉለበት	bälelläbät in his absence
በያለበት	bäyyalläbbät everywhere
ከያለበት	käyyalläbbät from all over
አላኝታ	allañta n. mainstay, reason for living
የለም	yälläm v.i there not (any); adv. no
ያለ የለለ	yallä yälellä in full force, all imaginable (things)
አለለ	ailälä v.i was frisky, aroused (mating donkey)
አለሉ	aläle adj. frisky, aroused (mating donkey); playboy, womaniser
አለል ዘለለ አለ	aläll zäläll alä v.i wandered about aimlessly
አለሉ	alällo n. pestle, round stone (used for crushing grain etc.)
አለመ	allämä v. t dreamed
አላሚ	allami n. dreamer, one who has dreams

እልም — *əlm* or ሕልም *həlm* n. dream

አለመጠ — *alämmäṭä* v.i slowed down (work); mocked (s/o) see also ለመጠ

አልጋጭ — *almač* n. one who slows down (at work); mocker

አለቀ — *alläqä* v.i finished; was consumed, terminated

አላቂ — *alaqi* adj. consumable

—እቃ — *—əqa* n. consumable goods

እላቂ — *əllaqi* n. remnants; tattered clothes

አልቂት — *əlqitt* n. extermination (of people)

እልት — *əlq* n. all or nothing (as a bet, wager)

እልት አለ — *ələqq alä* v.i was completely used up, finished

ተላለቀ — *tälalläqä* v.t killed each other off

አስተላለቀ — *astälalläqä* v.t caused to kill each other

አለቀሰ — *aläqqäsä* v.i wept, cried, see ለቀሰ

አልቃሽ — *alqaš* n. professional mourner

አልቃሻ — *alqašša* n/adj. (child) who cries continuously

ለቀስተኛ — *läqqästäñña* n. mourner

ልቅሶ — *ləqso* n. mourning, lamentation, crying

ግልቀሻ — *mälqaša* n. reliques (dead person's effects displayed at funeral)

አለቃቀሰ — *aläqaqqäsä* v.i cried a little

አላቀሰ — *allaqqäsä* v.t consoled, visited (bereaved person)

አላቃሽ — *allaqaš* n. visitors (to bereaved)

ተላቀሰ — *tälaqqäsä* v.i mourned for s/o

አስለቀሰ — *asläqqäsä* v.t caused s/o cry, weep

አስለቃሽ — *asläqqaš* n. s/t which causes grief, weeping

አለቃ — *aläqa* n. chief, head

አለቅነት — *aläqənnät* chiefdom

እልቅና — *əlqənna* n. chiefdom

አለበ — *alläbä* v.t milked; left marker (in book)

አላቢ — *alabi* n. milkmaid, milker

እለባት — *ələbat* n. bookmark

ግለቢያ — *malläbbiya* n. milking pail

ግለቢያ — *maläbiya* n. s/t used as bookmark

ታለበ — *talläba* v.i was milked

ታላቢ — *talabi* n. milk cow, dairy cow

አሳለበ — *asalläbä* v.i had (cow, goat etc.) milked

አለበለዚያ — *aläbälläzziya* adv. otherwise, also አለዚያ

አለት — *alät* n. rock, hard stone

አለንጋ — *alänga* n whip

አለኛታ — *alläññəta* n. moral support

አለከለከ — *aläkälläkä* v.i panted

አለክላኪ — *aläklaki* adj. panting

አለጉመ — *alägg°ämä* v.t worked slowly

አልጓሚ — *alg°ami* n.slow worker

አለጣ — *alläṭä* v.i was thin, flavourless (food, wäṭ)

አለጨ — *alläčča* n. pepperless wäṭ

አለፈ — *alläfä* v.t passed by; guaranteed (s/o)

አላፊ — *alafi* n/adj. passer-by; passenger; responsible

አላፊነት — *alafinnät* n. responsibility

እልፊት — *əlfitt* n. transgression, contempt (of court)

ግለፊያ — *mäläfiya* n. passage, corridor etc.; adj. acceptable, good

ታለፈ	*talläfä* v.i was passed, was ignored
ተላለፈ	*tälalläfä* v.i passed each other *(on the way)*; was postponed; trespassed, broke a law
ተላላፊ	*tälalafi* n. passer-by; traffic
—በሽታ	—*bäššəta* n. contagious disease
መተላለፊያ	*mättälaläfiya* n. way through; passageway
አሳለፈ	*asalläfä* v.t allowed to pass; acted as usher, a waiter
አሳላፊ	*asallafi* n. waiter
አስተላለፈ	*astälalläfä* v.t postponed; directed *(traffic, e,g policeman)*
አለፉ	see ለፉ
አለፈጨቀ	*alläfaččäqä* v.t squeezed out, squashed *(in the hand)*
አሉባልታ	*alubalta* n. gossip, hearsay, see also አለ
አሉማ	*aluma* n. amaranth
አሉታ	*aluta* n. negative, negation
አላመጠ	*allammäṭä* v.t chewed
ተላመጠ	*tälammäṭä* v.i was chewed
አላሰ	*alasä* v,i have s/o lick something *(e.g from fingers)*; diluted *ṭäǧ* with honey, *see* ላሰ
አላሸቀ	see ላሸቀ
አላባ	*alaba* n. produce, income *(from land)*
—ገለባ	—*gäläba* n. farm products
አላድ	*alad* n. half bərr *(arch.)*
አል—	*al*—pref. gram. negative marker
አልማዝ	*almaz* n. diamond
አለባለ	*aləbbale* adj. ordinary, unremarkable *(per·son)*; see also አለ
አልቦ	*albo* n. spacing bead *(annular, usu. silver)*

አልኮል	*alkol* n. alcohol
አልኮሰኮሰ	*alkosäkkosä* v.i worked haphazardly
አልኮስኳሽ	*alkoskʷaš* n. slovenly worker
አልጋ	*alga* n. bed; kingship
—ወራሽ	– *wäräš* n. crownprince
ድንክ—	*dənk*- n. truckle bed
ያልጋ ልብስ	*yalga ləbs* n. bed clothes
ባላልጋ	*balalga* n. occupant of the throne monarch
አልጐመጐመ	*algʷämäggʷämä* v.i grumbled *(over work)*
አልጐምጓሚ	*algʷämgʷami* n. grumbler
አልጼ	see አለጠ
አሉሉ	*alollo* n. pestle *(round stone for crushing grain)*, iron ball
አመለመለ	*amälämmälä* v.t rolled *(co..on in palms for ease of spinning)*
አመልማሉ	*amälmalo* n. wad of raw cotton *(rolled for spinning)*
አመለከተ	*amäläkkätä* v.t pointed at; applied *(e.g for work)*; turned ones attention, notified signifed see also ተመለከተ
አመልካች	*amälkač* n. applicant *(e.g. for work)*
—ተውላጠ ስም	—*ṭäwläṭä səm (gram.)* demonstrative pronoun
—ቅጽል	—*qəṣṣəl* n. *(gram.)* demonstrative adjective
ማመልካቻ	*mamälkäča* n. application *(for work)*
ምልክት	*mələkkat* n. sign mark; inᴄicaᴄion traᴄe, symptom; signal
የንግድ—	*yänəgd*—n. trade mark
አስመለከተ	*asmäläkkätä* v.t felt the inclination *(to do s/t)*
አመለከ	*amälläkä* v.t worshipped

156

እምላኪ.   amlaki n. worshipper
ጣዖት—   ṭa'ot—n. idolater
እምላክ   amlak n. God
እምልኮ   amləko a. woship
—ጣዖት   —ṭa'ot n. idolatry
ተመለከ   tämälläkä v.i was worshipped
ተመላኪ.   tämällaki n. object of worship
እመለጠ   see መለጠ
እመላለሰ   see መለሰ
እመል   amäl n. habit, character, bad temper
እመለኛ   amäläñña adj. moody, bad-tempered
ላመል   lamäl adv. barely, slightly, lightly, only
እመመ   ammämä v.i was sick, ill (usu.with pronominal suffix) e.g እመመኝ amämäññ I feel sick, I feel ill
እመም   əmäm or ሕመም həmäm n. disease, sickness
እመም‍ተኛ   əmämtäñña n. patient sick person
እማመመ   amammämä v.i had slight pain, felt a little ill
ታመመ   tammämä v.i was sick, ill
ታማሚ   tamami n. sick person, patient
እሳመመ   asammämä v.t hurt (s/o)
እመረረ   see መረረ
እመረቀዘ   see መረቀዘ
እመራ   see መራ
እመሰ   ammäsä v.t shuffled (e.g coffee beans on griddle); stirred (people up), agitated
እግሸ   ammaš n. one who stirs up trouble
እምስ   əmməs adj. lightly roasted (grain)
ማመሻ   mammäša n. spatula (stick) for turning, roasting grain etc.
ታመሰ   tammäsä v.i was turned, shuffled (roasting grain etc.); was troubled
እሳመሰ   asammäsä v.t had (s/t) turned, shuffled (roasting grain etc.)
እመስቃቀለ   ammäsäqaqqälä v.t put into disorder, disarranged
እመስቃቃይ   ammäsäqaqay n. one who causes disorder, confusion
እመሰኳ   amäsäkkʷa v.t chewed (cud)
የሚያመሰኳ እንሰሳ   yämmiyamäsäkkkʷa ənsəsa n. ruminant
እመሰገነ   amäsäggänä v.t praised, thanked
እመስጋኝ   amäsgañ n. one who is thankful, gives praise
ምስጋና   məsgana n. thanks, praise
ተመሰገነ   tämäsäggänä v.i was praised, was thanked
እመሰጋገነ   amäsägaggänä v.t thanked, praised sparingly
እስመሰገነ   asmäsäggänä v.t had (s/o) praised, thanked; did praiseworthy work
እመሳቀለ   see እመስቃቀለ
እመቀ   ammäqä v. forced by pressing, compressed
እመት   amät n. year also ዓመት
እመተ ምሕረት   amätä məhərät A.D
እመቾ   ammäččä v.i was comfortable; was obliging, honest (character)
እመቺ   amäččäi adj. comfortable; convenient (time)
ምቹ   məččäu adj. comfortable
ምቹነት   məččäunnät n. comfortability
ምቾት   məččäot n. comfort

157

ተመቸ	tämäččä v.i was convenient; was comfortable
ተመቻቸ	tämäčaččä v.i sat comfortably
አመቻቸ	ammäčaččä v.t set in order, arranged neatly, packed neatly
ኣመነ	ammänä v.t believed, trusted
አማኝ	amañ n. believer, one who believes,
እምነት	əmnät n. belief, trust; reliance, faith
ታመነ	tammänä v.i was trustworthy; was believed
ታማኝ	tammañ adj. loyal, trustworthy
መታመኛ	mättamäña n.guarantee
ተማመነ	tämammänä v.t trusted each other
መተማመኛ	mättämamäña n. guarantee
አስተማመነ	astämammänä v.t convinced, proved (s/t) genuine; established the truth (in a dispute, by third party)
ማስተማመኛ	mastämamäña n. evidence (to settle dispute)
አሳመነ	asammänä v.t convinced (s/o)
አሳማኝ	asammañ n. one who convinces (s/o)
ማሳመኛ	masammäña n. convincing reason, fact
አመነታ	ʾmänäta v.t doubted, wavered
አመንቺ	amänči adj. wavering, doubtful
አመነታታ	amänätatta v.i became a little doubtful
አስመነታ	asmänätta v.t caused (s/o) to doubt
አመነዘረ	ʾmänäzzärä v.i committed adultery
አመንዛሪ	amänzari n. adulterer; adj. adulterous
አመንዝራ	amänzəra n. adulterer

አመናቀረ	ammänaqqärä v.t treated rudely, impolitely see also መነቀረ
አመነቃቀረ	ammänäqaqqärä v.t put into complete disorder
ተመናቀረ	tämänaqqärä v.i behaved rudely
ተመነቃቀረ	tämänäqaqqärä v.i behaved rudely;was put into complete disorder
አመዛዘነ	ammäzazzänä v.t weighed up (in o/s mind) evaluated, see መዘነ
አመዛዛኝ	ammäzazañ adj. intelligent, perspicacious
አመካኘ	ammäkaññä v.i used as an excuse or pretext
ምክንያት	məknəyat n. reason, cause, excuse, justification
አመድ	amäd n. ashes, cinder
አመዳም	amädam adj. pale (complexion)
አመድ አደረገ	amäd adärrägä v.t turned to rubble, wrecked, destroyed completely
አመዳይ	amäday n. frost
አመገ	ammägä v.t crammed together
አመገለ	ammäggälä v.t squeezed out (pus), see also መገለ
አመጠጠ	amäṭṭätä v.t blotted; dried out a little, see also መጠጠ
ማምጠጫ	mamṭäča n. blotting paper
አሙስ	amus, also ሃሙስ hamus Thursday
አሚና	amina n. itinerant singer
አሚዶ	amido starch (stiffening)
አማ	amma v.t gossipped against (s/o), backbited
አሜት	amet or ሐሜት hamet n. malicious

158

አሜታ gossip
ameta or ሐሜታ hameta n. malicious gossip, backbiting

አሜተኛ ametāñña or ሐሜ ተኛ hametāñña n. backbiter

ታሞ ṭamma v.i was gossipped against

ተማሞ tämamma v.t spread tales about each other

አማረ amarä v.i was beautiful, attractive;

አምሮት amrot n. desire, appetite, pleasure; whim

አማራ amara n. Amhara
አማርኛ amarəñña n. Amharic; indirect suggestion

አግሰለ see መስለ

አማን aman n. peace, tranquility

አማተበ ammattäbä v.i crossed oneself, made the sign of the cross

አማታ see መታ
አማት amat n. mother-in-law, father-in-law

አማካኝ ammakañ n. average
አማካይ amakay adj. central, middle

አማች amač n. brother-in-law; relative by marriage

አማጠ amaṭä v.i was in labour, see also ምጥ

አሜሪካ amerika n. America
አሜሪካዊ amerikawi American
አሜን amen intej. Amen.
አሜከላ amekäla n. thistle

አምላክ amlak n. God, see አመለከ

አምሳ amsa n. fifty
—አለቃ —aläqa n. sergeant
—እገር —əgər n. centipede
አምሳኛ amsañña adj. fiftieth.
አምሳል amsal n. resemblance see also መስለ

አምሳያ amsayya n. resemblance
አምስት amməst adj. five
አምስተኛ amməstäñña adj. fifth
አምባል ambäll n. captain (sport)
ሻምባል šambäll n. captain (mil.)
አምቡላ ambulla n. sediment (of ṭäǧ)
አምቡላንስ ambulans n. ambulance
አምቧቧ ambʷabbʷa v.t allowed to pour, gush out (e.g from pipe)
አምባ amba n. flat-topped mountain (with village settlement); quarter, district (of town)
—ገነን —gännän n. demagogue
አምባጓሮ ambaguʷaro skirmish, affray, fight, fracas
አመባጓሮኛ ambäguʷaroñña adj. quarrelsome
አምባረቀ ambarräqä v.t shouted, roared like thunder; thundered see also ባረቀ
አምባራይሌ ambarayle n. lesser kudu
አምባር ambar or አንባር anbar n. bracelet
አምባሳዴር ambasadār n. ambassador
ባለሙሉ ሥልጣን— balämulu səlṭan-n. ambassador plenipotentiary
ኤምባሲ embasi n. embassy
አምባሻ ambašša n. flat bread (decorated)
አምባንር see አምባ
አምባዛ ambbazza n. catfish,
አምቦልክ amboləkk n. envelope also አምቦጥል and እንቦልክ
አምቦረቀቀ amboräqqäqä v.t was made to look baggily dressed
አምቦጨቦጨ ambočäbboča v.t slopped about (e.g halffull water pot)
ተምቦጫቦጨ tämbočabboča v.t slopped about

	(liquid), *also* ተንበጪ በጪ
አምታታ	see መታ
አምና	amna n. last year
አምፑል	ampul n. electric bulb
አጒሪት	see ሙዋርት
አጒ፟	am\"ašša v.t treated with oil and fat *(new clay cooking utensils)*
ተጒ፟	täm\"ašša v.i was treated *(new cooking pot, with oil)*
አምዘገዘገ	amzägäzzägä v.t flew shudderingly (*e.g spear)*
ተምዘገዘገ	tämzägäzzägä v.i was hurled shudderingly *(spear)*
አምለጪ	see ሞለጪ
አምሌ	amole n. bar of salt *(used as currency previously),* rock-salt
አምራ	amora n. bird of prey *(eagle, kite, crow etc.)*
አምቀምቀ	amoqämmoqä v.i swollen with moisture *(e.g grain) ;* was inflamed and watery *(e.g diseased eye)*
አምት	amot also ሐሞት *(hamot)* n. bile; courage
አምተቢስ	amotäbis adj.cowardly
አምት የሌ ለው	amot yälellaw adj. cowardly
አምቱ የፈ ሰሰ	amotu yäfässäsä adj. apathetic, lacking in spirit, fire
አምኘ	amoňňä v.t fooled, made a fool of, *see olso* ሞኘ
ማምኘ	mamoňňa n. placebo, means of distracting, fooling a child
አምፅ	amoč n. **arisaema**
አሠመረ	asämmärä v.t ruled *(a line);* did well, *see* ሠመረ

ማስመሪያ	masmäriya n. ruler, *(straight edge)*
አሠገመረ	asämammärä v.t drew *(several lines)* with a ruler
አሣግ	asama n. pig *(domestic)*
አሠሠ	assäsä v.i wiped round ənğara mə{ad with oil*);* swept *(an area, military)*
አሠሣ	asäsa n. sweeping *(military operation)*
ማሰሻ	massäša n.wiping cloth *(for ənğara mə{ad)*
ታሠሠ	tassäsä v.i was wiped round; was swept *(military)*
አሠረ	assärä v.t tied, tied up; imprisoned
አሣሪ	asari n. jailor
አሣር	asar n. trials, troubles, tribulation
አሣሪኘ	asaräňña adj trouble-prone
እሥረኘ	əsräňňa n. prisoner
እሥራት	əssərat n. imprisonment
እሥር	əssər n. bundle; imprisonment
—ቤት	-bet n. jail
ተሣሠረ	täsassärä v.i was entangled; was entangled with each other; had *(s/t)* in common
ታሠረ	tassärä v.i was imprisoned, tied up
ታሣሪ	tasari adj. condemned, sentenced
መታሣሪያ	mättasäriyä n. place of confinement
አሳሠረ	usassärä v.t had s/o imprisoned, had s/t, s/o tied up
አስተሣሠረ	astäsassärä v.t had *(people, things)* roped, chained together
አሠር	asär n. dregs; excrement
አሠገረ	asäggärä v.t fished; trotted *(horse, mule),* see also ሠገረ

160

አሥጋሪ asgari n. fisher-
man, also ዓሣ አሥጋሪ

ግሥጋሪያ masgäriya n. bait (for
fishing)

አረህ aräh n. spur, slope,
side of a mountain

አረሆ aräho or አረሐ aräho
n. chanteuse

አረመ arrämä v.t weeded;
corrected, marked
(e.g school exercises)

አረም aräm n. weed

አራሙቻ arramuçça n. dis-
carded weeds

አራሚ arrami n. one who
weeds; one who
corrects, marks
(papers)

እርማት ərrəmat n correction
(papers, exercises)

ታረመ tarrämä v.i was
weeded; was
corrected

ተራረመ tärarrämä v.t cor-
rected each other

አሳረመ asarrämä v.t had
(s/t) corrected; had
(s/t) weeded

አረሜኔ arämäne adj. heathen;
cruel

እረመኔነት arämänennät n.
heatheness; cruelty

አረሚ arämi ° adj. heathen,

አረማዊ arämawi n. pagan

አረረ arrärä v.i burnt black
(by cooking)

አረር arär n. bullet, ball
(of cartridge)

እራሪ ərrari n. very short
and thin person

አሳረረ asarrärä v.t caused
burn black (by
cooking)

አረሰ arräsä v.t ploughed;
tended a woman
after giving birth

አራስ aras newly born
baby

አራሽ araš n. plough-
man, farmer

እራሽ ərraš n. ploughed
land

እርሻ ərša n. farming,
tillage, agri-
culture

ማረሻ maräša n. plough

አራረስ ararräsä v.t
ploughed here and
there

ታረሰ tarräsä v.t was
ploughed; culti-
vated; was tended
(woman after
giving birth)

አሳረሰ asarräsä v.t had
(land) cultivated

አሳራሽ asarraš n. gentle-
man farmer

አስተራረሰ astärarräsä v.t
helped (s/o)
cultivate, plough

አረቀ arräqä v.t trained,
moulded (s/o's charac-
ter); straightened
out (an affair)

ታረቀ tarräqä v.i was re-
conciled; was sraight-
ened

አስታረቀ astarräqä v.t rec-
onciled

አረበደ arräbbädä v.i. busied
o/s (to curry
favour with s/o)

አረባጭ aräbbaǧ adj. n,
one who busies
himself (to curry
favour)

አርባጭ arbaǧ adj. n, (one)
who busies him-
self (to curry
favour)

ተርበደበደ tärbädäbbädä v.i
shivered with
fear

ተርበድባጭ tärbädbaǧ adj.
fearful, shaking

አረንጓደ arängʷade adj. green

አረደ arrädä v.t slaughtered

አራጭ araǧ n. slaughterer

እርድ ərd n. slaughtered
animal; turneric

ታረደ tarärdä v.i was
slaughtered

ታራጭ taraǧ n. animal
for slaughter

ተራረደ tärarrädä v.t killed
each other (with
knives, swords);

fooled, cheated each other

አሳረደ asarrädä v.t had (an animal) slaughtered

አረዳ arädda v.t broke bad news

አርኚ arǧi n. bringer of bad news

መርጃ märräǧa n. evidence, intelligence (secret information)

መርዶ märdo n. announcement of death

ተረዳ tärädda v.i was given, had bad news; was helped

አስረዳ asrädda v.t explaine' clarified, enlightened

አስረጅ asräǧǧ n. informant

ማስረጃ masräǧǧa n. evidence, proof; explanation

in **አረዳ መሬት** arädda märet cultivated land (several times)

አረጀ aräǧǧä v.i grew old

አሮጊ aroge adj. old

አሮጊት arogit old woman

እርጅና arǧanna n. old age

አስረጀ asräǧǧä v.t aged, caused to age

አረገዘ aräggäzä v.i was pregnant

እርጉዝ arguz adj. pregnant

እርግዝና argazanna n.pregnancy

ተረገዘ täräggäzä v.i grew in the womb

አስረገዘ asräggäzä v.t made s/o pregnant

አረገደ aräggädä v.i moved rhythmically, swayed (in mourning)

አርጋጅ argaǧ n. mourner(who sways rhythmically)

ማርገጃ margäǧa n. mourning area (in church yard)

አረገረገ arägärrägä v.i swayed rhythmically (priests etc.)

አረግራጊ arägragi n. swaying in rhythm

አረጋዊ arägawi n. old man. see also **አሯጊ** and **አሪጅ**

አረግ aräg n. creeper, shoot

አረጠ arräṭä v.i was sterile (human or animal)

አረጠረጠ aräṭärräṭä v.i loitered about aimlessly

አረጥራጭ araṭrač n. loiterer

አረፈ see under **ዐረፈ**

አረፈደ see **ረፈደ**

አረፉ aräfa n. froth, lather

አሪትሜቲክ aritmetik n. arithmetic

አራ arra v.t shitted, defecated, excreted (not polite)

አር ar n. shit, excrement; sediment (not polite)

አራስ aras woman in childbed

— **ልጅ** — laǧ n. newborn baby

አራት aratt adj. four

አራተኛ arattäñña adj. fourth

አራው see **አውራ**

አራጣ araṭa n. usury, unlawful interest

— **አበዳሪ** — abäddari n. usurer

አሬራ arera n. skimmed milk

አርማ arma n. badge, emblem, insignia

አርመን armän n. Armenia, Armenian

አርሲ arsi n. one of the Administrative regions, central Ethiopia (Arsi)

አርሸብ aršab or **አርሺብ** aršib n. archive

አርበኛ arbäñña n. warrior, patriot, partisan

አርበኝነት arbäññannät n.guerrilla warfare

አርባ arba adj. forty

አርባኛ arbañña adj. fortieth

አርቲቡርቲ artiburti n. hocus-pocus

አርነት arannät n. freedom

— **ወጣ** — wäṭṭa v.i became free

አርአያ ara'ya n. good example

አርአያነት ara'yannät n. good example

አርእስት	ar'əst n. title (of book etc.); headline, heading	ታሰበ	tassäbä v.i was thought—
አርከፋከፋ	arkäfäkkäfä v.t sprinkled, watered (seedlings etc.)	ታሰቦ ዋለ	tassəbo walä was commemorated
ማርከፍከፍያ	markäfkäfiya n. watering can	መታሰቢያ	mättasäbiya n. commemoration
ተከፋከፋ	tärkäfäkkäfä v.i was sprinkled, watered	ያልታሰበ	yaltassäbä adj. sudden; unexpected
አርኪዮሎጅ	arkiyoloği n. archaeology	ተሳሰበ	täsassäbä v.t made the reckoning; thought of each other
አርዘ ሊባኖስ	arzä libanos n. cedar	ተሳሳቢ	täsasabi n. creditor
አርድእት	ardə'ət n. disciples	አስተሳሰበ	astäsassäbä v.t had (s/o) made
አርጀና	arğano n. nile lizard		up the reckoning
አርገበገበ	argäbäggäbä v.t fanned o/s, waved (hand)	አሰባጠረ	(third party) assäbaṭṭärä v.t got people together;
አርገብገብ	ərgəbgəb adj. softhearted	አሰበጣጠረ	laid (s/t) crosswise assäbäṭaṭṭärä v.t
ተርገበገበ	tärgäbäggäbä v.i fluttered; was softhearted		mixed together; caused to get together
አርጋኖን	arganon n. organ (musical instrument)	አሰት	assät n. lie, falsehood also ሐሰት
አርጩሜ	arčumme n. lath, cane (for beating children)	አሰነበተ	see ሰነበተ
አርጌ	see አረጌ	አሰንክለ	see ሰነከለ
አሰላ	asälla v.i thought deeply, calculated see also ስሌት	አሰናዳ	assänadda v.t prepared (food, room, house), arranged
አሰሰ	assäsä v.t scoured the town; greased (a griddle)	አሰናጅ	assänağ n. one who prepares (s/t)
አሰሳ	ässäsa n. search	አሰነዳዳ	assänädadda v.t busied o/s with preparation, arrangement
አሰረ	see አሥረ	ተሰናዳ	täsänadda v.i was arranged, prepared
አሰበ	assäbä v.i thought, calculated	መሰናዶ	mässänado n. preparation, arrangement
አሳቢ	assabi adj. thoughtful, considerate	ተሰነዳዳ	täsänädadda v.i was arranged, prepared; got ready
አሳብ	assab n. thought		
—የለሽ	—yälläš adj. inconsiderate; devil-may-care	አሰኘ	assäññä v.i (used. with pronominal suffix) felt the urge to do s/t; e.g ወደ ቤት
ሒሳብ	hisab n. arithmetic, calculation bill (e.g in restaurant)	መሄድ አሰኘኝ	mäyhed assäññäññ I feel going home
አሳሰበ	asassäbä v.t reminded (s/o)	ተሰኘ	täsäññä v.i was named, called
አሳሳቢ	asassabi n. reminder, one who reminds; adj. critical, serious	ኡሰገገ	see ሰገገ
—ጉዳይ	—gudday serious matter	አሰጣ	asäṭṭa v.t spread out in sun (grain, clothes

163

ስጥ   etc. to dry)
səṭ n. s/t spread
out to dry

ግስጫ   masča n. place or
thing where s/t is
spread out to dry

አሰፈሰፈ   asäfässäfä v.i was
ravenous, anxious
to have (s/t)

አሰፍሳፊ   asäfsafi adj. ravenous, over-eager

አሱ   see ሱፉ
አሲድ   asid n. acid
አሲዳም   asidam adj. quickly
used up; insubstan-
tial

አሳለፈ   asalläfä v.t let (s/t)
pass by, see አለፈ

አሳማ   asama n. pig
ያሳማ ሥጋ   yasama səga n.
pork

አሳረረ   asarrärä v.t caused
to be burned black,
see. አረረ

አሳሰበ   see አሰበ
አሳሳ   see ሣሣ
አሳቀ   see ሣቀ
አሳሳቀ   see ሣቀ
አሰቀቀ   see ሰቀቀ
አሳበረ   see ሰበረ
አሳበቀ   see ሰበቀ
አሳበበ   see ሰበብ
አሳነስ   see አነሰ
አሳንሰር   asansär n. elevator, lift
አሳከረ   see ሰከረ
አሳዘነ   see አዘነ
አሳደረ   see አደረ
አሳጣ   assaṭṭa v.t betrayed
(confidence, friend-
ship, trust etc.)

አሳጪ   assači n. one who
betrays (confidence,
trust, friendship etc.)

አሴረ   see ሴራ
አስ—   as—(gram.) causative
pref.

አስመጣ   see መጣ
አስማ   asma n. asthma
አስማት   asmat n. spell, witchcraft, sorcery

አስማተኛ   asmatäñña n. master
of spells, sorcerer

አስረከበ   asräkkäbä v.t delivered, handed over

አስረካቢ   asräkkabi n. deliverer
ተረከበ   täräkkäbä v.i received
ተረካቢ   täräkkabi n. one who
receives, receiver

ተረካከበ   täräkakkäbä v.t
handed over (post,
keys, equipment
etc.)

ተረካካቢ   täräkakabi n. par-
ticipants in a hand-
over

አረካከበ   arräkakkäbä v.i took
part in hand-over

አረካካቢ   arräkakabi n. par-
ticipant in hand-over

ርከከብ   rəkəkkəb n. process
of handing-over

አስቀረ   see ቀረ
አስተማረ   astämarä v.t. taught
see also ተማረ

አስተማሪ   astämari n. teacher,
instructor

ማስተማሪያ   mästämariya n.
teaching aid, place

አስተባበለ   see አበለ
አስተናገደ   astänaggädä v.t. entertained (guests);
treated (customers)

አስተናጋጅ   astänagaǧ n. steward,
host, hostess

አስተናበረ   astänabbärä v.t. looked
after (guests)

አስታረቀ   see *አረቀ
አስተዋለ   astäwalä v.i. paid attention, took note of

አስተዋይ   astäway adj. wise,
intelligent, thought-
ful, observant,
prudent

አስታወሰ   astawwäsä v.t. remembered

ማስታወሻ   mastawäša n. mem-
orandum; remem-
brance; note

አስታጎለ   astaggu°älä v.i. hindered
interrupted

አስከረን   askären n. corpse, body
ያስከረን ሳጥን   yaskären saṭən n.
coffin

አስኮነነ   see ኮነነ
አስኳል   ask°al n. yolk
አስወደደ   see ወደደ
አስደረገ   asdärrägä v.t. had
(s/t) made, see

164

እስደራጊ

አስገባ

አስገነዘበ

አስገኘ

አስገኚ

አስፋልት
አሶመሰመ

አሶሙ ዒ ሚ

አሸ

ማሻ

አሻሸ

አሽታ

ታሸ

መታሻ

ተሻሸ

አሳሸ

አስተሻሸ

አሸመ

አሸም

ታሸመ

አሸረጠ

አደረጊ and *ደረጊ
asdärragi n. one who
has s/t made
see ገባ
asgänäzzäbä v.t. made
s/o understand;
called attention to
asgäññä v.t. discovered
caused to be found,
see also አገኘ
asgäñi n. discoverer,
finder
asfalt n. asphalt
asomässomä v.i cantered
(a horse), see also
*ሰመሰመ
asomsuʷami adj.
cantering
aššä v.t rubbed
massaged, kneaded;
rubbed between
the palms (i.e grain)
maša n: kneading
trough; embro-
cation, balm
ašaššä v.t rubbed
lightly, a little ˗
aššəta n. physio-
therapy
taššä v.i was
rubbed, massaged
kneaded; was
sluggish in work
mättaša n. oint-
ment, balm (for
rubbing into skin)
täšaššä v.t snuggled
up to; brushed
against
asaššä v.t had
s/o rubbed,
massaged
astäšaššä v.t brought
close to each other
aššämä v.t trimmed
(hair) perfectly
əššəm adj. perfectly
trimmed (e.g Afro
hair style)
taššämä v.i was
perfectly trimmed
ašärräţä v.t hitched
up (i.e towel round

waist), see also
ሸርጥ
ašär bašär adj. poor
(food)
aššäbbärä v.t caused
panic, disturbance,
terrorized see also
ሸብር
aššabbari n. one
who causes uproar.
disturbance
ašäbärräqä v.i was
decorated, adorned
up (person)
ašäbäššäbä v.t swayed
(priests in ritual
dancing)
ašäbšabi n. one who
sways gracefully
(priestly dance)
ašätä v.i began to
ripen, was nearly
ripe (just edible)
əšät n. unripe form
(peas, bean etc.)
see ሸተተ
aššännäfä or አቸነፈ
aččännäfä v.i/t.
beat, won, triumph-
hed over, was vic-
torious, conquered
aššännafi n. winner
täšännäfä v.i was
beaten, lost (game
etc.), was conquered
täšännafi n. loser,
defeated (one)
täšänannäfä v.t beat
each other
ašänkətab n. amulet
ašända n. gargoyle,
rainspout; drinking
trough (animals)
ašäwa n. sand
ašäwamma adj. sandy
ašäwannät n.
sandiness
aššägä v.t packed:
sealed
əššəg adj. sealed;
packed up

ኧሻር ባሻር

አሸበረ

አሸባሪ

አሸበረቀ

አሸበሸበ

አሸብሻቢ

አሸተ

እሸት

አሸተተ
አሸነፈ

አሸናፊ
ተሸነፈ

ተሸናፊ

ተሸናነፈ

አሸንከታብ
አሸንዳ

አሸዋ
አሸዋማ
አሸዋነት

አሸገ

እሸግ

ግሽገያ	*maššägiya* n. glue, tape, paper etc. (used for packing)
ታሽገ	*taššägä* v.i was sealed, packed up
አሳሽገ	*asaššägä* v.t had (s/t) sealed wrapped up, packed
አሽጋሽገ	*aššägaššägä* v.t packed (s/t) closer, closed up (ranks. people etc.)
ተሽጋሽገ	*täšägaššägä* v.t was packed up closer
አሹራ	*ašura* n. land sale tax
አሻራ	*ašara* n. fingerprint
የራስ—	*yäras-*n. light curls
የጅ—	*yägg̈-*n. lines (of palm of hand)
አሻለ	*aššalä* v.t improved, ameliorated see also *ሻለ
አሻሻለ	*aššašalä* v.t improved ameliorated
አሻቀበ	*ašaqqäbä* or አሸቀበ *ašäqqäbä* v.t went uphill, upwards
ሽቅብ	*šəqqəb* adj. uphill, upwards
አሻንጉሊት	*ašangullit* n. doll
አሻፈረኝ	*ašaffäräññ* excl. definitely no; definitely not
አሽሙር	*ašmur* n. veiled insult
አሽሙረኛ	*ašmuräñña* n. one who gives a veiled insult
አሽሟጠጠ	*ašmʷaṭṭäṭä* v.t insulted tacitly, criticised (esp. behind s/o's back)
አሽሟጣጭ	*ašmʷaṭačč* n. one who criticises, insults (especially in a hidden way or behind s/o' back); point of curved sword; decorative ball on scabbard tip
አሽሟጣ ጭነት	*ašmʷaṭačənnät* n. veiled criticism
አሽቀነጠረ	*ašqänäṭṭärä* v.t thrust aside

ተሽቀነጠረ	*täšqänäṭṭärä* v.i was thrust aside
አሽቆለቆለ	see አቆለቆለ
አሽበለበለ	*ašbäläbbälä* v.t tumbled over, rolled away (e.g whirlwind)
ተሽበለበለ	*täšbäläbbälä* v.i was whirled away, rolled away
አሽከረከረ	*aškäräkkärä* v.t bowled along (e.g child's hoop or wheel). drove (vehicle)
አሽከርካሪ	*aškärkari* n. driver; one who bowls. (hoop etc.)
(እ)ሽክርክ ሪት	*(ə)škərkərit* n. hoop (child's)
ተሽከረከረ	*täškäräkkärä* v.i was rolled, bowled along.
ተሽከርካሪ	*täškärkari* n. vehicle; s/t which is rolled along
አሽከር	*aškär* n. servant (male)
አሽከርነት	*aškärənnät* n. domestic service
አሽካካ	*aškakka* v.t clucked (laying hen)
አሽካኪ	*aškaki* adj. clucking (hen)
አሽኮረመመ	*aškorämmämä* v.t flirted with, courted, made up to
አሽኮርማሚ	*aškormami* n. flirt
ተሽኮረመመ	*täškorämmämä* v.t was seductive, agreeable to flirtation, coy
ተሽኮርማሚ	*täškormami* adj. coy, flirtatious
አሽጓጠጠ	*ašgʷaṭṭäṭä* also አንጓጠጠ *angʷaṭṭäṭä* v.i was uncouth, vulgar (in expression or speech)
አሾለ	*ašolä* v.t sharpened, made tapered, see also ሾለ
አፉን—	*afun –* v.i was over-talkative
አሾለቀ	*ašolläqä* v.i peeped at, round, through
አሾላቂ	*ašollaqi* n. peeper
ማሾለቂያ	*mašolläqiya* n. peep-hole

አሾለከ *see* ሾለከ

አሾቀ *ašoqä* v.t parboiled and sauted *(peas, beans etc.)*

አሹቅ *ašuq* n. sauted and parboiled *(beans etc.)*

አሾከሾከ *ašokäššokä* v.t gossipped against *(s/o)*

አሾክሿኪ *ašokšʷaki* n. gossipper

አሾፈ *ašofä* v.t mocked, laughed at

አሿፊ *ašʷafi* n. mocker

አቀለለ *see* ቀለለ

አቀለጠ *see* ቀለጠ

አቀላጠፈ *see* ቀለጠፈ

አቀመሰ *see* ቀመሰ

አቀማጠለ *aqqämaṭṭälä* v.t entertained royally, mangnificently

ቅምጥል *qəməṭṭəl* adj. treated lavishly, indulged

ተቀማጠለ *täqämaṭṭälä* v.i was entertained royally, lavishly

አቀረሸ *aqäräššä* v.t brought up *(vomitted a little, e.g babies)*

ቅርሻት *qəršat* n. vomit *(of children, small amount)*

አቀረቀረ *aqäräqqärä* v.t lowered one's gaze, looked away, bowed one's head

አቀረበ *see* ቀረበ

አቀበለ *aqäbbälä* v.t passed to *(s/o)*

ቅበላ *qəbbäla* n. Shrove Tuesday

ቅብብሎሽ *qəbəbbəloš* n. playing at "catch," playing ball

አቀባይ *aqäbbay* n. one who passes *(s/t)* to s/o

አቀባበለ *aqäbabbälä* v.t cocked *(fire-arm)*

ተቀበለ *täqäbbälä* v.t received

ተቀባይ *täqäbbay* n. recipient

ተቀባበለ *täqäbabbälä* v.t passed around, passed hand to hand, passed to each other

አስቀበለ *asqäbbälä* v.t had *(s/o)* receive *(s/t)*

አቀነበጠ *aqänäbbäṭä* v.t threw out shoots *(plant), see also* ቀንበጥ

አቀና *aqänna* v.t straightened developed *(barren country); see also* ቀና

አቅኚ *aqñi* n. settler, developer *(of land country);* seller of grain *(usu. farmer)*

አቃና *aqqanna* v.t straightened

አቀናበረ *aqqänabbärä* v.t compiled *(literature);* edited texts into one *see also* ቀነበረ

አቀናባሪ *aqqänabari* n. literary editor, compiler

አቀነባበረ *aqänäbabbärä* v.t compiled, edited, *see also* ቀነበረ

አቀነባባሪ *aqqänäbabari* n. compiler

አቀፈ *aqqäfä* v.t embraced; cradled *(a child in the arms);* brooded *(hen)*

ዓለም አቀፍ *aläm aqqäf* adj. international

አቃፊ *aqafi* adj. embracing

እቅፍ *əqqəf* n. bundle *(sticks, hay, grass)*

ያበባ— *yabäba*–n. bunch of flowers

ማቀፊያ *maqäfiya* n. swaddling cloth, *(for child)*

ታቀፈ *taqqäfä* v.t cradled *(a child in o/s arms);* held, caught *(s/t)* in o/s arms

መታቀፊያ *mätaqäfiya* n. swaddling cloth, shawl *(for child)*

ተቃቀፈ *täqaqqäfä* v. t embraced each other

አሳቀፈ *asaqqäfä* v.t gave a hen eggs to hatch

አስታቀፈ *astaqqäfä* v.t gave child to *(s/o)* to

	mind, hold
አቈግዳ	aqumada also አቅግዳ aqmada n. leather grain bag
አቃሬ	aqarä v.i (usu. with pron. suffic) had indigestion, see also ቃሬ
አቃሰተ	aqassätä v.i groaned, moaned (with pain); puffed, panted (due to over weight)
አቃቂር	aqaqir n. criticism, review (of a book)
—ማውጣት	- mawțat to criticize to (find fault with)
አቃተ	aqatä v.t (usu. with pron. suffix) become difficult e.g መራመድ አቃተው märramäd aqatäw he could not walk
አቃጠረ	ḋqqațțärä v.t pimped acted as a pimp,
አቃጣሪ	aqqațari n. pimp
ተቃጠሬ	täqațțärä v.i had an appointment
አቃጨለ	aqaččälä or አንቃጨለ anqaččälä v.t rang (handbell), see also ቃጭል
አቄለ	aqelä v.t treated (s/o) like a fool, see also ቄል
አቄመ	aqemä v.i had a grudge, see also ቂም
አቅለሸለሸ	aqläšälläšä v.i felt sick (nauseous), naʋsiated
አቅለሸላሸ	aqläšlaš adj. causing one to feel sick
አቅማማ	aqmamma v.i felt un-certain, hesitated
አቅማሚ	aqmami adj. un-certain, hesitant
አቅጣጫ	aqțačča or አግጣጫ agțačča n. direction (towards s/t)
አቆለቆለ	aqoläqqolä v.t went down-hill
አቆላለፈ	aqqolalläfä v.t en-tangled, see also ቆለፈ
አቆላመጠ	aqqolammäța v.t flattered

ቆልማጫ	qulmačča n flattery
አቆላማች	aqolamać n. flatterer
አቆመ	aqomä v.t halted (s/t, s/o), erected (s/t), made (s/o, s/t) to stand up, see also ቆመ
አቆጠቆጠ	aqoțäqqoäța v.i de-veloped shoots (plant), sprouted; took successfully
አቆራኘ	aqqoäraññä v.t tied (prisoner to guard)
ተቆራኘ	täqoraññä v.i. was tied (prisoner to guard)
አቋረጠ	aqq"arräța v.t inter-rupted; disturbed; made a short-cut, see ቋረጠ
አቋራጭ	aq"arać n/adj. (one) who interrupts; disturbs
—መንገድ	—mängäd n. a short-cut
እገር—	agär—n. globe-trotter
ማቋራጫ	maqq"aräča n. a short-cut
ተቋረጠ	täq"arräța v.i was stopped; was dis-continued
ሥራ—	səra - v.t undertook a contract
ተቋራጭ	täq"arać n. contractor
የሥራ—	yäsəra-- n. contractor
አቋቋመ	aqq"aq"amä v.t. estab-lished, set up; instituted; attended memorial, christening service, see ቆመ
አቋቋሚ	aqq"aq"ami n/adj. (one) who estab-lishes, sets up, institutes
ተቋቋመ	täq"aq"amä v.i was established, set up, instituted; was on firm grounds (business)
አበላ	abbälä v.i. told lies;

168

አባይ denied
አባይ abay n. liar
አባይነት abuyənnät n. untruthfulness

ታበለ tabbälä v.i. was denied
አስተባበለ astäbabbälä v.t. denied, declared untrue, rejected
አስተባባይ astäbabay n. one who denies s/t
ማስተባበያ mästäbabäya n. disclaimer

አበል aball n. stipend, salary, allowance, see also በላ
የውሎ— yäwəlo— n. per diem, also የቀን አበል
የጡረታ— yäturätä— n. pension, social security

አበረ abbärä v.t collaborated stood with; conspired against
in ግብረ አበር gəbrä abbär collaborator, accomplice

አባሪ abari n. enclosure (s/t enclosed), attachment (document)

አብሮ abro adv. together, along with
ተባበረ täbabbärä v.i. was united, cooperated, allied oneself, joined forces
ተባባሪ täbabari adj. cooperative, associate
ትብብር təbəbbər n. cooperation, coordination
አስተባበረ astäbabbärä v.t. co-ordinated
አስተባባሪ astäbabari n. coordinator

አበሰ abbäsä v.t. wiped, cleaned (with a rag)
አበሰረ abässärä v.t. announced good news, heralded
ብስራት bəsrat n. good news
አበሳ abäsa n. sin; misfor-

tune
አበባ abäbä v.i. blossomed flowered, bloomed
አበባ abäba n. flower, bloom
—ጎመን —gommän n. cauliflower
አበባማ abäbamma adj.flowery (full of flowers)
ያበባ ማስ yabäba masqämmäča n. vase
ቀመሟ
እቅፍ አበባ əqqəf abäba n. bouquet
አበባ ጉንጉን abäba gungun n. garland, wreath

አበጀ abäǧǧä v.t mended repaired, did well see also በጀ
አበጃጀ abäǧaǧǧä v.t. put in order; repaired, mended

አበጋዝ abägaz n. Ethiopian title (leader)
የጦር— yäṭor— n. war leader
አበጠ ιοιäṭä v.i was swollen
እበጥ əbäṭ n. swelling
እባጭ əbbač n. swelling
እብጠት əbṭät n. swelling
አባጣ abaṭa adj. swollen
—ጎባጣ —gobaṭa n. uneven land, broken ground, undulating (land)

አባበጠ ababbäṭä v.t. got slightly swollen
አሳበጠ asabbäṭä v.t. made (s/t) swell
አበጠረ abäṭṭärä v.t. combed; winnowed, see በጠረ

አበጣሪ abäṭṭari n. winnower
ማበጠሪያ mabäṭṭäriya n. comb; winnowing basket
አበጣጠረ abäṭaṭṭärä v.t. combed slightly
አስበጠረ asbäṭṭärä v.t. had (s/o) comb; winnow
ተበጠረ täbäṭṭärä v.i. was combed; was winnowed
ተበጣጠረ täbäṭaṭṭärä v.i. combed each other's hair
ብጣሪ bäṭṭari n. chaff

አቡን abun n. bishop, arch-bishop, patriarch (title of respect given to such people)

አቡጃዲ abuǧädid n. cotton (cloth), calico

አቡጊዳ abugida n. alphabet

አባ abba n. title of respect given to priests, monks

አባወራ abba wärra n. husband

አባጩንሬ abba ǧäggʷarre n. caterpillar (insect)

አባል abat n. member (of group, committee etc.)

አባለዘር abaläzär n. sperm; genital organ

አባልነት abaiәnnät n. member-ship

አባረረ abbarrärä v.t drove away, see also በረረ

አባራሪ abbarari adj/n. (one) who drives s/o away

አባራ abarra v.i stopped raining

አባበለ ababbälä v.t cajoled

አባባይ ababay adj/n. (one) who cajoles

አባባ see ባባ

አባባ abbaba interj. father! daddy!

አባት abbat n. father

ክርስትና— kәrәstәnna – n. God Father cf. ክርስትና እናት

ጡት— ṭut – n. adoptive father

የእንጀራ— yä'әnǧära—n. step father

አባከነ abakkänä v.t squan-dered, wasted, see also ባከነ

አባካኝ abakañ adj. squan-derer, wasteful

አባይ abaya adj. slothful, sluggardly

አባዬ abbayye interj. father! daddy !

አቤት abet interj. yes! yes sir !

አቤቱታ abetuta n. complaint, appeal (to superior)

አብረቀረቀ abräqärräqä v.i sparked;

shone, became luminous, see ባረቀ

አብረቅራቂ abräqraqi adj. spark-ling, luminous

አብሲት absit n. proving dough

—መጣል —mäṭal inf. to make proving dough

አብሶ abәso adj. especially

አብሽ abәš n. fenugreek

አብቃቃ see በቃ

አብነት abәnnät n. example

አቧለተ abuʷallätä v.i made jokes, see also ቧልት

አቦሬ abore n. gourd, water scoop

—አፍ —af adj. wide-mouthed

አቦካ see ቦካ

አቧራ abʷara n. dust

አቧራማ abʷaramma adj. dusty

አቦሻምኔ abbošämmane n. chee-tah, also ወቦሻምኔ

አተላ atäla n. sediment (in beer), lees, dregs

አተመ attämä v.t stamped; printed

አታሚ attami n. printer

እትም әttәm n. printing; issue (magazine etc.), edition

ማተሚያ mattämiya n. printing device, machine

—ቤት —bet n. printing press

ማኅተም mahәtäm n. seal, rubber stamp

አሳተመ asattämä v.t had (s/t) printed, stamped

አሳታሚ asattami n. publisher

ማሳተሚያ masattämiya n. print-ing cost

ታተመ tattämä v.i was stamped; printed

አተመታተመ atämättämä v.t scooped up (with bread), see also ተመታመሰ

ማተምተሚያ matämtämiya n. ground red pepper

አተራመሰ attärammäsä v.t threw into disorder, messed up; disturbed (people)

ትርምስ tәrәmmәs n. dis-turbance, disorder, chaos

170

አተራማሽ	*attäramaš* n. disturber
አተC	*atär* pea
አኩሪ—	*akuri—* n. soya bean
አተበ	*attäbä* v.t cut the ambilical cord
አታቢ	*attabi* n. one who cuts the ambilical cord *(professional)*
እትብት	*ətəbt* n. ambilical cord
እትብቱ የተቀበረበት	*ətəbtu yätäqäbbäräbbät* n. one's birthplace
አተተ	*attätä* v.i discussed at length
አተታ	*atäta* n. discussion *(lengthy)*
ታተተ	*tattätä* v.i was discussed at length
አተኮረ	*atäkkorä* v.t stared fixedly, gazed at
አታለለ	*attallälä* v.t deceived, cheated
አታላይ	*attalay* swindler, cheater, cheat
አታሞ	*atamo* n. small drum
አቴና	*atena* n. rush matting
አትሮንስ	*atronəs* n. bookstand, lectern
አቶ	*ato* n. Mr.
አቶሰቶሰ	*atosätosä* v. was inquisitive, interfering
ቶስቷሳ	*tostʷassa* adj. inquisitive, interfering
አቶስቷሽ	*atostʷaš* adj. inquisitive, interfering
አቻ	*ačča* adj. peer, of the same rank, of the same status
—ለአቻ	*—lä'ačča* matching pair, equals
አቻምና	*aččaməna* year before last *also* ሀቻምና
አገዜ ዓለም	*ahaze aläm* adj. all-powerful *(God)*
አነሳ	*anässa* v.t took up, lifted; withdrew *(a charge);* was very absorbent *(grain for brewing)*
ፎቶግራፍ አንሺ	*fotograf anši* n. photographer
—ማንሻ	*—marša* n. camera
ማንሻ	*manša* n. lifting

	device
አነሣሣ	*annäsassa* v.t encouraged, incited to action, inspired confidence in. *see also* ተነሣሣ
አነሣሽ	*annäsaš* n/adj. *(one)* who encourages, incites to action, inspires confidence in
አነC	*anär* n. stray, wild cat, serval
አነሰ	*annäsä* v.i diminished; became smaller; was reduced, *see also* ትንሽ
አነስተኛ	*anästäñña* adj. medium, rather small
አሳነሰ	*asannäsä* v.t made smaller, reduced
አነቀ	*annäqä* v.t choked, strangled
ማነቆ	*manäqo* n. **drawback,** stumbing-block
ታነቀ	*tannäqä* v.i was choked, strangled, hanged oneself
አሳነቀ	*asannäqä* v.t had *(s/o)* choked, strangled
ተናነቀ	*tänannäqä* v.t gripped at each other
እንባ ተና ነቀው	*ənba tänannäqäw* v.t was in melting mood
ትንቅንቅ	*tənəqnəq* n. struggle, fight
አነቀፈ	*anäqqäfä or* አደናቀፈ *addänaqqäfä* v.t caused *(s/o)* to stumble
አንቃፊ	*anqafi* n. stumbling-block
እንቅፋት	*ənqəfat* n. stumbling-block
አነቃ	*anäqqa* v.t awoke, wake *(s/o)* up, *see also* ነቃ
አንቂ	*anqi* adj/n *(one)* who awakes; stimulant; refreshing
ማንቂያ	*manqiya* n. stimulant; refreshing

አነቃቃ annäqaqqa v.t stirred (s/o) into action

አነቃቂ annäqaqi n. (s/t), (s/o) that stirs to action

ማነቃቂያ mannäqaqiya n. means of stirring (s/o) up

አነፀረ anäqq^wärä v.t plucked out (eye, boil etc.)

አነበበ anäbbäbä v.t read, see also ነበበ

አንባቢ anbabi adj/n. (one) who reads, reader

ምንባብ mənbab n. passage (of reading)

አነባበበ anäbabbäbä v.t read a few lines

አናባቢ annababi n. vowel

ማናባቢያ mannababiya n. vowel

አስነበበ asnäbbäbä v.t had (s/o) read

ተነበበ tänäbbäbä v.i was read

ተነባቢ tänäbbabi n. consonant

ተናበበ tänabbäbä v.t followed a reading (for comparison)

ተናባቢ tänabbabi adj. compounded (word)

አነበነበ anäbännäbä v.t murmmured

አነብናቢ anäbnabi adj/n. (one) who murmurs

አነባበረ annäbabbärä v.t superimposed

አነባበሮ annäbababro n. əňǧära sandwich

ተነባበረ tänäbabbärä v.i was superimposed

አነባ anäbba v.t wept

እንባ ənba or አምባ əmba n. tears

—አድርቅ —adrəq n. hypocritical mourner

አነከሰ anäkkäsä v.i limped

አንካሳ ankassa adj. limping

አንካሴ ankasse n. stick with pointed metal end

ማንከሻ mankäša n. stick to support a limp

አነካከሰ anäkakkäsä v.t limped slightly

አስነከሰ asnäkkäsä v.t made (s/o) limp

አነከተ anäkkätä v.t broke; ate up voraciously, cf. ነከተ

አነካከተ anäkakkätä v.t broke into pieces

ኡነኩረ anäkk^wärä n. broke up (cake, pancake etc. in pan)

እንኩሮ ənk^wuro n. flour mix (for brewing)

ማንኩርያ mank^wäriya n. stirring stick (for brewing flour)

አነኩተ änäkk^wätä v.t roasted beans, peas etc. (in shell)

እንኩቶ ənk^wəto n. roasted beans, peas etc. (in shell); riff-raff

ተነኩተ tänäkk^wätä v.i was roasted (in shell)

አነወረ anäwwärä v.t blamed

ነወር näwər n. indecency

አስነወረ asnäwwärä v.t, was indecent, impolite

አስነዋሪ asnäwwari n. indecency; impoliteness

አነዘረ anäzzärä v.i became numb, cramped, see also ነዘረ

አነደደ anäddädä v.i burned (s/t); lit, see also ነደደ

አነገሠ anäggäsä v.t crowned as king, see also ነገሠ

አነገበ anäggäbä v.t carried on one's shoulder

አንጋቢ angabi adj./n. (one) who carries (s/t) on his shoulder

እንገብ əngəb n. s/t carried on one's shoulder

አነገተ anäggätä v.t carried on one's shoulder, round one's neck, see አንገት

አንጋች angač n. bodyguard

ማንገቻ mangäča n. shoulder-strap

አስነገተ asnäggätä v.t had s/o shoulder (s/t)

ተነገተ tänäggätä v.i was

172

አነጉረ shouldered.
anäggʷärä v.t refined (butter)

ንጉር *nəgwər* adj. refined (butter)

ተነጉረ *tänäggʷärä* v.i was refined

አነጉተ *anäggʷätä* v.t baked small *ənǧära* (e.g for child)

እንጉቻ *əngʷäčča* n. small *ənǧära*

አነጠ *annäṭä* v.t did carpentry

አናጢ *anaṭi* n. carpenter

አናጢነት *anaṭinnät* n. wood work

አሳነጠ *asannäṭä* v.t had some carpentry done; had s/o build (house)

ታነጠ *tannäṭä* v.i was built

አነጠረ *anäṭṭärä* v.t refined; bounced (ball), see also ነጠረ

አንጣሪ *anṭari* adj/n. (one) who refines; works metal

ብር *bərr-* n. silver smith

ወርቅ— *wärq-* n. gold smith

አንጠራኛ *anṭäränña* n. -smith

ማንጠሪያ *mänṭäriya* n. refining device

አነጠሰ *anäṭṭäsä* v.i sneezed

አነጠነጠ *anäṭännäṭä* v.i showed thriving health (person)

አነጠፈ *anäṭṭäfä* v. spread carpet (on floor); made up a bed, see also ነጠፈ

ንጣፍ *nəṭaf* n. floor-covering

አንጣፊ *anṭafi* n. master of the Bedchamber

ምንጣፍ *mənṭaf* n. carpet

አነጣጠፈ *anäṭaṭṭäfä* v.t had rugs etc. spread about

አስነጠፈ *asnäṭṭäfä* v.t had s/o lay carpet

አናጠፈ *annaṭṭäfä* v.t helped (s/o) to spread carpets, make up beds

ተነጠፈ *tänäṭṭäfä* v.t was spread (with carpets); was made up (bed)

አነጣ *anäṭṭa* v.t whitened see also ነጣ

አነጣጠረ *annäṭaṭṭärä* v.i aimed at (target); made a comparison, also አነጻጸረ

አነጣጣሪ *annäṭaṭari* n. marksman

አነጻ see አነጠ

አነጻ *anäṣṣa* v.t. cleaned. see also ነጻ

አነጻጸረ *annäṣaṣṣärä* v.t compared also አነጣጠረ

ተነጻጸረ *tänäṣaṣṣärä* v.i was compared

ተነጻጻሪ *tänäṣaṣari* adj comparable

አነፈረ *anäffärä* v.t over-cooked, over boiled, see also ነፈረ

አነፈሰ *anäffäsä* v.t winnowed, see also ነፈሰ

አንፉሽ *anfaš* adj/n (one) who winnows

አነፈረቀ *anäfärräqä* see ነፈረቀ

አነፈነፈ *anafännäfä* v.i sniffed, nosed about (of dog)

አናረ *annarä* see ናረ

አናበበ *annabbäbä* v.t made a comparative reading; acted as a vowel see ነበበ

አናት *anat* n. head, top, summit of. ቀንጮ

አናከ *annakka* v.t caused (s/o) to be contaminated see ነካ

አናዘዘ *annazzäzä* v.t took (s/o's) will, see also ተናዘዘ

አናዛዥ *annazaž* adj/n (one) who takes (s/o's) will

ተናዘዘ *tänazzäzä* v.i made one's will

ተናዛዥ *tänazaž* adj/n (one) who makes his will

ኑዛዜ *nuzaze* n. will (before — death)

ቃለ *qalä*—n. testament (document of one's will)

አናደደ	annaddädä v.t vexed, enraged, maddened see ነደደ	
እናዳጅ	annadag̃ adj/n. (one, s/t) that causes rage	
ተናደደ	tänaddädä v.i was vexed, maddened	
ተናዳጅ	tänadag̃ adj/n one who is easily enraged, vexed	
አናገወ	annaggäsä v.t exaggerated, see also ነገወ	
እናጋሽ	annagaš adj/n (one) who exaggerates	
ተናገወ	tänaggäsä v.i was exaggerated	
አናገረ	nagggarä v.t made s/o speak ; talked to s/o, gave s/o an audience; had (s/o) on see ነገረ	
አናጋ	annagga v.t shook (upset); disrupted	
አናጊ	annagi adj/n (one) who shakes. disrupts	
ተናጋ	tänagga v.i was shaken, disrupted	
አናጠረ	anaṭṭärä v.i acted flamboyantly see also ነጠረ	
አናጠበ	annaṭṭäbä v.t thwarted, frustrated; hindered	
አናፋ	anaffa v.t brayed, (donkey), made a strident noise, see ነፋ	
አን—	an—pref. of active verb	
አንስታይ ጾታ	anəstay ṣota n. female gender	
አንሻተተ አንሻታች ተንሻተተ ተንሻታች	anšattätä v.i slipped anšatač adj. slippery tänšattätä v.i slipped tänšatač adj. slipping	
አንቀላፋ እንቅልፍ እንቅልፋም	anqälaffa v.i fell asleep ənqəlf n. sleep ənqəlfam adj. sleepy; inactive	
አንቀልባ	anqälba n. small leather for carrying infants on the back	
አንቀሳቀሰ	anqäsaqqäsä v.t set (s/t) into motion; reactivated; moved, see also ቀሰቀሰ	
አንቀሳቃሽ	anqäsaqaš adj/n	

		one who moves, sets into motion; reactivates
ማንቀሳቀሻ	manqäsaqäša n. means for setting (s/t) into motion	
ተንቀሳቀሰ	tänqäsaqqäsä v.i moved; was set into motion ; was reactivated	
ተንቀሳቃሽ	tänqäsaqaš adj. moving ; movable, mobile	
አንቀጠቀጠ	anqäṭäqqäṭä v.t caused to tremble; frightened quivered	
ነንቀጥቃጭ	anqäṭqač adj. shaking; frightening; quivering	
ተንቀጠቀጠ	tänqäṭäqqäṭä v.i trembled ; was frightened	
ተንቀጥቃጭ	tänqäṭqač adj. shaking; quivering	
ቀጥቃጣ	qäṭqaṭa adj. coward; fearful; stingy, miserly	
አንቀጽ	anqäṣ n. verb ; paragraph	
ርእሰ—	rə'əsä—n. editorial (newspaper)	
ቀዳማይ—	qädamay—n. perfect (verb)	
ካልአይ —	kalə'ay—n. imperfect (verb)	
ሣልሳይ—	saləsay—n. subjunctive (verb)	
ትእዛዝ—	tə'əzaz—n. imperative (verb)	
ንዑስ—	nə'us—n. infintive (verb)	
ቦዝ—	boz—n. gerund	
አንቃር	anqar n. soft palate	
አንቆረቆረ	anqoräqqorä poured water in a thin stream	
ማንቆርቆሪያ	manqorqoria n. pitcher	
አንባሪ	anbäri n. whale	
ዓሣ—	asa—n. whale	
አንበሳ	anbässa n. lion	
አንበጣ	anbäṭa n. locust	
አንቢተረ	anbu"aṭṭärä v.t splashed	
አንተ	antä pron. (you sing.m.)	
አንተላከሰ	antälakkäsä v.t muddled through, did one's job slovenly	

አንተገተገ	*antägättägä* v.t burnt brightly; glittered
አንቱ	*antu* pron. you *(poli e)*
አንቱታ	*antuta* n. addressing in a polite form
አንቴና	*antena* n. antenna
አንቺ	*anči* pron. you *(f.)*
አንቺዬ	*ančiyye* pron. you! *(f. exclamatory)*
አንከራተተ	*ankärattätä* v.t. made to wander from place to place
አንከረፈፈ	*änkäraffäfä* v.t. carried *(s/t)* slugishly, awkwardly, clumsily
ከርፋፋ	*kärfaffa* adj. sluggish, awkward, clumsy
ተንከረፈፈ	*tänkäraffäfä* v.t. behaved slugishly, awkwardly, clumsily
አንከበከበ	*ankäbäkkäbä* or አንከበ ከበ *ankäbakkäbä* v.t. handled carefully, affectionately, kindly, cherished *(treat with affection)*, took under one's wings see *ከበ ከበ
እንክብካቤ	*ənkəbəkkabe* n. careful handling, fostering
ተንከባከበ	*tänkäbakkäbä* v.i. fostered, cherished *(treated with affection)*; took care of
አንካላ	*ənkalla* adj. lame *(person)*, one who limps
አንካሴ	*ankasse* n. stick *(with pointed metal end)*, see also አነከሰ
አንኮላ	*ankola* n. large drinking vessel made of gourd ; adj. fool, moron
አንኳር	*ankʷar* n. cube *(of sugar)* lump *(of sugar)*
አንኳኳ	*ankuʷakkuʷa* v.t. tapped at, knocked
አንዞቀዘቀ	*anžaqäžžäqä* v.t. made to gush, run freely *(liquid)*, emitted a copious stream
አንዦት	*anžät* አንጀት *anžät*

	n. intestine; inner feeling, sympathy
አንዦት ቢስ	*anžätä bis* adj. indecisive ; cruel
አንዛበበ	*anžabbäbä* አንጃበበ *anǧabbäbä* v.i hovered
አንዛባቢ	*änžabbäbi* v.i hovering
አንደላቀቀ	*andälaqqäqä* v.t spoiled *(a child)*; indulged; treated sumptuously, lavishly, see also *ደለቀቀ
አንደላቃቂ	*andälaqaqi* adj/n *(one)* who spoils *(a child)*
ደልቃቃ	*dälqaqqa* adj. spoilt *(child)*
ተንደላቀቀ	*tändälaqqäqä* v.i lived sumptuously, lavishly
ተንደላቃቂ	*tändälaqaqi* adj/n *(one)* who lives sumptuously, lavishly
አንዳረበበ	*andäräbbäbä* v.t caused to become almost full, see also ደረበበ
አንዳበት	*andäbät* n. style of speech, language
አንዳበተ ቀና	*adäbätä qänna* adj. eloquent *(speaker)*
አንዳፈደፈ	*andäfaddäfä* v.t caused to writhe, see also *ደፈደፈ
ተንዳፈደፈ	*tändäfaddäfä* v.i writhed
አንድ	*and* adj. one
—ሁለቴ	or አንዴ ሁለቴ —*hulätte, ande hulätte* n. a couple of times, a few times
—ላይ	—*lay* adv. together
—ሰው	—*säw* pron. somebody, someone
—ቀን	—*qän* n. some day, one day
—ባንድ	—*band* adv. singly, point by point, in detail, one by one, one at a time
—ነገር	—*nägär* n. something, one thing
—አደረገ	—*adärrägä* v.t unified
—ጋ	—*ga* adv. together

175

—ጊዜ	—gize adv. once, sometime	
ባንድ	band adv. togetner	
—ጊዜ	—gize adv. at once	
አንዱጋ	anduga adv. somewhere	
አንደኛ	andäññä adj. first	
አንዴ	ande adv. once	
አንዲት	andit adj. one (f.)	
አንዳች	andačč n. s/t	
አንዳንድ	andand adj. some	
አንዳፍታ	andafta adv. one moment	
አንድላንድ	andland n. one to one	
አንድላይ	andəlay adv. together	
አንድም	andəmm pron. nobody, no one, either conj. or, also	
አንድነት	andənnät adv. together	
እያንዳንዱ	əyyandandu n. each one, everyone, everybody	
ባንድነት	bandənnät adv. together	
አንጀት	anžät አንጐት anžät intestine; heart (feeling), sympathy,	
አንጀተ ቢስ	see አንጐት	
አንጃ ግራንጃ	anža gəranža n. malicious remarks	
አንጃ	anža n faction	
አንጆ	ango adj. tough meat	
አንገራገረ	angäraggärä v.i faltered; behaved, spoke hesitantly, was indecisive	
አንገራጋሪ	angäragari adj. faltering, hesitant. indecisive	
አንገት	angät n. neck	
አንገተ ሰባራ	angätä säbara adj. timid, shy, humble, submissive, meek	
—ዳንዳና	—dändanna adj. obstinate	
አንገት የሌለው	angät yälelläw adj. selfish, inconsiderate	
አንገትጌ	angätge n. collar	
አንገዋለለ	angäwallälä v.t looked down upon s/o, belittled	
አንገዋላይ	angäwalay n. one who looks down upon s/o	
አንገደገደ	angädäggädä v.t caused (s/o, s/t) to totter, staggered	
ተንገደገደ	tängädäggädä or ተንገዳገደ tängädaggädä v.i tottered, staggered	
ተንገድጋጅ	tängädagag adj. tottering, staggering	
ገድጋዳ	gädgadda adj. tottering, staggering	
አንገፈገፈ	angäfäggäfä v.t caused to be fed up, disgusted	
አንገፍጋፊ	angäfgafi adj. disgusting, repulsive	
ተንገፈገፈ	tängäfäggäfä v.i was fed up, disgusted	
አንጋረ	angarre n. dry skin (sheeps, goats)	
አንጋደደ	angaddädä v.t slanted, deviated (line etc.) bent, curved,see also ገደደ	
ተንጋደደ	tängaddädä v.i tottered, staggered	
አንጋጋ	angagga v.t drove (cattle etc.) enmass	
ተንጋጋ	tängagga n. v.i was driven (cattle etc.) enmass	
ጋጋታ	gagata n. clamour, uproar	
አንጋፉ	angaffa n. first-born (son)	
አንጕል	angʷäl n. brain	
አንጕላም	angʷälam adj. intelligent	
አንጕለቢስ	angʷäläbis n. thoughtless, selfish	
አንጕራጕረ	angʷäraggʷärä v.t murmured, grumbled; hummed (a song)	
አንጕራጓሪ	angʷäragʷari adj/n (one) who murmurs, grumbles	
እንጕርጕሮ	əngʷərgʷəro n. humming song	
አንጕደጕደ	angʷädäggʷädä v.t poured abundantly, caused to gush	
አንጓ	anguʷa n. joint (finger), small separating point in sugar-cane

176

እንጓለለ   and bamboo stalks
      ang"allälä እንገዋለለ
      angäwallälä v.t
      looked down upon
      s/o, belittled
እንጓላይ   ang"alay n. one who
      looks down upon
      s/o, one who belittles
      others
እንጠለጠለ   anṭäläṭṭälä v.t sus-
      pended, hung
ማንጠልጠያ   manṭälṭäya n. hanger,
      support from which
      s/t can be hanged,
      handle
ተንጠለጠለ   tänṭäläṭṭälä v.t was
      suspended, hung
ተንጠልጣይ   tänṭälṭay adj. hang-
      ing, suspended
ተንጠላጠለ   tänṭälaṭṭälä v.i
      climbed (a tree etc.)
እንጠበጠበ   anṭäbäṭṭäbä እንጠባ
      ጠበ anṭäbaṭṭäbä v.t
      dropped
ተንበጠበጠ   täntäbäṭṭäbä or ተን
      ጠባጠበ tänṭäbaṭṭä-
      bä v.i dripped
እንጣጣ   anṭaṭṭa v.t caused to
      fizzle; snapped
      (break with a sharp
      crack)
ተንጣጣ   tänṭaṭṭa v.i fizzled;
      snapped, crackled;
      farted
እንጦርጦስ   anṭorəṭos n. abyss,
      inferno
እንጨጨ   ančačča v t caused to
      make a loud noise;
      squealed
ተንጨጨ   tänčačča v.i was
      noisy, cried in dis-
      agreement
ጫጫታ   čačata n. noise
እንጸባረቀ   anṣäbarräqä v.i re-
      flected see also *ጸበረቀ
እንጸባራቂ   ansäbaraqi adj. re-
      flecting
ተንጸባረቀ   tänṣäbarräqä v.i was
      reflected
እንጸር   anṣar n. direction
      (of thought); aspect
እንጸር ላንጸር   anṣar lanṣar facing
      one another, vis-a-vis
ከ... እንጸር   kä...anṣar in contrast

እንፈራጠጠ   to, in the direction of
      anfäraṭṭäṭä v.i sat with
      legs outstretched
እኛረ   anorä v.t put down,
      placed; kept (s/o)
      in one's house
      etc. see also ኛረ
እኛከ   aññäkä v.t chewed,
      masticated
ታኛከ   taññäkä v.i was
      chewed, masticated
እእምሮ   a'əməro n. knowledge,
      mind, thought, wit
—ሳተ   —satä v.i became
      insane
—ቢስ   —bis adj. thought-
      less, inconsiderate
—አጣ   —aṭṭa v.i was
      shameless, incon-
      siderate, selfish
—ው ረጋ   —w rägga v.i re-
      laxed, was tran-
      quilized
—አወቀ   —awwäqä v.i matured
      (mentaly), reached
      the state of reasoning
—ደከማ   —däkamma adj.
      feeble-minded
የእእምሮ   yää'əməro həmäm
ሕመም   n. mental disease
—ሕመምተኛ   —həmämtäñña adj.
      insane, mad
—ሐኪም   —hakim n. psy-
      chiatrist
—ሕክምና   —həkkəmənna n.
      psychiatry
አከለ   akkälä v.t put more,
      gave more; became
      equal to
እኩል   əkkul n. half, adj.
      equal
እኩል ሌሊት   əkkulä lelit n. mid-
      night
—ቀን   —qän r. midday
እኩል አደረገ   əkkul adärrägä v.t
      equated
እኩሌታ   əkkuleta adj/n half
እኩይ   əkkuyya adj. of the
      same age, the same
      rank or position, peer
ታከለ   takkälä v.i was put
      more ; was given
      more
ተከከለ   täkakkälä v.i was

አሳከለ equalized; had the same status

asakkälä v.t caused to be put more; caused to be given more; changed the form of e.g ትልቅ አሳከለ made big

አስተካከለ astäkakkälä y.t equalized; put into order; gave uniformity; trimmed; set (a watch); rectified

ጠጉር አስተካ ካይ ṭägur astäkakay n. hair-dresser; barber

አከመ akkämä v.t treated (patient)

አካሚ akkami adj/n (one) who treats (patient)

አኪም akim ሐኪም hakim n. physician, doctor

—ቤት —bet n. hospital

ሀከምና hakkəmənna n. treatment (medical)

ታከመ takkämä v.i was treated (patient)

ታካሚ takkami n. patient

አሳከመ asakkämä v.t had (s/o) treated

አሳካሚ asakkami n. one who cares for the treatment of a patient

አከምባሎ akämbalo n. lid of a məṭad (clay oven for baking ənğära)

አከረረ see ከረረ

አከርካሪ akärkari n. back-bone

አከሰለ see ከሰለ

አከሰመ see ከሰመ

አከበረ akäbbärä v.t honoured, respected, revered, see ከበረ

አከበደ akabbädä v.t made heavy; difficult see ከበደ

አከተ akkätä v.t packed (for journey)

ታከተ takkätä v.i was packed

አሳከተ asakkätä v.t had (s/t) packed

አከተመ akättämä v.i reached an end; ended

ማክተሚያ maktämiya n. climax

አከናነበ akkänannäbä v.t covered s/o's head with the šämma

ተከናነበ täkänannäbä v.i covered one's head with the šämma see also * ከናነበ

ክንብንብ kənəbnəb n. covering (of the head with the šämma)

አከናወነ akkänawwänä v.t completed

ተከናወነ täkänawwänä v.i was completed; was perfectly done

ክንውን kənəwwən n. completion; perfectly done work

አከከ akkäkä v.t scratched (one's body)

እከክ əkäk n. itch

እከካም əkäkam adj. full of itches, full of scratches (human being); wretched

ታከከ takkäkä v.i leaned, rested against (s/o, s/t)

ታካኪ takaki adj. leaning, resting, resting against (s/o, s/t)

አካከከ akakkäkä v.t scratched slightly

አስታከከ astakkäkä v.t made to rest against (s/o, s/t) ; hinted

አሳከከ asakkäkä v.t itched

አከፈለ akäffälä v.i fasted (for three days before Easter), see ከፈለ

አከፋይ akfay n. one who fasts (for three days)

አከፍሎት akfəlot n. fasting (of three days)

ማክፈያ makfäya n. present for (s/o) who has fasted

አካል akal n. body; organ; member

አካላት akalat n. members of the body

አካላዊ akalawi adj. pertaining to the body

አካለ መጠን akalä mäṭän n. man-

178

—ጎደሎ hood, full growth

—godälo adj. invalid, crippled

አካበተ akabbätä v.t accumulated (usually wealth illegally)

አካባች akabač adj/n. (one) who accumulates (e.g wealth)

አካፈለ akkafälä see ከፈለ

አካፋ akafa n. spade

አካፋ akaffa v.i drizzled

ካፍያ kaffya n. drizzle, shower (of rain)

አክሊል aklil n. crown

አከምባሎ akəmbalo n. cover of the griddle on which እንጀራ is made

አከ አለ akk alä v.i cleared one's throat

አከታ akkəta n. phlegm

አከ መባያ akk mäbaya spittoon

አከርማ akərma n. kind of grass from which baskets etc. are made

አክስት akəst n. aunt

አክሲዮን aksion n. share, stock

አኮላሸ akkolaššä v.t castrated (animal), emasculated

ኩልሸት kuləššət n. castration

ተኮላሸ täkolaššä v.i was castrated, emasculated

አስኮላሸ askolaššä v.t had (an animal) castrated, emasculated

 አኮማተረ akkomattärä v.t wrinkled, creased

ተኮማተረ täkomattärä v.i was wrinkled, creased

ኩምትርትር kumtərtər adj. severely wrinkled, creased

አኮማታተረ akkomätattärä v.t wrinkled, creased severely

አኮረፈ akorräfä v.i snored; was sulky; v.t foamed, produced foam, lathered

አኩራፊ akurafi adj/n. (one) who snores; irascible

ኩርፊያ kurfiya n. snoring;

irascibility, sulking

ተኮረፈ täkorräfä v.t became irascible, sulky, see also ኮረፈ

ተኮራፊ täkorrafi adj. irascible, sulky

ተካረፈ täkʷarräfä v.t became in unspeaking terms with (s/o)

አስኮረፈ askorräfä v.t angered

አኮራመተ akkorammätä v.t shrivelled; became crippled (with disease)

ኮርማታ kormatta adj. crippled, shrivelled

ኩርምትምት kurmətmət adj. crippled, shrivelled

ተኮራመተ täkorammätä v.i was shrivelled, crippled

አኮፋዳ akofada n. satchel, knapsack

አኮረተ akʷärrätä v.t produced bulb (e.g onion)

አኩራች akʷərač adj. bulbing (plants e.g onion)

ኩረት kʷärät n. pebble

አኩሰሰ akʷässäsä v.t made meagre, lean, thin; see also ኩሰሰ

አኩበከበ akʷäbäkkʷäbä v.t ran with short paces;

አኩቴት akkʷätet n. consecrated bread (sacrament), Host

አሁን ahun also ኡሁን ahun adv. now

አሁኑኑ ahununu adv. immediately

አወለቀ awälläqä v.t undressed, took off one's clothes, dismantled, see also ወለቀ

ልብ አውላቂ ləbb awlaqi adj. pestering, vexatious

ኪስ— kis—n. pick pocket

አወላለቀ awälalläqä v.t undressed completely; dismantled

አወለወለ awäläwwälä v.i had shining complexion,

179

አወላወለ   *see also* ወለወለ
አወላገደ   *see* * ወላወለ
አወረደ   *see* * ወለገደ
      awärrädä v.t took down, unloaded; *see also* ወረደ
አወራ   *awärra* v.t narrated, told, informed
አውሪ   *awri* n. narrator
ተወራ   *täwärra* v.i was told, narrated
አዋራ   *awwarra* v.t made s/o speak, made s/o divulge a secret
አስወራ   *aswärra* v.t caused to be talked about s/t
*አወሰ   *awwäsä
ታወሰው   *tawwäsäw* he thought of, he remembered
አወሳ   *awässa* v.t mentioned
ተወሳ   *täwässa* v.i was mentioned
አወቀ   *see* በወቀ
አወናብደ   *see* *ወነብደ
አወን   *awän* adv. interj. yes
አወንታ   *awänta* n. affirmative, positive
አወከ   *awwäkä* v.t troubled, disturbed; became difficult
አዋኪ   *awwaki* adj. troublesome, disturbing; difficult
እውከት   *əwkät* or ሀውከት *həwkät* n. trouble, disturbance; difficulty
ታወከ   *tawwäkä* v.i was disturbed, was put in difficult situation
አወካ   *awäkka* v.i shouted (*commotion*), uproared
ዋካታ   *wakata* n. shout, (*commotion*), uproar
ውካታ   *wəkata* n. shout (*commotion*), uproar
አወዛወዘ   *see* ወዘወዘ
አወደ   *awwädä* v.t perfumed
አወደስ   *see* ወደስ
አወዳደረ   *awwädaddärä* v.t caused to compete; compared
ውድድር   *wədəddər* n. com-

petition

አወዳዳሪ   *awwädadari* adj/n. one who supervises a competion
ተወዳደረ   *täwädaddärä* v.i competed
ተወዳዳሪ   *täwädadari* n. competitor; resemblance, equal
አወጋ   *awägga* v.i narrated, told stories, reported over (*s/t*)
ወግ   *wäg* n. tradition; narration, lore; usage
በወግ   *bäwäg* adv. properly
የወግ ልብስ   *yäwäg ləbs* n. regalia, uniform cf. የደንብ ልብስ
ወገኛ   *wägäñña* adj. conceited, vein
አውጊ   *awgi* adj. n (*one*) who narrates
አወጣ   *see* ወጣ
አዋለ   *see* ዋለ
አዋለደ   *see* ወለደ
አዋልደጊሻ   *awaldägešša* n. aardvark
አዋሐደ   *awwahädä* made one; mixed (*s/t*); caused to digest
ምግብ ማዋ ሐጃ   *məgəb mawwahaga* n. food digestive
ተወሐደ   *täwahädä* v.i became united, unified; was digested (*food*)
አዋረደ   *see* ወረደ
አዋራ   *awara* n. dust, also አቢራ
      see አወራ
አዋሰ   *awasä* v. lent, *see also* ዋስ *was*
አዋሽ   *awaš* adj/n. (*one*) who lends
ውሰት   *wəsät* n. lending
ተዋሰ   *täwasä* v.t acted as guarantor; v.i borrowed
ተዋዋሰ   *täwawasä* v.i lent from each other guaranteed each other
አዋሽከ   *awwaššäkä* v.t told tales
አዋዋለ   *awwawalä* v.t helped in drawing a contract, agreement,

180

አጣጣይ	see also ዋለ
	awwaway adj/n (one) who helps drawing contract, agreement
ውል	wəl n. contract, agreement
ተዋዋለ	täwawalä v.i drew a contract, agreement
ተዋዋይ	täwaway n. contractor
አዋዜ	awaze n. a mixture of red pepper and other spices used for eating raw meat
አዋየ	awwayyä v.t consulted, asked for advice
አዋደደ	see ወደደ
አዋጣ	see ወጣ
አውላላ	awlalla n. open ground
አውሎ ነፋስ	awlo näfas n.whirl wind
አውራ	awra n. main, leader chief, head
—መንገድ	—mängäd n. main road
—ጎዳና	—godana n. highway
—ዶሮ	—doro n. cock
—ጠላት	—ṭälat n. mortal enemy
—ጣት	—ṭat n. thumb
አውራሪስ	awraris n. rhinoceros
አውራጃ	awrağğa n. district, ወረዳ
አውሬ	awre n. ferocious animal; adj. inhuman, cruel, pl. አራዊት
አውሬነት	awrennät n. ferocity, savagery
አውሮፕላን	awroppälan n. airplane
አውሮፓ	auroppa n. Europe, also አውሮጳ
አውተረተረ	awtärättärä v.t. meddled through, did (s/t) imperfectly, slovenly
አውተርታሪ	awtärtari adj/n (one) who meddles through, does his job imperfectly, slovenly
ተውተረተረ	täwtärättärä v.i. staggered, walked unsteadily, tottered
አውተፈተፈ	awtäfättäfä v.t. did

	one's job slovenly, imperfectly, see ወተፈ
ተውተፈተፈ	täwtäfättäfä v.i. was done slovenly, imperfectly; pocked one's nose in every business
ተውተፍታፊ	täwtäftafi adj/n (one) who acts slovenly: dirty (mannerless)
አውታር	awtar n. cord of lyre
የድምጽ—	yädəmṣ—n. vocal cords
አውቶቡስ	awtobus n. bus
አውደለደለ	awdäläddälä v.i. vagabonded; roamed
አውደልዳይ	awdälday adj vagabond, tramp, roamer
አውድማ	awdəmma n. threshing floor
አዎ	awo particle, yes ! also አዎን awon
አወንታ	awänta n. affirmative
አዕማድ	a'əmad n. pillars; derived forms (of verb)
አዘለ	azzälä v. t. carried (child) on the back; carried fruits (tree)
ማዘያ	mazäya n s/t used for carrying a child on the back (cloth, tanned leather) cf. አንቀባ
ታዘለ	tazzälä v.t. was carried (child) on the back
አዘመመ	see ዘመመ
አዘመረ	see ዘመረ
አዘመተ	see ዘመተ
አዘራጠ	azärräṭä v.t farted
አዘረፈ	see ዘረፈ
አዘረ	see ዘረ
አዘነ	äzzänä v.i was sad, sorry; was sorrowful; mourned, deplored, had regrets, was in low spirit
አዛኝ	azañ adj. compassionate
አዘንተኛ	azäntäñña ሐዘንተኛ hazäntäñña n. mourner
አዛዘነ	azazzänä v.i was

ተዛዘነ somewhat sad *tāzazzänä* v.i had mutual compassion

አሳዘነ *asazzänä* v.t aroused compassion, was pitiable, pathetic

እሳዛኝ *asazzañň* adj. pitiable, pathetic

አዘወተረ *see* * ዘወተረ

አዘዘ *azzäzä* v.t ordered, commanded

አዛዥ *azzäž* adj/n commander, (one) who gives orders

ማዘዣ *mazäža* n. order (written direction)

የመድኃኒት— *yämädhanit*—n. prescription

የገንዘብ— *yägänzäb*—n. voucher

የፍርድ ቤት— *yúfərd bet*—n. warrant

ታዘዘ *tazzäzä* v.i. was ordered; obeyed

ታዛዥ *tazzaž* adj. obedient

ትእዛዝ *ta'zaz* n. order

ጸሐፊ— *ṣähfe*—n. minister of pen

አሳዘዘ *asazzäzä* v.t. had (s/o, s/t) ordered

አዘገመ *azäggämä* v.i. walked slowly, paced

ማዘገሚያ *mazgämia* n. (s/t that keeps (s/o) busy

አዘጋገመ *azägaggámä* v.i. walked rather slowly, paced rather slowly, did one's work very slowly

አዘጋጀ *azzägaggä* v.t. prepared, made ready; *see also under* *ዘጋጀ

አዘጠዘጠ *see* *ዘጠዘጠ

አዙሪት *azurit* n. whirlpool, *also* አዘዋሪት

አዛባ *azaba* n. dung

አዛባ *azzabba* v.t. made incompatible, created disharmony (between two things), made incoherent (sentence etc.)

ተዛባ *tāzabba* v.i. was

incompatible, was in disharmony, was incoherent

አዛውንት *azawənt* n. dignified elderly man

አዛጋ *azzagga* v.t/v.i. helped in closing; yawned, *see also* ዛጋ

አዜመ *azemä* v.i. chanted intoned, *see also* ዜማ

አዝሙድ *azmud* n. in
ጥቁር— *təqur*— n. black cumin
ነጭ— *näčč*— n. bishops weed

አዝራር *azrar* n. button (of clothes)

አዝዋሪ *see* ዞረ

አዞ *azzo* n. crocodile; mixture of beans, peas etc. flour and powdered mustard used as appetiser

አዞረ *see* ዞረ

አዠ *ažžä* v.i. oozed

አየ *ayyä* also ዐየ v.t. saw, looked at

አየለ *ayyälä* v.i became strong, over-powered, was predominant, was prevalent *see also* ኃይል

አየር *ayyär* n. weather, air
—መንገድ —*mängäd* n. airline
—ወለድ —*wälläd* n. airborne
— —ወታደር — —*wättaddär* n. paratrooper
—ኃይል —*hail* n. Air Force
የአየር ሁኔታ *yä'ayyär huneta* n. weather condition
—መልእክት —*mäla'əkt* n. airmail, airletter
—ንብረት —*nəbrät* n. climate
—ወራራ —*wärära* n. air raid
—ጠባይ —*ṭäbay* n. weather, climate
—ፖስታ —*posta* n. airmail

አያ *ayya* n. title of respect for an elderly person (male)

አያሌ *ayyale* adj. much, adv. very much. a

182

	good deal		station.
አያት	ayat n. grandfather, grandmother	አዳደለ	adaddälä v.t distributed here and
እያያ	ayyayya n. title of respect to an elder brother		there (in small quantity)
አዬ	aye interj. oh ! (exclamation of astonishment)	አሳደለ	asaddälä v.t had (s/t) distributed
		አደለ	adälla v.t was biased in favour of, treated with undue partiality
—ጉድ	—gud interj. what a pity ! oh my goodness !		
አይ	ay interj. oh! (exclamation of surprise)	አዳይ	adday adj/n (one) who treats with undue partiality
አይል	in ምንም አይል mən-əmmayəl it is tolerable, it is not bad	አድላዊ	adlawi n. one who treats with undue partiality, adj. biased
አይሁዳዊ	ayhudawi adj. Jewish		
አይሁድ	ayhud n. Jew, Jews	አድሎኛ	adloñña adj. biased (in favour of)
አይብ	ayb n. fresh cheese		
አይቦ	aybo n. white wheat	አደላለ	see ያለደለ
አይዞህ	ayzoh don't be afraid, be courageous, take it easy, never mind	አደመ	addämä v.t plotted, conspired
		አዳሚ	addami adj/n. (one) who takes part in a plot, conspiracy
አይድረስ	aydräs interj. that is awful !		
አይደለም	aydälläm v.t it is not	አድመኛ	admäñña n. conspirator, plotter,
አይጥ	ayt n. mouse		
አይጠ በላ	ayṭä bälla adj. mouse eater	አድማ	adma n. plot conspiracy
አይጣማ	ayṭamma adj. greyish, having the colour of a rat	እድመኛ	ədmäñña n. guests (in a wedding)
		ታደመ	taddämä v.i was plotted conspirated; was invited to a wedding (arch.)
አይጠ መጎጥ	ayṭä mägoṭ n. rat		
አይጠዳሽ	ayṭädaš adj. gloomy (person), melancholic		
አደለ	addälä v.t distributed; had good luck e.g ታድያለሁ täddäyyallähu I am lucky	አደመጠ	adämmäṭä v.t listened to ; followed an event carefully see also *ያመጠ
አዳይ	adday adj/n (one) who distributes	አድማጭ	admač adj/n (one) who listens; follows an e vent attentively
እድል	əddəl n. luck		
እድለ ቢስ	əddəlä bis adj. unlucky, unfortunate (person)	አዳመጠ	addammäṭä v.t listened to
		ማዳመጫ	maddamäča n. receiver (telephone)
ታደለ	taddälä v.i was distributed ; became lucky		
		አደረ	addärä v.t passed the night
ማደያ	in የነዳጅ ማደያ yänädag maddaya n. filling station, gas	ያደረ መሬት	yaddärä märet fallow land
		ለጌታ አደረ	lägeta addärä v.t entered into the service of a master

183

ሥርተ አደር *särto addär* n.
the working people

እንደት አደ *ər̰det addärk* good
ርh morning

ደጋና አደር *dähna ədär* good
night

አዳሪ *adari* adj/n *(one)*
who passes the
night at a place

—ተማሪ —*tämari* n. board-
ing student

—ትምህርት —*təmhərt bet* n.
ቤት boarding school

ሴተኛ አዳሪ *setäñña adari* n.
prostitute

በረንዳ— *bärända—* n. vaga-
bond, tramp

ዱር— *dur–*n. vagabond,
brigand, tramp

እዳሪ *əddari* n. fallow
land

—ወጣ —*wäṭṭa* v.i went to
the W.C

አዳር *adar* n. an over
night

አድሮ *adro* adv. finally
ወሎ— *wəlo—*adv. in the
long run, event-
ually, at last

አድር ባይ *ədər bay* adj. op-
portunist, servile

እድር *əddər* n. communal
self–help organization

እድርተኛ *əddərtäñña* n. member
of a self helping
organization

ማደርያ *madärya* n. lodg-
ing, place to pass
the night; military
serivice land

ተዳደረ *tädaddärä* v.i was
administered; *(in-
stitution etc.)*;
lived in harmony
with others

መተዳደሪያ *mättädadäriya* n.
means of subsistence

—ሕግ —*həgg* n. con-
stitution

አስተዳደረ *astädaddärä* v.t administered *(insiti-
tution)*; passed the
night together *(as*

companion)

አስተዳዳሪ *astädadari (m)*. adj
administrator; *(one)*
who passes the
night with *(s/o* as
companion)

አደረሰ *see ደረሰ*
አደረቀ *see ደረቀ*
አደረገ *see * ደረገ*
አደራ *adära* n. *(s/t)* entrusted to *(s/o)*

ያደራ *yadära däbdahbe* n.
ደብዳቤ letter of recommend-
ation; registered
letter

ባለ አደራ *balä'adära* n. trustee
አደራ *adärra* v.t formed webs
አደሰ *addäsä* v.t renewed
አዳሽ *addaš* adj. n. *(one)*
who renews, renewer

አዲስ *addis* adj. new
—አበባ —*ababa* n. Addis
Ababa *(capital of
Ethiopia)*
—ኪዳን —*kidan* n. New Tes-
tament

እደሳ *əddäsa* n. renewing,
renewal

አዳደሰ *adaddäsä* v.t renewed
slightly

ታደሰ *taddäsä* v.i was
renewed; was refre-
shed; was renovated

አሳደሰ *asaddäsä* v.t had
(s/t) renewed

አደቀቀ *see ደቀቀ*
አደበ *addäbä* n. became
polite, refrained from
becoming mischievous

አደብ *addäb* n. polite-
ness, good manners
—ገዛ —*gəza* be polite

አደበነ *see ደበነ*
አደባ *adäbba* v.i lurked,
stalked

አደባባይ *addäbabay* n. open
public place, square
(city); court
(judicial); formal
gathering place of
sovereign

አደባየ *adäbayyä* v.t hit force
fully

አደነ *addänä* v.t hunted

አደን	*addän* n. hunt, hunting
አዳኝ	*addañ* n. hunter
አደነቀ	see ደነቀ
አደነቆረ	*adänäqqorä* v.t deafened; annoyed *(s o)* by a loud voice or sound, made one's intelligence or faculties dulled, see ደነቆረ
አደናገረ	see * ደነገረ
አደነገዘ	see ደነገዘ
አደንጓሬ	*adängu"orre* n haricot beans
አደዘደዘ	*adäzäddäzä* v.t roamed, wandered aimlessly
አደዝዳኙ	*adzdaž* adj. n. *(one)* who roams aimlessly
አደይ አበባ	*adäy abäba* n. maskel flower *(wild flower that grows during the month of September, species of the ox-eye daisy)*
አደገ	*addägä* v.i grew up, became taller, developed physically; rose *(in rank)*
አብሮ አደግ	*abro addäg* n. childhood friend
ስድ አደግ	*sədd addäg* adj. impertinent *(child)*, rude, impolite
ማደጎ	*madägo* n. fosterchild
እድገት	*ədgät* n. growth; promotion
አሳደገ	*asaddägä* v.t fostered; promoted *(in rank)*
አሳዳጊ	*asaddagi* n. fosterparent
አስተዳደግ	*astädadäg* n. upbringing; breeding; education
አደገደገ	see*ደገደገ
አደፈ	*addäfä* v.i become dirty, filthy, was soiled
አደፍ	*adäf* n. menstruation
—ወረዳት	—*wärrädat* v.t menstruated
እድፍ	*ədəf* n. dirt, filth, stain
አሳደፈ	*asaddäfä* v.t polluted. made dirty

አደጋ	*adäga* n. danger, accident, peril
—ላይ. ወደቀ	—*lay wäddäqa* v.i was exposed to danger
—ጣላ	—*talä* v.t exposed to danger, imperilled
—ጣላ	—*talä* v.t attacked by surprise,
አደጋኛ	*adägäñña* n. dangerous, unsafe. hazardous, perilous
የእሳት አደጋ	*yä'sat adäga* n. fire hazard
—መከላከያ	—*mäkkälakäya* n. firebrigade
አዱኛ	*adduñña* n. world, wealth
ባለ—	*balä*—adj. wealthy
አዳም	*addam* n. **Adam**
አዳምና ሄዋን	*addamənna hewan* n. Adam and Eve
አዳራሽ	see ደረስ
አዳበለ	see ደባለ
አዳበረ	see ዳበረ
አዳከመ	see ደከመ
አዳነተ	see*ዳነተ
አዳጠ	see ዳጠ
አዳፈነ	see ደፈነ
አዳፋ	see ደፋ
አድማስ	*admas* n. horizon
አድባር	*adbar* n. guardian spirit *(G. mountains)*
አዶ	*addo* n. elephant hunter
አጇለ	*ağğälä* v.t soaked *(for a prolonged time)*
ታጇለ	*tağğälä* v.i was soaked
አሳጇለ	*asağğälä* v.t had *(s/t)* soaked
አጄንዳ	*ağända* n. agenda
አጅሬ	*ağğire* adj. ingenious, smart, high spirited
አጀበ	*ağğäbä* v.t escorted *(to give honour to s/o)*
አጀብ	*ağäb* n. entourage, suite, escort
አጃቢ	*ağğabi* n. entourage, suite, escort
ታጀበ	*tağğäbä* v.i was escorted
አሳጀበ	*asağğäbä* v.t had *(s/o)* escorted
አጃ	*ağğa* n. oats
አገለለ	see *ገለለ

አገለገለ see *ገለገለ
አገለደመ see *ገሰደመ
ኀገሰባበጠ see ገሰበጠ
አገላገሉ see ኀገገሉ
አገመ aggämä v.t cupped
አጋሚ aggami adj/n (one)
who performs
cupping operation
ወገምት wagämt n. cupping
instrument
አገሳ agässa v.i. roared
(lion); belched,
see also ገሳ
ገሳት ḡəsat n. roar (lion);
belch·
አገር agär country; native
land
አገሬ agäre n. natives,
indigenous people
አገር ቤት agär bet n. countryside
—አስተዳዳሪ —astädadari provin-
cial administrator
አገሬ ገዥ agärä gäž n. governor
ያገር ልጅ yagär ləǧ n. com-
patriot
አገር አስተዳ agär astädädar mini-
ደር ሚኒስ ster n. ministry
ቴር of interior
—ውስጥ —wəsṭ adj. dom-
estic, local
—ግዛት —gəzat ministry
ሚኒስቴር of interior (arch.)
—ፍቅር —fəqər n. patriotism
ቅኝ አገር qəňň agär n. colony
ውጭ— wəčč— n. abroad
የውጭ—ሰው yäwəčč— säw n.
foreigner
የሰው— yäsaw agär n. foreign
country
የትውልድ— yätəwələdd—n. native
country
ባላገር balagär n. country-
man ; country
(countryside)
አገረረ see ገረረ
አገሸሸ agäššäšä also ገሸሸ አደ
ረገ gäšäšš adärrägä
v.t got rid of; ignored
(intentionally)
አገበ see ገበ
አገባብ aggäbab n. syntax ;

አገበደደ procedure, see also ገበ
aggäbadäddädä v.t
brought to complet-
ion (work etc.), made
nearly completed
አገተ aggätä v.t. sequestrated
(cattle for grazing
in one's land)
አገነፈሰ see ገነፈሰ
አገነፉ see ገነፉ
እንገኝ see አገኝ and *ገኝ
አገናዘበ aggänazäbä v.t. auth-
enticated, verfied,
see ገንዘብ
አገናዛቢ aggänazabi adj.
possessive (gram.)
ተገናዘበ tägänazzäbä v.i.
possessed, made
one's own pro-
perty; was auth-
enticated, verified
አስገነዘበ asgänäzzäbä v.t.
drew the attention
of, made s/o under-
stand (an issue) ;
clarified
አገኝ agäňňä v.t. found, got
ግንኙነት gənəňňunnät n. re-
lation
ተገኝ tägäňňä v.i. was found
ተገናኘ tägänaňňä v.i. met
each other; had
sexual intercourse
(polite)
አገናኘ aggänaňňä v.t caused
to meet each other;
made to encounter
each other; let a calf
suck
አገናኝ aggänaň mäkʷännən n.
መኮንን liaison officer
አገዘ aggäzä v.t helped,
aided
አጋዥ aggaž adj/n (one)
who helps, aids
ራስ አገዝ ras aggäz adj.
self-helping
አገዛ əggäza n. helping
ተጋዘ tägaggäzä v.i helped
each other
ተጋጋዥ tägugaž adj. help-
ing each other, sup-
porting each other
አገደ aggädä v.t obstructed

stopped, hindered, blocked; made inactive, tended domestic herd

ወለድ አገድ **wälläd aggäd** n. mortgage

አጋጅ **aggaǧ** n. herdsman

እገድ **əggəd** adj. stopped, hindered, blocked

ግገኛ **maggäǧa** n. pasture; obstruction

ታገደ **taggädä** v.i was obstructed, stopped, hindered blocked; was tended (domestic herd)

አሳገደ **asaggädä** v.t caused to be obsructed, stopped etc; caused domestic herd to be tended

አገደም see * ገደም

አገደደ see * ገደደ

አገደፈ see ገደፈ

አገዳ **agäda** n. cane, stalk, stem

መህል— **mähal**—n. shin

ሽንኮር— **šänkor**—n. sugar cane

አገገመ **agäggämä** v.t recovered (from prolonged illness), convalesced

አገጋሚ **agäggami** adj/r convalescent

አገጠጠ see ገጠጠ

አገጭ **agač** n. chin

አጋጫም **agaǧam** adj/n one with big chin

አጋለ see ጋለ

አጋለጠ see *ገለጠ

አጋም see *ጋመ

አጋመስ see ገመስ

አጋም **agam** n. carisa edulis, hawthorn

አጋራ **aggarra** v.t shared (s/t) to (s/o)

አጋሪ **aggari** adj/n one who shares (s/t) to (s/o)

ተጋራ **tägarra** v.i shared (s/t) with (s/o) see also ጋራ

አጋር **aggar** n. helper; alliance

አጋሰስ **agassäs** n. pack-horse

አጋሰሰ **agassäsä** v.t collected, gathered indiscriminately

አጋበሰ **agabbäsä** v.t gathered collected indiscriminately

አጋተ see *ጋተ

አጋነነ see ገነነ

አጋና **agana** n. price, bid

አጋንዱራ **agandura** n. rough, coarse person, one lacking finesse

አጋዘ see * ጋዘ

አጋዝን **agazän** n. greater kudu

አጋደመ **aggaddämä** laid down horizontally

አግዳሚ **agdami** adj. horizontal

—ወንበር —**wänbär** n. bench

ጋድም **gadǝm** adj. horizontal

አጋደደ **agaddädä** v.t became of good service, became useful

አጋጠመ see ገጠመ

አጋፈረ **aggafärä** v.t ushered

አጋፋሪ **aggafari** n. usher

አጋፈፈ see ገፈፈ

አጊጠ see ጊጠ

አግባብ see ገባ

አግተለተለ see * ገተለተለ

አጎለመስ see ጎለመስ

አጎበር **agobär** n. canopy (covering over a bed)

አጎት **aggot** n. uncle

ያጎት ልጅ **yaggot ləǧ** n. cousin

አጎነበሰ see *ጎነበሰ

አጎዛ **agoza** n. dried sheep's skin (used for sitting on)

አጎጠጠ **agoṭṭäṭä** v.t made grimaces (to cause laughter), also አን ጎጠጠ

አጉጣጭ **aguṭač** adj/n (one) who makes grimaces

አጉለ see አስታጉለ

አጉላ see ጉላ

አጉለመስ see ጎለመስ

አጉረ **agguʷarä** v.t packed in (an enclosure); stuffed, crowded together, huddled; penned up

187

ታጉሬ	taggu*ärä v.i was packed in, stuffed, crowded together
አሳጉሬ	asaggu*ärä v.i had (s/t) stuffed packed, crowded together
አጉሬስ	see ጎሬስ
አጉሬበ	see ጎሬበ
አጉሬ	agu*ärra v.t cried, moaned in agony (usually s/o possessed by evil spirit)
አጉሳቀለ	see ጉሳቁለ
አጉበር	see አጎበር
አጓሬ	see አጉሬ
አጓት	aggu*at n. whey
አጓደደ	aggu*addädä v.t caused to relax, caused to depend with confidence
ተጓዳጅ	tägu*adağ adj/n (one) who relaxes, takes easy, slow in action
አጓጓ	see ጓጓ
አጠለለ	see ጠለለ
አጠለቀ	see ጠለቀ
አጠመቀ	see ጠመቀ
አጠመደ	see ጠመደ
አጠማ	see ጠማ
አጠሬ	aṭṭärä v.t became short; was brief; shrank
አጠሬኝ	aṭṭäränñ I am short of
እጥሬት	äṭrät n. shortage
አጭር	ačč*är adj. short
አሳጠሬ	asaṭṭärä v.i abridged, cut short, shortened
አጠሬ	aṭṭärä v.i made a fence around s/t, enclosed (with a fence)
ታጠሬ	taṭṭärä v.i was fenced; was surrounded
አጥር	aṭər n. fence
ግቢ	—gäbbi n. courtyard, compound, campus
አጠሬ	see ጠሬ
አጠሬቀመ	see *ጠሬቀመ
አጠሬጠሬ	see ጠሬጠሬ
አጠቀስ	see ጠቀስ

አጠቃ	see *ጠቃ
አጠቃሰለ	see ጠቀለለ
አጠበ	aṭṭäbä v.t washed; bathed; developed (a film); eroded (soil by water)
አጠብ	aṭäba n. washing
አጣቢ	aṭabi n. laundry man
እጣቢ	äṭṭabi n. wash (kitchen liquid with waste food)
እጥበት	äṭbä: n. washing
በዶሬቁ—	bädäräqu—n. dry laundry
እጥቤ	äṭṭäbbe usually followed by ሌባ n. shameless thief
ተጣጠበ	täṭaṭṭäbä v.i washed oneself (rashing)
ታጠበ	taṭṭäbä v.t washed oneself; was washed; was eroded
ታጣቢ	taṭabi adj. washable
መታጠቢያ	mättaṭäbiya n. basin (for washing)
—ቤት	—bet n. bathroom, W.C
አጣጠበ	aṭaṭṭäbä v.t washed slightly
አሳጠበ	asaṭṭäbä v.t had (s/t) washed
አስታጠበ	astaṭṭäbä v:t poured water on (s/o) while washing
አጠበቀ	see ጠበቀ
አጠበበ	see ጠበበ
አጠባ	see ጠባ
አጠነ	aṭṭänä v.t fumigated
አጣኝ	aṭañ adj/n (one) who fumigates
እጣን	äṭan n. incense
እጥነት	äṭnät n. fumigation
እጥን	äṭṭän adj. fumigated
ማእጠንት	ma'äṭänt n. fumes of incense
ማጠኛ	maṭäña n. herb used in fumigation
ታጠነ	taṭṭänä v.i was fumigated
አሳጠነ	asaṭṭänä v.t had (s/o) fumigate (place etc.)
አጠነከሬ	see ጠነከሬ
አጠነዛ	see ጠነዛ

አጠነጠነ	see *ጠነጠነ
አጠነፈፈ	see ጠነፈፈ
አጠኘ	see ጠኘ
አጠየቀ	see ጠየቀ
አጠደቀ	see ጠደቀ and ጸደቀ
አጠዳ	see ጠዳ and ጸዳ
አጠገብ	aṭägäb adv. close to
በ...	bä...adv. by, near, beside
እ...	ə...adv. by, near, beside
አጠጣ	see ጠጣ
አጠፈ	aṭṭäfä v.t folded, doubled
ቃሉን—	qalun aṭṭäfä v.t retracted one's statement, broke one's word
አጠፋታ	aṭäfeta adj. twofold
እጥፍ	əṭəf n. doublefold, times
እጥፋት	əṭəfat n. crease
ማጠፊያ	mäṭafiya n. hinge
ታጠፈ	taṭṭäfä v.i was folded, doubled
ታጣፊ	taṭṭafi adj. folding
ወንበር	—wänbär n. folding chair
መጣጠፊያ	mättaṭafiya n. curve (of a road), bend of road
አጣጠፈ	aṭaṭṭäfä v.t folded (clothes), foided up (a letter), rolled up (bed-clothes etc.)
አጣ	aṭṭa v.i became needy, poor; failed to find
እጦት	əṭot n. poverty, need, lack. shortage
ታጣ	taṭṭa v.i was absent, was not to be found
አሳጣ	asaṭṭa v.t deprived (s/o) of one's possessions, wealth etc.
አጠለቀ	see ጠለቀ
አጣሞመመ	see ጠሞሞ
አጣሞረ	see ጠሞረ
አጣሪ	aṭari n. one who sells spices
አጣራ	see ጠራ
አጣበቀ	see ጠበቀ

አጣና	aṭana n. rather thin stem of eucalyptus tree (used as fuel or for building)
አጣደፈ	see ጠደፈ
አጣጣሞ	see ጠሞሞ
አጣጣረ	see ጣረ
አጣጥ	aṭaṭ n. thorny bush
አጣፋረ	see ጠፈረ
አጣፈጠ	see ጣፈጠ
አጤ	see እጤ
አጤቀ	aṭeqä v.t mocked at; was scornful
አጤነ	aṭenä v.i pondered, thought deeply (about)
አጥያኝ	aṭyañ adj. n (one) who thinks deeply (about)
አጥለቀለቀ	see * ጠለቀለቀ
አጥመለመለ	see * ጠመለመለ and ተ'ታ መለመለ
አጥሚት	aṭmit n. gruel
አጥቅ	aṭq n. fringe (of rug or shawl)
አጥበረበረ	aṭbäräbbärä v.t dazzied
አጥበርባሪ	aṭbärbari adj. dazzling
አጥቢያ	aṭbiya n. quarter (division of a town or village)
—ኮከብ	—kokäb n. morning star
—ዳኛ	—dañña n. magistrate, Justice of the Peace
አጥናፍ	aṭnaf n. edge, boarder (for the world)
አጥናፈ ዓለም	aṭnafä aläm n. the far end of the world
አጥወለወለ	aṭwäläwwälä v.t nauseated
አጥወልዋይ	aṭwälway adj. nauseous
አጦሰ	aṭola v.t husked (using a fan)
ማጦያ	maṭoya n. fan (used for husking grain)
አጦዘ	aṭoza v.t hit (s/o) with a heavy blow
አጬ	see ዐጬ
እጨለጨለ	ačäläččälä v.i became green
አጨለገ	ačälläga v.t looked at

አጥላጊ   (s/t) stealthily; stole (coll.)
ǟǧlagi adj/n (one) who looks at (s/t) stealthily; a thief (coll.)

አጨማተረ   ač̣č̣ämattärä v.t wrinkled (one's face, cloth etc.), see ጨመተረ

አጨስ   see ጨስ

አጨቀ   ač̣äqa v.t made ● swampy; soaked

አጨቀ   ač̣č̣äqä v.t stuffed (push, thrust), crammed

አጨበጨበ   see ጨበጨበ

አጨነቆረ   ač̣änäquʷärä v.t peeped at (looked slyiy)

አጨደ   ač̣č̣ädä v.t mowed

አጨዳ   ač̣č̣äda mowing

አጫጅ   ač̣ag̃ adj/n (one) who mows

ታጨደ   tač̣č̣ädä v.i was mowed

ታጫጅ   tač̣ag̃ n. s/t ready for mowing

ማጨድ   mač̣äd n. sickle

—እግር   —əgər adj. bow-legged

አጫጨደ   ač̣ač̣č̣ädä v.t mowed here and there

እጥድ አደረገ   əč̣č̣əd adärrägä v.t mowed completely, entirely

አሳጨደ   asač̣č̣ädä v.t had (grass, hay etc.) mowed

አጫረተ   see * ጨረተ

አጫወተ   see * ጫወት

አጫፈረ   see ጨፈረ

አጥር   see አጠረ

አጥበረበረ   ač̣bäräbbärä v.t ; swindled, cheated, defrauded, embezzled, see also *ጨበረበረ

አጸፋ   aṣäfa n. reprisal, retaliation; (s/t) done in return (good or bad)

አጸፋውን መለሰ   aṣäfawən mälläsä n. did (s/t) by way of reprisal

አጸፋ ተወላጠ ስም   aṣäfa täwlaṭä səm n. reflexive pronoun

አጽቅ   aṣq n. joint (finger, bamboo, sugar cane

አጸ   etc.); knuckle
aṣe n. title of former Emperors of Ethiopia see ፈሳ

አፈሳ
አፈሳግ   afälama n. money paid by a cattle owner for damages done by his cattle

አፈሙዝ   afämuz n. muzzle (of fire-arm)

አፈረ   affärä v.i was ashamed; became embarassed; became modest; remained fruitless (farm land); backed out, went back on one's word, escaped from an agreement

አፋሪ   afari adj./n. (one) who is shy, embarassed

አፋር   affar adj. shy, embarassed

አፋሪም   affaram adj./n. one who backs out

እፍረት   əfrät n. embarassment, shyness, shame, humiliation

አፍረት ስጋ   afrätä səga, or ሐፍረት ሥጋ hafrätä səga n. genital organ (pol.)

ታፈረ   taffärä v.i was respected, honoured, revered

ታፋሪ   taffäri adj./n (one) who is respected, honoured, revered

አሳፈረ   asaffärä v.t disgraced, embarassed, humiliated

አሳፋሪ   asaffari adj. shameful, disgraceful

አፈረስ   see ፈረስ
አፈረጠ   see ፈረጠ
አፈረጠመ   see ፈረጠመ
አፈር   afär n. soil, earth
—በላ   —bälla v.i died
—ብላ   —bala go to hell!
—ይብላኝ   —yəblaññ what a pity !
የብረት—   yäbərät—n. iron ore, ore

አፈሰ   affäsa v.t scooped (with the hands or with

	a scoop)
አፈሳ	afäsa n. mass arrest
እፋሽ	əffaš n. grain scooped from the ground *(usually mixed with dirt)*
ታፈሰ	taffäsä v.i was scooped up
አሳፈሰ	asaffäsä v.t had grain etc. scooped up; had mass arrested
አፈሰሰ	see ፈሰሰ
አፈቀረ	see * ፈቀረ
አፈተለከ	see * ፈተለከ
አፈታ	see ፈታ
አፈነ	affänä v.t choked, suffocated; kidnapped; kept as a strict secret
አፍኖ ያዘ	affəno yazä v.t suppressed *(a smile)*
—ገደለ	—gäddälä v.t smothered
አፋኝ	afäna n. kidnappping
አፋኝ	affañ n. kidnapper
እፍኝ	əffəññ n. handful, fistful
ማፈኛ	maffäña n. gag, clip
ተፋፈነ	täjaffänä v.i was **overcrowded**, congested; thronged
ታፈነ	taffänä v.i was choked, suffocated, muffled *(the nose)*; was kidnapped; was kept as a strict secret
አሳፈነ	asaffänä v.t had s/o kidnapped
አፈነገጠ	afänäggäṭä v.i retreated, withdrew, receded
አፈንጋጭ	afängaç n. secessionist
አፈናጠጠ	see ፈነጠጠ
አፈዘዘ	afäzzäzä see ፈዘዘ
አፈገ	affägä v.t cramped
እፍግ	əffəg cramped, stuffed together
ታፈገ	taffägä v.i was cramped, was stuffed together
ተፋፈገ	täfaffägä v.t huddled together *(due to narrow space)*

እፍግፍግ አለ	əfəgfəgg alä v.i was very much cramped, huddled, congested, became over—crowded
እፍግፍግ አደረገ	əfəgfəgg adärrägä v.t cramped, huddled, congested
አፈገመ	see ፈገመ
አፈገፈገ	see ፈገፈገ
አፈጠነ	see ፈጠነ
አፈጠጠ	see ፈጠጠ
አፈፈ	affäfä v.t trimmed *(edges of book)*, scraped, *(skin, hide)*
እፋፊ	əffafi n. scraping *(small bits produced by scraping)*
አፈፍ አለ	afäff alä v.i stood up abruptly
አፈፍ አደረገ	afäff adärrägä v.t seized *(s/t)* abruptly, grabbed
አፏጨ	afuʷaččä v.t whistled, see also ፉጨት
አፉሰሰ	see ፈሰሰ
አፉረደ	see ፈረደ
አፉደሰ	afaddäsä v.i loitered around; wandered; vagabonded
አፉዳሽ	afadaš adj. loiterer; wanderer; vagabond
አፉፉ	see ፉፉ
አፉፍ	afaf n. edge of a mountain, cliff, hill top, summit
አፍ	af n. mouth; opening, inlet; language
አፈ ልስልስ	afä ləsləs adj. polite, courteous, unruffled
አፈሙዝ	afämuz n. muzzle *(of gun)*
አፈማር	afämär n. glib; suave
አፈቅቤ	afäqəbe adj. glib, suave
አፈታሪክ	afätarik also ያፍ ታሪክ yaf tarik n. legend, mythology
አፈኛ	afäñña adj. talkative
አፈንጉሥ	afänagus n. President of the Supreme Court
አፈጮሌ	afäçolle adj. smart aleck
አፈጮማ	afäčoma adj. glib,

191

አፍለኛ	suave	ባሕረ ኤርትራ	bāhrä erətra n. Red Sea

አፍለኛ

• ጦጣ አፍ

እኔሁ አፍ

suave

cfläñña n. unleavened *ənğära*

muti af ad. talkative

ašoh af n. one who makes malicious remarks

አፍላ — *afla* n. prime, youthfulness, youth, vigour

አፍላል — *aflal* n. large clay pot for boiling meat etc.

አፍሪቃ — *afriqa* n. Africa

አፍሪቃዊ / አፍርንጅ — *afriqawi* n. African — *afrəng* n. ground pepper (*appetizer*)

አፍታታ — see *ፈታ*

አፍንጫ / እፍንጫማ — *afənča* n. nose — *afənčamma* adj. long-nosed

አፍንጮ / አፋአ / አፋአዊ — *afənčo* adj. long-nosed — *afə'o* n. external (*G.*) — *af'awi* adj. external

አፎት / አፎቄ / አፍዮን — *afot* n. sheath — *afoqe* n. lance — *afyon* n. opium

አፓርትማ / ኡኡ አለ — *appartma* n. apartment — *'u'u alä* v.i cried for help

ኡጋንዳ / ኢሉባቦር — *uganda* n. Uganda — *illubbabor* n. one of the Administrative Regions, western Ethiopia (*Ilubbabor*)

ኢምንት — *imənt* n. nothing, not worth mentioning, unimportant

ኢትዮጵያ / ኢትዮጵያዊ — *itəyoppyəa* n. Ethiopia — *ityoppəyawi* n. Ethiopian (*m*)

ኢ.ትዮጵያዊት — *itəyoppəyawit* n. Ethiopian (*f.*)

ኢንሹ / ኢየሩሳሌም / ኢየሱስ / ኢየሱሳዊ / ኢየቤልዩ / ኢጣልያ / ኢጣልያነኛ / ኢጣልያዊ — *inšu* n. Gunther's dikdik — *iyyärusalem* n. Jerusalem — *iyyäsus* n. Jesus — *iyyäsusawi* n. Jesuit — *iyyobeləyu* n. jubilee — *italəya* n. Italy — *italyanəñña* n. Italian (*lauguage*) — *italyawi* Italian (*person*)

ኤሊ / ኤርትራ / ኤርትራዊ — *eli* n. tortoise — *erətra* n. Eritrea — *erətrewi* n. Eritrean

ኤክዌተር — *ekkwetär* n. equator also *የምድር ሰቅ* *yämədər säqq*

ኤጭ — *ečč* interj. exclamation of abhorence

ኤፒስ ቆጶስ — *epis qoppos* n. bishop

ኤጲፋንያ — *epifanəya* n. epiphany

እህ — *əh* interj. well (*expression of astonishment*), well! (*expression of relief*); well (*expression of consent*), e.g well go ahead; oh, yes!

እህል — *əhəl* n. grain, crops, food

እህላም — *əhlam* adj. rich in grain, full of crops

እህት / እህቶችማማች — *əhət* n. sister, *also* እኅ *əi* — *əhətəmmamuč* n. sisters

አላም አለ — *əiləm alä* v.i disappeared, vanished

አላቅት — *əliəqt* n. Adam's apple see *አለቀ*

አላቅና / አላባት / አላክ — *əlləbat* n. book-mark — *əllək* n. obstinacy, stubbornness *also* አላሁ

አልከኛ — *əlləkäñña* adj, stubborn, obstinate *also* አልከኛ

አላፍ — *əlf* adj. ten thousand (*arch.*)

አላፍኝ — *əlfəññ* n. living-room; porlour

— አስከልካይ — —*askälkay* n. chamberlain

—አሽከር — —*aškär* n. butler

እሑድ — *əhud* n. Sunday

እም ምኔት — *əmmä mənet* n. abbess; Mother Superior

እምር አለ — *əmmärr alä* v.i hopped, crossed (*a ditch etc.*) by hopping

እምቤት — *əmmäbet* n. lady, lady of the house

እምቤታችን — *əmmäbetaččən* Our Lady, the Virgin Mary

የቤት እምቤት — *yäbet əmmäbet* n. housewife

እምት — *əmmät* interj./n yes

አመኚት *(answer given when a woman is called by s/o or when s/o calls her)*

አመኚት *∂mmāčat* n. nursing mother

—ጽሕፈት —*ṣ∂hfāt* n. insertion *(writing)*

አማሆይ *∂mmahoy* n. term used to address a nun *(such as "mother! etc.")*

አሜቴ *∂mmete* interj. my lady!

አምር *∂mm∂r* adj. tiny, minute

—ታህል —*tah∂l* n. tiny thing

አምስ *∂ms* n. vagina, vulva

አምቡ-ሽቡ-ሽ *∂mbušbuš* n. unfermented beer

አምቡ ዋ አለ *∂mbu"a alä* v.i lowed *(cow)*

አምቡዋይ *∂mbu"ay* n. solanum incanum, solanum indicum

አምቡጥ *∂mbuṭ* n. pad, shell

አምቢልታ *∂mbilta* . n. large wind instrument like a fife

አምቢልተኛ *∂mbiltāñña* n. one who plays the አም ቢ.ልታ also አምቢ ልታ ነፊ

አምቢ አለ *∂mbi alä* v.i refused; became difficult to run , manipulate *(machine, gadget)*

አምቢ.ተኛ *∂mbitāñña* adj. disobedient, refractory, recalcitrant

አምቢ.ታ *∂mbita* n. refusal

አምብርት *∂mb∂rt* n. navel; centre, core *(most important part of anything)*

አምብዛም *∂mb∂zamm (followed by a negative verb)* adv. seldom, not often rarely, scarcely

አምቦሳ *∂mbossa* n. calf *(newly born)*

አሜ *∂mm∂yyä* interj. mother; *(lit. my mother)*

አምፉርፉር *∂mf∂rf∂r or* እንፉርፉ ∂nf∂rf∂r n. boiled dry ∂nǧ∂ra with wäṭ cf. ግንፉልፉል

አሠይ *∂ssäy* interj. hurrah

well done .

አሜት *∂sset* n. wage, value

አረኛ *∂rräñña* n. shepherd herdsman; impolite rude, boorish, illmannered, vulgar

አረኝነት *∂räññ∂nnät* n. herdsmanship

አረኛነት *∂rräññannät* n. impoliteness, rudeness, etc

(እ)ፉር *see* ፉር

(እ)ፉዝ *see* ፉዝ

(እ)ፉት *see* ፉ.ቀ

(እ)ሪዝ *see* ሪዝ

አሪይ *∂ryia* n. wild boar

አራሪ *∂rrari* adj. dwarfish

(እ)ራስ *see under* ራስ

(እ)ራቄት *see* ራቄት

አርሱ *∂rsu* pron. he, it

(እ)ርሳስ *see* ርሳስ

አርሳዎ *∂rsāwo* pron. you *(pol.)*

(እ)ርሳት *see* ርሳት *and* ወረሳ

አርሾ *∂ršo* n. leaven, yeast in አርቃን ሥጋ ∂rqanä s∂ga n. nakedness

አርባና *see* ረባ

አርቦ *∂rbo* n. one fourth *(product of land paid to landlord)*

አርኩም *∂rkum* n. stork

አርኩስ *see* ርኩስ

አርካን *∂rkän* n. degree *(solar measurement)*; staircase: terrace *(levelled area of slopping land)*

አርካብ *∂rkab* n. stirrup

አርኮት *∂rkot* n. water container *(made of hard leather)*

አርያ *∂rya* n. wild boar also አሪይ

አርይ አለ *∂rr∂y alä* v.i cried for help, also አረ አለ

አርድ *∂rd* turmeric; slaughtered animal see also አረደ

(እ)ርግብ *see* ርግብ

አርግብግቢት *∂rg∂bg∂bit* n. propeller; fontanelle see also *ረገብገብ

አርጋጥ *∂rgaṭ* adj. sure; with out any doubt, for granted see ረጋጠ

አርጋጠኛ *∂rgaṭäñña* adj. sure;

193

እርግጥ — without any doubt, for granted

እሰይ — ərrəmta n. barrage (continuous gunfire)
əssäy interj. (exclamation of joy, welcome, approval,) hurrah;

እሳ — əssa interj. oho!; (exclamation of surprise or triumph)

እሳት — əsat n. fire; adj. brilliant, intelligent

እሳተ ገሞራ — əsatä gämora n. volcano

እሳታዊ — əsatawi adj. pertaining to fire

እሳት አፍ — əsat af adj. talkative, chatty

—አደጋ — —adäga n. firehazard; fire brigade

እሳቸው — əssaččäw pron. he, she (polite)

እስላም — əslam n. Mohammedan, Muslim see also ሰለሞ

እስራኤል — əsra'el n. Israel
እስራኤላዊ — əsra'elawi n. Israelite
እስስት — əsəst n. chameleon; adj. spiteful, vicious

—አፍ — —af n. back-biting, slanderer

እስተ — or እስከ əstä, əskä prep. conj. until, tili

እስከዚህ — əskäzzih prep. until here

እስከዚያ — əskäzziya prep: until there; till then

እስከየት — əskäyät prep. until where?

እስካሁን — əskahun conj. until now

እስቲ — or እስኪ, əsti, əski well now, please?

—ለየው — —ləyäw please let me see it (him)

—አሳየኝ — —assayäññ please show me!

—ላሂድ — —ləhid let me go
—ትሂድና — —təhedənna let me see you dare go

እስትንፋስ — əstənfas n. breath, breathing; mere words not tangible, see also ነፈስ

እስክ — see እስተ
እስክስታ· — əskəsta n. shoulder dance (typical Ethiopian)

—ወረደ — —wärrädä v.t. danced (with shoulders)

እስክንድርያ — əskandərəya n. Alexandria

እስያ — əsya n. Asia
ትንሹ— — tənnəšu—Asia Minor
እስፓንያ — əspanəya n. Spain
እስፓንኛ — əspanəñña n. Spanish
(እ)ስፖርት — əsport n. sport
እሿት — see ሺት
እሺ — əšši yes, all right, O.K.

—አለ — —alä v.i. complied, agreed, consented

—ባይ — —bay adj. submissive, compliant

እሽ — əšš interj. hush! silence keep calm!

—አለ — əšš alä v.t. shooed (flies, birds, chickens etc)

እሽሩሩ — əššəruru n. lullaby
እሽኮላሌ — əškoläle n. altercation, squabble

እሾክ — əšoh n. thorn also እሾሁ
እሾኻም — əšoham adj. thorny
(እ)ቀጭ አለ — əqäčč alä v.i. snapped (break with a sharp crack)

እቀጭጭታ· — əqqäččəta n. snap (sound of breaking)

እበት — əbbät n. dung
እቡይ — əbbuy adj. wicked, evil minded, bad-hearted

እባብ — əbab n. serpent, snake
እባባም — əbabam adj. full of serpents, snakes

እባክህ — əbakkəh v.i. please? do me a favour?

እባክዎን — əbakkäwon v.i. please do me a favour? (polite)

እባካችሁ — əbakkaččəhu pl. of the above

እባክሽ — əbakkäš f. of the above

እብስ አለ — əbbəss alä v.i. left for good,' disappeared

194

	vanished *(out of sight)*
እብሪት	*əbrit* n. arrogance, conceit
እብሪተኛ	*əbritäñña* adj. arrogant, conceited
እብነ በረድ	*əbənä bäräd* n. marble
እብነ አድማስ	*əbənä admas* n. diamond
እቴቴ	*ətete* n. expression used to address an elder sister or an elder female relative
እቴዋ	*ətewwa* my sister *(expression used to address a female aquaintance or a sister)*
እቴጌ	*ətege* n. Empress
እት	or እህት *ət, əhət* n. sister
እትማማች	*ətəmmamač* n. sisters
እትማማችነቱ	*ətəmmamačənnät* n. sisterhood
እትዬ	*ətəyyä* n. my sister *(when addressing an elder sister or an elder acquaintance)*
እትፍ አለ	*əttəf alä* or እንትፍ አለ *əntəff alä* v.t spat
እቶን	*əton* n. furnace
እነ	*ənnä* plural marker pref. እነማ *ənnäma* who ?
እነኛ	*ənnäñña* or እነዚያ *ənnazziya* pron. adj. those
እነዚህ	*ənnäzzih* pron. adj. these
እነኋት	*ənnähuʷat* here she is *(arch.)*
እነሆ	*ənnäho* v.t behold here he is! here it is!
እና	*ənna* conj. and, and then, see ና *na*
እናት	*ənnat* n. mother
እናትነት	*ənnatənnät* n. motherhood
እናትና አባት	*ənnatənna abbat* n. parents
እናት አገር	*ənnat agär* n. motherland
የእንጀራ እናት	*ya'ənǧära ənnat* n. stepmother
የክርስትና—	*yäkərəstənna—* n.

	godmother
እንስላል	*ənsəlal* n. anise
እንሰት	*ənsät* n. false banana
እንስራ	*ənsəra* n. large water jar *(made of clay)*
እንስሳ	*ənsəsa* n. adj. animal
እንስሳነት	*ənsəsannät* n. animality
እንስሳት	*ənsəsat* n. fauna
እንስሳዊ	*ənsəsawi* adj. animal
የቤት እንስሳ	*yäbet ənsəsa* n. domestic animal
እንስት	*ənəst* adj. female
እንስትነት	*ənəstənnät* n. femininity
እንሽላሊት	*ənšəlalit* n. lizard
እንሽርት ውሃ	*ənsərt wəha* n. amniotic fluid
እንቃቅላ	*ənqaqəlla* n. small poisonous lizard
እንቅርት	*ənqərt* n. goitre
እንቅርታም	*ənqərtam* adj. goitrous
እንቅብ	*ənqəb* n. large basket for measuring grain
እንቆቅልሽ	*ənqoqəlləš* n. puzzle, riddle
እንቆቆ	*ənqoqqo* n. seed of a a plant used against tapeworm
እንቁላል —ጣለ (ች)	*ənqʷəlal* n. egg *ənqulal ṭallä(čč)* v.t laid an egg
እንቁራሪት	*ənqʷərarit* n. frog
እንቁጣጣሽ	*ənqʷəṭaṭaš* n. New Year's festival *(first of Mäskäräm)*
እንቡዋይ	see እምቡዋይ
እንቢልታ	see እምቢልታ
እንባ	or እምባ *ənba, əmba* n. tears
እንባም	*ənbam* adj. easily irritated to weep
እንባ አዘለ	*ənba azzälä* v.t was tearful, was teary
እንባ በእንባ ተራጨ	*ənba bänba täraččä* v.i lamented *(in group)*
እንተን	or እንትና *əntän, əntənna* n. what is his name? *(used when failing to remember s/o's name)*
እንትን	*əntən* what is the name?

195

እንተፉ፡ አለ   (used when failing to remember the name of s/t) *əntəff alä*. or **እትፉ አለ** *ətəff alä* v.t spat

እትፉታ   *əttəfta* n. spitting

እንቶ ፈንቶ   *ənto fänto* n. nonsense

እንቺ   *ənčči* imp. take, here you have see **እንኪ**

እንከን   *ənkän* n. defect, blemish (of reputation)

እንከናም   *ənkänam* adj. full of defect, imperfect

እንከን የማያጠፋው   *ənkän yämayaṭaw* adj. inacurrate, erroneous (perpetually)

እንከፉ   *ənkäf* adj. idiotic, imbecile, senile

እንካ   *ənka* imp. take! here you have (m.)

—በንካ   —*bánka* give and take

እንኪ   *ənki* or **እንቺ** *ənči* imp. take, here you have (f.)

እንከርት   *ənkərrit* n. brazier

እንከርዳድ   *ənkərdad* n. tares

እንከርዳዳም   *ənkərdadam* adj. full of tares

እንከብል   *ənkəbəll* n. tablet, pill, see also **ተንከባለለ**

እንኮኮ አለ   *ənkokko alä* v.t carried (child) on the shoulders

እንኮኮ   *ənkokko* n. carrying (a child) on the shoulders

እንኮይ   *ənkoy* n. plum

እንኳ   *ənku^a* adv. even

እንኳን   *ənku^an* (with negative verb) adv. not even

እንዘጥ አለ   or **እንዘጭ አለ** *ənzäṭ alä*, *ənzzäčč alä* v.i flopped (on the bottom)

እንዚራ   *ənzira* n. Ethiopian harp

(እ)ንዝህላላ   (*ə*)*nzəhlal* adj. slack, careless

(እ)ንዝህላ ልነት   (*ə*)*nzəhlalənnät* n. slackness, carelessness

እንዝርት   *ənzərt* n. spindle

እንዝዝ   *ənzəz* n. type of beeltle

ጥቋር—   *ṭəqur*—n. hornet

እንደ—   *əndä*—adj. prep. adv. like, as, according to, in accordance with

እንደልብ   *əndäləbb* as one wishes

እንደኔ   *əndäne* adv. according to me

እንደገና   *əndäggäna* adv. again

እንዲሁ   *əndihu* adv. and also, likewise

እንዲሁም   *əndihumm* adv. thus, likewise

እንዲህ   *əndih* adj. like this, such

እንዶታ   *əndeta* adv. surely

እንዶት   *əndet* adv. how?

እንዶድ   *əndod* n. phytolaca dodecandra (a plant whose fruit is used as a detergent, soap tc.)

እንጀራ   *ənğära* n. bread (usually Ethiopian)

እንጀራ አባት   *ənğära abbat* n. stepfather

—እናት   —*ənnat* n. stepmother

የንብ እንጀራ   *yänəb ənğära* n. honeycomb

የንጀራ ልጅ   *yänğära ləg* n. stepchild

እንጂ   *ənği* adv. conj. but, on the contrary,

ይሁን እንጂ   *yəhun ənği* adv. nevertheless

እንጃ   *ənğa* adv. I have no idea, I dont know, I wouldn't know

እንጃለት   *ənğallät* adv. I h ave no idea about him, I woudn't know about him (expression of indifference)

እንጃለህ   *ənğalləh* adv. I have no idea about you, I wouldn't know about you; (don't nag me)

እንጃለሽ   *ənğalləš* adv. (f. of the above)

እንጃለኝ   *ənğalləňň* adv. woe

me !
እንጃባቱ ənǧabbatu adv. to Hell with him; I wouldn't know about him
እንጀሪ ənǧorri n. raspberry
እንገር əngär n. colstrum
እንጉዳይ ənguday n. mushroom
እንግሊዝ əngəliz n. Englishman, English
እንግሊዛዊ əngəlizawi n. Englishman
እንግሊዘኛ əngliz ənña n. English (language)
እንግሊዝ አገር əngəliz agär n. England
እንግልጣር ənglṭar n. England (arch.)
እንግዲህ əngədih adv. therefore; hence, thus, now
እንግዲያማ əngədiyamma adv. well then, if that is the case
እንግዲያስ əngədiyass adv. (same as above)
ከእንግዲህ kängədih adv. hereafter
—ወዲህ —wädih adv. henceforth, from this time onward
—ወዲያ —wädiya adv. from this time on
እንግዳ əngəda n. guest, stranger; adj. odd, queer, unusual
—ነገር –nägär n. unusual thing
—ደራሽ —däraš n. sudden occurrence, unexpected happening
እንጉቻ əngočča n. small əngära (specially baked for children) see እነጉተ
እንጣጥ አለ ənṭaṭ alä v.i sprang
እንጥል ənṭəl n. uvula, tonsil
እንጨት ənčät n. wood
የእንጨት yä'ənčät adj. wooden
እንጫጭ ənčəč n. unripe, green
እንፋሎት ənfalot n. vapour, steam
እንፍሉ ənfəlle n. lightly boiled meat
እንፍ አለ ənf alä v.i blew one's nose (pol.)

እኛ əñña pron. we
እኝኝ ብላ əññəññ bəla n. a three days' continuous rain sometimes at the beginning of September
እከሉ əkäle, or እንሊ əgäle n. so-and-so, such-and-such
እከክ əkäk n. itch, see also አከክ
እከድዩ əkkädəyyä interj. oh no! (exclamation of surprise, astonishment, stupefaction)
እኩል əkkul adj/n equal, alike, half, uniform see also እኩለ
እከል əkkəl n. problem (personal), obstacle
እከላም əkkəlam adj. full of problems
እኮ əkko adv. indeed! yes; of course ! exactly, truly
እሽ əhə adv. yes! imp. go on (i.e I am listening)
እውልኝ əwəlləñña imp. see, look (what is happening)
እውነት əwnät n. truth, reality; adj. true, real
እውነተኛ əwnätäñña adj. truthful
እውነታ əwnäta n. reality
እውነተኛነት əwñätäññäññät n. truthfulness
እውነትም əwnätəmm adj. indeed, certainly, as a matter of fact
እውን əwn n. reality, truth
እዚህ əzzih adj. here
እዚያ əzziya adj. there
—እያ —əyyä pref. (used both with nouns) each, every (with a perfect verb) while, all the time that
እየቀሉ əyyäqəlu adj. different from one another
እያደር əyyaddär adv. later on, as time passes
እያንዳንዱ əyandandu adj. each

እየመጣ	one, every one *ʾyyāmāṭṭa* v.i he is coming
እዳ	*ʾda* n. debt
ባለዳ	*balāda* also ባለእዳ *balāʾʾda* n. creditoɪ, debtor
እድመኛ	*ʾdmāñña* n. invited guests *(at a wedding feast)*, see also አዳም
እድሜ	*ʾdme* n. age
እድም	*ʾdmo* n. fence *(of church);* churchyard
እጅ	*ʾǧǧ* n. hand
እጅ ሰፊ	*ʾǧǧā sāffi* adj. generous
—ብሉህ	*—bʾlʾh* adj. highly skilled *(in manual work)*
—ጠባብ	*—ṭābbab* n. tunic *(loose narrow sleeved shirt reaching the knees)*
እጀታ	*ʾǧǧāta* n. handle *(of an axe)*
እጅ ለእጅ	*ʾǧǧ lāǧǧ* hand in hand
—መንሻ	*—mānša* n. present *(to higher man in rank or position)*
—ሰጠ	*—sāṭṭā* v.i. capitulated ; surrendered
—ብጅ	*—bāǧǧ* n. cash *(payment);* act of working together to complete a piece of work quickly
—በዛ	*—beza* n. thimble
—ነሣ	*—nāssa* v.i bowed down *(to greet)*
—አደረገ	*—adārrāgā* v.i took over, **took** control over *(/st),* possessed
—ና እግር	*—na ʾgʾr* n. limbs
—እጅ አለ.	*—ʾǧǧ alā* v.i got fed up with; loathed
—ከፍንጅ ተያዘ	*—kāfʾnǧ tāyazā* was caught red–handed
ሁለት እጅ	*hulātt ʾǧǧ* twice as much
ባለጅ	*balāǧǧ* n. blacksmith, craftsman
የእጅ ሥራ	*yāʾʾǧǧ sʾra* n. manual

	work, handicraft
—ሰዓት	*—sāʾat* n. wristwatch
—ሹራብ	*—šurrab* n. glove
—ቦምብ	*—bomb* n. grenade
—ጠብብ	*—ṭʾbāb* n. handicraft
—ጽሕፈት	*—ṣʾhʾfāt* n. handwriting, penmanship
እጅግ	*.ʾǧǧʾge* n. sleeve
እጅግ	*ʾǧʾgg* adv. very much
—በጣም	*—bāṭam* adv. extremely, very much
እጅጉን	*ʾǧǧʾgun* adv. very well ? *(after having greeted s/o to ask such a question as "are things going very well ?*
እጋለ	*ʾgāle* n. so-and-so also አከሌ
እጋሊት	*ʾgālit* n. *(f)* so-and-so
እግር	*ʾgʾr* n. foot
እግረ መንገድ	*ʾgrā mängād* n. on one's way
የእግር—	*yāʾʾgʾr—* n. path, trail, track, footpath
እግረ ሙቅ	*ʾgrā muq* n. tight shackle
እግረኛ	*ʾgrāñña* n. pedestrian; adj. restless
እግር በግር	*ʾgʾr bāgʾr* adv. one after the other
—ብረት	*—bʾrāt* n. fetter, shackle
ልጅ እግር	*lāǧǧ ʾgʾar* n/adj. young man, young woman ; young
እጅና እግር	*ʾǧǧʾnna ʾgʾr* n. limbs
እግዚአብሔር	*ʾgzi'ābʾher* n. God
እግዚእነ	*ʾgzi'ʾnā* **Our** Lord
እግዚአታ	*ʾgzi'ota* n. name of prayer *(God have mercy upon us)*
እግዝእት	*ʾgzā't* n. **Our** Lady
እግዝእትነ ማርያም	*ʾgzā'tʾnā mariyam* n. Our Lady Mary
እጢ	*ʾṭi* n. gland
እጣን	*ʾṭan* n. incense see አጠበ
እጥቢ	
እጭ	*ʾčč* n. larva
እፉኝት	*ʾfuññit* n. viper
እፊያ	*ʾffiya* n. lid *(of a cooking pot, basket)*

198

እፍ አለ	əff alä v.t blew on the fire; lived high	ኦሪታዊ	oritawi adj. pertaining to the Old Testament; old fashioned
እፍ እፍ አለ	əff əff alä v.t blew on the fire repeatedly; lived in each others pocket	ሕን ኦሪት	həggä orit n. laws of Moses
አፍላ	afla n. time of full vigour, prime	ኦርቶዶክስ	ortodoks n. orthodox (belief)
—ጉረምሳ	afla gorämsa n. in the prime of youth	ኦርቶዶክሳዊ	ortodoksawi n. orthodox (believer)
እፎይ አለ	əffoy alä v.i sighed in or with relief, felt relief	ኦርቶዶክሳዊት	ortodoksawit n. Orthodox (church, or female Orthodox)
እፎይታ	əffoyta n. relief	አቶማቲክ	otomatik adj. automatic
ኦሪት	orit n. pentateuch; biblical times	አቶሞቢል	otomobil n. automobile
		ኦፐራሲዮን	operasiyon n. surgery, also ቀዶ ጥገና

ከ

ከ—	kä prep. from, at, out of		demarcated, appropriated
ከመጣ	kämäṭṭa if he comes	ተከለለ	täkullälä v.t demarcated (land border between neighbours or rivals)
ካልመጣ	kalmäṭṭa unless he comes		
ከሀዲ	see ካደ	ተከላይ	täkalay adj/n (one) who participates in solving border disputes
ከለለ	källälä v.i tinkled (ringing loud of a bell)		
ከለለ	källälä v.i screened, protected from view; staked out (a plot of land), appropriated (land for special purpose)	አስከለለ	askällälä v.t had (s/t or s/o) screened, protected from view; had (land, border)
ከለላ	käläla n. screen, cover (protecting from view)	ከለሰ	källäsä v.t diluted (a strong drink), added water (in a stew); reviewed (a lesson)
ከላይ	kälay adj/n (s/t) that screens, covers	ከለሽ	källaš n. revisionist
ከለላ	källala n. demarcation, appropriation (of land)	ከለሳ	källasa n. reviewing (a lesson), revision
ከለል	källäl n. boundary, confines, zone	ከልስ	källəs n. mulatto, half-caste
ብሔራዊ—	bəherawi—n. national park	መከለሻ	mäkälläša n. hot water added to stew
ተከለለ	täkällälä v.i was screened, protected from view ; was staked out; was appropriated (land for special purpose)	ተከለሰ	täkälläsä v.i was diluted; was reviewed
		ተካለሰ	täkalläsä v.i crossbred (with each other)
		አካለሰ	akkalläsä v.t caused

199

	to crossbreed
ከለበ	källäbä v.i became restless, bustled, hustled
ከላባ	källabba adj. graceless; busy-body
ከልብ	kälb n. dog *(Ar.)*
ከለበሰ	källäbbäsä v.t threw water at s/o, tossed out water
ተከለበሰ	täkäläbbäsä v.i was tossed out *(water)*
አስከለበሰ	askäläbbäsä v.t had water thrown at s/o
ከለቻ	källäčča n. helmet
ከለከለ	käläkkälä v.t prevented, hindered, forbade prohibited, impeded
ከልካይ	kälkay adj/n who prevents, hinders, forbids, impedes
ከልከል	kəlkəl adj. forbidden, prohibited, prevented
ተከለከለ	täkäläkkälä v.t was prevented, hindered, forbidden,
ተከላካይ	täkälakay adj/n *(one)* who defends, resists, withstands, defender, resistant
መከላከያ ሚኒስቴር	mäkkäläkäya minister Ministry of Defence
አከላከለ	akkälakkälä v.t caused to be prevented, forbidden, hindered, impeded
አስከለከለ	askäläkkälä v.t caused to be prevented, hindered, impeded
እልፍኝ አስከልካይ	əlfəññ askälkay n. chamberlain
ከለፈ	källäfä v.t became restless, nuisance
*ከለፈለፈ	*käläfälläfä
ከለፍላፋ	käläflaffa adj. mischievous, arch
ከለፍለፍ	kələfləf adj. mischievous, arch
ከለፍለፍ አለ	kələfləff alä v.i became too mischiev-

	ous, arch
ተከለፋለፈ	täkläfälläfä v.i become mischievous, arch
ተከለፍላፈ	täkläflafi adj. mischievous, arch
አከለፋለፈ	akläfälläfä v.t hustled, disturbed s/o's tranquility, serenity
ከል	käll n. mourning dress *(black, blue or yellow, usually white dress dyed in such colours)*
ከመረ	kämmärä v.t piled up stacked, put in a heap
ከማሪ	kämmari adj/n *(one)* who piles up, stacks, puts in a heap
ከመራ	kəmmära n. piling, stacking, heaping
ከምር	kemmər n. pile, heap *(usually of stones, etc.)*
አከመረ	akkammärä v.t helped *(s/o)* in piling up *(s/t)*
አስከመረ	askämmärä v.t had *(s/t)* piled up, stacked, heaped
*ከመቸ	* kämäčča
ከምቹ	kəməččú adj. assembled; collected, concentrated; self-sufficient
ከመቻት	kəməččət n. collection, concentration
ተከማቸ	täkamaččä v.i was assembled, gathered, concentrated
ተከመቻቸ	täkämäčaččä v.i became gradually gathered, assembled, collected concentrated
አከመቻቸ	äkkämäcaččä v.t assembled, collected, gathered, concentrated *(gradually)*
ከመከመ	kämäkkämä v.t patted into shape *(hair)*; raked together *(heap of hay)*
ከምከም	kəmkəm n. well-

ተከመከመ	shaped Afro hairstyle *täkämäkkämä* v.i was patted into shape *(hair)*; was raked together *(hay)*
ከሙን	*kämun* n. cumin *(spice)*
ከምሱር	*kämsur* n. primer *(of cartridge)*
ከሠተ	*kässätä* v.t made clear, manifested, revealed
ክሥተት	*kəstät* n. phenomenon
ተከሠተ	*täkässätä* v.i was clear, manifested, revealed
ከረመ	*kärrämä* v.i spent the year, spent the rainy season, spent a certain time of the year
ከራሚ	*kärami* adj/n. *(one)* who spends a year or part of the year at a certain place, one who lives long; s/t that lasts long
ከርሞ	*kärmo* n. next year
ከረምት	*kərämt* n. rainy season
መከረሚያ	*mäkrämiya* n. place, supply etc. for passing a year or part of a year
አከረመ	*akärrämä* v.t kept for a year, delayed for a year or a part of a year, kept for a long time
አከረመ	*akkarrämä* v.t lived with s/o *(e.g friend, relative)* for a year, or part of the year
ከረረ	*kärrärä* v.i was twisted tightly *(rope, string)*; became acute *(situation, crises etc.)* became grave *(quarrel)*
ከራራ	*kärara* adj. undersized, dwarfish *(person, animal)*
ከራር	*kərar* n. Ethiopian lyre *(with six strings)*
ክር	*kərr* n. thread; wick, ribbon *(typewriter)*
ተከረረ	*täkarrärä* v.i came to a head *(quarrel)*;

	was aggravated *(from both sides)*, reached a crisis
አከረረ	*akärrärä* v.t twisted tightly *(rope, string)*, made acute, grave *(situation, crisis quarrel)*
አከራሪ	*akrari* adj/n radical *(political)*; *(one)* who aggravates situations, quarrel
ቀኝ—	*qäññ*— n. right extremist
ግራ—.	*gəra*—- n. left extremist
ከረበበት	*käräbbätä* v.t knocked down *(with a blow or in wrestling)*
ተከረበበት	*täkäräbbätä* v.i was knocked down
ከርቡሽ	*kärbuš* n. water-melon
ከርቤ	*kärbe* n. myrrh
*ከረተተ	*kärättätä*
ከርታታ	*kärtatta* n. adj wanderer, roamer; wandering, roaming, vagrant
ተንከራተተ	*tänkärattätä* v.i wandered around, roamed, roved, became a vagrant
ተንከራታች	*tänkärataČ* adj/n same as ከርታታ
አንከራ ተተ	*ankärattätä* v.t caused to wander around, roam, rove
ከረተፈ	*kärättäfä* v.t hewed,
ተከረተፈ	*täkärättäfä* v.i was hewed
አስከረተፈ	*askärättäfä* v.t had *(s/t)* hewn
ከረከመ	*käräkkämä* v.t trimmed, shortened *(to give good shape)*; cut *(s/o's)* hair
ከርከማት	*kärkəmat* n. edge *(out of which the cut is made)*
ከርከም	*kərkəm* adj/n trimmed; cut *(hair)*; edge *(out of which the cut is made)*
የ ከርከም እ.ረ	*kərkkəm adärrägä*

201

ረገ

ተኸረከመ

እስከረከመ

ከረከረ

ማሲንቆ--

ከርከር

ከርከር

ተከረከረ

ተከራከረ

ዋጋ-

ተከራካሪ

አከራካሪ

የሚያከራክር

የማያከራክር

ከረዳዳ

ከርዳዳ

ከርዳድ

ከርድ
ከርድድ

ከራጢት

ከረፋፋ
ከራፋ

v.t trimmed well;
gave good shape;
(by shortening)
täkäräkkkämä v.i
was trimmed; was
shortened (to give
good shape); was
cut (hair)
askäräkkämä v.t had
(s/t) trimmed, cut
short; had (s/o's)
hair cut
käräkkärä v.i was
acrid (sharp stinging),
sawed
masinqo— played
the masinqo
kärkər n. chancroid
kərkər n. groove
level (of liquid
measure)
täkäräkikärä v.i was
sawed
täkärakkärä v.i
argued, debated
contended, contested
(challenge)
waga—v.i bargained,
haggled
täkärakari n.
disputant n. litigant
akkärakari adj. con-
troversial, debatable
yämmiyakkär'akkər
adj. controversial,
debatable
yämmayakkärakkər
adj. unquestionable,
beyond dispute
käräddädä v.i became
kinky; became coarse
(material, flour)
kärdadda adj. kinky;
coarse (material,
flour, powder etc.)
kərdad or እንከርዳድ
ənkərdad n. tares
kərədd same as ከርዳዳ
kərdəd adj. same as
ከርዳዳ
kärätit n. small bag,
pouch
see ተንከረፋፋ
käräffa v.i stank, have

ከርፋታም
ከርፋት
አከረፋ

ከራማ

ከርስ
ከርሡ ባሕር

—ምድር

ከርሳም

ከችከር
ከሰለ

ከሰልማ

ከሰል
ከሰይ

—እንጨት

ከሰይ

አከሰለ

አከሰይ

አስከሰለ

ከሰመ

አከሰመ

ከሰረ

ከሳራ

ኪሳራ

a horrid and of-
fensive smell
kərfatam adj. stinking
kərfat n. stink
akäräffa v.t caused
to stink, stank
kärama n. respect-
ability(Ar.), charisma
kärs n. belly, stomach
kärsä bahr n. bottom
of the sea
—mədər n. bottom
of the earth
kärsam adj. glutto-
nous
kärkärro n. warthog
kässälä v.i became
charcoal; was sun-
burnt, became
extremely dark
(pigmentation)
käsäləmma adj.
darkish, blackish
käsäl n. charcoal
käsay adj. easily
carbonized (type of
wood)
—ənččät n. wood that
can easily be trans-
formed into charcoal
kəssay adj. car-
bonized
akässälä v.t made
charcoal; sunburnt,
darkened completely
(pigmentation)
aksay adj/n (one)
who makes charcoal
askässälä v.t had
(s/o) make charcoal
kässämä v.i dried
(wound); withered,
faded (plant), be-
came sunburnt
akässämä v.t dried
(wound); faded,
withered (plant)
kässärä v.i became
bankrupt ; went
broke
kässara n. bank-
ruptcy
kisara n. expend-

	iture, expenses; costs; deficit
አክሰረ	akässärä v.t bankrupted; brought deficit, incurred unnecessary costs
አክሳሪ	aksari adj. bankrupting (business deal)
ከሰሰ	kässäsä v.t accused, brought a law suit,sued (s/o), brought a charge against (s/o)
ከሳሽ	käsaš n. plaintiff, accuser
ከስ	kəss n. charge (legal); accusation, suit (in court of law)
ተከሰሰ	täkässäsä v.i was charged (in a court of law), was sued
ተከሳሽ	täkässaš n. defendant, accused
ተካሰሰ	täkassäsä v.t accused each other, brought charges against each other, sued each other
ተካሳሽ	täkasaš n. parties accusing each other
አካሰሰ	akkassäsä v.t caused to accuse each other etc.
አስከሰሰ	askässäsä v.t had, (s/o) accused, sued, charged
ሰበ	kässäbä v.t earned (money in trade), profited; tilled (land)
ከሰብ	käsäb n. earning, profit
ወሰከሰ	käsäkkäsä v.t harrowed (ploughed ground); dashed to bits
ገንዘብ—	gänzäb — v.t squandered (money)
መከስከሻ	mäkäskäša n. harrow
ተከሰከሰ	täkäsäkkäsä v.t was harrowed; was dashed to bits
ተከሳከሰ	täkäsakkäsä v.t hit up each other; rained blows at each other
አከሰከሰ	akäsäkkäsä v.t gave

	plenty of food and drink
አስከሰከሰ	askäsäkkäsä v.t had (ground) harrowed; had (s/t) dashed to bits
ከሳ	kässa v.i became thin, became emaciated, lost weight, became skinny
ከሲታ	kässitta adj. thin, skinny
ከሳት	kəsat n. thinness, loss of weight
አከሳ	akässa v.t made thin, made skinny
ከሸነ	kāššänä v.t made excellent (usually for ወጥ), garnished
ከሸፈ	kāššäfä v.i misfired (gun); became abortive (plan, revolution)
*ከበለለ	see ተንከባለለ
ከበረ	käbbärä v.i was honoured, revered; was precious, became wealthy; got rich, was celebrated (holiday)
የከበረ ድንጋይ	yäkäbbärä dəngay n. precious stone, gem
ከበረታ	käbäreta n. honour, reverence
ከበርቴ	käbbärte adj. wealthy
የመሬት—	yämäret–n. land lord
ከቡር	kəbur adj. respectful; His honour, excellency
ክቡራን	kəburan gentlemen, your excellencies
ክቡራት	kəburat ladies
ክብረት	kəbrät n. wealth; riches
ክብር	kəbr n. honour, reverence, respect, prestige
ክብርና	kəbrənna n. virginity; celibacy
ከብረ በዓል	kəbrä bä'al n. celebration
ክብር ዘበኛ	kəbr zäbäñña n. bodyguard
ክብርና ገሠሠ	kəbrənna gässäsä

ተከበረ   v.t deflowered
täkäbbärä v.i was honoured; was venerated, commanded respect, became celebrated *(holiday)*

ተከባበረ   täkäbabbärä v.i gave mutual respect, respected each other

ተከባባሪ   täkäbabari adj. respecting each other

አከበረ   akäbbärä v.t honoured, venerated, gave respect to; celebrated *(holiday)*

ቃሉን—   qalun—he kept his word

አከባሪ   akbari adj. honouring, respecting

ቀጣሮ—   qäṭäro—adj. punctual

አከባባር   akkäbabär n. way of celebration, ceremony, celebration

አከብሮት   akbᵊrot n. veneration, respect, honour

አከባበረ   akäbabbärä v.t gave pretentious honour, respect etc.

አስከበረ   askäbbärä v.t had *(s/o, s/t)* honoured, respected

ሕግ አስከባሪ   hᵊgg askäbbari n. public prosecutor

ሥነ   sᵊna sᵊr'at—n. master
ሥርዓት —   of ceremonies; policeman

ፀጥታ—   ṣäṭṭᵊta—n. security man

ከበሮ   käbäro n. drum

—መታ   —mätta v.t played the drum

ከበሰ   käbbäsä v.i tied a. big turban around the head

ከበበ   käbbäbä v.t encircled., surrounded, besieged., encompassed, crowded around *(s/t)*

ከበባ   käbäba n. encirclement, surrounding

ከባቢ   käbabi adj. surrounding

—አየር   ayyär n. atmosphere

—ጋፊት   —gᵊffit n. atmospheric pressure

ከበብ   käbäb n. club, circle *(geometrical)*

የሙዚቃ—   yämuziqa— n. glee club

የከበብ   yäkᵊbäb aggamaš n.
አጋማሽ   semi-circle

ከብ   kᵊbb adj. round, circular

ከብነት   kᵊbbᵊnnät n. roundness

ከብብ አደረገ   kᵊbᵊbb adärrägä v.t encircled completely

ተከበበ   täkäbbäbä v.t was encircled, surrounded besieged completely

አካበበ   akkabbäbä v.t surrounded

አካባቢ   akkababi n. surrounding

አስከበበ   askäbbäbä v.t caused to be surrounded, encircled, besieged

ከበተ   käbbätä v.t accumulated *(wealth)*; hid one's ill-will

አካበተ   akabbätä v.t accumulated *(wealth)*

አካባች   akabač adj/n *(one)* who accumulates wealth

ከበደ .   käbbädä v.i was heavy: was grave, was difficult, became serious *(situation)*; was severe *(punishment)*; was pregnant *(animal)*

ከባድ   käbbada adj. heavy
ከባድ   käbbad adj. heavy: difficult; serious, grave; severe *(injury)*

ተከበደ   täkabbädä v.t was heavy

ተካባጅ   täkabaǧ adj. heavy
አከበደ   akäbbädä v.t made difficult, serious

*ከበከበ   *käbäkkäbä
ተንከባከበ   tänkabakkäbä v.t treated well, cherished, yielded to the wishes of, took under one's wing

እንከባከበ	ankäbakkäbä v.t same as above
ከብት	käbt n. animal, livestock; adj. imbecile
—እርቢ	—arbi n. breeder (cattle)
—እርባታ	—ᵃrbata n. breeding (cattle)
የጋማ—	yägamma n. equines (horses, donkeys, mules)
የቀንድ—	yäqänd—n. cattle, bovines
የጭነት—	yäčᵃnät — n. pack animal
*ከተለ	*kättälä
ከትትል	kᵃtᵃttᵃl n. keeping an eye on, watching, supervison
ምክትል	mᵃkᵃttᵃl n. vice-, acting (for another)
—ሚኒስትር	—ministr n. viceminister
ከተል አለ	kättäll alä v.t followed (s/o)
ከተል አደረገ	kättäll adärrägä v.t brought next
ተከተለ	täkättälä v.t followed; resulted from
ተከታይ	täkättay adj. following, follower, entourage
ተከታተለ	täkätattälä v.t kept an eye on ; kept up with ; pursued ; followed each other ; happened in succession
ተከታታይ	täkätatay adj/n. successive, consecutive; (one) who keeps (an eye on)
አስከተለ	askättälä v.t caused to follow ; incurred (cost etc); resulted in, gave rise to
አከታተለ	akkätattälä v.t caused to happen one after the other , gave rise to
ከተለበ	kätälläbä v.t snatched (thief)
ተከተለበ	täkätälläbä v.i was snatched
ከተመ	kättämä v.t founded a city
ከተሚ	kätäme n. city dweller, metropolitan
ከተማ	kätäma n. city
—ቀመስ	—qämmäs adj / n. (one) who is exposed to city life
መሀል—	mähal—n. city centre
ከተረ	kättärä v.i diked; harnessed (a water fall) , concentrated, gathered
ከተራ	kätära n. eve of Epiphany (lit. gathering)
ከትር	kᵃttᵃr adj. diked; concentrated, gathered
ተከተረ	täkättärä v.i was diked ; was gathered was concentrated
አስከተረ	askättärä v.t had a dike built up
ከተበ	kättäbä v.t vaccinated; enrolled (s/o) in the army
ከታቢ	kätabi adj/n (one) who vaccinates ; (one) who enrolls people (in the army)
ከታብ	kᵃtab n. talisman, amulet (charm)
አሽን—	ašän— n. talisman (amulet)
ከትባት	kᵃttᵃbat n. vaccination
ተከተበ	täkättäbä v.i was vaccinated, was enrolled (in the army)
አስከተበ	askättäbä v.t had ,(s/o) vaccinated, had (s/o) enrolled (in the army)
ከተተ	kättätä v.t put (into a bag, satchel etc.)
ከቶ	kätto adv. absolutely, completely, fully; never
ከቶውንም	kättowᵃnᵃmm adv. never
ከተት	kᵃtät n. mobilization (troops)
ከት	kᵃtt n. with ልብስ e.g የከት ልብስ yäkᵃtt lᵃbs

205

ተከተተ	n. sunday best
	täkättätä v.i was put in; was inserted ; was stored ; came to an end
አካተተ	akkattätä v.t helped in putting (s/t) into a bag etc.; included
አካቴ	akkate in እስከናካቴው əskännakkatïew adv. never, at all
አሰከተተ	əskättätä v.t had (s/t) put into a bag, satchel etc; had (troops) mobilized
ከተከተ	kätäkkätä v.t chopped (wood, meat etc.); inflicted (with sharp pain)
ከትካች	kətəkkač n. splinters
ተንከተከተ	tänkätäkkätä v.i shrieked with laughter, howled with laughter
ተንከታከተ	tänkätakkätä v.i crumbled (broke into pieces)
ተከተከተ	täkätäkkätä v.i was chopped (wood, meat etc.)
ተከታከተ	täkätakkätä v.t bit each other fiercely
አንከተከተ	ankätäkkätä v.t caused to shriek, howl with laughter
አንከታከተ	ankätakkätä v.t. crumbled, crushed
አሰከተከተ	askätäkkätä v.t had (s/t) chopped
ከተፈ	kättäfä v.t cut in little pieces (meat); minced meat, onions etc; chopped
ከትፎ	kətfo n. a dish of minced meat with butter flavoured with chilli (served usually raw)
መከተፊያ	mäktäfiya n. chopping board (meat onion etc.)
ተከተፈ	täkättäfä v.i was minced, chopped (meat, onion etc.) minced, chopped

ከት ብሎ ሳቀ	kätt bəlo saqä v.i burst into laughter
ከተ	see ከተተ.
ከቻረ	käččärä v.i dried (bread)
ከቾር	käčaro adj. dwarfish (person); dry (humour), dull
ከቻሪ	käčarra adj. dwarfish (person), dry (humour)
ከቻቻ	käččäčä v.i became dry (bread etc.), became dull (conversation, speech etc.)
ከቻቻ	käčača adj. dry (uninteresting), dull
ከቾቾ አለ	kəččəč alä v.i dried to excess; became extremely boring
ከቾ አለ	käčč alä v.i arrived suddenly, arrived unexpectedly
ከነ—	kännä—prep. including, with
ከነቤተሰቡ	kännä betäsäbu with his family, including his family
ከነአካቴው	känn'akkattew adv. in spite of these (circumstances)
ከነበለ	känäbbälä v.t caused to tumble off, tipped up (container)
ከነተረ	känättärä v.t tied fast ; gave a stunning blow
ከነነ	kännänä v.i became bone–dry
አከነነ	akännänä v.i. made bone-dry
ከነከነ	känäkkänä v.t. tickled (pepper in the nostrils), vexed (caused anxiety in one's mind)
*ከነወነ	* känäwänä
ከነወ	kənəwwen n. accomplishment
ተከናወ	täkänawwänä v.i. was accomplished; was successful (an undertaking)
አከና ነ	akkänawwänä v.t. accomplished; brought to success

ከነጻ   *kānädda* v.t. measured by cubits *(length of arm)*

ክንድ   *kənd* n. arm, forearm; cubit

አስከነጻ   *askänädda* v.t. had s/o measure by cubits

ከነፋ   *kännäfä* v.t. bustled; fluttered about *(moved from place to place aimlessly)*

ክንፋም   *kənfam* adj. winged

ክንፍ   *kənf* n. wing

አከነፋ   *akännäfä* v.t caused to move quickely, bustled

*ከነነበ   * *känannäbä*

ተከነነበ   *täkänannäbä* v.i. covered one's head *(with a šämma)*, pulled a blanket over one's head

አከነነበ   *akkänannäbä* v.t. covered with a šamma, pulled blanket over s/o head

ከንቱ   *käntu* vain, futile, useless

ከንቱነት   *käntunnät* n. vanity, uselessness

ከንቲባ   *käntiba* n. mayor

ከንች   *känč* n. beams *(in building)*, rafters

ከንፈር   *känfär* n. lip

ከንፈራም   *känfäram* adj. thick-lipped

ከንፈር ወዳጅ   *känfär wädağ* n. boy friend, girl friend

ከከ   *käkka* v.t. ground *(coarsely)*

ከካም   *kəkkam* adj. untidy, dirty

ከክ   *kəkk* n. split-peas, beans etc. *(used for wäṭ)*

ተከከ   *täkäkka* v.i was ground coarsely

አስከከ   *askäkka* v.t had peas, beans etc. ground coarsely

ከውታታ   *käwtatta* n. roamer, wanderer

ከውትት አለ   *käwtätt alä* v.i roamed, wandered

ተንከዋተተ   *tänkäwattätä* v.i roamed, wandered

ከውር   *käwr* n. crucible, melting-pot

ከውካዋ   *käwkawwa* adj. light, frivolous, not serious

ከዛራ   *käzära* n. walking-stick, cane

ከዚህ   *käzzih* adv. from here

— በኋላ   —*bähuʷala* adv. after this

ከዚያ   *käzziya* adv. from there

—በኋላ   —*bähuʷala* adv. after that

—ወዲያ   —*wädiya* adv. since then, ever since

ከይሲ   *käysi* n. devil; cruel mischievous person, imp

ከደነ   *käddanä* v.t covered with a lid; thatched house with grass;

ከዳን   *kədan* n. cover, covering; thatch; cap *(pen)*

ቤት—   *bet*—n. thatch

ተከደነ   *täkäddänä* v.i was covered; thatched

አከደነ   *akkaddänä* v.t helped in covering *(s/t)*; helped in thatching a house

አስከደነ   *askäddänä* v.t had s/t covered; had a house thatched

ከዳ   *kädda* v.t betrayed, deserted; abandoned; denied

ከዳተኛ   *kädatäñña* n. traitor, deserter

ከጂ   *käği* n. traitor

ከዳት   *kədat also* ከሕደት *kəhdät* n. denial, betrayal ; desertion

አስከዳ   *askädda* v.t had s/o desert *(the army etc.)*; caused s/o to deny a friend etc. abandon etc.

ከጀለ   *käğğälä* v.t coveted, had the inclination to do, to like s/t

ከጀላ   *kəğğäla* n. inclination

ከፈለ to do, to have s/t
ከፈል *käffälä* v.t paid out; divided

ከፊል *käfil* n. partial

በከፊል *bäkäfil* adv. partially

ከፋይ *käfay* n. payer

ከፋይ *kəffay* n. segment

ከፍል *kəfəl* n. portion; room (in a house); class-room; division; grade (class in school)

ከፍለ ሀገር *kəflä hagär* n. administrative region

—ቃል —qal n. syllable

—ዓለም —aläm n. hemisphere, continent

—ዘመን —zämän century

—ጊዜ —gize n. period, session (in class)

—ጦር —ṭor n. division (army)

ከፍያ *kəfəyya* n. payment, pay, share

የመፃመሪያ *yämäǧämmäriya*—n. down-payment

መከፈልት *mäkfält* n. meal served to the clergy after service

መከፈያ *mäkfäya* n. bed urinal

ከፋፈለ *käfaffälä* v.t divided up, divided, classified, distributed

ከፋፍሎ ገዛ *käfafläh gəza* divide and rule

ከፍልፋይ *kəfəlfay* n. fraction

ከፍልፍል *kəfəlfəl* adj. divided, allotted

ተከፈለ *täkäffälä* v.i was paid out; was divided

ተከፋይ *täkäffay* n. adj. payee; divisible

ተከፋፈለ *täkäfaffälä* v.i divided between each other; was divided into many parts; was segmented; was divided (in opinion)

ተካፈለ *täkaffälä* v.i took a share, participated, divided (s/t) with (s/o), shared with another; split (profit

etc.)

ተካፋይ *täkafay* adj. n one (who) participates in (s/t), one (who) takes part in (s/t)

አከፋፈለ *akkäfaffälä* v.t distributed; apportioned, portioned out

አከፋፋይ *akkäfafay* n. distributor

ማምረቻና *mamräčanna* makk- ማከፋፈያ *äfafäyo* n. production and distribution

አካፈለ *akkaffälä* v.t divided (total); distributed, allotted; imparted (one's ideas)

አካፋይ *akkafay* adj/n one (who) divides (a total) ; one (who) distributes, allots

የጋራ — *yägara*—n. common denominator

ማከፈል *makkafäl* n. division (arithmetic)

አስከፈለ *askäffälä* v.t charged with a payment; made s/o pay charges

ከፈተ *käffätä* v.t opened; unlocked; got brighter (colour)

ክፍት *kəft* adj. open; bright (colour)

ልብ ክፍት *ləbbä kəft* adj. frank

ክፍት አፍ *kəft af* adj. talkative

መከፈቻ *mäkfäča* n. key, opener (instrument)

ቆርቆሮ— *qorqorro*—n. tin opener

ከፋፈተ *käfaffätä* v.t threw (doors, windows etc.) open

ክፍት አደረገ *käffət adärrägä* v.t opened suddenly

ተከፈተ *täkäffätä* v.t was opened; started (meeting)

ተከፋች *täkäffač* n. s/t that can be opened

ተካፈተ *täkaffätä* usually preceded with አፍ eg. አፍ ተካፈተ *af täkaffätä* v.i insulted at each other.

ተከፋፈተ · blamed each other

ከፈነ · täkäfaffätä v.t was wide open

ከፈን · käffänä v.t wrapped up a corpse for burial

መከፈኛ · käfän n. shroud

ተከፈነ · mäkäffäña n. shroud

አስከፈነ · täkäffänä v.i was wrapped up (corpse)

ከፈከፈ · askäffänä v.t had (a corpse) wrapped

käfäkkäfä v.t compacted the thatch roof, raked together (thatch, heap of hay)

ከፍከፍ · kəfkəf adj. well raked and trimmed

ተከፈከፈ · täkäfäkkäfä v.i was compacted well (thatch, heap of hay), was raked together

አስከፈከፈ · askäfäkkäfä v.t had (thatch etc.) compacted well, (heap of hay etc. raked together)

ከፈይ · käfäy n. velvet

ከፈፈ · käffäfä v.t trimmed the edges of s/t (usually leather, edge of book etc.)

ከፈፍ · kəfäf n. edge (trimmed)

ተከፈፈ · täkäffäfä v.i was trimmed (edges of s/t)

አስከፈፈ · askäffäfä v.t had(the edges of s/t) trimmed

ከፋ · käfa n. one of the Administrative Regions, south western Ethiopia (Kafa)

ከፋ · käffa v.i became worse, wicked, became bad

ከፉ · kəfu adj. wicked, evil, vicious, mean

—ቀን · —qän n. hard time

ከፉኛ · kəfuñña adv. awfully, gravely, badly; seriously

ከፉተኛ · kəfatäñña adj. wicked, evil, bad

ከፉት · kəfat n. wickedness,

ምን ከፋኝ · evil
mən käffañ I have no objection, I agree, I am willing

ከፋ አለው · käfa aläw v.i was rather sad, became somewhat offended

ተከፋ · täkäffa v.i became offended, sad, was hurt (feeling)

ተከፊ · täkäfi adj/n (one) who is easily offended

አከፋ · akäffa v.t worsened

አስከፋ · askäffa v.t displeased, angered (s/o); caused to dislike

አስከፊ · askäffi adj. disgusting, offensive, repulsive; ugly

ከፍ አለ · käff alä v.i was elevated, high, raised

ከፍተኛ · käffətäñña adj. higher, high, advanced (course); important (matter, rank etc.); maximum

—ፍርድ ቤት · —fərd bet n. High Court

ከፍታ · käffəta n. high (mountain), altitude

ከፍ ከፍ አለ · käff käff alä v.i was raised, elevated gradually, grew higher gradually

ኩሊ · kuli n. coolie, porter

ኩሊነት · kulinnät n. work of a coolie, porter

ኩላሊት · kulalit n. kidney

ኩል · kul n. antimony dust, see also ኳል

ኩልል አለ · see ኩላሊ

ኩምቢ · kumbi n.trunk(elephant)

ኩራዝ · kurraz n. small kerosene lamp; dwarf

ኩሬ · kure n. pool, pond

ኩርማን · kurman n. one fourth of an əngära

ኩርሲ · kursi n. chair (Harar)

ኩርትም አለ · see ኩረተመ

ኩርፋድ · kurfad adj. pug-nosed and small-faced (person)

ኩስ · kus n. excrement (fowl)

ኩሽ   *kuš* n. Cush *(country in the Nile Valley)*

ኩሻዊ   *kušawi* n. Cushitic *(a sub-family of the Afro-Asiatic language)*

ኩበት   *kubät* n. dry cow dung *(used as fuel)*

ኩባያ   *kubbayya* n. cup, mug *(of metal)*

ኩብ ሜትር   *kubb metər* also ሜትር ኩብ *metər kubb* cubic metre

ኩብኩብ   *kubkubba* n. young locust

ኩታ   *kuta* n. toga *(white cotton loose garment)*

ኩታራ   *kutara* n. nipper *(small child)*

ኩክ   *kuk* n. earwax

ኩክኒ   *kukni* n. mange

ኩክኒያም   *kukniyam* adj. mangy

ኩየሳ   *kuyyəsa* n. termite hill

ኩዳዬ   *kudade* also ሁዳዬ *hudade* n. Lent

ኩዳድ   *kudad* also ሁዳድ *hudad* n. plantation

ኩፍ አለ   *kuff alä* v.i rose *(of dough)*

ኩፍ ኩፍ አለ   *kuff kuff alä* v.i became sullen *(person)*

ኩፍኝ   *kuffənn* n. measles, chicken-pox

ኩፍ ጫማ   *kuf čamma* n. shoes

ኪሎ   *kilo* n. kilo

—ሜትር   —*metər* n. kilometer

—ግራም   —*gram* n. kilogramme

—ዋት   —*wat* n. kilowatt

ኪራይ   *kiray* n. rent *(house, car etc. see also* ተከራየ)

ኪራየተኛ   *kirayätäñña* n. lessee

ኪስ   *kis* n. pocket; drawer *(box-like container)*

የኪስ ገንዘብ   *yäkis gänzäb* n. pocket-money

ኪን   *kin* n. skill

ኪነት   *kinät* n. art

ኪነ ጥበብ   *kinä ṭəbäb* n. work of art

ኪንታሮት   *kintarot* n. wart

ኪንታሮታም   *kintarotam* adj. infested with warts

የአህያ ኪን ታሮት   *yä'ahəyya kintarot* n. hemorrhoids

ኪያር   *kiyar* n. cucumber

ኪዮስክ   *kiyosk* n. kiosk, booth

ኪዳን   *kidan* n. treaty, pact, covenant *(Biblical)*

ሐዲስ—   *haddis*—n. New Testament

ብሉይ—   *bəluy*—n. Old Testament

ቃል—   *qal*—n. agreement, pact, covenant; promise

ካህን   *kahən* n. priest, pastor, clergyman *(pl.* ካህናት *see also* ካነ)

ካልእ   *kalə'* adj. second *(G.)*

ካሎስ   *kalos* n. satin

ካሜራ   *kamera* n. camera

ካሚዮን   *kamiwon* n. lorry, truck

ካም   *kam* n. Ham

ካማዊ   *kamawi* adj. Hamite

ካምፉር   *kamfur* n. camphor

ካራ   *karra* n. curved knife *(large)*

ካርቦን   *karbon* n. carbon

ካርታ   *karta* n. map; title deed. *(land);* playing cards

ካርቶን   *karton* n. cardboard

ካርኒ   *karni* n. receipt

ካሮት   *karot* n. carrot

ካሰ   *kasä* v.t compensated, paid damages, indemnified

ካሳ   *kasa* n. compensation, indemnity, restitution, reparation

ተካሰ   *täkasä* v.i was compensated, indemnified, paid damage

ተካካሰ   *täkakasä* v.i compensated, indemnified each other; equalized

አካካሰ   *akkakasä* v.t caused damage to be paid, had compensation paid, equalized

አስካሰ   *askasä* v.t had compensation, damage paid

ካስማ   *kasma* n. tent peg, stake *(for tent)*

ጀበ   *kabä* v.t piled up *(stones etc.);* praised

	(s/o) unduly
ካብ	kab n. pile (of stones etc.)
ከቦሽ	kəboš n. piling
ተካከበ	täkakabä v.i praised each other unduly
አካከበ	akkakabä v.t helped (s/o) in piling up (stones etc.)
አስካበ	askabä v.t had (stones etc.) piled up
ካባ	kaba n. quarry
ካባ	kabba n. mantle, cloak cape
ካቤላ	kabella adj. long-footed
ካብት	see ሀብት
ካቦ	kabbo n. foreman (It.)
ካቲካላ	kati kala n. arrack (strong colourless alcoholic drink)
ካታሎግ	katalog n. catalogue
ካቶሊክ	katolık n. catholic
ካቶሊካዊ	katolikawi n. a catholic (m.)
ካቶሊካዊት	katolikawit n. a catholic (f.)
ካች	kačč see also ሁች hačč adj/adv. yonder, over there
ካቻምና	käččamna also ሁቻምና haččamna n. the year before
ካነ	kanä v.t ordained (as a priest or deacon)
ካሀን	kahən n. priest, pastor, clergyman
ካሀነት	kəhnät n. ordination
ቤተ—	betä—n. clergy, the Church
ተካነ	täkanä v.i was ordained; became an expert in a field
አስካነ	askanä v.t had s/o ordained (as a priest or deacon)
ካንዴላ	kandella n. spark-plug (It.)
ካኪ	kaki n. khaki
ካካ	kakka n. excrement (a word used with children), adj. bad
ካወያ	kawəyya n. iron (for clothes)
ካዕብ	ka'əb n. second order

	of the alphabet (e.gሁ)
ካደ	kadä v.t forsook, denied, renounced, repudiated (a statement)
ካጂ	kaği adj/n (one) who forsakes, denies renounces, repudiates a statement
ክደት	kədat also ሁደት kəhdät n. denial, forsaking renouncement, repudiation (of a statement)
ተካደ	täkadä v.i was denied, renounced, repudiated (a statement), forsaken
አስካደ	askadä v.t caused to forsake, deny, renounce, repudiate (a statment)
ካደመ	kaddämä v.t served (coffee etc.)
ካዳሚ	kaddami adj/n (one) who serves (coffee etc.)
ካፍር	kafir n. Christian (word used by Moslems, meaning irreligious, unbelieving)
*ካፋ	*kaffa
ካፊያ	kaffiya n. drizzle, shower (of rain)
አካፋ	akaffa v.i drizzled
ካፖርት	kapport n. overcoat
ኬላ	kella n. toll station
ኬሻ	keša n. sack (cloth, bag)
ኬንትሮስ	kentros n. longitude
ኬንያ	kenya n. Kenya
ኬክሮስ	kekros n. latitude
ክሊኒክ	klinik n. clinic
ክላሰር	klasär n. file (folder)
ክላክስ	klaks n. hoot
ክልብሽ አለ	kəlbəšš alä v.t nauseated
ክልብሽት	kəlbəšta n. nausea
ክልተው አለ	kəltəw alä v.i collapsed (for persons due to a hard blow or heavy sleep)
ክረምት	kərämt n. rainy season see also ክረመ
ክራC	see ክረረ
ክራቫት	kravat n. necktie
ክC	see ክረረ
ክርስቲያን	kərəstiyan n. Christian

ቤተክርስትያን betäkrəstəyan Church
ክርስትና kərəstənna n.
Christianity
—አነሥ —anässa n. christened
(for godparents)
ክርስቶሳዊ krəstosawi n.
Christian
ክርስቶስ krəstos n. Christ
ክርታስ kərtas n. card board;
membrane
ክርን kərn n. elbow
ክርክር see ክሬከረ
ክሳድ kəsad n. collar
ክስ see ከሰሰ
ክብር see ከበረ
ክብሪት kəbrit n. matches
ክብርና see ከበረ
ክታብ kətab n. charm (amulet)
አሻን— ašän-amulet, talisman
ከው አለ kəww alä v.i was stun-
ned, was caught by
surprise; dried very
much
ክፉ see ከፋ
ክፍ አለ kəff alä word used
to chase away a cat
ክፍል see ከፈለ
ኮሚቴ komite n. committee
ኮመተረ see አኮማተረ
ኮምፓስ kompass n. compass
ኮረመተ see አኮራመተ
ኮረሪማ korärima n. cardamon
ኮራሸመ koräššämä v.t gorman-
dised
ኮረብታ koräbta n. hill
ኮረብታማ koräbtamma adj. hilly
ኮረጀ korrägä v.t corrected
(exam. papers) ;
cheated (exams)
ኩረጃ kurräga n. cheating
(exams.)
ተኮረጀ täkorrägä v.i was
corrected (exams)
አስኮረጀ askorrägä v.t had
(s/o) correct one's
exam. papers ; helped
(s/o) cheat (exams)
ኮረጆ korägo n. satchel
ኮረጠ korräṭä v.i was
piquant (food)
ኮራ korra v.i became proud,

showed off
ኩሩ kuru adj. proud;
gentle, high-spirited
ኩራተኛ kuratäñña adj. proud;
conceited
ኩራት kurat n. pride, conceit
ተኩራራ täkurarra v.i showed
off, was boastful
አኮራ akorra v.t caused to
become self-suf-
ficient, independent
ኮርማ korma n. bull
ኮርቻ koräčča n. saddle
ኮርፋ ኮርፋ አለ korfa korfa alä v.i
became somewhat
angry; moody, bad-
tempered
ኮሰመነ kosämmänä v.i became
emaciated, lean,
skinny
ኮስማና kosmanna adj. thin
lean, skinny
አኮሰመነ akosämmänä v.t
emaciated, made
lean, skinny
ኮሶ koso n. tape-worm;
taenia; taeniacide
—ታየው —tayyäw v.i became
infested with tape-
worms
—ጠጣ —ṭäṭṭa v.t took
taeniacide
ኮሸሸ አለ košäšš alä v.i rustled
ኮሸም košäm n. rumex abys-
sinica (kind of fruit
with sweet and sour
taste)
ኮበለለ kobällälä v.i deserted
(the army etc.), ran
away; eloped
ኩብለላ kubläla n. desertion;
elopement
ኮብላይ koblay n. deserter,
fugitive
አኮበለለ akobällälä v.t caused
(s/o) to desert, run
away; caused to elope
አስኮበለለ akobällälä v.t see
አኮበለለ
አስኮብላይ askoblay adj/n (one)

212

	who causes *(s/o)* to desert *(the army)*, run away
ኮባ	koba n. false banana
ኮተኮተ	kotäkkotä v.t hoed up weed
ኩትኳቶ	kutku"ato n. hoeing
ኩትኮታ	kutkota n. hoeing
መኮትኮቻ	mäkotkoča n. hoe
ተኮተኮተ	täkotäkkätä v. was hoed
አስኮተኮተ	askotäkkotä v.t had *(garden)* hoed
ኮቴ	kotte n. hoof
የኮቴ ገንዘብ	yäkotte gänzäb n. embarkation fee
ኮት	kot n. coat
ኮትጃ	kotəčča usually ኮትጃ መሬት kotəčča märet n. black cotton soil
*ኮነሰነሰ	* konäsännäsä
ኩንስንስ	kunəsnəs adj. stilted, unnatural, artifical *(behaviour)* pretentious
ተኮነሰነሰ	täkunäsännäsä v.t behaved unnaturally, artifically, pretentiously
ተኮነስናሽ	täkunsnaš adj. stilted, unnatural, artificial
ኮንትራት	kontrat n. contract
ኮንትሮባንድ	kontroband n. contraband
ኮከብ	kokäb n. star *(pl.* ከዋክብት *käwakəbt)*
—ቆጠራ	qoṭära n. astrology, horoscope
—ቆጣሪ	—qoṭari n. astrologer
አጥቢያ—	aṭbiya—n. morning star
ኮካን	kokän n. cockscomb *(red crest of cock)*
ኮክ	kok n. peach
*ኮደደ	* koddädä
ኩዳድ	kudad also ሁዳድ hudad n. plantation
ኮዳ	kodda n. water-bottle *(metal flask)*, canteen *(USA)*
ኮፈኮፈ	kofäkkofä v.i errupted

ኩወለለ	ku"ällälä v.i became crystal clear
ኩወለል አለ	ku"ällāl alä v.i became crystal clear
*ኩወለተፈ	* ku"älättäfä
ኩወልተፈ	ku"ältaffa adj. lisping
ኩወልትፍ	ku"əltəf adj. lisping
ተኩወለተፈ	täku"älättäfä v.i lisped, stuttered
ኩወለኩወለ	ku"äläku"älä v.t tickled; lined up *(caused to be in line)*; spurred
ኩወልኩወላ	ku"lku"äla n. tickling; lining up; spurring
ኩወልኩወል	ku"əlku"əl adj. lined-up
—መስማር	—mäsmär n. parallel lines
ተኩወለኩወለ	täku"äläku"älä v.i was tickled; was lined up; was spurred
አስኩወለኩወለ	asku"äläku"älä v.t caused to line up
ኩወላ	ku"älla v.t polished, made lustrous *(metal etc.)*
ኩወልኩወሎ	ku"älku"ällo n. lock *(hair)*
ኩወመኩወመ	ku"ämäkku"ämä v.t relished *(food, drink)*; gormandized
ኩወረት	ku"ärät see አኩወረት
ኩወረት	ku"ärät v. gravel
ኩወረተመ	ku"ärättämä v.t squatted *(on ones legs)*; crippled
ኩወረታተመ	ku"ärätattämä v.i squeezed s/t together; crippled
ተኩወረተመ	täku"ärättämä v.i squatted
ተኩወረታተመ	täku"ärätattämä v.i squatted down
ኩወረኩወመ	ku"äräkku"ämä v.t chipped off; rapped on the head with the knuckles
ኩወርኩወመ	ku"ärku"äma n. chipping off
ኩወርኩወም	ku"ärku"əm n. blow

ኩራኩራ	*kuʷäräkkuʷärä* v.t tickled, spurred *(a horse); cleaned the ears of wax* with knuckles		

ኩራኩራ *kuʷäräkkuʷärä* v.t tickled, spurred *(a horse);* cleaned the ears of wax

ኩራዳ *kuʷäräddä* n. maiden

ኩራፈ *kuʷärräfä* v.i bubbled, foamed

ኩራፌ *kuʷäräfe* adj. sparkling *(of wines and other drinks)*

ኩርፈኛ *kuʷərfäñña* n. one with whom one is not on speaking terms

ኩርፍተኛ *kurrəftäñña* adj. moody

ኩርፊያ *kuʷərfiya* n. snoring; grimace, sulks

ኩርፍ *kuʷərf* n. not on speaking terms

ኩራ *see* ኩራ

ኩሰሰ *kuʷässäsä* v.i emaciated, was lean and weak

ኩሰሰ *kuʷäsasa* a.dj emaciated, lean and weak

ኩሰሰነት *kuʷäsasannät* n. emaciation, weakness

አኩሰሰ *akuʷässäsä* v.t emaciated; belittled

አኳሰሰ *akuʷassäsa, or* አንኳሰሰ *ankuʷassäsä* v.t belittled

ኩሰተረ *kuʷäsättärä* v.t made a horrible face; trimmed *(wick of a lamp candle),* snuffed

ኩስታራ *kuʷästarra* adj. serious, thoughtful; not given to pleasure seeking; daring

መኩስተሪያ *mäkuʷästäriya* n. snuffers

ሲጋራ— *siḡara*—n. ash-tray

ተኩሰተረ *täkuʷäsättärä* v.i was trimmed *(wick of lamp etc.)*

ተኩሰተረ *täkuʷäsattärä* v.i frowned at, made a horrible face

ኩሰኩሰ *kuʷäsäkkuʷäsä* v.t itched *(of wool etc.);* caused discomfort *(cloth)*

ኩሰካሰ *kuʷäskuʷassa* adj. uncomfortable *(cloth)*

ኩሰ *kuʷässa* v.t excreted *(waste matter)*

ኩሰም *kuʷəsam* adj. dirty

ኩስ *kuʷəs* n. excrement

ኩሰበለለ *see* * ከበለለ

ኩነሰነሰ *see* *ኩነሰነሰ

ኩነነ *kuʷännänä* v.t condemned

ኩናኝ *kuʷännañ* adj. n *(one who condemns*

ኩነኔ *kuʷənäne* n. damnation, condemnation

ተኩነነ *täkuʷännänä* v.i was condemned

አስኩነነ *askuʷännänä* v.t showed pity for *(s/o),* became pitiful, abject, pathetic

አስኩናኝ *askuʷännañ* adj. pathetic, much to be pitied

ኩክ *see* ኩክ

ኩረንችት *kuʷərənčət* n. small thorny bush

ኩስኩስት *kuʷəskuʷəst* n. ewer, coffee, teapot

*ኩበኩበ *see* አኩበኩበ

ኳ አለ *kuʷa alä* v.i knocked *(short, sharp sound of metal etc.)*

ኳኳቴ *kuʷakuʷate* n. repeated sound of knocks

ተንኳኳ *tänkuʷakkuʷa* v.i tinkled; produced repeated sounds of knocks

አንኳኳ *ankuʷakkuʷa* v.t knocked at a door

ኳላ *kuʷalä* v.t made up one's eyelashes with antimony

ኩል *kul* n. antimony *(powder)*

ተኳኳላ *täkuʷakuʷalä* v.t painted one's eyelashes with antimony

214

ኳስ	kuʷas n. ball
ኳተ	kuʷatä v.t cultivated
መኳቻ	mäkuʷača n. small pick or cultivtor (instrument)

ኩንክ	kuʷank n. cockscomb, crest
ኹለተ	see ሁለት
ኹሉ	see ሁሉ
ፕን	or ፕን honä v.i became

ወ

ወሀ	wäha also ውሀ wəha n. water
—ፕን	—honä v.i was converted into liquid; was caught by surprise, was stunned
—ጆጠረ	—quʷaṭṭärä v.t formed blisters
—በላmeasure	—bällaw v.i was drowned; became useless, vain
—ወሀ አለ	—wäha alä v.t. became thirsty
—አጠጣ	—aṭäṭṭa v.t watered (plants)
—ወረደ	—wärrädä v.t went to fetch water
ወሀም	wähamma adj. watery
የወሀ ልክ	yäwäha lǝkk n. water-level; spirit-level
—ማጠራቀ ሚያ	—maṭṭäraqämiya n. water reservoir
—ተርብ	—tärb n. dragon-fly
እህል ወሀ	əhǝl—n. food and drink
የቧምቧ—	yäbuʷambuʷa—n. running water
የእንቁላል—	yä'ənqulal—n. white (of an egg)
የግብር—	yägəbr—n. douche (of women)
ፈረሰኛ—	färäsäñña—n. torrent (sudden)
ፍልወሃ	fəlwäha n. thermal springs
ወህኒ	wähni n. jail, penitentiary
—ቤት	—bet n. jail, penitentiary
ወለላ	wäläla n. honey (separated from wax)
ወለል አለ	wäläll alä v.i became

clear, brilliant

—አደረገ	—adärrägä v.t caused to become clear, brilliant (light etc.); opened wide
ወላም አለ	wälämm alä v.t sprained
ወላምታ	wälämta n. sprain, wrench
ወላም ዘላም አለ	wälämm zälämm alä v.i wavered, hesitated, became indecisive
ወለቀ	wälläqä v.i became disjointed, slipped off (got free from), was put out of joint; was pulled out (tooth)
ወላቂ	wälaqi adj. not fast enough, loose, easily disjointed
ውላቂ	wəllaqi n. s/t disjointed
ውልቃት	wəlləqat n. sprain, wrench
ወላለቀ	wälalläqä v.i became disjointed completely, was taken to pieces was dismantled
ውልቅልቅ	wəlqəlǝq adj. dismantled, disjointed
ወለቅ አደረገ	wäläqq adärrägä v.t disjointed slightly; undressed (oneself suddenly)
ውልቅ አለ	wəlläqq alä v.t became disjointed suddenly, slipped off suddenly
ውልቅ አደረገ	wəlläq adärrägä v.t disjointed suddenly;

215

	caused to slip off suddenly; took off clothes etc. *(suddenly)*
ተዋለቀ	*täwalläqä* v.i bit each other severely
አወለቀ	*awälläqä* v.t dismantled, disjointed; pulled out, took off *(one's clothes)*
ልብ አው·ላቂ	*ləbb awlaqi* adj. nagging, tiresome, wearing
ኪ.ስ—	*kis* — n. pick-pocket
አወላለቀ	*awälalläqä* v.t dismantled completely; took off one's clothes; took to pieces
አስወለቀ	*aswälläqä* v.t had s/t dismantled ,had s/t taken into pieces; had s/o take off clothes
ወለወለ	*wäläwwälä* v.t mopped up, wiped; polished
መወልወያ	*mäwälwäya* n. mop⸜
ወለወለ	*wälawwälä* v.i hesitated
ወላዋይ	*wälaway* adj. hesitating, hesitant
አወላወለ	*awwälawwälä* v.t help s/o in mopping up, in wiping; hesitated
አወላዋይ	*awwälaway* adj. hesitant, hesitating
ወለወልዳ	*wäläwälda* n. backbiter, dishonest, deceitful
ወለደ	*wällädä* v.t gave birth to ; deliverd *(child)*; engendered; accrued interest
ወለድ	*wälläd* n. interest *(bank etc.)*
ወላድ	*wällad* n. fertile *(woman)*, fecund
ወላጅ	*wälaǧ* n. parent
ው·ላጅ	*wəllaǧ* adj. halfcaste, bastard
ው·ልድ	*wəld* in የቤት ው·ልድ *yäbet wəld* n. slave, born in his master's house

ልደት	*lədät* n. Christmas; birth, birthday
ልጅ	*ləǧ* n. child, boy,
ወላለዳ	*wälallädä* v.t gave birth to a few offspring
ተወለደ	*täwällädä* v.i was born
ተወላጅ	*täwällaǧ* n. blood relation, kin
ትው·ልድ	*təwlədd* n. generation
ተዋለደ	*täwallädä* v.i intermarried *(thus producing offspring)*, multiplied *(human being)*; produced several shoots *(plant)*; was related through marriage
አዋለደ	*awwallädä* v.t acted as midwife
አዋላጅ	*awwalaǧ* n. midwife
አስወለደ	*aswällädä* v.t caused to give birth to a child
ወለገደ	*wäläggädä*
ወልጋዳ	*wälgaddä* adj. twisted bent, distorted, twisted out of shape
ተወላገደ	*täwälaggädä* v.i. became twisted, crooked
ተወለጋገደ	*täwälägaggädä* v.t became completely twisted, crooked
አወላገደ	*awwälaggädä* v.t twisted, crooked
አወለጋገደ	*awwälägaggädä* v.t twisted, distorted completely
ወለጋ	*wällägga* n. one of the Administrative Regions western Ethiopia *(Wollega)*
ወላንሳ	*wälansa* n. velvet; adj. amiable
ወላይታ	*wälayətta* n. Wolayitta *(nationality, living in Sidamo)*
ወላይትኛ	*wälayətəñña* n. the Wolayitta language
ወላፈን	*wälafän* n. blazing fire
ወል	*wäl* adj. common

የወል ስም   yäwäl səm n. common noun

ወሎ   wällo n. one of the Administrative Regions, north-eastern Ethiopia (Wollo)

ወሙቴ   wämmäte adj. riff-raff, vagabond, vagrant

ወምፈል   wämfäl also ወንፈል wänfäl n. work (farming) carried out by helping each other

ወምበር   wämbär also ወንበር n. wänbär n. chair; judge

ወረህ   wäräha n. cripple; adj. bow-legged

ወረረ   wärrärä v.t invaded (army), infested (vermin, insects etc.)

ወራራ   wärära n. invasion; infestation

ወረርሽኝ   wäräršəññ n. plague, epidemic

ወራሪ   wärari adj/n invading (army)

ወሮበላ   wärro bälla adj. vagbond, vagrant, tramp, hooligan

ውርር አደረገ   wərrər adärrägä v.t invaded completely; infested completely (vermin, insect)

ተወረረ   täwärrärä v.i was invaded (by an army); was infested (with vermin, insects etc.)

ፊት አውራሪ   fit awrari n. an Ethiopian title (general)

አስወረረ   aswärrärä v.t caused to be invaded; caused to be infested

ወረሰ   wärräsä v.t inherited; confiscated

ወራሽ   wäraš n. heir

አልጋ—   alga—n. crown prince, princess

ዋርሳ   warsa n. brother-in-law (term used among Muslims, since one can marry his sister-in-law ofter his brother's

death)

ርስት   rəst n. owned land

ያባት—   yabbat—n. heritage (of land)

ተወረሰ   täwärräsä v.i was inherited ; was confiscated

ተወራሽ   täwärraš adj/n (one) whose property is confiscated

ተወራረሰ   täwärarräsä v.t was recorded (e.g bills, vouchers etc. in a cash register)

አወረሰ   awärräsä v.t gave one's property as an inheritance

አወራረሰ   awärarräsä v.t recorded (bills, vouchers etc. in a cash register)

ወረቀት   wäräqät n. paper; letter

ወረብ   wäräb n. chant (church)

ወረቦ   wäräbbo n. small antelope

ወረት   wärät n. capital (money); liquid (finance); stock; temporal friendship; vogue

ወረተኛ   wärätäññä adj. inconsistent (in objectives, in wishes, in friendship); capricious (in personal behaviour); fickle

ወረንጦ   wäränṭo n. tweezers

—አፍ   —af n. s/o who uses biting words

ወረክራክ   wäräkrakka adj. shaky, unsteady

ወረወረ   wäräwwärä v.t threw; bolted (fastened with a bolt)

ውርወራ   wərwära n. throwing

መወርወሪያ   mäwärwäriya n. bolt; shuttle (in a loom)

ተወረወረ   täwäräwwärä v.i was thrown; spurted (in race); leaped

ተወርዋሪ   täwärwari adj. spurting, leaping

ተወራወረ tawärawwärä v.i threw s/t at each other

አሰወራወረ aswärawwärä v.t had s/o throw s/t

ወረዛ wäräzza v.t oozed through, moisted

አወረዛ awäräzza v.t caused to ooze, moist

ወረደ wärrädä v.i descended, went down, came down ; got off, dismounted

ትክሻ— takäšša— v.i suffered from shoulder cramp

ወረዳ wäräda n. district, zone

ምክትል— makattal— n. subdistict

ወራዳ wärradda adj. disgraceful, dishonourable, ignoble

ወራዳነት wärraddannät n. dishonour, shamefulness

ወራጅ wäräǧ adj. flowing, descending

—ወሀ —wäha n. flowing water

ወርድ wärd˅ n. breadth, width

ወርድ ሰፊ wärdä säffi adj. wide, broad (cloth, garment etc.)

—ጠባብ —ṭäbbab adj. narrow

ወርድና ስፋት wärdanna safat dimensions

ወርዳም wärdam adj. wide, broad

ወርዴ wärde n. s/o cured of V.D. (syphilis)

ወራጅ warraǧ n. rags, old clothes, worn-out

ወርዳት wardät n. humiliation, indignity, disgrace, degradation

ወርድ ward in ወርድ ንባብ ward nabab n. quicker style of reading (of pupil's thus trained)

—ከራሰ —kärase n. (expression used to declare that grave consequences are inevitable)

I warn you !

ውርጃ warǧa n. abortion

ውርጅብኝ warǧabbaññ n. a sudden disaster ; stream of invectives

ወራረደ wärarrädä v.i descended gradually

ውርርድ wararrad n. bet, wager

ተወረደ täwärrädä v.i accomplished one's duties, became contented

ተወራጅ täwärraǧ adj. inferior

ተወራረደ täwärarrädä v.i made a bet

ተዋረደ täwarrädä v.i was humiliated, debased dishonoured

አወረደ awärrädä v.t brought down ; caused to descend; led a choir

አውራጃ awraǧǧa n. province

አውራጅ awraǧ n. choir leader, song leader

አወራረደ awärarrädä v.t brought down repeatedly

አወራረደ awwärarrädä v.t helped s/o bring down s/t; caused to bet; cut meat in lumps

አዋረደ awwarrädä v.t humiliated, despised, dishonoured ; helped s/o bring s/t down

አሰወረደ aswärrädä v.t aborted ; had s/t brought down

ወረገኑ wärrägänu n. Royal Herdsmen

*ወረዉ see ተወራዉ

ወረፈ wärräfä v.t despised, scoffed at, taunted

ወራፊ wärrafi adj/n (one) who despises, scoffs at etc.

ዋሬ wäre n. news, rumour gossip ; story, see also አወራ

የመንደር— yämändär— n. gossip. the talk of the town

ወሬኛ wäreñña adj/n talkative, (one) who

218

	has a loose tongue
ወር	*wär* n. month
የወር መባቻ	*yäwär mäbačä* n. first day of the month
—አበባ	—*abäba* n. menstruation
ወርቅ	*wärq* n. gold
ወርቃማ	*wärqamma* adj. golden; precious (especially for time)
ወርቃ ወርቅ	*wärqawärq* adj. yellowish
ወርቅ አንጣሪ	*wärq anṭari* n. goldsmith
የወርቅ ቡቻላ	*yäwärq bučč̣alla* n. gold-bar, bullion
መሶብ ወርቅ	*mäsobä wärq* n. decorated mäsob
ራሰ—	*rasä*—n. crown
ሰምና—	*sämənna*—n. metaphorical speech, sentence, etc.
ወርች	*wärč* n. thigh
ወርጫ ከንበል	*wäräčä känbəl* adj. slanting (landscape)
ወርካ	*wärka* n. sycamore
ወሰለተ	*wäsällätä* v.i idled about; broke one's faith; prevaricated
ወስላታ	*wäslatta* n. dishonest, liar; rogue
ውስልትና	*wəslətənna* n. dishonesty, lie
አወሰለተ	*awäsällätä* v.t caused to become idle, dishonest
ወሰነ	*wässänä* v.i decided; limited, made a resolution
ወሰን	*wässän* n. boundary; limit
—የሌለው	—*yälelläw* adj. limitless, unlimited, boundless
ከብሬ—	*kəbrrä*—n. record (score not reached before)
ወሰንተኛ	*wäsäntäñña* n. bordering (country); neighbour (of land)
ወሳኝ	*wässañ* adj. decisive; limiting

ውሳኔ	*wəssane* n. resolution; decision
መወሰኛ	*mäwässäña* in የህግ መወሰኛ ምክር ቤት *yähəgg mäwässäña məkr bet* n. senate
ተወሰነ	*täwässänä* v.i was decided; was limited
የተወሰነ	*yätäwässänä* adj. limited, definite, specific
ያልተወሰነ	*yaltäwässänä* adj. unrestricted, unlimited, indefinite
ተዋሰነ	*täwassänä* v.i demarcated, bordered with s/o, s/t, shared a common border
ተዋሳኝ	*täwasañ* n. demarcating parties; bordering one another
አዋሰነ	*awwassänä* v.t demarcated; bordered
አዋሳኝ	*awwasañ* adj. bordering
አስወሰነ	*aswässänä* v.t had s/t decided; had resolution passed
*ወሰከ	**wässäkä
ተውሳክ	*täwsak* n. filth, dirt, parasite
ወሰካ	*wäsäka* n. stretcher
ወሰወሰ	*wäsäwwäsä* v.i pedalled (e.g bicycle, sewing mechine); put stitches in
ወስዋሳ	*wäswassa* adj. restless; undependable
ውስውስ	*wəswəs* adj. stitched
ውስወሳ	*wəswäsa* n. pedaling
መወስወሻ	*mäwäswäša* n. pedal
ወሰደ	*wässädä* v.t took
እንቅልፍ ወሰደው	*ənqəlf wässädäw* v.i fell asleep
ወሰድ አደ ረገው	*wäsädd adärrägäw* v.t became slightly crazy
ተወሰደ	*täwässädä* v.i was taken
አዋሰደ	*awwassädä* v.t helped s/o in taking s/t away
አስወሰደ	*aswässädä* v.t had s/t taken away; let

ወሳፍቻ s/t be stolen see ሰፋ

ወስከምቢያ wäskämbia n. cover (of basket, pot etc.)

ወስፈንጥር wäsfänṭər n. bow

ወስፋት wäsfat n. hookworm

ወስፋታም wäsfätam adj. lean, emaciated

ወስፋት ቁራጭ wäsfat quʷäraç adj. disgusting, repelent

ወስፈ see ሰፋ

ወሸለ wäššälä v.i did s/t slovenly, loosely

ወሸላ wäšäla adj. uncircumcized; coward

ውሻል wəšal n. wedge

ወሸመ wäššämä v.t took a woman as a mistress; took a man as a lover

ውሸማ wəšəmma n. mistress, lover, concubine

ወሸቀ wäššäqä v.t inserted, stuffed

ወሻቀ wäššaqqa adj. dependant, not self-supporting; lazy, sluggish

ወሸባ wäšäba n. carded cotton ready for spinning

ወሸከተ wäšäkkätä v.i told lies, told made-up stories

ወሸከት wäšäkät adj. liar
ወሸካታ wäškatta adj. liar
ወሽ wäš n. breast of a cow
ወሽመላ wäšmälla n. loquat
ወሽመጥ wäšmäṭ n. gusset
ወሽመጡ wäšmäṭu täqorräṭä ተቀረጠ was demoralized, frustrated, thwarted

የባሕር ወሽ yäbähər wäšmäṭ n. መጥ gulf

ወቀረ wäqqärä v.t chiselled carved (stone; millstone); tattooed

ውቅራት wəqqərat n. tattoo
ውቅራታም wəqəratam adj. tattooed

መዋቅር mäwaqər n. structure, framework

ላእላይ- la'əlay-n. superstructure

ታሕታይ— tahtay-n. infrastrcture

ተዋቀረ täwaqqärä v.i was erected (building)

አስወቀረ aswäqqärä v.t had stone etc. chiselled, carved; had s/o tattooed

ወቀሰ wäqqäsä v.t reprimanded, reproached, criticized

ወቀሳ wäqqäsa n. reprimand, reproach, criticism

ወቃሽ wäqaš adj. n. (one) who reprimand's reproaches, criticizes

ተወቀሰ täwäqqäsä vi was reproached, criticized

ተወቃቀሰ täwäqaqqäsä v.i reproached, criticied each other

ተዋቀሰ täwaqqäsä v.i reproached criticized each other

ወቀጠ wäqqäṭä v.t pounded, crushed to powder, pestled (with mortar); castrated (animal)

ወቀጣ wäqäṭa n. pounding, crushing (with mortar)

ውቃጭ wəqqaç n. left–over of a thing pounded

ውቅጥ wəqṭ adj. powdered; castrated

—በርበሬ —bärbärre n. pounded pepper

—ወይፈን —wäyfän n. castrated bull

ሙቀጫ muqäččä n. mortar
—ገልጋል —gəlgäl n. pestle

ተወቀጠ täwäqqäṭä v.i was pounded, crushed to powder; was castrated (animal)

አዋቀጠ awwaqqäṭä v.t helped s/o in pounding, in crushing s/t to powder

አስወቀጠ aswäqqäṭä v.t had s/t pounded, crushed to powder, had (an animal) castrated

220

ወታ	*wäqqa* v.t threshed; beat	
ውቂያ	*wəqqiya* n. threshing	
መውቂያ	*mäwqiya* n. thresher, threshing-machine	
ተወታ	*täwäqqa* v.i was threshed, was beaten	
አዋታ	*awwäqqa* v.t helped in threshing	
አስወታ	*aswäqqa* v.t had grain threshed	
ወቄት	*wäqet* n. ounce	
ወቅት	*wäqt* n. time, season, period	
ወቅቱ አይደ ለም	*wäqtu aydälläm* it is untimely	
በወቅቱ	*bäwäqtu* adv. on time	
በየወቅቱ	*bäyyäwäqtu* adv. periodically, frequently	
ወበረ	*wäbärra* v.i blustered *(of persons)*	
ወበቀ	*wäbbaqä* v.i became excessively hot	
ወበቅ	*wäbäq* n. excessive heat	
አወበቀ	*awäbbäqä* v.i felt excessive heat	
ወባ	*wäba* n. malaria; adj. skinny	
ወባማ	*wäbamma* adj. malaria district	
የወባ ትንኝ	*yäwäba tənəñň* n. mosquito	
ብጫ ወባ	*bəča wäba* n. yellow fever	
ወቦ ሻምኔ	*wäbbo šämmane* n. cheetah, *also* አቦሻምኔ	
ወተት	*wätät* n. milk	
ወተታም	*wätätam* n. full of milk *(of cow)*	
ወተት አንጀት	*wätät anǧät* n. intestine *(of an animal)*	
ወተወተ	*wätäwwätä* v.t pestered s/o with requests, importuned	
ወትዋታ	*wä: .atta* adj. importunate	
ወትዋች	*wätwač* adj. importunate	
ወተፈ	*wättäfä* v.t plugged *(a leak, a bottle etc.)*	
ወታፉ	*wättaffa* adj.	

	inactive, lazy	
ውታፍ	*wətaf* n. plug, cork, stopper	
ውትፍ	*wəttəf* adj. inactive, lazy	
ተወተፈ	*täwättäfä* v.i was plugged; became inactive, lazy	
አስወተፈ	*aswättäfä* v.t had a leakage plugged	
ወተፍታፉ	*wätäftaffa* adj. dirty, untidy; *see* አወተፈተፈ	
ወታቦ	*wätabo* adj. tottery	
ወታደር	*wätaddär* n. soldier	
ወታደራዊ	*wättaddärawi* adj. military	
ወታደርነት	*wätaddärənnät* n. military profession	
ወትሮ	*wätro* adv. long ago	
እንደ ወትሮው	*əndä wätrow* as always, as usual	
ያለወትሮው	*yalä wätrow* adv. unusually	
ወነበደ	*wänäbbädä* v.i became a brigand	
ወንበዴ	*wänbädé* n. brigand	
ውንበዳ	*wənbäda* n. brigandage	
ውንብድና	*wənbədənna* n. brigandage	
ተወነባበደ	*täwänäbabbädä* v.i deceived, deluded each other	
ተወናበደ	*täwänabbädä* v.i was deceived, deluded	
አወናበደ	*awwänabbädä* v.t deluded, misled s/o	
አወናባጅ	*awwänabaǧ* adj/r misleading, charlatan	
ወነከረ	*wänäkkärä* v.t entangled	
አወናከረ	*awwänakkärä* v.t entangled; did one's work slovenly	
ወነወነ	*wänäwwänä* in ጅራቱን ወነወነ *ǧərätun wänäwwänä* v.t wagged the tail	
ወነጀለ	*wänäǧǧälä* v.t incriminated, accused s/o of wrong doing	
ወንጃይ	*wänǧay* adj/n *(one)* who incriminates,	

	accuses s/o of wrong doing
ወንጀል	wänğäl n. crime
ወንጀለኛ	wänğälähñä adj/n criminal
ውንጀላ	wanğäla n. act of incriminating, accusation
ተወነጀለ	täwänäğğälä v.i was incriminated, was accused of wrong doing *
ተወነጻጀለ	täwänäžağğälä v.i incriminated each each other of wrong doing
አስወነጀለ	aswänäğğälä v.t had s/o accused of wrong doing
ወነጨፈ	wänäččäfä v.t slung (threw a stone with a sling)
ወንጭፍ	wänčäf n. sling (for throwing stones)
የላስቲክ—	yälastik—n. catapult
ወና	wäna adj. deserted (house)
ወናፍ	wänaf n, bellows
ወንባር	wänbär also ወምባር wämbär chair; judge
ታጣፊ—	tattafi— n. folding stool
ወንዝ	wänz n. river
የወንዝ ልጅ	yäwänze läğ n. compatriot, fellow country-man
ወንዛወንዝ	wänza wänz n. river-side
ወንድ	wänd adj. male; brave, daring
ወንደ ላጤ	wändä latte n. bachelor
ወንዳወንድ	wändawänd adj. tomboy; manly
ወንዳገረድ	wändagäräd adj. hermaphrodite
ወንዴ	wände' adj. male (plants etc.)
ወንድነት	wändännät n. bravery, daring
ወንድም ታላቅ—	wändämm n. brother tallaq—n. elder brother

ወንድማማችነት ግትነት	wändämmamaččännät n. brotherhood, fraternity
የወንድም ልጅ	yäwändämm läğ n. nephew, niece
ወንጌል	wängel n. Gospel
ወንጌላዊ	wängelawi adj. Evangelist
ወንጣፍት	wäntäft n. small strainer
ወንፈል ·	wänfäl n. communal labour see ጇጊ and ደበ
ወንፊት ወከለ	wänfit n. sieve see ነፋ wäkkälä v.t represented (s/o), acted on behalf; appointed s/o as one's representative; delegated
ወኪል	wäkkil n. representative, delegate
ወካይ	wäkkay adj/n (one) who delegates s/o
ውክላ ውክልና	wäkkäla n. mandate wäkkälänna n. representation, mandate
ተወከለ	täwäkkälä v.i was delegated, mandated, acted as s/o's agent (trade)
ተወካይ	täwäkkay n. representative delegate
ወዘተ.	wäzätä abbreviation for ወዘተረፈ wäzätärfä etcetera
ወዘተ	wäzzätä v.t put a can on an oven (for boiling water)
ወዛና	wäzäna n. beauty, charm, gloss
ወዛናም	wäzänam adj. beautiful, charming
ወዘወዘ	wäzäwwäzä v.t shook, waved (hand etc.)
ውዝዋዜ	wazwäza n. skaking, waving
ውዝዋዜ	wazäwwaze n. dance, sway
ተወዘወዘ	täwäzawwäzä v.i was shaken, waved, swayed
ተወዛዋዥ	täwäzawaž adj. shaking, waving (swaying hand etc.)

222

አወዛወዘ	awwäzawwäzä v.t shook, waved
ወዛፈ	wäzzäfä v.t put aside (work), made indolent
ውዝፍ	wəzzəf adj. used with እና 'əda overdue (payment)
ተወዛፈ	täwäzzäfä v.i sat idly
ወዛ	wäzza v.i transpired (face); brightened, had a lively look
ወዛም	wäzzam adj. bright (face), lively
ወዛደር	wäzaddär n. proletariat, worker
ወዝ	wäz n. transpiration;brilliance(face), sweat
ውዛት	wəzat n. brilliance
አዋዛ	awwazza v.t treated subtly, tried to convince subtly
ወዣብ	wäžäb n. windy torrent
ወየበ	wäyyäbä v.i became yellowish (tooth, nail etc.); became tainted
ወይባ	wäyba adj. yellowish, tainted
ውይባት	wəyyəbat n. taint
ወየው	wäyyäw interj. oh my God ! oh dear !
ወያኔ	wäyäyane n. occasional tribal war (in Wollo)
ወይ	wäy adv/conj. either ; or; interj; yes! (in response to s/o calling)
ወይም	wäyəmm adv. or, either
ወይራ	wäyra n. olive tree
ወይስ	wäyəss adv. or
ወይን	wäyn n. grape ; wine
ወይንግ	wäynəmma adj. violet
ወይናዴጋ	wäynadäga n. region with mild weather, temperate zone
ወይን ጠጅ	wäyn ṭäǧǧ n. wine; adj. violet
ወይኖ	wäyno adj. violet
ወይዘሮ	wäyzäro n. Madam, Mrs.

ወይጉድ	wäygud interj. oh !
ወይጉዴ	wäygude interj. oh me !
ወይፈን	wäyfän n. bull
ወዮ	wäyyo interj. alas !
ወዮታ	wäyyota n. lamentation
ወዳ	wädä prep. to, towards
ወዲህ	wädih or ወደዚህ wädäzzih adv. here
ወዲያ	wädiya or ወደዚያ wädäzziya adv. there; interj. away with it! away with you!
ወዲያልኝ	wädyalləňň interj. alas!
ወዴት	wädet adv. where
ወዲያው	wädyaw adv. immediately, soon after
ወዳለ	wäddälä v.i became stout, fat, corpulent
ወዳላ	wädälla adj. corpulent, fat, stout
ወዳል	wädäl adj. fat, stout, corpulent
—አህያ	—ahəyya n. jackass
አወዳለ	awäddälä v.t made fat, stout, corpulent
ወዳመ	wäddämä v.t was completely destroyed, annihilated
ውድማ	wədma n. forest, uninhabited deserted place, desert
አወዳመ	awäddämä v.t destroyed, annihilated
አውዳማ	awdəmma n. threshing ground
*ወዳረ	*wäddärä
ወዳር	wädär n. of the same kind, resemblance
—የለሽ	—yälläš adj. incomparable
ወዳረኛ	wädäräňňa adj. competitor, rival
ተወዳደረ	täwädaddärä v.i competed; was compared
ወዳሮ	wädäro n. rope
*ወዳሰ	*wäddäsä
ውዳሰ	wəddäsa n. praising
ውዳሴ	wəddase n. praise, laudation, eulogy

—ከንቱ   —kǎntu or ከንቱ— kǎntu—n. cajolery, flattery

አወደሰ   awäddäsä v.t praised

ወደቀ   wäddäqä v.i fell down; was killed in battle ; failed (exam. etc.); committed fornication

ውዳቂ   wǝddaqi n. scum (people), riff-räff; leftovers, rubbish

ውድቀት   wǝdqät n. sin

ውድቅ   wǝdq adj. overruled (claim, objection)

ተዋደቀ   täwaddäqä v.i killed each other (in battle-field)

ወደብ   wädäb n. harbour, haven, port

ወደደ   wäddädä v.i loved, liked; desired; was in love with

ወዳድ   wäddad adj/n (one) who likes s/o, s/t

አገር—   agär- n. patriot, nationalist

ወዳጅ   wädaǧ n. friend, lover

ወዳጅነት   wädagǝnnät n. friendship

ወዶ ዘማች   wäddo zämač n. volunteer (soldier)

—ገበ   gäbba—n. dog (who seeks refugee in s/o house)

ውድ   wǝdd adj. dear; expensive

ውድነት   wǝddǝnnät n. expensiveness

ወደድ አለ   wäddäd alä v.i became somewhat expensive

ተወደደ   täwäddädä v.i was loved, liked; became expensive

ተወዳጅ   täwäddaǧ adj. dear (person)

ተዋደደ   täwaddädä v.i loved, liked each other; was fixed (e.g spade, pickaxe etc. with the handle)

አዋደደ   awwaddädä v.t made to love, like each other; fixed instru-

ment with handle

አስወደደ   aswäddädä v.t made expensive; caused to like s/o, s/t

ወጀብ   wäǧäb n. storm, tide

ወገረ   wäggärä v.t stoned

ወጋሪ   wägari adj/n (one) who stones

ውግረት   wǝgrät n. stoning

ተወገረ   täwäggärä v.i was stoned

አስወገረ   aswäggärä v.t had s/o stoned

ወገብ   wägäb n. waist

—መሞከር   —mämokkär go to the toilet (pol.)

ወገን   wägän n. side, way, direction; party section

ባለወገን   bäläwägän adj. belonging to the high class, influential

*ወገደ   *wäggädä
ተወገደ   täwäggädä v.i was eliminated, was fired (from work)

አስወገደ   aswäggädä v.t eliminated, discarded, got rid of

ወገድ   wägǝd imp. get out of the way, go away

ወገግ አለ   wägägg alä v.i dawned, began to grow light

ወገጋታ   wäggägta n. early dawn illumination

ውጋገን   wǝgagän n. irradiation

ወገጠ   see ወቀጠ
ወጋ   wägga v.t pierced; stabbed; pricked; gave an injection to; combated

ወጊ   wägi in መርፌ ወጊ n. one who gives an injection to s/o

ውጋት   wǝgät n. sharp pain (stomach, back etc.)

ወጋጋ   wägagga v.i felt occasional pain (stomach, back etc.)

ተወጋ   täwägga v.i was pierced; was pricked was given an injection

ተዋጋ *täwagga* v.i fought, combated, fought, each other; gored

ተዋጊ *täwagi* n. fighter, warrior

—አውሮፕላን —*auroppəlan* n. fighter plane

አዋጋ *awwagga* v.t conducted war; caused to quarrel

አዋጊ *awwagi* adj/n (one) who conducts war; (one) who incites a quarrel

መኰንን —*mäkonnən* n. combatant officer

አስዋጋ *aswägga* v.t had s/o stabbed; had s/o given an injection

ወጋግራ *wägagra* n. beam (in a building)

ወጌሻ *wägešša* n. s/o trained in physiotherapy, masseur; surgeon

ወግ *wäg* n. custom; short story; chat, talk

ወገኛ *wägäñña* adj. braggart, assuming, presumptuous

—አክራሪ *wäg akrari* adj. conservative

—አጥባቂ *aṭbaqi* adj. conservative

ባለወግ *baläwäg* n. dignitary, man of rank, peer

ልብስ *yäwäg ləbs* n. uniform

ወጠረ *wäṭṭärä* v.t stretched, tightened

ወጣራ *wäṭṭarra* adj. puffed up

ውጥረት *wəṭrät* n. dilemma, pressure (compelling force), tension

ውጥር *wəṭər* adj. conceited
ውጥርጥር *wəṭərṭər* adj. puffed up

ተወጠረ *täwäṭṭärä* v.i was stretched, tightened; was conceited, puffed up

ተወጣጠረ *täwäṭaṭṭärä* v.i was completely stretched,

---

tightened

አዋጠረ *awwaṭṭärä* v.t helped s/o in stretching s/t tightly

አስወጠረ *aswäṭṭärä* v.t had s/t stretched

ወጠቀ *wäṭṭäqä* v.t stuffed (oneself with food)

ተወጠቀ *täwäṭṭäqä* v.i was stuffed (with food)

ወጠነ *wäṭṭänä* v.t started, began, commenced

ወጣኝ *wäṭṭañ* n. beginner
ውጥን *wəṭən* adj. s/t started; unfinished

ተወጠነ *täwäṭṭänä* v.i was started,, began, commenced

አስወጠነ *aswäṭṭänä* v.t had s/t started, began, commenced

ወጠጠ *wäṭäte* n. young goat(m.)
ወጣ *wäṭṭa* v.i went up, ascended, climbed

ወጣት *wäṭṭat* n. adj. young man; youth
ወጣትነት *wäṭṭatənnät* n. youth
ወጣ ገባ *wäṭṭa gäbba* adj. uneven (esp. landscape)

ወጥ *wäṭṭ* in አንድ ወጥ *andwäṭṭ* adj. uniformed

ወጭ *wäč* n. expenses
ውጤት *wəṭṭet* n. result, outcome; output; effect; mark (examination)

የእንሰሳት— *yä'ənsəsat*—n. animal products

ውጭ *wəčč* n. outside
—አገር —*agär* n. abroad
መዋጮ *mäwwaču* n. contribution (of money)

መውጫ *mäwča* n. outlet
ወጣ አለ *wäṭa alä* v.i went out

ወጣጣ *wäṭaṭṭa* v.i went out frequently

ተወጣጣ *täwäṭaṭṭa* v.i was contributed (money etc.), was raised (money, manpower)

ተዋጣ *täwaṭṭa* v.i was

225

	raised (money, man-power etc.); became successful (enter-prise, scheme)
አወጣ	awãṭṭa v.t made go out, took put; issued (coin, magazine), expelled; saved (s/o); spent (money)
እጅ—	əǧǧ—raised one's hand
እጁን—	əǧǧun—saved himself
ምሥጢር—	məsṭir—v.t divulged a secret
ገንዘብ—	gänzäb—v.t spent money; drew money
ራሱን—	rasun—v.t saved one-self
ተንድ—	qänd—v.t became very old; was infuriated
—አውጣ	—awṭa n. snail
ዓይን—	ayn— ad,. thick-skinned, shameless
አውጫጭኝ	awčaǧǧəññ n. judicial inquiry of a com-munity for offence committed by one of its members
ግውጫ	mawča n. table of contents
አወጣጣ	awwãṭaṭṭa v.t con-vinced, cajoled s/o to speak the truth
አዋጣ	awwaṭṭa v.t raised, contributed money; became enterprising (business)
አዋጪ	awwač n. con-tributor (money etc.)
አስወጣ	aswãṭṭa v.t made to go out; chased out, drove away
አስተዋጽኦ	astãwaṣ̣ə'o n. con-tribution
ወጥ	wäṭ n. sauce
—ቤት	—bet n. kitchen; cook
ወጭት	wäčit n. dish (con-tainer)
ወፈረ	wäffärä v.i became thick, fat, voluminous
ወፍራም	wäfram adj. fat, thick; voluminous

ውፍረ	wəffare n. fatness; thickness
ውፍረት	wəfrät n. fatness, thickness
ወፈር አለ	wäfärr älä v.i became slightly fat, thick
ወፋፈረ	wäfaffärä v.t got fat
አወፈረ	awäffärä v.t fattened, thickened
ወፈፈ	wäffäfä v.i with a pro-nominal suffix e.g
ወፈፈው	wäfäfäw v.i became slighty insane, eccen-tric
ወፈፈ	wäfäffe adj. eccen-tric, neurotic
ወፈፍተኛ	wäfäftäñña adj. eccentric, neurotic
ወፍ	wäf n. bird
የሌት—	yälet-n. bat
ወፈ ያሬድ	wäfä yared n. bird of paradise
ወፍ ዘራሽ	wäf zärraš n. wild (of plants)
—አራሽ	—arraš n. wild (of plants)
የወፍ በሽታ	yäwäf bäššəta n. jaundice ·
—ቤት	—bet n. cage ,nest
—ጎጆ	—goǧǧo n. nest
ወፍሙ	see ፈሙ
ወርፆ	see ወፈፆ
ዋለ	walä v.i passed, spent the day; did a favour to s/o
እንዴት ዋልክ	əndet walk how are you? good after-noon, good day
ውለታ	wəläta n. favour
ባለውለታ	bäläwəläta n. one who is indebted to s/o, one who has one's gratitude
ውለታ ቢስ	wəläta bis adj. thank-less, ungrateful
—ቢስነት	—bisənnät n. ingratitude
ውል	wəl n. agreement, pact; knot
ውለኛ	wəläñña adj. trust-worthy, dependable
ውሎ	wəlo n. a full day (12 Hrs.)

226

—አባል	—abäll n. per diem	
—አድር	—adro adv. in the long run, sooner or later	
—ገባ መንገድ	—gäbba mängäd n. a day's journey	
መ-ያ	muya n. special skill	
መ-ያተኛ	muyatäñña n. labourer	
ባለ መ-ዋል	balä mu"al n. favourite (person)	
ባለ መ-ያ	balä muya adj/ n highly skilled (person)	
ደኅና ዋል	dähna wal have a good day, bye-bye	
ተዋዋለ	täwawalä v.i made a pact, agreed with one another	
አዋለ	awalä v.t kept s/o, s/t for the whole day; used s/t for a particular purpose	
በሥራ ላይ—	bäsəra lay— put into practice, executed (a plan)	
አዋዋለ	awwawalä v.t helped to make an agreement, a pact; spent the day with s/o (as a company)	
አዋዋይ	awwaway adj/n one who helpes in making an agreement, a pact	
ዋለለ	wallälä v.i wavered, bacame unsteady, vacillated, became inconstant; hesitated	
ዋላላ	walala adj. wavering, unsteady	
ዋልያ	waliya n. walia ibex	
ዋልታ	walta n. pole; a round disc of wood in the inner top of a round roof where the rafters join together	
የሰሜን—	yäsämen— n. North Pole	
የደቡብ—	yädäbub— n. South Pole	
ዋልካ	walka n. black cotton	

	soil	
ዋርሳ	warsa n. brother-in-law (for a female) see also ወረሰ	
ዋርዳ	warda n. black mule	
ዋስ	was n. guarantor	
ዋሸ	waššä v.i told lies, lied ; told a falsehood promise	
ዋሾ	wašo adj liar	
ውሸት	wəšät n. lies	
ውሸታም	wəšätam adj. liar	
ዋሻ	wašša n. cave, den, cavern	
ዋሽንት	wašənt n. flute, fife	
—ናፊ	—näfi n. flute player	
ዋቢ	wabi n. guarantor	
—መጽሐፍት	—mäṣahəft n. bibliography	
*ዋበ	*wabä see ተዋበ	
ዋተተ	wattätä v.i roamed, wandered (hence became very tired)	
አውታታ	awtatta adj/n (one) who wanders, roams	
ዋነስ	wanäs n. turtle-dove	
ዋና	wana n. swimming see also ዋኘ	
የዋና ልብስ	yäwana ləbs n. bathing suit	
ዋነታኛ	wanätäñña n. swimmer	
ዋና	wanna adj. main essential, major, principal proprietor; capital investment	
—አዛዥ	—azzaž n. commander-in-chief	
—ከተማ	—kätäma n. capital city	
—ዲሬክተር	—direktär n. general director	
—ፀሐፊ	—ṣähafi n. secretary general ; executive secretary	
—ገንዘብ	—gänzäb n. capital investment	
ዋነኛ	wannäñña n. proprietor; chief	

ዋኔ	wane n. turtle-dove cf. ዋነስ
ዋንዛ	wanza n. cardia africana
ዋንጫ	wänča n. a drinking-horn, goblet
ዋኘ	wañña v.i swam
ዋና	wana n. swimming
የዋና ልብስ	yäwana ləbs n. bathing suit
ዋነተኛ	wanätäñña n. swimmer
ዋኚ	wäñi n. swimmer
መዋኛ	mäwaña n. swimming pool
አስዋኘ	aswaññä v.t had s/o swim
ዋካታ	wakata also ወካታ wəkata n. uproar, commotion, see አወከ
ዋዌ	wawe n. copula, conjunction (gram.)
ዋዛ	waza n. jest, scoff
—ፈዛዛ	—fäzaza n. joke, not serious, jest
ዋዜማ	wazema n. eve
ዋድያት	wadyat n. large shallow basin
ዋዤ	waǧǧä or ዋዠ wažžä v.t ransomed
ዋግሞት	see አገመ
ዋጋ	waga n. price, cost, value ; reward ; fee
በምንም—	bämənəmm— at any price
የጉልበት—	yägulbät—n. labour cost
ዋጋ ነሳ	waga nässa v.t discredited
—ቈረጠ	—quʷärräṭä v.t fixed a price
—ሰበረ	—säbbärä v.t cheapened (the price of s/t)
—ሰጠ	—säṭṭä v.t appreciated
—ቢስ	—bis adj. worthless
—አለው	—alläw is worthwhile, is important is of value
—አሳረረ	—assarrärä v.t bid against s/o
—አጣ	—aṭṭa v.t became discredited, useless

—ያለው	—yalläw adj. worthy, important, worth considering
—የለሽ	—yällaš n. worthless, useless ; priceless
የዋጋ ዝርዝር	yäwaga zərzər n. invoice, price-list
ዋግ	wag n. rust (plant disease)
ዋግሹም	wagšum n. title of former governors of Lasta
ዋጠ	waṭä v.t swallowed, gulped
ምራቁን የዋጠ	məraqun yäwaṭä adj. mature (person), serious
ተዋጠ	täwaṭä v.t was swallowed, gulped
አዋጠ	awaṭä v.t gave s/o, s/t to swallow
አስዋጠ	aswaṭä v.t gave s/o, s/t to swallow
ወሀ	see ወሀ
ውለታ	see ዋለ
ውላጅ	see ወለደ
ውል	wəl n. contract, agreement, see also ተዋ ዋለ and አዋዋለ
ውል አለ	wəll alä v.t had a sudden desire, nostalgia
ውልታ	wəlləta n. sudden desire, nostalgia, ardour
ውልምጥምጥ	wəlməṭməṭ adj. irresolute, unsteady; subservient, bootlicking
ውልብ አለ	wəlləbb alä v.t caught a glimpse of
ውልብልቢት	wəlbləbit n. propeller; tip of the tongue
ውልከፍከፍ አለ	wəlkəfkəff alä v.i. became entangled, see also ተወላከፈ
ውሪ	wəri n. kid (child)
ውራ	wərra n. last (in competition; examination etc.)
—ወጣ	—wäṭṭa he became last (in his class, contest etc.)
ውርባ	wərba n. dew
ውር ውር አለ	wərr wərr alä v.i

228

	fluttered, flew here and there; moved here and there suddenly in small numbers
ውርውርታ	*wərwərta* n. sudden movement in small numbers
ውርንጭላ	*wərənčəlla* ውርንጫ *wərənča* n. young donkey
ውርዴ	*see* ወረደ
ውርጅብኝ	*see* ወረደ
ውርጋጥ	*wərgaṭ* n. whipper-snapper
ውርጭ	*wərč* n. frost
ውስጥ	*wəsṭ* n/prep, interior, inside
ወደ—	*wädä–* adv. inside, in
ውስጥ አዋቂ	*wəsṭä awaqi* adj. well-informed
ውስጠ ደምብ	*wəsṭä dämb* n. by-law
—ዘ	*—zä* n. verbal adjective; adj. mysterious
ውስጣዊ	*wəsṭawi* adj. internal
ውስጥ ለውስጥ	*wəsṭ läwəsṭ* adv. secretly, stealthily
—ውስጡን	*—wəsṭun* adv. secretly
—እግር	*—əgər* n. sole *(human foot)*
እውስጥ	*əwəsṭ* adv. inside
ከውስጥ	*käwəsṭ* adv. underneath, inside
የውስጥ	*yäwəsṭ* adj. internal
በ...ውስጥ	*bä...wəsṭ* prep, in, inside
ከ...ውስጥ	*kä...wəsṭ* out of, from
እ...ውስጥ	*ə...wəsṭ* prep. in, inside
ውሻ	*wəšša* n. dog
ውሻነት	*wəššannät* n. filthiness, dishonourable behaviour
ውሽልሽል	*wəšəlšəl* adj. slovenly made, cf. ወሸለ
ውሽንፍር	*wəšənfər* n. rain accompanied by a strong wind
ውቃቢ	*wəqabi* n. guardian spirit
ውቃቤ ቢስ	*wəqabe bis* adj. graceless
—አምላክ	*—amlak* n. guardian spirit
—የራቀው	*—yäraqäw* adj. graceless
ውቅያኖስ	*wəqyanos* n. ocean
ውነት	*wənät also* እውነት *əwnät* n. truth, reality
ውነተኛ	*wənä täñña* adj. truthful, trustworthy
ውነታ	*wənäta* n. reality
ውን	*wən* እውን *əwən* adj. real
ውንድቢ	*wəndəbbi* n. eland *(taurotragus oryx)*
ውካታ	*wəkata* n. uproar, commotion, *see* አወካ
ውዳሴ	*see* ወደሰ
ውዴላ	*wəddella* n. saddle-blanket
ውድማ	*wədma* n. forest, uninhabited, deserted place, desert, *see* ወደመ
ውድድር	*wədəddər* n. competition *see* አወዳደረ
ውጅምብር	*wəǧəmbər* ውዥምብር n. choas, utter confusion
ውጥን	*see* ወጠነ
ውጥንቅጥ	*wəṭənqəṭ* n. jumble, medley
ዎፍ	*see* ወፍ

O

ዐልቅት	*allqətt* n. leech *(small blood-sucking worm)*
ዐመል	*amäl* n. habit, character
ዐመላም	*amälam* adj. n. moody; s/o with bad disposition
ዐመለኛ	*amälämña* adj/n. moody, s/o with a bad disposition; vicious *(horse, mule etc.)*
ዐመለቢስ	*amäläbis* adj/n bad-

	tempered; disagreeable, mannerless (person)
ላመል	lamäl adv. barely
ዐመቀ	ammäqä v.t. stuffed, crammed, forced in by pressing
ዕምቅ	əmməq n. stuffed, crammed
ታመቀ	tammäqä v.i was stuffed, crammed, forced in by pressing
አሳመቀ	asammäqä v.t had s/t stuffed, crammed etc.
ዐመጠ	ammäṭä or ዐመፀ ammäṣä v.i revolted, rebelled
ዐመጥ	amäṭ also ዐመፅ amäṣ n. revolution uprising, mutiny
ዐመጠኛ	aṃnäṭäññä also ዐመፀኛ amäṣäññä n. rebel, insurgent, lawless, criminal
ዐምድ	amd n. column, pillar
ዐምደ ወርቅ	amdä wärq n. arcade
ዐሞሌ	amole n. salt bar (used as currency in earlier days)
ዐሣ	asa n. fish
ዐሣነባሪ	asanäbari n. whale
ዐሣ አጥማጅ	asa äṭmäǧ n.— አሥ ጋሪ— asgari n. fisherman
ዐሥር	assər adj. ten
ዐሥረኛ	assəräñña adj. tenth
ዐረቀ	arräqä v.t straightened out (branch, back of a person etc.); molded (character)
ዐረበ	arräbä v.t tanned (of animal skin)
ዐራቢ	arṛabi n. tanner
ዐረብ	arab n. an Arab
ባሕር—	bahər—n. leather (tanned)
—ብረት	—bərät n. steel
—አገር	—agar n. Arabia
ዐረብኛ	aräbäñña n. Arabic language
ዐረብያ	aräbəya n. Arabia
ዐረንጓ ዐሮንቃ	aränqʷä aronqa n. marshy,

	boggy land
ዐረዘ	see ታረዘ
ዐረገ	arrägä v.t ascended
ዕርገት	ərgät n. Ascension
ዐረፈ	arräfä v.i rested, became quiet, reposed, landed (plane); was housed; died, passed away
ዐረፍተ ነገር	aräftä nägär n. sentence
ዕረፍት	əräft n. break, rest, repose, vacation, recess, pause, interval
ዕርፍ	ərf n. plow handle
ዕርፈ መስቀል	ərfä mäsqäl n. spoon for administering the Eucharist
ማረፊያ ቤት	maräfiya bet n. custody (imprisonment)
ምዕራፍ	mə'əraf n. chapter
አሳረፈ	asarräfä v.t had s/o rested, paused; landed (airplane)
ዐረፈ	aräfa n. lather
ዐርብ	arb n. Friday; weaver's frame
ዐቀበት	aqäbät n. steep, upward slope
—ቁልቁለት	—qulqulät n. ups and downs
ዐቃቢት	aqqabit n. woman who grinds the wheat for Eucharistic bread
ዐቃቤ ሕግ	aqqabe həgg n. prosecutor
—መጻሕፍት	—mäṣahəft n. librarian
ዐቀደ	aqqädä v.t planned, thought of a plan; projected, designed (a plan)
ዐቅድ	aqd n. plan, scheme
ዕቅዳ	əqqəda n. planning, scheming, projecting
ዕቅድ	əqqəd n. plan, scheme; project
ታቀደ	taqqädä v.t was planned; was projected etc.
አሳቀደ	asaqqädä v.t had s/t planned, schemed, projected
ዐቅል	aql n. mind; sense, brain

ዐቅም aqm n. force, power; ability, capacity; measure

ዐቅም ቢስ aqmä bis adj./ n weak , weakling

ዐበደ abbädä v.i went mad, became crazy, became insane; became frenzied

ዕብደት əbdät n. madness; insanity, lunacy

ዕብድ əbd adj. mad, crazy, insane, lunatic

—ውሻ —wəššsa n. rabid dog

አሳበደ asabbädä v.t maddened, drove crazy

ዐወቀ awwäqä v.i knew, was familiar with, recognized, realized; had sexual intercourse with (a woman)

ዐዉቀ ዐበድ awqo abbäd n. eccentric person

ዐዋቂ awaqi adj. knowledgeable, intelligent, wise; full-grown

ዕውቀት əwqät n. knowledge

ዕውቀተኛ əwqatäññä adj. knowledgeable, well-informed

ዕውቅ əwq adj. well-known

ዕውቅያ əwqiya n. acquaintance

ተዋወቀ täwawwäqä v.i became acquainted with one another, was introduced to each other

ታወቀ tawwäqä v.i was known, became famous

ታዋቂ tawaqi adj. known, famous

መታወቂያ mättawäqiya n. identification

—ወረቀት —wäräqät n. indentity card

አሳወቀ asawwäqä v.i made s/t known, informed

አስተዋወቀ astawäwwäqä v.t introduced (people)

አስታወቀ astawwäqä v.t in-

formed, notified, announced, declared

ማስታወቂያ mastawäqiya n. notice, information

—መለጠፊያ —mälättäfiya n. notice-board

ዐውደ ዓመት awədä amät n. festival (lit. turn of the year)

ዐዘቅት azäqt n. abyss, difficult, grave situation

ዐየ ayyä v.t saw; observed, looked at

ተያየ täyayyä v.i looked at each other; saw one another

ታየ tayyä v.i was seen. appeared, was shown; was displayed, was visible

አሳየ asayyä v.t showed demonstrated, displayed, exhibited; presented (a play)

አስተያየ astäyayyä v.t. compared

አስተያየት astäyayät n. observation, judgement, attitude, opinion, point of remark

—አደረገ —adärrägä took into consideration

ዐይን ayn n. eye

—ለዐይን —läyn face to face

ዐይነ ግዝ aynämaz n conjunctivitis

—ምድር —mədr n. excrement (human); a little hole in the ground used as water closet

—ርግብ —rəgb n. veil

—ሰባራ —säbara adj. shy; timid

—ሰብ —səb n. eye-orbit

—ስዉር —səwwər adj. blind

—ሾውራራ —šäwrarra adj. squint-eyed

—ኅሊና —həllina n. thought

—ደረቅ —däräq adj. impudent, shameless, cheeky

—ገመድ —gämäd n. approximate estimation

ዐይናማ aynamma adj. beautiful, pretty

231

ዐይናር	ayñar n. eye–discharge
ዐይን ለዐይን	ayn lä'ayn adv. face to face
—ዐዋጅ	—awⁱağ adj. be at loss in selecting one thing among many others
—አውጣ	—awṭa adj. impudent, saucy
—አፋር	—affär adj. shy, timid, bashful
—የሌለው	—yälelläw wⁱəšät adj.out-and-out (lie),complete (lie)
ለዐይን ሲይዝ	lä'ayn siyəz adv. in the dusk
ቅጽበተ ዓይን	qəṣbätä ayn n. moment, a split second
በዐይን ቄራኛ	bä'aynä qurañña keeping an eye on
ባንድ ዐይን ዐየ	band ayn ayyä treat alike, was impartial
የዐይን ምስክር	yä'ayn məsəkkər n. eye-witness
—ቆብ	— qob n. eyelid
—ብሌን	—bəlen n. pupil of the eye
አንዳይና	andayna adj. one-eyed
ዐይነት	aynät n. type, sort, kind, quality; colour
ዐጤ	aṭe ዐጤ n. title of a king (e.g emperor)
ዐጥንት	aṭənt n. bone; ancestry
ባለ ዐጥንት	balä aṭənt adj. bony; of good parentage
ዐጥንት የሌ ለው	aṭənt yälelläw adj weak (person, morally)
ዐጨ	aččä v.t was engaged, betrothed; recommended (s/o to a position)
ዕጩ	əču n. candidate
—መኰንን	—mäkkonən n. cadet
—መምህር	—mämhər n. teacher training school student
ዕጮኛ	əčoñña n. fiancée;
ግጨ	mača n. dowry
ተጫጨ	täčaččä v.i engaged to one another (for marriage)
ታጨ	taččä v.i was engaged betrothed; was

	recommended (to a position)
መታጫ	mättača n. dowry
አሳጨ	asaččä v.t caused s/o to be engaged (to marry); had s/o recommended
ዐጽም	aṣm n. skeleton, remains (dead body)
ዐጽም ርስት	aṣmä rəst n. family land
ዒላማ	ilama n. aim, target
ዔሊ	eli n. tortoise
ዓለም	aläm n. world
ዓለመኛ	alämäñña adj/n comfortable person (free from pain, anxiety etc.), euphoric, relieved; living luxuriously
ዓለማዊ	alämawi adj/n worldly (person); sensuous; secular
ዓለማዊነት	alämawinnät n. worldliness
ዓለሙን አየ	alämun ayyä enjoyed life
ዓላም አቀፍ	aläm aqqäf adj. international
ከፍለ ዓለም	kəfla aläm n. hemisphere
ዘለዓለም	zälä'aläm adv. forever ; always, eternally
ዘለዓለማዊ	zälä'alämawi adj. eternal
ዓጤ	see ዐጤ
ዓላማ	alama n. aim, goal, target, purpose, objective, intent
—ቢስ	—bis adj. aimless, purposeless
—የለሽ	—yälläš adj. aimless purposeless
ዓመት	amät n. year
ዐውዴ—	awdä—n. holiday (religious)
ዓመተ ምሕ ረት	amätä məhrät n. A.D, year of grace
ዓመታዊ	amätawi adj. annual
ዓመት በዓል	amät bä'al n. holiday anniversary

232

በዖ፤ዓመቱ	bäyyä amätu adv. yearly, annually	ture, utensil
ከዓመት	kä'amät amät year in, year out	የወንድ— yäwänd— n. penis (pol.)
ዓመት		የሴት— yäset—n. vagina(pol.)
ዕለት	ǝlät n. day	ጥሬ— ṭäre— n. raw material
ዕለታዊ	ǝlätawi adj. daily	ዕንቀ ǝnquʷ n. precious
ዕልል አለ	ǝlǝll alä v.i uttered cries of joy, jubilation	stone, jewelry
ዕልልታ	ǝlǝlta n. cries of joy, jubilation	ዕቀጣጣሽ ǝnquʷǝṭaṭaš n. New Year's Day
ዕርፈ መስቀል	ǝrfä mäsqäl n. spoon for administering the Eucharist	ዕውር ǝwwǝr adj. blind
		ዕንለ ግውታ ǝguʷalä mawta n. orphan
ዕቃ	ǝqa n. goods, thing, object, article: luggage; vessel, instrument; genital organs (pol.)	ዕጣ ǝṭa n. lot, chance (of lottery); fate, destiny
—ማጠቢያ	—maṭäbiya n. sink	—አወጣ —awäṭṭa also ዕጣ ጣለ ǝṭa ṭalä v.t cast lot
—ቤት	—bǝt n. store-house; storekeeper	—ደረሰው —därräsäw v.t drew the winning lot
—አዚሪ	—azuʷari n. peddler	
ሆድ እቃ	hod ǝqa n. entrails, guts	ዕጫገ ǝčäge n. title of the Abbot of the monastery of Däbrä Libanos
የሽክላ—	yäskla— n. earthenware	ዕፁብ ድንቅ ǝṣub dǝnq adj. marvellous, astonishing, breath-taking
የበቅሎ—	yäbäqlo— n. harness	
የቤት—	yäbet— n. furni-	ዕፅ ǝṣ n. herb (used as medicine); plant
		ዕፀ በላ ǝṣä bäll adj. herbivorous
		ዕፀዋት. ǝṣäwat n. flora

ዘ

ዘሆን	zähon also ዝሆን zǝhon n. elephant	ዝልል zǝllǝl n. beer must dissolved with water
ዘሆኔ	zähone n. elephantiasis	መዝለያ mäzläya n. springboard
የዘሆን ኩምቢ —ጆሮ ይስ ጣኝ አለ —ጥርስ	yäzähon kumbi n. tusk yäzähon ǧoro yäsṭäññ alä lend a deaf ear yäzähon ṭǝrs n. ivory	ተዘለለ täzällälä v.i was skipped over (a word etc.); was left aside; was dissolved with water (beer must)
ዘለለ	zällälä v.i jumped; leaped, climbed over; skipped over (a word etc·), left aside; gambolled; dissolved the must of beer with water	ተዘለለ täzallälä played cheerfully, gambolled
		አዘለለ azzälällä v.i had s/o jump, leap
ዘላይ	zälay n. jumper (sport)	ዘላለ zäläla n. bunch (grapes, strawberries etc.), cluster
ዝላይ	zǝllay n. jumping, leaping	የእንብ— yä'ǝnba- n. teardrops
ዝላያ	zǝlliya n. jump, leap	የወይን— yäwäyn- n. cluster, bunch of grapes

ዘለሰ	zälläsä v.t stooped (one's head)	እንዛላዞለ	anzälazzälä v.t carried s/t awkwardly
ዜሰለሰኛ	zäläsäñña n. type of poetry causing sadness or low spirit	ዘለግ አለ	zälägg alä v.i was high in stature, was tall, able-bodied, of manly appearance
ዝለሰ	zəlləs adj. stooped		
ዘለቀ	zälläqä v.i penetrated (water); completed (study, book reading); went through (difficulties etc.); appeared; lasted (ration etc.)	ዘለግላጋ	zäläglagga adj. tall, of manly appearance
		ዘለፈ	zälläfä v.t rebuked, blamed, reproached, reprimanded
ዘለቄታ	zäläqeta n. continuity, lasting, perpetuity, permanence	ዘለፋ	zäläfa n. rebuke blame, reproach, reprimand
ዘላቂ	zälaqi adj. perpetual, continuous, lasting	ዝልፈት	zəlfät n. rebuke, blame, reproach, reprimand
ተዘለቀ	täzälläqä v.i was completed	ዝልፊያ	zəlfiya n. rebuke, blame, reproach, reprimand
የሚዘለቅ አይደለም	yämizzälläq aydälläm it is unbearable, very difficult	ተዘለፈ	täzälläfä v.t rebuked blamed, reproached, reprimanded
አዘለቀ	azälläqä v.t brought to the end; caused to survive (difficulties), brought into view	ተዘላፊ	täzalafi adj/n (one) who rebukes, blames, reproaches
		አዘለፈ	azzälläfä v.t. have s/o rebuked, blamed, reproached, reprimanded
እዛለቀ የማያዛልቅ ክርክር	azzalläqä v.t lasted long yämmayazzalləq kərəkkər weak argument	ዘለፍለፈ ዝልፍልፍ	see ተዘለፈለፈ zəlfləf adj. fainting; exhausted, tired out
ዘለበት	zäläbät n. buckle (of belt)	ዘላለም	see ዓለም
ዘላዓለም	zälä'aläm adv. forever see ዓለም	ዘላበደ	zälabbädä v.i babbled, jabbered
ዘለዘለ	zäläzzälä v.t cut meat in small strips	ዘላባጅ	zälabağ adj/n (one) who jabbers
ዘልዛላ	zälzalla adj. careless, lax, unguarded	ዘላን	zällan n/ adj nomad; impolite, lawless (of person)
ዘልዛልነት	zälzallannät n. carelessness, laxity	ዘመመ	zämmämä v.t curved down, lent, inclined
ዝልዝል	zəlzəl n. meat cut into small strips	አዘመመ	azämmämä v.t curved down, lent, inclined
—ጥብስ	—ṭəbs n. roasted meat cut into small strips	አዝማሚያ	azmammiya n. inclination; tendency, direction
ተንዘለዘለ	tänzäläzzälä v.i was careless, lax ; was untidy, slovenly	ዘመሚት	zämämit n. a kind of red ant
		ዘመረ	zämmärä v.t sang (bird); sang a song, chanted

.234

ዘመረ	zəmmära n. singing	ዘማን	an army (to war)
ዘማሬ	zəmmare n. song, hymn		zämän n. date,epoch, period, era
መዘምር	mäzämmər n. singer (church), cantor	ዘማናዊ	zämänawi adj. modern, fashionable, up-to–date; sophisticated
መዘምራን	mäzämməran n. pl. choir		
መዝሙር	mäzmur n. hymn, song	ዘማናይ	zämänay also ዘበናይ, zabänay adj. sophisticated; up–to–date; parvenu
ብሔራዊ—	bəhərawi—n. national anthem		
መዝሙረ ዳዊት	mäzmurä dawit n. Psalms of David	ዘማን አመጣሽ	zämän amäṭṭaš adj vogue; latest (fashion)
ደቀ መዝሙር	däqqä mäzmur n. disciple pl: ደቀ መዝሙ- ርት	ዘመዘመ	zämäzzämä v.t embroidered (needlework)
አዘመረ	azämmärä v.t sang a song, sang a hymn	ዝምዝማ	zəmzämä n. needle-work
ዘመተ	zämmätä v.i went on a military mission, expedition; made a raid; campaigned; migrated	ዝምዝማት	zəmzəmat n. embroidery
		ተዘመዘመ	täzämäzzämä v.i was embroidered
ዘማች	zämäča n. raid, military expedition; campaign, fight	ዘማድ	zämäd n. relative, relation, kinsman, family, friend see under ተዘመደ
ዘማች	zämač n. compaigner (soldier, raider, fighter in war, etc.)	ሁሉ ዘማዴ	hullu zämäde adj. popular (person)
—ወፍ	—wäf n. migrating bird	ቅርብ ዘማድ	qərb zämäd n. close relative
ተዘመተ	täzammätä v.i became rampant (disease); spread (news, disease, fire)	ቤተ—	betä — n. relations (relatives)
		ዘማዳሞች	zämädamočč n. relatives
አዘመተ	azämmätä v.t led a campaign, a raid, led army to the front, led an expedition (war)	ዘማድ አዝማ ግድ	zämäd azmad n. relations (relatives)
		የሥጋ ዘማድ	yäsəga zämäd n. blood relation
አዝማች	azmač n. leader of an expedition (war); refrain (of a song)	የዘማድ አውራ	yäzämäd awra n. chief of a clan, a family
ቀኝ—	qäññ—n. old Ethiopian title (lit. commander of the right wing)	ዘማ	zämma n. adulteress; see also ዘሙት
ግራ—	gəra–n. old Ethiopian title (commander of the left wing)	ዘማዊ	zämmawi adj. adulterous, fornicator
አዘመተ	azzammätä v.t spread (news, disease)	ዘሙተኛ	zəmmutäñña adj. adulterous, fornicator
አዘመተ	azzämmätä v.t led	ዘምቢል	zämbil n. basket (of woven palm leaves)
		ዘምባባ	zämbaba n. palm tree
		ዘረረ	zärrärä v.t stretched s/t in full length;

	knocked s/o down; knocked out
ተዘረረ	*täzärrärä* v.i was stretched at full length; was knocked-down, was knocked out
ዘረነቀ	*zärännäqä* v.t stuffed in, forced in; inserted
ተዘረነቀ	*täzärännäqä* v.i was stuffed in, forced in, was inserted
ዘረከተ	*zäräkkätä.* v.t tore away *(made a rent in s/t)*; tore open s/o 's belly *(with a knife etc.)*
ዘርካታ	*zärkatta* adj. fattish
ዝርክት	*zərəkt* adj. torn
ዝርክት አለ	*zərkkətt alä* v.i was suddenly torn way
ዝርክት አደ ረገ	*zərkkətt adärrägä* v.t toré s/t away suddenly
ተዘረከተ	*täzäräkkätä* v.i was torn away suddenly
ዘረክራካ	*zäräkrakka* adj. messy, untidy *see* ተዝረክረከ
ዝርክርክ ያለ	*zərəkrəkk yalä* adj. messy, untidy
ዝርክርክ አደ ረገ	*zərəkrəkk adärrägä* v.t made messy, untidy
ዘረዘረ	*zäräzzärä* v.i .v.t developed ears *(of corn etc.)*; changed money *(into small denominations)*; enumerated; itemized; discussed in detail
ዘርዛራ	*zärzarra* adj. loose *(sieve, wire- netting etc.)*
ዘርዛሪ	*zərəzzari* n. change *(small denominations)*
ዝርዝር	*zərzər* n. change
ተዘረዘረ	*täzäräzzärä* v.i was changed *(money into small denomi- nations)*; was item- ized, was enumerated
አዘረዘረ	*azzäräzzärä* v.t had money changed into

	small denominations
ዘረጋፋ	*zäräggäfä* v.t poured out, emptied, tipped out
ዝርጋፍ ወርቅ	*zərgəf wärq* n. neck- lace *(golden)*
ዝርጋፍ አለ	*zərgəff alä* v.i was emptied; ,was tipped out
ዝ ርጋፍ አደ ረገ	*zərgəff adägärrä* v.t poured out; emp- tied; tipped out *(quickly)*
ተዘረጋፋ	*täzäräggäfä* v.i was emptied; was tipped out; flooded in
አዘረጋፋ	*azzäräggäfä* v.t had s/t emptied, s/t tipped
ዘረጋ	*zärägga* v.t stretched out, spread out, extended; unrolled *(carpet etc.)*
ዝርግ	*zərg* adj. flat
—ሳህን	— *sahən* n. flat dish
ዝርግ ነት	*zərgənnät* n. flatness
ተዘረጋ	*täzärägga* v.i was spread; was ex- tended
አዘረጋ	*azzärägu* v.t caused s/t to be spread, extended
አዘረጋጋ	*azzärägagga* v.t caused s/t to be spread extensively
*ዘረጠ	**zärräṭä*
ዘረጦ	*zäräṭo* adj. coward, weakling
ዝራጭ	*zərraç* adj. coward, weakling
አዘረጠ	*azärräṭä* v.t farted *(vulgar, impolite)*
በዱላ—	*bädulla*—hit severely with a stick
ዘረጥራጥ	*zäräṭraṭṭa* adj. cow- ard, weakling
ዝርጥርጥ	*zərəṭrəṭ* adj. coward
ተዝረጠረጠ	*täzräṭärräṭä* v.i was a coward, withdrew frightened
አንዘረጠ	*anzarräṭä* v.t lived a vagabond life
አዝረጠረጠ	*azräṭärräṭä* v.t caused fear, panic
ዘረጠጠ	*zäräṭṭäṭä* v.t caused to

236

ዘረጠጥ fall by pulling s/o's. legs; degraded s/o by not using a polite form of address *zäräṭäṭṭ* adj. stout *(person)*, pot-bellied

ዝርጣጥ *zärṭaṭṭa* adj. stout *(person)*, pot-bellied

ዝርጥጥ *zarṭaṭ* adj. stout *(person)*

ተንዘረጠጠ *tänzäräṭṭätä* v.t. grew too stout

ተዘረጠጠ *täzäräṭṭäṭä* v.i. was made to fall by pulling s/o's legs

አንዘረጠጠ *anzäräṭṭäṭä* v.t. grew too stout

ሆዱን— *ሆዱን* — he had a stout belly

አዘረጠጠ *az zäräṭäṭä* v.t had s/o fell by pullng his legs

* ዘረፈጠ * *zäräffäṭä*

ዝርፈጠ *zärfaṭṭa* adj. idle, lazy

ተንዘረፈጠ *tänzäraffäṭä* v.i. occupied a large space by sitting idly

ተዘረፈጠ *täzäräffäṭä* v.i. sat idly

ዘረፈ *zärräfä* v.t. plundered, ransacked; composed poetry impromptu

ዘረፋ *zäräfa* n. plundering, ransacking

ዘራፊ *zärafi adj/n* (one) who plunders

ቅኔ ዘራፊ *qane zärafi* n. one who composes poetry impromptu

ዘራፍ *zärraf* n. pillager

ዝርፊያ *zarfiya* n. pillage, plundering

ተዘረፈ *täzärräfä* v.i. was plundered, ransacked

ተዘራረፈ *täzärarräfä* v.i plundered, ransacked each other

አዘረፈ *azzärräfä* v.t. had s/t plundered, ransacked

* ዘረፈ * *zärräfä*

ዝርፍ *zärf* fringe of dress, garment

ዝርፍና በአቤት *zärfanna b aläbet* n. constructive state *(gram.)*

* ዘረፈረፈ * *zäräfärräfä*

ዘረፍራፋ *zäräfraffa* adj. untidy

ዝርፍርፍ *zərəfrəf a* dj. slovenly

አዘረፈረፈ *azräfärräf fä* v.t. put one's clo thes on carelessly

* ዘረፋፈ * *zäräffäf̣ị*

ዘረፋፍ *zäräfäf* adj. untidy

ዝርፋፍ *zärfaffị a* adj. untidy

ተንዘረፈፈ *tänzäri iffäfä* v.i hung loosel; y

አንዘረፈፈ *anzäri iffäfä* v.t. hung loosely, carried s/t c'lumsily

ዘራ *zärra* v.t so wed, see(led, gr ew *(wheat etc.)*

ዘሪ *zäri* adj./n.(one) who sows

ዘራም *zäram* adj. blessed with many descendar its

ዘር *zär n.* seed; noun

ጎመን— *gomi nän – n.* rapeseed

ዘረ መልካም *zärä mälkam* adj. of a decent family

—መጥፎ *—i näṭfo* adj. from a ba d family

—ቢስ *—-bis* adj. of low class

–ቡሩክ *--buruk* adj. from ?ᵡ 'olessed family

—ብዙ *—bazu* adj. rich in progeny

—ከፉ *—kạfu* adj. from bad familj

—ደግ *—dägg* adj. from a decent family

—ጥሩ *—ṭaru* adj. from good family

ዘር ቆጣሪ *zär qoṭari* adj. of blue blood

የዘር ግንድ *yäzär gạnd* n.family tree

ጥሬ ዘር *ṭare zär* n. noun *(derived from a verb)*

ተዘራ *täzärra* v.i was sown

አዘራ *azära* v.t winnowed

ማዘሪያ *mazriya* n. winnowing implement, tool

አዘራ *azzära* v.t had seed

sown

ዘርፉ *see* ዘረፈ.

ዘቀዘቀ zäqäzzäqä v.t turned up - side - down, over- turned

ዘቅዛቃ zäqzaqqa adj. sloping *(area)*

ዝቅዝቅ zəqzəq adv. down- wards

ተዘቀዘቀ täzäqäzzäqä v.i hung up - side - down, was overturned

አዘቀዘቀ azäqäzzäqä v.t went down, went down- wards

ፀሀይ—ት the sun went down

አዘቀዘቀ azzäqäzzäqä v.t made s/t go down

ዘቀጠ zäqqäṭä v.i settled to the bottom of a liquid; sank

ዝቃጭ zəqqač n. sediment, residue

ዝቅጣቃጭ zəqəṭqač n. sedi- ment, residue

አዘቀጠ azäqqäṭä v.i went down *(as residue, sediment)*

አዘቅት azäqt n. abyss

ዘቃቅቤ zäqaqəbe n. kind of aromatic plant, basil

ዘበለለ zäbällälä v.t emptied the bowels in great quantity

ዘበተ zäbbätä v.i derided, laughed scornfully at

ዘበት zäbät n. banter, firvolity

ተዘባበተ täzäbabbätä v.i de- rided ,laughed scornfully at each other

መዘባበቻ mäzzäbabäča n. laughing - stock, ridicule

ዘበነ zäbbänä v.i became sophisticated; mod- ernized *(people)*

ዘበናይ zäbänay ዘመናይ zämänay adj/n. sophisticated, modern, parvenu

ዘበናይነት zäbänayənnät n. sophistication

ዘበን also ዘመን zäbän n. time, era, epoch

ተዘባነነ täzäbannänä v.i be- came extremely self- confident, snobbish, conceited

ተዘባናይ täzäbanay adj. snobbish, conceited

አዘባነነ azzäbannänä v.t. treat s/o lavishly, sumptuously, treated s/o in grand style

ዘበዘበ zäbäzzäbä v.t was verbose, dwelt upon a subject

ነገር ዘብዛቢ nägär zäbzabi adj. importunate

ዘብዛባ zäbzabba adj. im- potunate

ዝብዝብ zəbəzzəb n. dwelling upon a subject, importunity

ዘበጠ zäbbäṭä v.i sloped downward

ዘባጠ zäbaṭa n. depression *(surface)*

ዘብጥ zäbṭ n. depression

ዘቢብ zäbib n. raisin, dried grape

ዘባ zäbba v.i warped, was bent

ተዛባ täzabba v.i. became incoherent *(sen- tence)*; was out of order; was distorted

አዛባ azzabba v.t. made incoherent *(sen- tence)*; distorted *(in- formation etc.)*

ዘባረቀ zäbarräqä v.i. talked nonsense, confused an issue, rambled on, wandered in one's talk

ዘባራቂ zäbaraqi adj/n *(one)* who talks nonsense, confuses an issue

ዘባረረቀ zäbärarräqä v.t. made messy, put in

238

ዝብርቅርቅ zəbrəqrəq n. mess
ተዘበራረቀ tāzābārarrāqā v.t.
was made completely messy, was put in a disorderly manner, was completely confused

ተዘባረቀ tāzābarrāqā v.i. was made messy, was put in a disorderly manner, was confused

አዘበራረቀ āzzābārarrāqā v.t. made completely messy, put in a disorderly manner, confused completely

አዘባረቀ āzzābarrāqā v.t. made messy, put in a disorderly manner, confused

ዘባተሉ zābatālo n. ragged-clothes

ዘብ zāb n. sentry
ዘበኛ zābāñña n. watchman, guard

ዘቦ zābo in ወርቅ-warqān. cloth interwoven with gold thread

ዘነቀ zānnāqā v.t. inserted forcefully
ተዘነቀ tāzānnāqā v.i. was forcefully inserted
በአእምሮየ ሐሳብ ተዘነቀ ብኝ an uneasy feeling sneaked into my mind

ዘነቆለ zānāqqolā v.t. poked s/o's eye(with a finger)
ተዘነቆለ tāzānāqqolā v.i. was poked with a finger (eye)

ዘነበ zānnābā also ዘነመ v.i. rained
ዝናብ zənab n. rain
ሌባ— leba— n. brief rain
ወጨፎ-- wāçāfo—n. rainstorm
ዶፍ— dof—n. heavy rain
የዝናብ ልብስ yāzənab ləbs n.

—መለኪያ —mālākkiya n. rain gauge
ዝናባም zənabam adj. rainy
አነነበ azānnābā v.t. caused to rain
* ዘነበለ *zānābbālā
ዘነባላ zānballa adj. slanting
ዝነባሌ zənābbale n. inclination, tendency, preference, trend
አዘነበለ azānābbālā v.i. slanted; stooped, inclined

ዘነተረ zānāttārā v.t. snatched with the teeth
ተዘነተረ tāzānāttārā v.i. was snatched with the teeth

ዘነነ zānnānā v.i. slanted
ዘነን ያለ zānānn yalā adj. slanting
ዘናና zānana adj. slanting
* ዘነከተ zānākkātā
ዘነካታ zānkatta adj. graceful, exuberant
ተዘናከታ tāzānakkātā v.t. behaved gracefully
ዘነዘና zānāzāna n. pestle
ዘነጋ zānāgga v.i forgot, became absent-minded
ዝንጉ zəngu adj. forgetful, scatter-brained
ዝንጋታ zəngata n. forgetfulness
ተዘነጋ tāzānāgga v.i. was forgotten
ተዘነጋጋ tāzānāgagga v.i. was forgotten; forgot each other
ተዘነጋ tāzānagga v.i. felt confident
አዘነጋ azānāgga v.t. caused to forget
አዘነጋ azzānagga v.t. caused to forget (with the intention of doing harm to s/o.)
ዘነጣ zānnāṭā v.i. became chic; showed an air of superior excel-

ዘናጭ — lence (behaviour) *zännač* adj. stylish; dandified

ዜንጥ — *zenṭ* n. chic; air of superior excellence

ዜንጠኛ — *zenṭäñña* adj. stylish

ዝነጣ — *zännäṭa* n. chic; air of superior excellence

ዘነጠለ — *zänäṭṭälä* v.t. cut s/t away (branch from a tree etc.); cut s/t open (e.g belly of an animal by a hyena); mispronounced a syllable (esp. its pitch)

ዝንጥል — *zənṭəl* n. branch (of tree freshly cut)

ዘነጣጠለ — *zänäṭaṭṭälä* v.t. cut s/t away in pieces; cut s/t open repeatedly

ተዘነጠለ — *täzänäṭṭälä* v.i. was cut away ; was cut open

ተዘነጣጠለ — *täzänäṭaṭṭälä* v.t. was cut into pieces; was ragged (clothes)

አዘነጠለ — *azzänäṭṭälä* v.t. had s/t cut into pieces

ዘነጠፈ — *zänäṭṭäfä* v.t. cut away (branch from a tree)

ዝንጣፈ — *zənəṭṭafi* n. twig, bough

ተዘነጠፈ — *täzänäṭṭäfä* v.i. was cut away (branch)

ዘነፈ — *zännäfä

ዝንፍት — *zənnəfat* n. overlapping

ተዘነፈ — *täzannäfä* v.i became of uneven length, overlapped

ተዘናፈ — *täzanafi* adj. of uneven length; overlapping

አዘነፈ — *azzannäfä* v.t. caused to be of uneven length, caused to overlap

ዘንፈላ — *zänfalla* adj. graceful, glamorous, exuberant

ተዘናፈለ — *täzänaffälä* v.i. behaved gracefully

ዘና — *zänna* v.i. relaxed, felt at ease

መዝናኛ — *mäznaña* n. means of amusement, entertainment

—ቦታ — *—bota* n. place of amusement, entertainment, recreation

ተዘና — *täzanna* v.i. felt at ease

ተዝናና — *täznanna* v.i. felt at home

አዝናና — *aznanna* v.t. entertained

አዝናኝ — *aznañ* adj. entertaining

ዘንቢል — *zänbil* n. basket

ዘንካታ — *zänkotta* adj. graceful

ዘንድ — *zänd* adv. near, besides, ት እኔው ዘንድ ነው he is near me, beside me, he is at my place (with simple imperfect, that... may) ይመጣ ዘንድ ነገርኩት I told him that he might come; prep. from ከእግዚአብሔር ዘንድ from God. adv since ከመጣ ዘንድ እኔ አነጋግረዋለሁ since he has come I shall talk to him

ዘንድ አንቀጽ — *zänd anqäṣ* n. jussive (gram.)

ዘንዶ — *zändo* n. larg snake

ዘንጋዳ — *zängada* n. sorghum

ዘንግ — *zäng* n. road, axis, goad, shaft (of spear)

የፈረስ ዘንግ — *yäfäräs zäng* n. kind of shrub

ዘከረ — *zäkkärä* v.t. commemorated (religious occasion) with a feast

ዝክር — *zəkər* n. commemoration with a banquet (in a religious occassion)

ዝክረ ነገር — *zəkrä nägär* n. memorabilia

መዘክር — *mäzäkkər* n. in ቤተ መዘክር museum

ተዘከረ   *täzäkkärä* v.i. gave
        alms to s/o
ተገከር   *täzkär* also ተዝካር n.
        feast or banquet in
        commemoration of
        a dead relative
--አወጣ   --*awäṭṭa* v.t. gave
        a feast or banquet
        in commemoration
        of a dead relative
አዘከረ   *äzäkkärä* v.t.prayed on
        at a feast or banquet
        in commemoration
        of a dead person
ዘከዘከ   *zäkäzzäkä* v.t. poured
        out in quantity;
        emptied completely
ምስጢር   *mäsṭir*— v.t. di-
        vulged a secret, had a
        loose tongue
ዘክዘካ   *zäkzäkka* adj. ex-
        travagant
ወንፊት   —*wänfit* n. loose sieve
ዝክዝክ   *zəkzək* adj. loose
        (fabrics)
ዝክዝክ አደረገ   *zəkzəkk ädärrägä* in
        ምስጢሩን ዝክዝክ አድ
        ርጎ አወጣ divulged
        all secrets
ተዘከዘከ   *täzäkäzzäkä* v.i. was
        poured out in
        quantity, was emptied
        completely
አዘከዘከ   *azzäkäzzäkä* v.t.
        had   s/t   emptied
        completely ምስጥሬን
        ሁሉ አዘከዘከኝ
        he made   me   tell
        him all my secrets
ዘካ(ት)   *zäka(t)* n. alms (used
        by Moslems only)
ዘኬ   *zäkke* n. food collected
        by church students
        from begging; meal
        eaten at church after
        mass service (brought
        by believers)
—ለቃሚ   —*läqami* adj. beggar
        (insult to students)
--ተማሪ   —*tämari* n. student
        who supports himself
        by begging
ዘወረ   *zäwwärä* v.t. turned
        a wheel

ዘዋሪ   *zäwwarra* in—በታ
—ቦታ   —*bota* n.   an
        out-of-the   way place
ዘወርዋራ   *zäwärwarra* adj.
        roundabout way
ዝውውር   *zəwəwwər* n. transfer
ማዘውወር   *mäzäwwər* n. pulley
ተዘወረ   *täzäwwärä* v.i. was
        turned (wheel)
ተዘዋወረ   *täzäwawwärä* v.i.
        moved around, trav-
        elled about; circulated
        (blood)
ተዘዋዋሪ   *täzäwawäri* adj.
        circulating, migrant,
        wandering,   errant,
        mobile
—ክሊኒክ   —*klinik* n.mobile clinic
ተዘወረ   *täzawwärä* v.i. was
        transferred
ተዘዋሪ   *täzawäri* adj.
        transferable,   mobile
አዘወረ   *azzäwwärä* v.t. had
        a wheel turned
አዛወረ   *azzawwärä* v.t. had
        s/o tranferred
ዘዋተረ   *zäwwättärä*
ዘወትር   *zäwätər* adv. always
        constantly, regularly
ተዘወተረ   *täzäwättärä* v.t.
        has become usual.
        habitual
አዘወተረ   *azäwättärä* v.t.
        frequented (a place),
        did s/t regulary,
        continued to do s t
        constantly
አዘውታሪ   *azäwtari* adj/n one
        who frequently does
        s/t
ዘው አለ   *zäww alä* v.i. came in
        suddenly,   entered
        abruptly
ዘው ዘው አለ   *zäww zäww alä*
        v.i. entered here and
        there
ዘውድ   *zäwd* n. crown
—አማከሪ   —*ammakari* n. crown
        counselor
—አገዛዝ   —*aggäzaz* n. king-
        dom
—ደፋ   —*däffa* v.t. was
        crowned, became a
        king, an emperor

241

—ጫነ v.t. see ዘወረ ዳቆ

ባለ— balä — n. legitimate heir to the throne

ዘዌ zäwe n. angle

ዘየረ zäyyärä v.t. greeted (used by Moslems only)

ዝየራ zəyyära n. greeting

ተዘያየረ täzäyayyärä v.i. greeted each other

ዘየነ zäyyänä v.t. embelished, decorated

ዝየና zəyyäna n. embelishment, decoration

ዘየደ zäyyädä v.i. was tactful, prudent

ዘያጅ zäyyag adj. tactful, prudent

ዝየዳ zəyyäda n. tact, prudence

ዘዬ zäye n. tact, prudence

—አዋቂ —awaqi adj. prudent, tactful

ዘዮቤ zäyəbe n. figure of speech, expression

ዘዮት zäyət n. oil

የምግብ— yäməgab-n. edible oil

የሞተር— yämotor-n. motor oil

የተልባ— yätälba-n. linseed oil

የኑግ— yänug— noug oil

የወይራ— yäwäyra- n. olive oil

የጉሎ— yägulo- n. castor oil

ዘዴ zäde n. method, way of doing s/t, ways and means of doing s/t

—አዋቂ —awaqi adj. tactful, prudent

ዘደኛ zədeñña adj. tactful, prudet, resourceful

በዘዴ bäzäde adv. carefully, artfully

ዘገመ zäggämä

ዘገምተኛ zägämtäñña adj./n (one) who walks slowly

ዘገምታ zägämta n. walking slowly

አዘገመ azäggäma v.i. walked; did s/t slowly plodded, made slow headway

አዝጋሚ azgami n. plodder

ዘገረረ zägärrärä v.t. knocked

ዘገባ zäggäbä v.t. aimed, took aim

ዘገባ zägäba n. report

ዘጋቢ zägabi n. reporter

መዝገብ mäzgäb n. register, roster, ledger, record

መዝገብ ቃላት mäzgäbä qalat n, dictionary, lexicon

መዝገብ ቤት mäzgäb bet n. archives, record office, registry

መዝጋቢ mäzgabi n. registrar

ምዝገባ məzgäba n. registration

ተመዘገበ tämäzäggäbä v.i. was registered

መመዝገቢያ mämmäzgäbiya n. registration fee, place

ተመዝጋቢ tämäzgabi n. registering candidate

አስመዘገበ asmäzäggäbä v.t. had s/o registered

ዘገነ zäggänä v.t. took handful (grain etc.)

ዝግን zəgən n. highly seasoned dish of minced meat cooked in butter

አዘገነ azzäggänä v.t. had s/o take a handful (grain etc.)

ዘገነነ zägännänä used with pronominal suffix such as -ኝ-ው-etc. e.g

ዘገነነው zägännänäw v.i. was disgusted (by a horrible scene), was horrified

ዘገናኝ zägnañ n. horrifying scene

ዘገየ zägäyyä v.i. was late, was delayed

ዘገይት አለ zägyätt alä v.i. came a little late

አዘገየ azägäyyä v.t. delayed, detained, postponed, kept late

ዘገይቶ መጣ zägyəto mäṭṭa he was late

ቢዘገይ ቢዘ ገይ bizägäy bizägäy at the latest

ቢዘገይም bizägäyyəm however

*ዘገ	late he/ it is *zägägga*
ዝግ፟	*zəgəggu* adj. ready, prepared *(to do s/t)*
ዝግጅት	*zəgəggət* n. preparation, arrangement
ተዘገጃጀ	*täzägäğğağä* v.i. was prepared, ᴗ was arranged
ተዘጋጀ	*täzägağğä* v.i. was ready, was prepared; prepared oneself; was put in order
አዘጋጃጀ	*azzägäğğağğä* v.t. prepared, arranged, put in order
አዘጋጀ	*azzägağğä* v.t. prepared, arranged, put in order
አዘጋጅ	*azzägağ* adj/ n. *(one)* who prepares, arranges, puts in order
መጽሔት—	*mäṣəhet—* n. editor of a periodical
ማዘጋጃ	*mazägaga in* ማዘጋጃ ቤት *municipality,* a city hall
ዘጋ	*zägga* v.t. closed, blocked, shut off, obstructed, blocked up
ዝግ	*zəg* adj. closed, blocked
መዝጊያ	*mäzgiya* n. door, gate, entrance
ዝግ ችሎት	*zəg čəlot* n. closed session of a court of law
ተዘጋ	*täzägga* v.i. was closed
ተዘጊ	*täzägi* adj. easy to close
አዘጋ	*azzägga* v.t. had s/t *(door, opening)* closed
አዛጋ	*azzagga* v.t. yawned
*ዘገረጎረ	*zägorägorä*
ዘጎርጓሮ	*zägorgʷarra* adj. stripped, multi-coloured
ዝጉርጉር	*zəgurgur* adj. stripped, multicoloured
ተዘጎረጎረ	*täzgoräggorä* v.i. became stripped,

	multicoloured
አዝጎረጎረ	*azgorägorrä, also* አዥጎረጎረ *ažgoräggorä* v.t. made stripes, made multicoloured
ዘጎነ	*zäggonä* v.i. was full of sores
ዘጠና	*zäṭäna* adj/n ninety
ዘጠናኛ	*zäṭänaňňa* adj/n ninetieth
ዘጠኝ	*zäṭäňň* adj. nine
ዘጠነኛ	*zäṭänäňňa* adj/n ninth
*ዘጠጠ	* *zäṭäzzäṭä*
ዘጠዘጠ	*zäṭazaṭ* adj. tramp, bum *(U.S.)*
ዘጥ ዘጥ አለ	*zäṭṭ zäṭṭ alä* v.i. loafed
አዘጠዘጠ	*azäṭäzzäṭä* v.t. loafed, wandered about doing nothing, bummed
አዘጥዛጥ	*azäṭzač* adj/n *(one)* who loafs, wanders about doing nothing, bum
ዘጭ አለ	*zäčč alä* also እንዘጭ አለ *ənzäčč alä* v.i. fell down abruptly, slumped
ዘፈቀ	*zäffäqä* v.i. dipped, soaked
ዝፍቅያ	*zəfqiya* n. dipping *(boys in swimming)*
ተዘፈቀ	*täzäffäqä* v.i. was dipped, soaked, plunged
ተዛፈቀ	*täzaffäqä* v.i. dipped each other *(in swimming)*
አዘፈቀ	*azäffäqä* v.t. had s/o dipped in water
ዘፈነ	*zäffänä* v.t. sang
ዘፈን	*zäfän* n. song
—አወረደ	—*awärrädä* v.t. led a choir *(in singing)*
ዘፋኝ	*zäfaň* n. singer
አዘፈነ	*azzäffänä* v.t. had s/o sing
አዛፈነ	*azzaffänä* v.t. accompanied s/o in singing
ዘፈዘፈ	*zäfäzzäfä* v.t. soaked in water; *(clothes, grain etc.)*, put aside

243

undone for a long time e.g.

ሰራውን ዘለዘለው he put his work aside for a long time

ዘፈዘፈ *zäfazäfo* adj. rounded, obese

ዝፍዝፍ *zəfzəf* adj. soaked (in water); lazy

ተዘፈዘፈ *täzäfäzzäfä* v.i. was soaked in water

ዘፈዘፈ *zäfäzzäfä*

ተንዘፈዘፈ *tänzäfäzzäfä* v.i. writhed (in pain); trembled (in terror)

አንዘፈዘፈ *anzäfäzzäfä* v.t. caused to tremble (in terror), shiver with fear

ዘፈጠጠ *zäfäṭṭäṭä*

ዘፈጠጥ *zäfäṭäṭ* adj. pot-bellied

ዝፍጣጥ *zäfṭaṭṭa* adj. stout, pot-bellied

ተንዘፈጠጠ *tänzäfäṭṭäṭä* v.i. had large prominent belly, became pot-bellied

አንዘፈጠጠ *anzäfäṭṭäṭa* v.t. appeared with a large belly

ዘፍ አለ *zäff alä* v.i. slumped

ዙረት see ዞረ

ዙሪያ see ዞረ

ዙር see ዞረ

ዙጥ አደረገ *zuṭṭ adärrägä* v.i. broke wind, farted

ዙፋን *zufan* n. throne

ለቀቀ —ለቀቀ *—läqqäqä* v.t. abdicated

—ቤት *—bet* n. throne room

—ወረሰ *—wärräsä* v.t. succeeded to the throne

—ላይ ወጣ *—lay wäṭṭa* v.t. came to the throne

ዚቀኛ *ziqäñña* n. an admirable person; a subtle person

ዛለ *zalä* v.i wearied (body limb); was exhausted (body, mind)

ዝለት *zələt* n. weariness

አዛለ *azalä* v.t. caused weariness, exhausted

ዛላ *zala* n. ear of corn; stature

ዛላው መልከም *zalaw mälkäm* adj. tall and handsome

ዛር *zar* n. kind of evil-spirit that possesses people

ባለ— *balä—* n. s/o possessed by an evil spirit

ዛራም *zäräm* adj. possessed by «zar»: easily irritated

የዛር ፈረስ *yäzär färäs* n. person attacked by «zar»

ዛሬ *zare* n. adv. & n to-day; at this present age, period

—ነገ *—nägä* n. procrastination

——አለ *——alä* v. procrastinated, stalled

ዛሬውኑ *zärewənu* adv. this very day

እስከ ዛሬ *əskäzare* until today, to date

ዛቀ *zaqä* v.t. scooped up, shovelled; removed s/t e.g. grain, ashes, dung, flour in great quantity

ዝቆሽ *zəqoš* adj. very cheap e g. ዋጋው ዝቆሽ ነው the price is very cheap

መዛቂያ *mäzaqiya* n. scoop

ተዛቀ *täzaqä* v.i. was scooped up, shovelled, removed in great quantity

አዛቀ *azzaqä* v.t. had s/t scooped up, shovelled etc.

ዛቢያ *zabiya* n. shaft (handle of an axe)

ዛተ *zatä* v.i. threatened

ዛቻ *začča* n. threat, menace

ተዛዛተ *täzazatä* v.i. threatened each other

ዛተለ *zättälä* v. became ragged

ዛተሉ *zatälo* n. rag

ዛኒጋባ *zanigabba* n. annex (building)

ዛዘነ *zazzänä* v.i. had a strong sexual desire (lusted)

ዛዠኝ *zazañ* adj. lustful

244

	(after a woman)
* ዛዛ	* zazza
ተንዛዛ	tänzazza v.i. was superfluous
አንዛዛ	anzazza v.t. made superfluous
ዛገ	zagä v.i. corroded, rusted
ዛገት	zagät n. rust
አዛገ	azagä v.t rusted
ዛጎል	zagol n. shell, coral
ዛጎልኛ	zagolǝñña ˙adj. coral
ዛፍ	zaf n. tree
ባሀር—	bahǝr—n. eucalyptus
ዛፉ	zafu n. dwarf *(ironical)*
ዜማ	zema n. chant, song, tune; church song
ዜመኛ	zemäñña n. person with a good voice, also ባለ ዜማ
ዜማ ሰበረ	zema säbbärä v.t. sang false notes
—አወረደ	—awärädä v.t. led a song
አዜመ	azemä v.t. sang, chanted
ዜሮ	zero n. zero; naught, nil; love *(in games)*
ዜሮ ለዜሮ	zero läzero nil-nil
ዜና	zena n. news
—መዋዕል	—mäwa'ǝl n. chronicle
—አቀባይ	—aqäbbay n. reporter
—አጠናቃሪ	—aṭṭänaqari n. correspondent *(newspaper)*
—እረፍት	—ǝräft n. obituary
አርእስተ—	ar'ǝstä—n. headlines *(news)*
ዜጋ	zega n. citizen, subject
የወጭ—	yäwǝčč—n. foreign national, expatriate
ዘሀ	zäha n. hank, also ሀይ
ዘሆን	zähon also ሀሆን zähon n. elephant
ዘሆኔ	zähone n. elephantiasis
የዘሆን ጥርስ	yäzähon ṭǝrs n. ivory
የ—ጆሮ	yä—ǧoro yasṭäñ ̃ alä
ይሰጠኝ አለ	lend a deaf ear
ዘሙት	zǝmmut n. adultery, lust, fornication
ዘሙተኛ	zǝmmutäñña n. adulterer, fornicator
ዘማ	zämma n. adulteress

ዘማም	zǝmam n. purified gold
ዘማሬ	see ዘመረ
ዝም አለ	zǝmm alä v.i. kept quiet, remained still, held still; was indifferent
ዝምተኛ	zǝmmǝtäñña adj. quiet, still, silent; reserved
ዝምታ	zǝmmǝta n. silence
ዝም ብሎ	zǝmm bǝlo adv. just so, without any reason ዝም ብሎ ይናደ ዳል he is irritated without any reason
ዝም አሰኘ	zǝmm assäñ ̃ä v.t silenced, hushed
ዘምብ	zemb also ዝንብ zǝnb n fly
ዝምቡን እሺ አለ	zǝmbun ǝ ̀šš alä v.t. swished away flies
ዝምባም	zǝmbam adj/n full of flies; inactive; a slowcoach
ዝምቦ	zǝmbo n. slowcoach
ዝምቤ ከልክል	zǝmbä kälkǝl n. mosquito-net
ዘር አለ	zǝrr alä v.i. appeared, came around ወፍ ዘር የማይልበት ቦታ an abandoned place, a deserted place
ዘርክርክ አለ	zǝrǝkrǝkk alä v.i. was littered, strewn, cluttered, untidy, messy
ዘርክራካ	zärkrakka adj. untidy; extravagant
ዘርክርክ	zärǝkrǝk adj. messy; untidy
ተዘርከረከ	täzräkärräkä v.i. was untidy, messy
አዘርከረከ	azräkärräkä v.t. made untidy, messy; littered
ዘርጋፍ አለ	see ዘረጋፈ
ዝቅ አለ	zǝqq alä v.i. lowered ; sank *(price)*, declined, became inferior
ዝቅተኛ	zǝqqǝtäñña adj. inferior
ዝቅታ	zǝqqǝta n. depression, condescension
ዝቅ ዝቅ አለ	zǝqq zǝqq alä v.i. deteriorated

ዝቅ ዝቅ አደረገ	zəqq zəqq adärrägä v.t. deteriotated	ዝግባ	zəgba podocarpo (podocarpus gracilior)
ዝባዘንኬ	zəbazənke n. trifle	ዝግ አለ	zəgg alä v.i. was slow, slowed down
ዝባድ	zəbad n. civet (substance)	ዝግተኛ	zəggətäñña adj. slow, tardy, slow-moving
ዝተት	zəttät n. coarse woollen cloth	ዝግታ	zəggəta n. slowness, tardiness
ዝተታም	zəttätam adj. raggcd, tattered, threadbare	ዝግን	see ዘገነ
ዝና	zənna n. fame, reputation	ዝፍት	zəft n. tar
		ዞረ	zorä v.i. turned around, rotated, went around, revolved
ዝነኛ	zənnäñña adj. famous, reputable, renowned, eminent, celebrated		
ዝናሟ	see ዝነኛ	ዞዋሪ	zäwari n. vagabond wanderer, vagrant
ዝናቢስ	zənna bis adj. without fame, reputation	ዙረት	zurät n. wandering, vagrancy ስራው ዙረት ነው he is leading a vagrant life
ዝና ወዳድ	zənna wäddad adj. anxious for fame		
ዝናር	zennar n. cartridge belt	ዙሪያ	zuria n. circumference, circuit; surrounding area
የዝናር ግፈኛ	yäzənnar maffäña n. belt strap		
ዝናብ ዘነበ	see ዘነበ		
ዝንባሌ	see ዘነበለ	ዙር	zur n. round(action) በመጀመሪያው ዙር in the first round
ዝንብ	see ዝምብ		
ዝንተ ዓለም	zentä aläm adv. from time immemorial		
ዝንጀሮ	zəngaro n. monkey, ape, baboon	ዙሮ ገጣም	zuro gäṭṭäm adj. roundish
ተራ—	tära—n. anubis baboon	ዞሮ ዞሮ	zoro zoro adv. at least, finally, in the end
ነጭ—	näčč—n. hamadryas baboon		
ጬላዳ—	čälada—n. gelada baboon	ተዙዙረ	täzuʷazuʷarä v.i. went around; misjoined
ዝንጅብል	zənǧəbəll n. ginger		
ዝንጉርጉር	zəngurgur adj. spotted, striped, multicoloured	አዞረ	azorä v.t.i took s/t around; was giddy ራሱን አዞረው he became giddy
ዝንጣል	see ዘነጠለ		
ዝከር	see ዘከረ		
ዝይ	zəyy n. goose, gander	አዟሪ	azuʷari n. peddler also ሽቀጣ / እቃ አዟሪ
ዝጉን	see ዘጋነ		
ዝጋ	see ዘጋ	አዙሪት	azurit n. whirlpool
		ማዞሪያ	mazoriya n. telephone operator, switch board

ዠ

ዠለጠ	žälläṭä v.t. hit (with a stick)	ዠመረ	see ጀመረ
		ዠምበር	see ጀምበር
ተዠለጠ	täžälläṭä v.i was hit (with stick)	ዠረር አለ	žärärr alä v.i. flowed abundantly
አዠለጠ	ažžälläṭä v.t. had s/o hit (with a stick)	ዠረገገ	žäräggägä v.t stripped off (the fruits from

246

	the branch)
ተንዣረገገ	tänžäräggägä v.i.
	bore abundantly;
	flew down (of hair)
*ዠረገዳ	*žäräggädä
ዠርጋዳ	žärgadda adj.
	graceful, elegant
ዠርባ	see ጀርባ
ዠቀዠቀ	žäqäžžäqä
ተንዠቀዠቀ	tänžäqäžžäqä v.i.
	flowed abundantly,
	gushed
አንዠቀዠቀ	anžäqäžžäqä v.t.
	caused to flow abun-
	dantly, caused to gush
*ዠበረረ	*žäbärrärä
ዠበረር	žäbärär adj. senile
ዠብራራ	žäbrarra adj. senile,
	feeble-minded
ዠብረር አለ	žäbrärr alä v.i. became
	senile, feeble-minded
ተንዠባረረ	tänžäbarrärä v.i. be-
	camد senile, feeble-
	minded
*ዠበበ/ጀበበ	*žäbbäbä also ǧäbbäbä
ተንዠበበ	tänžäbbäbä v.i. hovered
አንዠበበ	anžäbbäbä v.i.
	hovered
አንዠባቢ	anžäbabi adj. hovering
ዠበድ አደረገ	žäbädd adärrägä v.t.
	hit slightly
ዠብዱ	žäbdu also ጀብዱ
	ǧäbdu n. adventure
ዠንዲ	see ጀንዲ
ዠገነ	see ጀገነ
ዠጉሪ ሱሪ	see * ዘነሪ ሱሪ
*ዠጎደጎደ	*žägodäggodä
ተዠጎደጎደ	täžgodäggodä v.i. was
	plentiful
አዠጎደጎደ	ažgodäggodä v.t.
	gave, brought s/t
	abundantly
ዠርት	žart also ጀርት ǧart n.
	porcupine

ጛን—	žan also ጃን ǧan used
ጛንሆይ	in ጛንሆይ žanhoy, n.
	His Majesty
ጛንጠላ	ጃንጠላ žanṭäla also
	ganṭäla n. umbrella,
	parasol
ጛንጠራር	also ጃንጠራር žanṭäraa-
	ar, ganṭarar n. Old
	title of a Wollo feudal
ጛንደረባ	also ጃንደረባ žandär-
	aba, gandäräba n.
	eunuch
ኽማት	also ጀማት žämmat,
	gämmat n. tendon
ኽረት	also ጀረት žärät, ǧar-
	ät n. creek, brook,
	stream
ኽራት	also ጀራት žärat, ǧär-
	at n. tail
ኽራታም	žäratam kokäb n.
ኮከብ	comet
ኽራፍ	also ጀራፍ žäraf, ǧäraf
	n. whip (especially
	the kind used by men)
ኽብ	also ጀብ žäb, gäb n.
	hyena
ኽንፎ	also ጀንፎ žänfo, ǧan-
	fo- n. metal protection
	on the butt of
	a spear, walking-stick
	etc.
ኽዋ ኽዌ	also ጀዋጀዌ žäwwaže-
	wwe, ǧäwwaǧäwwe
	n. swing, pendulum
ኽው ያለ ገደል	žäww or ጀው ያለ ገደል
	ǧäww yalä gäddäl n.
	precipice (of moun-
	tain)
ኽግራ	also ጀግራ žägra, ǧäg-
	ra n. guinea fowl
ጛር	also ጀር žoro, ǧoro, n.
	ear
ጛፈ አሞራ	also ጀፈ አሞራ žoffe,
	ǧoffe amora n. vulture

የ

የ—	yä prep. of
	የሰው ልጅ ታሪክ the
	history of mankind;
	+personal pronoun
	የኔ (የእኔ) my, mine
	with perfect and im-

	perfect verb who, that,
	which
	የመጣው ሰው the man
	who came,
	የሚመጣው ሰው the
	man who will come

የለ—
—የለሸ
ልብ—
ስም—
ቅርፅ—

አመል—

የሌለው·

የለም

የሌት ወፍ
የመን
የመኒ
የሚ—

የማ—

የማን
የም—

የምስራች

የምር

የሰራ አካላት

የረር

የርሱ

የርሳቸው

yällä—
in *ləbb* —adj.
absent-minded
səm—adj. nameless
qərṣ—adj. shapeless,
amorphous
amäl—adj. cranky,
grouchy, moody
or የለለው· yälelläw
yälälläw prep. without,
free from, *suff.* less
e.g ቤት የሌለው·
homeless ጥርጣሬ
የሌለው· doubtless
yälläm n. there is not;
he is not around
yälet wäf n. bat
yämän n. Yemen
yamani n. Yemenite
yammi—with imper-
fect indicating third
person sing & pl.,
which, who, that
የሚናገር ወፍ
a bird that talks
yämma with imperfect
indicating negation,
that... who...
not, which... not
የማይሰራ ሰው· a man
that does not work
yämann pron. whose
yämm—with imperfect,
indicating first person
sing & pl., what, that
የምናገረው·ን አላወቀም
I don't know what
I am talking about
yäməssäračč n. good
news, good tidings,
hurrah !
yämärr adv. seriously,
earnestly
yässära akalat n. the
entire body
የሰራ አካላቴን ያመኛል
i feel pain in my
entire body
yärär n. name of a
mountain east of
Addis Ababa
also የሱ *yärsu*, *yässu*
pron. his
yärsaččäw, also የሳቸው·

የብስ

የት
የቱ

የትም

የትና የት

የትኛው·

የትየለ

የኔታ

የንሹ

የካቲት
የከት
የከት ልብስ

የወል
የዋህ

የዋህነት

የዚያ
የየ—

የይ
የዲያ

የግድ
የፍጥኝ

—ዲቱ

ያ

yässaččäw pron.
their, theirs
yäbs n. mainland, dry
land, land
yät pron. where
yätu⁻ pron. which,
which one
yätəmm adv. every-
where, anywhere,
any place
yätənnayät adj. long
(distance), inaccess-
ible
yätəññäw pron. which
one
yätəyyäläle adj. un-
attainable, beyond
one's reach
yäneta, (for የኔጌታ *yän-
egeta*) interj. master
(for a teacher or
an elderly person)
yänšu also ኢንሹ *inšu*
n. dikdik
yäkkatit n. February
(see also under ከተተ)
yäkətt ləbs n.
Sunday best
yäwäl adj. common
yäwwah adj. innocent,
simple, meek, harm-
less
yäwwahənnät n.
innocence, simplicity
see እዚህ
yäyyä pron. every/every-
one የየሰው·ን ታሪክ
ንገረኝ tell me the
story of every man
yäyy n. jackal
yädiya, also እዲያ *ädiya*
(expression of abhor-
rence) away with it
see ገደደ
yäfiṭṭəㇺ in የፈጥኝ አሰረ
tied the hands
behind the back
—*yitu* def. art. feminine
marker e.g. ልጅ+
ዪቱ= ልጅቱ *ləጅitu*
the girl
ya adj. pron. that
ያ ሌላ ይህ ሌላ that
is a different thing

248

ያህል	yahəl see ..o under አክለ adv. about, nearly, approximately ዋጋው ይህን ያህል ነው· ለማለት አልችልም I cannot tell the price exactly
ያም	yam adj. that
-ሆነ ይህ	—honä yəh adv. nevertheless, in any case
--ቢ.ሆ'ን	--bihon adv. whatever it is, even at that
ያኔ	yanne, also ያን ጊዜ yangize adv. at that time; then
ያን	yannən adj. acc. that
ያንም	yannəmma but that
ያንን	yann adj. acc. that
ያኛው	yaññaw the other one
ያች	yačč pron/adj. f. that
ያቻትና	yaččutənna there she is
ያው	yaw there he is
ያውልህ	yawəlləh here it is
ያውና	yawənna there he is
ያውኮ	yawəkko but there he/ it is !
ያዘ	yazä v.t. caught; grasped, held, seized;started መናገር ከያዘ አያ ቆምም after having started to talk he never stops
ያዘት	yəzät n. content, volume
ያዞታ	yazota n. tenure የመሬት ይዞታ land tenure
ያዝ ለቀቅ	yazz läqqäq not serious ሥራውን ያዝ ለቀቅ ያደርጋል He is not serious at his duty/work.
መያዣ	mäyaža n. container; pawn, mortgage; hostage
ተያዘ	täyazä v.i. was caught; was arrested; was impounded; was occupied (place), was busy (telephone)
ተያዥ	täyaž n. guarantor
ተያያዘ	täyayazä v.i. was connected; was coherent; was inflamed. caught fire

አያያዘ	ayyayazä v.t. joined together, connected. united; kindled
አያያዝ	ayyayaz n. handling. management; behaviour
አስያዘ	asyazä v.t. had s/o arrested, caught; impounded
ማስያዣ	masyaža n. bail
ዬ	—ye poss. pron. suff. used after nouns ending with vowels; e.g. በሬ+ዬ=በሬዬ my ox
--ዬ	yye suff. pron. added to name of countries to denote birth place e.g. ወሎዬ Wolloyan, ጅሩዬ Gərruyan
--ዩው	—yäw def. art. m. the, ሰውዩው the, man
ዩጭ	yečč, also ኤጭ ečč (expression of abhorence) away with it!
ይ---	yə—pron. suff. imperfect marker e.g. ይ+verb + አል =ይመጣል he will come
ይሁዳ	yəhuda n. Judea
ይሁዲ	yəhudi n. Jew;
ይህ	yəh adj. this
·ይህማ	yəhamma but this, well, this
ይህም	yəhəmm and this
ይህን	yəhənn this
ይህን ያህል	—yahəl this much, all these
ይህኛው	yəhaññaw this one
ይኸው	yəhäw here he/ it is
·ይሉኝታ	yəluññta (see also under አለ) concern about public opinion
--ቢ.ስ	—bis adj. unscrupulous
ይሉኝ አይል	yəluññ ayəl adj. unscrupulous
ይላማ	yəlama, also ኢላማ ilama n. target, aim
ይልቅ	y.ələq see also ላቀ adv. rather than, more
ይልቁን	yələqun adv. rather
ይልቁንም	yələqunəmm adv.

ይልቀንስ   ...pecially. on the contrary
yaləqunəss adv. rather, by preference or choice

ይልቅስ   *yaləqəss* adv. rather, by preference or choice

ይማም   *yəmam*, also ኢማም *imam* n. Imam (*title of Muslim leader, especially of the one that leads the prayer in the forefront*)

ይቅርታ   *yəqərta*, see also under ቀረ excuse, ይቅርታ አድርግልኝ excuse me, ይቅርታ ያድርጉ ልኝ excuse me (*pol.*)

ይበል   *see* አለ
ይብላኝ   ይብላኝ *see* በላ
ይብራ   *yəbra* n. duck
ይብስ   *see* ባሰ
ይቶት   *yətot* n. title of an old widow
ይኸው   *see* ይህ
ይድረስ   *see also* under

ይገባኝ

ይፋ
 · ሆነ
 ·· ወጣ
በይፋ
··ዎ
··ዎዋ

ዮርዳኖስ
ማየ ዮርዳኖስ

··ዮሽ

ዮድ

ደረሰ used in የይ ረስ የይ.ድረስ done in a hurry, hastily done *yəgəbaňň see also* ገባ n. appeal (*in court*). petition
yəfa n. s/t official
—*hona* v.i. became official
—*wäṭṭa* v.i. was declared officially
bäyəfa adv. openly. publicly
-*yyo* dem. pron. f. that, ያቾ ሴትዮ that woman
—*yəwa* def. ፡ rt. f. the, ሴትዮዋ the woman
yordanos n. Jordan
mayä—n. sacred water of the River Jordan
yyoš dis. adv. *used in* ሁለትዮሽ pairs, አራ ትዮሽ in fours etc.
yod n. iodine

ደ

ደኸየ
ደኸ
··ሰብ ሳቢ
··አደግ
ድኸነት
አመለ ደኸ
አደኸየ
ደለለ
ደላላ
ደላይ
ድለላ

dähäyyä v.i. was impoverished, became poor
ደኸ *däha* (also ድኸ፣ ደህ ፣ ድህ) adj./n poor
—*säbsabi* n. philanthropist
—*addäg* n. orphan
dəhənnät n. poverty, penury
amälä däha adj. of bad charcter, grouchy, sulky
adähäyyä v.t. impoverished
dällälä v.t. cajoled, flattered
dällala n. broker, middleman
dällay n. flatterer
dəllälu n. flattering;

ድለል
ተደለለ
መደለያ
መደለያ
ደለል
ደለቀ
ድልቂያ
ተደለቀ
°ደለቀቀ

brokerage
የድለላ ዋጋ brokerage
dəlləl adj. easily cajoled, flattered, persuadable, gullible
tädällälä v.i. was cajoled, flattered, persuaded
mäddäläya n. bribe
mädälläya n. blandishment
däläl n. alluvial soil, silt
dälläqä v.t. hit with the fist (*especially one's chest in a funeral*); ደረቱን ደለቀ he hit his chest with the fist
dəlqiya n. dance (*with leaps*)
täddälläqä v.i. danced (*with jumps*)
°*däläqqäqä*

250

ደለቀት   däläqäq adj. spoilt
(usually child)

ደልቃቃ   dälqaqqa adj. spoilt:
lavishly living

መንደላቀቂያ   mändälaqāqiya n.
lavish items

ተንደላቀቀ   tändälaqqäqä v.i.
lived lavishly

ተንደላቃቂ   tändälaqaqi adj./n·
one who lives
lavishly, luxuriously

አንደላቀቀ   andälaqqäqä v.t.
lavished, treated s/o
generously

ደለበ   dälläbä v.i got fat *(ox)*

ደልብ   dəlb adj. fatted
(ox)

—ሥንጋ   —sänga n. fatted
(ox)

አደለበ   adälläbä v.t. fattened
(ox)

አድላቢ   in ስንጋ–n. one
who fattens cattle

ደለኸ   dällähä v.t. pounded
red pepper with
garlic, onion, salt and
other spices

ድልኸ   dəlləh n. red pepper
pounded with garlic,
onion, salt and other
spices

ደለዘ   dälläzä v.t. pounded
soaked pepper;
thrashed *(with a
stick)*; crossed out
(a line), deleted

ድልዝ   dəlləz n. pounded
soaked pepper; de-
letion

ደለደለ   däläddälä v.t. leveled
(road, ground);
devided s/t into equal
parts; assigned to
various places *(pupils in
class-rooms, soldiers to
different posts etc.)*

ደልዳላ   däldalla adj. well-
built *(person)*; well-
established *(in life)*;
well - balanced *(scale)*

ድልደላ   dəldäla n. distribution, assignment

ድልድል   dələddəl n. distri-

bution, assignment

ድልደይ   dəldəy n. bridge

ተደለደለ   tädäläddälä v.i. was
leveled; was divided
into equal parts;
assigned in various
places *(pupils in
class-rooms, soldiers to
different post)*

ተደላደለ   tädäladdälä v.i was
well settled *(in life)*;
sat comfortably

አደላደለ   addäladdälä v.t. helped
s/o to settle well

አስደለደለ   asdäläddälä v.t. had s/t
leveled; had s/t
divided into equal
parts etc.

ደለፈሰ   däläffäsä v.t. scooped
out in great quantity

ደላ   dälla v.i. was comfortable, agreeable, happy

ድሎት   dəlot n. comfort,
happiness, luxury,
opulence

ድሎተኛ   dəlotäñña adj/n
(one) who lives
a happy, luxurious,
opulent· life

ተድላ   tädla n. pleasure

—ደስታ   —dästa n. pleasure
and happiness

*ደላ   dälla

አደላ   adälla v.t. was
partial, showed
favour, was biased

አድልዎ   adləwo n. partial-
ity, bias, favour-
itism

አዳላ   addalla v.t. was
partial, showed favour

ደላለ   see ደለለ

ደላጎ   dälago n. piece of
discarded old leather;
imbecile

—ለባሽ   —läbaš adj. ragged

ደመመ   dämmämä v.i. used
with pron. suff. i.e.
ደመመው· he was
astonished

ደማሚ   dämami adj.· astonishing

ተደመመ   tädämmämä v.i. was

	astonished
ይ.መሬ	dämmärä v.t. added (math.), summed up
ይ.ኦሜሬ.	also dämära, ደመሬ damära) n. a heap of poles and sticks to be used as a bonfire at Mascal cross) feast
ደ.ሙሬ.	dəmmära n. addition
ደ.ማሬ	dəmmari n. s.t that is added to .
ደ.ሞ፤	dəmmər n. sum, total
ተይ.መሬ	tädämmärä v.i. was added, summed up; joined with s o
ተይ.ማሬ	tädämmari n. s t that is added to
ተዳመሬ	tädammärä v.i.
ሰስቱ ቁጥሮች ተዳም፤ረው ውጤታ ቻው ፴፪ ሆነ	was added together the three figures were added and the result was 32
አዳመሬ	addammärä v. t. added together
አስደመሬ	asdämmärä v.t. had s/t added toegther
ደመሰሰ	dämässäsä v.t. destroyed, annihilated, exterminated; stamped out
ድም.ሰሳ	dəmsäsa n. destruction, annihilation, extermination
ተደመሰሰ	tädämässäsä v.i. was destroyed, annihilated, exterminated, stamped out
አስደመሰሰ	asdämmässäsä v.t. had s/t, s/o, destroyed, killed, exterminated
ደመቀ	dämmäqä v.i. was brightened (light, colour), became lively (gathering, party, game etc.)
ደማቃ	dämmaqa adj. bright (colour)
ደማቅ	dämmaq adj. bright (colour); lively (party, social occasion); gay or loud (colour)
ድም.ቀት	dəmqät n. brightness (colour, light)
ድም.ቅ	dəmq adj. bright
አደመቀ	adämmäqä v.t. en-

	livened
አደ.ማቂ.	admaqi in. ዘፋኝ zäfän— n. a good leader of singing
አዳመቀ	addammäqä v.t. enlivened
አዳማቂ.	addamaqi n. one who sings well
ደ.መ፤	see ደመ፤
ደመወዝ	dämäwäz n. salary, wage, (see also under ደማ)
ደመወዝተኛ	dämäwäztäñña n. salaried worker, employee
ባለደመወዝ	balädämäwäz n. salaried worker, employee
ደመደመ	dämäddämä v.t. finished, ended, terminated, (a speech)
ድም.ዳማ	dəmdäma n. conclusion (of a speech)
ድም.ድ.ማት	dəmdəmat n. upper parts of walls that are joined to the roof
መደም.ደሚያ	mädämdämya n. conclusion (of speech)
ተደመደመ	tädämäddämä v.t. was concluded; finished building the walls of a building
*ደመጠ	see also under ድም.ጅ
ድም.ጥ	dəmt n. voice, sound
ድም.ጣም	dəmtam also ድም ጻም n. a good singer
ድም.ጥ መልካም	dəmtä mälkam n. one with a sweet voice
—ሰላላ	—sälala n. one with a thin voice
—ጎርናና	—gornnana n. one with hoarse, rough voice
ድም.ጥማጥ	dəmatamat n. whereabouts
ድም.ጥማጡ ጠፋ	dəmatmatu taffa no one knows his whereabouts
ተደመጠ	tädämmäta v.i. was listened
ተደማጭ	tädämmač adj. influential, powerful
ተደማመጠ	tädämammäta v.i. list

-252-

አደመጠ ened to each other
adämmäṭä v.t.
listened to

አዳመጠ addammäṭä v.t.
listened to; waited for
eagerly

ማደመጫ maddamäča n. receiver (telephone)

ደማ dämma v.i. bled

ድማት dəmat n. bleeding

ዳም däm n. blood

ደመ መራራ dämä märara adj.
offensive, allergic
(of person), unsympathetic

—መራር —märrar (same as above)

—በራድ —bärrad adj. cool, unexcited

—ቢስ —bis adj. cowardly

—ነፍስ —näfs n. instinct

ደመኛ dämäñña n. enemy, foe, mortal enemy

ደመ ከልብ dämä kälb adj/n (one) who dies a dog's death, s/o unprotected by the law

ደመወዝ dämäwäz n salary, wage

ደመግቡ dämä gəbu adj. charming, handsome

ደማም dämam adj. charming, attractive

ደም መላሽ dämmälläš n. avenger also ደመላሽ

—መሰለ —mässälä v.i. turned red (from anger); reddened

—ማነስ —manäs n. anaemia

የ—ስር yä-sər n. blood vessel, vein

—ሸተተው —šättätäw v.t. became agressive, became blood thirsty

—በደም ሆነ —bädäm honä v:i. was stained with blood

—ብዛት —bəzat b. high blood pressure

—ተበቀለ —täbäqqälä v.t. avenged

—ተቃባ —täqabbä v.i. was in enmity with

—አስተኬ —astne adj. reddish

—አስተሬ —astäffi n. inedible poisonous mushroom

—አፈላ —afälla v.t. vexed, provoked

—አፈሰሰ —afässäsä v.t. shed blood
)

—አፈታ —afätta v.i. bled continuously

—ወረዳት —wärrädat she had her menses (irregularly)

—ደም አለው —aläw v.i. was infuriated, was blood-thirsty

—ጋን —gan n. artery

—ጣት —gəbat n. good complexion

—ፍላት —fəlat n. blind anger

በደም ፍላት he killed him
ገደለው in blind anger
አደማ adämma v.i. bled hurt, injured

ደማሚት dämamit n. dynamite

ደምበኛ dämbäñña, also ደንበኛ dänbañña n. client, customer; government soldiers that have settled in hostile areas of Ethiopia; adj. regular, correct

የደምበኛ ልጅ yädämbäñña ləǧ n. offspring of a ደምበኛ

ደምበኛን dämbägan n. demijohn also ደንበኛን

ደምባራ dämbara see ደንበረ

ደምብ dänb (see also under ደነባ) n. regulation, law, principle, rule, provision, procedure

ደምቦጭ አለ dämbočč alä v.i. had round cheeks

ደራመን därämän n. itching skin disease (such as dandruff, scurf)

ደራመናም därämänam n. scruffy person

ደረሰ därräsä v.i. reached (a place), arrived; happened; was ready (food etc.); reached (maturity)

መጽሐፍ— mäṣhaf — v.t. wrote

ደረሰለት *därräsällät* v.i. came
to his help

ደረሰበት *därräsäbät* v.t.
learnt (found out);
caught up with;
befell him (bad sense)

ደረሰኝ *därräsäññ* n. receipt

ደራሲ *därasi* n. author,
composer, writer

ደራሲነት *därasinnät* n.
authorship

ደራሽ ውሃ *däraš wäha* n. flash
flood

ደርሶ መልስ *därso mäls* n. round
trip

—ቲኬት —*ticket* n. round-
trip ticket ,

ደራሹ ጠፋ *därrašu ṭäffa* v.i.
no one knows his
whereabouts

ድርሰት *därsät* n. compo-
sition, essay, treatise

ድርሳን *därsan* n. a homily
book

ድርስ *därs* adj. *in*—እርጉዝ
—*ärguz* n. a preg-
nant woman whose
days are near for
delivery

መድረሻ *mädräša* n. arrival,
time or place of
arrival, destination;
haven

—ቢስ —*bis* n. tramp,
vagrant

ባእድ መድረሻ *ba'äd*— n. suffix

ድርሷ አይ *därräšš ayläm* he
አለም never shows up (due
to bad consequences)

ተደረሰ *tädärräsä* v.i. was
composed, was
written (book, essay
etc.)

ተዳረሰ *tädarräsä* v.i. was
distributed, allocated
(to several people)

አደረሰ *adärräsä* v. t. de-
livered (consignment);
brought forward
(message)

ፀሎት— *ṣälot* — v.t. said his
prayers

አያድርስ *ayadärs* interj. God
save! God forbid!

እድራሻ *adrašša* n. address

አዳረሰ *addarräsä* v.t. has
distributed, allocated
(to several people)

አዳራሽ *addaraš* n. hall

የማዘጋጃ *yämäzzägaga bet*—
ቤት— n. the Town Hall

ደረሰመ *därässämä* v.t. demol-
ished (building); sunk
(foundation)

ተደረሰመ *tädärässämä* v.i. was
sunk (foundation)

ደረቀ *därräqä* v.i. was dry,
dried out; was stiff-
ened; was stubborn,
obstinate, persist-
ent; got strong
(beverage)

ደረቅ *däräq* adj. dry,
dried; stiff; stubborn,
obstinate, persist-
ent; pigheaded

—ሌሊት —*lelit* n. midnight

—ምች —*mäčč* n. disease with
a severe headache
and high temperature

—ትንቢት —*tänbit* n. an im-
minent prophesy

—እንጀራ —*änğära* n. änğära
without wäṭ ወጥ

—ወዝ —*wäz* n. dandruff

—ግንባር —*gämbar* adj.
unlucky, chanceless

—ጉንፋን —*gunfan* n. dry
influenza

—ጦር —*ṭor* n. emergency
troop (without pro-
visions and heavy
weapons)

ደረቆት *däräqot* n. boiled and
dried (barely, wheat,
etc. used in brewing
ṭäla ጠላ)

ደረቀ *däräqa* adj. lean,
emaciated

ድርቀት *därqät* n. dryness;
stubbornness

ሆድ:— *hod*—n. constipation

ድርቅ *därq* n. drought

— ቦባለ —*qäbäle* n. drought
affected area

ደረቅ ብዬ *därräqq bäyyä* adj.

obstinate, wilful, stubborn

ድርቅና *dərqənna* n. wilfulness

ድርቆሽ *dərqoš* n. hay; dried ənğära

ደረቅ ዐይነ *därāq ayn* adj. shameless, immodest (behaviour)

ተዳረቀ *tädarrāqä* v.t. tried to say or do s/t in vain

ተዳረቀረቀ *tädərāqärräqä* v.i. was obstinate, wilful

አደረቀ *adärräqä* v.t. dried

አስደረቀ *asdärräqä* v.t. had s/t dried

ደረበ *därräbä* v.t. put s/t on top of s/t ; put on a blanket, a sheet of cloth

ደርብ *därb* n. storey

ደርብ *dərrəb* adj. compound (word); double

—ሰረዝ *—säräz* n. semicolon (፤)

—ኩታ *—kuta* n. double *kuta* ኩታ

ድርብርብ *dərəbrəb* adj. laminated

ማደርቢያ *mädärräbiya* n. general name for ኩታ or blanket etc.

ተደረበ *tädärräbä* v.i. concurred, co-operated (in inflicting harm to s/o)

ተደራቢ *tädärrabi* n. accomplice

ተደራረበ *tädärarräbä* v.i. came one on the top of the other (work incident); laminated; was redundant

ተደራራቢ *tädärarabi* adj. redundant

*ደረበበ *däräbbäbä*

ደርባባ *därbabba* adj. gentle, graceful

ድርባብ *dərbäb* n. measure (for grain) not quite full a measure of grain and a second not quite full

ደርባብ አለ *därbäbb alä* v.i. was gentle, graceful; withdrew from the

discussion bashfully

ተንደረባባ *tändäräbbäbä* v.i. was rather full, was rather quiet, calm

አንደረባባ *andäräbbäbä* v.t. caused to become almost full

ደረተ *därrätä* v.t. patched

ድሪት *dərito* n. patched material

ድሪቱዋም *dərituʷam* adj. ragged (person)

ድርት *dərrət* adj. patchy

ተደረተ *tädärrätä* v.i. was patched

አስደረተ *asdärrätä* v.t. had torn clothes patched

ደረት *därät* n. chest (body), breast

ደረተሰ ሰፊ *därätä säfi* adj. strongly-built (person)

ደረታም *därätam* adj. (one) with a broad chest

ሱቅ በደራቴ *suq bädäräte* n. pedlar

*ደራከከ *däräkkäkä*

ደርካከ *därkakka* adj. glowing (embers, charcoal)

ተንደራከከ *tändäräkkäkä* v.i. glowed; fruited well

ደራደረ *däräddärä* v.t. set in rows, arranged in order, aligned; enumerated

በገና— *bägäna—* v.t. played the harp

ድርዳራ *dərdära* n. setting in rows

ድርድር *dərdər* n. orderly arrangement

ድርድር *dərəddər* n. negotiation

በገና ድርዳራ *bägäna dərdära* n. playing the harp

ማድርዳሪያ *mädärdäriya* n. shelf

ተደራደረ *tädäräddärä* v.i. was set in rows, was arranged in order

ተደራደረ *tädäräddärä* v.i. negotiated

ተደራዳሪ *tädäradari* n. negotiator

ተንደራደረ *tändäräddärä* v.i.

255

መንደርደሪያ **mändärdäriya** *hassab*
ሐሳብ n. main idea

—አረፍተ ነገር —**aräftä nägär** n. topic sentence

አደራደረ **addäraddärä** v.t. conducted negotiation

አስደረደረ **asdäräddärä** v.t. had things set in rows

ደረጀ **däräğğä** v.t. developed (financially, physically), prospered

ድርጁ **dərəğğu** adj. stable (financially)

ድርጅት **dərəğğət** n. organization, firm (business), institution

ተደራጀ **tädäraǧǧä** v.i. was organized, institutionalized

አደራጀ **adäraǧǧä** v.t. developed, stabilized; made prosperous v.t. organized, institutionalized

አደራጅ **addäraǧ** comite n. organizing committee
ኮሚቴ

°ደረገ **därrägä*

ድርጊት **dərggitt** n. action, happening, episode, incident: behaviour

ተደረገ **tädärrägä** v.i. was done, has happend, occurred

ተደረጊ ግሥ **tädärragi gəss** n. passive verb

አደረገ **adärrägä** v.t. has done, did

አድራጊ **adragi** adj/n (one) who does s/t

—ግስ —**gəss** n. active verb

—ፈጣሪ —**fäṭari** adj. omnipotent, dictator

አኳኳንት **adragot** n. action, deed

በጎ— **baggo**— n. philanthrophy, charity

——ድርጅት ——**dərəǧǧit** n. philanthropic institution, charitable institution

አድርጎ **adrəgo**—used (with a preceding adj.) as

ደህና— **dähna**—well e.g.
ደህና አድርጎ መታ፣ he bit him well

አ.ደራረግ **addäraräg** n. way, manner of doing, using things

እስደረገ **asdärrägä** v.t. had s/t done

ኣስደራጊ ግሥ **asdärragi gəss** n. causative verb

ደረጘመ **däräggämä** v.t. slammed (door)

ድርግም አለ **dərgəmm alä** v.i. went out suddenly (fire, light); went suddenly dark

ተደረገመ **tädäräggämä** v.i. slammed (door); went out suddenly (fire, light), became suddenly dark

ደረፎጭ **däräfoṭč** adj. ugly

ደራ **därra** v.i. was lively (market); was successful (marriage) e.g.
ትዳሩ ደርቷል his marriage was/is successful

የደራ ገበያ **yädärra gäbäyä** n. lively market

ድሪያ **dərriya** n. flirtation

ተዳራ **tädarra** v.t. flirted

°ዳራ **därra*

አደራ **adärra** v.t. made webs

ድር **dər** n. web; warp

ድርና ማግ **dərənna mag** n. warp and weft

——ሆኑ ——**honu** v.i. they lived together in complete harmony

የሸረሪት ድር **yäšärärit dər** n. spider's web

ደራጎን **däragon** n. dragon

ደርቡሽ **därbuš** n. Sudanese; the Mahdi's soldiers

ዳርብ **därb** n. storey, see also ደረበ

—ቤት —**bet** n. storeyed building

ዳርዝ **därz** n. selvedge; hem; ደርዝ ያለው ሰው ነው he is a principled man

ደርግ **därg** n. committee (G.) ንኡስ— **nə'us**— n. subcommittee

ዳሰመ **dässämä** v.t. made lunge

256

ደሰሰ	*dässäsä* v.i. became squalid, shabbily *(hut)*		illegitimate child; child *(euphemistically)*
ደሳሳ	*dāsasa* adj. squalid, sh.bby *(hut)*	ድቀላ	*dəqäla* n. crossbreeding
—ንጅ	· vəǧǧo n. a shabby !ut	ተዳቀለ	*tädaqqälä* v.i. was crossbred
ደሴት	.፡፡፡ n. island	አዳቀለ	*addaqqälä* v.t. crossbred
ደሴት	·-nkkäl n. peninsula	ደቀቀ	*däqqäqä* v.i. was fine, minute
ደስ አለ	*däss alä* v.i. was pleasing, attractive, was charming	ደቂቃ	*däqiqa* n. minute
—ተሰኘ	—*täsäññä* v.i. was happy, pleased	ደቃቃ	*däqaqa* adj. weak, feeble
—አለው	—*aläw* v.i. was contented, pleased	ደቃቃ	*däqqaqa* adj. fine
ደስታ	*dässəta* n. pleasure, happiness, delight.	ደቀቅ	*däqqaq* adj. fine, minute
በ—	*bä—* adv. with pleasure, gladly	ተዳቀቀ	*tädaqqäqä* v.i. became weak *(body: due to exhaustion, disease)*
ደስተኛ	*dässətäñña* adj. joyful, happy	አደቀቀ	*adäqqäqä* v.t. pounded; made weak *(fatigue, disease)*
የደስደስ	*yädäsdäss* n. charm, attraction	አስደቀቀ	*asdäqqäqä* v.t. had s/t pounded, powdered
የደስደስ አላት	*yädäsdäss* she is charming, attractive	ደቀነ	*däqqänä* v.t. put under the tap *(bucket, kettle etc.)*
ተደሰተ	*tädässätä* v. enjoyed oneself, was pleased, amused oneself	ድቅን	*dəqqən* n. s/t put under the tap *(e.g. bucket, kettle)*
ተደሳች	*tädässač* adj. cheerful, enjoying oneself, happy	ድቅን አለ	*dəqqənn alä* v.i. blocked s/o's way
መደሰቻ ቦታ	*mädäsäča bota* n. place of entertainment	ተደቀነ	*tädäqqänä* v.i. blocked s/o's way
አስደሰተ	*asdässätä* v.t. amused, made happy, entertained, pleased	ደቀደቀ	*däqäddäqä* v.t. ploughed virgin land; stamped *(repeatedly one's foot)*
አስደሳች	*asdässač* adj. enjoyable, pleasing, lovely	ደቅደቂት	*däqdäqqit* n. motorcycle
*ደሸደሸ	*däšäddäšä*	ዱቅዱቅ	*duqduq* n. pounded pepper
ደሸደሸ	*däšädäš* adj. loitering, dawdling	ድቅድቅ	*dəqdəq* n. ploughed virgin land
አደሸደሸ	*adäšäddäšä* v.t. loitered around, bummed around	ተንደቀደቀ	*tändäqäddäqä* v.i. produced a sound like that of a motor-cycle
አደስዳሽ	*adäsdaš* n. loiterer, bum		
ደቀመዝሙር	*däqqämäzmur* n. student, desciple, pl.	ደቂቃ	*däqiqa* see ደቀቀ
	ደቀ መዝሙርት *däqqä mäzamurt*	ደቃ	*däqqa* v.t. hit severely
ደቀለ	*däqqälä* v.t. had an illegitimate child	ደቆሰ	*däqqosä* v.t. grounded, pounded
ዲቃላ	*diqala* n/adj. bastard,	ድቁስ	*dəqqus* n. powdered pepper

257

መደቈሻ mädäqqoša n. mill-stone

ደቈቈስ däqu^waqqosä v.t. battered

ደቈስቈሳ däqosqu^wassa adj. feeble, weak

ተደቈሰ tädäqqosä v.i. was powdered

ደበለለ däbällälä v.t. threw down (in wrestling)

ተደበለለ tädäbällälä v.i. was thrown down (in wrestling)

ተንደንባለለ tändänballälä v.i. rolled (in the dust like a donkey)

አንደባለለ andäballälä v.t. rolled down, threw s/o down

*ደበለበለ also ደበለበለ *däbäläbbälä, *däboläbbolä

ደበለባላ däbälballa adj. oval

ድቡልቡል dəbulbul adj. round (ball-shaped)

ድብልብል dəbelbəl adj. fat and roundish

ተድበለበለ tädbäläbbälä v.i. was fat and roundish; rounded out (figure)

አድበለበለ adbäläbbälä v.t formed into a ball

ደበለቀ däbälläqä v.t. mixed; confounded also ደበለቀ

ድብልቅ dəbəlləq n/adj. mixture, mixed; compound

ደበላለቀ däbälalläqä v.t. mixed up, amalgamated

ድብልቅልቅ dəbləqləq n. confusion; uproar; anarchism (confusion)

ተደበለለቀ tädäbälläqä v.i. joined others, mixed with others

ተደባለቀ tädäballäqä v.i. was mixed; joined others

ተደበላለቀ tädäbälalläqä v.i. was thrown into utter confusion, was mixed up; was disorganized

አደባለቀ addäballäqä v.t. mixed; confused

አስደባለቀ asdäbälläqä v.t. caused to be mixed; caused s/o to join others

አስደባለቀ asdäballäqä v.t. caused to be mixed

ደበሎ däbälo n. tanned sheep skin (worn by students of the traditional school and shepherds)

—ለባሽ —labaš adj. of humble parents

ደበሰሰ däbässäsä v.i. faded (colour), was dim

ደብሳሳ däbsassa adj. faded, dim

*ደበሰበሰ * däbäsäbbäsä

ደበሰበሰ däbäsbassa adj ambiguous

ተድበሰበሰ tädbäsäbbäsä v.i. was ambiguous

አድበሰበሰ adbäsäbbäsä v.t. made ambiguous

ደበቀ däbbäqä v.t. hid, concealed; sheltered (hide)

ደባቃ däbbaqqa adj. out-of-the-way

ደባቃ በታ an out-of-the-way place

ድብቃ dəbbäqa n. concealment

ድብቅ dəbbəq adj. hidden, concealed; secret

በድብቅ ሄደ he left secretly

ድብብቆሽ dəbəbbəqoš n. hide-and-seek

ተደበቀ tädäbbäqä v.i. was hidden, concealed; was kept secret

ተደባበቀ tädäbabbäqä v.i. hid from each other

አስደበቀ asdäbbäqä v.t. had s/t hidden

ደበበ däbbäbä v.i. overhung

ድባብ dəbab n. large processional umbrella

ደብብ አለ däbäbb alä v.i. discoloured

258

ደበተ	däbbätä v.t. depressed (less active)	ራቅ	east
ደባች	däbbač adj. depressing (less active)	—ምዕራብ	—mə'rab southwest
ድብት አደረገ	dəbbət adärrägä v.t. made depressed (inactive)	—ዋልታ	—walta n.South Pole
		ደባ	däba n. intrigue
ደበነ	däbbänä v.i./v.t. was over roasted; was infuriated; was tightly tied	—ሠራ	—särra v.t. intrigued
		—ዋለ	—walä v.t. intrigued
		አደባ	adäba v.i lurked
		ደባለቀ	see ደበለቀ
ድባና	dəbbano adj. dwarfish, undersized	ደባል	n. däbbal room-mate
ድብን ያለ እንቅልፍ	debbənn yalä ənqəlf n. heavy, sound sleep	ደብር	däbər n. sanctuary (church,) pl. አድባራት adbarat
አደበነ	adäbbänä v.t. infuriated, burnt with fury	የደብር አለቃ	yädäbər aläqa n. vicar
		ደብተራ	däbtära n. unordained but highly - trained clergyman
ደበናንሳ	däbänansa n. tanner; blacksmith		
ደበዘዘ	däbäzzäzä v.i. was dim; faded, tarnished (lost lustre)	ደብተር	däbtär n. exercise book copy-book
		ደብዳቤ የሹመት	däbdabbe n. letter yäšumä letter of accreditation (diplomatic)
ደብዛዛ	däbzazza adj. dim, gloomy; blurred (print), vague, indistinct		
		ደብዛ	däbza n. trace, whereabouts
አደበዘዘ	adäbäzzäzä v.t faded, blurred	ደብዛው ጠፋ	däbzaw ṭäffa n. all trace was lost of him, no one knows his whereabouts
ደበደበ	däbäddäbä v.t beat, attacked, assaulted		
		ደቦ	däbo see also ዣጀ and ወንፈል n. communal labour
ደባደቦ	däbadäbo n. stitched rag		
ድብደባ	dəbdäba n. beating, striking, assaulting	*ደቦለቦለ	* däboläbbolä
		ደቦልቧላ	däbolbu"alla adj. round
ድብደብ	dəbdab n. pack saddle (usually goat or sheepskin)	ድቡልቡል	dəbulbul adj. round, ball-shape, spherical
ተንደበደበ	tändäbäddäbä v. i. was full of inflammation (body)	ተደቦለቦለ	tädboläbbolä v.i was made round, was rolled (dough etc.)
ተደበደበ	tädäbäddäbä v.i. was beaten, attacked assaulted	አደቦለቦለ	adboläbbolä v.t rounded (made round), rolled (dough etc.)
ተደባደበ	tädäbaddäbä v.i. beat each other up	ደቦል	däbbol n. cub
ተደባዳቢ	tädäbadabi adj. quarrelsome, aggressive (physically)	ያንበሳ- *ደሀረ	yanbässa— n. lion-cub *däharä
		ደሀራይ	däharay n. cantle (of a saddle)
ደቡብ	däbub n. south		
ደቡባዊ	däbubawi n. adj. southern	አድኃሪ (የ)አድኀሮት ኃይላት	adhari n. reactionary (yä) adhərot hailat n. reactionary forces
ደቡብ ምሥራ	däbub məsraq south-	ደነሰ	dännäsä v.t. danced
		ደናሽ	dännaš n. dancer

ዳንስ — dans n. dance

—ቤት —bet n. dance-hall

ዳንሰኛ dansäñña n. dancer

አስደነሰ asdännäsä v.t danced with s/o

ደነቀ dännäqä v.i with pronominal suffix e.g. ደነቀው was astonished, admired, surprised

ደንቅ dənq n/adj wonder, astonishment, marvel; wonderful, astonishing, marvellous

ደንቅ አለው dənnəq aläw v.i. was astonished; admired, surprised; was perplexed; was amused

ተደነቀ tädännäqä v.i. was astonished, wondered

ተደናቂ tädännaqi adj. astonishing, surprising; superb, marvellous

ተጋነቀ tädannäqä v.i was exaggerated

አደነቀ adännäqä v.t. admired, wondered, was impressed

አድናቂ adnaqi n. fan

አድናቆት adnaqot n. admiration, appreciation, astonishment

አስደነቀ asdännäqä v.t. astonished, surprised

አስደናቂ asdännaqi adj. impressive, admirable, magnificent

ደነቀረ dänäqqärä v.t. inserted forced in, knocked into, wedged in

ደንቃራ dänqara n. stumbling-block, nuisance, obstacle

ተደነቀረ tädänäqqärä v.i was inserted ; acted as a stumbling block, an obstruction

ነገር ተደነቀረ nägär tädänäqqäräbäñ I was obstructed ረብኝ

ደነቀፈ *dänäqqäfä see also ነቀፈ and እነቀፈ

ደንቀፈ dänqaffa adj. wobbly, staggering

ተደናቀፈ tädänaqqäfä v.i. stumbled, faltered, staggered; was interrupted, obstructed

አደናቀፈ addänaqqäfä v.t. made to stumble, interrupted, hampered the movement; thwarted, obstructed

ደነቆለ dänäqqolä v.t. poked s/o's eye (with the finger)

ደነቆረ dänäqqorä v.i. was deaf, was stupid see also አደነቆረ

ደንቆሮ dänqoro adj. deaf; ignorant, stupid

ድንቁርና dənqurənna n. stupidity, ignorance, deafness

ደነበረ dänäbbärä v.i. shied, bolted (of a horse); jumped (startled)

ደንባሪ dänbari adj. shy, skittish

ደንበራ dänbarra adj. weak-sighted; excitable, restless

ተደናበረ tädänabbärä v.i. groped

አደነበረ adänabbärä v.i. caused to bolt (horse)

አደናባሪ addänabari n/adj. crook ; misleading

አስደነበረ asdänäbbärä v.t. caused to bolt (horse); frightened, alarmed, stupefied

አስደንባሪ አስደንባሪ alarming news
ወሬ

ደነበ dänäbba v.t. set rules and regulations, established procedures

ደንብ dänb n. rule, regulation, procedure, provision

የደንብ ልብስ yädänb ləbs n. uniform

ሰላ ደንብ sälä dänb n. point of order

በደንብ bädänb adv. prop-

260

እንደ ደንቡ   erly, perfectly *əndä dänbu* as is the rule, according to the rules and regulations

ውስጠ ደንብ   *wəsţä dänb* n. by-law

ደንበኛ   *dänbäñña* adj/n. regular, correct; genuine; customer, client

ደንብ ሠራ   *dänb särra* v.t. set rules and regulations

—አልባ   —*alba* adj. chaotic, disorderly

—አወጣ   —*awäţţa* v.t. set rules and regulations

በደንቡ መሰረት   *bädänbu mäsärät* according to the rules and regulations

ደነበዘ   *dänäbbäzä* v.i. was discoloured

ደነበዝ   *dänäbäz* adj. weak-minded

ደንበዛ   *dänbazza* adj. weak-minded

ተደነበዘ   *tädänabbäzä* v.i. was in a smoky haze

ደነነ   *dännänä* v.i. slanted *(tree etc.)*

ደናና   *dänana* adj. slanting

ደነዘ   *dännäzä* v.i. became blunt *(blade);* was dull *(intellect)*

ደነዝ   *dänäz* adj. blunt *(blade);* dull *(blade, intellect)*

አደነዘ   *adännäzä* v.t. dulled; stupified *(with drinks)*

ደነዘዘ   *dänäzzäzä* v.i grew numb; was dull *(intellect)*

አደነዘዘ   *adänäzzäzä* v.t. made insensitive, stupefied, be numbed

ደነደነ   *dänädännä* v.i. was plump, fat; was conceited

ደንዳና   *dändanna* adj. plump, fat; sturdy

ደንዴነ   *dändanne* n. large intestine

*ደነገረ   * *dänäggärä*

ደንጋራ   *dängarra* adj. perturbed, perplexed; puzzled

ተደናገረ   *tädännaggärä* v.i. was perturbed, perplexed

አደናገረ   *addänaggärä* v.t. perturbed, perplexed, confused, puzzled

አደናጋሪ   *addänagari* adj. perturbing, puzzling; fraudulent

አደነጋገረ   *addänägaggärä* v.t. threw into[1] utter confusion, disorder

ደነገዘ   *dänäggäzä* v.i. became weak-sighted *(due to old age)*

ደንጋዛ   *dängazza* adj. weak-sighted

ድንግዝግዝ አለ   *dəngəzgəzz alä* v.i. became dusk

ደነገገ   *dänäggägä* v.t. instituted, decreed by-law

ድንጋጌ   *dənəggage* n. legislative decree, law, regulation

ደነገጠ   *dänäggäţä* v.i. was alarmed, startled, shocked, was taken aback

ደንጋጣ   *dängaţţa* adj. shy, timid; amenable *(person)*

ድንጉጥ   *dənguţ* adj. shy, timid; amenable *(person)*

ድንጋጤ   *dənəggaţe* n. shock, alarm, fright

ተደናገጠ   *tädänaggäţä* v.i. was alarmed, startled, shocked

አስደነገጠ   *asdänäggäţä* v.t. startled, frightened, terrified, shocked

አስደንጋጭ   *asdängaç* adj. terrifying, shocking, frightening

ደነገረ   *dänäggora* v.t. dug up land; brought an irrelevant topic into a

ደንጎራ   discussion
dängora n. spear headed digging implement, also መደን ጎሪያ

ደንጉርጉር መንገድ   dəngurgur mängäd n. rough road

ደነፈፈ   dänäffäfä v. i. was slow, stupid, obtuse

ደንፋፍ   dənfäf adj. slow, stupid, obtuse

ደነፋ   dänäffa v.i. bragged, boasted, blustered, vaunted

ደነፊ   dänfi adj. braggart, boastful, big-mouthed

ደንፋታ   dənfata n. bragging, boast

ደን   dänn n. forest, woods
ደናማ   dännamma adj. forested, wooded

ደንቃራ   see ደንቀራ
ደንባኝን   dänbägan n. demijohn also ደምባኝን

ደንብ   see ደነባ
ደንታ   dänta n. care
—ቢስ   —bis adj. careless
—የለሽ   —yälläš adj./ careless
ደንዳሮ   dändärro n. stupid fat woman

ደንዳስ   dändäss n. backbone
ደንዳሳም   dänddässam adj. strong, vigorous, sturdy (physical)

ደንደነ   see ደነደነ
ደንገላሳ   dängälasa n. trot (horse)
ደንገሎ   dängällo n. animal feed (bread of impure flour)

ደንጋጡር   dängäṭur n. lady-in waiting, lady of the bed-chamber

ደህና   dähna adj. good, safe, well, fine, all right see also ጸን

በደህና ያግባህ   bädähəna yagbah Bon Voyage!

ደህና ሁን   —hun goodbye
—ሰንብት   —sänbət bye-bye!
—ቀን   —qän peaceful time
—አምሽ   —amš Good evening! (when departing)

—እዳር   —ədär Good night!
—ከረም   —käräm Goodbye! (for a longer time)
—ዋል   —wal have a good day!

ደህንነት   dähnännät n. safety, well-being
የሕዝብ—   yähəzb–public security

ደከመ   däkkämä v.i. got tired fatigued; was weak; strove, endeavoured
ደካማ   däkama adj. weak. feeble, weary
ደኩም   dəkum adj. handicapped pl. ደኩማን dəkumman
ደካም   dəkam n. exhaustion, weakness
ደክመት   dəkmät n. weakness. imperfection
ተደከመ   tädäkkämä v.i. exhausted all possibilities
ተዳከመ   tädakkämä v. i. became exhausted, was tired out
አደከመ   adäkkämä v.t. weakened, tired, fatigued
አዳከመ   addakkämä v.t. exhausted, fatigued
አድካሚ   adkami adj. exhausting
*ደከደከ   *däkäddäkä
ተንደከደከ   tändäkaddäkä v. i. boiled (thick liquid e.g polenta, pudding etc.)
አንደከደከ   andäkäddäkä v.t. boiled (thick liquid;.
ደኸየ   dähäyyä v.i. was poor was impoverished
ድኽ   dəha n./adj. poor
ድኽነት   dəhənnät n. poverty, penury
አደኸየ   adahäyya v.t. impoverished
ደወለ   däwwälä v.t. rang bell); struck (a clock) dialled, called on the telephone; hit strongly
ደወል   däwäl n. bell!

ደዋይ dāwway n. bell ringer
ድወላ dǝwwäla n. ringing
ተደወለ tädäwwälä v.i. was
rung
አስደወለ asdäwwälä v.t. had a
bell rung
*ደወረ *dāwwärä
ድወር dǝwwǝr n. spool
አዳወረ adawwärä v.t wound
on the spool
ማዳወሪያ madawäriya n. distaff
ደዌ dāwe n. disease, sick-
ness, illness
—ስጋ —sǝga n. leprosy
—ነፍስ —näfs n. sin
ድወይ dǝwwǝy n. midget,
dwarf
*ደዘደዘ *dāzäddāzä
ደዘደዘ dāzädäz n. tramp,
wanderer
አደዘደዘ adäzäddäzä v.t.
wandered, bummed
አደዝዳዥ adäzdaž adj. vaga-
bond
ደይን däyn n. judgement
እለተ— ǝlätä— n. the Day of
Judgement
ዳዳሆ dädäho n. juniper
ዳደረ däddärä v.i. hardened,
solidified
ድድር dǝddǝr adj. hard,
solid
ዳደቀ däddäqä v.t. dug up
land
ድድቅ dǝddǝq adj. dug up
(land)
ዳደበ däddäbä v.i. was dull,
stupid, moron
ድደብ dǝddäb adj. dull,
stupid, idiot
አዳደበ adäddäbä v.t. dulled
ዳጅ dāǧǧ n. outside, out
of doors, entrance
ዳጅ ሰላም dāǧǧä sälam n. gate-
way of a church
compound; place
where churchmen
eat after services
—ጣኝ —ṭāñi n. applicant
waiting for a certain
post
ዳጅ ጠናት dāǧǧ ṭǝnat n. wait-

ing patiently to be
employed
ዳጅ አዝማች also dāǧǧ azmač
governor of pro-
vince, general of an
army (old usage)
ዳጃፍ dāǧǧaf n. front
of house, entrance,
doorway
ዳጀን dāǧän n. rearguard
—ጦር —ṭor n. rear of an
army
ዳጃች dāǧǧačč short form of
ዳጅ አዝማች see above
ዳገመ däggämä v.t. repeated;
recited (a prayer),
gave a second time
ዳጊማ ፊዳል dägimä fidäl n. re-
petitive letters e.g
ደበበ, ጠበጠበ
ዳግሞ dägmo adv. also ደግም
moreover, besides
furthermore, also,
again
ዳግመኛ dagmäñña adv.
again, another time,
once again
ዳግማይ dagmay, also ዳግማዊ
dagmawi adj. sec-
ond (preceding the
name of a king) e.g
ዳግማይ/ዊ ዮሐንስ
Yohannis II
ዳግማይ ተን dagmay tänsai n. the
ሣይ Sunday after Easter
ዳግማዊ dagmawi see ዳግማይ
ዳገም dagäm adj. second
—አራቂ —aräqi n. re-
distilled arrack
ዳግሞሽ dagmoš adv. second
time
ድጋሚ dǝggami adj. repeated
በድጋሚ bädǝggami adv. re-
peatedly
ድግመት dǝgǝmt n. recitation
(charm)
ተዳገመ tädäggämä v.i. was
recited
ተዳጋገመ tädägaggämä v.i. was
done, happened
repeatedly, became

ተደጋጋሚ tädägagami adj. frequent

አስደገመ asdäggämä v.t. had s/t repeated

ረገሰ däggäsä v. t. gave a feast, made preparation for banquet

ድግስ dəggəs n. banquet, festive meal

ተደገሰ tädäggässä v.i. was prepared (banquet), was in store (of trouble)

አስደገሰ asdäggäsä v.t. had a festive meal prepared

*ደገተ *däggätä

ዳገት dagät n. uphill road, slope

አዳገተ adaggätä v.i. was difficult, was hard; was impossible

አዳጋች adagač adj. difficult, hard, arduous

ደገነ däggänä v.t. pointed (a gun, an arrow)

ደጋን dägan n. bow for carding cotton, wool

—እግር —əgər adj. bandy-legged

ድገና dəggäna n. pointing (a gun etc.)

ድጉን dəggən adj. pointed (gun, arrow)

—መትረየስ —mäträyyäs n. tri-poded - machine-gun

—መጋዝ —mägaz n. hack-saw

ተደገነ tädäggänä v.i. was pointed (a gun, an arrow)

ደገኝ ደጋ see

ደገደገ dägäddägä v.i. was weak-sighted; was weak, emaciated

ደግዳጋ dägdagga adj. lean, emaciated, feeble

አደገደገ adägäddägä v.t wore the šämma down over the shoulder and round the waist as a sign of respect

አደግዳጊ adägdagi adj. ser-

---

vile, subservient, obsequious

አስደገደገ asdägäddägä v.t. had complete control over others

ደገፈ däggäfä v.t. supported (an opinion, a motion), favoured; backed

ደጋፊ däggafi n. partisan supporter; backer; benefactor

ደግፍ däggəf in ጆሮ ደግፍ ǧoro däggəf n. mumps

ድጋፍ dəgaf n. support, backing, endorsement

መደገፊያ mädäggäfiya n. support, buttress, bracket

ተደገፈ tädäggäfä v.i. was supported; leant on; propped oneself against

መደገፊያ mäddägäfiya n. arm (of chair), s/t used to lean on

ተደጋገፈ tädägaggäfä v.i. supported, backed each other

ተደጋጋፊ tädägagafi adj. supporting each other, complementary to each other

አስደገፈ asdägäfä v.t. rested

ደጋ däga n. highland

ወይና— wäina — n. temperate zone

ደገኛ dägäñña n. highlander

ደጋን see ደገነ

ደግ dägg adj. good-hearted, kind, nice

ደጋደግ däggadägg adj. good-hearted, generous

ደግ ነው dägg näw interj.O.K! good!

—ሥራ —səra n. benevolence

ደግነቱ dəggənnätu adv. luckily, fortunately e.g ደግነቱ አልሞተም luckily he did not die

ደግነት däggənnät n.

264

ደጎመ	goodness, kindness *däggomä* v.t. sub- sidized	ጠፅ	*ṭälla* —*ṭägg* n. unfiltered *ṭägg*
ድጎማ	*dəggoma* n. subsidy	አደፋረሰ	*addäfäräsä* v.t. stirred
መደጎሚያ	*mädäggomiya* n. sub- sidy		up, agitated *(liquid)*; disturbed, put in a state of chaos
ተደጎመ	*tädäggomä* v.i. was subsidized		
ደጎሰ	*däggosä* v.t. decorated the cover of a book	ደፈቀ	*däffäqä* v.t. dipped, dunked
ድጉስ	*dəgʷs* n. leather dec- oration	አረፋ—	*aräfa* — v.t. foamed
ድጉሳት	*dəggʷsat see* ድጉስ	ድፍቂያ	*dəfqiya* n. dipping *(boys in swimming)* cf.
ደጎባ	- *däggoba* adj. un- educated and servile; n. pupa, chrysalis *(of locust)*	ዝፍቂያ	
		ተደፈቀ	*tädäffäqä* v.i. was dipped
ደፈረ	*däffärä* v.i. was bold, dared; was disre- spectful; violated; was courageous	ተዳፈቀ	*tädaffäqä* v.i. dipped each other *(in swimming)* cf. ተዛፈቀ
		አስደፈቀ	*asdäffäqä* v.t. had s/o dipped *(in swimming)*
ደፋር	*däffar* adj. cour- ageous, bold, fearless, adventurous; disre- spectful, uncouth, rude; insolent		
		ደፈነ	*däffänä* v.t. filled up *(hole in the ground)*; stopped a leak; closed *(eyes)*
ድፍረት	*dəfrät* n. courage, boldness; impudence, rudeness, insolence	ደፈና	*däfänä* in በደፈናው *bädäfänaw* adv. in general, by and large
ተደፈረ	*tädäffärä* v.i. was violated, trespassed upon	ዳፈን	*dafän* n. absence of a clergyman from a service
ተዳፈረ	*tädaffärä* v.i. took liberties with ,treated with impudence; be- haved rudely	የዳፈን ገንዘብ	*yädafän gänzäb* n. penalty paid by clergyman for absenting himself from a service
ተዳፋሪ	*tädafari* adj. impu- dent, rude, insolent		
ተደፋፈረ	*tädäfaffärä* v.i. took courage	ድፍን	*dəfən* adj. solid *(not hollow)*; entire
አደፋፈረ	*addäfaffärä* v.t. em- boldened, encouraged	—ቅል	—*qəl* n. *(lit.)* solid gourd; stupid, blockhead
አስደፈረ	*asdäffärä* v.t. had s/o violate s/t or s/o	—አበሻ	—*abäša* n. the entire Ethiopian population
ደፈረሰ	*däfärräsä* v.i got muddy, became turbid	ደፈንፋና	*däfänfanna* adj. vague, obscure, am- biguous
ድፍርስ	*dəfrəs* adj. muddy, turbid	ድፍንፍን	*dəfənfən* adj. vague, obscure, ambiguous
—አይን	—*ayn* adj. bloodshot	ዳፍንት	*dafənt* n. hemeralopia
—ጠላ	—*ṭälla* n. unfiltered		

265

ዳፍንታም *dafəntam* n s/o suffering from hemeralopia; adj. slow, sluggish

ተደፈነ *tädäffänä* v.i. was filled up (hole in the ground), was stopped (a leak); was closed (eyes)

ተዳፈነ *tädaffänä* v.i. was choked (fire), did not take place (church service)

ተድፈነፈነ *tädfänäffänä* v.i. was kept secret

አዳፈነ *addaffänä* v.t. choked up fire

አዳፍኔ *addafne* n. mortar (gun)

አድፈነፈነ *adfänäffänä* v.t made ambiguous (intentionally)

አስደፈነ *asdäffänä* v.t.had a hole filled up

ደፈደፈ *däfäddäfä* v.t. mixed beer must with water

ደፍደፍ *dəfədəf* n. beer must
ተንደፋደፈ *tändäfaddäfä* v.i. writhed

*ደፈጠ * *däffäṭa*
ደፈጣ *däfäṭa* n. ambush
—ተዋጊ —*täwagi* n. guerrilla fighter

አደፈጠ *adäffäṭä* v.t. lay in ambush, lurked

አስደፈጠ *asdäffäṭä* v.t. caused s/o to be in ambush

ደፋጠጠ *däfäṭṭäṭä* v.t. squashed flat, rolled (made flat)

ደፍጠጠ *däfṭaṭṭa* adj. flatly squashed

ድፍጥ *dəfəṭṭ* adj. flatly squashed

—አፍንጫ —*afənča* adj. flat-nosed

ተደፋጠጠ *tädäfäṭṭäṭä* v.t. was flatly squashed

ደፋ *däffa* v.t. spilt (liquid) bent (the neck) made s/o fall flat on his face; fornicated

ዘውድ— *zäwd*–v.t. was crowned

ዳቦ *dabbo*–v.t. baked bread

አንጋተን— *angätun*–v.t. became meek, became mild and patient

ድፋት *dəfat* n. Ethiopian mark of low pitch of sound

ድፍ ዳቦ *dəfo dabbo* n. large baked loaf of bread

ዳፋ አለ *däfa alä* v.i. died suddenly; stooped

ዳፋ ቀና አለ *däfa qäna alä* v.i. bustled about

ተዳፋ *tädäffa* v.i. was spilt; died suddenly

ተዳፋ መሬት *tädafa märet* n. sloping ground

ተዳፋት *tädäfat* n. slope

አዳፋ *addaffa* v.t. drove (cattle) downhill

አድፋፋ *adfaffa* v.t. spent money extravagantly

አድፋፊ *adfafi* adj. extravagant

ደፍ *däf* n. door-sill

ደፍ አለ *däff alä* v.i thudded to the ground

ዱለት *dulät* n. spiced dish of chopped sheep or goat's tripe and liver mixed with butter eaten as a first course; conspiracy

ዱለቻ *dulläčča* n. an old bull

ዱላ *dulla* n. club, stick
ዱለኛ *dulläñña* n. quarrelsome, aggressive, disposed to attack

ዱላ ቀረሽ *dulla qärräš* in ዬ ቀረሽ ጥል fierce quarrel

ዱልዱም
ዱC see ዬለደሮ
ዱCዩ *dur* n. forest, wood *durəyye* adj. hooligan, hoodlum, vagabond

ዱC *duro* also ድሮ *dəro* adv. in the past, in olden times, long ago

—ዘመን —zämän in olden times, long ago, in the past

ዱሽ duš n. stump (of the limb).

ዱቄት duqet, also ዶቄት doqet n. flour, powder

ዱባ dubba n. pumpkin, squash

ዱቤ dube n. credit

ዱቤ dubbe in ዱቤ ባቄላ dubbe baqela n. broad beans

ዱብል dubl adj. double

ዱብ አለ dubb alä v.t. came suddenly; tumbled down

ዱብ ዱብ አለ dubb dubb alä v.i. trickled (tears); toddled (child)

ዱብ እዳ dubb əda n. unexpected incident, a surprise

ዱካ duka n. trace, trail, track, footprint

ዱዳ duda also ድዳ dəda adj. dumb, mute

ዲቶና see under ዲያቆን

ዲቆላ see under ደቆላ

ዲብ dib n. knoll

ዲናሞ dinamo n. dynamo

ዲናሚት dinamit n. dynamite

ዲካ dikka n. limit

ዲያብሎስ diablos n. devil

ዲዳ dida adj. dumb, mute, also ዱዳ ፡ ድዳ

ዲግሪ digri n. degree (diploma)

ዲፕሎማ diploma n. diploma

ዳለጠ dallätä v.i. slipped, slided

አዳለጠ adallätä v.t. slipped, slided

ዳለቻ daləčča adj. grey

ዳሌ dalle n. hips (woman's)

ዳልጋ አንበሳ dalga anbäsa n. caracal

ዳመነ dammänä v.i. was cloudy

ዳመና dammäna n. cloud

ዳመናማ damännamma also ዳመናም dammänam adj. cloudy

ዳመጠ dammäṭä v.t crushed (with a roller), crushed cotton to separate the seeds

ዳመጦ damäṭo n. cotton whose seeds are separated

ዳምጣው damṭäw n. road-roller

መዳመጫ ብረት mädamäča bərät n. metal rod used to separate seeds from cotton

—ድንጋይ —dəngay n. smooth flat stone used for crushing cotton to separate seeds

ተዳመጠ tädämmäṭä v.i. was crushed (with a roller)

ዳማ dama n. checkers

ዳማ ፈረስ dama färäs n/adj reddish-brown horse; bay

ዳምጣው see ዳመጠ
ዳሞትራ damotəra n. big venomous kind of spider

ዳረ darä v.t. gave s/o in marriage, married, married off

ተዳረ tädarä v.i. was married .

ትዳር tədar n. married life, home life

—ያዛ —yazä v.t. was married, started a home

—ፈታ —fätta v.t. was divorced

ባለትዳር balä tədar n. married

ዳረገ darrägä v.t. donated

ዳረጎት darägot n. donation

ድርጎ dərgo n. endowment

ተዳረገ tädarrägä v.i. was donated

ዳሩ ግን daru gən adv. but, nonetheless, however

ዳር dar n. border, bank (of lake, river), edge

ዳራጋር daragär n. border countries, frontier

ዳርቻ daračča adv. edge, end

ከዳር እዳር kädar ədar from end to end; throughout, entirely

267

ጻር ጻር አለ	dar dar alä v.i. beat around the bush, hesitated		wheat), loaf of bread
ጻርና ጻር	darənna dar two extreme ends	—ቆሎ	—qollo n. small round dough balls roasted and eaten as provisions on a journey
ከጻር ጻር	kädar dar from all sides, also ከጻር እስከጻር	ዶሮ—	doro—n. large loaf of bread baked with chicken stew
ጻሰ	dasä v.t. tramped upon, stamped s/t out	ዳነ	danä v.i. was cured, was healed, recovered, was
ተጻሰ	tädasä v.i. was tramped upon, was stamped out		saved
ጻሰሰ	dassäsä v.t. touched; felt with the hands; caressed	መድሃኒት	mädhanit n. medicament; medicine; remedy; cure; drug; poison
ጻስ	das n. booth, shelter (hut)	የሚያስተኛ—	yämiyastäñña- n. anesthetic
ጻሸቀ	daššäqä v.i. was stamped, was stamped out	መድሃኒተኛ	mädhanitäñña n. healer; poisoner (person)
*ጻበለ	*dabbälä n.	መድሃኒታም	mädhanitam n. poisoner
ደባል	däbbal room-mate		
ተጻበለ	tädabbälä v.i. roomed with s/o	መድሃኒት ቀመሰ	mädhanit qämmäsä v.t. took a purgative
አጻበለ	addabbälä v.t. let s/o room with s/o	—ቀማሚ	—qämmami n. pharmacist, druggist
ጻበረ	dabbärä v.i. thrived, was enriched	—ቤት	—bet n. pharmdrugstore
አጻበረ	adabbärä v.t. enriched, fertilized (soil, developed (muscle)	መድሃኔ ዓለም	mädhane aläm n Saviour of the W (Christ)
ማጻበሪያ	madabäriya n. fertilizer	መድን	mädən n. guarantee, security; bail
ጻበሰ	dabbäsä v.t. touched lightly, felt (touch), felt one's way, groped	የመድን ድርጅት	yämädən dərəğğət n. insurance (company)
ጻበሳ	dabbäsa n. groping	አዳነ	adanä v.t. saved, rescued; cured, healed;
ደባበሰ	däbabbäsä v.t. caressed, fondled, patted (child)		redeemed
ጻቢት	dabit n. sirloin	ዳተኛ	datañña adj.slack, remiss
ጎድን ተጻቢት	godən tädabit n. sirloin with ribs	ዳንስ	dans see ደነሰ
ጻባ	dabba n. yellowish tanned cow skin (worn by monks and hermits etc. as an over coat)	ዳንኪራ	dankira n. dance (hitting the ground with the feet), war-dance
		ዳንዴ	dande adj. strong and stupid
በለ ጻባ	balädabba adj./ poor, usually used together with በለ ጻባና በለከበ the poor and the rich	ዳንጎለ	dangəlle n. ram
		ዳኘ	daññä v.t judged, arbitrated
ጻቦ	dabbo n. bread (of	ዳኛ	dañña n. judge; umpire
		ዳኝነት	daññənnät n. arbitration, judgeship, judgement

268

ዳኛ ረገጠ   (ability to judge)
dañña räggäṭä
court defiance

—ተሰየመ   —täsäyyämä v.i.
acted as a judge

አጥቢያ ዳኛ   aṭbiya dañña n.
Justice of the Peace

የውሃ ወራጅ ዳኛ   yäwᵊha wärag dañña n. temporary arbitrator

የዘመድ ዳኛ   yäzämäd dañña n. family arbitrator

ተዳኘ   tädaññä v.i. was brought to court (person)

ዳከረ   dakkärä v.i. worked hard, fatigued

ዳከዩ   dakkᵊyᵧe n. duck

ዳኸ   dahä v.i. crawled (baby), walked on all fours (like a baby)

ዳዊት   dawit n. David; the Psalms of David

—ደገመ   —däggämä v.t. recited the psalter of David

መዝሙረ--   mäzmurä— n. Psalms of David

ዳዋ   dawwa n. undergrowth, shrub

—ለበሰ   —läbbäsä v.t was full of shrubs

—በላው   —bällaw v.t. was covered with shrubs, sank into oblivion

ዳውላ   dawᵊlla n. twenty qunnas (grain measure appr. 100 kg.)

ዳዴ   dade n. toddling (child)

—አለ   —alä v.i. toddled (child)

ዳዶ   dado n. nut

*ዳገተ   *daggätä

ዳጋታም   dagätam adj. sloping, hilly

ዳገት   dagät n. slope, uphill road, ascent

አዳገተ   adaggätä v.i. was difficult, was impossible

አዳጋች   adagač adj. difficult, impossible

   (understanding)

ዳጠ   daṭä v.t. ran over, rolled over s/t; mashed (vegetables etc.)

ዳጣ   däṭa n. slippery

ዳጥ   daṭ n. slippery

ተዳጠ   tädaṭä v.i. was run over e.g. በመኪና ተዳጠ he was run over by a car

አዳጠ   adaṭä v.t. caused to slip

ዳጨ   daččä v.t. ran over

ዳፈነ   see ዳፈነ

ዳፉ   dafa used as በ...ዳፉ bä... däfa prep. because of, due to someones fault; በርሱ ዳፉ ተቀጣሁ I was punished due to his fault

ዳፍንት   däfnᵊt n. hemeralopia (eye disease that causes visibility at night difficult) see also ደፈነፈነ

ዳፍንታም   dafᵊntam n. s/o suffering from hemeralopia; adj. slow, sluggish

ድል   dᵊl n. victory, triumph

—ሆነ   —honä v.i. was conquered, was defeated

—መታ   —mätta v.t. defeated, vanquished, overcame, subdued

—ነሳ   —nässa see ድልመታ

—አዳረገ   —adärrägä see ድል መታ and ድል ነሳ

ባለድል   balädᵊl adj. victorious, triumphant

ድል ያለ   dᵊll yalä used with ድግስ dᵊggᵊs n. sumptuous banquet

ድልኽ   dᵊllᵊh n. sauce of spiced pepper

ድልድይ   see ደለደለ

ድመት   dᵊmmät n. cat

—ዓይን   —ayn adj. blond-eyed

የድ_{መት} ጓል yädəmmät gəlgäl
ጓል n. kitten
ድንቡሎ dənbullo adj. pretty
(girl) ; 5 cents (in
rural areas)
ድምቡሽ dəmbuš adj. plump
(woman)
ድምቡሼ ጓላ dəmbušše gäla adj.
fat in a pleasant-
looking way
ድምቡጭ አለ dəmbučč alä v.i. was
plump, was rounded
(cheeks)
ድምቢጥ dəmbiṭ n. type of
small bird (sylvia
lugens)
ድምብላል dəmbəlal n. coriander
ድምድግት see ደመደመ
ድምጥግጥ dəməṭmaṭ used as
ድምጥግጡ ጠፋ
dəmṭmatu ṭäffa was
annihilated, destroyed
completely, disapeared
completely
ድምጽ dəmṣ n. sound voice,
tone; vote
—ማጉያ —maguya n. loud-
speaker
—ሰጠ —säṭṭä v.t. voted
ድምፈፅ also ድንፈፅ
see ደነፈፈ
ደሪ dəri n. necklace, string
(of pearls)
ድራት see ደረት
ድራማ dərama n. drama
ድር dər see also ደራ n.
warp; web
ድርና ማግ dərənna mag n. warp
and weft ድርና ማግ
ሆኑ they agreed
completely, they
lived in complete
harmony
ድርስ see ደረስ
ድርብ see ደረብ
ድርግ see ደረገ
ድርጭት dərčč̣ət n. quail
(alanda cristata)
ድሮ dəro also ዱሮ duro adv.
in the past, formerly,
in olden times, pre-
viously, long ago,

already
ድስት dəst n. saucepan (clay)
ብረት— bərät— n. saucepan (metal)
ሰታቴ— sätate— n. large
saucepan (clay)
አፈድስት afädəst bərälle n.
ብርሌ small bell-mouthed
flask (used for
drinking mead and
beer)
ድበላ see ደበላ
ድቡሽት dəbbušt n. sand
ድብ dəbb n. bear (animal)
ድባብ see ደበበ
ድብኛት dəbəññät n. small
cylindrical granary
made of mud, earth
ድንባር dənbär also ድምባር
dəmbär n. boundary,
borderline, border
ድንባርተኛ dənbärtäññä, ድንባራተኛ
also dəmbärätäñña n.
one whose land is
adjoining s/o's land
ድንቡሼ see ድምቡሽ
ድንቢጥ see ድምቢጥ
ድንች dənnəčč n. potatoes
ስኳር— səkuʷar— n. sweet
potatoes
ድንክ dənk n. dwarf; midget
--አልጋ —alga n. couch
ድንከዬ dənkəyyä adj. dwar-
fish
ድንኳን dənkuʷan n. tent
—ተከለ —täkkälä v.t.
pitched a tent
ድንጋት dəngät adv. suddenly,
by chance; perhaps,
in case
ድንጋተኛ dəngätäñña adj.
sudden, unexpected;
emergency
በድንጋት bädəngät adv. sud-
denly, accidentally,
unexpectedly
ድንጉላ ፈረስ dəngulla n. stallion
ድንጉል dəngul n. worker bee
ድንጋይ dəngay, also ድንጊያ
dängiya n. stone
—ልብሱ —ləbsu n. tortoise
—ራስ —ras adj. stupid

270

—ሸበት	—šabät also የደንጋይ ሸበት yädəngay šabat n. moss
—ወቃሪ	—wäqari n. stone-mason
—ከሰል	—käsäl n. coal
(የ)—ዘመን	(yä)—zämän n. stone age
(የ) ኩላሊት—	(yä) kulalit— n. stone in the kidney
ባህ—	bäha— n. soapstone
ባሪያ—	bariya — n. black stone
ወፍጮ—	wäfčo — n. millstone
ደንጋል	dəngəl n. virgin
ደንገላይ	dəngəlay adj/n celibate
ደንገላዊ	dəngəlawi adj/n celibate
ደንገልና	dəngələnna n. celibacy
ደኝ	dəññ n. sulphur
ድኩላ	dəkkula n. bushbuck (tragelaphus scriptus)
ድኽ	see ደኸየ
ደው አለ	dəww alä v.i. was perplexed, was in a stupor
ደዳ	dəda, also ዴዳ adj. dumb, mute (unable to speak)
ደድ	dədd n. gum (of teeth)
ደዳም	dəddam n. one with protruding gums
ደድት	see ደደቀ
ደጀን	dəgäno n. crowbar (used for moving out stones)
ደጋፍ	see ደገፈ
ደግ	dəg n. long cloth band (worn wrapped tightly around the waist), sash
ደገር	dəgər n. ploughshare
ደገስ	see ደገሰ
ደጓ	dəguʷa n. Ethiopian hymn book
ደፈርሳ	dəfarsa n. defassa waterbuck, common waterbuck (kobus defassa, kobus ellipsiprymnus)
ድፍ	ድፍ see ደፈ
ዶላ	dolä v.t. inserted, put in (feeling)

ዶላት	dollätä v.i. conspired, plotted, intrigued
*ዶላዶለ	* doläddolä
ዶልዷላ	dolduʷalla adj. generous
ዶልዷሌ	dolduʷalle adj. generous
አባ—	abba—adj. generous
ተንዶላዶለ	tändoläddolä v.i. gushed
ዶለዝ	doläz adj. dead (to all feeling)
ዶለዶመ	doläddomä v.i. became blunt (point, sharp edge); was dull
ዶልዷማ	dolduʷamma adj. blunt (point, sharp edge), dull (pencil)
ዱልዱም	duldum adj. blunt, dull
አዶለዶመ	adoläddomä v.t, made blunt, dull
ዶማ	doma n. pickaxe
ዶማኛ	domäñña n. one who uses a pickaxe for cultivating land (not a plough)
ዶሮ	doro n. hen, chicken
—ወጥ	—wäṭ n. stew made with chicken
—ዳቦ	—dabbo n. large loaf of raised bread baked with chicken stew
—ጩኸት	—ǯuhät n. early in the morning, cock-crow, dawn, day-break
ቄብ—	qeb—n. pullet
አውራ—	awra—n. cock, rooster
ዶቃ	doqa n. glass bead
ዶቄት	doqet, also ዱቄት duqet n. flour, powder
የፉርኖ—	yäfurno— n. white flour
ዶኬ	dokke n. ordinary powdered legume stew, also ዶዮ
ዶክተር	doktär, also ዶክቶር doktor n. doctor, medical doctor, physician
ዶዮ	oyyo n. ordinary powdered legume stew
ዶጮ	doččo n. small glass or clay container

271

ዶፈር *dofär* n. idoform
ዶፈዶፈ *dofäddofä* v.t. became fat
ዶፈዶፍ *dofädof* adj. fattish
ዶፍዷፋ *dofduʷaffa* adj. fattish
ዶፍ *dof* used as ዶፍ ዝናብ
—ዝናብ *—zənab* n. heavy rain

ጀ

*ጀለ **ǧälä*
ጀላንጀል *ǧəlanǧǧəl* adj. imbecile stupid, silly
ጀላጀል *ǧəlaǧəl* adj. naive, silly
ጀል *ǧəl* fool, imbecile, stupid, foolish, naive
ጀልነት *ǧələnnät* n. stupidity, silliness, naivety
ተጃጃለ *täǧaǧalä* v.i. behaved naively, stupidly
አጃጃለ *aǧǧaǧalä* v.t. made fun of, ridiculed
*ጀለጀለ **ǧäläǧǧälä*
ተንጀላጀለ *tänǧälaǧǧälä* v.i. was poorly dressed, shabby
ጀለጠ *see* ዠለጠ
ጀሌ *ǧäle* n. combatant without firearms
ጀልባ *ǧälba* n. small boat
ጀመረ *ǧämmärä* v.t. started, commenced
ጀማሪ *ǧämari* n. beginner; novice
ከ...ጀምሮ *kä..ǧämmәro* beginning from, since
ጀምር *ǧəmmər* adj. started
በጀምር የቀረ adj. incomplete
መጀመሪያ *mäǧämmäriya* n. beginning, start, first, front
ተጀመረ *täǧämmärä* v.i. was started
አስጀመረ *äsǧämmärä* v.t. had s/t started
ጀምብ *ǧämb* n. one of two parts of loads of an animal
ጀምበር *ǧämbär also* ዠምበር n. sun
ጀረገገ *ǧärägägä also* ዠረገገ v.t. stripped off *(fruits from branches)*
ተንጀረገገ *tänǧäräggägä* v.i. bore abundantly *(fruits)* bore a heavy crop
አንጀረገገ *anǧäräggägä* v.t. bore abundantly *(fruit)*, bore a heavy crop *(fruit tree)*
ጀሶ *ǧässo* n. gypsum
ጀርመን *ǧärmän* n. German Germany, German Language
ጀበርቲ *ǧäbärti* n. name given by Arabs to Ethiopian Moslems
ጀበና *ǧäbäna* n. kettle, coffee pot
ጀበደ *ǧäbbädä also* ዠበደ v.t. struck *(hit)* s/o with a stick
ጀባ *ǧäba* word used when offering s/t to s/o, especially cup of coffee
ጀብዱ *ǧäbdu* n. act of bravery, adventure, heroic act
ጀብደኛ *ǧäbdäňňä* adj. adventurous
ጀቦነ *ǧäbbonä* v.t. covered s/o or oneself with a piece of cloth; muffled
*ጀነነ **ǧännänä*
ጀናና *ǧänana* adj. extremely proud
ጀነን *ǧənnən* adj. proud, conceited
ተጀነነ *täǧännänä* v.i. became proud, conceited

ጀንዲ	*ğāndi* n. tanned hide of an ox or a cow (*used for sleeping on*)
ገጀነ	*gäğğänä* v.i. was courageous,
ጀግና	*ğägna* adj. courageous, brave, hero gallant, valourous,
ጀግንነት	*ğägnənnät* n. courage bravery, valour
አጀገነ	*ağğäggänä* v.t. emboldened, put heart to, made a man of
ጁህ	*ğuh* n. cloth made of soft wool
ጂኦሜትሪ	*ğiometry* n. geometry
ጂኦሜትራ	*ğiometra* n. land-surveyor
ጂኦግራፊ	*ğiografi* n. geography
ጂገ	*ğige* n. communal labour
ጃል	*ğal* exclamatory word marking agreement, joy, or surprise e.g ንገረኝ እንጂ ጃል Oh! please tell me እንዲህ ነው እንጂ ጃል that is marvellous! ምነው ጃል! what is going around!
ጃርት	*ğart* n. porcupine
ጃንሆይ	*ğanhoy* n. title used in addressing a monarch
ጃንደርባ	*ğandaräba* n. eunuch
ጃንጥላ	*ğanṭala* n. parasol, umbrella, parachute
ጃኖ	*ğano* n. tunic with broad red band (*näṭäla with broad red band*)
ጃኬት	*ğakket* n. jacket
ጃዊ	*ğawwi* n. piece of red cloth
ጃውሳ	*ğawwusa* n. highway robber, a lawless-man; uncouth person
ጃየ ጃገረ	*ğaggä* v.i. became senile in ጋሻጃገረ *gašša ğagre* n. body-guard; shield-bearer
ጃጎን	*ğappan* n. Japan

ጃፓናዊ	*ğappanawi* n/adj. Japanese
ጄኔራል	*ğeneral* n. general
ጅማት	*ğəmmat* n. sinew, nerve, tendon
ጅማታም	*ğəmmatam* adj. skinny, bony
ጅምሩክ	*ğəmruk* also ጉምሩክ n. custom house
ጅምናስቲክ	*ğəmnastik* n. gymnastics, athletics
ጅራፍ	*ğəraf* n. plough-man's whip
ጅብ አለ	*ğəbb alä* also እጅብ አለ *əğğib alä* v.i. agglomerated, clustered
ጅብ —አፍ	*ğəb* n. hyena —*af* n. s/o having a large mouth
ጅንጀር	see also ዝንጀር *ğənğäro zänğäro* monkey, ape, baboon
ጅንፎ	*ğənfo*, also ዠንፎ ዠንፎ metal protection on the butt of a spear, a walking-stick
ጅዋጅዌ ጅዋጅዌ ተጫወተ	*ğəwwağəwwe* n. swing *ğəwwağəwwe täčäww-ätä* v.i. played on the swing, swung
ጅው —ያለ ገደል	used as ጅው አድርጎ ጠጣ *ğəww adrəgo täṭṭa* v.t. gulped down —*yälä gädäl* n. precipice
ጅጊ	*ğəgi* n. communal labour cf. ወንፈል፡ ደቦ
ጅግራ	*ğəgra* n. guinea hen
ጆሮ —ሰጠ —ዳግፍ —ጎንድ —ጠቢ ለምለም—	*ğoro* n. ear ; handle of (*a cup*) *goro säṭṭä* v.i. listened attentively —*däggəf* n. mumps —*gənd* n. area around the ears —*ṭäbbi* n. informer *lämläm*— n. lobe
ጆነያ	*ğonəyya* n. sack
ጆፈ አሞራ	*ğoffe amora* n. vulture
ጆፍጆፈ	*ğofğoffe* n. hair-tuft

273

ጎሀነም gähannäm n. Gehenna, Hell

ጎሀነም እሳት gähannämä əsat n. inferno, Hell

ጎሀድ gǎhad adj. open, clear, visible

ጎሀዱ ዓለም gǎhadu aläm the visible world

በጎሀድ bäghad adv. openly, evidently

*ጎለለ *gällälä

ጎለልተኛ gälältäñña adj. aloof secluded, isolated

—አገሮች —agäročč n. neutral states

ጎለልተኛነት gälältäññannät n. neutrality, seclusion

ጎል gəll adj. private exclusive; personal

በጎል bägəll adv. privately

በየጎል bäyyägəll adv. individually

ጎለኛ gəllaňňa adj. individualistic, unsociable

ጎላዊ gəllawi adj. private

—ሀብት —habt n. private property

ጎለል አለ gäläll alä v.i. moved aside, stood aside, gave way; avoided situations

—አደረገ —adärrägä v.t. made to give way, got rid of; segregated

ተጎለለ tägällälä v.i. was segregated, was made to give way; was excluded

አጎለለ agällälä v.t. kept in the background, secluded, got rid of

ራሱን— rasun— v.t. secluded oneself, kept onself aloof, avoided situations

ጎለመ gälämma v.i. became rancid *with pron. suff.*

ጎለመኝ gälämmaňň I have had enough, I got fed up

ጎለሞተ gälämmotä v.i. became a widower

ጋለሞታ galämota n. a widow

ጎልሙትና gəlmutənna n. unmarried life *(after divorce)*

አጎለሞተ agälämmotä v.t. gave shelter to a widow

ጎለበ gälläbä v.t. denudated, stripped off *(s/o's or ones clothes)*

ጎልብ gəlb adj. superficial

ጎልብነት gəlbənnät n. superficiality

ጎለበጠ gäläbbäṭä v.t. turned upside-down ; poured liquid from one container to another; copied *(book)*; overthrew; turned over *(a page)*

ጎልባጭ in አፈር ጎልባጭ äfär gälbač dump-truck

ጎልባጭ gəlläbbač n. copy *(of a book, a letter, a passage etc.)*

ተጎለብባጠ tägälälbbäṭä v. i. was turned upside-down, was overthrown, was copied *(book)*; was turned over, was tipped over; was capsized *(boat etc.)*

ተጎለባበጠ tägäläbabbäṭä v. i. turned over *(changed position)*; changed one's mind *(frequently)*

ተጎላበጠ tägälabbäṭä v.i. turned this way and that

አጎላበጠ aggälabbäṭä v. t. turned this way and that; leafed through *(a book); scrutinised*

274

ጉዳዩን በጥን he scrutinized the
ቃቴ እገላ matter carefully
ብሎ እያ
አስገለበበጠ asgäläbbäṭä v.t had
a book, article etc.
copied
ገለባ gäläba n. straw, chaff,
hull (of peanut etc.);
adj. shallow (not
serious)
ገለታ gäläta n. favour,
gratitude
—ቢስ —bis adj. ungrateful
ገለወደ * gäläwwädä
ገልዋዳ gälwadda n. loafer
ተንገላወደ tängälawwädä v.i.
loafed about
ገለደመ * gäläddämä
ገልድም gäldəm n. skirt (worn
by men; similar to a
kilt)
አገለደመ agäläddämä v.t. wore
a skirt
ገለጃጃ gäläǧǧäǧä v.i. became
senile
ገለጃጅ gäläǧäǧ adj. senile;
awkward
ገልጃጃ gälǧaǧǧa adj. senile;
awkward
ተንገላጃጃ tängälaǧǧäǧä v.i. became senile; became
awkward
ገለገለ * gäläggälä
ገልጋሎት gälgalot n. service
ተገለገለ tägälägälä v. i. was
served; made use of,
employed
ተገልጋይ tägälgay n. clientele
አገለገለ agälägälä v.t. served,
rendered service; was
valid, was in use
አገልጋይ agälgay n. servant
አገልጉሎት agälgəlot n. ser-
vice; use, benefit
አገልገል agälgəl n. a round.
basket for carrying
food etc, during
a journey
ያገለገለ yagäläggälä adj.
second-hand, used
e.g ያገለገለ መኪና
second-hand car
ገለጠ also ገለፀ gälläṭä

v.t. unveiled, un-
covered; explained,
opened (a book)
ገለጠ also ገለፀ gäläṣa,
gäläṣa n. expla-
nation
ገላጣ gäläṭa adj. open
(space without trees)
ገላጭ gäläč in ገላጭ ድር
ሰት —gäläč dərsät
n. expository com-
position
ገላጭ in በገላጭ bägəllač
adv. openly
የደመና— yädämmäna gəllač
n. clear sky (after
being cloudy)
ገልጥ gəlṭ adj. clear,
open; sincere also
ገልጽ ገልጥነት or
ገልጽነት gəltənnät,
gäləsənnät n,
clarity; sincerity
መገለጫ mägläča n. state-
ment, declaration,
communique;expla-
nation, demonsrat-
tion
—ሰጠ —säṭṭä he made
a statement, he
declared
—አወጣ —awäṭṭa he issued
a statement
ገላለጠ gälalläṭä v.t. dis-
closed (a secret);
exposed
ተገለጠ tägälläṭä v.i. was
unveiled, un-
covered; was ex-
plained; was opened
(book); was dis-
closed;was declared
ተጋለጠ tägalläṭä v.i. was
exposed (by reveal-
ing the guilt or
wrong doing); was
exposed(uncovered)
አጋለጠ aggalläṭä v.t. ex-
posed (a plot,wrong
doing)
ገለፈተ * gäläffätä
ገለፈት gäläfät n. bark, rind
ገለፋታም gäläfätam adj. dirty,

275

ገለፈጠ untidy
ገለፈጥ *gäläffäṭä* v.i. smirked
ገልፋጭ *gäläfäṭ* n. smirker
ገለፈፈ *gälfaç* n. smirker
ግልፋፊ *gäläffäfä* v.t. peeled, stripped
ተገለፈፈ *gəläffafi* n. peel
ገላ *tägäläffäfä* v.i. peeled, was stripped
ገላ ነክ *gäla* n. body
  gäla näkk n. underwear
የገላ ሳሙና *yägäla samuna* n. toilet-soap
ገላመጠ *gälammäṭä* v.t. glared at ,stared fiercely
ገልማጫ *gälməççä* n. angry, fierce look
ተገለማመጠ *tägälämammäṭä* v. i. looked here and there *(due to fear)*
ተገላመጠ *tägälammäṭä* v.i. glared at, stared fiercely; looked here and there *(due to fear)*
*ገላታ * *gälatta*
ገልቱ *gältu* adj. unskilled, ignorant, lay
ተንገላታ *tängälatta* v.i. was maltreated, suffered *(hardship)*, was handled roughly
አንገላታ *angälatta* v.t. maltreated, handled roughly
እንግላት *əngələtt* adj. maltreated
ገላገለ *gälaggälä* v.t. intervened between two quarreling, fighting people; relieved from danger; arbitrated
ገላጋይ *gälagay* n. peacemaker
ገልግል *gäləggäl* n. peacemaking; relief
መገላገያ ገን *mäggälagäya gänzäb* n. arbitration fee
ዘብ
ተገላገለ *tägälaggälä* v.i. was arbitrated; delivered (a child) አጅዋን ያለ ችግር ተገላገለች she delivered her child

without difficulty
ጋል *gäl* n. piece of broken earthenware
ገመለ *gämmälä* v.t. baked a large loaf of unleavened bread
ግምል *gəmməl* n. large unleavened bread
ገመል *also* ግመል n. camel
ገመሰ *gämmäsä* v.t. divided into two; ploughed for the first time
ገመሳ *gämäsa* n. ploughing for first time
ገሚስ *gämis* adj. half
ግማሽ *gəmmaš* adj. half
ተገመሰ *tägämmäsä* v. was divided, split into two
ተጋመሰ *tägammäsä* v.i. was. halfway finished
አስገመሰ *asgämmäsä* v.t had land ploughed for the first time; had divided into two
አጋመሰ *aggammäsä* v.t. reached halfway; did half of s/t
አጋማሽ *aggamaš* adj/n. half, middle; halfway
ገመተ *gämmätä* v.t. estimated, evaluated, rated; valued, assessed; assumed, presumed
ዝቅ አድርጎ— *zəqq adärgo*—v.t. underestimated
ከፍ አድርጎ— *käf adärgo*— overestimated
ገማች *gämmač* n. evaluator,
ግምት *gəmmət* n. estimation, assessment, evaluation; guess, assumption
በግምት *bägəmmət* adv. approximately, roughly
ያለግምት ·*yalägəmmət* without estimating; without proper thinking
ተገመተ *tägämmätä* v.i. was estimated, assessed, evaluated, assumed; have a low opinion of s/o

276

አስገመተ	asgämmätä v.t. had s/t, s/o evaluated, rated, assessed	ገም	smell, putrid
ገምና	gämäna n. faults, mistakes		gäm adj. stinking
—ከታች	—kätač one who hides the faults of others	ገማገም	gämagäm n. worthless fellow
		ተጋጋ	tägamma v.i. mis_ treated each other. led a horrible life
ገምናው ተገ ለጠ	gämänau tägällätä he was exposed (his wrong doings were revealed)	ተገማጋ	tägmamma see ተጋጋ
		አገማ	agämma v.t rot, caused to become putrid; put aside to be destroyed
—ወጣ	—wätta his villainy was exposed		
ገመደ	gämmädä v.t. twisted a rope, made a rope; entwined, made (issue) more diffcult	ገምቦ	gämbo also ገንቦ n. amphora, clay pot (medium sized opposed to ጋን and እንስራ.)
ነገር መገመድ ይወዳል	he likes to make things more difficult	የዳም—	yädäm—adj. pretty
ገመድ	gämäd n. rope	ገሞራ	gamora in እሳተ
—አፍ	—af adj. inarticulate		ገሞራ əsatä gämora n. volcano
—ጣለ	—talä v.t. measured land (by means of a rope)	ገሞራው	gämora" n. a tough person (only used by braggarts)
ገመደለ ተገመደለ	gämäddälä v.t. hacked tägämäddälä v.i. was hacked	ገሠሠ	gässäsä in ግሥ ገሠሠ gäss gässäsä v.t. conjugated a verb
ገመገመ	gämäggämä v.t. evaluated, appraised, assessed	ገሣዊ ስም	gässawi səm n. verbal noun
ገ ምጋሚ	gämgami n. evaluator, assessor	ግሠሪያ ገሥ	masàriya gəss finite verb
ግምገማ	gəmgäma n. evaluation, assessment, appraisal	ገሠጸ	gässäsä v.t. reprimanded, rebuked, reproved
ተገመገመ	tägämäggämä v.i. was evaluated, appraised	ግሣጸ	gəssase n. reprimand, rebuke
አስገመገመ	asgämäggämä v.t. had s/o, s/t, evaluated etc; came in torrents (rain)	ተግሣጽ	tägsas n. admonition, reproof, reprimand, also ገሠጠ
ገመጠ	gämmatä v.t. tore off a mouthful, tored chunk off	ገረመ	gärrämä used with. suf.
ግ ግጥ	gəmmač n. chunk	ገረመኝ	gärrämäññ I was astonished, amazed, perplexed
ገጋ	gämma v.i. stank, smelt bad, was putrid	ገሩም	gərum adj. wonderful, marvellous, splendid, magnificient
ግጋት	gəmat n. stink, bad smell		
ግጋታም	gəmatam adj. stinking, having a bad	—ድንቅ	—dənq adj. splendid, marvellous
		ገርማ	gərma n. majesty, dignity
		—ሌሊት	—lelit dreadfulness of the night
		—መለኮት	—mäläkot n. divine power

.277

—መንግሥት	—mängəst n. stately condition
—ሞገስ	mogäs n. respectability
ገርማዊ	gərmawi adj. majestic
ገርማዊ ንጉሠ ነገሥት	Imperial Majesty
ባለገርማ	balägərma adj. respectable
ተገረመ	tägärrämä v.i. was astonished, surprised, amazed, impressed
አስገረመ	asgärrämä v.t. caused to be astonished, surprised, amazed, impressed
አስገራሚ	asgärrami adj. astonishing, amazing, impressive
ገረመመ	gärämmämä v.t. looked maliciously at, looked fiercely at
ገረረ	gärrärä v.i. became scorching (sun); became extremely heated (oven)
ገራራ	gärara adj. scorching
ገረሸ	* gäräššä
ገርሻ	gərša n. relapse
አገረሸ	agäräššä v.i. relapsed
አገረሸበት	agäräššäbbät suffered a relapse
° ገረበበ	* gäräbäbä
ገርባባ	gärbabba adv. ajar
ገርበብ አለ	gärbäbb alä v,i. was ajar; kept quiet, withdrew from discussions
ተንገረበበ	tängäräbäbä v.i. was ajar
ገረኑግ	gäränug n. gerenuk (litocranius walleri)
ገረዘ	gärräzä v.t. circumcised; grafted (plant)
አንደበቱ ያለ ተገረዘ	andäbatu yaltägärräzä adj. ill - mannered, insolent, rude, vulgar
ገረዛ	gərräza n. act of circumcising
ገርዛት	gərzät also ገዝራት gəzrät n. circumcision
ገርዘት	gərrəzat n. circumcision (manner of)
ተገረዘ	tägärräzä v.i. was circumcised
አስገረዘ	asgärräzä had s/o circumcised, had a plant grafted
ገረደፈ	gäräddäfä v.t. pounded coarsely
ገርደፍ	gərddəf adj./n. coarsely pounded (flour)
ገረድ	gäräd n. maid-servant, house-maid
ልጃገረድ	ləǧagäräd n. girl
ወንዳገረድ	wändagäräd n. hermaphrodite (human being)
የቁን ገረድ	yäčən gäräd n. concubine, mistress
ገርድና	gərdənna n. position of maidservant
ገረጀፈ	gäräǧǧäfä v.i. grew old, aged ; became senile ; was tough (meat)
ገርጃፋ	gärǧaffa adj. aged: tough (meat)
ገረገረ	* gäräggärä
ገርጋራ	gärgarra adj . restive (horse); wilful, obstinate
ገርገር	gərrəgərr n. disturbance, panic, turmoil ; riot; commotion; hustle and bustle
አንገራገረ	angäraggärä v.t. became restive (horse); was wilful, obstinate
አንገራጋሪ	angäragari adj. wilful, obstinate
° ገረገበ	* gäräggäbä
ገርገብ	gərgəb adj. lightly boiled (beans peas etc.)
ተንገረገበ	tängäräggäbä v.i. was lightly boiled (beans, peas etc.); was (morally) tortured
አንገረገበ	angäräggäbä v.t

278

boiled lightly *(beans)*;
tortured *(morally)*

ገረገደ **gäräggädä** v.t. fenced;
erected a wall
(wooden)

ገርገድ **gərgəd** n. erected
wooden wall

ገረፈ **gärräfä** v.t. whipped
lashed, flagellated

ገራፊ **gärafi** n. flagellant

ገርፍያ **gərfiya** n. whipping,
flagellating, lashing

ገርፈት **gərrəfat** n. skin
eruption

ገርፍ **gərf** in አሻዋ ገርፍ
n. *ašäwa gərf*
cemented mud wall

ተገረፈ **tägärräfä** v.i. was
whipped, lashed,
flagellated

ገራ **gärra** v.t. tamed,
trained a beast

ጋሪ **gäri** n. animal-
tamer

ጋር **gär** adj. simple-
hearted, good-
natured

ገራጋር **gäragär** adj. naive

ተገራ **tägärra** v.i. was
tamed; trained
(beast)

ያልተገራ **yaltägärra** adj. savage; ill-mannered,
uncouth

አስገራ **asgärra** v.t. had a
beast tamed, trained

ገራም **gärram** adj. pacific,
peaceful; gentle
(horse)

ገሰሰ **gässäsä** violated *in*
መብቱ አይገሰስም *mäbtu
ayəggäsässəm* his
rights are not to be
violated

ሕግ ተገሰሰ **həggᵘa tägässäsä**
she was deflowered

ገሰረ **gässärä** v.t. gulped
(liquid)

ገሰገሰ **gäsäggäsä** v.i. hurried,

walked rapidly,
walked fast

ገሰገሰ **gəsəggase** n. rapid
advance, fast walk
also ገስገሰ

* ጋሰ **gässa**

ገሳት **gəsat** n. belch;
roar *(lion)*

አገሳ **agässa** v.t. belched;
roared *(lion)*

ገሸለጠ **gäšällätä** v.t. peeled off

ተገሸለጠ **tägäšällätä** v.i was
peeled off

ገሸረ **gäššärä** v.t. dumped
(placed)

ገሸር **gaššər** adj. conceited

ተገሸረ **tägäššärä** v.i. sat
idle; was conceited

እንደ ድንጋይ **don't sit over**
አትገሸር there like a stone

*ገሸገሸ **gäšäggäšä**

ተገንሸገሸ **tängäšäggäša** v.i. felt
disgusted, disliked
greatly; had an
aversion to, had
enough of

እንገሸገሸ **angäšäggäšä** v.t.
loathed

ገባሎ **gäbälo** n. type of lizard

ገበረ **gäbbärä** v.t. paid
tribute *(in kind and
money)*

ገባር **gäbbar** n. tenant
farmer

—ወንዝ —**wänz** n. tributary
(river)

ገብረ ሥጋ **gəbrä səga** n. sexual
relations

—መርፈ —**märfe** n. fine
woollen carpet

—ሰዶም —**sädom** n. sodomy

—በላ —**bälla** n. dependants
of a person of
high rank

—አበር —**abbär** n. ac-
complice, partner in
crime, confederate

—ገብ —**gäbb** n. morals

—ጣል —**täll** n. land whose
tax is not paid for
several years and
thus could be claimed
for transfer by

279

	anyone
ግብር	gəbər n. tax, income tax; banquet, feast
ግብር አበላ	gəbər abälla v.t. feasted, gave a feast to
—ዋጓ	—wäha n. douche (for women)
—ከፋይ	—gəbər käfay n. tax-payer
ምግባር	məgbar n. virtue
ተግባር	tägbar n. act, practice; occupation
በተግባር	bätägbar adv. in practice, practically
ተግባራዊ	tägbarawi adj. practical
ገባሬ	gäbäre n. farmer, peasant
(የ)— ግገበር	yä — mähəbär farmers' association, peasants association
ግብርና	gəbrənna n. agriculture, farming
የ— ሚኒስቴር	yä—minister Ministry of Agriculture
ገበር	gäbär n. lining of a garment
ገበርዲን	gäbärdin n. gabardine
*ገበሰበሰ ግብስብስ	* gäbäsäbbäsä gəbəsbəs adj. trash (material)
አግበሰበሰ	agbäsäbbäsä v.t. accumulated indiscriminately
ገበታ	gäbäta n. large wooden bowl (for kneading); dining-table
—ቀረበ	—qärräbä the table is set
—አስደንጋጭ	—asdängaç n. big eater, see ደነገጠ
—ተነሣ/ ከፍ አለ (የ)ገበታ ልብስ	—tänässa/käff alä the table is cleared yä/gäbäta ləbs n. table-cloth
ገበታው ዳነ ገጠ	gäbätaw dänäggäṭä have little food on the table
ገበቴ	gäbäte n. wooden bowl
ገበዝ	gäbäz n. administrator of a church
ግብዝና	gəbəzmna n. the post
	of a gäbäz ገበዘ
ገበየ	gäbäyyä v.t. shopped, went marketing; acquired
ገበያ	gäbäya n. market; market-place
(የ) —ቀን	(yä)—qän n. market-day
ገበያ ቆመ	gäbäya qomä the market is underway
—ተበተተነ	—täbättänä v.t. the market is over
—አለው	—alläw there is demand for (goods); he does a good business
—ዳራ	—därra the market is in full swing
—ወጣ	—wäṭṭa went to the market
ገበያተኛ	gäbäyatäñña n. shopper
ገብይ	gäbyi n. shopper, customer
ተገበያየ	tägäbäyayyä v.t. transacted; made a deal
*ገበደደ ተገባደደ	* gäbäddädä tägäbaddädä v.i. was almost completed (assignment)
አገባደደ	aggäbaddädä v.t. has almost completed
*ገበገበ ገብጋብ	* gäbäggäbä gäbgabbä adj. greedy, stingy, parsimonious
ተስገበገበ	tässgäbäggäbä v.i. was greedy, stingy
ተንገበገበ	tängäbäggäbä v.i. was greedy, stingy; was scorched; suffered (morally)
አንገበገበ	angäbäggäbä v.t scorched; caused to suffer (morally): inflicted pain
አንገብጋቢ ጥያቄ (ጉዳይ)	angäbgabi ṭəyyaqe (gudday) a burning question (issue)
ገበጣ	gäbäṭa n. a game consisting of a board with

280

ገበ	a double row of twelve holes played with pebbles or beads *gäbba* v.i. entered, went in, came in, got in
ልብሱ	*ləbsu qäläm*—have a dress dyed
ቀለም—	
ሸፍታው—	*šəftaw* — the rebel submitted to the authorities
ቃል—	*qal*— he made a promise, he pledged, he guaranteed
ትዝቃዜ ገባው	*qəzəqqaze gäbbaw* he froze *(felt very cold)*
ነገሩ—	*nägäru*—he understood the issue
በነገሩ ገባ	*bänägäru gäbba* he interfered in the matter
ትምህርት ገባው	*təmhərt gäbbaw* he understood, followed, comprehended his subject, lesson
ንስሐ—	*nəssəha* he repented
እሳት ገባው	*əsat gäbbaw* was almost burnt *(by cooking or roasting)*
ከመንገድ ገባ	*kämängäd gabba* he came home from a journey
ወዶ—	*wäddo*— n. volunteer *(military)*
ድህነት ገባው	*dəhnnät gäbbaw* he was impoverished
ጋዶል ገባ	*gädäl gəbba* he was precipitated; he was lost *(had bad luck)*
ጉድጓድ ገባ	*gudguʷad*—he fell into a ditch
ገራ ገባው	*gəra gäbbaw* he was confused, perplexed, was in difficulty, was at a loss
ገብር ገባ	*gəbər gäbba* meal is served *(in the palace or in homes of dignitaries)*
ጣልቃ—	*ṭalqa*—he interfered, meddled

ፀሐይ ገባች	*ṣähay gäbbaččʼ* the sun has set
ገቢ	*gäbi* n. income
—ሽቀጥ	—*šäqäṭ* n. import
—ቀረጥ	—*qäräṭ* n. income-tax
—ገንዘብ	—*gänzäb* n. income
ገቢና ወጭ	*gäbinna wäči* income and expenditure
ገባት	*gəbat in* ገባት መሬት *gəbaṭä märet.* burial
የዶም ገባት	*yädäm gəbat* n. good complexion
ገብ	*gäbb in* ሁለ ገብ *hulä gäbb* adj. comprehensive, versatile
ሰርጎ—	*särgo*–n. infiltrator
ባሕረ—	*bährä*–n. cape
ወሃ— መሬት	*wəha–märet* land with irrigation canals
ወሎ — መንገድ	*wälo–mängäd* one day's roundtrip journey
ዐይነ—	*aynä gäbb* adj. attractive; handsome
ገብረ—	*gəbra gäbb* n. morals adj. polite
ጋብቻ	*gabəčča* n. marriage, matrimony
ገቢ	*gəbbi* n. palace; compound; enclosure; premises
ቅጥር—	*qəṭər*–n. campus
ገቢ ነፍስ ውጪ ነፍስ	be in great trouble
ገብ	*gəb* n. score *(in a game)*, goal *(soccer);* aim, objective
መግቢያ ተገቢ	*mägbiya* n. entrance *tägäbbi* adj. proper appropriate; right *(person)*, appropriate *(choice);* fitting
ተጋባ	*tägabba* v.i. married one another
ገራ—	*gəra*–v.i. he was confused, was at a loss was perplexed
ተገባባ	*tägbabba* v.i. reached an agreement, consented

281

ተግባቢ tägbabi adj. agreeable (ready to agree)

አገባ agäbba v.t. brought in, put into, inserted; scored (a goal); paid back; married

ይግባኝ አለ yəgbaññ älä submitted an appeal (to a law of court)

አገቦ agbo n. veiled insult, sarcasm cf. **አሽሙር**

አጋባ aggabba v.t. emptied a container; arranged marriage, unpacked

ገራ– gära—v.t. confused bedevilled, muddled

አስገባ asgäbba v.t. inserted; let in, admitted; put in; introduced (bring s/t into use for the first time)

አስተጋባ astägabba v.i. echoed, reverberated

ገባሬ ሥናይ gäbare sännay n. priest or deacon who plays major role during the Mass

ገበር see **ገበሬ**

ገብር * gäbr

ገብረ ጉንዳን gäbrä gundan n. skilful type of ant

ገብስ gäbs n. barley

ገተለተለ * gätälättälä

ገትልትል gətəltəl adj. jumbled, disordered

ተገተለተለ tägtälättälä v.i. came, went disorderly

አገተለተለ agtälättälä v.t. carried away or brought with disorderly

ገተረ gättärä v.t. pulled tight, stretched tight

ገታራ gättara adj. stubborn, obstinate

ገትር gəttər adj. stubborn, obstinate, persistent

ተገተረ tägättärä v.i. was stretched tight; stuck around

ተገታተረ tägätattärä v.i. was stretched tighly

ተጋተረ tägattärä v.ik. started one's duties seriously

አጋተረ aggattära v.t. gave a serious assignment

ገተገተ *gätäggätä in **ቁስሉ ገተገተው** his wound throbbed with pain

ገትጋታ gätgatta adj. nagging

ገታ gätta v.t. reined a horse; constrained (temper); repressed (laughter)

ራሱን– rasun-controlled oneself

ተገታ tägätta v.i. was constrained, repressed

ገነባ gänäbba v.t. built (a house etc.),

ገንቢ in **ገንቢ ሂስ** gänbi his n. constructive criticism

ገንባታ gänbata n. bulding up

ገንብ gänb also **ግምብ** gəmb, stone wall

–ቤት —bet n. stone house, concrete building

ገንባኛ gänbäñña also **ግምባኛ** gəmbäñña n. mason, bricklayer

ገነተረ gänättärä v.i. became tougher or leathery (meat for not being well-cooked)

ገንታራ gäntarra adj. wilful

ገንትር gəntər leathery meat

ገነት gännät n. paradise

ምድራ– mədrä - earthly paradise

ገነነ gännänä v.i. was famous, grew (of fame), became illustrious

ገነን in **አምባ ገነን** amba gännän n. dictator, tyrant

ገናና gänana adj. famous, illustrious

ተጋነነ tägannänä v.i. was exaggerated

አጋነነ aggannänä v.t. exaggerated; maximized, overstated

ቃለ አጋኖ qalä agganno n. exclamation

የ–ምልክት yä-mǝləkkǝt exclamation mark

ገነዠ gännäzä v.t. shrouded (a corpse)

ገንዘት gənzät n. putting in a shroud

መገነዣ mägännäža n. shroud

ገነዘበ *gänäzzäbä

ግንዛቤ gənəzzabe n. realisation, awareness

ተገነዘበ tägänäzzäbä v.i. realized, was aware, perceived

አገናዘበ agänazzäbä v.t. compared, counter-checked

አገናዛቢ. ተው ላጠ ስም aggänazabi täwlaţä-səm possessive pronoun

—አፃፋ —aṣäfa – reflexive pronoun

ገነደሰ gänäddäsä v.t cut down (a big tree)

ገነገነ gänäggänä v.i hesitated, was suspicious

ገንጋኝ gängañ adj. hesitant, suspicious

ገነጠለ gänäţţälä v.t. broke-off (branches); detached (the stub)

ግንጣይ gənäţţay cut off branch

ገነጠል gänäţäl n. stick (freshly cut)

—ጌጥ —geţ n. not going with, not matching (clothes)

ገነጣጠለ gänäţaţţälä v.t. cut in pieces

ተገነጠለ tägänäţţälä v.i. was broken off (branch); seceded

ተገንጣይ tägänţay n. sessesionist; faction

ተገነጣጠለ tägänäţaţţälä v.i. fell into pieces

ገነፈለ gänäffälä v.i. boiled over

በቁጣ— bäquţţa–burnt out in anger, was filled with fury

ገንፈል gänfäl adj. boiled

ገንፈልፈል (meat) gänfälfäl əngära boiled in wäţ

*ገነፈ *gänäffa

ገንፎ gänfo n. porridge (of wheat, barley oats etc.)

አገናፈ agänäffa v.t. cooked porridge

ጋና gäna adj. adv. still, yet, but

አሁን ጋና መጣ ahun gäna mäţţa he came just now, he came at this very moment

እንደጋና əndägäna adv. again

ጋና ነው gäna näw it is early, it is not yet

—ናኝ —näññ I am not ready

—ለጋና —längäna on the pretext that s/t will happen

ጋና ለጋና ይመ ጣል ብለህ ተኮን መሉ ተተምጠሀ ትውላለሀ ? Are you going to sit down all day on the pretext that he will come?

ጋና ዞጎ ተበርቄ there is still a long way to go (not at this time)

ጋና ጥዶ same as above

ጋና ጋም ጋና gänna n. Christmas; name of a game played during advent (s/t like hockey); bat (used in the game)

ሰብከተ— səbkätä— advent

also ገምባለ gänbale, gamballe n. boot-tree, legging, puttee

ገንበ see ገምበ

ገንዘብ gänzäb n. money, currency, property see *ገነዘበ

—ሰብሳቢ —säbsabi n. money collector

—ቤት —bet n. treasurer

—ተቀባይ —täqäbbay n. cashier ; receiving teller

—አወጣ —awäţţa spent money

—አይሆንም —ayhonəm he, it is useless

ልጅ ገንዘብ አይሆንም he is a useless boy

—አደረጋ —adärrägä pos-

283

—እጠፉ   sessed, acquired
—aṭäffa squandered money
—hፋይ   —käfay n. paying teller; payer, pay master
ተጠባባቂ   tāṭäbabaqi gänzäb n. reserve fund
ግንዘብ
ዋና ገንዘብ   wanna gänäzb n. capital
ፕሬ—   ṭäre— cash
—ያዥ   —yaž n. treasurer
ገንዳ   •   gända n. trough (for animals to drink from)
ገንጋበት   gängäbät adj. miserly, stingy
• ገኘ   • gäññä
ገንኙነት   gänäññunnät n. relationship, contact, association; communication; intercourse
ገኘት   gäññät n. discovery
ተገኘ   tägäññä v.i. was found; was recovered
ተገናኘ   tägänaññä v.i. met each other; was compatible; had sexual intercourse
አገናኘ   aggänaññä v.t. brought together
አገናኝ መኮ   aggänaññ mäkonnän liaison officer
ንን
አገኘ   ägäññä v.t. found, discovered; earned; came across, met; acquired
አስገኘ   asgäññä v.t. brought in (money, wealth); produced, resulted in
• ገዋለለ   • gäwällälä
ተንገዋለለ   tängäwallälä v.i. was looked down upon, was belittled
አንገዋለለ   angäwallälä v.t. looked down, belittled
ገዉዝ   gäwz n. nut
ገዘረ   see ገረዘ
ገዘተ   gäzzätä v.t. anathematised; applied sanctions against
ገዝት   gäzzät n. sanction, ban
ተገዘተ   tägäzzätä v.i. swore

አስገዘተ   gave one's words asgäzzätä v.t. had (s/o) swear
ገዘገዘ   gäzäggäzä v.t. sawed ; cut with difficulty (with dull blade); weakened (of prolonged illness)
ገዘጋዛ   gäzgazza adj. stammering; stubborn, heavy-headed
ገዘፈ   gäzzäfä v.i. was stout, was fat
ገዘፍ   gäzäf n. stoutness, fatness, massiveness
ገዙፍ   gäzuf adj. tall and fat; gigantic; massive
ግዘፈት   gäzfät n. massiveness ; stoutness, fatness
አገዘፈ   agäzäfä in ልቡን— läbbun–v.t. was conceited,
ገዛ   gäzza v.t. bought, purchased ; ruled over, dominated; hired a lawyer
ነፍስ—   näfs–became conscious (aware of)
አዳብ—   adäb–became polite
ገዥ   gäž n. buyer ; master ; ruler
ገዛት   gäzat n. area of jurisdiction, territory of a state, realm
ቀዥ—   qäžž— n. colony (territory)
የገዛ ልጁ   yägäzza läžu his own son
—ራሴ   —rase I myself
በገዛ እጁ   bägäzza äžže by myself
—ፈቃዴ   bägäzza fäqade on my own accord , by myself
ገዥ   gäžž n. bargain, buy, transaction
ተገዛ   tägäzza v.i. was ruled, was subdued
ተገዥ   tägäž n. subject (under s/o's rule)

ተገዛዛ	tägäzzazza v.i. transacted
ተጋዛ	tägazza v.i. occupied land as a tenant, leased (land as a tenant)
ተጋዥ	tägaž n. tenant
መጋዞ	mäggazo n. rent (of land)
አጋዛ	aggazza v.t. leased land to a tenant
ገደለ	gäddälä v.t. killed, massacred, murdered, put to death
ራሱን—	rasun— committed suicide
ገዳይ	gäday n. killer
ነፍስ—	näfsä — n. murderer, killer
ገድል	gädl n. saint's life (acta sanctorum)
ገድለኛ	gäläñña adj. miraculous
ባለገድል	balägädl adj. miraculous
ግዳይ	gädday n. trophy; booty (captured from the enemy)
—ቆጠረ	—qoṭṭärä displayed one's booty (captured from the enemy)
ግድያ	gädäyya ʳ. killing
ተገደለ	tägäddälä v.i. was killed
ተጋደለ	tägaddälä v.i. killed one another; fought
ተጋድሎ	tägadälo n. fighting; campaign (against social evils)
ተጋዳይ	tägaday n. warrior
አስገደለ	asgäddälä v.t. had s/o killed
ገደል	gädäl n. precipice, cliff
ገደላማ	gädälamma adj. precipitous
ገደላገደል	gädälagädäl adj. full of precipices
ገደል ሰደደ	gädäl säddädä v.t. got s/o into trouble
—ገባ	—gäbba see ገባ

የገደል ማሚት	yägädäl mammito n. echo
* ገደመ	*gäddämä
ገደማ	gädäma adv. approximately, roughly; hereabout
እዚህ ገደማ	hereabouts, round
ወደ ስድስት ሰዓት ገደማ	towards 12 o'clock
ጋድም	gadəm in ጋድም ወንበር gadəm wänbär n. bench
ግድም	gədəm n/adv᷄ area, place; near, around
ጋድሚያ	gadmiya n. heavy sleeper
አገደመ	agäddämä v.t. passed by
አግድመት	agdəmät n. plane
አግድም	agdəm adj. horizontal, transverse
አግድሞሽ	agdəmoš adv. horizontally
አግድም አየዉ	agdəm ayyäw he looked at him spitefully
አጋደመ	aggaddämä v.t. laid (s/o), (s/t) down
አግዳሚ ወንበር	agdami wänbär n. bench
—ጠረጴዛ	—ṭäräppeza n. desk (long)
አላፊ አግዳሚ	alafi agdami n. passers-by
* ገደረደረ	*gädäräddärä
ገድርዳራ	gädärdarra adj. pretentious
ግድርድር	gədərdər adj. pretentious
ተገደረደረ	tägädäräddärä v.i. pretended (not to want, or like s/t)
ተግድርዳሪ	tägdärdari adj. pretentious
ገደበ	gäddäbä v.t. made a dam, dammed
ገደብ	gädäb n. limit, limitation; probation
—አደረገ	—adärrägä v.t. stipulated
—የሌለዉ	—yälelläw absolute (limitless)
ያፍ—	yaf—limit of what one should say

285

ግድብ   gəddəb n. dam, dike, barrage

*ገደደ
ገዳዳ   *gäddädä
gäddada adj. twisted, crooked, bent

ተንጋደደ   tängäddädä v.i. became twisted, bent

አንጋደደ   angaddädä v.t. twisted, bent

*ገደደ   *gäddädä with pron suff. in mən gäddädäñ ምን ገደደኝ I agree with, o.k., I have no objection

ገዳጅ   gəddağ n. duty, obligation

ገዴታ   gəddeta n. duty, obligation compulsory; condition (stipulation)

በግድ   bägədd adv. by force, unwillingly

ያለውድ በግድ   yaläwədd bägədd by force

ገድ ሆነበት   gədd honäbbät he was forced, he couldn't do otherwise

—የለም   —yälläm never mind
—የለውም   —yälläwəm he is careless, he does'nt mind
—የለሽ   —yälläš adj. careless
ምን ገደ   mən gädde what do I care?

ተገደደ   tägäddädä v.i. was compelled, was forced; was obligated

አጋደደ   aggaddädä v.t. was useful, was helpful
ምን አገደኝ   mən agäddoññ I am not against it

አስገደደ   asgäddädä v.t. forced, brought pressure on, compelled

ገዳገደ   gädäggädä v.t. erected a wooden wall
ገድጋዳ   gədgadda n. wall
*ገዳገደ   *gädäggädä
ተንጋዳገደ   tängädaggädä v.i. staggered
አንጋዳገደ   angädaggädä v.t. staggered
ገደፈ   gäddäfä v.t. broke the

fast; made a mistake omitted

ገድፈት   gədfät n. a non-fasting day; omission, error

አገደፈ   agäddäfä v.t. made s/o break the fast; had s/o err (while writing etc.)

አስገደፈ   asgäddäfä v. t. had s/o made a mistake (while writing etc.)

ገዶ   gädde n. buzzard (kind of falcon)

ገድ   gädd n. good luck, good omen

ገድ ቢስ   gäddä bis adj. ill-omened, unlucky

ገዳማ   gäddamma adj. lucky (things e. g. number)

ገዳም   gäddam adj. lucky (person)

ገድ በለኝ   gädd bäläññ wish me good luck
—የለሽ   —yälläš adj. ill-omened, unlucky

ገድለ   see ገደለ
*ገገመ   * gäggämä
ገገምተኛ   also ገመምተኛ gämämtäñña n. convalescent

አገገመ   agäggämä v.i. convalesced

ገገረ   gäggärä v.i. became hard, solid (liquid)
ገገር   gəggər adj. hard, solid

ገጠመ   gäṭṭämä v.t. fitted together, joined together; fitted in, joined (bad people); fixed, repaired; matched (game); engaged (the enemy;) wrote poetry; rhymed

ገጠም   gäṭṭäm in ኩታ ገጠም መሬት plots of land adjoining one another

ገጠሚ   gäṭami in ገጥም—gəṭəm–poet

ገጥሚያ   gäṭmiya n. match (game); confrontation, engagement (battle)

ኳስ—   kuʷas-football match

ግጥም   gäṭäm n. poetry, poem

ግጥም አለ   gäṭṭämm alä died suddenly

ገጣጠመ   gäṭaṭṭämä v.i. reassembled (machinery etc.)

ግጥም—   gäṭäm-scribbled poetry

ተጋጠመ   tägäṭaṭṭämä v.i. was fitted together; was assembled (car etc.); confronted each other

መገጣጠሚያ   mäggäṭaṭämiya n. joint (of body etc.)

ተጋጠመ   tägaṭṭämä v.i. met (teams); confronted

ፊት ለፊት-   fit läfit-was confronted with (enemy); coincided (events)

ተጋጣሚ   tägaṭami n. contestant, adversary (in contest of any kind)

አገጣጠመ   aggäṭaṭṭämä v.t. assembled (car etc.); made people confront each other (to settle disagreements or misunderstandings)

አጋጠመ   aggaṭṭämä v.t. brought together

ምን አጋጠ መህ ፤   what has happened to you ?

አንድ አንጂሳ አጋጠመኝ፤   I ran across a lion

አጋጣሚ ነገር፤ በአጋጣሚ   an unexpected thing bä'aggaṭami adv. by chance, unexpectedly

የአጋጣሚ ነገር   yä'aggaṭami nägär just by chance

ገጠር   gäṭär n. rural area, countryside

የገጠር መሬት   yägäṭär märet rural land

ገጠሬ   gäṭäre 'n. countryman (person living in rural land)

ገጠበ   gäṭṭäbä v.t wounded (especially the back of a beast of burden)

ገጣባ   gäṭaba adj. wounded (back of a beast of burden)

ተገጋጠበ   tägäṭaṭṭäbä v.i. was full of scratches and wounds

ገጠገጠ   gäṭäggäṭä v.t. built houses close together

ገጥገጥ ያለ መንደር   a dense village

ገጠጠ   gäṭṭäṭä in ጥርሱ ገጠጠ ṭärsu gäṭṭäṭä had teeth too long

ገጣጣ   gäṭaṭa adj. bucktoothed

ገጦ   in ገጦ ለጣይ gäṭṭo läṭay one who cannot close his mouth because of his protruding teeth (insult)

ተንጋጠጠ   tängaṭṭäṭä v.i. was bent

አንጋጠጠ   angaṭṭäṭä v.i. looked upwards; lifted up one's eyes

ገጥ   *gäṭṭ

ገጥታ   gäṭṭäta n. direction

ገጠ ቢስ   gäṭṭä bis adj. grace less

ገጨ   gäǯǯä v.t. bumped, knocked against; run over (vehicle)

ገጨኸኝ   gäǯǯähäññ adj. crude, coarse (manners, person)

ግጭት   gäǯǯät n. collision; crash, clash, friction conflict misunderstanding

ገጭ አለ   gäǯǯ alä v.i. came suddenly

ተገጨ   tägäǯǯä v.i. bumped on s/t

ተጋጨ   tägaǯǯä v.i. knocked, against, crashed had a conflict with, clashed (be in disagreement)

አገጫጨ   aggäǯaǯǯä in ብርቀቁ አገጫጨ bärčäqqo

287

አጋሙ

	aggäčäččä toasted (raising glasses)
	aggaččä v. t. clashed (objects); hit s/o violently; created a conflict, animosity between
*ገጪገጪ	*gäčäggäčä
ተንገጫገጪ	tängäčaggäčä v.i rattled, jerked along
አንገጫገጪ	angäčaggäčä v.t. rattled; jolted
ገጽ	gäṣṣ n. face (of earth); page (of book)
ገጸ መልካም	gäṣṣä mälkam adj. beautiful, handsome
—ቢስ	—bis adj. ugly
—ባሕርይ	—bähräy n. character (in a novel, short story)
ገጽታ	gaṣṣäta n. appearance, look
ገፋተ	* gäffätä
ገፋት	gäfät n. scum
ገፋተረ	gäfättärä v.t. pushed s/o violently, shoved
ተገፋተረ	tägäfättärä v.i. pushed at
ገፋገፋ	gäfäggäfä v.t. spent a miserable life አስር ዓመት እስር ቤት ገፍ ግፍ ወጣ was released after ten miserable years in prison
ተንገፋገፋ	tängäfäggäfä v.i. was disgusted, had a strong aversion to
አንገፋገፋ	ängäfäggäfä v.t. had a strong dislike to, was filled with dismay; disgusted
*ገፋጠጠ	* gäfäṭṭätä
ገፋጠጥ	gäfäṭäṭ adj. protuberant
ገፍጣጣ	gäfṭaṭṭa adj. protuberant
ተንገፋጠጠ	tängäfäṭṭäṭä v.i. became big-bellied
አንገፋጠጠ	angäfäṭṭäṭä v.t. bellied
ገፋፋ	gäffäfä v.t. stripped off (garment); divested (an official of

	power and authority); skimmed
ገፋፋ	gäfäffa n. exploitation , exorbitant (price)
ገፋፊ	gäfafi n. exploiting (selfish)
ተገፋፋ	tägäffäfä v.i. was stripped off; was skinned; was divested; was skimmed
ገፋ	gäffa v.t. pushed, shoved; mistreated
ሥራውን—	särawən—he made good progress (in ones duties)
ትምህርት—	təmhərt—he advanced in studies
እድሜ—	ədmew—he has advanced in years
ወሰን—	wäsän–trespassed (land
ወተት—	wätät— v.t. churned
ቢገፋ ቢገፋ ገፋ	bigäfa bigäfa utmost in አፋር ገፋ afär gäfi peasant (insult)
በገፍ	bägäf adv. abun‿ dantly, in great quantity
ግፊት	gəffit n. pressure (power), impulse
ግፊያ	gffəya n. crush (persons; pushing, pressing)
ገፋ ቢል	gəfa bil if the worst comes
ግፍ	gəf n. injustice, unfairness, violence, atrocity
—ሥራ	—särra did an injustice
—ዋለ	—walä committed evil
—ፈጸመ	—fäṣṣämä committed an atrocious crime
ግፈኛ	gəfäñña adj. wicked, cruel; atrocious
ገፋፋ	gäfaffa v.t. instigated, pressed strongly, motivated, put pressure

ተገፋ on *tägäffa* v.i. went forward *(work)*; was maltreated

ተገፊ *tägäfi* adj. maitreated

ተጋፋ *tägaffa* v.i. shoved one another, pressed *(push)*

ሥልጣን — *səlṭan*— was disrespectful, he went over his head

ተጋፍቶ አለፈ *tägafto älläfä* he forced his way through

ተገፋፋ *tägäfaffa* v.i. was instigated, motivated

ጉላንጆ *gulunǧo* n. gristle tough *(meat)*; ugly

ጉልላት *gulləlat* n. dome, cupola

ጉልማ *guləmma* n. plot of land *(given to s/o)*

ጉልባን *gulban* n. thickly boiled beans and wheat *(served on Good Friday)*

ጉልት *see* ጎለት

ጉሎ *gulo* n. castor plant

—ፍሬ —*fəre* n. castor bean

—ዘይት —*zäyət* n. castor oil

ጉማ *guma* n. blood money, ransom

—በላ —*bälla* took blood money

ጉማሬ *gumarre* n. hippopotamus

—አለንጋ —*alänga* lash made of hippopotamus skin

ጉም *gum* n. mist, fog

የጉም ሽንት *yägum šənt* n. drizzle

—ጅብ —*ǧəb* adj. stingy, niggardly

ጉማም *gumam* adj. foggy, misty

ጉምሩክ *gumruk* n. customs office, customs house

የጉምሩክ *yägumruk qärät*

ቀረጥ duty paid at the customs

ጉም ጉም አለ *gumm gumm alä* v.i. grumbled *(complained)*; grumbled *(thunder)*

ጉምጉምታ *gumgumta* n. grumbling *(complaint; thunder)*

ጉረኛ *guränno* n. enclosure *(for sheep and goats)*

ጉራ *gurra* n. bragging, boasting, show-off

—ነዛ —*näzza* bragged, boasted

—ነፋ —*näffa* bragged, boasted

ጉረኛ *gurränña* n. braggart, boaster

ጉራማይሌ *quramaile* n. type of black-bird, *(black and green coloured)*; tattoo *(of the gum of the teeth at intervals)*

ጉራቻ *gurračča* adj. black *(for horse)*

ጉራች *gurračč* name given to a black horse

ጉራንጉር *gurangur* adj. rugged, rough *(place)*

ጉራጌ *gurage* Gurage land, Gurage people

ጉሬ *gure, also gore* ጎሬ n. den, lair

ጉሬዛ *gureza* n. colobus monkey *(Colobus abysinicus)*

ጉሬዛማ *gurezamma* adj. black and white coloured

ጉርጥ *gurṭ* n. toad

ጉርር *gurorro; also* ጉረሮ *gurärro* n. throat

ጉሽርጥ *gušrəṭṭ* n. plant with oblong tubers used by women for colouring their hands and feet

ጉብት *gubbät* n. liver

የጉብት በሽታ *yägubbät bäššita* n. liver cancer

ጉባኤ *guba'e* n. conference, assembly, congregation

—ቃና —*qana* ge'ez poem of two stanzas

—ነገረ —*näggärä* taught the commentary of the Bible

ቃለ— *qalä*— n. minutes (of a meeting)

—ተቀመጠ —*täqämmäţä* sat in a conference

—አደረገ —*adärrägä* held a conference

አፈ— *afä*—n. chairman (arch.)

ጠቅላላ— *ţäqlalla*—General Assembly

ጉብታ *gubbţa* n. hillock

ጉብ አለ *gubb alä* v.i. sat tight

ጉባኛ *gubäñña* n. spy (arch.)

ጉቦ *gubbo* n. bribe

—ሰጠ —*säţţä* v.t. bribed

—በላ —*bälla* v.t. took bribes

ጉቦኛ *gubboñña* n. one who takes bribes

ጉትቻ *gutəčča* n. car-ring

ጉትያ *gutəyya* n. crest (of bird), tuft of hair on children's head

ጉቶ *gutto* n. tree stump

ጉኒና *gunina* n. cap (head-covering)

ጉንዳን *gundan* n. ant

ጉንፋን *gunfan* n. common cold

ጉንፋን ያዘው *gunfan yazäw* he caught cold

ጉያ *guyya* n. lap

ጉዳይ *gudday* n. matter, business ; problem

—የለኝም *gudday yälläññəm* I don't care a pin

ጉዳዬ አይደለም *guddaye aydälläm* it is not my business

ጉዳይ ፈጻሚ *gudday fäşşami* solicitor, chargé d'affaires

ባለጉዳይ *balägudday* person with a case in the court, person who

has problem to be discussed with an official

ጉዳይ *gudday* less, to ለሦስት አሥር ጉዳይ ten to three

ጉድ *gud* adj. strange surprising, unusual

ወይ *wäy*—what a strange thing, how strange, what a wonder

ጉዳኛ *gudäñña* adj. surprising strange

ጉድ አወጣ *gud awäţţa* divulged

—አደረገ —*adärrägä* deluded

—ፈላ —*fälla* something strange has happened

ጉድ ጉድ አለ *gudd gudd alä* v.i. bustled about

ጉድብ *gudba* n. ditch

ጉዶ *guddo* n. short curved sword, scimitar

ጉጉት *guggut* n. owl ; anxiety see ጓጓ

ጉጉት *gugut* see ጓጓ

ጉጉ *gugu* ጓጉ see ጓጓ

ጉግማንጉግ *gugmangug* n. Gog and Magog

ጉግስ *gugs* n. polo-type game

ጉጠት *guţät* n. pincers, pliers forceps cf. ፈቻል

ጉጥ *guţ* n. stump (of a branch)

ጉፍታ *gufta* n. scarf (hair-covering used by Moslem women)

ጊንጥ *ginţ* n. scorpion

ጊዜ *gize* n. time

—የወለደው —*yäwällädäw* adj. recent, transitory; haphazard; modern

—ያለ — —*yalä* –late at night ባጊዜ *bägize* adv. on time, early

ጊዜው አይደለም ለም *gizew aydälläm* it is unseasonal, premature

ጊዜያዊ *gizeyawi* adj. provisional, tentative,

290

ሁ-ልጊዜ	interim, temporary
ሌላ—	hullgize adv. always
	lela— adv. another time
መን—	mən— adv. when? at what time
—ጊዜም	—gizemm adv. always, all along; at any time
በሆነ ጊዜ	bahonä gize adv. at a certain stage; sometimes; any time
በቅርብ—	bäqərb—adv. in the near future, shortly
በዛሬ—	bäzare—adv. nowadays
በየጊዜው	bäyyägizew adv. often, constantly, from time to time, regularly
ባሁኑ ጊዜ	bähunu gize adv. nowadays
ባለ—	balä—a man of the world; powerful, influential man
ባንድ—	band—adv. at once; simultaneously; immediately
ብዙ—	bəzu— adv. often
ብዙወን—	bəzuwən— adv, most of the time
ትርፍ—	tərf spare time; leisure
ትንቢት—	tənbit—future tense
ኅላፊ—	halafi—perfect (past) tense
አለ—	alä—adv. late, untimely
አንድ—	and—adv. once
አብዛኛውን	abazññawən—adv. most of the time
ከቅርብ— ወዲህ	käqərb—wädih adv. in recent times
ከ—ወደ—	ka—wädä—adv. from time to time
ከፉ ጊዜ	kəfu gize n. famine
ከፍላ—	kəflä—n. period
የዚህን—	yäzihən—adv. at this time, then
የዚያን—	yäzziyan–at that time, then

ያለ—	yalä—untimely, inopportunely, prematurely
ያን—	yann—adv. at that time, then
ጥቂት—	təqit—adv. for a short while
ጊዳር	gidär n. heifer
ጋለ	galä v.i. was hot, was red from heating (metal); was heated (discussion, argument)
የጋለ ብረት	yägalä bərät heated metal
—ስሜት	səmmet enthusiasm, ardour, fervent desire
ግለት	gəlät n. heat, hotness
የፀሐይ—	yäṣähay—the heat of the sun
ተጋጋለ	tägagalä v.i. was heated (discussion, argument)
አጋለ	agalä v.t. made hot (metal etc.)
አጋጋለ	aggagalä v.t. heated up (discussion); instigated
ጋለበ	galläbä v.t. rode (a horse, bicycle etc.); made to gallop
	ልበ አበሻ ፈለገ he wanted to have full control over me
ግልቢያ	gəlbiya n. horse riding, galloping
ጋመ	gamä v.i. heated up
ተጋጋመ	tägagamä v.i. be on fire
አጋጋመ	aggagamä v.t. fired (caused to begin burning)
ጋማ	gamma n. mane (of horse, mule)
የጋማ ከብት	yägamma käbte n. beast of burden
ጋሜ	gamme n. hair-do of a girl
ጋሞ ጎፋ	gamogofa n. one of the Administrative Regions, southern Ethiopia
ጋረ	garä v.i. toiled; tried

ጋር
በጋር በግር

ግረት ጥረት

ጋረደ

ግርዶሽ
የጨረቃ—

የፀሐይ—

ተጋረደ

መጋረጃ

ጋረጠ

ጋረጥ

ተጋረጠ

ጋሪ

የእጅ—
ጋሪ ነጂ
ጋራ
ጋራማ

ጋራዥ

ጋሬ

ጋሻበ

ጋሻ
—ዣግሬ
—መሬት

one's best
gar n. toil
bagär bäṭar with
tremendous toil
and agony
gərät ṭärät toil and
agony
garrädä v.t. veiled,
covered, concealed,
screened; curtained
off; blinded
gərdoš n. screen,
veil: eclipse
yäčäräqa—lunar
eclipse
yäṣähay—solar
eclipse
tägarrädä v.i. was
veiled, covered,
concealed, screened,
was covered by
curtains
mäggaräǧa n. cur-
tain
garräṭä v.t. pricked
(for thorns and
stubs of pointed wood)
gareṭa n. prickle (of
plants), thorns
tägarräṭä v.i. stood
in one's way
gari n. carriage, horse-
drawn car, cart
yä'ǧǧ--n. wheelbarrow
gari näǧi n. carter
gara n. mountain
garamma adj. moun-
tainous
see ጋር
garaǧ n. garage,
hangar
garre n. ǝnǵera made
out of flower of
mixed grains (in-
ferior quality)
gaššäbä v.i. grew pre-
cociously (plants)
gašša shield
—ǧagre n. equerry
—märet land measur-
ing appr. 40

ጋሺ/ጋሼ

ጋበዘ

ጋባዥ

ግብዣ

ተጋበዘ

ጋተ

ተጋተ

አጋተ

ጋነን

ጋነናም

ጋነን ጐታች

ጋን

የደም—
የጠምነጃ—

ጋንደያ

ጋንጢጥ

*ጋዘ

ግዘት

ግዘተኛ

hectares
gašše, or gaššayye term
used by a younger
brother or sister to
address an older
brother (also used
to address any
person older than
oneself) cf. እትዬ
gäbbäzä v.t. invited to
a meal; treated to;
offered (drinks,
cigarettes etc.)
gabaž n. host, host-
ess (woman en-
tertaining guests)
gǝbžža n. invitation,
reception, party,
feast
tägabbäzä v.i. was
invited; threatened
to beat, kill s/o;
bid defiance to
gatä v.t. let a child
drink out of the hand
tägatä v.i. made to
drink (unwillingly,
e.g medicine)
agatä v.t. started
having a larger
udder
ganen n. demon, evil
spirit adj. wicked (pl.
አጋንንት aganǝnt)
ganenam adj. moody,
bad-tempered
ganen gottač n.
sorcerer
gan n. very large
pitcher used in
making beer
yädäm—n. artery
yäṭämänǧa — n.
chamber (of gun)
gandǝyya n. a fat lazy
person
ganṭiṭ adj. scornful,
contemptuous, sniffy
* gazä
gǝzot n. banishment,
confinement
gǝzotäñña person in
banishment

ግዞት ቤት	gəzot bet n. banishment *(place)*	
መጋዣ	mägažža n. beast of burden *(horse)*	
ተጋዘ	tägazzä v.i. was banished, was put in prison, was under house arrest	
አጋዘ	agazä v.t. banished, exiled; carried away, transported	
ጋዝ	gaz n. petroleum, kerosene, gas	
ጋየ	gayyä v.t. was set on fire	
አጋየ	agayyä v.t burnt off, set on fire	
*ጋደለ	*gaddälä also አጋደለ agaddälä v.i. leaned to one side, inclined	
ጋዲ	gadi n. strip of leather etc., for tying the hind legs of a cow when milking	
ጋገረ	gaggärä v.t. baked bread	
ጋጋሪ	gagari in ዳቦ ጋጋሪ dabbo — n. baker	
እንጀራ—	ənğära—ənğära baker	
ዳቦ መጋገሪያ	dabbo mägagariya n. oven; bakery	
ተጋገረ	tägaggärä v.i. baked formed a thick layer; was sticky	
ጋጋ	gagga v.i. slapped *(someone's face)*	
*ጋጋ	*gagga	
ጋጋታ	gagata n. uproar, clamour, haste	
ተንጋጋ	tängagga v.i. flocked together	
አንጋጋ	angagga v.t. drove flock	
ጋጋኖ	gagano n. water-hen	
ጋጠ	gaṭä v.t. grazed, pastured; gnawed a bone	
ጋጠ ወጥ	gaṭä wäṭ adj. impolite, rude	
ግጦሽ	gəṭoš n. pasture, grazing land	
ግጣህ ውጣ	gəṭäh wəṭa move heaven and earth,	

stick it out
ሰው መጋጥ ይወዳል
he likes to backbite people

ራብ ጋጠኝ	rab gaṭäññ I am terribly hungry	
አጋጠ	agaṭä v.t. pastured, grazed	
መጋጫ	mägaça n. grazing land	
ጋጠጠ	gaṭṭäṭä v.t. cut s/t back; cut badly, cut very short	
ጋጣ	gaṭa, also ጋጥ gaṭ n. stable, pen *(cattle)*, stall *(horse)*	
ጌሾ	gešo n. a plant, the leaves of which are used in the preparation of beer and mead ሆፕ hop, buckthorn	
ጌታ	geta n. lord, master; owner; adj. rich *(having much money or property)*	
ጌታው	getaw n. Sir! Mr.!	
ጌታዬ	getaye My Lord!	
ጌቶች	getočč Master	
ጌትነት	getənnät wealthiness, richness	
ለጌታ አደራ	lägeta addärä was in someones service	
የጌታ	yaneta term used in addressing one's teacher, master	
ጌጅ	geğğ n. gauge, gage	
ጌጥ	geṭ n. decoration ornament, adornment, jewelery	
ጌጣኛ	geṭäñña adj. well decorated	
ጌጣጌጥ	geṭageṭ n. jewelery	
ተጊያጊያጠ	tägiyagiaṭä n. put ornaments on, decorated oneself	
አጌጠ	ageṭä v.t. was decorated; well-dressed	
ግላስ	gəlas n. caparison *(of a horse)*	
ግል	see ገለለ	

ገልጋል **gəlgāl** n. lamb, kid, cub (young of animals)

ገልጋል እንግ **gəlgāl ansa** type of eagle that snatches kids, lambs

ገልባጥ see ገለበጠ

ገልምጣ see ገለመጠ

ገልደም see *ገለደም

ገልጥ see ገለጠ

ገልፍ አለዉ **gəlləff allāw** v.i. he got mad (suddenly)

ገልፍተኛ **gəlaftāñña** adj. hot-blooded, ill-tempered, ill-natured

ገልፍታም **gəllaftam** adj. same as above

ገልጽ see ገለጠ or ገለጸ

ገመል also ገመል **gəmāl**, ¦ **gāmāl** n. camel

ገግደ መስቀል **gəmmadā māsqāl** piece of the cross on which Christ was crucified

ገም see ገግ

ገምሩክ **gəmruk** ገምሩክ also **gumruk** n. customs office, customs house

ገምባር **gəmbar**, also ገንባር **gənbar** n. forehead; brow; front (military); luck

—ለገምባር —**lāgəmbar** face to face, vis-a-vis cf. ፊት ለፊት

ገምባረ ቦታ **gəmbarā boqa** adj. white spotted (cow on the forehead)

ገምባሩን ቋጠረ **gənbarun qʷəṭṭārā** v.i. frowned

ገምባሩ የማይታጠፍ **gəmbaru yāmmayəttaṭṭāf** adj. daring, bold

ገምባራም **gəmbaram** adj. lucky

ገምባር የለለዉ **gəmbar yālellāw** unlucky, unfortunate

—ቀዳም —**qāddām** n. fore-front, vanguard

—አስመታ —**asmātta** v.i. waited at someone's house or office for favour

ባለገምባር **balāgəmbar** adj. lucky, fortunate

የጦር ገምባር **yāṭor gəmbar** front line; battle field

ገም ገም አለ **gəmm gəmm alā** v.i. thundered (from a distance); started uprising, rebellion

ገምገምታ **gəmgəmta**, thunder; starting of an uprising, a rebellion

ገምት see ገመተ

ገምጅ **gəmǧa** n. silk or velvet cloth with embroidery; muslin

ገምጅ ቤት **gəmǧa bet** n. treasury, storehouse

ገሥ see ገሠሠ

ገሹም see ገረመ

ገራ **gəra** n. left adj. difficult

ገራም ነፈሰ ተነ **gəram nəfāsā tānni** whatever may happen

ገራ ተመስ **gəra qāmmās** left oriented, tending left (politically)

—ቀኝ —**qāññ** n. drill (military)

—ቢስ —**bis** adj. clumsy, ungraceful

—አክራሪ —**akrari** ultra-leftist

ገራዝማች **gərazmač** commander of the left (title)

ገራ እጋባ **gəra aggabba** v.t. bewildered, puzzled, perplexed

—ክንፍ —**kənf** n. left-wing

—ወንበር —**wānbar** one of the three judges in a court sitting on the left side

—ገባዉ —**gābbaw** v.i. was bewildered, puzzled, perplexed

—ጌታ —**geta** a church authority who stands in the outermost corridor of the

294

	church
—ጎንደር	—gondär n. slave (euphemism)
ግራኝ	gᵊrañ ñ adj. left-handed
graማፎን	gᵊramafon n. gramophone, phonograph
ግራም	gram n. gramme
ኪሎ—	kilo— n. kilo-gramme
ግራC	gᵊrar n. acacia abessinica
ግራዋ	gᵊrawwa n. vernonia mycrocephala
ግራጫ	gᵊraččʼa adj. grey (only for donkeys and mules)
ግርግ	see ግረም
ግር አለ	gᵊrr alä v.i. was confused
ግር ግር አለ	gᵊrr gᵊrr alä v.i was in a state of confusion
ግርኝ	see ግረኘ
ግርዶሽ	see ጋረደ
—ግ በስተ—	gᵊrge n. foot (of bed) ŏästä— adv. at the foot of
ግርግር	see * ገረገረ
ግሣ	gᵊssᵊlla n. panther
ግሽንግስ	gᵊssangᵊs n. junk, hodge-podge, rubbish.
ግቢ	see ገባ
ግበC	see ገበረ
—ግባዝ	gᵊbbᵊz n. hypocrite adj. not strong enough (construction)
ግብጥ	see ግብዐ
ግብዐ	gᵊbş n. Egypt
ግብጻዊ	gᵊbşawi n. Egyptian
ግተልተል	see* ገተለተለ
ግትC	see ገተረ
ግተት	gᵊttät adj. naïve, foolish n. an old basket
ግታቻ	gᵊtᵊ ččʼa adj. stupid, inactive; worth nothing
ግጫ	gᵊ ččʼa n. tuft of hard grass
ግን	gᵊn (sometimes) ግና adv. prep. rel. pron., conj. but, however

ነገC—	nägär—but
ዳሩ—	daru—but
ግንበኝ	see ገነባ
ግንባC	see ግምባC
ግንቦት	gᵊnbot n. May
ግንዘት	see ገነዘ
ግንዲላ	see ግንድ
ግንድ	gᵊnd n. trunk (of tree); block (of wood)
ግንደቆርቁር	gᵊndä qorqur n. woodpecker
ግንዲላ	gᵊndilla n. log (of tree)
የዘር ግንድ	yäzär gᵊnd n. genealogy
ጾር ግንድ	goro gᵊnd n. temple
ግንጥል	see ግንጠለ
ግንጭል	gᵊnčʼäl n. jaw
ግኡዝ	gᵊ'uz n. inanimate
—ዮታ	—şota n. neuter gender
ግዕዝ	gᵊ'ᵊz n. Geez language (a classical language of Ethiopia)
ግዘት	see ጋዘ
ግዳይ	see ገደለ
ግዳጅ	see ገደደ
ግድጋጅ	see ገደገደ
ግግ	gᵊgg n. milk-teeth (before they appear)
ግፍ	see ገፋ
ግፍፍል	see ተግፈለፈለ
ጎህ	goh n. dawn, day-break
—ሲቀድ	—siqädd adv. at daybreak
ጎለመሰ	golämmäsä v.i. developed, matured (phsyically, mentally)
ጎልማሳ	golmassa n. adult, youngman
የጎልማሶች ትምህርት	yägolmasočč tᵊmhᵊrt adult education
አጎላመሰ	agolammäsä v.t. complemented (gram.)
አጎላማሽ	aggolamaš adj. complementary (gram.)
ጎለበተ	goläbätä v.i. became

ጉልበት strong
gulbät n. strength, energy ; knee

ጉልበተኛ gulbätäñña adj. strong, sturdy; aggressive

ጎምላላ gomlalla adj. graceful

ተጎማለለ tägomallälä v.i. walked gracefully

ጎመን gommän n. greens

—ዘር —zär n. rape seed

ጎመዘዘ gämäzzäzä v.i. tasted sour

ጎምዛዛ gomzzaza adj. sour

ተጎማዘዘ tägomazzäzä v.i. -tasted sour

አጎመዘዘ agomäzzäzä v.t. turned sour

ጎመጀ see ጎመጀ

ጎመደ gommädä v.t. cut into chunks

ጉማጅ gummag n. chunk

ጎመድ gomäd n. pole (wood), cane(used for beating s/o)

ጎማዳ gomada adj. cut ugly

ጎመጀ gomäggä v.i. had an appetite for; desired eagerly

አስጎመጀ asgomäggä v.t. looked delicious and appetising; tempted (attracted)

ጎማ gomma n. tire; rubber; wheel (vehicle)

ጎረመሰ gorämmäsä v. i. reached adolescence (male)

ጉርምስና gurmasanna n adolescence

ጎረምሳ gorämsa n. adj. adolescent

ጎረሰ gorräsä v. t. took a mouthful; v.i. was loaded (gun)

ጉራሽ gurraš n. mouthful

ጉርሻ gurša n. mouthful; tip (for service)

አጎረሰ agorräsä v.t. gave a mouthful; loaded (a gun) ; tipped

ጎረበ gorräbä v. i. crushed, wrinkled (dress etc.)

ተጉረበረበ täguräbärräbä v.i was wrinkled (dress etc.)

*ጎረበተ * goräbbätä

ጉርብትና gurbatanna n. neighbourhood

ጎረቤት goräbet n. neighbour

ጎረቤታም goräbetam n. neighbours

ተጎራበተ tägorabbätä v.i. lived in neighbourhood

ተጎራባች tägorabač adj. neighbouring

አጎራበተ aggorabbätä v.i. allowed s/o to be one's neighbour

ጎረበጠ see ጉረበጠ

ጉረደ gorrädä v.t. cut, chopped

ጉራጅ gurrag n. stub (of wood)

ጉርድ gurd n. s/t cut off

—ቀሚስ n. skirt

ጎራዳ gorada n. ugly

ጎራጅ gorag in ጉራጅ ቃል gorag qal contracting word (gram.)

ጎራረደ gorarrädä v.t. cut into pieces, chopped

ጎረደመ goräddämä v.t. munched

ጎረዶማን gorädoman n. driver of a ̃merchants caravat (beast of buraen)

ጎራ gora n. mountain

ጎራ አለ gora alä v.i stopped over, dropped in (on one's way)

ጎራዴ gorade n. sword

ጎሬ see ጎራ

ጎርመጥ gormat n. crab

ጎርደድ አለ gordädd alä v.i perambulated, walked to and for

ተንጎራደደ tängoraddädä v.i perambulated, walked to and for

ጎሳ gosa n. clan

ጎሸ goššä n. buffalo; interj. well done! bravo!

ጎበበ gobbäbä v.i. towered,

ጎባባ overtopped, over-
hanged
gobaba adj. towering,
overtopping, over-
hanging

ጎበዘ *gobbäzä* v.i became
successful; became
smart, was brave

ጉብዝና *gubzənna* n. success;
bravery, courage

ጎበዝ *gobäz* adj. success-
ful; smart, brave; n.
young man, fine
young man

የጎበዝ አለቃ የጎበዝ አለቃ *yägobäz*
aläqa n.leader of
warriors

ጎተራ *gotära* n. granary,
grain storage

—ሆድ —*hod* adj. big-bellied

ጎታ *gota* n. small granary

* ጎነጠፈ * *gonäṭṭäfä* also ተጎናጸፈ

ተጎናጠፈ *tägonaṭṭäfä, tägonaṣ-*
ṣäfä v.i. was wrapped
up, wrapped oneself
up *(with shawl,*
toga etc.)

መጎናጠፊያ also መጎናጸፊያ *maggo-*
naṭäfiya, mäggo-
naṣäfiya n. shawl,
toga

ጎነጸፈ see ጎነጠፈ

ጎን *gonn* n. side, flank *(of*
body); adv. by the
side of, beside

እ...ጉን *ə...gonn* adv. beside

ከ...ጉን *kä...gonn* adv. close
to, beside

ወደጎን *wädä gonn* adv. aside,
abreast

ጉን ለጉን *gonn lägonn* adv.
close to, beside,
alongside

ጎንደር *gondär* n. one of the
Administrative Re-
gions, north-western
Ethiopia *(Gondar)*

ጎንደሬ *gondäre* n. Gonderian

ጎንደርኛ *gondärəñña* n. the
dialect of Gondar

ጎዘጎዘ *gozzäggozä* v.t. spread
out s/t on the floor

(mattress, straw etc.
as bedding)

ጉዝጉዝ *guzgu*ʷ*az* n. bedding

ጎደለ *goddälä* v.i. subsided
(of flood water),
diminished; decreased
was incomplete; was
short in; fell short

ጉድለት *guddlät* n. defect, deficiency, lack, short-
coming; fault, mistake

ጎደሎ *godälo* adj. not full;
incomplete, lacking;
weakling

—ቀን —*qän* evil day

—ቁጥር —*quṭər* odd number

የቀን ጎደሎ *yäqän godälo* evil day

ቀን የጎደለበት *qän yägoddäläbbät*
adj. wretched, heart-
broken

አካለ ጎደሎ *akalä—*n. crippled,
invalid

እምነተ ጎደሎ *əmnätä —* adj. dishonest

ጉዳይ *gudday in* ሩብ ጉዳይ
rub gudday quarter to

ተጎዳለ *tägu*ʷ*addälä* v.i.
failed to fulfil

አጎደለ *agoddälä* v.t. de-
creased; diminished;
stood in need of

ጎዳ *goda* adj. plain *(not*
coloured, ordinary)

—ሸማ —*šämma* plain šämma

—በሬ —*bäre* a bull of
ordinary colour

ጎ. *godda* v.t. harmed, injured, damaged, hurt;
overcharged
e.g. በዋጋ ተጎዳን
we are overcharged
(price)

ጉዳት *gudat* n. harm, injury,
damage; suffering;
disadvantage

ጉዳተኛ *gudatäñña* adj. suffering, harmed, in-
jured ill-conditioned

ጎጂ *goǧi* adj. harmful

ተጎዳ *tägodda* v.i. was
harmed, injured,
damaged, hurt; suf-
fered; was overcharged

297

ገዳኒሳ godanissa n. scar

ጎጆ ǧoǧǧo also ጎጘ gožžo n. small hut; booth, cottage

ደሳሳ— dässasa — n. shack

—ቀለሰ —qälläsä v.t. built a small house

—ወጣ —wäṭṭa v.t. married

ጎጆና ጉለቻ goǧǧonna gulləčča married life

የወፍ ጎጆ yäwäf goǧǧo.n. cage (birds) n. nest

ጎፈረ goffärä v.i. was large and bushy (hair)

ጎፈሬ gofäre n. Afro style (hair-cut)

ጎፈር goffär n. mane of a lion

ጎፈሪያም gofäriyam adj. bushy hair

አጎፈረ agoffärä v.t. grew large bushy hair

ጎፈንነ ǧofännänä v.t averted one's eyes from; was repellant (food), was disgusting

*ጎፈፈ *goffäfä

ጎፈፈ gofäfa adj. lubberly; blockhead

ጎፍላ gofla n. tuft of hair

*ጉለመመ *golämämä

ጉለመመ gu*älmæmma adj. stately, graceful

ተጉለመመ tägu*älammämä v.i. walked gracefully

ጉለተ gu*ällätä v.i. placed three stones above a fire-place in order to make the cooking pot rest; endowed (land to a church)

ጉልተኛ gultäñña n. big land owner

ጉልት in ርስት ጉልት rəstä gult n. fief, land given by a ruler to an individual or to the church as an endowment

ጉልት gu*əllət n. back-street market

ጉለቻ gu*əlləčča n. three stones or earthen-

ware tripod on which the cooking pot rests above the fire

ተጉለተ tägu*ällätä v.i. sat idly (for a long time)

*ጉለደፈ *gu*äläddäfä

ጉልደፍ gu*əldəf adj. lisping; lacking dexterity

ጉልደፋ gu*äldaffa adj. lacking dexterity

ተጉለደፈ tägu*äladdäfä v.i. lisped

ጉለጉለ gu*äläggu*älä v.t. cleaned ploughed land of weeds; emptied out (a sack, a suit-case)

ምስጢር— məsṭir – let the cat out of the bag; let one into the secret

ጉልጉሎ gu*əlgu*alo n. cleaning ploughed land of weeds also ጉልጓ

ጉለ gu*älla v.i. was magnified (appeared larger), stood out; was clear

ጉለህ gu*ələh adj. clear, evident, obvious; gross (error)

አጉለ agu*älla v.t. magnified (made to appear larger); amplified

ደምጥግ ጉያ dəmṭ magu*ya n. amplifier; megaphone

አጉይ መነጥር ag*yi mänäṭṭər n. microscope

ጉመረ gu*ämarra v.i. started ripening (fruit, grain)

ጉመተመተ *gu*ämätämmätä
አጉመተመት agu*mätämmätä v.i. murmured (complained in a murmur)

*ጉመዘዘ see ጎመዘዘ

*ጉመጠመጠ *gu*ämäṭämmäṭä
ተጉመጠመጠ tägu*mäṭämmäṭä v.i. rinsed (the mouth)

ጉግ see ጎግ

*ጉረመረመ *gu*ärämärrämä
ጉርምርምታ gu*ərəmrəmta n.

298

አጕረመረመ growling
aguʷərämärrämä
v.t. murmured,
grumbled; grunted,
complained

አጕረምረሚ aguʷərämrami adj.
grumbling, mur-
muring

*ጕረመስ see ጎረመስ

ጕርምጥ guʷärməṭ n. incurable
skin ulcer

ጕረስ see ጎረስ

ጕረበጠ guʷäräbbäṭä v.t. was
uncomfortable, was
hard (sitting or
sleeping place)

ሆዱን ጕረበ hoden guʷäräbbäṭ-
ጠኝ äññ I feel unwell
in my stomach

ጕርበጣ guʷärbaṭṭa adj.
uncomfortable, hard
(sitting, sleeping
place)

*ጕረነነ *guʷärännänä

ጕርነነ guʷärnanna adj. rough
(voice)

ጕረነ guʷäränna v.i. tasted
burnt

ጕርነት guʷərnat n. burnt
taste

አጕረነ aguʷäränna v.t.
burnt (the food)

ጕረጸመ see ጎረጸመ

ጕረጕረ guʷärägguʷärä v.t.
searched (a house
etc.); poked

አንጕረጕረ anguʷäragguʷärä
v/t sang melan-
choly song

እንጕርጕሮ ənguʷərgguʷəro n.
melancholy song

*ጕረጠ *guʷärräṭä

ጕርጥ guʷərṭ also ጎርጥ n.
frog

ጕርጥ ዐይን guʷərṭ ayn adj.
ox-eyed

ጕረጥረጣ guʷäräṭraṭṭä n. one
with bulging eyes

አጕረጠረጣ aguʷräṭärräṭä v. t.
looked furiously
at s/o

አጕርጥ aguʷərṭ adj. sar-
donic, scornful

ጕረፈ guʷärräfä v.i. flooded,
flew in abundance;
gushed (of tears);
lathered

ጕርፍ guʷärf n. flood,
torrent

*ጕረ *guʷärra

አጕረ aguʷärra v.t. groaned,
screamed (hysteri-
cally)

አጓረ aguʷarra v.t. bel-
lowed (ox)
groaned; boomed
(cannons)

ጕሰመ guʷässämä, also ጕሸመ
guʷäššämä, v.t.
thumped (s/o on the
side to bring s/t to
his attention); jerked
(with sudden push);
nudged

ነጋሪት— nägarit- v.t. drum-
med

ጕስም guʷssäma n. nudge

ጕሰረ guʷässärä v.t. · stuffed
into; stuffed (one-
self with food)

ጕሰቀለ guʷäsäqquʷälä v.t.
was in a miserable
condition, was
wretched

ጕስቀላ guʷ əsquʷällä n.
wretchedness, misery

ጕስቋላ guʷäsquʷalla adj.
miserable, wretched

ተጕሰቀለ täguʷäsaqquʷälä v.i
suffered greatly;
was mishandled

አጕሰቀለ aguʷäsaqquʷälä v.t
mistreated, misused,
mishandled; rendered
haggard (of suffering)

ጕሰጕሰ guʷäsägguʷäsä v.t.
crammed, stuffed
into, stuffed (oneself
with food)

*ጕሸ *see ጎሸ

ጕሸመ see ጎሰመ

ጕበኘ guʷäbäňňä v.t. visited,
toured; inspected,
reviewed (troops)

ጕብኝት guʷəbəňňət n. visit;
tour

ጉብኒ *guʷäbñi* n. visitor
አገር— *agär-* n. tourist
አስጎብኝ *asguʷäbäññä* v.t.
showed around:
guided (visitors,
tourists)
አስጎብኒ *asguʷäbñi* n. tourist
guide
ጉብበ see ጎብበ
ጉብዘ see ጎብዘ
*ጉብደደ * *guʷäbäddädä*
አጉብደደ *aguʷäbäddädä* v.i.
bowed to, demeaned
onself, licked the
boots
አጉብዳጅ *aguʷäbdağ* adj.
boot-licking
*ጉብጉብ * *gaʷäbägguʷäbä*
አጉብጉብ *aguʷäbägguʷägbä* v.i.
acted as a stooge
for
አጉብጓቢ *aguʷäbguʷabi* n.
stooge
ጉብጣ *guʷäbbäṭä* v.i. was
bent; was humped,
was curved
ጉባጣ *guʷäbaṭa* adj. curved,
hunched, bent
ጉቢጥ *guʷäbiṭ* n. hump-
back (insult)
ጉብጠት *guʷbṭät* n. bend
አጉብጣ *aguʷäbbaṭä* v.t.
bent, forced into
a curve
ጉብን *guʷäbban* n. one who
has taken s/o's
husband or wife
*ጉተመ * *guʷättämä*
አጉተመተመ *aguʷtämättämä* v.i.
murmured (com-
plained)
ጉተተ *guʷättätä* v.t. pulled,
dragged, drew to-
ward, tagged on
guʷattäta in የገመድ
ጉተታ yägämäd
guʷattäta tug of war
ጉታታ *guʷätata* n/adj.
sluggard, slacker,
sluggish, slow (in
work)
ጉትት *guʷattat* adj. slow
ጉትጃ *guʷatačča* also yä-

ጎሮ \ጉ̈ʷatäčča n.
ear-ring
ተጉተተ *täguʷattätä* v.i. was
pulled, dragged;
lagged behind
ተጉታች *täguʷättač* n. trailer
ተጓተተ *täguʷattätä* v.i.
slackened; lagged be-
hind, delayed (work),
took a long time
*ጉተነ * *guʷättänä*
ጉተና *guʷatäna* n. bushy
hair
አጉተነ *aguʷättänä* v.t. grew
bushy hair
ጉተጉተ *guʷätägguʷätä* v.t. bad-
gered, kept nagging
ጉትጉታ *guʷatguʷäta* n.
badgering, nagging
ጉነቀለ *guʷänäqquʷälä* v.i. germinated
.ጉነቀል *guʷänqul* n. soaked
and germinating
beans used as food
አጉነቀለ *aguʷänäqquʷälä* v.t.
germinated
*ጉነበሰ * *guʷänäbbäsä*
ጉንበስ ቀና *guʷänbäss qäna alä*
አለ v.i. toiled (at a task)·
አጉነበሰ *aguʷänäbbäsä* v.i.
bent, stooped;
bowed to
አጉንባሽ *aguʷänbaš* adj.boot-
licking also አፋሽ
አጉንባሽ
አስጉነበሰ *asguʷänäbbäsä* v.t.
subdued (brought
under control)
*ጉነዘለ * *guʷänäzzälä*
ጉንዛላ *guʷänzalla* adj. undulating (field of
wheat etc.)
ተጉናዘለ *täguʷänazzälä* v.i.
undulated (a field of
wheat in the breeze)
ጉነጉነ *guʷänägguʷänä* v.t.
plaited (hair, rope),
braided
ጉንጛኝ in ነገር ጉንጛኝ nägär
guʷänguʷañ n.
schemer, intriguer
ጉንጉን *guʷänguʷan* n. plait,
braid

300

ያበባ—	yabāba— n. wreath, garland	
ተጕነጕነ	tägu^wänäggu^wänä v.t. was plaited	
ጕነጠ	gu^wännäṭä v.t. jerked cf. ጕስመ	
በነገር—ኝ	bänägär—ñ passed rude remarks about me, that was a dig at me	
ጕነጣ	gu^wännäṭa n. jerk (sudden push)	
*ጕነ጑	gu^wänäččä	
ጕንጭ	gu^wənč n. cheek	
—ሙሉ	—mulu adj. mouthful	
ጕንጩም	gu^wənčam s/o with fat cheeks	
ተጕነ጑	tägu^wänäččä v.t. took a gulp, sipped	
ጕነጠፈ	see ነነጠፈ.	
ጕነፈ.	gu^wännäfä v.t. soaked in hot water	
ጕደሪ	gu^wädärri n. taro	
*ጕደኘ	* gu^wädäññä	
3ደኛ	gu^waddäñña n. friend, companion, colleague	
የሥራ—	yäsəra—n. co-worker, colleague	
የትምህርት ቤት—	yätəmhərt bet—n. school mate	
የክፍል—	yäkəfəl—n. classmate	
የጦር 3ደ	yäṭor gu^wadd n. ally	
3ደኛሞች	gu^waddäññamoč n. pl. friends, companions, associates	
3ደኝነት	gu^waddäññənnät n. friendship, fellowship	
3ደ.	gu^wadd n. comrade	
ተጕዳኘ	tägu^wädaññä v.i became friend to; joined	
*ጕደደ	*gu^wäddädä	
ጕዳዳ	gu^wädada adj. graceful (in movement)	
ተንጓደደ	tängu^waddädä v.i. moved gracefully	
ጕደጕደ.	gu^wädäggu^wädä v.i. became hollow, deep; sank in (soil, road etc.)	
ጕድጓዳ	gu^wädgu^wadda adj/n hollow, deep; depression	
ጕድጓድ	gu^wədgu^wad n. pit,	

		hole, cavity; well, depression, ditch
—ማስ	—masä n.t. plotted, conspired, pulled wires
አጕደጕደ.	agu^wädäggu^wädä v.t. hollowed out, deepened
ጕጃም	gu^wäǧǧam n. one of the Administrative Regions western Ethiopia (Gojam)
ጕጃሚ	gu^wäǧǧame n. Gojamite
ጕፈያ	gu^wäfäyyä v.i. was lean (meat); was thin (ox)
ጕፋያ	gu^wfayya adj. lean (meat), thin
ጕፉ	see ጕፉ
3 አለ	gu^wa alä v. i. banged (made a loud noise)
*3ለለ	*g^wallälä
ጕላይ	gu^wəllay n. husk
ተንጓለለ	tängu^wallälä v.i. was raked
አንጓለለ	angu^wallälä v.t. raked; paid no attention to (consciously)
3ል	gu^wal n. clod (lump of earth)
*3መጠ	*gu^wammäṭä
አ3መጠ	agu^wammäṭä v.t. gormandized, devoured
3ር	gu^waro n. backyard
አምባ—	ʾmbba—n. quarrel
አምባ 3ርኛ	—gu^waroñña adj. quarrelsome
*3ሽ	*gu^waššä
ጕሽ	gu^wəš n. unfiltered beer
3ነ	gu^wanä v.i. bonded, rebounded, bounced (ball etc.)
አ3ነ	agu^wanä v. t. rebounded, bounced
*3ዘ	*gu^wazä
ጕዞ	gu^wəzo n. journey, trip, travel, voyage, itinerary
ጕዞኛ	gu^wəzoñña n. traveller
ተ3ዘ	tägu^wazä v. i. travelled, journeyed

ተጓዥ tagu‴az n. ʊ ᴄɪᴇr; passenger

ተጓጓዘ tāgu‴agu‴azä v. i. was transported

መጓጓዣ mäggu‴agu‴aža n. means of transportation, vehicle

አጓጓዘ aggu‴agu‴azä v. t transported

አስጓዘ asgu‴azä v.t. had goods transported

ጓያ gu‴ayya n. vetch

*ጓደደ *gu‴addädä

ተጓደደ tägu‴addädä v.i. was slow (intentionally)

ጓዳ gu‴ada n. store-room

አዋቅ —awwäq adj. well informed, privy to, in the know

ጓድ see ጉደኝ

ጓጉለ gu‴aggu‴älä v.i. clotted (cream, soup etc.)

ሰውነቱ— säwənnätu—have muscle-bound

ጓጓላ gu‴aggu‴ala n. clot

አጓጉለ agu‴aggu‴älä v.t.

አጓጉል agu‴agul adj. improper, indecent, incorrect, unbecoming

—እምነት —əmnät n. superstition

ጓጉረ gu‴aggu‴ärä v.t. groaned (.made a deep sound)

ጓጉጠ gu‴aggu‴äṭä v.t. poked (with a stick or finger); vomited

ጓጉንቻር gu‴agunčär n. toad

ጓጓ gu‴aggu‴a v.i. wished strongly, have a fervent desire, was anxious, curious, eager; yearned, looked forward

ጐጉ gu‴əggu adj. desirous, curious

ጐጉት gu‴ggut n. longing curiously, fervent desire

ጐንፉን see ጉንፉን

ጐድብ see ጉድብ

ጠ

ጠለለ ṭällälä v.i. was purified; was pure; was filtered

ጠለላ ṭäläla n. shelter, shed

ጠላላ in ጠላላ ሜዳ tälaḷa meda n. open landscape

ተንጣለለ tänṭallälä v.i. spread (water on a flat land)

አጠለለ aṭällälä v.t. purified, filtered; strained (passed liquid through a cloth)

ማጥለያ maṭläya n. sifter, filter, strainer

*ጠለለ *ṭällälä

ጠል ṭäll n. dew; rain; verdure

ጠላ ṭäla n. shade. shadow umbrella

—ቢስ —bis adj. graceless, undignified; airy,

---

light- hearted

—የሌለው —yälelläw adj. undignified

—የቀለለው —yäqälläläw adj. lightminded

ጥላማ ṭälamma adj. shady

ዓይነ ጥላ aynäṭäla n. phobia, aversion

ተጠለለ täṭällälä v.i. took shelter; sought refuge; took cover

መጠለያ mäṭṭäläya n. shed, shelter; refugee camp

አስጠለለ asṭällälä v.t. gave shelter to, sheltered

*ጠለመ see ጸልመት

ጠለቀ ṭälläqä v.i. was deep; dived; sank; submerged, be profound

302

የጠለተ
ትምህርት
—እውቀት
ጠላቂ
ጣልቃ
—ገባ

—ገብ

—ገብነት

መጥለቂያ
ጥልቀት
—የሌለው
የፀሐይ/
የጀንበር—
ጥልቅ

ጥልቅ አለ

ጥልቅ ብዪ

ጥልፋ
መጥለቂያ

ተጣለተ

ተጥለቀለቀ

አጠለቀ

ላብ አጠለቀው

አጥለቀለቀ

ጠለዘ

	yäṭälläqä təmhərt profound learning
	—əwqät profound knowledge
	ṭälaqi n. diver
	ṭalqa adv. in between
	—gäbba v.t meddled, interfered; broke into conversation; intruded
	—gäbb n. meddler, intruder
	—gäbbənät n. interference, intrusiveness
	mäṭläqiya n. dipper
	ṭəlqät n. depth
	—yälelläw adj. shallow
	yäṣahay/yägänbär—ṭəlqät n. sundown
	ṭälq adj. deep, profound; expert (knowledge)
	ṭälləqq alä v.t. intruded, mixed in, interfered
	ṭälləqq bəyyä n. busy–body
	ṭälləqqo n. small axe mäṭläqiya n. bucket, can etc. for dipping water out
	täṭalläqä v.i. ducked each other cf. ተዛፈቀ
	täṭläqälläqä v.i. was flooded, was overflowing, was overwhelmed
	aṭälläqä v.t. put on (shirt, trousers etc.); wore (a chain around the neck)
	lab aṭälläqäw he was drenched with sweat
	aṭläqälläqä v.t. flooded, overflowed; overwhelmed (gratitude, joy etc.)
	ṭälläzä v.t. hit, kicked

ጆር የሚጠ
ልዝ መዝቃ
*ጠለጠለ
ተንጠለጠለ

የተንጠለጠለ
—ጉዳይ

አንጠለጠለ

ማንጠልጠያ

ጠለፈ

ጠለፋ

ጠላፊ

ጥልፊያ

ጥልፍ

ጥልፍልፍ

መጥለፊያ

ተጠለፈ

ተጠላለፈ

ጠላ

	strongly deafening music
*	ṭäläṭṭälä ənṭäläṭṭälä v.i. was hung, was suspended; swung
	yäṭänṭäläṭṭälä gudday a pending case, issue
	anṭäläṭṭälä v.t. hung up; suspended
	manṭälṭäya n. handle (of suitcase), hook, peg (for coat, hat); staple (of padlock)
	ṭälläfä v.t. tripped (up); tied the legs of animal; entangled; kidnapped (a girl, a slave); hijacked; embroidered; connected (wire,rope)
	ṭäläfa n. hijacking, kidnapping, abduction
	ṭäläfi n. hijacker, kidnapper
	ṭəlfiya n. hijacking, abduction; catching and pulling s/o's leg
	ṭəlf n. needlework, embroidery
	ṭələfləf n. entanglement
	in መጥለፊያ ቋንቋ mäṭläfiya quʷanquʷa a language from which translation is made
	täṭälläfä v.i. was abducted, hijacked; was tripped (up)
	täṭälalläfä v.i. was entangled (thread), interlocked; interlinked
	ṭälla n. common

Ethiopian beverage (beer)
guš—young beer
ṭälla v.i. hated, disliked
ṭälat n. enemy, foe, adversary
ṭəlaččä n. hatred, dislike, hostility, antagonism, animosity
ṭəl n. quarrel, fight, enmity
ṭəläñña n. person who is not on speaking terms with someone
täṭälla v.i. was hated, became unpopular
yätäṭälla adj. unpopular; hated
täṭalla v.i. quarreled with, fought with; disputed
aṭṭalla v.t. set two people at variance
aṭlalla v.t. spurned, contemned
asṭälla v.t. disgusted
masṭällo adj. ugly, hideous
asṭäyy adj. disgusting, abhorrent
ṭälsäm n. amulet (with colourful designs)
see ጸለየ
see ተጥመለመለ
ṭämmämä v.i. was crooked, twisted, curved, deformed was stubborn, played against, refused
ṭämama adj. crooked, bent, curved; uncooperative, stubborn
täṭammämä v.i. was crooked, distorted
aṭṭammämä v.t. distorted; twisted, bent
*ṭämmärä
:n ጣምራ ጠላት **ṭamra ṭälat** n. joint

enemy
ṭämmər adj . affixed
—qal affixed word; compounded word
täṭammärä v.i. was combined, coupled
täṭamari n. noun in apposition (gram.)
aṭṭammärä v.t. combined, coupled; folded, crossed (the arms), joined
mästäṣamər n. conjunction (gram.)
ṭämärrärä v.i. became exceedingly hot (sun, fire); became very severe (war)
see ተጥመሰመሰ
ṭämässäsä v.t. trampled (crushed under the feet)
ṭämmäqä v.t. brewed beer; immersed in water , soaked (clothes)
ṭəmqät n. baptism, Epiphany
ṭəmqätä bahər open space where the feast of Epiphany is celebrated
məṭmaq n. baptismal font
täṭämmäqä v.i· was brewed (beer) ; immersed oneself in water
I was in a sweat
aṭämmäqä v.t. baptized, christened
mäṭmäqiya n. baptismal font
ṭämäne n. chalk (for writing)
ṭämänža /ga n. gun, rifle
ṭämänga mäfča n. screw-driver
*ṭämäzämmäzä
ṭämäzmazza adj/n.

ተጥመዠመዠ	sinuous, zigzag *täṭmäzämmäzä* v.i. twisted *(road)*	አጣመደ	trap *aṭṭammädä* v. t. joined up *(oxen)*
አጥመዠመዠ	*aṭmäzämmäzä* v.t. twisted	አጣግጅ	in አጣግጅ በሬ *aṭṭamäǧ bäre* one
ጠመዠዘ	*ṭämäzzäzä* v.t. wrung, twisted	አስጠመደ	of the pair of oxen *asṭämmädä* v.t.
ጠምዛዛ	*ṭämzazza* adj/ʌ tortuous *(road)*, winding, spiral; zigzag		caused *(s/o)* to be looked at with hatred
ጥምዝ	*ṭəmәzz* adj. twisted	ጠመጠመ	*ṭämäṭṭämä* v. t. wrap- ped *(a scarf round*
ተጠመዠዘ	*täṭämäzzäzä* v.i. twisted		*the head)*; wound, *(bandage)*; coiled
መጠምዠሻ	*mäṭṭämzäža* n. curve, turn *(in a road)*	ጠምጣግ ጠምጣሚ	up *ṭämṭamma* adj· sturdy *ṭämṭami* n. priest,
ተጠመዘዘ	*täṭämazzäzä* v.i. bent, wound		clergyman *(pejor- ative)*
ጠመዥ	*ṭämäž* n. type of barley *(whose husk can be easily removed)*	ጥምጣም	*ṭәmṭәm* n. turban, headband
ጠመደ	*ṭämmädä* v.t. yoked *(oxen together)*; looked at s/o with hatred	ጥምጥም አለ	*ṭәmṭәmm alä* v.i. be- came sturdy; v.t em- braced *(forcefully)*; curled up
ጠማድ	*ṭämmad* n. team *(of oxen)*	ጥምጥም ያለ	*ṭәmṭәmm yalä* adj. sturdy
ጥንድ	*ṭәnd also* ጥምድ n. couple, pair·	ተጠመጠመ	*täṭämäṭṭämä* v.i. was entwined, clung to
ወጥመድ	*wäṭmäd* n. snare, trap *(for animals)*		*(e.g. à child to his mother etc.)*; coiled
—ገባ	—*gäbba* v.t. was caught in a snare, was ensnared, was trapped	ጠማ(ው)	*ṭämma(w)* v.i. was thirsty, had a thirst for
ተጠመደ	*täṭämmädä* v.i. was yoked *(oxen)*: was looked at with hatred	ጥማት ጥም ተጠማ	*ṭәmat* n. thirst *ṭәm* n. thirst *täṭämma* v.i. was thirsty ; had a fer- vent desire to
በሥራ—	*bäsәra*—was very busy	አጠማ	*aṭämma* v.t. blotted *(dried up wet ink)*
ተጣመደ	*täṭammädä* v.i. have animosity against each other	ማጥሚያ አስጠማ	*maṭmiya* n. blotter *asṭämma* v.t. made thirsty
አጠመደ	*aṭämmädä* v.t. set traps, entrapped, laid snares; caught *(fish)*	ጠምበላል ጠረመሰ	*ṭämbäläl* n. jasmine *ṭärämmäṣä* v.t. smashed down *(wall, door etc.)*
አጥማጅ	in ዓሣ አጥማጅ *asa aṭmaǧ* n. fisherman	ተጠረመሰ	*täṭärämmäsä* v.i. got smashed
ማጥመጃ	*maṭmäǧa* n. snare,	ጠረረ	*ṭärrärä* v.i. was very strong *(sun)*
		ጠራራ	*ṭärara* n. blazing

305

የጠራራ ፀሐይ (sun) yäṭärara ṣähay midday sun

ጠረሰ ṭärräsä v.i. became blunt (knife, razor)

ጥርስ ṭərs n, tooth, tusk

የዝሆን— yäzəhon—n. tusk, ivory

—ሻረፈ —šärräfä v.i. lost one's milk-tooth

ጥርስ በረዶ ṭərsä bärädo adj. with snow-white teeth

—ወላቃ —wälaqa adj. toothless

—ጓጣጣ —gäṭaṭa adj. bucktoothed

ጥርሱን ነከሰ ṭərsun näkkäsä v.t. had patience, perseverance

—ነከሰብኝ —näkkäsäbbäññ he threatened me

ጥርሱን ነከሶ ṭərsun näkso adv. patiently, with perseverance

ጥርሳም ṭərsam adj. bucktoothed

ጥርስ አፋጨ ṭərs afäččä v.t. gnashed (the teeth)

—አወጣ —awäṭṭa v.t. cut a tooth

—ጓባ —gäbba v.t. became antipathetic

አጠረሰ aṭärräsä v.t. dulled (edge of a blade, razor)

የጥርስ ሐኪም yäṭərs hakim n. dentist

—ሳሙና —samuna n. toothpaste

ጠረቀመ ṭäräqqämä v.t. slammed (the door)

ጥርቅም አድርጎ በላ ṭərqəmm adərgo bälla ate well

—አሳረ —assärä v.t. tied s/t fast

*ጠረቀመ *ṭäräqqämä

ጥርቃሚ ṭəräqqami n. the riffraff, the rubble

ጥርቃሞ ṭəräqqamo n. the riff-raff, the rubble

ጥርቅም ṭərəqqəm n. collection

ጥርቅምቅም ṭərqəmqəm n. rubble

ተጠረቃቀመ (disorderly crowd); hotch-potch, jumble täṭäräqaqqämä v.i. gathered together, was gathered together

ተጠራቀመ täṭäraqqämä v.i. was collected; gathered (people); accumulated

አጠራቀመ aṭṭäraqqämä v.t. collected, gathered accumulated; saved (money)

ጠረበ ṭärräbä v.t. carved, hewed (shaped by chopping)

ጠራቢ ṭarabi in ድንጊያ ጠራቢ dängiya ṭärabi n. stonemason

ጠርብ ṭärb n. lumber, board, plank

ጠርብ የሚያህል ሰው ṭärb yämmiyahəl säw a gigantic man

ጥራቢ ṭərrabi n. shavings

ጥርብ ድንጊያ ṭərb dängiya n. hewn stone

መጥረቢያ mäṭräbiya n. hatchet, axe

*ጠረበበ *ṭäräbbäbä

ጠርባባ ṭärbabba adj. sulky

ተንጠረበበ tänṭäräbbäbä v.i. sulked

ጠረነቀ ṭärännäqä v.t tied firmly

ጠረን ṭärän n. odour

*ጠረወዘ *ṭäräwwäzä

ተንጠራወዘ tänṭäräwwäzä v.i. walked feebly

ጠረዘ ṭärräzä v.i. bound (a book)

ጠርዝ ṭärz n. fringe, hem, edge, border

ጥራዝ ṭəraz n. volume (book); binding

—ነጠቅ —näṭṭäq adj. superficial, shallow, semi-learned

*ጠረዘዘ *ṭäräzzäzä

ጠርዛዛ ṭärzazza adj. gloomy, depressed

ተንጠረዘዘ tänṭäräzzäzä v.i. was

ጠረገ	gloomy, depressed *ṭärrägä* v.t. swept, wiped, cleaned; shined *(shoes)*; mopped *(the forehead)*
መንገድ—	*mängäd*—v.t. opened a road to, cleaned a road to, paved the way for
ጠራጊ	*in ጫማ ጠራጊ žamma ṭäragi* n. shoeshine boy
ጥራጊ	*ṭərragi* n. rubbish, sweepings
ጥርጊያ	*in ጥርጊያ መንገድ ṭərgiya mängäd* n. cleared road *(not paved)*
ጥርጊያ ጎዳና	*ṭərgiya godana* sée ጥርጊያ መንገድ
መጥረጊያ	*mäṭrägiya* n. broom, sweeper
ተጠረገ	*in ተጠርጎ ሄደ ṭäṭärgo hedä* left for good *(only for an unwanted person)*
ተጠራረገ	*in ተጠራርጎ ጠፋ ṭäṭärargo ṭäffa* disappeared together completely *(only for unwanted person)*
ጠረጠረ	*ṭäräṭṭärä* v.i. suspected; mistrusted, doubted, had suspicions
ጠርጣሪ	*ṭärṭari* adj. suspicious, doubtful; sceptic, distrustful
ጥርጣሬ	*ṭərəṭṭare* n. suspicion, distrust, doubt
ጥርጥር	*ṭərəṭṭər* n. doubt, suspicion
ያለ—	*yalä*—adv. unquestionably, undoubtedly
ተጠረጠረ	*ṭäṭäräṭṭärä* v.i. was suspected *(of being guilty)*
ተጠራጠረ	*ṭäṭäraṭṭärä* v.i. was in doubt about, called into question, coudn't believe
እትጠራጠር	*attəṭṭäraṭär* be sure, take my word
ተጠራጣሪ	*ṭäṭäraṭari* adj. scep-tical, distrustful
አጠራጠረ	*aṭṭäraṭṭärä* v.t. was questionable, doubtful, equivocal
አጠራጣሪ	*aṭṭäraṭari* adj. questionable, doubtful, equivocal
ጠረጠረ	*ṭäräṭṭärä* c.t removed husks with the teeth *(of cooked beans etc.)*
ጥርጣሪ	*ṭərəṭṭari* n. husks removed in the above way
ጠረጠሰ	*ṭäräṭṭäsä* v.i. got blunt *(of sharp edge)*
ጥርጥስ	*ṭərṭəs* adj. blunt
ተጠረጠሰ	*tänṭäraṭṭäsä* v.t. got blunt *(sharp edge)*
ጠረጴዛ	*ṭäräppeza* n. table; desk
የጠረጴዛ ልብስ	*yäṭäräppeza ləbs* n. table-cloth
ጠረፍ	*ṭäräf* n. border *(line dividing two states or countries)*, coast, frontier
የጠረፍ ክላል	*yäṭäräf kəlləl* n. border line *(line dividing two countries)*
ጠረፍ ጠባቂ	*ṭäräf ṭäbbaqi* n. border patrol
ጠራ	*ṭärra* v.t. called, called up; named; mentioned
ግብዣ—	*gəbža*—v.t. invited *(to a party, feast etc.)*
ስም—	*səm*—v.t. took attendance
—ጠሪ	*—ṭäri* one who takes the attendance
ጥሪ	*ṭərri* n. call, invitation
የፍርድ ቤት ጥሪ	*yäfərd bet ṭərri* n. summons *(order to appear before a judge or magistrate)*
የጥሪ ወረቀት	*yäṭərri wäräqät* n. invitation card
የናት አገር ጥሪ	*yännat agär ṭərri* call of the Motherland
ተጠራ	*täṭärra* v.i. was called. summoned

ሰሙ—	səmu—v.i became famous, found recognition
ተጣሪ	tätäri n. representative, patron
ቋሚ—	qu"ami—n. permanent secretary
ተጣራ	tätarra v.i. called out 'summoned)
አስጠራ	astärra v.t. had (s/o) called, summoned
ሰሙን—	səmmun—won a good name for oneself
ጠራ	tärra v.i. was pure, was clear; brightened (sky); cleared up (weather)
ጥራት	tərat n. purity, pureness
ጥሩ	təru adj. good, fine, nice
ሰመ—	səmä — dj. famous, reputable
ጥር	in ሰመ ጥር səmä tər adj. famous, reputable
ተጣራ	tätarra v.i. was filtered, refined, purified; was verified; was sold out
ጉዳዩ—	guddayu—the case was cleared up
የተጣራ ገቢ	yätätarra gäbi net income
—ወሬ	—wäre authentic news
አጠራ	atärra v.t. cleaned, purified, made clear
አጣራ	attarra v.t. purified distilled, filtered, clarified; cleared up; verified; sold out
ማጣሪያ	mattaria n. filter; strainer
ጠራራ የጠራራ ፀሐይ	tärara n. blazing sun yätärara şähai midday sun
*ጠራራ	*tärarra
ተንጠራራ	täntärarra v.i. reached out; streched one's arms (legs, oneself); aspired too much

አንጠራራ	in አንጠራራኝ antärarrañ I felt like stretching myself
ጠር	see ፀር
ጠርሙስ·ስ(ዝ)	tärmus (z) n. bottle
ጠርቡሽ	tärbuš n. tarboosh, fez
ጠሰቀ	tässäqä v.t. tied tightly
ጥስቅ አድርጎ ይበላል	tässəqq adərgo yəbälal he is a big eater
ጠሰቆ አሰረ	tässəqo assärä he tied fast
ጥስቅ ያለ ሰውነት	tässəqq yalä säwənnät strongly built body
ጠቀለለ	täqällälä v.t. coiled; wrapped, wrapped up; (a rug etc.); enveloped
አገሪቱን ጠቅ ልሉ ገዛ	he ruled over the entire country
ንዙን ጠቀለለ	gu"azun täqällälä he packed up his things
ጠቅልሎ አገባት	täqləlo agäbbat he married her (after having a woman as a mistress for a long time)
ቀርበቱን ጠቅ ልሎ ሄደ	qurbätun täqləlo hedä he left for good
ጠቅላላ	täqlalla adj. total; overall; general; rough (idea)
—ድምር	—dəmmər grand total, sum, total
—ጉባኤ	—guba'e general assembly
ጠቅላላውን/ በጠቅላላው	täqlallawən/ bätäqlallaw adv. in general, generally
በጠቅላላ አነጋገር	bätäqlalla annägagär generally speaking
ጠቅላይ	in ጠቅላይ መምሪያ täqlay mämriya headquarters
—ሚኒስቴር ጽሕፈት ቤት	—ministeṛ şəhfät bet office of the Prime Minister
—ሚኒስትር	—ministər n. Prime Minister, premier
—አቃቤ ሕግ	—aqqabe həgg n. Procurator Genera

—አዛዥ —azzaž n. commander- in- chief

—ፍርድ ቤት —fərd bet Supreme Court

ጥቅል ṭəqqəl n. parcel, package, coil

—ጎመን —gommän. head of a cabbage

የጥቅል ስም yäṭəqqel səm n. collective noun

ጥቅል ብራና ṭəqəll bəranna n. scroll (of parchment)

መጠቅለያ ወረቀት mäṭäqläya wäräqät n. wrapping paper

ተጠቃለለ täṭäqallälä v.i. was summed up, was concluded; was covered (subject), was aggregated

ግጠቃለያ maṭṭäqaläya n. conclusion

አጠቃለለ aṭṭäqallälä v.t. concluded, brought to an end.

አጠቃላይ aṭṭäqalay adj. comprehensive, general, inclusive

—ሕግ —həgg n. universal law

ጠቀመ ṭäqqämä v.t. benefitted, rendered service; v.i. was beneficial, was useful, helpful; stitched (clothes)

ጠቀሚታ ṭäqämeta n. benefit, advantage

ጣቃሚ ṭäqami adj. useful, beneficial, advantageous, valuable; profitable important (advice)

ጥቅም ṭəqəm n. benefit, profit, use, usefulness

ተጠቀመ täṭäqqämä v.i. used, made use of; benefitted; took the advantage of; drove a profit

ተጠቃሚ täṭäqqami n. beneficiary; user

ተጠቃሚ ሕዝብ —həzb consumers

ጠቀስ ṭäqqäsä v.t. winked at; cited, quoted; referred to; dipped a pen into ink

ሰማይ ጠቀስ sämay ṭäqqäs n. skyscraper

ጥቅስ ṭəqs n. citation, quotation

ትእምርት— tə'mərtä — n. quotation mark

ጥቅሻ ṭəqša n. wink

ተጠቃሽ in ተጠቃሽ ተሳቢ. täṭäqqaš täsabi n. direct object (gram.)

ተጠቃቀሰ täṭäqaqqäsä v.i. called by winking at each other

አጠቀሰ aṭäqqäsä v.t. dunked (bread)

አጣቀሰ aṭṭaqqäsä v.t. gave a comparative reference

ጠቀጠቀ ṭäqäṭṭäqä v.t. stuffed, pressed down ; compressed

ጢቃጠቆ ṭäqaṭäqo n. scar (from smallpox); spots, speckle, freckle

ጥቅጥቅ ṭäqṭäq adj. compacted, compressed, stuffed

*ጠቃ *ṭäqqa

ጥቃት ṭəqat n. oppression, assault, maltreatment

ተጠቃ täṭäqqa v. i. was oppressed, assaulted, maltreated; mated (for animals)

ተጠቂ täṭäqi adj. oppressed, maltreated

አጠቃ aṭäqqa v.t. oppressed, assaulted, maltreated, mated (for animals)

ብቸኝነት ያጠቃዋል bəčäññənnät yaṭäqawal he suffers from loneliness

እጥቂ aṭqi n. oppressor, aggressor

ጠቆመ ṭäqomä v.t. gave a hint, pointed out ; informed on; pointed at; nominated (for election)

ጠቋሚ ṭäquʷami n. informer, stool-pigeon (persoᵑ)

309

ጥቆግ ፣ ጠበረረ ... *ṭaqqoma* n. hint, information; nomination *(for election)*

ጥቁም ፣ ተጠቆመ *ṭaqqum* n. nominee *täṭäqqomä* v.i. was nominated; was pointed out

ጠቆረ *ṭäqqorä* v.i. turned black; grew dark

ጠቍራ *ṭäquʷara* adj. dark *(skin)*, Negro

ጥቁራ in ጥቁራ ዝንጀሮ *ṭəqure ẓəngäro* n. kind of dark baboon

ጥቁር *ṭəqur* adj. dark *(skin)*, black, Negro

—ራስ —ras n. layman

—ሰሌዳ —säleda n. blackboard

—አባይ —abbay n. Blue Nile

—አዝሙድ —azmud n. cumin *(black)*

—እንግዳ —əngəda n. an unexpected special guest

—እንጨት —ənčät n. ebony

—ገበያ —gäbäya n. black market

አጠቆረ *aṭäqqorä* v.t. blackened, blacked, darkened

ገንዘብ— *gänzab—* v.t. bought or sold currencies in the black market

ፊቱን— *fitun—* v.i. frowned, looked black, made a face

ጠበል *ṭäbäl* n. holy water; mineral water

—ቀመስ —*qämmäsä* partook in a ጠበል ceremony

—ተነከረ —*tänäkkärä* v.t. immersed oneself *(in holy water)*

—ተጠመቀ —*täṭämmäqä (same as above)*

—ጠዲቅ —*ṭädiq* n. monthly, celebration with food and drinks in honour of saints

ጠበልተኛ *ṭäbältäñña* n.

people who immerse themselves in holy water

ṭäbärrärä

ተንጠባራሪ *tänṭäbarari* adj. conceited

ṭäbäräbbärä

አጠበረበረ *aṭbäräbbärä* v.t. blinded *(by sun)* glared *(light)*, bedazzled

ጠበሰ *ṭäbbäsä* v.t. roasted *(meat, maize)*, fried, grilled; toasted; scorched

ጠብሳ *ṭäbasa* n. scar

ጥብስ *ṭəbs* n. fried, roast

—ሥጋ —*səga* n. roasted meat

—ወጥ —*wäṭ* n. stew

መጥበሻ *mäṭbäša* n. frying or roasting pan

ጠበሰቀ *ṭäbässäqä* v.t. hit violently *(with a stick)*

ጠበቀ *ṭäbbäqä* v.t. waited for; looked after, watched, took care of; expected; waited for; preserved

ቃሉን *qalun*—he kept his promise

አፉን *afun*—was cautious *(in expressing what one wants to say)*

ጊዜ— *gize—* waited for an opportune time

ጠበቃ *ṭäbäqa* n. advocate, lawyer, attorney

—ገዛ —*gäzza* n. hired a lawyer

ጠባቂ *ṭäbbaqi* n. keeper, guardian, custodian

በር— *bärr—* n. doorkeeper

በግ— *bäg—* n. shepherd

የበላይ— *yäbälay ṭäbbaqi* n. patron

ጥበቃ *ṭəbbäqa* n. watching, guarding; protection, conservation

የሕዝብ ጤና — ሚኒስቴር Ministry of Public Health

የሕዝብ ደህን ነት—ሚኒስቴር Ministry of Public Security

310

ጥብቅ ṭəbbəq adj . acting ; mistress (concubine)

ጥብቅና ṭəbqənna n. advocacy, power of attorney

ተጠበቀ tāṭäbbäqä v.i. -was expected; was kept; was looked after; was taken care of

ተጠባበቀ tāṭäbabbäqä v.i. expected; awaited, looked forward to

ተጠባባቂ tāṭäbabaqi adj. acting

—ሹም —šum n. acting head

ጠበቀ ṭäbbäqä v. t. was tightened, was firm, was fastened; was stressed (syllable)

ጠባቃ ṭäbäqa adj . tight, fast; firm

ጥብቅ ṭəbq adj . tight tied; severe, strict, rigid ; drastic

ግስጠን ቀቂያ —masṭänqäqiya n. strict warning

—ግሳሰቢያ —masassäbiya n. cautionary notice

—ትእዛዝ —tə'əzaz n.strict order

ጥብቆ ṭəbbəqo n. long children's shirt

መጣብቅ mäṭabq n. glue

አጠባበቀ aṭäbbaqä v.t. tightened, fastened; put emphasis

አጥባቂ in ወገ አጥባቂ wäg aṭbaqi adj. conservative

አጥብቆ aṭbəqo adv. strongly, very much

ተጣበቀ tāṭabbäqä v.t. was glued, was stuck together, adhered to; clung to

አጣበቀ aṭṭabbäqä v.t. glued; stuck together

አጣብቂኝ aṭṭabqiññ n. very narrow passage (way through)

ማጣበቂያ maṭṭabäqiya n. glue, gum , adhesive

ጠበበ ṭäbbäbä v.i. was narrow ; was tight (clothes)

ጠባብ ṭäbbab adj. narrow, tight

አስተሳሰበ— astäsasäbä— adj. narrow-minded

እጅ— əggä—n. long Ethiopian shirt

ጥበት ṭəbbät n. constriction (for limited space)

ተጠበበ in ተጨነቀ ተጠበበ tāǧännäqä ·tāṭäbbäbä v.i. was preoccupied, worried, was careworn

ተጣበበ tāṭabbäbä v.i. was crammed with; was crowded

አጠበበ aṭäbbäbä v.t. narrowed, tightened

አጣበበ aṭṭabbäbä v.t. crowded, jammed

*ጠበበ *ṭäbbäbä

ጠቢብ ṭäbib n. wise ; artisan

ጠይብ ṭäyib n. one with the evil eye

ጥበበኛ ṭəbäbäñña adj. wise skillful, clever, sapient, sagacious

ጥበብ ṭəbäb n. wisdom, technique

ሥነ— sənä — n. fine arts

ኪነ— kinä—n. art, work of art, technology

የእጅ— yä'əǧǧ—n. handicraft

—ቀሚስ —qämis n. dress with a coloured hem

ጥበብ ፈለክ ṭəbäb fäläk n. astrology

ጠበደለ ṭäbäddälä v.i. became fat

ጠብደል ṭäbdäl adj. fat, large

—እንጀራ —ənǧära n. large ənǧära

ጠበጠበ ṭäbäṭṭäbä v.t. patted, (a ball), patted (hit gently with the open hand)

ጥብጠባ ṭəbṭäba n. act of patting a ball

ነጠብጣብ näṭäbṭab n. dots

ተንጠባጠበ tänṭäbaṭṭäbä v.i.

አንጠባጠበ dripped, dribbled, trickled *(of water)*, was scattered *anṭäbaṭṭäba* v.t. dribbled, dropped one by one, dripped, let fall one by one, scattered

ጠባ *ṭäbba* v.t. sucked, suckled,

መስከረም ሲጠባ *mäskäräm siṭäba* at the end of the rainy season, at the beginning of autumn

ነጋ ጠባ *nägga ṭäbba* adv day in day out

ጠቢ *ṭäbi* in ጀሮ ጠባ *goro ṭäbi* n. spy, stool–pigeon, nark, informant

ጥቢ *ṭabbi* n. spring

ጥቦት *ṭabbot, or* ጠቦት *ṭäbbot* n. lamb

ተጠባ in ኮሶ ተጠባ *kosso täṭabba* v.i have tapeworms

አጠባ in ጡት አጠባ *ṭut aṭäbba* v.t. adopted a child

አጥቢ in አጥቢ እንሰሳት *aṭbi ansasat* n. mammals

ጠባይ *ṭäbay* n. charac er, conduct, behaviour, manners; nature *(character)*

ልዩ — *layyu*–n. peculiarity
ጠባየ
መልካም *ṭäbayä mälkam* adj. good - natured, courteous

— መጥፎ *mäṭfo*—adj. ill-natured

ጠብ *ṭäb* n. quarrel
ጠበኛ *ṭäbäññä* adj. quarrelsome, quick-tempered

ጠብ አለ *ṭäbb alä* v.i. dripped,

ጠብ የማ ይለው *ṭäbb yämmayläw* adj. stingy, mean, niggardly

ሥራው ጠብ አይልም *saraw ṭäbb aylamm* futile exercise, fruitless work

ጠብ in ጠብ እርግፍ አለ *ṭäbb argaff alä* v.i. toiled, hustled and bustled, was submissive

ጠብታ *ṭäbbata* n. drop; speck
ጠቦት *see* ጠባ
ጠንሰሰ *ṭänässäsä* v.t. mixed hop and yeast for brewing beer

ጥንስስ *ṭansas* n. the mixture of the above

ጠነቆለ *ṭänäqqolä* v.t. engaged in sorcery, was a soothsayer; pricked some one's eye *(with the finger)*

ጠንቋይ *ṭänqu"ay* n. wizard, magician, witchdoctor, sorcerer

ጥንቆላ *ṭanqola* n. witchcraft, magic, sorcery

ተጠናቆለ *täṭänaqqolä* v.i. was a dare-devil

*ጠነቀረ *ṭänäqqärä
አሰናቀረ *aṭṭänaqqärä* v.i. compiled *(news report etc.)*

ጠነቀቀ *ṭänäqqäqä* v.t. took care *(in orthography)*

ጥንቃቃ *ṭänqaqqa* adj. careful, prudent, cautious, meticulous

ጥንቁቅ *ṭanquq* adj. careful; meticulous; cautious, thorough, scrupulous, prudent

ጥንቃቄ *ṭanaqqaqe* n. care, carefulness, precaution, prudence

ተጠነቀቀ *täṭänäqqäqä* v.i. was careful, took care, watched- out, took precautions, was prudent

ተጠናቀቀ *täṭänaqqäqa* v.i. was completed, was finished, was brought to an end; was ready

አጠናቀቀ *aṭṭänaqqäqä* v.t. completed, finished, brought to an end; made ready

አስጠነቀቀ   *asṭänäqqäqä*   v.t. warned, alarmed, put on the alert, cautioned

ማስጠንቀቂያ   *masṭänqäqiya*   n. warning, alarm, notice *(warning)*

*ጠነበረ   **ṭänäbbärä*

ጠንባራ   *ṭänbarra also* ጠምባራ adj. one-eyed, weaksighted *(insul·)*

*ጠነበሰ   **ṭänäbbäsä*

ጠንባሳ   *ṭänbassa* adj. weaksighted *(insult)*

ጥንብስብስ   *ṭənbəsbəs* adj. weaksighted

ተጠናበሰ   *täṭänabbäsä* v.i. was weak-sighted; walked unsteadily *(due to weak sight)*

ጠነበዘ   *ṭänäbbäzä* v.i drunk oneself to death

እስኪ. ጠነብዝ ጠጣ ጠንባዥ   he drunk far too much

ጠንባዥ   *ṭänbäzzä* n. drunkard

ጠነባ   *ṭänäbba* v.i. stank, became putrid

ጥምባት   *ṭənbat, also* ጠምባት *ṭəmbat* n. stink

ጥንባታም   *ṭənbaṭam* adj. stinking, fetid, malodorous

ጥንብ   *also* ጥምብ *ṭənb, ṭəmb* adj.stinking, fetid; n. carcass, dead body *(of animal)*

-አንሣ   *– ansa* n. vulture, scavenger

አጠነባ   *aṭänäbba* v.t. putrefied

ጠነነ   *ṭännänä* v.i. became difficult

ጠነነኝ   *ṭännännäññ* I found it difriult *(to understand)*

አጠነነ   *aṭännänä* v.t. made difficult

ጠነከረ   *ṭänäkärä* v.i. was strong, rigorous; was hard, was solid, was tough

ጠንካራ   *tänkkära* adj. strong, hard, solid: firm, tough, robust

ጥንካሬ   *ṭənəkkare* n. strength, toughness, firmness

ተጠናከረ   *täṭänakkärä* v.i. was reinforced, was envigorated, recuperated; was consolidated; was emphasized

ማጠናከሪያ   *maṭṭänakäria* n. reinforcement

አጠነከረ   *aṭänäkkärä* v.t. reinforced; fortified; consolidated

አጠናከረ   *aṭṭänakkärä* v.t. reinforced; emphasiz·d consolidated

*ጠነወተ ተጠናወተ   **ṭänäwwätä täṭänawwätä* v.t. attacked *(disease)*

ጠነዘ   *ṭänäzza* v.i. burnt due to lack of water *(cooking food)*

ወሬው ጠነዘ   *wärew ṭänäzza* the story became boring *(due to hearing repeatedly)*

ጠናዛ   *ṭänaza* ad; feeble and ugly

*ጠነጋ አጠናጋ   **ṭänägga in* በጥፊ አጠናጋ *baṭəffi aṭṭänagga* v.t . slapped s/o's face violently

*ጠነጠነ ጥንጥን   **ṭänäṭṭänä ṭənṭən* adj. *(s/t)* coiled

ተጠነጠነ   *täṭänäṭṭänä* v.i. was coiled

አጠነጠነ   *aṭänäṭṭänä* ?.t. coiled ; pondered over, put one's thinking cap on

ጠነፈፈ አጠነፈፈ ማጠንፈፊያ   *ṭänäffäfä* v.i. was sifted *aṭänäffäfä* v.t. sifted *maṭänfäfiya* n. sifter

*ጠና ጠኘ ጥናት ጠና   **ṭänna see* ደጅ ጠኘ *ṭänat see* ደጅ ጥናት *ṭänna* v.i. was strong was firm

ጥኑ | *ṭənu* adj. strong, firm

ጥናት | *ṭənat* n. strength, steadfastness; study, research; survey *(assessment)*

ተጠና | *tāṭänna* v. i. was studied, was surveyed, was considered

ጉዳዩ እየተ ጠና ነው· | *guddayu əyyätāṭänna näw* the case is being considered, studied

አጠና | *aṭänna* v.t. made strong, hardened; studied; surveyed

ተጥናና | *tāṭnanna*, also ተጸና *tāṣnanna* v.i. found solace, was encouraged

አጥናና | *aṭnanna*, also አጸና *aṣnanna* v.t. consoled, gave comfort, encouraged, gave solace

አጥናኝ | *aṭnaň* n. consoler

አስጠና | *asṭänna* v.t. tutored

አስጠኚ | *asṭäňňi* n. tutor

ጠኔ | *ṭänne* n. famished condition

—ይዞኛል | *—yəzoňňal* I am famished for food

ጠኔያም | *ṭännəyam* n. starveling

ጠንቅ | *ṭänq* n. cause *(of s/t bad)*

ጠንቀኛ | *ṭänqäňňa* adj. harmful, disastrous, evil; vicious *(spiteful)*

ጠንበለል | *see* ጠምበለል

ጠንፍ | *ṭänf* n. border, edge

*ጠወለወለ | *ṭäwäläwwälä*

አጥወለወለ | *aṭwäläwwälä* v.t. felt giddy; nauseated

ጠወለገ | *ṭäwällägä* v.i. faded, withered; fatigued, wearied; wilted

ጠውላጋ | *ṭäwlagga* adj. withered; fatigued; weary *(body)*

*ጠወረ | *see* ጠሬ

ጠዘጠዘ | *ṭäzäṭṭäzä* v.i. smarted *(sharp pain)*

ጠዝጣዛ | *ṭäzṭāza* n. smart *(sharp pain)*

ጥዘጥዜ | *ṭäzäṭṭaze* n. smart *(sharp pain)*

ጠየመ | *ṭäyyämä* v.i. became dark brown

ጠይም | *ṭäyyəm* adj. dark-brown *(person's complexion)*

ጠየቀ | *ṭäyyäqä* v.t. asked, inquired, demanded; entailed, questioned; paid a visit, called on someone

ጠያቂ | *ṭäyyaqi* in በሽተኛ— *bäššəttäňňa —* n. visitor *(of sick person)*

ጥያቄ | *ṭäyyäqa* n. visiting; questioning

ጥያቄ | *ṭäyyaqe* n. question, request, query, interrogation

የጥያቄ ምልክት | *yäṭäyyaqe mäläkkät* n. question mark

የቃል ጥያቄ | *yäqal ṭäyyaqe* n. interview

መጠይቅ | *mäṭäyyəq* n. questionnaire

ተጠየቀ | *tāṭäyyäqä* v.i. was asked

ተጠየቅ | *tāṭäyyäq* n. logic

ተጠያቂ | *tāṭäyyaqi* adj. responsible, accountable

መጠየቂያ ቅፅ | *mäṭäyyäqiya qəṣṣ* n. requisition form

ተጠያየቀ | *tāṭäyayyäqä* v.t. sought information

አጠየቀ | *aṭäyyäqä* v.t. proved, gave evidence

አጠያየቀ | *aṭṭäyayyäqä* v. t. collected information; became doubtful

አጠያያቂ | *aṭṭäyayaqi* adj. doubtful

አጣየቀ | *aṭṭayyäqä* v.t. became questionable, disputable

*ጠያፈ | *ṭäyyäfä*

ጥያፍ | *ṭäyyaf* also ፀያፍ *ṣäyyaf* adj. distasteful, unbecoming, repugnant; vulgar; taboo

314

ጥዩፍ **ṭəyyuf** adj. fastidious, squeamish *(easily disgusted)*

ጥይፉተኛ **ṭəyyəftäñña** adj. fastidious, squeamish *(easily disgusted)*

ተጠየፈ **täṭäyyäfä** v.i. abhorred; was fastidous, squeamish

ተጠያፈ **täṭäyyafi** adj. fastidious, squeamish

አጠያየፈ **aṭṭäyayyäfä** v. t. disliked, disrelished, distasted

አሰጠየፈ also **አጸየፈ asṭäyyäfä aṣṣäyyäfä** v.t. was disgusting

አሰጠያፈ also **አጸያፊ asṭäyyafi**, **aṣṣäyyafi** adj, disgusting, nasty *(remarks)*; vulgar, repellent

ጠያር ግመል **ṭäyyar gəmäl** n. dromedary

ጠየብ **ṭäyəb** n. cottage artisan *(used in derogatory sense)*

ጠየቀ **täddäqä** see also ፀደቀ v.i. took root *(transplated plant)*

ጠዲቅ **ṭädik** n. loaf of raised bread served on a Christian religious occasion

ጠበል— **ṭäbäl**—n. food and drinks served on a Christian religious occasion

*ጠደፈ *ṭädäffä

ጥድፊያ **ṭədfiya** n. haste, hurry, rush

ተጣደፈ **täṭaddäfä** v.i. hastened, hurried, rushed

አጣደፈ **aṭṭaddäfä** v.t. hastened, hurried, rushed

በጥያቄ assailed him with አጣደረው questions

አጣዳፊ **aṭṭadafi** adj. urgent, pressing

አጣዳፊ ሥራ **aṭṭadafi səra** n. pressing business, urgent task

ጠዳ **ṭädda** see also ፀዳ v.i.

---

was clean, was neat

ጥዱ **ṭädu** adj. clean, neat

የማይጠዳው **yämmayṭädaw** adj. gloomy, cheerless *(person)*

ተጣዳ **täṭadda** v.t. cleaned oneself

ጠድከል **ṭädkäl** n. a pair of compasses

ጠጅ **ṭäǧǧ** n. hydromel, mead

—ቤት — **bet** n. bar where ṭäǧǧ is served; person in charge of the distribution of ṭäǧǧ *(in a royal palace)*

—ጣለ —**ṭalä** v.t. prepared ṭäǧǧ

የወይን— **yäwäyən**— n. wine

ጠገራ in ጠገራ ምሳር **ṭägära məssar** n. hatchet, axe

—ብር —**bərr** n. thaler

ጠገበ **ṭäggäbä** v.i. was satiated, was full *(from food)*; was arrogant, conceited

ጥጋብ **ṭəgab** n. satiety; plenty; arrogance, conceit

ጥጋበኛ **ṭəgabäñña** adj. arrogant, conceited

አጠገበ **aṭäggäbä** v.t. satiated;

አጥጋቢ **aṭgabi** adj. satisfactory, adequate, convincing

—መልስ —**mäls** n. saisfactory answer

አጣገበ **aṭṭaggäbä** v.t. supplied plentifully

ጠገነ **ṭäggänä** v.t. repaired, mended, fixed, patched up, treatd a fracture or dislocation

ጠጋኝ **ṭäggañ** n. craftsman

ጥገና **ṭəggäna** repair, fixing

—ክፍል —**kəfəl** n. maintenance shop

ቀዶ— **qäddo**—n. opertion *(surgical)*, surgery

ጥጉን **ṭəggən** adj. mended

ተጠጋገነ **täṭägaggänä** v.i. helped each other; backed each other up

አስጠገነ	*asṭäggänä* v.t. had s/t repaired, mended
*ጠገገ	*ṭäggägä* v.i. cicatrised, healed up, skinned over
ጠጉር	*ṭägur* n. hair
ጠጉረ ሉጭ	*ṭägura luččä* smooth-haired
ከርዳዳ	—*kärdadda* woolly haired
ጠጉራም	*ṭäguram* adj. hairy
ጠጉር ቆራጭ	*ṭägur qoräč* n. barber, hair-dresser
አስተካካይ	—*astäkakay* barber, hair-dresser
ማስተካከያ ቤት	—*mastäkakäya bet* n. barber-shop
አሰዳር	—*assäṭar* n. hairdo,
የበግ	*yäbäg* n. wool
ጠግ	*ṭägä* see also በግ n. wealth; grace
ጠጋቢስ	*ṭäggabis* adj. grace-less
ባለጠጋ	*baläṭägga* adj. wealthy
*ጠጋ	*ṭägga
ጠግ	*ṭägg* n. side; corner adv. close to; vicinity
ያዘ	—*yazä* v.t. took cover, cornered onself
ጠጋኛ	*ṭäggäñña* a dj./n dependant, subject (not independant)
ጠጋኝነት	*ṭäggäññännät* n. dependency
ጠጋኝ ሀረግ	*ṭägägñña ḥaräg* n. subordinate clause
ሀገር	—*hagär* n. protectorate
ባለጠግ	*baläṭägg* n. protègè
ተጠጋ	*täṭägga* v.i. got near, advanced upon, drew close, approached; took shelter, sought protection
መጠጊያ	*mäṭṭägiya* n refuge, shelter
ተጠጋጋ	*täṭägagga* v.i. came close to each other, was contiguous, were put close togther
አጠጋጋ	*aṭṭägaga* v.t. cause to come close to each

	other, put close together
አስጠጋ	*asṭägga* v.t. sheltered (protected); harboured (gave shelter); brought close
ጠጠረ	*ṭäṭṭärä* v.i. hardened; solidified
ጠጠር	*ṭäṭär* n. gravel, pebble
ጣይ	—*ṭay* n fortune teller (using pebbles)
ጥጥር	*ṭəṭṭər* adj solid, hard
አጠጠረ	*aṭäṭṭärä* v.t. hardened, solidified; made difficult
ጥያቄውን አጠጠረው	*ṭəyyaqewən aṭäṭṭäräw* he made the question difficult
*ጠጠተ	*ṭäṭṭätä, see also ጸጸተ *säṣṣätä, with pronominal suffix e.g. ጠጠተኝ *ṭäṭṭätäññ* I regreted; I was filled with remorse
ጠጠት	*ṭäṭät* n. regret, remorse
ተጠጠተ	*täṭäṭṭätä* v.i. regretted, repented, was sorry
ጠጣ	*ṭäṭṭa* v.t. drunk; smoked (cigarettes)
እቁብ	*əqqub* —joined a money saving association
ጠጭ	*ṭäč̣č̣* n. drinker, drunkard
መጠጥ	*mäṭäṭṭ* n. beverage, drink, strong drink. liquor
ውሃ መጠጫ	*wəha mäṭäč̣č̣ä* n. drinking vessel; tip
ተጣጣ	*täṭaṭṭa* vi. was added to, was supplemented
አጠጣ	*aṭäṭṭa* v.t. gave to drink; irrigated, watered (a plant)
አጣጣ	*aṭṭaṭṭa* v.t. joined s/o for a drink
አጣጭ	*aṭṭač̣* n. drinking partner

ጠፈረ	*ṭäffärä* v.t. wrapped and tied tighty
ጠፈር	*ṭäfər* n. leather, strip, thong
--ነካሽ	--*näkaš* itinerant merchant *(who uses beast of burden for transporting goods; pejoraive)*
አጠፈረ	*aṭṭafärä* in በጥፊ አጠ ፈረ *bäṭəfi aṭṭaffärä* slapped on the face
ጠፈር፡	*ṭafar* n. firmament, space *where the universe exists)*
ጠፈረታኛ	*ṭäfäratäñña* n astronaut, cosmonaut
የጠፈር መን ኮራኩር	*yäṭäfär mänkorakur* n. space-ship
ጠፈጠፈ	*ṭäfäṭṭäṭä* v.t. levelled, flattened out *bäṭəffi ṭäfäṭṭäfäw* he slapped him on the face repeatedly
በጥፊ ጠፈጠፈው	
ጠፍጣፋ	*ṭäfṭaffa* adj. flat, level
ጥፍጥፍ፡	*ṭəfṭəf* n. animal dung flattened with the hands in order to dry to be used as fuel
* ጠፈጠፈ	* *ṭäfäṭäffa*
ጠፈጠፈ ተንጠፈጠፈ	*ṭäfäṭäf* n. drips *tänṭäfäṭṭäfä* v.t. dripped. trickled, streamed *(sweat)*
አንጠፈጠፈ	*anṭäfäṭṭäfä* v.t dripped *(sweat)*, dripped-dry
ጠፋፋ	*ṭäfṭafa* v.t. started draining *(became less wet)*
ጠፍ አለ	*ṭäff alä* v.i. became clean, neat, tidy, spruce
አጠፈፈ	*aṭäffäfä* v.t. drained
ጠፋ	*ṭäffa* v.i disappeared, was lost, went astray, vanished, was missing; was extinguished; go out *(of light, fire, electricity)*; died *(of engine)*, was eradicated; was spoilt *(child;)* was

	destroyed *(country)* in ስሙ ጠፋኝ I forgot his name
ጠፋኝ	
ስሙ ጠፋ መንገዱ ጠፋው	he was discredited he lost his way
ብላይቱ ጠፋኝ አገሩቱ ጠፋች	I am at a loss the country was destroyed
የሚያያርገው ጠፋው ይሆ ጠፋ	he was puzzled, perplexed run away with *(absconded with)*
ገንዘብ ጠፋ ው ጠፋበት	he lost money
ጠፋ ሆነ	was abandoned, deserted *(country)*
መሬት	--*märet* n. waste land, undeveloped land, unclaimed or abandoned land
በብት	--*käbt* n. strayed animal
ጨረቃ	*čäräqa* n. moonless night
ጥፉ	in መልክ ጥፉ *mälkä-ṭəfu* adj. ugly
ጥፉት	*ṭəfat* n. mistake, fault; offense, guilt, damage, destruction
ምን ጥፉት አጠፋህ	what wrong did you commit?
ጥፉተኛ	*ṭəfatäñña* n. wrogdoer. offender, guilty
መጥፎ	*mäṭfo* adj. bad, wicked, evil,
ሽታ	*šəta* repugnant odour, bad smell
ተጠፋፋ	*täṭäfaffa* v.. lost each other
ተጣፋ	*täṭaffa* v.i. desroyed each other
አጠፋ	*aṭäffa* v.t. committed a crime, did wrong, committed an offense; exterminatd, eradicated; extinguished, turned off *(light)*, blew out *(candle)*

ራሱን አጠፋ	did away with himself
ስም አጠፋ	defamed (s/o's reputation)
ድንግል አጠፋ	deflowered
ገንዘብ አጠፋ	wasted money, squandered money
በላጲስ አጠፋ	erased with a rubber
አጥፊ	aṭafi n. wrongdoer, offender, guilty
አጥፊና ጠፊ	aṭfinna ṭafi mortal enemies
አጣፋ	aṭṭaffa v.t. robed oneself (with šämma); exceeded in rank. character, achievment etc.
ጡሌ	ṭulle n. gourd (Bottle)
ጡል ጡል አለ	ṭull ṭull alä v.i. walked in a fast and graceless manner; meddled in
ጦልጡላ	ṭolṭuʷalla adj. meddlesome
ተንጦለጦለ	tänṭoläṭṭolä v.i. was meddlesome
ጡር	ṭur n. wrongdoing
ነፍሰ —	näfsä— adj. pregnant
—ጡርነት	—ṭurǝnnät n. pregnancy
ጡረኛ	ṭuräñña n. a wrongdoer
ጡር ሰሪ	ṭur säri n. wrongdoer
ጡብ	ṭub n. brick , tile
ጡብ ጡብ አለ	ṭubb ṭubb alä v.i. hopped about (children, birds etc.)
ጡት	ṭut n. breast, teat
የጡት ጫፍ	yäṭut čaf n. nipple; spout
ጡት ተወ	was weaned
ጡት አጠባ	adopted a child
ጡት ጣለ	was weand
ጡት አስጣለች	weaned
የጡት ልጅ	adopted child
የጡት አባት	foster father
የጡት እናት	foster mother
ጡንቻ	ṭunča n. muscle
ጡንቻኛ	ṭunčäñña aj. hefty, strong; quarrelsome
ጡንቻም	ṭunčamma adj. muscular (having much muscle)

ጡዋት	also ጥዋት ṭuwat, ṭawat n. morning
ነገ ጢት	tomorrow morning
ዛሬ ጢት	this morning
ጡዋትና ግታ	everyday, always
ጡዋት ጡዋት	every morning
ጡጥ አደረገ	ṭuṭṭ adärrägä v.t. sent out wind (farted)
ጡጦ	ṭuṭṭo n. baby's bottle.
የጡጦ ጫፍ	nipple of baby's bottle
ጡጫ	ṭuččʼa n. fist, punch
በጡጫ መታ	bäṭuččʼa mätta gave a blow with the fist, punched
ጢም	ṭim also ጺም ṣim n. beard
ባፉ ጢም ተደፋ	fell on one's face
ጢም አለ	ṭimm alä v.i. was filled to the brim, was filled to capacity
ጢም ብሎ ጥላ	ṭimm bǝlo molla v.i. was filled to capacity
ጢት አለ	ṭiqq alä v.t. spat between the teeth (as a sign of disgust or contempt)
ጢታ	ṭiqqǝta n. spittle, spit
ጢን አለ	ṭinn alä v.i. overflowed; was full; was conceited
ጢን ብሎ ሰከረ	he was dead drunk
ጢጥ	in ጢጥ መሬት ṭiṭṭ märet n. plot of land
ጣለ	ṭalä v.t. threw away, threw out, threw down; dropped, lost; discarded
መልህት—	—anchored
መሠረት—	—laid the foudation
ተላይ—	—measured land (for distribution or to impose a land tax)
ተረጥ—	imposed a tax
በረደ—	hailed
ተስፋ—	placed hope
አደጋ ላይ—	exposed to danger, imperiled
አደጋ—	attacked by surprise

318

እጣ—	drew lots
እምነት—	placed confidence
እንቁላል—(ች)	laid eggs
ዐይኑን—	set eyes on, have an eye to
ዕቁብ—	paid the əqqub money (see ዕቁብ)
ድንኳን—	pitched (a tent)
ዳስ—	erected a booth
ዝናብ—	rained
ጠጅ—	prepared hydromel
ጡት—	was weaned
ጥሎሽ—	gave a dowry (by fiancé to his fiancée)
ጥንቡን—	hit rock bottom (price)
ጨርቁን—	he was stark raving mad
ጣይ	in ጣይ በሽታ ṭay bāššəta n. epilepsy (also የሚጥል በሽታ)
ጥለት	ṭəlät n. embroidered fringe of dress
ጥሎ ግለፅ	ṭəlomaläf n. knockout (game)
ጥሎሽ	ṭəloš n. dowry (money the fiancé gives to his fiancée)
የእግዚአ ብሔር—	ya'əgziabəher — the wrath of God
መጣያ	in ቀሻሻ መጣያ qušaša māṭaya n. dump
ተጣጣለ	in እጣ ተጣጣለ əṭa ṭäṭaṭalä v. i. drew lots also እጣ ጣለ
ጣልቃ	see ጠለቀ,
ጣመ	ṭamä v.i. tasted pleasant, was savoury, was tasty
ጣም	ṭam n. taste also ጣዕም
ጣመ ቢስ	ṭamä bis adj . tasteless, crude (not having grace, taste or rifinement)
ጣም የለሽ	ṭam yälläš adj. tasteless; crude (not having grace, taste or refinement)
—እጣ	—aṭṭa v.i. was tasteless (food)
አጣመ	aṭamä v.t. made

	tasty ; spiced
አጣጣመ	aṭṭaṭamä v.t. tasted
ጣሙን	ṭamän n. muscular fatigue
ጣጣ	ṭama n.toil
—ገንዘብ	— gänzäb n. hard earned money, property
ጣረ	ṭarä v.i. tried hard, toiled, made an effort
—ሞት	—mot n. death throes. agony
ጥረት	ṭərät n. effort, endeavour
መጣር መጋር	māṭar māgar inf. to toil, work hard
ተጣጣረ	tāṭaṭarä v.. endeavoured, strove for, tried hard
ተጣጣሪ	tāṭaṭari adj. enterprising
አጣጣረ	aṭṭaṭari v.t . was in death throes
ጣሰ	ṭasä v. broke through (a fence etc.); tres passed, breached, violated (the law); pounded coarsely
ጥሻ	ṭəša n. bush, thicket
የማይጣስ ህግ	inviolable law
ጣሰሰ	ṭassäsä v.t trampled down
ጣሳ	ṭasa n. can, tin
በጣሳ አሻገ	bāṭasa aššägä v.t. canned (food)
የጣሳ ምግብ	yāṭasa məgab n. canned-food
ጣቃ	ṭaqa n. bolt of cloth
ጣባ	ṭaba n. small clay dish (container)
ጣት	ṭat n finger
ሌባ—	leba-. index finger
ግህል—	mahəl-n. middle finger
ትንሽ—	tənnaš - n. little finger
አውራ—	awra - n. thumb
የተለበት—	yäqäläbät — n. ring finger
የእግር—	ya'əgər - n. toe
የጣት ቢዛ	yäṭat beza n. thimble
—እንጓ	—angu"a n. knuckle
ጣእም	ṭa'əm n. taste, flavour
ጣእመ ቃል	ṭa'əmä qal n. elo-

319

—ዘማ
ጣአስ
ጣኦት
—አምላኪ
—አምልኮ
ጣወንት

ጣዝማ
—ማር

ጣይ
ጣያ

ምጣድ

ብረት ምጣድ

ጣጣ

ጣጠኛ

ባለ ብዙ ጣጣ

ጣጣ የለሽ

*ጣጣ
ጣጣቴ
ተንጣጣ

ጣፈ

ጥፈት
መጣፊያ

መጣፍ
ጣፈጠ

quence
—*zema* n. melody
ṭa'os n. peacock
ṭa'ot n. idol
—*amlaki* adj.
idolatrous
—*amləko* n. idolatry
ṭawənt n. one that has
taken someone's wife
or husband
ṭazma n. bee-like insect
—*mar* n. honey of
such an insect
see ፀሀይ
ṭadä v.t. put a cooking
pot, a kettle, a pan
etc. on the fire
məṭad n. griddle, disc
*(of clay in which
bread is made)*
bərät — n. disc *(of
iron on which coffee
etc. is roasted)*
ṭaṭa n. trouble, complication, nuisance
ṭaṭäñña adj. trouble-
some, problematic,
complicated
bulä bəzu ṭaṭa full of
problems
ṭaṭa yälläš adj. ir-
reproachable, perfect,
unimpeachable
*ṭaṭṭa
ṭaṭate n. talkative
tänṭaṭṭa v.i. snapped
(as of burning wood),
crackled *(as of burn-
ing dry sticks);* was
loquacious
ṭafä see also ጻፈ v.t.
wrote; patched/up
(a garment)
ṭəfät n. writing
mäṭafiya n. a patch
*(piece of material put
on a hole or damaged
part of a garment)*
mäṭaf n. book also
መጽሐፍ
ṭaffäṭä v.i. was sweet,
was tasty; was de-
licious, was savoury

ጣፈጠ

ጣፈጭ

መጣፈጥ

ነጭ—

ጥቁር—

አጣፈጠ

ጣሪያ
ጢስ

ጢስ
የመርዝ—

ጢሰኛ

ጢሳም
አጢሰ

ቤቱን አጢሰ
ኩብት
አጢያሽ
ጤና
የሕዝብ ጤና
ጥበቃ
ሚኒስቴር
ጤና ቢስ

—ነፍ

—አዳም

—አጣ

ይስጥልኝ

የጤና ጠንቅ

ለጤናም

ጤነኛ

ጤናማ

ṭafaṭa adj. sweet,
tasty, delicious
ṭafač̣ adj. sweet, tasty,
delicious
mäṭafäṭ n.niggela seed,
fennel-flower cf. አዝ
ሙድ
näč̣č̣ — n. bishop's
weed. cf. ነጭ አዝሙድ
ṭəqur — n. black
cummin cf. ጥቁር
አዝሙድ
aṭaffäṭä v.t. sweet-
ened, flavoured, made
tasty
ṭaffiya n. spleen, milt
ṭesä v.i. smoked; was
infuriated
ṭis n. smoke, fume
yämärz— n. poison
gas
ṭisäñña n. tenant far-
mer
ṭisam adj. smoky
aṭesä v.t. smoked
(cigarettes)
I have fumigated
the house
aṭiyaš n. smoker
ṭena n. health
yähəzb ṭena ṭəbbäqa
minister Ministry of
Public Health
ṭena bis adj. sick,
ill; disturbing *(person)*
nässa v.t dis-
turbed
addam, or ጤናዳም
ṭenaddam n. rue *(ruṭa
hortensis)*
—*aṭṭa* v.t. was in
poor health
yosṭəlləññ how are
you? good-bye, good
morning, good
evening, good night
yäṭena ṭänq insani-
tary
läṭenawo to your
health
ṭenäñña adj. healthy
(person)
ṭenamma adj. healthy

320

ጤዛ   *ṭeza* n. dew

ጤፍ   *ṭef* n. millet-like cereal whose flour is used for *ǝngära*

ማኛ—   *mañña*— very white ṭef

ሰርገኛ —   *särrgäñña*— *ṭef* of mixed colour

ቡንኝ   *bunnǝññ*— rapidly growing *ṭef*

ጥቁር—   *ṭǝqur ṭef* brown *ṭef*

ጥለት   see ጣለ

ጥላ   *ṭǝla* n. umbrella; shade, shadow

ጥላማ   *ṭǝlamma* adj. shady

ጥላ ቢስ   *ṭǝla bis* adj. graceless

ጃን ጥላ   *ǧanṭǝla* n. parasol

ዓይነ ጥላ   *ayǝnä ṭǝla* n. phobia

ጥሉ ማለፍ   see ጣለ

ጥሞና   *ṭǝmmona* n. calm

በጥሞና   *bäṭǝmmona* adv. calmly

ጥሩምባ   *ṭǝrumba* n. trumpet, auto horn

ጥሩምባኛ   *ṭǝrumbäñña* n. trumpeter

ጥሩምባ ነፋ   *ṭǝrumba näffä* v. t. played the trumpet; praised himself; bragged

ጥሪት   *ṭǝrit* n. property, possession

—ሰበሰበ   —*säbässäbä* v.t. accumulated wealth

ባለጥሪት   *balä ṭǝrit* n. a well-to-do person

ጥሬ   *ṭǝre* n. green *(grain)*; crude

—ሥጋ   —*sǝga* n. raw meat

—እቃ   —*ǝqa* n. raw material

—ዘር   —*zär* n. verbal noun

—ዘይት   —*zäyǝt* n. crude oil

—ገንዘብ   —*gänzäb* n. cash

ጥሬጥሬ   *ṭǝraṭǝre* n. cereals

ጥር   *ṭǝrr* n. January

ጥርስ   see ጠረስ

ጥርኝ   *ṭǝrǝññ* n. civet-cat

—ፈረስ   —*färäs* white spotted horse

ጥርጊያ   see ጠረገ

ጥሻ   see ጣሰ

ጥቀርሻ   *ṭǝqärša* n. soot *(from*

ጥቁር   see ጠቆረ

ጥቂት   *ṭǝqit* adj. some, a little, a few, small *(amount)*

ጥቃቅን   *ṭǝqaqqǝn* n. minute, minor, tiny

ጥቅል   see ጠቀለለ

ጥቅምት   *ṭǝqǝmǝt* n. October

ጥብብ   see ጠበበ

ጥብስ   see ጠበሰ

ጥብኛ   *ṭǝbbǝñña* n. small round loaf of bread

ጥንት   *ṭǝnt* n. former days, ancient times, earlier days

ጥንታውያን   *ṭǝntawǝyan* n. people of the past

ጥንት የሌለው   *ṭǝnt yälelläw* that who or which has no beginning

የጥንት ሰው   *yäṭǝnt säw* n. early man

ጥንቸል   *ṭǝnčäl* n. rabbit, hare

ጥንዚዛ   *ṭǝnzizza* n. kind of beetle

ጥንድ   see ጠመደ

ጥንፍ   *also* ጽንፍ *in* አጥናፈ ዓለም *aṭnafä aläm* remotest part of the world

ከጥንፍ እስከ አጥናፍ   *kǝṭǝnf askä aṭnaf* from here to eternity

ጥዋ   see ጽዋ

ጥዋት   see ጡዋት

ጥይት   *ṭǝyyǝt* n. bullet, ammunition, cartridge; adj. intelligent, skillful

—የማይበሳው   —*yämmaybäsaw* adj. bullet- proof

ጥድ   *ṭǝd* n. juniper tree

ጥጃ   *ṭǝǧǧa* n. calf *(young of cow)*

ጥጋት   *ṭǝggäṭ* n. milking-cow

ጥግ   see ጠጋ

ጥጥ   *ṭǝṭ* n. cotton

ጥጥፉሬ   *ṭǝṭfäre* n. cotton seed, *also* ጥፍጥሬ

ጥፊ   *ṭǝffi* n. slap

በጥፊ መታ   *bäṭǝffi mätta* v.t. slapped

—ጠፈጠፈ   —*ṭäfäṭṭäfä* v.t. slapped repeatedly

ጥፍር | ṭəfər n. fingernail, claw

ጥፍረኛም | ṭəfram adj. impolite. insolent (lit. one with uncut finger-nails)

* ጠላ | *ṭolä

ጠለጠል | ṭolätol adj. light-footed, fleet; inquisitive, meddlesome, nosey

ጠልጣይ | ṭoltuʷalla adj. light-footed, fleet; inquisitive, meddlesome, nosey

ጠመ | ṭomä, also ጾመ ṣomä v.i. fasted

ጦም | ṭom n. fast

—ቀን | —qän n. fast-day

ጠማኛ | ṭomäñña n. one who fasts

ጧሚ | ṭuʷami n. one who fasts

ጦም አደረ | ṭom addärä v.t. went without supper

—አዳሪ | —adari n. one living in wretched poverty

—ፈታ | —fätta v.t. broke one's fast

ጦረ | ṭorä v.t. cared for aged people (especially for parents or relatives)

ጡረታ | ṭuräta n. pension, social security

—አስገባ | —asgäbba v.t. pensioned off

—አወጣ | —awṭṭa v.t. pensioned off

—ወጣ | —wäṭṭa v.t. retired

—ገባ | —gäbba v.i. retired

የጡረታ ቤት | yäṭuräta bet n. home for the aged, old folks' home

—አባል | —aball n. pension, social security

ጦር | ṭor n. war; army; spear, lance

—ኃይሎች | —hailočč n. armed forces (the army)

—አዛዥ | —azzaž n. army commander

—አዝማች | —azmač n. commander of battle-field

የ—ካሣ | yä—kasa n. war reparations

ግምባር | —gəmbbar n. war front (military)

የ—ኅይኞ | ya—guʷaddäñña n. ally

ምድር | mədər-- n. ground forces

አፍላ ጦር | afla n. active army

ከለፍ | käflä—n. division (army unit)

ደረቅ | däräq—n. emergency troop (without provisions and heavy weaponry)

ጦረኛ | ṭoräñña n. warrior, fighter

ጦርነት | ṭorənnät n. war, battle, warfare

የጦር መሣሪያ | yäṭor mässariya n. weapon, armament

ጦር መሪ | ṭor märi n. commander (military)

የ—መርከብ | yä—märkäb n. warship, fleet

ሚኒስቴር | —minister Ministry of War

ሜዳ | —meda n. battlefield

የጦር ሜዳ መነፅር | yäṭor meda mänäṭṭər n. field-glasses, binoculars

ጦር ሠራዊት | särawit n. army

—ሰፈር | säfär n.military camp

—ስልት | —salt strategy, tactics

—ተፈታ | —täfätta v.i. has surrendered, yielded (army)

* ጦስ | *ṭos

በርሱ ጦስ ነው ከሥራ የወጣሁት | it is due to him that I have been dismissed from my job

ጦሰኛ | ṭosäñña adj. troublesome

ጦሰኝ | ṭosäññ n. wild thyme;

ጦሽ አለ | ṭošš alä v.i. snapped

ጦቢያ | ṭobbiya n. Ethiopia (arch.)

ጦጣ | ṭoṭa n. ape, monkey

ጦጢት | ṭoṭit n. word used

322

ሙፈ	for calling an ape	ጧፈ	ṭuʷaf n. candle
	ṭofä v.i. flew into a rage; sky-rocketed (of price)	ተጧጧፈ	(rather thin type) täṭuʷaṭṭuʷafä in ጥሉ ተጧጧፈ the quarrel
በንይ.ት—	bänəddet—was enraged, flew into a temper	ጧ. ኣለ	has been aggravated ṭuʷa alä v.i. cracked

ጨ

ጨለመ	čällämä v.i. got dark, was dark (room)	ጨመለቀ	baláꞌǝng)
ጨለግ	čälläma, also ጥለግ	ጨመለት	* čämälläqä
	čəlläma n. darkness; night		čämälläq adj. filthy, bedraggled
—ፊት	—fit adj. gloomy (person)	ጨምለቃ	čämlaqqa adj. filthy; bedraggled, slovenly;
መጨለም	in የፀሐይ መጨለም		dirty (unclean in thought or talk)
	yäṣähai mäččälläm n. eclipse	ተጨመላለቀ	täčämalälläqä v.i. was besmeared, was bis-
አጨለመ	in ፊ.ቱን አጨለመ fitun ačällämä		mirched; was arrogant
	he put on a long face	ተጨግለቀ	täčämalläqä v.i. was smeared, was bedrag-
ጨለጠ	čälläṭä v.t. drank to the last drop		gled; was arrogant
ጨላጭ	čälläč n. drinker cf. ጠጪ	አጨመላለቀ	ačämälalläqä v.t. besmeared, bismirched made a mess of
ጥላጭ	čəllač n. last drop (of beverage)	አጨግለቀ	aččämalläqä v.t. smudged; made a
ጥላጥ ብሎ ሄደ	čəlläṭṭ bəlo hedä he left for good, disappeared	ጨመረ	mess of čämmärä v.t. added,
—አደርጎ ዋሸ	—adəgo waššä he told lies shamelessly		increased; gave, put, had some more; raised
— ጠጣ	—ṭäṭṭa he drank to the last drop	ጥመሪ	čəmmari n. increment, increase
አጨላጭ	aččalač n. drinking companion	የደመወዝ—	yädämäwäz—n. salary increment
ጨለፈ	čälläfä v.t. ladled out, dipped out	የዋጋ—	yäwaga— n. price increase
ጥልፉ	čəlfä n. ladle, dipper	ጥምር	čəmmər adj. in addition, including
ጨለ	čälle n. green (area of land with growing grass); glass-bead, necklace	ተጨመረ	täččämmärä v.i. was added, was included; was raised (salary);
—ጥይ	—ṭai n. sorcerer		joined others
ጨለ	čälle n. roan antelope (usually followed with	ተጨመሪ	täčämmari adj. extra, additional; more
		በተጨመሪ	bätäčämmari adv. moreover, further-

more, in addition, among other things
asǯämmärä v.t. has s/t added, increased had (salary) raised

ǯämmäqä v.t. squeezed; wrung (wet clothes); made a resume, made an abstract

ǯämmaqi n. juice
yäbärtukan- n. orange juice
yäfäre nägäru- n. gist
mäǯmäqiya n. mangle
täǯämmäqä v.t. was squeezed; was wrung
asǯämmäqä v.t. had s/t squeezed; had wet clothes wrung
ǯämmätä v.i. became taciturn, reserved
ǯämmət adj. taciturn, reserved
*äǯmättärä
ǯämtarra adj. wrinkled
täǯämätattärä v.i. was full of wrinkles
täǯämattärä v.i. was wrinkled
in ግምባሩን —
gämbarun- wrinkled ones forehead
ǯämäddädä v.t. grabbed (made a sudden snatch)
ǯämdadda adj. wrinkled, creased; dwarfish and lean
täǯämädaddädä v.i. was completely creased, wrinkled cf. ተጨመታተረ
täǯämaddädä v.i. creased, was wrinkled
aǯǯämaddädä v.t. creased, wrinkled
gämbarun— wrinkled one's forehead
ǯämäǯǯämä v.t. kissed

repeatedly
täǯämaǯǯämä v.i. kissed each other repeatedly
*ǯärämmämä
ǯärmamma adj. deformed
täǯärammämä v.i. was deformed
aǯǯärammämä v.t. deformed
*ǯärämmätä
ǯärmatta adj. deformed cf. ጨርማማ and ጨርማዳ
täǯärämammätä v.i. was deformed; creased
täǯärammätä v.i. was deformed, creased
ǯärär n. ray, stream of light
yäṣähai- n. sunbeam
*ǯärämmädä
ǯärmadda adj. deformed, creased
täǯärammädä v.i. was deformed; creased
äǯǯärammädä v. t. deformed; creased
ǯärräsä v.t. finished completed, ended, terminated; consumed; exterminated; ate up; used up
ǯärräso adv. completely, quite; through and through
I don't quite understand
ǯärraš adj. completely, altogether
äskännä ǯärrašu altogether, completely
bäǯärraš adj. absolutely not; never; not at all
täǯärräsä v.i. was completed, was finished; was consumed
täǯǯärräsä v.t. killed each other

324

አጫረሰ	aččarräsä v.t. helped in finishing s/t
ጨረቂት	čäräqit n. type of sorghum
ጨረቃ	čäräqa n. moon
ሙሉ—	mulu— n. full moon
ጨፍ—	täf- n. moonless night
የጨረቃ	yäčäräqa gordoš
ግርዶሽ	lunar eclipse
ጨርቋ	also ጨርቋ, čärquʷa, čorqa adj. immature (crop) in የጨረቃ ተዘካር yäčäräba täzkar full of confusion, full of turmoil
*ጨረተ	*čärrätä also *ጨረተ čarrätä
ጨረታ	čarräta n. auction : tender
የጨረታ ዋጋ	yäčäräta waga n. bid
ተጫረተ	täčarrätä v.i. bid (made bid)
ተጫራች	täčärač n. bidder
አጫረተ	aččarrätä v.t. put s/t up to auction
አጫራች	aččarač n. auctioneer
ጨረገደ	čäräggädä v t. cut (with a spade or a sickle etc.)
*ጨረጨረ	*čäräččärä
ተንጨረጨረ	tänčäräččärä v t. broiled
አንጨረጨረ	ančäräččärä v. t. broiled
ጨረጨሰ	čäräččäsä v.t. became very old
ጨርጻሳ	čärčassa adj. very old
ጨረፈ	čärräfä v.t. touched slightly
ጨረፍታ	čäräfta n. glimpse
በጨረፍታ አየ	bäčäräfta ayyä caught a glimpse of
*ጨረፈፈ	*čäräffäfä
አንጨረፈፈ	ančäräffäfä v.i. in ጠጉ ሩን—had unkempt hair
ጨርቅ	čärq n. cloth, fabric, rag
ጨርቋ ጨርቅ	čärqa čärq n. textiles, fabrics
ጨርቁን ጣለ	čärqun ṭalä v.i. became mad
ጨርቅ ሰፊ	čärq säfi n. tailor
ጨሰ	see ጨሰ
ጨቀየ	čäqäyyä v i. was muddy, was covered with mud
ጭቃ	čəqa n. mud , mire
ጭቃም	čəqamma adj muddy, miry
ጭቃ ሹም	čəqa šum n. village headman
—ቤት	-čet n. mud-house
—ጀራፍ	-ǧəraf unexpected odd thing
አጨቀየ	ačäqäyyä v.t. turned into mire
ጨቀጨቀ	čäqäččäqä v.t. nagged, pestered
ጨቃጫቃ	čäqčaqqa adj. pestring, nagging
ጭቅጭቅ	čəqəččəq n. dispute, quarrel, argument
ተጨቃጨቀ	täčäqaččäqä v.i. disputed; quarreled
ተጨቃጫቂ	täčäqačaqi adj. pestering, nagging
አጨቃጨቀ !	aččäqaččäqä v.t. was disputable. caused quarrel
አጨቃጫቂ	aččäqačaqi adj. problematic; insoluble (problem)
ጨቅላ	čäqla n. baby, infant
ጨቅላነት	čäqlannät n. babyhood, infancy
ጨቆነ	čäqqonä v.t. oppressed domineered
ጨቋኝ	čäqquʷañ n. oppressor, tyrant; domineering, cruel
ጭቁን	čəqqun adj. oppressed
—መደብ	—mädäb oppressed class
ጭቆና	čəqqona n. oppression, tyranny
ተጨቆነ	täčäqqonä v.i. was oppressed
ተጨቋኝ	täčäqquʷañ adj. oppressed
—መደብ	---mädäb oppressed class
*ጨበረረ	*čäbärrärä

325

ጨበረር ፤ čäbärär adj. unkempt
ጨብራራ ፤ čäbrarra adj. unkempt

*ጨበረበረ ፤ *čäbäräbbärä
ተጨበረበረ ፤ täčbäräbbärä v.i was cheated, embezzled
አጫበረበረ ፤ ačbäräbbärä v.t.dazzled; cheated, swindled, embezzled
አጫበርባሪ ፤ ačbärbari n. cheat, swindler, crook, imposter

ጨበጠ ፤ čäbbäṭä v.t. squeezed, clutched, clenched (the fist); clasped; grabbed; grasped

ጨበጣ ፤ in የጨበጣ ውጊያ yäčäbäṭa wäggiya hand-to-hand combat
ጨባጣ ፤ čäbbaṭṭa n. midget
ጨብጥ ፤ čäbṭ also ጨባጦ čäbaṭo n. gonorrhea
ጭብጭ ፤ čǝbbač n. handful
ጭብጥ ፤ in የነገሩ ጭብጥ yänägäru čǝbṭ the main point, the gist
ጭብፕ ፤ čǝbbäṭ n. handful, fistful, bunch
ጭብጦ ፤ čǝbbäṭo n. round, rather heavy loaf of bread (carried as provisions)
ተጨበጠ ፤ täčäbbäṭä v.i. was squeezed; was grabbed; grasped
ተጨበጭ ፤ täčäbbač adj. comprehensible; concrete
—ምክንያት ፤ —mäknäyat n. concrete fact
ተጨባበጠ ፤ täčäbabbäṭä v.i. wrinkled, creased
እጅ ፤ ለጅ ፤ ተጨባበጡ ፤ äǧǧ läǧǧ täčäbabbäṭu they shook hands
አጫባበጠ ፤ ačäbabbäṭä v.t. wrinkled, creased
ጨበደ ፤ čäbbodä v.t. grabbed
ጨብጥ ፤ see ጨበጠ
*ጨበጨበ ፤ *čäbäččäbä
ጭብጭባ ፤ čǝbčäba n. applause, hand clapping
አጫበጨባ ፤ ačäbäččäbä v.t. clapped, clapped hands, applauded

አጫብጣቢ ፤ ačäbčäbi n. henchman
አስጨበጨበ ፤ asčäbäččäbä, or ተጨ በጨበለት ፤ täčäbäččäb-ällät he was acclaimed, was received with applause
ጨበጨበ ፤ čäbäččäbä v.i. bǝcame verdant, sent forth leaves
ጨነቀ ፤ čännäqä with pron. suff. e.g ጨነቀኝ ፤ čännäq-äñ I am at a loss, I am embarrassed, I am in a difficulty
ጭንቀት ፤ čanqät n. worry, concern, disturbance, anguish
ጭንቅ ፤ čǝnq n. worry, hardship, difficulty
ተጨነቀ ፤ täčännäqä v.i. showed concern, was embarassed, was in a dilemma
—ተጠበበ ፤ —täṭäbbäbä v.i. was in great straits, was puzzled
ተጨናነቀ ፤ täčänannäqä v.i. was crowded, was congested
አስጨነቀ ፤ asčännäqä v.t. molested, nagged, pestered; put s/o in a great difficulty, worry
አስጨናቂ ፤ asčännaqi adj. puzzling, full of difficulties, harrowing
*ጨነቆረ ፤ *čänäqqorä
ጨንቋራ ፤ čänquwarra adj. crosseyed
አጨነቋረ ፤ ačänäqquwärä v.i. peeped (took a look at)
*ጨነበሰ ፤ *čänäbbäsä
ጨንባሳ ፤ čänbassa, also ጨምባሳ čämbassa adj. weaksighted
ጨነገፈ ፤ čänäggäfä v.i. aborted (miscarried); went wrong, was thwarted
ጭንጋፍ ፤ čǝngaf n. abortion (creature produced by abortion)
ተጨናገፈ ፤ täčänaggäfä v.i. mis-

326

አጨናገፈ carried (plans etc.) ; was thwarted, failed aččänaggäfä v.t. foiled, thwarted, hindered

*ጨነጎለ *čänäggolä
ተጨናጎለ täčänaggolä v.i. miscarried (plans etc.) was thwarted, failed, cf. ተጨናገፈ

አጨናጎለ aččänaggolä v.t. foiled, thwarted, hindered, cf. አጨናገፈ

ጨንገር čängär n. twig, stick (for punishing children)

ጨከነ čäkkänä v.i. was cruel, ruthless, severe, harsh

ጨካኝ čäkkañ adj. cruel, ruthless, merciless, brutal

ጭከና čəkkäna n. cruelty brutality, atrocity

ጭካኔ čəkkane n. cruelty, brutality, atrocity

በጭካኔ ገደለው bäčəkkane gäddäläw he killed him in cold blood

ተጨካከነ täčäkakkänä v.i. treated each other infavourably

ጨዋ čäwa n. person of good breeding, not a slave adj. well-behaved, well mannered, gentleman; illiterate, layman

ጨዋነት čäwannät n. good breeding, politeness, decency

የጨዋ ልጅ yäčäwa ləǧ n. free person (not a slave)

—ቤተ ሰብ —betäsäb n. of good family

ውናና čäwnanna adj. small-eyed

ገግ with pron. suff. e.g
ጨገገኝ čäggägäññ I am feeling uneasy, I grew uneasy

ጭጋግ čəgag n. mist, haze, fog

ጭጋጋም čəgagam adj. misty, hazy, foggy

ጭጋግ ፊት čəgag fit adj. unpleasant, cheerless, gloomy (person)

ጨጨብሳ čäččäbsa n. unleavened bread cut into pieces and mixed with butter

ጨፈለቀ čäfälläqä v.t. crushed, squashed; ploughed virgin land for the second time; amalgamated (business etc.)

ጭፍለቃ čəfläqa n. ploughing virgin land for the second time

ጭፍልቅ čəfləq n. virgin land ploughed for the second time

ተጨፈለቀ täčäfälläqä v.i. was crushed, squashed; was ploughed for the second time (virgin land)

አስጨፈለቀ asčäfälläqä v.t. had s/t crushed, squashed; had virgin land ploughed for the second time; was amalgamated (business)

ጨፈረ čäffärä v.i. danced

ጨፋሪ čäffari n. dancer

ጭፈራ čəffära n. dance

ጭፍራ čəfra n. accompaniment; escort, suite; soldier, subbordinate

ተጫፈረ täčaffärä v.i. joined others, mixed with others

ተጫፋሪ täčafari n. accomplice

አጫፈረ aččaffärä v.t. mixed, brought together

አጫፋሪ aččafari n. suite, escort; accomplice

አስጨፈረ asčäffärä v.t. had s/o dance

*ጨፈረረ *čäfärrärä

ጨፈረር čäfärär adj. unkempt

ጨፍራራ čäfrarra adj. unkempt

ጨፈቀ čäfäqa n. bundle of wood

ተጨፋፈቀ täčäfaffäqä v.i. was overcrowded, was congested

ጨፈነ čäffänä v.t. shut (the

ጨፋኛ *ǧäffanna* adj. poor-sighted

ጯፍን *ǧəffən* adj. with eyes shut

በጯፍን *bäǧəffən särraw* he ሥራው did it blindly *(thoughtlessly)*

ጨረገገ *ǧäfäggägä* v.t. frowned

ጨፍጋጋ *ǧäfgagga* adj. gloomy

—ቀን —*qan* n. muggy day

ጨረጨረ *ǧäfäǧǧäfä* v.t. cut into pieces, chopped off, cut down, lopped; exterminated

ጯፍጨፋ *ǧəfǧäfa* n. chopping off, cutting down; extermination

ጯፍጫፊ *ǧəfəǧǧafi* n. cut off pieces

ተጨፋጨፋ *täǧäfäǧǧäfä* v.i. was cut into pieces; was chopped off; was cut down; was exterminated

ተጨፋጨፋ *täǧäfaǧǧäffä* v.i. exterminated each other, killed each other

ጨፌ *ǧäffe* n. lush meadow

ጩረር አለ *ǧurərr alä* v.i. trickled *(flowed as a little stream)*

መንጮራር *mänǧorär* n. spout

ጩቅ *ǧuq* adj. greedy

ጩቤ *ǧube* n. small dagger

ጩስ *see* ጢስ

ጫማ *ǧamma* n. shoe, foot *(measurement)* ; sole *(of foot)*

—ሰሪ —*sāri* n. cobbler

—ስፊ —*säfi* n. shoemaker

—ሳመ —*samä* v.t. kissed s/o's foot *(as a sign of respect or gratitude)*

—ጣራጊ —*ṭäragi* n. shoeblack

ላስቲክ — *lastik—or* ጎማ-*gomma*-n. rubbers

ቡት— *but*—n. boots

ነጠላ— *nätäla*—n. sandals

ኩፍ— *kuf*—n. boots *(arch.)*

የቢት— *yäbet*—n. slippers

የጫማ ማሰሪያ *yäǧamma mäsäriya* n. shoelace, shoestring

—ማንኪያ —*mankiya* n. shoe horn

—ቀለም —*qäläm* n. shoe cream, shoe polish

ተጫማ *täǧamma* v.t. put on shoes *(arch.)*

መጫሚያ *mäǧǧamiya* n. shoes *(arch.)*

ጫረ *ǧarä* v.t. scribbled; scraped; scratched; struck *(a match)*

እሳት— *əsat*— v.t. got fire from a neighbour

ጫር ጫር *ǧarr ǧarr adärrägä* v.t. አደረገ scraped out slightly

ጫጫረ *ǧaǧärä* v.t. scribbled, scrawled

ጭረት *ǧərät* n. scratch, stroke *(in writing)*, dash, accent *(accent mark)*

ንኡስ— *nə'us*—n. hyphen

ተጫጫረ *täǧaǧarä* v.i. was full of scratches

አጫረ *aǧarä* in ጠብ አጫረ *ṭäb aǧärä* v.t. started a fight.

ጠብ አጫሪ *ṭäb aǧari* adj. aggressive, troublemaker

ጫት *ǧat* n. leaves with mild narcotic quality *(chewed mostly by Muslims)*

—ቀመ —*qamä* v.t. chewed *ǧat*

ጫነ *ǧänä* v.t. loaded *(beast of burden, truck)*, burdened; put the saddle on

ጫና *ǧänna* n. burden *(fig.)*

ጭነት *ǧänät* n. load, burden, cargo, freight

— ማርከብ — *märkäb* n. freighter

— ማኪና — *mäkina* n. truck, lorry

—ከብት —*käbt* n. beast of burden, pack animal

መጫኛ *mäǧañña* n. strap of leather used in fastening a load, thong

ጫነ አለ *ǧann alä* v.t. pressed *(a button etc.)*; overcharged

ተጫነ *täǧanä* v.t. was loaded; pressed *(a button)*

ተጫጫነ
ተጫጫነው
አጫጫነ

አስጫነ

ጫንቃ
ጫካ

ጫካ ለጫካ
ሄደ

ጫካማ

*ጫወት
ጨዋታ

-ያዘ

የጨዋታ ሜዳ

ጮውውት

ተጫወተ

ተጫዋች

መጫወቻ

ተጨዋወተ

አጫወተ

አጫዋች

ተጫወተበት

ጫጉላ
ጫጨት
የወፍ:--
*ጫጫ
ጫጫታ
ተንጫጫ

depress *(the gas pedal)*; suppressed täčačanä v.i. oppressed *(of weather, sleep)* täčačanäw felt drowsy äččačanä v.t. helped in loading asčanä v.t. had s/t loaded čanqa n. shoulder čakka n. forest, woods, jungle čakka läčakka hedä he went through the forest čakkamma adj. wooded *čawwätä čäwata n. play; entertainment, amusement; conversation —yazä v.t. was engaged in conversation yäčawata meda n. playing field čäwäwwät n. entertainment, friendly conversation, *(with a friend or friends)* täčawwätä v.t. played, chatted, had a friendly conversation täčawač adj. playful; sociable; player mäččawäča n. toy, plaything täčawawwätä v.i. conversed, had a friendly discussion aččawwätä v.t. entertained s/o, amused s/o, kept s/o company aččawač n. referee *(in game)*; entertainer, jester täčawwätäbbät he played tricks on him, he ridiculed him čagula n. nuptual house čačutt n. chick yäwäf— n. baby bird *čaçça čaçata n. noise, row tänčaçça v.i. was

noisy; made a loud noise, cried in disagreement

እንጫጫ — anžaçça v.t. caused to make a loud noise, to squeal

ጫጫ — čaçča v.i. stopped growing, was emaciated

አጫጫ — ačaçça v.t. emaciated

ጫፍ — čaf n. top; edge, tip, summit; point *(knife)*; hem

ጫፍና ጫፍ — čafənna čaf n. two ends of s/t

ጫፍ ጫፉን ነገረኝ — čaf čafun näggäräññ He told me some part of the story. He gave me a hint.

ጮላት — čəlat n. hawk, falcon cf. ጮላሪት

ጮላንጮል — čəlančəl n. spark *(of light)*; gleam, glimmer

የተስፋ— yätäsfa— n. glimmer, ray *(of hope)*

ጮላዳ — čəlada, or ጮላዳ čälada n. gelada baboon

ጮልፊት — čəlfitt n. sparrow, hawk cf. ጮላት

ጮልፉ — see ጮለፈ
ጮምሬ — see ጮመረ
ጮምቲ — see ጮመቀ
ጮምት — see ጮመት
ጮምጮምታ — čəmčəmta n. rumour
—ሰማ — —sämma v.t. got wind of
ስለሱ ምንም — sälässu mänemm
—የለ — —yällä nothing has been heard about him
ጮረት — see ጮረ
ጮሬ — čəra n. hair at the end of an animal's tail; fly-whisk, fly-swatter
—ቀረሽ — —qärräš n. madcap
—ቆላ — —qolla v.t. wagged *(the tail;)* licked the boots of
ጮሬው ጮሌ — čəraw čolle adj. cunning
ጮራር — čəraro n. dry sticks
—እንር — —əgär adj. thin-legged
ጮራቅ — čəraq n. cannibal
ጮራቅነት — čəraqənnät n. cannibalism

ጭር አለ   *č̣ǝrr alä* v.i. was calm, still *(surrounding)*, was silent, deserted *(streets etc.)*

ጭርታ   *č̣ǝrrǝta* n. calmness, stillness

ጭርንቁስ   *č̣ǝrǝnqus* n. rag *(piece of old and torn cloth)*

ጭርንቁሳም   *č̣ǝrǝnqusam* adj. ragged

ጭስ   *see* ጨሰ

ጭቄን   *see* ጨቆነ

ጭቅቅት   *č̣ǝqǝqqǝt* n. dirt, filth *(on one's body and clothes)*

ጭቅቅታም   *č̣ǝqǝqqǝtam* adj. dirty, filthy *(of people)*

ጭቃ   *see* ጨቀየ

ጭቅና   *č̣ǝqqǝnna* n. fillet, sirloin

የጭቅና ጥብስ   *yäč̣ǝqqǝnna ṭǝbs* n. fillet steak

ጭብጠ   *see* ጨበጠ

ጭቦ   *č̣ǝbbo* n. injustice, unfairness

ጭቦኛ   *č̣ǝbboňňa* adj. unfair, unjust

ጭን   *č̣ǝn* n. lap, thigh

የጭን ቅልጥም   *yäč̣ǝn qǝlṭǝm* n. tibia

—ገረድ   —*gäräd* n. mistress *(concubine)*

ጭንቅ   *see* ጨነቀ

ጭንቅላት   *č̣ǝnqqǝlat* n. skull

ጭንቅላታም   *č̣ǝnqǝllatam* n. one with a small face and a big head

ጭንጫ   *č̣ǝnč̣a* n. stony ground

ጭኮ   *č̣akko* n. flour made of roasted barley mixed with butter (usually taken with as provisions for a long journey)

ጭው አለ   *č̣ǝww alä* v.i. rang *(of the ear)*

ጭው አለብኝ   *č̣ǝww aläbbǝňň* I feel dizzy

ጭው ያለ በረሃ   *č̣ǝww yalä bäräha* n. a vast expanse of desert

—ገደል   ——*gädäl* n. precipice

ጭድ   *č̣ǝd* n. ṭef straw

እሳትና ጭድ   *ǝsatǝnna č̣ǝd* adj. irreconcilable, antagonistic *(lit. fire and straw)*

ጭገር   *č̣ǝgär* n. hair *(of a person)* other than that of the head

ጭገራም   *č̣ǝgäram* adj. hairy

ጭጭ አለ   *č̣äč̣č̣ alä* v.i. hushed, remained dumb, lapsed into silence

ጭፍን   *see* ጨፈነ

ጮለ   *č̣olä* v.i. schemed, was crafty

ጮሌ   *č̣olle* n./adj schemer, crafty

*ጮለ   *č̣olä*

እጮለ   in በጥፊ አጮለ *bäṭǝffi ač̣olä* smacked, slapped

ጮማ   *č̣oma* adj. fat *(meat)*

—ከብት   —*käbt* fat animal

አፈ—   *afä*— n. flatterer

ጮረረ   *č̣orrärä* v.i. trickled *(flowed as a small stream)* cf. ጨረር አለ

ጮራ   *č̣orra* n. ray of the sun

ጮርቃ   *č̣orqa* adj. immature *(crop)*

ጮቅ   *č̣oq* n. chap *(of the skin)*

ጮቤ   in ጮቤ መታ *č̣obbe mätta* v.t .leapt with joy

—ረገጠ   —*räggäṭä* v.t. leapt with joy

—ዘለለ   —*zällälä* v.t. leapt with joy

ጮኸ   *č̣ohä* v.i. cried *(shouted)*, yelled, shouted in a loud voice; screamed, cried out; barked *(dog)*; appealed *(to a sovereign etc,)*

ጩኸት   *č̣uhät* n. shout, cry, scream, yell, noise howl; clamour, appea

—ትርፉ   —*tǝrfu* adj. effort-wasting, futile

ዶር—   *doro*— n. early morning

ተጯጯኸ   *täč̣uʷač̣ʷahä* v.i. made repeated demands; clamoured repeatedly

አጮኸ   *ač̣ohä* v.t. cracked *(whip etc.)*

በጥፊ—   *bäṭǝffi*— v.t. smacked, slapped the face

አስጮኸ   *asč̣ohä* v.t. caused to cry, shout

ጰ

ጰልቃን *pālqan* n. pelican
ጰራቅሊጦስ *päraqliṭos* n. the Paraclete, the Holy Spirit
ጰንጠቆስጤ *pänṭäqosṭe* n. Pentecost, Whitsunday
ጳጉሜ(ን) *pagume(n)* n. intercalary month *(5-10 September)*

ጳጳስ *pappas* n. bishop
ሊቀ ጳጳስ *liqä pappas, liqä pappasat* n. archbishop
ጳጶሰ *päppäsä* v.i. was ordained bishop
አጳጶሰ *apäppäsä* v.t. ordained bishop

ጸ

*ጸለመ *ṣällämä*
ጽልመት *ṣəlmät* n. darkness
ጸለየ *ṣälläyä* v.i. prayed, recited prayers
ጸሎት *ṣälot* n. prayer, service
ጸሎተኛ *ṣälotäñña* adj. religious, pious
የጸሎት ቤት also ቤተ ጸሎት *yäṣälot bet, betä ṣälot* n. chapel
ጸሎት አደረሰ *ṣälot adärräsä* v.t. prayed
ጸሎተ ሃይማኖት *ṣälotä haimanot* n. the Creed
ጸሎተ ማእድ —*ma'əдd* n. say grace
—ማኅበር —*mähəbär* n. communal prayer
—ኃሙስ —*hamus* n. Maundy Thursday
መታሰቢያ ጸሎት *mättäsäbita ṣälot* n. memorial service
ተጸለየ *täṣälläyä* v.i. was prayed
አጸለየ *aṣṣälläyä* v.t. had prayer made
ጸሐይ see ፀሐይ
ጾር see ፆር
*ጸበረቀ *ṣäbärräqä*
ተንጸበረቀ *tänṣäbarräqä* v.i. was sparkled, shimmered, was reflected
ነጸብራቅ *näṣäbraq* n. glare; reflection
አንጸባረቀ *anṣäbarräqä* v.t. sparkled, glittered,

glared, glistened; reflected
አንጸባራቂ *anṣäbaraqi* adj. glaring; brilliant
ጸነነ *ṣännänä* v.i. was difficult
ጸና *ṣänna see* ጠና
ጽኑ(እ) *ṣənu(')* adj. stable, firm; acute, severe
—እሥራት —*əssərat* n. hard labour
ጽኑአን ግሥች *ṣənu'an gəssoč* n. strong verbs
ጽኑነት *ṣənunnät* n. strength, firmness
ተጸናና *täṣnanna* v.i. was consoled, found solace; was comforted; cheered up
አጸና *aṣänna* v.t. ratified, put into effect
አጽናና *aṣnanna* v.t. consoled, gave comfort, gave solace; encouraged
ጸናጽል *ṣänaṣəl* n. sistrum
*ጸያፈ *ṣäyyäfä*
ጸያፍ *ṣäyyaf* adj. disgusting, base; gross *(language)*, obscene *(language)*
ተጸያፈ *täṣäyyäfä* v.i. abhored, loathed
አጸያፈ *aṣṣäyyäfä* v.t. was offensive, filled with disgust
አጸያፊ *aṣṣäyyafi* adj. base,

ጸደቀ   dishonourable, disgusting, loathsome *ṣäddäqä* v.i. was declared righteous, was pious; was ratified *(bill)*; was approved

ጽድቅ   *ṣadəq* adj. righteous, pious, just

ጽድቅ   *ṣədq* n. righteousness

ተመጸደቀ   *tämäṣaddäqä* v.i. behaved hypocritically; aggrandized oneself

ተመጸዳቂ   *tämäṣadaqi* adj. hypocritical

መመጸደቅ   *mämmäṣadäq* inf. self-aggrandizement

አጸደቀ   *aṣäddäqä* v.t. ratified, approved

ጸደይ   *ṣädäy* n. spring *(season)*

ጸዳ   *ṣädda* v.i. was cleaned, was disinfected

ጽዱ   *ṣədu* adj. clean

ጽዳት   *ṣədat* n. sanitation, cleanliness

የጽዳት ዘመቻ   *yäṣədat zämäča* sanitation campaign

ተጸዳዳ   *täṣädadda* v.i. cleaned up; went to the lavatory

መጸዳጃ   *mäṣṣädaǧa* n. lavatory

አጸዳ   *aṣäddda* v.t. cleaned; cleaned up

ጸጉር   *ṣägur* n. hair, fur, *also* ጠጉር

ጸጋ   *ṣägga* n. grace

—ቢስ   —*bis* adj. graceless

ባለ—   *balä*— n. ,rich, wealthy, well-to-do

ጸጥ አለ   *ṣäṭṭ alä* v.i. was silent, calm, quiet; quieted down *(wind, storm, wave etc.)*; was secure

ጸጥ ለጥ አለ   *ṣäṭṭ läṭṭ alä* v.i. surrendered, was subdued. yielded, gave in, admitted, defeated

ጸጥተኛ   *ṣäṭṭətäňňa* adj. quiet *(gentle; not rough in disposition)*

ጸጥታ   *ṣäṭṭəta* n. quiet, tranquility, calm, silence,

stillness; security

—አስከበረ   *askäbbära* restored order. kept peace; suppressed, subdued rebellion

—አስኮብሪ   —*asʌäbbari* security forces

በጸጥታ   *b. ṭṭəta* adv. quietly

የጋራ ጸጥታ   .ägara ṣäṭṭəta ɔlective security

የጸጥታ ምክር ቤት   *yäṣäṭṭəta məkər bet* Security Council *(UNO)*

ጸጥ አሰኘ   *ṣäṭṭ assäňňä* v.t. quietened, silenced suppressed

—አደረጓ   —*adärrägä* quietened, suppressed, quelled *with pronominal suff.* e.g. ጸጸተኝ *ṣäṣṣätäňň* I felt sorry, i regretted

ጸጸተ

ጸጸት   *ṣäṣät* n. remorse, sorrow, repentance, regret

ጸጸተኛ   *ṣäṣätäňňä* adj. sorrowful, remorseful

ተጸጸተ   *täṣäṣṣätä* v.i. regretted, repented, was sorry

ጻፈ   *ṣafä*, *also* ጣፈ *ṭafä* v.t. wrote, wrote down

ጸሐፊ   *ṣähafi* n. writer, clerk, secretary, scribe; author

ጸሐፊ ትእዛዝ   *ṣähafe tə'əzaz* n. Minister of the Pen

ልዩ ጸሐፊ   *ləyyu ṣähafi* n. private secretary

ቄም—   *qum*— n. calligrapher

ዋና—   *wanna*— n. secretary general

ጽሑፍ   *ṣəhuf* n. writing *(anything written)*

ሥነ—   *sənä*— n. literature

አፋዊ ሥነ ጽሑፍ   *afawi sənä ṣəhuf* n. oral literature

—ጽሑፋዊ   —*ṣəhufawi* adj. literary

በራሪ ጽሑፍ   *bärari ṣəhuf* n. leaflet

ጽሕፈት   *ṣəhəfät* n. writing

ቄም—   *qum*—n. calligrpahy

የቃል—   *yäqal*— n. dictation

አጭር—   *ačč̣ər* — n. stenograpy, short-hand

የእጅ—   *yä'əǧǧ*— n. hand—

writing
yäṣəhəfät mākina n. typewriter
mäṣhaf n. book
mäṣahəft bet n. library
mäṣhaf qədus n. Bible, Scripture
betä mäṣahəft n. library
(yä) mäṣahəft suq/ mädäbbər book-shop, book-store
täṣafä v.i. was written, was recorded *(in writing)*
täṣaṣafä v.i. corresponded with one another
aṣṣafä v.t. had a letter, a book written, dictated
ṣahəl n. paten
ṣəllat n. tablet of wood or stone used as a *tabot*
ṣəllatä muse n. Tablet of the Law
see ጸም
see ጸኝ and ጠኝ
pl. አጽናፍ *in* አጽናፈ ዓለም

aṣnafä aləm remote place of the world
ṣawwa n. chalice, cup
—*anässä* v.i. drank a toast
ṣəyon in አክሱም—*aksum* --the church of St. Mary in Axum
ṣəyonawi adj. Zionist
ṣəgge räda n. rose *(flower)*
see also ጾም *somä, ṭomä* v.t. fasted
ṣawami ጾሚ *ṣuʷami* n. faster
ṣomäñña n. faster
ṣom n. fast, fasting
—*addärä* v.i. went without supper
—*adäri* adj. very poor
--*gäddäfä* v.t. broke one's fast
ṣota n. gender, sex
täba'tay— masculine gender
anstay— feminine gender
yäwäl— common gender
gə'uz— neuter gender

ፀ

ṣähay n. sun
ṣähayamma adj. sunny, bright *(day)*
ṣähay wäṭṭač the sun rose
—*ṭälläqäčč* the sun set
bərhanä ṣähay n. sunlight
yäṣähay mänäṣṣər/ mänäṭṭər sun-glass
—*čärär* n. sun-beam
—*gərdoš* n. eclipse
ṣar n. enemy
ṣärä— pref. against,

anti—
ṣärä həzb adj. anti-people
—*märz* adj. antidote
—*maryam* n. protestant *(lit. anti-Mary)*
—*täbay* n. insecticide
—*tank* n. antitank
—*auroppəlan* n. anti-aircraft
—*imperialism* n. anti-imperialism
—*fiwdal* n. anti-feudal
ṣännäsäčč v.t. became pregnant

ፅንስ	ṣəns n. pregnancy, embryo		
ፅንስ ሐሳብ	ṣənsä hassab n. meaning, connotation, concept	ተፀነሰ	abortion . täṣännäsä v.i. conceived (of pregnancy)
ፅንስ ማስወገድ	ṣəns maswärräd n.	ፀዳል	ṣädal n. brilliance (of light)

ፈ

'ፈለመ	*fällämä	ፈላስፋ	fälasfa, or ፈላስማ
ፍልሚያ	fəlmiya n. duel (any two-sided contest)		fälasma n. philosopher
ተፋለመ	täfallämä v.i. fought duels	ፍልስፋ	fəlsäfa n. discovery, invention
ተፋላሚ	täfalami n. dueller	ፈልሳፊ	fälsafi n. inventor, discoverer
አፋለመ	affallämä v.t. caused (s/o) to fight a duel	ፍልስፍና	fəlsəfənna n. philosophy
ፈለሰ	fälläsä v. was uprooted (plant); immigrated, migrated	ተፈላሰፈ	täfälassäfä v.i. philosophised
ፈላሻ	fälläša n. Ethiopian Jew	ፈለቀ	fälläqä v.i. sprung from, gushed out (liquid), originated (idea)
ፍልሰታ	fəlsäta n.the Assumption (of Mary)	አፈለቀ	afälläqä v.t. generates produced (idea); caused to spring from
ፍልስለስ	fəlsləs adj. destroyed, dilapidated		
ፍልስልሱ ወጣ	fəlsləsu wäṭṭa v.t. fell into pieces	*ፈለቀለቀ	*fäläqälläqä
ተፋለሰ	täfalläsä v.i. went wrong, was disrupted	ፍልቅልቅ	fələqləq adj. jovial, smiling, cheerful
አፈለሰ	afälläsä v.t. uprooted (a plant)	ተፍለቀለቀ	täfläqälläqä v.i. bubbled (boiling liquid)
አፋለሰ	affalläsä v.t.disrupted, destroyed; caused (s/t) to come to nothing	የፊቱ ወዝ ተፍለቀለቀ	yäfitu wäz täfläqälläqä had a glossy complexion
ፈለሰመ	see ፈለሰፈ	አፍለቀለቀ	afläqälläqä v.t. caused to bubble
*ፈለሰሰ	*fälässäsä		
ፈለሰሰ	fäläsäs adj/n .(one) who lives in luxurious surroundings	ፈለቀቀ	fäläqqäqä v.t. broke loose
ፈልሳሳ	fälsassa adj/n.(one) who lives in luxurious surroundings	ጥጥ—	ṭəṭ— v.t. treated cotton in a gin, or with the fingers
ተንፈላሰሰ	tänfälassäsä v.i. lived luxuriously	in የጥጥ ፍልቃቂ	yäṭəṭ fəlləqqaqi n. cotton seed cf. ጥጥ ፍሬ
ፈለሰፈ	fälässäfä, also ፈለሰመ fälässämä v.i. philosophized; made a discovery; invented	ጥጥ ፈልቃቂ መኪና	ṭəṭ fälqaqi mäkina n. gin (for treating cotton)
		in የወርቅ ፍልቃቂ	yäwärq fələqqaqi n. gold foil, gold leaf

334

መፈልቀቂያ	in የብረት መፈልቀቂያ yäbərät mäfälqäqiya n. crowbar	**ፈሊጥ**	fäliṭ n. method, style, mode; sagacity
ተፈለቀቀ	täfäläqqäqä v.i. broke loose	**አዲስ—**	addis— n. new style
* ፈለከለከ	* fäläkälläkä	**ፈሊጠኛ**	fäliṭäňňa adj. sagacious; tactful, artful, resourceful, clever, ingenious (in), adroit

* ፈለከለከ fäläkälläkä
ተፍለከለከ täfläkälläkä v.i. swarmed (ants etc.)
ፈለክ fäläk n. planet
ፈለገ fällägä v.t. wanted, desired, wished, liked; looked for, searched for, sought, expected; was interested in
ፈላጊ fällagi n. one who wants, desires; searcher
ዕቃው ፈላጊ የለ ውም ʾəqaw fällagi yälläwəm the commodity has no demand
ፈለግ fäläg n. trail, trace track; path; example
ፍላጎ fəlläga n. search, quest
ፍላጎት fəllagot n. wish, desire, want (need), will, interest; inclination
ተፈለገ täfällägä v.i. was sought, desired, wanted
ተፈላጊ täfällagi adj. necessary, essential, required, desirable
ተፈላለገ täfälallägä v.i. looked for one another; had a mutual interest
አፈለገ affallägä v.t. helped s/o in searching for s/t
አስፈለገ asfällägä v.t. was important, necessary, imperative
ግርፍ አስፈለገኝ märäf asflällägäňň I felt like resting
ፈለጠ fällätä v.t. split (wood), quarry (marble, stone etc.); v.i. feel a headache e.g. ራሴን ፈለጠኝ rasen fällätäňň I feel a headache. I have a headache.
ፈለጣ in እንጨት ፈለጣ ʾənčät fälätа act of splitting wood, wood chopping

in እንጨት ፈላጭ ʾənčät fälač n. wood-chopper
ደንጊያ— dängiya—n. quarryman
ፈላጭ ቆራጭ fälač qorač n. dictator, authoritarian, absolute ruler, tyrant
ፍልጥ fəlṭ n. split wood
ተፈለጠ täfällätä v.i. was split (wood), was chopped
ተፈላጭ täfällač adj. easily split (wood)
ፈለፈለ fäläffälä v.t. hatched (chicken); bored into, hollowed out; shelled (beans); husked (corn)
ፈልፋላ fälfäla adj. extremely wicked (person)
ፍልፈል in ፍልፈል አፋር fəlfäl afär n. mole
ፍልፍል fəlfəl adj. shelled (beans etc.)
መፈልፈያ in የቡና መፈልፈያ yäbunna mäfälfäya n. coffee pulper
ተፈለፈለ täfäläffälä v.i. was hatched; was hollowed, was shelled; was husked
አስፈለፈለ asfäläffälä v.t. had (s/t) shelled; hollowed, husked
ፈሊጥ see ፈለጠ
ፈላ fälla v.i. boiled; was fermented; swarmed (moved in large numbers)
ፍላት fəlat n. boiling
ፍል fəl adj. boiled
ፍል ወሃ fəlwäha n. hot spring, thermal springs
ተፈላ täfällä v.i. was boiled
አፈላ afälla v.t. boiled, made to boil

335

? ?	gud—v.t. created trouble	

ፍዳቃል af... medium sized cooking pot

አንፋሎት ənfalot c. steam, vapour

አስፈላ asfälla v.t. had (s/t) boiled

ፈረማ färrämä v.t. signed (a document); endorsed (a check)

ፈራሚ färrami adj./n. (one) who signs (a document); one (who) endorses (a check) signatory

ፈርማ firma n. signature

ተፈረማ täfärrämä v.i. was signed (a document); was endorsed (a check)

ተፈራረማ täfärarrämä v.i. concluded an agreement, ratified (on both sides)

ተፈራራሚ täfärarami n. signatories

አስፈረማ asfärrämä v.t. had (s/o) signed

ፈረሰ färräsä v.t. fell in ruins, fell apart, collapsed; was destroyed; was violated (pact); was abrogated (contract)

ፈረሽ färaš adj. liable to fall apart; legally invalid

ፈረሽ በስባሽ färaš bäsbaš dj. mortal

ፍራሽ fəraš n. mattress

ፍርሽ fərraš n. ruins, remains

ፈረረሰ färarräsä v.i. fell to pieces, fell in ruins

ፍስራሽ fərsraš n. ruins, remains

ፍስርስ fərsrəs adj. dilapidated

ፍስርሱ ወጣ fərsrəsu wätta v.i. fell into pieces, was dilapidated

ተፈረሰ täfarräsä v.i. disagreed (on price)

አፈራረሰ afärarräsä v.t. wreck-

ed, destroyed, ruined

ፈራሱላ färäsulla n. 17 kilos

ፈራስ färäs n. horse, stallion

መዳ — n. Greyer's zebra

ፈራሰኛ färäsäñña n. horseman, cavalry; cavalryman; torrent

ለጣ ፈራስ läta färäs n. barebacked horse

(ፈ) ስለጣን yäsäytan färäs adj. moody

(ፈ) ፈረስ ጉልበት yäfäräs gulbät n. horsepower

—ግልጎ -galgö n. colt

ፈራቄ färäqe

ፈራቄ järäqe n. shift system (in schools etc.)

ፈርቅ färq n. difference (price)

ፈረቀረቀ färäqärräqä

ተፈረቀረቀ täfräqärräqä v.i. suppurated; oozed with pus

ፈራንሳይ färänsay n. France

ፈራንሳዊ färänsawi adj. French, Frenchman

ፈራንሳየኛ färänsayäñña n. French (language)

ፈራከረከ färäkärräkä

ፈራክራክ färäkrakka adj. falling apart

ፍራክርክ fərakrak adj. falling apart

ተፈራከረከ täfräkärräkä v.i. fell apart; trembled with fear

ፈራከሰ färäkkäsä v.t. cracked

ፍርክስ färkəs n. a crack

ተፈራከሰ täfäräkkäsä v.i. was cracked

ፈረደ färrädä v.t. judged, pronounced sentence, rendered judgement

ፈረደለት färrädällät he ruled in his favour

ፈረደበት färrädäbbät he ruled against him

ፈራጅ färäǧ adj./n. one who judges, pronounces sentence

ፍርጃ färǧa n. disaster, calamity; punishment

ፍርድ

of God
ፈርድ n judgement;
award (decision given
by a judge or arbi-
trator)

ፍርድ ጋንደል
ፈርዳ gändäl n.
biased judge

ፍርድ ሚኒስ
ፈርድ minister n.
Ministry of Justice

ቱር
—ሚኒስትር
—ministr n. Minister
of Justice

ሽንጎ
—šango n. people's
tribunal

ቤት
—bet n. court, tri-
bunal, court of justice

አውራጃ ፍር
awrajja fərd bet n.
awrajja court (pro-
vincial court)

ድ ቤት

ከፍተኛ
käffətäñña — n. high-
court

ወረዳ
wäräda — n. district-
court

መታደር
wättadär— n. court-
martial

ጠቅላይ
ţäqlay— n. supreme
court

ተፈረደ
täfärrädä v.i. was
judged; was evaluated

ተፋረደ
täfarrädä v.i. brought
one's case to the court
of justice

ተፋራጅ
täfaraž adj./ n. (one)
who brings his case
to the court of justice

አፋረደ
affarrädä v.t. arbi-
trated, saw the case
of opponents
asfärrädä was decided
in his favour

አስፈረደ

ፈረገረገ
°färägärägä
fərəgrəg adj. inter-
woven, n grid, grating

ፍርግርግ

 ፈራገጠ
°färäggäţä
tänfäragäţä v.i. wrig-
gled

ፈራጠ
färräţä v.i. broke open,
burst

ፈርጥ
färţ a stone in a set-
ting

ፍርጥ አድርጎ
färräţţ adəgo tänag-
gärä he spoke bluntly,
he spoke straight out

አፋረጠ
afärräţä v.t. broke

ተፍረጠረጠ
täfräţärräţä v.i. was
squeezed out (boil
etc.)

አፍረጠረጠ
in አፍርጥርጦ ተናገረ
afräţrəţo tänaggärä
he spoke bluntly, he
spoke straight out

ፈራጠመ
färäţţämä v.i. became
fleshy, strong

ፈርጠመ
färţamma adj. well-
built, strong (person),
corpulent

አፈራጠመ
afäräţţämä v.t.became
fleshy, strong

ፈራጠጠ
färäţţäţä v.i. ran away
(horse); deserted

ፈርጣጭ
färţač n. deserter

ፍርጣጣ
färţäţa n. desertion

°ፈራጠጠ
°färäţţäţä

ተንፈራጠጠ
tänfäraţţäţä v.i. was
stretched (legs while
sitting)

አንፈራጠጠ
anfäraţţäţä v.t.
stretched one's legs
(while sitting)

ፈረፈረ
färäffärä v.t.crumbled,
broke into small pieces

ፍርፋሪ
färəffari n. crumbs

ፍርፍር
färfər n crumbled
əngära mixed in wät

ተፈረፈረ
täfäräffärä v.i.
crumbled

°ፈረፈረ
°färäffärä

ተንፈረፈረ
tänfäraffärä v.i. flop-
ped around, writhed

ፈሪሳዊ
färisawi n. hypocrite,
self-righteous person.
Pharisee

ፈራ
färra v.i. was afraid.
feared, was fearful,
was frightened

ፈሪ
färi adj. coward,
timid, fearful

ፈሪህ እግዚአ
färiha gzi'abəhēr n. the
fear of God

ብሔር

ፈሪነት
färinnät n. cowardice

ፍራት
färat n. fright, fear,
scare, ፍራት ፍራት
አለው färat färat
aläw v.i hesitated

337

ፍራቻ	due to fear
	färačča n. fear
ተፈራ	*täfärra* v.i. was feared, respected, honoured
ተፈሪ	*täfäri* adj./n. *(one)* who is feared, respectful, honourable
ተፈራረ	*täfärarra* v. i. feared each other; had mutual respect
አስፈራ	*asfärra* v.t. frightened, terrified, scared
አስፈሪ	*asfärri* adj. fearful, fierce, ferocious
አስፈራረ	*asfärarra* v.t. terrified, scared, threatened
ፈረ	*färra*
ፍሬ	*färe* n. fruit, seed, berry
—ሰጠ	—*säṭṭä* v.t. was productive; bore fruits *(of work)*
ፍሬያማ	*färeyamma* adj. fruitful
ፍረፍሬ	*färäfäre* n. fruits *(of all kind)*
ፍሬ ቢስ	*färe bis* adj. useless, pointless, fruitless, absurd, futile, ridiculous
—ነገር	—*nägär* n. gist, main point, central ideas; essence; summary *(of an article)*
የሥራ—	*yäsära* — n. output, result *(of one's activities)*
የብልት—	*yäbällät* — n. testicle
አፈራ	*afärra* v.t. produced fruits, bore fruits
ፈር	*fär* n. furrow *(of a —plough)*
—ለቀቀ	—*läq ṇäqä* v.i. missed the point
—ያዘ	—*yazä* v.t. stuck to the point
ፈርስ	*färs* n. chyme and chyel
ፈርሳም	*färsam* adj. big-bellied
ፈርኝ	*färǧ* n. fringe, ruffle *(of skirt)*
ፈርጥ	*see* ፈረጠ

ፈሰሰ	*fässäsä* v.i. poured out, spilled over; flew
ሐሞቱ—	*hamotu*— lost courage, lost hope
ሞልቶ—	*molto*— v.i. overflew
ፈሰሰ	*fäsäse* n. one with long hanging hair *(woman)*
ፈሰስ	*fäsäs* n. gutter *(of a roof)*
—አደረገ	—*adärrägä* reimbursed unspent goverment money to the central treasury
ፈሳሽ	*fäsaš* n. liquid, fluid
—ወይ	—*wäha* n. running water
ፍሳሽ	*fässaš* n. sewage; leakage
የውሃና የፍሳሽ ባለ ስልጣን	*yäwähanna yäfässaš baläsälṭan* water and sewage authority
ፍስስ አለ	*ṇn* ልቡ ፍስስ አለ *läbbu fäsäss alä* his heart sank; became lazy
በውነቱ ፍስስ አለ ተፋሰሰ	*säwännätu fäsäss alä* felt sluggish *in* ደም ተፋሰሰ *däm täfassäsä* v.i. killed each other, injured each other
አፈሰሰ	*affässäsä* v.t.spilled, leaked, poured
ደም—	*däm*— shed blood
አፋሰሰ	*affassäsä* v.t. spilled here and there
ፈሰከ	*fässäkä* v.t. broke the fast
ፋሲካ	*fasika* n. Easter
ፍስክ	*fässäk* n. non-fasting day
ፈሰፈሰ	*fäsäffäsä* v.t. thrashed soundly, gave a thorough beating
ፈሳ	*fässa* v.t. broke wind, farted
ፈሳም	*fäsam* n. farter; coward
ፈስ	*fäs* n. fart
ፈሱን ጠበሰ	*fäsun ṭäbbäsä* ran away quickly from;

338

	(people) to be stupi-fied	·ፌጋፈገ	*täfägaffägä* v.i. pressed against
ፈያደ	*fäyyädä* v.i. became use-ful	፤ ፈገፈገ	*afägäffägä* v.t. drew back; retreated; gave ground; withdrew
ፋይዳ	*fayda* n. usefulness, value, importance	ፈበ መ	*see also* ፈጸመ
—ቢስ	—*bis* adj. useless, worthless	ፍ፥ጥምጥም	*fäṭämṭäm* n. engage-ment *(agreement to marry)*
—የለሽ	—*yälläš* adj. uselsss, valueless	ተፈጠመ	*täfäṭṭämä* v.i. gave a promise in front of a judge
ፈጀ	*fäggä* v.t. consumed, ate up; exterminated; took *(time);* burnt *(of hot liquid)*	ተፈጣጠመ	*täfäṭaṭṭämä* v.i. be-came engaged *(to get married)*
ነገረ ፈጅ	*nägärä fägg* n. re-presentative *(in legal affairs)*	ፈጠረ	*fäṭṭärä* v.t. created, devised *(a scheme);* invented
ፍጀታ	*fägota* n. consumption; floor *(in a debate)*	ፈጠራ	*fäṭära* n. invention
—ይሰጠኝ	—*yassäṭäňň* May, I take the floor?	የፈጠራ ወሬ	*yäfäṭära wäre* fabrication *(false story of events)*
ፍጀት	*fäggät* n. massacre; uproar, disturbance, tumult	—ጽሑፍ	—*ṣähuf* creative writing
ተፈጀ	*täfäggä* v.t. was con-sumed, was eaten up	ፈጣሪ	*fäṭari* n. creator
ተፋጀ	*täfaggä* v.i. destroyed one another; was hot *(pepper);* burnt *(hot liquid)*	ፍጡር	*fäṭur* n. creature, being *(creature)*
አፋጀ	*affaggä* v.t. caused to destroy one another	ፍጥረት ሥነ—	*fäṭrät* n. creature *sänä—* n. nature
አስፈጀ	*asfäggä* v.t. had s/o destroyed	ተፈጠረ	*täfäṭṭärä* u.i. was created
ፈገመ	*fäggämä* v.i. tumbled down	ተፈጥሮ	*täfäṭro* n. nature, natural state
ፍገም አለ	*fäggämm alä* v.i. tumbled down; died suddenly	የተፈጥሮ ሀብት	*yätäfäṭro habt* n. natural resources
አፈገመ	*afäggämä* v.t. let s/o tumble down	ፈጠነ	*fäṭṭänä* v.i. was quick, hurried, went fast, was fast, speeded up
ፈገገ	*fäggägä* v.i. smiled	ፈጣን	*fäṭṭan* adj. quick, swift, rapid
ፈገግታ	*fägögta* n. smile	ፍጡን	*in* ፍጡን ረድኤት *fäṭu-nä rädə'et* patron saint
—ቢስ	—*bis* adj. cheerless		
*ፈገጠ	*fäggäṭä*	ፍጥነት	*fäṭnät* n. speed, velocity, rapidity
ፈገጠው	*fäggäṭäw* to Hell with it	—ጨመረ	—*čämmärä* v.t. accelerated
ፈገፈገ	*fägäffägä* v.t. rubbed; scraped	በፍጥነት	*bäfäṭnät* adv. im-mediately, rapidly,fast
ፍገፋጊ	*fägäffagi* n. scrapings	ተፋጠነ	*täfaṭṭänä* v.i. hurried
ተፈገፈገ	*täfägäffägä* v.i. was rubbed, scraped	አፋጠነ	*affaṭṭänä* v.t. speeded, quickened, hastened
*ፈገፈገ	*fägäffägä*	አፋጣኝ	*affaṭaň* adj. urgent

ፈታሽ   *fättaš* n. inspector

ፍተሻ   *fəttäša* n. inspection, search

ተፈተሸ   *täfättäša* v.i. was checked; was inspected; was searched

ተፈታተሸ   *täfätattäša* v.i. tried out one another

አስፈታሸ   *asfättäša* v.t. had s/t, s/o inspected; searched

.ተነ   *fättänä* v.t. examined, tested, experimented, put to the test; tempted

ፈተና   *fätäna* n. examination, test; trial, temptation

ፈታኝ   *fättan* n. examiner, invigilator

ፍቱን   *fətun* adj efficacious (remedy), efficient (e.g. way of teaching), tried

ፍቱንነት   *fətunənnät* n. efficacy

መፈተኛ   *mäfättäña* adj. experimental

ተፈተነ   *täfättänä* v.i. was examined, tested; was put to the test

ተፈታኝ   *täfättañ* n. candidate (in an examination), examinee

ተፈታተነ   *täfättatänä* v.i. tempted s/o, put temptation in somebody's way

ተፈታታኝ   *täfätatañ* n. tempter

አፈታተነ   *affätattänä* v.t. caused to compete against each other

አስፈተነ   *asfättänä* v.t. had s/o examined, had s/t tested

ፈተገ   *fättägä* v.t. rubbed, removed the hulls; scrubbed (pans)

ፍተጋ   *fəttäga* n. rubbing

ፍትግ   *fəttəg* n. wheat, barley etc. whose hulls are removed

ተፈተገ   *täfättägä* v.i. was rubbed; was scrubbed

ተፋተገ   *täfattägä* v.i. made

---

friction (by rubbing); quarrelled

አፋተገ   *affattägä* v.t. caused to rub against each other

አስፈተገ   *asfättägä* v.t. had the hulls removed; had s/t scrubbed

ፈተፈተ   *fätäffätä* v.t. crumbled up s/t soft (bread in sauce); was impertinent, was intrusive

ፈትፋች   in ነገር ፈትፋች *nägär fätfač* adj. impertinent, intrusive

ፍትፍት   *fətfət* n. scrambled bread (ənǧarä) mixed in pepper sauce

ፈታ   *fätta* v.t. released, untied unfastened; undid (a knot); divorced; solved; deciphered; gave absolution

ሥራ   *səra –* v.t. was idle, was out of work

ፈት   *fätt* n. divorced (mainly for woman) also ፍትሕት *fətat*,

ፍታት   *fəthat* n. prayer for the dead

ፍትሕ   *fəth* n. justice

ፍትሕ   *fətha bəher həgg*

ብሄር ሕግ   civil code

ፍች   *fəčč* n. interpretation; solution; meaning; divorce

መፍትሂ   *mäftəhe* n. solution; remedy

መፍቻ   *mäfča* n. spanner; key

የጠመንጃ   *vätämänǧa — n. screwdriver

ፈታታ   *fätatta* v.t. dismounted, dismantled

ዕድሜ   *ədme yəftah* n. life

ይፍታህ   imprisonment

ተፈታ   *täfätta* v.i was released; was untied, was divorced; was solved

ጦር–   *tor—* v.t. was routed (for an army)

ተፋታ   *täfatta* v.i. divorced one another

ተፍታታ	*täftatta* v.i. was disentangled *(a thread)* in ሰውነቱን አፍታታ *säwənnätun aftatta* v.t. limbered up
እግሩን—	*əgrun—* v.t. stretched one's legs
አፋታ	in ደም አፋታብት *däm afättabbät* bled heavily
አፋታ	*affatta* v.t. divorced *(of s/o pronouncing a divorce)*
አስፋታ	*asfätta* v.t. had s/o released *(from prison, detention)*; had s/t untied, freed
ፋቸል	*fäčäl* n. pincers
ፋነቀለ	*fänäqqälä* v.t. pulled out, ripped out *(pulled out)* in መፋንቀለ መንግሥት *mäfänqälä mängəst* n. coup d'etat
መፋንቀል	
ተፋነቀለ	*täfänäqqälä* v.i. was pulled out
ተፋናቀለ	in ከሥራው ተፋናቀለ *käsəraw täfänaqqälä* he lost his job
አፋናቀለ	in ከሥራ አፋናቀለ *käsəra affänaqqälä* caused s/o to lose his job
• ፋነቸረ	• *fänäččärä*
ተፋነቸረ	*täfänäččärä* v.i. died instantly
ፋነከተ	*fänäkkätä* v.t. broke open, threw open, broke into pieces
ፍነካች	*fənəkkač* n. moiety
ፍንከት	*fənkət* adj. broken open; full of scars *(on the head)*
ፍንከች አለ	*fənkəčč alä* v.i. flinched
ወይ ፍንከች	*wäy fənkəčč* I will never flinch
ተፋነከተ	*täfänäkkätä* v.i. was broken open
ተፋናከተ	*täfänakkätä* v.t. hit each other's heads
ፋነዳቀ	*fänäddäqä* v.i. was jubilant, cheerful, viva-

	cious
ፍንደቃ	*fəndäqa* n. exaltation, ecstasy, spiritual uplift
ፍንድቅ አለ	*fənddəqq alä* v.i. was jubilant, cheered up
• ፋነደደ	• *fänäddädä*
ፋንዳዳ	*fändadda* adj. big-bottomed
አፋነደደ	*afänäddädä* v.t. stooped *(immoral)*; lowered oneself morally
ፋነዳ	*fänädda* v.i. exploded, blew up, burst; blew up *(of fire)*; erupted *(of volcano)*; was open *(of flower)*, bloomed
ፋንጂ	*fänǧi* n. explosive dynamite, also ዲና ሚት
ፍንዳታ	*fəndata* n. out-break, irruption
ፋንዳ ፋነዳ አለ	*fända fända alä* v.i. cheered up
አፋነዳ	*afänädda* v.t. exploded, blew up, burst
ፋነገለ	*fänäggälä* v.t. overthrew, overturned
ፋንጋላ	*fängalla* adj. unsteady in ባሪያ ፋንጋይ barəya *fängay* n. slave trader
ፋንጋይ	
ፍንገላ	in ባሪያ ፍንገላ bärəya *fəngäla* n. slave trading
ተፋነገለ	*täfänäggälä* v.i. was overthrown, overturned
• ፋነጠረ	see አፋነጠጠ
ፋነጠረ	*fänäṭṭärä* v.t. flicked
ፋንጠር አለ	*fänṭṭär alä* v.i. was secluded, kept oneself aloof, withdrew oneself
ፋንጣራ	in ፋንጣራ ቦታ *fänṭarra bota* n. remote place
ፍንጣሪ	*fənəṭṭari* n. spark *(given off by flint)*
ፍንጥር	*fänṭər* n. drink after doing some business
ወስፋንጥር	*wäsfänṭər* n. bow
ተፋናጠረ	*täfänaṭṭärä* v.i. flipped

341

ተስፈናጠረ	back *täsfänäṭṭärä* v.i. was ejected, was projected (shell)	ፈንታ	also ፋንታ *fänta, fanta* n. share, portion, turn
ተስፈንጣሪ	*täsfänṭari* adj. extremist (politics)	በ...—	*bä...—*instaad of, in place of
አፈናጠረ	*affänaṭṭärä* v.t. projected (shell)	በፈንታቸው	*bäfäntaw* in his turn
አስፈናጠረ	*asfänäṭṭärä* v.t. flipped; projected (shell)	ፈንዜ	*fänze* n. curved sword
ፈነጠቀ	*fänäṭṭäqä* v.t. projected (beam of light); splashed water	ፋንጣጣ	*fänṭaṭa* n. small-pox.
ፍንጣቂ	*fǝnäṭṭaqi* n. spark; splotch (of ink, sauce etc.)	ፈከፈከ አፈከፈከ	*fäkäffäkä* *afäkäffäkä* v.t. erupted (skin)
ተፈናጠቀ	*täfänaṭṭäqä* v.i. was splashed; was plattered	ፈካ	*fäkka* v.i. blossomed (flower); brightened (face, colour); brightened,was alight(face), smiled; burst open (popcorn)
አፈናጠቀ	*affänaṭṭäqä* v.t. splashed		
ፈነጠዘ	*fänäṭṭäzä* v.i. was merry, was excited and happy, exalted	ፍካት	*fäkat* n. brightness (colour, face)
በደስታ—	*bädässäta—* was full of joy	ፍክ አፈከ	*fäk* adj.bright (colour) *afäkka* v.t. animated; blossomed
ፈንጠዣ	*fänṭäzäyya* n. merry-making, jubilance, exaltation	ፈወሰ	*fäwwäsä* v.t. healed, cured
—በፈንጠዣ ሆነ	*—bäfänṭäzäyya honä* was in great joy and merriment	ፈዋሽ ፈውስ ፈውስ ቢስ	*fäwwaš* n. healer *fäws* n. healing *fäwsä bis* adj. incurable
አስፈነጠዘ	*asfänäṭṭäzä* v.t. treated s/o lavishly	ፈውስ የለሽ	*fäws yällaš* adj. incurable
ፈነጠጠ ተፈናጠጠ	*fänäṭṭäṭä* *täfänaṭṭäṭä* v.i. rode pillion	ተፈወሰ	*täfäwwäsä* v.i. was healed, cured
ተፈናጣጭ	*täfänaṭač* n. pillion rider	አስፈወሰ	*asfäwwäsä* v.t. had s/o healed, cured
አፈናጠጠ	*affänaṭṭäṭä* v.t. had s/o ride pillion	ፈዘዘ	*fäzzäzä* v.i. became dull (eye); stared; was glassy (eyes); was dazed (by a blow); was numb (limbs); was in a stupor
ፈነጨ	*fänäččä* v.i. gambolled; pranced (of a horse); frolicked, capered		
ፈነፈነ ተፈናፈነ	*fänäffänä* *täfänaffänä* v.i. got close to one another, huddled	ፈዛዛ ዋዘ—	*fäzazza* adj. slow; feeble (eye) *waza—*aimless pursuit, lacking seriousness, trivial
መፈናፈኛ ቦታ ፈናፈነ አፈናፈነ	*mäffänafäña botta* place to stand on *fänäffänä* *afänäffänä* v.t. smelt, sniffed (of an animal)	ተፋዘዘ አፈዘዘ	*täfazzäzä* v.i. gazed at each other *afäzzäzä* v.t. dazed (by a blow); made listless; bewitched (charmed)
		አፋዘዘ	*affazzäzä* v.t. caused

(people) to be stupified

ፈየደ fäyyädä v.i. became useful

ፋይዳ fayda n. usefulness, value, importance

--ቢስ —bis adj. useless, worthless

—የለሽ —yälläš adj. uselsss, valueless

ፈጀ fäǧǧä v.t. consumed, ate up; exterminated; took (time); burnt (of hot liquid)

ነጋሪ ፈጅ nägärä fäǧǧ n. representative (in legal affairs)

ፍጆታ fəǧota n. consumption; floor (in a debate)

—ይሰጠኝ —yəssäṭäññ May, I take the floor?

ፍጅት fəǧǧət n. massacre; uproar, disturbance, tumult

ተፈጀ täfäǧǧä v.t. was consumed, was eaten up

ተፋጀ täfaǧǧä v.i. destroyed one another; was hot (pepper); burnt (hot liquid)

አፋጀ affaǧǧä v.t. caused to destroy one another

አስፈጀ asfäǧǧä v.t. had s/o destroyed

ፈገመ fäggämä v.i. tumbled down

ፍግም አለ fəggəmm alä v.i. tumbled down; died suddenly

አፈገመ afäggämä v.t. let s/o tumble down

ፈገገ fäggägä v.i. smiled

ፈገግታ fägägta n. smile

—ቢስ —bis adj. cheerless

*ፈገጠ *fäggäṭä

ፈገጠው fäggäṭäw to Hell with it

ፈገፈገ fägäffəgä v.t. rubbed; scraped

ፍግፈጊ fəgəffagi n. scrapings

ተፈገፈገ täfägäffägä v.i. was rubbed, scraped

*ፈገፈገ *fəgäffägä

·ፈጋፈገ täfägaffägä v.i. pressed against

ፈገፈገ afägäffägä v.t. drew back; retreated; gave ground; withdrew

ፈጠመ see also ፈጸም

ፍጥምጥም fäṭəmṭəm n. engagement (agreement to marry)

ተፈጠመ täfäṭṭämä v.i. gave a promise in front of a judge

ተፈጣጠመ täfäṭaṭṭämä v.i. became engaged (to get married)

ፈጠረ fäṭṭärä v.t. created, devised (a scheme); invented

ፈጠራ fäṭära n. invention

የፈጠራ ወሬ yäfäṭära wäre fabrication (false story of events)

—ጽሑፍ —ṣəhuf creative writing

ፈጣሪ fäṭari n. creator

ፍጡር fəṭur n. creature, being (creature)

ፍጥረት fəṭrät n. creature

ሥነ— sənä— n. nature

ተፈጠረ täfäṭṭärä u.i. was created

ተፈጥሮ täfäṭro n. nature, natural state

የተፈጥሮ ሀብት yätäfäṭro habt n. natural resources

ፈጠነ fäṭṭänä v.i. was quick, hurried, went fast, was fast, speeded up

ፈጣን fäṭṭan adj. quick, swift, rapid

ፍጡን in ፍጡን ረድኤት fəṭunä rädə'et patron saint

ፍጥነት fəṭnät n. speed, velocity, rapidity

—ጨመረ —čämmärä v.t. accelerated

በፍጥነት bäfəṭnät adv. immediately, rapidly, fast

ተፋጠነ täfäṭṭänä v.i. hurried

አፋጠነ affäṭṭänä v.t. speeded, quickened, hastened

አፋጣኝ affaṭaň adj. urgent

ፈጠጠ   *fäṭṭäṭä* v.i. popped (of eyes)

ፈጠጠ   *fäṭaṭa* adj. pop-eyed

ፍጥጥ ብሎ   *fǝṭǝṭṭ bǝlo ayyä* v.i.

አየ   stared at, gazed at

ተፋጠጠ   *täfaṭṭäṭä* v.i. were stupified; struck each other speechless; confronted each other

አፋጠጠ   *affaṭṭäṭä* v.t. caught (s/o) out (e.g. with difficult question); put (s/o) on the spot

ፈጠፈጠ   *fäṭäffäṭä* v.t. squashed (press out of shape)

ፈጥርቅ መጠጥ   *fäṭrǝq mäṭäṭṭ* n. very strong drink

ፈጨ   *fäččä* v.t. ground (grain), milled flour, crushed (rock)

ፈጫይ   *fäčay* n. grinder (woman who earns her living by grinding grain for other people)

ወፍጮ   *wäfčo* n. mill, grinding slab

—ቤት   —*bet* n. mill

ተፋጨ   *täfaččä* v.i. was sharpened (a knife against another knife)

አፋጨ   *affaččä* v.t. sharpened (a knife against another knife); gnashed (of the teeth)

*ፈጨረጨረ   *fäčäräččärä*

ተፍጨረጨረ   *täfčäräčärä* v.i. floundered, made frantic efforts

ተፍጨርጫሪ   *täfčärčari* a man of great enterprise

ፈጸመ   *fäṣṣämä*, see also ፈጠመ *fäṭṭämä*, v.t. ended, fulfilled, finished, carried out, completed, accomplished

ፈጽሞ   *fäṣṣǝmo* adv. entirely, completely, utterly

—አልመጣም   —*almäṭṭamm* he has never come

ፍጹም   *fǝṣṣum* adj. complete, absolute, perfect

በፍጹም   *bäfǝṣṣum* adv.

absolutely, entirely

—አልመጣም   —*almäṭṭamm* he has never come

ፍጹምነት   *fǝṣṣumǝnnät* n. perfection

ፍጻሜ   *fǝṣṣame* n.ending, end, completion, fulfilment

ተፈጸመ   *täfäṣṣämä* v.i. came to an end, was completed; came true

አስፈጸመ   *asfäṣṣämä* v.t. executed, carried out, got s/t finished

አስፈጻሚ   *asfäṣami* n. executor

ጉዳይ—   *gudday*— n. solicitor, barrister

አፈጻጸም   —*affäṣaṣäm* n. procedure

ፈፈ   *fäfa* n. rivulet, brook

ፉሎ   *fulo* n. headstall

ፉርኖ   *furno* n. bread (European style)

—ቤት   —*bet* n. bakery

—ዱቄት   —*duqet* n. white flour

ፉርጎ   *furgo* n. car (train)

ፉትቦል   *futbol* n. football also እግር ካስ

ፉት አለ   *futt alä* v.i. sipped

ፉንጋ   *funga* adj. ugly

ፉካ   *fuka* n. opening in a wall see ፍhረ

ፉጨት   *fučät* n. whistling (with the mouth etc.)

አፉጨ   *afuʷaččä* v.t. whistled (with the mouth)

ፉጋ   *fuga* n. cabinet-maker (a derogatory word)

ፊላ   *fila* n. kind of grass, used as roof covering

ፊር ፊር አለ   *firr firr alä* v.i. writhed helplessly

ፊሽካ   *fiška* n. whistle

—ነፋ   —*näffa* v.t. whistled

ፊት   *fit* n. face, front; adv. at first, before

በ—   *bä*— adv. before, early

ከ—   *kä*— adv. infront of

እ—   *ǝ*— adv. in front of

ከሁሉ በፊት   *kähullu bäfit* first of all

344

ከፊት ለፊት	käfit läfit in front of, opposite, face to face
ከሰዓት በፊት	käsä'at bäfit n. forenoon
ከዚህ—	käzzih— adv. previously, before
ወደ—	wädä— in the future, later on
የፊት እግር	yäfit əgər n. foreleg
—ጥርስ	—ṭərs n. incisor
ፊተኛው	fitäññäw the earlier one
ፊት ልሙጥ	fitä ləmuṭṭ adj. plain (ordinary, without ornament)
—ማጣጣ	—mäṭaṭa adj. leanfaced
ሰልካካ	—sälkakka adj. handsome (good-looking
—ከባድ	—käbbad adj. with an unpleasant face
ፊቱ ተኮማተረ	fitu täkomattärä v.i. frowned
—ደም መሰለ	—däm mässälä v.i. blushed
—ደነጋጣ	—dänäggäṭä v.i. was disconcerted
—ገረጣ	—gäräṭṭa v.i. became pale
—ጭር አለ	—čarr alä v.i. was melancholy
ፊቱን ጳጣረ	fitun qu"aṭṭärä v.t. frowned
—አዞረ	—azorä v.t. ignored
—ኮሶ አስመሰለ	—koso asmässälä v.t made a terrible face
—ኮሰተረ	—kosättärä v.t. showed seriousness, frowned
ፊት ለፊት	fit läfit adv. face to face, in front of, opposite to
ፊትና ኋላ	fitənna hu"ala one following the other
ፊት ነሣ	fit nässa v.t. refused, treated s/o in an unfriendly way
ፊታውራሪ	fitawrari old Ethoipian title
ኮሶ ፊት	koso fit adj. making grimaces
ወደፊት	wädä fit interj. forward! in the future

ጫጉራ ፊት	čäggu"arra fit adj. pimply
የፊታችን	yäfitaččən the coming (e.g. Tuesday)
ፊና	in በየፊናው bäyyäfinaw in their various ways, each in his own way
ፊናንስ	finans n. finance
የፊናንስ ዘበኛ	yäfinance zäbäñña n. customs official
ፊን አለ	finn alä v.i. spouted
ፊንጢጣ	finṭiṭṭa n. anus
ፊኛ	fiñña n. bladder; balloon
ፊውዳል	fiwdäl adj. feudal
ፊደል	fidäl n. alphabet, letter (syllabary), character (letter)
—ለያ	—läyyä v.t. mastered the alphabet
—ቆጠረ	—qoṭṭärä v.t. mastered the alphabet
—አስቆጠረ	—asqäṭṭärä v.t. taught the alphabet
ፊጥ አለ	fiṭṭ alä v.t. mounted a horse, mule etc. quickly
ፊጥኝ	in የፊጥኝ አሰረ yäfiṭṭaññ assärä v.t. tied the hands behind the back
ፋመ	famä v.i. got red hot; became glowing, became live (coals, fire)
ፍም	fäm n. ember, hot coals
ፊቱ— መሰለ	fitu—mässälä v.i. blushed
ተፋፋመ	täfafamä v.i. glowed, burnt up, flamed up; reached a climax; was in full swing; raged (battle)
አፋፋመ	affafamä v.t. made (s/t) flare up; made (s/t) reach a climax
ፋረ	farä v.t. hollowed out
ፋርማሲ	farmasi n. pharmacy
ፋርስ	fars n. Persia
ፋሮ	faro n. white-tailed mongoose also ፋሲ.ጋ see ፈሰከ
ፋሲካ	
ፋስ	fas n. axe
ፋሽኮ	fašco n. flask

345

ፈቀ faqä v.t. scraped; tanned (hide; rubbed (teeth);) scaled (a fish); wrote off (debt)

ፋቂ faqi n. tanner

ፍቅፋቂ fəqəffaqi n. scrap in ጥርስ መፋቂያ ţərs mäfaqiya n. stick of a particular tree used to brush the teeth

ፈብሪካ fabrika n. factory, plant

ባለ— balä — n. manufacturer

ፈታ fata n. moment of rest, lull

—ሰጠ —säţţä v.t. gave time

—ነሣ —nässa v.t. kept busy

—የለውም —yälläwənm v.i he is tied down (by work)

ፈነነ fannänä v.i. was led astray (child etc.)

ፈኖ fanno n. volunteer (fighter arch.)

ፈና fana n. torch

ፈንታ fanta n. portion, share; turn

በኔ— bäne — in place of me

ፈንዳያ fändəyya ŋ. excrement (of horse, mule, donkey)

ፈና see ፈነነ

ፈኖስ fanos n. lamp, lantern, oil lamp

ፈካልቲ fakälti n. faculty

ፈክቱር faktur n. receipt, bill, invoice

ፈይል fail n. file (record)

ፈየለ fäyyälä v.t. filed

ፈይዳ fäyda n. use, value, importance

—ቢስ —bis adj. useles

—የለሽ —yällä̀ adj. useless, unimportant

ፈዳት fadät n. weasel

ፈግ see ኢፈገ

ፈጉሎ fagullo n. oil-cake, expeller

ፈፈ faffa v.i. thrived (of

children), grew fa...

ፈቆ feqo n. oribi (ourebia ourebi)

ፈንጣ fenţa n. grasshopper, cricket

ፈዝ fez n. joke, mockery, jest

ፈዘኛ fezzäñña adj./n.(one) who jokes, mocker

አፈዘ afezä v.i. joked, mocked, derided, made fun of

አፍያዥ afyaž adj./n. (one) who jokes, mocker

ፍላፃ fəlaşşa n. arrow

ፍሥሐ fəssəha n. joy, happiness

ፍሩስካ fruska n. bran

ፍሪዳ fərida n. fattened bullock

ፍራሽ faraš n. mattress

ፍራት see ፈራ

ፍሬ fare n. fruit, berry, seed

—ሰጠ —säţţä v.t. gave good results, bore fruit (work)

—ቢስ —bis adj. useless, pointless, fruitless; futile

—ነገር —nägär n. central idea, gist, summary, essence

የሥራ— yäsəra— n. output

የብልት— yäbəllət— n. testicle

ፍራፍሬ farafare n. fruits

ፍሬያማ fareyamma adj. fruitful

ፍርምባ farəmbba n. chest (of animal)

ፍትሐት fathat n. absolution

ጸሎተ— şäl(tä— n. funeral ceremony

ፍትሕ fath n. justice, judgement

ፍትሕ ብሔር ሕግ fətha bəher hagg n. civil code

ፍትወት fatwät n. lust (sexual)

ፍትወተ ሥጋ fatwätä səga n. the lusts of the flesh

ፍትወተኛ fatwätäñña adj. lustfu'

ፍናፍንት fənafənt n. hermaphrodite also መንታዊ

ፍንክት see ፈንከተ

ፍንጃል fənğal n. porcelain cup

ፍንጅ   *in* እጅ ከፈንጅ *ə̆gg* kāfənğğ adj. red-handed

ፍንጥር   see ፈነጠረ

ፍንጭ   fənč n. hint, clue, key (to a mystery)

ፍየል   fəyyäl n. goat

—ማላስ   —mālas adj. talkative

የሜዳ—   yämeda— n. gazelle

ፍዳ   fədda n. hardship, misery, tribulation

ፍዳውን አየ   fəddawən ayyä he suffered greatly

ፍጃታ   see ፈጀ

ፍግ   fəg n. manure, dung

ፍጥረት   see ፈጠረ

ፎሌ   folle n. drinking vessel made of a dried gourd

ፎላፎል   foläfol adj. cheerful (person), jovial vivacious

ፎልፉዋላ   folfuʷalla adj. cheerful (person), jovial, vivacious

ፎረሸ   forräšä v.i. failed, was unsuccessful (col.)

ፉርሽ   furš n. failure (col.)

ፎረፎር   foräfor n. dandruff, scurf

*ፎቀቀ   *foqqäqä

ፎቃቃ   foqaqa n. tattle-tale, informer

ፎቀቅ አለ   foqqäq alä v.i. stood aside, got out of the way; *also* ፈቀት አለ

ተንፉዋቀቀ   tänfuʷaqqäqä v.i. dragged oneself along the ground

አንፉዋቀቀ   anfuʷaqqäqä v.t.

pushed a little

አንፉዋቃቂ   anfuʷaqaqi n. tattle-tale, informer

ፎቅ   foq n. storey

—ቤት   —bet n. a building with saveral storeys (floors)

ባለስድስት   bäläsəddəst foq bet ፎቅ ቤት   a six-storeyed building

ፎነነ   fonnänä v.t. cut off someone's nose

ፎና   fonana n. one with the nose cut; short-nosed

ፎከረ   fokkärä v.t. uttered war boasts, bragged, boasted

ፉከራ   fukkära n. bragging boasting

ፉካከር   fukəkkər n. competition, rivalry

መፈከር   mäfäkkər n. slogan

ተፎካከረ   täfokakkärä v.i. competed with each other

ተፎካካሪ   täfokakari n. competitor, rival

አፎካከረ   affokakkärä v.t. caused (s/o) to compete

ፎከተ   fokkätä v.t. scratched (the body)

ፎካት   fokät n. itch

ፎጣ   fota n. towel

ፏፏቴ   fuʷafuʷate n. waterfall, cataract, falls

*ፏጨ   *fuʷaččä

ፏጨት   fuččät n. whistling (with the mouth)

አፏጨ   afuʷaččä v.t. whistled (with the mouth)

ፐ

ፒራሚድ   piramid n. pyramid

ፒያኖ   piyano n. piano

ፒጃማ   piğama n. pyjamas

ፓርላማ   parlama n. parliament

ፓርቲ   parti n. party

ፓትርያርክ   patrəyark n. patriarch

ፓኮ   pakko n. packet, box (matches)

ፓይለት   pailät n. pilot (air plane)

ፓፓዬ   pappaye n. papaya

ፐርሙዝ   permuz n. thermos flask

ፕላስተር   plastär n. adhesive tape

347

ፕላስቲክ	plastik n. plastic
ፕላኔት	planet n. planet
ፕላን	plan n. plan
ፕሬስ	pres n. press
ፕሬዚዴንት	prezident n. president
ፕሮባ	proba n. fitting *(by a tailor)*
ፕሮብለም	problem n. problem
ፕሮቶኮል	protokol n. protocol
ፕሮጀ	prože n. project
ፕሮግራም	program n. programme
ፕሮፌሰር	profesär n. professor
ፕሮፓጋንዳ	propagandda n. propaganda
ፖለቲካ	politika n. politics
ፖለቲከኛ	politikäñña n. politician; liar

የፖለቲካ ሰው	yäpolitika säw n. statesman
—ቡዴን	—budən n. party *(political)*
ፖሊሲ	polisi n. policy
ፖሊስ	polis n. policeman, police
የፖሊስ ሠራዊት	yäpolis särawit n. police force
ፖሊስ ጣቢያ	polis ṭabiya n. police station
ፖምፕ	pompa n. pump
ፖስታ	posta n. letter, mail, envelope
ፖስተኛ	postäñña n. postman, mailman
ፖስታ ሳጥን	posta saṭən n. post-office box, mail box
—ቤት	—bet n. post-office

ENGLISH - AMHARIC

a
’ኤይ’ ፣’ እ -ያተሙ- አንድ

abandon
እ’ባንደን -ግ- እርግፍ አርጎ መተው [ተወ] ፣ መክዳት [ከ’ዳ]

abandoned
እ’ባንደንድ -ቅ- የተተወ
immoral
-ቅ- ልቅ ፣ ስ’ድ (ለጠባይ)

abasement
እ’ቤይስመንት -ስ- ውርደት

abate
እ’ቤይት -ግ- ጸጥ ማለት [አለ] (ለማዕበል ወዘተ) ፣ ማነስ [አ’ነስ] ፣ መድከም [ደ’ከመ]

abbey
’አቢ -ስ- ገዳም ፣ ደብር

abbreviate
እብ’ሪቪዩይት -ግ- ማሳ’ጠር [አሳ’ጠረ] (ለ,ታ ላት)

abbreviation
እብሪቪ’ዩይሽን -ስ- ማሳ’ጠር (ለቃላት)

abdicate
’አብዲኬይት -ግ- ሹመት በፈቃድ መተው [ተወ]

abdomen
’አብደመን -ስ- ሆድ

abduct
እብ’ደክት -ግ- መጥለፍ [ጠ’ለፈ] ፣ መፈን ገል [ፈነ’ገለ] (ለሰው)

abet
እ’ቤት -ግ- ጥፋት እንዲሠሩ ማ’ደፋፈር [አ’ደፋ’ፈረ] ፣ መገፋፋት [ገፋ’ፋ]

abetter
እ’ቤተ -ስ- ለመጥፎ ሥራ የ’ሚገፋ’ፋ ፣ የ’ሚ ያ,ደፋ’ፍር

abeyance
እ’ቤየንስ -ስ- እሥራ ላይ እንዳይውል የተ ደ’ረገ ሕ’ግ .

abhor
እብ’ሆር -ግ- መጥላት [ጠ’ላ] (ፈ’ጽሞ) ፣ መ’ጸየፍ [ተጸ’የፈ]

abide
እ’ባይድ -ግ- መኖር [ኖረ] ፣ ባንድ ሥፍራ መ’ቀመጥ [ተቀ’መጠ] ፣ መ’ታገሥ [ታ’ገሠ]

abiding
እ’ባይዲንግ -ቅ- ለረ’ጅም ጊዜ የ’ሚቆ’ይ

ability
እ’ቢሊቲ -ስ- ችሎታ

abject
’አብጀክት -ቅ- የተዋ’ረደ ፣ ወ’ራ’ዳ

ablaze
እብ’ላይዝ -ቅ- የ’ሚ’ቃ’ጠል ፣ የ’ሚንበለ’በል (ቤት ወዘተ)

able
’ኤይበል -ቅ- ችሎ,ታ ያ’ለው ፣ የሠለ’ጠነ ፣ የ’ሚችል

abnormal
አብ’ኖ;መል -ቅ- ያልተለ’መደ ፣ እንግዳ (ለነ ገር)

aboard
እ’ቦ:ድ -ቅ- በመርከብ ፣ በባቡር ፣ በአውሮ’ ፕላን ላይ (ተሳፍሮ)

abode
እ’በውድ -ስ- መኖሪያ ቦታ

abolish
እ’ቦሊሽ -ግ- መደምሰስ [ደመ’ሰስ] ፣ መሠ’ ረዝ [ሠ’ረዘ]

abolition
አቦ’ሊሽን -ስ- መደምሰስ

abominable
እ’በሚነበል -ቅ- አ’ሥ’ቃቂ ፣ የ’ሚያስጠ’ላ ፣ እ’ጸ’ያፊ

abomination
እበሚ’ኔይሽን -ስ- አ’ሥ’ቃቂ ነገር

aboriginal
አቦ’ሪጂነል -ቅ- ጥንታዊ ነዋሪ (ያንድ አገር የመሠረት ሕዝብ)

aborigine
አቦ’ሪጂኒ -ስ- ያንድ አገር ጥንታዊ ነዋሪ ሰው

abortion
እ’ቦ:ሽን -ስ- ልጅ ማስወ’ረድ

abound

እ'ባውንድ -ግ- መትረፍረፍ [ተትረፈ'ረፈ]

about

እ'ባውት -ተግ- ገደማ ፣ ያህል ፣ ወዲያ'ና ወዲህ (መሄድ)

above

እ'በቭ -ተግ- ላይ ፣ በላይ

abrasion

እብ'ሬይዠን -ስ- መፋቅ

abreast

እብ'ሬስት -ተግ- ጐ'ን ለጐ'ን

abridge

እብ'ሪጅ -ግ- ማሳ'ጠር [አሳ'ጠረ] (መጽሐፍ)

abridgement

እብ'ሪጅመንት -ስ- ማሳ'ጠር ፤ ያ'ጠረ ጽሑፍ

abroad

ኢ'ብሮ'ድ -ተግ- በው'ጭ አገር ፤ ባሕር ማዶ

abrupt

እብ'ረፕት -ቅ- ቁር'ጥ ቁር'ጥ ያለ (ለንግ'ግር) ፤ ድንገተ'ኛ (ለነገር) ፣ ያልታ'ሰበ

abruptness

እብ'ረፕትነስ -ስ- ቁር'ጥ ቁር'ጥ ማለት (ለንግ'ግር) ፤ ድንገተ'ኛነት (ለነገር)

abscess

'አብሴስ -ስ- እ'ባጭ ፣ እበጥ (መግል የተ'ጠረ)

abscond

እ'ብስኮንድ -ግ- መሸሽ [ሸ'ሸ] ፤ መ'ደበቅ [ተደ'በቀ] (ጥፋት አጥፍቶ ቅጣት እን'ዳይደር ስ'በት)

absence

'አብሰንስ -ስ- አለመ'ገኘት ፣ መቅረት

absent

'አብሰንት -ቅ- ያልተገ'ኘ (እሥራ ላይ) ፣ ቀሪ፣ የሌ'ለ

vague

-ቅ- ሐ'ሳብ ብኩ'ን

absentee

አብሰን'ቲ: -ስ- እሥራ ያልተገ'ኘ

absolute

'አብሰሉ:ት -ቅ- ፍ'ጹም ፣ የተሟ'ላ (ለጠባይ ወዘተ)

absolution

አብሰ'ሉ:ሽን -ስ- መንጻት (ከኃጢአት) ፣ ሥር የት

absolve

እብ'ዞልቭ -ግ- ማንጻት [አነ'ጻ] ፣ ነጻ ማው ጣት [አወ'ጣ] (ከወንጀል ተግባር)

absorb

እብ'ሶ:ብ -ግ- መምጠጥ [መ'ጠጠ] (እንደ ሰፍ ነግ)

absorbent

እብ'ሶ:በንት -ቅ- መጣጭ ሳቢ (ፈሳሽ ወዘተ)

absorbing

እብ'ሶ:ቢንግ -ቅ- መጣጭ ፣ አስጐያያት ግራኪ

abstain

እብስ'ቴይን -ግ- ራስን መከልከል [ከለ'ከለ]፣ አንድ ነገር ከማድረግ ራስን ማገ'ድ [አ'ገደ]

abstemious

እብስ'ቲምየስ -ቅ- ራሱን ከብዙ መብል'ና መጠ'ጥ የ'ሚጋታ

abstinence

'አብስቲነንስ -ስ- በመጠኑ መኖር

abstract

'አብስትራክት -ቅ- የ'ማይ'ጨ'በጥ ፣ የ'ማይ 'ጻ'ስስ ፣ ረቂቅ

summary

-ስ- አሕጽሮተ ጽሑፍ

abstract

እብስት'ራክት -ግ- ማውጣት [አወ'ጣ] ፤ ከነ ድ ነገር ወይን'ም ከሐ'ሳብ መውሰድ [ወ'ሰደ]

abstruse

እብስት'ሩ:ስ -ቅ- አዳጋች ፣ በቀ'ላሉ የማ'ይ ገባ ፤ ጥልቅ ፣ የተሸ'ሸገ

absurd

እብ'ሰ:ድ -ቅ- የ'ማይመስል ፣ የተጃጃለ

abundance

እ'በንደንስ -ስ- ብዛት ፣ የተትረፈ'ረፈ

abundant

እ'በንደንት -ቅ- ብዙ

abuse

እብ'ዩ:ዝ -ግ- ለመጥፎ ነገር ማዋል [አዋለ] (ሥልጣንን ፣ መብትን ወዘተ)

curse

-ግ- መ'ሳደብ [ተሳ'ደበ]

abus

እብ'ተ:ኒዥ -ቅ- ተሳዳቢ ፣ ጸራፊ ፣ አ'ዋራጅ (በመ'ሳደብ)

350

abysmal

እ'ቢዝመል -ቅ- በጣም መጥፎ (ለነገር፣ለሁናቴ)

abyss

እ'ቢስ -ስ- ከል'ክ ያ'ለፈ ጥልቀት ፣ አንጦር ጥስ ፣ ጄ'ው ያለ ገደል

academic

አከ'ደሚክ -ቅ- የቀለም (ት፣፣ሀርት ወዘተ) ፣ የምሁራን (ማነበር)
not practical
-ቅ- በ፣ራ ላይ ያልዋለ (ዕውቀት)

academy

እ'ካደሚ -ስ- ከ'ፍተ'ኛ ፣ምሀርት ቤት የሙዚቃ ከ'ፍተ'ኛ ትምሀርት ቤት

accede

ኡ ያ'ሲይድ -ግ- መስማማት [ተስማ'ማ] ፣ ከ'ፍተ'ኛ ሥራ መያዝ [ያዘ]

accelerate

እክ'ሴለሬይት -ግ- ፍ፡፣፣ኑ መጨ'መር [ጨ'መረ]

acceleration

እክሴለ'ሬይሸን -ስ- ፍጥነት መጨ'መር ፣በጣም መፍጠን

accent

'አክሰንት -ስ- ያ'ነጋገር ፣ምንድ (ጉንደር'ኛ፣ ሸዋ'ኛ ፣ ጉ'ጀም'ኛ ወዘተ)
stress
-ስ- በቃላት ላይ የ'ሚ'ደ'ረግ ይዘት

accept

እክ'ሴፕት -ግ- መ'ቀበል [ተቀ'በለ]

acceptable

እክ'ሴፕተብል -ቅ- የ'ሚ'ቀ'በሉት ፣ ተስማሚ

access

'አክሴስ -ስ- ሊያደርስ የ'ሚያስችል መንገድ፣ ዘዴ

accessory

እክ'ሴሰሪ -ስ- የጥፋት ረ'ዳት
car
-ስ- የተሽከርካሪዎ'ች መለ'ወጫ
jewellery
-ስ- የሴቶ'ች ጌጣ ጌጥ

accident

'አክሲደንት -ስ- ድንገት
unpleasant
-ስ- አደጋ

accidental

አክሲ'ዴንተል -ቅ- ድንገተ'ኛ

accidentally

አክሲ'ዴንተሊ. -ተግ- በድንገት

acclaim

እክ'ሌይም -ግ- በእልልታ መ'ቀበል [ተቀ' በለ]

acclamation

አክለ'ሜይሸን -ስ- የደ'ስታ አ'ቀባበል

accommodate

እ'ኮመዴይት -ግ- ማረፊያ ማ'ዘጋጀት [አ'ዘ ጋ'ጀ] ፣ መርዳት [ረ'ዳ]

accommodation

እክመ'ዴይሸን -ስ- ማረፊያ (በሆቴል)

accompaniment

እ'ከምፐኒመንት -ስ- አብሮ መ'ጫወት (ሙ ዚቃ ፣ ዘፈን)

accompanist

እ'ከምፐኒስት -ስ- አብሮ ተጫዋች

accompany

እ'ከምፐኒ -ግ- ለዘፋኝ ሙዚቃ መምታት [መ'ታ]
go with
-ግ- አብሮ መሄድ [ሄደ]

accomplice

እ'ከምፕሊስ -ስ- የጥፋት ረ'ዳት ፣ ግብረ አ'በር

accomplish

እ'ከምፕሊሽ -ግ- ፍ'ጸሜ ማድረስ [አደ'ረ ስ] ፣ መፈ'ጸም [ፈ'ጸመ] ፣ማ'ከናወን [እ'ከና' ወነ]

accomplished

እ'ከምፕሊሽድ -ቅ- የተፈ'ጸመ ፣ የተከና ጎነ፣ ባለሞያ

accomplishment

እ'ከምፕሊሽመንት -ስ- ክን'ውን ፣ ሞያ ፣ ስጦታ ፣ ተውህቦ

accord

እ'ኮ፡ድ -ስ- ስምም'ነት

accordingly

እ'ኮ፡ዲንግሊ. -ተግ- በ . . . መሠረት ፣ ስለ'ዚህ

351

accost

እኮስት -ግ- ማነጋገር [አነጋገረ] (የማያ
ውቁትን ሰው)

rudely

-ግ- በጉ'ሸማ መጥራት [ጠ'ራ]

account

እካውንት -ስ- ሒሳብ

credit

-ስ- ዱቤ

story

-ስ- ታሪክ

accountable

እካውንተብል -ቅ- ጎላፊ (ተወ'ቃሽ ሊሆን
የሚችል)

accountant

እካውንተንት -ስ- የሒሳብ መዝገብ ያዥ

accumulate

እክ'ዩምዩሴይት -ግ- መሰብሰብ [ሰበ'ሰበ] ፣
ማከማቾት [አ'ከማ'ቸ] ፣ አ'ጠራ'ቀመ [ማ'ጠ
ራቀም]

accumulator

እክ'ዩምዩሴይተ -ስ- በኤሌክትሪክ የሚ'ሞ'
ላ ባትሪ

accuracy

አክዩረሲ -ስ- ፍ'ጹም'ነት ፣ ል'ክ'ነት

accurate

አክዩረት -ቅ- ል'ክ ፣ ፍ'ጹም

accursed

እ'ከስት -ቅ- የተረ'ገመ ፣ እርጉም ፣ የማይ
ሳ'ካ'ለት

accusation

አከዩ'ዜይሽን -ስ- ክ'ስ

accusative

እክ'ዩ፡ዘቲቭ -ቅ- ተሳቢ (ሰዋስው)

accuse

እክ'ዩ፡ዝ -ግ- መክሰስ [ከ'ሰሰ] ፣ መወንጀል
[ወነ'ጀለ]

accustom

እ'ከስተም -ግ- መልመድ [ለ'መደ] ፣ ራስን
ማልመድ [አለ'መደ]

ace

'ኤይስ -ስ- በካርታ ጨዋታ አንደ'ኛው ቁጥር

very good

-ቅ- በጣም ጥሩ ፣ የሠለ'ጠነ (ለአው'ሮ
'ፕላን ነጇ ፣ ለሽቅ'ድ'ድም መኪና ነጇ)

ache

'ኤይክ -ስ- ውጋት ፣ ሕመም

head-

-ስ- ራስ ምታት

achieve

እ'ቺይቭ -ግ- ያ'ቹትን ማግኘት [አገ'ኘ] ፣
ወ'ዳ'ቀዱት ግብ መድረስ [ደ'ረሰ]

achievement

ቾ'ቺይቭመንት -ስ- የሥራ ክን'ውን ፣ አንድ
ተግባር መፈ'ጸም

acid

'አሲድ -ስ- አሲድ ፣ አቾዶ

-ቅ- መጣጣ ፣ ኮምጣ'ጣ

acidity

አ'ሲዲቲ -ስ- ቃር ፣ የአቾዶ'ነት ጣዕም ፣ ጠባይ
ያለው

acknowledge

እክ'ኖለጅ -ግ- ዋጋ መስጠት [ሰ'ጠ] (ለሥ
ራ ፣ ለአድራጉት) ፤ ራስ በመነካቅነት ሰላምታ
መስጠት [ሰ'ጠ] ፤ የተላክ ዕቃ መድረሱን
ማ'ረጋገጥ [አ'ረጋ'ገጠ]

acknowledgement

እክ'ኖለጅመንት -ስ- ያንድ ሰው ድርሰት
እንዲታ'ወቅ ማድረግ

greeting

-ስ- ሰላምታ

acoustics

እ'ኩስቲክስ -ስ- የድምፅ ጥናት ፤ ባን'ድ ሕን
ፃ ውስጥ የድምፅ ማስተጋባት ሁናቴ

acquaint

እክ'ዌይንት -ግ- ሰው ማስተዋወቅ [አስተ
ዋ'ወቀ] ፣ ማ'ለማመድ [አ'ለማ'መደ] (ካንድ
ሁናቴ ጋር)

acquaintance

እክ'ዌይንተንስ -ስ- የሚያውቁት ሰው ፣ ዕው
ቲያ ፤ ዕውቀት

acquiesce

አከዊ'ዩስ -ግ- መስማማት [ተስማ'ማ] (ያለ
መ'ጠራጠር)

acquiescence
አክዊ'ዩሰንስ -ስ- ስምም'ነት (በፈቃደ'ኛ'ነት)

acquire
እክ'ዋየ -ግ- ማገኘት [አገ'ኘ]

acquisition
አክዊ'ዚሽን -ስ- አ'ዲስ ንብረት

acquit
እክ'ዊት -ግ- ነጻ መልቀቅ [ለ'ቀቀ] (በፍርድ ቤት)

acquittal
እክ'ዊተል -ስ- ነጻ የመልቀቅ ሥርዓት

acre
'ኤከ -ስ- ፬ሺ፱፻ ሜትር ካሬ (የመሬት ስፋት ል'ክ)

acrid
'አክሪድ -ቅ- የ'ሚሰነ'ፍጥ (ሽ'ታ)

acrimonious
አክሪ'መውኒየስ -ቅ- መራራ ፡ ጎይለ'ኛ (ክ ር'ክር)

across
እክ'ርስ -ተግ- በግዶ ፡ በእ'ሻጋሪ

act
'አክት -ግ- ማድረግ [አደ'ረገ]
drama
-ስ- የቲያትር ክፍል ፡ ገቢር

acting
'አክቲንግ -ቅ- ተጠባባቂ ፡ እንደራሴ (ያንድ ሥራ)
theatre work
-ስ- በቲያትር ተካፋይ መሆን

action
'አክሽን -ስ- ግብር ፡ ሥራ

active
'አክቲቭ -ቅ- ጉብዝ ፡ ንቁ (ሠ'ራተ'ኛ)

activity
አክ'ቲቪቲ -ስ- ሥራ

actor
'አክተ -ስ- የቴአትር ተጫዋች (ተባዕት) ፡ ተዋናይ

actress
'አክትረስ -ስ- የቴአትር ተጫዋች (እንስት) ተዋናይት

actual
'አክቹል -ቅ- ል'ክ'ኛ ፡ እውነተ'ኛ (ለትር ጉም ፡ ለፍ'ች) ፤ በእሁን ጊዜ ያ'ለ

actually
'አክቹሊ -ተግ- በውነቱ

acumen
'አክዮሜን -ስ- ጉብዝ ነ'ጋዴ የመሆን ችሎታ
mental acuteness
-ስ- ማስተዋል

acute
እክ'ዩ፡ት -ቅ- ጎይለ'ኛ (ሕመም) ፡ አስቸ'ጋሪ (ጉ'ዳይ)

adamant
'አደመንት -ቅ- ጽኑእ (የው'ሳኔ)

Adam's apple
አደምዝ 'አፐል -ስ- ማንቁርት

adapt
እ'ዳፕት -ግ- እንዲስማ'ማ ማድረግ [አደ'ረገ] (በመለዋወጥ) ፡ ለእ'ዲስ ሁናቴ እንዲ'መ'ች አመል ፡ ጠባይ ፡ ሁናቴ መለወጥ [ለ'ወጠ]

adaptability
እዳፕተ'ቢሊቲ -ስ- ራስን የማስማማት ች ሎታ ፡ ሁናቴ

add
'አድ -ግ- መጨ'መር [ጨ'መረ]
mathematical
-ግ- መደ'መር [ደ'መረ]

addiction
እ'ዲክሽን -ስ- ሱስ ፡ መጥፎ ልማድ (ሜት ፡ ሲጃራ ፡ መጠ'ጥ ወዘተ)

addition
እ'ዲሽን -ስ- ድ'ምር

address
እድ'ረስ -ግ- መ'ናገር [ተና'ገረ] (በስብሰባ ውስጥ)
-ስ- አድራሻ

adept
እ'ዴፕት -ቅ- ሥልጡን ፡ ባለሞያ

adequate
'አደክወት -ቅ- በቂ ፡ ተመጣጣኝ

adhere
እድ'ሒየ -ግ- መ'ጣበቅ [ተጣ'በቀ] ፡ መደ ገፍ [ደ'ገፈ] (ሐሳብ ፡ ዐላማ)

353

adherent

እድ'ሔረንት -ስ- ተከ'ታይ (ለፖለቲካ ክፍል)

adhesion

እድ'ሂገን -ስ- መ'ጣበቅ (አንድ ነገር ከሌላው ጋር በመጣብቅ)

adhesive

እድ'ሂዚቭ -ቅ- ተጣባቂ ፣ መጣብቅ

adjacent

እ'ጀይሰንት -ቅ- ቅርብ ፣ ጉ'ን ፣ ቀ'ጥሎ ያ'ለ

adjective

'አጀክቲቭ -ስ- ቅ'ጽል (ሰዋስው)

adjoining

እ'ጀይኒንግ -ቅ- ተ'ጥሎ ያ'ለ ፣ ቅርብ

adjourn

እ'ጀ፡ን -ግ- መቅ'ጠር [ቀ'ጠረ] (ስብሰባ ፣ ጉባኤ ፣ ላልተወ'ሰነ ጊዜ)

adjournment

እ'ጀ፡ንመንት -ስ- ቀጠር (የስብሰባ ፣ የጉባኤ)

adjudicate

እጅ'ዩዲኬይት -ግ- መፍረድ [ፈ'ረደ] (ለውድ'ድር)

adjust

እ'ጀስት -ግ- ማስተካከል [አስተካ'ከለ] ፣ በደምብ ማድረግ [አደ'ረገ]

administer

እድ'ሚኒስተ -ግ- መምዛት [ገ'ዛ] (ላገር) ፣ ማስተዳደር [አስተዳ'ደረ]

-to

-ግ- መስጠት [ሰ'ጠ]

administration

አድሚኒስት'ሬይሽን -ስ- አገር አ'ገዛዝ ፣ የአስተዳደር ሥራ

admirable

'አድሚረበል -ቅ- አስገ'ራሚ ፣ አስደ'ናቂ ፣ ድንቅ ፣ ግሩም

admiral

'አድሚረል -ስ- የባሕር ጎይል ከ'ፍተ'ኛ መኰ'ንን

admiration

አድመ'ሬይሽን -ስ- አድናቆት

admire

እድ'ማየ -ግ- ማድነቅ [አደ'ነቀ] ፣ መ'ገረም [ተገ'ረመ]

admissible

እድ'ሚሰበል -ቅ- የ'ሚ'ቀ'በሉት ፣ ነውር ያልሆነ

admission

እድ'ሚሽን -ስ- የሠ'ራትን በደል አምኖ መ'ቀበል

entry

-ስ- መግባት

-fee

-ስ- የመግቢያ ዋጋ

admit

እድ'ሚት -ግ- ማመን [አ'መነ] (ጥፋትን) ፣ እን'ዲገባ መፍቀድ [ፈ'ቀደ]

admonish

አድ'ሞኒሽ -ግ- መገ'ሠፅ [ገ'ሠፀ] ፣ መቆ'ጣት [ተቆ'ጣ] (ሰውን ፣ ልጅን ወዘተ)

adolescence

አደ'ሴሰንስ -ስ- የጉርምስ'ና ጊዜ

adolescent

አደ'ሴሰንት -ስ- ጉረምሳ

adopt

እ'ዶፕት -ግ- ጉ'ዲፈ'ቻ መውሰድ [ወሰደ]፣ማደጉ ማሳ'ደግ [አሳ'ደገ] ፣የሰውን ልጅ እንደ ልጅ አድርጎ ማሳ'ደግ [አሳ'ደገ] ፣የጡት ልጅ ማድረግ [አደ'ረገ] ፣የሌላውን ሰው ነገር ፣ ሐ'ሳብ ወስዶ እሥራ ላይ ማዋል [አዋለ]

adoration

አደ'ሬይሽን -ስ- በጣም መውደድ ፣ በጣም ማፍቀር (እግዚአብሔርን ወዘተ) ፣ ው'ዳሴ

adore

እ'ዶ፡ -ግ- በጣም መውደድ [ወ'ደደ] (እንደ እግዚአብሔር) ፣ ማመ'ደስ [አመ'ደሰ]

adorn

እ'ዶ፡ን -ግ- ማስጌጥ [አስጌጠ] ፣ መሽ'ለም [ሽ'ለመ]

adrift

እድ'ሪፍት -ቅ- የሚዋ'ልል ፣ ቁጥ'ጥር የሌ'ለ በት (መርከብ በባሕር)

adroit

እድ'ሮይት -ቅ- ቅልጡፍ ፣ ቀልጣ'ፋ ፣ ሥል ጡን

adult

አ'ደልት -ቅ- ጉልማ'ሳ

adult

'አደልት -ስ- ጉልማ'ሳ

354

adulterate

እ'ደልተሪት -ግ- መጥፎ ነገር በንጹሕ ላይ መደባለቅ [ደባል'ቀ]፣ በክ'ለሳ ጥራት መቀ'ነስ [ቀ'ነስ]

adultery

እ'ደልተሪ -ስ- ዝ'ሙት

advance

እድ'ቫ፡ንስ -ግ- ወደፊት መግፋት ·[ገ'ፋ] (ለ ወ'ታ'ደር) ፤ መ'ራመድ [ተራ'መደ]

advancement

እድ'ቫ፡ንስመንት -ስ- መ'ራመድ (የግዕረግ ዕድገት)

advantage

እድ'ቫ፡ንቲጅ -ስ- ቅድሚያ ፤ ክ'ፉ ያለ ቦታ፣ ጥሩ ዕ'ድል

advent

'አድቬንት -ስ- መድረስ ፤ ምጽአት

festival

-ስ- ክልደት በፊት ያ'ሉት ሳ'ምንቶ'ች፣ ስብከት ገ'ና

adventure

እድ'ቬንቸ -ስ- አደገ'ኛ ሁናቴ ፤ አደጋ ያ'ለ' በት ጉዞ

adverb

'አድቨብ -ስ- ተውሳከ ግ'ሥ (ሰዋስው)

adversary

'አድቨሰሪ -ስ- ጠላት ፤ ባላንጣ

adverse

'አድቨ፡ስ -ቅ- እ'ዌኪ ፣ ም'ቾ ያለሆነ (ሁናቴ)

adversity

እድ'ቨ፡ሲቲ -ስ- መጥፎ ጊዜ ፤ የቾ'ገር ጊዜ

advertisement

እድ'ቨ፡ቲስመንት -ስ- ማስታወቂያ (የገገድ ሽ ቀጠሽቀጥ)

advertiser

'አድቨታይዘ -ስ- ማስታወቂያ አውጪ (የነ ገድ ሽቀጣሽቀጥ)

advertise

'አድቨታይዝ -ግ- ማስታወቅ [አስታ'ወቀ] (የነገድ ዕቃ)

advice

እድ'ቫይስ -ስ- ምክር

advisable

እድ'ቫይዘበል -ቅ- የተሻለ (ቢያደርጉት ጥሩ ው'ጤት የ'ሚያስገ'ኝ)

advise

እድ'ቫይዝ -ግ- መምከር [መ'ከረ]

advisory

እድ'ቫይዘሪ -ቅ- መካሪ

advocate

'አድቮኬይት -ግ- መደ'ገፍ [ደ'ገፈ] (ሐሳብ) -ስ- ጠበቃ

aerial

'ኤሪየል -ስ- አንቴና

aerodrome

'ኤረድርውም -ስ- የአውሮ'ፕላን ማረፊያ ፣ የአውሮ'ፕላን ጣቢያ

aeronautics

ኤረ'ኖቲክስ -ስ- የአውሮ'ፕላን በረራ ትም ህርት

aeroplane

'ኤርፕሌይን -ስ- አውሮ'ፕላን

afar

እ'ፋ፡ -ተግ- በሩቅ

affable

'አፈበል -ቅ- ረገጠተ'ኛ

affair

እ'ፌየ -ስ- ጉ'ዳይ

love-

-ስ- ው'ሽ'ም'ነት ፣ ድ'ብቅ ፍቅር (በ ወንድ'ና በሴት መካ'ከል)

affect

እ'ፌክት -ግ- መንካት [ነ'ካ] (ጉ'ዳይ ወዘተ)፣ የሰውን ልግግድ መገልበጥ [ገለ'በጠ]

affected

እ'ፌከተድ -ቅ- የተለ'ወጠ ፤ የ'ሚገ'ደው *exaggerated*

-ቅ- ነ'ኝ ባይ ፣ ክመጠን የበ'ለጠ

affection

እ'ፈክሸን -ስ- ፍቅር ፤ ዝን'ባሌ

affiliate

እ'ፈሊዬይት -ግ- ገን'ኙ'ነት ማድረግ [አደ 'ረገ]

affinity

እ'ፈኒቲ -ስ- የቀ'ረበ ገንኙ'ነት ፣ ተመሳሳ ይ'ነት

affirm

እ'ፈ፡ም -ግ- ማ'ረጋገጥ [አ'ረጋ'ገጠ]

355

affirmation
አፈ'ሜይሽን -ስ- ግ'ፈጋገጥ

affirmative
እ'ፈ:መቲቭ -ት- የአወንታ

affix
እ'ፌክስ -ግ- መለ'ጠፍ [ለ'ጠፈ] (በግደግ'ጸ ላይ)

afflict
እፍ'ሊክት -ግ- ግ'ሠቃየት [አ'ሠቃየ]

affliction
እፍ'ሊክሽን -ስ- ከ'ባድ ሕመም ፣ ከ'ባድ መከራ

affluent
'አፍሉወንት -ት- ሀብታም ፣ ባለጸ'ጋ

afford
እ'ፎ:ድ -ግ- መቻል [ቻለ] (ለመከፈል፣ለግ ድረግ ፣ ለግለት)

affray
እፍ'ፈይ -ስ- ጥል ፣ ብጥ'ብጥ

affront
እፍ'ረንት -ስ- ስድብ ፣ ሰውን የ'ሚያስተ' ይም ተግባር

aflame
እፍ'ሌይም -ት- የ'ሚንበለ'በል

afloat
እፍ'ለውት -ት- የ'ሚንሳ'ፈፍ ፣ ተንሳፋፊ

afore-said
አ'ፎ:ሴድ -ት- ቀደ'ም ብሎ የተነ'ገረ (ለጽ ሑፍ)

afraid
እፍ'ፈይድ -ግ- መፍራት [ፈ'ራ]

afresh
እፍ'ፈሽ -ተግ- እንደገና (መጀ'መር)

after
'አ:ፍተ -መዋ- ከ . . . በኋላ

aftermath
'አ:ፍተግይ -ስ- ያንድ አደጋ ፣ መቅሠፍት ፣ መዐት ው'ጤት (ፍርስራሽ ፣ ብጥ'ብጥ መዘተ)

afternoon
አ:ፍተ'ኑ:ን -ስ- ከሰዓት ፣ ከቀትር በኋላ

afterwards
'አ:ፍተወድዝ -ተግ- በኋላ

again
እ'ጌን -ተግ- እንደገና

against
እ'ጌንስት -መዋ- (ተቃውሞን መግለጫ) በ . . . እጠገብ ፣ ከ . . . ጋር (ጦር'ነት)

age
'ኤይጅ -ስ- ዕድሜ ፣ ዘመን

aged
'ኤይጅድ -ት- በዕድሜ ገፋ ያለ ፣ ሽማግ'ሌ

agency
'ኤይጀንሲ -ስ- ውክል'ና፣ያንድ መካይል ሥራ፣ ቢሮ መዘተ

agenda
እ'ጀንደ -ስ- ዝርዝር (በስብሰባ ላይ የ'ሚ'ወ ያ'ዩ'ባ'ቸው ጉ'ዳዮ'ች)

agent
'ኤይጀንት -ስ- ወ'ኪል

agglomeration
እግሎመ'ፈይሽን -ስ- መ'ከማቸት ፣ መ'ሰብ ሰብ

aggravate
'አግሬቬይት -ግ- ግባስ [አባሰ]

aggregate
'አግረጌይት -ት- ድ'ምር (ጠቅላ'ላ)

aggression
እግ'ሬሽን -ስ- የጠላት'ነት ስ'ሜት ፣ ጥል (ያለምክንያት)

aggressive
እግ'ሬሲቭ -ት- ጥለ'ኛ ፣ ማጋደ'ኛ

aggressor
እግ'ሬሰ -ስ- ጥል ያ'ነሣ'ሣ ፣ ጠብ አጫሪ መዘተ

agile
'አጃይል -ት- ፈ'ጣን ፣ ቀልጣ'ፋ

agility
እጂሊቲ -ስ- ፍጥነት

agitate
'አጇቴይት -ግ- መነቅነት [ነተ'ነተ] (ለመደ ባለት)
make trouble
-ግ- መበጥበጥ [በጠ'በጠ]፣ ግ'ወከ [አ'ወከ]

aglow
እግ'ለው -ት- የፋም ፣ የተጋጋለ ፣ የተንተር' ከከ (ከስል ፣ እሳት)

ago
እ'ገው -ተግ- ከ . . . በፊት

agony
'አጐኒ -ስ- ሕግም (ታ'ላቅ) ፣ ሥቃይ

agrarian
እግ'ሬሪየን -ቅ- የእርሻ

agree
እግ'ሪ፡ -ግ- መስማማት [ተስማ'ማ]

agreeable
እግ'ሪየበል -ቅ- ተስማሚ

agreement
እግ'ሪ:መንት -ስ- ውል ፣ ስምም'ነት

agriculture
'አግሪከልቸ -ስ- እርሻ ፣ ግብር'ና

ahead
እ'ሐድ -ተግ- ወደፊት

aid
'ኤይድ -ግ- መርዳት [ረ'ዳ]

ail
'ኤይል -ግ- መ'ታመም [ታ'መመ]

ailment
'ኤይልመንት -ስ- ሕመም ፣ በ'ሽታ

aim
'ኤይም -ግ- ግ'ነጣጠር [አ'ነጣ'ጠረ]
-ስ- ግብ ፣ ተምኔት

air
'ኤየ -ስ- አ'የር

aircraft
'ኤከራ:ፍት -ስ- አውሮ'ፕላን

airfield
'ኤፈይልድ -ስ- ያውሮ'ፕላን ግረሪያ (በተለ'ይ ለጦር አውሮ'ፕላን)

air force
'ኤር:ስ -ስ- ያ'የር ጓይል

airline
'ኤላይን -ስ- ያ'የር መንገድ (የንግድ)

airmail
'ኤጋይል -ስ- ያ'የር ደብዳ'ቤ ፣ በአውሮ'ፕላን የ'ሚላክ ደብዳ'ቤ

airman
'ኤመን -ስ- ያ'የር ጓይል ወ'ታ'ደር ፣ የግ'ል አውሮ'ፕላን ነጂ

airport
'ኤፖ:ት -ስ- ያውሮ'ፕላን ግረሪያ

airtight
'ኤታይት -ቅ- አ'የር የ'ግያስገ'ባ

airy
'ኤሪ -ቅ- ነ'ፋ'ሻ

aisle
'አይል -ስ- ቅኔ ግሕሌት ፣ በተደረ'ደሩ ወንበ ር'ች መሀል ጠ'ባብ መ'ተላለፊያ

ajar
እ'ጃ: -ቅ- በከፈል ክፍት ፣ ገርበ'ብ ያለ

akin
እ'ኪን -ቅ- የ'ሚ'መሳ'ሰል

alacrity
እ'ላክሪቲ -ስ- ፍጥነት (ለሥራ)

alarm
እ'ላ:ም -ግ- ግስደንገጥ [አስደነ'ገጠ]
-ስ- ምል'ከት (ያደጋ)

alas
እ'ላስ -ቃኣ- ወይኔ

album
'አልበም -ስ- ፎቶግራፉ ፣ ቴምብር መዘተ የ'ሚ'ሰበ'ሰብ'በት ደብተር

alcohol
'አልከሆል -ስ- አልኮል (አስካሪ መጠ'ጥ)

alcove
'አልከውቭ -ስ- ት'ንሽ ቅ'ሥት (በግርግ'ዳ ውስጥ)

ale
'ኤይል -ስ- ጠ'ላ (መጠ'ጥ)

alert
እ'ለ:ት -ቅ- ንቁ
-ስ- ግስጠንቀቂያ

alias
'ኤይሊየስ -ስ- የተለ'ወጠ ስም (በወንጀለ ኞ'ች ዘንድ)

alibi
'አለባይ -ስ- ወንጀል በተደ'ረገ'በት ቦታ አለ መኖርን ለግ'ረጋገጥ የ'ሚ'ስጥ ግስረ'ጃ

alien
'ኤይሊየን -ስ- እንግዳ ፣ የው'ጭ አገር ሰው ፣ ባዕድ

alight
እ'ላይት -ቅ- የ'ሚ'ታ'ጠል ፣ የተያያዘ (በሳት)
-ግ- መውረድ [ወ'ረደ] (ከንድ ነገር ላይ)

align

እ'ላይን -ግ- ማስተካከል [አስተካ'ከለ]

alike

እ'ላይክ -ት- መሳይ

alimentary

አሲ,'ሜንታሪ -ት- ምግብነ'ት ያለው

alive

እ'ላይቭ -ት- በሕይወት ያለ ፣ ነዋሪ

all

'ኦ:ል -ት- ሁ'ሉ

all right

ኦ:ልራይት -ተግ- መልካም ፣ ጥሩ ፣ ደኅና

allay

እ'ሌይ -ግ- ማ'ረጋጋት [አ'ረጋ'ጋ] (ጥር'ጣሬ፣
ፍርሐት)

allegation

አለ'ጌይሸን -ስ- ክ'ስ (ገና ማስረ'ጃ ያልተ'ረ
በ'በት)

allege

እ'ሌጅ -ግ- መ'ናገር [ተና'ገረ] (ያለማስረ'
ጃ)

allegiance

እ'ሊይጀንስ -ስ- ጓላፊ'ነት መያዝ ፣ በጦር'
ነት ጊዜ ለማግልገል ውለታ መግባት ፣ ግ'ዴታ
መግባት

allegory

'አሌጎሪ -ስ- ምሳ'ሌያዊ ተረት (በሰው ፣ በእ
ንስሳት አስመ'ስሎ የ'ሚ'ነ'ገር)

alleviate

እ'ሊ:ቪዬት -ግ- ሥቃይን መቀ'ነስ [ቀ'ነሰ] ፣
ሕመምን ማሳ'ነስ [አሳነ'ሰ]

alley

'አሊ, -ስ- ጠ'ባብ መንገድ ፣ ስርጥ መንገድ

alliance

እ'ላያንስ -ስ- የሞር ጓ'ድ አገር'ች ፣ የመ'ረዳ
ዳት ቃል ኪዳን (በአገር'ች መከ'ከል)

allied

'አላይድ -ት- የተስማ'ማ ፣ የተባ'በረ

alligator

'አለጌይተ -ስ- ዐ'ዞ ፣ አርጀና

allocate

'አለኬይት -ግ- መስጠት [ሰ'ጠ] ፣ መቆ'ነን
[ቆ'ነነ] ፣ ማ'ካፈል [አ'ካ'ፈለ] ፣ መደልደል
[ደለ'ደለ]

allot

እ'ሎት -ግ- ማ'ካፈል [አ'ካ'ፈለ] ፣ ግ'ደል
[አ'ደለ]

allotment

እ'ሎትመንት -ስ- መቁነን ፣ እ'ዳሪ ፣ እቤት
አጠገብ የ'ሚ'ገ'ን'ኝ ቦታ

allow

እ'ላው -ግ- መፍቀድ [ፈ'ቀደ]

allowance

እ'ላወንስ -ስ- የኪስ ገንዘብ ፣ ል'ዩ ውጭ

alloy

'አሎይ -ስ- ቅል'ቅል (ግዕ'ድን)

allude

አ'ሉ:ድ -ግ- ማውሳት [አወ'ሳ] ፣ መጥቀስ
[ጠ'ቀሰ]

alluring

እል'ዩ:ሪንግ -ት- አስተያየት ግራኪ

allusion

እ'ሉዠን -ስ- ማውሳት ፣ መጥቀስ

ally

'አላይ -ስ- ጓ'ድ ፣ ተባባሪ (በጦር'ነት ጊዜ)

almighty

ኦ:ል'ማይቲ -ት- ሁ'ሉን የ'ሚችል (ለእግዚ
አብሔር)

almond

'አ:መንድ -ስ- ለውዝ

almost

'ኦ:ልመውስት -ተግ- ል ፣ ሊ . . . ነቢ.

alms

'አ:ምዝ -ስ- ምጽዋት ፣ ለበ'ን አድራጎት የ'ሚ
ሰጥ ገንዘብ

aloft

እ'ሎፍት -ተግ- በላይ

alone

እ'ለውን -ተግ- ብ'ቻ

along

እ'ሉንግ -ተግ- ከ . . . ጋር
-መዋ- በ . . .

alongside

እሉንግ'ሳይድ -ተግ- ቀ'ጥሎ

aloof

እ'ሉ:ፍ -ት ፣ -ተግ- ገለልተ'ኛ (ከሰዎ'ች በወ
ራት ወዘተ) ፣ በሩቅ ፣ ኩሩ

358

aloud
ኧ'ላውድ -ተግ- በጩኸት ፣በከ'ፍተ'ኛ ድምፅ

alphabet
'አልፈቤት -ስ- ፊደል

alphabetical
አልፈ'ቤቲከል -ቅ- በፊደል ተራ

already
ኦ:ል'ሬዲ -ተግ- ቀድሞ ፣ [illegible]ራት (ከተወ'ሰነ ጊዜ)

also
'ኦ:ልሰው -ተግ- ደግሞ ፣ ደ[illegible]ም
-መዋ- -ም ፣ እ'ና

altar
'ኦ:ልተ -ስ- መንበር ፣ ምሥዋዕ

alter
'ኦ:ልተ -ግ- መለ'ወጥ [ለ'ወጠ]

alteration
ኦ:ልተ'ሬይሽን -ስ- ለውጥ

altercation
ኦ:ልተ'ኬይሽን -ስ- ክር'ክር

alternate
'ኦ:ልትኔይት -ግ- መ'ለዋወጥ [አ'ለዋ'ወጠ]

alternate
ኦ:ል'ተ:ነት -ቅ- [illegible] የ'ሚመጣ፣ የ'ሚያሥ'ልስ

alternative
ኦ:ል'ተ:ነቲቭ -ስ- [illegible] (ከሁ[illegible]ት ነገር)

although
ኦ:ል'ዘው -መዋ- ምን'ም እ[illegible]

altitude
'አልቲትዩድ -ስ- ከ'ፍታ'ነት ፣ ከ'ፍታ

altogether
ኦ:ልተ'ጌዘ -ተግ- በፍ'ጹም ፣ ፈ'ጽሞ ፣ በጭ'ራሽ

aluminium
አሉ'ሚንየም -ስ- አ'ሉሚንየም

always
'ኦ:ልዌይዝ -ተግ- ሁ'ል ጊዜ ፣ ዘወትር ፣ ሠርክ

amalgamate
ኧ'ማለገሜይት -ግ- ማ'ዋሐድ [አ'ዋሐደ]

amass
ኧ'ማስ -ግ- መሰብሰብ [በበ'ሰበ] ፣ ማ'ከማቸት [አ'ከማ'ቸ] ፣ ማግበስበስ [አግበሰ'በሰ]

amateur
'አመተ -ቅ- የ'ማይ'ከ'ፈለው ሙዚቀ'ኛ ፣ ስፖርተ'ኛ ወዘተ

amaze
ኧ'ሜይዝ -ግ- መ'ገረም [ተገ'ረመ]

ambassador
አም'ባሰደ -ስ- የመንግሥት መልእክተ'ኛ (ወደ ሌላ መንግሥት የ'ሚ'ላክ) ፣ አም'ባሳደር

amber
'አምበ -ስ- ሙ'ጫ (ደረቅ) ፣ ጠቈር ያለ ብጫ ቀለም ፣ ል'ባልማ (ል'ብ-አልማ) ዛጐል ፣ የዛጐል'ነት ባሕርይ ያ'ለው

ambidextrous
አምቢ'ዴክስትረስ -ቅ- ግራ'ኝ'ና ቀ'ኜ የሆነ፣ በግራው በቀ'ኙ'ም መሥራት የ'ሚሆን'ለት

ambiguity
አምቢግ'ዩዊቲ -ስ- አ'ጠራጣሪ ትርጉም ፣ ግልጽ ያልሆነ'ና በሁለ'ት መንገድ ሊ'ፈታ የ'ሚ'ችል ነገር ፣ ሁናቴ

ambiguous
አም'ቢግዮወስ -ቅ- አ'ሻሚ ፣ ግልጽ ያልሆነ (ለትርጉም)

ambition
አም'ቢሽን -ስ- የጋለ ፍ'ላጐት ፣ ል'በ ት'ልቅ''ነት ፣ ተምኔት

ambulance
'አምብዩለንስ -ስ- የሕመምተ'ኞ'ች ማ'መላለሻ መኪና

ambush
'አምቡሽ -ግ- አደጋ ለመጣል ማድፈጥ [አደ'ፈጠ]

amelioration
አሚሊየ'ሬይሽን -ግ- ማ'ሻሻል [አ'ሻሻለ]

amenable
ኧ'ሜነበል -ቅ- ተቀ'ባይ (ትእዛዝ) ፣ ሐ'ረብ ፣ ትእዛዝ የ'ማይ'ቃ'ወም

amend
ኧ'ሜንድ -ግ- ማስተካከል [አስተካ'ከለ]

amendment
ኧ'ሜንድመንት -ስ- ማ'ሻሻል (ሕ'ግ ወዘተ

amenity
ኧ'ሜንቲ -ስ- ባንድ ቀበሌ የ'ሚ'ገ'ኝ ጠቅላላ የሕዝብ አገልግሎት

amiable
'ኧይሚየበል -ቅ- ተወ'ዳጅ ፣ ሰው ወዳጅ

amicable
’አሚከበል -ት- ተወ'ዳጅ ፣ ሰው ወዳጅ ፣
የመ'ዋደድ ስ'ሜት

amid (st)
እ’ሚድ (ስት) -ተግ- በመካ'ከል

amiss
እ’ሚስ -ት- የተበላ'ሸ ፣ ብል'ሹ ፣ በስሕተት
የተሠ'ራ

ammunition
አምዩኒሽን -ስ- ጥ'ይት

amnesty
’አምነስቲ -ስ- ምሕረት (ለእስረ ኛ)

among (st)
እ’መንግ (ስት) -ተግ- በመካ'ከል

amorous
’አመረስ -ት- የፍቅር'ና የመውደድ ስ'ሜት
የያዘው (በፍትወተ ሥጋ)

amount
እ’ማውንት -ስ- መጠን
          -ግ- መድረስ [ደ'ረሰ] ፣ ግ'ከል [አ'ከለ]
(ለመጠን ፣ ለብዛት)

amphibious
አም’ፈቢየስ -ት- በየብስ'ም በወ'ሃ'ም ውስጥ
መኖር የ'ሚችል ፍጡር

ample
’አምፕል -ት- በቂ ፣ ስ'ፊ

amplify
’አምፕሊፋይ -ግ- ግጉላት [አጉ'ላ]

amplifier
’አምፕሊፋየ -ስ- ማጉያ

amputate
’አምፐዩቴይት -ግ- መቁረጥ [ቁ'ረጠ] (እ'ጅ፣
እግር)

amuse
እም’ዩ:ዝ -ግ- ግስደ'ስት [አስደ'ሰተ]

an
’እን -ያተመ- አንድ

analogy
እ’ናለጂ -ስ- ተመሳሳይ'ነት (ባን'ዳንድ ሁኔቱ
በሁለ'ት ነገር'ች መካከል) ፣ በከፊል ተመሳሳ
ይ'ነት

analyse
’አነላይዝ -ግ- መተንተን [ተነ'ተነ]

analysis
እ’ናለሲስ -ስ- ትንተ'

anatomy
እ’ናተሚ -ስ- አናተሚ (የሰው'ነት ክፍሎ'ች
ጥናት) I አካል ፣ ሰው'ነት

ancesiors
’አንሴስተዝ -ስ- ትውል'ድ ፣ አያት ቅድግ
ያት ፣ ዘር ግንዘር

anchor
’አንከ -ስ- መልሕቅ

ancient
’ኤይንሸንት -ት- ጥንታዊ

anecdote
’አኔክደውት -ስ- በንግ'ግር ውስጥ አንደም'
ሳሌ የ'ሚ'ጠ'ቀስ ታሪክ (የ'ሚያ'ሥቅ)

and
’አንድ -መዋ- እ'ና - ና - ም

angel
’ኤይንጀል -ስ- መልአክ

anger
’አነገ -ስ- ቁ'ጣ

angle
’አንገል -ስ- ማዕዘን

angry
’አንገሪ -ት- ቁ'ጡ

anguish
’አንገዊሽ -ስ- ታ'ላት ሐዘን ፣ ት'ልት ሥቃይ

angular
’አንገዩለ -ት- ቀ'ጭን ፣ መንግ'ና (ለሰው) I
የማዕዘን መ'ታጠሪያ ነጥብ

animal
’አኔመል -ስ- እንሰሳ ፣ አውሬ

animosity
አኒ’ሞሰቲ -ስ- ጠላት'ነት ፣ ጥላ'ቻ

ankle
’አንከል -ስ- ቁርጭም'ጭሚት

annex
’አኔክስ -ግ- የሌሎ'ችን አገር ከገዛት ጋር
ግ'ዋሐድ [አ'ዋሐደ]

annexe
አ’ኔክስ -ስ- ት'ጥያ (ለቤት)

annihilate
እ’ናየላይት -ግ- መደምሰስ [ደመ'ሰሰ] ፣ ማጥ
ፋት [አጠ'ፋ]

360

anniversary
አኒ'ቨ:ሰሪ -ስ- ዓመት በዓል ፣ ክብረ በዓል

annotate
'አነቴይት -ግ- ትርጉም መስጠት [ሰ'ጠ] (ለ መጽሐፍ) ፣ መግለጽ [ገ'ለጸ] ፣ ማብራራት [አብራ'ራ]

announce
እ'ናውንስ -ግ- ማስታወቅ [አስታ'ወቀ] ፣ ማ' ወጅ [ዐ'ወጀ]

announcement
እ'ናውንስመንት -ስ- ማስታወቂያ ፣ ዐዋጅ

annoy
እ'ኖይ -ግ- ማስቆ'ጣት [አስቆ'ጣ] ፣ ማ'በሳ ጨት [አ'በሳ'ጨ]

annual
'አነዉወል -ቅ- ዓመታዊ

annuity
እን'ዩዊቲ -ስ- በ'ያመቱ የ'ሚ'ከ'ፈል የተወ' ሰነ ገንዘብ

annul
እ'ነል -ግ- ሕ'ግን መሥ'ረዝ [ሠ'ረዘ]

annunciation
እ'ነንሲ'ዬይሸን -ስ- ብሥራት

anoint
እ'ኖይንት -ግ- በዘይት ራስን መቀ'ባት [ቀ'ባ] (በተለ'ይ ለክህነት፣ ለንጉሥ ፣ ለክርስቶስ)

anomaly
እ'ኖመሊ -ስ- ከልምድ'ና ከሥርዓት ው'ጭ መሆን ፣ ሕ'ግ አለማክበር

anonymous
እ'ኖነመስ -ቅ- ስም የሌለ'በት መጽሐፍ ፣ ደብዳ'ቤ ፣ ስጦታ ፣ ወዘተ

another
እ'ነዘ -ቅ ፣ ተሱ- ሌላ

answer
'አ:ንሰ -ግ- መልስ መስጠት [ሰ'ጠ]
-ስ- ም'ላሽ ፣ መልስ (የተ'ያቄ)

ant
'አንት -ስ- ጉንዳን ፣ ገብረ ጉን'ዳን ፣ ቁ‑ጭም

anteater
'አንቲተ -ስ- ወልደጊ'ዛ

antagonism
አን'ታገነዘም -ስ- ጠላት'ነት ፣ ባላንጣ'ነት

antagonist
አን'ታገኒስት -ስ- ተቃዋሚ ፣ ባላን'ጣ

antelope
'አንተለውፕ -ስ- አጋዘን ፣ ሚዳ'ቋ ወይን'ም የሚዳ ፍ'የል የ'ሚመስሉ እንሰሳት

antenna
አን'ቴና -ስ- አንቴና ፣ የራዲዮ'ና የቴሌቪዥን ማዕበል መ'ቀበያ

anterior
አን'ቲሪየ -ቅ- ቀደም ብሎ የመ'ጣ

anthem
'አንሰም -ስ- የቤተ ክርስቲያን መዝሙር ፣ መዝሙ‑C (ያንድ አገC)

anthology
አን'ሶለጂ -ስ- ምርጥ ምንባቦ'ች ፣ የምንባብ መጽበል

antic
'አንቲክ -ስ- እ'የዘ'ለሉ መጫ‑ኸ ፣ መቦ'ረቅ ፣ ጅላጅል

anticipate
አን'ቲሲጌይት -ግ- ይሆናል ብሎ መጠ'በቅ [ጠ'በቀ] ፣ ሳይሆን አይቀር'ም ብሎ መሥራት [ሠ'ራ]

antidote
'አንቲደውት -ስ- የመርዝ ማርከሻ

antipathy
አን'ቲፐሲ -ስ- ጥላ'ቻ

antique
አን'ቲይክ -ቅ- ጥንታዊ ፣ ታሪካዊ

antiquity
አን'ቲክዊቲ -ስ- የጥንት ጊዜ (በታሪኩ የታ‑ ወ'ቀ)

antiseptic
አንቲ'ሴፕቲክ -ስ- የቁስል መድኃኒት

antler
'አንትለ -ስ- የሚዳ'ቋ፣ የሚዳ ፍ'የል ወይን'ም ያጋዘን ቀንድ

anus
'ኤይነስ -ስ- የሰገራ መውጫ ቀዳዳ ፣ (የሰው፡ የእንስሳት ወዘተ) ፊንጢ'ጣ ፣ ሙ'ኒ

anvil
'አንቪል -ስ- ብረት የ'ሚ'ቀጠቀጥ'በት ብረት፡ መስፍ

anxiety
አንግ'ዛየቲ -ስ- መሥጋት ፣ ሥጋት ፣ ጭንቀት

361

anxious
’እንክሽስ -ቅ- የተጨነቀ ፣ ሥጉ-

any
’ኤኒ -ቅ- ማ’ነ’ኛው’ም ፣ እንዳ’ች

anybody
’ኤኒቦዲ -ተስ- ማ’ነ’ኛው’ም ሰው

anyhow
’ኤኒሀወ -ተግ- በማ’ነ’ኛው’ም ሁናቴ ፣ ያ’ም
ሆነ ይህ
-ቅ- እንደነገሩ-

anyone
’ኤኒወን -ተስ- ማ’ነ’ኛውም ሰው

anything
’ኤኒሲ’ንግ -ተስ- ማ’ና’ቸውም ነገር

anyway
’ኤኒዌይ -ተግ- በማ’ና’ቸውም ሁናቴ

anywhere
’ኤኒዌየ -ተግ- የት’ም

apart
’እ’ፓ፡ት -ተግ- ተለ’ይቶ ፣ በተለ’ይ

apartment
’እ’ፓ፡ትመንት -ስ- እ’ፓርትማ ፣ብዙ ቤተሰብ
የ’ሚያኖር ሕንፃ

apathetic
አፐ’ሴቲክ -ቅ- የ’ማይነ’ደው

apathy
’አፐሲ -ስ- የስ’ሜት ማጣት፣ግ’ዴ’ለሽ መሆን

ape
’ኤፕ -ስ- የዝንጀሮ’ና የጦጣ በይነት እን
ስሳ ነገር ግን ጅራት የሌ’ለው

aperient
’እ’ፔሪየንት -ስ- የ’ሚያስቀ’ምጥ መድኃኒት

aperitif
’እ’ፔረቲፍ -ስ- ከምግብ በፊት የ’ሚ’ጠ’ጣ
መጠ’ጥ (እንዲያስርብ) ፣ ከሥቴ ከርሥ

aperture
’አፐቸ -ስ- ት’ንሽ ቀዳዳ ፣ ብስ

apex
’ኤይፔክስ -ስ- ጫፍ

apiary
’ኤይፕየሪ -ስ- የንብ ቀፎዎ’ች ቦታ

apologetic
’እ፣ለ’ጄቲክ -ቅ- ይቅርታ ጠ’ያቂ ፣ ተፀ’ፀች

apologize
’እ’ፖለጃይዝ -ግ- ይቅርታ መጠ’የቅ [ጠ’የቀ]

apology
’እ’ፖለጂ -ስ- ይቅርታ-

apostle
’እ’ፖስል -ስ- ደ’ቀ መዝሙር ፣ ሐዋርያ

apostrophe
’እ’ፖስትረፊ -ስ- ጭረት (የነጥብ ዓይነት) (’)

appal
’እ’ፖ፡ል -ግ- ማስደንገጥ [አስደነ’ገጠ] ፣ ማ’ጸ’
የፍ [አ’ጸ’የፈ]

appalling
’እ’ፖ፡ሊንግ -ቅ- አስደንጋጭ ፣ አ’ጸ’ያፊ

apparatus
’አፐራይተስ -ስ- መ’ቀላጠፊያ መ’ሣሪያ (በላ
ይንስ ላቦራትሪ)

apparel
’እ’ፓረል -ስ- ልብስ

apparent
’እ’ፓረንት -ቅ- ግልጽ ፣ የ’ማያ’ጠራ’ጥር

apparently
’እ’ፓረንትሊ -ተግ- በግልጽ

apparition
’አፐ’ሪሽን -ስ- የተከ’ሰተ መንፈስ

appeal
’እ’ፒል -ግ- ይግባኝ መጠ’የቅ [ጠ’የቀ]
-ስ- ቁንጅ’ና ፣ ደግም’ነት ፤ የተፈድሊ
ገንዘብ ስብሰባ

appear
’እ’ፒየ -ግ- ብ’ቅ ማለት [ብ’ቅ አለ] ፣ መም
ሰል [መ’ሰለ] ፤ መ’ታየት [ታ’የ]

appease
’እ’ፒይዝ -ግ- ማስደ’ስት [አስደሰተ] ፣ ማ-
በያ መስጠት [ሰ’ጠ] ፣ ማስታገሥ [አስታ
ገሥ] ፣ መ’ለማመጥ [ተለማ’መጠ]

appellant
’እ’ፔለንት -ስ- ባለይግባ’ኝ ፣ ይግባ’ኝ ባይ

append
’እ’ፔንድ -ግ- መቀ’ጠል [ቀ’ጠለ]

appendicitis
አፔንዲ’ሳይቲስ -ስ- የትርፍ አንጀት ሕመም

appertain
’አፐ’ቴይን -ግ- መ’ገናዘብ [ተገና’ዘበ]

appetite
’እፐታይት -ስ- የመብላት ፍላጎት

applaud
እፐ’ሎ፡ድ -ግ- ማጨብጨብ [አጨብ’ጨበ]

applause
እፐ’ሎ፡ዝ -ስ- ጭብጨባ

apple
’እፐል -ስ- ፖም (የፍራፍሬ ዓይነት)

appliance
እፐ’ላየንስ -ስ- መ’ሣሪያ

applicable
እፐ’ሊከበል -ቅ- ጉ’ዳዩ የ’ሚ’መለ’ከተው

applicant
’እፕሊከንት -ስ- ጠ’ያቂ (የሥራ) ፣ አመል
ካች

application
እፐሊ’ኬይሽን -ስ- ማመልከቻ ፣ እሥራ ላይ
ማዋል

apply
እፐ’ላይ -ግ- መጠ’የቅ [ጠ’የቀ] (ሥራ) ፡
ማመልከት [አመለ’ከተ]

appoint
እ’ፖይንት -ግ- መቅጠር [ቀ’ጠረ] ፣ መሾም
[ሾመ]

appointment
እ’ፖይንትመንት -ስ- ሥራ ፣ ማዕረግ

apportion
እ’ፖ፡ሽን -ግ- መቆ’ነን [ቆ’ነነ]

apposite
’እፐሲት -ቅ- ተስማሚ (ለንግ’ግር)

appraise
እፐ’ሬይዝ -ግ- መመርመር [መረ’መረ] ፣
መገ’መት [ገ’መተ]

appreciate
እፐ’ሪሺዬይት -ግ- መውደድ [ወ’ደደ] ፣ ደ’ስ
መ’ሰኘት [ተሰ’ኘ]

apprehend
እፐሪ’ሄንድ -ግ- መያዝ [ያዘ]
understand
-ግ- መ’ረዳት [ተረ’ዳ]

apprehension
እፐሪ’ሄንሽን -ስ- መፍራት ፣ መ’ጨነቅ (ለመ
ጨ ሁኔታ)

’apprentice
እፐ’ሬንቲስ -ስ- ሞያ ተማሪ (የአ’ጅ)

approach
እፐ’ረውች -ግ- መቅረብ [ቀ’ረበ]
-ስ- መንገድ (ያ’ቀራረብ)

approbation
እፐረ’ቤይሽን -ት- መስማማት ፣ ማመስገን ፡
እበ’ጀህ ማለት

approve
እፐ’ሩ፡ቭ -ግ- መስማማት [ተስማ’ማ] ፣ ማጽ
ደቅ [አጸ’ደቀ]

approximate
እፐ’ሮክሲመት -ቅ- አቅራ’ቢያ ፣ ያህል ፡
ገደማ
-ግ- መቅረብ [ቀ’ረበ]

appurtenance
እ’ፐ፡ተነንስ -ስ- ንብረት ፣ የግ’ል ዕቃ ፣ ያንድ
ነገር አባሪ የሆነ

April
ኤይፕረል -ስ- ሚያዝያ

apron
ኤይፕረን -ስ- ሽ’ርጥ

apt
’እፕት -ቅ- ተስማሚ ፣ ትክ’ክል ፣ ደምበ’ኛ

aptitude
’እፕቲትዩ፡ድ -ስ- ችሎታ ፣ ተስማሚ’ነት ፣
የተፈጥሮ ችሎታ

aquarium
እክ’ዌሪየም -ስ- ያሣ ማስቀ’መጫ ገንዳ (ሰው
ሠ’ራሽ)

aquatic
አክ’ዋቲክ -ቅ- የውሃ (ወገን)

aqueduct
’አክዌደክት -ስ- የመጠ’ጥ ወሃ የ’ሚሄድ’በት
ቦይ

aquiline
’አክወላይን -ቅ- ንሥር መ’ሰል ፣ ቀ’ጭን’ና
ጎባጣ (ለአፍንጫ)

arable
’አረበል -ቅ- ለእርሻ ተስማሚ (መሬት)

arbiter
’አ፡ቢተ -ስ- ሽማግ’ሌ ፣ አስታራቂ

363

arbitrary

’ኣ:ቢትረሪ -ቅ- በጣም ያልታ'ሰበ'በት ፣ በች
ኮ'ላ የተደ'ረገ (ው'ሳኔ) ፣ ያለ በቂ ምክንያት
የተወ'ሰነ (ው'ሳኔ) I ተቀናቃኝ የሌ'ለው (በሥ
ልጣኑ)

arbitrate

’ኣ:ቢትሬይት -ግ- መሸምገል [ሸመ'ገለ] (ግስ
ታረት)

arbitration

ኣ:ቢት'ሬይሽን -ስ- ሽምገላ

arbitrator

’ኣ:ቢትሬይተ -ስ- ሸማግ'ሌ ፣ አስታራቂ

arbour

’ኣ:በ -ስ- ጥላ'ማ ቦታ (እዛፍ ሥር መዘተ)

arc

’ኣ:ክ -ስ- ቅ'ሥት (ቅርስ)

arch

’ኣ:ች -ስ- ቅ'ሥት

archaic

ኣ:'ኬይክ -ቅ- ጥንታዊ ፣ ታሪካዊ

archangel

’ኣ:ኬንጀል -ስ- ሊቀ መላእክት

archbishop

ኣ:ች'ቢሾፕ -ስ- ሊቀ ጳጳሳት

archaeology

ኣ:ኪ'ዎለጂ -ስ- በመሬት ውስጥ የተቀ'በሩ
የታሪክ ቅርሶ'ች ጥናት

archer

’ኣ:ች -ስ- ቀስተ'ኛ ፣ በቀስት'ና በፍላ'ጻ የ'ሚ
ዋ'ጋ

archipelago

ኣ:ቺ'ፐለገው -ስ- የተጫ'ፈሩ ደሴቶ'ች

architect

’ኣ:ኪተክት -ስ- አርኪቴክት (የቤት ፕላን ነ
ዳፊ)

archives

’ኣ:ካይቭዝ -ስ- ሰነዶ'ች (አርኬ)
office

-ስ- ቤተ መዛግብት

ardent

’ኣ:ደንት -ቅ- በጉ'ዳዩ በጣም የ'ሚያ'ስብ'በት ፣
ስ'ሜቱ በጉ'ዳዩ የተቀስ'ቀስ ፣ ጥልቅ ስ'ሜት
ያ'ለው (ስለአንድ ጉ'ዳይ)

ardour

’ኣ:ደ -ስ- ፍቅር ፣ ጥሩ ስ'ሜት ፣ ጥልቅ ስ'ሜት

arduous

’ኣ:ድዩወስ -ቅ- አስቸ'ጋሪ ፣ አሰልቺ ፣ አ'ዋኪ
(ሥራ)

area

’ኤሪያ -ስ- ቦታ (የተወ'ሰነ) ፣ ሥፈር
measure

-ስ- ስፋት

arena

ኧ'ሪ:ን -ስ- ሰፊ ክ'ብ ቦታ (የስፖርት መዘተ)

argue

’ኣ:ገዩ -ግ- መከራከር [ተከራ'ከረ]

argument

’ኣ:ግዩመንት -ስ- ክር'ክር

arid

’ኣሪድ -ቅ- ደረት

arise

ኧ'ራይዝ -ግ- መነሣት [ተነ'ሣ]

aristocracy

ኣሪስ'ቶክረሲ -ስ- ባላ'ባቶ'ች

arithmetic

ኧ'ሪስመቲክ -ስ- ሒሳብ

ark

’ኣ:ክ -ስ- ታቦት
ship

-ስ- የኖሕ መርከብ

arm

’ኣ:ም -ስ- ክንድ

armament

’ኣ:መመንት -ስ- የጦር መ'ሣሪያዎ'ች ፣ ትጥቅ

armchair

ኣ:ም'ቼየ -ስ- ባለመ'ደገፊያ ወምበር (የእ'ጅ
መ'ደገፊያ ያ'ለው)

armistice

’ኣ:ሚስቲስ -ስ- ጦር'ነት ለጊዜው ለማቆም
መስማማት

armour

’ኣ:መ -ስ- የብረት ልብስ ፣ ጥሩር

armpit

’ኣ:ምርት -ስ- ብ'ብት

arms

’ኣ:ምዝ -ስ- የጦር መ'ሣሪያ

364

army

'አ:ሚ -ስ- ጦር ሠራዊት ፣ ወ'ታ'ደር

aroma

ኧ'ረውመ -ስ- መዓዛ

aromatic

አረ'ማቲክ -ቅ- መዓዛ ያ'ለው

around

ኧ'ራውንድ -ተግ- ባ'ካባቢ

arouse

ኧ'ራውዝ -ግ- ማስነ'ሣት [አስነ'ሣ]

arrange

ኧ'ሬይንጅ -ግ- ማ'ዘጋጀት [አ'ዘጋ'ጀ]

array

ኧ'ሬይ -ስ- ሰልፍ

arrears

ኧ'ሪየዝ -ስ- የተወ'ዘፈ ፣ ያልተከ'ፈለ የቤት ፣ የመሬት ፣ የሥራ ወዘተ እዳ

arrest

ኧ'ረስት -ግ- መያዝ [ያዘ] (ለፖሊስ)

arrive

ኧ'ራይቭ -ግ- መድረስ [ደ'ረሰ]

arrogant

'አረጎንት -ቅ- ዘላፊ ፣ ደ'ፋር ፣ እብሪተ'ኛ

arrow

'አረው -ስ- ፍላ'ፃ ፣ ወስፈን'ጥር

arsenal

'አ:ሰነል -ስ- የጦር መ'ሣሪያ ዕቃ ቤት ፣ የመ'ሣሪያ ፋብሪካ

arsenic

'አ:ሰኒክ -ስ- አሰኒክ (ነይል'ኛ መርዝ)

arson

'አ:ሰን -ስ- የሰው ቤት ማ'ቃጠል

art

'አ:ት -ስ- ጥበብ ፣ አንድ ነገር የማድረግ ችሎታ ፣ አንድ ነገር የመፍጠር ተስጥዖ

creative

-ስ- ኪነ ጥበብ

arterial

አ:'ቲሪየል -ቅ- ዋ'ና ፣ አውራ ፣ የደም ሥር ወገን

artery

'አ:ተሪ -ስ- ት'ልቅ የደም ሥር

artful

'አ:ትፉል -ቅ- ብልጎነተ'ኛ ፣ ዘዴኛ ፣ ጮ'ሌ

article

'አ:ቲክል -ስ- ዕቃ

literary

-ስ- ጽሑፍ(ጋዜጣ)

grammatical

-ስ- መስተአ'ምር (ሰዋስው)

articulate

አ:'ቲክዮሌይት -ግ- ጋልጾ አድርጎ መ'ናገር [ተና'ገረ]

articulate

አ:'ቲክዮሌት -ቅ- ጥሩ ተናጋሪ ፣ ነገር ዐዋቂ

artificial

አ:ቲ'ፊሻል -ቅ- ሰው ሠ'ራሽ

artillery

አ:'ቲለሪ -ስ- መድፈ'ኛ

artisan

'አ:ቲዛን -ስ- በእ'ጅ ሥራ ዕውቀት የሠለ'ጠነ

artist

'አ:ቲስት -ስ- ሠዓሊ ፣ የኪነ ጥበብ ሰው

as

'አዝ -መገ- እንደ

as ... as

-መገ- ከሆነ

ascend

ኧ'ሴንድ -ግ- መውጣት [ወ'ጣ] (ወደላይ)

ascendancy

ኧ'ሴንደንሲ -ስ- ድል ፣ ሥልጣን፣የበላይ'ነት ፣ መግዛት ፣ የመግዛት ነይል (ሥልጣን)

ascendant

ኧ'ሴንደንት -ቅ- ወጪ (ወደላይ)

ascension

ኧ'ሴንሸን -ስ- ዕርገት

ascent

ኧ'ሴንት -ስ- መውጣት

ascertain

አሰ'ቴይን -ግ- ማ'ረጋገጥ [አ'ረጋ'ገጠ]

ascetic

አ'ሴቲክ -ቅ- ባሕታዊ

ascribe

እስክ'ራይብ -ግ- ማ'ሳበብ [አ'ሳ'በበ] ፣ አንድ ነገር የሌላ መሆኑን መግለጽ [ገ'ለጸ]

365

ash

'አሽ -ስ- አመድ ፤ የዛፍ ዓይነት

Ash Wednesday

-ስ- የጾም አርባ መጀ'መሪያ ቀን

ashamed

እ'ሼይምድ -ቅ- ያ'ፈረ

ashen

'አሽን -ቅ- የገረ'ጣ (መልክ)

ashore

አ'ሾ: -ተግ- በወደብ ላይ ፤ በባሕር ዳር

ash-tray

'አሽ-ትሬይ -ስ- መተርኮሻ (የሲ፮ራ)

aside

እ'ሳይድ -ተግ- በስተጐ'ን

-ስ- የምሥጢር ንግ'ግር

ask

'አ:ስክ -ግ- መጠ'የቅ [ጠ'የቀ]

askance

እስ'ካንስ -ተግ- በመ'ታዘብ

askew

እስክ'ዩው -ቅ ፤ ተግ- ጐባጣ

asleep

እስ'ሊይፕ -ቅ- የተኛ

aspect

'አስፔክት -ስ- አቅጣ'ጫ ፤ አግጣ'ጫ፤ ትር

እይት

aspersion

እስ'ፐ:ሽን -ስ- ስድብ ፤ ሰውን ባልሡ'ራው

ሥራ ማ'ዋረድ

asphalt

'አስፋልት -ስ- የሬንጅ'ና የጠጠር ድብ'ልቅ

(ለመንገድ መሥሪያ)

asphyxia

እስ'ፊክሲያ -ስ- መ'ታፈን (የመ'ታፈን ሞት)

aspirant

'አስፒረንት -ቅ- ከፍ ወዳለ ማዕርግ ለመድ

ረስ የ'ሚ'መኝ

-ስ- ከፍ ያለ ም'ኞት ያለው

aspiration

አስፒ'ሬይሽን -ስ- ከፍ ያለ ተስፋ

aspire

አስ'ፓየ -ግ- ከፍ ወዳለ ማዕረግ ፤ ም'ኞት

ለመድረስ መ'መኘት [ተ'መኘ]

ass

'አስ -ስ- አህ'ያ

assail

እ'ሴይል -ግ- መግጠም[ገ'ጠመ] (ለጦር'ነት) ፤

መ'ጨነቅ [ተጨ'ነቀ] (ፍርሃት)

assailant

እ'ሴይለንት -ስ- በጐይል አደጋ የ'ሚጥል በ

ላት ፤ ተከራካሪ ጠላት

assassin

እ'ሳሲን -ስ- ነፍስ ገዳይ (ሹም)

assassinate

እ'ሳሲኔይት -ግ- መግደል (ገ'ደለ) (ሹምን)

assassination

እሳሲ'ኔይሽን -ስ- መግደል (ሹም)

assault

እ'ሶልት -ግ- አደጋ መጣል [ጣለ]

assay

አ'ሴይ -ግ- መሞ'ከር [ሞ'ከረ]

gold

-ግ- መፈ'ተን [ፈ'ተነ] (ወርቅ)

assemble

እ'ሴምበል -ግ- መ'ሰብሰብ [ተሰብ'ሰበ]

assembly

እ'ሴምብሊ -ስ- ስብሰባ

assent

እ'ሴንት -ግ- መስማማት [ተስማ'ማ]

-ስ- ስምም'ነት

assert

እ'ስ:ት -ግ- መብት እንዲ'ጠ'በቅ'ለት መ'ና

ገር [ተና'ገረ]

say

-ግ- ማለት [አለ]

assess

እ'ሴስ -ግ- መመርመር [መረ'መረ] ፤ ግ'ጠ

ዛዙን [አ'መዛ'ዘነ]

assets

'አሴትስ -ስ- የተቆ'መጠ ገንዘብ ፤ ዋጋ ያ'ላ

ቸው ንብረቶ'ች

assignment

እ'ሳይንመንት -ስ- ተግባር (የ'ሚ'ፈ'ጸም)

assimilate

እ'ሲሚሌይት -ግ- መ'ዋሐድ [ተዋሐደ] (አነ

ስተ'ኛው ከከ'ፍተ'ኛው)

366

assist
እ'ሲስት -ግ- መርዳት [ረ'ዳ]

associate
እ'ሰውሲዬይት -ግ- መ'ተባበር [ተባ'በረ]
-ስ- ጓ'ደኛ ፣ የሥራ ጓ'ደኛ

association
እ'ሰውሲዬይሽን -ስ- ማኅበር

assorted
አ'ሶ፥ቲድ -ቅ- ል'ዩ ል'ዩ

assume
እስ'ዩ፥ም -ግ- ማ'ሰብ [አ'ሰበ] ፣ መገ'መት
[ገ'መተ] ፣ መምሰል [መ'ሰለ]

assurance
እ'ሾ፥ረንስ -ስ- ዋስት'ና ፤ መጽናናት

assure
እ'ሾ፥ -ግ- ማ'ረጋገጥ [አ'ረጋ'ገጠ]

asterisk
'አስተሪስክ -ስ- ኮከባዊ ምል'ክት (በጽሑፍ)

asthma
'አስመ -ስ- አስም ፣ መተንፈስ የ'ሚያ'ግድ
በ'ሽታ

astonish
እስ'ቶኒሽ -ግ- መገረም [ተገ'ረመ] ፣ መ'ደ
ነቅ [ተደ'ነቀ]

astonishment
እስ'ቶኒሽመንት -ስ- መገረም ፣ መ'ደነቅ

astound
እስ'ታውንድ -ግ- መገ'ረም [ተገ'ረመ] ፣ መ'
ደነቅ [ተደ'ነቀ]

astray
እስት'ሬይ -ተግ- በመጥፋት ፣ በመኰብለል

astride
እስት'ራይድ -ተግ- አንፈራ'ጦ (መሄድ ፣ መ
'ቀመጥ)

astrology
እስት'ሮለጅ -ስ- ኮከብ ቆጠራ

astronomy
እስት'ሮነሚ -ስ- የፈለክ ጥናት

astute
እስት'ዩ፥ት -ቅ- ብልህ ፣ ሩጩ'ሉ

asunder
እ'ሰንደ -ተግ- ለያይቶ ፣ ተለያይቶ

asylum
እ'ሳይለም -ስ- መ'ጠጊያ ፣ መ'ሰደጃ
mental-
-ስ- የእብዶ'ች ሐኪም ቤት

at
'አት -መ፯- በ . . .
-*two o'clock*
በሁለ'ት ሰዓት
-*home*
በቤት ፣ እቤት
-*last*
በመጨ'ረሻ
-*once*
ባንድ ጊዜ ፣ ወዲያውኑ

atheism
'ኤይሲይዝም -ስ- ከሂዶተ እግዚአብሔር

atheist
'ኤይሲይስት -ስ- በእግዚአብሔር መኖር የ'ማ
ያምን ሰው

athlete
'አዕሊይት -ስ- የስፖርት ሰው ፣ እስፖርተ'ኛ

atlas
'አትለስ -ስ- አትላስ ፤ የዓለምን ካርታ የ'ያዘ
መጽሐፍ

atmosphere
'አትመስፈየ -ስ- አ'የር ፣ ነፋስ

atone
እ'ተውን -ግ- መ'ታረቂያ መስጠት [ሰ'ጠ] ፣
መካሥ [ካሠ] ፤ መዋጀት [ዋ'ጀ]

atrocious
እት'ረውሸስ -ቅ- አ'ሠ'ቃቂ

atrocity
እት'ሮሲቲ -ስ- አ'ሠ'ቃቂ ወንጀል ወይን'ም
ሥራ

attach
እ'ታች -ግ- ማ'ጣበቅ [አ'ጣ'በቀ] ፣ ማ'ያያዝ
[አ'ያያዘ]

attachment
እ'ታችመንት -ስ- የማ'ያያዝ ተግባር ፣ ማ'ያ
ያዝ ፣ አባሪ ጽሑፍ

367

attack
ኧ'ታክ -ግ- አደጋ መጣል [ጣለ] ፣ መግጠም [ገ'ጠመ] (ጦር'ነት)
of sickness
-ግ- በሽታ መያዝ [ያዘ]
-ስ- አደጋ ፤ መ'ያዝ (በበ'ሽታ)
attain
ኧ'ቴይን -ግ- መድረስ [ደ'ረሰ] (ም'ኞት)
attempt
ኧ'ቴምት -ግ- መሞ'ከር [ሞ'ከረ]
attend
ኧ'ቴንድ -ግ- አተ'ኩሮ ማ'ሰብ [አ'ሰበ]
be present
-ግ- መ'ገኘት [ተገ'ኘ]
wait for
-ግ- መጠ'በቅ [ጠ'በቀ]
function
-ግ- ማሳ'ለፍ [አሳ'ለፈ] (ምግብ ፣ ግብ ዣ)
attendance
ኧ'ቴንደንስ -ስ- በስብሰባ የነ'በረ (ሕዝብ)
attendant
ኧ'ቴንደንት -ስ- አሳ'ላፊ ፣ ቋሚ
attention
ኧ'ቴንሽን -ስ- አተ'ኩሮ ማ'ሰብ
-ግ- ተጠንቀቅ (ትእዛዝ ፣ ለወ'ታ'ደር)
attentive
ኧ'ቴንቲቭ -ቅ- ጥንቁቅ ፣ ንቁ
attenuated
ኧ'ቴንዩዌይተድ -ቅ- መንማ'ና ፣ የከ'ሳ (በበ 'ሽታ ምክንያት)
attest
ኧ'ቴስት -ግ- መ'ረጃ መስጠት [ሰ'ጠ] (በፍ ርድ ቤት)
attic
'አቲክ -ስ- ት'ንሽ ክፍል (ከጣራ በታ'ች)
attire
ኧ'ታየ -ስ- ልብስ
attitude
'አቲትዩ:ድ -ስ- የሰው'ነት አ ቋቋም ፤ አስተያ የት ፣ አስተሳሰብ
attorney
ኧ'ተ:ኒ -ስ- ወ'ኪል (ያንድን ድር'ጅት ጉ' ዳይ የ'ሚፈ'ጽም) ፣ ጠበቃ

attract
ኧት'ራክት -ግ- መሳብ [ሳበ] ፣ አስተያየትን መውሰድ [ወ'ሰደ] ፣ መማረክ [ማ'ረከ]
attribute
'አትሪብዩት -ስ- መ'ታወቂያ ፣ ጠባይ
credit
ኧት'ሪብዩት -ግ- መስጠት [ሰ'ጠ] (የሚ'ገ'ባ ው መሆኑን በማመን)
auction
'ኦ:ክሽን -ስ- ሀ'ራጅ
auctioneer
ኦ:ክሽ'ኒየ -ስ- ዕቃ በሀ'ራጅ የ'ሚሸጥ
audacious
ኦ:'ዴይሸስ -ቅ- ደ'ፋር ፣ ጉበዝ
audacity
ኦ:'ዳሲቲ -ስ- ድፍረት ፣ ጉብዝ'ና
audible
'ኦ:ዲበል -ቅ- የ'ሚ'ሰ'ማ
audience
'ኦ:ዲየንስ -ስ- ተመልካች (ሕዝብ)
audit
'ኦ:ዲት -ግ- መ'ቆጣጠር [ተቆጣ'ጠረ]
audition
ኦ:'ዲሽን -ስ- መፈ'ተን (ቲያትር ሠ'ራተ'ኞን)
auditor
'ኦ:ዲተ -ስ- ሒሳብ ተቆጣጣሪ
auditorium
ኦ:ዲ'ቶ:ሪየም -ስ- ታ'ላቅ አ'ዳራሽ (የሙዚቃ የንግ'ግር)
augment
ኦ:ግ'ሜንት -ግ- ማብዛት [አበ'ዛ] ፤ ከ'ፍ ማድ ረግ [አደ'ረገ] (በመጠን ፣ በቁጥር)
august
ኦ:'ገስት -ቅ- የተከ'በረ ፣ ባለግርማ
August
'ኦ:ገስት -ስ- ነሐሴ
aunt
'ኦ:ንት -ስ- አክስት
auspices
'ኦ:ስፒሲዝ -ስ- ተጠባባቂ'ነት ፣ መሪ'ነት ፣ ረዳ ት'ነት
auspicious
ኦ:ስ'ፒሸስ -ቅ- ባለተስፋ

austere
አስ'ቲየ -ቅ- ያሳጌጠ ፡ ተራ

authentic
አ:'ቴንቲክ -ቅ- እውነተኛ ፡ ግ'ታለል የሌ'
ለ በት

author
'አ:ሰ -ስ- ደራሲ

authoritative
አ:'ሶረተቲቭ -ቅ- ሥልጣን የተመረ'ኮዘ ፡
ባለሥልጣን ፤ እምነት የ'ሚ'ጣል በት

authority
አ:'ሶረቲ -ስ- ሥልጣን

authorize
'አ:ሰራይዝ -ግ- ሥልጣን መስጠት [ሰ'ጠ]

autobiography
አ:ተባ'ዮግራፊ -ስ- በባለቤቱ የተጻፈ የራስ
ታሪክ

autocracy
አ'ቶክረሲ -ስ- ለሥልጣኑ ወሰን የሌ'ለው ያን
ድ ሰው አስተዳደር (የመንግሥት)

autograph
'አ:ተግራፍ -ስ- ፊርማ ፡ ያንድ ሰው የራሱ
የእ'ጅ ጽሑፍ

automatic
አ:ተማቲክ -ቅ- አውቶማቲክ ፡ በራሱ የ'ሚ
ሠራ

autonomous
አ:'ቶነመስ -ቅ- ነጻ (መንግሥት)

autonomy
አ:'ቶነሚ -ስ- ነጻ'ነት ያ'ለው (መንግሥት)

autumn
'አ:ተም -ስ- መፀው (በእንግሊዝ አገር መስከ
ረም'ና ጥቅምት) ፡ በልግ (በኢትዮ'ጵያ)

auxilliary
አ:ክ'ዚልየሪ -ቅ- ረጂ ፡ አባሪ ፡ መ'ጠባበቂያ

avail
እቬይል -ግ- መርዳት [ረ'ዳ] ፡ ራስን ለርዳታ
ማ'ዘጋጀት [አ'ዘጋ'ጀ]

available
እ'ቬለበል -ቅ- የ'ሚ'ገኝ ፡ ለማግኘት የ'ማ
ያስቸ'ግር

avarice
'አቨሪስ -ስ- የገንዘብ ጉ'ጉት ፡ ንፍገት

avenge
እ'ቬንጅ -ግ- መ'በቀል [ተበ'ቀለ]

avenue
'አቨኑዩ -ስ- ጉዳና

average
'አቨረጅ -ስ- መካ'ከለኛ ፡ አማካ'ኝ ፡ ል'ዩ
ል'ዩ ቁጥሮ'ች ተደ'ምረው በብዛታ'ቸው ሲ'ከ
ፈል የ'ሚደርሰው (ምሳሌ፡ 4+5+9=18÷3=6)

averse
እ'ቨ:ስ -ቅ- የሚጠላ ፡ ጠዪ

aversion
እ'ቨ:ሽን -ስ- ጥላቻ

avert
እ'ቨ:ት -ግ- ማ'ገድ [አ'ገደ] (ለአደጋ) ፡ ማስ
ወ'ገድ [አስወ'ገደ]

aviary
'ኤይቫየሪ -ስ- የተሰበ'ሰቡ ሕይወት ያ'ላ'ቸ
ው ወፎ'ች ፤ የወፍ ጎ'ጆ

aviation
ኤይ'ቬይሽን -ስ- አቪያሲዮን ፡ የመብረር
ጥበብ

avid
'አቪድ -ቅ- ጉ'ጉ ፡ ጠንካ'ራ ምኞ'ት ያ'ለው

avoid
እ'ቮይድ -ግ- ራስን መከልከል [ከለ'ከለ] ፡
በጉ'ዳዩ አለመግባት [-ገ'ባ] አንድ ነገር እንዳ
ይደርስ ገለ'ል ማለት [አለ]

avow
እ'ቫው -ግ- በሐሳብ ድ'ርቅ ማለት [አለ] ፡
አንድ ነገር ለመተው መ'ሣል [ተሣለ] ፡
መማል [ማለ]

await
እ'ዌይት -ግ- አንድ ነገር መጠ'በቅ [ጠ'በቀ]
(ይደርሳል ብሎ)

awake
እ'ዌይክ -ግ- መ'ነሣት [ተነ'ሣ] ፡ መንቃት
[ነ'ቃ] (ከመ'ኝታ)
-ቅ- ንቁ

award
እ'ዎ:ድ -ግ- መሸ'ለም [ሸ'ለም]

aware
እ'ዌየ -ቅ- የ'ሚያውቅ ፡ የተጠነ'ቀቀ

away
እ'ዌይ -ተግ- ወዲያ

369

awe
’አ: -ስ- አክብሮት

awful
’አ:ፉል -ቅ- አስፈ'ሪ ፣ የ'ሚያስጠ'ላ

awfully
’አ:ፊሊ -ተግ- በጣም ፣ ከፉ'ኛ

awhile
እ'ዋይል -ተግ- ጥቂት ጊዜ ፣ አንዳፍታ

awkward
’አ:ክወድ -ቅ- አ'ዋኪ ፣ አስፈ'ሪ (ለሁናቴ)

awl
’አ:ል -ስ- መብሻ ፣ መሰርሰሪያ ብረት

awning
’ኦ:ኒንግ -ስ- ዳስ ፣ ከለላ

awry
እ'ራይ -ቅ- ዝብርቅርቅ

axe
’አክስ -ስ- መጥረቢያ ፣ ጥ'ል'ቆ ፣ ፋስ

axle
’አክሰል -ስ- መንኮራኩሮ'ች የ'ሚይዝ ጋድ
ሚያ ብረት

azure
’አዡር -ቅ- ሰማያዊ

B

babble
’ባበል -ግ- መለፍለፍ [ለፈ'ለፈ] ፣ ማልጎም
ጎም [አልጎመ'ጎመ]

baboon
በ'ቡን -ስ- ግመሬ ዝንጀሮ

baby
’ቤይቢ -ስ- ሕፃን

babyish
’ቤይቢይሽ -ቅ- ያልበ'ሰለ (ለሰው)፣ የልጅ
'ነት ጠባይ ያለው

baby-sitter
’ቤይቢ ሲተ -ስ- ሕፃናት ጠ'ባቂ (ወላጆ'ች
በሌ'ሉ ጊዜ)

bachelor
’ባቸለ -ስ- ያላገ'ባ ፣ ወንደላ'ጤ

back
’ባክ -ስ- ጀርባ
-ተግ- ወደ ኋላ
-ቅ- የኋላ ፣ ዘመናዊ ያልሆነ ፣ ወደኋላ
የቀ'ረ ፣ ዝ'ቅተተ'ኛ

backbite
’ባክባይት -ስ- ሐሜት

backbone
’ባክበውን -ስ- ደንደ'ስ ፣ የ'ማያወላ'ውል ጠባይ፣
ያንድ ነገር ዋ'ናው ክፍል

background
’ባክግራውንድ -ስ- በስተኋላ ያ'ለ ነገር (የሥ
ዕል ፣ የፎቶግራፍ)፣ ቤተሰብ ፣ አስተዳደግ ወዘተ

backward
’ባክወድ -ቅ- ያልሠለ'ጠነ ፣ ወደኋላ የቀ'ረ

backwards
’ባክወድዝ -ተግ- ወደኋላ ፣ የኋሊት

backwater
’ባክዋ፡ተ -ስ- በወንዝ አጠገብ የ'ሚ'ገኝ የረ
'ጋ ኩሬ (ወንዙ የ'ማይደርስ'በት)

bacon
’ቤይከን -ስ- በእንፋሎት የደ'ረቀ ያሣማ ሥጋ

bacteria
’ባክ'ቴሪየ -ስ- በ'ሽታ የ'ሚያመጡ ጥቃ'ቅን
ፍጥረቶ'ች

bad
’ባድ -ቅ- መጥፎ ፣ ከፉ

badge
’ባጅ -ስ- የመ'ለያ ምል'ክት ፣ መ'ለ'ዮ (በል
ብስ ላይ ፣ በባርኔጣ ላይ ወዘተ)

badger
’ባጀ -ግ- መጨቅጨቅ [ጨቀ'ጨቀ] ፣ መጎት
ጎት [ጎተ'ጎተ]

baffle
’ባፈለ -ግ- ማስቸ'ገር [አስቸ'ገረ] ፣ ማ'ወክ
[አ'ወከ]፣ መጽነን [ጸ'ነነ]
-ስ- ክል'ል ፣ ጋርዶሽ

370

bag
’ባግ -ስ- ከረጢት ፣ አቅማዳ

baggage
’ባጌጅ -ስ- የጉዞ ዕቃ

bail
’ቤያል -ግ- በመ፡ዋስ ግሲለ፡ተቅ [አስለ፡ተቀ]
(እስረ፡ኛን) -ስ- መ፡ተማመኛ ገንዘብ

bait
’ቤይት -ስ- የሆነ ማጥመጃ ምግብ ፤ ወጥመድ
(ሥዕላዊ)

bake
’ቤይክ -ግ- መጋገር [ጋ፡ገረ]

baker
’ቤይከ -ስ- ዳቦ ፣ እንጀራ ጋጋሪ

bakery
’ቤይከሪ -ስ- ዳቦ መጋገሪያ (ሱቅ ፣ ቦታ)

balance
’ባለንስ -ግ- መመዘን [መ፡ዘነ]
-ስ- ሚዛን

balcony
’ባልከኒ -ስ- ሰገነት

bald
’ቦልድ -ቅ- መላጣ ፣ በራ ራስ ፣ ራሰ በራ

baldness
’ቦልድነስ -ስ- መላጣነት ፣ በራነት

baleful
’ቤይልፉል -ቅ- በጥላ፡ቻ የተመላ

baulk
’ቦ፡ልክ -ግ- ማ፡ደናቀፍ [አደና፡ቀፈ]
-ስ- የተቆ፡ረጠ ግንድ

ball
’ቦ፡ል -ስ- ኳስ

ballad
’ባለድ -ስ- ከጥንት የመ፡ጣ ዘፈን ፣ ግጥም ፣
ተረት (በግጥም መልክ)

ballet
’ባሌ -ስ- በወገዝ፡ዋዜ የሚ፡ገ፡ለጽ ቴያትር
(በመ፡ዚቃ የታ፡ጀበ)

balloon
በ’ሉ፡ን -ስ- የተነ፡ፋ ቆዳ ወይን፡ም ላስቲክ

ballot
’ባለት -ስ- የምርጫ ካርድ ፣ ወረቀት

ballpoint
’ቦ፡ልፖይንት -ስ- እስክሪፕቶ ፣ የጭቃ ብዕር

balm
’ባ፡ም -ስ- የእበጥ ፣ የቁስል ቅባት

balustrade
’ባሉስትሬይድ -ስ- በግራ፡ና በቀ፡ኝ ያለ የመ
ወጣጫ መ፡ደገፊያ ፣ በሰገ፡ነት ላይ ያለ መ፡ደ
ገፊያ

bamboo
ባም’ቡ፡ -ስ- ሽመል ፣ ቀርከሃ

ban
’ባን -ግ- ማቆም [አቆመ] ፣ መከልከል [ከለ
፡ከለ] (እንድ ድር፡ጅት ፣ ነገር ወዘተ እንዳይቀ
ጥል)
-ስ- ማ፡ገጃ ሕ፡ግ

banal
በ’ናል -ቅ- ተራ ፣ ል፡ዩ ያልሆነ ፣ አስተያየት
የ፡ማይ፡ማ፡ርክ

banana
በ’ና፡ን -ስ- ሙዝ

band
’ባንድ -ስ- ስብሰባ ፤ የሙዚቃ ጓ፡ድ ፣ መጠቅ
ለያ (የወረቀት ፣ የሻሽ)

bandage
’ባንዴጅ -ስ- የቁስል መጠቅለያ ፣ የቁስል
ማሰሪያ (ሻሽ)

bandit
’ባንዲት -ስ- ሽፍታ ፣ ወምበዴ ፣ ቀ፡ማ፡ኛ

baneful
’ቤይንፉል -ቅ- ክፉ ፣ መጥፎ ፣ ጉጅ

bang
’ባንግ -ግ- ድ፡ም ማለት [አለ]
-ስ- ከ፡ፍ ያለ ድምፅ

bangle
’ባንገል -ስ- አምባር

banish
’ባኒሽ -ግ- ማ፡ጋዝ [አጋዘ] (እ፡ሥር ቤት)

banishment
’ባኒሽመንት -ስ- ግዞት

banister
’ባኒስተ -ስ- የቤት ደረጃ ገደብ

bank
’ባንክ -ስ- በወንዝ ዳር፡ቻ ያፈር ፣ ያሸዋ ቁ
ልል
money
-ስ- ባንክ (የገንዘብ)

371

bankrupt
’ባንክረፕት -ስ- መክሰሩን ሕ'ግ ያ'ረጋ'ገጠ'ለት
ሰው ፣ ንብረቱ ተሸጦ ለእዳ እንዲ'ከፈ'ል የተወ
'ሰነ'በት ሰው
-ቅ- እዳውን መክፈል የ'ማይችል

bankruptcy
’ባንክረፕሲ -ስ- ከሳራ ፣ መክሰር

banner
’ባነ -ስ- ሰን'ደቅ ዓላማ ፣ የጨርቅ ምል'ክት
(በሰልፍ)

banquet
’ባንክዌት -ስ- ግብር (ግብዣ)

bantam
’ባንተም -ስ- ል'ዩ ዓይነት ትን'ንሽ ዶሮ

banter
’ባንተ -ስ- ቀልዳቀልድ

baptism
’ባፕቲዝም -ስ- ጥምቀት (ሥርዓቱ)

baptize
ባፕ'ታይዝ -ግ- ማጥመቅ [አጠ'መቀ] ፣ ክር
ስት'ና ማንሣት [አነ'ሣ]

bar
’ባ፡ -ግ- መከልከል [ከለ'ከለ] ፣ ማ'ገድ [አ'ገደ]
pole
-ስ- ማ'ገጃ ብረት
drinking
-ስ- መጠጥ ቤት ፣ መሸታ ቤት ፣ ቡ'ና
ቤት

barb
’ባ፡ብ -ስ- የመንጠ'ቆ ፣ የፍላ'ፃ ጫፍ (ወደኋላ
የተመ'ለሰው ስለት)

barbarian
ባ፡'ቤሪየን -ስ- አረመኔ (ሰው)

barbaric
ባ፡'ባሪክ -ቅ- አረመኔ\(ተገባር)

barbarity
ባ፡'ባሪቲ -ስ- አረመኔነት

barbarous
’ባ፡በረስ -ቅ- ያልሠለ'ጠነ ፣ ጨ'ካኝ

barbecue
’ባ፡ቢክዩ -ስ- የፍም ጥብስ (ከቤት ው'ጭ የ'ሚ
'ጠ'በስ)

barber
’ባ፡በ -ስ- ጠጉር ቆራጭ ፣ ጠጉር አስተካካይ ፣
ጢም ላጭ

bare
’ቤየ -ቅ- ባዶ ፣ የተራ'ቆተ ፣ ያልተሸ'ፈነ ፣
ገላጣ ፤ ለች'ንገር ያህል የ'ሚበቃ

barely
’ቤሊ -ተግ- በጥቂቱ ፣ በጨረፍታ ፣ በግልጥ ፣
በይፉ

bargain
’ባ፡ጌን -ግ- ዋጋ መ'ከራከር [ተከራ'ከረ]
በዋጋ ውጣ ውረድ ማለት [አለ]
-ስ- የዋጋ ክር'ክር ፣ የዋጋ ውጣ ውረድ

barge
’ባ፡ጅ -ስ- ታንኳ ፣ ት'ንሽ መርከብ

bark
’ባ፡ክ -ግ- መጮኸ [ጮኸ] (ለው'ሻ)
-ስ- የው'ሻ ጩኸት
of tree
-ስ- ልጥ (የዛፍ)

barley
’ባ፡ሊ -ስ- ገብስ

barn
’ባ፡ን -ስ- ጎተራ

barometer
በ'ሮመተ -ስ- ባሮሜትር (ያ'የር መለ'ኪያ
መ'ሣሪያ)

baron
’ባረን -ስ- «ባሮን» (ዝ'ቅተ'ኛ የሹ
መት ስም)

barrack
’ባረክ -ስ- የመ'ታ'ደር'ች መኖሪያ ቤት ፣ የወ
'ታ'ደር ሠፈር
heckle
-ግ- መበጥበጥ [በጠ'በጠ] ፣ ማ'ወክ
[አ'ወከ] (በንግ'ግር ጊዜ)

barrage
’ባራ፡ጅ -ስ- የተፋፋመ ተኩስ (ወደ አንድ
አቅጣ'ጫ የ'ሚ'ተ'ኮስ)
river
-ስ- ግ'ድብ (የውሃ)

barrel
’ባረል -ስ- በርሜል (በተለ'ይ የእንጨት) ፣
አፈሙዝ (ጠመንጃ)

barren

’ባረን -ት- ድርት (እገር)

of female

-ት- መካን ፣ መ‘ካን

barricade

ባሪ’ኬይድ -ስ- መ‘ሽሸጊያ ፤ መ‘ከላከያ ፣ መስ ናክል (ለጦር’ነት)

barrier

’ባሪየ -ስ- ግ’ንጸ

barrister

’ባሪስተ -ስ- የሕ’ግ ጠበቃ

barter

’ባ:ተ -ግ- መ‘ላወጥ [ተላ‘ወጠ] (ለንግድ ፣ ም‘ሳሌ ዕቃ በቃ)

base

’ቤይስ -ስ- መሠረት ፤ መሥሪሪያ ቦታ ፣ ሠፈር

low

-ት- ወ‘ራ‘ዳ

baseless

’ቤይስለስ -ት- መሠረተቢስ ፣ መሠረት የሌ ‘ለው

basement

’ቤይስመንት -ስ- ከምድር ቤት በታ’ች ያ‘ለ ክፍል

baseness

’ቤይስነስ -ስ- ወ‘ራ‘ዳነት

bashful

’ባሽፉል -ት- ተሽኮርማሚ ፣ አ‘ፋር

basic

’ቤይሲክ -ት- መሠረታዊ

basin

’ቤይሰን -ስ- ነድን‘ዳ ሳሕን ፣ ገበታ (ግቡ ኪያ) ፤ ገንዳ

basis

’ቤይሲስ -ስ- መሠረት

bask

’ባ:ስክ -ግ- መ‘ዘርር [ተዘ‘ረረ] (እፀሐይ ላይ)

basket

’ባ:ስኪት -ስ- ቅርጫት

bass

’ቤይስ -ት- ዝ‘ቅተ‘ኛ (ለድምፅ)፣ ዝ‘ቅተ‘ኛ የድ ምፅ ስልት

bastard

’ባ:ስተድ -ስ- ዲቃላ

colloquial

-ስ- የታ‘ባ’ከ

baste

’ቤይስት -ግ- ቅባት ማፍሰስ [አፈ‘ሰሰ] (በጥ ብስ ሥ’ጋ ላይ)

bat

’ባት -ስ- ገ’ና (ለጨዋታ)

animal

-ስ- የሌሊት ወፍ

batch

’ባች -ስ- ስብስብ ፣ ቁ‘ልል

bath

’ባ:ፅ -ግ- ሰው‘ነትን መ‘ታ‘ጠብ [ታ‘ጠብ]

-ስ- መ‘ታጠቢያ ክፍል ፣ ባ‘ኞ

bathe

’ቤይዝ -ግ- በውሃ ማጠብ [አ‘ጠበ] ፣ መዋ ’ኘት [ዋ‘ኘ]

bather

’ቤይዘ -ስ- ዋኝ ፣ ዋነተ‘ኛ

bathroom

’ባ:ፅሩም -ስ- የመ‘ታጠቢያ ክፍል ፣ መ‘ታጠ ቢያ ቤት

baton

’ባተን -ስ- አ‘ጭር በ‘ትር

battalion

በ’ታልየን -ስ- የሻለቃ ጦር

batter

’ባተ -ግ- መቆርቆር [ቆረ‘ቆረ] ፣ መምታት [መ‘ታ] (ለበ‘ር)

-ስ- የዕንቁላል‘ና የዱቄት ድብ‘ልቅ

battery

’ባተሪ -ስ- የኤሌክትሪክ ኃይል የተከማ‘ቸ‘በት ዕቃ ፣ የባትሪ ደንጊያ

battle

’ባተል -ስ- ጦር‘ነት ፣ ው‘ጊያ

bawl

’ቦ:ል -ግ- መጮ‘ኽ [ጮ‘ኸ] ፣ ማልቀስ [አለ‘ቀ ሰ] (በከ‘ፍተ‘ኛ ድምፅ)

bay

ቤይ -ግ- መጮ‘ኽ [ጮ‘ኸ] (ለእንስሳት)

geographical

-ስ- የባሕር ወሽመጥ

373

bayonet

’ቢየኔት -ስ- ሳንጃ

bazaar

በ’ዛ: -ስ- የገበያ ቦታ ፣ ሱቆ'ች የ'ሚ'ገ'ኙ'በት የከተማ ክፍል ፣ የብዙ ል'ዩ ል'ዩ ዕቃዎ'ች ር'ካሽ ሽ'ያጭ

be

’ቢይ -ግ- መሆን [ሆነ]

beach

’ቢይች -ስ- የባሕር ፣ የሐይቅ ዳር

beacon

’ቢይከን -ስ- በተራራ ጫፍ ላይ ያለ እሳት (ለምል'ክት)

bead

’ቢይድ -ስ- ዶቃ ፣ ግርዳ (አንዱ እንክብ'ል)፣ ጨ'ሌ

beak

’ቢይክ -ስ- የወፍ አፍ:

beaker

’ቢይክ -ስ- ት'ልቅ ብርጭ'ቆ (ካፉ ላይ ባንድ ወገን ወጣ ያለ ከንፈር ያ'ለው)

beam

’ቢይም -ስ- አግዳሚ ፣ ተሸካሚ ፣ ወፍራም አራት ማዕዘን'ነት ያ'ለው እንጨት

bean

’ቢይን -ስ- ባቄላ

bear

’ቤየ -ስ- ድ'ብ

carry

-ግ- መ'ሸከም [ተሸ'ከመ]

bearable

’ቤረበል -ት- የ'ማይ'ውክ ፣ ቀ'ላል

beard

’ቢየድ -ስ- ጢም

bearer

’ቤረ -ስ- ተሸካሚ ፣ ኩሊ ፣ ሽ'ቃይ ፣ ሐ'ማል

bearing

’ቤሪንግ -ስ- አቋቋም ፣ ጠባይ ፣ ተሸካሚ ብረት ፣ ኩፔኔ'ታ (የመኪና)

beast

’ቢይስት -ስ- አውሬ

beastly

’ቢይስትሊ -ት- ያውሬነት ጠባይ ያ'ለው ፣ አስቀ'ያሚ

beat

’ቢይት -ግ- መምታት [መ'ታ]

at sport

-ግ- ማ'ሸ'ነፍ [አ'ሸ'ነፈ]

beautiful

ብ'ዩቲፉል -ት- ቆንጆ ፣ ውብ ፣ ያማረ

beauty

ብ'ዩቲ -ስ- ቆንጆ'ና

because

ቢ'ኮዝ መሣ ፣ ተግ- ስለ ፣ በ ... ምክንያት

beckon

’ቤከን -ግ- መጥቀስ [ጠ'ቀሰ] (በእ'ጅ ፣ በራስ)

become

በ'ከም -ግ- መሆን [ሆነ]

becoming

በ'ከሚንግ -ት- ቆንጆ ፣ ውብ

bed

’ቤድ -ስ- አልጋ

bedding

’ቤዲንግ -ስ- ያልጋ ልብስ

bedeck

በ'ዴክ -ግ- ማስጌጥ [አስጌጠ]

bedroom

’ቤድሩም -ስ- መ'ኝታ ቤት

bee

’ቢይ -ስ- ንብ

beef

’ቢይፍ -ስ- የበሬ ፣ የላም ሥጋ

beehive

’ቢሐይቭ -ስ- የንብ ቀፎ

beer

’ቢየ -ስ- ጠ'ላ ፣ ቢራ

beeswax

’ቢይዝዋክስ -ስ- የማር ሰፈፍ

beetle

’ቢይተል -ስ- ጢንዚዛ

befall

በ'ፎል -ግ- መሆን [ሆነ] ፣ ሙድረስ [ደ'ረሰ] (ሁናቴ)

before

በፎ: -ተግ- በፊት ፣ አስተ'ድም

in time

-መዋ- ከ ... በፊት

374

befriend
በፍሬንድ -ግ- መ'ወዳጀት [ተወዳ'ጀ]

beg
'ቢግ -ግ- መለመን [ለ'መነ] ፣ መቢገት [ቢ'ገ
ተ]

beggar
'ቢገ -ስ- ለ'ማኝ ፣ ቢጋች

begin
ቢ'ጊን -ግ- መጀ'መር [ጀ'መረ]

beginner
ቢ'ጊነ -ስ- ጀ'ማሪ ፣ አላዋቂ

beginning
ቢ'ጊኒንግ -ስ- መጀ'መርያ

begrudge
ቢገ'ረጅ -ግ- መ'መቅኘት [ተመቀ'ኘ] ፣ መን
ቆጥቆጥ [ተንቆጠ'ቆጠ] (ለመስጠት)

beguile
ቢ'ጋይል -ግ- ማ'ታለል [አ'ታ'ለለ] ፣ ማ'ወ
ና'በድ [አ'ወና'በደ]

behalf
ቢ'ሃፍ -ስ- ፈንታ

behave
ቢ'ሄይቭ -ግ- ራስን መምራት [መ'ራ] ፣ ራስን
ከከፉ ሥራ ማራቅ [አራቀ]

behaviour
ቢ'ሄቭየ -ስ- ጠባይ

behead
ቢ'ሄድ -ግ- መሰ'የፍ [ሰየፈ] (የሰውን ራስ)

behind
በ'ሃይንድ -ተግ- ወደኋላ
-መዋ; ከ . . . ኋላ

behold
በ'ሀውልድ -ግ- መ'መልከት [ተመለ'ከተ]
exclamation
-ቃአ- እ'ነሆ

being
'ቢያንግ -ስ- ሕያው ፍጡ'ር

belch
'ቤልች -ግ- ማግሳት [አገ'ሳ] (ከመጥገብ የተ
ነ'ሣ)
-ስ- ግሳት

belief
በ'ሊይፍ -ስ- እምነት ፣ ሃይማኖት

believe
በ'ሊይቭ -ግ- ማመን [አ'መነ]

bell
'ቤል -ስ- ደወል ፣ ቃጭል

belligerent
በ'ሊጀረንት -ቅ- ጠብ'ኛ ፣ በጥባጭ

bellow
'ቤለው -ግ- እንደ በሬ ማግሳት [አገ'ሳ] ፣
በቁ'ጣ መጮኽ [ጮኸ]

bellows
'ቤለውዝ -ስ- ወናፍ

belly
'ቤሊ -ስ- ሆድ ፣ ከርስ

belong
በ'ሎንግ -ግ- መ'ገናዘብ [ተገና'ዘበ]

belongings
በ'ሎንጊንግዝ -ስ- ንብረት ፣ ዕቃ

beloved
በ'ለቭድ -ቅ- ው'ድ ፣ የተወ'ደደ

below
በ'ለው -ተግ- በታ'ች

belt
'ቤልት -ስ- ቀበ'ቶ ፣ መ'ታጠቂያ

bench
'ቤንች -ስ- ረ'ጅም ወምበር ፣ አናዳሚ. ወም
ብር

bend
'ቤንድ -ግ- መጉበጥ [ጎ'በጠ]
of road
-ስ- መ'ጠምዘዣ መንገድ ፣ ትክ'ክል
ያልሆነ ጎባጣ መንገድ

beneath
በ'ኒይ‌ዝ -ተግ- በታ'ች

benediction
ቤኔዲክሽን -ስ- ቡራኬ ፣ ጸሎተ ቡራኬ

benefactor
'ቤነፋክተ -ስ- ቸር ሰው ፣ መጽዋች (ገንዘብ
የ'ሚሰጥ) ፣ በ'ጎ አድራጊ

beneficial
ቤነ'ፊሸል -ቅ- ደ'ግ ፣ ጥሩ

benefit
'ቤነፊት -ግ- ማትረፍ [አተ'ረፈ] ፣ መ'ጠ
ቀም [ተጠ'ቀመ]
-ስ- ጥቅም

375

benevolent
በ'ኔቨለንት -ቅ- ለሌሎች በ'ጎ አድራጊ.

benign
በ'ናይን -ቅ- ርኅሩኅ ፣ ቸር

benzine
'ቤንዚን -ስ- ቤንዚን ፣ ነዳጅ

bequeathe
ቢ.ክ'ዊይዝ -ግ- ማውረስ [አወ'ረስ]

bequest
ቢ.ክ'ዌስት -ስ- ውርስ ዕቃ ፣ ገንዘብ

bereaved
በ'ሪቭድ -ቅ- ሐዘንተ'ኛ
-ስ- ሐዘንተ'ኛ

berry
'ቤሪ -ስ- እንጀ'ሪ

berth
'በ፡ስ -ስ- መ'ኝታ ቦታ (በመርከብ ላይ)

beseech
ቢ.'ሲይች -ግ- መለ'መን [ለ'መነ]፣ መ'ለማመጥ
[ተለማ'መጠ]

beside
በ'ሳይድ -መዋ- በ ... አጠገብ
-me
በኔ አጠገብ

besides
በ'ሳይድገ -ተግ- ደግሞ ፣ ከ'ዚህ በላይ

besiege
ቢ.'ሲይጅ -ግ- መክበብ (ለጦር'ነት)

best
'ቤስት -ቅ- የበ'ለጠ ፣ ተወዳዳሪ የሌ'ለው

bestial
'ቤስቲየል -ቅ- አረመኔ ፣ ጨ'ካኝ ፣ ሰብአዊ
ስ'ሜቱን የተገ'ፈፈ ፣ አራዊት መሰ'ል

bestow
በስ'ተው -ግ- መስጠት [ሰ'ጠ] (ከበላይ)

bet
'ቤት -ግ- መ'ወራረድ [ተወራ'ረደ]
-ስ- ውር'ርድ

betray
በት'ሬይ -ግ- መክዳት [ከ'ዳ] ፣ አሳ'ልፎ መስ
ጠት [ሰ'ጠ] (ለጠላት)

betrayal
በት'ሬየል -ስ- ክዳት ፣ አሳ'ልፎ መስጠት

betroth
በት'ረውዝ -ግ- ማጨት [አ'ጨ]

betrothal
በት'ረውዘል -ስ- ማጨት ፣ ቀለበት ማድረግ
(ለእጮኛ'ኛ)

better
'ቤተ -ቅ- የተሻለ

between
በት'ዊይን -መዋ- በ ... መካ'ከል

bevel
'ቤቨል -ስ- በሰ'ያፍ የተቆ'ረጠ ነገር

beverage
'ቤቨሪጅ -ስ- መጠ'ጥ (ሙ-ቅ)

bevy
'ቤቪ -ስ- ስብስባ (በተለ'ይ የሴቶ'ች)

bewail
ቢ.'ዌይል -ግ- ማልቀስ [አለ'ቀስ]፣ ወይ ማለት
[አለ]

beware
ቢ.'ዌየ -ግ- መ'ጠንቀቅ [ተጠነ'ቀቀ]

bewilder
ቢ.'ዊልደ -ግ- ማስጨ'ነቅ [አስጨ'ነቀ] ፣ ማ'
ደናገር [አ'ደናገረ]

bewitch
ቢ.'ዊች -ግ- በአስማት ማደንዘዝ [አደነ'ዘዘ]

beyond
ቢ.'ዮንድ -መዋ- በስተኋላ ፣ አልፎ

bias
'ባየስ -ስ- ማዘንበል ፣ ወዳንድ ወገን ማዘ
ላት ፣ ጠግማ ፍርድ ፣ አድልዎ

bib
'ቢብ -ስ- በሕፃናት አንገት ላይ የ'ሚ'ታ'ሰር
ፎጣ ወይን'ም መሐ'ረም

Bible
'ባይበል -ስ- መጽሐፍ ት'ዱስ

biblical
'ቢ.ብሊ.ከል -ቅ- የመጽሐፍ ት'ዱስ

bibliographical
ቢ.ብሊየግ'ራፊከል -ቅ- የመጻሕፍት ዝርዝር

bibliography
ቢ.ብሊ.'የግራፊ -ስ- የመጻሕፍት ዝርዝር

biceps
'ባይሴፕስ -ስ- ጡንቻ (የእ'ጅ)

376

bicker

'ቢከ -ግ- ላ'ረባ ነገር መጨ'ታጨት [ተጨ
ታ'ጨቀ]

bicycle

'ባይሲከል -ስ- ቢስኪሌት

bid

'ቢድ -ግ- ዋጋ መንገር [ነ'ገረ]

-ስ- መግዣ ዋጋ

bier

'ቢየ -ስ- ቃሪዛ

big

'ቢግ -ቅ- ት'ልቅ ፣ ታ'ላቅ

bigamy

'ቢገሚ -ስ- ሁለ'ት ሴት ማግባት ፣ በሚስት
ላይ ሁለ'ተ'ኛ ሴት የማግባት ወንጀል

bigoted

'ቢገተድ -ቅ- ዐዋቂ ነ'ኝ ባይ ፣ ጠ'ባብ አስተ
ያየት ያ'ለው ፤ ቸ'ኮ

bilateral

ባይ'ላተረል -ቅ- ከሁለ'ት ወገን ፣ ሁለ'ቱን
ወገን የ'ሚነካ

bile

'ባይል -ስ- ሐሞት ፤ ቁ'ጣ

bilingual

ባይ'ሊንግዌል -ቅ- ሁለ'ት ቋንቋዎ'ች አስተ
ካክሎ የ'ሚ'ና'ገር

bill

'ቢል -ስ- ደ'ረሰ'ኝ ፣ ሒሳብ

billet

'ቢለት -ስ- የወ'ታ'ደር ቤት፤የጦጨት ቁ'ራጭ

billion

'ቢልየን -ስ- ቢልዮን (ሚሊዮን ጊዜ ሚሊ
ዮን)

billow

ጋ'ቢለው -ስ- ማዕበል

billy-goat

'ቢሊ ገውት -ስ- ወንድ ፍ'የል

bin

'ቢን -ስ- የእንጀራ ፣ የጥራጥሬ ወዘተ ማስቀ
'መጫ በርሜል

bind

'ባይንድ -ግ- ማሰር [አ'ሰረ]

binder

'ባይንደ -ስ- ጠ'ራዥ ፣ ደ'ጋሽ ፤ የመ፣ነ'ረዝ
ዕቃ

binding

'ባይንዲንግ -ስ- ጥራዝ

biography

ባ'የግረፊ -ስ- የሕይወት ታሪክ

biology

ባ'ዮለጂ -ስ- ሕይወት ያ'ላቸው ፍጡሮ'ች
ጥናት ፤ ባዮሎጂ

birch

'በ፡ች -ስ- ል'ምጭ

bird

'በ፡ድ -ስ- ወፍ

birth

'በ፡ስ -ስ- ልደት

birthday

'በ፡ስዴይ -ስ- የልደት በዓል

birthmark

'በ፡ስማክ -ስ- ማርያም የሳመ'ቸው ምል'ክት
(በሰው'ነት ላይ)

birthplace

'በ፡ስፕሌይስ -ስ- የተወ'ለደ'በ'ት አገር

biscuit

'ቢስኪት -ስ- ብስኩት

bisect

'ባይ'ሴክት -ግ- ለሁለ'ት ትክ'ክል ክፍሎ'ች
መክፈል [ከ'ፈለ] (በመቁረጥ)

bishop

'ቢሸፕ -ስ- ጳ'ጳስ

bit

'ቢት -ስ- ቁ'ራሽ

horse's

-ስ- ልጓም

bitch

'ቢች -ስ- ሴት ው'ሻ

bite

'ባይት -ግ- መንከስ [ነ'ከስ]፣ መነደፍ [ነ'ደፈ]

biting

ባ'ይቲንግ -ቅ- ብርጻም ነፋስ

of comment

-ቅ- የ'ሚያሳ'ዝን ነቀፌታ

bitter

'ቢተ -ቅ- መራራ

377

black

ብ'ላክ -ቅ- ጥቁር

black-beetle

ብ'ላክቢ.ተል -ስ- ጥቁር ጢንዚ'ዛ

blackboard

ብ'ላክቦ:ድ -ስ- ጥቁር ሰሌዳ

blackmail

ብ'ላክሜይል -ግ- ገንዘብ ለመውሰድ ግስ ፈራራት [አስፈራ'ራ] (ስም አጠፋ'ለሁ፣ ምስ ጢር አወጣ'ለሁ በማለት)

blacksmith

ብ'ላክስሚ,ስ -ስ- ብረት ሠሪ ፤ ቀጥቃጭ ፤ ባለ'ጆ

bladder

ብ'ላደ -ስ- ፊ.'ኛ

blade

ብ'ሌይድ -ስ- ስለት ፤ ምላ'ጭ

blame

ብ'ሌይም -ግ- ጥፋተ'ኛ ማድረግ [አደ'ረገ] ፤ ማ'መካኘት [አመካ'ኘ]

blank

ብ'ላንክ -ቅ- ንጹህ ወይ.

blanket

ብ'ላንኬት -ስ- ብርድ ልብስ

blasphemy

ብ'ላስፈ.'ሚ -ስ- በእግዘ አብ ኤር ላይ መጥፎ መናገር ፤ አዝአብላሔርን መድፈር

blast

ብ'ላ:ስት -ስ- ኃይለ'ኛ ነፋስ ፣ የመፈንዳት ድምፅ

blatant

ብ'ሌይተንት -ቅ- ሐፍረት ቢስ

blaze

ብ'ሌይዝ -ግ- መንበልበል [ተንበለ በለ] (ለአ ላ ን)

bleach

ብ'ሊይች -ግ- ማንጣት (አነ'ጣ)
-ስ- ማንጫ ዱቄት

bleak

ብ'ሊይክ -ቅ- ገላጣ ፤ ባዶ ፤ ድርቅ (ለመሬት)

bleat

ብ'ሊይት -ግ- መጮኽ [ጮኽ] (ለበግና ለፍ 'የል)

bleed

ብ'ሊይድ -ግ- መድማት [ደ'ማ]

blemish

ብ'ሌሚሽ -ስ- መጥፎ ምል'ክት ፤ (መልክ የ'ሚያጠፋ)

blend

ብ'ሌንድ -ግ- ማ'ደባለቅ [አ'ደባ'ለቀ]

bless

ብ'ሌስ -ግ- መባረክ [ባ'ረክ]

blessed

ብ'ሌሰድ -ቅ- የተባ'ረከ ፣ ቡሩክ፣ የተቀ'ደሰ

blight

ብ'ላይት -ስ- የአትክልት በ'ሽታ (እንዲጠወ 'ልግ የ'ሚያደርግ)

blind

ብ'ላይንድ -ግ- ዓይን ማጥፍበበር [አጣበረ' በረ]
-ቅ- ዕ'ውር
-ስ- መ'ጋረጃ

blindfold

ብ'ላይንድፎልድ -ግ- የሰው ዓይን በጨርቅ መሸፈን [ሸ'ፈነ]

blink

ብ'ሊንክ -ግ- ዓይን ማርገብገብ [አርገበ'ገበ]

bliss

ብ'ሊስ -ስ- ታ'ላቅ ደስታ

blister

ብ'ሊስተ -ስ- ወያ የጿ'ጠረ ቁስል

blithe

ብ'ላይዝ -ቅ- ደ'ስ ያለው ፤ የተደ'ሰተ

blizzard

ብ'ሊዘድ -ስ- ኃይለ'ኛ ነፋስ (በረዶ የያዘ)

blob

ብ'ሎብ -ስ- ትንሽ ን'ጣቢ ፤ ትንሽ ጠብ'ታ

block

ብ'ሎክ -ግ- ማ'ገድ [አ'ገደ]
-ስ- የጫጨት ጉ'ማጅ ፤ የደንጊያ ፍን'ካች

blockade

ብሎ'ኬይድ -ግ- አንድ ቦታ መክበብ [ከ'በበ] (ጠላትን ጋንኙ'ነት ለማሳ'ጣት) ፣ ማ'ገድ [አ'ገደ] (ጋንኙ'ነት ለመከልከል)

blockhead

ብ'ሎክሄድ -ስ- ደ'ደብ ሰው

378

blonde

ብ'ሎንድ -ቅ- ወርቅ'ማ ጠጉር ያለው፣ያ'ላት

blood

ብ'ለድ -ስ- ደም

bloodthirsty

ብ'ለድሲስቲ -ቅ- ደም ለማፍሰስ የ'ሚቺ'ኩል፡ ጨ'ካኝ

bloom

ብ'ሉ:ም -ግ- ማ'በብ [አ'በበ]

blossom

ብ'ሎሶም -ግ- ማ'በብ [አ'በበ]
-ስ- አበባ

blot

ብ'ሎት -ስ- የቀለም እንነብ'ጣበ.

blotch

ብ'ሎች -ስ- በቆዳ ላይ ያ'ለ መጥፎ ምል'ክት

blouse

ብ'ላውዝ -ስ- ብሉዝ ፣ የሴቶ'ች ሸሚዝ

blow

ብ'ለው -ግ- መንፋት [ነ'ፋ]
-ስ- ጡ'ሚ

blubber

ብ'ለበ -ስ- የዓሣ አንበሪ ሥራ
-ቅ- ያ'በጠ (ለከንፈር)

bludgeon

ብ'ለጀን -ስ- ዱ'ላ (የበረት ፣ የንጨት)

blue

ብ'ሉ: -ቅ- ሰማያዊ

bluff

ብ'ለፍ -ግ- ማንንላል [አንን'ለለ] (የሰውን ሓሳብ)

blunder

ብ'ለንደ -ግ- ሥራ አልኮስተሮ መሥራት [ሠ'ራ]፣ ሥራ ማ'ጨማለቅ [አ'ጨማ'ለቀ]

blunt

ብ'ለንት -ቅ- ደነዝ ፣ ዱልዱም ፣ ደ'ፋር

blur

ብ'ለ: -ስ- ጨረፍታ ፣ ው'ልብታ

blurt

ብ'ለ:ት -ግ- ሳያ'ስቡ በድንንት ሙ'ናገር [ተና'ገረ]

blush

ብ'ለሽ -ግ- ከሃፍረት የተነ'ሣ ፊት መቅላት [ቀ'ላ]

bluster

ብ'ለስተ -ግ- መፎ'ከር [ፎ'ከረ]፡ ማዛት [ዛተ]፡ መደንፋት [ደን'ፋ]
-ስ- ድፍ…ታ ፣ የነፋስ ታወኻት

boar

'ቦ: -ስ- ወንድ ዐሣማ (ያልተኮላ'ሸ) ፣ ኮርማ ዐሣማ

board

'ቦ:ድ -ስ- ጠፍጣ'ፋ.የንጨት ቁ'ራጭ፣ ሣንታ
ship, train etc.
-ግ- መውጣት [ወ'ጣ]፣ መ'ሣፈር [ተሣ ፈረ]
- and lodging
-ስ- የመኝሪያ'ና የቁ'ለብ ዋ.ጋ
- card
-ስ- ወፍራም ካርቶን

boarder

'ቦ:ደ -ስ- እሰው ቤት ለምግቡ'ና ለመኝርያው እ'የከ'ፈለ የ'ሚኖር ፣ ቀ'ለብተ'ኛ

boarding-house

'ቦ:ዲንግ 'ሃውስ -ስ- በኪራይ የ'ሚ'ታ'ደር'በት ቤት

boarding-school

'ቦ:ዲንግ ስ'ኩ:ል -ስ- አዳሪ ተማሪ ቤት

boast

'በውስት -ግ- መፎ'ከር [ፎ'ከረ]፣ ጉ'ራ መን ዛት [ነ'ዛ]፣ መ'መካት [ተመ'ካ]

boat

'በውት -ስ- ጀልባ

bobbin

'ቦቢን -ስ- በከሪ ፣ ማጠንጠኛ እንጨት ፣ አነ ከር'ት

body

'ቦዲ -ስ- ሰው'ነት ፣ አካል

bodyguard

'ቦዲጋድ -ስ- የክብር ዘበኛ'፣የገ'ል ጠ'ባቂ፣ አሽከር

bog

'ቦግ -ስ- አርንቃ

bogus

'በውገስ -ቅ- ግ'ብዝ

boil

'ቦይል -ግ- መፈ'ቀል [ፈ'ቀለ]
-ስ- ብጉንጅ

379

bold
’ቦልድ -ቅ- ደ'ፋር ፣ ኅበዝ ፣ ጀግና
bolster
’ቦልስተ -ግ- መደ'ገፍ [ደ'ገፊ.] ፣ መርዳት
[ረ'ዳ]
pillow
-ስ- ትራስ
bolt
’ቦልት -ግ- መደንበር [ደነ'በረ]
food
-ግ- መጉስጉስ [ጉስ'ጉስ] (ምግብ)
lock
-ስ- መቀርቀሪያ ፣ መደንቀሪያ
bomb
’ቦም -ስ- ቦም'ብ ፣ ፈንጂ
bombastic
ቦም’ባስቲክ -ቅ- ትዕቢተ'ኛ ፣ የ'ሚ'ነ'ፋ. ፣
ጉ'ረ'ኛ
bombard
ቦም’ባ:ድ -ግ- ቦምብ መጣል [ጣለ] (ከእ'
የር) ፣ በቦምብ መደብደብ [ደብ'ደበ]
bomber
’ቦመ -ስ- ቦምብ ጣይ አውሮ'ፕላን
bond
’ቦንድ -ስ- ሕ'ጋዊ ስምም'ነት ፣ ስለወ'ሰዱት
ገንዘብ የ'ሚ'ሰጥ ፈርማ ያ'ለ'በት ደ'ረሰኝ
tying rope
-ስ- ማሠሪያ
bondage
’ቦንዲጅ -ስ- ባር'ነት ፣ ግዞት
bone
’ቦውን -ስ- ዐጥንት
bonfire
’ቦንፋየ -ስ- ደመራ ፣ የቁሻሻ ቃጠሎ
bonnet
’ቦነት -ስ- የሴት ባርኔጣ
bonus
’ቦውነስ -ስ- ጉርሻ (ገንዘብ)
book
’ቡክ -ስ- መጽሐፍ
-ግ- አስቀ'ድሞ በመክፈል ፣ በመንገር
ቦታ መያዝ [ያዘ] (በባቡር በአውሮ'ፕላን ፣
በቴያትር ወዘተ)

booking
’ቡኪንግ -ስ- አስቀ'ድሞ በመክፈል፣ በመንገር
ቦታ ቀድሞ መያዝ (በቴያትር ፣ በባቡር ወዘተ)
bookish
’ቡኪሽ -ቅ- መጽሐፍት በብዛት የ'ሚያ'ነብ ፣
መጽሐፍት በብዛት መጥቀስ የ'ሚ'ወ'ድ
book-keeper
’ቡክኪፐ -ስ- መዝገብ ያዥ (የገንዘብ)
booklet
’ቡክለት -ስ- ት'ንሽ መጽሐፍ
boom
’ቡ:ም -ግ- ድ'ም ማለት [አለ] (አንድ ነገር
ሲወድቅ)
-ስ- የኤኮኖሚ ደረጃ መዳበር ፣ ድ'ምታ
(ድምፅ) ፣ ረ'ጅም ግንድ
boon
ቡ:ን -ስ- በራኬ ፣ ማመስገኛ ነገር
-ቅ- የተደ'ሰተ ፣ ደ'ስተ'ኛ
-ስ- ውለታ
boot
ቡ:ት -ስ- ቦት ጫ'ማ
booth
ቡ:ፅ -ስ- ኪዮስክ
booty
’ቡ:ቲ -ስ- በጦር'ነት ላይ የተዘ'ረፈ ዕቃ ፣ ሰለ
ባ ፣ ማርጣ ፣ የምርኮ ንብረት
booze
’ቡ:ዝ -ግ- ብዙ መጠጣት [ጠ'ጣ] (አስካሪ
መጠ'ጠ'ች)
-ስ- መጠ'ጥ ፣ አልኮል
border
’ቦ:ደ -ስ- ወሰን
bore
’ቦ: -ግ- መፈልፈል [ፈለ'ፈለ] ፣ መብሳት
[በ'ሳ] ፣ መንገፍገፍ [ተንገፈ'ገፈ.] ፣ መሰል
ቸት [ሰለ'ቸ]
boredom
’ቦ:ደም -ስ- መንገፍገፍ ፣ መሰልቸት
boring
’ቦ:ሪንግ -ቅ- አሰልቺ ፣ አንገፍጋፊ
born
’ቦ:ን -ቅ- የተወ'ለደ
borough
’ቡረ -ስ- ሠፈር ፣ የከተማ ክፍል

380

borrow

'በረው -ግ- መ'በደር [ተበ'ደረ]

bosom

'ቡዘም -ስ- ደረት ፤ የጡት አ'ካባቢ.

boss

'ቦስ -ስ- አለቃ ፤ ሹም ፤ የጋ'ሻ ጉጥ

both

'በውስ -ቅ- ሁለ'ቱም

bother

'በዘ -ግ- ማስቸ'ገር [አስቸ'ገረ] ፣ ማስጨ'ነቅ [አስጨ'ነቀ] ፤ ማ'ወክ [አ'ወከ]

bottle

'ቦተል -ስ- ጠርሙዝ ፤ ጠርሙስ

bottom

'ቦተም -ስ- ሥር ፤ መ'ቀመጫ (ቂጥ) ፣ ዳ'ሌ
-ቅ- ታ'ች

bough

'ባው -ስ- ቅርንጫፍ (የዛፍ)

boulder

'ቦለደ -ስ- ታ'ላቅ ቋጥ'ኝ

bounce

'ባውንስ -ግ- ማንጠር [አነ'ጠረ] (ኳስ)

bound

'ባውንድ -ግ- እ'መር እ'መር ማለት [አለ] ፤ ማንጠር [አነ'ጠረ]
limit
-ስ- ወሰን
forced
-ቅ- የተገ'ደደ
on the way to
-ቅ- ጉዞ'ጀ (ለመሄድ)
tied up
-ቅ- የታ'ሠረ (በገመድ ፣ በሰንሰለት ወዘተ)

boundary

'ባውንደሪ -ስ- ወሰን(ፃገር)

bountiful

'ባውንቲፉል -ቅ- ለ'ጋስ ፤ ቸር

bounty

'ባውንቲ -ስ- ለ'ጋስነት ፤ ቸር'ነት

bout

'ባውት -ስ- የቦክስና የትግል ጨዋታ ውድ 'ድር ፤ የተወ'ሰነ ጊዜ (እንድ ሥራ የተፈ'ጸመ 'በት)

bow

'ባው -ግ- እ'ጅ መንሣት [ነ'ሣ]
of ship
-ስ- የመርከብ ፊት

bow

'በው -ስ- ባለውል እስር (ቀር.ጋሳ)
weapon
-ስ- ቀሥት

bowel

'ባውል -ስ- ደንዳኔ (እሥር የ'ሚ'ጠራ'ቀም 'በት የአንጀት ክፍል)

bowl

'በውል -ስ- ሰ'ፊ ሳሕን

box

'ቦክስ -ግ- በጡጫ መምታት [መ'ታ]
container
-ስ- ሣጥን ፤ ካርቶን

boxer

'ቦክስ -ስ- ቦክስ'ኛ

boxing

'ቦክሲንግ -ስ- የቦክስ ጨዋታ

boy

'ቦይ -ስ- ልጅ (ወንድ)

brace

ብ'ሬይስ -ግ- በንጨት ማጠንከር [አጠነ'ከረ] ማጥበቅ [አጠ'በቀ]
tool
-ስ- መስርሰሪያ (መ'ሣሪያ)

bracelet

ብ'ሬይስለት -ስ- አም'ባር

bracket

ብ'ራከት -ስ- ቅ'ንፍ ፤ ድጋፍ ፤ ማስደ'ገፊያ (የዕቃ መደርደሪያ ወዘተ)

brackish

ብ'ራኪ.ሽ -ቅ- ከ'ባድ (ለውሃ ጣዕም)

brag

ብ'ራግ -ግ- መፎ'ከር [ፎ'ከረ]

braid

ብ'ሬይድ -ስ- የወርቅ ፤ የብ'ር ጥልፍ

brain

ብ'ሬይን -ስ- አንጎል ፤ አእምሮ

381

brake
ብ'ሬይክ -ግ- ...ግታት [ገ'ታ] ፣ ፍሬን መያዝ
[ያዘ]
    -ስ- ፍሬን ፣ ሙ-ግቻ
branch
ብ'ራ:ንች -ስ- ቅርንጫፍ
brand
ብ'ራንድ -ግ- ምል'ክት ግድረግ [አደ'ረገ] (በ
ጋለ ብረት ፣ ለእንስሳት)
    animals
    -ስ- ምል'ክት (የእንስሳት)
    trade mark
    -ስ- ምል'ክት (የንግድ)
brandish
ብ'ራንዲሸ -ግ- መቃጣት [ቃ'ጣ] (ፉ'ላ)
brass
ብ'ራ:ስ -ስ- ነሐስ
brave
ብ'ሬይቭ -ቅ- ጎበዝ ፣ ጀግና
brawl
ብ'ሮ:ል -ግ- አም'ባጓሮ ማንሣት [አነ'ሣ]
bray
ብ'ሬይ -ስ- የአህ'ያ ጩኸት
braze
ብ'ሬይዝ -ግ- መበየድ [በ'የደ]
breach
ብ'ሪይች -ግ- መጣስ [ጣሰ] (ለሕ'ግ)
bread
ብ'ሬድ -ስ- ዳቦ
breadth
ብ'ሬድስ -ስ- ስፋት
break
ብ'ሬይክ -ግ- መስበር [ሰ'በረ]
    bad news
    -ግ- ማርዳት [አረ'ዳ]
    rest
    -ስ- ዕረፍት
breakdown
ብ'ሬይክዳውን -ግ- መ'ሰበር [ተሰ'በረ] ፣ መ
'ሰናከል [ተሰና'ከለ] (ለመኪና ወዘተ)
    mental
    -ስ- የአእምሮ ፣ የሰው'ነት ጤና ድንገ
ተ'ኛ መ'ናወጥ

breakfast
ብ'ሬክፈስት -ስ- ቁርስ
breast
ብ'ሬስት -ስ- ጡት
    bosom
    -ስ- ደረት
breath
ብ'ሬስ -ስ- ትንፋሽ ፣ እስትንፋስ
breathe
ብ'ሪይዝ -ግ- መተንፈስ [ተነ'ፈሰ]
breeches
ብ'ሪቺዝ -ስ- ጠ'ባብ ሱ'ሪ
breed
ብ'ሪይድ -ግ- መርባት [ረ'ባ] (ለእንስሳት)
breeder
ብ'ሪይደ -ስ- ከብት አርቢ
breeze
ብ'ሪይዝ -ስ- ነፋስ (ቀ'ላል) ፣ የነፋስ ሽ'ውታ
breezy
ብ'ሪይዚ -ቅ- ነፋሳም (ሳይበዛ ሽ'ው የ'ሚል)
brethren
ብ'ሬዝረን -ስ- ወን'ድ'ሞ'ች ፣ ወን'ድ'ማማ
ች'ች
brevity
ብ'ሬቪቲ -ስ- አ'ጭር'ነት (ለንግ'ግር)
brew
ብ'ሩ: -ግ- መጠመቅ [ጠ'መቀ] (መጠ'ጥ)
brewery
ብ'ሩወሪ -ስ- መጠመቂያ (ቦታ)
bribe
ብ'ራይብ -ግ- ጉ'በ መስጠት (ሰ'ጠ)
    -ስ- ጉ'በ
bribery
ብ'ራይበሪ -ስ- ጉ'በ መስጠት
brick
ብ'ሪክ -ስ- ጡብ ፣ ሽክላ
bridle
ብ'ራይድል -ስ- ልጓም
bridegroom
ብ'ራይድግሩም -ስ- ወንድ ሙሽ'ራ
bridesmaid
ብ'ራይድዝሜይድ -ስ- ሴት ሚዜ

382

bridge
ብ'ሪጅ -ጉ- ድልድይ መሥራት [ሠ'ራ]
-ስ- ድልድይ

brief
ብ'ሪይፍ -ቅ- አ'ጭር (ንግ'ግር)
legal
-ስ- መ'ረጃ ወረቀት (የክ'ስ)

briefcase
ብ'ሪይፍኬይስ -ስ- የ'ጅ ቦርሳ

brigade
ብሪ'ጌይድ -ስ- ቢሪጌድ

brigand
ብ'ሪገንድ -ስ- በመዝረፍ'ና ሰውን እያ'ፈነ
በመያዝ ገንዘብ የ'ሚያገኝ ወንበዴ

bright
ብ'ራይት -ቅ- ብሩህ ፣ ያልጨ'ለመ ፣ ፀሐያ'ማ

brilliant
ብ'ሪልየንት -ቅ- የ'ሚያበራ ፣ የ'ሚያንጸባ'ርቅ፣
ብልጕ

brim
ብ'ሪም -ስ- የዕቃ ፣ የስኒ አፍ

brine
ብ'ራይን -ስ- ጨው ያ'ለ'በት ውሃ ፣ የጨው
ው'ሃ

bring
ብ'ሪንግ -ጉ- ማምጣት [አመ'ጣ]

brink
ብ'ሪንክ -ስ- ዳር

brisk
ብ'ሪስክ -ቅ- ፈ'ጣን

bristle
ብ'ሪሰል -ጉ- መገንፈል (ገነ'ፈለ) (በቁ'ጣ)
-ስ- ያቀbefመ'ቀመ ጠጉር

British
ብ'ሪቲሽ -ቅ- ብሪጣንያዊ ፣ ብሪታንያዊ

brittle
ብ'ሪተል -ቅ- ተሰ'ባሪ ፣ በቀ'ላሉ የ'ሚ'ሰ'በር

broach
ብ'ረውች -ጉ- መክፈት [ከ'ፈተ] (ጠርሙዝ ፣
በርሜል) ፣ ወይ'ይት ፣ ንግ'ግር መጀ'መር [ጀ'
መረ]

broad
ብ'ሮ:ድ -ቅ- ሰ'ፊ

broadcast
ብ'ሮ:ድካ:ስት -ጉ- በራዲዮ መ'ናገር [ተና'ገረ]
-ቅ- የተበታ'ተነ ጥራጥሬ

broaden
ብ'ሮ:ደን -ጉ- ማስፋት [አስ'ፋ]

brocade
ብረ'ኬይድ -ስ- ጥልፍ (ልብስ)

broken
ብ'ረውከን -ቅ- የተሰ'በረ

broker
ብ'ረውከ -ስ- ደ'ላላ ፣ አ'ሻሻጭ
stock-
-ስ- የአክሲዮን አ'ሻሻጭ

bronze
ብ'ሮንዝ -ስ- ነሐስ

brooch
ብ'ረውች -ስ- የልብስ ፈርጥ (ጌጥ)

brood
ብ'ሩ:ድ -ጉ- መተ'ከዝ [ተ'ከዘ]
-ስ- ጫጩ'ቶች

brook
ብ'ሩክ -ስ- ጅረት

broom
ብ'ሩም -ሰ- መጥረጊያ (የቤት)

broth
ብ'ሮስ -ስ- ተ'ጥነ ሾርባ ፣ መረቅ

brothel
ብ'ሮ̱ል -ስ- የሴተ'ኛ አዳሪ ቤት (የሽር兀ጣ
ቤት)

brother
ብ'ረ̱ -ስ- ወን'ድ'ም

brotherhood
ብ'ረ̱ሁድ -ስ- ወን'ድ'ም'ነት ፣ ወን'ድ'ማማ
ች'ነት

brother-in-law
ብ'ረ̱ሪንሎ: -ስ- አማች ፣ የሚስት ወንድ'ም

brow
ብ'ራው -ስ- ገምባር

brown
ብ'ራውን -ቅ- ቡ'ና'ግ

bruise
ብ'ሩ:ዝ -ስ- ስም'በር (ከተመ'ቱ በኋላ እሰው'ነ
ት ላይ የ'ሚ'ታ'ይ ምል'ክት)

383

brush

ብ'ረሽ -ግ- መጥረግ [ጠ'ረገ] ፣ መቦ'ረሽ [ቦ'ረሽ]

-ስ- ብሩሽ

brutal

ብ'ሩ:ተል -ቅ- ጨ'ካኝ ፣ አረመኔ ፣ አውሬ (ለጠ ባይ)

brute

ብ'ሩ:ት -ስ- አውሬ ፣ ጨ'ካኝ ሰው

bubble

'በበል -ግ- መፍለቅለቅ [ተፍለቀ'ለቀ] (ለፍ ላት)

-ስ- የአረፋ ኳስ

buck

'በክ -ስ- ወንድ አጋዘን

bucket

'በኪት -ስ- ባልዲ ፣ ሽንክ'ሎ

buckle

'በከል -ስ- ዘለበት

bud

'በድ -ስ- እምቡጥ

budge

'በጅ -ግ- መንቀሳቀስ [ተንቀሳ'ቀሰ] ፣ ገለ'ል ማለት [አለ]

budget

'በጀት -ስ- ባጀት ፣ የመንግሥት ገቢ'ና ለ'የ መሥሪያ ቤቱ የሚ'ደለ'ደል የገንዘብ ድርሻ

buff

'በፍ -ግ- መወልወል [ወለ'ወለ] (ወርቅ ፣ ብረ ታብረት)

-ቅ- ነጣ ያለ ብጫ

buffalo

'በፈለው -ስ- ጎ'ሽ (እንስሳ)

buffer

'በረ -ስ- ክ'ብ በባቡር ፊት ያለ የግ'ጭት መ'ከላከያ ብረት ፣ ፓራውልት (የባቡር)

buffoon

በ'ፉ:ን -ስ- ቂል ፣ በሁናቴው የ'ሚያ'ሥቅ ሰው

bug

'በግ -ስ- ትን'ንሽ ነፍሳት (ትኋንተባይ ወዘተ)

bugbear

'በግቤየ -ስ- የ'ሚፈሩት ነገር

bugle

ብ'ዩ:ገል -ስ- ጥሩምባ (የወ'ታ'ደር)

bugler

ብ'ዩ:ግለ -ስ- ጥሩምባ ነፊ (ወ'ታ'ደር)

build

'ቢልድ -ግ- መገንባት [ገነ'ባ]

builder

'ቢልደ -ስ- ቤት ሠሪ ፣ ተጳራጭ (ቤት ለመ ሥራት)

building

'ቢልዲንግ -ስ- ግንብ ፣ ሕንጻ

bulb

'በልብ -ስ- አምፑል

plant

-ስ- ሥር (ያትክልት)

bulge

'በልጅ -ግ- መ'ወጠር [ተወ'ጠረ] ፣ መ'ነፋት [ተነ'ፋ]

-ስ- የተወ'ጠረ የተነ'ፋ ነገር

bulk

'በልክ -ስ- ክብደት

bull

'ቡል -ስ- በሬ

bullet

'ቡለት -ስ- ጥ'ይት

bullion

'ቡለየን -ስ- የወርቅ የብ'ር ነዶ

bullock

'ቡለክ -ስ- ወይፈን (የተኮላ'ሽ)

bully

'ቡሊ. -ስ- ደካማ አጥቂ ፣ በጥባጭ ጠብ'ኛ

bump

'በምፕ -ግ- በጎይል መውደቅ [ወ'ደቀ] ፣ ዱ'ብ ማለት [አለ]

-ስ- እበጥ

bumper

'በምፕ -ቅ- በጣም ት'ልቅ

of car

-ስ- የግ'ጭት መ'ከላከያ (የመኪና) ፣ ፓራውልት

bumptious

'በምሸስ -ቅ- ኩሩ

bun

'በን -ስ- ክ'ብ ኬክ

bunch

'በንች -ስ- እ'ቅፍ (በተለ'ይ የአበባ)

384

bundle
’በንደል -ስ- እሥር ፣ ሪብጣ

bung
’በንግ -ስ- ውታፍ ፣ መወ’ተፊያ

bungalow
’በንገለው -ስ- ጎ’ጆ

bungle
’በንገል -ግ- አደበስብሶ ሥራ ራት [ሠራ’]

bunk
’በንክ -ስ- የንጨት አልጋ (ነመርከብ ፣ በባ
ቡር ላይ)

bunting
’በንቲንግ -ስ- ል’ዩ ል’ዩ ቀነም ያለው ሰን
ደቅ ዓላማ የ’ሚ’ሠ’ራ’በት ብ’ጉን ጨርቅ ፣
ሰንደቅ ዓላማ ፣ ሰንደቶ ዓላማ’ች

buoy
’ቦይ -ስ- እደ፡ጋ ለ’ግልሥራሰ፡በተ በባሕር ላይ የ’ሚ
ንሳ’ፈፍ ነገር (የጎ’ን ጣጣተ መ፡ሃፉን የ’ሚያም
ለ’ከት)

buoyant
’ቦየንት -ቅ- ተንሳፋፊ
happy
 -ቅ- ደ’ስታ፡ም

burden
’በ፡ደን -ስ- ሸክም™
 -ግ- መጫን [·⋯]

burglar
’በ፡ግለ -ስ- ቤት ሰርሳሪ ፣ ሴሳ

burglary
’በ፡ግለሪ -ስ- ቤት ሰርሳሪ’ነት ፣ ሌብ’ነት ፣
ቤት ሥርሥሪ

burial
’ቤሪየል -ስ- ሥርዓተ ቀብር

burly
’በ፡ሊ -ቅ- ጎይለ’ኛ ፣ ደልዳ’ላ

burn
’በ፡ን -ግ- ማ’ቃጠል [አ’ቃ’ጠለ] ፣ መፍጀት
[ፈ’ጀ] (ለእሳት)

burnish
’በ፡ኒሽ -ግ- መወልወል [ወለ’ወለ] (ብረት)

burr
’በ፡ -ስ- ጫጎነት (ልብስ የ’ሚይዝ)

burrow
’በረው -ግ- ጉድጓድ መቆ’ፈር [ቆ’ፈረ]
 -ስ- ጉድጓድ (የጥንቸል መኖሪያ)

burst
’በ፡ስት -ግ- መፈንዳት [ፈነ’ዳ]
 -ስ- ድንገተ’ኛ ድምፅ (የጠመንጃ ወዘተ)

bury
’ቤሪ -ግ- መቅበር [ቀ’በረ]

bus
’በስ -ስ-ˆ አውቶቡስ

bush
’ቡሽ -ስ- ቁጥቋጦ

bushel
’ቡሸል -ስ- የእህል መሥፈሪያ

bushy
’ቡሺ. -ቅ- ች’ፍ’ግ ያለ

business
’ቢዝነስ -ስ- ንግድ ፣ ሞያ ፣ ድር’ጅት

businesslike
’ቢዝነስላይክ -ቅ- የተሟ’ላ ፣ ሥርዓት ተከ
’ታይ ፣ ብቁ

bustle
’በሰል -ግ- መ’ቻኮል [ተቻኮ’ለ]
 -ስ- ዋካታ

busy
’ቢዚ. -ቅ- ሥራተ’ኛ ፣ ባለ ብዙ ሥራ ፣ ሥራ
ያልፈ’ታ ፣ ባተሌ

but
’በት -መዋ- ግን ፣ ነገር ግን

butcher
’ቡቸ -ስ- ከብት አራጅ ፣ ሥካን’ዳ ነ’ጋዴ

butler
’በትለ -ስ- የልፍ’ኝ አሽከር

butt
’በት -ስ- የወሃ በርሜል
of gun
 -ስ- ሰደፍ (ጠመንጃ)
of goat
 -ግ- መውጋት [ወ’ጋ] (ለቀንድ ከብት)

butter
’በተ -ስ- ቅቤ

butterfly
’በተፍላይ -ስ- ቢ’ራቢ’ሮ

385

buttock
'በተክ -ስ- መ'ቀመጫ (ቂጥ) ፡ ዳ'ሴ

button
'በተን -ስ- ቁልፍ (የልብስ)

buttonhole
'በተንሆውል -ስ- የቁልፍ (መግቢያ) ቀዳዳ
-ግ- መነዝነዝ [ነዘ'ነዘ] ፡ ማሰልቸት
[አሰለ'ቸ]

buttress
'በትረስ -ግ- መደ'ገፍ [ደ'ገፈ]
-ስ- ድጋፍ (ለቤት)

buy
'ባይ -ግ- መግዛት [ገ'ዛ]

buzz
'በዝ -ግ- ጥ'ዝ ማለት [አለ] (ለንብ)

by
'ባይ -መቀ- በ . . .
near-
በ . . . አጠገብ
-*car*
በመኪና

bygone
'ባይጎን -ቅ- ያ'ለፈ

bystander
'ባይስታንደ -ስ- ተመልካች ፡ ታ'ዛቢ

byway
'ባይዌይ -ስ- ጠ'ባብ መንገድ

cab
'ካብ -ስ- ታክሲ

cabbage
'ካቢጅ -ስ- ጎ'መን

cabin
'ካቢን -ስ- ጉ-ጆ
of ship etc.
የተሳፋሪዎ'ች መ'ቀመጫ (በአ
ውር'ፕላን ፡ በመርከብ ወዘተ)

cabinet
'ካቢኔት -ስ- የሚኒስቴሮ'ች ምክር ቤት
furniture
-ስ- ት'ንሽ ቁም ሣጥን ፡ (የጌጣጌጥ፡ የስ
ኒና የሳሕን ወዘተ ማስቀ'መጫ)

cable
'ኬይበል -ስ- የብረት ገመድ
telegram
-ስ- ቴሌግራም

cackle
'ካከል -ግ- መንጫጫት [ተንጫ'ጫ] (ለዶ
ሮ'ት)

cadet
ከ'ዴት -ስ- እፈሪ መኮ-'ንን

cadge
'ካጅ -ግ- መለ'መን [ለ'መነ] (ገንዘብ)

cafe
'ካፌ -ስ- ቡ'ና ቤት

cafeteria
ካፈ'ቴሪየ -ስ- ተመ'ጋቢዎ'ች ራሳ'ቸው ምግ
ባ'ቸውን የ'ሚያነሡ'በት የምግብ ቤት

cage
'ኬይጅ -ስ- የወፍ ፡ ያንበሳ ወዘተ ቤት (ከብ
ረት ወይን'ም ከሽቦ የተሠ'ራ)

cajole
ከ'ጆውል -ግ- ማባበል [አባ'በለ]

cake
'ኬይክ -ስ- ኬክ ፡ ዳ'ቦ

calamity
ከ'ላሚቲ -ስ- መቅሠፍት ፡ ጥፋት ፡ መከራ

calculate
'ካልክዩሌይት -ግ- ማ'ሰብ [አ'ሰበ] ፡ መቁ
'ጠር [ቆ'ጠረ]

calculation
ካልክዩ'ሌይሸን -ስ- ሒሳብ

calendar
'ካለንደ -ስ- ቀን መቀጠሪያ

calf
'ካ:ፍ -ስ- ጥ'ጃ

call
'ኮ:ል -ግ- መጥራት [ጠ'ራ] (ሰው እንዲመጣ
ግያ፡ረግ)

caller
'ኮ:ለ -ስ- ጐብኝ ፣ ጠ'ያቂ

calling
'ኮ:ሊንግ -ስ- ሞያ

callous
'ካለስ -ስ- የደ'ረቀ ቆዳ
-ት- ጨ'ካኝ ፣ ርኅራኄ የሌ'ለው

callow
'ካለው -ት- ያልሠለ'ጠነ ፣ ልምድ የሌ'ለው

calm
'ካ:ም -ት- ዝ'ምተ'ኛ ፣ ጸ'ጥተ'ኛ

calumny
'ካለምኒ -ስ- የውሸት ሐሜት ፣ የውሸት ክ'ስ

camel
'ካመል -ስ- ግመል

camera
'ካምረ -ስ- ፎቶግራፍ ማንሻ

camouflage
'ካመፍላ:ጅ -ስ- ግ'ሳሳቾ (የጠላትን ወ'ታ'ደ
ሮ'ች) ፣ ማስመ'ሰያ

camp
'ካምፕ -ስ- ሠፈር

campaign
ካም'ፔይን -ግ- መ'ዋጋት [ተ'ዋጋ] ፤ መ'ወ
ጻ'ደር] (ለምርጫ)
-ስ- የተደጋ'ገመ ው'ጊያ ፤ ውድ'ድር
(ለምርጫ)

camp-bed
'ካምፕ'ቤድ -ስ- የመንገድ አልጋ

camping
'ካምፒንግ -ስ- በአንድ ቦታ ላይ መሠፈር

campus
'ካምፐስ -ስ- የዩኒቨርስቲ ግ'ቢ

can
'ካን -ስ- ቆርቆ'ር
-ግ- መቻል [ቻለ]

canal
ከ'ናል -ስ- ቦይ ፣ መስኖ

cancel
'ካንሰል -ግ- መፋት [ፋተ] ፣ ግጥፋት [አጠ
'ፋ]

cancer
'ካንሰ -ስ- ነቀርሳ

candid
'ካንዲድ -ት- ግልጥ ፣ እውነተ'ኛ (ለሰው)

candidate
'ካንዲዴይት -ስ- እጩ

candied
'ካንዲድ -ት- በሱ'ካር የተሸ'ፈነ

candle
'ካንደል -ስ- ሻማ

candlestick
'ካንደልስቲክ -ስ- መቅረዝ

candour
'ካንደ -ስ- ግልጥ'ነት ፣ እውነተ'ኛ'ነት

candy
'ካንዲ -ስ- ከረሜ'ላ

cane
'ኬይን -ስ- አገዳ
walking stick
-ስ- በ'ትር ፣ ምርኩዝ

canine
'ኬይናይን -ት- የው'ሻ ዘር ፣ ው'ሻ የ'ሚመ
ስል
tooth
-ስ- የው'ሻ ክራንቻ ፣ ተንጣ'ጤ

canker
'ካንከ -ስ- አጣቆ (የተክል በ'ሽታ)

canned
'ካንድ -ት- የታ'ሸገ (ቆቆ'ር)

cannibal
'ካኒበል -ስ- ጥራት

cannon
'ካነን -ስ- መድፍ

cannon-ball
'ካነን'ቦ:ል -ስ- የመድፍ ጥ'ይት

canoe
ከ'ኑ: -ስ- ታንኳ

canon
'ካነን -ስ- የቤተ ክርስቲያን ሕ'ግ ፣ ሥርዓተ
ቤተ ክርስቲያን

canopy

'ካነፒ -ስ- ዳስ ፣ ከለላ ፣ አጎበር

canteen

ካን'ቲይን -ስ- የምግብ አ'ዳራሽ (በፋብሪካ ፣
በዩኒቨርስቲ ወዘተ)

canter

'ካንተ -ግ- ደንገላሳ መምታት [ሡ'ታ]
-ስ- ደንገላስ

canvas

'ካንቫስ -ስ- ሸራ

cap

'ካፕ -ስ- ቆብ

capable

'ኬይተብል -ቅ- ሬ ፖቂ ፣ የ'ሚችል

capacious

ከ'ፔይሸስ -ቅ- ሰ'ፊ ፣ ብዙ ቦታ ያ'ለው

capacity

ከ'ፓሲቲ -ስ- አንድ ነገር የ'ሚይዘው መጠን
ability
-ስ- ችሎታ

cape

'ኬይፕ -ስ- ካ'ባ
geographical
-ስ- ርእስ ምድር

caper

'ኬይፐ -ስ- ሚጥሚጣ
trick
-ስ- ግ'ታለያ
-ስ- የሕፃናት ጠባይ በጨዋታ (ዋዛ ፣
ረሣሣ) ፣ መዝለል

capital

'ካፒተል -ቅ- በሞት ፍርድ የ'ሚ'ቀ'ጣ የወን
ጃል)
city
-ስ- ዋ'ና ከተማ ፣ መዲና
money
-ስ- ተቀ'ማጭ ገንዘብ ፣ መ'ነሻ ገንዘብ
(የሥራ ፣ የንግድ ወዘተ)
very good
-ቅ- በጣም ጥሩ ፣ ድንቅ

capitulate

ከ'ፒትዮሌይት -ግ- ድል በመ'ነሣት ምክን
ያት ለባላድሩ አገር አ'ገዛዙን ማስረ'ከብ [አስ
ረ'ከበ]

caprice

ከፕ'ሪይስ -ስ- አምሮት (ጥቃ'ቅን'ና የ'ግይ
ረባ ፣ ም'ሳሌ ፣ የርጉዝ ሴት)

capricious

ከፕ'ሪሸስ -ቅ- ስለጥቃ'ቅን ነገር ላጥብቆ አ
'ሳቢ

capsize

ካፕ'ሳይዝ -ግ- መ'ገልበጥ [ተገለ'በጠ] (ለመ
ርከብ ፣ ለጀልባ)

capsule

'ካፕሱል -ስ- ደረቅ እምቡጥ ፤ የመድኃኒት
ሙልሙል ቢልቃጥ

captain

'ካፕቴን -ስ- ሻምበል

caption

'ካፕሽን -ስ- ከሥዕል በግርጌ የ'ሚ'ጻፍ መግ
ለጫ ፣ ከሥዕል በታ'ች የተመለ'ከተ ጽሑፍ
(በጋዜጣ ወዘተ)

captive

'ካፕቲቭ -ስ- ምርኮ'ኛ

captivity

ካፕ'ቲቪቲ -ስ- ምርኮ

capture

'ካፕቸ -ግ- መማረክ [ማ'ረከ] ፣ መያዝ [ያዘ]

car

'ካ: -ስ- መኪና ፣ አውቶሞቢል

carbon

'ካ:በን -ስ- ጥላት ፣ ጥላሽት ፣ ከሰል (የጢጫት)

carbon-paper

'ካ:በን 'ፔይፐ -ስ- የካርቦን ወረቀት

carbuncle

'ካ:በንከል -ስ- እበጥ (ት'ልቅ) ፤ ቀ'ይ የ'ሚ
ያብረቀ'ርቅ ዕንቁ

carcass

'ካ:ከስ -ስ- ጥምብ (በድን ፣ የእንሰሳ)

card

'ካ:ድ -ስ- ካርድ ፣ ወረቀት

cardboard

'ካ:ድቦ:ድ -ስ- ካርቶን

cardigan

'ካ:ዲገን -ስ- የሱፍ ኮት (ጨርቁ በእ'ጅ የተ
ሠ'ራ)

388

care

ኬየ -ግ- መ'ጠንቀቅ [ተጠነ'ቀቀ]
-ስ- ጥን'ቃቄ

career

ከ'ሪየ -ስ- ሥራ (የሕይወት ሙሉ)

careful

ኬፉል -ቅ- ጥንቁቅ

careless

ኬሌስ -ቅ- የ'ማይ'ጠነ'ቀቅ ፤ ንዝህላል ፤ ዝር
ክርክ (በሥራው)

caress

ከ'ሬስ -ግ- መዳሰስ [ዳ'ሰሰ] ፤ መዳበስ [ዳ'በሰ]
ማሻሸት [አሻ'ሸ] (በፍቅር)

caretaker

ኬቴይከ -ስ- ቤት ጠ'ባቂ (ባለቤቱ በሌ'ለ
በት ጊዜ) ፤ ያንድ ሕንፃ ጓላሬ ፤ ጊዜያዊ አስተ
ዳዳሪ (ለመንግሥት)

cargo

'ካ፡ገው -ስ- ጭነት (የአውሮ'ፕላን ፤ የመርከብ)

carnal

'ካ፡ነል -ቅ- ሥጋዊ (መንፈሳዊ'ነት የሌ'ለው)

carnivorous

ካ፡'ኒቨረስ -ቅ- ሥጋ ተመ'ጋቢ ፤ ሥጋ በ'ል

carol

'ካረል -ስ- የልደት መዝሙር (የክርስቶስ) ፤
የገ'ና መዝሙር

carpenter

'ካ፡ፐንተ -ስ- አናጺ

carpentry

'ካ፡ፐንትሪ -ስ- አናጺ'ነት

carpet

'ካ፡ፐት -ስ- ምንጣፍ ፤ ስጋ'ጃ

carriage

'ካሪጅ -ስ- ሰረገ'ላ

carrier

'ካሪየ -ስ- ተሸ'ካሚ ፤ ኩሊ ፤ ዕቃ በመኪና
አ'ጓጓዥ

carrot

'ካረት -ስ- ካሮት

carry

'ካሪ -ግ- መ'ሸከም [ተሸ'ከመ]

cart

'ካ፡ት -ስ- ጋሪ

cart-horse

'ካ፡ት'ሆ፡ስ -ስ- ጋሪ ጎ'ታች ፈረስ

carton

'ካ፡ተን -ስ- የካርቶን ሣጥን

cartoon

ካ፡'ቱ፡ን -ስ- የ'ሚያ'ሥቅ የጋዜጣ ሥዕል

cartridge

'ካ፡ትሪጅ -ሬ- ተኩሀ

carve

'ካ፡ቭ -ግ- መቅረብ [ቀ'ረፀ] (ደንጊያ ፤ እን
ጨት ፤ እብነ በረድ ወዘተ)
meat
-ግ- መቁረጥ [ቆ'ረጠ] (ለሥጋ)

cascade

ካስ'ኬይድ -ስ- የውሃ ፏፏቴ

case

ኬይስ -ስ- ሻንጣ
legal
-ስ- ክ'ስ
example
-ስ- ም'ሳሌ

cash

'ካሽ -ስ- ጥሬ ገንዘብ

cashier

ካ'ሺየ -ስ- ገንዘብ ተቀ'ባይ ፤ ከፋይ ፤ መንዛሪ

cask

'ካ፡ስክ -ስ- የንጨት በርሚል

cast

'ካ፡ስት -ግ- [መጣልጣል] ፤ መወርወር [ወረ
'ወረ] ፤ ሊቴያትር ሠ'ራተ'ኞች የ'ሚሠሩትን
ድርሻ ማ'ደል [አ'ደለ]
plaster
-ስ- ጀፕስ
theatrical
-ስ- ቴያትር ተ-ዛዎች ፤ ተዋናዪያን
-ግ- ፈሳሽ ማዕ'ድን ቅርፅ እን'ዲይዝ
በ፡ድንጋ ውስ-ት ማፍሰስ [አፈ'ሰስ]

castigate

'ካስቲጌይት -ግ- መቅጣት [ቀ'ጣ] (በመ
ታት)

casting
'ካ:ስቲንግ/ -ስ- መጣል
theatrical
        -ስ- በፊልም ፣ በቲያትር የሚሠሩ
ሰዎች ምድባ
castle
'ካ:ሰል -ስ- ግንብ ፣ ምሽግ
castor
'ካ:ስተ -ስ- ተሽከርካሪ (ለወንበር ፣ ለቁም
ሣጥን ወዘተ)
casual
'ካዥዩወል -ቅ- ድንንተኛ ፣ ሳይጠባ በቁት
የሆነ ፣ እንደፈቃደው ይሁን የሚል ፣ የማይ
ጠነቀቅ ፣ ደንታ ቢስ
casualty
'ካዝዩወልቲ -ስ- በከባድ አደጋ የተነጻ ሰው ፣
በጦርነት የቆሰሉ ፣ የሞቱ ወታደሮች
cat
'ካት -ስ- ድመት
catalogue
'ካተሎግ -ስ- በቤተ መጻሕፍት ያሉ የመጻ
ሕፍት ዝርዝር ፣ ለሽያጭ የቀረበ የዕቃ ዝር
ዝር ፣ እሱቅ ውስጥ የዕቃውን ዓይነት የሚገ
ልጽ ዝርዝር ጽሑፍ
cataract
'ካተራክት -ስ- የውሃ ፏፏቴ
disease
        -ስ- ዓይንን የሚያለብስ በሽታ ፣ ዓይነ
ሞራ
catarrh
ከ'ታ፥ -ስ- አ'ክታ'ና ንፍጥ በብዛት እንዲወጣ
የሚያደርግ በሽታ ፣ ጉንፋን
catastrophe
ከ'ታስትረፊ -ስ- መቅሠፍት ፣ ድንንተኛ አ
ደጋ
catch
'ካች -ግ- መያዝ [ያዘ] ፣ መቅለብ [ቀለበ]
catching
'ካቺንግ -ቅ- ተላላፊ (ለበሽታ)
catechism
'ካተኪዝም -ስ- ምስጢረ ሥላሴ ፣ ትምህርተ
ክርስቲያን (በመጠመቅ በፊት የሚማሩት)
categorical
ካተጎሪከል -ቅ- እርግጠኛ ፣ ፍጹም (የማ
ያሻሚ'ጥር)

category
'ካተጎሪ -ስ- መደብ ፣ የወል መታወቂያ
(ለብዙ ነገሮች)
cater
'ኬተተ -ግ- ምግብ ማዘጋጀት [አ'ዘጋጀ]
caterpillar
'ካተርፒለ -ስ- አ'ባ ጨጓሬ ፣ የነፍን ትል
catgut
'ካትገት -ስ- የደ'ረቀ አንጀት ፣ ጅማት
cathedral
ከ'ቴድረል -ስ- ት'ልቅ ደብር (ጳጳስ የሚቀ
መጥ'በት)
cattle
'ካተል -ስ- ከብት
cauliflower
'ኮሊፍላወ -ስ- አበባ ጎመን
cause
'ኮዝ -ግ- እንዲሆን ማድረግ [አደ'ረገ]
reason
        -ስ- ምክንያት
cauterize
'ኮተራይዝ -ግ- መተኮስ [ተኮሰ] (ለሰው'ነ
ት በጋለ መሣሪያ)
cautious
'ኮሽስ -ቅ- ጥንቁቅ ፣ ሥጉ
cavalry
'ካቨልሪ -ስ- ፈረሰኛ ወታደር
cave
'ኬደቭ -ስ- ዋሻ
cavity
'ካቪቲ -ስ- ጎድጓዳ ነገር ፣ ጉድጓድ ፣ ሥር
ሥር
cease
'ሲደስ -ግ- ማቆም [አቆመ] (ሥራን ፣ ንግግ
ርን ወዘተ)
cedar
'ሲደ -ስ- አርዘ ሊባኖስ (የዛፍ ዓይነት)
cede
'ሲይድ -ግ- መልቀቅ [ለ'ቀቀ] (ለምብት) ፡
ማመን [አ'መነ] ፣ መቀበል [ተቀ'በለ] (አስተ
ያየት)
ceiling
'ሲይሊንግ -ስ- ጣሪያ (የውስጡ ክፍል)

celebrate

’ሴለብራይት -ግ- በዓል ማክበር [አከ'በረ]

celebration

ሴለብ’ሬይሽን -ስ- ክብረ በዓል

celebrity

ሴ’ሌብሪቲ -ስ- ባለዝና'ና የታ'ወቀ ፤ የተከ'በረ

celestial

ሰ’ሌስቲየል -ቅ- ሰማያዊ ፣ የሰማይ

celibacy

’ሴለበሲ -ስ- ምንኩስ'ና ፣ ንጽሕ'ና (ለወን'ድ ብ'ቻ)

celibate

’ሴለበት -ቅ- የመነ'ኮሰ ፣ በንጽሕ'ና የ'ሚ ኖር

cell

’ሴል -ስ- ት'ንሽ ክፍል (የእስረ'ኛ ፣ የመነ ኮሳ)

battery

-ስ- የባትሪ ደንጊያ

cellar

ሴለ -ስ- የዕቃ ቤት (ከወለል በታ'ች የ'ሚ'ገ'ኝ)

cement

ሰ’ሜንት -ስ- ሲሚንቶ

cemetery

’ሴመትሪ -ስ- መቃብር (ቦታ)

censor

’ሴንሰ -ግ- መ'ቆጣጠር [ተቆጣ'ጠረ]

person

-ስ- ተቆጣጣሪ ፣ ሳንሱር

censorship

’ሴንሰሺፕ -ስ- ተቆጣጣሪ'ነት

censure

’ሴንሸ -ግ- መ'ታወፅ [ተቃ'ወመ]

-ስ- እለመስማማት

census

’ሴንሰስ -ስ- የሕዝብ ቆጠራ

cent

’ሴንት -ስ- ሳንቲም (የብ'ር አንድ መቶ'ኛ)

centenarian

ሴንተ’ኔሪየን -ስ- መቶ ዓመት ዕድሜ ያ'ለው

centenary

ሴን’ቲነሪ -ስ- የመቶ'ኛ ዓመት በዓል

centimetre

’ሴንቲሜተ -ስ- ሳንቲሜትር

centipede

’ሴንቲፒይድ -ስ- አምሳ እግር (የትል ዓይነት)

central

’ሴንትረል -ቅ- ማዕከላዊ ፣ ጠቅላይ

centralize

’ሴንትረላይዝ -ግ- ማማከል [አማ'ከለ] ፣ ግ እኩላዊ ማድረግ [አደ'ረገ] ፤ መጠቅለል [ጠቀ' ለለ]

centre

’ሴንተ -ስ- መካ'ከል ፣ መሀል

century

’ሴንቸሪ -ስ- አንድ መቶ ዓመት

ceramic

’ሴራሚክ -ቅ- የሸክላ ሥራ

cereal

’ሲሪየል -ስ- እህል (ስንዴ ፣ ጤፍ ፣ ገብስ መሀተ)

ceremonial

ሴረ’ሞኒየል -ቅ- የክብረ በዓል ፣ በዓላዊ ፣ ሥነ ሥርዓታዊ

-ስ- በዓል

ceremony

’ሴረመኔ -ስ- በዓላዊ ሥነ ሥርዓት

certain

’ሰ፡ተን -ቅ- እርግጥ

certainly

’ሰ፡ተንሊ -ተግ- በርግጥ

certainty

’ሰ፡ተንቲ -ስ- እርግጠ'ኛነት ፣ እርግጠ'ኛነት

certificate

ሰ’ቲፊከት -ስ- የምስ'ክር ወረቀት

certify

’ሰ፡ቲፋይ -ግ- መመስከር [መሰ'ከረ] ፣ ግ'ረጋ ገጥ [አ'ረጋ'ገጠ]

cesspool

’ሴስፑ፡ል -ስ- የሰገራ መ'ጠራቀሚያ ጉድጓድ

chafe

’ቼይፍ -ግ- እ'ጅ ማ'ፋተግ [አ'ፋ'ተገ] (መቶት ለማግኘት)

be impatient

-ስ- አለመ'ታገሥ ፣ ትዕግሥት ማጣት

chaff

’ቻፍ -ስ- እ'ብቅ ፣ ት'ቢያ

391

chagrin
'ቻግሪን -ስ- ማዘን ፣ ደ'ስ አለመ'ሰኘት

chain
'ቼይን -ስ- ሰንሰለት

chair
'ቼ: -ስ- ወንበር

chairman
'ቼ:መን -ስ- አፈ ጉባኤ ፣ ሊቀ መንበር

chalice
'ቻሊስ -ስ- ጽ'ዋ (የሥ'ጋ ወደሙ)

chalk
'ቾ:ክ -ስ- ጠመኔ ፣ (ቾክ) አስተማሪ በጥቁር
ሰሌዳ ላይ የ'ሚጽፍ'በት

challenge
'ቻለንጅ -ግ- መ'ጿጿም [ተጿጿመ] ፣ መ'ወዳ
ደር [ተወዳ'ደረ]
-ስ- መ'ጿጿም ፣ ውድ'ድር

chamber
'ቼይምበ -ስ- አ'ዳራሽ ፣ ምክር ቤት

chambermaid
'ቼይምበሜይድ -ስ- ሴት አገልጋይ (አል.ጋ
አንጣፊ ወዘተ)

champion
'ቻምፒየን -ስ- አ'ሸ'ናፊ (ነ ኀ'ድር)

chance
'ቻ:ንስ -ስ- ዕ'ድል

change
'ቼይንጅ -ግ- መለ'ወጥ [ለ'ወጠ]
money
-ስ- ለውጥ ፣ ምን'ዛሪ

channel
'ቻነል -ስ- ቦይ ፣ ጠ'ባብ የባሕር መ'ተላለ
ፊያ ፣ ወሃ መ'ተላለፊያ ፈረፈር

chant
'ቻ:ንት -ግ- ማሕሌት መቆም [ቆመ]

chaos
'ኬዮስ -ስ- ብጥ'ብጥ ፣ ሕ'ገ ወ'ጥነት

chapel
'ቻፐል -ስ- የጸሎት ቤት ፣ ት'ንሽ ቤተ ክርስ
ስቲያን

chaperon
'ሻፐረውን -ስ- የደ'ረስ'ች ልጅ ጠ'ባቂ ሴት
(ምግዚት)

chapter
'ቻፕተ -ስ- ምዕራፍ (የመጽሐፍ)

char
'ቻ: -ስ- ቤት ጠራጊ ሴት

character
'ካረክተ -ስ- ጠባይ ፣ መ'ለያ
letter
-ስ- ፊደል

charcoal
'ቻ:ከውል -ስ- ከሰል (የንጨት)

charge
'ቻ:ጅ -ግ- መ'ክሰስ [ከ'ሰሰ]
fee
-ስ- ክ'ስ
battle
-ስ- ጉጥሚያ ፣ መግጠም (ለጦር'ነት)
fire-arm
-ግ- ማጉረስ [አን'ረስ] (መ'ሣርያ)
money
-ግ- ማስከ'ፈል [አስከ'ፈለ]
fill
-ግ- የ'ሚችለውን ያህል መሙላት
[ሞ'ላ]

charitable
'ቻሪተብል -ቅ- ቸር ፣ ለ'ጋስ

charity
'ቻሪቲ -ስ- በ'ን አድራጎት

charm
'ቻ:ም -ስ- ውበት ፣ የደስ ደ'ስ

charming
'ቻ:ሚንግ -ቅ- አስደ'ሳች ፣ ውብ ፣ የደስ ደ'ስ
ያ'ለው

chart
'ቻ:ት -ስ- የባሕር ካርታ (ለመርከብ ጉዞ የ'ሚ
ያገለ'ግል) ፤ ሠንጠረዥ

charter
'ቻ:ተ -ስ- ንጉሣዊ ትእዛዝ (አንድ ነገር ለመ
ፍቀድ)
hire
-ግ- በሙሉ መ'ከራየት [ተከራ'የ] (አው
ሮ'ፕላን ፣ መርከብ ወዘተ)

charwoman
'ቻ:ውመን -ስ- ቤት ጠራጊ ሴት

chase

’ቼይስ -ግ- ማ'ሳደድ [አሳ'ደደ]

chasm

’ካዝም -ስ- ጥልቅ'ና ጠ'ባብ ሽለቆ

chaste

’ቼይስት -ቅ- ድንግል'ና ፣ ንጽሕ'ና ያ'ለው
(ለሴት)

chastise

ቻስ'ታይዝ -ግ- መቅጣት [ቀ'ጣ] (በመምታ
ት ፣ በመገረፍ) ፣ መቅሠፍ [ቀ'ሠፈ]

chastity

’ቻስቲቲ -ስ- ድንግል'ና ፣ ንጽሕ'ና (ከፈቃደ
ሥጋ)

chat

’ቻት -ግ- መ'ጫወት [ተጫ'ወተ] ፣ ግውራት
[አወ'ራ]

chatter

’ቻተ -ግ- መለፍለፍ [ለፈ'ለፈ] ፤ ጥርስ ማን
ቀጥቀጥ [አንቀጠ'ቀጠ](ከብርድ ፣ ከፍርሃት የተ
ነ'ሣ)

chauffeur

’ሸውፈ -ስ- ሾፌር ፣ ለሰው የተቀ'ጠረ አውቶ
ሞቢል ነጂ

cheap

’ቺይፕ -ቅ- እር'ካሽ

cheat

’ቺይት -ግ- ማ'ታለል [አ'ታ'ለለ]

check

’ቼክ -ግ- መ'ቆጣጠር [ተቆጣ'ጠረ] ፣ ማቆም
[አቆመ] ፣ መገታት [ገ'ታ] (ፈረስ ወዘተ)

cheek

’ቺይክ -ስ- ጉንጭ

cheekbone

’ቺይክበውን -ስ- የጉንጭ አጥንት

cheeky

’ቺይኪ -ቅ- ባለጌ ፣ ያልታ'ረመ ፣ ለበላይ አክ
ብሮት የ'ማያሳ'ይ

cheer

’ቺየ -ግ- በደ'ስታ መጮኸ [ጮኸ]

cheerful

’ቺየፉል -ቅ- ደ'ስተ'ኛ ፣ ደ'ስ ያለው ፣ ተደ
'ሳች

cheese

’ቺይዝ -ስ- የደ'ረቀ ሐይብ (ፎርማጆ)

chef

’ሼፍ -ስ- በሆቴል ውስጥ የወጥ ቤቶ'ች አለቃ

chemical

’ኬሚካል -ስ- ጥንተ ንጥር
-ቅ- ጥንተ ንጥራዊ

chemist

’ኬሚስት -ስ- ቀ'ማሚ (መድኃኒት ፣ ጥንተ
ንጥር)

chemistry

’ኬሚስትሪ -ስ- ጥንተ ንጥር ቅ'መማ (ኬሚ
ስትሪ)

cheque

’ቼክ -ስ- አንድ ባንክ ላንድ ሰው ገንዘብ እን
ዲከፍል የ'ሚ'ታ'ዘዝ'በት ወረቀት ፣ ቼክ

cherish

’ቼሪሽ -ግ- ማፍቀር [አፈ'ቀረ] ፣ መ'ከባከብ
[ተከባ'ከበ]

chest

’ቼስት -ስ- ደረት ፣ ት'ልቅ ሣጥን

chew

ቾ'ዩ -ግ- ማ'ላመጥ [አ'ላ'መጠ] ፣ ማ'ኘክ
[አ'ኘክ]

chicken

’ቺከን -ስ- ጫጩ'ት

chicken-pox

’ቺከን ፖክስ -ስ- ጉድፍ (በ'ሽታ)

chick-pea

’ቺከፒ -ስ- ሽምብራ

chief

’ቺይፍ -ስ- አለቃ ፣ ዋ'ና

chieftain

’ቺይፍተን -ስ- አለቃ ፣ ሹም (የነገድ ፣ የጎሳ)

child

’ቻይልድ -ስ- ሕፃን

childhood

’ቻይልድሁድ -ስ- ሕፃን'ነት ፣ ልጅ'ነት

childish

’ቻይልዲሽ -ቅ- የልጅ ሥራ ፣ ፍሬ ቢስ

chill

’ቺል -ስ- ብርድ
a cold
-ስ- ጉንፋን

chilli

’ቺሊ -ስ- ሚጥሚ'ጣ (በርበ'ሬ)

393

chilly

ˈቺሊ -ት- ብርዳም ፣ ተዝታ'ዣ

chime

ˈቻይም -ስ- የደወል ድምፅ

chimney

ˈቺምኒ -ስ- የጢስ መውጫ (ለቤት)

chin

ˈቺን -ስ- አገጭ

chink

ˈቺንክ -ስ- ጥላን'ጥል

chip

ˈቺፕ -ስ- ስ'ባሪ ፣ ስን'ጣሪ (የንጨት)

potato

-ስ- የድ'ን'ች ጥብስ

chirp

ˈቸ፡ፕ -ስ- የወፍ ድምፅ

chisel

ˈቺዜል -ስ- መር

chivalrous

ˈቺሸልረስ -ት- የተቀ'ጣ ፣ የታ'ደበ (ለሴት) ፤ የደካሞ'ች የተጠ'ቁ ረ'ዳት

chock

ˈቻክ -ስ- ወፍራም እንጨት (ያንድ ነገር ግፋ ሚያ)

chocolate

ˈቻክለት -ስ- ቾኮላታ

choice

ˈቾይስ -ስ- ምርጫ

choir

ክ'ዋየ -ስ- መዘምራን

choke

ˈቾውክ -ግ- ግነት [እነ'ቀ] ፣ ጉር'ሮን ፈርጦቆ መያዝ [ያዘ]

choose

ˈቾ፡ዝ -ግ- መምረጥ [መ'ረጠ]

chop

ˈቻፕ -ግ- መክተፍ [ከ'ተፈ] ፣ መቆራረጥ [ቆ ራ'ረጠ]

chopper

ˈቻፕ -ስ- ት'ንሽ መጥረቢያ ፣ ፋስ

chorus

ˈኩረስ -ስ- መዘምራን ፣ ዘፋኞ'ች

Christ

ክ'ራይስት -ስ- ክርስቶስ ፣ መሲሕ

christen

ክ'ሪሰን -ግ- ማጥመቅ [አጠ'መቀ] ፣ ክርስ ት'ና ማስነ'ሣት [አስነ'ሣ]

christian

ክ'ሪስትየን -ት- ክርስቲያን

Christmas

ክ'ሪስመስ -ስ- የገ'ና በዓል ገ'ና

chronic

ክ'ሮነክ -ት- ብዙ ጊዜ የ'ሚቆይ (በ'ሽታ)

chronicle

ክ'ሮነክል -ስ- ዜና መዋዕል

chubby

ˈቻቢ -ት- ክ'ብ ፈት'ና ጉንጓዳም (ሰው)

chuckle

ˈቻክል -ግ- በቀ'ስታ መንከትከት [ተንከተ 'ከተ] (ለሣቅ)

chunk

ˈቻንክ -ስ- ት'ልቅ ቁ'ራጭ ፣ ሙ'ዳ

church

ˈቸ፡ች -ስ- ቤተ ክርስትያን ፣ ቤተ እግዚአብ ሔር

churn

ˈቸ፡ን -ግ- ወተት መገፋት [ገ'ፋ] ፣ መናጥ [ና ጠ]

chute

ˈሹ፡ት -ስ- መንሸራተቻ

cigar

ሲ'ጋ፡ -ስ- ሲጋር (ጥቅ'ል ትምባሆ)

cigarette

ሲገ'ሬት -ስ- ሲጋራ ፣ ትምባሆ

cinder

ˈሲንደ -ስ- ረመጥ

cinema

ˈሲነማ -ስ- ሲኒማ

cinnamon

ˈሲነመን -ስ- ቀረፋ

circle

ˈሰ፡ክል -ስ- ክበብ ፣ ክ'ብ ነገር

circular

ˈሰ፡ክዩለ -ት- ክ'ብ

circulate

ˈሰ፡ክዩለይት -ግ- ማ'ደል [አ'ደለ] ፤ መዞር [ዞረ] ፣ ከቦታ ወደ ቦታ በነጻ መ'ዘዋወር [ተዘ ዋ'ወረ]

394

circumcise
'ሰ:ከምሳይዝ -ግ- መግረዝ [ገ'ረዝ]

circumference
' ሰ'ከምፈረንስ -ስ- ዙሪያ ፡ ከበብ (ያንድ
ነገር)

circumstance
'ሰ:ከምስታንስ -ስ- ሁናቴ ፡ ሁኔታ

circumstantial
ሰከምስ'ታንሻል -ቅ- ቀጥተ'ኛ ግስረ'ጃ የሌ
'ለው (ምስክር'ነት በፍርድ ቤት)፡ምክንያታዊ
ወይን'ም አ'ሳባቢ ግስረ'ጃ

circus
'ሰ:ከስ -ስ- ሰርከስ ፡ የእንስሳት ጨዋታ ትር
ኢት

cite
'ሳይት -ግ- መጥቀስ [ጠ'ቀስ] (ለማስረ'ጃ ፡
ለማ'ረጋገጫ)፡እርግድ ቤት ማቅረብ [አቀ'ረበ]

citizen
'ሲቲዘን -ስ- ዜጋ

city
'ሲቲ -ስ- ከተማ

civic
'ሲቪክ -ቅ- የማ'ዘጋጃ ቤት

civilian
ሲ'ቪልየን -ስ- ሲቪል ፡ (ወታ'ደር ያልሆነ)

civilization
ሲቪሊ'ዜይሽን -ስ- ሥ'ል'ጣኔ

claim
ክ'ሌይም -ግ- መብቴ ነው ብሎ መጠ'የቅ
[ጠ'የቀ] ፡ የኔ ነው ማለት [አለ]
-ስ- ማመልከት (መብት ለመጠ'የቅ)

claimant
ክ'ሌይመንት -ስ- አመልካች ፡ አቤት ባይ

clamber
ክ'ላምበ -ግ- መንጠላጠል [ተንጠላ'ጠለ] ፡
መውጣት [ወ'ጣ] (ተራራ ፡ ዛፍ ወዘተ)

clammy
ክ'ላሚ -ቅ- እርጥብ (ከላብ የተነ'ሣ)

clamour
ክ'ላመ -ስ- ጩኸት

clamp
ክ'ላምፕ -ግ- ማ'ያያዝ [አ'ያያዘ]
-ስ- ማ'ያያዣ

clan
ክ'ላን -ስ- ጎሳ

clandestine
ክ'ላንደስታይን -ቅ- ምስጢራዊ

clap
ክ'ላፕ -ግ- ማጨብጨብ [አጨበ'ጨበ]

clarify
ክ'ላሪፋይ -ግ- ጉልህ ማድረግ [አደ'ረገ] ፡
መግለጽ [ገ'ለጸ] ፡ ንጹሕ ማድረግ (አደ'ረገ) ፡
ግብራራት [አብራ'ራ]

clarity
ክ'ላሪቲ -ስ- ግልጽ'ነት ፡ ጉልህ'ነት

clash
ክ'ላሽ -ግ- መ'ላተም [ተላ'ተመ] ፡ መ'ጋጨት
[ተጋ'ጨ] ፡ መ'ከራከር [ተከራ'ከረ]

clasp
ክ'ላ:ስፕ -ግ- መጨ'በጥ [ጨ'በጠ] ፡ መቆ'ለፍ
[ቆ'ለፈ] ፡ ማ'ያያዝ [አ'ያያዘ]

class
ክ'ላ:ስ -ስ- ክፍል (በትምህርት ቤት)
category
-ስ- ደረጃ ፡ መደብ (በማነባራዊ ኑር)

classify
ክ'ላሲፋይ -ግ- በደምብ መከፋፈል [ከፋ'ፈለ]
(በ'ያይነቱ ፡ በ'የወገኑ)

clatter
ክ'ላተ -ስ- ኳኳቴ (ድምፅ)

clause
ክ'ሎ:ዝ -ስ- አንቀጽ (የውል)
grammatical
-ስ- ዐረፍተ ነገር (አንድ ግሰሪያ አን
ቀጽ ብ'ቻ ያ'ለው)

claw
ክ'ሎ: -ስ- ጥፍር (የእንስሳት)

clay
ክ'ሌይ -ስ- ሸክላ

clean
ክ'ሊይን -ግ- ማጽዳት (አጸ'ዳ) ፡ መጥረግ [ጠ
'ረገ] (ለቤት)
-ቅ- ንጹሕ ፡ የጸ'ዳ

cleanliness
ክ'ሌንሊነስ -ስ- ንጽሕ'ና ፡ ጽዳት

395

clear

ክ'ሊየ -ቅ- ግልጽ

liquid

-ቅ- በውስጡ የሚያሳ'ይ

cleft

ክ'ሌፍት -ስ- ስንጥቅ

clemency

ክ'ሌመንሲ -ስ- ምሕረት ፣ በጥፋት ላይ ልል
መሆን ፣ ጥፋትን አክብዶ አለማየት

clench

ክ'ሌንች -ግ- መጫ'በጥ [ጫ'በጠ] (እ'ጅን)

clergy

ክ'ለ:ጂ -ስ- ካህናት

clergyman

ክ'ለ:ጂመን -ስ- ካህን

clerical

ክ'ሌሪከል -ቅ- የጸሐፊ (ሥራ)

priestly

-ቅ- የካህን

clerk

ክ'ላ:ክ -ስ- ጸሐፊ

clever

ክ'ሌቨ -ቅ- ብልጎ

cleverness

ክ'ሌቨነስ -ስ- ብልጎነተ'ኛ'ነት

click

ክ'ሊክ -ስ- ተ'ጭታ (ድምፅ)

client

ክ'ላየንት -ስ- ደምበ'ኛ (የገፀ)

clientele

ክላየን'ቴል -ስ- ደምበ'ኞች

cliff

ክ'ሊፍ -ስ- ገደል ፣ ኻ'ው ያለ ገደል

climate

ክ'ላይመት -ስ- ያንድ ቦታ ጠቅላ ያ'የር'ና
የነፋስ ሁናቴ

climax

ክ'ላይማክስ -ስ- አንድ ታሪክ ፣ ድርጊ'ት ፣
ሁናቴ አስተያየት የሚማ'ርኸበት ደረጃ

climb

ክ'ላይም -ግ- መውጣት [ወ'ጣ] ፣ መንጠላ
ጠል [ተንጠላ'ጠለ]

cling

ክ'ሊንግ -ግ- መያዝ [ያዘ] (አጥብቆ)

clinic

ክ'ሊኒክ -ስ- ክሊኒክ ፣ የጤና ጣቢያ

clip

ክ'ሊፕ -ስ- ትን'ንሽ ዕቃዎ'ች ማ'ያያዣ
ነገር

clique

ክ'ሊይክ -ስ- እርስ በእርሳ'ቸው የሚ'ደጋ'ገፉ
የግ'ል ግን'ኙ'ነት ያ'ላ'ቸው ሰዎ'ች

cloak

ክ'ለውክ -ስ- ካ'ባ

cloakroom

ክ'ለውክሩም -ስ- ልብስ ግስቀ'መጫ ክፍል
(ካ'ፖርት ፣ ባርኔጣ ወዘተ)

clock

ክ'ሎክ -ስ- የጠረ'ጴዛ ሰዓት

clog

ክ'ሎግ -ግ- መ'ደፈን [ተደ'ፈነ] (በቆሻሻ)

close

ክ'ለውስ -ቅ- ቅርብ ፣ የተጠ'ጋ

close

ክ'ለውዝ -ግ- መዝጋት [ዘ'ጋ] (ለበ'ር) ፣ ማ
ጠፍ [አ'ጠፈ] (መጽሐፍ)

cloth

ክ'ሎስ -ስ- ብ'ትን ጨርቅ

clothe

ክ'ለውዝ -ግ- ማልበስ [አለ'በሰ]

clothes

ክ'ለውዝስ -ስ- ልብስ

cloud

ክ'ላውድ -ስ- ደ'መና

cloudy

ክ'ላውዲ -ቅ- ደ'መና'ማ

clove

ክ'ለውቭ -ስ- ቅርንፉድ

clown

ክ'ላውን -ስ- አ'ዝቂ ሰው ፣ ሰውን ባ'ነጋጋሩ'ና
በመ'ላ ሁናቴው የሚያ'ሥቅ ሰው

club

ክ'ለብ -ስ- ክበብ ፣ ማነበር

stick

-ስ- ዱ'ላ ፣ በ'ትር

clue

ካ'ሉ: -ስ- ፍንጭ ፣ ምል'ክት

396

clumsy
ክ'ለምዚ -ት- እ'ረግመዱ የ'ሚያስጠ'ላ ፡ ቶር
ፉ'ፉ
roughly made
-ት- ጥሩ ሆኖ ያልተሠ'ራ ፡ የ'ግደፍር

coach
'ኮውች -ግ- ግሠልጠን [አሠለ'ጠነ] (ለስፖ
ርት)
trainer
-ስ- አሠልጣኝ
vehicle
-ስ- ሠረገ'ላ

coagulate
ክ'ዋገዩሌይት -ግ- መርጋት [ረ'ጋ] (ለፈሳሽ)

coal
'ኮውል -ስ- ከሰል (የደንጊያ)

coarse
'ኮ:ስ -ት- ሻካራ ፡ ኮስኳ'ሳ ፡ ግርድፍ' ፤ ያ'ለ
መ
behaviour
-ት- ያልታ'ረመ (ለጠባይ)

coast
'ኮውስት -ስ- የባሕር ዳር

coat
'ኮውት -ስ- ካ'ፖርት ፡ ኮት

coax
'ኮውክስ -ግ- ማባበል [አባ'በለ] ፡ ማግባባት
[አግባ'ባ]

cobbler
'ኮብለር -ስ- ጫ'ማ አ ዳሽ

cobra
'ኮብረ -ስ- እ'ፉ'ኝት

cock
'ኮክ -ስ- አውራ ዶር

cockerel
'ኮክረል -ስ- አውራ ዶር (በእድሜ አነ'ስ ያለ)፣
ስ'ራን ዶር

cockroach
'ኮክሮውች -ስ- በረር

cocoa
'ኮውኮው -ስ- ካካዎ

code
'ኮውድ -ስ- ሕ'ግ መንግሥት ፤ በልምድ ፡ በባ
ህል ላይ የተመሠ'ረተ ሕ'ጎ'ች
secret writing
-ስ- ምስጢራዊ ጽሑፍ

coffee
'ኮፈ -ስ- ቡን ፡ ቡ'ና

coffee-pot
'ኮፈ ፖት -ስ- ጀበና ፡ ቡ'ና ማፍያ ፡ መቀጄ

coffin
'ኮፊን -ስ- የሬሳ ሣጥን

coherent
ክ'ሂረንት -ት- የተያያዘ (ለንግ'ግር)

coil
'ኮይል -ግ- መጠምጠም [መመ'መ] ፡ መጠ
ትለል [ጠቀ'ለለ]
-ስ- ጥምጥም ነገር ፡ ጥ'ቅል

coin
'ኮይን -ስ- መሐ'ለቅ ፡ ዝርዝር ፍራንክ

coincide
ክሮን'ሳይድ -ግ- በአንድ ጊዜ መሆን [ሆነ]
(ለሁለ'ት ነገር'ች)

coincidence
ክ'ዎንሲደንስ -ስ- ድንገተ'ኛ ድርጊ'ት ፡ ድን
ገተ'ኛ አ'ጋጣሚ

cold
'ኮልድ -ስ- ብርድ
-ት- ብርዳም ፡ ተዝቃ'ዛ
sickness
-ስ- ጉንፋን

collaborate
ክ'ላበሬይት -ግ- መ'ረዳዳት [ተረዳ'ዳ] ፡ ተጋ
ግዞ መሥራት [ሠ'ራ]
with enemy
-ግ- ከጠላት ጋር መ'ተባበር [ተባ'በረ]

collapse
ክ'ላፕስ -ግ- መ'ደምሰስ (ተደመ'ሰሰ) ፡ መፍ
ረስ [ፈ'ረሰ] ፤ ተዝለፍልፎ መውደቅ [ወ'ደቀ]

collar
'ኮላ -ስ- አንገትጌ ፡ ክሳድ

colleague
'ኮሊይግ -ስ- የሥራ ጓ'ደ'ኛ

397

collect

ከ'ሌክት -ግ- መሰብሰብ [ሰበ'ሰበ] ፣ ግ'ከግ
ቾት [እ'ከግ'ች]

collection

ከ'ሌክሽን -ስ- የተሰበ'ሰበ ፣ የተከግ'ች ነገር

collector

ከ'ሌክተr -ስ- ሰብሳቢ ፣ እ'ከጋች

college

'ኮላጅ -ስ- ኮ'ሌጅ ፣ ከ'ፍተ'ኛ ትምህርት ቤት

collide

ከ'ላይድ -ግ- መ'ጋጨት [ተጋ'ጨ] ፣ መ'ላ
ተም [ተላ'ተመ]

collision

ከ'ሊጀን -ስ- ግ'ጭት ፣ መ'ላተም

colloquial

ከ'ለውክዊል -ት- የተራ ሰው ፣ የመንገድ
ቋንቋ ፣ (የጽሑፍ ያልሆነ)

colloquialism

ከ'ለውክዊሊዝም -ስ- ተራ እ'ነጋገር ፣ ተራ
ቃል

colon

'ኮውለን -ስ- ሁለ'ት ነጥብ (፡)

colonel

'ከ፡ነል -ስ- ኮሎኔል

colony

'ኮለኒ -ስ- ቅኝ ግዛት ፣ ቅኝ አገር

colossal

ኮ'ሎሰል -ት- ታ'ላቅ ፣ በጣም ት'ልቅ ፣ በጣ
ም ግዙፍ

colour

'ከለ -ስ- ቀለም

colouring

'ከለሪንግ -ስ- እ'ተላለም ፣ መልክ

colt

'ኮልት -ስ- የፈረስ ግልገል

column

'ኮለም -ስ- ረ'ጅም ዓምድ
   of house
      -ስ- ምሰ'ሶ
   of newspaper
      -ስ- ዓምድ (የጋዜጣ)

comb

'ከውም -ግ- ግበ'ጠር [አበ'ጠረ] (ለጠጉር)
   -ስ- ግበ'ጠሪያ ፣ ሚዶ

combat

'ኮምባት -ግ- መ'ዋጋት [ተዋ'ጋ] ፣ መግጠም
[ገ'ጠመ] (ለጦር'ነት)
   -ስ- ው'ጊያ ፣ ጦር'ነት

combatant

ከም'ባተንት -ስ- ተዋጊ

combination

ኮምቢ'ኔይሽን -ስ- መ'ጣመር ፣ መ'ገናኘት
(የሁለ'ት ነገር'ች)

combine

ከም'ባይን -ግ- ግ'ጣመር [አ'ጣመረ]

combine

'ኮምባይን -ስ- ያንድ'ነት ግኅበር ፣ ጎብረት
(የንግድ)

combustion

ከም'በስቸን -ስ- መ'ቃጠል

come

'ከም -ግ- መምጣት [መ'ጣ]

comedian

ከ'ሚይዲየን -ስ- አ'ሣቂ ፣ ቀ'ላጅ (ሰው)

comedy

'ኮመዲ -ስ- አ'ሣቂ ፣ ቀላጅ ቴያትር ፣ አ'ሥ
ቲ'ኝ ቴያትር (ፍጻ'ሜው የደ'ስታ የሆነ)

comely

'ከምሊ -ት- መልከ ቀ'ና ፣ ውብ ፣ ቆንጆ (ለል
ጃገረድ)

comet

'ኮመት -ስ- ጅራታም ኮከብ

comfort

'ከምፈrት -ስ- ም'ቾት ፣ ድሎት

comfortable

'ከምፈrተብል -ት- ም'ቹ ፣ ድሎት ያለው

comical

'ኮሚካል -ት- አ'ሥቂ'ኝ

comma

'ኮመ -ስ- ነጠላ ሠረዝ (፣)

command

ከ'ማንድ -ግ- ግዘዝ [አ'ዘዘ]

commander

ከ'ማንደ -ስ- አ'ዛዥ

commanding

ከ'ማንዲንግ -ት- አ'ዛዥ
   impressive
      -ት- ባለግርግ ፣ ግርግ ዋገስ ያለው

398

commandment

ከ'ማ፡ንድመንት -ሱ- ትእዛዝ

commemorate

ከ'ሜመሪይት -ጉ- የማስታወሻ በዓል ግድ ረገ [አደ'ረገ]

commence

ከ'ሜንስ -ጉ- መጀ'መር [ጀ'መረ]

comment

'ኮሜንት -ጉ- አስተያየት መስጠት [ሰ'ጠ] -ሱ- አስተያየት

commentary

'ኮመንትሪ -ሱ- ትርጓሜ ፣ አስተያየት (ስለአ ንድ ሁናቴ ፣ ድርጊ'ት) *radio* -ሱ- ስለአንድ ድርጊ'ት በራዲዮ የሚ 'ሰጥ ሐተታ ፣ ት'ችት (ስፖርት ወዘተ)

commentator

'ኮመንቴይተ -ሱ- አስተያየት ሰጪ ፣ መፈ'ክር

commerce

'ኮመ፡ስ -ሱ- ንግድ

commercial

ከ'መ፡ሻል -ቅ- የንግድ

commission

ከ'ሚሽን -ጉ- ግዝዘ [አ'ዘዘ] ፣ አንድ ነገር እንዲፈ'ጸሙ ሥልጣን መስጠት [ሰ'ጠ] *payment* -ሱ- የደ'ላላ'ነት ዋጋ ፣ ለደ'ላላ የሚ'ከ 'ፈል ገንዘብ

commit

ከ'ሚት -ጉ- መፈ'ጸም [ፈ'ጸመ] ፣ ግድረገ [አ'ደረገ] (መጥፎ 'ራ) *to prison* -ጉ- እሥር ቤት ማስገ'ባት [አስገ'ባ] (ለዳ'ኛ)

committee

ከ'ሚቲ -ሱ- ደርጓ (ጉባኤ)

commodity

ከ'ጥረቲ -ሱ- የንግድ ዕቃ ፣ ሽቀጣሽቀጥ ፣ የርሻ'ና የግዕ'ድን ው'ጤት

common

'ኮመን -ቅ- ተራ ፣ የጋራ ፣ የተለ'መደ ፣ እን ግዳ ያልሆነ *low class* -ቅ- ዝ'ቅት'ኛ (በማኅበራዊ ኑር) ፣ ዓለጉ ስ'ድ

| | |

commonplace

'ኮመንፕሌይስ -ቅ- ተራ የሆነ

commotion

ከ'መውሽን -ሱ- ብጥ'ብጥ ፣ ሁከት ፣ ፅ'ጥታ መንሣት

communal

'ኮምዩኗል -ቅ- ጉብረ ሰብአዊ

communicate

ከ'ምዩኒኬይት -ጉ- መ'ገናኘት [ተገና'ኘ] ፣ ግ'ገናኘት [አ'ገና'ኘ] ፤ ግስተላለፍ [አስተ'ላ ለፈ] (በሽታ ፣ መልእክት)

communication

ከምዩኒኬይሽን -ሱ- መ'ገናኛ

communion

ከም'ዩንየን -ሱ- ቁርባን

community

ከም'ዩኒቲ -ሱ- ጉብረት ሰብ

compact

'ኮምፓክት -ቅ- ደጎና ሆና የታ'ሸገ ፣ የተ ጠጋ'ጋ

companion

ከም'ፓንየን -ሱ- ጓደ'ኛ ፣ ባለንጀራ

company

'ከምፓኒ -ሱ- ኩ'ባን'ያ ፣ ሽርካ *social* -ሱ- በግብዣ ላይ ያ'ሉ ሰዎ'ች ፣ እንግ ዶ'ች

compare

ከም'ፔየ -ጉ- ግ'መዳደር [አ'መዳ'ደረ] ፣ ግ'ነ ፃየር (አ'ነፃ'ፀረ)

comparison

ከም'ፓሪስን -ሱ- ግ'ነፃፀር ፣ ግ'መዳደር

compartment

ከም'ፓ፡ትመንት -ሱ- ክፍል ፣ በባቡር ውስጥ የተጓፈሪዎ'ች መ'ቀመጫ ክፍል

compass

'ከምፐስ -ሱ- ኮም'ፓስ ፣ ያቅጣ'ጫ መምሪያ መ'ሣሪያ (ጣደካል)

compassion

ከም'ፓሽን -ሱ- ርኅራኄ

compatible

ከም'ፓቲበል -ቅ- አንድ ላይ መኖር የሚ ቻል ፣ ተስማሚ ፣ ከሌላ ሰው ጋር በደ'ስታ መኖር የ'ሚችል

399

compel

ከም'ፔል -ግ- ግስን'ደድ [አስን'ደደ]

compensate

'ኮምፐንሴይት -ግ- መካሥ [ካሥ] ፣ መተ'ካት
[ተ'ካ] (ባጠ'ፉት በወ'ሰዱት ዕቃ ፋንታ)

compete

ከም'ፒይት -ግ- መ'ወዳደር [ተወዳ'ደሪ]

competent

'ኮምፐተንት -ት- ችሎታ ያ'ለው ፣ ለሥራ
ተገቢ የሆነ ሰው

competition

ኮምፐ'ቲሽን -ስ- ውድ'ድር

competitor

ከም'ፔቲተ -ስ- ተወዳዳሪ

compile

ከም'ፓይል -ግ- ግ'ዘጋጀት [አዘጋ'ጀ] (ለመ
ጽሐፍ)

complain

ከም'ፕሌይን -ግ- መ'ነጫነጭ [ተነጫ'ነጨ] ፣
አቤቱታ ማቅረብ [አቀ'ረበ] ፣ በሰው ላይ ስሕ
ተት ማግኘት [አገ'ኘ]

complaint

ከም'ፕሌይንት -ስ- አቤቱታ ፣ ክ'ስ

complete

ከም'ፕሊይት -ግ- መጨ'ረስ [ጨ'ረሰ] ፣ መፈ
'ጸም [ፈ'ጸመ]
-ት- ሙሉ ፣ ፍ'ጹም

complex

'ኮምፕለክስ -ት- የተወሳ'ሰበ ፣ ድብልቅልቅ
አስቸ'ጋሪ ፣ ዘንግ

complexion

ከም'ፕለክሽን -ስ- የመልክ ቀለም ፣ መልክ

complicate

'ኮምፕሊኬይት -ግ- ማ'ጣመም [አ'ጣ'መመ]
አ'ዋኪ ማድረግ [አደ'ረገ] የተወሳ'ሰበ ማድረግ
[አደ'ረገ]

complicated

'ኮምፕሊኬይተድ -ት- አ'ዋኪ ፣ አስቸ'ጋሪ

complication

ኮምፕሊ'ኬይሽን -ስ- የተወሳ'ሰበ ፣ የተዘባ
'ረተ ነገር (ሁናቴ)

compliment

'ኮምፕለሚንት -ግ- ማመስገን [አመሰ'ገነ]
-ስ- ምስጋና ፣ መሙያ (ለዋሰው)

comply

ከም'ፕላይ -ግ- መስማማት [ተስማ'ማ] ፣ አ
ንዱ በጠ'የቀው ነገር ታ'ዛዥ መሆን [ሆነ]

compose

ከም'ፐውዝ -ግ- መድረስ [ደ'ረሰ] (መዚቃ
መጽሐፍ ፣ ትነ)

composer

ከም'ፐውዘ -ስ- መዚቃ ደራሲ

composition

ኮምፐ'ዚሽን -ስ- ድርሰት (የጽሐፍ ፣ የመ
ዚቃ)

compound

'ኮምፐውንድ -ስ- አጥር ግ'ቢ
chemical mixture
-ስ- የተደባ'ለቃ ጥንት ንጥር

comprehend

ኮምፕረ'ሀንድ -ግ- መ'ረዳት [ተረ'ዳ] ፣ ግስ
ተዋል [አስተዋለ]

comprehension

ኮምፕረ'ሀንሽን -ስ- ግስተዋል ፣ መ'ረዳት

comprehensive

ኮምፕረ'ሀንሲቭ -ት- አ'ጠቃላይ ፣ ብዙ ነገር
የያዘ

compress

ከም'ፕረስ -ግ- መ'ጫን [ተጫነ] ፣ መጠት
ጠት [ጠቀ'ጠቀ]

compromise

'ኮምፕረማይዝ -ግ- ሁለ'ት ወገኖች በ'የበ
'ኩላ'ቸው አንዳንድ በመተው አለመ
ግባባትን ማስወ'ገድ [አስወ'ገደ]

compulsion

ከም'ፐልሽን -ስ- ግ'ዴታ ፣ ያለ ወ'ድ

compulsory

ከም'ፐልሰሪ -ት- የ'ሚያስገ'ድድ

compute

ከም'ፒዩት -ግ- ግ'ሰብ [አ'ሰበ] (ለሒሳብ)

comrade

'ኮምራድ -ስ- ጓደ'ኛ ፣ ባልንጀራ

comradeship

'ኮምራድሺፕ -ስ- ጓደ'ኛነት ፣ ባልንጀር'ነት

conceal

ከን'ሲይል -ግ- መ'ሸሸግ [ተሸ'ሸገ] ፣ መደ
'በቅ [ደ'በቀ]

400

concede
ከን'ሲይድ ፥ መ'ሸነፍን መገለጽ [ገ'ለጸ]

conceive
ከንሲ'ይቭ ፥ ግርዘM [አረ'ገዘ]
think
፥ ግሰብ [አ'ሰበ]

concentrate
ኮንሰንትሬይት ፥ ባንድ ነገር ላይ እተ'ኩር ግ'ሰብ [አ'ሰበ] ፤ ግ'ከማቸት [አ'ከማ'ቸ]

concentration
ኮንሰንት'ሬይሽን -ስ- እተ'ኩር ግ'ሰብ
gathering
-ስ- ስብሰባ ፣ ባንድ ሥፍራ መ'ሰብሰብ፣ መ'ከማቸት

concept
ኮንሴፕት -ስ- ሐ'ሳብ

conception
ከን'ሴፕሽን -ስ- ሐ'ሳብ
pregnancy
-ስ- እርግዝ'ና ፣ መፀነስ

concern
ከን'ሰን -ስ- የ'ሚገ'ድ ፣ የ'ሚያሳ'ስብ ነገር ፣ ቻ'ል የ'ግይሉት ተ'ዳይ ፣ የ'ሚያገባ ጉ'ዳይ

concert
ኮንሰት -ስ- ኮንሰርት (ሙዚቃዊ ትርኢት)

concise
ከን'ሳይስ ፥ የተመ'ጠነ ፣ አ'ጭርና ግልጽ (ለንግ'ግር)

conclude
ከንክ'ሉ፡ድ ፥ መደምደም [ደመ'ደመ] ፣ መጨ'ረስ [ጨ'ረስ]
decide
፥ መ'ወሰን [ወ'ሰነ]

conclusion
ከንክ'ሉ፡ዠን -ስ- መደምደሚያ ፣ ግሥሪያ
decision
-ስ- ው'ሳኔ

concord
ኮንኮ፡ድ -ስ- ስምም'ነት ፣ ሰላማዊ ግን'ኙ'ነት

concrete
ኮንክሪይት ፥ ገ'ዝ የ'ሚ'ጨ'በጥ ፣ የ'ሚ'ጻ'ሰስ
building material
-ስ- ሲሚንቶ

condemn
ከን'ዴም ፥ መፍረድ [ፈ'ረደ] ፣ ጥፋተ'ኛ ነው ግለት [አለ] ፣ ግውገዝ [አወ'ገዘ]

condense
ከን'ዴንስ ፥ ግሳ'መር [አሳ'መረ] (ለጽ'ሑፍ)
scientific
፥ ወደ ፈሳሽ'ነት መ'ለወጥ [ተለ'ወጠ]

condition
ከን'ዲሽን -ስ- ሁናቴ ፣ ሁኔታ ፣ እ'ካን

condole
ከን'ደውል ፥ ግስተዛዘን [አስተዛ'ዘነ]

conduct
ኮንዳክት -ስ- አመል ፣ ጠባይ

conduct
ከን'ዳክት ፥ መምራት [መ'ራ]

cone
'ከውን -ስ- ድፍ ጎን'ማ

confectioner
ከን'ፌክሽነ -ስ- ጣፋጭ ምግብ ሠሪ

confectionery
ከን'ፌክሽነሪ -ስ- ጣፋጭ ምግብ

confer
ከን'ፈ፡ ፥- መስጠት [ሰ'ጠ] (ለግዕርግ) መ'መከከር [ተመከ'ከረ]

conference
'ኮንፈረንስ -ስ- ጉባኤ ፣ ስብሰባ

confess
ከን'ፌስ ፥ ን'ሥሐ መግባት [ገ'ባ] ፣ ጥፋትን ግመን [አ'መነ]

confide
ከን'ፋይድ ፥ ች'ግርን ግ'ዋየት [አ'ዋ'የ] ፣ እምነት በሰው ላይ መጣል [ጣለ]

confidence
'ኮንፈደንስ -ስ- እምነት
secret
-ስ- ምስጢር

confidential
ኮንፈ'ዴንሽል ፥- ምስጢራዊ ፣ ድ'ብቅ

confine
ከን'ፋይን ፥ ግጋዝ [አጋዘ] ፣ እሥር ቤት ግስገ'ባት [አስገ'ባ]

401

confinement

ከን'ፋይንመንት -ስ- ግዞት ፣ እ'ሥራት birth of child

-ስ- የወሊድ ጊዜ

confirm

ከን'ፈ፡ም -ግ- ግጸደቅ [አጸ'ደቀ] ፣ ማ'ረጋገጥ [አ'ረጋ'ገጠ]

confirmation

'ኮንፈ'ሜይሸን -ስ- ግጸደቅ ፣ ማ'ረጋገጥ

confiscate

'ኮንፌስኬይት -ግ- መውረስ [ወ'ረሰ] (ሀብት በመንግሥት)

conflict

ከንፍ'ሊክት -ግ- መ'ጣላት [ተጣ'ላ] ፣ አለመ ግባባት [-ተግባ'ባ]

conflict

'ኮንፍሊክት -ስ- አለመስማማት ፣ ጥል ፣ አለ መግባባት

conform

ከን'ፎ፡ም -ግ- ሌሎችን መምሰል [መሰለ] (በጠ ባይ ወዘተ) ፣ መ'ከተል [ተከ'ተለ]

confront

ከንፍ'ረ,ንት -ግ- መግጠም [ገ'ጠመ] (አደጋ ፣ ዛ'ቻ)

confrontation

ኮንፍረን'ቴይሸን -ስ- መግጠም (አደጋ ፣ ዛ'ቻ)

confuse

ከንፍ'ዩ፡ዝ -ግ- ማ'ደናገር [አ'ደና'ገረ] ፣ መ'ደ ናገር [ተደና'ገረ]

confusion

ከንፍ'ዩ፡ዠን -ስ- መ'ደናገር ፣ ድንገርገር ፣ ብጥ'ብጥ

congeal

ከን'ጂይል -ግ- መርጋት [ረ'ጋ] (ለፈሳሽ)

congenial

ከን'ጂይኒየል -ቅ- በምርጫ ፣ በስ'ሜት የ'ሚ ስማ'ማ ፣ ተስማሚ

congestion

ከን'ጄስቸን -ስ- መ'ተፋፈግ ፣ መ'ጨጓቆን

congratulate

ከንግ'ራትዩሌይት -ግ- የም'ሥራ'ች ግለት [አለ]

congratulation

ከንግራትዩ'ሌይሸን -ስ- የም'ሥራ'ች ግለት

congregate

'ኮንግረጌይት -ግ- መ'ሰብሰብ [ተሰበሰ'በ]

congress

'ኮንግረስ -ስ- ስብሰባ ፣ ጉባኤ

conjecture

ከን'ጄክቸ -ስ- ግምት ፣ የሌ'ለው ሐሳብ ፣ መላ

conjugation

ኮንጅዩ'ጌይሸን -ስ- እርባታ (የግ'ሥ) ፣ መ'ጣ መር ፣ መ'ያያዝ

conjunction

ከን'ጀንክሸን -ስ- መስተፃምር (ሰዋሰው)

conjure

'ከንጀ -ግ- ምትሀት መሥራት [ሠ'ራ] (በእ'ጅ ቅልጥፍ'ና)

conjurer

'ከንጀረ -ስ- ምትሀተ'ኛ

connect

ከ'ኔክት -ግ- ማ'ገናኘት [አ'ገና'ኘ]

connection

ከ'ኔክሸን -ስ- ግን'ኙ'ነት

connive

ከ'ናይቭ -ግ- መዶ'ለት [ዶ'ለተ]

connubial

ከን'ዩ፡ቢየል -ቅ- የጋብ'ቻ

conquer

'ኮንከ -ግ- ማ'ሸ'ነፍ [አ'ሸ'ነፈ] ፣ ድል መን ሣት [ነ'ሣ]

conqueror

'ኮንከረ -ስ- ድል ነሺ ፣ ባለድል ፣ አ'ሸ'ናፊ

conscience

'ኮንሽን -ስ- ጎ'ሊና ፣ ክፉ'ና ደ'ግን መለ'ያ ውሳጣዊ ስ'ሜት

conscientious

ኮንሺ'ዩንሸስ -ቅ- ሥራውን በውቄ የ'ሚሠራ ፣ ጎላፈ'ነት የ'ሚ'ስ'ግው ፣ ጠንካ'ራ (ለሥራ)

conscious

'ኮንሸስ -ቅ- የነ'ቃ ፣ ንቁ ፣ ሊያ'ስብ ፣ ሊ'ረ'ዳ የ'ሚችል

conscript

'ኮንስክሪፕት -ግ- በግ'ዶታ ወ'ታ'ደር ነት ው'መልመል [ተመለ'መለ]

-ስ- በግ'ዶታ የ'ሚያገለ'ገል ወ'ታ'ደር

402

consecutive
ከን'ሴክዩቲቭ ቅ- ተከታታይ ፡ ቅደም ተከ
'ተል'ነት ያ'ለው

consent
ከን'ሴንት ጉ- መስማማት [ተስማ'ማ]
-ስ- ስምም'ነት

consequence
ኮንሲክዌንስ -ስ- የ'ሚ'ነ'ባ መደምደሚያ ፡
መፈጸሚያ
result
-ስ- ው'ጤት ፡ እንድ ሁናቴ የ'ሚያስከ
'ትለው ነገር

consequently
ኮንሲክዌንትሊ -ተገ- በጂላ
therefore
-ተገ- ስለ'ዚህ ፡ በ'ዚህ ምክንያት

conservative
ከን'ሰ፡ሸቲቭ ቅ- ለውጥ የ'ማይ ወ'ድ ፡ በተ
ነቀ ልግድ የጸ'ና

conserve
ከን'ሰ፡ሸ ጉ- ጋቆ'የት [አቆ'የ] (ዕቃ እንዳ
ይ'በላ'ሸ በ ማድረግ)

consider
ከን'ሲደ ጉ- መመርመር [መረ'መረ] ፡ በነ
ገሩ ፡ በጉ'ዳዩ ማ'ሰብ [አ'ሰበ]

considerable
ከን'ሲደረበል ቅ- በጣም ት'ልቅ ፤ ሊያስተ
ውሉት የ'ሚ'ነ'ባ

considerate
ከን'ሲደረት ቅ- ርኅሩኅ ፡ ለሰው አ'ሳቢ

consideration
ከንሲደ'ሬይሸን -ስ- ሐ'ሳብ (ጥን'ቃቄ ያ'ለ'በት)
thoughtfulness
-ስ- ርኅራኄ ፡ ለሰው ማ'ሰብ

consign
ከን'ሳይን ጉ- ማስረ'ከብ [አስረ'ከበ]
entrust
-ጉ- አደራ መስጠት [ሰ'ጠ]
send
-ጉ- መላክ [ላከ]

consignment
ከን'ሳይንመንት -ስ- ጥነት (የተላከ)

consist of
ከን'ሲስት አቭ ጉ- ከ...መ'ሠራት [ተሠ'ራ]

consistent
ከን'ሲስተንት ቅ- ተመሳሳይ ፡ (እንድ ዓይ
ነት የሆነ) ፡ የ'ግይ'ለ'ወጥ ፡ የተወ'ሰነ

consolation
ከንሶ'ለይሸን -ስ- ማጽናኛ

consolidation
ከንሶሊ'ዴይሸን -ስ- ማጠንከር ፡ ማ'ዋሐድ ፡
የጠ'ና ግድረጋ

consonant
'ኮንሰነንት -ስ- ድምፅ ተ'ተ'ባይ ፈደል (ሰጥ
ሰው)
-with
ቅ- የ'ሚስማ'ማ ፡ ጎብር'ነት ያ'ለው

conspicuous
ከንስ'ፒከዩወስ ቅ- በቀ'ላሉ የ'ሚ'ታ'ይ
ያልተሠ'ወረ ፡ ለዓይን ግልጽ የሆነ

conspiracy
ከንስ'ፒረሲ -ስ- መሻ'መቅ ፡ ሴራ

conspirator
ከንስ'ፒረተ -ስ- ሻ'ማቂ ፡ ሴረ'ኛ

constable
'ኮንስተበል -ስ- ተራ የፖሊስ ወ'ታ'ደር

constant
'ኮንስተንት ቅ- የ'ማይ'ለ'ወጥ ፡ የተወ'ሰነ ፤
የ'ግያ'ጸ'ርጥ

constipation
ኮንስቲ'ፔይሸን -ስ- የሆድ ድርቀት (ሥገራ
የ'ሚከለ'ከል በ'ሽታ)

constitution
ኮንስቲት'ዩ፡ሽን -ስ- ሕ'ገ መንግሥት ፤ አ'ቀነ
ባበር ፤ አ'መሠራረት ፤ የሰው'ነት ጤን'ነት

construct
ኮንስት'ረክት ጉ- መገንባት [ገነ'ባ] ፡ መሥ
ራት [ሠ'ራ] (ቤት ወዘተ)

constructive
ኮንስት'ረክቲቭ ቅ- ጠቃሚ ፡ መ'ሻሻል
የ'ሚያመጣ ፡ አልሚ

consul
'ኮንሰል -ስ- ቆንሲል (በው'ጭ አገር የአገሩን
ጉ'ዳይ የ'ሚ'ጠባ'በት ሹም)

consult
ከን'ሰልት ጉ- ማ'ማከር [አ'ማከረ] ፡ ምክር
መጠ'የቅ [ጠ'የቀ]

403

consultant

ከን'ሰልተንት -ስ- አ'ማካሪ ፣ ምክር ሰጪ ፣
ምክር ተቀ'ባይ

consume

ከንስ'ዩ፡ም -ግ- መጨ'ረስ [ጨ'ረስ] ፣ መፍ
ጀት [ፈ'ጀ] (ለምግብ ወዘተ)

consumer

ከንስ'ዩ፡መ -ስ- ደምበ'ኛ (የንግድ)
final user
-ስ- በ'ላተ'ኛ (ገዝቶ ለራሱ ጥቅም የ'ሚ
ያውል)

consumption

ከን'ስምሽን -ስ- መጨ'ረስ ፣ መፍጀት (ምግብ ፣
ነዳጅ ወዘተ)

contact

ኮን'ታክት -ግ- መ'ገናኘት [ተገና'ኘ] ፣ መ'ነ
ካካት [ተነካ'ካ]
a person
-ስ- የ'ሚያውቁት ሰው (በሥልጣን ላይ
ያ'ለ)

contagious

ከን'ቴይጀስ -ቅ- በመ'ነካካት የ'ሚ'ተላ'ለፍ፣
ተላላፊ (በ'ሽታ)

contain

ኮን'ቴይን -ግ- መያዝ [ያዘ] (ለዕቃ)

container

ከን'ቴይነ -ስ- መያዣ (ለዕቃ)

contaminate

ከን'ታሚኔይት -ግ- መ'ነካካት [ተነካ'ካ]፣ በ
'ሽታ ማስተላለፍ [አስተላ'ለፈ]

contemplate

'ኮንተምፕሌይት -ግ- ማ'ሰላሰል [አ'ሰላ'ሰለ]፣
አጥልቆ መመርመር [መረ'መረ]፣ማውጣት
ማውረድ [አወ'ጣ አወ'ረደ]፣አሰት'ኩር መ'መ
ልከት [ተመለ'ከተ]

contemplation

ኮንተምፕ'ሌይሽን -ስ- ማ'ሰላሰል ፣ ጥልቅ
ምርመራ

contemporary

ከን'ቴምፐራሪ -ቅ- በአንድ ዘመን አብሮ የኖረ
(ሰው ወዘተ)

contempt

ከን'ቴምፕት -ስ- ማ'ዋረድ ፣ ማሬዝ ፣ ንቀት

content

ከን'ቴንት -ት- የተደ'ሰተ ፣ ያልከ'ፋው ፣ ት'ር
ያላለው

content

'ኮንቴንት -ስ- ይዞታ

contest

'ኮንቴስት -ስ- ውድ'ድር

continent

'ኮንቲነንት -ስ- አህጉር

continual

ኮን'ቲነዋል -ት- የ'ጊያጿርጥ ፣ የ'ሚተ
'ጥል

continuation

ከንቲንዩ'ዌይሽን -ስ- መቀ'ጠል ፣ የ'ሚከ
'ተል ነገር

contingent

ከን'ቲንጀንት -ት- ሊደርስ የ'ሚችል ፣ እርግ
ጠ'ኛ ያልሆነ
close to
-ት- ወደፊት ሊሆኑ ከ'ሚችሉ ነገር'ች
ጋራ የተያያዘ
body of troops
-ስ- የጦር ክፍል

contortion

ከን'ቶሽን -ስ- መ'ጠማዘዝ (የሰውነ'ት ወዘተ)

contour

'ኮንቱወ -ስ- ቅርፅ ፣ መልክ

contraband

'ኮንትራባንድ -ስ- ኮንትሮባንድ ፣ ቀረጥ ያልተ
ከ'ፈለ'በት ሸቀጥ (በድ'ብቅ የ'ሚ'ሸጥ)

contraceptive

ኮንትረ'ሴፕቲቭ -ስ- የርግዝ'ና መከላከያ

contract

'ኮንትራክት -ስ- ስምም'ነት ፣ ውል ፣ ኮንት
ራት

contract

ከን'ትራክት -ግ- መ'ኮማተር [ተኮማ'ተረ]
a disease
-ግ- በ'ሽታ መያዝ [ያዘ]

contractor

ከን'ትራክተ -ስ- ተጫራጭ ፣ ተዋዋይ (የሥራ)

contradict

ኮንትረ'ዲክት -ግ- መ'ቃወም [ተቃ'ወመ] ፣
መ'ቃረን [ተቃ'ረነ]

404

contrary
ኮንትራሪ -ት- ተቃራኒ

contrast
ኮንትራስት -ጉ- ል'ዩ'ነት ለማግኘት ግ'ነ
ፀሮ [እ'ነገ'ፀሪ] ፤ ል'ዩ'ነት ግግኘት [እጊ'ኘ]
-ስ- ጉልህ የሆነ ል'ዩ'ነት

contribute
ኮንት'ሪብዩት -ጉ- ገንዘብ ግ'ዋጣት[እ'ዋ'ጣ]፤
አንድ ነገር ለመፍሩ ፣ ለመ'ሠራቱ ምክንያት
መሆን [ሆነ]

contribution
ኮንትሪብ'ዩሽን -ስ- አስተዋጽኦ ፣ መ'ዋጮ

contributor
ኮንት'ሪብዩተ -ስ- ገንዘብ እ'ዋጭ ፣ መ'ዋጮ
የ'ሚያደርግ ሰው

contrivance
ኮንት'ራይቫንስ -ስ- ለል'ዩ ተገባር የተሠ'ራ
መኪና ፤ መ'ተላጠሪያ

control
ኮንት'ሮል -ጉ- ሥልጣን መያዝ [ያዘ]

controversial
ኮንትረ'ቨ:ሸል -ት- የ'ግይስግ'ው'በት ፣ የ'ሚ
ያ'ከራ'ክር

controversy
ኮንት'ሮቨሲ -ስ- ክር'ክር ፣ የ'ግይስግ'ውበ
ት ጉ'ዳይ

convalescent
ኮንቨ'ሌሰንት -ት- አገ'ጋሚ ፣ ገመምተ'ኛ

convene
ኮን'ቪይን -ጉ- ጉባኤ መሰብሰብ [ሰበ'ሰበ]

convenient
ኮን'ቪይኒየንት -ት- ተስግሚ ፣ ም'ቹ

convent
ኮንበንት -ስ- ገዳም (የሴቶ'ች)

convention
ኮን'ቪንሽን -ስ- ት'ልቅ ስብሰባ
custom
-ስ- ባህል

conventional
ኮን'ቬንሽነል -ት- ባህል አክባሪ ፤ በባህል
ላይ የተመሠ'ረተ ፣ የተለ'መደ ነገር

converge
ኮን'ቨ:ጅ -ስ- መ'ጋጠም [ተጋ'ጠመ] ፣ መ'ገና
ኘት [ተገና'ኘ]

conversant
ኮን'ቨ:ሰንት -ት- ዐዋቂ ፣ ልምድ ያ'ለው

conversation
ኮንቨ'ሴይሽን -ስ- ንግ'ግር

converse
ኮን'ቨ:ስ -ጉ- መ'ነጋገር

converse
ኮንቨስ -ስ- ተቃራኒ ፣ ተቃዋሚ ነገር

conversion
ኮን'ቨ:ሽን -ስ- ሃይማኖት መለ'ወጥ

convertible
ኮን'ቨ:ተበል -ት- መ'ዛወር ፣ መ'ለወጥ የ'ሚ
ች'ል

convey
ኮን'ቪይ -ጉ- ግ'ዘዋወር [አ'ዘዋ'ወሪ] (ካንድ
ቦታ ወደ ሌላው)

convict
ኮን'ቪክት -ጉ- መፍረድ [ፈ'ረደ] (ሲ'ፈ'ረድ
'በት)

convict
ኮንቪክት -ስ- እሥረ'ኛ ፣ የተፈ'ረደ'በት
ሰው

conviction
ኮን'ቪክሽን -ስ- ጽኑ እምነት

convince
ኮን'ቪንስ -ጉ- ግላ'መን [አሳ'መነ]

convivial
ኮን'ቪቪየል -ት- የደ'መቀ (ግብዣ) ፣ ግገበ
ራዊ ፤ ምቃ ያ'ለው (በመ'ጠጥ)

convoy
ኮንቮይ -ስ- ሠልፍ (የጦር መኪናዎ'ች)

convulsion
ኮን'ቨልሽን -ስ- ወፈ'ፍ ግድረግ (ድንገተ'ኛ
የሰው'ነት) ፣ መባተት

cook
ኩክ -ጉ- ወጥ መሥራት [ሠ'ራ]
chef
-ስ- ወጥ ቤት (ሰው) ፣ ወጥ ሠሪ

cookery
ኩከሪ -ስ- ወጥ አ'ሠራር

cooker
ኩክ -ስ- ምድ'ጃ

405

cool
'ኩ፥ል -ግ- ማቀዝቀዝ [አቀዝ'ቀዘ]
-ት- ቀዝቃ'ዛ

cooperate
ከ'ዎፐሬይት -ት- መ'ተባበር [ተባ'በረ] ፣ መ
'ረዳዳት [ተረዳ'ዳ]

cooperation
ከዎፐ'ሬይሽን -ስ- ጉብረት ፣ ተራድኦ

coordinate
ከ'ዎ፥ዲኔይት -ግ- በትክ'ክለ'ኛ መንገድ እንዲ
'ሠ'ራ ማስተባበር [አስተባ'በረ]

cope with
'ከውፕ ዊዝ -ግ- አንድ አስቸ'ጋሪ ሥራ ደጣና
አድርጎ ማ'ካሄድ [አ'ካሄደ] ፤ ብቁ ሆኖ መ'ገኘት
[ተገ'ኘ]

copious
'ከውፒየስ -ት- ብዙ ፣ የተትረፈ'ረፈ

copper
'ኮፐ -ስ- መዳብ

copulate
'ኮፕዩሌይት -ግ- መ'ገናኘት [ተገና'ኘ] (በፈ
ቃደ ሥጋ)

copy
'ኮፒ -ግ- መገልበጥ [ገለ'በጠ] ፣ መቅዳት
[ቀ'ዳ] (ጽሑፍ ወዘተ)
-ስ- ቅ'ጇ ፣ ግል'ባጭ

cord
'ኮ፥ድ -ስ- ገመድ ፣ ሲባጎ

cordial
'ኮ፥ዲየል -ት- ደግ'ነት የተሞ'ላ ፤ ል'ባዊ

cordon
'ኮ፥ደን -ስ- የግዕረግ ምል'ክት (እንደ መቀ
'ነት ያ'ለ) ፤ መከበብ (በፖሊስ)

core
'ኮ፥ -ስ- ቡጥ ፣ ማእከላዊ ቦታ

co-respondent
ከውረስ'ፖንደንት -ስ- በዝ'ሙት የተከ'ሰሰ
ሰው (ያና ካለተፈ'ታ'ች ከሰው ሚስት ጋር በመ
'ገናኘት)

coriander
'ኮሪያንደ -ስ- ድምብላል

cork
'ኮ፥ክ -ስ- ቡሽ

corkscrew
'ኮ፥ክስክሩ -ስ- የቡሽ መንቀያ

corn
'ኮ፥ን -ስ- የስንዴ ዓይነት እህል

coronation
ኮሮ'ኔይሽን -ስ- የንግሥ በዓል ፣ በዓለ ንግሥ

corner
'ኮ፥ነ -ስ- ማዕዘን

corps
'ኮ፥ -ስ- ጓ'ድ

corpse
'ኮ፥ፕስ -ስ- ሬሳ ፣ በድን

corporal
'ኮ፥ፐረል -ስ- ያ'ሥር አለቃ
-ት- የሰውነ'ት

corporation
ኮፐ'ሬይሽን -ት- የማ'ዘጋጃ ቤት መ'ማክርት
company
-ስ- ኩ'ባን'ያ

correct
ከ'ሬክት -ግ- ማረም [አ'ረመ] (የተሳሳተውን)
-ት- ል'ክ ፣ ያልተሳሳተ

correction
ከ'ሬክሽን -ስ- እ'ርማት

correctness
ከ'ሬክትነስ -ስ- ሕ'ግ አክባሪ'ነት ፣ ትክ'ክለ
'ኛ'ነት

correspond
ኮረስ'ፖንድ -ግ- መ'ጻጻፍ [ተጻጻፈ]
be equal
-ግ- መ'ተካከል [ተካ'ከለ] ፣ መ'መሳሰል
[ተመሳ'ሰለ]

correspondent
ኮረስ'ፖንደንት -ስ- ደብዳ'ቤ የ'ሚ'ጻጻፉት
ሰው
newspaper
ወ'ኪል (የጋዜጣ)

corridor
'ኮሪዶ፥ -ስ- መ'ተላለፊያ (የቤት)

corrode
ከ'ረውድ -ግ- መ'በላት [ተበ'ላ] (ብረታ ብረ
ት)

corrosion
ከ'ረውገን -ስ- መ'በላት ፣ መዛግ

corrugated iron
ኮረጌተድ'አየን -ስ- የቤት ክዳን ቆቆ'ር

406

corrupt
ከ'ረፐት -ግ- ግ'በላሸት [አ'በላ'ሽ] ፣ ግጥ
ፉት [አጣ'ፉ]
-ቅ- ብል'ሹ ፣ ጥፉ

cost
'ኮስት -ግ- ግውጣት [አወ'ጣ] (ለዋጋ)
በ . . . መ'ገዛት [በ . . . ተገ'ዛ]

costly
'ኮስትሊ -ቅ- ው'ድ

costume
'ኮስትዩም -ስ- ልብስ

cot
'ኮት -ስ- የሕፃን አልጋ

cottage
'ኮተጅ -ስ- ት'ንሽ የመኖሪያ ቤት (በባላገር) ፣
ዛጎ'ባ

cotton
'ኮተን -ስ- ጥጥ

couch
'ካውች -ስ- ድንክ አልጋ

cough
'ኮፍ -ግ- መሳል [ሳል] (ለጉንፋን)

council
'ካውንስል -ስ- መማከርት ፣ ደርግ

councillor
'ካውንስለ -ስ- የደርግ ፣ የጉባኤ አባል

counsellor
'ካውንስለ -ሱ- አ'ማካሪ

count
'ካውንት -ግ- መቁጠር [ቆ'ጠረ] ፣ ግ'ሰብ
[አ'ሰበ] (ለሒሳብ)

countenance
'ካውንተነንስ -ስ- ፊት ፣ በፊት ላይ ያ'ለ ሲ'ሜ
ት (የሐዘን ፣ የደ'ስታ ወዘተ)

counter
'ካውንተ -ስ- ዕቃ ለሽ'ያጭ የ'ሚቀርብ'በት
ረ'ጅም የሱቅ ጠረ'ጴዛ
games
-ስ- ፈሽ (የመ'ጫወቻ)
mechanical
-ስ- መቁጠሪያ (መ'ሣሪያ)

counterfeit
'ካውንተፈት -ቅ- ትክ'ክለ'ኛ ያልሆነ ፣ ለግ
'ታለል አስመ'ስሎ የተሠ'ራ ገንዘብ

counterfoil
'ካውንተርፎይል -ስ- ጉርድ (የካርኒ ወዘተ)

countless
'ካውንትሌስ -ቅ- ቁጥር የሌ'ለው ፣ በጣም
ብዙ ፣ ተቆጥሮ የ'ማያልቅ

country
'ከንትሪ -ስ- አገር

countryman
'ከንትሪመን -ስ- ባላገር (ሰው) ፤ ያገር ልጅ

countryside
'ከንትሪሳይድ -ስ- ባላገር (አገር)

couple
'ከፕል -ስ- ሁለ'ት የሆነ ነገር ፣ ጥንድ ፣ 'ባልና'
ሚስት
-ግ- ግ'ጣመር [አ'ጣ'መረ]

courage
'ከሪጅ -ስ- ድፍረት ፣ ጀግን'ነት

courageous
ከ'ሬይጀስ -ቅ- ደ'ፋር ፣ ጀግና ፣ ጎበዝ

courier
'ኩሪየ -ስ- መልከተ'ኛ

course
'ኮስ -ስ- ትምህርት ፣ በተወ'ሰነ ጊዜ የ'ሚ'ግ
ሩት ትምህርት
race-
-ስ- የሽቅ'ድ'ም ሜዳ

court
'ኮት -ስ- የታ'ጠረ ቦታ ፣ አጥር ግ'ቢ
legal
-ስ- ፍርድ ቤት
palace
-ስ- ቤተ መንግሥት
personnel
-ስ- በቤተ መንግሥት የ'ሚኗሩ ሰዎ'ች

courteous
'ኮቲየስ -ቅ- የታ'ረመ ፣ ጥሩ ጠባይ ያ'ለው
ሰው አከባሪ ፣ ትሑት

courtesy
'ከተሲ -ስ- የታ'ረመ ጠባይ ፣ ትሕት'ና

court-martial
ኮት'ግሻል -ስ- የወ'ታ'ደር ፍርድ ቤት

courtyard
'ኮትያይድ -ስ- አጥር ግ'ቢ ፣ ትጥር ግ'ቢ

407

cousin
'ከዝን -ስ- ያ'ጎት ፣ ያክስት ልጅ

cover
'ከሸ -ግ- መሽ'ፈን [ሽ'ፈነ] ፣ መከደን [ከ'ደነ]
-ስ- መሽ'ፈኛ ፣ ክዳን

covet
'ከሸት -ግ- የሰው ንብረት ለመውሰድ መከ
'ጀል [ከ'ጀለ] ፣ በሰው ንብረት መቅናት [ቀ'ና]፣
መሌ'ሰን [ሌ'ሰነ]

cow
'ካው -ስ- ላም

coward
'ካውድ -ስ- ፈሪ ፣ በቅቢ'ታ

cowardice
'ካወዲስ -ስ- ፍርሀት

cowl
'ካውል -ስ- የመነኩሴ ቆብ ፣ ሽፋን (የራስ)

coy
'ኮይ -ቅ- ሲያሽኮረ'ምሙት ዓይነ አ'ፋር የ'ሚ
መስል

crab
ክ'ራብ -ስ- ስ'ምንት እግር'ች ያ'ሉት ደንጊያ
ለ'በስ ዐሣ

crack
ክ'ራክ -ግ- መንቃት [ነ'ቃ] (ጉድጓ'ዳ ፣ ዕቃ
መዘተ)
    one's fingers
-ግ- ማንጨጭት [እንጨ'ጨ] (ጣት)

cracker
ክ'ራክ -ስ- መስበሪያ ፣ መፈርከሻ
    biscuit
-ስ- ደረቅ ብስኩት

crackle
ክ'ራክል -ግ- መንጣጣት [ተነጣ'ጣ] ፣ መን
ጨጨት [ተነጨ'ጨ] (ለድምዕ)

cradle
ክ'ሬይደል -ስ- የሕፃን አልጋ

craft
ክ'ራ፡ፍት -ስ- ጥበብ (የእ'ጅ)
    ship
-ስ- መርከብ

craftsman
ክ'ራ፡ፍትስመን -ስ- የእ'ጅ ጥበብ ያ'ለው ፣
በተገባረ እድ የሠለ'ጠነ

crafty
ክ'ራ፡ፍቲ -ቅ- አ'ታላይ ፣ ሙ'ሌ ፣ ብልጥ ፣ ተን
ኮለ'ኛ

crag
ክ'ራግ -ስ- ቋጥ'ኝ ፣ የቋጥ'ኝ ጫፍ

cram
ክ'ራም -ግ- መጎስጎስ [ጎስ'ጎሰ] ፣ ግ'መት
[ዐ'መቀ]

cramp
ክ'ራምፕ -ስ- ድንዛዜ ፣ መ'ጨበጥ (የሰው'ነት)

crane
ክ'ሬይን -ስ- ረ'ጅም እግር'ና አንገት ያለው
ቶመታም ወፍ ፣ ክ'ባድ ሸክም የ'ሚያነሣ
መኪና

crank
ክ'ራንክ -ስ- መዞ'ወር [ዞ'መረ]

crash
ክ'ራሽ -ግ- ወድቆ መ'ሰበር [ተሰ'በረ]
-ስ- ወድቆ የተሰ'በረ ነገር ፣ ስብርባሪ
(በመውደቁ ምክንያት)

crate
ክ'ሬይት -ስ- ት'ልቅ የእንጨት ሣጥን

crater
ክ'ሬይተ -ስ- ሰ'ፊ ጉድጓድ (እንድ ነገር በመ
ፈንዳቱ የተቆ'ፈረ)

crave
ክ'ሬይብ -ግ- ለማግኘት መጓጓት [ጓ'ጓ]

crazy
ክ'ሬይዚ -ቅ- እብድ

creak
ክ'ሪክ -ግ- ሲ'ጥ ሲ'ጥ ግላት [አለ] (ለበ'ር፣
ለመንበር መዘተ)

cream
ክ'ሪይም -ስ- ቅባት ፣ ስልባቦት

crease
ክ'ሪይስ -ስ- እ'ጥፋት

create
ክሪ'ዬይት -ግ- መፍጠር [ፈ'ጠረ]

creation
ክሪ'ዬይሸን -ስ- ፍጥረት ፣ ፍጡር

creative
ክሪ'ዬይቲብ -ቅ- ፈጣሪ ፣ አንቺ (ለሓሳብ)

creator
ክሪ'ዬይተ -ስ- ፈጣሪ

408

creature
ክ'ሪይቸ -ስ- ፍጥረት

credence
ክ'ሪይደንስ -ስ- እምነት ፤ እውነት መሆኑን መቀ'በል

credentials
ክረ'ዴንሸልዝ -ስ- መ'ታወቂያ ወረቀት

credible
ክ'ሬዲበል -ቅ- የ'ሚ'ታ'መን

credit
ክ'ሬዲት -ስ- ዱቤ
-ግ- ገንዘብ በሌላ ሒሳብ ማስቀ'መጥ
[አስቀ'መጠ]

creditor
ክ'ሬዲተ -ቅ- አበ'ዳሪ

credulity
ክሬድ'ዩሊቲ -ስ- እምነት (ያለማ'ሰብ) ፤ በቂ ያልሆነ ማስረ'ጃ መ'ቀበል

credulous
ክ'ሬድዩለስ -ቅ- በቀ'ላሉ አማኝ

creed
ክ'ሪይድ -ስ- እምነት
liturgical
-ስ- ጸሎተ ሃይማኖት

creek
ክ'ሪይክ -ስ- ት'ንሽ ወንዝ ፤ ጅረት

creep
ክ'ሪይፕ -ግ- መዳከ [ዳከ]

creepy
ክ'ሪይፒ -ቅ- የ'ሚያስፈ'ራ ፤ የ'ሚያስደነ'ግጥ ፤ የ'ሚዘገ'ንን

cremation
ክረ'ሜይሸን -ስ- በድን ማ'ቃጠል

crematoriu
ክሬመ'ቶ፡ሪየም -ስ- በድን የ'ሚ'ታ'ጠል'በት ቦታ

crescent
ክ'ሬሰንት -ስ- ሙሉ ያልሆነ'ች ጨረቃ
shape
-ስ- ማጭድ ቅርፅ

cress
ክ'ሬስ -ስ- ጉ'ጉብሌ (እንደሰላጣ ያለ በወንዝ ዳር የ'ሚበቅል ተክል)

crest
ክ'ሬስት -ስ- ጉተና ፤ ተ'ራ ፤ ቁንጮ ፤ ፥ ንክ
sign
-ስ- አርማ

crevasse
ክረ'ቫስ -ስ- ሥንጥቅ (የመሬት)

crevice
ክ'ሬቪስ -ስ- ቀ'ጭን ሥንጥቅ (የተባይ መ'ሸ ሸጊያ) ፤ ንቃቃት

crew
ክ'ሩ፡ -ስ- በመርከብ በአውሮ'ፕላን ውስጥ የ'ሚሠሩ ሠራተኞ'ች

cricket
ክ'ሪከት -ስ- ክሪኬት (የእንግሊዝ ጨዋታ)
insect
-ስ- ዋዝንቢት

crime
ክ'ራይም -ስ- ወንጀል

criminal
ክ'ሪሚነል -ቅ- ወንጀለ'ኛ

crimson
ክ'ሪምዘን -ቅ- ብሩህ ቀ'ይ

cringe
ክ'ሪንጅ -ግ- በፍርሃት ማፈግፈግ [አፈግ'ፈገ]

crinkle
ክ'ሪንክል -ግ- መ'ጨማደድ [ተጨማ'ደደ] ፤ መ'ኮማተር [ተኮማ'ተረ]

cripple
ክ'ሪፕል -ቅ- አካለ ስንኩል ፤ ድ'ውይ

crisis
ክ'ራይሲስ -ስ- የብጥ'ብጥ ፤ የሁከት ጊ.'

crisp
ክ'ሪስፕ -ቅ- ደረቅ'ና ቀ'ጭን

critical
ክ'ሪቲከል -ቅ- ስሕተተ የ'ሚያገ'ኝ ፡፡ '፯
dangerous
-ቅ- አሥጊ ፤ አ'ሠ'ጊ

criticism
ክ'ሪቲሲዘም -ስ- ት'ችት ፤ ስሕተት ማግኘት ፤ ሂስ

criticize
ክ'ሪቲሳይዝ -ግ- ስሕተት ማግኘት [አገ'ኘ] ፤ መተ'ቸት [ተ'ቸ]፤በሰው ላይ መፍረድ [ፈ'ረደ]፤ አስተያየት መስጠት [ሰ'ጠ]

409

croak
ክ'ረዉክ -ስ- የእንቁራሪት ዉሸት

crocodile
ክ'ሮከዳይል -ስ- ዐ'ዞ

crockery
ክ'ሮከሪ -ስ- ሳሕን ፣ ፈንጃል'ና የመሳ'ሰለው

crooked
ክ'ሩከድ -ት- ጠማጣ (ለቅርፅ ፣ ለአመል)

crop
ክ'ሮፕ -ስ- ሰብል ፣ አዝመራ
  whip
  -ስ- አለንጋ

cross
ክ'ሮስ -ግ- መ'ሻገር [ተሻ'ገረ]
  crucifix
  -ስ- መስቀል
  angry
  -ት- ቁ'ጡ

crossbar
ክ'ሮስባ፡ -ስ- አግድም ብረት (በተለ'ይ በሁለ'ት ብረቶ'ች የቁም የተያዘ)

crossing
ክ'ሮሲንግ -ስ- መ'ሻገሪያ ፣ አንድ መንገድ ሌላውን የ'ሚያ'ጸ'ርጥ በት ቦታ

cross-roads
ክ'ሮስሮውድዝ -ስ- መስቀል'ያ መንገድ

crouch
ክ'ራዉች -ግ- በእንገር ቁጢ'ጥ ብሎ መ'ቀመጥ [ተቀ'መጠ]፣ ተጎንብሶ መ'ቀመጥ [ተቀ'መጠ]፣ ግድባት [አደ'ባ]

crow
ክ'ሮው -ግ- መጮህ [ጮህ] (ለዶሮ)

crow
ክ'ሮው -ስ- ቁራ
  cock
  -ስ- የዶሮ ዉሸት

crowbar
ክ'ሮውባ፡ -ስ- የማጥን መከፈቻ ብረት

crowd
ክ'ሮውድ -ስ- የተሰበ'ሰበ ሰው ፣ የሰው ክም'ችት

crowded
ክ'ራውዲድ -ት- የተሰበ'ሰበ ፣ የታ'ፈገ

crown
ክ'ራውን -ስ- ዘውድ

crucial
ክ'ሩ፡ሸል -ት- በጣም አስፈ'ላጊ

crucible
ክ'ሩ፡ሲበል -ስ- ግፍያ ዕቃ

crucifixion
ክሩ፡ሲ'ፈክሽን -ስ- ስቅለት

crucify
ክ'ሩ፡ሲፋይ -ግ- መስቀል [ሰ'ቀለ]

crude
ክ'ሩ፡ድ -ት- ያልነ'ጠረ
  of person
  -ት- ባለጌ ፣ ያልተቀ'ጣ
  roughly made
  -ት- መና'ኛ

cruel
ክ'ሩወል -ት- ዉ'ካኝ ፣ አረመኔ (ርኅራኄ በግ ጣት)

cruelty
ክ'ሩወልቲ -ስ- ዉ'ካኔ ፣ አረመኔ'ነት (ርኅራኄ በግጣት)

cruet
ክ'ሩወት -ስ- የቅማም ቅመም መያዣ ዕቃ (እንግ'ድ ላይ የ'ሚቀርብ)

cruise
ክ'ሩ፡ዝ -ግ- በመርከብ መንሸራሸር [ተንሸራ 'ሸረ] ፣ የጦላት መርከብ መ'ከታተል [ተከታ 'ተለ]

cruiser
ክ'ሩ፡ዘ -ስ- ት'ልቅ የጦር መርከብ

crumb
ክ'ረም -ስ- ፍር'ፋሪ (የዳቦ)

crumble
ክ'ረምበል -ግ- መፈርፈር [ፈረ'ፈረ]

crumple
ክ'ረምፕል -ግ- መጨባበጥ [ጨባ'በጠ]

crunch
ክ'ረንች -ግ- መጉረጨደም [ጉረጨ'ደም] ፣ መ ቀርጠም [ቀረ'ጠመ]

crusader
ክሩ'ሴደረ -ስ- የመስቀል ጦር'ነት ወ'ታ'ደር

crush
ክ'ረሽ -ግ- ግድተት [አደ'ታተ]

410

crust

ክ'ረስት -ስ- የዳ'ቦ ቅር'ፈት ፣ የደረቀ ዳ'ቦ ቁ'ራሽ

crusty

ክ'ረስቲ -ት- ደረት ፣ ትርፊ'ት የጥ'ላ'በት

crutch

ክ'ረች -ስ- መ'ደገሬያ እንጨት (ለእግር ሰባራ ሰው) ፣ ምርኩዝ

cry

ክ'ራይ -ግ- ግልቀስ [አለ'ቀሰ] shout

-ስ- ጩኸት

crying

ክ'ራይንግ -ት- አልቃ'ሻ

crypt

ክ'ሪፕት -ስ- ከቤተ ክርስቲያን በታ'ች ያለ የመቃብር ቦታ

cryptic

ክ'ሪፕቲክ -ት- በተ'ላሉ የ'ግይገባ ፣ ምስ ጢር የጥ'ላ'በት

crystal

ክ'ሪስተል -ስ- መስተዋት (የ ጋው የከ'በረ) ፣ ብር'ሌ (ግዕ'ድን) geological

-ስ- ባለጩ'ት

cub

'ከብ -ስ- ያንበሳ ግልገል

cube

ክ'ዩ፡ብ -ስ- ስ'ድስት ግዕዘን ያ ለው ቅርፅ

cubic

ክ'ዩ፡ቢክ -ት- ኩ'ብ

cubicle

ክ'ዩ፡ቢከል -ስ- ባንድ ክፍል ውስጥ ትን'ንሽ ክፍሉ'ች

cucumber

ክ'ዩከምብ -ስ- ክያር

cud

'ከድ -ስ- እንሰሳት የ'ሚያመነ'ዥኩት ግር ፣ ምግብ

cuddle

'ከደል -ግ- አቀብቆ ማቀፍ [አ'ቀፈ]

cudgel

'ከጀል -ስ- 'ዱላ ፣ በ'ትር (መምቻ)

cue

ክ'ዩ: -ስ- የቢልያርድ መ'ጫወቻ ዘንግ sign

-ስ- ምል'ክት (አንድ ነገር ለመ'መ42 kት)

cuff

'ከፍ -ስ- እ'ጅጌ

culinary

'ከሊነሪ -ት- የወጥ ቤት ፣ ከወጥ ጋር ግን'ኙ 'ነት ያ ለው

culminate

'ከልሚኔይት -ግ- መጨ'ረስ [ጨ'ረስ]

culmination

ከል ሚ'ኔይሽን -ስ- ተፍጻሜት ፣ መጨ'ረሻ

culpable

'ከልፐበል -ት- ሊ'ወ'ቀስ የ'ሚ'ገ'ባው ፣ ተወ 'ቃሽ

culprit

'ከልፐሪት -ስ- ጥፋተ'ኛ ሰው ፣ ወንጀለ'ኛ ፣ በወንጀል የተከ'ሰሰ ሰው

cult

'ከልት -ስ- አምልኮ (ጣዖት)

cultivate

'ከልቲቬይት -ስ- ግረስ [አ'ረስ] ፣ ግሳ'ደግ [አሳ'ደገ] (ለአትክልት)

cultivation

ከልቲ'ቬይሽን -ስ- እርሻ

cultural

'ከልቸረል -ት- የትምህርት ፣ ባህል ነ'ክ

culture

'ከልቸ -ስ- ባህል ፣ ትምህርት

cumbrous

'ከምብረስ -ት- እ'ጅግ ከ'ባድ'ና ምቹ ያልሆነ (ለመ'ሸከም)

cumin

'ኩሚን -ስ- ከመ'ን

cumulative

ክ'ዩምዩለቲቭ -ት- የ'ሚያደግ ፣ እ'የጨ'መረ የ'ሚሄድ

cunning

'ከኒንግ -ት- ተ'ለ ፣ ብልጥ

cup

'ከፕ -ስ- ስኒ

411

cupboard
'ከበድ -ስ- ቁም ሣጥን

cupidity
ከዩ'ፒዲቲ -ስ- ሥ'ሥት

cur
'ከ: -ስ- ባለቤት የሌ'ለው ውሻ ፤ ልክስክስ

curable
ከ'ዩረበል -ቅ- ሊድን ፤ ሊ'ፈ'ወስ የ'ሚ'ቾል

curacy
ከ'ዩረሲ -ስ- ሰበካ (የንፍቅ ቄስ)

curate
ከ'ዩረት -ስ- ንፍቅ ቄስ (ረ'ዳት ቄስ)

curative
ከ'ዩረቲቭ -ቅ- መድኃኒት'ነት ያ'ለው

curator
ከዩ'ሬይተ -ስ- የምዱዚየም ኃላፈ

curb
'ከ:ብ -ግ- መ'ቆጣጠር [ተቆጣ'ጠረ]
-ስ- ዛብ ፤ መገቻ (ለፈረስ ፤ ለበቅሎ)

curdle
'ከ:ዶል -ግ- መርጋት [ረ'ጋ] (ወተት)

cure
ከ'ዩወ -ግ- ማዳን [አዳነ] ፤ መፈ'ወስ [ፈ'ወሰ]

curfew
'ከ:ፍዩ -ስ- ከተወ'ሰነ ጊዜ በኋላ መ'ዘዋወር
የ'ሚከለ'ክል ትእዛዝ (የመንግሥት)

curio
ከ'ዩሪዮ -ስ- ያንድ አገር ግስታወሻ ዕቃ

curiosity
ከዩሪ'ዮስቲ -ስ- ሁ'ሉን የማወቅ ፍ'ላጎት ፤
ቸ'ኩልነ'ት

curious
ከ'ዩሪየስ -ቅ- ሁ'ሉን ለማወቅ የ'ሚቸ'ኩል ፤
እንግዳ ፤ ያልተለ'መደ

curl
'ከ:ል -ግ- መጠቅለል [ጠቀ'ለለ]

currant
'ከረንት -ስ- ዘቢብ

currency
'ከረንሲ -ስ- ገንዘብ

current
'ከረንት -ቅ- ያሁን ጊዜ
of river
-ስ- ጉርፍ
electric
-ስ- ኮ'ረንቲ ፤ ኤሌክትሪክ

curriculum
ከ'ሪከዩለም -ስ- ሥርዓተ ትምህርት

curse
'ከ:ስ -ግ- መርገም [ረ'ገመ]
-ስ- እርግማን

cursed
'ከ:ስት -ቅ- የተረ'ገመ

cursive
'ከ:ሲቭ -ቅ- የተያያዘ (ጽሕፈት)

cursory
'ከ:ሰሪ -ቅ- ቸ'ኩል ፤ ፍጥነት ያ'ለ'በት

curtail
ከ'ቴይል -ግ- ማሳ'ጠር [አሳ'ጠረ]

curtain
'ከ:ተን -ስ- መ'ጋረጃ ፤ አነበር

curtsy
'ከ:ትሲ -ግ- እ'ጅ መንሣት [ነ'ሣ] (ለሴት)

curvature
'ከ:በቸ -ስ- ቆልማ'ማ'ነት ፤ መ'ቆልመም ፤
ቆልምም

curve
'ከ:ብ -ስ- ቆልማ'ማ ፤ ጠማ'ማ ነገር

cushion
'ኩሽን -ስ- መ'ከ'ዳ

custodian
ከስ'ተውዲየን -ስ- ጠ'ባቂ ፤ ኃላፈ ፤ አሳ'ዳጊ

custody
'ከስተዲ -ስ- ጠ'ባቂ'ነት ፤ አሳ'ዳጊ'ነት

custom
'ከስተም -ስ- ልምድ ፤ ልግድ

customs
'ከስተምዝ -ስ- ጉምሩክ ፤ ኪ'ላ

customary
'ከስተመሪ -ቅ- የተለ'መደ 、

customer
'ከስተመ -ስ- ደምበ'ኛ (የገበያ)

custom-house
'ከስተም 'ሀውስ -ስ- ጉምሩክ

412

cut

'ከት   ⟶ መቁረጥ [ቆረጠ]
    -ሱ- ቁርጥ ፣ ቁስል (በመ'ቁረጥ)

cute

ክ'ዩ፡ት ⟶ የ'ሚያምር ፣ ቆንጆ ፣ እ'ተ'ር ም'ተ'ን ያለ

cutlery

'ከትለሪ -ሱ- ቢ'ላዋ ፣ ሹ'ካ'ና ማንካ መዘተ

cutlet

'ከትሌት -ሱ- የጉድን ሥጋ ፣ ኮትሌት

cutter

'ከተ -ሱ- ሥለት ፣ ቆራጭ

cutting

'ከቲንግ -ሱ- ተቆርጦ የ'ሚ'ተ'ከል ተከል
newspaper
       -ሱ- ከጋዜጣ ላይ ተቆርጦ የወ'ጣ ጽሑፍ

cycle

'ሳይክል -ሱ- ተከታትሎ በተመ'ሰነ ጊዜያት የ'ሚ'ደጋ'ገም ነገር ፤ ዑደት
bicycle
       -ሱ- ቢስክሌት

---

cyclist

'ሳይክሊስት -ሱ- ቢስክሌት ነጂ

cyclone

'ሳይክለመን -ሱ- ታ'ላቅ አውሎ ነፋስ

cylinder

'ሲሊንደ -ሱ- ክ'ብ ወምድ

cylindrical

ሲ'ሊንድሪከል -ት- ባለክ'ብ ወምድ

cymbals

'ሲምበዝ -ሱ- ከነሐስ የተሠ'ሩ ሁለ'ት ስ ሐን መ'ሰል የሙዚቃ መ'ሣሪያዎ'ች

cynic

'ሲኒክ -ሱ- የነ'ገሩትን የ'ገያም ሰው ፣ ጠ ግግ ትርጉም የ'ሚሰጥ ሰው ፣ ተጠራጣሪ

cynical

'ሲኒከል -ት- የነ'ገሩትን የ'ገያም ፣ ጠጣግ ትርጉም ሰጥ

---

dab

'ዳብ ⟶ መተምተም [ተመ'ተመ]

dad

'ዳድ -ሱ- አ'ባቴ ፣ አ'ባ'ቴ ፣ አ'ብ'ዬ

daft

'ዳ፡ፍት -ት- ቂል ፣ ደካማ አእምሮ ያ'ለው

dagger

'ዳገ -ሱ- መጪ ፣ ጉ'ዶ

daily

'ዴይሊ -ተተ- በ'የቀኑ
        -ት- የቀን

dainty

'ዴይንቲ -ሱ- የ'ሚያስጉመ'ጅ ምግብ ፣ አ'ጅ የ'ሚያስቆረ'ጥጥ ምግብ
        -ት- የ'ሚያስጉመ'ጅ ፣ አ'ጅ የ'ሚያስ ቆረ'ጥጥ (ምግብ) ፤ ሁ'ሉ ነገር የ'ማይጥመው
        -ት- አ'ተ'ር ም'ተ'ን ያለ (ለሴት)

---

dairy

'ዴሪ -ሱ- የወተት ፋብሪካ

dais

'ዴይስ -ሱ- ሉዓላዊ ቦታ ፣ ት'ንሽ የእንጨት መድረክ ፣ ሉዓላዊ መድረክ

dam

'ዳም -ሱ- የውሃ ግ'ድብ
animal
        -ሱ- ያረ'ገዘ'ች እንስሳ(ፈረስ ፣ በግ መዘተ)

damage

'ዳሚጅ ⟶ ግ'በላሸት (አ'በላ'ሸ)
        -ሱ- ብል'ሽት

damn

'ዳም ⟶ መኩ'ነን [ኩ'ነነ]

damnation

ዳም'ኔይሸን -ሱ- ጥፋት ፣ ኩነኔ

damp

'ዳምፕ -ት- እርጥብ

413

dance
'ዳንስ -ግ- እስክስታ መውረድ [ወ'ረድ] ፣
መደ'ነስ [ደ'ነሰ]

dancer
'ዳንስ -ስ- እስክስታ ወራጅ ፣ ደ'ናሽ ፣ ጨ'ፋሪ

dancing
'ዳንሲንግ -ስ- እስክስታ መውረድ ፣ ዳንስ ፣
ጭ'ፈራ

danger
'ዴይንጅ -ስ- አደጋ

dangerous
'ዴይንጀረስ -ት- አደገ'ኛ

dangle
'ዳንገል -ግ- ማንጠልጠል [አንጠለ'ጠለ] ፣
መንጠልጠል [ተንጠለ'ጠለ]

dare
'ዴየ -ግ- መድፈር [ደ'ፈረ]
challenge
-ግ- መ'ፍከር [ተፍካ'ከረ]

daring
'ዴሪንግ -ት- ደ'ፋር

dark
'ዳክ -ስ- ጨ'ለማ
-ት- ጥቁር (የልብስ ፣ የሰው መልክ
ወዘተ)

darken
'ዳከን -ግ- ማጥቆር (አጠ'ቆረ) ፣ መጨ'ለም
[ጨ'ለመ]

darkness
'ዳክኔስ -ስ- ጭ'ለማ ፣ ጨ'ለማ

darn
'ዳን -ግ- መጥቀም [ጠ'ቀመ] (በተለይ'ይ ለሰủ
ልብስ)

dart
'ዳት -ግ- መ'ፈትለክ [ተፈተ'ለከ]
-ስ- በእ'ጅ የ'ሚ'ወረ'ወር በጣም ት'ን
ሽ ፍላ'ፃ

dash
'ዳሽ -ግ- መርጥ

dashing
'ዳሺንግ -ት- ሎጋ ፣ አስደ'ሳች ፣ መልክ መል
ካም
running
-ት- ሩ'ጫ

date
'ዴይት -ስ- ቀን ፣ ዘመን (ም'ሳሌ ፣ መስከረም
፮ ቀን ፲፱፻፷'ን ም)

daub
'ዶብ -ግ- መምረግ [መ'ረገ] (በጭቃ)

daughter
'ዶተ -ስ- ልጅ (ሴት)

daughter-in-law
'ዶተሪንሎ: -ስ- ምራት

dauntless
'ዶንትሌስ -ት- ደ'ፋር

dawdle
'ዶ:ደል -ግ- ወደኋላ መቅረት [ቀ'ረ] ፣ በከ
ንቱ ጊዜ ማባከን [አባ'ከነ] ፣ ያለ ዓላማ በመን
ገድ ላይ መንከራተት [ተንከራ'ተተ]

dawn
ዶ:ን -ስ- ንጋት

day
'ዴይ -ስ- ቀን

daylight
'ዴይላይት -ስ- የቀን ብርሃን

dazed
'ዴይዝድ -ት- የደነዘ'ዘው ፣ ለጥቂት ጊዜ
ስ'ሜቱን ያ'ጣ (በወ'መታት ምክንያት)

dazzle
'ዳዘል -ግ- ዓይን ማንጸባረቅ [አንጸባ'ረቀ]

dazzling
'ዳዝሊንግ -ት- የ'ሚያንጸባ'ርቅ

deacon
'ዲይከን -ስ- ዲያቆን

dead
'ዴድ -ት- የሞተ ፣ ም'ውት

deaden
'ዴደን -ግ- ሕመም መቀ'ነስ [ቀ'ነሰ] ፣ ድም
ፅን ማብረድ [አብ'ረደ]

dead-line
'ዴድ ላይን -ስ- የተወ'ሰነ ጊዜ (አንድ ሥራ
የ'ሚ'ፈ'ጸም'በት)

deadly
'ዴድሊ -ት- ለሕይወት አስጊ

deaf
'ዴፍ -ት- ደንቆር (ጆሮው የ'ማይሰማ)

deafen
'ዴፈን -ግ- ማደንቆር [አደነ'ቆረ] (በድምፅ)

414

deafness
'ዴፍነስ -ስ- ደንቁር'ና

deal
'ዲደል -ግ- መነ'ገድ [ነ'ገደ]
playing cards
-ግ- የመ'ጫወቻ ካርታ ማ'ደል [አ'ደለ]

dealer
'ዲደለ -ስ- ነ'ጋዴ
cards
-ስ- ካርታ አ'ዳይ

dear
'ዲየ -ቅ- የተወ'ደደ ፤ ው'ድ
price
-ቅ- ው'ድ (ለዋጋ)

dearest
'ዲየረስት -ቅ- እ'ጅግ የተወ'ደደ

death
'ዴስ -ስ- ሞት

debar
ዲ'ባ፡ -ግ- ማ'ገድ [አ'ገደ] ፤ መከልከል [ከለ 'ከለ]

debased
ዲ'ቤይስድ -ቅ- ዝ'ቅ ያለ ፤ የተዋ'ረደ
money
-ቅ- ሌላ ብረታብረት የተጨ'መረ'በት
(መሐ'ለት)

debatable
ዲ'ቤይተብል -ቅ- የ'ሚያ'ከራ'ክር ፤ አ'ከራ ካሪ

debate
ዲ'ቤይት -ግ- መከራከር [ተከራ'ከረ]

debauchery
ዲ'ቦ፡ቼሪ -ስ- በግብረ ገ'ብ ዝ'ቅተ'ኛነት
ዝ'ሙት ፤ ምግብ'ና መጠ'ጥ ወዘተ ግብዣት

debility
ዲ'ቢሊቲ -ስ- ድካም (የሰው'ነት)

debris
'ዴብሪ -ስ- ፍርስራሽ (የቤት)

debt
'ዴት -ስ- እ'ዳ ፤ ብ'ድር

debtor
'ዴተ -ስ- ተበ'ዳሪ ፤ ባለዳ

decade
ዲኬይድ -ስ- 0'ሥር ዓመት

decadent
'ዴከደንት -ቅ- ወ'ራዳ

decapitate
ዲ'ካፒተይት -ግ- የሰው አንገት መሥ'የፍ [ሡ'የ ፈ]

decay
ዲኬይ -ግ- መሻገት [ሻ'ገተ] ፤ መ'በላት- [ተበ'ላ]

deceased
ዲ'ሲይስት -ቅ- ሙት

deceit
ዲ'ሲይት -ስ- ማ'ታለል

deceitful
ዲ'ሲይትፉል -ቅ- አ'ታላይ

deceive
ዲ'ሲይቭ -ግ- ማ'ታለል [አ'ታ'ለለ]

December
ዲ'ሴምበ -ስ- ታኅሣሥ

decent
'ዲሰንት -ቅ- ጨዋ ፤ የተከ'በረ

deception
ዲ'ሴፕሸን -ስ- ማ'ታለል

deceptive
ዲ'ሴፕቲቭ -ቅ- አ'ታላይ

decide
ዲ'ሳይድ -ግ- መቁረጥ [ቆ'ረጠ] (ለሐሳብ)

decipher
ዲ'ሳይፈ -ግ- አ'ዋኪ ጽሑፍ ማንበብ [አነ 'በበ]

decision
ዲ'ሲዠን -ስ- ው'ሳኔ

decisive
ዲ'ሳይሲቭ -ቅ- የመጨ'ረሻ ፤ ጽኑእ (በው'ሳኔው)
of person
-ቅ- ቆራጥ

deck
'ዴክ -ግ- ማስጌጥ [አስጌጠ]
of ship
-ስ- የመርከብ ወለል

declaim
ዲክ'ሌይም -ግ- በሕዝብ ፊት መ'ናገር [ተና 'ገረ]

415

declamation
ደክለ'ሜይሸን -ስ- በሕዝብ ፊት ስ'ሜት
የ'ሚቀሰ'ቅስ ንግ'ግር ግድረገ

declaration
ደክለ'ሬይሸን -ስ- ንግ'ግር ፡ ዐዋጅ

declare
ዲክ'ለየ -ግ- መግለጽ [ገ'ለጸ] ፣ ግ'ወጅ
[ዐ'ወጀ]

decline
ዲክ'ላይን -ግ- ማነስ [አ'ነሰ]
refuse
-ግ- እም'ቢ ማለት [አለ]

decompose
ዲከም'ፐውዝ -ግ- መበስበስ [በሰ'በሰ]

decorate
'ዴከሬይት -ግ- ማጌጥ [አጌጠ]
house
-ግ- ቤት ቀለም መቀ'ባት [ቀ'ባ]

decoration
ዴከ'ሬይሸን -ስ- ጌጥ
medal
-ስ- ኒሻን

decorative
'ዴከረቲቭ -ቅ- ያጌጠ ፣ ያጌረ

decorator
'ዴከሬይተ -ስ- ቤት የ'ሚቀ'ባ ሰው

decorous
'ዴከረስ -ቅ- የተከ'በረ ፡ ጥሩ ጠባይ የ'ሚያሳ'ይ

decoy
'ዲኮይ -ስ- መሳቢያ ፡ ወጥመድ ማጥበያ ነገር፣
ማጥመጃ

decrease
ዲክ'ሪይስ -ግ- ማነስ [አ'ነሰ]

decree
ዲክ'ሪይ -ግ- ትእዛዝ ማውጣት [አወ'ጣ] (ንጉ
ሣዊ)
-ስ- ትእዛዝ ፣ ዐዋጅ

decrepit
ዲክ'ሬፒት -ቅ- በዕድሜ ምክንያት ያረጀ ፣
የተበላ'ሸ

decry
ዲክ'ራይ -ግ- መ'ቃወም [ተቃ'ወመ]

dedicated
'ዴዲኬይቲድ -ቅ- ሕይወቱን ላንድ ተግባር
ያዋለ

dedication
ዴዲኬይሸን -ስ- ሕይወትን ላንድ ተግባር
ማዋል

deduce
ዲድ'ዩስ -ግ- በሁናቴው መሠረት ፍርድ መስ
ጠት [ሰ'ጠ] (ለሕ'ሳብ)

deduct
ዲ'ደክት -ግ- መቀነስ [ቀ'ነሰ] (ከደመወዝ
ወዘተ)

deduction
ዲ'ደክሸን -ስ- የሕ'ሳብ ው'ጤት
money
-ስ- ት'ናሽ

deed
'ዲይድ -ስ- ሥራ ፡ ተግባር

deem
'ዲይም -ግ- ማሰብ-[አ'ሰበ] ፣ ግመን [አ'መነ]

deep
'ዲይፕ -ቅ- ጥልቅ

deepen
'ዲይፐን -ግ- ማጥለት [አጠ'ለተ] ፣ ጥልቅ
ማድረግ [አደ'ረገ]

deer
'ዲየ -ስ- አጋዘን

deface
ዲ'ፌይስ -ግ- ትርዕ ማጥፋት [አጠ'ፋ] ፣
ጽሑፍ እንዳይ'ነ'በብ መድ'ለዝ [ደ'ለዘ]

defamation
ዴፈ'ሜይሸን -ስ- የስም ማጥፋት ወንጀል

default
ዲ'ፎልት -ግ- በተጠር አለመ'ገኘት [-ገኘ'ኘ]
(በፍርድ ቤት)
in debt
-ግ- የተብ'ደሩትን ገንዘብ በጊዜ አለመ
ክፈል [-ከ'ፈለ]

defaulter
ዲ'ፎልተ -ስ- በተጠረው ያላተገ'ኘ (በፍርድ
ቤት)

defeat
ዲ'ፌይት -ግ- ማ'ሸነፍ [አ'ሸነፈ]
-ስ- ማ'ሸነፍ

416

defect
’ዲፌክት -ሱ- ጉድለት ፣ እንከን

defective
ዲ’ፌክቲቭ -ት- ጉድለት ያ'ለ'በት

defence
ዲ’ፌንስ -ሱ- መ'ከላከያ

defend
ዲ’ፌንድ -ግ- ለራስ መ'ከላከ ነ [ተከላ'ከለ]

defendant
ዲ’ፌንደንት -ሱ- ተከ'ሳሽ

defender
ዲ’ፌንደ -ሱ- ተከላካይ

defensive
ዲ’ፌንሲቭ -ት- የመ'ከላከያ (ዘዴ)

defer
ዲ’ፌ፣ -ግ- ግስተላለፍ [አስተላ'ለፈ] (ለሌላ
ተን)

deferential
ዲፈ’ረንሸል -ት- ሥልጣን አክባሪ

defiant
ዲ’ፋየንት -ት- ተጻጻሚ ፣ መ'ካች
child
    -ት- የ'ግይ ታዛ'ዝ (ነሌ ፭)

deficiency
ዲ’ፊሸንሲ -ሱ- ጉድለት ፣ እንከን

deficient
ዲ’ፊሸንት -ት- ጎን'ደለው ፣ ምሉ ያልሆነ ፣
እንከን ያ'ለ'በት

deficit
’ዴፊሲት -ሱ- የገንዘብ ግነስ ፣ ከገቢ ሰ—
መብዛት (በንግድ)

defile
ዲ’ፋይል -ግ- ግርኩስ [አረ'ኩስ]

define
ዲ’ፋይን -ግ- መወ'ሰን [ወ'ሰነ] (የቃል ፍ'ች
ለመስጠት)

definite
’ዴፊኒት -ት- የተወ'ሰነ ፣ ቁርጥ ፣ ግልጽ

definition
ዴፊ’ኒሽን -ሱ- ው'ሳኔ ፣ ያንድ ነገር ሁናቴ ፣
ጠባይ መግለጫ

deformed
ዲ’ፎ፡ምድ -ት- ሰው'ነቱ የተበላ'ሸ ፣ ቅርጹ
የጠ'ፋ

deformity
ዲ’ፎ፡ሚቲ -ሱ- የሰው'ነት ፣ የቅርጽ መ'በላሸት

defraud
ዴፍ’ሮ፡ድ -ግ- ግ'ታለል [አ'ታ'ለለ](ለንንዘብ)

defray
ዴፍ’ሬይ -ግ- መከፈል [h'ፈለ]

deft
’ዴፍት -ት- ተልጣ'ፋ ፣ ባለሙያ

defunct
ዲ’ፈንክት -ት- የሞተ ፣ ም'ውት ፣ የ'ግይ
ሥራ (ለግነበር መዘተ)

defy
ዲ’ፋይ -ግ- መ'ጻጸም [ተጻጸመ]
orders
    -ግ- አለመ'ታዘዝ [-ታ'ዘዘ]

degenerate
ዲ’ጀነሪት -ግ- መ'ዋረድ [ተዋ'ረደ]

degrade
ዲግ’ሬይድ -ግ- ግ'ዋረድ [አ'ዋ'ረደ] ፣ ዝ'ት
ግድረግ [አደ'ረገ]

degrading
ዲግ’ሬይዲንግ -ት- አ'ዋራጅ ፣ ዝት አድራጊ

degree
ዲግ’ሪይ -ሱ- ግዐርግ ፣ ደረጃ ፣ ተዋረድ

deity
’ዴይቲ -ሱ- አምላክ'ነት ፣ አምላካዊ ጠባይ
ወይን'ም ባሕርይ

dejected
ዲ’ጀክተድ -ት- ያ'ዘነ ፣ በፍ'ጹም ያልተደ
'ሰተ

delay
ዴ’ሌይ -ግ- መዘግየት [ዘገ'የ]
    -ሱ- መዘግየት

delegate
’ዴሊጌይት -ግ- ሥልጣን ለበታ'ች እንዲሠ
ራ'በት መስጠት [ሰ'ጠ] ፣ መወ'ከል [ወ'ከለ]

delegate
’ዴለገት -ሱ- በብዙ ሰዎ'ች ስም የተወ'ከለ
መልእክተ'ኛ

delegation
ዴለ’ጌሽን -ሱ- መልእክተ'ኞች

delete
ደ’ሊይት -ግ- መፋቅ [ፋቀ] (ቃላት መዘተ)

417

deletion
ደ'ሊይሽን -ስ- የተፋተ ፣ የተደ'ለዘ ጽሑፍ

deliberate
ደ'ሊበረት -ት- የታ'ሰበ'በት ፣ በግወቅ የተ
ደ'ረገ ፣ ሆነ ተብሎ የተደ'ረገ

deliberation
ደሊበ'ሬይሽን -ስ- ውይ'ይት ፣ አንድ ነገር
በጥን'ቃቄ ግምናት ፤ በንግ'ግር ፣ በእንቅስ'ቃሴ
መዘተ ፣ ዝ'ግተ'ኛ'ነት

delicacy
'ዴሊከሲ -ስ- ረቂቅ'ነት
food
-ስ- ጣዕም ያ'ለው ምግብ
politeness
-ስ- ጥን'ቃቄ

delicate
'ዴሊከት -ት- እስደ'ሳች ፣ በረቂቅ'ነት የተ
ሠ'ራ ፣ አደን የ'ግይችል

delicious
ደ'ሊሽስ -ት- ጣፋጭ ፣ ጣዕም ያ'ለው

delight
ደ'ላይት -ግ- መ'ደሰት [ተደ'ሰተ] ፣ ግስደ
'ሰት [አስደ'ሰተ]
-ስ- ደ'ስታ

delightful
ደ'ላይትፉል -ት- በጣም የተደ'ሰተ

delineate
ዲ'ሊኔዩይት -ግ- ሥዕል መንደፍ [ነ'ደፈ]

delinquency
ዲ'ሊንክወንሲ -ስ- ግ'ዳጅ አለመፈ'ጸም ፤
ሕ'ገ ወ'ጥ'ነት (ለመ'ጣቶ'ች) ፣ ብልግ'ና

delinquent
ዲ'ሊንክወንት -ት- ወንጀለ'ኛ (ለመ'ጣቶ'ች) ፣
ግ'ዳጁን የ'ግይፈ'ጽም ፣ ባለጌ

delirious
ዲ'ሊሪየስ -ት- ትዝታታም (በበ'ሽታ ምክንያት)

deliver
ዲ'ሊቨ -ግ- ግስረ'ከብ [አስረ'ከበ]

deliverance
ዲ'ሊቨረንስ -ስ- ድነነት (የእግዚአብሔር) ፣
ነጻ መውጣት ፣ መዳን

delivery
ዲ'ሊቨሪ -ስ- ርክ'ክብ
of child
-ስ- መውለድ ፣ መ'ገላገል (ለሕፃን)

dell
'ዴል -ስ- ት'ንሽ ሸለቆ ብዙ ዛፍ ያ'ለ'በት

delude
ደል'ዩ:ድ -ግ- ግ'ታለል [አ'ታ'ለለ] ፣ ግጥ
በርበር [አጥብረ'በረ]

deluge
'ዴልጅ -ስ- ድንገተ'ኛ የወሃ ሙላት

delusion
ደል'ዩ:ዠን -ስ- ግ'ታለል፤ የተሳሳተ ስ'ሜት
ወይን'ም እምነት (ከሕመም የተነ'ሳ)

de luxe
ዲ'ለክስ -ት- በጣም ያግረ ፣ በጣም ጥ'ቾት
ያ'ለው

delve
'ዴልቭ -ግ- መቆ'ፈር [ቆ'ፈረ] (በአካፋ)

demagogue
'ዴመጎግ -ስ- በገገሮ'ች ላይ ሕዝብ የ'ሚ
ያሥነ'ሣ የፖሊቲካ መሪ

demand
ዲ'ማንድ -ግ- መጠ'የቅ [ጠ'የቀ]

demeanour
ደ'ሚ:ነ -ስ- አመል ፣ ጠባይ ፣ ሁናቴ

demented
ደ'ሜንቲድ -ት- ያ'በደ ፣ እብድ

demise
ዲ'ማይዝ -ስ- ጥት

democracy
ደ'ሞክራሲ -ስ- ዴሞክራሲ ፣ የሕዝብ ገዛት

demolish
'ደሞሊሽ -ግ- ግተፋት [አጠ'ፋ] ፣ ግውደም
[አወ'ደም]

demolition
ደሞ'ሊሽን -ስ- መፍረስ (የቤት ፣ የሕንፃ)

demon
'ዲይመን -ስ- ርኩስ መንፈስ ፣ ሠይጣን

demonstrate
'ዴመንስትሬይት -ግ- ግሳ'የት [አሳ'የ]፤ ግስ
ረ'ጃ እ'ያ'ረቡ መግለጽ [ገ'ለጸ]
political
-ግ- ሰላግዊ ሠልፍ ግድረግ [አደ'ረገ]

demonstration

ዴመንስት'ሬይሽን -ስ- በም'ሳሌ ፣ በማስረ'ጃ ማሳ'የት ፤ ወ'ታ'ደራዊ ሰልፍ
political

-ስ- ሰላማዊ ሠልፍ

demonstrative

ደ'ሞንስትረቲቭ -ቅ- ገላጭ ፣ እመልካች (ሰዋ ሰው)

demonstrator

'ዴመንስትሬይተ -ስ- አሳዪ ፣ ገላጭ (ሰው)
political

-ስ- ሰላማዊ ሠልፈ'ኛ

demoralize

ደ'ሞረላይዝ -ግ- ቅስም መስበር [ሰ'በረ]

demur

ዲ'መ: -ግ- መ'ጠራጠር [ተጠራ'ጠረ] (መ'ልስ ለመስጠት)

demure

ዲም'ዩወ -ቅ- ዓይን አ'ፋር (በተለ'ይ ለልጃገ ረድ ፣ ለሴት)

den

'ዴን -ስ- ጉድጓድ ፣ መ'ሸሸጊያ (ያውሬ)

denial

ዲ'ናየል -ስ- ክህደት ፣ ተቃውሞ ፣ አለመ'ቀ በል (ሐ'ሳብ) ፣ ማስተባበል

denomination

ዲኖሚ'ኔሽን -ስ- በእንድ ሃይማኖት የ'ሚያ ምኑ ሰዎ'ች የ'ሚ'ጠሩ'በት ስም ፤ አንድ ዓይ ነት የሆኑ የ'ሚ'ጠ'ሩበት (ምሳሌ ፣ ሃይ ማኖት ፣ ገንዘብ ፣ መለ'ኪያ)
money, stamps

-ስ- የመሐ'ለቅ ፣ የቴምብር ዋጋ

denominator

ዲ'ናሚነተ -ስ- የጋራ አ'ካፋይ (በሒሳብ)

denote

ዲ'ነውት -ግ- ማመልከት [አመለ'ከተ]

denounce

ዲ'ናውንስ -ግ- [ከ'ሰሰ] ፣ በሕዝብ መሀል መወንጀል [ወን'ጀለ] ፤ የስምም'ነት ውል ለማ ፍረስ ማ'ሰብን ማስታወቅ [አስታ'ወቀ]

dense

'ዴንስ -ቅ- ጥቅጥ'ቅ ያለ ፣ ች'ፍ'ግ ያለ

density

'ዴንሲቲ -ስ- ውፍረት (ለፈሳሽ)
population

-ስ- በእንድ ቀበሌ የነዋሪ ሕዝብ ብዛት

dent

'ዴንት -ስ- ሥርጉዳት

dental

'ዴንተል -ቅ- የጥርስ

dentifrice

'ዴንቲፈሪስ -ስ- የጥርስ ሳሙና

dentist

'ዴንቲስት -ስ- የጥርስ ሐኪም

denture

'ዴንቸ -ስ- ሰው ሠ'ራሽ ጥርስ

denunciation

ዲነንሲ'ዩሬሽን -ስ- መወንጀል ፣ በሰው ላይ መ'ናገር

deny

ዲ'ናይ -ግ- መካድ [ካደ] ፣ ማስተባበል [አስ ተባ'በለ]

depart

ዲ'ፓ:ት -ግ- መሄድ [ሄደ] ፣ መተው [ተወ] ፣ መሞት [ሞተ]

department

ዲ'ፓ:ትመንት -ስ- ክፍል ፣ ቅርንጫፍ ፣ ንኡስ ክፍል

departmental

ዲፓ:ት'ሜንተል -ቅ- የክፍል (የአስተዳደር)

departure

ዲ'ፓ:ቸ -ስ- ጉዞ ፣ ጉዞ መጀ'መር

depend (on)

ዲ'ፔንድ -ግ- መ'መካት [ተመ'ካ] ፣ ሐ'ሳብ እሰው ላይ መጣል [ጣለ]

dependable

ዲ'ፔንደበል -ቅ- የ'ሚ'መ'ኩ'በት ፣ የ'ሚያ ምኑት ፣ እምነት የ'ሚ'ጣል'በት

deplore

ዲፕ'ሎ: -ግ- በጣም ማዘን [አ'ዘነ] ፣ ዋይ ማለ ት [አለ] ፤ አለመስማማት [-ነ ነግ'ማ]

deploy

ዲፕ'ሎይ -ግ- ወ'ታ'ደር በ'የጦር ግምባር ማ 'ሰ'ለፍ [አ'ሰ'ለፈ] ፤ ቦታ ቦታ መስጠት [ሰ'ጠ]

419

deport
ዲ'ፖ:ት -ግ- ካገር ግስወ'ጣት [አስወ'ጣ] (ወ ዳጉ ወይን'ም ወደ ሴላ አገር እንዲዪዴድ)

deportation
ዲፖ'ቴይሽን -ስ- ካገር ግስወ'ጣት ፣ እንዳን ሕዝብ በጊዶል ካገር ግ'ባረር

deportment
ዲ'ፖ:ትመንት -ስ- ያ'ረግመድ ሁናቴ ፣ ጠባይ

depose
ዲ'ፐውዝ -ግ- ከዙፋን ግውረድ [አወ'ረደ]

deposit
ዲ'ፖዚት -ግ- ግስተ'መጥ [አስተ'መጠ] (ለገ ንዘብ)
bank account
-ስ- ተቀ'ግጭ ገንዘብ (በባንክ ወዘተ)
guarantee
-ስ- መያዣ ገንዘብ ፣ ተብድ

depositor
ዲ'ፖዚተ -ስ- አስተ'ግጭ (ገንዘብ በባንክ)

depository
ዲ'ፖዚትሪ -ስ- ዋጋ ያላ'ቸው ዕቃዎ'ች የ'ሚ 'ተ'መጡ'በት ቤት ፣ ያደሪ ዕቃ ግስተ'መሜ ቤት

depot
'ዴፐው -ስ- ገምጃ ቤት (የወ'ታ'ደር ወዘተ)

depraved
ዲፕ'ሬይቭድ -ተ- ፍ'ዴፕ ሕ'ገ ወጥ ፣ የተበ ላሸ ፣ ብል'ሹ

depravity
ዲፕ'ራቪቲ -ስ- ሕ'ገ ወ'ጥነት ፣ ብል'ሹነት፣ ከግብረ ገ'ብነት መራ ቅ

depreciate
ዲፕ'ሪ ሼዶይት -ግ- ግርጀት [አረ'ጀ] (ለዕቃ)፣ ዋጋ መቀ'ነስ [ቀ'ነሰ]

depreciation
ዲፕረሺ'ዶይ ሽን -ስ- ዋጋ መቀ'ነስ (በእርጅ'ና ምክንያት)

depredation
ዲፕሬ'ዴይሽን -ስ- ዘረፋ

depression
ዲፕ'ሬሽን -ስ- ረ'ባ'ዳ አገር
mood
-ስ- ጭፍግ'ግ ግለት (ለስ'ሜት)

deprive
ዲፕ'ራይቭ -ግ- መ'ከልከል [ተከል'ከለ]

depth
'ዴፕ -ስ- ጥልቀት

deputation
ዴፑ'ቴይሽን -ስ- ወ'ከላ'ነት ፣ አቤት ባዮ 'ች (የተወ'ከሉ)

depute
ዲፑ'ፑውት -ግ- አንድ ሥራ እንዲሠራ ሰው መወ'ከል [ወ'ከለ]

deputize
'ዴፑፑታይዝ -ግ- መ'ወከል [ተወ'ከለ]

deputy
'ዴፑፑቲ -ስ- ረ'ዳት (ናንድ ሹም)
parliament
-ስ- የሕዝብ እንደራሴ

derailment
ዲ'ሬይልመንት -ስ- የባቡር ሐዲድ ለ'ቆ መ'ገልበጥ

deranged
ዲ'ሬይንጅድ -ተ- እብድ ፣ አእምሮው የተና 'ወጠ ፣ የተግ'ታ'በት

derangement
ዲ'ሬይንጅመንት -ስ- እብደት ፣ የአእምሮ መ 'ናወጥ ፣ መ'ግታት

derelict
'ዴሬሊክት -ተ- የተተወ ፣ ለመ'በላሸት የደ 'ረሰ ፣ የተረ'ሳ

deride
ዲ'ራይድ -ግ- ለግሪዝ መ'ግት [ግት] ፣ መ'ግ ለት [ተግ'ለቀ]

derision
ዴ'ሪገን -ስ- የፌዝ ግት

derisive
ዴ'ራይሲቭ -ተ- ፌዝ'ኛ

derivation
ዴሪ'ቬይሽን -ስ- የወ'ግ ፣ ከአንድ ነገር

derivative
ዲ'ሪቨቲቭ -ተ- የወ'ግ ፣ ከአንድ ነገር የተ'ገ'ኘ

derive
ዲ'ራይቭ -ግ- መውጣት (ወ'ግ) ፣ ካንድ ነገር ሴላ ነገር ግግኘት [አገኘ] (ም'ሳሴ ፣ ቃላት ከቃል ግውጣት)

derogatory
ደ'ሮገትሪ -ቅ- አ'ዋራጅ ፣ ክብር የ'ሚነሣ

descend
ዲ'ሴንድ -ግ- መውረድ [ወ'ረደ] ፣ ግቆልቆል
[አቆለ'ቆለ]

descendant
ዲ'ሴንደንት -ቅ- የልጅ ልጅ ፣ ሲወር'ድ ሲ'ዋ
'ረድ የመ'ጣ

descent
ዲ'ሴንት -ስ- ወደታ'ች መውረድ ፣ ግቆል
ቆል
heredity
-ስ- ትውል'ድ ፣ ዘር

describe
ዲስክ'ራይብ -ግ- ስለአንድ ነገር ሙሉ መግ
ለጫ መስጠት [ሰ'ጠ]

description
ደስክ'ሪፕሽን -ስ- ሙሉ መግለጫ

desert
'ዴዘት -ስ- ምድረ በዳ ፣ ሰው የ'ማይኖር'በት
ክፍለ ሀገር

desert
ዲ'ዘ፡ት -ግ- መተው [ተወ] ፣ መክዳት [ክ'ዳ]
(ለወ'ታ'ደር)

deserter
ዲ'ዘ፡ተ -ስ- የክ'ዳ ወ'ታ'ደር ወይን'ም መርh
በ'ኛ

deserve
ዲ'ዘ፡ሽ -ግ- የተገ'ባው መሆን [ሆነ]

design
ዲ'ዛይን -ስ- ዕ'ቅድ ፣ ፕላን
-ግ- ዕ'ቅድ መሥራት [ሠ'ራ]

designate
'ዴዚግኔይት -ግ- ግመልከት [አመለ'ከተ] ፣
መወሰን [ወ'ሰነ] ፤ ለአንድ ሥራ መሾም [ሾመ]

desirable
ዲ'ዛይረበል -ቅ- ሊመርጡት የ'ሚ'ገባ ፣
አስተያየት ግራኪ ፣ አስደ'ሳች ፣ ክል'ብ
የ'ሚ'ፈ'ለግ

desire
ዲ'ዛየ -ግ- መ'መኘት [ተመ'ኘ] ፣ በጣም
መፈ'ለግ [ፈ'ለገ] ፣ ክል'ብ መፈ'ለግ [ፈ'ለገ]

desk
'ዴስክ -ስ- የማንበቢ'ና የጽሕፈት ጠ'ረጴዛ

---

desolate
'ዴዘለት -ቅ- ሰው የ'ማይኖር'በት ፤ በጣም
ያ'ዘነ (በብ'ቸ'ኝ'ነት ምክንያት)

despair
ዲስ'ፔየ -ግ- ተስፋ መቁረጥ [ቆ'ረጠ] ፣ ያለ
ተስፋ መቅረት [ቀ'ረ]

despatch
ዲስ'ፓች -ግ- መላክ [ላከ] (ዕቃ)

desperate
'ዴስፕረት -ቅ- ተስፋ ቢስ ፣ ተስፋ የቆ
'ረጠ

despicable
ዲስ'ፒከበል -ቅ- ፍ'ጹም ክብር የ'ማይ'ገ'ባው

despise
ዲስ'ፓይዝ -ግ- መዝለፍ [ዘ'ለፈ] ፣ መንቀፍ
[ነ'ቀፈ]

despite
ደስ'ፓይት -መዋ- ም'ንም እንኳ(ን) . . . በ

despoil
ደስ'ፖይል -ግ- ሀብት ፣ ገንዘብ መቀ'ማት
[ቀ'ማ] ፣ መዝረፍ [ዘ'ረፈ]

despondency
ደስ'ፖንደንሲ -ስ- ማዘን ፣ መ'ከፋት

despondent
ደስ'ፖንደንት -ቅ- ያ'ዘነ ፣ የh'ፋው

despot
'ዴስፖት -ስ- ተቀናቃኝ የሌ'ለው ጨ'ቋኝ
ገዥ

dessert
ዲ'ዘ፡ት -ስ- ከዋ'ና ምግብ በኋላ የ'ሚቀርብ
ጣፋጭ ምግብ ፣ ፍራፍሬ ወዘተ

destination
ዴስቲ'ኔይሽን -ስ- የ'ሚ'ንዙ'በት ፣ የ'ሚሄ
ዱ'በት ቦታ

destined (for)
'ዴስቲንድ -ቅ- ለ . . . የታ'ሰበ

destiny
'ዴስቲኒ -ስ- ተምኔት ፣ አንድ ሰው ወደፊት
የ'ሚገጥመው ዕ'ድል (ጥሩ ወይን'ም መጥፎ)

destitute
'ዴስቲትዩ፡ት -ቅ- ያ'ጣ ፣ የቸ'ገረው ፣ በጣም
የደh'የ

421

destroy

ዲስትሮይ -ግ- መደምሰስ [ደመ'ሰሰ] ፣ ግፈ
ራረስ [አፈራ'ረስ]፤መግደል [ገ'ደለ] ፣ መፍጀት
[ፈ'ጀ] (መግደል)

destroyer

ዲስትሮየ -ስ- የ'ሚደም'ስስ ሰው ፣ የ'ሚያ
ፈራ'ርስ ሰው ፤ የጦር መርከብ (መከ'ከለ'ኛ
መጠን ያ'ለው)

destruction

ዲስት'ራክሽን -ስ- ጥፋት ፣ መፈራረስ ፣ እል
ቂት ፣ ፍርስራሽ

destructive

ዲስትራክ'ቲቭ -ት- አጥፊ ፣ አፍራሽ ፣ አ'በላሽ

detach

ዲ'ታች -ግ- መነጣጠል [ነጣ'ጠለ] ፣ መፍ
ታት [ፈ'ታ]

detached

ዲ'ታችት -ት- የተነጣ'ጠለ ፣ ለብ'ቻው ተለ
'ይቶ ያ'ለ

detail

'ዲቴይል -ግ- ስለአንድ ነገር ጥቃ'ቅን ጠባይ
ሁሉ መ'ናገር [ተና'ገረ]
-ስ- ዝርዝር ነገር

detain

ዲ'ቴይን -ግ- እን'ዳይሄድ መከልከል [ከለ
'ከለ] ፣ ግቆ'የት [አቆ'የ] ፤ በእስር ቤት ግቆ
'የት [አቆ'የ]

detect

ዲ'ቴክት -ግ- ፈ'ልጎ ግገኘት [አገ'ኘ]

detective

ዲ'ቴክቲቭ -ስ- መርማሪ (በተለ'ይ የወንጀል)
-story
-ስ- የወንጀለ'ኛ'ና የምር'ምሩ ታሪክ ያ'ለ
'በት መጽሐፍ

detention

ዲ'ቴንሽን -ስ- እሥር ቤት ግቆ'የት

deter

ዲ'ተ: -ግ- የ'ሚመጣውን ፈርቶ ከመሥራት
(ሰው ግ'ገድ [አ'ገደ]

detergent

ዲ'ተ:ጀንት -ስ- ዱቄት ወይን'ም ፈሳሽ የሆነ
ግጽጃ ፣ ንጹሕ ግድረጊያ

deteriorate

ዲ'ቲሪየሬይት -ግ- እ'የከ'ፋ ፣ እ'የተበላ'ሸ
መሄድ [ሄደ]

determination

ዲተ:ሚ'ኔይሽን -ስ- ቁርጥ ሐሳ'ብ

determine

ዲ'ተ:ሚነ -ግ- መቁረጥ [ቆ'ረጠ] (ሐ'ሳብነ)

deterrent

ዲ'ተረንት -ስ- ከፍርሃት የተነ'ሣ የ'ሚ'ው'ራን
የሚያ'ገድ ነገር

detest

ዲ'ቴስት -ግ- አጥብቆ መጥላት [ጠ'ላ]፣ መ'ጸ
የፍ [ተጸ'የፈ]

dethrone

ዲ'ዐ'ረውን -ግ- ከአልጋ ግውረድ [አወ'ረደ]
(ንጉሥ)

detonate

'ዴተኔይት -ግ- ግፈን'ዳት [አፈነ'ዳ] ፣ በ'ነ
ይል መፈን'ዳት [ፈነ'ዳ]

detour

'ዲቱወ -ግ- ከዋ'ናው መንገድ መውጣት [ወ
'ጣ] (ዋ'ናው መንገድ ስለታ'ገደ ወይን'ም እስ
ኪ'ው'ራ)
-ስ- ተለ'ዋጭ ሌላ መንገድ (ዋ'ናው መን
ገድ ስለታ'ገደ ወይን'ም እስኪ'ው'ራ)

detract

ዲት'ራክት -ግ- ግሳ'ነስ [አሳ'ነስ] ፣ መቀ'ነስ
[ተ'ነሰ] (የሰው ስም ፣ ዕቃ ፣ ዋ.ጋ ወዘተ)

detrimental

ዴትሪ'ሜንተል -ት- ጎጂ

devaluation

ዲቫልዩ'ዌይሽን -ስ- ዋ.ጋ ግ'ውረድ (በተ
ለ'ይ የገንዘብ)

develop

ዲ'ቬለፕ -ግ- እንዳይድግ ግድረግ [አደ'ረገ]፣
ግስፋፋት [አስፋ'ፋ]

development

ዲ'ቬለፕመንት -ስ- እድገት ፣ መስፋፋት

deviate

'ዲቪዬይት -ግ- ከተለ'መደው ሥርዓት መው
ጣት [ወ'ጣ]

device

ዲ'ቫይስ -ስ- መ'ቀላጠፊያ መ'ሣሪያ ፤ ዕ'ቅድ:
አንድ ነገር ለመሥራት የታ'ሰበ ዘዴ ወይን'ም
የተው'ራ መ'ሣሪያ

devil

'ዴቨል -ስ- ዲያብሎስ ፣ ሰይጣን

422

devil-may-care
ኔቪል ሜይ'ኬየ -ቅ- ግ'ዴ'ለሽ

devilry
'ዴቪልሪ -ስ- የሰይጣን ሥራ

devious
'ዲቪየስ -ቅ- ጠምዛዛ
person
-ቅ- ል'ቡ የ'ማይ'ገን'ኝ

devise
ዲ'ቫይዝ -ግ- መፈልሰፍ [ፈለ'ሰፈ] (መ'ሣ
ሪያ ፣ ዕ'ቅድ)

devoid
ዲ'ቮይድ -ቅ- ባዶ ፣ የተራ'ቆተ ፣ የሌ'ለ በት

devote
ዲ'ቮውት -ግ- ጊዜን ፣ ኃይልን ፣ ኃ.ዖ.ወትን
ላንድ ተግባር ማዋል [አዋለ]

devoted
ዲ'ቮውተድ -ቅ- ጊዜውን ፣ ኃይሉን ፣ ሕይወ
ቱን ላንድ ተግባር ያዋለ
loving
-ቅ- በጣም የ'ሚያፈቅር

devotion
ዲ'ቮውሽን -ስ- ጊዜን ፣ ኃይልን ፣ ሕይወትን
ላንድ ተግባር ማዋል

devour
ዲ'ቫወ -ግ- መዋጥ [ዋጠ] (ለታላ'ላቅ እንስ
ሳት) ፣ መስልቀጥ [ሰለ'ቀጠ]

devout
ዲ'ቫውት -ቅ- ሃይማኖተ'ኛ

dew
ድ'ዩ: -ስ- ጤዛ

dexterity
ዴክስ'ቴሪቲ -ስ- ቅልጥፍ'ና (የእ'ጅ ፣ የሰው
'ነት)

dexterous
'ዴክስትረስ -ቅ- እ'ጅ ቀልጣ'ፋ

diabetes
ዳያ'ቢቲዝ -ስ- የሱ'ካር በ'ሽታ

diabolical
ዳያ'ቦለካል -ቅ- ሰይጣናዊ ፣ በጣም ክፉ

diagnose
'ዳየግኖውዝ -ግ- መመርመር [መረ'መረ] (ሐ
ኪም በ'ሽታ)

diagnosis
ዳየግ'ኖውሲስ -ስ- ምርመራ (በ'ሽታ ለማወቅ
በሐኪም)

diagonal
ዳ'ያገነል -ስ- አ'ገናኝ መሥመር (ከማዕዘን ማዕ
ዘን የ'ሚያ'ገና'ኝ
-ቅ- አ'ገናኝ (ለመሥመር ፣ ከማዕዘን
ማዕዘን)

diagram
'ዳያግራም -ስ- ንድፍ (የማስረ'ጃ ሥዕል)

dial
'ዳየል -ስ- ክበብ ፣ የሰዓት ወይን'ም የሌላ
መሣ'ሪያ ክ'ብ መልክ
telephone
-ስ- የቴሌፎን ግዞሪያ (ቁጥር ያ'ለበ'ት)
-ግ- የቴሌፎን ጥሪ ለማድረግ. ቁጥር
ማዞር [አዞረ]

dialect
'ዳየለክት -ስ- የቋንቋ ዲቃላ ፣ ባንድ ቋንቋ
ውስጥ ያንድ ወገን ሕዝብ ወይን'ም ቀበሌ የ'ሚ
'ና'ገር'በት የቋንቋ ዘየ (ም'ሳሌ ፣ ጎንደር'ኛ ፣
ሸዉ'ኛ ፣ ወሎ'ኛ ወዘተ)

dialectic
ዳያ'ሌክቲክ -ስ- በክር'ክር መልክ እውነትን
ለማግኘት መ'መራመር

dialogue
'ዳየሎግ -ስ- ንግ'ግር ፣ በንግ'ግር መልክ
የተዘጋ'ጀ ጽሑፍ ፣ ውይ'ይት

diameter
ዳ'ያሜተ -ስ- ክበብን ለሁለ'ት የ'ሚከፍል
መሥመር (ዲያሜትር)

diamond
'ዳየመንድ -ስ- አልማዝ

diaper
'ዳየፐ -ስ- የቀዘን ጨርቅ (የሕፃን) ፣ የሕፃን
የንጽሕ'ና ጨርቅ

diarrhoea
ዳያ'ሪየ -ስ- ተቅማጥ ፣ ቅዘን

diary
'ዳየሪ -ስ- ማስታወሻ መያዣ ደብተር (የዕለ
ኑን ሁናቴ ጽፈው የ'ሚይዙ'በት)

dice
'ዳይስ -ስ- ዛሁራ

423

dictate

ዲክ'ቴይት -ግ- የቃል ጽሑፈት ማ'ጸፍ [አ'ጸፈ]
ጎይል ሥልጣን ተመርኩዞ ማዘዝ [አ'ዘዘ]

dictation

ዲክ'ቴይሽን -ስ- የቃል ጽሑፈት ፤ ጎይል ፤
ሥልጣን የተመረ'ከዘ ትእዛዝ

dictator

ዲክ'ቴይተ -ስ- ተቀናቃኝ የሌ'ለው ንጉሥ

dictatorial

ዲክተ'ቶሪየል -ቅ- ትእዛዝ አብጋሪ ፣ ማዘዝ
የ'ሚወ'ድ ፤ ተቀናቃኝ የሌ'ለው (ንጉሥ) ፣ ጎይ
ል ሥልጣን የተመርኩዘ

diction

'ዲክሽን -ስ- የአ'ነጋገር ግልጽ'ነት ፤ የቃላት
አ'መራረጥ (በንግ'ግር)

dictionary

'ዲክሽነሪ -ስ- መዝገበ ቃላት

die

'ዳይ -ግ- መሞት [ሞተ]

diet

'ዳየት -ስ- ምግብ
regimen
-ስ- ል'ዩ ምግብ (የሕመምተ'ኛ)

differ

'ዲፈ -ግ- መ'ለየት [ተለ'የ]

difference

'ዲፈረንስ -ስ- ል'ዩ'ነት

different

'ዲፈረንት -ቅ- ል'ዩ (የተለ'የ)

differentiate

ዲፈ'ረንሺዬይት -ግ- መለ'የት [ለ'የ] ፣ ለ'
ቶ ማወቅ [ዐ'ወቀ]

difficult

'ዲፊኩልት -ቅ- አስቸ'ጋሪ ፣ አ'ዋኪ

difficulty

'ዲፊኩልቲ -ስ- ችግር ፤ መከራ ፤ ሁከት

diffuse

ዲፈ'ዩስ -ቅ- የተበታ'ተነ ፤ የተሰራ'ጨ
የተደባ'ለቀ (በመ'ዋሐድ)

diffusion

ዲፈ'ዩዠን -ስ- መ'በታተን ፤ መ'ሰራጨት
መ'ደባለቅ (በመ'ዋሐድ)

dig

'ዲግ -ግ- መቆ'ፈር [ቆ'ፈረ]

digest

ዳይ'ጄስት -ግ- ማንሸራሸር [አንሸራ'ሸረ]
(ለምግብ)

digestible

ደ'ጄስትብል -ቅ- የ'ሚንሸራ'ሸር በቀ
ከሰው'ነት የ'ሚስማ'ማ (ምግብ)

digestion

ደ'ጄስቸን -ስ- ማንሸራሸር (ምግብ)

digestive

ደ'ጄስቲቭ -ቅ- ምግብን ለማንሸራሸር የ'
ሪዳ

digit

'ዲጂት -ስ- አንድ አኃዝ
finger
-ስ- ጣት

dignified

'ዳግኒፋይድ -ቅ- የተከ'በረ ፣ ክብሩን ጠ'ባቀ

dignify

'ዲግኒፋይ -ግ- ማክበር [አክ'በረ] ፣ በማዕረ
ክ'ፍ ማድረግ [አደ'ረገ]

dignitary

'ዲግኒተሪ -ስ- ት'ልቅ ሹመት ያ'ለው ሰው
(በተለ'ይ በቤተ ክህነት)

dignity

'ዲግኒቲ -ስ- ክብር ፣ የታ'ላቅ'ነት ስ'ሜት
ታ'ላቅ ሹመት ፣ ማዕረግ

digress

ዳይግ'ሬስ -ግ- ከመንገድ ማጎለል [አጎ'ለለ] ፣
ከአርእስት መውጣት [ወ'ጣ] (ለንግ'ግር)

dike

'ዳይክ -ስ- ያፈር ቁ'ልል (ውሃን የ'ሚይዝ
የ'ሚገ'ድብ)
dam
-ስ- ግ'ድብ

dilapidated

ዲ'ላፒዴይተድ -ቅ- የተለያ'የ ፣ የፈረ'ረሰ ፣
የወ'ላለቀ (ለሕንፃ ፣ ለቤት ዕቃ ወዘተ)

dilate

ዳይ'ሌይት -ግ- በሰ'ፈው መ'ከፈት [ተከ'ፈተ]
ማስፋት [አስ'ፋ] ፤ በረ'ጅም መጻፍ [ጻፈ]
ወይን'ም መ'ናገር [ተና'ገረ]

dilatory

'ዲለተሪ -ቅ- ጊዜ አባካኝ ፣ የ'ሚያዘገ'ይ ፣
ዝ'ግተ'ኛ

424

diligence	ትጋት	u. ct,	መራ አሳየ አዘዘ
diligent	ትጉ ትጉህ ተጋ		ተቆጣጠረ ቀጥተኛ
dilute	አቀጠነ	direction	አቅጣጫ መሪነት ተቆጣ
dim	ቀነሰ ደብዛዛ		ጣሪነት መመሪያ
dimensions	ውርድና ፡ ስፋት	directive	መምሪያ መሪ ፡ ቃል
diminish	ቀነሰ አሳነሰ ተቀነሰ	directly	በቀጥታ
	አነሰ ጉደለ	director	ዲሬክተር አስኪያጅ
diminution	ቅነሳ	directory	ማውጫ የስም ፡ ማውጫ
dine	እራት ፡ በላ	dirge	ሙሾ
uuug)	ቆሽሽ ፡ ያለ	dirt	ቆሻሻ እድፍ ጉድፍ
dining room	መብል ፡ ቤትቀም ግብ ፡ ቤት		መስሎ ፡ ታየ
dinner	ራጉ እራት	dirty	ቆሻሻ አደፈ
dip	አጠለቀ አጠ ቀሰ	disability	ጉድለት
diploma	የምስክር ፡ ወረቀት	disable	ሰነከለ
diplomacy	ዲፕሎማሲ		
diplomatic	ዘዴኛ የዲፕሎማሲ		

425

disabled
ዲ'ሴይብልድ -ቅ- አካለ ስንኩል

disadvantage
ዲሰድ'ቫ:ንቲጅ -ስ- እንቅፋት ፡ መሰናክል

disagree
ዲስግ'ሪ -ግ- አለመስማማት [-ተስማ'ማ]

disagreeable
ዲስግ'ሪየበል -ቅ- የ'ማይስማ'ማ ፡ ደ'ስ የ'ማ
ያ'ለ'ኝ ፡ ?ወዳጅ'ነት ስ'ሜት የ'ማያሳ'ይ ፡
ቁ'ጡ

disagreement
ዲስግ'ሪ:ይመንት -ስ- አለመስማማት

disallow
ዲስ'ላው -ግ- መከልከል [ከለ'ከለ] ፡ አለመ
'ቀበል [-ተቀ'በለ]

disappear
ዲስ'ፒየ -ግ- መጥፋት [ጠ'ፋ] ፡ መ'ሠወር [ተሠ
'ወረ]

disappearance
ዲስ'ፒረንስ -ስ- መጥፋት ፡ መ'ሠወር

disappoint
ዲስ'ፖይንት -ግ- ማሳ'ዘን [አሳ'ዘነ] ፡ የሰ'ጡ
ትን ተስፋ አለመፈ'ጸም [-ፈ'ጸመ]

disappointment
ዲስ'ፖይንትመንት -ስ- አለመ'ደሰት ፡ ማዘን
(የፈ'ለጉትን ነገር ባለማግኘት)

disapprove
ዲስፕ'ሩ፡ቭ -ግ- አለመስማማት [-ተስማ'ማ]

disarm
ዲ'ሳ:ም -ግ- መ'ሣሪያ ፡ መ'ከላከያ ሙቀ'ማት
[ቀ'ማ]

disaster
ዲ'ዛ:ስተ -ግ- ሙ'ጋት ፡ ጥፋት

disastrous
ዲ'ዛ:ስትረስ -ቅ- ድንገተ'ኛ ጥፋት የ'ሚያ
ስከ'ትል

disband
ዲስ'ባንድ -ግ- ማነበር መፍታት [ፈ'ታ] ፡
ማነበር መበ'ተን [በ'ተነ] ፡ ከወ'ታ'ደር አገል
ግሎት ማ'ሰናበት [አ'ሰና'በተ]

disbelieve
ዲስበ'ሊይቭ -ግ- አለማመን [-አ'መነ]

disburse
ዲስ'ብ:ስ -ግ- ገንዘብ መክፈል [ከ'ፈለ]

---

disbursement
ዲስ'ብ:ስመንት -ስ- መክፈል

disc
'ዲስክ -ስ- ክ'ብ ጠፍጣ'ፋ ነገር
record
-ስ- የሙ-ዚቀ ሸክላ

discard
ዲስ'ካ:ድ -ግ- መጣል [ጣለ] ፡ የ'ማያፈ'ልጉ
ትን የመ'ጫወቻ ካርታ እመሬት ላይ መጣል
[ጣለ] ፡ ማስወ'ገድ [አስወ'ገደ]

discern
ዲ'ስ፡ን -ግ- መለ'የት [ለ'የ] (በማየት)

discerning
ዲ'ስ፡ኒንግ -ቅ- ከፋ'ና ደ'ጉን መለ'የት የ'ሚ
ችል ፡ አስተዋይ

discharge
ዲስ'ቻ:ጅ -ግ- መልቀቅ [ለ'ቀቀ] ፡ መፍ፡ታት
[ፈ'ታ] (እሥረ'ኛ) ፡ ከሥራ ማስወ'ጣት [አስ
ወ'ጣ]

disciple
ዲ'ሳይፐል -ስ- ደ'ቀ.መዝሙር ፡ ተማሪ

discipline
'ዲሲፕሊን -ስ- ሥርዓት ፡ ሥነ ሥርዓት

disclose
ዲስክ'ለውዝ -ግ- መግለጽ [ገ'ለጸ] ፡ (የተደ
'በቀ ነገር)

disclosure
ዲስክ'ለውዠ -ስ- መግለጽ ፡ የተደ'በቀውን
ይፋ ማድረግ

discolour
ዲስ'ካለ -ግ- ማደብዘዝ [አደብ'ዘዘ] (ለቀለም)፡
ቀለም መለ'ወጥ [ለ'ወጠ] ፡ መበ'ከል [በ'ከለ]
(በቀለም)

discomfiture
ዲስ'ከምፈቸ -ስ- ማፈር

discomfort
ዲስ'ከምፈት -ስ- ደ'ስ አለመ'ሰኘት ፡ ቀ'ላል
ሕመም

disconcert
ዲስከን'ስ፡ት -ግ- ማሳ'ፈር [አሳ'ፈረ] ፡ ማ'ደና
ገር [አ'ደና'ገረ]

disconnect
ዲስክ'ኔክት -ግ- መለያየት [ለያ'የ]

disconsolate
ዲስ'ኮንሶለት -ቅ- ያልተደ'ሰተ ፡ የ'ማይጽና'ና

426

discontented
ዲስከን'ቴንተድ -ቅ- ያልተ'ደ'ሰተ፣ቅ'ር ያለው-

discontinue
ዲስከን'ቲንዩ -ግ- ማ'ቋረጥ [አ'ቋ'ረጠ] ፣ አለ
መቀ'ጠል [-ቀ'ጠለ]

discord
'ዲስኮ፡ድ -ስ- አለመስማማት ፣ ጎብረት ማጣት

discordant
ዲስ'ኮ፡ደንት -ቅ- የ'ማይስማ'ማ

discount
'ዲስካውንት -ስ- የዋጋ ቅ'ናሽ ፣ እ'ጅ በ'ጅ
ለ'ሚከፍል የ'ሚ'ደ'ረግ የዕዳ ፣ የብ'ድር
ቅ'ናሽ

discourage
ዲስ'ከሬጅ -ግ- ማስፈራራት [አስፈራ'ራ] ፣
አለማ'ጀገን [-አ'ጀ'ገነ]፣ ተስፋ ማስቆ'ረጥ [አስ
ቆ'ረጠ]

discourse
'ዲስኮ፡ስ -ስ- ንግ'ግር

discover
ዲስ'ከቨ -ግ- ማግኘት [አገ'ኘ] ፣ ቀድሞ ያል
ታ'ወቀ ነገር መፈልሰፍ [ፈለ'ሰፈ]

discovery
ዲስ'ከቨሪ -ስ- ፍልሰፋ'ና፣ ቀድሞ ያልታ'ወቀ
ነገር ማግኘት

discredit
ዲስክ'ሬዲት -ግ- ዋጋ ማሳ'ጣት [አሳ'ጣ]

discreet
ዲስክ'ሪይት ጠንቃ'ቃ (በንግ'ግር)

discrepancy
ዲስክ'ሬፐንሲ -ስ- የሒሳብ ጉድለት፣ጉድለት

discretion
ዲስክ'ሬሽን -ስ- ጠንቃ'ቃ'ነት (በሥራ ፣ በአ
'ነጋገር) ፣ ነጻ'ነት (አእምሮ የፈረ'ደውን ለመሥ
ራት)

discriminate
ዲስክ'ሪሚኔይት -ግ- ለ'ይቶ ማወቅ [ዐ'ወቀ]
socially
-ግ- የዘር ል'ዩ'ነት ማድረግ [አደ'ረገ]

discrimination
ዲስክሪሚ'ኔይሽን -ስ- ል'ዩ'ነት ፣ ነገር ፣
በውናቲዎ'ች መካ'ከል ያ'ለውን ጥቃ'ቅን ል'ዩ
'ነት የማወቅ ችሎ፡ታ
racial
-ስ- የዘር ል'ዩ'ነት

discuss
ዲስ'ከስ -ግ- መ'ወያየት (ተወያ'የ) ፣ አንድ
ጉ'ዳይ መመርመር'ና ማጥናት [አጠ'ና]

discussion
ዲስ'ከሽን -ስ- ውይ'ይት

disdain
ዲስ'ዴይን -ግ- ማንቋሸሽ [አንቋ'ሸሸ] ፣ በን
ቀት ዓይን መ'መልከት [ተመለ'ከተ]

disease
ዲ'ዚይዝ -ስ- በ'ሽታ ፣ ሕመም

disembark
ዲሴም'ባ፡ክ -ግ- (ከመርከብ ካውሮ'ፕላን) መው
ረድ [ወ'ረደ]

disengage
ዲሴን'ጌይጅ -ግ- ወደ'ኋላ መ'መለስ [ተመ'ለሰ]
(በጦር'ነት) ፣ ራስን ነጻ ማድረግ [አደ'ረገ] (ከን
ቡ'በት ነገር)

disentangle
ዲሴን'ታንገል -ግ- መፈታታት [ፈታ'ታ] ፣
መለያየት [ለያ'የ] (ለተወሳ'ሰበ ነገር)

disfigure
ዲስ'ፊገ -ግ- መልክ ቅርዕ ማጥፋት [አጠ'ፋ]
(በማቁሰል ፣ በማ'በላሸት)

disgorge
ዲስ'ጎ፡ጅ -ግ- ማስታወክ [አስታ'ወከ] (ለአን
ስሳት) ፣ በ'ሚ'ገባ ያልተገ'ኝ ትርፍ መመ'ለስ
[መ'ለሰ]

disgrace
ዲስግ'ሬይስ -ስ- ነውረት ፣ በሰዎ'ች ዘንድ
መ'ከበርን ማጣት (ከመጥፎ አመል የተነ'ሣ)

disgraceful
ዲስግ'ሬይስፉል -ቅ- ነውረት'ኛ ፣ አሳፋሪ

disguise
ዲስ'ጋይዝ -ግ- መልክን ድምዕን መለ'ወጥ
[ለ'ወጠ] (እንዳ'ይ;ታ'ወቁ)
-ስ- መልክን ድምዕን መለ'ወጥ (እንዳ
ይ;ታወቁ)

disgust
ዲስ'ገስት -ግ- መጥላት [ጠ'ላ] ፣ መ'ጸየፍ
[ተጸ'የፈ]
-ስ- ጥላ'ቻ፣ መ'ጸየፍ

disgusting
ዲስ'ገስቲንግ -ቅ- አ'ጸያፊ ፣ ማስጠ'ለ-

427

dish
’ዲሽ -ስ- የምግብ ማቀረቢያ ሳሕን (ጎድጓ'ዳ)
food
-ስ- ምግብ
dishcloth
’ዲሽክሎስ -ስ- የሳሕን መወልወያ ጨርቅ
dishearten
ዲስ'ሀ፡ተን -ግ- ማስፈራራት [አስፈራ'ራ]
dishonest
ዲ'ሶኔስት -ት- የ'ማይ'ታመን ፣ አ'ታላይ ፤
አጭበርባሪ ፣ ወስላ'ታ
dishonour
ዲ'ሶነ -ግ- አለማክበር [-አክ'በረ] ፣ ማ'ዋረድ
[አ'ዋ'ረደ]
dishonourable
ዲ'ሶነረበል -ት- የ'ማይ'ክ'በር ፣ ነፍረተ ቢስ
disinfect
ዲሲ'ን'ፌክት -ግ- በ'ሽታ ከ'ሚያመጡ ነፍ
ሳት ነጻ ማድረግ
disinfectant
ዲሲ'ን'ፌክተንት -ስ- ?ተባይ መግደያ መድ
:ኃኒት
disinherit
ዲሲ'ን'ኄሪት -ግ- ልጅ ከውርስ መከልከል
[ከለ'ከለ] ፣ መካድ [ካደ]
disintegrate
ዲ'ሲ'ንቲግሬይት -ግ- መ'ሰባበር [ተሰባ'በረ]
disintegration
ዲሲ'ንቲግ'ሬይሽን -ስ- መ'ሰባበር
disinterested
ዲ'ሲ'ንትሬስተድ -ት- የ'ማይ'ዳ'ላ ፣ አድልዎ
የ'ሌ'ለ'በት
dislike
ዲስ'ላይክ -ግ- አለመውደድ [-ወ'ደደ]
dislocate
’ዲስለኬይት -ግ- መለያየት [ለያ'የ] ፣ ከቦታ
ማ'ናወጥ [አ'ና'ወጠ] (ለሰውነት መ'ጋጠሚያ)
dislocation
ዲስለ'ኬይሽን -ስ- መለያየት
dislodge
ዲስ'ሎጅ -ግ- በታ ማስለ'ተት [አስለ'ተተ] ፣
ካ'ለ'በት ቦታ በ'ነይል ማስለ'ተት [አስለ'ተተ]

disloyal
ዲስ'ሎየል -ት- የ'ማይ'ታ'መን ፣ እምነት የ'ማ
ይ'ጣል'በት ፣ ከሓዲ
dismal
’ዲዝመል -ት- የ'ማያስደ'ስት ፣ የጨፈ'ገገው ፣
ያ'ዘነ
dismantle
ዲስ'ማንተል -ግ- መፈታታት [ፈታ'ታ] ፣
መበታተን [በታ'ተነ] ፣ መለያየት [ለያ'የ]
(መ'ሣሪያ)
dismay
ዲስ'ሜይ -ስ- አለመ'ደሰት
dismiss
ዲስ'ሚስ -ግ- ማስወ'ገድ [አስወ'ገደ] ፣ ማ'ባ
ረር [አ'ባ'ረረ]፣ማስወ'ጣት [አስወ'ጣ] (ከሥራ)
dismount
ዲስ'ማውንት -ግ- መውረድ [ወ'ረደ] (ከፈ
ረስ ወዘተ)
disobedience
ዲሰ'ቢዲየንስ -ስ- አለመ'ታዘዝ ፣ እም'ቢ'ተ
'ኝ'ነት
disobedient
ዲስ'ቢዲየንት -ት- የ'ማይ'ታ'ዘዝ ፣ እም'ቢ
ተ'ኛ ፣ አሻ'ፈረኝ ባይ
disobey
ዲስ'ቢይ -ግ- አለመ'ታዘዝ [-ታ'ዘዘ]
disorder
ዲ'ሶ፡ደ -ስ- ሕ'ገ ወ'ጥነት ፣ ብጥ'ብጥ ፣ የሕ
ዝብን ወ'ጥታ ማ'ወክ
disorderly
ዲ'ሶ፡ደሊ -ት- ሕ'ገ ወጥ ፣ በጥባጭ
disorganize
ዲ'ሶ፡ጎናይዝ -ግ- ያለሥርዓት ማስቀ'ረት [አስ
'ቀረ] ፣ መደበላለቅ [ደበላ'ለቀ] ፣ ሥርዓት ማ
ሳ'ጣት [አሳ'ጣ]
disown
ዲ'ሰውን -ግ- ከውርስ ማ'ገድ [አ'ገደ] ፣ ነላ
ፈ'ነትን ማስወ'ረድ [አስወ'ረደ]
disparage
ዲስ'ፓሪጅ -ግ- ማንቋሸሽ [አንቋ'ሸሸ]፣ ማ'ታ
ለል [አ'ታ'ለለ] (ሰው'ን)
disparity
ዲስ'ፓሪቲ -ስ- ል'ዩ'ነት ፣ አለመ'መሳሰል

428

dispatch
ዲስ'ፓች -ግ- መላክ [ላከ] ፣ ፈጥኖ መላክ [ላከ] ፣ በፍጥነት መጨ'ረስ [ጨ'ረስ]

dispel
ዲስ'ፔል -ግ- መበታተን [በታ'ተነ]

dispensable
ዲስ'ፔንሰበል -ቅ- ሊቀር የ'ሚችል ፣ ቢቀር የ'ማይጎዳ

dispensary
ዲስ'ፔንሰሪ -ስ- የመድኃኒት ቤት (በሆስፒ ታል)

dispensation
ዲፐንን'ሴይሸን -ስ- መስጠት ፣ ማ'ደል ፣ የ'ሚ'ታ'ደል ነገር

dispense
ዲስ'ፔንስ -ግ- መስጠት [ሰ'ጠ] ፣ ማ'ደል [አ'ደለ] (መድኃኒት ፣ ምፅዋት (ወዘተ)
    medicine
    -ግ- መድኃኒት መቀ'መም [ቀ'መመ]

dispersal
ዲስ'ፐ፡ሰል -ስ- መ'በታተን ፣ የተበታ'ተነ መሆን

disperse
ዲስ'ፐ፡ስ -ግ- መበታተን [በታ'ተነ] ፣ መ'በታ ተን [ተበታ'ተነ]

displace
ዲስፕ'ሌይስ -ግ- ከቦታ ማ'ቃወስ [አ'ቃ'ወሰ] ፣ ያለቦታው ማስቀ'መጥ [አስቀ'መጠ]

display
ዲስፕ'ሌይ -ግ- ማሳ'የት [አሳ'የ] (ለዕቃ)
    -ስ- ትርኢት ፣ ለመ'ታየት የተዘረ'ጋ ዕቃ

displease
ዲስፕ'ሊይዝ -ግ- ማስከ'ፋት [አስከ'ፋ] ፣ ማስ ቀየም [አስቀ'የመ]

disposal
ዲስ'ፐውዘል -ስ- መጣል (ቴሻሻ ፣ ጉድፍ)
    order
    -ስ- ትእዛዝ

disposition
ዲስፐ'ዚሸን -ስ- ጠባይ ፣ ዝን'ባሌ ፣ አ'ቀማ መጥ

dispossess
ዲስፐ'ዜስ -ግ- ያዞታ ፣ ንብረት በተለ'ያ መሬት ማስለ'ቀቅ [አስለ'ቀቀ]

disproportionate
ዲስፐረ'ፖ፡ሽነት -ቅ- ያልተመዛ'ዘነ ፣ ብልጫ ያ'ለው

disprove
ዲስፕ'ሩ፡ቭ -ስ- ልክ' አለመሆኑን ማስረ'ዳት [አስረ'ዳ]

disputable
ዲስፕ'ዩ፡ተበል -ቅ- የ'ሚያ'ከራ'ክር ፣ የ'ሚ ያ'ጠራ'ጥር

dispute
ዲስፕ'ዩ፡ት -ስ- ጥል ፣ ክር'ክር

disqualify
ዲስክ'ዎሊፋይ -ግ- ያንድ ሰው ችሎታ በቂ አለመሆኑን መግለጽ [ገ'ለጸ] ፣ ከውድ'ድር ግስ ወ'ጣት [አስወ'ጣ] (አስ፞ርት)

disquiet
ዲስክ'ዋየት -ግ- ማ'ወክ [አ'ወከ] ፣ መበጥበጥ [በጠ'በጠ] ፣ ሰላም መንሣት [ነ'ሣ]
    -ስ- ጭንቀት ፣ ሁከት ፣ ብጥ'ብጥ(የፖላ ቲካ ወዘተ)

disregard
ዲስረ'ጋ፡ድ -ግ- ቸ'ል ማለት [አለ] ፣ ዋጋ አለ መስጠት [-ስ'ጠ]

disreputable
ዲስ'ሬፑዩተበል -ቅ- ወ'ራ'ዳ ፣ ክብር የ'ማይ 'ስ'ጠው

disrespect
ዲስረስ'ፔክት -ስ- አለማክበር ፣ ብልግ'ና

disrespectful
ዲስረስ'ፔክትፉል -ቅ- ባለጌ ፣ ያልተቀ'ጣ ፣ አመለቢስ

disrupt
ዲስ'ረፕት -ግ- መበጥበጥ [በጠ'በጠ] (ዕ'ቅ ድን) ፣ ሕግ'ና ሥርዓትና የሌ'ለው ማድረግ [አደ'ረገ]

disruption
ዲስ'ረፕሸን -ስ- ብጥ'ብጥ ፣ ሁከት ፣ ሕግ'ና ሥርዓት ማጣት

dissect
ዲ'ሴክት -ግ- መበ'ለት [በ'ለተ]

dissection
ዲ'ሴክሸን -ስ- ብ'ልት ማውጣት (በደን ወዘተ በሕ'ክም'ና)

disservice
ዲ'ሰ፡ቪስ -ስ- ውለታ ቢስ ሥራ

429

dissipate
'ዲሲፓይት -ግ- ማባከን [አባ'ከነ] (ጊዜ ፣ ገን
ዘብ) ፣ ማስወ'ገድ [አስወ'ገደ] (ፍርሃት ፣ ድን
ቄር'ና ወዘተ)

dissipated
'ዲሲፓተተድ -ቅ- ኑርው በመጥፎ ልም ድ
የተበላ'ሸ ፤ ብኩን ፣ የተበታ'ተነ

dissolute
'ዲሰሉት -ቅ- አውደልዳይ ፣ እንደ'ሻው የ'ሚ
ኖር (መሻተ'ኛ ፣ ቅንዝረ'ኛ)

dissolution
ዲስ'ሉሸን -ስ- የምክር ቤት መ'ዘጋት ፤ መ'ለ
ያየት

dissolve
ዲ'ዞልቭ -ግ- መቅሚ ጒት [ቒ'ቒ] ፣ ማቅሚ ጒት
[አቒ'ቒ]

dissonant
'ዲሰነንት -ቅ- ጣዕም ዜማ የሌ'ለው ፣ ጓኽራ
(ድምፅ)

dissuade
ዲስ'ዌይድ -ግ- አንድ ነገር እንዳያደርጉ መም
ከር [መ'ከረ] ፣ መገፋፋት [ገፋ'ፋ]

distance
'ዲስተንስ -ስ- ርቀት

distant
'ዲስተንት -ቅ- ሩቅ

distasteful
ዲስ'ቴይስትፉል -ቅ- ለ'ዛ ቢስ ፣ ጣዕም ቢስ

distend
ዲስ'ቴንድ -ግ- መ'ነፋት [ተነ'ፋ] ፣ መንፋት
[ነ'ፋ]

distil
ዲስ'ቲል -ግ- ማ'ጣራት [አ'ጣራ] (ለውሃ
በመ-ቀት)

distillation
ዲስቲ'ሌይሸን -ስ- ማ'ጣራት

distiller
ዲስ'ቲል -ስ- አ'ጣሪ

distillery
ዲስ'ቲለሪ -ስ- ማ'ጣሪያ ቦታ

distinct
ዲስ'ቲንክት -ቅ- የተለ'የ ፤ የ'ማያ'ሳስት ፣ ተለ
'ይቶ የ'ሚ'ታ'ወቅ

distinction
ዲስ'ቲንክሽን -ስ- ል'ዩ'ነት ፣ የተለ'የ መ'ታ
ወቂያ (ለማዕረግ)

distinctive
ዲስ'ቲንክቲቭ -ቅ- ል'ዩ

distinguish
ዲስ'ቲንገዊሽ -ግ- ለ'ይቶ ማወቅ [ዐ'ወቀ]

distinguished
ዲስ'ቲንገዋሽት -ቅ- የተለ'የ ፤ የተከ'በረ

distort
ዲስ'ቶ፡ት -ግ- ማ'ጣመም [አ'ጣ'መመ] ፣ ማ'በ
ላሸት [አ'በላ'ሸ] ፣ ማ'ወላገድ [አ'ወላ'ገደ]

distortion
ዲስ'ቶ፡ሽን -ስ- ማ'ጣመም ፣ ማ'ወላገድ ፣ ማ'በ
ላሸት

distract
ዲስት'ራክት -ግ- ሐ'ሳብ ወደ ሌላ አቅጣ'ጫ
መግረክ [ግ'ረከ] ፤ አተ'ኩረው እንዳያ'ስቡ
ማ'ሰናከል [አ'ሰና'ከለ] ፤ ሐ'ሳብ ማባከን [አባ
'ከነ]

distraction
ዲስት'ራክሽን -ስ- ሐ'ሳብ የ'ሚወስድ ነገር ፣
ሐ'ሳብ አባካኝ ነገር

distress
ዲስት'ሬስ -ስ- ጭንት ፣ ሐዘን

distribute
ዲስት'ትሪብዩት -ግ- ማ'ደል [አ'ደለ]

distribution
ዲስትሪብ'ዩሽን -ስ- ማ'ደል

district
'ዲስትሪክት -ስ- ወረዳ ፣ ክፍለ ሀገር

distrustful
ዲስት'ረስትፉል -ቅ- ሰው የ'ማያምን ፣ ተጠ
ራጣሪ

disturb
ዲስ'ተ፡ብ -ግ- ማ'ወክ [አ'ወከ] ፣ መበጥበጥ
[በጠ'በጠ]

disturbance
ዲስ'ተ፡በንስ -ስ- ብጥ'‥ጥ ፣ ህውከት

disunite
ዲስዩ'ናይት -ግ- መለያየት [ለያ'የ] ፣ ጉብረት
ማ'ላ'ጣት [አላ'ጣ]

disused
ዲስ'ዩ፡ዝድ -ቅ- ከአገልግሎ- ው'ጭ የሆነ ፣
የ'ማይ'ው'ራ'በት

430

ditch

’ዲች -ስ- ቦ'ይ ፣ ረ'ጅም ቁ'ፍር (ለመ'ከላከ.ያ፣ ለውሃ መውረጃ)

dive

’ዳይቭ -ግ- መጥለቅ [ጠ'ለቀ] (እራ-ስን አስቀ 'ድሞ እውሃ ውስት)

diver

’ዳይቨ -ስ- ጠላቂ ሰው (እ ሥ-ሃ ውስጥ)

diverge

ዳይ'ቨ:ጅ -ግ- ወደ ል'ዩ ል'ዩ አቅጣ'ጫ መሄድ [ሄደ] ፣ ከባህል ፣ ከአስተያየት የተለ'የ መሆን [ሆነ]

diverse

ዳይ'ቨ:ስ -ቅ- ል'ዩ ል'ዩ (በጠባይ ፣ በዐይነት)

diversion

ዳይ'ቨ:ሽን -ስ- አቅጣ'ጫ መለ'ወጥ [ለ'ወጠ] (ለም'ሳሌ መንገድ ሲ'ዘጋ)

divert

ዳይ'ቨ:ት -ግ- አስተያየት ፣ አቅጣጫ መለ ወጥ [ለ'ወጠ] ፣ ማስደ'ሰት [አስደ'ሰተ]

divide

ዲ'ቫይድ -ግ- መክፈል [ከ'ፈለ] ፣ መከፋፈል [ከፋ'ፈለ]

dividend

’ዲቪዴንድ -ስ- ድርሻ ፣ ክፍ'ያ (ለባለአክሲ ዮኖ'ች የ'ሚ'ከፈል)

divination

ዲቪ'ኔይሸን -ስ- ወደፊት የ'ሚሆነውን መ'ና ገር ፣ መ'ነበይ

divine

ዲ'ቫይን -ቅ- መለኮታዊ ፣ የእግዚአብሔር

diving

’ዳይቪንግ -ስ- መስጠም

divinity

ዲ'ቪኒቲ -ስ- መለኮት ፣ አምላክ ፣ መለኮታዊ ነገል

divisible

ዲ'ቪዚበል -ቅ- ሊ'ከፈል የ'ሚችል

division

ዲ'ቪዠን -ስ- ክፍል ፣ ማ'ከፈል ፣ መ'ከፈል ፣ አለመስማማት ፣ በሐ'ሳብ መ'ለያየት

divorce

ዲ'ቮ:ስ -ግ- መፍ:ታት [ፈ';ታ] (ሚስት ፣ ባል)

---

divulge

ዳይ'ቫልጅ -ግ- ምስጢር ማውጣት [አው'ጣ]

dizziness

’ዲዚነስ -ስ- ራስ መክበ.ድ ፣ ራስ መዞር ፣ ማጥ ወልወል

dizzy

’ዲዚ -ቅ- ራሱ የከ'በደው ፣ አእምሮው የታ'ወከ

do

’ዱ -ግ- መሥ-ራት [ሠ'ራ] ፣ ማድረግ [አደ'ረገ]

docile

’ደውሳይል -ቅ- በቀ'ላሉ ሊያስተምሩት ሊ'ቆ ጣ'ጠሩት የ'ሚ'ቻል

dock

’ዶክ -ስ- የመርከብ ወደብ (መርከብ የ'ሚ'ሠ 'ራ'በት ቦታ)

docker

’ዶክ -ስ- የመርከብ ዕቃ አውራጅ

docket

’ዶክት -ስ- ደ'ረሰ'ኝ

doctor

’ዶክተ -ስ- ሐኪም

academic

-ስ- ዶክተር

doctorate

’ዶክተረት -ስ- የዶክተር'ነት ማዕረግ

doctrine

’ዶክትሪን -ስ- የሃይማኖት ትምህርት ፣ የሕይ ወት ወይም የእምነት መምሪያ ትምህርት

document

’ዶክዩመንት -ስ- ማስረ'ጃ ጽሑፍ

documentary

ዶክዩ'ሜንተሪ -ቅ- ማስረ'ጃነት ያ'ለው (የተ ጻፈ)

dodge

’ዶጅ -ግ- ማምለጥ [አም'ለጠ] (ከአደጋ ም'ሳሌ ፣ ከተወረ'ወረ ነገር)

doe

’ደው -ስ- ሴት አጋዘን ፣ ሴት ተንቸላ

doe-skin

’ደውስኪን -ስ- የጋዘን ቆዳ

dog

’ዶግ -ስ- ው'ሻ

431

dogged
’ዶገድ -ቅ- ቸኩ ፤ ተስፋ የማይቆርጥ

dogma
’ዶግመ -ስ- የሃይማኖት ሕ'ንጋት (ግስረ'ጀ የሌ
'ለው ፣ ለም'ላሌ ፣ ከሃይማኖት ሰ ም'ች የታ'ዘዘ)

doll
’ዶል -ስ- አሻንጉ'ሊት

dollar
’ዶለ -ስ- ብ'ር (ገንዘብ)

dolorous
’ዶለረስ -ቅ- በጣም ያ'ዘነ ፣ የሚያሳ'ዝን ፣
የ'ሚያ'ያም

dolt
’ዶልት -ቅ- ቂል ፣ ሞ'ኝ ፣ ደንቆሮ ፣ ደ'ደብ

domain
ደ'ሜይን -ስ- የመሬት ሀብት ፤ ግዛት

dome
’ደውም -ስ- ክ'ብ ጣራ

domestic
ደ'ሜስቲክ -ቅ- የቤት

domesticate
ደ'ሜስቲኬይት -ግ- እንሰሳን ግልመድ [አለ
'መደ]

domicile
’ዶሚሳይል -ስ- መኖርያ ቤት

dominant
’ዶሚነንት -ቅ- የሚገዛ ፣ ባለሥልጣን
የማዘዝ መብት ያ'ለው ፣ የሰ'ፈነ

dominate
’ዶሚኔይት -ግ- መግዛት [ገ'ዛ] (በሥልጣን)

domination
ዶሚ'ኔይሽን -ስ- ሥልጣን

domineer
ዶሚ'ኒየ -ግ- በጉይል ግሳ'ደር [አሳ'ደረ]

dominion
ደ'ሚንየን -ስ- ሥልጣን ፣ ጉይል ፣ ግዛት (አገ
ር)

donate
ደ'ኔይት -ግ- መስጠት [ሰ'ጠ] ፣ መለ'ገሥ
[ለ'ገሠ] (ለበ'ጉ አድራጉት)

donation
ደ'ኔይሽን -ስ- ስጦታ (የእርዳታ)

donkey
’ዶንኪ -ስ- አህ'ያ

donor
’ደውን -ስ- ሰጪ ፣ ለ'ጋሽ (በተለ'ይ ደሙን
ለሕመምተ'ኛ)

doom
’ዱ፡ም -ስ- ዕ'ድል ፣ ፍርድ ፣ ጥፋት ፣ ሞት

doomsday
’ዱ፡ምዝደይ -ስ- የመጨ'ረሻ የፍርድ ቀን ፣
ምጽአት

door
’ዶ፡ -ስ- በ'ር ፣ ደ'ጃፍ

door-keeper
’ዶ፡ኪፐ -ስ- በ'ረኛ ፣ በ'ር ጠ'ባቂ

door-mat
’ዶ፡ማት -ስ- የገር መጥረጊያ ጨርቅ (እበ'ር
ላይ የ'ሚ'ነ'ጠፍ)

dormant
’ዶ፡መንት -ቅ- እንቅልፍም (ለጊዜው ሥራ
የማይሠራ)

dormitory
’ዶ፡መትሪ -ስ- የመ'ኝታ አ'ዳራሽ

dormouse
’ዶ፡ማውስ -ስ- ዐይጠ መጉጥ

dose
’ደውስ -ስ- ል'ክ (ለአንድ ጊዜ የ'ሚሆን መድ
ኃኒት)

dot
’ዶት -ስ- ነቁጥ ፣ ነጥብ

dotage
’ደውተጅ -ስ- የእእምሮ ድካም (ከእርጅ'ና
የተነ'ሣ) ፣ መጃጀት

double
’ደበል -ቅ- እጥፍ

doubt
’ዳውት -ግ- መ'ጠራጠር [ተጠራ'ጠረ]
-ስ- ጥር'ጥር

doubtful
’ዳውት-ፉል -ቅ- የሚያ'ጠራ'ጥር ፣ አ'ጠራ
ጣሪ

doubtless
’ዳውትለስ -ቅ- የማ'ያ'ጠራ'ጥር

douche
’ዱ፡ሽ -ስ- ግብር ውሃ ፣ ግብር ውሃ መውጣት ፤
ዘላይ እሰው'ነት ላይ የ'ሚፈ'ስ ውሃ (ሰው'ነት
ለመ'ታጠብ) ፤ ውሃውን የ'ሚያፈስ'ው መ
ሣሪያ

432

dough
ˈደው -ስ- ሊጥ (የዳቦ)

dove
ˈደቭ -ስ- እርግብ

dovecote
ˈዳቭኮት -ስ- የርግብ ቤት

down
ˈዳውን -ተግ- ወደ ታች

downcast
ˈዳውን፡ካ፡ስት -ቅ- ያዘነ ፣ ያልተደ'ሰተ

downfall
ˈዳውንፎ፡ል -ስ- ድቀት ፣ ውድቀት ፣ ፍርስራሽ ከ'ባድ ዝናም

downpour
ˈዳውንፓ፡ -ስ- ከ'ባድ ዝናም (የ'ማያ'ቋ'ርጥ)

downright
ˈዳውንራይት -ቅ- ቀጥተ'ኛ ፣ ግልጽ ፣ ጥን ቁቅ

downward(s)
ˈዳውንወድ(ዝ) -ተግ- ወደታ'ች

dowry
ˈዳውሪ -ስ- ጥሎሽ (ሴት የም'ትሰጠው)

doze
ˈደውዝ -ግ- ማሽ'ለብ [አሽ'ለበ] (እንቅልፍ፣) ማንጎላጀት [አንጎላ'ጀ]

dozen
ˈደዘን -ስ- ደርዘን ፣ ቁጥሩ በሥራ ሁ'ለት የሆነ (ዕቃ)

drab
ድˈራብ -ቅ- ብሩህ ቀለም የሌ'ለው ፣ የ'ማያምር (ለልብስ)

draft
ድˈራ፡ፍት -ስ- ረቂቅ (ጽሑፍ) ፣ ንድፍ (ሥዕል)

draftsman
ድˈራፍ፡ትስመን -ስ- ንድፍ ነዳፊ ፣ (የመሀን 'ዲስ)

drag
ድˈራግ -ግ- መጎ'ተት [ጎ'ተተ]

dragon
ድˈራገን -ስ- ደራጎን (ክንፍ ያ'ለው'ና እሳት የ'ሚተፋ ፍጡር)

dragonfly
ድˈራገንፍላይ -ስ- የውሃ ተርብ

drain
ድˈሬይን -ስ- የውሃ መሄጃ (በመንገድ ዳር ፣ የቁሻሻ'ና የእድፍ)

drainage
ድˈሬይነጅ -ስ- የፍ'ሳሽ መሄጃ ቦዮ'ች

dramatic
ድሪˈማቲክ -ቅ- አስደ'ናቂ ፣ አስገ'ራሚ (ሕያው ታሪክ ፣ ቴያትር)

dramatist
ድˈራመቲስት -ስ- የቴያትር መጽሐፍ ደራሲ

drape
ድˈሬይፕ -ግ- ማልበስ [አለ'በሰ] ፣ መሸ'ፈን [ሸ'ፈነ] ፣ ማ'ጠፋት .[አ'ጣ'ፈ] (ኩ-ታ ወዘተ)

draper
ድˈሬይፕ -ስ- ጨርቃ ጨርቅ ነ'ጋዴ

drapery
ድˈሬይፕሪ -ስ- የግድግ'ዳ ልባስ ጨርቅ

drastic
ድˈራስቲክ -ቅ- ከ'ባድ ው'ጤት የ'ሚያስከ ትል

draught
ድˈራ፡ፍት -ስ- ከው'ለት ትይ'ዩ አቅጣ'ጫየ'ሚ ገባ ጎደለ'ኛ አ'የር ፣ መጎተት ፣ መሳብ
drink
-ስ- ባንድ ትንፋሽ የ'ሚ'ጠ'ጣ መጠ'ጥ
game(pl.)
-ስ- ዳማ (የጨዋታ ዓይነት)

draught board
ድˈራ፡ፍትቦ፡ድ -ስ- የዳማ መ'ጫወቻ ገበ፣
engineering
-ስ- የንድፍ መንደፊያ ገበ፣ (የመሀን ዲስ)

draughtsman
ድˈራ፡ፍትስመን -ስ- የሕንፃዎ'ችን ፣ፕላን'ና ን ድፍ የ'ሚሠራ ሰው

draw
ድˈሮ፡ -ግ- መሣል [ሣለ] (ለሥዕል)
pull
-ግ- መሳብ [ሳበ] ፣ መጎ'ተት [ጎ'ተተ] ፣ ውሃ መቅዳት [ቀ'ዳ] (ከጉድጓድ) ፣ መምዘዝ [መ'ዘዘ] (መ'ሣሪያ ከአፎ፡ት ወዘተ)

drawback
ድˈሮ፡ባክ -ስ- እንቅፋት ፣ መጥፎ ዕ'ድል

433

drawer
ድ'ሮ:ወ -ስ- የጠረ'ጴዛ መሳቢያ

drawing
ድ'ሮ:ዊንግ -ስ- ሥዕል

dread
ድ'ሬድ -ስ- ት'ልቅ ፍርሃት ፡ ጭንቅ

dreadful
ድ'ሬድፉል -ቅ- በጣም የ'ሚያስፈ'ራ ፡ በጣም የ'ሚያስጨ'ንቅ

dream
ድ'ሪይም -ግ- ማ'ለም [አ'ለመ]
-ስ- ሕልም

dreamy
ድ'ሪይሚ -ቅ- ሐ'ሳበ ብኩን ፡ እንዳ'ለመ የ'ሚኖር

dreary
ድ'ሪየሪ -ቅ- የ'ሚቀ'ፍ ፡ የ'ሚያሳ'ዝን ፡ የ'ሚሰለ'ች

dregs
ድ'ሬግዝ -ስ- አተላ ፡ ዝ'ቃጭ

dress
ድ'ሬስ -ግ- መልበስ [ለ'በሰ]
women's
-ስ- ቀሚስ

dresser
ድ'ሬሰ -ስ- አልባሽ ፡ የቀዳጅ ሐኪም ረ'ዳት

dribble
ድ'ሪበል -ግ- መላገግ [ላ'ገገ] ፡ ማንጠብ ጠብ [አንጠበ'ጠበ] (ለውሃ)፡ኳስ ደጋግሞ ማንጠር [አን'ጠረ]
-ስ- ለጋግ

drift
ድ'ሪፍት -ስ- መዋለል [ዋ'ለለ] (እባሕር ላይ አቅጣ'ጫ ሳይጠ'ብቁ)

drill
ድ'ሪል -ግ- መብሳት [በ'ሳ] ፡ መሠርሠር [ሠረ'ሠረ]
-ስ- መሠርሠሪያ ፡ መብሻ መ'ሣሪያ
military
-ግ- ማሠልጠን [አሠለ'ጠነ] (ለወ'ታ'ደር)
-ስ- የሰልፍ ትምህርት
material
-ስ- የጥጥ ጨርቅ

drink
ድ'ሪንክ -ግ- መጠጣት [ጠ'ጣ]
-ስ- መጠጥ

drip
ድ'ሪፕ -ግ- መንጠብጠብ [ተንጠበ'ጠበ]
-ስ- ጠ'ብታ

drive
ድ'ራይቭ -ግ- መንዳት [ነ'ዳ] (የመኪና ወዘተ)
-out
-ግ- ማስወ'ጣት [አስወ'ጣ] ፡ ማ'ባረር [አባ'ረረ]

driver
ድ'ራይቨ -ስ- መኪና ነጂ ፡ ሾፌር

droop
ድ'ሩ:ፕ -ግ- መሸ'ጎብ [ሸ'ጎበ]

drop
ድ'ሮፕ -ግ- መጣል [ጣለ] ፡ መውደቅ [ወ'ደቀ]
-ስ- ጠ'ብታ

droppings
ድ'ሮፒንግዝ -ግ- ፍግ ፡ ፋንድ'ያ ወዘተ

drought
ድ'ራውት -ቅ- ድርቅ ፡ የዝናም ማነስ ፡ ጥም

drown
ድ'ራውን -ግ- መስጠም [ሰ'ጠመ]

drowsy
ድ'ራውዚ -ቅ- ያንቀላ'ፋ ፡ የ'ሚያንጎላ'ጅ

drudge
ድ'ረጅ -ስ- የተንገላ'ታ አገልጋይ ፡ ከ'ባድ የ'ሚያስለ'ች ሥራ የ'ሚሠራ አሽከር

drug
ድ'ረግ -ስ- ለመድኃኒት'ነት የ'ሚያገለ'ግል ጥንተ ንጥር ፡ አስካሪ ቅጠላቅጠል (ጫት ፡ ሐሺሽ ፡ አፕየም ወዘተ)

drum
ድ'ረም -ስ- ከበሮ ፡ አታሞ ፡ ታምቡር

drummer
ድ'ረመ -ስ- ከበሮ መቺ ፡ አታሞ መቺ

drunk
ድ'ረንክ -ቅ- የሰ'ከረ

drunkard
ድ'ረንከድ -ስ- ሰ'ካራም

drunkenness
ድ'ረንከንኔስ -ስ- ሰ'ካራም'ነት ፡ ስካር

dry
ድ'ራይ -ግ- መድረቅ [ደ'ረቀ]
-ት- ደረቅ ፡ ድርቅ

duck
'ደክ -ስ- ዳ'ክ'የ
avoid
-ግ- በድንንት ራስን ወ'ይም ሰው'ነትን
ማዝንበል [አዘን'በለ] (ከመ'ታየት ለመዳን)

dull
'ደል -ት- ደ'ደብ ፡ በፎሉ የ'ማይገባው
weather
-ት- የ'ሚቀ'ፍ ፡ ጭፍግ'ግ ያለ (ቀን)

dumb
'ደም -ት- ድዳ

dump
'ደምፕ -ግ- መጣል [ጣለ]
-ስ- ቁሻሻ መጣያ ፡ አመድ ማፍሰሻ

dune
ድ'ዩ፡ን -ስ- ያሸዋ ክ'ምር (በነፋስ የተከ'መረ)

dung
'ደንግ -ስ- እበት ፡ ፍግ

dungeon
'ደንጀን -ስ- ወህኒ ቤት ፡ ጨ'ለማ ክፍል
(ምድር ቤት ያ'ለ)

dunghill
'ደንግሂል -ስ- የእበት ፡ የፍግ ቁ'ልል

duplicate
ድ'ዩፕሊኬይት -ግ- ጽሑፍ ማ'ባዛት [አ'ባ
'ዛ] (በማ'ባገ መኪና ወዘተ) ፤ በሁ'ለት ማ'ባ
ዛት [አ ባ'ዛ] ፤ በትክ'ክል መገልበጥ [ገለ'በጠ]
(ጽሑፍ)

duplicate
ድ'ዩፕሊከት -ስ- የተበ'ዛ ጽሑፍ (አንድ ግል
'ባጭ)

durable
ድ'ዩረብል -ት- ጠንካ'ራ ፡ ረ'ጅም እድሜ
ያ'ለው

during
ድ'ዩሪንግ -መዋ- በ . . . ጊዜ ውስጥ

dusk
'ደስክ -ስ- ማምሻ (የጀምበር መጥለቂያ ጊዜ)

dust
'ደስት -ስ- አቧራ ፡ ት'ቢያ

duster
'ደስተ -ስ- አቧራ መጥረጊያ ፡ አቧራ ማ'ራ
ገፊያ

dustpan
'ደስትፓን -ስ- የቁሻሻ መሰብሰቢያ ዕቃ

dusty
'ደስቲ -ት- አቧራ ያለ'በሰው ፡ ቡ'ላ

dutiful
ድ'ዩ፡ቲፉል -ት- ታ'ዛዥ ፡ ሰው አክባሪ

duty
ድ'ዩ፡ቲ -ስ- ተግባር
customs
-ስ- ቀረጥ

duty-free
ድ'ዩ፡ቲ ፍሪይ -ት- ከቀረጥ ነጻ የሆነ (ዕቃ ፡
ሽቀጣሽቀጥ)

dwarf
ድ'ዎ፡ፍ -ስ- ድንክ ሰው ፡ እንስሳ ወዘተ

dwell
ድ'ዌል -ግ- መኖር [ኖረ]

dwelling
ድ'ዌሊንግ -ስ- መኖሪያ ቦታ

dwindle
ድ'ዊንደል -ግ- እ'ያነሰ ፡ እ'የተ'ነሰ መሄድ
[ሄደ]

dye
'ዳይ -ግ- ቀለም መንከር [ነ'ከረ]
-ስ- ቀለም (ልብስ መንከሪያ)

dyer
'ዳየ -ስ- ቀለም ነካሪ

dying
'ዳይንግ -ት- የ'ሚሞት

dynamic
ዳይ'ናሚክ -ት- ንቁ ፡ ጉይል ያ'ለው ፡ እንት
ስ'ቃሴ የ'ሚፈጥር

dynamite
'ዳይነማይት -ስ- ፈንጂ ፡ ዲናሚት

dynasty
'ዲነስቲ -ስ- የነገሥታት የዘር ሐረግ ፡ ሥርወ
መንግሥት

435

E

each
'ኢይች -ቅ- እ'ያንዳን'ዱ

eager
'ኢገር -ቅ- ጉ'ጉ

eagle
'ኢይገል -ስ- ንሥር

ear
'ኢየ -ስ- ጆሮ

early
'ኧሊ -ተግ- በማለዳ ፣ ቀደ'ም ብሎ ፣ ማልዶ

earn
'ኧን -ግ- ማትረፍ [አት'ረፈ] (ገንዘብ) ፤ ማግ
ኛት [አገኘ] (ዝ'ና ፣ ጥሩ ስም ወዘተ)

earnest
'ኧኔስት -ቅ- ቁም ነገረ'ኛ ፣ በነገሩ ያ'ሰበ'በት ፣
የቆ'ረጠ (አንድ ነገር ለመሥራት)

earnings
'ኧኒንግዝ -ስ- ትርፍ ፣ ደመዎዝ

ear-ring
'ኢየሪንግ -ስ- ጉትቻ

earth
'ኧስ -ስ- መሬት
  globe
         -ስ- ዓለም
  dust
         -ስ- አፈር

earthenware
'ኧስንዌየ -ስ- የሸክላ ዕቃ

earthquake
'ኧስክዌይክ -ስ- የመሬት መንቀጥቀጥ

ease
'ኢይዝ -ስ- ም'ቾት ፣ መዝናናት ፣ የመንፈስ
ፀ'ጥታ

easel
'ኢይዘል -ስ- ማስቀ'መጫ (የጥቁር ሰሌዳ ፣
የሥዕል መዘተ)

east
'ኢይስት -ስ- ምሥራቅ

Easter
'ኢይስተ -ስ- በዓለ ትንሣኤ

eastern
'ኢይስተን -ቅ- ምሥራቃዊ ፣ የምሥራቅ

easy
'ኢይዚ -ቅ- ቀላል

eat
'ኢይት -ግ- መብላት [በ'ላ] ፣ መ'መገብ [ተመ
'ገበ]

ebony
'ኤበኒ -ስ- ጥቁር እንጨት ፣ ዞ'ጺ

eccentric
ኤክ'ሴንትሪክ -ቅ- የተለ'የ ጠባይ የ'ሚያሳ'ይ
(ሰበው) ፣ ወፈ'ፈ

ecclesiastic
ኤክለዚ'ያስቲክ -ስ- ካህን

echo
'ኤከው -ስ- የገደል ማ'ሚቶ (ነገር ግን ይህ'ን
ለመሳ'ሰለው ድምፅ ሁ'ሉ)

eclipse
ኢክ'ሊፕስ -ስ- የፀሐይ መጨ'ለም (ጨረቃ በር
ፀ'ና በመሬት መካከል በም'ትሆን'በት ጊዜ)

economics
ኤክኖ'ሚክስ -ስ- የአገር ሀብት ው'ጤት'ና
የማ'ከፋፈል ጥናት ፣ ኢኮኖሚክስ

economical
ኤክኖ'ሚከል -ቅ- ቆጣቢ ፣ ር'ካሽ

economize
ኢኮነማይዝ -ግ- በቁ'ጠባ መኖር [ኖረ] ፣
ወጪን መቀ'ነስ [ቀ'ነስ]

ecstasy
'ኤክስተሲ -ስ- ታላቅ ደስታ ፣ ሐ'ሤት

edge
'ኤጅ -ስ- ጠርዝ ፣ ዳር'ቻ

edible
'ኤደበል -ቅ- የ'ሚ'በ'ላ

edifice
'ኤዲፊስ -ስ- ታ'ላቅ ሕንፃ

edit
'ኤዲት -ግ- ለማ'ተም የሌላውን ሰው ጽሑፍ
ማ'ዘጋጀት [አዘጋጀ] (እ'ርም አስተካክሎ
ወዘተ)

436

editor
'ኤዲተር -ስ- ጋዜጣ አ'ዘጋጅ፣ መጽሐፍ አ'ቀና
ባሪ ፣ መጽሐፍ አ'ጠናጻሪ

educate
'ኤጅዩኬይት -ግ- ማስተማር [አስተማረ] ፣
ማሥልጠን [አሥለ'ጠነ]

education
ኤጅዩ'ኬሸን -ስ- ትምህርት ፣ አስተዳደግ
(በዕውቀት በግብረ ገ'ብ'ነት)

effect
ኢ'ፌክት -ስ- ው'ጤት ፣ በእንምሮ ላይ የቀ'ረ
ስ'ሜት

effective
ኢ'ፌክቲቭ -ቅ- ው'ጤት ሊያስገ'ኝ የ'ሚችል
ብቁ፣ በእንምሮ ላይ ት'ልቅ ስ'ሜት የ'ሚተው

effeminate
ኤ'ፌሚነት -ቅ- ሴታ ሴት

efficient
ኤ'ፊሸንት -ቅ- በቂ ችሎታ ያ'ለው ፣ አጥጋቢ
ው'ጤት የ'ሚሰጥ፣ የሥራ'ጠነ

effigy
'ኤፊጂ -ስ- ምስል (የሰው ፣ በደንጊያ በእን
ጨት ላይ ወዘተ)

effort
'ኤፈት -ስ- ጥረት ፣ ትግል (አንድ ነገር ለመ
ፈ'ጸም) ፣ ሙ'ከራ

effrontery
ኤፍ'ረንተሪ -ስ- ማንጓጠጥ ፣ የ'ማይ'ገ'ባ ድፍ
ረት

egg
'ኤግ -ስ- እንቁላል

egoistic
ኤጎ'ዊስቲክ -ቅ- ራሱን ወ'ዳድ

eight
'ኤይት -ቅ- ስምንት

eighteen
ኤይ'ቲይን -ቅ- ዐሥራ ስ'ምንት

eighteenth
ኤይ'ቲንቲ -ቅ- ዐሥራ ስ'ምንተ'ኛ

eighth
'ኤይትቲ -ቅ- ስምንተ'ኛ

eightieth
'ኤይቲየቲ -ቅ- ሰማንያ'ኛ

eighty
'ኤይቲ -ቅ- ሰማንያ

either
'አይዘ -መዋ- ወይን'ም
-ቅ- ከሁለ'ት አንዱ

ejaculate
ኢ'ጃክዩሌይት -ግ- ሰውን ጨሀ መ'ጣራት [ተ
ጣ'ራ] ፣ በደንገት መ'ናገር ፣ [ተና'ገረ]፤በድ
ንገት ማስፈንጠር [አስፈን'ጠረ]
-ስ- ድንገተ'ኛ ዋይታ

eject
ኢ'ጄክት -ግ- ማስፈን'ጠር [አስፈነ'ጠረ] ፣
ገፍትሮ ማስወ'ጣት [አስወ'ጣ]

elaborate
ኢ'ላበረት -ቅ- በብዙ ጥን'ቃቄ'ና በተሟ'ላ
ሁኔታ የተሠ'ራ ፣ ጊጥ ጌጥ የበ'ዛ'በት
-ግ- በዝርዝር መግለጥ [ገ'ለጠ]

elapse
ኤ'ላፕስ -ግ- ማለፍ [አ'ለፈ] (ለጊዜ)

elastic
ኢ'ላስቲክ -ስ- ላስቲክ
expanding
-ቅ- የላስቲክ
-ቅ- የ'ሚ'ለ'ጠጥ

elated
ኢ'ሌይተድ -ቅ- በጣም የተደ'ሰተ (አንድ
ተግባር በመፈ'ጸም)

elbow
'ኤልበው -ስ- ክርን

elder
'ኤልደ -ስ- በዕድሜ የበ'ለጠ (በቤተ ሰብ
ውስጥ)

elect
ኢ'ሌክት -ግ- መምረጥ [መ'ረጠ] (ድምፅ በመ
ስጠት)

election
ኢ'ሌክሸን -ስ- ምርጫ

elector
ኤ'ሌክተ -ስ- መራጭ

electorate
ኤ'ሌክተረተ -ስ- መራጮ'ች

electricity
ኤሌክት'ሪሲቲ -ስ- ኤሌክትሪክ

electrician
ኤሌክት'ሪሸን -ስ- ኤሌክትሪክ ሠ'ራተ'ኛ

437

eleven
ኢ'ሌቨን -ቅ- ዐሥራ አንድ

eleventh
ኢ'ሌቨንስ -ቅ- ዐሥራ አንደ'ኛ

elegant
'ኤሌገንት -ቅ- ያማረ'በት (ለልብስ)

element
'ኤለመንት -ስ- ጥንተ ነገር (ያልተከፋ'ፈለ እንደተፈ'ጠረ ያ'ለ ነገር)

elementary
ኤለ'ሜንታሪ -ቅ- ቀ'ላል ፤ የ'ማያ'ውክ
education
-ስ- የአንደ'ኛ ደረጃ ትምህርት

elephant
'ኤለፈንት -ስ- ዝሆን

elevate
'ኤለቬይት -ግ- ከ'ፍ ማድረግ [አደ'ረገ]

elevator
'ኤለቬይተ -ስ- አሳንሰር

elicit
ኢ'ሊሲት -ግ- ነገር ማ'ዋጣት [አዋ'ጣ] (እውነት ፤ ምስጢር ፤ ወሬ ወዘተ)

eligible
'ኤሊጀበል -ቅ- ላንድ ሥራ የደ'ረሰ፤የተገ'ባ፤ መ'መረጥ የ'ሚችል
for marriage
-ቅ- ለጋብ'ቻ የደ'ረሰ

eliminate
ኢ'ሊመኔይት -ግ- ማስወ'ገድ [አስወ'ገደ] መፋቅ [ፋቀ] (ስም)

elite
ኤ'ለይት -ስ- በግዕዘን ፤ በትምህርት ፤ በሀብት እ'ጅግ የላቁ ሰዎ'ች

elongate
'ኢሎንጌይት -ግ- ማስረ'ዘም [አስረ'ዘመ]

elope
ኢ'ለውፕ -ግ- መኩብለል [ኩብ'ለለ] (ሴት ከወዳጅ ጋር ለመ'ጋባት)

eloquence
'ኤለኩወንስ -ስ- ል'ሳነ ቅን'ነት ፤ አንደበተ ርቱዕ'ነት

eloquent
'ኤለኩወንት -ቅ- ል'ሳነ ቅን ፤ አንደበተ ርቱዕ

else
'ኤልስ -ቅ- ሌላ
otherwise
-ተግ- አለበለ'ዚያ ፤ ያለ'ዚያ

elsewhere
ኤልስ'ዌየ -ተግ- በሌላ ቦታ

elucidate
ኢ'ሉሲዴይት -ግ- ያንድ ነገር ፍ'ች ጉልህ አድርጎ መግለጽ [ገ'ለጸ] ፤ ማስረ'ዳት [አስረ'ዳ]

elude
ኢ'ሉድ -ግ- ማምለጥ [አመ'ለጠ] (ከመያ'ዝ ፤ ከመታ'የት ወዘተ በማ'ታለል)

elusive
ኢ'ሉሲቭ -ቅ- ለመያዝ የ'ሚያ'ውክ ፤ ለመ'ረዳት'ና ለማስታወስ የ'ሚያ'ውክ

emaciated
ኢ'ሜይሲዬተድ -ቅ- የመነ'መነ ፤ እ'ጅግ የከ'ሳ

emancipate
ኢ'ማንሲፔይት -ግ- ነጻ ማውጣት [አወ'ጣ] ፤ ከባር'ነት አር'ነት ማውጣት [አወ'ጣ]

embalm
ኤም'ባ:ም -ግ- በድን እን'ዳይበሰ'ብስ መድኃኒት ማድረግ [አደ'ረገ]

embankment
ኤም'ባንክመንት -ስ- ያፈር ቄ'ልል (ለውሃ መ'ያ ደቢያ)

embargo
ኤም'ባ:ገው -ስ- የንግድ ግን'ኙ'ነት ክንያ አገር ጋር ማ'ጿረጥ

embark
ኤም'ባ:ክ -ግ- መ'ሣፈር [ተሣ'ፈረ] (በመር ከብ ፤ በአውሮ'ፕላን ፤ በባቡር)

embarrass
ኤም'ባረስ -ግ- ማሳ'ፈር [አሳ'ፈረ]

embarrassment
ኤም'ባረስመንት -ስ- ጉፍረት

embassy
'ኤምባሲ -ስ- ኤም'ባሲ ፤ በው'ጭ አገር ያሉ መልእክተ'ኛ የሆነ ሰው መሥሪያ ቤት

embellish
ኤም'ቤሊሽ -ግ- ማጌጥ [አጌጠ] (አንድ ነገር)

ember
'ኤምብ -ስ- ፍም

embezzle

ኤም'በዚል -ግ- ገንዘብ ማጭበርበር [አጭብ
ረ'በረ] ፡ ገንዘብ ማጉደል [አጓ'ደለ] (አደራ
የተሰ'ጠውን ፡ መዝገብ በማ'ቃወስ)

embitter

ኤም'ቢተ -ግ- ማስመ'ረር [አስመ'ረረ]

emblem

'ኤምብለም -ስ- አርማ (የቤተ ሰብ ፡ የደር
'ጅት)

embody

ኤም'ቦዲ -ግ- ጨ'ምሮ መያዝ [ያዘ] ፡ እ*ራ
ላይ መዋል [አዋለ]

embrace

ኤምብ'ሬይስ -ግ- ማቀፍ [አ'ቀፈ]

embroider

ኤምብ'ሮይደ -ግ- ጥልፍ መጥለፍ [ጠ'ለፈ]

embryo

'ኤምብሪየው -ስ- ፅንስ ፡ ሽል

emerald

'ኤመረልድ -ስ- በ'ለር
colour
-ት- አረንጓዴ

emerge

ኢ'መ፡ጅ -ግ- ብ'ቅ ማለት [አለ] (ከተደ'በቀ
'በት)

emergency

ኢ'መ፡ጀንሲ -ስ- ያልጠ'በቁት አደገ'ኛ ሁናቴ ፡
አስቸ'ካይ ውሳኔ የ'ሚያ'ሻው

emery-cloth

'ኤመሪ ክሎ፟ዝ -ስ- የብርጭ'ቆ ወረቀት

emetic

ኢ'ሜቲክ -ስ- የሚያስታ'ውክ መድኃኒት

emigrant

'ኤሚግራንት -ስ- አገሩን ለ'ቆ ወደሌላ አገር
የ'ሚሄድ ሰው (ለመኖር)

emigration

ኤሚግ'ሬይሸን -ስ- አገር ለ'ቆ ወደሌላ አገር
ለመኖር መሄድ

eminent

'ኤሚነንት -ት- ከ'ፍተ'ኛ ፡ ባለ ክብር ፡ ስመ
ጥር (ሰው)

emissary

'ኤሚሰሪ -ስ- መልእክተ'ኛ

emit

ኢ'ሚት -ግ- ከራሱ ማውጣት [አወ'ጣ]
(ፀሐይ ብር'ሃን) ፡ ማሥረጽ [አሠ'ረጸ]

emotion

ኢ'መውሽን -ስ- ኀይለ'ኛ ስ'ሜት (ውስጣዊ)

emperor

'ኤምፐረ -ስ- ንጉሠ ነገሥት

emphasise

'ኤምፈሳይዝ -ግ- የበ'ለጠ ዋ.ጋ መስጠት [ሰ'ጠ]
(ለቃል ፡ ለሐ'ሳብ ወዘተ)

emphatic

ኤም'ፋቲክ -ት- የበ'ለጠ ዋ.ጋ ሰ'ቶ የተገ'ለጠ
(ቃል ፡ ሐ'ሳብ ወዘተ)

empire

'ኤምፓየ -ስ- የንጉሠ ነገሥት ግዛት

employ

ኤምፕ'ሎይ -ግ- መቅጠር [ቀ'ጠረ] (ለሥራ)

employee

ኤምፕ'ሎይ -ስ- ተቀጣሪ ፡ ሠ'ራተ'ኛ

employer

ኤምፕ'ሎየ -ስ- ቀጣሪ

employment

ኤምፕ'ሎይመንት -ስ- ሥራ

empower

ኤም'ፓወ -ግ- ሥልጣን መስጠት [ሰ'ጠ]

emptiness

'ኤምፕቲነስ -ስ- ባዶ'ነት

empty

'ኤምቲ -ቅ- ባዶ

emulate

'ኤምዩሌይት -ግ- ለመ'ተካከል መሞ'ከር [ሞ
'ከረ] ፡ የበ'ለጠ አድርጎ ለመሥራት መሞ'ከር
[ሞ'ከረ]

enable

ኤን'ኤይብል -ግ- ማስቻል [አስቻለ] (ችሎ'ታ)

enamel

ኢ'ናመል -ስ- ብርጭ'ቆ የ'ሚመስል ነገር ፡ ብ
ረት'ላሕን ወዘተ የ'ሚ'ቀ'ባ'በት (ለጌጥ ወዘተ)

enchant

ኤን'ቻ፡ንት -ግ- ከል'ክ በላይ ማስደ'ሰት [አስ
ደ'ሰተ]

enchantment

ኤን'ቻ፡ንትመንት -ስ- ከል'ክ ያ'ለፈ ደ'ስታ

439

enchantress

ኤን'ቻ፡ንትሪስ -ስ- ሴት ጠንቋይ

encircle

ኤን'ሰ፡ከል -ግ- መክበብ [ከ'በበ]

enclose

ኤንክ'ለውዝ -ግ- ማጠር [አ'ጠረ]

shut in

-ግ- ባንድ ነገር ውስጥ መዝጋት [ዘ'ጋ]፣
ማ'ነር [አ'ነረ]

enclosure

ኤንክ'ለውዠ -ስ- ግ'ቢ ፣ የታ'ጠረ ቦታ

encounter

ኤን'ካውንተ -ግ- መግጠም [ገ'ጠመ] (ያል
ጠ'በቁትን ነገር)

encourage

ኤን'ከሪጅ -ግ- ማ'በረታታት [አ'በረታ'ታ]

end

'ኤንድ -ግ- መጨ'ረስ [ጨ'ረሰ] ፣ ማብቃት
[አበ'ቃ]
-ስ- መጨ'ረሻ

endanger

ኤን'ዴይንጀ -ግ- አደጋ ላይ መጣል [ጣለ]

endeavour

ኤን'ዴቫ -ግ- በጣም መሞ'ከር [ሞ'ከረ]
-ስ- ሙ'ከራ

ənding

ኤን'ዲንግ -ስ- መጨ'ረሻ ፣ ግዛቆሚያ ፣ ባዕድ
መድረሻ (ሰዋሰው-)

endless

ኤንድ'ሌስ -ቅ- ግለቂያ የሌ'ለው

endorse

ኤን'ዶ፡ስ -ግ- በፊርማ ማ'ረጋገጥ [አ'ረጋ'ገጠ]፣
መፈ'ረም [ፈ'ረመ] (ለቼክ ወዘተ) ፣ መደ'ገፍ
[ደ'ገፈ] (ያንድ ሰው ሐ'ሳብ ወዘተ)

endow

ኤን'ዳው -ግ- መስጠት [ሰ'ጠ] (ገንዘብ ፣
ሀብት ፣ መስጠት [ሰ'ጠ] (ተውህቦ ፣ የተፈጥሮ
ስጦታ ወዘተ) \

endurance

ኤንድ'ዩ፡ረንስ -ስ- ትዕግሥት ፣ ቻይ'ነት (መከ
ራ)

endure

ኤን'ድዩወ -ግ- መ'ታገሥ [ታ'ገሠ] ፣ መቻል
[ቻለ] (መከራ)

enemy

'ኤነሚ -ስ- ጠላት ፣ ባላንጣ

energy

'ኤነጂ -ስ- ኀይል

enforce

ኤን'ፎ፡ስ -ግ- ማስገ'ደድ [አስገ'ደደ]

engaged (become)

ኤን'ጌይጅድ -ግ- ማጨት [አ'ጨ]

engagement

ኤን'ጌይጅመንት -ስ- መ'ተጫጨት
work
-ስ- ሥራ
appointment
-ስ- ቀጠሮ

engine

'ኤንጂን -ስ- መኪና
locomotive
-ስ- ባቡር ሳቢ መኪና

engineer

ኤንጂ'ነየ -ስ- መሀንዲስ

engineering

ኤንጂ'ነየሪንግ -ስ- መሀንዲስ'ነት

English

'ኢንግሊ'ሽ -ቅ- እንግሊዛዊ
language
-ስ- እንግሊዝ'ኛ ቋንቋ

Englishman

'ኢንግሊሽመን -ቅ- እንግሊዛዊ (ሰው)

engrave

ኤንግ'ሬይቭ -ግ- ስም ፣ ቅርፅ ወዘተ በወ
ርቅ ፣ በብ'ር ላይ ፈልፍሎ መጻፍ [ጻፈ]

enjoy

ኤን'ጆይ -ግ- በአንድ ነገር መ'ደሰት [ተደ
'ሰተ]

enjoyment

ኤን'ጆይመንት -ስ- ደ'ስታ

enlarge

ኤን'ላ፡ጅ -ግ- ማስፋት [አሰ'ፋ] ፣ ማሳ'ደግ
[አሳ'ደገ] (ለፎቶግራፍ)

enlighten

ኤን'ላይተን -ግ- ማብራራት [አብራ'ራ]፣ማስ
ረ'ዳት [አስረ'ዳ]

440

enormous

ኢ'ኖ:መስ -ቅ- በጣም ት'ልቅ ፣ በጣም ሰ'ፊ

enough

ኢ'ነፍ -ቅ- በቂ

enquire

ኢንክ'ዋየ -ግ- መጠ'የቅ [ጠ'የቀ] (ስለአንድ ነገር ለማወቅ)

enrich

ኤን'ሪች -ግ- ግበልጸግ [አበለ'ጸገ] ፣ ግዳበር [አዳ'በረ]

enrol

ኤን'ሮል -ግ- መ'መዝገብ [ተመዘ'ገበ]

enrolment

ኤን'ሮልመንት -ስ- ስም ግስመዝገብ

ensure

ኤን'ሾ: -ግ- ግ'ረጋገጥ [አ'ረጋ'ገጠ] ፣ ካደጋ የራቀ ግድረግ [አደ'ረገ]

entail

ኤን'ቴይል -ግ- መጠ'የቅ [ጠ'የቀ] (አንድ ሥራ የ'ሚያስፈ'ልገው ጊዜ ፣ ድካም ገንዘብ ወዘተ)

entangle

ኤን'ታንገል -ግ- ግ'ወሳሰብ [አ'ወሳ'ሰበ] ፣ እች'ግር ላይ መጣል [ጣለ]

enter

'ኤንተ -ግ- መግባት [ገ'ባ]

enterprise

'ኤንተፕራይዝ -ቅ- ዕ'ቅድ (የሥራ) ፣ ሊያ 'ቋ'ጣ ወይንም ላይ'ቋ'ጣ የ'ሚችል የሥራ ዕ'ቅድ

enterprising

'ኤንተፕራይዚንግ -ቅ- ባለ ዕ'ቅድ (የሥራ) ፣ ያ'ቋ'ጣ'ኛ ብሎ ሥራ የ'ሚጀ'ምር

entertain

ኤንተ'ቴይን -ግ- እንግዳ ግ'ሥዌት [አ'ሥ 'ወተ] ፣ ግስተናገድ [አስተና'ገደ]

enthusiasm

ኤንስ'ዩ:ዚያዝም -ስ- ታ'ላቅ ፍ'ላጎት ፣ ጽኑእ ሞ'ኞት

enthusiastic

ኤንስዩ:ዚ'ያስቲክ -ቅ- ጽኑእ ም'ኞት ያ'ለው

entice

ኤን'ታይስ -ግ- ለመሳብ ፣ ለግ'ሳሳት ፣ ለግባ በለ መሞ'ከር [ሞ'ከረ]

entire

ኤን'ታየ -ቅ- መ'ላ ፣ ሙ'ሉ ፣ ድፍን

entrails

'ኤንትሬይልዝ -ስ- ሆድ ዕቃ

entrance

'ኤንትረንስ -ስ- መግቢያ ፣ በ'ራፍ ፣ በ'ር

entrance

ኤንት'ራ:ንስ -ግ- በጣም ግስደ'ስት [አስደ'ሰ ተ]

entreat

ኤንት'ሪይት -ግ- መ'ለማመጥ [ተለማ'መጠ]፣ መ'ለማመን [ተለማ'መነ]

entrust

ኤንት'ረስት -ግ- ጋላፊ'ነት መስጠት [ሰ'ጠ] ፣ አደራ ግለት [አለ]

envelope

'ኤንቨለውፕ -ስ- አንፎል'ፕ

envious

'ኤንቪየስ -ቀቅ- ቀ'ናተኛ ፣ ቀናኢ

environment

ኤን'ቫየረንመንት -ስ- አ'ካባቢ (አንድ ፍጡር የ'ሚኖር'በት)

envoy

'ኤንቮይ -ስ- መልእክተ'ኛ (የመንግሥት)

envy

'ኤንቪ -ስ- ም'ቀ'ኝነት ፣ ቅናት

epic

'ኤፒክ -ቅ- ታሪካዊ (ጀግና)

poem

-ስ- ያንድ ጀግና ገብዝና የ'ሚተ'ርክ ረ'ጅም ግጥም

epidemic

ኤፒ'ዴሚክ -ስ- ተላላፊ በ'ሽታ (ተስቦ ፣ ወረ ርሽ'ኛ)

epilepsy

'ኤፒሌፕሲ -ስ- የ'ሚጥል በ'ሽታ ፣ የባሪያ በ'ሽታ

episode

'ኤፒሰውድ -ስ- ከተከታታይ ሁናቴ'ዎች አ ንዱ

epistle

ኢ'ፒሰል -ስ- መልእክት ፣ ደብዳ'ቤ (የመ ጽሐፍ ቅ'ዱስ)

epitaph

'ኤፒታፍ -ስ- ለሞተ ሰው የ'ሚ'ደ'ረግ ንግ 'ግር ፣ በሞተ ሰው መቃብር ላይ የ'ሚ'ጻፍ ጽሑፍ

441

epoch
'ኤይፖክ -ስ- ዘመን ፣ ጊዜ (ታሪካዊ ፣ የሕይ
ወት ወዘተ)

equal
'ኢይክወል -ቅ- ተመሳሳይ ፣ ትክ'ክል ፣(አ'ቻ
(በብዛት ፣ በመጠን በማዕረግ)

equality
ኢክ'ዎሊቲ -ስ- ተመሳሳይ'ነት ፣ ትክ'ክል
'ነት

equalize
'ኤይክወላይዝ -ግ- ማስተካከል [አስተካ'ከለ]፣
እ'ኩል ማድረግ [አደ'ረገ]

equanimity
ኤክወ'ኒሚቲ -ስ- የመንፈስ ጸ'ጥታ

equation
ኤክ'ዌይዝን -ስ- ማስተካከል ፣ መ'ተካከል

equator
ኢክ'ዌይተ -ስ- የምድር ወገብ

equine
'ኤክዋይን -ቅ- የፈረስ ፣ ፈረስ የ'ሚመስል

equip
ኢክ'ዊፕ -ግ- የ'ሚያስፈ'ልግ ዕቃ ማ'ዘጋጀት
[አ'ዘጋ'ጀ] ፣ የጦር ትጥቅ ማቅረብ [አቀ'ረበ]

equipment
ኢክ'ዊፕመንት -ስ- የ'ሚያስፈ'ልግ ዕቃ ማ
'ዘጋጀት ፣ ለሥራ የ'ሚያስፈ'ልግ ዕቃዎ'ች ፣
የጦር መ'ሣሪያዎ'ች ወዘተ

equivalent
ኢክ'ዊቨለንት -ቅ- ተመሳሳይ ፣ ተወዳዳሪ (ባ
ዋጋ ፣ በመጠን ፣ በቁጥርም)

equivocal
ኢክ'ዊቨከል -ቅ- ግልጽ ያልሆነ ፣ ትርጉሙ
ጉልህ ያልሆነ ፣ አ'ጠራጣሪ ትርጉም ያ'ለው

era
'ኢረ -ስ- ዘመን ፣ ጊዜ (በታሪክ)

eradicate
ኢ'ራዲኬይት -ግ- ነቅሎ ማጥፋት [አጠ'ፋ] ፣
ማስወ'ገድ [አስወ'ገደ] ፣ መደምሰስ [ደመ'ሰሰ]

erase
ኢ'ሬይዝ -ግ- መፋቅ [ፋቀ] ፣ ማጥፋት [አጠ
'ፋ] (በላ'ጺ.ስ)

eraser
ኢ'ሬይዘ -ስ- ላ'ጺስ

erect
ኢ'ሬክት -ግ- ቀጥ ማድረግ [አደ'ረገ] ፣ ማ
ቆም [አቆመ] (ለሕንጻ ወዘተ)

erection
ኢ'ሬክሽን -ስ- መቆም ፣ ቀ'ጥ ማለት ፣ ሕንጻ

erosion
ኢ'ረውዠን -ስ- የመሬት በጉርና መ'ሠርሠር ፣
እ'ያ'ለተ መሄድ (የመሬት)

err
'ኧ፡ -ግ- መ'ሳሳት [ተሳሳተ] ፣ ጥፋት መሥራት
[ሠ'ራ]

erratic
ኢ'ራቲክ -ቅ- እምነት የ'ማይጥሉ'በት ፣ ጠ
ባዩ የ'ሚ'ለዋ'ወጥ

error
'ኤረ -ስ- ስሕተት ፣ ግድፈት

eruption
ኢ'ረፕሽን -ስ- መፈንዳት (ለእሳተ ጎሞራ)

escape
ኢስ'ኬይፕ -ግ- ማምለጥ [አመለ'ጠ]

escort
'ኤስኮት -ግ- ማ'ጀብ [አ'ጀበ]

especially
ኤስ'ፔሽል -ተግ- በተለ ይ፡ ይልቁንም

espionage
'ኤስፒየናዥ -ስ- ስ'ለላ

essay
'ኤሰይ -ስ- ጽሑፍ ፣ ድርሰት ፣ ያብቃሙን ጊዜ
አጠ'ር ያለ)

essential
ኢ'ሴንሸል -ቅ- አስፈ'ላጊ

establish
ኢስ'ታብልሽ -ግ- መመሥረት [መሠ'ረተ] ፣
ማቋቋም [አቋቋመ]

estate
ኢስ'ቴይት -ስ- እርስት

esteem
ኢስ'ቲይም -ግ- ማክበር [አከ'በረ]

estimate
'ኤስቲሜይት -ግ- መገ'መት [ገ'መተ] ፣ መገ
ምገም [ገመ'ገመ]

estuary
'ኤስትዩወሪ -ስ- ወንዝ ወደ ባሕር የ'ሚፈ'ስ
'በት ቦታ

442

eternal

ኢ.'ተ፡ኅል -ት- ዘለዓለማዊ ፣ መጨ'ረሻ የሌ
'ለው

ethical

'ኤ,ስከል -ት- ግብረ ገ'ባዊ (ለጠባይ) ፣ ከግ
ብረ ገ'ብ'ነት ጋር ግን'ኙ'ነት ያ'ለው

ethics

ኢ.ስ,ክስ -ስ- የግብረ ገ'ብ'ነት ጥናት

Ethiopia

ኢ.ሲ,'የው፡ፒ.ያ -ስ- ኢ.ትዮ'ጵያ

Ethiopian

ኢ.ሲ,'የው፡ፒ.የን -ት- ኢ.ትዮ ጵያዊ ·

eucalyptus

የክ'ሊ,ፕተስ -ስ- ባሕር ዛፍ·

Eucharist

'ዩ፡ከሪስት -ስ- ሥ'ጋ ወደሙ ፡ ቁርባን

eunuch

'ዩ፡ነክ -ስ- ጃንደረባ ፡ ስልብ

European

ዩረ'ፒ.የን -ት- አውሮ'ጳዊ

evade

ኢ.'ቬይ.ድ -ግ- ማምለጥ [እመ'ለጠ] ፣ ገለል
ማለት [አለ] ፣ መልስ ለመስጠት አለመፈ'ለግ
[-ፈ.ለ ገ]

evacuate

ኢ.'ባክዩዌይ.ት -ግ- ማስለ'ቀቅ [አስለ'ቀቀ]
(ሕዝብ ከሀገር)

evaluate

ኢ.'ቫልዩዌይ.ት -ግ- መገ'መት [ገ'መተ]

evaporate

ኢ.'ቫፐሬይ.ት -ግ- መትነን [ተ'ነነ]

evasive

ኢ.'ቬይ.ዚቭ -ት- ማምለጫ ፣ ካንድ ሁኔቴ
መረቅያ (መልስ ወዘተ)

eve

'አይ.ቭ -ስ- ዋዜማ

even

'አይ.ቨን -ተግ- እንኳን ፡ በ . . . ም
-ት- ለ'ጥ ያለ ፡ የተስተካ'ከለ ፣ የተመ
ዛ'ዘነ ፡ ለሁለ'ት በትክ'ክል ሊ.'ከ'ፈል የ'ሚ
'ቻል

evening

'አይ.ቭኒንግ -ስ- ም'ሽት

event

ኢ.'ቬንት -ስ- ድር'ጊት ፡ ሁናቴ

eventful

ኢ.'ቬንትፉል -ት- አዳ'ዲስ ነገር ያ'ለ'በት ፡
አስደ'ሳች

ever

'ኤ ቨ -ተግ- መ'ቼም ፡ ምንጊዜም ፡ ሁል ጊዜ

everlasting

ኤ ቨ'ላ፡ስቲንግ -ት- መ'ጨ'ረሻ የሌ'ለው ፡
ዘለዓለማዊ

every

'ኤ ቨሪ -ት- ሉ ያንዳንዱ

everybody

'ኤ ቨሪቦ,ዲ -ስ- እ'ያንዳንዱ ሰው

everyday

ኤ ቨሪ'ዴይ. -ት- በ'የተኑ ፡ የ'የተኑ

everyone

'ኤ ቨሪወን -ስ- እ'ያንዳንዱ ሰው

everything

'ኤ ቨሪሲ,ንግ -ስ- ግ'ን'ኛው'ም ነገር ፡ ሁ'ሉ'ም
ነገር

everywhere

'ኤ ቨሪዌየ -ተግ- የት'ም

evict

ኢ.'ቪ.ክት -ግ- ማስወ'ጊድ [አስወ'ጊደ] (በሕ'ግ)፣
መንቀል [ነ'ቀለ] (ሰው'ን ከርስት)

evidence

'ኤ ቪ.ደንስ -ስ- ማስረ'ጃ

evil

'ኢ.ቪል -ስ- ክፋት

ewe

'ዩ፡ -ስ- ሴት በግ

exact

ኤ.ግ'ዛክት -ት- በትክ'ክል ፡ ል'ክ

exactly

ኤ.ግ'ዛክትሊ -ተግ- በትክ'ክል
-ቃአ- ል'ክ እንደ'ዚህ

exaggerate

ኤ.ግ'ዛጀሬይ.ት -ግ- ማ'ጋነን [አ'ጋ'ነነ]፣ ከ'ሚ
'ገ'ባ በላይ ስለአንድ ነገር መ'ናገር [ተና'ገረ]

examination

ኤ.ግዛሚ'ኔይ.ሽን -ስ- ፈተና

443

examine
እን'ዛመን -ግ- መፈ'ተን [ፈ'ተነ] ፡ መመር
መC [መረ'መረ]

example
እን'ዛ:ምፐል -ስ- ም'ሳሌ ፡ ማስረ'ጃ

excavate
'ኤክስከቬይት -ግ- መቆ'ፈር [ቆ'ፈረ] (የተደ
'በቀ ነገC ለማግኘት)

exceed
ኤክ'ሲይድ -ግ- መብለጥ [በ'ለጠ] ፡ መላቅ
[ላቀ]

excellent
'ኤክሴለንት -ቅ- በጣም ጥ'ሩ ፡ እ'ጅግ የላቀ

except
ኤክ'ሴፕት -ተግ- ከ . . . በስተቀC

exception
ኤክ'ሴፕሽን -ስ- ያልተለ'መደ ነገC ፡ ሁናቴ ፡
እ'ጠቃላይ ሕ'ግን የማይ'ከ'ተል ነገC ፡ ሁናቴ

exceptional
ኤክ'ሴፕሽነል -ቅ- ያልተለ'መደ ፡ በጣም ጥሩ

excerpt
'ኤክስ፡ፐት -ስ- አስተዋፅአ ፡ እ'ጭC ምን
ባብ (የመጽሐፍ ፡ የፊልም ፡ የቴያትC መዘተ)

excess
ኤክ'ሴስ -ስ- ከል'ክ ማ'ለፍ ፡ ማትረፍ ፡ ማትረ
ፍረፍ

excessive
ኤክ'ሴሲቭ -ቅ- ከል'ክ ያ'ለፈ ፡ የተትረፈ'ረፈ

exchange
ኤክስ'ቼይንጅ -ግ- መ'ለዋወጥ [ተለዋ'ወጠ]

excise
'ኤክሳይዝ -ግ- መቅረጥ [ቀ'ረጠ] (በአገር ው
ስጥ የ'ሚ'ሸጡ ዕቃዎ'ችን)
tax
-ስ- ቀረጥ (በአገር ውስጥ በ'ሚ'ሸጡ
ዕቃዎ'ች ላይ የ'ሚ'ጣል)
take out
-ግ- መቁረጥ [ቆ'ረጠ] (ከመጽሐፍ አን
ዱን ክፍል)

excite
ኤክ'ሳይት -ግ- ማስደ'ሰት [አስደ'ሰተ] ፡ ስ'ሜ
ትን መቀስቀስ [ቀስ'ቀስ]

excitement
ኤክ'ሳይትመንት -ስ- ደ'ስታ ፡ የስ'ሜት ፡ መ'ቀ
ስቀስ

exclaim
ኤክስክ'ሌይም -ግ- በድንገት መጮኽ [ጮኸ]
(ከሥቃይ ፡ ከ'ቁጣ ፡ ከድን'ጋጤ ወዘተ የተ
ነ'ሣ)

exclamation
ኤክስክለ'ሜይሽን -ስ- የማ'ጋነን ጩኸት ፡
የአንክሮ ድምፅ

exclude
ኤክስክ'ሉ:ድ -ግ- ለ'ይቶ ማስተ'ረት [አስተ'ረ]

exclusive
ኤክስክ'ሉ:ሲቭ -ቅ- የተለ'የ ፡ ል'ዩ

excrement
'ኤክስክረመንት -ስ- ዓይነ ምድC ፡ ኩስ

excretion
ኤክስክ'ሪይሽን -ስ- የወ'ጣ ነገC (ከሰው'ነት ፡
አሰC ፡ አC ፡ ላቦት ወዘተ)

excruciating
ኤክስክ'ሩ:ሺዬይቲንግ -ቅ- በጣም የ'ሚያ'ም ፡
የ'ሚያ'ሠቃ'ይ

excursion
ኤክስ'ከ:ሽን -ስ- አ'ጭC የሽ'CሽC ጉዞ

excuse
ኤክስክ'ዩ:ዝ -ግ- ይቅC ማለት [አለ] ፣ ስጎተ
ትን ቻ'ል ማለት [አለ]

excuse
ኤክስክ'ዩ:ስ -ስ- ይቅርታ ፡ ምክንያት (የሠ'ሩት
ሥራ ል ክ መሆኑን ለማስረ'ዳት)

execute
'ኤክሲከዩ:ት -ግ- መፈ'ጸም [ፈ'ጸመ] (የተጠ
'የቁትን ፡ የታ'ዘዙትን ነገC)

execution
ኤክሲክ'ዩ:ሽን -ስ- መፈ'ጸም (አንድ ጉ'ዳይ) ፣
መግደል (ሞት የተፈ'ረደ'በትን)

executive
ኤክ'ዜከዩቲቭ -ስ- ባለሥልጣን

exempt
ኤክ'ዜምፕት -ግ- ከግ'ዴ,ታ ነጻ መሆን [ሆነ]
-ቅ- ሕ'ግ የማያስገ'ድደው

exercise
'ኤክሰሳይዝ -ስ- መልመጃ ፡ መ'ለማመጃ
-ግ- መሥራት [ሠ'ራ] ፡ ማድረግ [አደ
'ረገ]

exert
ኤክ'ዘ:ት -ግ- በጣም መሥራት [ሠ'ራ] ፡
እሥራ ማዋል [አዋለ]

444

exhale

ኤክስ'ሄይል -ግ- መተንፈስ [ተነ'ፈሰ] (ወደ ው'ጭ)

exhaust

ኤግዞ፡ስት -ግ- ማድከም [አደ'ከመ]
-ስ- የመኪና ጢስ መውጫ ቧምፖ

exhibit

ኤግዚቢት -ግ- ማሳ'የት [አሳ'የ]

exhibition

ኤክሲ'ቢሸን -ስ- ኤክዚቢሽን ፣ ለመ'ታየት የቀ'ረቡ ዕቃዎ'ች ፣ ትርኢት (የዕቃዎ'ች)

exile

'ኤክሳይል -ግ- ማጋዝ [አጋዘ] (ለቅጣት)
-ስ- ግዞተ'ኛ ፣ የግዞት ቦታ

exist

'ኤግዚስት -ግ- መኖር [ኖረ]

existence

ኤግ'ዚስተንስ -ስ- መኖር ፣ ሀ'ላዌ

exit

ኤግዚት -ስ- መውጫ በ'ር

expand

ኤክስ'ፓንድ -ግ- መ'ለጠጥ [ተለ'ጠጠ] ፣ መ'ሳብ [ተሳበ]

expect

ኤክስ'ፔክት -ግ- መ'ጠባበቅ [ተጠባ'በቀ] (አንድ ሁናቴ ፣ ነገር ወዘተ እን'ደ'ሚሆን)

expectant

ኤክስ'ፔክተንት -ቅ- በጉጉ'ት በተስፋ የ'ሚጠ'በቅ

expedition

ኤክስቴ'ዲሸን -ስ- የጥናት ፣ የምርመራ ጉዞ ፣ አንድ ዓላማ ያ'ለው ጉዞ

expel

ኤክስ'ፔል -ግ- ማስወ'ጣት [አስወ'ጣ] ፣ ማስወ'ገድ [አስወ'ገደ]

expend

ኤክስ'ፔንድ -ግ- ገንዘብ ፣ ጊዜ ጉልበት ወዘተ ላንድ ተግባር ማዋል [አዋለ]

expenditure

ኤክስ'ፔንዲቸ -ስ- ወጭ (የገንዘብ)

expense

ኤክስ'ፔንስ -ስ- ወጭ (የገንዘብ)

expensive

ኤክስ'ፔንሲቭ -ቅ- ው'ድ (ለዋጋ)

experience

ኤክስ'ፒሪየንስ -ስ- የሥራ ልም'ምድ (በማየት'ና በመሥራት የተገ'ኘ)

experiment

ኤክስ'ፔሪመንት -ግ- መፈ'ተን [ፈ'ተነ] (ያንድ ነገር ሁናቴ ለማጥናት)
-ስ- ሙ'ከራ (የጥናት)

expert

'ኤክስፐ፡ት -ቅ- ዐዋቂ ፣ ባለሙያ

expire

ኤክስ'ፓየ -ግ- ማለቅ [አ'ለቀ] (ለጊዜ)

explain

ኤክስፕ'ሌይን -ግ- መግለጽ [ገ'ለጸ] ፣ ማስረ'ዳት [አስረ'ዳ]

explanation

ኤክስፕለ'ኔይሸን -ስ- አ'ገላለጽ

explode

ኤክስፕ'ለውድ -ግ- መፈንዳት [ፈነ'ዳ] ፣ ማፈንዳት [አፈነ'ዳ]

exploit

ኤክስፕ'ሎይት -ግ- ያገር ሀብት እሥራ ላይ ማዋል [አዋለ] ፤ ያለ አግባብ የሰው ጉልበት መብዝላት [በ'ላ]

exploit

'ኤክስፕሎይት -ስ- የጉብዝ'ና ሥራ ፣ ተግባር (በጦር'ነት ወዘተ)

explore

ኤክስፕ'ሎ፡ -ግ- መርምሮ ማግኘት [አገ'ኘ]

explosion

ኤክስፕ'ለውዠን -ስ- መፈንዳት

export

'ኤክስፖ፡ት -ግ- የንግድ ዕቃ ወደውጭ አገር መላክ [ላከ]

exposed

ኤክስ'ፐውዝድ -ቅ- ግልጽ የሆነ ፣ ያልተሰ'ወረ

exposure

ኤክስ'ፐውዠ -ስ- ተገልጦ መ'ታየት

expound

ኤክስ'ፓውንድ -ግ- ማስረ'ዳት [አስረ'ዳ]

express

ኤክስፕ'ሬስ -ግ- በድር ጊት በቃላት ፣ በእ'መ ለካከት ማስረ'ዳት [አስረ'ዳ]
-ቅ- ፈ'ጣን

445

expression

ኤክስፕ'ሬሽን -ስ- መልክ ፣ ፊት ፣ የመልክ
ሁናቴ (ቁ'ጣ ፣ ሐዘን ፣ ደ'ስታ ወዘተ)

extend

ኤክስ'ቴንድ -ግ- መዘርጋት [ዘረ'ጋ] ፣ ግር
ዘም [አረ'ዘመ] ፣ ማስፋ'ዘም [አስፋ'ዘመ]

extension

ኤክስ'ቴንሽን -ስ- ተጨ'ማሪ ነገር

extensive

ኤክስ'ቴንሲቭ -ቅ- ት'ልቅ ፣ የተዘረ'ጋ ፣ ስ'ፊ

extenuate

ኤክስ'ቴንዩዌይት -ግ- የሙ'ሩትን ጥፋት ቀ'ላል
አድርጎ ማሳየ'ት [አሳ'የ] ፣ ጥፋትን ማቅለል
[አቀለ'ለ]

exterior

ኤክስ'ቲሪየ -ቅ- የውጭ ፣ አፍአዊ

exterminate

ኤክስ'ተ፡ሚኔይት -ግ- መፍጀት [ፈ'ጀ] ፣ መ
ጨ'ረስ [ጨ'ረሰ] ፣ መደምሰስ [ደመ'ሰሰ]

external

ኤክስ'ተ፡ናል -ቅ- የው'ጭ ፣ አፍአዊ

extinct

ኤክስ'ቲንክት -ቅ- ያለፈ ፣ የጠ'ፋ ፡ዘሩ የ'ማ
ይ'ገ'ኝ (ለእንስሳት ዓይነት)

extinguish

ኤክስ'ቲንግዊሽ -ግ- ማጥፋት [አጠ'ፋ-] (ለእ
ሳት)

extort

ኤክስ'ቶ፡ት -ግ- በዛቻ፣ በኃይል መውሰድ [ወ
'ሰደ] (ገንዘብ)

extra

'ኤክስትረ -ቅ- ሌላ ፣ ተጨ'ማሪ

extract

ኤክስት'ራክት -ግ- ማውጣት [አወ'ጣ] (በን
ይል) ፣ መንቀል [ነ'ቀለ]

extraordinary

ኤክስትሮ፡ዲነሪ -ቅ- ያልተለ'መደ ፣ እንግዳ
የሆነ

extravagant

ኤክስት'ራቫገንት -ቅ- ገንዘብ አባካኝ

extreme

ኤክስት'ሪይም -ቅ- ከባድ (ለሕ'ግ ፣ ለድህ'ነት
ወዘተ) ፤ ወደ አንድ ወገን ፈ'ጽሞ ያያ'ለ

exult

ኤክ'ዘልት -ግ- በጣም መ'ደሰት [ተደ'ሰተ]

eye

'አይ -ስ- ዓይን

eyebrow

'አይብራው -ስ- ቅንድብ

eyeglasses

'አይግላሲዝ -ስ- መነ'ጥር ፣ መነ'ጽር

eyelash

'አይላሽ -ስ- ሽፋ፡ሽፍት ፣ ሽፋሉ

eyelid

'አይሊድ -ስ- ያይን ቆብ

eyesight

'አይሳይት -ስ- ያይን ብርሃን

eye witness

'አይዊትነስ -ስ- ምስ'ክር ፣ ያይን ምስ'ክር

fable

'ፌይብል -ስ- ተረት

fabric

'ፋብሪክ -ስ-.አካል ፣ ቅርፅ (ያንድ ነገር)
ጨርቃ ጨርቅ ፣ ድር'ና ማግ (የጨርቅ)

fabricate

'ፋብሪኬይት -ግ- መሥራት [ሠ'ራ] (ዕቃ) ፣
ፈጥሮ ማውራት [አወ'ራ]

face

'ፌይስ -ግ- መግጠም [ገ'ጠመ] (ዓይን ለዓ
ይን)

-ስ- ፊት ፣ መልክ

facetious

ፈ'ሲሽን -ቅ- ፈዝ የ'ሚያበዛ (ያለቦታው)

facilitate

ፈ'ሲሊቴይት -ግ- ቀ'ላል ማድረግ [አደ'ረገ] ፣
ች'ግር ማ'ቃለል [አ'ቃለለ]

446

facility
ፈ'ሲ.ሊ.ቲ -ስ- ሥራ የ'ሚያ'ቀላ'ጥፍ፣ መ'ሣሪያ ፤ አገልግሎት ወዘተ ፤ ሥራ ፤ ትምህርት ለማ'ከናወን የ'ሚረዳ ዘዴ።

fact
'ፋክት -ስ- እውነት ፤ እርግጠ'ኛ ነገር

factor
'ፋክተr -ስ- ምክንያት ፤ የተለ'የ ው'ጤት ለማስገ'ኘት የነ'በረ ሁኔቴ

factory
'ፋክትሪ -ስ- ፋብሪካ

faculty
'ፋከልቲ -ስ- ል'ዩ ስጦታ ፤ ተውህቦ ፤ ችሎታ፣ በዩኒቨርስቲ ውስጥ ል'ዩ የትምህርት ክፍል ፤ የዩኒቨርስቲ መምህራን

fade
ፈይድ -ግ- መደብዘዝ ፤ [ደብ'ዘዘ] ፤ ቀለም መልቀቅ [ለ'ቀቀ]

fail
ፌይል -ግ- መውደቅ [ወ'ደቀ]፤ (ፈተና ወዘተ)፤ ማቆት [አቆተ] (አንድ ሥራ ፤ ሙ'ከራ)

faint
ፌይንት -ግ- መዝለፍለፍ [ተዝለፈ'ለፈ] -ቅ- ጉ-ልህ ያልሆነ ፤ ደካማ

fair
'ፌየ -ቅ- ነጭ ያለ ፤ አድልዎ የሌ'ለ'በት ፤ የ'ሚያ'ጋ'ላ ፤ ደረቅ'ና ጥሩ (ለአ'የር)

faith
'ፌይስ -ስ- እምነት

faithful
'ፌይስፉል -ቅ- ታ'ማኝ፣ እሙ'ን

fake
'ፌይክ -ስ- እውነተ'ኛ ያልሆነ ፤ ማስመ'ሰያ ነገr

fall
'ፎ፡ል -ግ- መውደቅ [ወ'ደቀ]

fallacy
'ፋለሲ -ስ- ወሸት

fallow
'ፋለው -ቅ- ታርሶ ያ'ደረ መሬት

false
'ፎልስ -ስ- ውሸት ፤ የተሳሳተ (ለንግ'ግr)

falter
'ፎ፡ልተr -ግ- ፌራ ተ'ባ ማለት [አለ] (በንግ'ግr ፤ በርም'ጃ ፤ በሥራ ወዘተ)

fame
'ፌይም -ስ- ዝ'ና ፤ ጥሩ ስም

familiar
ፈ'ሚልየ -ቅ- የታ'ወቀ ፤ የተለ'መደ ፤ ብዙ ጊዜ ያ'ይ፡ት ፤ የሰ'ሙ፡ት ወዘተ

family
'ፋመሊ -ስ- ቤተ ሰብ

famine
'ፋሚን -ስ- ረኃብ (ባን'ድ አገr) ፤ ቀጠና

famous
'ፌይመስ -ቅ- ዝነ'ኛ ፤ ስመ ጥሩ ፤ ስመ ጥr

fan
'ፋን -ስ- ማራገቢያ

fanatic
ፈ'ናቲክ -ቅ- አንድ ነገr ፤ ሐ'ሳብ በመደ'ገፍ ፤ በመ'ቃወም የ'ሚ'መና'ቸክ ሰው ፤ እምነቱን (ሐ'ሳቡን) አለቅጥ የ'ሚያጤን ሰው

fancy
'ፋንሲ -ስ- ከእውነት የራቀ እምነት ፤ ሐ'ሳብ

fangs
'ፋንግዝ -ስ- የው'ሻ ክራንቻ ፤ እባቦ መርዝ'ን የ'ሚያስተላ'ልፍ'በት ጥርስ

fantastic
ፋን'ታስቲክ -ቅ- ድንቅ ፤ ሊሠሩት የ'ማይ'ቻል (ዕ'ቅድ ፤ ሐ'ሳብ)

fantasy
'ፋንተሲ -ስ- ከእውነት የራቀ እምነት ፤ በሕ'ሳብ እንጂ እሥራ ላይ ሊውል የ'ማይቸል ነገr

far
'ፋ፡ -ቅ- ሩቅ

fare
'ፌየ -ስ- የጉዞ ዋጋ
food
-ስ- ምግብ

farewell
ፈ'ዌል -ቃአ- ደኅና ይሁኑ (ሁን)

farm
'ፋ፡ም -ስ- እርሻ (ቦታ)

farmer
'ፋ፡መ -ስ- ገበሬ ፤ አራሽ

farther
'ፋ፡ዘ -ቅ- የራቀ፣ ሩቅ

fascinate
'ፋስኔይት -ግ- ማስደ'ነቅ [አስደ'ነቀ]

447

fashion

’ፋሽን -ግ- መቅረብ [ተ'ረብ]

style

-ስ- ሞድ

fast

’ፋ፡ስት -ግ- መጦም [ጦመ] ፣ መጾም [ጸመ]

-ስ- ጦም ፣ ጾም

fast

ፋ፡ስት -ቅ- ፈ'ጣን ፣ የተጣበቀ ፣ በቀ'ላሉ የማ

ይነቃነ'ቅ

fasten

’ፋ፡ሰን -ግ- ማጥበቅ [አጠ'በቀ]

fastener

’ፋ፡ስነ -ስ- ማጥበቂያ

fat

’ፋት -ቅ- ወፍራም

of meat

-ስ- ስብ

fatal

’ፌይተል -ቅ- ሞት የ'ሚያስከ'ትል ፣ አደገ'ኛ

fate

’ፌይት -ስ- ዕ'ድል ፣ እጣ

father

’ፋ፡ዘ -ስ- አ'ባት

father-in-law

-ስ- አማት (ለወንድ)

fatigue

ፈ'ቲይግ -ስ- የሰው'ነት ዝለት ፣ መድከም

(በሥራ ምክንያት)

fatten

’ፋተን -ግ- ማወ'ፈር [አወ'ፈረ] ፣ መቀ'ለብ

[ቀ'ለበ] (ለማስባት)

fault

’ፎልት -ስ- ስነተት

faultless

’ፎልትሌስ -ቅ- እንከን የሌ'ለው

faulty

’ፎልቲ -ቅ- ስሕተት የሞ'ላ'በት

favour

’ፌይቨ -ግ- መወደድ [ወ'ደደ]

-ስ- ውለታ

favourable

’ፌይቨረበል -ቅ- ጥሩ ፣ ተስማሚ

favourite

_’ፌይቨሪት -ቅ- ተስማሚ ፣ አብልጠው የ'ሚ

ወ'ዱት

fawn

’ፎ፡ን -ግ- ጅራት መቁላት [ቆ'ላ] (ለውሻ) ፣

ማ'ቆላመጥ [አ'ቆላ'መጠ]

colour

-ቅ- ግራ'ጫ

fear

’ፊየ -ስ- ፍርሃት

fearful

’ፊየፉል -ቅ- ፈሪ ፣ አስፈሪ

fearless

’ፊየሌስ -ቅ- የ'ማይፈራ ፣ ደ'ፋር

feasible

’ፊይዘበል -ቅ- እሥራ ላይ ሊውል የ'ሚችል

feast

’ፊይስት -ግ- በዓል ማክበር [አክ'በረ]

-ስ- በዓል

feat

’ፊይት -ስ- ጀብዱ ፣ ከል'ክ ያ'ለፈ የጉብዝ'ና

ሥራ

feather

’ፊዘ -ስ- ላባ (የወፍ ፣ የዶሮ ወዘተ)

features

’ፊይቸዝ -ስ- መልክ ፣ ያንድ ነገር የተለ'የ

ጠባይ

February

’ፌብሩወሪ -ስ- የ'ካቲት

federation

ፌደ'ሬይሽን -ስ- ፌደራሲዮን ፣ ባንድ ጠቅ

ላይ እ'ገዛዝ የ'ሚ'ገ'ዙ ነጻ የውስጥ ደምብ

ያ'ላ'ቸው ያንድ መንግሥት አገር'ች

fee

’ፊይ -ስ- ለማገባርተ'ኛ'ነት ፣ ለትምህርት፡ለሕ

'ክም'ና ወዘተ የ'ሚ'ከ'ፈል ያገልግሎት ዋጋ

feeble

’ፊይበል -ቅ- ደካማ

feed

’ፊይድ -ግ- መመ'ገብ [መ'ገበ] ፣ ማብላት

[አብ'ላ]

feeder

’ፊይደ -ስ- መ'ጋቢ (እንስሳት ፣ አትክልት)

ተከባካቢ ፣ መ'ጋቢ (መንገድ)

448

feel
'ፊይል -ግ- መዳሰስ [ዳ'ሰስ]
emotion
-ግ- መ'ሰማት [ተሰ'ማ] (ለስ'ሜት)
felicity
ፌ'ሊሲቲ -ስ- ደ'ስታ ፣ ሐ'ሜት
feline
'ፊይላይን -ቅ- የድመት ወገን
fell
'ፊል -ግ- መቁረጥ [ቆ'ረጠ] (ለዛፍ) ፣ መጣል
[ጣለ]
fellow
'ፌለው -ስ- ጓ'ደ'ኛ ፣ ሰው
fellowship
'ፌለውሺፕ -ስ- ጓ'ደ'ኝ'ነት ፣ ማኅበር
felon
'ፌለን -ስ- ወንጀለ'ኛ (ከ'ባድ)
felony
'ፌለኒ -ስ- ከ'ባድ ወንጀል
felt
'ፌልት -ስ- ወፍራም ጨርቅ
female
'ፊይሜይል -ቅ- እንስት
feminine
'ፌመኒን -ቅ- አነስታይ
fen
'ፌን -ስ- ረግረግ ፣ ጨቀጨቅ
fence
'ፌንስ -ስ- አጥር
ferment
ፈ'ሜንት -ስ- ብጥ'ብጥ ፣ ሀውከት (የፖሊቲካ)
ferment
'ፈ:ሜንት -ግ- መፍላት [ፈ'ላ] (ለጥንስስ) ፣
መቡካት [ቦ'ካ] (ለቡኮ ፣ ለሲጥ)
ferocious
ፈ'ረውሽስ -ቅ- ጨ'ካኝ ፣ ጎይለ'ኛ ፣ አውሬ
fertile
'ፈ:ታይል -ቅ- ለም (ለመሬት)
fertility
ፈ'ቲሊቲ -ስ- የመሬት ልማት ፤ መ'ራባት
(ለሰው ፣ ለእንስሳ)
fertilizer
'ፈ:ቲላይዘ -ስ- የመሬት ማዳበሪያ

fertilize
'ፈ:ቲላይዝ -ግ- እንዲ'ራ'ባ ማድረግ [አደ'ረገ]
fervour
'ፈ:ሸ -ስ- ጥልቅ ስ'ሜት ፣ ታ'ላቅ ፍ'ላጎት ፣
የመንፈስ መ'ቃጠል
fester
'ፌስተ -ግ- መነፍረቅ [ነፈ'ረቀ] (ለቁስል)
festival
'ፌስቲቨል -ስ- በዓል ፣ ክብረ በዓል
fetch
'ፌች -ግ- ሄዶ ማምጣት [አመ'ጣ]
feud
ፍ'ዩ:ድ -ስ- ክ'ባድ የ'ቆየ ጥል (በሁለ'ት ቤተ
ሰብ ፣ ሰዎ'ች መካ'ከል)
fever
'ፊይቨ -ስ- ት'ኩሳት (ሕመም)
few
ፍ'ዩው -ቅ- ጥቂት
fiance
ፌ'ያንሴ -ስ- እጮ'ኛ
fickle
'ፊከል -ቅ- እምነት የ'ማይ'ጣል'በት ፣ ከ'ዳ
ተ'ኛ ፣ ተለዋዋጭ
fiction
'ፊክሽን -ስ- ል'ብ ወ'ለድ ታሪክ
fiddle
'ፊደል -ግ- መ'ጫወት [ተ'ጫ'ወተ] (እንደ
ነገር በእ'ጅ ይዞ ባለማተዋል)
cheat
-ግ- ማጭበርበር [አጭበረ'በረ]
fidget
'ፊጀት -ግ- መቁነጥነጥ [ተቁነጠ'ነጠ]
field
'ፊይልድ -ስ- ሜዳ ፣ መስክ ፤ የተወ'ሰነ የት
ምህርት ዓይነት
fiend
'ፊይንድ -ስ- ሰይጣን ፣ ርኩስ መንፈስ ፣ በጣም
ክፉ'ና ጨ'ካኝ ሰው
fierce
'ፊየስ -ቅ- አውሬ ፣ ጨ'ካኝ ፣ ጎይለ'ኛ
fifteen
ፊፍ'ቲይን -ቅ- ዐሥራ አ'ምስት
fifteenth
ፊፍ'ቲንፅ -ቅ- ዐሥራ አ'ምስተ'ኛ

449

fifth
'ፊፍስ -ቅ- አ'ምስተ'ኛ

fiftieth
'ፊፍቲየስ -ቅ- አምሳ'ኛ

fifty
ֵ'ፊፍቲ -ቅ- አምሳ

fig
'ፊግ -ስ- የበለስ ፍሬ

fight
'ፋይት -ግ- መ'ዋጋት [ተዋ'ጋ] ፣ መ'ታገል
[ታ'ገለ]
-ስ- ው'ጊያ ፣ ትግል

figure
'ፊገ -ስ- ቅርፅ ፣ መልክ ፣ አኃዝ

file
'ፋይል -ስ- ዋረድ ፣ ፋይል ፣ የሰለፉ መሥ
መር

filings
'ፋይሊንግዝ -ስ- ሙ'ራጅ ፣ ብ'ናኝ

fill
'ፊል -ግ- መሙላት [ሞ'ላ]

filling
'ፊሊንግ -ስ- በተሰ'በረ ጥርስ ውስጥ የ'ሚ'ሞ
'ላ ነገር

filly
'ፊሊ -ስ- ያልተጠ'ቃ'ች ፈረስ

film
'ፊልም -ስ- ፊልም
layer
-ስ- ሥሥ ሽፋን

filter
'ፊልተ -ግ- ማ'ጣራት [አ'ጣ ራ] (ለፈሳሽ)
-ስ- ማ'ጣሪያ

filth
'ፊልስ -ስ- ተውሳክ ፣ እድፍ ፣ ቈሻሻ

filthy
'ፊልሲ -ቅ- እድፋም ፣ ቈሻሻ

filtration
ፊልት'ሬይሽን -ስֵ ማ'ጣራት

fin
'ፊን -ስ- የዐሣ ክንፍ

final
'ፋይነል -ቅ- የመጨ'ረሻ

finance
ፋይ'ናንስ -ግ- በገንዘብ መርዳት [ረ'ዳ] ፣ ለአ
ንድ ዕ'ቅድ ገንዘብ ማውጣት [አወ'ጣ]
-ስ- የመንግሥት ገንዘብ አስተዳደር

find
'ፋይንድ -ግ- ማግኘት [አገ'ኘ]

finding
'ፋይንዲንግ -ስ- ተፈ'ልጎ የተገ'ኘ ነገር ፣
ሕ'ጋዊ ው'ሳኔ(ዎ'ች)

fine
'ፋይን -ስ- መቅጣት [ቀ'ጣ]
punishment
-ስ- ቅጣት
thin
-ቅ- ረቂቅ ፣ ሥሥ
good
-ቅ- ጥሩ ፣ መልካም

finery
'ፋይነሪ -ስ- ጌጣ ጌጥ ያ'ለ'በት ልብስ

finger
'ፊንገ -ስ- ጣት

finger-print
'ፊንገፕሪንት -ስ- አሻራ

finish
'ፊኒሽ -ግ- መጨ'ረስ [ጨ'ረሰ]

fir
'ፈ፡ -ስ- የዛፍ ዓይነት (አርዘ ሊባኖስ የ'ሚ
መስል)

fire
'ፋየ -ስ- እሳት
dismiss
-ግ- ከሥራ ማስወ'ገድ [አስወ'ገደ]

fire brigade
'ፋየብሪጌይድ -ስ- የሳት አደጋ መ'ከላከያ ድር
'ጅት

fireman
'ፋየመን -ስ- የእሳት አደጋ መ'ከላከያ ወ'ታ
'ያር
stoker
-ስ- ማገዶ አቅራ-ቢ. (በባቡር ላይ)

fireplace
'ፋየፕሌይስ -ስ- ምድ'ጃ

450

fireproof
'ፋየፕሩፍ -ቅ- እሳት የማያቃጥለው ፡ እሳት
የማይጎዳው

firewood
'ፋየውድ -ስ- ማገዶ

fireworks
'ፋየወ፡ክስ -ስ- ርችት

firm
'ፈ፡ም -ቅ- ጽኑእ ፡ ጠንካራ

firmament
'ፈ፡መመ፡ንት -ስ- ጠፈር ፡ ሰማይ

firmness
'ፈ፡ምኔስ -ስ- ጽኑእነት ፡ ጠንካራነት

first
'ፈ፡ጎት -ቅ- አንደኛ ፡ የመጀመሪያ

firstborn
'ፈ፡ስትቦ፡ን -ስ- የበኩር ልጅ

fiscal
'ፊስከል -ቅ- የመንግሥት (ገንዘብ)

fish
'ፊሽ -ስ- ዐሣ

fisherman
'ፊሸመን -ስ- ዐሣ አጥማጅ ፡ ዐሣ አሥጋሪ

fishmonger
'ፊሽመንገ -ስ- ዐሣ ነጋዴ

fishy
'ፊሺ -ቅ- ዐሣ ዐሣ የሚሽት
suspicious
-ቅ- የሚያ ጠራጥር (ነገር ፡ ሁናቴ)

fissure
'ፊሸ -ስ- ስንጥቅ (በደንጊያ ወዘተ)

fist
'ፊስት -ስ- ቡጢ

fit
'ፊት -ግ- መስማማት [ተስማማ]
-ስ- የሚጥል በ'ሽታ ፡ ድንገተኛ ቁ'ጣ፡
ቅናት ወዘተ

fitness
'ፊትኔስ -ስ- መስማማት

fitter
'ፊተ -ስ- ገጣሚ (ዕቃ ፡ መኪና ወዘተ)

fitting
'ፊቲንግ -ስ- የሚ'ገጠም ነገር ፡ እቤት ውስ
ጥ የሚገባ ነገር
suitable
-ቅ- የሚስማማ

five
'ፋይቭ -ቅ- አምስት

fix
'ፊክስ -ግ- መለ'ጠፍ [ለ'ጠፈ]
mend
-ግ- ማበ'ጀት [አበ'ጀ] ፡ መጠ'ገን
[ጠ'ገነ]

fixed
'ፊክስት -ቅ- የተለ'ጠፈ
mended
-ቅ- የተበ'ጀ

fizz
'ፊዝ -ግ- መፍላት [ፈ'ላ] (የታ'ሸገ መጠ'ጥ፡
ሲ'ከ'ፈት)

fizzy
'ፊዚ -ቅ- የ ሚፈላ

flabby
ፍ'ላቢ -ቅ- ማለዋ'ልል ፡ ጠንካራ ያልሆነ ፡
ደካማ (ለሰውነት ሥጋ)

flag
ፍ'ላግ -ስ- ባንዲራ ዐላማ
-ግ- ቶስፉ መቀረጥ ፡ [ቆ'ረጠ] ፡ መድ
ከም [ደ'ከመ

flagon
ፍ'ላገን -ስ- ትልቅ ጠርሙዝ (የመጠ'ጥ መ
ያዣ)

flagrant
ፍ'ሌይግረንት -ት- ደ'ፋር ፡ የማያፍር ፡ ዓይነ
ደረቅ

flagstaff
ፍ'ላግስታ፡ፍ -ስ- የባንዲራ ዐላማ እንጨት ፡
ሰን'ደቅ

flail
ፍ'ሌይል -ግ- መውቃት [ወ'ቃ] (እበ'ትር)
-ስ- መውቂያ በትር

flair
ፍ'ሌየ -ስ- የተፈጥሮ ስጦታ ፡ ተውህቦ

flamboyant
ፍላም'ቦየንት -ቅ- እጅ'ኝ እጅ'ኝ ባይ ፡ ጉ'ረኛ፡
ጊጣ ጊጥ የበ'ዛ'በት

451

flame

ፍ'ሌይም -ስ- ነበልባል

flange

ፍ'ላንጅ -ስ- ዘርፍ

flank

ፍ'ላንክ -ስ- ሽንጥ

flannel

ፍ'ላነል -ስ- ወፈ'ር ያለ የሱፍ ልብስ

flap

ፍ'ላፕ -ግ- መውለብለብ [ተውለበ'ለበ]
-ስ- ክዳን

flare

ፍ'ሌየ -ግ- ቡ'ግ ማለት [አለ] (ለጥቂት ጊዜ)

flash

ፍ'ላሽ -ግ- ቡ'ግ ማለት [አለ] ፣ ማብለጥለጥ
[አብለጨ'ለጨ]
-ስ- ድንገተ'ኛ ብርሃን

flask

ፍ'ላ:ስክ -ስ- ኮ'ዳ

flat

ፍ'ላት -ቅ- የተዘረ'ጋ ፣ አሰልቺ
-ስ- በፎቅ ላይ አንድ መኖሪያ ቤት
tyre የፈነ'ዳ ፣ የተነ'ፈሰ ጎ'ማ

flatiron

ፍ'ላታየን -ስ- ካው'ያ

flatten

ፍ'ላተን -ግ- መደምጥ [ዳ'መጠ]

flatter

ፍ'ላተ -ግ- ማ'ቆላመጥ [አ'ቆላ'መጠ] ፣ ግስ
ደ'ስት [አስደ'ሰተ]

flattery

ፍ'ላተሪ -ስ- ቁልም'ጫ

flaunt

ፍ'ሉ:ንት -ግ- በግልጽ አለመ'ታዘዝ [-ታዘ'ዘ]

flavour

ፍ'ሌይቨ -ስ- መዓዛ ፣ ጣዕም

flaw

ፍ'ሉ: -ስ- እንከን

flaxen

ፍ'ላክሰን -ቅ- የገረ'ጣ (ለጠጉር)

flay

ፍ'ሌይ -ግ- ቆዳ መግፈፍ [ገ'ፈፈ] (ለቅጣት)

flea

ፍ'ሊይ -ስ- ቁን'ጫ

fleck

ፍ'ሌክ -ስ- ነቁጥ ፣ ጉድፍ

flee

ፍ'ሊይ -ግ- መሸሽ [ሸ'ሸ] ፣ መጥፋት [ጠ'ፋ]

fleece

ፍ'ሊይስ -ስ- የበግ ጠጉር

fleet

ፍ'ሊይት -ስ- የጦር መርከቦ'ች
-ቅ- በፍጥነት የ'ሚርጥ

flesh

ፍ'ለሽ -ስ- ሥጋ

fleshy

ፍ'ሌሺ -ቅ- ወፍራም

flex

ፍ'ሌክስ -ግ- ግጠፍ'ና መዘርጋት [አ'ጠፈ ፣
ዘረ'ጋ]
-ስ- የተሸ'ፈነ ሽቦ

flexibility

ፍላክሲ'ቢሊቲ -ስ- የመታጠፍ ችሎታ ፤ ግ'
ትር አለመሆን ፣ ሐ'ሳብን በቀ'ላሉ የመለ'ወጥ
ችሎታ

flexible

ፍ'ሌክሲበል -ቅ- መ'ታጠፍ የ'ሚችል ፣
ግ'ትርያልሆነ ፣ ሐ'ሳቡን በቀ'ላሉ የ'ሚለው'ጥ

flick

ፍ'ሊክ -ግ- በጣት ማስፈን'ጠር [አስፈን'
ጠረ] ፣ ጣት ማጮኽ [አጮኸ] (ለመጥራት)

flicker

ፍ'ሊክ -ግ- መደብዘዝ [ደበ'ዘዘ] (ዉፍ ፣ ሻማ)

flier

ፍ'ላየ -ስ- በራሪ ፣ አውሮ'ፕላን ነጂ

flight

ፍ'ላይት -ግ- ሽ'ሽት ፤ መብረር

flighty

ፍ'ላይቲ -ቅ- የ'ማይ'ታ'መን

flimsy

ፍ'ሊምዚ -ቅ- በጣም ቀ'ጭን'ና ቀ'ላል ፣
በቀ'ላሉ ሊበላ'ሽ ፣ ሊ'ጎ'ዳ የ'ሚችል

flinch

ፍ'ሊንች -ግ- ወደኋላ ማፈግፈግ [አፈገ'ፈገ]
(ከፍርሃት ፣ ከበ'ትር የተነ'ሣ)

452

fling
ፍ'ሊ.ንግ -ግ- መወርወር [ወረ'ወረ]

flint
ፍ'ሊ.ንት -ስ- ደን'ጊ ያ (የሲጃራ ማ'ቀጣጠያ ወ
ዘ፡ተ)

flippant
ፍ'ሊ.ፐንት -ቅ- የ'ማይነ'ደው ፤ ደንታ ቢስ

flirt
ፍ'ለ፡ት -ግ- ማሽኮርመም [አሽኮረ'መመ]

flirtation
ፍለ'ቴይሸን -ስ- ማሽኮርመም

flit
ፍ'ሊ.ት -ግ- ብ'ር ብ'ር ማለት [አለ]

float
ፍ'ለው፡ት -ግ- መንሳፈፍ [ተንሳ'ፈፈ]

flock
ፍ'ሎክ -ስ- መንጋ (የበግ)

floe
ፍ'ለው -ስ- የ'ሚንሳ'ፈፍ የበረዶ ቁ'ራጭ

flog
ፍ'ሎግ -ግ- መግረፍ [ገ'ረፈ]

flood
ፍ'ለድ -ስ- ጎርፍ

floodlight
ፍ'ለድላይት -ስ- ት'ልቅ መብራት (በቤት
ው'ጭ)

floor
ፍ'ሎ፡ -ግ- መጣል [ጣለ] (መ'ቱ)
-ስ- ወለል
storey
-ስ- ፎቅ ፤ ደርብ

floral
ፍ'ሎ፡ረል -ቅ- የአበባ

florid
ፍ'ሎሪድ -ቅ- የቀ'ላ (ለመልክ) ፤ በጣም ያጌጠ

florist
ፍ'ሎሪስት -ስ- አበባ ሻጭ

flotsam
ፍ'ሎትሰም -ስ- በወሃ ላይ የተንሳ'ፈፈ ነገር
(ቆሻሻ ፤ የመርከብ ስ'ባሪ ወዘተ)

flour
ፍ'ላወ -ስ- ዱቄት

flourish
ፍ'ለሪሽ -ግ- ማማር [አማረ] ፤ መሥ፨መር
[ሠ'መረ]

flow
ፍ'ለው -ግ- መፍሰስ [ፈ'ሰሰ]

flower
ፍ'ላወ -ስ- አበባ

fluctuate
ፍ'ለክቸዌይት -ግ- መ'ለዋወጥ [ተለዋ'ወጠ]
(ለእንቅስ'ቃሴ) ፤ መድከም [ደ'ከመ] ፤ መበር
ታት [በረ'ታ]

flue
ፍ'ሉ፡ -ስ- የጢስ መውጫ (በቤት ውስጥ)

fluent
ፍ'ሉወንት -ቅ- አንደበተ ቀ'ና

fluff
ፍ'ለፍ -ስ- የተጠቀ'ለለ የሱፍ የጥጥ ወዘተ
ብ'ናኝ

fluid
ፍ'ሉዊድ -ስ- ፈሳሽ (ውሃ ፤ ወተት ፤ ወዘተ)

fluke
ፍ'ሉ፡ክ -ስ- አ'ጋጣሚ ዕ'ድል

flurry
ፍ'ለሪ -ስ- ድንገተ'ኛ ሩ'ጫ ፤ መበርገግ ፤
ድንገተ'ኛ የነፋስ ሽ'ውታ

flush
ፍ'ለሽ -ግ- መቅላት [ቀ'ላ] (ቀለም)
wash away
-ግ- ጠርጎ መሄድ [ሄደ]

fluster
ፍ'ለስተ -ግ- ማ'ደናበር [አ'ደና'በረ] ፤ ማ'ደ
ናገር [አ'ደና'ገረ]

flute
ፍ'ሉ፡ት -ስ- ዋሽንት

flutter
ፍ'ለተ -ግ- ብ'ር ብ'ር ማለት [አለ]

fly
ፍ'ላይ -ግ- መብረር [በ'ረረ]
-ስ- ዝምብ

foal
'ፎውል -ስ- የፈረስ ግልገል ፤ የአህ'ያ ውር
ንጭላ ፤ ውርንጭ'ላ

453

foam

’ፈውም -ግ- አረፋ መድረቅ [ደ'ፈቀ]
-ስ- አረፋ ፣ ኮረፉ

fodder

’ፎደ -ስ- የደ'ረቀ የእንስሳት ምግብ (ድርቆሽ፣
ገለባ ወዘተ)

foe

’ፈው -ስ- ጠላት ፣ ባላንጋራ

foetus

’ፈተስ -ስ- ሽል

fog

’ፎግ -ስ- ጉም ፣ ጭጋግ

foggy

’ፎጊ -ቅ- ጭጋጋም

foil

’ፎይል -ግ- ወንጀል እንዳይሠራ ማቆም [አ
ቆመ]
tin-
-ስ- የብ'ር መልክ ያለው ወረቀት

fold

’ፎልድ -ግ- ማጠፍ [አጠ'ፈ]

folder

’ፎልደ -ስ- ዶሴ

foliage

’ፈውሊየጅ -ስ- ቅጠላ ቅጠል

folk

’ፈውክ -ስ- ሕዝብ

folk-lore

’ፈውክሎ: -ስ- ያ'ባቶ'ች ተረት ፣ እምነት ፣
ባህል (ጥናት)

follow

’ፎለው -ግ- መ'ከተል [ተከ'ተለ]

follower

’ፎለወ -ት- ተከ'ታይ ፣ ደ'ጋፊ (የእምነት
ወዘተ)

folly

’ፎሊ -ስ- ቂል'ነት ፣ ጅል'ነት

foment

ፈ’ሜንት -ግ- መፍላት [ፈ'ላ] (ጥንስስ) ፣ ብጥ
'ብጥ ማንሣት [አነ'ሣ]

fond

’ፎንድ -ት- አፍቃሪ ፣ የ'ሚወ'ድ

fondle

’ፎንደል -ግ- ማሻሽት [አሻ'ሸ] ፣ መደባበስ
[ደባ'በሰ]

font

’ፎንት -ስ- ማጥመቂያ ገበታ (በቤተ ክርስቲ
ያን ውስጥ)

food

’ፉ:ድ -ስ- ምግብ

fool

’ፉ:ል -ስ- ቂል ሰው ፣ ሞ'ኟ ሰው
-ግ- ማ'ታለል [አ'ታ'ለለ] ፣ ማቄል
[አቄለ]

foolish

’ፉ:ሊሽ -ቅ- ቂል ፣ ሞ'ኟ

foot

’ፉት -ስ- እግር

foothold

’ፉትሆውልድ -ስ- የእግር መቆናጠጫ ፣ መ'ቆ
ናጠጫ ቦታ

footman

’ፉትመን -ስ- አ'ጀቢ (ፈረስ'ኛን ወዘተ) ፣ አገ
ልጋይ (እንግዳ በማስተ'ባት'ና በማስተናገድ)

footpath

’ፉትፓ:ፕ -ስ- የግር መንገድ

footprint

’ፉትፕሪንት -ስ- ዱካ

for

’ፎ: -መዋ- ለ . . .
-መገ- ስለ

forage

’ፎረጅ -ግ- ቀ'ለብ መሰብሰብ
-ስ- የእንስሳት ምግብ ፣ መ'ና

forbear

ፎ’ቤየ -ግ- አንድ ነገር ከመሥራት ራስን
መግታት [ገ'ታ]

forbear

’ፎቤየ -ስ- አያት ቅድም አያት

forbid

ፈ’ቢድ -ግ- መከልከል [ከለ'ከለ]

force

’ፎ:ስ -ግ- ማስገ'ደድ [አስገ'ደደ]
-ስ- ጉይል

forceps

’ፎ:ሴፕስ -ስ- ወረንጦ

454

ford

'ፎ:ድ -ግ- ጥልቅ ባልሆነ ቦታ ወንዝ መ'ሻገር [ተሻ'ገረ]

-ስ- ወንዝ መ'ሻገሪያ ቦታ

forearm

'ፎ:ራ:ም -ስ- ክንድ

foreboding

ፈ'በውዲንግ -ስ- ፍርሃት (ለ ሚመጣ ሁናቴ)

forecast

'ፎ:ካስት -ግ- መ'ንበይ [ተን' የ] ፡ ወደፊት የ'ሚያጋጥመን ነገር መ'ናገር [ና'ገረ]

forefather

'ፎ:ፋ:ዘ -ስ- አያት ቅድም አያት

forefinger

'ፎ:ፊንገ -ስ- ሌባ ጣት

forehead

'ፎረድ -ስ- ግንባር ፡ ግምባር

foreigner

'ፎረነ -ስ- የውጭ አገር ሰው

foreman

'ፎ:መን -ስ- የሠራተ'ኞ'ች ተቆጣጣሪ ፡ አለቃ

foremost

'ፎ:መውስት -ቅ- የመጀ'መሪያ ፡ በ ግም አስ ፈ'ላጊ

forenoon

'ፎ:ኑ:ን -ስ- ጧት ፡ ከቀትር በፊት

forerunner

'ፎ:ረነ -ስ- መንገድ ጠ (አንድ ነገር መም ጣቱን የ'ሚነግር)

foresee

ፎ'ሲ -ግ- የ'ሚመጣውን ማወቅ [ዐ'ወቀ] ፡ ወደፊት ለ'ሚመጣው ሁናቴ መ'ዘጋጀት [ተዘ ጋ'ጀ]

foreshadow

ፎ'ሻደው -ግ- ቀድሞ ማስጠንቀቅ [አስጠን 'ቀቀ] ፡ ማመልከት [አመለ'ከተ]

foresight

'ፎ:ሳይት -ስ- ለ'ሚመጣ ች'ግር አስቀ'ድሞ ማ'ሰብ ፡ ሁናቴዎ'ችን ቀድሞ የማየት ተግባር

forest

'ፎረስት -ስ- ደ'ን ፡ ዱር

forestall

ፎስ'ቶ:ል -ግ- አንድ ነገር ቀድሞ በመሥ ራት ሌላው እንዳይሠራው ማድረግ [አደረ'ገ]

forester

'ፎረስተ -ስ- ደ'ን ጠባቂ

forestry

'ፎረስትሪ -ስ- የደ'ን አ'ያያዝ ትምህርት

forewarn

ፎ'ዎ:ን -ግ- በቅድሚያ ማስጠንቀቅ [አስጠ ን'ቀቀ]

foreword

'ፎወ:ድ -ስ- የመጽሐፍ መቅድም (ብዙ ጊዜ ከደራሲው ያልሆነ)

forfeit

'ፎፊት -ግ- በቅጣት መልክ አንድ ነገር ማጣት [አ'ጣ] (በሕ'ግ ፡ በስፖርት)

-ስ- ቃል የገ'ቡ'በትን ነገር ለመፈ'ጸም መያዣ ገንዘብ ፡ የዋስት'ና ገንዘብ

forge

'ፎ:ጅ -ግ- ብረት መቀጥቀጥ [ቀጠ'ቀጠ] (ቅር ፅ ለመስጠት) ፡ ለማ'ታለል አስመ'ስሎ መሥ ራት [ሠ'ራ] (ፊርማ ፡ ገንዘብ)

forgery

'ፎ:ጀሪ -ስ- ሕ'ገ ወ'ጥ ገንዘብ መሥራት ፡ ማስረ'ጃ ፡ መዝገብ ወዘተ ማ'ቃወስ (ለማጭ በርበር)

forget

ፈ'ጌት -ግ- መርሳት

forgive

ፈ'ጊቭ -ግ- ይቅር ማለት [አለ]

forgo

ፎ'ገው -ግ- መተው [ተወ]

fork

'ፎ:ክ -ስ- ሹ'ካ ፡ ባ'ላ

pitch-

-ስ- መንሽ

forlorn

ፈ'ሎ:ን -ቅ- ያ'ዘነ ፡ የተ'ከዘ ፡ የከ'ፋው

form

'ፎ:ም -ስ- ቅርፅ

formal

'ፎ:መል -ቅ- የተወ'ሰነ ሕ'ግ የተከተ'ተለ ፡ ሥነ ሥርዓታዊ ፡ ጠባዩ የ'ማያ'ወላ'ውል

formality

ፎ'ማሊቲ -ስ- ሥነ ሥርዓት ፡ ወግ

former

'ፎ:መ -ቅ- የቀድሞ

formerly
'ፎ.መርሊ. -ተግ- ባ'ለፈው ጊዜ

formidable
'ፎ'ሚደብል -ት- አስፈ'ጋሪ ፡ ኃይለ'ኛ ፡ መስ
ጓኽል የበ'ዛ'በት

formulate
'ፎ:መዩለይት -ግ- መሥረት [ሥ'ራ] (ፅ'ቅድ)

forsake
ፈ'ሴይክ -ግ- መካድ [ካ'ደ] ፡ መተው [ተ'ወ]

forthcoming
ፎ:ስ'ከሚንግ -ት- ወደፊት የ'ሚመጣ

fortification
ፎ:ቲፈ'ኬይሽን -ስ- ም'ሽግ

fortify
'ፎ:ቲፋይ -ግ- መመሽግ [መ'ሸገ]

fortitude
'ፎ:ቲትዩድ -ስ- ጀግን'ነት ፡ ለችግር ለሥቃይ
አለመ'በገር

fortnight
'ፎ:ትናይት -ስ- ሁለት ሳምንት

fortress
'ፎ:ትረስ -ስ- ም'ሽግ ፡ አምባ

fortunate
'ፎ:ትዩነት -ት- ዕ'ድለ'ኛ

fortune
'ፎ:ትዩን -ስ- ዕ'ድል ፡ ሀብት ፡ ብዕል

forty
'ፎ:ቲ -ት- አርባ

forward
'ፎወድ -ተግ- ወደፊት

fossil
'ፎስል -ስ- እመረት ላይ የ'ሚ ገኝ የተደፈነ
ታሪክ ምስክት (የየ'ረቱ ሕይወት የነበረ
ችው ዓፍረ'ች)

foster
'ፎስተ -ግ- ማበረታታት [አበረታ'ታ] ፡ ማሳ
ደግ [አሳ'ደገ]

foster-father
'ፎስተፋ:ዘ -ስ- የጡት አባት

foster-mother
'ፎስተመዘ -ስ- የጡት እናት

foul
'ፋውል -ት- በጣም የቆ'ሸሸ ፡ አስቀ'ያሚ ፡
መጥፎ ሽ'ታ'ና ጣዕም ያ'ለው ፡ ሽ'ረ'ኛ
sport
-ስ- ስሕተት ፡ ጥፋት

found
'ፋውንድ -ግ- መመሥረት [መሠ'ረተ]

foundation
'ፋውን'ዴይሽን -ስ- መሠረት

founder
'ፋውንደ -ስ- መሥራች

foundling
'ፋውንድሊንግ -ስ- ወድቆ የተገ'ኘ ሕፃን

foundry
'ፋውንድሪ -ስ- የብረት ማቅለሚያ

fount
'ፋውንት -ስ- ምንጭ (የውሃ)

fountain
'ፋውንተን -ስ- ምንጭ (የውሃ)

four
'ፎ: -ት- አራት

fourteen
ፎ:'ቲደን -ት- ዐሥራ አራት

fourteenth
ፎ:'ቲደንስ -ት- ዐሥራ አራተ'ኛ

fourth
'ፎ:ስ -ት- አራተ'ኛ

fowl
'ፈውል -ስ- ወፍ ፡ ዶሮ

fox
'ፎክስ -ስ- ቀበሮ

fraction
ፍ'ራክሽን -ስ- ስብራ ፡ ያንድ መሉ ነገር
ክፍል (ለሒሳብ)

fracture
ፍ'ራክቸ -ስ- ስ'ብረት (የዐጥንት)

fragile
ፍ'ራጃይል -ት- በቀላሉ የ'ሚ ሰበር

fragment
ፍ'ራግመንት -ስ- ስ'ባሪ

fragrance
ፍ'ራይግረንስ -ስ- መዓዛ ፡ ጥሩ ሽ'ታ

456

fragrant

ፍ'ሬይግረ`ንት -ቅ- ጥሩ ሽ'ታ'ያ'ለው ፣ ሽ'ታው
የ'ሚ'ያ'ውድ

frail

ፍ'ሬይል -ቅ- ደካማ (በሰው'ነት ጠባይ) ፣ በቀ
'ላሉ የ'ሚ'ሰ'በር

frame

ፍ'ሬይም -ስ- ክፈፍ ፣ ሰው'ነት ፣ አካል

framework

ፍ'ሬይምወ፡ክ -ስ- ቅርፅ በመስጠት ፣ ድጋፍ
በመሆን የ'ሚያገለ'ግል መ'ዛሪያ ፣ ሥርዓት ፣
መሠረት (ለመንግሥት ፣ ለፅ'ቅድ ወዘተ)

franchise

ፍ'ራንቻይ`ዝ -ስ- የመምረጥ ሙሉ መብት (የ
ሕዝብን እንደራሴዎ'ች ወዘተ)

frank

ፍ'ራንክ -ቅ- ግልጽ ፣ እውነተ'ኛ ፣ ቀ'ጥተ'ኛ
(ነገር የ'ማያድበሰ'ብስ)

frantic

ፍ'ራንቲክ -ቅ- የተደና'ገረው (ከሥቃይ ፣ ከህ
ፍረት ወዘተ የተነ'ሣ)

fraternal

ፍረ'ተ፡ነል -ቅ- የወንድ'ም'ነት

fraternity

ፍረ'ተ፡ኒቲ -ስ- ወንድ'ም'ነት

fraternize

ፍ'ራተናይዝ -ግ- መ'ወዳጀት [ተወዳ'ጀ]

fraud

ፍ'ሮ፡ድ -ስ- ማጭበርበር (ለገንዘብ)

fray

ፍ'ሬይ -ግ- መንተብ [ነ'ተበ]
fight

-ስ- ጦል ፣ ጭቅ'ጭቅ

freak

ፍ'ሪይክ -ስ- ያልተለ'መደ ትርዕ ፣ መልክ ፣
ጄል ሐሳብ ያ'ለው ሰው

freckles

ፍ'ሬክልዝ -ስ- በሰው'ነት ቆዳ ጥቁ'ቁር ምል
'ክቶ'ች

free

ፍ'ሪይ -ግ- ነጻ ማውጣት [አወ'ጣ]
without payment

-ቅ- ነጻ ፣ ያለ ዋጋ

freedom

ፍ'ሪይደም -ስ- ነጻ'ነት

freeze

ፍ'ሪይዝ -ግ- ወደ በረዶ'ነት መ'ለወጥ [ተለ'ወ
ጠ] ፣ ወደ በረዶ'ነት መለ'ወጥ [ለ'ወጠ]

freight

ፍ'ሬይት -ስ- በየብስ ፣ በመርከብ ፣ ባውር'
ገላን የ'ሚ'ላክ ጭነት ፣ ለጭነት የ'ሚከ'ፈል
ኪራይ

French

ፍ'ሬንች -ቅ- ፈረንሳይ
language

-ስ- ፈረንሳይ'ኛ

frenzy

ፍ'ሬንዚ -ስ- የእብድ'ነት ሥራ

frequent

ፍሪክ'ወንት -ግ- ማዘውተር [አዘወ'ተረ]
ፍ'ሪክወንት -ተግ- ሁል ጊዜ

fresh

ፍ'ሬሽ -ቅ- ት'ኩስ ፣ ተዘ'ጋዠ (ለነፋስ)

freshman

ፍ'ሬሽመን -ስ- በዩኒቨርስቲ ያንደ'ኛ ዓመት
ተማሪ

fret

ፍ'ሬት -ግ- ለት'ንሽ ነገር መጨ'ነት [ተጨ
'ነተ]

fretful

ፍ'ሬትፉል -ቅ- ያልተደ'ሰተ ፣ ቅር ያለው

friar

ፍ'ራይ -ስ- መነኩሴ (የተለ'የ ሥርዓት ወገን
የሆነ)

friction

ፍ'ሪክሽን -ስ- መ'ፋተግ
trouble

-ስ- አለመስማማት ፣ በሐ'ሳብ መ'ለያ
የት

Friday

ፍ'ራይደይ -ስ- ዓርብ

friend

ፍ'ሬንድ -ስ- ወዳጅ ፣ ጓ'ደ'ኛ ፣ ረዳት

friendship

ፍ'ሬንድሺፕ -ስ- ወዳ'ጅ'ነት

fright

ፍ'ራይት -ስ- ፍርሃት (ከልቅ'ና ድንጋጤ'ኛ

457

frightful
ፍራይትፉል -ቅ- በጣም የሚያስፈራ፤ የሚ
ያስደነግጥ

frigid *
ፍሪጂድ -ቅ- የቀዘቀዘ (ለወሲያዊ ነት)
woman
-ቅ- ቀዝቃዛ (ለአነጋር ፡ ለስሜት)

frill
ፍራል -ስ- የልብስ ጌጥ (የጫፍት ፡ ተጉረብ
ርቦ የተሰፋ)

fringe
ፍሪንጅ -ስ- ዘርፍ ፡ መጨረሻ (የልብስ)

frisky
ፍሪስኪ -ቅ- ጨፋፊ ፡ ዘንጣዒ

fritter
ፍሪት -ግ- መሰባበር [ሰባበረ] ፡ ማድቀቅ
[አደቀቀ] ፡ ቀስ በቀስ ማባከን [አባከን] (ለገ
ንዘብ ለጊዜ መሳሰ)

frivolous
ፍሪቮለስ -ቅ- ዋጋ ቢስ ፡ እርባን የሌ ለው
ሞኝ ፡ ባዶ አንጎል

frock
ፍሮክ -ስ- መጉናጸፊያ ፡ ተጎባ

frog
ፍሮግ -ስ- እንቁራሪት

frolic
ፍሮሊክ -ግ- መፈንጠዝ [ፈነጠዘ]

from
ፍሮም -ተግ- ከ . . .

front
ፍሮንት -ስ- ፊት

frontier
ፍሪንቲየ -ስ- ያገር ወሰን

frost
ፍሮስት -ስ- ውርጭ

froth
ፍሮዝ -ስ- አረፋ

frown
ፍራውን -ግ- ፊት ማኮሳተር [አኮሳተረ]

frozen
ፍሪውዝን -ቅ- ውሃ በረዶ ነት የሆለ ወይ

frugal
ፍሩጋል -ቅ- ገንዘብ ቆጣቢ (ለምግብ)

fruit
ፍሩት -ስ- ፍራፍሬ

fruitful
ፍሩትፉል -ቅ- ፍሬ የሚሰጥ ፡ ለወልድ
የሚችል ፡ ዋጋ ያለው

fruition
ፍሩዊሽን -ስ- ፍሬ ማፍራያ ጊዜ ፡ መክፈወን
(ያቀዱት ዕቅድ) ፡ የሥራ ክንውን

fruitless
ፍሩትሌስ -ቅ- ፍሬ የማይሰጥ

frustrate
ፍረስትሬይት -ግ- ማደናቀፍ [አደናቀፈ] ፡
(ለሥራ ፡ ለዕቅድ) ፡ ማጓተት [አጓተተ] ፡
ማጨናገፍ [አጨናገፈ]

frustration
ፍረስትሬይሽን -ስ- ተስፋ መቁረጥ ፡ መጓ
ተት ፡ መጨናገፍ

fry
ፍራይ -ግ- መጥበስ [ጠበሰ]

frying-pan
ፍራይንግ ፓን -ስ- መጥበሻ

fuel
ፍዩወል -ስ- ማገዶ ፡ ነዳጅ

fugitive
ፍዩጂቲቭ -ስ- የተሸሸ ፡ የተባ ረረ ሰው ፡
ኮብላይ

fulfil
ፉልፊል -ግ- ሥራ ማከናወን [አከናወነ] ፡ ዕቅ
ድ እንዲፈጸም ማድረግ [አደረገ]

fulfillment
ፉልፊልመንት -ስ- መፈጸም (ተስፋ ፡ ግዴ
ታ መወጣት) ፡ መከወን (የዕቅድ ፡ የተመኘት)

full
ፉል -ቅ- መላ

fully
ፉሊ -ተግ- በሙላ

fumble
ፈምብል -ግ- መደባበስ ፡ ዳብሶ [ዳበሰ] (እንደ
ነገር ለመፈለግ) ፡ እንደ ነገር ይዞ ማድረግ
(እጅ ጅ መያዝ አለመቻል [ፈል]

fume
ፍዩም -ስ- ጢስ (ማታከ ሽታ ያለው ም ጢያ ት)

fumigate
ፍዩሚጌይት -ግ- በጢስ ማጥበስ [አጠበሰ] (በ
ባይ ለመጠዳል)

458

fun
'ፈን -ስ- ደ'ስታ ፣ ጨዋታ ፣ ቀልድ

function
'ፈንክሽን -ስ- ሥራ ፣ ተግባር

fund
'ፈንድ -ስ- የተሰበ'ሰበ ገንዘብ (ላንድ ተግባር እንዲውል) ፣ በብዛት የ'ሚ'ገ'ኝ ነገር

fundament
'ፈንደሜንት -ስ- መሠረት ፣ ቂ.ጋር

fundamental
ፈንደ'ሜንተል -ቅ- መሠረታዊ

funeral
ፍ'ዩ፡ነረል -ስ- ሥርዓተ ቀብር

fungus
'ፈንገስ -ቅ- የእንጉዳይ ዓይነት ተክል

funnel
'ፈነል -ስ- የጢስ መውጫ (የመርከብ ፣ የባ ቡር)፣ማንቆርቆርያ (የድፍ ዋንጫ ቅርፅ ያ'ለው)

funny
'ፈኒ -ቅ- የ'ሚያ'ሥቅ
strange
-ቅ- የ'ሚያስገ'ርም

fur
'ፈ፡ -ስ- ለምድ ፣ ፀጉሮ

furious
ፍ'ዩ፡ሪየስ -ቅ- ቁ'ጡ

furl
'ፈ፡ል -ግ- መጠቅለል [ጠቀ'ለለ] (ለሰን'ደቅ ዓላማ መዘተ)

furnace
'ፈ፡ነስ -ስ- እቶን ፣ ከውር

furnish
'ፈ፡ኒሽ -ግ- ቤት በዕቃ መሙላት [ሞ'ላ]
provide
-ግ- ማቅረብ [አቀ'ረበ]

furniture
'ፈ፡ኒቸ -ስ- የቤት ዕቃ

furrow
'ፈ፡ረው -ስ- ትልም ፣ ፈረ

further
'ፈ፡ዘ -ቅ- ተጨማሪ ፣ ራ'ቅ ያለ
-ተግ- እ'ዚህ በላይ ፣ ደግሞ

furtive
'ፈ፡ቲቭ -ቅ- ተንኮለ'ኛ ፣ የ'ሚያደርገውን የ 'ሚደ'ብቅ

fury
ፍ'ዩ፡ሪ -ስ- ቁ'ጣ ፣ ኃይለ'ኛ ን'ዴት

fuse
ፍ'ዩ፡ዝ -ስ- ፊልቦላ (የኤሌክትሪክ)

fuss
'ፈስ -ግ- ለጥቃ'ቅን ነገር በጣም መ'ጨነቅ [ተጨ'ነቀ]

fussy
'ፈ.ሲ -ቅ- በጣም ጠንቃ'ቃ (ለጥቃ'ቅን ነገር)

fusty
'ፈስቲ -ቅ- መጥፎ ሽ'ታ ያ'ለው

futile
ፍ'ዩ፡ታይል -ቅ- እርባን የሌ'ለው ፣ ጥቅም ቢስ

future
ፍ'ዩቸ -ስቅ- ተምኔት ፣ የ'ሚመጣ ጊዜ ፣ የመ ደረት

fuzzy
'ፈዚ -ቅ- በእ'ጅቅር ጠገር የተሸ'ፈነ ፣ ጠጉረ ክርዳ'ዳ ፣ ግልጽ ያልሆነ

---

gabble
'ጋብል -ግ- መለፍለፍ [ለፈ'ለፈ] ፣ መቀባ ጠር [ቀባ'ጠረ]

gadget
'ጋጀት -ስ- ት'ንሽ መ'ሣሪያ ወይን'ም የመ 'ሣሪያ መለ'ዋወጫ

gag
'ጋግ -ግ- አፍ መ'ለጉም-[ለ'ጉመ] (እንዳ ይና'ገሩ)

gaiety
'ጌየቲ -ስ- በደ'ስታ መፈንደቅ

gaily
'ጌይሊ -ተግ- በደ'ስታ ፡ በ'ሚያስደ'ስት ሁኔታ

gain
'ጌይን -ግ- ማትረፍ [አተ'ረፈ]
-ስ- ትርፍ

gait
'ጌይት -ስ- ያረ'ማመድ ሁኔታ ፡ የ'ኋኋት ሁኔታ

galaxy
'ጋለክሲ -ስ- ባንድ'ነት የተሰበ'ሰቡ ከዋክብት ፡ የከዋክብት ክምች'ት

gale
'ጌይል -ስ- በጣም ጠንካ'ራ ነፋስ

gall
'ጎ:ል -ግ- ማቁሰል [አቆ'ሰለ] ፡ ማስቆ'ጣት [አስቆ'ጣ] ፡ ማ'ናደድ [አ'ና'ደደ]
bile
-ስ- ሐሞት

gallant
'ጋለንት -ቅ- ጎበዝ ፡ ጀግና ፡ ጨዋ ፡ ያማረ (ለመርከብ)

gall-bladder
'ጎ:ል ብ'ላደ -ስ- የሐሞት ከረጢት

gallery
'ጋለሪ -ስ- በፎቅ ላይ ያ'ለ ሰገ'ነት
picture-
-ስ- የሥዕል ማሳ'ያ አ'ዳራሽ

galley
'ጋሊ -ስ- በመርከብ ውስጥ ያ'ለ ወጥ ቤት

gallon
'ጋለን -ስ- ጋሎን (የፈሳሽ መለ'ኪያ)

gallop
'ጋለፕ -ግ- መጋለብ [ጋ'ለበ]

gallows
'ጋለውዝ -ስ- ሰው መስቀያ ዕንጨት

galore
ጋ'ሎ: -ተግ- በመትረፍረፍ ፡ በብዛት

gamble
'ጋምበለ -ግ- ቁማር መ'ጫወት [ተጫ'ወተ]

gambler
'ጋምብለ -ስ- ቁማርተ'ኛ

gambol
'ጋምበል -ግ- መፈንጨት [ፈነ'ጨ] ፡ በደ'ስታ መዝለል [ዘ'ለለ] ፡ መቦ'ረቅ [ቦ'ረቀ]

game
'ጌይም -ስ- ጨዋታ

gander
'ጋንደ -ስ- ወንድ ዳ'ክ'ዬ

gang
'ጋንግ -ስ- ወ'ሮበ'ላ ፡ ወንበዴዎ'ች

gangster
'ጋንግስተ -ስ- ኀይለ'ኛ ወንጀል ሠሪ (መ'ሣሪያ የያዘ)

gangway
'ጋንግዌይ -ስ- ጠ'ባብ መ'ተላለፊያ

gaol
'ጄይል -ስ- እሥር ቤት

gailer
'ጄይለ -ስ- የወህኒ ቤት ፡ ዘበ'ኛ ፡ የወህኒ ቤት ኀላፊ

gap
'ጋፕ -ስ- ክፍት ቦታ (በሁለ'ት ነገሮ'ች መካ'ከል ያ'ለ)

gape
'ጌይፕ -ግ- አፍ ከፍቶ ማየት [አ'የ] (በመ'ደነቅ)

garage
'ጋራ:ዥ -ስ- ጋራዥ ፡ ተሽከርካሪዎ'ች የ'ሚ ያርፉ'በት ቦታ

garb
'ጋ:ብ -ስ- የልብስ ስፌት ዓይነት ፡ ልብስ

garbage
'ጋ:በጅ -ስ- ው'ዳቂ ነገር ፡ ቆሻሻ ፡ ጥ'ራጊ

garden
'ጋ:ደን -ስ- የትክልት ቦታ ፡ ዐፀድ

gargle
'ጋ:ገል -ግ- ጉሮ'ሮን ፡ አፍን በውሃ መጉመጥመጥ [ተጉመጠ'መጠ]

garland
'ጋ:ለንድ -ስ- ያበባ ጉጥ

garlic
'ጋ:ሊክ -ስ- ነ'ጭ ሽንኩርት

garment
'ጋ:መንት -ስ- ልብስ

garnish
'ጋኒሽ -ግ- ማስጌጥ [አስጌጠ] ፤ ምግብ ውስጥ ቅመማ ቅመም መጨ'መር [ጨ'መረ] ፤ መከ 'ሽን [ከ'ሽነ]

garrison
'ጋሪሰን -ስ- አንድ ከተማ ወይን'ም ም'ሽግ የ'ሚጠ'ብቁ ወ'ታ'ደሮ'ች

garrulous
'ጋረለስ -ቅ- ለፍላፊ ፤ ስለጥቃ'ቅን ነገር መዘ ላበድ የ'ሚወ'ድ

garter
'ጋ፡ተ -ስ- የግር ሹ'ራብ መወ'ጠሪያ ላስቲክ (የሴቶ'ች)

gas
'ጋስ -ስ- ጋዝ ፤ አ'የር

gaseous
'ጌይሲየስ -ቅ- ጋዝ የ'ሚመስል

gasoline
'ጋሰሊይን -ስ- ቤንዚን

gash
'ጋሽ -ስ- ጥልቀት ያለው ቁስል ፤ የሰው'ነት ብጣት

gasp
'ጋ፡ስፕ -ግ- ወደላይ ወደላይ መተንፈስ

gastric
'ጋስትሪክ -ቅ- የሆድ

gate
'ጌይት -ስ- በ'ር

gather
'ጋዘ -ግ- መሰብሰብ [ሰበ'ሰበ]
think
-ግ- ማ'ሰብ [አ'ሰበ]

gauge
'ጌይጅ -ግ- በጥን'ታቂ መለ'ካት [ለ'ካ]
measure
-ስ- መለ'ኪያ

gaunt
'ጎ፡ንት -ቅ- በጣም ቀ'ጨጨ ፤ ከ'ሲ'ታ ፤ ማስ ጠ'ሉ

gauze
'ጎ፡ዝ -ስ- የሐ'ከምና ጥጥ

gay
'ጌይ -ቅ- ደ'ስተ'ኛ ፤ የተደ'ሰተ

gaze
'ጌይዝ -ግ- አተ'ኩሮ መ'መልከት [ተመለ 'ከተ]

gazelie
ገ'ዘሌ -ስ- ፌቆ

gear
'ጊያ -ስ- ማርሽ ፤ ፍጥነት መለ'ወጫ (የመ ኪና)

gearbox
'ጊያቦክስ -ስ- ካምቢዮ ፤ የፍጥነት መለ'ወጫ መ'ሣሪያ ያለ'በት ግጥን (በመኪና ሞቶር ውስጥ)

gem
'ጀም -ስ- ዕንቁ ፤ የተከ'በረ ደንጊያ (የተወለ 'ወለ'ና የተቦ'ረቀ) ፤ ከ'ፍ ያለ ዋጋ ያ'ለው ዕቃ

gender
'ጀንደ -ስ- ጾታ

general
'ጀነረል -ቅ- ጠቅላ'ላ
military
-ስ- ጀኔራል (ደ'ጃዝማች ፤ ፈ'ታውራሪ)

generally
'ጀነረሊ -ተግ- በጠቅላ'ላው
. *usually*
-ተግ- ሁል ጊዜ

generate
'ጀነሬይት -ግ- ማውጣት [አወ'ጣ] ፤ ካለመ ኖር ወደ መኖር ማምጣት [አመ'ጣ]

generation
ጀነ'ሬይሽን -ስ- ትውል'ድ

generosity
ጀነ'ሮሲቲ -ስ- ልግ'ስ'ና ፤ ችሮታ

generous
'ጀነረስ -ቅ- ለ'ጋሥ ፤ ቸር

genesis
'ጀነሲስ -ስ- ፍጥረት ፤ ልደት ፤ አራት ዘፍጥ ረት

genial
'ጂንየል -ቅ- ፈገግተ'ኛ ፤ ርኅሩኅ ፤ ገራገር ፤ ደ'ጋደ'ግ ፤ ተባባሪ

genius
'ጂንየስ -ስ- የላቀ የአእምሮ ፤ የኪነ ጥበብ ስጦታ ፤ የተፈጥሮ ተውህቦ

461

gentle
'ጄንተል -ቅ- ጨዋ ፡ የተከ'በረ ፡ ርኅሩኅ ፡ ተ
ወ'ዳጅ

genuflect
'ጄንዩፍሊክት -ግ- ለጸሎት መንበርከክ [ተን
በረ'ከከ]

genuine
'ጄንዩወን -ቅ- እውነተ'ኛ ፡ መ'ሳሳት የሌ'ለ
'በት ፡ የታ'መነ

geography
ጂ'የግራፊ -ስ- መልክዐ ምድር

geology
ጂ'የሎጂ -ስ- ጂኦሎጂ (የመሬት ሁናቴ'ና
ጠባይ የናት)

germ
'ጄ'ም -ስ- ጀርም ፡ በ'ሽታ የ'ሚያመጡ ጥቃ
'ቅን ፍጥረቶ'ች

germicide
'ጄ'ሚሳይድ -ስ- የተባይ መግደያ መድኃኒት

germinate
'ጄ'ሚኔይት -ግ- ማቆንጎል [አቆነ'ጎለ] ፡
መብቀል [በ'ቀለ]

gesticulate
ጀስ'ቲክዩሌይት -ግ- ሰ'ና'ገሩ እ'ጅን ፡ አካ
ልን ማ'ወዛወዝ [አ'ወዛ'ወዘ]

gesture
'ጄስቸ -ስ- የሰው'ነት የእ'ጅ ንቅ፞ናቴ (ሐ'ሳ
ብ ለመግለጽ)

get
'ጌት -ግ- ማምባት [አመ'ጣ]
obtain
-ግ- ማግኘት [አገ'ኘ]

geyser
'ጊያዘ -ስ- ፍልውሃ (ከመሬት የ'ሚፈልቅ)

ghastly
'ጋስትሊ -ቅ- አስፈ'ሪ ፡ አስደንጋጭ

ghost
'ገውስት -ስ- የሙታን መንፈስ (ለሕያዋን
የ'ሚታ'ይ) ፡ መንፈስ

giant
'ጃየንት -ስ- በጣም ረ'ጅም ፍጡር ፡ ከሰው
ቁመት የላቀ ርዝመት ያ'ለው ሰው ፡ ወይን'ም
ሌላ ትልቅ ፍጡር

giblet
'ጂብለት -ስ- የዶሮ ወይን'ም የሌሎ'ች አዕ
ዋፍ ሆድቃ (የ'ሚ'በ'ላው ክፍል)

giddy
'ጊዲ -ቅ- ራሱን የ'ሚያዞረው ፡ የ'ሚያጥወ
ለ'ውለው ፡ ጎላፈ'ነት የ'ማይ'ሰማው

gift
'ጊፍት -ስ- ስጦታ ፡ ሽ'ልማት

gifted
'ጊፍተድ -ቅ- ተውህቦ ያ'ለው

gigantic
ጃይ'ጋንቲክ -ቅ- ጎ'ያለ (ሰው ፡ ከመጠን
በላይ የሆነ ፍጡር)

giggle
'ጊገል -ግ- እ'የተሽኮረ'መመ መሣቅ [ሣቀ]

gill
'ጊል -ስ- የዐሣ መተንፈሻ (ሳምባ)

gilt
'ጊልት -ቅ- ወርቅ ቅብ

gimlet
'ጊምለት -ስ- መሠርሠሪያ (መ'ሣሪያ)

gin
'ጂን -ስ- ጂ'ን (፡ ጠ) ፡ የጥጥ መፈልቀ
ቂያ መከና

ginger
'ጂንጅ -ስ- ዝንጅብ ፡

gipsy
'ጂፕሲ -ስ- በሁረት የ'ሚኖር አንድ ነገድ
(በአውሮ'ጳ ውስጥ) ፡ ዘዋሪ ፡ ቤት ያ'ለሽ ፡
ክርታ'ታ

giraffe
ጂ'ራፍ -ስ- ቀ'ጭኔ

girder
'ጊ፡ደ -ስ- ጠንካ'ራ የብረት ፡ የእንጨት ዘንግ

girdle
'ጊ፡ደል -ግ- መ'ታጠቅ [ታጠ'ቀ] (በመ'ታጠ
ቂያ)
-ስ- መ'ታጠቂያ

girl
'ጊል -ስ- ልጃገረድ

girth
'ጊፀ -ስ- መቀ'ነቻ (የጭነት ፡ የኮር'ቻ)

gist
'ጂስት -ስ- ዋ'ና ሐ'ሳብ (የክር 'ክር)

462

give

'ጊቭ -ግ- መስጠት [ሰ'ጠ]

glacier

ግ'ላሲየ -ስ- የበረዶ ወንዝ

glad

ግ'ላድ -ቅ- ደ'ስታ

glade

ግ'ሌይድ -ስ- በደ'ን መካ'ከል ያለ ገላጣ ቦታ

glamour

ግ'ላም -ስ- የ'ሚግግ'ር\h ቁንጅ'ና ፡ ደማም'ነት

glance

ግ'ላንስ -ግ- መልከት ማድረግ

gland

ግ'ላንድ -ስ- እጢ.

glare

ግ'ሌየ -ግ- አፍ'ጦ መ'መልከት [ተመለ'ከተ]
(በቁ'ጣ)
strong light
-ስ- ዓይን የ'ሚያጥበረ'ብር (የ'ሚ
ያጥበረ'ብር) ብርሃን

glass

ግ'ላ፡ስ -ስ- ብርጭ'ቆ
material
-ስ- መስተዋት

gleam

ግ'ሊይም -ስ- የብርሃን ጥላንጥል ፡
የ'ሚያብለጨ'ልጭ ብርሃን (በተለ'ይ ብ'ል'ጭ
ድር'ግ'ም የ'ሚል)

glean

ግ'ሊይን -ግ- መቃረም [ቃ'ረመ]

glee

ግ'ሊይ -ግ- ደ ስታ ፡ ፈንጠ'ዝያ

glen

ግ'ሌን -ስ- በተራራ መሀ'ከል ያ'ለ ጠ'ባብ
ሸለቆ

glib

ግ'ሊብ -ቅ- ቋንቋው የ'ሚገራ'ለት (ነገር ግን
የ'ሚለው የ'ማይ'ታ'መን)

glide

ግ'ላይድ -ግ- መንሸራተት [ተንሸራ'ተተ]

glimmer

ግ'ሊመ -ግ- ጥል ጥል ማለት [አለ]
-ስ- ጥላንጥ'ል

glimpse

ግ'ሊምስ -ግ- ማየት [አ'የ] (ነገር ግን የታ'
የው ነገር ቶሎ ሲጠፋ)
-ስ- ው'ልብታ

glisten

ግ'ሊሰን -ግ- ማንጸባረቅ [አንጸባ'ረቀ] (ለው-ሃ)

glitter

ግ'ሊተ -ግ- ማንጸባረቅ [አንጸባ'ረቀ] ፡ መን
ቆጥቆጥ [ተንቆጠ'ቆጠ] (ለጌጣጌጥ)

gloat

ግ'ለውት -ግ- በሰው ሥቃይ መ'ደሰት [ተደ
'ሰተ]

globe

ግ'ለውብ -ስ- ዮብልቡል የሆነ ነገር ፡ መሬት፡
ሉል (መልክዐ ም'ድር)

globular

ግ'ሎብዩለ -ቅ- ድቡልቡል

globule

ግ'ሎብዩ፡ል -ስ- ጠ'ብታ (የውሃ ፡ የደም ወ፡ዛተ)

gloom

ግ'ሉ፡ም -ስ- ጨለምለ'ም ማለት ፡ ደብዛ ፡ ዝ
ማለት
sadness
-ስ- ሐዘን ፡ አለመ'ደሰት ፡ መ'ከፋት

gloomy

ግ'ሉ፡ሚ -ቅ- ደብዛ'ዛ ፡ ጨለ'ም ያለ
sad
-ቅ- ያልተደ'ሰተ ፡ ያ'ዘነ ፡ የተከ'ፋ ፡
ጥፍ'ግ ያለው

glory

ግ'ሎሪ -ስ- ክብር ፡ ስብሐት

glorious

ግ'ሎሪየስ -ቅ- ባለክብር ፡ ክቡር ፡ ስመ ጥር

gloss

ግ'ሎስ -ስ- የ'ሚያበራ የ'ሚያንጸባ'ርቅ ነገር

glossy

ግ'ሎሲ -ቅ- የ'ሚያበራ ፡ የ'ሚያንጸባ'ርቅ

glove

ግ'ለቭ -ስ- የእ'ጅ ሹ'ራብ ፡ ጐዋንቲ

glow

ግ'ለው -ግ- መፋም [ፋ.ም]

glow-worm

ግ'ለወ፡ም -ስ- የ'ሚያበራ ትል ፡ ትለበ'ራ

463

glue
ግ'ሉ፥ -ስ- መጣብቅ ፣ ማ'ጣበቂያ ሙቅ ፣ ማ'ሸ
ጌያ

glum
ግ'ለም -ቅ- ያ'ዘነ ፣ የተከ'ፋ

glut
ግ'ለት -ስ- የተትረፈ'ረፈ ነገር

glutton
ግ'ለተን -ስ- ሆዳም ሰው ፣ ከመጠን በላይ
የ'ሚበላ ሰው

gnash
'ናሽ -ግ- ጥርስ መቆርጠም [ቆረ'ጠመ] ፣
ጥርስን ማ'ፏጨት [አ'ፏ'ጨ] (በቁ'ጣ)

gnat
'ናት -ስ- ቢምቢ ፣ የወባ ትን'ኝ

gnaw
'ና፥ -ግ- መነርደም [ነረ'ደመ]

go
'ገው -ግ- መሄድ [ሄደ]

goad
'ገውድ -ግ- መኮልኮል [ኮለ'ኮለ] (ለፈረስ
ወዘተ)
-ስ- ከብት መንጃ ል'ም'ጭ

goal
'ገውል -ስ- ግብ ፣ ዐላማ

goat
'ገውት -ስ- ፍ'የል

gobble
'ጎበል -ግ- በቾ'ኮላ መብላት [በላ] ፣ መስገ
ብገብ [ተስገበ'ገበ] (ለምግብ)

go-between
'ገውብትዊይን -ስ- አ'ቃጣሪ (ሴት) ፣ አስታ
ራቂ

goblet
'ጎብለት -ስ- ዋንጫ

god
'ጎድ -ስ- አምላክ

God
'ጎድ -ስ- እግዚአብሔር

godchild
'ጎድ ቻይልድ -ስ- የክርስት'ና ልጅ

goddess
'ጎደስ -ስ- እንስት አምላክ

godfather
'ጎድፋ፥ -ስ- የክርስት'ና አ'ባት

godmother
'ጎድመ፥ -ስ- የክርስት'ና እ'ናት

godsend
'ጎድሴንድ -ስ- ድንገተ'ኛ ዕ'ድል

goggles
'ጎገልዝ -ስ- የነፋስ ፣ የአቧራ መነ'ጥር (በተ
ለ'ይ ቢሲክለት ነጂዎ'ች የ'ሚያደርጉት)

goitre
'ጎይተ -ስ- እንቅርት

gold
'ጎውልድ -ስ- ወርቅ
colour
-ቅ- ብጫ

goldsmith
'ጎውልድስሚዽ -ስ- ወርቅ አንጣሪ ፣ ወርቅ
ሠሪ

good
'ጉድ -ቅ- ጥሩ ፣ መልካም

good-bye
ጉድ'ባይ -ቃአ- ደኅና ይሁኑ (ሁን)

goods
'ጉድዝ *-ስ- ሸቀጣ ሸቀጥ

goodwill
ጉድ'ዊል -ስ- በ'ጎ ፈቃድ

goose
'ጉ፥ስ -ስ- ዝ'ዬ

gore
'ጎ፥ -ግ- መውጋት [ወ'ጋ] (በቀንድ)
-ስ- የ'ሚፈ'ስ ደም

gorge
'ጎ፥ጅ -ግ- እ'የተስገበ'ገቡ መብላት [በ'ላ]
-ስ- ሸለቆ (በሁለ'ት ገደል መሀ'ከል
ያ'ለ)

gorgeous
'ጎ፥ጀስ -ቅ- በጣም የ'ሚያምር ፣ በቀለም ያሸ
በ'ረቀ

gospel
'ጎስፐል -ስ- ወንጌል

gossamer
'ጎሰመ -ስ- የሸረሪት ድር

464

gossip

’ጎሲፕ -ግ- ያልተረጋ'ገጠ ወሬ ግ'ዋራት [ኦ
ዋ'ራ]

-ስ- ሐሜት ፡ ያልተረጋ'ገጠ ወሬ ፡ ጭም
ጭምታ

gouge

’ጋውጅ -ግ- መበርበር [በረ'በረ] ፡ መሰርሰር
[ሰረ'ሰረ]

gourmand

’ጎ፡መንድ -ቅ- ሆዳም

govern

’ገቨን -ግ- መግዛት [ገዛ] (በሥልጣን)

government

’ገቨንመንት -ስ- ግዛት ፤ መንግሥት

governor

’ገቨነ -ስ- ገዥ

gown

’ጋውን -ስ- ረ'ጅም ቀሚስ

grab

ግ'ራብ -ግ- አፈ'ፍ አድርጎ መያዝ [ያዘ] ፡ ጠ
'ፍሮ መያዝ [ያዘ] ፤ መንጠቅ [ነ'ጠቀ]

grace

ግ'ሬይስ -ስ- ረድኤት ፡ ውበት ፡ ያ'ረጣመድ
ማማር

prayer

-ስ- ከማዕ'ድ በፊት'ና በኋላ የ'ሚ'ጸ'ለ
ይ ጸሎት

graceful

ግ'ሬይስፉል -ቅ- ረድኤት ያ'ለው ፡ ሲ'ራ
'መድ የ'ሚያምር'በት ፡ ዝርጋ'ዳ

gracious

ግ'ሬይሸስ -ቅ- ቸር ፡ ለ'ጋሥ

grade

ግ'ሬይድ -ስ- ማዕረግ ፡ ደረጃ

gradient

ግ'ሬይዲየንት -ስ- ቁልቁለት'ነት ያ'ለው ቦታ

gradual

ግ'ራጁወል -ቅ- ዝ'ግተ'ኛ ፡ ቀ'ስ በቀ'ስ የ'ሚ
'ደ'ረግ

graduate

ግ'ራጁዌይት -ግ- መ'መረቅ [ተመ'ረቀ] (በት
ምህርት)

graft

ግ'ራ፡ፍት -ግ- መክተብ [ከ'ተበ] (ለአትክልት)

grain

ግ'ሬይን -ስ- እህል ፡ ጥራጥሬ ፡ ቅንጣት

grammar

ግ'ራመ -ስ- ሰዋስው

granary

ግ'ራነሪ -ስ- የእህል ጎተራ

grand

ግ'ራንድ -ቅ- ት'ልቅ ፡ አስደ'ናቂ

grandeur

ግ'ራንድዮ -ስ- ት'ልቅ'ነት ፡ ገናና'ነት

grandfather

ግ'ራንድፋ:ዘ -ስ- ወንድ አያት

grandmother

ግ'ራንድመዘ -ስ- ሴት አያት

grange

ግ'ሬይንጅ -ስ- በትናን'ሽ ቤቶ'ች የተከ'በበ
የባለቤቱ መኖሪያ (በባላገር) ፤ የእህል ጎተራ

granite

ግ'ራኒት -ስ- ጥቁር ደንጊያ

grape

ግ'ራይፕ -ስ- ወይን

grant

ግ'ራ፡ንት -ግ- መስጠት [ሰ'ጠ] (የ'ጠ'የቁትን)

graphic

ግ'ራፊክ -ቅ- አ'ገላለጹ ሕያው የሆነ ፡ በ'ሚ
'ታይ ምል'ክቶ'ች የተገ'ለጸ ፤ የጽሑፍ ፡ የሥ
ዕል ወዘተ

grapple

ግ'ራፕል -ግ- ጨ'ብጦ መያዝ [ያዘ] ፡ ለተ'ም
ማድረግ [አደ'ረገ] ፤ መ'ታገል [ታገለ]

grasp

ግ'ራ:ስፕ -ግ- መያዝ [ያዘ] ፤ መጨ'በጥ [ጨ
'በጠ]

understand

-ግ- መ'ረዳት [ተረ'ዳ]

grasping

ግ'ራ:ስፒንግ -ቅ- ሥ'ሥታም (የገንዘብ) ፤ ለሥ
ልጣን ፡ ለገንዘብ ትርፉ የ'ሚን'ን

grass

ግ'ራ:ስ -ስ- ሣር

grasshopper

ግ'ራ:ስሆፐ -ስ- ፌንጣ

465

grate

ግ'ሬይት -ግ- መፋቅ [ፋቀ] (ም'ሳሌ፡ፎርማጃ)

-ስ- እሳት የ'ሚነ'ድ'በት ፍርግርግ ብረት

grateful

ግ'ሬትፉል -ቅ- ባለውለታ

grater

ግ'ሬተ -ስ- መፋቂያ ፣ መፈርፈሪያ (መ'ሠ ሪያ)

gratify

ግ'ራቲፋይ -ግ- የፈ'ለጉትን መስጠት [ሰ'ጠ] ግስደ'ሰት [አስደ'ሰተ]

gratitude

ግ'ራቲትዩ፡ድ -ስ- ምስጋና (ለተደ'ረገ'ለት ው ለታ የ'ሚ'ደ'ረግ)

gratuity

ግ'ረትዩዊቲ -ስ- ጉርሻ ፣ ስጦታ ፣ ያገልግሎት ገንዘብ (ለወ'ታ'ደሮ'ች ያገልግሎታ'ቸው ጊዜ ሲ'ፈ'ጸም የ'ሚ'ሰ'ጥ)

grave

ግ'ሬይቭ -ስ- መቃብር

serious

-ቅ- ከ'ባድ ፣ አ'ዋኪ

gravedigger

ግ'ሬይቭዲጋ -ስ- መቃብር ቆ'ፋሪ

gravel

ግ'ራቨል -ስ- ጠጠር

gravestone

ግ'ሬይቭስተውን -ስ- የመቃብር ደንጊያ (ጽ ሑፍ የ'ሚ'ጻፍ'በት)

graveyard

ግ'ሬይቭያ፡ድ -ስ- የመቃብር ቦታ

gravity

ግ'ራቪቲ -ስ- የመሳብ ኃይል ፤ አስቸ'ጋሪ'ነት

gravy

ግ'ሬይቪ -ስ- ቅባት (የተጠ'በሰ ሥጋ)

gray

ግ'ሬይ -ቅ- ግራ'ጫ ፣ አመድ'ማ

graze

ግ'ሬይዝ -ግ- መጋጥ [ጋጠ] (ለእንስሳት)

wound

-ስ- ጭረት (ለቁስል)

grease

ግ'ሪይስ -ስ- የቀ'ለጠ ጥራ ፣ ቅባት

greasy

ግ'ሪይሲ -ቅ- ቅባታም ፡ አዳላጭ

great

ግ'ሬይት -ቅ- ት'ልቅ ፣ ታ'ላቅ

greatcoat

ግ'ሬይትከውት -ስ- ካ'ፖርት (ከበ'ድ ያለ)

greatly

ግ'ሬይትሊ -ተግ- በጣም ፣ በብዛ'ሚ

greatness

ግ'ሬይትነስ -ስ- ት'ልቅ'ነት

greed

ግ'ሪይድ -ስ- ሥ'ሥት (ለምግብ ፣ ለገንዘብ)

greedy

ግ'ሪይዲ -ቅ- ት'ቅታም ፣ ሥ'ሥታም (ለም ግብ ፣ ለገንዘብ ወዘተ)

green

ግ'ሪይን -ቅ- አረንጓዴ ፣ ገና ያልበ'ሰለ ፣ ጥሬታ (ለአትክልተ)

greet

ግ'ሪይት -ግ- ሰላምታ መስጠት [ሰ'ጠ]

greeting

ግ'ሪይቲንግ -ስ- ሰላምታ

grenade

ግረኔይድ -ስ- የእ'ጅ ቦምብ

grey

ግ'ሬይ -ቅ- ግራ'ጫ ፣ አመድ'ማ

grid

ግ'ሪድ -ስ- የወንፈት መልክ ያ'ለው የብረት መ'ሠሪያ

grief

ግ'ሪይፍ -ስ- ሐዘን

grievance

ግ'ሪይቫንስ -ስ- የአቤቱ'ታ ሥ'ክንያት ፣ አቤ ቱታ

grieve

ግ'ሪይቭ -ግ- ማዘን [አ'ዘነ]

grievous

ግ'ሪይቨስ -ቅ- አሳዛኝ ፣ ከ'ባድ

grill

ግ'ሪል -ስ- ጥብስ ሥ'ጋ ፣ መጥበሻ ፤ የወንፈት መልክ ያ'ለው የብረት ፡ ወ'ሠሪያ (ለሥ'ጋ መጥ በሻ)

grim

ግ'ሪም -ቅ- የጨፈ'ገገው ፣ ጥላ'ቻ ያ'ደረ'በት

466

grimace

ግ'ሪመስ -ግ- ፊትን በጥላ'ቻ ግ'ኮፋተር [አ'ኮ ፉ.'ተሪ] ፣ መ'ኮሳተር [ተኮሳ'ተሪ]

grime

ግ'ራይም -ስ- እንሽቅ ፣ እድፍ

grin

ግ'ሪን -ግ- ፈገ'ግ ግለት [አለ]

grind

ግ'ራይንድ -ግ- መፍጨት [ፈ'ጨ]

grindstone

ግ'ራይንድስተውን -ስ- የወፍጮ ደንጊያ

grip

ግ'ሪፕ -ግ- መጨ'በጥ [ጨ'በጠ] ፣ መያዝ [ያዘ]

gripe

ግ'ራይፕ -ስ- የሆድ ቁርጠት

gristle

ግ'ሪስል -ስ- አንጀ ነት)

grit

ግ'ሪት -ስ- የደ'ቀቀ ጠጠር

groan

ግ'ረውን -ግ- መጓጎር [ጓ'ጎረ] ፣ ማቃሰት [አቃ'ሰተ]

grocer

ግ'ረውሰ -ስ- የምግብ ሸቀጥ ነ'ጋዴ

grocery

ግ'ረውሰሪ -ስ- የምግብ ሸቀጥ ሱቅ

groggy

ግ'ሮጊ -ቅ- ተንገድጋጅ ፣ ተንገዳጋጅ ፣ ለመ ውደቅ የደ'ረሰ

groin

ግ'ሮይን -ስ- ሙላ

groom

ግ'ሩ፦ም -ግ- መጥረግ [ጠ'ረገ] (ፈረስን) servant
-ስ- ፈረስ አጣቢ well-ed
ልብሱ ያግራ'በትና ጠጉሩ'ም በደምብ የተ በ'ጠረ

groove

ግ'ሩ፦ሽ -ስ- ስንጥቅ

grope

ግ'ረውፕ -ስ- መዳበስ [ዳ'በሰ] (እንደ ዕ'ውር ወዘተ)
-ቅ- ዶፈደፍ ፣ ወፍራም

gross

ግ'ረውስ -ቅ- ባለጌ ፣ ያልታ'ረመ ፣ ደ'ደብ number
-ስ- በሥራ ሁ'ለት ደርዘን

ground

ግ'ራውንድ -ስ- መሬት

groundless

ግ'ራውንድለስ -ቅ- መሠረተ ቢስ ፣ በቂ ምክ ንያት የሌ'ለው

group

'ግሩ፦ፕ -ስ- የተሰበ'ሰበ (ሰው)

grouse

ግ'ራውስ -ግ- ግጉ ምሪም [አጉረመ'ረመ]

grove

ግ'ረውቭ -ስ- አነስተ'ኛ ደ'ን

grovel

ግ'ሮቨል -ግ- ራስን ዝ'ቅ ግድረግ [አደ'ረገ] (በትሕት'ና)

grow

ግ'ረው -ግ- ማደግ [አ'ደገ] make-
-ግ- መትከል[ተ'ከለ] ፣ መዝራት [ዘ'ራ]

growl

ግ'ራውል -ግ- መጓጎር [ጓ'ጎረ] ፣ መጮኸ [ጮ'ኸ]

growth

ግ'ረውስ -ስ- እድገት

grub

ግ'ረብ -ስ- ትል (ወዲያው የተፈለ'ፈለ) food
-ስ- ምግብ (ተራ ቃል)

grubby

ግ'ረቢ -ቅ- ያልጸ'ዳ ፣ ያ'ደፈ

grudge

ግ'ረጅ -ግ- መ'መቅኘት [ተመቀ'ኘ] ፣ መን ፈግ [ነ'ፈገ]

gruel

ግ'ሩ፦ወል -ስ- ሙቅ ፣ አጥሚት

467

gruesome
ግሩ:ሰም -ቅ- አስቀ'ያሚ ፤ ለማየት የ'ሚያ
'ሠ'ቅቅ

gruff
ግ'ረፍ፡ -ስ- ሻካራ'ነት ፤ ነጭና'ሳ'ነት ፤ አመ
ለቢስ'ነት

grumble
ግ'ረምበል -ግ- ማጉረምረም [አጉረመ'ረመ]

grunt
ግ'ረንት -ስ- ማኩረፍ (በተለ'ይ ለወሣማ ድ
ም'ፅ)

guarantee
ጋረን'ቲ: -ግ- ተያዥ መሆን [ሆነ]፤ ዋስ መሆን
[ሠነ]
-ስ- ዋስት'ና ፤ ተያዥ'ነት

guarantor
'ጋረንቶ: -ስ- ዋስ ፤ ተያዥ ፤ ዋቢ.

guard
'ጋ:ድ -ግ- መጠ'በቅ [ጠ'በቀ] (እንዳይመልጥ)
-ስ- ጠ'ባቂ ፤ ዘበ'ኛ

guardian
'ጋ:ድየን -ስ- አሳ'ዳጊ. ፤ ጎላፊ (ለሕፃን)

guerilla
ገ'ሪለ -ስ- የደፈጣ ጦር'ነት ፤ በደፈጣ የ'ሚ'ዋ
'ጉ ሰዐ''ች

guess
'ጌስ -ግ- ማ'ሰብ [አ'ሰበ] (በግ'ምት) ፤ መገ
ም'ገም ['ገመ'ገመ]
-ስ- የግ'ምት ሐ'ሳብ

guest
'ጌስት -ስ- እንግዳ (ሰው)

guidance
'ጋይደንስ -ስ- አ'መራር ፤ የመምራት ሥራ

guide
'ጋይ:ድ -ግ- መምራት [መ'ራ]
person
-ስ- መሪ

guile
'ጋይል -ስ- ሪኮ'ሌ'ነት ፤ አ'ታላይ'ነት

guilt
'ጊልት -ስ- ጥፋት ፤ ሕ'ግን የመጣስ ሁኔቴ ፤
ስ'ሜት

guinea fowl
'ጊነፋ ውል -ስ- ጅግራ

guinea-pig
'ጊኒ'ፒግ -ስ- መድኃኒት ወዘተ መፈ'ተኛ (ለ
ው፡እንስሳ ወዘተ)

guise
'ጋይዝ -ስ- ያልሆነትን መስሎ መ'ታየት ፤
የልብስ ዓይነት ቅ'ድ ፤ ሞድ

gulf
'ገልፍ -ስ- የባሕር ሠ'ላጤ

gullet
'ገለት -ስ- የምግብ መ'ተላለፊያ ቧንቧ. (ከጉ
ሮ'ሮ እስከ ሆድ ያ'ለው)

gullible
'ገለበል -ቅ- የ'ዋህ ፤ በቀ'ላሉ የ'ሚ'ሞ'ኝ

gulp
'ገልፕ -ግ- መ'ጉጔ ጭት [ተጉጔ'ጨ]
-ስ- ጉንጭ ቡሎ

gum
'ገም -ስ- ድ'ድ
adhesive
-ስ- መጣብቅ ፤ ማ'ጣበቂያ ፤ ማ'ሸጊያ
of a tree
-ስ- ሙ'ጫ

gumboil
'ገምቦይል -ስ- የድ'ድ እብጠት

gun
'ገን -ስ- ጠበንጃ (ጠመንጃ)

gunner
'ገነ -ቅ- መድፈ'ኛ

gunpowder
'ገንፓውደ -ስ- ባሩድ

gunsmith
'ገንሰሚዝ -ስ- ጠበንጃ ሠሪ

gurgle
'ገ:ገል -ስ- የውሃ ድምፅ (ጠ'ባብ አፍ ካ'ለው
ጠር፡ሙዝ ሲ'ቀ'ዳ) ፤ መንዶቅዶቅ

gush
'ገሽ -ግ- በብዛት መፍሰስ [ፈ'ሰሰ] ፤ መጉረፍ፡
[ጎ'ረፈ]

gust
'ገስት -ስ- የነፋስ ሽ'ውታ

gut
'ገት -ስ- አንጀት
cat
-ስ- የከ'ረረ ጅማት፣የግን'ነት ነትሳ፡ብዝ'ና

468

gutter
’ጉተ -ስ- የውሃ መ'ተላለፊያ (በመንገድ ዳር) ፣
የውሃ መውረጃ ቧን'ቧ (ከጣራ ላይ)

guttural
’ጉተረል -ቅ- የጉሮ'ሮ (ፊደል ወዘተ) ፤ የጎባባ
ጉር'ና

guy
’ጋይ -ስ- ሰው

guzzle
’ጋዘል -ግ- መግ'ጠም [ገ'ጠመ] (ለመጠ'ጥ)

gymnastics
ጅም’ናስቲክስ -ስ- የሰው'ነት ማጠንከሪያ እን
ቅስ'ቃሴ ፤ ጅምናስቲክ

habit
’ሀቢት -ስ- ልማድ
dress
-ስ- የመነኮሳት ል'ዩ ል'ዩ ልብስ

habitable
’ሀበተብል -ቅ- በውስጡ ሊኖሩ'በት የ'ሚ
ቻል

habitation
ሀበ’ቴይሽን -ስ- መኖሪያ ቤት

habitual
ሀ’ቢቹውል -ቅ- የተለ'መደ፤ባልማድ የተሠ'ራ

hack
’ሀክ -ግ- መቆራረጥ [ቆራ'ረጠ] ፣ መተፍ
ተፍ [ተፈ'ተፈ]
horse
-ስ- ያረጀ ፈረስ ፤ ኪ'ና፣ የ'ሚ'ከራ'ይ
ፈረስ

hackneyed
’ሀክነይድ -ቅ- የተለ'መደ ፣ ተራ (ለንግ'ግር ፣
ለጽሑፍ)

haemorrhage
’ሄመሬጅ -ስ- የደም ሥር መ'በጠስ'ና የደም
በሰው'ነት መፍሰስ

haft
’ሀፍት -ስ- እ'ጀታ (የቢ'ለዋ ወዘተ)

haggard
’ሀገድ -ቅ- የጠወ'ለገ ፣ የደ'ከመው (ለሰው)

hail
’ሄይል -ግ- መ'ጣራት [ተጣ'ራ] (ሰው ሰላ
ም'ታ ለመስጠት)
-ስ- በረዶ (የዝናብ)

hailstone
’ሄይልስተውን -ስ- በረዶ (አንድ ጠጠር)

hair
’ሄየ -ስ- ጠጉር

hairdresser
’ሄድሬሰ -ስ- ጠጉር አስተካካይ ፤ ጠጉር ቆራጭ

hairy
’ሄሪ -ቅ- ጠጉራ'ም

hale
’ሄይል -ቅ- ጤና'ማ

half
’ሀፍ -ስ- ግ'ማሽ ፣ እ'ኩል

hall
’ሆል -ስ- አዳራሽ

hallmark
’ሆልማክ -ስ- የወርቅ'ነት'ና የብር'ነት ማ
'ረጋገጫ ምል'ክት (እንጣሪው የ'ሚጸፈው
ጽሑፍ)

hallo
ሀ’ለው -ቃአ- እንዴት ነዎት (ነህ)

halo
’ሄለው -ስ- በራስ ዙሪያ የ'ሚ'ታ'ይ የቀ'ደ ሳን
ምል'ክት

halt
’ሆልት -ግ- መቆም [ቆመ] ፣ ማቆም [አቆመ]

halve
’ሀቭ -ግ- ለሁለ'ት መቁረጥ [ቆረጠ] ፣ ለሁ
ለ'ት መግመስ [ገ'መስ]
-ቅ- ለሁለ'ት የተከ'ፈለ ፣ የተገ'መስ

ham
'ሀም -ስ- በጨስ የደ'ረቀ'ና ጨው ያለ'በት
ያ፟ፘፘ ወርች ሥጋ

hamlet
'ሀምለት -ስ- ት'ንሽ መንደር

hammer
'ሀመ -ስ- መዶሻ

hammock
'ሀመክ -ስ- በዛፍ'ና በዛፍ መካ'ከል የ'ሚን
ጠለ'ጠል የ'ሚ'ተ'ኛ'በት ጨርቅ (እንደ አልጋ)

hamper
'ሀምፐ -ስ- ት'ልቅ ቅርጫት
handicap
-ግ- መግታት [ገ'ታ] ፣ እንዳይንቀሳ'ቀስ
ማድረግ [አደ'ረገ]

hand
'ሀንድ -ስ- እ'ጅ

handbill
'ሀንድቢል -ስ- ለሕዝብ የ'ሚ'በ'ተን የንግድ
ማስታወቂያ ወረቀት

handbook
'ሀንድቡክ -ስ- መምሪያ መጽሐፍ

handcuff
'ሀንድከፍ -ስ- የእ'ጅ እግር ብረት

handicap
'ሀንዲካፕ -ስ- እንቅፋት ፣ መሰናክል

handicraft
'ሀንዲክራፍት -ስ- የእ'ጅ ሥራ

handkerchief
'ሀንክቺፍ -ስ- መሐ'ረብ

handle
'ሀንደል -ግ- መያዝ [ያዘ] ፤ መ'ቆጣጠር መቻል
[ቻለ]
-ስ- ማንጠልጠያ ፣ ጀሮ (የዕቃ)

handsome
'ሀንሰም -ቅ- ያማረ ፣ የተዋበ (ለወንድ)

handwriting
'ሀንድራይቲንግ -ስ- የእ'ጅ ጽሕፈት

handy
'ሀንዲ -ቅ- ተስማሚ ፣ ቅልጥ'ፍ ያለ (ለዕቃ)

hang
'ሀንግ -ግ- መስቀል [ሰ'ቀለ] ፤ ማንጠልጠል
[አንጠለ'ጠለ]

hangar
'ሀንገ -ስ- ያውሮ'ፕላን ጋራዥ

hanger
'ሀንገ -ስ- የልብስ መስቀያ

hangman
'ሀንግመን -ስ- ሰቃይ (የተፈ'ረደ'በትን ሰው)

hank
'ሀንክ -ስ- ጥ'ቅል ገመድ ፣ ጥ'ቅል ሱፍ ፣ ድር

hanker
'ሀንከ -ግ- መ'መኘት [ተመ'ኘ]

haphazard
ሀፕ'ሀዘድ -ቅ- በድንገት የሆነሳያ'ስ'ቡት የተ
ደ'ረገ

happen
'ሀፐን -ግ- መሆን [ሆነ]

happiness
'ሀፒነስ -ስ- ደ'ስታ ፣ ፍ'ሥሐ

happy
'ሀፒ -ቅ- ደ'ስተ'ኛ ፣ ተደ'ሳች

harlot
'ሀለት -ስ- ሴተ'ኛ አዳሪ ፣

harrass
'ሀረስ -ግ- በ'የጊዜው ማስፈራራት [አስፈ
ራ'ራ] ፤ መነዝነዝ [ነዘ'ነዘ] ፣ ማልፋት [አለ'ፋ]

harbour
'ሀ፡በ -ስ- ወደብ (የመርከብ ማቆሚያ)

hard
'ሀ፡ድ -ቅ- ጠንካ'ራ

harden
'ሀ፡ደን -ግ- ማጠንከር [አጠነ'ከረ]

hardly
'ሀ፡ድሊ -ተግ- በች'ግር ፣ በመ'ቻገር

hardship
'ሀ፡ድሺፕ -ስ- መከራ ፣ ች'ግር

hardware
'ሀ፡ድዌየ -ስ- የወጥ ቤት ቁሳቁስ (ብረታብረት)

hardy
'ሀ፡ዲ -ቅ- መከራ ቻይ ፣ ጀግና

hare
'ሄየ -ስ- ጥንቸል (የሜዳ)

harelip
'ሄየሊፕ -ስ- የተከፈለ የላይ'ኛው ከንፈር

470

hark
’ሀ፡ክ -ስ- ግ'ዳሟጥ [አ'ዳ'መጠ]

harm
’ሀ፡ም -ግ- መጉዳት [ጎ'ዳ]

harmonious
ሀ:'መውኒየስ -ት- ሲሰሙት የ'ሚያስደ'ስት ፡ ግዕመ ዜማ ያ'ለው ፡ ስምም'ነት ያ'ለው

harness
’ሀ:ነስ -ስ- የፈረስ ዕቃ

harp
’ሀ:ፕ -ስ- በገና

harrow
’ሀረው -ስ- አፈር መከስከሻ መ'ሣሪያ (የእ ርሻ)

harsh
ሀ:ሽ ’-ት- ሻካራ ፡ ያልተስግ'ግ ፤ ጎደለ'ኛ (ለጠባይ)
sound
-ት- ሻካራ ድምፅ ፤ ጪ'ካኝ

harvest
’ሀ፡ቨስት -ግ- ግምረት [አመ'ረተ] ፡ ሰብል መሰብሰብ [ሰበ'ሰበ[
-ስ- ምርት

hasp
’ሀ:ስፕ -ስ- ግጠፊያ (ለበ'ር ፡ ለሻንጣ ፡ ለግ ጥን ወዘተ)

haste
'ሄይስት -ስ- ፍጥነት ፡ ቸ'ኩል'ነት ፡
-ግ- ግ'ጣደፍ [አ'ጣ'ደፈ] ፡ መቸ'ኩል [ቸ'ኩለ]

hat
’ሀት -ስ- ባርኔጣ

hatch
’ሀች -ስ- የመርከብ ክዳን (የዕቃ መጫ'ኛውን ክፍል የ'ሚከድነው)
-ግ- መፈልፈል [ፈለ'ፈለ] ፡ መ'ፈል 'ፈል [ተፈለ'ፈለ] (የዕንቁላል)

hatchet
’ሀቸት -ስ- ጥ'ልቆ ት'ን'ሽ መጥረቢያ

hate
'ሄይት -ግ- መጥላት [ጠ'ላ]

haughty
’ሀ:ቲ -ስ- ኩሩ ፡ ሰው ናቂ ፡ ደ'ፋር (በን ግ'ግር)

haul
’ሀ:ል -ግ- መጎ'ተት [ጎ'ተተ]

haunch
’ሀ:ንች -ስ- ዳ'ሌ

haunt
’ሀ:ንት -ግ- በርከስ መንፈስ መ'ባረር [ተባ 'ረረ]
-ስ- ሁልጊዜ የ'ሚሄዱ'በት ቦታ ፡ ቤት

have
’ሀቭ -ግ- መ'ገናዘብ [ተገና'ዘበ] ፤ መኖር [እ'ለ]

haven
'ሄይቭን -ስ- የረ'ጋ ወደብ ፡ መ'ጠጊያ ቦታ

havoc
’ሀቨክ -ስ- ብጥ'ብጥ ፡ ሽ'ብር

hawk
’ሀ:ክ -ስ- ጭላ'ፊ'ት
-ግ- ከቦታ ቦታ እየተዘዋ'ወሩ ዕቃ መነ'ገድ [ነ'ገደ]

hay
'ሄይ -ስ- ድርቆሽ

haystack
’ሄይስታክ -ስ- የድርቆሽ ክ'ምር

hazard
’ሀዘ፡ድ -ስ- አደጋ ፡ ዕ'ድል

hazardous
’ሀዘደስ -ት- አደገ'ኛ

haze
'ሄይዝ -ስ- ብርሃን የ'ሚሸ'ፍን ቀለ'ል ያለ ደ'መና ፡ ጭ,ጋግ

he
'ሂይ -ተስ- እርሱ ፡ እርሳ'ቸው ፡ እ'ሱ ፡ እ'ሳ ቸው

head
'ሄድ -ስ- ራስ
chief
-ስ- አለቃ ፡ ሹም

headache
'ሄደይክ -ስ- ራስ ምታት

headland
'ሄድለንድ -ስ- ወደ ባሕር ውስጥ ገባ ያለ ጎደል

471

headlight
'ሄድላይት -ስ- የመኪና የፊት መብራት ፡ በመርከብ አናት ላይ ያ'ለ መብራት

headmaster
ሄድ'ማ:ስተ -ስ- የትምህርት ቤት ዲሬክተር

headquarters
ሄድክ'ዎ:ተዝ -ስ- ጠቅላይ መምሪያ (የወ'ታ'ደር) ፤ ያንድ ድር'ጅት ጠቅላይ መሥሪያ ቤት

headstrong
'ሄድስትሮንግ -ቅ- በፍ'ላጎቱ የ'ሚ'መ'ራ ፡ ች'ኮ ፡ መንቻ'ካ

headway
'ሄድዌይ -ስ- ወደፊት የመሄድ እንቅስ'ቃሴ (በተለ'ይ የመርከብ)

heal
'ሂይል -ግ- መፈ'ወስ [ፈ'ወሰ] ፡ ማዳን [አዳነ]

health
'ሄልስ -ስ- ጤና

healthy
'ሄልሲ -ቅ- ጤና'ማ

heap
'ሂይፕ -ግ- መቆ'ለል [ቆ'ለለ]
-ስ- ቁ'ልል

hear
'ሂየ -ግ- መስማት [ሰ'ማ]

hearsay
'ሂየሴይ -ስ- ወሬ (አፈ ታሪክ)

hearse
'ኸ:ስ -ስ- የሬሳ መኪና

heart
'ሀ:ት -ስ- ል'ብ
good-ed
-ቅ- ርኅሩኅ

heartbeat
'ሀ:ትቢይት -ስ- የልብ ት'ርታ

heartburn
'ሀ:ትበ:ን -ስ- ቃር

hearten
'ሀ:ተን -ግ- ማጽናናት [አጽና'ና] ፡ ማ'በረታታት [አ'በረታ'ታ] ፡ ማ'ደፋፈር [አ'ደፋ'ፈረ]

hearth
'ሀ:ስ -ስ- ምድ'ጃ

heartily
'ሀ:ተሊ -ተግ- ከል'ብ

heartless
'ሀ:ትለስ -ቅ- ጨ'ካኝ ፡ የርኅራኄ ስ'ሜት የሌ'ለው

heat
'ሂይት -ግ- ማሞቅ [አሞቀ]
-ስ- ሙቀት

heath
'ሂይስ -ስ- የከብት ማ'ሠማሪያ ቦታ (የማ'ንም ያልሆነ)

heathen
'ሂይዘን -ቅ- አረመኔ

heave
'ሂይቭ -ግ- መጎተት [ጎ'ተተ] ፡ ማንሣት [አ'ነ'ሣ] ፤ መግፋት [ገ'ፋ]

heaven
'ሄቨን -ስ- ሰማይ
religious
-ስ- መንግሥተ ሰማያት

heavy
'ሄቪ -ቅ- ከ'ባድ

hectic
'ሄክቲክ -ቅ- ሥራ የ'ማያስፈ'ታ ፡ ፋታ የ'ማይሰጥ ፡ የተፋ'ጠነ

hedge
'ሄጅ -ስ- በድንበር ዙሪያ የ'ሚ'ገ'ኝ ተክል

heed
'ሂይድ -ግ- ማስተዋል [አስተዋለ]
-ስ- ጥን'ቃቄ ፡ ማስተዋል

heel
'ሂይል -ስ- ተረከዝ

hefty
'ሄፍቲ -ቅ- ወፍራም ፡ ከ'ባድ'ና ኀይለ'ኛ

heifer
'ሄፈ -ስ- ጊደር

height
'ሀይት -ቅ- እርዝማኔ

heighten
'ሀይተን -ግ- የበ'ለጠ ማድረግ [አደ'ረገ] ፡ ከ'ፍ ማድረግ [አደ'ረገ]

heir
'ኤየ -ስ- ወራ'ሽ (ወንድ)

heiress
'ኤየሬስ -ስ- ወራ'ሽ (ሴት)

hell

’ሄል -ስ- ሲኦል

helm

’ሄልም -ስ- የመርከብ መሪ (መ’ዣሪያ) ፤ ጥሩር

help

’ሄልፕ -ግ- መርዳት [ረ’ዳ]

helpful

’ሄልፕፉል -ቅ- ረጂ ፤ ለመርዳት የተዘጋጀ

helpless

’ሄልፕለስ -ቅ- ደካማ ፤ ረ’ዳት የሌ’ለው

hem

’ሄም -ስ- የልብስ ጠርፍ ፤ የልብስ ጠርዝ (በተ
ለ’ይ ታጥፎ የተሰ’ፋ)

hemisphere

’ሄመስፊየ -ስ- የዓለም አ’ጋማሽ

hemp

’ሄምፕ -ስ- አእምሮ የ’ሚያደነ’ዝዝ መድኃ
ኒት የ’ሚወጣ’በት ተክል ፤ ቃ’ጫ የ’ሚወ
ጣ’በት ተክል

hen

’ሄን -ስ- ዶሮ

hence

’ሄንስ -ተግ- ስለ’ዚህ ፤ ከ’ዚህ የተነ’ሣ

her

’ኸ: -ተስ- እርሷ ፤ የርሷ

herald

’ሄረልድ -ስ- የንጉሥ መልእክተ’ኛ ፤ ዐዋጅ
ነጋሪ

herb

’ኸብ -ስ- የሚ’በ’ላ ቅጠላቅጠል ፤ የምግብ
ማጣፈጫ ተክል

herd

’ኸ:ድ -ስ- መንጋ

herdsman

’ኸ:ድዝመን -ስ- ከብት አ’ጋጅ ፤ ከብት ጠ’ባቂ

here

’ሂየ -ተግ- እ’ዚህ

hereafter

ሂየ’ራ:ፍተ -ተግ- ከ’ዚህ በላይ ፤ ከእንግዲህ
ወዲህ ፤ ወደፊት

hereby

ሂየ’ባይ -ተግ- በ’ዚህ

hereditary

ኸ’ሬደትሪ -ቅ- የተወ’ረሰ (ጠባይ ወዘተ)

heresy

’ሄረሲ -ስ- ጥር’ጣሬ (የሃይማኖት) ፤ ሐራጥ
ቃ’ነት

herewith

ሂየ’ዊዝ -ተግ- ከ’ዚህ ጋር

heritage

’ሄረተጅ -ስ- ካ’ባቶች የተወ’ረሰ ነገር

hermit

’ኸ:ሚት -ስ- ባሕታዊ

hermaphrodite

ኸ’ማፍሮዳይት -ስ- ፍናፍንት

hernia

’ኸ:ኒየ -ስ- እበጥ (የሆድ)

hero

’ሂረው -ቅ- ጀግና (ለወንድ)

heroine

’ሄረዊን -ቅ- ጀግና (ለሴት)

heroism

’ሄረዊዝም -ስ- ጀግን’ነት

herself

ኸ’ሴልፍ -ተስ- እርሷ እራ’ዋ ፤ እ’ሷ ራ’ዋ

hesitate

’ሄዘቴይት -ግ- መ’ጠራጠር [ተጠራ’ጠረ]
ፈ’ራ ተ’ባ ማለት [አለ]

hew

ሆ’የው -ግ- መፈልፈል [ፈለ’ፈለ] ፤ መጥረብ
[ጠ’ረበ] (ለያ’ንጊያ)

hibernate

’ሃይበኔይት -ግ- ማንቀላፋት [አንቀላ’ፋ] (የክ
ረምትን ጊዜ ፤ ለእንቡራሪት መዛተ)

hidden

’ሂደን -ቅ- የተሸ’ሸገ ፤ የተደ’በቀ

hide

’ሃይድ -ግ- መደ’በቅ [ደ’በቀ]

hideous

’ሂዲየስ -ቅ- መልከ ጥፉ ፤ ማስጠ’ሎ ፤ አስቀ
’ያሚ

high

’ሃይ -ቅ- ከፍ ያለ

highly

’ሃይሊ -ተግ- በት’ልቁ ፤ በብዙ‐ው

highness

’ሃይነስ -ስ- ልዑል’ነት

473

highway
'ሀይዌይ -ስ- አውራ ጎዳና

hike
ሃይክ -ግ- በግር ረጅም መንገድ መንሸራ
ሸር [ተንሸራ'ሸረ]

hilarious
ሂ'ሌሪየስ -ት- በጣም አስደ'ሳች [ጊዚ] ፣ ሣቅ'ና
ዶ'ስታ የሞ'ላ'በት ·

hilarity
'ሂላሪቲ -ስ- ደ'ስታ

hill
'ሂል -ስ- ዐቀበት ፣ ኮረብታ

hillock
'ሂለክ -ስ- ጉ'ብታ ፣ ት'ንሽ ኮረብታ

hilt
'ሂልት -ስ- የጎራዴ ፣ የሰይፍ እ'ጀታ

him
'ሂም -ተስ- እርሱን ፣ እ'ሱን

himself
ሂም'ሴልፍ -ተስ- እርሱ ራሱ ፣ እ'ሱ ራሱ

hind
'ሀይንድ -ስ- ኋላ (ጀርባ)

hinder
'ሂንደ -ግ- ማ'ወክ [አ'ወከ] ፣ መከልከል [ከለ
'ከለ]

hindrance
'ሂንድረንስ -ስ- እንቅፋት ፣ መሰናክል

hinge
'ሂንጅ -ስ- ማጠፊያ (የበ'ር ፣ የመስኮት መዘጋት)

hint
'ሂንት -ስ- አ'ጭር ጠቃሚ ምክር

hip
'ሂፕ -ስ- ዳሌ

hippopotamus
ሂፖ'ፖተመስ -ስ- ጉማሬ

hire
'ሀየ -ግ- መከራየት [ተከራ'የ]
employ
-ግ- መቅጠር [ቀ'ጠረ]

hireling
'ሀየሊንግ -ስ- በገንዘብ የተቀ'ጠረ ሞያተ'ኛ፣
ለገንዘብ ሲል የ'ሚ'ሠ'ራ ወ'ታ'ደር

his
'ሂዝ -ተስ- የርሱ ፣ የ'ሱ

hiss
'ሂስ -ስ- እ'ስ ማለት (እንደ እባብ) ፣ አለመስ
ማማትን ለመግለጽ "እ'ስ" ማለት

historian
ሂስ'ቶሪየን -ት- ባለታሪክ ፣ ታሪክ ዐዋቂ ፣
ታሪክ ጸሐፊ ፣ የታሪክ ሊቅ

historic
ሂስ'ቶሪክ -ት- ታሪካዊ

history
'ሂስተሪ -ስ- ታሪክ

hit
'ሂት -ግ- መምታት [መ'ታ]

hitch
'ሂች -ግ- አንድ ነገር ላይ ማሰር [አ'ሰረ] ፣
ወደ ላይ ከ'ፍ ማድረግ [አደ'ረገ]

hitherto
ሂዘ'ቱ: -ተግ- እስካሁን ድረስ

hive
'ሀይቭ -ስ- የንብ ቀፎ

hoard
'ሆ:ድ -ግ- ማ'ከማቸት [አ'ከማ'ቸ] ፣ ማድለብ
[አደ'ለበ] (ገንዘብ ፣ ምግብ መዘተ)

hoarse
'ሆ:ስ -ት- ጎርና'ና (ለድምፅ)

hoax
ሆውክስ -ስ- ማሞ'ኘት (በቀልድ'ና በጨ
ዋታ)

hobble
'ሆበል -ግ- እያነከሱ በዝ'ግታ መ'ራመድ
[ተራ'ሙ'ደ] ፣ መቀየድ [ቀ'የደ]

hobby
'ሆቢ -ስ- የትርፍ ጊዜ ሥራ (ገንዘብ የ'ማይ'ከ
'ፈሉ'በት ለመ'ደሰት ፣ የ'ሚሠሩት ሥራ)

hoe
ሆው -ስ- መኩትኩቻ

hog
'ሆግ -ስ- የተከላ'ሸ ዐሣማ (ለእርድ የ'ሚ'ቀ
'ለብ)

hoist
'ሆይስት -ስ- እየተንጠጓ'ጎዱ ማንሣት [አነ'ሣ]

hold
'ሆውልድ -ግ- መያዝ [ያዘ]

holder
'ሆውልደ -ስ- መያዣ

474

hole
’ሆውል -ስ- ቀዳዳ ፣ ሽን቉ር

holiday
’ሆለዴይ -ስ- በዓል ፣ የዕረፍት ቀን ፣ ዐውደ
ዓመት

hollow
’ሆለው -ቅ- ውስጡ ባዶ የሆነ ፣ ቡርቡር

holy
’ሆውሊ -ቅ- ቅ’ዱስ

homage
’ሆመጅ -ስ- አክብሮት ፣ የበታ’ች’ነትን ፣ ታ’ዛ
ዥ’ነትን መግለጽ

home
’ሆውም -ስ- መኖሪያ ቤት ፣ የተወ’ለ’ዱበት
ቦታ ፣ የትውል’ድ አገር

homeless
’ሆውምለስ -ቅ- ቤት የሌ’ለው

homely
’ሆውምሊ -ቅ- እንግዳ ተቀ’ባይ ፣ ብሩኽ
ገ’ጽ

homesick
’ሆውምሲክ -ቅ- አገሩ የና’ፈቀው

homespun
’ሆውምስፐን -ቅ- እቤት የተፈ’ተለ ፣ ተራ ፣
ግልጽ
-ስ- እቤት የተፈ’ተለ ጨርቅ

homestead
’ሆውምስተድ -ስ- ባለቤቱ የ’ሚያርሰው እር
ስት ፣ በርሻ ቦታ ላይ ያ’ለ የመኖሪያ ቤት

homicide
’ሆመሳይድ -ስ- ያንድ ሰው በሌላ መ’ገደል ፣
ነፍስ ግ’ዳይ

homogenous
ኸ’ሞጅነስ -ቅ- ተመሳሳይ ፣ ከመጅ’መሪያ
እስከ መጨ’ረሻ አንድ ዓይነት የሆነ

honest
’አነስት -ቅ- ታ’ማኝ ፣ እውነተ’ኛ

honey
’ሀኒ -ስ- ማር

honeycomb
’ሀኒከውም -ስ- የማር እሽት

honeymoon
’ሀኒሙ፡ን -ስ- የሚጓላ ጊዜ ፣ የመ’ዋዋሪያ
ጊዜ (ጋዞ ወደላላ አገር ፣ ከተ‑ማ)

honorary
’አነረሪ -ቅ- የ’ማይ’ከ’ፈለው (ያንድ ድር’ጅት
አባል) ፣ የክብር አባል ወዘተ

honour
’አነ -ግ- ማክበር [አክ’በረ]
-ስ- ክብር

honourable
’አነረበል -ቅ- የተከ’በረ ፣ ክቡር

hood
’ሁድ -ስ- ከልብስ ጋር የተያያዘ ሾጣጣ ቆብ

hoodwink
’ሁድዊንክ -ግ- ማ’ታለል [አ’ታ’ለለ] ፣ ማ’ሳ
ሳት [አ’ሳሳተ] ፣ ዓይን መሸ’ፈን [ሸ’ፈነ] (የፈ
ረስ)

hoof
’ሁ፡ፍ -ስ- ኮ’ቴ (እንጓር)

hook
’ሁክ -ስ- ሜንጦ

hooligan
’ሁ፡ሊገን -ስ- አ’ሽ’ባሪ ፣ በጥባጭ ፣ ወ’ርበ’ላ

hoop
’ሁ፡ፕ -ስ- ክ’ብ ነገር (የብረት ፣ የእንጨት)

hoot
’ሁ፡ት -ስ- የጉላክስ ድምፅ ፣ የመኪና ጥሩምባ
ድምፅ

hooter
’ሁ፡ተ -ስ- ክላክስ (የመኪና ጥሩም’ባ)

hop
’ሆፕ -ግ- ባንድ እግር እ’የዘ’ለሉ መሄድ
[ሄደ] ፣ እንጣ’ጥ እንጣ’ጥ ማለት [አለ]

hope
’ኸውፕ -ግ- መ’መኘት [ተመ’ኘ] ፣ ተስፋ
ማድረግ [አደ’ረገ]
-ስ- ም’ኞት ፣ ተስፋ

hopeful
’ኸውፕፉል -ቅ- ባለም’ኞት ፣ ሙሉ ም’ኞት
ያ’ለው ፣ ባለተስፋ

hopeless
’ኸውፕለስ -ቅ- ዋጋ ቢስ ፣ ተስፋ ቢስ ፣ መድ
ጋን የሌ’ለው

horde
’ሆ፡ድ -ስ- መንጋ ፣ መዐት (ም’ሳሌ፣ የወ’ታ
’ደር መዐት)

horizon
ኸ’ራይዘን -ስ- አድማስ

475

horizontal
ሆሪ'ዞንተል -ቅ- አግድም ፣ ጋድሞሽ
horn
'ሆ:ን -ስ- ቀንድ
trumpet
-ስ- ቀንደ መለከት
car-
-ስ- ክላክስ
hornet
'ሆ:ነት -ስ- ተርብ
horrible
'ሆሪበል -ቅ- አስፈሪ ፣ አስደንጋጭ
horror
'ሆሬ -ስ- ፍርሃት ፣ ድን'ጋጤ ፤ መ'ጸየፍ
horse
'ሆ:ስ -ስ- ፈረስ
horsecloth
'ሆ:ስክሎⷆ -ስ- ቀሚስ (የፈረስ)
horseman
'ሆ:ስመን -ስ- ፈረሰ'ኛ
horseradish
'ሆ:ስሬዲሽ -ስ- ፍጅል
horseshoe
'ሆ:ሹ -ስ- የፈረስ ጫ'ማ
horticulture
'ሆ:ቲክልቸ -ስ- ያበባ መትከል ዋያ ፣ ያትክልት ቦታ አ'ያያዝ
hose
'ኾውዝ -ስ- ያትክልት ማጠጫ ጉ'ማ ፣ ሹራ ፣ ፕላስቲክ (ቀ'ጭን ረጅም ውስጡ ባዶ የሆነ ፣ የቢምቢ ዓይነት)
hospitable
ሆስ'ፒተበል -ቅ- እንግዳ ተቀ'ባይ
hospital
'ሆስፒተል -ስ- የሐኪም ቤት ፣ ሆስፒታል
hospitality
ሆስፒ'ታለቲ -ስ- እንግዳ ተቀ'ባይነት
host
'ኾውስት -ስ- አስተናጋጅ ፣ እንግዳ ተቀ'ባይ (ወንድ) ፤ የሰው መኖት (ብዙ ሰው)
host
'ኾውስት -ስ- ጉብስት (ለሥጋ ወደሙ የሚ ቀርብ) ፣ አ'ኮቴት

hostage
'ሆስተጅ -ስ- መያዣ የ'ሚሆን የጦር እስረ'ኛ
hostel
'ሆስተል -ስ- በል'ዩ ድር'ጅት የ'ሚ'ወ'ራ መኖርያ ቤት (የተማሪዎ'ች ፣ የሠ'ራተ'ኞ'ች ወዘተ)
hostess
'ሆውስተስ -ስ- እንግዳ ተቀ'ባይ (ሴት) ፣ ሴት አስተናጋጅ
hostile
'ሆስታይል -ቅ- ጠላት'ነት የ'ሚያሳይ ፣ የጠ ላት
hostility
ሆስ'ቲለ.ቲ -ስ- ጠላት'ነት
hot
'ሆት -ቅ- ሙቅ
hotel
ሆው'ቴል -ስ- ሆቴል
hound
'ሀውንድ -ስ- ው'ሻ (በተለ'ይ የአደ'ን ፣ የሸቅ ድ'ድም)
hour
'አወ -ስ- ሰዓት ፤ ጊዜ
hourly
'አወለ. -ተግ- በ'የሰዓቱ (የተደ'ረገ ፣ የሆነ)
house
'ሀውስ -ስ- ቤት
household
'ሀውስኾውልድ -ስ- ቤተሰብ
housekeeper
'ሀውስኪፐ -ስ- ገረድ (በዕድሜ የጎ'ፈ'ች)
housemaid
'ሀውስሜይድ -ስ- ገረድ (በዕድሜ አነ'ስ ያለ'ች)
hovel
'ሆቨል -ስ- መና'ኛ ት'ንሽ ጉ'ጆ
hover
'ሆቨ -ግ- ማንጓበብ [አንጓ'በበ]
how
'ሀው -ተግ- እንዴት
however
ሀ'ዌቨ -ተግ- ቢሆን'ም ፣ ይሁን'ና ፣ በምን'ም ሁናቴ ፣ በምን'ም መንገድ

476

howl
’ሀዉል -ግ- በከ'ፍተ'ኛ ድምፅ መጮኽ
[ጮኸ] (ለዉ'ሻ ፡ ለቀበሮ)

hub
’ኸብ -ስ- የመንኮራኩር መካ'ከል ክፍል

hubbub
’ኀበብ -ስ- ዋካታ

huddle
’ኸደል -ግ- መ'ታፈግ [ታ'ፈገ] (እንደበግ) ፡
መ'ሾጋሸግ [ተሾጋ'ሸገ] (ለሙቀት)

hue
ህ’ዩው -ስ- ቀለም ፡ መልክ (ቀ'ይ ፡ አረንጓዴ፡
ብጫ'ና ፡ ሰማያዊ)

hug
’ኸግ -ግ- ማቀፍ [አ'ቀፈ]

huge
ህ’ዩጅ -ቅ- በጣም ት'ልቅ

hum
’ኸም -ስ- ድምፅ (እፍን ዘግቶ የ'ሚ'ሰ'ማ)
ህ’ምታ ፡ ማንጉራገር (ዘፈን)

human
ህ’ዩ፡መን -ቅ- ሰብአዊ
-ስ- ሰው

humane
ህዩ’ሜይን -ቅ- ርኅሩኅ ፡ ሰብአዊ

humanity
ህዩ’ማነቲ -ስ- ሰብአዊ’ነት ፡ የሰው ልጅ ፡
ርኅራኄ

humble
’ኸምብል -ቅ- ትሑት

humdrum
’ኸምድረም -ቅ- አሰልቺ ፡ ተራ ፡ ትርኪ ምርኪ

humid
ህ’ዩ፡ሚድ -ቅ- እርጥብ

humidity
ህዩ’ሚደቲ -ስ- እርጥበት

humiliate
ህዩ’ሚሊዩይት -ግ- ማ'ዋረድ [አ'ዋ'ረደ]
ማሳ'ፈር [አሳ'ፈረ]

humility
ህዩ’ሚለቲ -ስ- ትሕት'ና

hummock
’ኸመክ -ስ- ት'ንሽ ጉ'ብ'ታ

humour
ህ’ዩመ -ስ- ዛቅ ፡ ቀልድ ፡ ቧልት

humourous
ህ’ዩመረስ -ቅ- ዛ'ቂተ'ኛ ፡ ቀልደ'ኛ ፡ ቧል
ተ'ኛ ፡ አ'ሥቂ'ኝ

hump
’ኸምፕ -ስ- ሻ'ኛ (የግመል ወዘተ)

humpback
’ኸምፕባክ -ስ- እጀርባው ላይ ጉ'በታ ያለ
’በት ሰው

hunch
’ኸንች -ግ- ሰዉ'ነትን ሸም'ቅቅ ማድረግ
[አደ'ረገ] (ክብርድ የተነ'ሣ)
-ስ- ጥር'ጣሬ

hunchback
’ኸንችባክ -ስ- እጀርባው ላይ ጉ'ብ'ታ ያለ'በ
ት ሰው

hundred
’ኸንድረድ -ቅ- መቶ

hundredth
’ኸንድረድስ -ቅ- መ'ቶኛ

hunger
’ኸንገ -ስ- ረኅብ

hungry
’ኸንግሪ -ቅ- ረኅብተ'ኛ ፡ የራበው

hunt
’ኸ፡ንት -ግ- ማ'ደን [አ'ደነ]

hunter
’ኸንተ -ስ- አዳ'ኝ

hurl
’ኸ፡ል -ግ- ዘነዶል መወርወር [ወረ'ወረ] ፡
በነዶል መ'ናገር [ተና'ገረ]

hurricane
’ኸረከን -ስ- በጣም ኃያለ'ኛ ነፋስ (በሰዓት
ከ፸፪ ኪ.ሜ በላይ ፍጥነት ያ'ለዉ)

hurry
’ኸሪ -ግ- መፍጠን [ፈ'ጠነ]

hurt
’ኸ፡ት -ግ- መጉዳት [ጎ'ዳ] ፡ ማቁሰል [አቆ
'ሰለ]

husband
’ኸዝበንድ -ስ- ባል ፡ ባለቤት (ተባዕት)

hush
’ኸሽ -ስ- ፀ'ጥታ ፡ (ትእዛዝ ፡ ፀ'ጥ በል)

477

husk
’ኸስከ -ስ- ሽፋን (የእህል) ፣ ል'ጣጭ (የፍሬ
ፍሬ)

husky
’ኸስኪ. -ቅ- ወፍራም ጠንካ'ራ (ለሰው)
voice
-ቅ- ወፍራም ድምፅ

hustle
’ኸሰል -ግ- በፍጥነት መሄድ [ሄደ]

hut
’ኸት -ስ- ጎ'ጆ

hutch
’ኸች -ስ- የትን'ንሽ እንሰሳት ማስቀ'መጫ
ሣጥን (ባንድ በ'ኩል የሽቦ ወንፈት ያለ'በት)

hybrid
’ሀይብሪድ -ስ- ክ'ልስ (ለእንስሳት ፣ ለአትክ
ልት)

hydrophobia
’ሀይድረ’ፈውቢየ -ስ- የው'ሻ በ'ሽታ ፣ ውሃ
የ'ማያስጠ'ጣ ፣ ውሃ የ'ሚያስፈ'ራ በ'ሽታ

hyena
’ይነ -ስ- ጅብ

hygiene
ሀይ’ጂይን -ስ- የጤና አ'ጠባበቅ ትምህርት ፣
የንጽሕ'ና መሠረታዊ ልምዶ'ች ፣ ንጽሕ'ና

hygienic
ሀይ’ጂይኒክ -ቅ- ጤና'ግ ፣ ንዱሕ ፣ ለጤና
አ'ጠባበቅ ተስማሚ

hymn
’ሂም -ስ- መዝሙር (መንፈሳዊ) ፣ ማሕሌት

hyphen
’ሃይፈን -ስ- አገድም ሠረዝ (—)

hypnotise
’ሂፕነታይዝ -ግ- ማደንዘዝ [አደነ'ዘዘ] ፣ እኔ
ምር መስ'ወር [ስ'ወረ] ፣ ማናዘዝ [አፈ'ዘዘ]

hypocrisy
ሂ’ፖክሪሲ -ስ- ግ'ብዝ'ነት ፣ መ'መጻደቅ

hypocrite
’ሂፐክሪት -ቅ- ግ'ብዝ ፣ ተመጻዳቂ

hypothesis
ሃይ’ፖፀሲስ -ስ- መላ ምት ፣ የምልዓባት
ሐ'ሳብ

hysterical
ሂስ’ቴሪከል -ቅ- አንድ ነገር አእምሮውን
ያ'ና'ወጠው ፣ ግ'ልፍተ'ኛ

ib.s
’አይቢስ -ስ- ጋጋኖ

ice
’አይስ -ስ- በረዶ (የረ'ጋ ውሃ)

ice cream
አይስክሪይም -ስ- አይስ ክሪም   ጀላ'ቲ
(ከበረዶ የተሠ'ራ ጣፋጭ ምግብ)

icy
’አይሲ -ቅ- በጣም ብርዳም

idea
አይ’ዲየ -ስ- ሐ'ሳብ

ideal
አይ’ዲይል -ቅ- የ'ሚስማ'ማ ፣ ፍ'ጹም የሆነ ፣
እንከን የሌ'ለ'በት

identical
አይ’ዴንተከል -ቅ- ተመሳሳይ ፥ በምን'ም
ሁናቴ ል'ዩ'ነት የ'ማያሳ'ይ

identify
አይ’ዴንተፋይ -ግ- ለ'ይቶ ማወቅ [ዐ'ወቀ]

identity
አይ’ዴንተቲ -ስ- መ'ታወቂያ

idiom
’ኢድየም -ስ- ያ'ነጋገር ዘየ ፣ ያ'ገላለጽ መን
ገድ (ያንድ ቋንቋ)

idiot
’ኢድየት -ስ- ደ'ደብ ሰው

idiotic
ኢድ’ዮቲክ -ቅ- ደንቆር ፣ ደ'ደብ

478

idle
’አይደል -ቅ- ሥራ ፈት ፣ ሰነፍ ፣ እሥራ ላይ
ያልዋለ

idleness
’አይደለኔስ -ስ- ሥራ ፈት'ነት

idol
’አይደል -ስ- ጣኦት

idolize
’አይደላይዝ -ግ- ከ'ሚ'?'ባው በላይ መው
ደድ ፣ ግድነቅ'ና ክብር መስጠት [ሰ'መ]

if
’ኢፍ -መተ- በ ... ፣ ከ፣ ...

ignite
ኢግናይት -ግ- መለ'ኮስ [ለ'ኮሰ] ፣ ግ'ቶ
ጠል [እ'ቃ'ጠለ]

ignition
ኢግኒሽን -ስ- መለ'ኮስ ፣ ግ'ቃጠል
engine
-ስ- ሞቶር ግስነ'ሻ

ignoble
ኢግኖውብል -ቅ- ወ'ራዳ ፣ ክብር የሌ'ለው

ignominy
’ኢግኖመኒ -ስ- ውርደት (በሕዝብ መካ'ከል) ፣
የ'ሚያሳ'ፍር ሥራ

ignorance
’ኢግኖረንስ -ስ- ደንቁር'ና ፣ አለማወቅ

ignorant
’ኢግኖረንት -ቅ- ደንቁር ፣ አላዋቂ

ignore
ኢግኖ፡ -ግ- 'ቸል ግለት [አለ]

ill
’ኢል -ግ- መ'ታመም [ታ'መመ]

illegal
ኢ'ሊይገል -ቅ- ሕገ ወ'ጥ

illegible
ኢ'ሌጀብል -ቅ- የ'ማይ'ነ'በብ

illegitimate
ኢለ'ጂተመት -ቅ- ዲቃላ ፣ ሕ'ጋዊ ያልሆነ

illicit
ኢ'ሊሲት -ቅ- ሕ'ጋዊ ያልሆነ ፣ የ'ማይ'ፈ'ቀድ

illiteracy
ኢ'ሊተረሲ -ስ- ማንበብ'ና መጻፍ አለመቻል

illiterate
ኢ'ሊተረት -ቅ- ማንበብ'ና መጻፍ የ'ማይቻል

illness
’ኢልነስ -ስ- ሕመም ፣ በ'ሽታ

ill-tempered
ኢል'ቴምፐድ -ቅ- የ'ማይ'ታ'ገሥ ፣ ቢቶ ላሉ
የ'ሚ'ቆ'ጣ ፣ ግ'ልፍተ'ኛ

illuminate
ኢል'ዩ:መኔይት -ግ- ማብራት [አበ'ራ]

illusion
ኢ'ሉ:ዠን -ስ- ሰዓይን የ'ሚመስል ነገር (ነገር
ግን እውነት ያልሆነ) ፣ ምትሀት

illustrate
’ኢለስትሬይት -ግ- በሥዕላ ሥዕል ግስጌጥ
[አስጌመ] (ለመጽሐፍ)
use examples
-ግ- በም'ሳሌ ማስረ'ዳት [አስረ'ዳ]

illustration
ኢለስት'ሬይሽን -ስ- ሥዕል
example
-ስ- ም'ሳሌ

illustrious
ኢ'ለስትሪየስ -ቅ- ዝ'ነ'ኛ ፣ የታ'ወቀ ፣ ስሙ'ጥር

image
’ኢመጅ -ስ- ቅርፅ ፣ ምስል

imaginary
ኢ'ማጂነሪ -ቅ- ሐ'ሳባዊ ፣ የ'ሚያ'ስቡቱ ነገር
ግን እውነት ያልሆነ

imagination
ኢ'ማጂ'ኔሽን -ስ- ሐ'ሳብ ፣ ግ'ምት

imagine
ኢ'ማጂን -ግ- ማ'ሰብ [አ'ሰበ] ፣ ሊሆ ይች
ላል ብሎ መገ'መት [ገ'መተ]

imbecile
’ኢምበሲይል -ቅ- ነሀላ'ላ ፣ ደንቆር ፣ አእ
ምሮ ደካማ

imbibe
ኢም'ባይብ -ግ- መጠ'ጣት [ጠ'ጣ] ፣ መቅ
ሰም [ቀ'ሰመ] (ሐ'ሳብ)

imitate
’ኢመቴይት -ግ- አስመ'ስሎ መሥራት [ሠ'ራ]

imitation
ኢመ'ቴይሽን -ስ- ማስመ'ሰል ፣ አምሳ'ያ

immaculate
ኢ'ማክዩለት -ቅ- ንጹሕ ፣ ያላ'ደፈ ፣ ጤእት
ያሠ'ራ ፣ ያልተበ'ከለ

immaterial
ኢመ'ቲሪየል -ቅ- አግባብ የሌ'ለው ፣ ከነገር
ው'ጭ የሆነ ፣ አስፈ'ላጊ ያልሆነ

immature
ኢመ'ቼወ -ቅ- ያልበ'ሰለ (ለሰው)

immediate
ኢ.'ሚይዲየት -ቅ- የአሁን ፣ በመካ'ከል ያል
ተጳ'ረጠ ፣ ወዲያው

immemorial
ኢመ'ሞ፡ሪየል -ቅ- የ'ማያስታ'ውሱት ፣ የጥ
ንት ፣ የቀድሞ (ጊዜ)

immense
ኢ.'ሜንስ -ቅ- ት'ልቅ ፣ በጣም ሰ'ፊ

immerse
ኢ.'መ፡ስ -ግ- መዝፈቅ [ዘ'ፈቀ] ፣ ማጥመቅ
[አጠ'መቀ]

immersion
ኢ.'መ፡ሽን -ስ- ዝፍቀት ፡ ጥምቀት

immigrate
'ኢ.መግሬይት -ስ- ለመኖር እንድ እገር ውስጥ
መግባት [ገ'ባ] (የራስን እገር ለ'ቆ)

immigration
ኢመግ'ሬይሽን -ስ- ፍልሰት ፣ እገር ለ'ቆ
መሄድ (በሌላ እገር ለመኖር)

imminent
'ኢ.መነንት -ቅ- በቅርብ ጊዜ የ'ሚሆን፡መሆኑ
የ'ማይቀር (በተለ'ይ ለአደጋ)

immobile
ኢ.'መውባይል -ቅ- የ'ማይንቀሳ'ቀስ ፣ እንድ
ቦታ ላይ የጸ'ና

immodest
ኢ.'ሞደስት -ቅ- ደ'ፋር ፣ ዓይን አውጣ

immoral
ኢ.'ሞረል -ቅ- ግብረ ገ'ብ'ነት የሌ'ለው ፣ ወ
'ራ'ዳ

immorality
ኢ.መ'ራለቲ -ስ- ግብረ ገ'ብ'ነት የሌ'ለው መ
ሆን

immortal
ኢ.'ሞ፡ተል -ቅ- ሕያው ፣ ዘላዓለም ነዋሪ

immovable
ኢ.'ሙ፡ቨበል -ቅ- የ'ማይንቀሳ'ቀስ ፣ እንድ
ቦታ ላይ ቀዋሚ የሆነ

immune
ኢ.ም'ፉ፡ን -ቅ- ም'ን'ም ነገር የ'ማይነካው
(በ'ሽታ)

imp
'ኢ.ምፕ -ስ- ት'ንሽ ሠይጣን (ብዙ የ'ማይ
ጉዳ) ፣ ቅልብልብ ልጅ

impact
'ኢ.ምፓክት -ስ- ግ'ጭት
influence
-ስ- ተጽእኖ

impair
ኢ.ም'ፔየ -ግ- ማድከም [አደ'ከመ] ፣ ዋጋ
መቀ'ነስ [ቀ'ነሰ] ፤ መጉዳት [ጉ'ዳ]

impart
ኢ.ም'ፓ፡ት -ግ- ማካፈል [አ'ካፈለ] ፣ መስ
ጠት [ሰ'ጠ] (ለምክር ፣ ለዕውቀት)

impartial
ኢ.ም'ፓ፡ሻል -ቅ- የ'ማይ'ጻ'ላ ፣ እንዱን ወገን
ከሌላው አብልጦ የ'ማያይ

impassable
ኤ.ም'ፓ፡ሰበል -ቅ- ሊ.'ሻ'ገሩት የ'ማይ'ቻል ፣
ሊ.ሄዱ'በት የ'ማይስችል (መንገድ ወዘተ)

impasse
'ኢ.ፓ፡ስ -ስ- መውጫ መንገድ የሌ'ለ'በት ቦታ፣
ሁናቴ

impatience
ኢ.'ፔይሽንስ -ስ- አለመ'ታገሥ ፣ መ'ቆጣት ፣
መ'ጣደ'ፍ

impeach
ኢ.ም'ፒ፡ች -ግ- መክሰስ [ከ'ሰሰ] (በታ'ላቅ
ወንጀል) ፣ የጥር'ጣሬ ጥ'ያቄ መጠየ'ቅ [ጠ'የቀ]
(ስለሰው ጠባይ ወዘተ)

impeccable
ኢ.ም'ፔስበል -ቅ- ስሕተት የሌ'ለ'በት ፣ ጉድ
ለት የ'ሌ'ለ'በት ፣ ንጺእት የ'ማይሠራ

impede
ኢ.ም'ፒ፡ድ -ግ- ማ'ደናቀፍ [አ'ደና'ቀፈ]
መከልከል [ከለ'ከለ]

impediment
ኢ.ም'ፔደመንት -ስ- እንቅፋት
speech
-ስ- ያ'ነጋገር ጉድለት (ም'ሳሌ ፣ መ'ን
ፈናፍ)

impending
ኢም'ፔንዲንግ -ቅ- በቅርብ ጊዜ ይሆናል
ተብሎ የ'ሚ.ያ'ሥ'ጋ

impenetrable
ኢም'ፔነትረበል -ቅ- ሊገቡበት የ'ማይ'ቻል
(ደ'ን ወዘተ)

impenitent
ኢም'ፔነተንት -ቅ- ን'ስሐ የ'ማይገባ ፣ የ'ማ
ያርመው

imperative
ኢም'ፔረቲቭ -ቅ- አ'ዛዥ ፣ ትእዛዝ ሰጪ.

imperceptible
ኢምፐ'ሴፕተበል -ቅ- ባይን የ'ማይ'ታይ

imperfect
ኢም'ፐ፡ፈክት -ቅ- ፍ'ጹም ያልሆነ ፣ ጉድለት
ያ'ለ'በት

imperial
ኢም'ፒሪየል -ቅ- ንጉሥ ነገሥታዊ

imperil
ኢም'ፔረል -ግ- አደጋ ላይ መጣል [ጣለ]

imperishable
ኢም'ፔረሽበል -ቅ- የ'ማይሞት ፣ የ'ማይጠፋ

impermeable
ኢም'ፐ፡ሚየበል -ቅ- ዝናብ የ'ማያስገ'ባ (የዝ
ናብ ልብስ ዓይነት)

impersonal
ኢም'ፐ፡ሰነል -ቅ- የ'ማያ'ዳ'ላ ፣ የተ'ለየ
ሰው'ን የ'ማይነካ

impersonate
ኢም'ፐ፡ሰኔይት -ግ- ሌላ ሰው መ'መሰል [ተ
መ'ሰለ] (ለማ'ታለል ወይን'ም ለቀልድ)

impertinence
ኢም'ፐ፡ቲነንስ -ስ- አስቸ'ጋሪ'ነት ፣ አ'ዋኪ.
'ነት (በንግ'ግር) ፣ ብልግ'ና

imperturbable
ኢምፐ'ተ፡በበል -ቅ- ለማ'ነ'ኛው'ም ነገር ደ
ን'ታ የሌ'ለው ፣ የ'ማይ'ጨነቅ

impervious
ኢም'ፐ፡ቪየስ -ቅ- ውሃ የ'ማይገባው

impetuous
ኢም'ፔትዩወስ -ቅ- ሳያ'ስብ በ'ጎይል የ'ሚ
ሠራ ፣ ች'ኩል ፤ በፍጥነት የታ'ሰበ ፣ የተሠ'ራ ፤
በ'ጎይል የ'ሚንቀሳ'ቀስ

impiety
ኢም'ፓየቲ -ስ- ሃይማኖት ተቃዋሚ'ነት ፣
ምግባረ ቢስ'ነት ፣ እግዚአብሔርን አለመፍ
ራት

implacable
ኢመፕ'ላከበል -ቅ- ሐ'ሳቡን የ'ማይለ'ውጥ፣
ች'ኮ ፣ መንቻ'ካ ፤ በጥላ'ቻ የተሞ'ላ

implement
'ኢምፕለመንት -ስ- መ'ሣሪያ

implicate
'ኢምፕለኬይት -ግ- አንድ ሰው የጥፋት ተካ
ፋይ መሆኑን ማሳ'የት [አሳ'የ]

implication
ኢምፕለ'ኬይሽን -ስ- እውነተ'ኛ ፍርድ ፣ ሌላ
ውን ጥፋተ'ኛ ማድረግ

implicit
ኢምፕ'ሊሲት -ቅ- ሳይ'ነገር የታ'ወቀ ፣ መጠ
'የቅ የ'ማያስፈ'ልገው

implore
ኢም'ፕ'ሎ፡ -ግ- መለ'መን [ለ'መነ] ፣ መ'ለማ
መጥ [ተለማ'መጠ]

imply
ኢም'ፕ'ላይ -ግ- ሐ'ሳብ ማቅረብ [አቀ'ረበ]

impolite
ኢም'ፕ'ላይት -ቅ- ያልተቀ'ጣ ፣ ያልታ'ረመ

import
ኢም'ፖ፡ት -ግ- ማስመ'ጣት [አስመ'ጣ] (ሸቀ
ጣ ሸቀጥ ከው'ጭ አገር)
'ኢምፖ፡ት -ስ- ጠቅላ'ላ ሐ'ሳብ ፣ ትርጉም

importance
ኢም'ፖ፡ተንስ -ስ- ዋጋ (ላንድ ነገር) ፣ አስፈ
'ላጊ'ነት

impose
ኢም'ፖወዝ -ግ- መሥፈን [ሠፈነ] (ቀረጥ ወዘተ)፣
ማስቀ'መጥ [አስቀ'መጠ] ፣ እንዲ'ቀ'በሉ ማስ
ገ'ደድ [አስገ'ደደ] (ሕ'ግን ወዘተ)

imposing
ኢም'ፖወዚንግ -ቅ- አስደ'ናቂ (በመጠኑ፣
በጠባዩ ፣ በመልኩ፣ ምክንያት)

imposition
ኢም'ፐ'ዚሽን -ስ- ጭነት (የቀረጥ)፣ በቅጣት
መልክ ለተጣገረ የ'ሚ'ሰጥ የቤት ሥራ ፣ የ'ማይ
'ገ'ባ ማስቸ'ገር

impossible
ኢም'ፖ'ሰበል -ቅ- የ'ማይ'ቻል

481

impostor
ኢም'ፖስት -ስ- ሌላውን መስሎ መ'ታየት
(ለማ'ታለል) ፣ ያልሆነውን ነ'ኝ እ'ያለ የ'ሚ
ያ'ታልል

impotence
'ኢምፐተንስ -ስ- ድካም ፣ አለመቻል

impoverish
ኢም'ፖቨሪሽ -ግ- ማደኸየት [አደኸ'የ]

impregnable
ኢምፕ'ሬግነበል -ቅ- መከራ የ'ማይበ'ገረው፣
መከራ የ'ማይፈታታው

impregnate
ኢምፕ'ሬግኔይት -ግ- ማስረ'ገዝ [አስረ'ገዘ]
soak
-ግ- ማጥለቅለቅ [አጠለቀ'ለቀ] (እፈ
ሳሽ ውስጥ)

impress
ኢምፕ'ሬስ -ግ- ማስደ'ነቅ [አስደ'ነቀ]፣ ስ'ሜ
ት መማረክ [ማ'ረከ]

impression
ኢምፕ'ሬሽን -ስ- ስ'ሜት ፣ ምል'ክት (የማ
ጎተም መዘተ)

impressionable
ኢምፕ'ሬሽነበል -ቅ- በቀ'ላሉ የ'ሚያምን

impressive
ኢምፕ'ሬሲቭ -ቅ- አስገ'ራሚ ፣ ስ'ሜት የ
ሚቀስ'ቅስ ፣ ስ'ሜት ማራኪ

imprint
'ኢምፕሪንት -ስ- ምል'ክት ፣ (የማጎተም መ
ዘተ)

imprison
ኢምፕ'ሪዘን -ግ- እሥር ቤት ማስገ'ባት [አስ
ገ'ባ]

imprisonment
ኢምፕ'ሪዘንመንት -ስ- መ'ታሠር ፣ እሥር
ቤት መግባት ፣ እሥር ቤት ውስጥ ያሳ'ለፉት
ጊዜ

improbable
ኢምፕ'ሮበበል -ቅ- የ'ሚያ'ጠራ'ጥር ፣ እው
ነት ሊሆን የ'ማይችል ፣ እውነት ሊ'ደ'ረግ የ'ማ
ይችል

impromptu
ኢምፕ'ሮምትዩ -ቅ- ያልተዘጋ'ጁ'በት ፣ በድ
ንገት ያደ'ረጉት ፣ ያሉት

improper
ኢምፕ'ሮፐ -ቅ- ሕ'ገ ወ'ጥ ፣ ባለጌ ፣ ሊ'ና'ገ
ሩት የ'ማይ'ገ'ባ

impropriety
ኢምፕረፕ'ራየቲ -ስ- ብልግ'ና ፣ ሊ.ሡሩት
የ'ማይ'ገ'ባ ሥራ

improve
ኢምፕ'ሩ:ቭ -ግ- ማ'ሻሻል [አ'ሻሻለ]

improvise
'ኢምፕረ'ቫይዝ -ግ- ድንገተ'ኛ አ'ጋጣሚን
እንደም'ንም መ'ወጣት [ተወ'ጣ]

imprudent
ኢምፕ'ሩ:ደንት -ቅ- ች'ኩል ፣ የ'ማያ'ስብ

impudence
'ኢምፕዩደንስ -ስ- ድፍረት (ሰውን ባለማ
 በር)

impulse
'ኢምፐልስ -ስ- ም'ኞት ፣ ፍ'ላጎት ፣ በል በ
የ'ሚል ስ'ሜት ፣ የ'ሚገፋ'ፋ ስ'ሜት

impulsive
ኢምፕ'ልሲቭ -ቅ- በስ'ሜት ብ'ቻ የ'ሚሠ

impunity
ኢም'ዩ:ነቲ -ስ- ከቅጣት ነጻ መሆን

impure
ኢምፕ'ዩወ -ቅ- ንጹሕ ያልሆነ ፣ ቆሻሻ ፣ የ
ደባ'ለቀ ፣ ውጥንቅጥ

impurity
ኢምፕ'ዩሪቲ -ስ- አለመጥራት ፣ ያ'ያፈ መሆን

in
'ኢን -መዋ- በ ... ውስጥ ፣ እ ... ውስጥ

inability
ኢነ'ቢላቲ -ቅ- አለመቻል

inaccessible
ኢነክ'ሴሰበል -ቅ- የ'ማይ'ደ'ረስ'በት ፣ የራቀ

innaccuracy
ኢ'ናክዩረሲ -ስ- ስሕተት ፣ የተነ'ቃቀ ጉደ
ለት

inaction
ኢ'ናክሽን -ስ- ሥራ አስ መሥረት ፣ ሥራ
መፍታት

nadequate
ኢ'ናዲክወት -ቅ- በቂ ያልሆነ ፣ ብቁ'ነት የለ
'ለው

inadmissible
ኢነድ'ሚሰበል -ቅ- የ'ማይ'ተ'በሉት

inadvertent
ኢነድ'ቨ፡ተንት -ቅ- ዝንጉ ፣ የ'ግይ'ጠነ'ተቅ ፣ ድንገተ'ኛ

inane
ኢ'ኔይን -ቅ- ጅል ፣ ጥ'ኝ

inanimate
ኢ'ናነመት -ቅ- ግዑዝ ፣ ሕይወት የሌ'ለው

inapplicable
ኢነፕ'ሊከበል -ቅ- እሥራ ላይ ሊውል የ'ማ ይችል

inappropriate
ኢነፕ'ረውፕሪየት -ቅ- የ'ማይስማ'ማ ፣ የ'ማ ይ'ገ'ባ

inarticulate
ኢና'ቲከዩለት -ቅ- በቀ'ላሉ መ'ናገር የ'ማ ይችል ፣ ግልጽ ሆኖ ያልተነ'ገረ ፣ ያ'ነጋገር እ'ስ ካክ የነ'ደለው

inattentive
ኢነ'ቴንቲቭ -ቅ- ሐ'ሳቡ የባ'ከነ ፣ ሐ'ሳብ ብኩን

inaudible
ኢ'ኖ፡ ደበል -ቅ- ሊ'ሰማ የ'ማይ'ቻል

inaugurate
ኢ'ኖ፡ግዩሬይት -ቅ- መ'ርቆ መክፈት [ክ'ፈተ] ግስተዋወቅ [አስተዋ'ወቀ] (አ'ዲስ መምህር ሹ'ም ወዘተ በስብሰባ ላይ)

inborn
ኢን'ቦ፡ን -ቅ- የተፈጥሮ ፣ ሲ'ወ'ለዱ አብሮ የተገ'ኘ (ጠባይ ወዘተ)

incalculable
ኢን'ካልከዩለበል -ቅ- ሊቆ'ጠር የ'ማይ'ቻል ፣ በጣም ብዙ

incandescent
ኢንካን'ዴሰንት -ቅ- በ'ግ ያለ ፣ የደ'መቀ ብር ሃን

incapable
ኢን'ኬይ፡ተበል -ቅ- የ'ማይ'ችል ፣ ችሎታ የሌ'ለው ፣ ደካማ

incense
'ኢንሴንስ -ስ- እጣን

incentive
ኢን'ሴንቲቭ -ቅ- አ'ነሣሽ (ሥራ እንዲሠሩ የ'ሚያደርግ)

---

inception
ኢን'ሴፕሽን -ስ- መጀ'መር ፣ መወ'ጠን

incessant
ኢን'ሴሰንት -ቅ- የ'ማያ'ቋርጥ ፣ ያልተ'ቋ'ረ ጠ ፣ ተ'ጣይ

inch
'ኢንች -ስ- ሁለ'ት ሳንቲሜትር ተ'ኩል (ለመ ለ'ኪያ)

incident
'ኢንሲደንት -ስ- ሁናቴ ፣ ድርጊ'ት

incidental
ኢንሲ'ዴንተል -ቅ- አብሮ ያ'ለ ገን ከፍረ ነገሩ ው'ጤ የሆነ ፣ ትንሽ'ና ዋጋ ቢስ የሆነ

incinerator
ኢን'ሲነሬይተ -ስ- ቄሻሻ ማ'ቃጠያ በርሜፈ (ከቆቆ'ር የተሠ'ራ)

incite
ኢን'ላይት -ግ- ማ'ደፋፈር [አ'ደፋ'ፈረ] ፣ መ ገፋፋት [ገፋ'ፋ] (አንድ ነገር እንዲያደርጉ)

inclement
ኢንክ'ሌመንት -ቅ- መጥፎ ፣ አስቸ'ጋሪ (አ' ር) ፤ ምሕረት የሌ'ለው

inclination
ኢንክሊ'ኔይሽን -ስ- ዝን'ባሌ

incline
ኢንክ'ላይን -ግ- ማዘንበል [አዘነ'በለ]

incline
'ኢንክላይን -ስ- ዘቅዛ'ቃ ቦታ

include
ኢንክ'ሉ፡ድ -ግ- መጨ'መር [ጨ'መረ]

inclusive
ኢንክ'ሉ፡ሲቭ -ቅ- አ'ጠቃላይ ፣ የ'ሚጨ'ም (ሁ'ሉን ነገር)

incoherent
ኢንክ'ሄረንት -ቅ- ያልተያያዘ (ለንግ'ግር)

income
'ኢንከም -ስ- ገቢ (ለገንዘብ)

incomparable
ኢን'ኮምፐረበል -ቅ- ተወዳዳሪ የሌ'ለው ተመሳሳይ የሌ'ለው

incompatibility
ኢንከምፓተ'ቢሊቲ -ስ- አለመስማማት

incompatible
ኢንከም'ፓተበል -ቅ- የ'ማይስማ'ማ

483

incompetence
ኢን'ኮምፒተንስ -ስ- የችሎታ ጉድለት ፤ የዕ
ውቀት ማነስ

incomplete
ኢንኮም'ፕሊይት -ቅ- ሙሉ ያልሆነ ፤ ጉድ
ለት ያለው

incomprehensible
ኢንኮምፕሪ'ሄንስበል ቅ- ሊ'ረዱት የ'ማይ
'ቻል ፤ የ'ማይገባ

inconceivable
ኢንከን'ሲይቨበል -ቅ- የ'ማይ'ታ'ሰብ

inconsiderate
ኢንከን'ሲደረት -ቅ- ለሌሎ'ች የ'ማያ'ስብ ፤
ይሎኝታ ቢስ

inconsistent
ኢንኮንሲስ'ተንት -ቅ- የ'ሚ'ለዋ'ወጥ (በሐ
ሳብ ወዘተ) ፤ አንድ መሥመር ወዘተ ተከ'ትሎ
የ'ማይሄድ ፤ ራሱን በራሱ የ'ሚ'ቃ'ወም

inconspicuous
ኢንኮንስ'ፒክዩወስ -ቅ- በቀ'ላሉ ጎልቶ የ'ማ
ይ'ለ'ይ ፤ አ.ምንት

inconvenience
ኢንከን'ቪይኔየንስ -ስ- ሃውከት ፤ ች'ግር ፤
አለመ'መቸት

incorporate
ኢን'ኮፐረይት -ግ- ማ'ዋሐድ [አ'ዋሐደ] ፤
በአንድ አካል ውስጥ ሌላ ነገር መጨ'መር
[ጨ'መረ]

incorrigible
ኢንኮሪጀበል -ቅ- የ'ማይታ'ረም

increase
ኢን'ሪይስ -ግ- መጨ'መር [ጨ'መረ] ፤ ማብ
ዛት [አበ'ዛ] ፤ ማተ'ለቅ [አተ'ለቀ]

incredible
ኢን'ሪደበል -ቅ- የ'ማይ'ታ'መን

incredulity
ኢንክሪድ'ዩለቲ -ስ- አለማመን ፤ ማመን አለ
መቻል

incriminate
ኢን'ሪመኔይት -ግ- ጥፋተ'ኛ ማድረግ [አደ
'ረገ] ፤ መወንጀል [ወነ'ጀለ]

incubate
'ኢንክዩቤይት -ግ- ዕንቁላል እንዲ'ፈለ'ፈል
እመፈልፈያ መኪና ውስጥ ማስቀ'መጥ [አስቀ
'መጠ] ፤ መፈልፈል [ፈለ'ፈለ] (ለዕንቁላል)

incur
ኢን'ክ፡ -ግ- ማምጣት [አመ'ጣ] (በራስ ላይ
ዕዳ ፤ መከራ ጥላ'ቻ ወዘተ)

incurable
ኢንክ'ዩረበል -ቅ- የ'ማይድን ፤ ፈውስ የሌ
'ለው (ለበ'ሽታ)

incursion
ኢን'ክ፡ሽን -ስ- ድንገተ'ኛ ወረራ ፤ ጉዋሚያ
(ለሥር'ነት)

indebted
ኢን'ዴተድ -ቅ- ባለውለታ ፤ ባለዕዳ (የገንዘብ)

indecent
ኢን'ዲይሰንት -ቅ- ባለጌ ፤ ነውረ'ኛ

indecision
ኢንዲ'ሲዠን -ስ- ው'ሳኔ መስጠት አለመቻል፤
ለመወ'ሰን ማመንታት

indecisive
ኢንዲ'ሳይሲ.ቭ -ቅ- ው'ሳኔ መስጠት የ'ማይ.
ችል ፤ ተጠራጣሪ

indeed
ኢን'ዲይድ -ተግ- በርግጥ

indefinite
ኢን'ዴፈኒት -ቅ- ያልተወ'ሰነ ፤ ጉልህ ያል
ሆነ ፤ እርግጠ'ኛ'ነቱ ያልታ'ወቀ

indelible
ኢን'ዴለበል -ቅ- ሊጠፋ የ'ማይችል ፤ ሊ'ፋቅ
የ'ማይ'ቻል

indemnity
ኢን'ዴምነቲ -ስ- ካሣ ፤ ዋስት'ና

indent
ኢን'ዴንት -ግ- አ'ዲስ አንቀጽ መጀ'መር
[ጀ'መረ]

independence
ኢንዲ'ፔንደንስ -ስ- ነጻ'ነት ፤ ራሱን መቻል
ከማ'ንም በታ'ች አለመሆን

indestructible
ኢንዲስት'ረክተበል -ቅ- የማይ'ደመ'ሰስ

indeterminate
ኢንዲ'ተ፡መነት -ቅ- ያልተወ'ሰነ ፤ ግልጽ ያል
ሆነ ፤ እርግጠ'ኛ ያልሆነ

index
'ኢንዴክስ -ስ- ያርእስት ማውጫ ፤ አመል
ካች

index-finger
'ኢንዴክስ'ፊንገ -ስ- ሌባ ጣት

484

indicate
ኢንዲኬይት -ግ- ማመልከት [አመለ'ከተ]

indication
ኢንዲኬይሸን -ስ- ምል'ክት ፣ ማመልከቻ

indicator
ኢንዲኬይተር -ስ- አመልካች ፣ አሳ'ይ

indict
ኢን'ዳይት -ግ- መ'ክሰስ [ተከ'ሰሰ]

indictment
ኢን'ዳይትመንት -ስ- ክ'ስ ፣ የክ'ስ ደብዳ'ቤ

indifference
ኢንዲፈረንስ -ስ- ግ'ዶ'ለሽ'ነት (ከማ'ነ'ኛ ው'ም ወገን አለመሆን)

indigenous
ኢንዲጄነስ -ቅ- ያንድ አገር ተወ'ላጅ ፣ አገሬ (ሕዝብ)

indigestion
ኢንዲ'ጀስቸን -ስ- የምግብ አለመንሸራሸር

indignant
ኢን'ዲግነንት -ቅ- ቁ'ጡ

indirect
ኢንዳ'ሬክት -ቅ- ቀ'ጥተ'ኛ ያልሆነ

indiscreet
ኢንዲስክ'ሪይት -ቅ- ምስጢር የ'ማይደ'ብቅ

indiscretion
ኢንዲስክ'ሬሸን -ስ- ምስጢር ማውጣት ፣ ምስጢር መደ'በቅ አለመቻል

indiscriminate
ኢንዲስክ'ሪመነት -ቅ- አለመለ'የት (ክፉ'ና ደ'ጉን)

indispensible
ኢንዲስ'ፔንስበል -ቅ- በጣም አስፈ'ላጊ ለ'ተው የ'ማይ'ቻል

indisposition
ኢንዲስፐ'ዚሸን -ስ- ሕመም (ቀ'ላል) ፣ ጥላ ች አለመሻት

indistinct
ኢንዲስ'ቲንክት -ቅ- ግልጽ ያልሆነ (ለዕ ' ለይ የ'ማይ'ቻል

individual
ኢንዲ'ቪጁወል -ስ- ሰው
-ቅ- የ'ያንዳንዱ

indofence
ኢንደለገንስ -ስ- ስንፍ'ና

indomitable
ኢንዶሚተብል -ቅ- የ'ማይ'ሸ'ነፍ ፣ የ'ማይ 'በ'ገር

indoor
'ኢንዶ፡ -ስ- የቤት ውስጥ ፣ እቤት ውስጥ ያ'ለ

induce
ኢንድ'ዩ፡ስ -ግ- ማሳ'መን [አሳ'መነ] (አንድ ነገር እንዲያደርግ)

inducement
ኢንድ'ዩ፡ስመንት -ስ- አንድ ነገር ለመሥ ራት መገፋፋት

indulge
ኢን'ደልጅ -ግ- አንድ ነገር ከመጠን በላይ ማድረግ [አደ'ረገ]

indulgence
ኢን'ደልጀንስ -ስ- የፈ'ለጉትን ማድረግ የ'ማይ'ወ'ይድ ተግባር በብዛት መፈ'ጸም
permission
-ስ- ፈቃድ

industrial
ኢን'ደስትሪየል -ቅ- የእንዱስትሪ

industrious
ኢን'ደስትሪየስ -ቅ- ትጉህ ው'ራተ'ኛ

industry
'ኢንደስትሪ -ስ- ሥራ ፣ ኢንዱስትሪ

inedible
ኢ'ኔደበል -ቅ- የ'ማይ'በ'ላ

ineffective
ኢ'ኔፈክቲቭ -ቅ- የ'ማይ'ሠራ ፣ የ'ማይረባ

inefficient
ኢ'ኔፊሸንት -ቅ- አጥጋቢ ያልሆነ (በሥ'ራ)

ineligible
ኢ'ኔለጀበል -ቅ- በቂ ችሎ'ታ የሌ'ለው (ለመ 'መረጥ)

inept
ኢ'ኔፕት -ቅ- እ'ጀ የተሳ'ሰረ ፣ ጉልደ'ፋ (እሥ'ራ ላይ) ፣ ሥራ የ'ማያልቅለ'ት ከፉ

inert
ኢ'ነ፡ት -ቅ- ለመሥራት ፣ ለመንቀሳቀስ ንቁ ል የሌ'ለው

inestimable
ኢ'ኔስቲመብል -ቅ- የ'ማይ'ገ'መት ፣ ዋጋው እ'ጅግ ከ'ፍ ያለ

485

inevitable
ኢ'ኔቪተበል -ቅ- የ'ማያመልጡት ፣ ግ'ዴታ
ያ'ለ'በት ፣ የ'ማይሽሽት

inexhaustible
ኢኔ'ዞ:ስተበል -ቅ- የ'ማያልቅ ፣ የ'ማያ'ጿ'ርጥ

inexplicable
ኢኔክስፕ'ሊከበል -ቅ- ሊ'ን'ለጽ የ'ማይ'ቻል

infallible
ኢን'ፋለበል -ቅ- እንከን የ'ሌለው ፣ ጎጢኣት
የ'ማይሠራ

infamous
'ኢንፈመስ -ቅ- በኃጢኣት የተበ'ከለ ፣ በጣም
ተንኮለ'ኛ ፣ ሐፍረተ ቢስ

infant
'ኢንፈንት -ስ- ሕፃን

infantile
'ኢንፈንታይል -ቅ- የሕፃን

infantry
'ኢንፈንትሪ -ስ- እግረ'ኛ ወታ'ደር

infatuated
ኢን'ፋትዩዌይተድ -ቅ- በ'ማይረባ ፍቅር አእ
ምሮውን ያ'ጣ

infatuation
ኢንፋትዩ'ዌይሽን -ስ- አእምሮ የ ሚያሳ'ጣ
ፍቅር

infect
ኢን'ፌክት -ግ- በ'ሽታ ማስያዝ (ለበ?ዘ) ፣
በ'ሽታ ማስተላለፍ [አስተላ'ለፈ]

infection
ኢን'ፌክሽን -ስ- በ'ሽታ መያዝ (የተላ'ለፈ)

infectious
ኢንፌክሽስ -ቅ- የ'ሚ'ተላ'ለፍ ፣ ተላላፊ
(በ'ሽታ)

infer
ኢን'ፈ: -ግ- ከመረ'መሩ በኋላ አስተያየት
መስጠት [ሰ'ጠ]

inferiority
ኢፌሪ'ዮረቲ -ስ- ዝ'ቅተ'ኛ'ነት

infernal
ኢን'ፈ:ናል -ቅ- ገሀ'ነማዊ ፣ ሰይጣናዊ

inferno
ኢን'ፈ:ነው -ስ- ገሀ'ነም ፣ አቶን

infest
ኢን'ፌስት -ግ- መውረር (ወ'ረረ) (ሠ:ጥ ፣
ትል ፣ ወዘተ)

infidel
'ኢንፊደል -ቅ- አረመኔ ፣ አላማኒ ፣ ጣኦት
አምላኪ

infiltrate
'ኢንፊልትሪየት -ግ- ቀስ በቀ'ስ እ'የገ'በ
መውረር (ወ'ረረ)

infinite
'ኢንፊነት -ቅ- መጨ'ረሻ የሌ'ለው

infinitive
ኢን'ፊነቲቭ -ስ- ንኡስ አንቀጽ (ሰዋሰው)

infinitesimal
ኢንፊነ'ቴሲመል -ቅ- በጣም ት'ንሽ ፣ ደ

infinity
ኢን'ፊነቲ -ስ- መጨ'ረሻ የሌ'ለው ጊዜ ፣ ቦ:
ወይ'ን'ም ቁጥር

infirm
ኢን'ፈ:ም -ቅ- ደካማ (በእርጅ'ና ምክንያት) ፣
አእምሮ ደካማ

infirmity
ኢን'ፈ:መ:ቲ -ስ- ደካም ፣ አለመጽናት

inflammable
ኢንፍ'ላመበል -ቅ- የ'ሚ'ቃ'ጠል (:
ወዘተ)

inflammation
ኢንፍለ'ሜይሽን -ስ- እብጠት ፣ እበጥ (የ'
ያ'ቃ'ጥል)

inflate
ኢንፍ'ሌይት -ግ- መንፋት [ነ'ፋ] ፣ በአ'
መሙላት [ሞ'ላ]

inflict
ኢንፍ'ሊክት -ግ- ክፉ ነገር እንዲደርስ ማ:
ረግ [አደ'ረገ] ፣ ማ'ሠቃየት [አ'ሠቃ'የ] (በ
ምታት ፣ በመቅጣት ወዘተ)

influence
'ኢንፍሉወንስ -ግ- ማግባባት [አግባ'ባ]
-ስ- አግባብ ፣ ተጽእኖ

influential
ኢንፍሉ'ዌንሻል -ቅ- አግባብ ያ'ለው ፣ ሥረ
ጣን ያ'ለው

influenza
ኢንፍሉ'ዌንዛ -ስ- ኢንፍሉዌንዛ ፣ ጉንፋን

486

influx
ኃእንፍለክስ -ግ- በብዛት መግባት [ገ'ባ] (እገ
ር ውስጥ)

inform
ኢን'ፎ:ም -ግ- ማስታወቅ [እስታ'ወቀ]፣ መን
ገር [ነ'ገረ]

informal
ኢን'ፎ:መል -ቅ- በይፋ ያልሆነ ፣ ሥርዓት ፣
ደምብ ያልተከ'ተለ ፣ መዝናናት ያለ'በት

informant
ኢን'ፎ:መንት -ስ- ተጠ'ያቂ ፣ አስረ'ጂ

information
ኢንፈ'ሜይሽን -ስ- ማስታወቂያ ፣ ወሬ ፣ ከሌላ
ሰው ያገ'ኙት ዕውቀት

informative
ኢን'ፎ:መቲቭ -ቅ- አስታዋቂ ፣ አስረ'ጂ

informer
ኢን'ፎ:መ -ስ- ሰ'ላይ (ለፖ'ሊስ የ'ሚነግር) ፣
ጠ'ቋሚ

infrequent
ኢንፍ'ሪይክወንት -ቅ- የ'ማያዘወ'ትር ፣ አል
ፎ አልፎ የ'ሚ ደ'ረግ

infringe
ኢንፍ'ሪንጅ -ግ- መጣስ [ጣሰ] (ሕ'ግ ፣ ውል፣
ደምብ)

infuriate
ኢንፍ'ዩሪዩሪት -ግ- ማ'ናደድ [አ'ና ደደ] ፣
ማስቆ'ጣት [አስ'ቆጣ]

ingenious
ኢን'ጂኒየስ -ቅ- ብልጎን ፣ በዋቂ (መ'ተላጠፈ
ያ በመሥ'ሪት)

ngenuity
ኢንጀን'ዩወቲ -ስ- ብልኀት ፣ ዕውቀት

ingot
'ኢንጎት -ስ- ወፍራም ወርቅ ወይን'ም ብረት
(የጠብ ቅርፅ ያ'ለው)

ingratitude
ኢንግ'ራትቱዩድ -ስ- ምስጋና ቢስ'ነት
ውለታ ቢስ'ነት

ingredient
ኢንግ'ሪይዲየንት -ስ- ምግብ ሲ'ሠ'ራ የ'ሚ
'ጨ'መር'በት ነገር ው'ለ

inhabitant
ኢን'ሀበ.ተንት -ስ- ያገር ነዋሪ

inhabit
ኢ.ን'ሀቢ.ት -ግ- መኖር [ኖረ] (ባንድ ቦታ ፣
ባንድ አገር)

inhale
ኢ.ን'ሄይል -ግ- አ'የር ወደ ውስጥ መሳብ [ሳበ]

inherent
ኢ.ን'ሂሪንት -ቅ- አብሮ የተፈ'ጠረ

inherit
ኢ.ን'ሄሪት -ግ- መውረስ [ወ'ረስ]

inhuman
ኢ.ህ'የ:መን -ቅ- ጨ.'ካኝ ፣ ከሰብአዊ ስ'ሜት
የተራ'ቆተ

inimitable
ኢ.'ኒመተበል -ቅ- አምሳ'ይ የሌ'ለው ፣ ል'ዩ

iniquity
ኢ.'ኒክወቲ -ስ- ኃጢአት ፣ በደል

initial
ኢ.'ኒሸል -ቅ- የመጀ'መሪያ
-ስ- የስም መጀ'መሪያ ፊደሎ'ች

initiate
ኢ.'ኒሸ.ዩዶ.ት -ግ- ሐ'ሳብ ማፍለቅ [አፈ'ለቀ]

initiation
ኢ.ኒሸ.'ዩዶ.ሽን -ስ- በማኅበራዊ ኑሮ ውስጥ
ተካፋዩ እንዲሆን ማግባት ፣ ሐሳ'ብ ማፍለቅ

initiative
ኢ.'ኒሸ.የቲ.ቭ -ስ- ሐሳ'ብ አፍላቂ'ነት

inject
ኢ.ን'ጀክት -ግ- መውጋት [ወ'ጋ] (መርፈ.)

injection
ኢ.ንጀክሽን -ስ- ትእዛዝ፣ የሰው መብት እንዳ
ይ.'ነ'ካ የ'ሚደ'ገግ የፍርድ'ቤት ትእዛዝ

injunction
ኢ.ን'ጀንክሽን -ስ- መርፈ. (መድኃ'ኒት)

injure
'ኢ.ንጀ -ግ- መጉዳት [ጎ'ዳ]

injury
'ኢ.ንጀሪ -ስ- ጉዳት ፣ ቁስል

injustice
ኢ.ን'ጆስቲ.ስ -ስ- አድልዎ (ለፍርድ)

ink
'ኢ.ንክ -ስ- ቀለም (መጻፊያ)

inkstand
'ኢ.ንክስታንድ -ስ- የቀለም ቢ.ልቃ.ጥ.
ለም ተንደ.

487

inland
'ኢን'ላንድ -ቅ- የአገር ውስጥ

inlet
'ኢንሌት -ስ- መፍሰሻ ፣ መሄጃ ፣ መግቢያ
(የውሃ ፣ የአ'የር)

inmate
'ኢንሜይት -ስ- ሆስፒታል ውስጥ የተ'ኛ ሕ
መም'ተ'ኛ (የአእምሮ)

inmost
'ኢንመውስት -ቅ- በጣም እውስጥ ያ'ለ
ጥልቅ

inn
'ኢን -ስ- ት'ንሽ ሆቴል ቤት

innate
ኢ'ኔይት -ቅ- አብሮ የተፈ'ጠረ ፣ በተፈጥሮ
ያ'ለ

inner
'ኢነ -ቅ- የውስጥ ፣ ማእከላይ

innermost
'ኢነመውስት -ቅ- ጥልቅ ፣ የውስጥ

innkeeper
'ኢንኪፐ -ስ- ባለት'ንሽ ሆቴል

innocence
'ኢነሰንስ -ስ- ንጽሕ'ና (ከጥፋት) ፣ ከደ'ሙ
ንጹሕ ፣ የማይነዳ

innumerable
ኢ'ኒ:መረበል -ቅ- የ'ማይ'ቆ'ጠር

innovate
'ኢነቬየት -ግ- አ'ዲስ ነገር መፍጠር [ፈ'ጠረ]፤
ለውጥ ማድረግ [አደ'ረገ]

inoculate
ኢ'ኖክዩሌይት -ግ- መርፈ መውጋት [ወ'ጋ]
(በ'ሽታ ለመ'ከላከል)

inoffensive
ኢ'ነፈንሲብ -ቅ- ክፉት የሌ'ለው ፣ የማይነዳ

inopportune
ኢኖፖት'ዩን -ቅ- የ'ማይስማ'ማ (ጊዜ)

inordinate
ኢ'ኖደነት -ቅ- የ'ሚያበዛ ፣ መጠን የ'ማየ
ውቅ ፣ መጠን የ'ለሽ

inquest
'ኢንክዌስት -ግ- ፍርድ ማ'ጣራት [አ'ጣ'ራ]
(በተለ'ይ የነፍስ ግ'ዳይ)

inquire
ኢ'ንክ'ዋየ -ግ- መጠ'የቅ [ጠ'የቀ]

inquiry
ኢ'ንክ'ዋሪ -ስ- ጥ'ያቄ ፣ ምርመራ

inquisitive
ኢ'ንክ'ዊዘቲብ -ቅ- ሁ'ሉን ለማወቅ የ'ሚ.ሻ ፣
ወሬ አ'ሳዳጅ

insane
ኢ.ን'ሴይን -ቅ- እብድ

insanity
* ኢ.ን'ሳነቲ -ስ- እብደት

insatiable
ኢ.ን'ሴይሸበል -ቅ- የ'ማይጠግብ ፣ በ'ቃ'ኝ
የ'ማይል

inscribe
ኢ.ንስክ'ራይብ -ግ- መጻፍ [ጻፈ] ፣ መቅረብ
[ቀ'ረበ] (ለጽሑፍ)

inscription
ኢ.ንስክ'ሪፕሽን -ስ- ጽሕፈት ፣ ጽሑፍ

insect
'ኢንሴክት -ስ- ተባይ

insecure
ኢ.ንስክ'ዩወ -ቅ- ያል'ረጋ ፣ አደጋ ያ'ለ'በት
ለሕይወት የ'ሚያ'ሰ'ጋ

insert
ኢ.ን'ሰ:ት -ግ- ማግባት [አገ'ባ] (ነገድ ነገ
እሌላው ውስጥ)

inset
'ኢንሴት -ግ- በተጨ'ማሪ ማግባት [አገ'ባ]
-ስ- በተጨ'ማሪ'ነት የገ'ባ ነገር

inside
ኢ.ን'ሳይድ -ተግ- በ ... ውስጥ

insidious
ኢ.ን'ሲዲየስ -ቅ- እየተጎ'ተተ የ'ሚገባ (ለሰፉ
ነገር) ፣ ለማጥፋት በድ'ብቅ የ'ሚሠራ

insight
'ኢንሳይት -ስ- ማስተዋል ፣ አስተዋይ'ነት ፣
ጠልቆ የመ'ረዳት ችሎታ

insignificant
ኢ.ንሲግ'ነፈክንት -ቅ- ዋጋ የሌ'ለው (ለነገር)

insinuate
ኢ.ን'ሲነዩዌይት -ግ- ተ'ጥተ'ኛ ባልሆነ መን
ገድ ሐሳ'ብ መግለጽ [ገ'ለጸ]

488

insinuation

ኢንሲነዩ'ዌይሽን -ስ- ሳይ'ና'ገሩ ሐ'ሳብ መግ ለጽ

insist

ኢን'ሲስት -ግ- ሐ'ሳብ አለመለ'ወጥ [-ለ'ወጠ]፡ አጥብቆ ማዘዝ [አ'ዘዘ]፡ መጠ'የቅ [ጠ'የቀ]

insolent

'ኢንሰለንት -ቅ- ተሳዳቢ፡ ደ'ፋር፡ ባለጌ

insolence

'ኢንሰለንስ -ስ- ብልግ'ና፡ ድፍረት

insoluble

ኢን'ሶልዩበል -ቅ- ፍ'ች የ'ማይ'ገ'ኝ'ለት

insolvent

ኢን'ሶልቨንት -ቅ- የከ'ሰረ፡ እዳውን መክ ፈል የ'ማይችል

insomnia

ኢን'ሶምኒየ -ስ- እንቅልፍ ማጣት

inspect

ኢንስ'ፔክት -ግ- ማየት [አ'የ]፡ መመርመር [መረ'መረ]

inspection

ኢንስ'ፔክሽን -ስ- ምርመራ፡ ጥን'ቃቄ ያ'ለ 'በት ቁጥ'ጥር

inspector

ኢንስ'ፔክተ -ስ- መርማሪ፡ ተቆጣጣሪ

inspiration

ኢንስፒ'ሬይሽን -ስ- መ'ነሣሻ ሐ'ሳብ፡ ድንገት የፈ'ለቀ ጥሩ ሐ'ሳብ

inspire

ኢንስ'ፓየ -ግ- ሐ'ሳብ መስጠት [ሰ'ጠ]፡ ማ'ነሣሣት [አ'ነሣ'ሣ]

instability

ኢንስተ'ቢለቲ -ስ- አለመ'ረጋጋት

install

ኢንስ'ቶ፡ል -ግ- መግጠም [ገ'ጠመ] (መ'ሣ ሪያ)

instalment

ኢንስ'ቶ፡ልመንት -ስ- ለገ'ዙት ዕቃ ዋጋውን በ'የጊዜው መክፈል

instance

'ኢንስተንስ -ስ- ሁኔታ፡ ም'ሳሌ (ለአንድ ነገር ማስረ'ጃ የ'ሚሆን)

instant

'ኢንስተንት -ስ- አ'ጭር ጊዜ
-ቅ- ወድያው የተደ'ረገ፡ የሆነ

instantaneous

ኢንስተን'ቴይኒየስ -ቅ- ወዲያውኑ የ'ሚሆን

instantly

'ኢንስተንትሊ -ተግ- አሁኑኑ፡ በፍጥነት

instead

ኢንስ'ቴድ -ተግ- በ . . . ፋንታ፡ በ . . . ምት'ክ

instep

'ኢንስቴፕ -ስ- የእግር ጉ'ብታ፡ የላይ'ኛው የግር ክፍል (በጣቶ'ች'ና በተረከዝ መሀል ያ'ለ)

instigate

'ኢንስቲጌይት -ግ- ማ'ነሣሣት [አ'ነሣ'ሣ]

instil

ኢንስ'ቲል -ግ- ቀስ በቀ'ስ ማስተማር [አስተማረ]፡ ማንጠባጠብ [አንጠባ'ጠበ]

instinct

'ኢንስቲንክት -ስ- በተፈጥሮ ስ'ሜት የ'ሚ'ሠ'ራ ሥራ፡ ደመ ነፍስ

institute

'ኢንስቲትዩ፡ት -ስ- የትምህርት ድር'ጅት

instruct

ኢንስት'ረክት -ግ- ማስተማር [አስተማረ]፡ ማሠልጠን [አሠለ'ጠነ]

order

-ግ- ማዘዝ [አ'ዘዘ]

instruction

ኢንስት'ረክሽን -ስ- ትምህርት

order

-ስ- ትእዛዝ

instructor

ኢንስት'ረክተ -ስ- አስተማሪ፡ አሠልጣኝ

instrument

'ኢንስትሩመንት -ስ- መ'ሣሪያ

insubordination

ኢንሰቦ፡ዶ'ኔይሽን -ስ- አለመ'ታዘዝ፡ እምቢ ተ'ኛ'ነት

insufficient

ኢንሰ'ፊሸንት -ቅ- የ'ማይበቃ፡ ያልተ'ሟላ

insular

'ኢንሹለ -ቅ- የደሴት፡ ደሴት መ'ሰል፡ የራ ሱን ጎሳብ'ቻ የ'ሚያስጠ'ጋ፡ አስተያየተ ጠባብ

insulate

’ኢንሹሌይት -ግ- ማ'ገድ [አ'ገደ] (ሙቀት ፡ ኤሌክትሪክ ወዘተ)

insulation

ኢንሹ'ሌይሽ -ስ- ማ'ገጃ (ሙቀት ፡ ኤሌክ ትሪክ ወዘተ)

insulator

’ኢንሹሌተር -ለ- ማ'ገጃ ፡ መ'ከላከያ መ'ሣ ሪያ (የሙቀት ፡ የድምፅ ወዘተ) ፡ የኤሌክትሪክ ሽቦ የ'ሚያልፍ'በት ሲኒ የመ'ሰል መ'ሣሪያ

insult

’ኢን'ሰለት -ግ- መስደብ [ሰ'ደበ] ፡ ማ'ዋረድ [አ'ዋ'ረደ]

insurance

ኢን'ሾ፡ረንስ -ስ- ዋስት'ና ፡ ኢንሹራንስ

insure

ኢን'ሾ፥ -ግ- ማ'ረጋገጥ [አ'ረጋ'ገጠ] ፤ ኢንሹ ራንስ መግባት [ገ'ባ]

insurgent

ኢን'ሰ፡ጀንት -ቅ- ሽ'ፍቾ ፡ ዐመፀ'ኛ (በመን ግሥት ላይ ወዘተ)

insurmountable

ኢንስ'ማውንተበል -ቅ- ሊ'ሸ'ነፍ የ'ማይ'ቻ ል ፡ የ'ማይ'ዞ'ለቅ

insurrection

ኢንሰ'ሬክሽን -ስ- ማ'መፅ ፡ የሕዝብ በመን ግሥት ላይ ብጥ'ብጥ ማንሣት

intact

ኢን'ታክት -ቅ- አደጋ ያልደ'ረሰ'በት ፡ ያል ተነ'ጻ ፡ ያልተነ'ካ

intake

’ኢንቴይክ -ስ- በተወ'ሰነ ጊዜ የ'ሚገባ የሰው፡ የተማሪ ወዘተ ብዛት

intangible

ኢን'ታንጀበል -ቅ- የ'ማይ'ጻ'ሰስ ፡ ገ዗ዝ ያልሆነ ፤ በግልጽ የ'ማይ'ረ'ዱት ፡ ደብዛ'ዛ

integral

’ኢንተግረል -ቅ- ዋ'ና ፡ እ'ጅግ አስፈ'ላጊ ፡ የ'ማይ'ነ'ጠል

integrity

ኢን'ቴግሪቲ -ስ- ቀ'ጥተ'ኛ'ነት ፡ ታ'ማኝ'ነት፡ ፍ'ጹም'ነት ፡ ሙሉ'ነት

intellect

’ኢንተሌክት -ስ- የአእምሮ ግስተዋል ችሎታ ፡ የማወቅ ችሎታ ፡ ብልሀ'ነት

intellectual

ኢንተ'ሌክቸወል -ቅ- በዋቂ ፡ ማእምር ፡ ምሁር

intelligence

ኢን'ቴሊጀንስ -ስ- ዕውቀት ፡ ል'ቡና

intelligible

ኢን'ቴለጀበል -ቅ- ሊ'ረ'ዱት የ'ሚ'ቻል

intemperance

ኢን'ቴምፐረንስ -ስ- ከመጠን በላይ የሆነ ነገር ፡ ከመጠን በላይ ማድረግ ፤ ስ'ካራም'ነት

intend

ኢን'ቴንድ -ግ- ማ'ሰብ [አ'ሰበ] ፡ ማ'ቀድ [ዐ'ቀደ]

intense

ኢን'ቴንስ -ቅ- ኃይለ'ኛ ፡ ከ'ባድ ፡ ጥልቅ (ለስ 'ሜት)

intent

ኢን'ቴንት -ስ- ዐቅድ

intention

ኢን'ቴንሽን -ስ- ሐ'ሳብ

intercede

ኢንተ'ሲይድ -ግ- ማ'ማለድ [አ'ማ'ለደ]

intercept

ኢንተ'ሴፕት -ግ- እፈ'ለጉት ቦታ እንዳይደ ርስ ማ'ስናከል [አ'ስና'ከለ] ፡ ማ'ገድ [አ'ገደ] (ሰው ፡ ደብዳ'ቤ ፡ ጠላት ወዘተ)

intercession

ኢንተ'ሴሽን -ስ- ማ'ማለድ ፡ ምልጃ

interchange

ኢንተ'ቼይንጅ -ግ- መለ'ዋወጥ [ተለ'ዋወጠ]

intercommunication

ኢንተኮምዩኒ'ኬይሽን -ስ- የእርስ በርስ ግን 'ኙ'ነት

intercourse

’ኢንተኩ፡ስ -ስ- እርስ በርስ መ'ገናኘት ፤ በፊ ቃደ ሥጋ ማወቅ

interdependent

ኢንተደ'ፔንደንት -ቅ- መ'ረዳዳት የ'ሚፈ 'ሊግ

interdict

ኢንተ'ዲክት -ስ- የማ'ገጃ ሕ'ግ

interest

’ኢንተረስት -ስ- ዝን'ባሌ

money

-ስ- ትርፍ ፡ አራጣ (በገንዘብ)

interesting
'ኢንተሪስቲንግ -ቅ- አስተያየት የሚስብ ፤
ቾ'ል የ'ማይሉት

interested
'ኢንተሪስተድ -ቅ- አስተያየቱን ወዳንድ ነገ
ር ያዘነ'በለ ፤ ዝን'ባሌ ያ'ለው

interfere
ኢንተ'ፈየ -ግ- ጣልቃ መግባት [ገ'ባ]

interference
ኢንተ'ፈረንስ -ስ- ጣልቃ ገ'ብ'ነት

interim
'ኢንተሪም -ቅ- ጊዜያዊ

interior
ኢን'ቲሪየ -ቅ- ውስጣዊ ፤ የውስጥ

interjection
ኢንተ'ጀክሽን -ስ- ቃለ አ'ጋ'ና (ሰዋሰው)

interlude
'ኢንተልዩ:ድ -ስ- በሁለ'ት ድርጊ'ቶ'ች መህ'
ከል አ'ጭር ጊዜ (የዕረፍት)

interlock
ኢንተ'ሎክ -ግ- ማ'ያያዝ [አ'ያያዘ]

intermarriage
ኢንተ'ማሪጅ -ስ- በል'ዩ ል'ዩ ጎሳዎ'ች መህ
'ከል የ'ሚ'ደ'ረግ ጋብቻ ፤ በቅርብ ዘመድ መህ
'ከል የ'ሚ'ደ'ረግ ጋብቻ

intermediate
ኢንተ'ሚይዲየት -ቅ- መካ'ከለ'ኛ ፤ ግዕከ
ላዋ፤በሁለ'ት ሁናቴዎ'ች መህ'ከል ያ'ለ ፤ የ'ሚ
'ፈ'ጸም ድር'ጊት

interment
ኢን'ተ:መንት -ስ- ሥርዓተ ቀብር

intermission
ኢንተ'ሚሽን -ስ- ት'ንሽ ዕረፍት

intermittent
ኢንተ'ሚተንት -ቅ- በ'የጊዜው የ'ሚያ'ቋ'ር
ጥ ወይን'ም እያ'ነሰ የ'ሚሄድ

intern
ኢን'ተ:ን -ግ- እሥር ቤት ማስገ'ባት [አስገ'ባ]

internal
ኢን'ተ:ነል -ቅ- ውስጣዊ

international
ኢንተ'ናሽነል -ቅ- ኢንተርናሲዮናል (ብዙ መ
ንግሥታትን የ'ሚ'መለ'ክት

internee
ኢንተ:'ኒ -ስ- ግዞተ'ኛ ፤ እሥረ'ኛ (ለጊዜው)

internment
ኢን'ተ:ንመንት -ስ- መ'ታሠር (ለጊዜው)

interpolate
ኢን'ተ:ፖሌይት -ግ- ምል'ከት ማድረግ [አደ
'ረገ] (በድርሰት ላይ አስተያየትን በመጨፍ)

interpret
ኢን'ተ:ፕሪት -ግ- መተርጐም [ተረ'ጐመ] ፤
'ፍ'ች መስጠት [ሰ'ጠ]

interpretation
ኢንተፕረ'ቴይሽን -ስ- ትርጉም ፤ ፍ'ች

interpreter
ኢን'ተ:ፕሪተ -ስ- አስተርጓሚ ፤ ትርጉማን

interrogate
ኢን'ቴረጌይት -ግ- መመርመር [መረ'መረ]
(ለፖሊስ ፤ ለዳ'ኛ ወዘተ)

interrogation
ኢንቴረ'ጌይሽን -ስ- ጥ'ያቄ

interrogative
ኢንተ'ሮገቲቭ -ቅ- መጠ'ይቅ

interrupt
ኢንተ'ረፕት -ግ- ማ'ቋረጥ [አ'ቋ'ረጠ]

interruption
ኢንተ'ረፕሽን -ስ- ማ'ቋረጥ

intersect
ኢንተ'ሴክት -ግ- ለሁለ'ት መከፈል [ከ'ፈለ]፤
መግሠስ [ገ'መሰ]

intersperse
ኢንተስ'ፐ:ስ -ግ- አልፎ አልፎ ማስቀ'መጥ
[አስቀ'መጠ]

interval
'ኢንተቨል -ስ- የዕረፍት ጊዜ (በሁለ'ት ድር
ጊ'ቶ'ች መህ'ከል) ፤ በሁለ'ት ነገሮ'ች መህ'ከል
ያ'ለ ክፍት ቦታ

intervene
ኢንተ'ቪይን -ግ- በመካ'ከል መግባት [ገ'ባ]
ጥ'ልቅ ማለት [አለ]

intervention
ኢንተ'ቬንሽን -ስ- ጣልቃ ገ'ብ'ነት

interview
'ኢንተቭዩ: -ስ- ጥ'ያቄ'ና መልስ

intestate
ኢን'ቴስቴይት -ቅ- ሳይ'ና'ዘዝ የሞተ

intestinal
ኢንቴስ'ታይነል -ት- የአንጀት ፣ የሆድቃ

intestine
ኢን'ቴስቲን -ስ- አንጀት

intimacy
'ኢንቲመሲ -ስ- የቅርብ ወዳጅ'ነት ፣ የግ'ል የሆነ ጉ'ዳይ

intimate
'ኢንቲመት -ት- የቅርብ ወዳጅ

intimation
ኢንቲ'ሜይሽን -ስ- ት'ንሽ ሐ'ሳፍ መስጠት ፣ ማስታወቅ

intimidate
ኢን'ቲሚዴይት -ግ- ማስፈራራት [አስፈራ'ራ]፣ መዛት [ዛተ]

intimidation
ኢንቲመ'ዴይሽን -ስ- ማስፈራራት ፣ ዛ'ቻ

into
'ኢንቱ -ተግ- ወደ ፣ ወደ ... ውስጥ

intolerable
ኢን'ቶለረበል -ት- የማይ'ታ'ገሡት

intolerance
ኢን'ቶለረንስ -ስ- አለመ'ታገሥ

intonation
ኢንተ'ኔይሽን -ስ- የድምፅ መውደቅ'ና መ'ነሣት (የንግ'ግር)

intoxicate
ኢን'ቶክሲኬይት -ግ- ማስከ'ር [አስ'ከረ]

intoxication
ኢንቶክሲ'ኬይሽን -ስ- ስካር

intoxicated
ኢን'ቶክሲኬይተድ -ት- የሰ'ከረ ፣ ስ'ካራም ፣ የጠ'ጣ

intransitive
ኢንት'ራንሲቲቭ -ት- የማይ'ሻ'ገር (ግ'ሥ ፣ ነዋሰው)

intrepid
ኢንት'ሬፒድ -ት- ደ'ፋር ፣ የማይፈራ

intricate
'ኢንትሪከት -ት- የተወሳ ሰዚ ፣ ግልጽ ያልሆነ

intrigue
'ኢንትሪግ -ግ- መደ'ለት [ደ'ለተ] ፣ ነገር መሥራት [ሠ'ራ]
-ስ- ዱ'ለታ

intrinsic
ኢንት'ሪንሲክ -ት- እውነተ'ኛ (ዋ.ጋ ወዘተ)

introduction
ኢንትረ'ደክሽን -ስ- መቅድም ፣ ማስተዋወቅ

introductory
ኢንትረ'ደክተሪ -ት- የመጀ'መሪያ ፣ አስተዋ ዋቂ

introspection
ኢንትረስ'ፔክሽን -ስ- ግ'ስላሳል ፣ ስ'ሜትን፣ ሐ'ሳብን መመርመር

intrude
ኢንት'ሩ.ድ -ግ- ጥ'ልቅ ማለት [አለ]

intrusion
ኢንት'ሩዠን -ስ- ጥ'ልቅ ማለት ፣ ግል.ቃ ጉ'ብ 'ነት

intuition
ኢንትዩ'ዊሽን -ስ- ብዙ ባለማ'ሰብ የተገ'ኘ ዕውቀት ፣ የተፈጥሮ ዕውቀት

inundate
'ኢነንዴይት -ግ- ማጥለቅለቅ [አጥለቀ'ለቀ]

inure
ኢን'ዩወ -ግ- ከእንግዳ ነገር ጋር መ'ለማመድ [ተለማ'መደ]

invade
ኢን'ቬይድ -ግ- መውረር [ወ'ረረ]

invalid
ኢን'ቫለ.ድ -ት- ዋ.ጋ ቢስ

invalid
'ኢንቫለ.ድ -ስ- ድ'ውይ ፣ አካለ ጉዳሎ ፣ አካለ ስንኩል

invaluable
ኢን'ቫልዩወበል -ት- ባለ ብዙ ዋ.ጋ ፣ ዋ.ጋው ሊ.'ገ'መት የማይ'ቻል

invariable
ኢን'ቬሪየበል -ት- የማይ'ለ'ወጥ

invasion
ኢን'ቬይዠን -ስ- ወረራ (ለመር'ነት)

invent
ኢን'ቬንት -ግ- አ'ዲስ ነገር ማውጣት [አወ 'ጣ] ፣ መፈልሰፍ [ፈለ'ሰፈ]

invention
ኢን'ቬንሽን -ስ- አ'ዲስ ነገር ወይን'ም ሐ'ሳብ ፣ አ'ዲስ የተ'ፈ'ራ; የተፈለ ስፈ ነገር

492

inventor

ኢን'ቬንተ -ስ- አ'ዲስ ነገር ወይን'ም ሐሳ'ብ ፈጣሪ

inventory

'ኢንሸንትሪ -ስ- የዕቃ ዝርዝር (የቤት ወዘተ)

inverse

'ኢንቨ:ስ -ት- ተቃራኒ ፤ የተገለ'በጠ (የውስጡ ወደ ው'ጭ)

invert

ኢን'ቨ:ት -ግ- መገልበጥ [ገለ'በጠ] (የውስጡን ወደ ው'ጭ)

invest

ኢን'ቬስት -ግ- ገንዘብ ግውጣት [አወ'ጣ] (ጥቅም ፤ ትርፍ ለ'ሚያመጣ ተግባር)

investigate

ኢን'ቬስትጌይት -ግ- መመርመር [መረ'መረ]

investigation

ኢንቬስተ'ጌይሸን -ስ- ምር'ምር

investigator

ኢን'ቬስቲጌይተ -ስ- መርማሪ

investment

ኢን'ቬስትመንት -ስ- እንግድ ላይ የዋለ ገን ዘብ

investor

ኢን'ቬስተ -ስ- ገንዘብ የሚያወጣ (ጥቅም ፤ ትርፍ ለ'ሚያመጣ ተግባር)

inveterate

ኢን'ቬተረት -ት- መሠረቱ የቆ'የ፤ ሥር የተ'ከለ (ልምድ ፤ አደ ልም ወዘተ) ፤ ች'ኮ ፤ ደረቅ

invidious

ኢን'ቪዲየስ -ት- መጥፎ ስ'ሜት ፤ ም'ቀ'ኝ ነት የ'ሚፈጥ'ርስ

invigilate

ኢን'ቪጂሌይት -ግ- ተፈ'ታኞች መጠ'በቅ [ጠ'በቀ] (ለመ'ቆጣጠር)

invigorating

ኢን'ቪገሬይ:ቲንግ -ት- የ'ሚያ'ነሣ'ግ ፤ የ'ሚ ያ'ነት'ታ

invincible

ኢን'ቪንሲበል -ት- የ'ግይ'ሸ'ነፍ

invisible

ኢን'ቪዘበል -ት- የ'ግይ'ታ'የ

invitation

ኢን'ቪ'ቴይሽን -ስ- ግብዣ

invite

ኢን'ቫይት -ግ- መጋበዝ [ጋ'በዘ]

invoice

'ኢንቮይስ -ስ- የዋጋ ዝርዝር

invoke

ኢን'ቮውክ -ግ- እርዳታ መጠ'የቅ [ጠ'የቀ] ፤ ምስ'ክር'ነት መጥራት [ጠ'ራ]

involuntary

ኢን'ቮለንትሪ -ት- ያለፈቃድ የሆነ ፤ ላይ'ታ 'ሰብ የሆነ

involve

ኢን'ቮልቭ -ግ- ማስገ'ባት [አስገ'ባ] (ጣን ድ ጉ'ዳይ ውስጥ)

invulnerable

ኢን'ቮልነረበል -ት- ጉዳት የ'ግይደርስ'በት

inward

'ኢንወድ -ት- ውስጣዊ

iodine

'አየዳይን -ስ- አዮዲን ፤ በት'ኩስ ቁስል ላይ የ'ሚፈ'ስ የ'ሚቆጣ'ቁጥ መድኃኒት

irate

አይ'ሬይት -ት- የተቆ'ጣ ፤ የተና'ደደ

iris

'አይሪስ -ስ- ያይን ብረት ፤ የአበባ ዓይነት (ቅጠሉ የሠይፍ ቅርጽ ያ'ለው)

irksome

'እ:ክሰም -ት- የ'ሚሰለ'ች ፤ ች'ኮ የ'ሚል ፤ አ'ዋኪ

iron

'አየን -ስ- ብረት

clothes-

-ስ- ካው'ያ

ironical

አ'ሮኒከል -ት- ውስጠ ፈዝ ያ'ለ'በት፤ፈዘ'ኛ፤ ም'ፀት ያ'ለ'በት (ንግ'ግር)

irony

'አረኒ -ስ- ውስጠ ፈዝ ንግ'ግር፤ ፈዝ፤ ም'ፀት

irrational

ኢ'ራሽነል -ት- ላይ'ታ'ሰብ የተሠ'ራ ፤ አስተ ካክሎ የማ'ሰብ ችሎታ የሌ'ለው ፤ በጣም ሞኝ

irreconcilable

ኢሬከን'ሳይለበል -ት- የ'ግይ'ታ'ረቅ ፤ የ'ግ ይስማ'ማ

493

irredeemable

ኢረ'ዲይመበል -ቅ- ሊያስተካ'ከሉት የ'ማይ
'ቻል ፤ ሊጠ'ገኑት የ'ማይ'ቻል

irregular

ኢ'ሬግዩላ -ቅ- ሕ'ገ ወ'ጥ ፤ ያልተስተካ'ከለ ፤
ከተለ'መደው ሥርዓት ው'ጭ የሆነ

irrelevant

ኢ'ሬለቨንት -ቅ- ከጉ'ዳዩ የራቀ ፤ አግባብ
የሌ'ለው

irreparable

ኢ'ሬፐረበል -ቅ- ሊ'ጠ'ገን የ'ማይ'ቻል

irrepressible

ኢሪፕ'ሬሰበል -ቅ- ሊ'ቆጣ'ጠሩት የ'ማይ'ቻ
ል ፤ ሊገቱት የ'ማይ'ቻል

irreproachable

ኢረፕ'ረውቸበል -ቅ- እንከን የሌ'ለው ፤ ጥ
ፋት የሌ'ለው

irresistible

ኢረ'ዚስተበል -ቅ- የ'ማይመ'ከቱት ፤ ስ'ሜ
ትን የ'ማያስገ'ታ ፤ ማራኪ

irresolute

ኢ'ሬዘለዩት -ቅ- አ'ወላዋይ ፤ ተጠራጣሪ

irresponsible

ኢረስ'ፖንሰበል -ቅ- ኃላፊ'ነት የ'ማይ'ሰ'ማ
ው ፤ አእምሮው ያልበ'ሰለ

irretrievable

ኢረት'ሪይቨበል -ቅ- ሊ'መ'ለስ የ'ማይ'ቻል፤
ሊ'ጠ'ገን የ'ማይ'ቻል

irreverent

ኢ'ሬቨረንት -ቅ- በሃይማኖት የ'ሚያፌዝ ፤ እን
ቋሻሽ

irrevocable

ኢ'ሬቭከበል -ቅ- የ'ማይ'ለ'ወጥ

irrigate

'ኢሪጌይት -ግ- በመስኖ ውሃ ማጠ'ጣት [አጠ
'ጣ] (አትክልት)

irrigation

ኢረ'ጌይሽን -ስ- የመስኖ ውሃ

irritable

'ኢሪተበል -ቅ- በቀ'ላሉ የ'ሚ'ና'ደድ

irritate

'ኢሪቴይት -ግ- ማስቆ'ጣት [አስቆ'ጣ] ፤ መተ
ንኳኩስ [ተነኳ'ኩስ] (ሰው'ነት)

irritation

ኢረ'ቴይሽን -ግ- ቁ'ጣ ፤ መብላት (ሰው'ነት
ለ'ሚያሳ'ክክ)

island

'እይለንድ -ስ- ደሴት

isle

'አይል -ስ- ደሴት

islet

'አይለት -ግ- ት'ንሽ ደሴት

isolate

'አይሰሌይት -ግ- ለ'ይቶ ማኖር [አኖረ]

isolation

አይሰ'ሌይሽን -ስ- ተለ'ይቶ መኖር ፤ ብ'ቸ'ኛ
'ነት

issue

'ኢሹ -ግ- መውጣት [ወ'ጣ] (ለፈሳሽ ወዘተ)፣
እ'ትም ማውጣት [አወ'ጣ] (መጽሔፍት ወዘተ)
-ስ- ልጅ ፤ ዘር ፤ እ'ትም

isthmus

'ኢስመስ -ስ- ል'ሳነ ምድር

it

'ኢት -ተስ- እርሱ ፤ እርሷ (ሰው ላልሆነ ፤ ለግ
ዑዝ ጸታ)

itch

'ኢች -ስ- መብላት (ሊያሳ'ክክ) ፣ እከክ

item

'አይተም -ስ- ከዝርዝር ጽሑፍ ውስጥ አንድ
ዕቃ

itinerary

ኢ'ቲነሪ -ስ- በጉዞ የጉብ'ኝት ዝግ'ጅት

its

'ኢትስ -ተስ- የርሱ ፤ የርሷ (ሰው ላልሆነ ፤
ለግዑዝ ጸታ)

itself

ኢት'ሴልፍ -ተስ- እራሱ ፤ እራሷ (ሰው ላል
ሆነ ፤ ለግዑዝ ጸታ)

ivory

'አይቨሪ -ስ- የዝሆን ጥርስ

J

jab
’ጃብ -ግ- መውጋት [ወ'ጋ] ፣ መጎ'ሰም [ጎ'ሰም]

jack
’ጃክ -ስ- ክሪከ ፣ የመኪና ጎ'ማ ማንሻ

jackal
’ጃኩ፧ል -ስ- ቀበር

jackass
’ጃካስ -ስ- አህ'ያ (ወንድ) ፤ ቂል

jacket
’ጃከት -ስ- ጉርድ ኮት

jack-knife
’ጃክናይፍ -ስ- ት'ልቅ ሰንጢ.

jade
’ጄይድ -ስ- አረንጓዴ ደንጊያ ፤ ጊ'ና

jaded
’ጄይደድ -ቅ- የደ'ከመው ፣ የዛለ

jag
’ጃግ -ስ- የሾለ ነገር ፤ ቡ'ጭቅ (የልብስ ወዘተ)

jail
’ጄይል -ስ- እሥር ቤት

jailer
’ጄይለ -ስ- እሥር ቤት ጠ'ባቂ

jam
’ጃም -ግ- መ'ታፈግ [ታ'ፈገ]
-ስ- ማርማላታ

janitor
’ጃኒተ -ስ- ቤት ጠራጊ ፣ ቤት ጠ'ባቂ ፣ በ'ረ'ኛ፣
ቤት ተከባካቢ

January
’ጃንዩወሪ -ስ- ጥር (የወር ስም)

Japan
ጄ'ፓን -ስ- ጃ'ፓን

jar
’ጃ: -ግ- መ'ጋጨት [ተጋ'ጨ]
-ስ- የዕቃ መያዣ (ከሽክላ ወይን'ም ከብ
ርጭ'ቆ የተሠ'ራ)

jaundice
’ጆንዲስ -ስ- የወፍ በ'ሽታ (ዓይን ብጫ የሚ
ያደርግ በ'ሽታ)

jaunt
’ጆ፡ንት -ስ- ሽ'ርሽ'ር

jaw
’ጆ: -ስ- መንጋጋ ፣ መንጋጫ'ላ

jealous
’ጄለስ -ቅ- ቀናተ'ኛ

jealousy
’ጄለሲ -ስ- ቅናት

jeer
’ጄየ -ግ- ማፈዝ [አፈዘ]

jelly
’ጄሊ -ስ- የረ'ጋ (ፈሳሽ) ፣ ዝልግልግ ነገር

jellyfish
’ጄሊፊሽ -ስ- ዝልግልግ ዐሣ

jemmy
’ጄሚ -ስ- የሥጥን መክፈቻ ብረት (በተለ'ያ
የሌባ'ች)

jeopardize
’ጄፓዳይዝ -ግ- አደጋ ላይ መጣል [ጣለ]

jeopardy
’ጄፓዲ -ስ- አደጋ

jerk
’ጀ:ክ -ስ- ድንገተ'ኛ እንቅስ'ቃሴ ፣ ብርጋ፣
ወዘተ

jerky
’ጀ:ኪ -ቅ- የሚያንገጫ'ግጭ ፣ ድንገተ'ኛ (ብር
ጋጋ)

jersey
’ጀ:ዚ -ስ- ሹ'ራብ (የጓላ)

jest
’ጄስት -ግ- መቀ'ለድ [ቀ'ለደ]

jet
’ጄት -ስ- ት'ንሽ ቀዳዳ ውሃ'ና አ'የር በጉይል
የ'ሚወ'ጣ'በት ፤ ጄት አውሮ'ፕላን
-ቅ- በጣም ጥቁር

jettison
’ጄቲሰን -ግ- መጣል [ጣለ] (ዕቃ ከመርከብ
ላይ ማዕበል ሲ'ነ'ሣ ለማቅለል)

jetty
’ጄቲ -ስ- የመርከብ መቆሚያ (በወደብ)

Jew
ጅ'ዩ: -ቅ- ይሁዲ

495

jewel

ጁ'ወል -ስ- ዕንቁ

jeweller

ጁ'ወለ -ስ- ዘጣጠፕ ነ'ጋዲ ፣ ዘጣጠፕ ሥራ ተ'ኛ

jewelry

ጁ'ወልሪ -ስ- ዘጣጠፕ

Jewish

ጁ'ዊሽ -ቅ- የአይሁዲ

jig

'ጂግ -ግ- መጨ'ፈር [ጨ'ፈረ]

jilt

'ጂልት -ግ- የጋብቻ ወል አለመፈ'ጸም [-ፈ'ጸመ] (ቃል ከ'ሠሩ በኋላ)

jingle

'ጂንገል -ግ- መንቃጨል [ተንቃ'ጨለ] -ስ- መንቃጨል

job

'ጆብ -ስ- ሥራ ፣ ተግባር

jocular

'ጆክዩለ -ቅ- ተሳዋች ፣ ተ'ላጅ

jog

'ጆግ -ግ- መሥገር [ሠ'ገረ] ፤ መነ'ሽም [ነ'ሸመ]

join

'ጆይን -ግ- ግ'ጋጠም [አ'ጋጠመ] (ሁለት ነገር'ች) ፤ ግገበረት'ኛ መሆን [ሆነ]

joiner

'ጆይነ -ስ- አናጢ

joinery

'ጆይነሪ -ስ- ያናጢ'ነት ሥራ

joint

'ጆይንት -ስ- መ'ጋጠሚያ ፣ እንን (የማት ፣ የእ'ጅ ወዘተ) ፣ ብ'ልት (የሥ'ጋ) -ቅ- የጋራ

jointly

'ጆይንትሊ -ተግ- ባንድ'ነት ፣ የጋር'ዮሽ

joist

'ጆይስት -ስ- ወጋግራ

joke

'ጆውክ -ስ- ቀልድ

joker

'ጆውከ -ቅ- ተሳዋች ፣ ተ'ላጅ

cards

-ስ- የተለ'የ የመ'ጫወቻ ካርታ ስም ፣ ጆከር

jolly

'ጆሊ -ቅ- ደስተ'ኛ

jolt

'ጆልት -ግ- መንዘፍዘፍ [ተንዘፈ'ዘፈ] -ስ- ድንገተ'ኛ እንቅስ'ቃሴ

jostle

'ጆስል -ግ- መ'ጋፋት [ተጋ'ፋ]

jot

'ጆት -ቅ- በጣም ትንሽ -ግ- ግስታውሻ ጽሑፍ መያዝ [ያዘ]

journal

'ጀ:ናል -ስ- በየተን የተፈ'ጸመ ሥራ ግስ ረ'ጂ ጽሑፍ

newspaper

-ስ- ጋዜጣ

journalism

'ጀ:ናሊዝም -ስ- ጋዜጣ የማ'ዘጋጀት ሞያ

journalist

'ጀ:ናሊስት -ስ- ጋዜጠ'ኛ

journey

'ጀ:ኒ -ስ- ጉዞ (ረ'ጅም)

jovial

'ጆውቪያል -ቅ- የተደ'ሰተ

jowl

'ጆወል -ስ- ወፍራም ጉንጭ (የተንጠለ'ጠለ)

joy

'ጆይ -ስ- ደስታ

joyful

'ጆይፉል -ቅ- ደስተ'ኛ

jubilant

'ጅዩቢለንት -ቅ- በጣም የተደ'ሰተ ፣ በደ'ስታ የፈነ'ደተ

jubilation

ጅዩቢ'ሌይሽን -ስ- ታላቅ ደስታ

jubilee

'ጅዩቢሊ -ስ- ኢ'ዮቤልዩ

judge

'ጀጅ -ግ- መዳኘት [ዳ'ኘ] -ስ- ዳኛ ፣ ፈራጅ

496

judgement
'ጀጅመንት -ስ- ፍርድ

judicial
ጁ'ዲሸል -ቅ- ሕ'ጋዊ

judicious
ጁ'ዲሸስ -ቅ- አ'መዛዛኝ ፡ ብልኀተ'ኛ ፡ ፍርድ ዐዋቂ

jug
'ጀግ -ስ- ማንቆርቆሪያ ፡ ማብረጃ

juggle
'ጀገል -ግ- እ'የወረ'ወሩ'ና እ'የቀ'ለቡ መ'ጫወት [ተጫ'ወተ]

juggler
'ጀግለ -ስ- እ'የወረ'ወረ'ና እ'የቀ'ለበ የ'ሚ'ጫ'ወት ሰው

juice
ጁ'ስ -ስ- ጭ'ማቂ (የፍሬ ወዘተ)

juicy
ጁ'ሲ -ቅ- ውኃ የሞ'ላ'በት (ፍሬ ወዘተ)

July
ጁቡ'ላይ -ስ- ሐምሌ

jumble
'ጀምበል -ግ- ያለ ሥርዓት መደበላለቅ [ደበ ላ'ለቀ]
-ስ- የተደበላ'ለቀ ነገር ፡ ዥርጓር ፡ ቅቤ የተጨ'መረ'በት አይብ

jump
'ጀምፕ -ግ- መዝለል [ዘ'ለለ]
-ስ- ዝ'ላይ

jumper
'ጀምፐ -ስ- ዘላይ
sweater
-ስ- ሹ'ራብ (የገላ)

junction
'ጀንክሽን -ስ- መ'ጋጠሚያ (የመንገድ ፡ የባቡር ሐዲድ)

juncture
'ጀንክቸ -ስ- መ'ጋጠሚያ ቦታ

June
ጁ፡ን -ስ- ሰኔ (የወር ስም)

jungle
'ጀንገል -ስ- ደ'ን

junior
ጁ'ንየ -ቅ- አነስተ'ኛ

junk
'ጀንክ -ስ- ው'ዳቂ ነገር ፡ ቆሻሻ ፡ የሲና'ች መርከብ

junket
'ጀንከት -ግ- በዐል ማድረግ [አደ'ረገ]

juror
'ጁረ -ስ- ዳ'ኛ

jury
'ጁሪ -ስ- ዳ'ኞ'ች

just
'ጀስት -ቅ- ል'ክ

justice
'ጀስቲስ -ስ- ትክ'ክለ'ኛ ፍርድ ፡ ቅን ፍርድ

jut
'ጀት -ግ- ወጣ ብሎ መ'ታየት [ታ'የ]

juvenile
ጁ፡ቨናይል -ቅ- ወ'ጣት ፡ የወ'ጣት ፡ የወ'ጣት'ነት ጠባይ ያ'ለው

juxtaposition
ጀክስተፐ'ዚሽን -ስ- ጎ'ን ለጎ'ን መ'ቀመጥ ወይን'ም ማስቀ'መጥ

K

keel
'ኪይል -ስ- መርከብ ሲ'ሠ'ራ እርስበርሱ የ'ሚያ'ያይዘው እንጨት ፡ ብረት

keen
'ኪይን -ቅ- በንቁ ያ'ሰበ'በት ፡ ኀይለ'ኛ (ነፋስ ወዘተ)

keenness
'ኪይነስ -ስ- በንቁ ማ'ሰብ

keep
'ኪይፕ -ግ- መጠ'በቅ [ጠ'በቀ]

keeper
'ኪይፐ -ስ- ጠ'ባቂ

keeping
'ኪይፒንግ -ስ- ጥበቃ

keepsake
'ኪይፕሴይክ -ስ- ማስታወሻ (የስጦታ ዕቃ)

keg
ኬግ -ስ- ት'ንሽ የንጨት በርሚል

kennel
ኬ:ነል -ስ- የው'ሻ ቤት

kerb
'ከ:ብ -ስ- የመንገድ ጠርፍ ፣ በመንገድ ዳር'ና ዳር ያ'ለ አገድም ጥርብ ደንጊያ

kerchief
'ከቺይፍ -ስ- የጠጉር ሻሽ

kernel
'ከነል -ስ- በፍራፍሬ ውስጥ የ'ሚገ'ኝ ጠን ካ'ራ ፍሬ (ም'ሳሌ ፣ የቶክ)

kettle
ኬተል -ስ- ጀበና

key
'ኪይ -ስ- ቁልፍ

keyhole
'ኪሆውል -ስ- የቁልፍ ቀዳዳ

keystone
'ኪስተውን -ስ- የማዕዘን ደንጊያ

kick
'ኪክ -ስ- መርገጥ [ረ'ገጠ] (በግር መምታት)

kid
'ኪድ -ስ- የፍ'የል ግልገል
child
-ስ- ት'ንሽ ልጅ

kidnap
'ኪድናፕ -ስ- ማፈን [አ'ፈነ] (ሰው ለመስ ረቅ)

kidnapper
'ኪድናፕ -ስ- አ'ፋኝ

kidney
'ኪድኒ -ስ- ኩላሊት

kill
'ኪል -ግ- መግደል [ገ'ደለ]

kiln
'ኪልን -ስ- የሸክላ መተኮሻ ምድ'ጃ

kilo
'ኪይለው -ስ- ኪሎ (መለ'ኪያ)

kin
'ኪን -ስ- ተወ'ላጅ (ዘመድ)

kind
'ካይንድ -ቅ- ርኅሩኅ
-ስ- ዓይነት

kindle
'ኪንደል -ግ- መለ'ኩስ ፣ [ለ'ኩስ]፣ማ'ቀጣጠል [አ'ቀጣ'ጠለ]

kindling
'ኪንድሊንግ -ስ- እሳት መለ'ኩሻ እንጨት

kindness
'ካይንድነስ -ስ- ርኅራኄ

kindred
'ኪንድረድ -ስ- ተ'ወላጅ ፣ ዘመድ

king
'ኪንግ -ስ- ንጉሥ

kingdom
'ኪንግደም -ስ- መንግሥት ፣ የንጉሥ ግዛት

kink
'ኪንክ -ስ- መ'ጣመም (የሽቦ ፣ የገመድ የጠጉር) ፣ መ'ቆጣጠር

kiosk
'ኪዮስክ -ስ- የተቃ'ቅን ዕቃዎ'ች መሸ'ጫ ት 'ንሽ ሱቅ ፣ ኪዮስክ

kiss
'ኪስ -ግ- መሳም [ሳመ]
-ስ- መሳም

kit
'ኪት -ስ- መ'ሣሪያ (የአንድ የእ'ጅ ሥ'ራተ'ኛ ፣ የጉዞ ዕቃ (የው'ታ'ደር ወዘተ)

kitbag
'ኪትባግ -ስ- ማሲኖዳ

kitchen
'ኪቸን -ስ- ወጥ ቤት ፣ ማድቤት

kite
'ካይት -ስ- ጥልፈ'ት ፣ ውልብልቢት (መ'ጫ ወኛ)

kitten
'ኪተን -ስ- ት'ንሽ ድ'መት

knack
'ናክ -ስ- ል'ዩ ችሎታ ፣ ጥያ

knapsack
'ናፕሳክ -ስ- ስ'ል'ቻ (በጀርባ የ'ሚ'ሸ'ከሙ-ት)

498

knave

ኔይቭ -ስ- የ'ማይ'ታ'መን ሰው ፣ ወ'ራ'ዳ ሰው
    cards
    -ስ- ወለድ (በካርታ ጨዋታ)

knead

ኒይድ -ግ- ማቡካት [አቦ'ካ]

kneading trough

ኒይዲንግ ት'ሮፍ -ስ- ገበታ ፣ ማቡኪያ

knee

ኒይ -ስ- ጉልበት

kneecap

ኒይካፕ -ስ- ሱሚ (የጉልበት)

kneel

ኒይል -ግ- መንበርከክ [ተንበረ'ከከ]

knell

ኔል -ስ- በቀብር ጊዜ የ'ሚ'ሰ'ማ የመሬዓ
    ድምፅ

knick-knack

ኒክናክ -ስ- ተራ ጌጣ ጌጥ

knife

ናይፍ -ስ- ቢ'ላዋ ፣ ካ'ራ

knight

ናይት -ስ- ማዕረግ ያ'ለው ሰው

knit

ኒት -ግ- ሹ'ራብ መሥራት [ሠ'ራ]

knitting

ኒቲንግ -ስ- የሹ'ራብ ሥራ

knob

ኖብ -ስ- ት'ንሽ ክ'ብ ነገር ፣ የመዝጊያ መክ
    ፈቻ መያዣ

knock

ኖክ -ግ- ማንኳካት [አንኳ'ኳ]

knocker

ኖክ -ስ- በ'ር የ'ሚያንኳ'ኳ

knockout

ኖካውት -ስ- ተጋጣሚን ከጨዋታ የ'ሚያስ
    ወ'ጣው በ'ትሩ (በቦክስ ጨዋታ) ፣ የተሉ ማላፍ
    ጨዋታ (በስፖርት)

knot

ኖት -ስ- ቄጥር (የገመድ ወዘተ)

know

ኖው -ግ- ማወቅ [ዐ'ወቀ]

knowledge

ኖለጅ -ስ- ዕውቀት ፣ ማወቅ

knowledgeable

ኖለጅበል -ቅ- ዐዋቂ

knuckle

ነከል -ስ- የጣቶ'ች መ'ጋጠሚያ (ለእ'ጅ)

label

ሌይብል -ስ- ምል'ክት (በጠርሙስ ወዘተ)

laboratory

ለ'ቦረትሪ -ስ- ላቦረተሪ

laborious

ለ'ቦ:ሪየስ -ቅ- ለመሥራት የ'ሚያስቸ'ግር

labour

ሌይብ -ስ- ሥራ
    childbirth
    -ስ- ምጥ

labourer

ሌይብረ -ስ- ሠ'ራተ'ኛ ፣ የቀን ሞያተ'ኛ

lace

ሌይስ -ስ- ጥልፍ ሥራ፣ሲ.ር'የጭ'ማ ማሠርያ

lacerated

ላሰራይተድ -ቅ- የተበጣ'ጠሰ (ለሰው'ነት)

lack

ላክ -ስ- እጦት

lacquer

ላከ -ስ- ቀለም (ወፍ;ራ'ም)

lactic

ላክቲክ -ቅ- የወተት

lad

ላድ -ስ- ወንድ ልጅ ፣ ጉብል

ladder

ላደ -ስ- መሰላል

ladle

ሌይደል -ስ- ጭልፋ

lady

’ሌዲ -ስ- ወይዘር

lag

’ላግ -ግ- ወደኃላ መትረት [ተ'ረ]
-ስ- መዘግየት

lair

’ሌየ -ስ- ጎሬ (የእውሬ)

laity

’ሌይቲ -ስ- ተራ ሕዝብ ፣ መያ'ይምናን

lake

’ሌይክ -ስ- ሐይት

lamb

’ላም -ስ- ጠ'ቦት ፣ ጥ'ቦት

lame

’ሌይም -ቅ- የሰ'ለለ (ለእንጐር) ፣ ሽባ

lament

ለ’ሜንት -ግ- ወ'ዮ ግለት [አለ]

lamentable

’ላመንተብል -ቅ- የ'ሚያሳ'ዝን

lamentation

ላመን’ቴይሸን -ስ- ስቆታው ፣ ወ'ዮታ

lamp

’ላምፕ -ስ- ፋኖስ ፣ እም'ፑል

lampblack

’ላምፕብላክ -ስ- ጥቀርሻ

lamp-post

’ላምፕውስት -ስ- የመብራት እንጨት (ኤሌ
ክትሪክ)

lamp-shade

’ላምፕሼይድ -ስ- የእምፑል ሽፋን

lance

’ላንስ -ስ- ጦር

land

’ላንድ -ስ- መሬት ፣ አገር
-ግ- ግረፍ [ዐ'ረፈ] (ለአውሮ'ፕላን ወ
ዘተ)

landing

’ላንዲንግ -ስ- ግረፍ ፣ ግሳ'ረፍ ፣ የእውሮ'ፕ
ላን ግረሪያ'ና መ'ነሻ ቦታ ፣ በቤት ደረጃ መከ
ክል የ'ሚ'ገ'ኝ ጠፍጣ'ፋ ቦታ ፣ ደረጃ ካስ'ተ
በጓል እስ'ሩ እጠገብ የ'ሚ'ገ'ገ'ኘው ጠፍጣ'ፋ
ቦታ

landlady

’ላንድሌይዲ -ስ- የቤት ባለቤት ፣ ቤት አ'ከ
ራይ (ሴት)

landlord

’ላንድሉ'ድ -ስ- የቤት ባለቤት ፣ ቤት አ'ከራይ
(ወንድ)

landmark

’ላንድግ'ክ -ስ- ያገር ምል'ክት ፣ የመሬት
ወሰን መለ'ያ ምል'ክት

landowner

’ላንደውን -ስ- ባለመሬት ፣ ባለርስት

landscape

’ላንድስኬይፕ -ስ- ያገር አ'ከባቢ

landslide

’ላንድስላይድ -ስ- ናዳ

lane

’ሌይን -ስ- ጠ'ባብ መንገድ ፣ ስርጥ መንገድ

language

’ላንጓጅ -ስ- ቋንቋ

languid

’ላንጓዊድ -ቅ- የዛለ ፣ ደካግ ፣ ፈዛዛ

languish

’ላንጓሺ -ግ- መናዘዝ [ፈ'ዘዘ] ፣ መደከም
[ደ'ከመ] ፣ መዛል [ዛለ]

languor

’ላንገ -ስ- ድካም ፣ መዛል ፣ መናዘዝ

lanky

’ላንኪ -ቅ- ተ'ዋን'ና ረ'ጅም ፣ ስላላ መላላ ፣
መንገ'ና

lantern

’ላንተን -ስ- ፋኖስ

lap

’ላፕ -ስ- ጭን
-ግ- መላከለክ [ለከ'ለከ] (ለመጠ ጥ)

lapel

ለ’ፔል -ስ- የኮት የደረት ታ'ግራ (ከእንገተገው
ጋር የ'ሚ'ያያዝ)

lapse

’ላፕስ -ግ- ተስ በተ'ስ እየተረ'ሳ መሄድ
[ሄደ] (ለሕ'ግ ፣ ለባህል)
-ስ- ተስ በተ'ስ እ'የተ'ረ መሄድ ፣ (ለሕ
'ግ ለባህል) ፣ በንግ'ግር ት'ንሽ ስ‌ተ‌ተ

larceny

’ላ:ስኒ -ስ- ስርቆት (ለጥ‌ቃ'ቶን ነገር)

500

lard
’ላ:ድ -ስ- ያማግ ስብ

larder
’ላ:ዶ -ስ- ጓዳ (የምግብ ማስተ'ማጫ)

large
’ላ:ጅ -ት- ሰ'ፊ ፣ ት'ልቅ

largely
’ላ:ጅሊ -ተግ- በብዛት ፣ ይበልጡን

lark
’ላ:ክ -ግ- መ'ቃለድ [ተቃ'ለደ]

larva
’ላ:ቫ -ስ- ትል (ወዲያው እንደተፈለ'ፈለ) ፣
እጭ

larynx
’ላሪንክስ -ስ- ግንቁርት

lash
’ላሽ -ግ- መግረፍ [ገ'ረፈ]

lass
’ላስ -ስ- ልጃገረድ ፣ የከንፈር ወዳጅ

lassitude
’ላሲትዩ:ድ -ስ- ድካም ፣ መታከት

last
’ላ:ስት -ግ- መቆ'የት [ቆ'የ]
final
-ት- መጨ'ረሻ

lasting
’ላ:ስቲንግ -ት- የ'ሚቆ'ይ ፣ ነዋሪ ፣ ዕድሜ
ያ'ለው

lastly
’ላ:ስትሊ -ተግ- በመጨ'ረሻ

latch
’ላች -ስ- መወርወርያ ፣ መቀተቀርያ (የበ'ር ፣
የመስኮት)

late
’ሌይት -ት- የዘገ'የ ፣ ከጥቂት ጊዜ በፊት የነ
'በረ ፣ ያ'ረፈ (የሞተ)

lately
’ሌይትሊ -ተግ- ከጥቂት ጊዜ በፊት ፣ በቅርብ
ጊዜ

latent
’ሌይተንት -ት- የተደ'በቀ ፣ የ'ግይሠራ ፣
የ'ግይነተሳ'ተሰ

lateral
’ላተረል -ት- የጐ'ን ፣ በስተጐን'ን ያ'ለ ፣ ከጐ'ን
ያ'ለ

latest
’ሌይተስት -ት- አ'ዲስ ፣ ዘመናዊ

lath
’ላስ -ስ- ሳንቃ

lather
’ላዠ -ስ- አረፋ ፣ ኮረፋ

latitude
’ላቲትዩ:ድ -ስ- ነጻ'ነት (የሐሳ'ብ መዘተ) ፣ ኬን
ትርስ (መልክዐ ምድር)

latrine
ለት'ሪይን -ስ- (የተቆ'ፈረ የሰገ- ጉድጓድ)

latter
’ላተ -ት- የኋለ'ኛ ፣ የአሁን (ጊዜ) ፣ በመጨ
'ረሻ የተጠ'ቀሰ መዘተ

latterly
’ላተሊ -ተግ- በቅርብ ጊዜ ፣ በአሁኑ ዘመን

lattice
’ላቲስ -ስ- እንደ ወገራት የተሠ'ራ የሽቦ ፣
የእንጨት አጥር

laud
’ሉ:ድ -ግ- ግመስገን [አመሰ'ገነ]

laudible
’ሉ:ደበል -ት- የ'ሚመሰ'ገን ፣ ምስጋና የ'ሚ
'ገ'በው

laugh
’ላ:ፍ -ግ- መሣቅ [ሣቀ]

laughable
’ላ:ፈበል -ት- የ'ሚያ'ሥቅ

laughter
’ላፍተ -ስ- ሣቅ

launch
’ሉ:ንች -ስ- ት'ንሽ በሞተር የ'ሚነ'ዳ ጀልባ
-ግ- እንደንተሳ'ተስ ግድረን [አደ'ረገ] ፣
መጀ'መር [ጀ'መረ]

laundress
’ሉ:ንድረስ -ስ- ልብስ አጣቢ ሴት

laundry
’ሉ:ንድሪ -ስ- የልብስ ግጠቢያ ቦታ ፣ የልብስ
ንጹሕ'ና መስጫ

lavatory
’ላቨትሪ -ስ- የንጽሕ'ና ቦታ ፣ ሽንት ቤት

501

lavish
'ላቪሽ -ግ- በብዙ መስጠት [ስ'ጠ] ፣ ማባከን
[አባ'ከነ]

law
'ሎ: -ስ- ሕ'ግ

law-court
'ሎ:'ኮ:ት -ስ- ፍርድ ቤት

lawful
'ሎ:ፉል -ቅ- ሕ'ጋዊ

lawn
'ሎ:ን -ስ- መስክ ፣ ጨ'ፌ

lawsuit
'ሎ:ሱት -ስ- ክ'ስ

lawyer
'ሎ:የ -ስ- ጠበቃ (ሕ'ግ የተማሪ)

lax
'ላክስ -ቅ- ልል (ለሕ'ግ)

laxative
'ላክሰቲቭ -ስ- የ'ሚያስቀ'ምጥ መድኃኒት ፣
ሆድ የ'ሚያዳ'ላ መድኃኒት ፣ የሆድ ድርቀት
የ'ሚያስ'ወግድ መድኃኒት

lay
'ሌይ -ግ- ማ'ጋደም [አ'ጋደመ] ፣ መጣል
[ጣለ] (ለዕንቁላል)

layer
'ሌየ -ስ- ውፍረት (የዝርግ ነገር) ፣ መሥ
መር (በጡጥ'ኝ ወዘተ) ፣ እሻል (ለመሬት)

layman
'ሌይመን -ስ- ተራ ሰው (ከህነት የሌ'ለው) ፣
መያ'ይምን

laze
'ሌይዝ -ግ- ጊዜን በከንቱ ማሳ'ለፍ [አሳ'ለፈ]፣
ማውደልደል [አውደል'ደለ]

laziness
'ሌይዚነስ -ስ- ስንፍ'ና

lazy
'ሌይዚ -ቅ- ሰነፍ

lead
'ሌድ -ስ- እርሳስ (ማዕ'ድን)

lead
'ሊይድ -ግ- መምራት [መ'ራ]

leader
'ሊይደ -ስ- መሪ

leading
'ሊይዲንግ -ስ- መሪ ፣ ዋ'ና

leaf
'ሊይፍ -ስ- ቅጠል

leaflet
'ሊይፍለት -ስ- ት'ንሽ ጽሑፍ

league
'ሊይግ -ስ- ማኅበር

leak
'ሊይክ -ግ- ማንጠብጠብ [አንጠብ'ጠበ] (ው
ሃ) ፣ መስረቅ [ስ'ረቀ] (ለውሃ)

leakage
'ሊይከጅ -ስ- ቀዳዳ ፣ ሽንቁር (ውሃ የ'ሚያ
ፈ'ስ ፣ የ'ሚሰርቅ)

leaky
'ሊይኪ -ቅ- የ'ሚያንጠብ'ጥብ ፣ የ'ሚያፈ'ስ፣
የ'ሚሰርቅ (ውሃ)

lean
'ሊይን -ግ- መ'ደገፍ [ተደ'ገፈ]
not fat
-ቅ- ቀ'ጭን ፣ ያልስ'ባ

leap
'ሊይፕ -ግ- መዝለል [ዘ'ለለ]

learn
'ለ:ን -ግ- መ'ማር [ተማረ] ፣ ማወቅ [ዐ'ወቀ]

learned
'ለ:ነደ -ቅ- የተማረ ፣ ዐዋቂ

learner
'ለ:ነ -ስ- ተማሪ

learning
'ለ:ኒንግ -ስ- ትምህርት

lease
'ሊይስ -ግ- ቤት ወይን'ም መሬት ለረ'ጅም
ጊዜ ማ'ከራየት [አ'ከራ'የ]

leaseholder
'ሊይስሀውልደ -ስ- ቤት ወይን'ም መሬት
ለተወ'ሰነ ጊዜ የተከራ'የ

leash
'ሊይሽ -ስ- ማሠሪያ (ጠፍር ፣ ስንስለት ፣ ለ
ው'ሻ)

least
'ሊይስት -ቅ- የመጨ'ረሻ ፣ ያነሰ

leather
'ሌዘ -ስ- ቆዳ

502

leave
'ሊይቭ -ግ- መተው [ተወ] ፤ መሄድ [ሄደ]

leaven
'ሌቨን -ስ- እርሾ

leavings
'ሊይቪንግዝ -ስ- ፍር'ፋሪ ፤ ትርፍራፊ

lecherous
'ሌቸረስ -ቅ- ቅንዝረ'ኛ ፤ ሴሰ'ኛ

lecture
'ሌክቸ -ስ- ንግ'ግር ፤ ትምህርት (ለብዙ ሰው፤
ተግሪ የ'ሚ'ደ'ረግ ፤ የሚነገር)

lecturer
'ሌክቸረ -ስ- ተናጋሪ ፤ አስተማሪ

ledger
'ሌጀ -ስ- የሒሳብ መያዣ መዝገብ

leech
'ሊይች -ስ- አልቅ'ት

leer
'ሊየ -ግ- በፌቃደ ሥጋ አስተያየት መ'መል
ከት [ተመለ'ከተ] ፤ በከፉ አስተያየት ማየት
[አ'የ]

left
'ሌፍት -ቅ- ግራ (አቅጣ'ጫ) ፤ የተተወ

left-handed
ሌፍት'ሀንደድ -ቅ- ግራ'ኛ (በግራ እ'ጁ መሥ
ራት የ'ሚቀናው)

leg
'ሌግ -ስ- ባት ፤ ቅልጥም

legacy
'ሌገሲ -ስ- ቅርስ ፤ ውርስ (በኑዛዜ የተገ'ኘ)

legal
'ሊይገል -ቅ- ሕ'ጋዊ

legality
ሊ'ጋለቲ -ስ- ሕ'ጋዊነት

legalize
'ሊይገላይዝ -ግ- ሕ'ጋዊ ማድረግ [አደ'ረገ]

legate
'ሌገት -ስ- መልእክተ'ኛ (የሮማው ፓ'ፓ)

legation
ለ'ጌይሸን -ስ- ሌጋሲዮን

legend
'ሌጀንድ -ስ- አፈ ታሪክ

leggings
'ሊጊንግዝ -ስ- ገምባ'ሌ

legibility
ሌጀ'ቢሊቲ -ስ- ለመ'ነበብ መ'ቻል

legible
'ሌጀበል -ቅ- የ'ሚ'ነ'በብ

legion
'ሊይጀን -ስ- የጦር ሠራዊት ክፍል ፤ ማኅበር፤
እልቆ መሣፍርት የሌ'ለው ሰው

legislate
'ሌጂስሌይት -ግ- ሕ'ግ ማውጣት [አወ'ጣ]

legislation
ሌጂስ'ሌይሸን -ስ- ሕ'ግ

legitimate
ለ'ጂተመት -ሕ- ሕ'ጋዊ ፤ ተገቢ

leisure
'ሌዠ -ስ- የዕረፍት ጊዜ ፤ የመዝናኛ ጊዜ

leisurely
'ሌዠሊ -ቅ- ዝ'ግተ'ኛ ፤ ተዝናኝ

lemon
'ሌመን -ስ- የባሕር ሎሚ

lemonade
ሌመ'ኔይድ -ስ- ሎሚናት

lend
'ሌንድ -ግ- ማበ'ደር [አበ'ደረ]፤ ማዋስ [አዋሰ]

lender
'ሌንደ -ስ- አበ'ዳሪ ፤ አዋሽ

length
'ሌንግስ -ስ- እርዝመት ፤ እርዝግኔ

lengthen
ሌንግሰን -ግ- ማርዘም [አረ'ዘመ]

lengthy
'ሌንግሲ -ቅ- በጣም ረ'ጂም

lenient
'ሊይኒየንት -ቅ- ትዕግሥተ'ኛ ፤ ልል (እ'ሳበ
ግ'ትር ያልሆነ)

lens
'ሌንዝ -ስ- የካሜራ ፤ የመነ'ጥር መስተዋት

Lent
'ሌንት -ስ- ጾም አርባ ፤ ሑዳዴ

lentil
'ሌንተል -ስ- ም'ስር (የእህል ዓይነት)

leopard
'ሌፐድ -ስ- ነብር ፤ ነምር

503

leper
'ሌፐ -ስ- ቆማጣ ፣ ሥጋ ደዌ ያ'ደረ'በት ሰው

leprosy
'ሌፕረሲ -ስ- ቁምጥ'ና ፣ ሥጋ ደዌ በ'ሽታ

less
'ሌስ -ቅ- ያ'ነሰ

lessen
'ሌሰን -ግ- ማሳ'ነስ [አሳ'ነሰ]

lesson
'ሌሰን -ስ- ትምህርት ፣ የ'ሚ'ማሩት ነገር ፣
ማስጠንቀቂያ

let
'ሌት -ግ- መልቀቅ [ለ'ቀቀ] ፣ መተው [ተወ]

letter
'ሌተ -ስ- ደብዳ'ቤ

lettuce
'ሌተስ -ስ- ሰላጣ

level
'ሌቨል -ቅ- ደልዳ'ላ ፣ ዝርግ ፣ ለ'ጥ ያለ

lever
'ሊያቨ -ስ- ሰቅስቆ ማንሻ (ብረት ፣ እንጨት)

levity
'ሌቨቲ -ስ- ያለቦታው የ'ሚ'ደ'ረግ ዋልታ ፣
ቁም ነገር እ'ቃ'ሉ ማየት

levy
'ሌቪ -ግ- ቀረጥ መሰብሰብ [ሰብ]
-ስ- በወዋጅ የተሰጠ ቀረጥ

lewd
ል'ዩ:ውድ -ቅ- ባለጌ ፣ ሐፍረተ ቢስ (በፈቃደ
ሥጋ ነገር)

liability
ላየ'ቢሊ:ቲ -ስ- ኃላፊ'ነት የመኖር ስ'ሜት ፣
የ'ሚያ'ግድ ነገር (ለሥራ መዘተ) ፣ የመከፈል
ኃላፊ'ነት

liable
'ላየበል -ቅ- በገ'ጸ/የ'ሚያ'ገባው (ሊ'ወ'ቀስ
የ'ሚ'ገ'ባው) ፣ ሊሆን የ'ሚችል

liaison
ሊ'ዩፈዞን -ስ- ግን'ኙ'ነት ፣ ጋብረት

liar
'ላየ -ቅ- ውሸታም ፣ ዋሾ

libel
'ላይበል -ስ- የሰው ክብር ነ'ክ የሆነ ጽሑፍ፣

---

liberal
'ሊበረል -ቅ- ነጻ አ'ሳቢ ፣ አስተሳሰብ ሰ'ፊ
generous
-ቅ- ቸር

liberate
'ሊበረይት -ግ- ነጻ ማውጣት [አወ'ጣ]

liberty
'ሊበቲ -ስ- ነጻ'ነት

librarian
ላይብ'ሬሪየን -ስ- o'ቃቤ መጻሕፍት

library
'ላይብረሪ -ስ- ቤተ መጻሕፍት

licence
'ላይሰንስ -ስ- ፈቃድ (የመኪና መንጃ ፣ የመ
'ጻያ መዘተ)

license
'ላይሰንስ -ግ- የሥራ ፈቃድ መስጠት [ሰ'ጠ]

licensed
'ላይሰንስት -ቅ- ፈቃድ ያ'ለው

licentious
ላይ'ሴንሸስ -ቅ- ሐፍረተ ቢስ (በፈቃደ ሥጋ
ነገር)

lick
'ሊክ -ግ- መላስ [ላሰ]

lid
'ሊድ -ስ- ሽፋን ፣ እ'ፈያ ፣ ክዳን

lie
'ላይ -ግ- መዋሸት [ዋ'ሸ]
-down
-ግ- መ'ጋደም [ተ'ጋ'ደመ] ፣ ማ'ጋም
[አ'ጋ'ደመ]

life
'ላይፍ -ስ- ሕይወት ፣ ኑር

lifebelt
'ላይፍቤልት -ስ- ከመስጠም የ'ሚያድን መ
'ጻያ (ከቡ'ሽ የተሠ'ራ)

lifeless
'ላይፍለስ -ቅ- ሕይወት የሌ'ለው ፣ የሞተ ፣
ም'ውት

lift
'ሊፍት -ግ- ማንጣት [አነ'ሣ]
-ስ- አሳንሰር

ligament
'ሊገመንት -ስ- ጅማቶ'ች ፣ ማ'ያያዝ ጋመ ደ

light
  'ላይት -ስ- ብርሃን ፣ መብራት
  not heavy
    -ቅ- ቀ'ላል

lighting
  'ላይቲንግ -ስ- መብራት (የቤት)

lighter
  'ላይተ -ስ- ሲጋራ ማ'ቃጠያ፣ማ'ቀጣጠያ (መ
  'ሣሪያ)

lighthouse
  'ላይትሀውስ -ስ- መርከቦ'ች ከጭ'ጥ'ኝ ጋር እን
  ዳይ'ጋ'ጩ የ'ሚያመለ'ክት ብርሃን ያ'ለ'በት
  ሕንጻ

lightning
  'ላይትኒንግ -ስ- መብረቅ

lights
  'ላይትስ -ስ- የከብት ሆድቃ

like
  'ላይክ -ግ- መውደድ [ወ'ደደ]
    -ቅ- የ'ሚመስል

likely
  'ላይክሊ -ቅ- ሊሆን የ'ሚችል ፣ ምናልባት
  'ነት ያለው

likeness
  'ላይክነስ -ስ- አምሳ'ያ

lilt
  'ሊልት -ስ- የዜማ አ'መታት

limb
  'ሊም -ስ- እግር'ና እ'ጅ

lime
  'ላይም -ስ- ሎሚ ፣ ኖራ

limestone
  'ላይምስተውን -ስ- በሀ ወይም ተፈርኵች ድን
  ጋይ

limit
  'ሊሚት -ግ- መወ'ሰን [ወ'ሰነ]
    -ስ- ወሰን

limitation
  ሊሚቴይሸን -ስ- ወሰን ፣ ድ'ካ

limp
  'ሊምፕ -ግ- ማንከስ [አነ'ከሰ]

limpid
  'ሊምፕድ -ቅ- የጠ'ራ ፣ ኩል'ል ያለ ፣ በው
  ስጡ የ'ሚያሳ'ይ (ውሃ ፣ አ'የር ፣ ዓይን)

line
  'ላይን -ስ- መሥመር

linen
  'ሊነን -ስ- ከተልባ እግር የተሠ'ራ ጨርቅ

liner
  'ላይነ -ስ- ታ'ላቅ መርከብ (ለመንገደ'ኞ'ች)

linger
  'ሊንገ -ግ- ወደኋላ ማለት [አለ] ፣ መቆ'የት
  [ቆ'የ]

linguist
  'ሊንግዊስት -ስ- የቋንቋዎ'ች ጥናት ሊቅ

liniment
  'ሊነመንት -ስ- መ'ታሻ ቅባት (ለአ'በጠ'ና
  ለጐ'ዳለ ሰው'ነት)

lining
  'ላይኒንግ -ስ- ገበር

link
  'ሊንክ -ስ- ማ'ያያዣ

lint
  'ሊንት -ስ- ጥጥ (የቁስል)

lion
  'ላየን -ስ- አንበ'ሳ

lip
  'ሊፕ -ስ- ከንፈር

liquid
  'ሊክዊድ -ስ- ፈሳሽ ነገር

liquidate
  'ሊክዊዴይት -ግ- መደምሰስ [ደመ'ሰሰ] ፣ መ
  ክፈል [ከ'ፈለ] (እዳ) ፣ የንግድ ድር'ጅት
  ገንዘቡን ለዕዳ በመክፈል መዝጋት [ዘ'ጋ]

liquor
  'ሊክ -ስ- አልኮል'ነት ያ'ለው መጠ'ጥ

lisp
  'ሊስፕ -ስ- መንተባተብ [ተነተባ'ተበ] ("ስ"
  ንና "ዘ" ን ደጋና አድርጐ ባለመ'ናገር)

list
  'ሊስት -ስ- ዝርዝር

listen
  'ሊሰን -ግ- ማ'ዳመጥ [አ'ዳ'መጠ]

listener
  'ሊሰነ -ስ- አድማጭ ፣ ሰሚ

listless
  'ሊስትለስ -ቅ- ደካማ ፣ ስልቹ

505

literacy
’ሊ.ተረሲ -ስ- የማንበብ'ና የመጻፍ ችሎታ

literal
’ሊ.ተረል -ቅ- ያለ ትርጓሜ ፤ እንደ ጽሑፉ ፤
ል'ክ ፤ ፍ'ጹም ስሕተት የሌ'ለ'በት

literary
’ሊ.ተረሪ -ቅ- የሥነ ጽሑፍ ፤ ሥነ ጽሑፋዊ

literate
’ሊ.ተሪት -ቅ- የማንበብ'ና የመጻፍ ችሎታ ያ
'ለው

literature
’ሊ.ትሪቸ -ስ- ሥነ ጽሑፍ

litre
’ሊ.ይተ -ስ- ሊ.ትር (የፈሳሽ መለ'ኪያ)

litter
’ሊ.ተ -ስ- ው'ዳቂ ፤ ል'ቃሚ ፤ ቁሻሻ

little
’ሊ.ተል -ቅ- ት'ንሽ ፤ አ'ጭር ፤ ጥቂት

live
’ላይቭ -ቅ- ንቁ ፤ ሕይወት ያ'ለው

live
’ሊ.ቭ -ግ- መኖር [ኖረ]

livelihood
’ላይቭሊ.ሁድ -ስ- ወረት የ'ሚ'ገ'ኝ'በት ሥራ፣
መ'ተዳደሪያ ሥራ

lively
’ላይቭሊ. -ቅ- ንቁ ፤ የተደ'ሰተ በፍን ነት የ'
ሚንቀሳ'ቀስ

liver
’ሊ.ቨ -ስ- ጉ'በት

liverish
’ሊ.ቨሪሽ -ቅ- ጉ'በቱ በመ'ታመም የ'ሚ'ሠ
ቃ'ይ

livery
’ሊ.ቨሪ -ስ- የቤት አገልጋይ መ'ለ'ዮ ልብስ

livestock
’ላይቭስቶክ -ስ- ከብት (የከብት ሀብት)

livid
’ሊ.ቪ.ድ -ቅ- መልኩ የጠ'ቆረ'ጣ (በቁ'ጣ ፤ በሕ
መም)

living
’ሊ.ቪንግ -ቅ- የ'ሚኖር ፤ ሕያው
-ስ- ወረት የ'ሚ'ገ'ኝ'በት ሥራ

living-room
’ሊ.ቪንግ ሩም -ስ- የእንግዳ መ'ቀበያ ክፍል ፤
እልፍ'ኝ (ሳሎን)

lizard
’ሊ.ዘድ -ስ- እንሽላሊ.ት

load
’ለውድ -ስ- ሸክም

loaf
’ለውፍ -ስ- ዳ'ቦ

loan
’ለውን -ስ- ብ'ድር ፤ ውሰት

loath
’ለውስ -ቅ- ወደኋላ የ'ሚል ፤ ፈቃድ የሌ'ለው
(እንደ ነገር ለማድረግ)

loathe
’ለውዝ -ግ- በጣም መጥላት [ጠ'ላ] ፤ መ'ጸ
የፍ [ተጸ'የፈ]

lobby
’ሎቢ. -ስ- ት'ንሽ አ'ዳራሽ ፤ በቤት ውስጥ
መ'ተላለፊያ ቦታ

lobe
’ለውብ -ስ- ለምለም ጆሮ ፤ ጆሮ ልም

local
’ለውከል -ቅ- ያንድ ቦታ ፤ ያገሬው

locality
ለው'ካለቲ -ስ- አንድ ነገር ያ'ለ'በት ቦታ ፤
አንድ ድርጊ.'ት የተፈ'ጸመ'በት ቦታ

locate
ለው'ኬይት -ግ- አንድ ነገር ያ'ለ'በትን ቦታ
ማግኘት [አገ'ኘ]

location
ለው'ከይሽን -ስ- ቦታ ፤ ሥፍራ

lock
’ሎክ -ግ- መቆ'ለፍ [ቆ'ለፈ]
-ስ- የበ'ር ቁልፍ ፤ የጠጉር ቁ'ጥራት

locker
’ሎከ -ስ- ቁልፍ ያ'ለው ት'ንሽ ቁም ሣጥን ፤
ሣጥን

locket
’ሎከት -ስ- እንደ አሽንክታብ በአንገት ላይ
የ'ሚንጠለ'ጠል የማስታወሻ ስጦታ

locksmith
’ሎክስሚ.ስ -ስ- ቁልፍ ሠ'ራተ'ኛ (የቤት)

506

locomotion

ለውከ'መኩሽን -ስ- ወደፊት መሄድ ፤ መንቀ
ሳቀስ ፤ ካንድ ቦታ ወደ ሌላው መሄድ መቻል

locomotive

ለውከ'መውቲቭ -ስ- የ'ሚያንቀሳ'ቅስ ፤ ባቡር
ጎ'ታች ሞተር

locust

'ለውከስት -ስ- አንበጣ ፤ አምበጣ

lodge

'ሎጅ -ግ- መኖር [ኖረ] ፤ (በሰው ዘንድ ለጊ.
ዜው'ና ገንዘብ እ'የከ'ፈሉ)

lodger

'ሎጀ -ስ- ገንዘብ እ'የከ'ፈለ በላላ ሰው ቤት
ደ'ባል ሆኖ የ'ሚኖር ሰው

lodging

'ሎጂንግ -ስ- ካንድ መኖሪያ ቤት ውስጥ የተከ
ራ'ዩት ክፍል

lodging-house

'ሎጂንግ 'ሀውስ -ስ- ፓንሲዮን፤ ለቀን ወይ'ንም
ለሳ'ምንት የ'ሚ'ከራዩት የቤት ክፍል

loft

'ሎፍት -ስ- በጣራ'ና በኮርኒስ መካ'ከል ያ'ለ
ው ክፍት ቦታ

lofty

'ሎፍቲ -ቅ- ረ'ጅም (ለቤት ፤ ለተራራ)

log

'ሎግ -ስ- የግንድ ቱ'ማጅ

logic

'ሎጂክ -ስ- የማስተዋል ጥበብ ፤ ትምህርት ፤
የመ'ከራከር'ና የማሳ'መን ችሎታ

logical

ሎጂከል -ቅ- ጉልህ ፤ ትክ'ክል (ለሐሳ'ብ)
አስተዋይ አእምሮ የ'ሚ'ቀ'በለው አሰተያየት፡

loin

'ሎይን -ስ- ሽንጥ ፤ የሽንጥ ሥጋ

loiter

'ሎይተ -ግ- ያለሥራ በ'የቦታው መ'ገተር [ተ
ገ'ተረ]

loneliness

'ለውንሊነስ -ስ- ብ'ቸ'ኝ'ነት

lonely

'ለውንሊ -ቅ- ብ'ቸኛ

long

'ሎንግ -ቅ- ረ'ጅም
-ግ- መናፈቅ [ና'ፈቀ

longevity

ሎን'ጄቬቲ -ስ- ረ'ጅም ዕድሜ

longing

'ሎንጊንግ -ስ- ናፍቆት

longitude

'ሎንጊትዩድ -ስ- ቀ'ጥ ያለ መሥመር ፤ ኬን
ትሮስ (መልክአ ምድርC)

longsighted

ሎንግ'ሳይተድ -ቅ- የወደፊቱን የ'ሚያ'ስብ ፤
አርቆ አ'ሳቢ ፤ ዓይኑ ቅርብ ማየት የ'ማይ'ችል

longstanding

ሎንግስ'ታንዲንግ -ቅ- የናረ ፤ የቆ'የ

look

'ሉክ -ግ- መ'መልከት [ተመለ'ከተ] ፤ አተ
ኩ'ሮ ማየት [አ'የ]

looking-glass

'ሉኪንግ ግ'ላ:ስ -ስ- መስታወት (የመልክ ማያ)

lookout

'ሉካውት -ስ- ዘበ'ኛ (አገC የ'ሚጠ'ብቅ) ፤
መጠ'በቂያ ቦታ

loom

'ሉ:ም -ስ- የሽ'ማኔ ዕቃ
-ግ- ብ'ቅ ማለት [አለ] (በ'ሚያስፈራ
ሁኔ'ቴ)

loop

'ሉ:ፕ -ስ- ቀለP (የገመድ ፤ የሽ'ቦ) ፤ ቀ'ጥራት

loophole

'ሉ:ፕሆውል -ስ- ከሕ'ግ ማምለጫ ምክንያት፡
ከም'ሽግ ውስጥ ለመተ'ኩሽ የተበ'ጀ ቀዳዳ

loose

'ሉ:ስ -ቅ- የተፈ'ታ ፤ የላ'ላ ፤ ልል

loosen

'ሉ:ሰን -ግ- መፍታት [ፈ'ታ] ፤ ማላላት [አላ'ላ]

loot

'ሉ:ት -ግ- መዝረፍ [ዘ'ረፈ]
-ስ- የተዘ'ረፈ ዕቃ

lop

'ሎፕ -ግ- መቀርጠፍ [ቀረ'ጠፈ] ፤ ማስተካ
ከል [አስተካ'ከለ] (የዛፍ ቅርንጫ'ፄ ወዘተ)፤
መጣል [ጣለ] (ለእንጨሳት ጆC)

lop-sided

ሎፕ'ሳይደድ -ቅ- የተዛ'ባ ፤ ያልተስተካ'ከለ

loquacious

ለውከ'ዌይሸስ -ቅ- ለፍላፊ ፤ ቀባጣሪ

507

lord
'ሎ፡ድ -ስ- ገ'ዥ ፣ ጌታ

lordly
'ሎ፡ድሊ -ቅ- የተከ'በረ ፣ ግርማ ያለው ፣ ቀብ
ራ'ራ

lore
'ሎ፡ -ስ- አፈ ታሪክ

lorry
'ሎሪ -ስ- የጭነት መኪና

lose
'ሉ፡ዝ -ግ- ማጥፋት [አጠ'ፋ] ፣ መጣል [ጣለ]
game
-ግ- ውር'ርድ መ'ሸነፍ [ተሸ'ነፈ]

loser
'ሉ፡ዘ -ስ- ተሸ'ናፊ (በውር'ርድ)

loss
'ሎስ -ስ- ከሳራ ፣ ማጣት ፣ የጠ'ፋ ነገር ፣ ጉዳት ፣
ሐዘን

lot
'ሎት -ስ- ብዛት ያለው ነገር ፤ በሀ'ራጅ የሚ
'ሸጥ ዕቃ ፤ ቁ'ራጭ መሬት
fate
-ስ- እጣ ፣ ዕ'ድል

lotion
'ለውሽን -ስ- ቅባት (ለጠጉር ፣ ለፈት)

lottery
'ሎተሪ -ስ- ሎተሪ

loud
'ላውድ -ቅ- ከ'ፍተ'ኛ (ለጩኸት)

lounge
'ላውንጅ -ስ- ማረፊያ ክፍል
-ግ- ተዝናንቶ መ'ቀመጥ [ተቀ'መጠ]

louse
'ላውስ -ስ- ቅማል

lousy
'ላውዚ -ቅ- ቅማላም ፤ በጣም መጥፎ ፤ ወ'ራዳ

love
'ለቭ -ግ- ማፍቀር [አፈ'ቀረ] ፣ መውደድ
[ወ'ደደ]

loveliness
'ለቭሊነስ -ስ- ቆንጆ'ና ፣ ውብ'ነት ፣ ተወ'ዳ
ጅ'ነት

lovely
'ለቭሊ -ቅ- ያማረ ፣ ቆንጆ ፣ ውብ ፣ ተወ'ዳጅ

lover
'ለቨ -ስ- አፍቃሪ ፣ ወዳጅ ውሽ'ማ

loving
'ለቪንግ -ቅ- ወ'ዳድ ፣ የ'ሚወ'ድ ፣ የ'ሚያፈ
ቅር

low
'ለው -ቅ- ዝ'ቅ ያለ ፣ ወ'ራ'ዳ

lower
'ለወ -ግ- ዝ'ቅ ማድረግ [አደ'ረገ]

loyal
'ሎየል -ቅ- ታ'ማኝ

loyalty
'ሎየልቲ -ስ- ታ'ማኝነት

lubricant
'ሉብሪከንት -ስ- ቅባት (ለመኪና ፣ ለዕቃ)

lubricate
'ሉብሪኬይት -ግ- ቅባት መቀ'ባት [ቀ'ባ] (ብ
ረት ብረት ፣ መኪና)

lubrication
ሉብሪ'ኬይሽን -ስ- የመኪና ቅባት

lucid
'ሉሲድ -ቅ- ግልጽ (ለንግ'ግር)

luck
'ለክ -ስ- ዕ'ድል

lucky
'ለኪ -ቅ- ዕ'ድለ'ኛ

lucrative
'ሉክራቲቭ -ቅ- ብዙ ገንዘብ የ'ሚያስገ'ኝ

ludicrous
'ሉዲክረስ -ቅ- አ'ሥቂ'ኝ ፣ የ'ጥሀ

luggage
'ለጌጅ -ስ- የመንገድ ጓዝ (ሻንጣ'ና የመሳ
'ሰለው)

luke-warm
ሉ፡ክ'ዋ፡ም -ቅ- ለ'ብ ያለ (ለውሃ ወዘተ)

lull
'ለል -ግ- ጸጥ ማድረግ [አደ'ረገ] ፣ እ'ሽሩሩ
ማለት [አለ]
-ስ- ጸ'ጥታ (ለጥቂት ጊዜ)

lullaby
'ለለባይ -ስ- እ'ሽሩሩ (ልጅ ለማስተ'ኛት
የ'ሚዘ'ፈን ዘፈን)

lumbago
ለም'ቤይገው -ስ- የጀርባ ቁርጥማት

508

lumber
’ለምበ -ስ- መርብ

luminous
’ሉ፡ሚነስ -ተ- የ’ጊያበራ

lump
’ለምፕ -ስ- ቶራጭ (ት’ልቃ) ፤ እበጥ

lumpy
’ለምፒ -ተ- የን’ ጉላ (ለበከ ፤ ለገንፎ)

lunacy
’ሉ፡ነሲ -ስ- እብደት

lunar
’ሉ፡ነ -ተ- የጨረቃ

lunatic
’ሉ፡ነቲክ -ተ- እብድ

lunch
’ለንች -ስ- ምሳ

luncheon
’ለንቸን -ስ- ጉበር (የምሳ)

lung
’ለንግ -ስ- ሳምባ

lunge
’ለንጅ -ግ- መሻጥ [ሻጠ] (በመር መዘተ)

lure
’ሉ፡ወ -ግ- እባብሉ እደጋ ላይ መማል [ማለ]፤ ግ’ታለል [አ’ታ’ለለ]

lurid
’ሉ፡ሪድ -ተ- አስፈ’ሪ ፤ እ’ሥታቲ ፤ ተለመ ደ’ግነት

lurk
’ለክ -ግ- ግድፈጥ [አደ’ፈጠ] ፤ ግደዋት [አደ’ዓ]

luscious
’ለሸስ -ተ- አስጎምጂ ፤ በጣም የጣሰል’ና የ’ሚ ግ’ፍጥ ግዕም ያ’ለመ (አፍራፍራ)

lust
’ለስት -ስ- ፍትወተ ሥጋ ፤ ጠንካ’ራ ፍ’ላጐት

lustre
’ለስተ -ስ- አንጸባራቂ ፤ ጽርፎት

luxuriant
’ለክዠ፡ሪየንት -ተ- ተትጐ’ት ብሉ የበ’ተለ (ግር ፤ ጣጐC) ፤ የተትራፈ’ረፈ

luxurious
ለክ’ዠ፡ሪየስ -ተ- ደሱታም ፤ ም’ቹት ያ’ለመ

luxury
’ለክዠሪ -ስ- ደሱት ፤ ም’ቹት

lynch
’ሊ፡ንች -ግ- መ’ገደል [ተገ’ደለ] (ታ’ፍና በመ መ’ሰድ ፤ በሕዝብ ያለ ፍርድ)

lyric
’ሊሪክ -ስ- የዘፈን ታላት ፤ ለዘፈን የተመ’ቹ አጫ’ጭር ግጥሞ’ች

mace
’ሜይስ -ስ- በትረ አርጉን

machine
መ’ሺይን -ስ- መኪና

machinery
መ’ሺይነሪ -ስ- የመኪና ዕታ ፤ የመኪና ሥራ

mackintosh
’ማኪንቶሽ -ስ- የዝናም ልብስ

mad
’ማድ -ተ- እብድ

Madam
’ማደም -ስ- እ’ግቲ ፤ እ’መቤቲ

madman
’ማድመን -ስ- ያ’በደ ሰመ

madness
’ማድነስ -ስ- እብደት

magazine
ማጋዚን -ስ- መጽሔት

of firearms
-ስ- የጥ’ይት ክፈታ ፤ የመር መ’ግሪያ ፤ የጥ’ይት መተ ዕታ ቤት

maggot
’ማጐት -ስ- የፍራፍረ ፤ የሥጋ ትል

magic
’ማጂክ -ስ- ጥንቆላ

magician

መ'ጄሽን -ስ- ጠንቋይ

magistrate

'ማጀስትሬይት -ስ- ዳኛ (በዝ'ቅተ'ኛ ፍርድ ቤት)

magnanimity

ማግነ'ነመቲ -ስ- ቸር'ነት ፣ ባለ ጥሩ ባ'ኽር ይ'ነት

magnet

'ማግነት -ስ- መግነጢስ

magnetic

ማግ'ኔቲክ -ቅ- መግነጢሳዊ

magnificent

ማግ'ኔፈሰንት -ቅ- ት'ልቅ ፣ ድንቅ

magnify

'ማግነፋይ -ግ- ማጉላት [አጎ'ላ] ፣ ት'ልቅ ማድረግ [አደ'ረገ]

magnifying-glass

'ማግነፋይንግ ግላ:ስ -ስ- ማጉያ መነ'ጥር

magnitude

'ማግኒትዩ:ድ -ስ- መጠን ፣ ት'ልቅ'ነት

mahogany

መ'ሆገኒ -ስ- ጥቁር እንጨት

maid

'ሜይድ -ስ- ገረድ

maiden

'ሜይደን -ስ- ልጃገረድ ፣ ሳዱ'ላ

mail

'ሜይል -ስ- ደብዳ'ቤ ፣ ፖስታ

maim

'ሜይም -ግ- የሰው ገላ መቆራረጥ [ቆራ'ረ ጠ] ፣ አካለ ስንኩል ማድረግ [አደ'ረገ]

main

'ሜይን -ቅ- ዋ'ና

mainland

'ሜይንለንድ -ስ- አገር ፣ አህጉር (ደሴት ያል ሆነ)

mainly

'ሜይንሊ -ተግ- ይበልጡን

maintain

ሜይን'ቴይን -ግ- መ'ከባከብ [ተከባ'ከበ] ፣ መጠ'በቅ [ጠ'በቀ]

say

-ግ- መ'ናገር [ተና'ገረ]

maintenance

'ሜይተነንስ -ስ- አ'ያያዝ ፣ አ'ጠባበቅ (በተ ለ'ይ ለሕይወት መጠ'በቂያ)

maize

'ሜይዝ -ስ- በ'ቆ'ሎ ፣ ባርማሽ'ላ

majestic

መ'ጄስቲክ -ቅ- ግርማዊ

majesty

'ማጀስቲ -ስ- ግርማ

major

'ሜይጅ -ቅ- ዋ'ና

military

-ስ- ሻለቃ

majority

መ'ጀረቲ -ስ- የ'ሚበልጠው ፣ አብዛ'ኛው ፣ ሕዝብ ወዘተ

make

'ሜይክ -ግ- መሥራት [ሠ'ራ] ፣ ማድረግ [አደ'ረገ]

make-believe

'ሜይክ ፣ በሊይቭ -ስ- ማስመ'ሰል

maker

'ሜይክ -ግ- አድራጊ

makeshift

'ሜይክሺፍት -ስ- ጊዜያዊ 'ምት'ክ (የተሻለ አስኪ'ገ'ኝ)

make-up

'ሜይከፕ -ስ- የመልክ ማሳ'መሪያ ቅባት ወዘተ

malady

'ማለዲ -ስ- ሕመም ፣ በ'ሽታ

malaria

ማ'ሌሪያ -ስ- ወባ ፣ ንዳድ

male

'ሜይል -ቅ- ተባዕት

malevolent

መ'ሌቨለንት -ቅ- ክፉ አ'ሳቢ ፣ ተንኮለ'ኛ

malice

'ማሊስ -ስ- ክፉ ሐሳ'ብ ፣ ሰውን የመጉዳ ፍ'ላጎት ፣ ተንኮል

malicious

መ'ሊሸስ -ቅ- ክፉ ፣ ክፉ አድራጊ ፣ ተንኮለ'

malignant

መ'ሊግነንት -ቅ- በሰው ላይ ክፋት የ'ሚ 'ስብ ፣ በጥላ'ቻ የተሞ'ላ

510

malleable
'ማሊየብል -ቅ- በቀላሉ ቅርፁ ሊ'ሰ'ጠው የ'ሚ'ቻል

mallet
'ማለት -ስ- የንጨት መዶሻ

malnutrition
ማልን‍ዮት'ሪሽን -ስ- በደምብ ባለመ'መገብ የ 'ሚ'ፈ'ጠር ሁናቴ

malt
'ሞልት -ስ- ብቅል (የጠ'ላ ፤ የቢራ)

maltreat
ማልት'ሪይት -ግ- መበ'ደል [በ'ደለ]

mammal
'ማመል -ስ- የ'ሚያጠቡ እንሰሳት ፤ ጡት ያ'ላ 'ቸው እንሰሳት

mammoth
'ማመፅ -ቅ- በጣም ት'ልቅ

man
'ማን -ስ- ሰው

manage
'ማነጅ -ግ- ማስተዳደር [አስተዳ'ደረ] ፤ መምራት [መ'ራ] (ለሥራ) ፤ በ'ሚ'ገ'ባ መያዝ [ያዘ]

management
'ማነጅመንት -ስ- አስተዳደር ፤ አ'መራር

manager
'ማነጀ -ስ- አስተዳዳሪ ፤ ሥራ መሪ

mane
'ሜይን -ግ- ጋ'ማ (የፈረስ ፤ የአንበሳ)

manger
'ሜይንጀ -ስ- የከብት መ'መገቢያ ፤ ግርግም

mangle
'ማንገል -ስ- የልብስ መጭመቂያ ፤ መጠም ዘገርያ መኪና
-ግ- መቆራረጥ [ቆራ'ረጠ] ፤ መበጣጠስ [በጣ'ጠሰ]

✝ **manhood**
'ማንሁድ -ስ- ጉልምስ'ና ፤ አካለ መጠን ፤ ጉብዝ'ና

• **mania**
'ሜይኒየ -ስ- እብደት ፤ ላንድ ነገር ከ'ሚ'ገ'ባ በላይ ማ'ሰብ

maniac
'ሜይኒያክ -ስ- አእምሮውን የሳተ ሰው ፤ በ ጣም ያ'በደ ሰው

manicure
'ማኒክዩው -ስ- እ'ጅን ፤ ጥፍር'ችን መ'ከ ባከብ

manifest
'ማኒፌስት -ግ- መግለጽ [ገ'ለጸ] ፤ ማሳ'የት [አሳ'የ]
-ቅ- ግልጽ

manifold
'ማኒፈውልድ -ቅ- ብዙ ቅርፅ ያ'ለው ፤ ል'ዩ ል'ዩ አገልግሎት የ'ሚሰጥ

manipulate
መ'ኒፑዩሌይት -ግ- በ'ጅ መሥራት [ሠ'ራ] ፤ መ'ቆጣጠር [ተቆጣ'ጠረ] ፤ አሳ'ምሮ መሥራት [ሠ'ራ]

mankind
ማንካይንድ -ስ- የሰው ዘር

manly
'ማንሊ -ቅ- ጀግና ፤ ጎበዝ

manner
'ማነ -ስ- ሁናቴ ፤ ጠባይ

manoeuvre
መ'ኑሽ -ስ- የጦር'ነት እንቅስ'ቃሴ ፆ'ቅድ

manor
'ማነ -ስ- የባለመሬቱ ቤት የ'ሚ'ገ'ኝ'በት ርስት

mansion
'ማንሽን -ስ- ታ'ላቅ ቤት ፤ አ'ዳራሽ

manslaughter
'ማንስሎ:ተ -ስ- በስሕተት ነፍስ መግደል

mantle
'ማንተል -ስ- ካ'ባ ፤ የማሽ ክ'ር

manual
'ማነዉል -ቅ- የእ'ጅ
book
-ስ- መምሪያ መጽሐፍ

manufacture
ማንዩ'ፋክቸ -ግ- በብዛት ሠርቶ ማውጣት

manufacturer
ማንዩ'ፋክቸረ -ስ- ባለፋብሪካ

manure
መን'ዩወ -ስ- የመሬት ማዳበሪያ መድኃኒት ፡ ፍግ

manuscript
'ማንዩስክሪፕት -ስ- የእ'ጅ ጽሑፍ

511

many
'ብዙ ት- ብዙ ፡ እ'ያሌ

map
'ማፕ -ስ- ካርታ (የሙሬት)

mar
'ማ: -ት- ግ'በላሸት [እ'በላ'ሸ] ፡ ማጥፋት
[እጠ'ፋ] ፡ ግረረርስ [እረረ'ርስ]

marble
'ማ:ብል -ስ- እብነ በረድ

march
'ማ:ች -ት- በሰልፍ መ'ሄጃ [+ጓዘ]

March
'ማ:ች -ስ- መ'ጋቢት (የወር ስም)

mare
'ሜየ -ስ- ሴት ፈረስ ፡ ባዝራ

margin
'ማ:ጂን -ስ- ህ'ዳግ (የመጽሐፍ መዘተ) ፡ ዳር
(የሐይት መዘተ)

marine
መ'ሪይን -ስ- የሙር መርከበ'ኛ
-ት- የባሕር

marital
'ማሪተል -ት- የጋብ'ቻ

maritime
'ማሪታይም -ስ- የባሕር ጉዳይ

mark
'ማ:ክ -ት- ምል'ክት ማድረግ [አደ'ረገ]
-ስ- ምል'ክት

market
'ማ:ከት -ስ- ገበያ

market-place
'ማ:ከትፕላይስ -ስ- ገበያ

marksman
'ማ:ክስመን -ስ- ጥሩ እ'ነማሪ ፡ ተኩሶ የማ
ይስት

maroon
መ'ሩ:ን -ት- ወደ ተፈ'ይነትፍ የማይደላ በ'ና'ግ
ተለየተ
leave stranded
-ት- ሰውን በችግር ላይ ጥሎ መሄድ
[ሄደ] (ም'ሳሌ ፡ ሰው በለ'ል'በት ደሴት መዘተ)

marquee
'ማ:ኪይ -ስ- ዳስ ፡ ት'ልቅ ድንኳን

---

marriage
'ማሪጅ -ስ- ጋብ'ቻ

married
'ማሪድ -ት- ያገ'በ ፡ ባለትዳር

marrow
'ማሪው -ስ- ዱ'ባ ፡ መጥነመጥን (የትልቁም
ትልቱም

marry
'ማሪ -ት- ማግባት [አገ'ባ]

marsh
'ማ:ሽ -ስ- ረግረግ

marshal
'ማ:ሻል -ስ- ሰልፍ መ'ባቲ ፡ ሰልፍ ተቆጣጣሪ

mart
'ማ:ት -ስ- ገበያ ፡ ሕ'ረጅ የ'ሚ'ባ'በት በት

martial
'ማ:ሻል -ት- የወ'ታ'ደር ፡ ወ'ታ'ደራዊ

martyr
'ማ:ተ -ስ- ሰማዕት

marvel
'ማ:ቨል -ት- መ'ደነት [ተደ'ነተ] ፡ መ'ደነቅ
[ተደ'ነቀ] (በመ'ደነት)

marvellous
'ማ:ቨለስ -ት- እስደ'ናቂ ፡ ጉ-ም (በመ'ደነት)

masculine
'ማስክዩለን -ስ- ተባዕት ፡ ወንድ

mash
'ማሽ -ት- ማድቀት [አደ'ቀተ] ፡ መደፍመጥ
[ደፈ'መጠ] (እመ ምግብ'ች)

mask
'ማ:ስክ -ስ- ጭምብ (የፊት መ'ሸ'ሸጊ'ና ልል
ትርዕ የ'ሚሰተ)

mason
'ሜይሰን -ስ- ደንጊያ ጠራቢ

masquerade
'ማስከረይድ -ት- ግ'ታለል ፡ እውነት ያልሆነ

mass
'ማስ -ስ- ክብደት
religious service
-ስ- ት'ዳሴ
majority
-ስ- ያብላጡ ሕዝብ ፡ ግንድ ቦታ የተከ
ግ'ች ሕዝብ

512

massacre
'ግስክ -ጉ- መጋደል [ገ'ደለ] ፤ መፍጀት
[ፈ'ጀ] (ለሰው)

massage
'ግሳ፤ጅ -ጉ- ግሸት [አ'ሸ] (ሰው'ነት)

massive
ግሲ፡ቭ -ት- በጣም ተ'ልቅና ከ'ባድ

mast
'ግ፡ስት -ሱ- የመርከብ ተራ-ዴ

master
'ግ፡ስተ -ሱ- ጌታ ፤ መሪ ፤ አ'ዛዥ

masterful
'ግ፡ስተፉል -ት- ጉደለ'ኛ (ነገር) ፤ ሥልጣኑን
በሌሎ'ች ላይ መጫገቃት የ'ሚ፡ወ'ድ ፤ የ'ሚ
ችል ፤ ታ'ላት ችሎታ ያ'ለው

masticate
ግስቲኬይት -ጉ- ግ'ነክ [አ'ነክ] ፤ ግ'ላ
መጥ [አ'ላመጠ]

mat
'ግት -ሱ- ሰሌን (የመለል ምንጣፍ)

match
'ግች -ሱ- ክብሪት
resemble
-ጉ- መ'መሳሰል [ተመሳ'ሰለ]
sport
-ሱ- ጉተግያ (ስፖርት)

match-maker
'ግች ሜይክ -ሱ- አ'ባባይ ፤ አ'ግቡ (ለጋብ'ቻ)

mate
'ሜይት -ሱ- የሥራ ጓ'ደ'ኛ ፤ ጓ'ደ'ኛ ፤ ሚስት ፤
ባል

material
መ'ቲሪየል -ሱ- ጨርቅ ጨርቅት ፤ አንድ ዕቃ
የ'ሚ፡ሠራ'በት ነገር

materialize
መ'ቲሪየላይዝ -ጉ- እፍ'ጸሜ ግድረስ [አደ'ረሰ]፤
እሥራ ላይ ግዋል [አዋለ]

maternal
መ'ተ፡ናል -ት- የእ'ናት ፤ እ'ናታዊ

maternity
መ'ተ፡ናቲ -ሱ- እ'ናት'ነት

mathematics
ግ፡'ግ፡ቲክስ -ሱ- የሒሳብ ትምህርት ፤ የሒ
ሳብ ዕሎ-ተት

matriculation
መ'ትሪኩ'ሌይሸን -ሱ- የዩኒ'ተ'ኛ ደረጃ ትም
ህርት ቤት መልተኛ ፈተና

matrimony
'ግትሪመኒ -ሱ- ጋብ'ቻ

matron
'ግይትረን -ሱ- ፀትዳር ብዙ ጊዜ የናረ'ች
ሴት ፤ ያንድ ድር'ጅት ጉዳይ የሆነ'ች ሴት (በሆ
ስፒታል መዘተ)

matter
'ግተ -ሱ- ነገር ፤ ጉ'ዳይ

matter-of-fact
ግተረ'ፋክት -ት- ተራ (ሁኔታ) ፤ ደንታ የለ
'ሰው ፤ እውነቱ ብ'ቻ የ'ሚ'ነ'ደው

matting
'ግቲንግ -ሱ- ሳዋሪ ፤ ሰሌን መዘተ

mattress
'ግትረስ -ሱ- ፍራሽ

mature
መ'ቸወ -ት- የበ'ሰለ (ለሰው)

maturity
መ'ቸሪቲ -ሱ- እደገት ፤ መብሰል (ለዕድ'ሜ)

maul
'ሞ፡ል -ጉ- መበ'ጨወት [በ'ጨተ] ፤ የፚ'ክ
ኔ ተገባር መፈ'ጸም [ፈ'ጸም]

mauve
'መውቭ -ት- ጠቆ'ር ያለ ሰግያዊ

May
'ሜይ -ሱ- ግንቦት

may
'ግይ -ጉ- መቻል [ቻል] ፤ ፈቃድ መ'ተበል
[ተፈ'በለ] (እንደ ረ'ዳት ግ'ሥ ግሪን ፤ ም
'ትትን'ና ፈተደን ይገልጣል)

maybe
'ግይቢ -ተጉ- ሊሆን ይችላል ፤ ምናልባት

mayor
'ግይ -ሱ- ከን'ተባ ፤ የከተማ ጋ'ዥ

maze
'ግይዝ -ሱ- መገበያ'ና መውጫው የ'ግይ
ታ'ወ'ት መንገድ ፤ የተመሳ'ሰበ ጉ'ዳይ፤ሕ'ሳብ

me
'ግይ -ተሱ- እኔን ፤ ለኔ

meadow
'ግይው -ሱ- መስሁ

meagre
'ሚገ -ቅ- ት'ንሽ ፡ የ'ማይበቃ (ምግብ ወዘተ)

meal
'ሚይል -ስ- ምግብ (የተዘጋ'ጀ)

mean
'ሚይን -ቅ- ገብጋ'ባ ፡ ቆጥቋ'ጣ (ለገንዘብ
ወዘተ) ፤ አስቀ'ያሚ ፤ የ'ማይ'ገ'ባ (ለጠባይ)

meaning
'ሚይኒንግ -ስ- ትርጉም ፡ ፍ'ች

means
'ሚይንዝ -ስ- መንገድ ፡ ብልጎት

meantime
'ሚይንታይም -ተግ- ወዲያው'ም፡በ'ዚያው'ም
ጊዜ ፡ በ'ዚሁ'ም መካ'ከል

meanwhile
ሚይን'ዋይል -ተግ- ወዲያ'ው'ም ፡ በ'ዚያው
'ም ፡ በ'ዚሁ'ም መካ'ከል

measles
'ሚይዘልዝ -ስ- ኩ'ፍ'ኝ

measure
'ሜገር -ግ- መለ'ካት [ለ'ካ]

meat
'ሚይት -ስ- ሥጋ

mechanic
ሚ'ካኒክ -ስ- ሜካኒክ

medal
'ሜዳል -ስ- ኒሻን ፡ ሊሻን

meddle
'ሜዶል -ግ- ጥ'ል'ቅ ማለት [አለ] (በሰው
ጉ'ዳይ)

mediate
'ሚ'ዲዬይት -ግ- መሸምገል [ሸመ'ገለ](ለማ
(ታረቅ)

medical
'ሜዲካል -ቅ- የመድኃኒት

medication
ሜዲ'ኬይሽን -ስ- መድኃኒት ፡ ሕ'ክም'ና

medicinal
መ'ዲሰነል -ቅ- መድኃኒት'ነት ያለው

medicine
'ሜዲሰን -ስ- መድኃኒት

medieval
ሜ'ዲይቫል -ስ- ማእከላዊ ዘመን (ከ፱ሺ፳፻ እ
ስከ ፩ሺ፭፻ ዓ ም ገደማ ያ'ለው የአውሮ'ፓ
ታሪክ)

meditate
'ሜዲቴይት -ግ- አጥልቆ ማ'ሰብ [አ'ሰበ] ፡
ከል'ብ ማ'ሰላሰል [አ'ሰላ'ሰለ]

medium
'ሚይዲየም -ቅ- መካ'ከለ'ኛ ፡ ደልዳ'ላ (ለቁ
መት)

meek
'ሚይክ -ቅ- ትሑት ፡ ታ'ዛዥ ፡ መከራን ታ
'ጋሽ

meet
'ሚይት -ግ- መ'ገናኘት [ተገና'ኘ]

meeting
'ሚይቲንግ -ስ- ስብሰባ ፡ መ'ገናኘት

melancholy
'ሜለንኮሊ -ስ- ጥልቅ ሐዘን ፡ ጭንት

mellow
'ሜለው -ቅ- የበ'ሰለ ፡ ለስላ'ሳ'ና ጣፋጭ ፤
ዕድሜ ያስተማረው ፤ የተዝና'ና

melodious
መ'ለውዲየስ -ቅ- ጣዕመ ዜማ ያ'ለው

melody
'ሜለዲ -ስ- ጣዕመ ዜማ

melon
'ሜለን -ስ- ከርቡሽ ፡ በ'ጢኪ

melt
'ሜልት -ግ- መቅለጥ [ቀ'ለጠ] ፡ ማቅለጥ
[አቀ'ለጠ]

member
'ሜምበ -ስ- አባል

membrane
'ሜምብሬይን -ስ- ሥሥ ሽፋን (የሰውን ፡
የእንስሳን ሥጋ የ'ሚያ'ገና'ኝ ፡ የ'ሚሸ'ፍን)

memento
መ'ሜንተው -ስ- የማስታወሻ ዕቃ (ያንዱን
ሰው የተለ'የ ሁናቴ የ'ሚያስታ'ውሱ'በት)

memoir
'ሜምዋ -ስ- የራስ ታሪክ ፡ የሰው ታሪክ (ያ'ዩት
በጽሑፍ መልክ)

memorable
'ሜመረበል -ቅ- የ'ሚታ'ወስ የ'ማይረ'ሳ

514

memorial

መ'ሞ፡ሪየል -ስ- መ'ታ ሰቢያ (የጦር'ነት ፣ የታላ'ላቅ ሰዎ'ች)

memorize

'ሜመራይዝ -ግ- ማስ ታወስ [አስ ታ'ወስ] ፣ በቃል ግጥናት [አጠ'ና]

memory

'ሜመሪ -ስ- ት'ዝ ታ

menace

'ሜነስ -ግ- መዛት [ዛተ] ፣ ማስፈራራት [አስ ፈራ'ራ]

menacing

'ሜናሲንግ -ስ- አስፈ'ሪ ፣ የ'ሚዝት

menagerie

ሞ'ናጀሪ -ስ- የዱር እንስሳት ማናሪያ ቦታ (በተለ'ይ ካገር አገር እ'የተዘዋ'ወሩ ለሰው የ'ሚ 'ታ'ዩ)

mend

'ሜንድ -ግ- መጠ'ገን [ጠ'ገነ]

menial

'ሚይኒየል -ቅ- ወ'ራ'ጻ (ሥራ) -ስ- የቤት አገል ጋይ

menstruation

ሜንስትሩ'ዌይሽን -ስ- አደፍ ፣ እንግዳ (የቤት ደም)

mental

'ሜንተል -ቅ- የአእምሮ

mentality

ሜን'ታለቲ -ስ- አእምሮ ፣ አስ ተሳሰብ

mention

'ሜንሽን -ግ- መጥቀስ [ጠ'ቀሰ]

mercantile

'መ፡ከን ታይል -ቅ- የንግድ ፣ የን'ጋዴ

mercenary

'መ፡ሰነሪ -ስ- በገንዘብ የተገ'ዛ ወ'ታ'ደር greedy -ቅ- ስለገንዘብ ብ'ቻ የ'ሚያ'ስብ ፣ ቆጥ ቋ'ጣ

merchandise

'መ፡ቸን ዳይዝ -ስ- የንግድ ዕቃ

merchant

'መ፡ቸንት -ስ- ነ'ጋዴ

merciful

'መ፡ሲፉል -ቅ- መሐሪ ፣ ርኅሩኅ

mercury

'መ፡ከዩሪ -ስ- ባዜ ታ

mercy

'መ፡ሲ -ስ- ምሕረት

mere

'ሚየ -ቅ- ተጨ'ማሪ'ም ፣ ተቀ'ናሽ'ም የሌ'ለ 'በት ፣ ቀ'ላል (ብ'ቻ)

merely

'ሚየሊ -ተግ- እን ጂየው ፣ ብ'ቻ ፣ በቀ'ላሉ

merge

'መ፡ጅ -ግ- መ'ዋሀለቅ [ተደባ'ለቀ]

merger

'መ፡ጀ -ስ- የቡሉ'ት ድር'ጅቶ'ች መ'ዋሐድ (የነ ግድ)

merit

'ሜሪት -ሰ- ሽ'ልማት የሚ ያሸልም ተገቢ'ነ ፣ ፣ የመ'መስገን ተገቢ'ነት

mermaid

'መ፡ሜይድ -ስ- ጀራቱ የዐሣ የተቀ'ረው ሰው 'ነቱ ግን የሰው ቅርፅ ያ ለው ፍጡር

merriment

'ሜሪሜንት -ስ- ደ'ስ ታ

merry

'ሜሪ -ቅ- ደ'ስ ተ'ኛ

mesh

'ሜሽ -ስ- መረብ ፣ መርበብ (ዕሣ ማጥመጃ)

mess

'ሜስ -ስ- ዘረክራ'ክ'ነት ፣ የንጽሕ'ና ጉድለት አለመ'ሰተር

message

'ሜሰጅ -ስ- መልእክት

messenger

'ሜሰንጀ -ስ- መልእክተ'ኛ ፣ ተላላኪ

metal

'ሜተል -ስ- ብ'ረት ብረት

metallic

ሜ'ታሊክ -ቅ- ብረት መ'ሰል ፣ የብረት ፣ ብ ረት ያ'ለ'በት

meter

'ሚይተ -ስ- መቴጠሪያ (የኤሌትሪክ ፣ የውሃ ወዘተ)

method

ሜ ሰድ -ስ- መንገድ (የአ'ሠራር)

methodical

ሜ'ሶዲከል -ተ- ሥርዓት መ'ባቲ፣ በደምብና
በሥርዓት የተሠ'ራ

meticulous

ሜ'ቲከዩለስ -ተ- ለጥቃ'ቅን ነገር ሁ'ሉ የ'ሚ
'ጠነ'ተ'ቅ ፣ በጣም ጥንቁቅ

metre

'ሜይተ -ስ- ሜትር (መለ'ኪያ)

metropolis

ሜት'ሮፖሊስ -ስ- ዋ'ና ከተማ ፣ መዲና

metropolitan

ሜትሪ'ፖሊተን -ተ- የዋ'ና ከተማ ፣ የሊቀ
ጳ'ጳሳት ወይን'ም የስብከት ሀገሩ

mettle

'ሜተል -ስ- ጉብዝ'ናመከራን መቻል (ለሰው ፣
ለፈረስ)

microbe

'ማይክረውብ -ስ- ሜክሮብ ፣ ረቂቅን ነፍሳት

microscope

'ማይክረስከውፕ -ስ- ሜክሮስኮፕ ፣ ጥቃ'ቅን
ነገሮ'ች እጅግ አፍ የ'ሚያሳ'ይ መነ'ጽር

midday

ሜድ'ዴይ -ስ- ቀትር ፣ ተሲዓት

middle

'ሜደል -ተ- መካ'ከለ'ኛ

middleman

'ሜደልማን -ስ- ጆሮ ነ'ጋዴ ፣ አገናኝ ሰው
(እንደ ደ'ላላ ያ'ለ)

middling

'ሜድሊንግ -ተ- መካ'ከለ'ኛ (ለዓይነት ፣ ለመ
ጠን)

midge

'ሜጅ -ስ- ትንኝ

midget

'ሜጄት -ስ- ድንክ

midnight

'ሜድናይት -ስ- እኩለ ሌሊት

midst

'ሜድስት -ስ- መካከል

midsummer

ሜድ'ሰመ -ስ- የበጋ አጋማሽ

midwife

'ሜድዋይፍ -ስ- አዋላጅ

might

'ማይት -ስ- ኃይል

mighty

'ማይቲ -ተ- ኃይለ'ኛ ፣ ት'ልቅ

migrant

'ማይግረንት -ስ- ስ'ደተኛ (ወደ ሌላ አገር
የ'ሚሄድ)

migrate

ማይግ'ሬይት -ግ- አገሩን ለ'ቆ ወደሌላ አገር
መሄድ [ዶደ] (ለመኖር)

mild

'ማይልድ -ተ- ለስላ'ሳ ፣ ጠን'ካራ የለ'ለው ፣
ተ'ላላ (ትግስት ወዘተ)

mildew

'ማይልዱው -ስ- አግቶ

mile

'ማይል -ስ- ማይል (የርቀት መለ'ኪያ)

milestone

'ማይልስተውን -ስ- የመንገድ ርቀት መንገ
ሪ ደንጋይ (አኅፄ አፄ በመንገድ ዳር የተ
ተ'ከለ)

militant

'ሜሊተንት -ተ- ተማይ ፣ ተዋጊ (ለእምነት
ወዘተ)

military

'ሜሊተሪ -ተ- ወታ'ደራዊ

milk

'ሜልክ -ስ- ወተት

milkmaid

'ሜልክሜይድ -ስ- ወተት አላቢ ሴት

milky

'ሜልኪ -ስ- ወተት የ'ሚመስል (ፈሳሽ)

mill

'ሜል -ስ- ወፍጮ

millennium

ሜ'ሌኒየም -ስ- አንድ ሺህ ዓመት ፣ ክርስ
እት በንጉ ክርስቶስ በመሬት ላይ የ'ሚነግሥ
በት ዘመን ፣ የስላምና የደኅንነት ዘመን

miller

'ሜለ -ስ- ባለወፍጮ ፣ በወፍጮ ቤት የ'ሚ
ሠራ

millet

'ሜሊት -ስ- የዳጉሳና የጤፍ ዓይነት እህል

516

milliner
’ሚሊነ -ስ- የሴት ባርኔጣ ሠሪና ሻጭ

million
’ሚልየን -ስ- ሚሊዮን ፡ እልፍ አእላፉት

millstone
’ሚልስተውን -ስ- የወፍጮ ደንጊያ

mimic
’ሚ'ሚክ -ግ- ሰው መቀ'ጸል [ቀ'ጸለ] ፡ ሰው
መቀንጠጥ [ቀነ'ጠጠ] ፡ የሰው አ'ነጋገር አስ
መ'ስሎ መ'ናገር [ተና'ገረ]

mimicry
’ሚ'ሚክሪ -ስ- ሰውን ቅ'ጸላ (ለአ'ነጋገር) ፡
ቅንጠጣ

mince
’ሚንስ -ግ- መክተፍ [ከ'ተፈ]

mincing machine
’ሚንሲንግ ፡ መ'ሺይን -ስ- የሥጋ መፍጫ
መኪና

mind
’ማይንድ -ስ- አእምሮ ፡ አንጎል ፡ አስተሳሰብ
-ግ- መ'ቃወም [ተቃ'ወመ] ፡ መ'ጠን
ቀቅ [ተጠነ'ቀቀ]

mine
’ማይን -ተስ- የኔ

mineral
’ሚነራል -ስ- የማዕድን'ን ቦታ (የተቆ'ፈረ)
ማዕ'ድን

mingle
’ሚንገል -ግ- መ'ደባለቅ [ተደባ'ለቀ] ፡ ማ'ደ
ባለቅ [አ'ደባ'ለቀ]

miniature
’ሚኒቸ -ስ- በጣም ት'ንሽ ሥዕል ፡ ያንድ ቅር
ፅ ት'ንሽ ምስል

minimize
’ሚኒማይዝ -ግ- ማሳ'ነስ [አሳ'ነሰ]

minimum
’ሚኒመም -ቅ- በተቻለ መጠን ያነሰ

mining
’ማይኒንግ -ስ- የማዕ'ድን ሥራ

minister
’ሚኒስተ -ግ- ማገልገል [አገለ'ገለ] ፡ መርዳት
[ረዳ]
-ስ- ሚኒስትር ፡ ካህን

ministerial
ሚኒስ'ቴሪየል -ቅ- የ'ሚኒስትር ፡ የ'ሚኒስቴር

ministry
’ሚኒስትሪ -ስ- ሚኒስቴር (መሥሪያ ቤት)

minor
’ማይነ -ቅ- ዝ'ቅተ'ኛ ፡ ያ'ነሰ ፡ ዋጋ የሌ'ለው
-ስ- ከሃያ ዓመት በታ'ች ያ'ለ ሰው

minority
ማይ'ኖሪቲ -ስ- ጥቂቶ'ች ፡ በቁጥር ያነሱ

minstrel
’ሚንስትረል -ስ- እ'የዞረ የ'ሚዘፍን አዝማሪ

mint
’ሚንት -ስ- ገንዘብ የ'ሚ'ሠ'ራ'በት ቦታ
herb
-ስ- ሚንታ

minus
’ማይነስ -ቅ- ያ'ነሰ ፡ የተቀ'ነሰ'ለት

minute
’ሚኒት -ስ- ደቂቃ ፡ ቃለ ጉባኤ

minute
ማይን'ዩ፡ት -ቅ- በጣም ት'ንሽ ፡ ዲ'ቃቅ

miracle
’ሚራክል -ስ- ተአ'ምር ፡ የ'ሚያስደ'ንቅ ነገር
ያልተለ'መደ ነገር

miraculous
ሚ'ራክዩለስ -ቅ- አስገ'ራሚ ፡ ታአ'ምራዊ

mire
’ማየ -ስ- ጭቃ ፡ አሮንቃ ፡ ቆሻሻ

mirror
’ሚረ -ስ- መስታዎት (ማየ)

mirth
’መ፡ስ -ስ- መ'ደሰት ፡ ሣቅ

misapprehension
ሚሳፕረ'ሄንሽን -ስ- በትክክል አለመ'ረዳት

misbehave
ሚስቢ'ሄቭ -ግ- አመለቢስ መሆን [ሆነ] ፡
መጥፎ አመል ማሳየት [አሳ'የ] ፡ መባለግ [ባ
ለገ]

miscalculate
ሚስ'ካልክዩሌይት -ግ- ስሕተት ማድረግ [አ
ደ'ረገ] (ባ'ሰበት ፡ በ'ገ'መተ'ት ነገር)

miscarriage
’ሚስካረጅ -ስ- ማስ'ረድ (ፅንስ)

miscarry
ሚስ'ካሪ -ግ- እፍ'ጸሜ አለመ'ድረስ [-ደ'ረስ]
ማስወ'ረድ [አስወ'ረደ] (ለእርግዝ'ና)

517

miscellaneous

ሚስ'ሌይኔየስ -ቅ- ል'ዩ ል'ዩ ፣ ድብልቅልቅ

mischief

'ሚስቺፍ -ስ- እ'ዋኪ'ነት ፣ ክልፍልፍ'ነት ክፉት ፣ በጥባጭ'ነት

mischievous

'ሚስቺቨስ -ቅ- ቅልብልብ ፣ እ'ዋኪ ፣ በጥ ባጭ

misdemeanour

ሚስደ'ሚይን -ስ- መጥፎ ሥራ ፣ ተላላፈ'ነት (ሕ'ግን)

miserly

'ማይዘሊ -ቅ- ሥ'ሥታም ፣ ገብጋ'ባ ፣ ቆጥ ቋ'ጣ

miserable

'ሚዘረብል -ቅ- በጣም ያልተደ'ሰተ ፣ መከራ ያጠ'ቃው ፣ መከሪ'ኛ

misery

'ሚዘሪ -ስ- መከራ ፣ ች'ግር

misfortune

ሚስ'ፎቹን -ስ- መጥፎ ዕ'ድል

misgiving

ሚስ'ጊቪንግ -ስ- ጥር'ጣሬ ፣ ፍርሀት

mishap

'ሚስሀፕ -ስ- ድንገተ'ኛ አደጋ (ቀለ'ል ያለ)

mislay

ሚስ'ሌይ -ግ- ዕቃ ያኖሩ'በትን ቦታ ማጣት [አ'ጣ] ፣ ለጊዜው ማጣት [አ'ጣ]

mislead

ሚስ'ሊይድ -ግ- ማ'ታለል [አ'ታለለ] ፣ ማ'ሳ ሳት [አ'ሳሳተ]

misplace

ሚስፕ'ሌይስ -ግ- ያለቦታው ማስቀ'መጥ [አ ስቀ'መጠ]

misrepresentation

ሚስሬፕሪዘን'ቴይሽን -ስ- እ'ያ'ወቁ የ'ሚያቀር ቡት ማ'ሳሳያ ፣ ትክ'ክል ያልሆነ ወሬ

miss

'ሚስ -ግ- ለመድረስ ፣ ለመምታት ፣ ለማግ ኘት ወዘተ አለመቻል [-ቻለ]

Miss

'ሚስ -ስ- ወይዘሪት

missile

'ሚሳይል -ስ- ተወርዋሪ የጦር መ'ሣሪያ ፣ ተስፈንጣሪ መ'ሣሪያ

missing

'ሚሲንግ -ቅ- የጠ'ፋ

mission

'ሚሺን -ስ- ተግባር ፣ መልእክት ፣ መልእክተ 'ኞች ፣ በሕይወት ሙሉ የ'ሚፈ'ጸም ተግባር *religious* -ስ- ሚስዮን (የሃይማኖት ስብከት ድር 'ጅት)

missionary

'ሚሽነሪ -ስ- የወንጌል መልእክተ'ኛ ፣ ሚስ ዮናዊ ሰው

mist

'ሚስት -ስ- ጭጋግ

mistake

ሚስ'ቴይክ -ግ- መ'ሳሳት [ተሳሳተ]

mistaken

ሚስ'ቴይከን -ቅ- የተሳሳተ

Mister

'ሚስተ -ስ- አቶ

mistress

'ሚስትረስ -ስ- ው'ሽማ (ሴት) ወዳጅ *employer* -ስ- እ'መቤት

mistrust

ሚስት'ረስት -ግ- አለማመን [-አ'መነ] ፣ መ'ጠ ራጠር [ተጠራ'ጠረ]

misunderstanding

ሚስንደስ'ታንዲንግ -ስ- አለመግባባት

misuse

ሚስ'ዩዝ -ግ- ማ'በላሸት [አ'በላ'ሸ] ፣ ያለ ቦታው ማዋል [አዋለ]

misuse

ሚስ'ዩስ -ስ- ማ'በላሸት ፣ አንድ ነገር በ'ሚ 'ገባው ቦታ አለማዋል

mite

'ማይት -ስ- በጣም ት'ንሽ ነገር ፣ ት'ንሽ ሕፃን

mitigate

'ሚቲጌይት -ግ- ማ ሳሳል [አ'ሳሻለ] ፣ ማለ 'ዘብ [አለ'ዘበ]

mitten

'ሚተን -ስ- የሱፍ እ'ጅ ቡ'ራብ (አራ'ቱን ጣት ለብ'ቻ አውራ ጣት ለብ'ቻ የ'ሚሸ'ፍን)

518

ር̣ክስ -ግ- መደባለቅ [ደባ'ለቀ]፣ መ'ደባለቅ
[ተደባ'ለቀ]

ιture
ሚከስቸ -ስ- የተደባ'ለቀ ነገር ፤ ማ'ደባለቅ

ix-up
'ሚክሰፕ -ስ- አለመግባባት ፤ መ'ሳሳት

noan
'መውን -ግ- ማቃሰት [አ቏'ሰተ] (ከሥቃይ
የተነ'ሣ)

moat
'መውት -ስ- በቤት ዙሪያ ያ'ለ የውሃ አጥር
(ለመ'ከላከያ)

mob
'ሞብ -ስ- ሕ'ገ ወ'ጥ ሰዎ'ች ፣ የተሰበ'ሰቡ
ሰዎ'ች (ብጥ'ብጥ ለማንሣት ፣ አንድ ሁኔቴ
ለመ'መልከት)

mobile
'መውባይል -ቅ- የ'ሚንቀሳ'ቀስ

mock
'ሞክ -ግ- ማፌዝ [አፌዘ]

mockery
'ሞከሪ -ስ- ፌዝ

mode
'መውድ -ስ- ያ'ደራረግ ወይን'ም ያ'ሠራር መን
ገድ ፣ ዘዴ ፤ ሞድ (የልብስ)

model
'ሞደል -ስ- ያንድ ነገር ት'ንሽ ቅርፅ ፣ እንደ
ም'ሳሌ የ'ሚ'ገለ'በጥ ነገር ፤ ሞድ የ'ምታሳ'ይ
ሴት ልጅ ፤ ጥሩ ም'ሳሌ (ሊ'ገለ'በጥ የ'ሚ'ገ
'ባው)

moderate
'ሞደረት -ቅ- መካ'ከለ'ኛ

modern
'ሞደን -ቅ- ዘመናዊ ፤ አ'ዲስ ሐ'ሳብ ያ'ለው

modest
'ሞደስት -ቅ- ትሑት ፤ ጭ'ምት

modification
ሞዲፊ'ኬይሽ'ን -ስ- ማ'ሻሻል ፤ ት'ንሽ ለውጥ

modify
'ሞዲፋይ -ግ- ማ'ሻሻል [አ'ሻሻለ] ፤ ት'ንሽ
ለውጥ ማድረግ [አደ'ረገ]

moist
'ሞይስት -ቅ- እርጥብ ፤ ዝናማም

moisten
'ሞይሰን -ግ- ማርጠብ [አረ'ጠበ]

moisture
'ሞይስቸ -ስ- እርጥበት

mole
'መውል -ስ- ፍልፈል ፤ ግርያም የሳመ'ችው
ም'ል'ክት (በሰው'ነት ላይ)

molest
'መለስት -ግ- ጥ'ልቅ ማለት [አለ] (በሰው
ሥራ) ፤ ማ'ወክ [አ'ወከ] (እ'ያ'ወቁ)

molten
'ሞለተን -ቅ- የቀ'ለጠ (ለብረታ ብረት)

moment
'መውመንት -ስ- ቅጽበት ፤ አፍታ

momentary
'መውመንትሪ -ቅ- አንድ አፍታ የቆ'የ

momentous
መ'ሜንተስ -ቅ- በጣም አስፈ'ላጊ

monarch
'ሞነክ -ስ- የበላይ ንጉሥ ፤ ንጉሥ

monarchy
'ሞነኪ -ስ- ንጉሣዊ አ'ገዛዝ ፣ ግዛቱ በአንድ
ከ'ፍተ'ኛ ሥልጣን ሥር ያ'ለ መንግሥት

monastery
'ሞነስትሪ -ስ- ገዳም

Monday
'መንደይ -ስ- ሰ'ኞ

monetary
'መነትሪ -ቅ- የገንዘብ

money
'መኒ -ስ- ገንዘብ

mongrel
'ሞንግረል -ስ- መጢቃ ፣ ዘሩ የተደባ'ለቀ
እንስሳ (ው'ሻ ፣ ወዘተ)

monitor
'ሞኒተ -ስ- መካሪ ፣ አስጠንቃቂ ሰው ፤የትም
ህርት ክፍል አለቃ (ተማሪ)

monk
'መንክ -ስ- መነኩሴ

monkey
'መንኪ -ስ- ዝንጀሮ

monopoly
መ'ኖፕሊ -ስ- አንድ ዓይነት ንግድ ያለ ተወ
ዳዳሪ መያዝ

519

monotonous
መ'ኖተነስ -ቅ- አሰልቺ

monster
'ሞንስተ -ስ- ታ'ላቅ አስፈ'ሪ ፍጡር፤ ወይን'ም
ት'ልቅ ተክል

monstrous
'ሞንስትረስ -ቅ- በጣም ት'ልቅ ፣ አስደንጋጭ፣
አስፈ'ሪ

month
'መንስ -ስ- ወር

monument
'ሞኒዩመንት -ስ- ሐውልት

mood
'ሙ:ድ -ስ- አ'ኳኳን ፣ ስ'ሜት

moody
'ሙ:ዲ -ቅ- አመለ'ኛ ፣ ነጭና'ጭ ፣ አመለቢስ

moon
'ሙ:ን -ስ- ጨረቃ

moonlight
'ሙ:ንላይት -ስ- የጨረቃ ብርሃን

moor
'ሙ: -ስ- ሰ'ፊ ጠፍ ሜዳ ፤ ቱርክ ፤ (የቱርክ አገር
ሰው)
-ግ- ጀልባ እወንዝ ዳር ማሠር [አ'ሠረ]

moot
'ሙ:ት -ቅ- አ'ጠራጣሪ ፣ አ'ከራካሪ
-ግ- ለመ'ነጋገር ማቅረብ [አቀ'ረበ]
(አንድ ጉዳ'ይ)

mop
'ሞፕ -ስ- ወለል መጥረጊያ ፣ ብት'ቱ (በን
ጨት ላይ ቀታ'ሠረ)

mope
'መውፕ -ግ- ስላንድ እ'ክል ማ'ሰላሰል [አ'ሰ
ላ'ሰለ]

moral
'ሞረል -ቅ- ጥሩ ፣ የተቀ'ጣ ፣ ግብረ ገ'ባዊ ፣
ባለ ምግባር

morale
መ'ራ:ል -ስ- ውስጣዊ ስ'ሜት (ስለ ድፍረት ፣
መ'ተማመን)

morals
'ሞረልዝ -ስ- ግብረ ገ'ብ'ነት

morality
መ'ራሊ.ቲ -ስ- ግብረ ገ'ብ'ነት

morbid
'ሞ:ቢድ -ቅ- አእምሮው ያልተተካ'ከለ ፣
'መመ ፤ በሰው ሥቃይ የ'ሚ'ደ'ሰት

more
'ሞ: -ቅ- ተጨ'ማሪ ፣ ይበልጥ

moreover
ሞ'ረውቨ -ተግ- ከ'ዚህ በላይ

morning
'ሞ:ኒንግ -ስ- ጧት ፤ ንጋት

morose
መ'ረውስ -ቅ- ጭፍግ'ግ ያለው ፤ ሊ'ነ
የ'ማይሽ ፣ የማይጠዳው ፣ አይጠዴ

morsel
'ሞ:ሰል -ስ- ቁ'ራሽ (ምግብ)

mortal
'ሞ:ተል -ቅ- መዋቲ

mortar
'ሞ:ተ -ስ- የተደባ'ለቀ ሲሚንት
military
-ስ- አ'ጻፍኔ (የጦር መ'ሣሪያ ዓ)
utensil "
-ስ- ሙቀ'ጫ

mortgage
'ሞ:ጊጅ -ስ- ንብረትን ዋስ በማድረግ ገን
መ'በደር

mortify
'ሞ:ቲፋይ -ግ- በሰው ፊት ማሳ'ፈር [አሳ'ፈ
ሰው ማሳ'ዘን [አሳ'ዘነ] ፤ ሰው'ነት በ
በጸሎት ማድከም [አደ'ከመ]

mortuary
'ሞ:ትዩወሪ -ስ- ሬሳ እስኪ'ቀ'በር የ'ሚ'ቀ
ጥ'በት ቦታ (በሐኪም ቤት ግ'ቢ) ፤ የሬሳ (

mosque
'ሞስክ -ስ- መስጊድ (የእስላሞ'ች ቤተ መ
ደስ)

mosquito
ሞስ'ኪተው -ስ- ቢምቢ ፤ የወባ ትን'ኝ

moss
'ሞስ -ስ- የደንጊያ ፣ የእንጨት ሽበት (በደ
ጊያ ፣ በእንጨት ወይን'ም በርጥብ ቦታ ላ
የ'ሚበቅል አረንጓዴ ወይን'ም ብጫ ተክል

most
'መውስት -ቅ- የ'ሚበልጥ

520

stly
ሞውስትሊ -ተግ- ይበልጡ፡ን

th
ሞ፟ስ -ስ- ብል ፣ ቁንቁን

ther
ሞዘ -ስ- እ'ናት

ther-in-law
ሞዘሪንሎ፡ -ስ- አማት (የባል ወይን'ም የሚ ስት እ'ናት)

tion
ሞውሽን -ስ- እንቅስ'ቃሴ

tive
ሞውቲቭ -ስ- የ'ሚያ'ነዃ'ሣ ምክንያት (እን ድ ነገር ለማድረግ)

tor
ሞውተ -ስ- ሞቶር

tor-car
ሞውተ'ካ፡ -ስ- መኪና ፣ አውቶሞቢል

ttled
ሞተልድ -ቅ- ል'ዩ ል'ዩ ቀለም በገላው ላይ የጣለ'በት

otto
'ሞተው -ስ- አ'ጭር ም'ሳለያዊ እ'ነጋገር (የ ጠባይን ሕ'ግጋት የ'ሚ'ና'ገር) ፣ ሕይወት የ'ሚ 'መ'ራ'በት ም'ሳሌ

ould
ሞልድ -ግ- ቅርፅ መስጠት [ሰ'ጠ] ፣ መልክ መስጠት [ሰ'ጠ]

ult
ሞልት -ግ- የላባ መርገፍ [ረ'ገፈ] (አዲስ ለማ ብቀል)

ound
'ማውንድ -ስ- ት'ንሽ የደንጊያ ፣ የአፈር ቁ'ልል

ount
'ማውንት -ግ- መውጣት [ወ'ጣ] (እንድ፡ነገር ላይ)

ountain
'ማውንቴን -ስ- ተራራ

ountainous
'ማውንተነስ -ቅ- ተራራ'ማ

ourn
'ሞ፡ን -ግ- ማልቀስ [አለ'ቀሰ] (ለሞተ ሰው)

---

mourner
'ሞ፡ነ -ስ- አልቃሽ

mournful
'ሞ፡ንፉል -ቅ- ያ'ዘነ

mourning
'ሞ፡ኒንግ -ስ- ልቅሶ ፣ ለቅሶ

mouse
'ማውስ -ስ- አይጥ

mousetrap
'ማውስትራፕ -ስ- ያይጥ ወጥመድ

moustache
መስ'ታ፡ሽ -ስ- ሪዝ

mouth
'ማውፅ -ስ- አፍ

mouthful
'ማውስፉል -ስ- አፍ ሙሉ

mouthpiece
'ማውፅፒደስ -ስ- ዋቢ ፣ ጠበቃ ፣ የሌላውን ሐሳ'ብ የ'ሚገልጽ ሰው ፣ ጋዜጣ ወዘተ፤ወደደአፍ የ'ሚ'ደ'ረገው የሙዚቃ መሣሪያ (ዋሽንት) ወዘተ ክፍል

movable
'ሞ፡ቫበል -ቅ- የ'ሚንቀሳ'ቀስ

move
'ሙ፡ቭ -ግ- ማንቀሳቀስ [አንቀሳ'ቀሰ]፣ መንቀ ሳቀስ [ተንቀሳ'ቀሰ]

movement
'ሙ፡ቭመንት -ስ- እንቅስ'ቃሴ

moving
'ሙ፡ቪንግ -ቅ- ተንቀሳቃሽ

mow
'መው -ግ- ማጨድ [አ'ጨደ]

much
'መች -ቅ- ብዙ ፣ አ'ያሌ

muck
'መክ -ስ- ቆሻሻ ፣ ጉድፍ

mucus
'ምዩከስ -ስ- ንፍጥ

mud
'መድ -ስ- ጭቃ

muddle
'መደል -ስ- ሥርዓት የሌ'ለው ፣ ዝብርቅርቅ ነገር

521

muddy
’መዲ -ቅ- ጭቃ'ማ

muffin
’መፊን -ስ- ቂጣ (ጠ.ቃጠቆ ያ'ለ'በት)

muffle
’መፈል -ግ- ማ'ፈን [አ'ፈነ] ፤ ማድከም [አደ.
'ከመ] (ድምፅ) ፤ መ'ሸፋፈን [ተሸፋ.'ፈነ]

muffler
’መፍለ -ስ- ሻል (ወፍራም)

mug
’መግ -ስ- ኩ'ባ'ያ

mule
’ምዩ:ል -ስ- በቅሎ

multiple
’መልቲፕል -ቅ- ል'ዩ ል'ዩ ክፍል ያ'ለው ፤
ብዙ

multiplication
መልቲፕሊ'ኬይሸን -ስ- ማብዛት ፤ ማ'ባዛት

multiply
’መልቲፕላይ -ግ- ማብዛት [አበ'ዛ] ፤ ማ'ባ
ዛት [አ'ባ'ዛ]

mumble
’መምብል -ግ- ማነብነብ [አነበ'ነበ] ፤ ጉን'ግ
ርን ግልጽ አድርጎ አለመ'ናገር [-ተና'ገረ]

mummy
’መሚ -ስ- በመድኃኒት እንዳይፈርስ'ና እንዳ
ይበሰ'ብስ የተደ'ረገ አስከሬን

mumps
’መምፕስ -ስ- ጆሮ ደ'ግፍ

munch
’መንች -ግ- አጥብቆ ማ'ላመጥ [አ'ላ'መጠ] ፤
ማ'ኘክ [አ'ኘከ]

municipal
ምዩ'ኒሲፕል -ቅ- ከከተማ አስተዳደር ጋር
ግን'ኙ'ነት ያለው

municipality
ምዩኒሲ'ፓሊቲ -ስ- ማ'ዘጋጃ ቤት

munitions
ምዩ'ኒሸንዝ -ስ- የጦር መ'ሣሪያ ሙዳ'ብር
(የጥ'ይት መዘተ)

mural
ምዩራል -ስ- እግድግ'ዳ ላይ የተሣለ ሥዕል
-ቅ- የግድግ'ዳ

murder
’መ:ደ -ግ- መግደል [ገ'ደለ] (ሰው)
-ስ- ነፍስ ግ'ዳይ.

murderer
’መ:ደረ -ስ- ነፍስ ገዳይ

murky
’መ:ኪ. -ቅ- ጥቁር ፤ ያልጠ'ራ ፤ የደበ'ዘዘ

murmur
’መ:መ -ግ- ማጉረምረም [አጉረመ'ረመ]

muscle
’መስል -ስ- ጡንቻ

muscular
’መስክዩለ -ቅ- ጡንቻ'ማ ፤ የጡንቻ

museum
መዩ'ዚየም -ስ- ቤተ መዘከር (ታሪካውያን
ቅርሶ'ች የሚ'ቀ'መጡበት'ና ለሕዝብ የሚ.
'ታ'ዩ'በት ቤት)

mushroom
’መሸሩም -ስ- እንጉዳይ

music
ምዩዚክ -ስ- ሙዚቃ

musket
’መስከት -ስ- መስኪ.'ት (ጠመንጃ)

muslim
’መዝሊም -ቅ- እስላም

muslin
’መዝሊን -ስ- ቀ'ጭን የጥጥ ጨርቅ

must
’መስት -ግ- መ'ገባት [ተገ'ባ]

mustard
’መስተድ -ስ- ሰናፍ'ጭ

muster
’መስተ -ግ- መሰብሰብ [ሰበ'ሰበ] (ወ'ታ'ደር
መዘተ ለቁጥ'ጥር)

musty
’መስቲ -ቅ- የሻገተ ፤ የሻ.ጋታ ሽ'ታ ያ'ለው

mutation
ምዩ'ቴይሸን -ስ- ለውጥ ፤ ል'ዩ'ነት

mute
ምዩ:ት -ቅ- ደዳ

mutilate
ምዩ:ቲሌይት -ግ- የሰው አካል መቆራረጥ
[ቆራ'ረጠ] ፤ አካል ስንኩል ማድረግ [አደ'ረ.

mutiny

ም'ዩ፡ተኒ -ስ- ብጥ'ብጥ ፡ አድማ (የመርከበ
'ኞ'ች ፡ የሰር ሠራዊት)

mutter

'መ፡ተ -ግ- ማነብነብ [አነብ'ነበ] ፡ ማጉረም
ረም [አጉረመ'ረመ]

mutton

'መ፡ተን -ስ- የበግ ሥጋ

mutual

ም'ዩቸዩወል -ቅ- የወል ፡ የጋራ ፡ የርስበርስ

muzzle

'መዘል -ስ- አፍ'ና አፍንጫ (የው'ሻ ፡ የቀ
በር፡ወዘተ) ፡ አፈ. ሙዝ (የጠመንጃ)

my

'ማይ -ተስ- የኔ

myself

ማይ'ሴልፍ -ተስ- (እኔ) ራሴ

mysterious

ሚስ'ቲሪየስ -ቅ- ምስጢራዊ ፡ የተሸ'ሸገ ፡ መፍ
ትሔ የሌ'ለው ሊ.ረ'ዱት የ'ማይ'ቻል

mystery

'ሚስተሪ -ስ- ምስጢር ፡ ድብቅ ፡ ሊ.ረ'ዱት
የማ'ይቻል ነገር

myth

'ሚ፡ስ -ስ- የጥንት ታሪክ ፡ አፈ.ታሪክ

mythical

'ሚ፡ሲ.ከል -ቅ- ል'ብ ወ'ለድ'ነት ያ'ለው (የጥ
ንት ታሪክ) ፡ አፈ.ታሪካዊ

N

nag

'ናግ -ግ- መጨቅጨቅ [ጨቀ'ጨቀ] ፡ መነዝ
ነዝ [ነዘ'ነዘ]

nail

'ኔይል -ስ- ምስማር ፡ ሚስማር ፡ ችንካር
finger-
-ስ- ጥፍር (የእ'ጅ)

naive

ና'ይቭ -ቅ- ተላቂ ፡ ጅል ፡ ጥ'ኝ ፡ የ'ጋየ'ግ

naked

'ኔይከድ -ቅ- ራቁት ፡ የተራ'ቆተ ፡ ዕርቃኑን
ያለ ፡ ያልተሸ'ፈነ

name

'ኔይም -ስ- ስም

namely

'ኔይምሊ. -ተግ- ማለት ፡ ይኸው'ም

namesake

'ኔይምሴይክ -ስ- ጥላሽ

nanny

'ናኒ -ስ- ልጅ አሳ'ዳጊ ፡ ሞግዚት (ሴት)

nanny-goat

'ናኒገውት -ስ- ሴት ፍ'የል

nap

'ናፕ -ስ- ተ'ኝቶ እ፡ንታልፍ፡ ሸለብታ

nape

'ኔይፕ -ስ- ማጅራት

napkin

'ናፕኪ.ን -ስ- የብብታ ርጣ ፡ አፍ መጥረጊያ
ርጣ

narcotic

ና፡ክትቲክ -ቅ- የ'ሚያደን'ዝዝ ፡ የ'ሚያስተኛ
መድኃኒት

narrate

ና'ሬይት -ግ- ታሪክ ማውራት [አወ'ራ] ፡ መ
ተ'ረክ [ተ'ረክ]

narration

ና'ሬይሸን -ስ- ታሪክ ፡ መተ'ረክ (ያንድ አገር
ወይ'ንም መንግሥት)

narrative

'ናረቲቭ -ስ- ታሪክ

narrator

ና'ሬይተ -ስ- አውራ፡ ተረት ተራች

narrow

'ናረው -ቅ- ጠ'ባብ

nasal

'ኔይዘል -ቅ- የአፍንጫ

523

nasty
'ና:ስቲ -ቅ- አስቀ'ያሚ ፣ ሸ'ታው ወይን'ም
ጣዕሙ የ'ሚያስጠ'ላ ፣ የ'ማይስማ'ማ
natal
'ኔተል -ቅ- የልደት ፣ የመ'ወለድ
nation
'ኔይሽን -ስ- አገር'ና ሕዝብ
national
'ናሽነል -ቅ- ብሔራዊ
nationality
ናሽ'ናለቲ -ስ- ዜግ'ነት
native
'ኔይቲቭ -ቅ- ያገር ተ'ወላጅ
natural
'ናቸረል -ቅ- ጠባያዊ ፤ የተለ'መደ
naturalization
ናቸረላይ'ዜይሽን -ግ- የሌላ አገር ዜግ'ነት
መያዝ [ያዘ]
naturally
'ናቸረሊ -ተግ- በርግጥ ፤ በተለምዶ
nature
'ኔይቸ -ስ- ሥነ ፍጥረት
naught
'ኖ:ት -ስ- ምን'ም ነገር
zero
-ስ- ዜሮ
naughty
'ኖ:ቲ -ቅ- ቅልብልብ ፤ የ'ማይታ'ዘዝ (ሕፃን)፣
በጥባጭ
nausea
'ኖ:ሲየ -ስ- የትውከቢያ ፣ የማስታወክ ስ'ሜት ፣
ቅልሽልሽታ
nautical
'ኖ:ቲከል -ቅ- ከባሕር ጉዞ ጋር ግን'ኙ'ነት
ያ'ለው
naval
'ኔይቨል -ቅ- የባሕር ኃይል
nave
'ኔይቭ -ስ- ፣ በቤተ ክርስቲያን መካ'ከለ'ኛው
ቦታ (ሕዝቡ የ'ሚቆም'በት) ፣ ቅኔ ማሕሌት
navel
'ኔይቨል -ስ- እም'ብርት

navigable
'ናቪገበል -ቅ- መርከብ ሊሄድ'በት የ'ሚችል
(ወንዝ)
navigate
'ናቪጌይት -ግ- መርከብ መንዳት [ነ'ዳ]
navvy
'ናቪ -ስ- የ'ጅ ሠ'ራተ'ኛ (ከባ'ድ ሥራ የ'ሚ
ሠራ) ፣ የጉልበት ሥራ የ'ሚሠራ
navy
'ኔይቪ -ስ- የባሕር ኃይል
navy-blue
ኔይቪ ብ'ሉ: -ቅ- ጥቁር ሰማያዊ
near
'ኒየ -ተግ- ቅርብ
nearly
'ኒየሊ -ተግ- ያህል
nearsighted
ኒየ'ሳይቲድ -ቅ- እሩቅ ማየት የ'ማይችል
neat
'ኒይት -ቅ- ንጹሕ ፣ ሥርዓት ያ'ለው ፣ የተሰ
'ተረ
nebulous
'ኔብዩለስ -ቅ- ደብዛ'ዛ ፣ ጉልህ ያልሆነ
necessary
'ኔሰሰሪ -ቅ- አስፈ'ላጊ
necessity
ነ'ሴሲ.ቲ -ስ- አስፈ'ላጊ ነገር
neck
'ኔክ -ስ- አንገት
necklace
'ኔክለስ -ስ- ድሪ ፣ ያንገት ጌጥ
necklet
'ኔክለት -ስ- ድሪ ፣ ያንገት ጌጥ
necktie
'ኔክታይ -ስ- ክራባት
need
'ኒይድ -ስ- ፍ'ላጎት ፣ እጦት ፣ ች'ግር
-ግ- መፈ'ለግ [ፈ'ለገ]
needle
'ኒይዶል -ስ- መርፌ
needy
'ኒይዲ -ቅ- ድሃ ፣ የተቸ'ገረ ፣ ምስኪን ፣ ች'ግ
ረ'ኛ

524

negative
'ኔገቲቭ -ቅ- አፍራሽ ፡ አሉታ

neglect
ነግ'ሌክት -ግ- ቸ'ል ማለት [አለ] ፣ ቸ'ላ ማለት [አለ]

negligence
'ኔግሊጀንስ -ስ- ቸ'ልተ'ኛነት

negligent
'ኔግሊጀንት -ቅ- ቸ'ልተ'ኛ ፣ ጥንቁቅ ያልሆነ

negligible
'ኔግሊጀበል -ቅ- ቸ'ል የ'ሚሉት፣ዋጋ የሌ'ለው

negotiate
ነ'ገውሺዬይት -ግ- ወደ ስምም'ነት ለመድ ረስ መ'ወያየት [ተወያ'የ] ፣ የስምም'ነት ድር' ድር ማድረግ [አደ'ረገ]

negro
'ኔይግረው -ቅ- ሻንቅ'ላ

neigh
'ኔይ -ግ- እንደ ፈረስ መጮኸ [ጮኸ]
-ስ- የፈረስ ጩኸት

neighbour
'ኔብ -ስ- ጎረቤት ፣ መንደርተ'ኛ

neighbourhood
'ኔበሁድ -ስ- አቅራ'ቢያ (በቤት)

neighbouring
'ኔበሪንግ -ቅ- ቅርብ ፣ አ'ካባቢ

neither
'ናይዘ -ተግ- ሆነ ... ወይም (በአፍራሽ'ነት)

nephew
'ኔፍዩ -ስ- የወንድ'ም ፣ የእነት ልጅ

nerve
'ነ:ቭ -ስ- የስ'ሜት ሥሮ'ች

nervous
'ነ:ቨስ -ቅ- በቀ'ላሉ የ'ሚደነ'ግጥ

nest
'ኔስት -ስ- የወፍ ጎ'ጆ

nestle
'ኔሰል -ግ- መ'ፈጋፈግ [ተፈጋ'ፈገ] (ሙቀ ትና ም'ቾት ለማግኘት)

nestling
'ኔስሊንግ -ስ- ገና መብረር የ'ማይችል ወፍ

net
'ኔት -ስ- መርበብ ፣ መረብ

nettle
'ኔተል -ስ- ሳ'ማ ፣ አለብላቢት

network
'ኔትወክ -ስ- የአንድ መሥሪያ ቤት ቅርንጫ ፎ'ች ፣ ግን'ኙነት ያ'ላቸው የራዲዮ ጣቢያዎ' ች ፣ የተጠላ'ለፈ ነገር (እንደ መርበብ)

neuter
'ን'ዩተ -ቅ- ግ0ዝ (ጾታ)

neutral
'ን'ዩትረል -ቅ- አማካኝ የሆነ ፣ ከሁለ'ቱ'ም ወገን ያልሆነ ፣ ገለልተ'ኛ

never
'ኔቨ -ተግ- በፍ'ጹም ፣ በምን'ም ጊዜ

nevertheless
ኔቨዘ'ሌስ -ተግ- ቢሆን'ም ፣ ይሁን'ና ፣ ሆ ኖ'ም

new
'ን'ዩው -ቅ- አ'ዲስ

newcomer
'ን'ዩከመ -ስ- አ'ዲስ ገ'ብ ፣ አ'ዲስ መጪ

news
'ን'ዩዝ -ስ- ወሬ ፣ ዜና

newspaper
'ን'ዩዝፔይፐ -ስ- ጋዜጣ

next
'ኔክስት -ቅ- የ'ሚቀ'ጥል ፣ ቀ'ጣይ

nearest
'ኒሬስት -ቅ- የቅ'ርብ ፣ በጣም ቅርብ የሆነ

nib
'ኒብ -ስ- የብዕር ጫፍ

nibble
'ኒበል -ግ- ጥ'ቂም ጥ'ቂም እ'ያደ'ረጉ- መብ ላት [በ'ላ] (ለትና'ንሽ እንስሳት) ፣ (ሁ'ለት ል'ብ መሆን [ሆነ] (ለማድረግ ለመ'ቀበል እየ'ፈ'ለጉ)

nice
'ናይስ -ቅ- ጥሩ ፣ ያማረ

nick
'ኒክ -ስ- ጭረት (ለቁስል)

nickname
'ኒክኔይም -ስ- በስም ላይ ተጨ'ማሪ የቁል ም'ጫ ፣ የመቀ'ለጃ ፣ የማፈዝ ስም (ም'ሳሌ ፣ አ'ጭሩን ሰው 'ዛፍ' ማለት)

niece
'ኒይስ -ስ- የወን'ድም ፣ የእነት ልጅ (ሴት)

525

niggard
'ኒገድ -ቅ- ሥ'ሥታም ፣ ገብጋባ

nigger
'ኒገ -ስ- ጥቁር ቡና'ማ (ቀለም) ፣ ጠቋራ (የጥ
ላ'ቻ መ'ጠሪያ)

night
'ናይት -ስ- ሌሊት ፣ ጭለማ

nightcap
'ናይትካፕ -ስ- የመ'ኝታ ቆብ ፣ ከመ'ኝታ
በፊት የ'ሚ'ጠ'ጣ መጠ'ጥ

nightfall
ናይትፎ፡ል -ስ- ምሽት

nightmare
'ናይትሜየ -ስ- ቅዠት

nil
'ኒል -ቅ- ምን'ም ፣ ዜሮ

nimble
'ኒምበል -ቅ- ፈ'ጣን ፣ ንቁ (በቶሎ የ'ሚገ
ባው)

nine
'ናይን -ቅ- ዘጠኝ

nineteen
'ናይን'ቲይን -ቅ- ዐሥራ ዘጠኝ

nineteenth
'ናይን'ቲንፅ -ቅ- ዐሥራ ዘጠነኛ

ninetieth
'ናይንቲየፅ -ቅ- ዘጠናኛ

ninth
'ናይንፅ -ቅ- ዘጠነኛ

ninety
'ናይንቲ -ቅ- ዘጠና

nip
'ኒፕ -ግ- መቆንጠጥ [ቆን'ጠጠ] ፣ መንከስ
[ነ'ከሰ]

nipple
'ኒፕል -ስ-` የጡት አፍንጫ ፣ የጡት ጫፍ፣

no
'ነው -ተግ- አይደ'ለም ፣ የ'ለም

nobility
ነ'ቢሊቲ -ስ- ባለክብር'ነት ፣ መሳፍንት

noble
'ነውበል -ቅ- የተከ'በረ ፣ ገበዝ ፣ የ'ሚ'ደ'ነቅ፣
ከ'ፍ ያለ ማዕረግ ያለው

nobody
'ነውበዲ -ቅ- ማን'ም

nod
'ኖድ -ቅ- ራስ መነቅነቅ [ነቀ'ነቀ] (ለመስ
ማማት ፣ ሰላምታ ለመስጠት)

noise
'ኖይዝ -ስ- ዋካታ

nominal
'ኖሚነል -ቅ- ለስሙ ያህል ፣ በጣም ት'ንሽ

nominate
'ኖሚኔይት -ቅ- መሰየም [ሰ'የመ]

nominative
'ኖሚነቲቭ -ቅ- ሳቢ (በሰዋሰው)

nominee
ኖሚ'ኔይ -ስ- በምርጫ ላይ የ'ሚደ'ገፉት ፣
ለመ'መረጥ የታ'ጩ

nonchalant
'ኖንሻለንት -ቅ- የ'ማይገ'ደው ፣ ግ'ዴ'ለሽ ፣
ስ'ሜቱ የቀዘቀዘ

non-commital
ኖንከ'ሚተለ -ቅ- እ'ሺ'ም እም'ቢ'ም የ'ማ
ይል ፣ አስተያየቱን የ'ሚሸ'ሽግ ፣ ከማ'ን'ኛው
ም ወገን ያልሆነ (በጥል)

none
'ነን -ተስ- ማን'ም

nonsense
'ኖንሰንስ -ስ- ትርኪ ምርኪ ፣ የ'ማይረባ

nook
'ኑክ -ስ- ራ'ቅ ያለ ቦታ (ገለ'ል ብለው የ'ሚ'ቀ
'መጡ'በት)

noon
'ኑን -ስ- ቀትር

noose
'ኑስ -ስ- ሽምቀ'ቆ (የስው መስቀያ)

nor
'ኖ፡ -መሣ- ወይ'ም ፣ ወይን'ም

normal
'ኖ፡መል -ቅ- የተለመ'ደ ፣ ያ፡መ'መው ፣ ያል
ተበላ'ሸ (ለአእምሮ)

north
'ኖፅ -ስ- ሰሜን

northern
'ኖፅን -ቅ- ሰሜናዊ

526

nose
'ነውዝ -ስ- አፍንጫ

nosegay
'ነውዝጌይ -ስ- ያበባ እቅፍ:

nostalgia
ኖስ'ታልጅየ -ስ- ያገር ናፍቆት ፣ ያለፈ ሁናቴ
ትዝታ

nostril
'ኖስትረል -ስ- ያፍንጫ ቀዳዳ

not
'ኖት -ተግ- አይደ'ለም

notable
'ነውተብል -ቅ- የታ'ወቀ

notch
'ኖች -ስ- የተፋረ ነገር (በሰንጢ) ፣ ስርጓዶት

note
'ነውት -ስ- ማስታወሻ (እ'ጭር ጽሑፍ)
-ግ- ጠንቅቆ ማስተዋል [አስተዋለ]

note-book
'ነውትቡክ -ስ- ማስታወሻ መጻፊያ ደብተር

noted
'ነውተድ -ቅ- የታ'ወቀ ፣ ዝ'ነ'ኛ

notepaper
'ነውትፔይፐ -ስ- ረቂቅ ማውጫ ወረቀት ፣
ደብዳ'ቤ መጻፊያ ወረቀት

nothing
'ነሲንግ -ተግ- ምን'ም

notice
'ነውቲስ -ግ- ማስተዋል [አስተዋለ]
-ስ- ማስታወቂያ

noticeable
'ነውቲሰብል -ቅ- በቀ'ላሉ የ'ሚ'ታ'ይ ፣ ገ
ልህ

notify
'ነውቲፋይ -ግ- ማመልከት [አመለ'ከተ] ፣
ማስታወቅ [አስታ'ወቀ]

notion
'ነውሸን -ስ- ሐ'ሳብ ፣ አስተያየት

notoriety
ነውተ'ራየቲ -ስ- መጥፎ ዝ'ና

notorious
ነ'ቶሪየስ -ቅ- በመጥፎ ተግባር የታ'ወቀ

notwithstanding
ኖትዊዝ'ታንዲንግ -ተግ- ቢሆን'ም ፣ ሆኖ'ም

nought
'ኖ፡ት -ስ- ምን'ም ነገር ፣ ዜሮ

noun
'ናውን -ስ- ስም ፣ ነ'ባር ፣ ዘር

nourish
'ነሪሽ -ግ- መመ'ገብ [መ'ገበ]

novel
'ኖቨል -ስ- ረ'ጅም ል'ብ ወለ'ድ ታሪክ (በስ
'ድ ጽሑፍ የተጻፈ)
-ቅ- አ'ዲስ'ና አስገ'ራሚ

novelty
'ኖቨልቲ -ስ- አ'ዲስነት

November
ነ'ቬምበ -ስ- ኅዳር

novice
'ኖቪስ -ቅ- ልምድ የለ'ለው ፣ ጀ'ማሪ
-ስ- በተባሕትዎ ዓዘ ገ.ዜ ያልቆ'የ(ች)

now
'ናው -ተግ- አሁን

nowadays
'ናወዴይዝ -ተግ- ዛሬ'ጉ ገ.ዜ ፣ በዚ'ኸ ዘመን

nowhere
'ነዌየ -ተግ- የት'ም

noxious
'ኖክሸስ -ቅ- መርዝም ፣ የ'ሚጎዳ ፣ ጎጂ

nozzle
'ኖዝል -ስ- የፈ'ሳ'ሹ መፈ'ረሻ (ውሃ የ'ሚፈ.
ስ'በት) ፣ የፈ'ሳ'ሹ አፈ መገ፤

nucleus
ን'ዩክሊየስ -ስ- የአቶም እምብርት ፣ ያገ
ነገር መሀሉ (እምብርቱ)

nude
ን'ዩ፡ድ -ቅ- ረቀ.

nudge
'ነጅ -ግ- መገን'ተል [ገን'ተለ] ፣ በክር
ን'ስም ማድረግ [አደ'ረገ]

nudity
ን'ዩ፡ዲቲ -ስ- ረቁት'ነት

nuisance
ን'ዩሰንስ -ስ- አ'ዋኪ ፣ በተባባይ ሰው

null
'ነል -ቅ- ዋጋ ቢስ

527

numb
’ነም -ቅ- የደነ’ዘዘ
-ግ- ማደንዘዝ [አደነ’ዘዘ]

number
’ነምበ -ስ- ቁጥር

numeral
ን’ዩመረል -ስ- አኀዝ

numerical
ንዩ’ሜሪከል -ቅ- የቁጥር

numerous
ን’ዩመረስ -ቅ- ብዙ ፣ እ’ያሌ

nun
’ነን -ስ- መነኩሲት

nunnery
’ነነሪ -ስ- የመነኩሳዩያት ገዳም

nuptial
’ነነሸል -ቅ- የሠርግ ፣ የጋብ’ቻ

nurse
’ነ፡ስ -ግ- ማስታመም [አስታ’መመ]

nursemaid
’ነ፡ስሜይድ -ስ- ልጅ አሳ’ዳጊ (ሴት)

nurture
’ነ፡ቸ -ግ- ማሳ’ደግ [አሳ’ደገ] (ለሕፃን)

nut
’ነት -ስ- ለውዝ

nutriment
ን’ዩትሪመንት -ስ- ምግብ (ለጤና ተስማሚ)

nutrition
ንዩት’ሪሸን -ስ- ምግብ

nutshell
’ነትሼል -ስ- የለውዝ ቅር’ፈት

nutty
’ነቲ -ቅ- የለውዝ ጣዕም ያ’ለው

nuzzle
’ነዘል -ግ- ባፍንጫ መ’ታከክ [ታ’ከከ] (በተ ለ’ይ ለእንሰሳት)

O

oaf
’ኦውፍ -ቅ- ባለጌ ፣ ያልሠለ’ጠነ ፣ ጅላጅል ፣ ሞኝ ሞ’ኝ

oak
ኦውክ -ስ- ባ’ሉጥ (የዛፍ ዓይነት)

oar
’ኦ፡ -ስ- መቅዘፊያ

oasis
ኦ’ዌይሲስ -ስ- የምድረ በዳ ኩሬ ውሃ

oath
’ኦውስ -ስ- መሐላ ፣ ስድብ ፣ እርግማን

oatmeal
’ኦውትሚይል -ስ- የአ'ጃ ዱቄት

oats
’ኦውትስ -ስ- አ’ጃ

obdurate
’ኦብጅዩረት -ቅ- ች'ኮ ፣ መንቻ'ካ

obedient
ኦ’ቢይዲየንት -ቅ- ታ’ዛዥ

obeisance
ኦ’ቢይሰንስ -ስ- በአክብሮት እ’ጅ መንሣት ፣ መ’ታዘዝ

obelisk
’ኦበሊስክ -ስ- ከደንጊያ ተጠርቦ የተሠ’ራ አራ’ት ማዕዘን ያ’ለው ሐውልት

obese
ኦ’ቢይስ -ቅ- በጣም ወፍራም (ለሰው)

obesity
ኦ’ቢይሲቲ -ስ- ያለመጠን ውፍረት

obey
ኦ’ቤይ -ግ- መ’ታዘዝ [ታ’ዘዘ]

obituary
ኦ’ቢቹሪ -ስ- የሙት ታሪክ (በጋዜጣ ወዘተ)

object
ኦብ’ጄክት -ግ- መ’ቃወም [ተቃ’ወመ]

object
’ኦብጀክት -ስ- ነገር ፣ ዐላማ

528

objection
እብ'ጄክሽን -ስ- መ'ቃወም

objectionable
እብ'ጄክሽነበል -ቅ- የ'ማያስደ'ስት ፣ የ'ሚ
'ቃ'ወሙት

objective
እብ'ጄክቲቭ -ስ- ግብ ፣ ዐላማ

obligation
አብሊ'ጌይሽን -ስ- ግ'ዴታ

obligatory
እብ'ሊጋትሪ -ቅ- አስገ'ዳጅ ፣ ግ'ዴታዊ

oblige
እብ'ላይጅ -ግ- ውለታ መዋል [ዋለ] ፤ ማስገ
'ደድ [አስገ'ደደ]

oblique
እብ'ሊያክ -ቅ- ሠ'ያፍ (መሥመር) ፣ ቀ'ጥ
ተ'ኛ ያልሆነ ፣ ዝቅ'ል ያለ ፣ ያዘ'መመ

obliterate
እብ'ሊተሬይት -ግ- መደምሰስ [ደመ'ሰሰ] ፣
መፋቅ [ፋቀ]

obliteration
እብሊተ'ሬይሽን -ስ- መደምሰስ ፣ ድምሰሳ ፣
መፋቅ

oblivion
እብ'ሊቪየን -ስ- መ'ረሳት ፣ መ'ዘንጋት

oblivious
እብ'ሊቪየስ -ቅ- የረ'ሳ ፣ የዘነ'ጋ ፣ ዝንጉ

oblong
'አብሎንግ -ቅ- አራት ማዕዘን (ሁለ'ት ጎ'ኑ
በርዝመት የ'ሚ'መሳ'ሰል) ፣ ምላሳ

obnoxious
እብ'ኖክሸስ -ቅ- የ'ሚያስጠ'ላ ፣ ደ'ስ የ'ማያ
'ሰ'ኝ (ለጠባይ)

obscene
እብ'ሲይን -ቅ- ባለጌ ፣ አስቀ'ያሚ ፣ ስለፈቃደ
ሥጋ በይፋ የ'ሚ'ና'ገር ፣ ነውር የ'ማያውቅ

obscenity
እብ'ሴነቲ -ስ- ብልግ'ና ፣ አስቀ'ያሚ'ነት ፣
ነውር አለማወቅ

obscure
እብስክ'ዩወ -ቅ- ግልጽ ያልሆነ ፣ የተሠ'ወረ

obsequious
እብ'ሲይክዊየስ -ቅ- ተለማማጭ

observant
እብ'ዘ፡ቨንት -ስ- ተመልካች ፣ አስተዋይ ፣
ታ'ዛቢ

observation
አብዘ'ቬይሽን -ስ- መ'መልከት ፣ ማስተዋል

observe
እብ'ዘ፡ቭ -ግ- መ'መልከት [ተመለ'ከተ] ፣ ማስ
ተዋል [አስተዋለ]

observer
እብ'ዘ፡ቨ -ስ- ተመልካች ፣ ታ'ዛቢ

obsession
እብ'ሴሽን -ስ- ሐሳብን መ'ማረክ (ከፍርሃት ፣
ትክክል ካልሆነ ሐሳብ የተነ'ሣ)

obsolete
'አብሰሊይት -ቅ- ዘመናዊ ያልሆነ ፣ ያረጀ ፣
እሥራ ላይ የ'ማይውል

obstacle
'አብስተክል -ስ- መሰናክል ፣ ዕንቅፋት

obstinate
'አብስቲነት -ቅ- ች'ኮ ፣ በእንዶ ሐሳብ ች'ካ
የ'ሚል

obstruct
እብስት'ረክት -ግ- ማ'ደናቀፍ [አ'ደና'ቀፈ] ፣
እንቅፋት መሆን [ሆነ]

obtain
እብ'ቴይን -ግ- ማግኘት [አገ'ኘ]

obtrusive
እብት'ሩዚቭ -ቅ- ል'ታይ ባይ ፣ ሥ'ሱጥ

obtuse
እብ'ትዩስ -ቅ- ፈዛዛ ፣ ደ'ደብ ፣ ቶሎ የ'ማይ
ገባው

obverse
'አብቨስ -ስ- የንጉሥ መልክ ፣ ዘውድ ያ'ለ'በት
የመሐ'ለቅ መልክ ፣ ዘውድ (የ'መሐ'ለቅ)

obvious
'አብቪየስ -ቅ- ግልጽ

occasion
እ'ኬይዠን -ስ- ጊዜ (ት'ልቅ) ፣ በዐል

occasionally
እ'ኬይዠነሊ -ተግ- አልፎ አልፎ

occult
አ'ክልት -ቅ- የአስማት

occupant
'አክዩፐንት -ስ- ነዋሪ ፣ ያዥ (ሥፍራ)

occupation
አኮፕሽን -ስ- ተግባር ፣ ሥራ
occupy
ኦክዩፓይ -ግ- መያዝ [ያዘ] ፣ መውረር [ወረ
ረ] (ላገር)
occur
ኦከ፡ -ግ- መሆን [ሆነ] ፣ መድረስ [ደረስ]
(ለነገር) ፣ ትዝ ማለት [አለ]
ocean
ኦውሽን -ስ- ውቅያኖስ
octagon
ኦክተገን -ስ- ስምንት ጎን ያለው ቅርፅ
October
ኦክተውበ -ስ- ጥቅምት
oculist
ኦክዩሊስት -ስ- ያይን ሐኪም
odd
ኦድ -ቅ- ለሁለት የማይከፈል (ለሒሳብ) ፣
ጥንድ ያልሆነ ፣ ያልተለመደ ፣ እንግዳ (ለ
ሁኔታ)
oddment
ኦድመንት -ስ- ርዝራዥ ፣ ቁርጥራጭ
odds
ኦድዝ -ስ- ልዩነት ፣ አለመመጣጠን ፣
ዕድል (የተፋ ወይ ንም የመተቤ)
ode
ኦውድ -ስ- ረዢም ያለ ግጥም (ረጃጅም ና
አጫጭር ስንኞች ያለበት)
odious
ኦውዲየስ -ቅ- የሚጠላ
odour
ኦውዱ -ስ- ሽታ ፣ መዓዛ
of
ኦቭ -መዋ- የ...
off
ኦፍ -ተግ- ወዲያ ፣ ወዲውጭ
offal
ኦፈል -ስ- ሆድቃ (የእንስሳት)፣ ቁሻሻ ፣ ው
ዳቂ
offence
ኦፈንስ -ስ- ሕግ መጣስ
offend
ኦፈንድ -ስ- ማስቀየም [አስቀየመ] ፣ መስ
ደብ [ሰደበ]

offensive
ኦፈንሲቭ -ቅ- አናዳጅ ፣ አሳ'ዛኝ ፣ አስቀ
ያሚ
offer
ኦፈ -ግ- ለስጦታ ማቅረብ [አቀረበ] ፣ ለም
ሽጥ ማስማማት [አስማማ] ፣ መሥዋዕት ማቅ
ረብ [አቀረበ]
offering
ኦፈሪንግ -ስ- መሥዋዕት
alms
-ስ- ለምጽዋት የወጣ ገንዘብ
offhand
ኦፍሀንድ -ቅ- ያለመ'ዘጋጀት ፣ ሳያስብ የደ
ፍረት ንግግር የሚያደርግ
careless
-ቅ- ግዴለሽ ፣ የማይ'ጠነቀቅ
office
ኦፊስ -ስ- ሥራ ፣ ተግባር
building
-ስ- ቢሮ ፣ መሥሪያ ቤት
officer
ኦፊሰ -ስ- ዓለ ሥልጣን
military
-ስ- የጦር መኮንን
official
ኦፊሻል -ስ- ሹም ፣ ዓለሥልጣን
-ቅ- ይፋ ፣ የመንግሥት
offshoot
ኦፍሹ፡ት -ስ- ቅርንጫፍ
offspring
ኦፍስፕሪንግ -ስ- ልጆች
often
ኦፈን -ተግ- ሁልጊዜ ፣ ዘወትር
Oh
ኦው -ቃአ- እንዴ! ወይጉድ!
oil
ኦይል -ስ- ዘይት
oilcan
ኦይልካን -ስ- የዘይት ማንቆርቆርያ ቆርቆ
(ባለ ቡት)
oilcloth
ኦይልክሎስ -ስ- ውሃ የማይዘልቀው ጨርቅ
oily
ኦይሊ -ቅ- በቅባት የተበከለ

530

ointment
'አይንትመንት -ስ- ቅባት

old
'ኦልድ -ቅ- አሮጌ ፣ ሽማግ'ሌ

old-fashioned
ኦልድ'ፋሽንድ -ቅ- ዘመናዊ ያልሆነ ፣ ጊዜ
ያ'ለፈ'በት ፤ ባሀልን ተከ'ታይ

olive
'ኦሊ.ቭ -ስ- ወይራ ፤ ወደ ብጫ'ነት ያዘነበለ
አረንጓዴ ቀለም

omen
'ኦውሜን -ስ- ገ'ድ ፣ ምል'ክት (መጪውን
ሁናቴ የ'ሚያሳ'ይ)

ominous
'ኦሚነስ -ቅ- አደጋ ሊያመጣ የ'ሚችል

omission
ኦ'ሚሽን -ስ- መግደፍ ፣ ግድፈት

omit
ኦ'ሚት -ግ- መተው [ተወ] ፤ መግደፍ [ገ'ደፈ]

omnibus
'ኦምነበስ -ስ- አውቶብስ

omnipotent
ኦም'ኒፐተንት -ቅ- ሁ'ሉን የ'ሚችል ፣ ከሃሉ
ኮሉ (ለእግዚአብሔር)

omniscient
ኦም'ኒሲየንት -ቅ- ሁ'ሉን የ'ሚያውቅ (ለእግ
ዚአብሔር)

on
'ኦን -መዋ- በ . . . ላይ ፣ በ

once
'ወንስ -ተግ- አንድ ጊዜ ፣ አንዲት ጊዜ

one
'ወን -ቅ- አንድ ፣ አንዲት

onerous
'ኦነረስ -ቅ- አስቸ'ጋሪ ፣ አ'ዋኪ. (ለሥራ)

oneself
ወን'ሴልፍ -ተስ- ራስ

onion
'ኦንየን -ስ- ሽንኩርት

onlooker
'ኦንሉከ -ስ- ተመልካች

only
'ኦውንሊ -ቅ- ብ'ቻ ፣ የተለ'የ ፣ መ'ስል የሌ
ለው

onslaught
'ኦንስሎ:ት -ስ- ከ'ባድ ግጥሚያ (ለጠላት)

onus
'ኦውነስ -ስ- ኃላፊ'ነት ፣ ሸክም

onward
'ኦንወድ -ተግ- ወደፊት

onyx
'ኦኒክስ -ስ- መረግድ

ooze
'ኡ:ዝ -ግ- ማዘፍት [አ'ዘፈ]

opaque
ኦ'ፔይክ -ቅ- በውስጡ የ'ማያሳ'ይ ፣ ብርሃን
የ'ማያስገ'ባ ፣ ጥቅጥ'ቅ ያለ

open
'ኦውፐን -ግ- መክፈት [ከ'ፈተ]

opening
'ኦውፐኒንግ -ስ- ቀዳዳ

operate
'ኦፐሬይት -ግ- መሥራት [ሠ'ራ] ፤ ማ'ው'ራት
[አ'ው'ራ]
-on
-ግ- መቅደድ [ቀ'ደደ] (ሕ'ክም'ና)

operation
ኦፐ'ሬይሽን -ስ- ሥራ
medical
-ስ- አፐራሲዮን ፤ ሰው'ነትን ለህ'ክም'
ና መቅደድ

operative
'ኦፐረቲቭ -ቅ- ሠራ
-ስ- ሠ'ራተ'ኛ (ይበልጡን የፋብሪካ ፤
ሚካኒክ)

opinion
ኦ'ፒንየን -ስ- አስተያየት ፤ ፍርድ ፣ እምነት ፤
ግ'ምት

opponent
ኦ'ፖነንት -ስ- ጠላት ፤ ተቃዋሚ ፣ ባላንጣ

opportune
'ኦፐቹ:ን -ቅ- ተስማሚ.

opportunity
ኦፐ'ቹነቲ -ስ- ም'ቹ ጊዜ (ሥራ ለመሥራት)

oppose
ኦ'ፖውዝ -ግ- መ'ቃወም [ተቃ'ወመ]

opposite
’ኦፐሲት -ቅ- ፊት ለፊት የሆነ ፣ ተቃራኒ ፣
የ’ሚይስማ’ማ ፣ አቅጣ’ጫው የተለያ’የ

opposition
ኦፐ’ዚሸን -ስ- መ’ቃወም ፣ ተቃዋሚ ክፍል

oppress
እፐ’ሬስ -ግ- መጨ’ቆን [ጨ’ቆን]

oppressive
እፐ’ሬሲቭ -ቅ- ጨ’ቋኝ

oppressor
እፐ’ሬሰ -ስ- ጨ’ቋኝ (ሰው)

optical
’ኦፕቲከል -ቅ- የዓይን

optician
ኦፕ’ቲሸን -ስ- መነ’ጥር ሠ’ራተ’ኛ (መነ’ጽር
ሠ’ራተ’ኛ)

optimist
’ኦፕቲሚስት -ስ- በጥሩ ተምኔት የ’ሚያምን
ሰው ፣ ሁኔታዎ’ችን ሁሉ በቅን የ’ሚያይ ሰው

option
’ኦፕሸን -ስ- የፈ’ለጉትን የመምረጥ መብት

or
’ኦ -መተ- ወይን’ም ፣ ወይ’ም

oral
’ኦረል -ቅ- የቃል ፣ የአፍ

orange
’ኦሬንጅ -ስ- ብርቱካን

oration
ኦሬይሸን -ስ- ንግ’ግር (በሕዝብ ፊት)

orator
’ኦሬተ -ስ- ንግ’ግር ዐዋቂ ፣ አንደበተ ርቱእ ፣
ጥሩ ተናጋሪ

oratory
’ኦረተሪ -ስ- ንግ’ግር የማድረግ ሀብት

orb
’ኦብ -ስ- ሉል (ንጉሥ በ’ጁ የ’ሚይዘው ፣ መስ
ቀል ያ’ለ በ’ላይ) ፣ ክ’ብ ነገር (ም’ሳሌ ፣ ፀሐይ ፣
ጨረቃ ፣ ክከብ ፣ ምድር)

orbit
’ኦብት -ግ- አንደን ነገር መዞር [ዞረ] (በፊለክ)
-ስ- አንድ ፈለክ በሌላው ዙሪያ የ’ሚያ
ደርገው መዞር ፣ ዑደት

orchard
’ኦቸድ -ስ- የፍራፍሬ ተክል ቦታ

orchestra
’ኦከስትረ -ስ- የሙዚቃ ጓ’ድ

ordain
ኦ’ዴይን -ግ- ክህነት መስጠት [ሰ’ጠ] ፣ መካን
[ከነ] ፣ ማዘዝ [አ’ዘዘ]

ordeal
ኦ’ዲይል -ስ- አ’ዋኪ የገብዝ’ና መለ’ኪያ
ፈተና

order
’ኦደ -ግ- ማዘዝ [አ’ዘዘ]
instruction
-ስ- ሥርዓት
sequence
-ስ- ቅደም ተከ’ተል

orderly
’ኦደሊ -ቅ- ጥሩ ሥርዓት ያ’ለው ፣ የተሻ’ከፈ፣
የተሰ’ተረ
servant
-ስ- የሆስፒታል ተላላኪ ፣ ያንድ መኮ
ን’ን ተላላኪ

ordinance
’ኦዲነንስ -ስ- ትእዛዝ ፣ ሕ’ግ ፣ ዐዋጅ ፣ ሃይማ
ኖታዊ ክብረ በዓል

ordinary
’ኦዲነሪ -ቅ- ተራ ፣ የተለ’መደ ፣ መና’ኛ

ordination
ኦዲ’ኔይሸን -ስ- መ’ሾም ፣ መሾም (መነ’ፈ
ሳዊ)

ordnance
’ኦድነንስ -ስ- መድፈ’ኛ ክፍል ፣ የጦር መ’ሣ
ሪያ’ና የምግብ መሣ’ብር (የወ’ታ’ደር)

ore
’ኦ -ስ- የብረ’ታ ብረት አፈር (ገና ያልነ’ጠረ)

organ
’ኦገን -ስ- የሰውነት ክፍል
musical
-ስ- አርጋኖን (ጓዳ ፒያኖ ያ’ለ የሙዚቃ
መ’ሣሪያ)

organic
ኦ’ጋኒክ -ቅ- የሰው’ነት ፣ የአካል ፣ ሕይወት
ያ’ለው

organization
ኦጋናይ’ዜይሸን -ስ- ድር’ጅት

532

organize
'ኦርጋናይዝ -ግ- ማ'ደራጀት [አ'ደራ·'ጀ] ፣ መ
ልክ መስጠት [ሰ'ጠ]

orgy
'ኦጂ -ስ- መ'ሳከር ፣ ቅጥ ማጣት (በታ'ላቅ
ግብገ ላይ) ፣ መፈንጠዝ

Orient
'ኦሪዩንት -ስ- ምሥራቃዊ የዓለም ክፍል

orientate
'ኦሪዩንቴይት -ግ- ማልመድ [አለ'መደ] ፣ አ
ንድ ነገር ማሳ'ወቅ [አሳ'ወቀ]

orifice
'ኦሪፊስ -ስ- ት'ንሽ ቀዳዳ ፣ የዋ'ሻ እፍ ወዘተ

origin
'ኦሪጂን -ስ- መጀ'መሪያ ፣ ምንጭ ፣ ትው
ል'ድ

original
'ኧ'ሪጂናል -ቅ- የመጀ'መሪያ ፤ ለመጀ'መሪያ
ጊዜ የተሠ'ራ ፣ አዲ'ስ ፣ አንቄ

originate
'ኧ'ሪጂኔይት -ግ- ማስገ'ኘት [አስገ'ኘ] ፣ መፍ
ጠር [ፈ'ጠረ]

ornament
'ኦ:ነመንት -ስ- ጌጣጌጥ

ornate
ኦ':ኔይት -ቅ- ያጌጠ

orphan
'ኦ:ፈን -ስ- እናለ ማውታ ፣ የሙት ልጅ

orphanage
'ኦ:ፈኔጅ -ስ- የሙት ልጆ'ች የ'ሚ'ረ'ዱ'በት
ድር'ጅት

orthodox
ኦ:ሰዶክስ -ቅ- በአስተያየቱ ትክ'ክለ'ኛ ፣ እም
ነቱ ያልተቃ'ወሰ
church
-ስ- ኦርቶዶክሳዊት ቤተ ክርስቲያን

orthography
ኦ:'ሰግራፊ -ስ- ትክ'ክለ'ኛ አ'ጻጻፍ (ፊደሉ
ያልተሳሳተ)

oscillate
'ኦሲሌይት -ግ- መ'ወዛወዝ [ተወዛ'ወዘ] ፣
ማ'ወዛወዝ [አ'ወዛ'ወ]

ostensible
ኦስ'ቴንሲበል -ቅ- እውነተ'ኛውን ምክንያት
ለመሸ'ፈን የቀ'ረበ (ምክንያት)

ostentation
ኦስቴን'ቴይሸን -ስ- ል'ታይ ል'ታይ ማለት ፣
ል'ታወቅ ል'ታወቅ ማለት

ostracize
'ኦስትረሳይዝ -ግ- ለ'ይቶ ማስቀ'ረት [አስ
ቀ'ረ] ፣ ማ.ገዝ [አገዘ] (ግዞት)

ostrich
'ኦስትሪች -ስ- ሰጎን

other
'አዘ -ቅ- ሌላ ፣ ል'ዩ ፣ ተጨ'ማሪ

otherwise
'አዘዋይዝ -ተግ- አለበለ'ዚያ

our
'አወ -ቅ- የ'ኛ

ours
'አወዝ -ተስ- የ'ኛ

ourselves
አወ'ሰልቭዝ -ተስ- (እ'ኛ) ራሳ'ችን

oust
'አውስት -ግ- ማስወ'ገድ [አስወ'ገደ] ፣ ወደ
ውጪ ማ'ባረር [አ'ባ'ረረ]

out
'አውት -ተግ- እው'ጭ ፣ ወደ ው'ጭ

outburst
'አውት'በስት -ስ- ስ'ሜት ለመግለጽ መገን
ፈል

outcast
'አውት'ካስት -ስ- የተጣ'ላ ፣ የተባረ'ረ
ከማኅበራዊ ኑሮ ው'ጭ የሆነ

outcome
'አውትከም -ስ- ው'ጤት

outcry
'አውትክራይ -ስ- አቤቱታ ፣ ጨኸት (የብዙ
ሰዎ'ች)

outdoor
አውት'ዶ: -ቅ- የው'ጭ (ከቤት)

outer
'አውተ -ቅ- የው'ጭ

outfit
'አውትፊት -ስ- ለተለ'የ ነገር የ'ሚ.ውል ሙሉ
ልብስ ፣ መ'ሣሪያ
organization
-ስ- ድር'ጅት ፣ ጓ'ድ ፣ ወ'ሮ'ላ

533

outhouse
'አውትሀውስ -ስ- ከዋ'ናው ቤት የተለ'የ ፡
የዕቃ ፡ የእንሰሳት ቤት

outing
'አውቲንግ -ስ- ሽ'ር'ሽር

outlandish
አውት'ላዲሸ -ቅ- እንግዳ የ'ሚመስል ፡ ያለ
ተለ'መደ

outlaw
'አውትሎ፡ -ስ- ሽፍታ ፡ ወንበዴ ፡ ደመ ከልብ

outlay
'አውትሌይ -ስ- ወጭ (ገንዘብ)

outlet
'አውትሌት -ስ- መውጫ ፡ መፍሰሻ (ለፈሳሽ
ነገር)

outline
'አውትላይን -ስ- ዋና ዋናውን ሐሳብ መግ
ለጫ እ'ጭር ጽሑፍ

outlook
'አውትሉክ -ስ- ካንድ ቦታ የ'ሚታ'ይ ትእ
'ይንት ፡ ወደፊት የ'ሚፈ'ጸም ፡ የ'ሚሆን ነገር
ያስተሳሰብ መንገድ

outnumber
አውት'ነምበ -ግ- በቁጥር መብለጥ [በ'ለጠ] ፡
ብዛት ማ'ብለጥ [አ'በ'ለ]

outpost
'አውትፖውስት -ስ- ፈን'ጠር ያለ መንደር ፡
ከሥራ'ዝኔ ራ'ቅ ያለ መንደር ፡ ራቅ ያለ ት'ንሽ
የጦር ሠፈር

output
'አውትፑት -ስ- ው'ጤት (ከፋብሪካ መዘተ
የ'ሚ'ገ'ኝ)

outrage
'አውትሬይጅ -ስ- ታ'ላቅ ወንጀል ፡ ታ'ላቅ
የጭ'ካኔ ተግባር

outrageous
አውት'ሬይጀስ -ቅ- አ'ወ'ቃቂ ፡ አስደነጋጭ

outset
'አውትሴት -ስ- መጀ'መሪያ

outside
አውት'ሳይድ -ስ- ው'ጭ
                     -ቅ- የው'ጭ

outsider
አውት'ሳይዳ -ስ- ያንድ ማኅበር አባል ያል
ሆነ ፡ ብዙ ተስፋ የሌ'ለው ሰው (በውድ'ድር)

outskirts
'አውትስክትስ -ስ- የከተማ ዳር'ቻ

outspoken
አውት'ስፖ‌ውክን -ቅ- ግልጽ ፡ እውነት ተና
ጋሪ ፡ የ'ማያ‌ይ'ብት

outstanding
አውት'ስታንዲንግ -ቅ- በጣም ጥሩ ፡ መ'ስሎ
የሌ'ለው ፡ ገና ያልተፈ'ጸም ፡ ያል'ለቀ
unpaid
                     -ቅ- ያልተከ'ፈለ (ዕዳ መዘተ) ፡ ው'ዝፍ
(ሒሳብ)

outstretched
አውት'ስት'ሬችድ -ቅ- የተዘረ'ጋ

outward
'አውትወይ -ተ-ግ- ወደ ው'ጭ

outwit
አውት'ዊት -ግ- ከ'ፍ ባለ ብል'ጠት ማ'ሸ'ነፍ
[አ'ሸ'ነፈ]

oval
'አውብል -ቅ- የእንቁላል ትርስ ያ'ለው ፡ ክ'ብ
ልመል

oven
'አቨን -ስ- ም'ድ'ጃ

over
'አውቨ -ተ-ግ- በ . . . ላይ
                     -ቅ- ያ'ለቀ ፡ የተፈ'ጸመ

overall
አውቨ'ር‌ል -ቅ- ጠቅላ'ላ ፡ አ'ጠቃላይ
garment
                     -ስ- የሥራ ልብስ ፡ ቱ'ታ

overcast
አቨ'ካስት -ቅ- በደ'መና የተሸ'ፈነ ፡ የጨ'ለ
'መ

overcoat
'አውቨኮውት -ስ- ካ'ፖርት

overcome
አቨ'ከም -ግ- ማ'ሸ'ነፍ [አ'ሸ'ነፈ]

overcrowded
'አቨ'ክ‌ራውደድ -ቅ- የተጣ'በበ (በሰዎ'ች)
መ'ፈናፈኛ የሌ'ለው

overdraft
'አውቨድ‌ራ‌ፍት -ስ- የባንክ እ'ላፊ እዳ ፡ ካለ
'ቀ መጠ‌ን በላይ ያው‌ጡ‌ት ገንዘብ (ከባንክ)

534

overdue
እኡ·ቨድ'ዩ: -ቅ- የዘገ'የ ፣ በጊዜው ያልተከ'ፈለ
(ው·'ገፍ፡ እዳ)

overflow
እr·ቨፍ'ለው -ግ- ሞልቶ መፍሰስ [ፈ'ሰሰ]

overgrown
እኡ·ቨግ'ረውን -ቅ- አለመጠን ያ'ደገ ፣ ያረ'ጀ
(ለአትክልት ወዘተ) ፣ በልምላሜ የተሸ'ፈነ ፣
ያለ ዕድሜው በጣም የረ'ዘመ (ለልጅ)

overhang
እኡ·ቨ'ህንግ -ግ- ማንጠልጠል [አንጠለ'ጠለ]

overhaul
እኡ·ቨ'ሆ:ል -ግ- ማ'ዶስ [አ'ደሰ] ፣ መቅደም
[ቀ'ደመ] (በፉ·'ጫ)

overload
እኡ·ቨ'ለውድ -ግ- ያለመጠን መጫን [ጫነ]

overlook
እወ·ቨ'ሉ·ክ -ግ- ቸ'ል ማለት [አለ] ፣ ትይ'ዩ
መሆን [ሆነ]

overpower
እኡ·ቨ'ፓወ -ግ- ማ'ሸ'ነፍ [አ'ሸ'ነፈ] ፣ ከሥ·
ልጣን ሥር ማድረግ [አደ'ረገ]

overrun
እኡ·ቨ'ረን -ግ- መውረር [ወ'ረረ] (በፍጥነት)

overseas
እኡ·ቨ'ሲይዝ -ስ- ባሕር ማዶ

overseer
'እኡ·ቨሲየ -ስ- ተቆጣጣሪ (የሥ'ራተ'ኞ'ች)

oversight
'እኡ·ቨ'ሳይት -ስ- ግድፈት ፣ ስሕተት

oversleep
እኡ·ቨስ'ሊይፕ -ስ- ከተወ'ሰነው ጊዜ ይበልጥ
መተ'ኛት ፣ ጋድሚያ'ነት

overtake
እኡ·ቨ'ቴይክ -ግ- መቅደም [ቀ'ደመ]

overthrow
እኡ·ቨ'ረው -ግ- መገልበጥ [ገለ'በጠ] (መ·ን
ግሥት) ፣ ማ'ሸ'ነፍ [አ'ሸ'ነፈ]

overtime
'እኡ·ቨታይም -ስ- ከተወ'ደበው የሥራ ጊዜ
በላይ ያ'ለፈ የሥራ ጊዜ ፣ ለ'ዚህ ጊዜ የ'ሚ'ከ
'ፈል ገንዘብ

overture
'እኡ·ቨቸ -ስ- ለአቴራ ወይን'ም ለትያትር መቅ
ድም የ'ሚሆን ሙ·ዚቃ

overturn
እኡ·ቨ'ተ:ን -ግ- መገልበጥ [ገለ'በጠ]

overweight
እኡ·ቨ'ዌይት -ቅ- ብዙ ክብደት ያ'ለው
-ስ- ከመጠን በላይ የሆነ ጭነት

overwhelm
እኡ·ቨ'ዌልም -ግ- ማ'ሸ'ነፍ [አ'ሸ'ነፈ] (ተ
ወዳዳሪ በሌ'ለው ·ኃይል) ፣ ማጥለቅለቅ [አጥለ
ቀ'ለቀ]

owe
'እው· -ግ- ባለዳ መሆን [ሆነ]

owl
'አውል -ግ- ጉ·'ጉ·ት (የወፍ ዓይነት)

own
'እኡ·ን -ግ- መ·'ገናዘብ [ተገና'ዘበ] ፣ ባለቤ·ት·
መሆን [ሆነ]

owner
'እኡ·ነ -ስ- ባለቤት ፣ ባለመብት·

ownership
'እኡ·ነሺ'ፕ -ስ- ባለቤት'ነት

ox
'አክስ -ስ- በሬ

oyster
'አይስት -ስ- አይስተr (የ'ሚ'በ'ላ ደንጊያ
ለ'በስ በሣ)

P

pace
'ፔይስ -ስ- ፍጥነት (የርም'ጃ፣የፉ·'ጫ)፣እርም'ጃ

pacific
ፐ'ሲፊክ -ቅ- ጸ'ጥ ያለ ፣ ሰላማዊ

Pacific
ፐ'ሲፊክ -ቅ- ፓ'ሲፊክ (የውቅያኖስ ስም)

pacify
'ፓሲፋይ -ግ- ጸ'ጥ ማድረግ [አደ'ረገ]

pack
'ፓክ -ስ- እሥር ፣ ረብጣ
-ግ- ዕቃ ለጉዞ ማሣሠር [አሣ'ሠረ]

package
'ፓክጅ -ስ- ት'ንሽ እሥር ፣ ረብጣ

packet
'ፓከት -ስ- ት'ንሽ እሥር ፣ ፓ'ኮ

packing
'ፓኪንግ -ስ- ማሥሪያ ጉዝጓዝ ፣ ማ'ሽጊያ
ጉዝጓዝ

packed
'ፓክድ -ቅ- የታ'ሠረ ፣ የታ'ሸገ (ዕቃ)

pad
'ፓድ -ስ- ዕቃ እንዳይ'ጎ'ዳ ለጉዝጓዝ የ'ሚሆን
ለስላ'ሳ ጨርቅ ፣ ገበር

padding
'ፓዲንግ -ስ- የማ'ሽጊያ ጉዝጓዝ (ዕቃ እንዳ
ይ'በላ'ሽ)

paddle
'ፓደል -ግ- ጥልቀት በሌ'ለው ውንዝ በግር
መሄድ [ሄደ] ፣ መቅዘፍ [ቀ'ዘፈ]
-ስ- መቅዘፊያ

paddock
'ፓደክ -ስ- የፈረሶ'ች ማሠልጠኛ ወይን'ም
መኖሪያ መስክ

padlock
'ፓድሎክ -ስ- ጎጉ-ንጉፍር ቀልፍ

paediatrics
ፒዲ'ያትሪክስ -ስ- የሕፃናት በ'ሽታ'ና የሕ
'ክም'ናው ጥናት

pagan
'ፔይገን -ስ- አረመኔ ፣ በብዙ አማልክት የ'ሚ
ያምን ሰው

page
'ፔጅ -ስ- ገጽ (የመጽሐፍ,
servant
-ስ- ተላላኪ ፣ አሽከር (በሆቴል ፣ በክ
ብብ ወዘተ)

pageant
'ፓጀንት -ስ- የበዓል ሰልፍ (የጥንት ባሀል
የ'ሚያሳ'ይ)

pail
'ፔይል -ስ- ባልዲ ፣ ሽንከ'ሎ

pain
'ፔይን -ስ- ሕማም ፣ ሥቃይ (የሰው'ነት)

painful
'ፔይንፉል -ቅ- የ'ሚያ'ም ፣ የ'ሚያ'ሠቃ'ይ

painstaking
'ፔይንዝቴይኪ'ንግ -ቅ- ጥንቁቅ (በሥራ) ፣
ባተሌ

paint
'ፔይንት -ግ- መቀ'ባት [ቀ'ባ] (ለቀለም) ፣
መሣል [ሣለ] (ለሥዕል)
-ስ- ቀለም (የቤት ወዘተ)

painter
'ፔይንተ -ስ- ቀለም ቀ'ቢ ፣ ሥዕል ሠዓሊ.

painting
'ፔይንቲንግ -ስ- ሥዕል

pair
'ፔየ -ስ- ሁለ'ት ፣ ጥንድ

pal
'ፓል -ስ- የቅርብ ጓ'ደ'ኛ

palace
'ፓለስ -ስ- ቤተ መንግሥት

palatable
'ፓለተብል -ቅ- የ'ሚጥም ፣ የ'ሚጣ'ፍጥ (ለ
ጣዕም ፣ ለአእምሮ)

palate
'ፓለት -ስ- ት'ናጋ

pale
'ፔይል -ቅ- የገረ'ጣ
-ስ- የሾለ ረ'ጅም የአጥር እንጨት

paling
'ፔይሊ'ንግ -ስ- የጎጨት አጥር

palisade
ፓለ'ሴይድ -ስ- በሾለ እንጨት ወይን'ም የብ
ረት ዘንግ የታጠ'ረ አጥር

pall
'ፖል -ግ- መሰልቸት [ሰለ'ቸ]
-ስ- ግምጃ (የሬሳ መሸ'ፈኛ)

pallid
'ፓሊድ -ቅ- የገረ'ጣ

palm
'ፓም -ስ- መዳፍ ፣ ዘምባባ

palmist
'ፓ:ሚስት -ስ- ጠንቋይ (መዳፍ ተመልክቶ
የ'ሚነግር)

536

palpable
’ፓልፐበል -ቅ- በቀ'ላሉ ሊ'ዳ'ሰስ የ'ሚችል ፤ ለእእምሮ ጉልህ የሆነ

palpitation
ፓልፒ'ቴይሽን -ስ- የል'ብ በፍጥነት መም ታት

palsy
’ፓ፡ልዚ -ስ- የእ'ጅ እንቅጥ'ቃጤ (በ'ሽታ)

paltry
’ፓ፡ልትሪ -ቅ- ዋጋ ቢስ

pamper
’ፓምፐ -ግ- ማንቀባረር [አንቀባ'ረረ]

pamphlet
’ፓምፍለት -ስ- ት'ንሽ መጽሐፍ

pan
’ፓን -ስ- መጥበሻ ፤ ድስት (ወዘተ)

pancake
’ፓንኬይክ -ስ- ከዱቄት ከዘይት'ና ከወተት የ'ሚ'ሥ'ራ ኬክ (ት'ኩሱን የ'ሚ'በላ)

pancreas
’ፓንክሪያስ -ስ- ጣ'ፊያ

pander
’ፓንደ -ግ- ማ'ቃጠር [አ'ቃ'ጠረ] (ለሴት) ፤ ማ'በረታታት [አ'በረታ'ታ] (ክፋን ሰው)

pane
’ፔይን -ስ- መስተዋት (የመስኮት ፡ አንድ ክፍል)

panel
’ፓነል -ስ- የግድግ'ዳ እንዱ ክፍል ፤ አራ'ት ማእዘን የሆነ እንጨት ፤ ለመፍረድ የተጠ'ሩ (በእንግሊዝ አገር) ሰዎ'ች የስም ዝርዝር ፤ በውይ'ይት የ'ሚ'ካ'ፈሉ ሰዎ'ች

pang
’ፓንግ -ስ- ውጋት ፡ ድንገተ'ኛ ሕማም

panic
’ፓኒክ -ስ- መ'ሸበር ፡ ሽ'ብር (ከፍርሃት የተ ነ'ሣ)

panorama
’ፓኖራ፡መ -ስ- ጠቅላ'ላ የመሬት አ'ቀማመጥ ፤ ትእ'ይይንት

pant
’ፓንት -ግ- ማለክለክ [አለክ'ለከ]

panther
’ፓንሰ -ስ- ግ'ሥ'ላ

pantry
’ፓንትሪ -ስ- ማጀት ፡ የምግብ ቤት መ'ዛሪያ የ'ሚ'ቀ'መጥ'በት ክፍል

pants
’ፓንትስ -ስ- የውስጥ ሱ'ሪ

paper
’ፔይፐ -ስ- ወረቀት
    news -ስ- ጋዜጣ

par
’ፓ፡ -ስ- የዋጋ መ'ተካከል

parable
’ፓረበል -ስ- ም'ሳ

parachute
’ፓራሹት -ስ- ጃንጥላ (ከአውሮ'ፕላን የ'ሚ 'ወ'ረድ'በት)

parade
ፐ'ሬይድ -ግ- በሰልፍ መ'ጓዝ [ተጓዘ]
    -ስ- ሰልፍ

paradise
’ፓረዳይስ -ስ- ገ'ነት

paradox
’ፓረዶክስ -ስ- ለመጅ'መሪያ ሲሰሙት ሐው ነት የ'ማይመስል ነገ ግን እውነት ሊሆን የ'ሚ ችል

paraffin
’ፓረፊን -ስ- ናፍታ

paragraph
’ፓረግራ፡ፍ -ስ- አንቀጽ (በጽሑፍ)

parallel
’ፓረሌል -ቅ- ጎ'ን ለጎ'ን የተ'ኩለ'ኩለ ትይ'ዩ (መሥመር)

paralyse
’ፓረላይዝ -ግ- ማስለል [አስ'ለለ] ፤ ሽባ ማድ ረግ [አደ'ረገ] ፤ አቅም ማሳ'ጣት [አሳ'ጣ]

paralysis
ፐ'ራለሲስ -ስ- ሽባ'ነት ፡ መስለል

paramount
’ፓረማውንት -ቅ- በጣም አስፈ'ላጊ ፡ ላ'ቅ ያለ

parapet
’ፓረፔት -ስ- በጣራ ፡ በመ'ነገድ ፡ በድልድይ ዳር'ና ዳር ያ'ለ ግንብ

paraphrase

paraphrase
'ፓራፍሬዝ -ግ- አንድ ጽሑፍ በቀላል
አነጋገር ፈትቶ መናገር [ተናግሬ]

parasite
'ፓራሳይት -ስ- ሰውነት የሚበሉ ተባዮች ፣
ለሰው ሸክም ሆኖ የሚኖር ሰው

parasol
'ፓርሶል -ስ- ጃንጥላ (ለፀሐይ መከላከያ)

parcel
'ፓ፡ሰል -ስ- እሥር ፡ ረብጣ

parched
'ፓ፡ችድ -ቅ- ቡና ፡ ደረቅ

parchment
'ፓ፡ችመንት -ስ- ብራና

pardon
'ፓ፡ዶን -ግ- ይቅር ማለት [አለ]
-ስ- ይቅርታ

pare
'ቴየ -ግ- መፋቅ [ፋቀ] (እንጨት) ፡ መከር
ከም [ከረከመ] ፡ መላጥ [ላጠ]

parent
'ቴሬንት -ስ- ወላጆች (አባት ወይንም እናት)

parenthesis
ቴ'ሬንሲሲስ -ስ- ቅንፍ (በጽሑፍ)

parenthood
'ቴሬንትሁድ -ስ- ወላጅነት

paring
'ቴሪንግ -ስ- ቆራጭ ፡ ፍቅፋቂ

parish
'ፓሪሽ -ስ- ሰበካ (ያንድ ቄስ)

parity
'ፓሪቲ -ስ- እኩልነት (የማዕረግ)

park
'ፓ፡ክ -ግ- መኪና ቦታ አስይዞ ማቆም [አ
ቆመ]
place
-ስ- ሜዳ

parley
'ፓ፡ሊ. -ስ- የእርቅ ድርድር (በውለ ት መሪዎች
መካከል)

parliament
'ፓ፡ለመንት -ስ- የምክር ቤት (ያንድ መንግ
ሥት)

parlour
'ፓ፡ለ -ስ- ልዩ የእንግዳ መቀበያ ክፍል

arochial
ፐ'ረውኪየል -ቅ- ሐሳብ ውሱን ፣ ጠባብ
አስተያየት ያለው

parole
ፐ'ሮል -ግ- ቃል በመቀበል አሥሬኛ መፍ
ታት [ፈታ]
-ስ- ቃል መስጠት

parrot
'ፓረት -ስ- በቀቀ 't (የወፍ ዓይነት)

parry
'ፓሪ -ስ- መመከት [መከተ] (ለበትር)

parsimonious
ፓ፡ሲ'መውኒየስ -ቅ- ሥሥታም ፡ ንፉግ
(ገንዘብ) ፡ ንፉግ

parson
'ፓ፡ሰን -ስ- ካህን

part
'ፓ፡ት -ስ- ክፍል

partake
ፓ'ቴይክ -ግ- መሳተፍ [ተሳተፈ]

partial
'ፓ፡ሻል -ቅ- በከፊል የሆነ ፣ ያልተፈጸመ
አ'ዳዪ ፡ አድልዎ የሚያደርግ

participate
ፓ'ቲሲፔይት -ግ- መካፈል [ተካፈለ] (ለ
ሥራ)

particle
'ፓ፡ቲክል -ስ- ትንሽ ቀ'ራጭ ፡ ስብርባሪ
እ'ጓባብ (ስዋስው)

particular
ፐ'ቲክዩለ -ቅ- ልዩ ፡ የተለየ
fussy
-ቅ- በጣም ጥንቁቅ

parting
'ፓ፡ቲንግ -ስ- መለያየት

partisan
'ፓ፡ቲዛን -ስ- ነፍ ሰባሽ ፡ ተዋጊ ፡ አርበኛ

partition
ፓ'ቲሽን -ስ- መከፈያ ፡ መከፈል ፡ ውለት
ክፍሎች የሚለዩ ግድግ'ዳ ፣ ግንቱ መዘጋ

partly
'ፓ፡ትሊ. -ተግ- በከፊል

partner
ፓርትነ -ስ- የሥራ ጓ ደ ኛ ፣ ሽርካ

party
ፓርቲ -ስ- ግብ ኘ
political
-ስ- የፓ ለቲካ ማኅበ ር

pass
ፓስ -ግ- ማለፍ፡ [አ ለፈ]
a law
-ግ- ሕ ግ ማውጣት [አወ ጣ]
give
-ግ- ማተ በል [አተ በለ]
ticket
-ስ- በነጻ የመግቢ ያ መ ታ ወቂ ያ ወረ
ቀት

passage
ፓሰጅ -ስ- መ ተላለፊ ያ
fare
-ስ- የጉዞ ዋ ጋ (የመርከብ)

passenger
ፓሰንጀ -ስ- መንገደ ኛ

passer-by
ፓሰ ባይ -ስ- ተላላፊ ፣ መንገደ ኛ

passion
ፓሽ ን -ስ- ታ ላቅ ስ ሜት ፣ ጥልቅ ስ ሜት ፣
ፍ ላጎት

passive
ፓሲቭ -ቅ- የ ማ ይሠራ ፣ ተገ ብ ሮ (ሰዋሰው)

passport
ፓ ስ ፖ ት -ስ- የይለፍ ወረቀት

past
ፓ ስ ት -ቅ- ያ ለፈ
-ስ- ያ ለፈ ጊዜ

paste
ፔ ይ ስ ት -ስ- መ ጣ ብ ቅ ፣ ማ ሽ ጊ ያ

pasteboard
ፔ ይ ስ ት ቦ ድ -ስ- ነ ጭ ጠ ና ፍ ራ ም ወ ረ ቀ ት ፣
ክ ር ታ ስ

pastime
ፓ ስ ታ ይ ም -ስ- የ ጊ ዜ ማ ሳ ለ ፊ ያ ሥ ራ (ለ መ
ዝ ና ኛ ፡ ለ መ ዝ ና ኛ)

pastoral
ፓ ስ ተ ረ ል -ቅ- ከ ከ ብ ት እ ረ ኛ ና ከ ሕ ይ ው ቱ
ጋ ር ግ ን ኙ ነ ት ያ ለ ው ፣ የ እ ጾ ስ

pastry
ፔ ይ ስ ት ሪ -ስ- ኬ ክ

.pasture
ፓ ስ ቸ -ስ- የ ከ ብ ት ማ ዋ ዬ መ ስ ክ ፣ የ ግ ጦ ሽ
ቦ ታ

pat
ፓ ት -ግ- መ ጠ ብ ጠ ብ [ጠ በ ጠ በ] (ሕ ፃ ና ት ን)

patch
ፓ ች -ስ- መ ጣ ፊ ያ (ጨ ር ቅ)

patchy
ፓ ቺ -ቅ- ጥ ሩ ነ ቱ ሙ ሉ ያ ል ሆ ነ ፣ በ መ ጠ ኑ ፣
ሆ ነ በ ዓ ይ ነ ት ያ ል ተ ስ ተ ካ ከ ለ

patent
ፔ ተ ን ት -ስ- አ ን ድ ነ ገ ር ባ ን ድ ሰ ው ፣ ባ ን ደ
ኩ ባ ን ያ የ ተ ሠ ራ የ ተ ፈ ለ ሰ ፈ መ ሆ ኑ ን ማ ረ
ጋ ገ ጫ ሰ ነ ድ

paternal
ፓ ተ ነ ል -ቅ- አ ባ ታ ዊ

path
ፓ ጵ -ስ- የ ግ ር መ ን ገ ድ ፣ የ ግ ረ ኛ መ ን ገ ደ ፣
ስ ር ጥ መ ን ገ ድ

pathetic
ፓ ጴ ቲ ክ -ቅ- አ ሳ ዛ ኝ

pathos
ፔ ይ ዞ ስ -ስ- የ ሐ ዘ ን ስ ሜ ት የ ሚ ቀ ስ ቅ ስ
ነ ገ ር ፣ ሁ ኔ ቱ

pathway
ፓ ጵ ዌ ይ -ስ- መ ተ ላ ለ ፊ ያ ፣ ጠ ባ ብ መ ን ገ ድ

patient
ፔ ይ ሸ ን ት -ስ- ሕ መ ም ተ ኛ
-ቅ- ታ ይ ፣ ት ዕ ግ ሥ ተ ኛ

patriotic
ፓ ት ሪ ዮ ቲ ክ -ቅ- ያ ገ ር ፍ ቅ ር ያ ለ ው ፣ ለ ሀ ገ ሩ
ተ ቆ ር ቋ ሪ

patrol
ፓ ት ረ ው ል -ግ- መ ፈ ተ ሽ [ፈ ተ ሽ] (አ ን ደ
ቦ ታ በ መ ታ ደ ር) ፣ ዘ ብ መ ቆ ም [ቆ መ]

patron
ፔ ይ ት ረ ን -ስ- ጠ ባ ቂ ፣ ተ ከ ባ ካ ቢ ፣ ረ ዳ ተ
customer
-ስ- ይ ም ብ ኛ (የ ን ግ ድ)

patronize
'ፓትረናይዝ -ግ- በዝ'ቅተ'ኛ መንፈስ እ'የተ
መለ'ከቱ መርዳት [ረ'ጻ] ፤ የበላይ ተጠባባቂ
መሆን [ሆነ] (የድር'ጅት ወዘተ)
a shop
-ግ- ደምብ'ኛ መሆን [ሆነ] (የሱ-ቅ)

patter
'ፓተr -ስ- የመንጠብጠብ ድምፅ ፤ የፈ'ጣን
እርምጃ ድምፅ ፤ ፈ'ጣን አ'ነጋገር (ያ'ሥቂ'ኝ
ሰው-)

pattern
'ፓተን -ስ- ሐረግ ፤ አንድ ነገr ለመሥ‌ራ‌ል
የ'ሚ'ገለ'በጥ ቅርፅ ፤ መንገድ ፤ ዓይነት ፤ ም'ሳ
ሌ ወዘተ

paunch
'ፓንች -ስ- ቦርጭ

pauper
'ፖ:ፐr -ስ- ደሃ ፤ በተራድኦ ገንዘብ የ'ሚኖr
ድሃ ሰው-

pause
'ፖ:ዝ -ግ- ለጥቂት ጊዜ ማረፍ [ዐ'ረፈ]

pave
'ፔይቭ -ግ- መደልደል [ደለ'ደለ] (መንገድ)

pavement
'ፔይቭመንት -ስ- በመኪና መንገድ ዳር'ና
ዳር ያ'ለ የእግረ'ኛ መሄጃ ፤ የግr'ኛ መንገድ

pavilion
ፐ'ቪልየን -ስ- ዳስ

paving
'ፔይቪንግ -ስ- ንጣፍ ደንጊያ (የመንገድ)

paw
'ፖ: -ስ- መዳፍ (የእንስሳት)

pawn
'ፖ:ን -ስ- መያገ ዕቃ (ለገንዘብ ብ'ድር)
chess
-ስ- ወ'ታ'ደr (በሰንጠረጅ ጨዋታ)
agent
-ስ- መ'ሣሪያ (ለክፉ ሥራ ፤ ለሰው-)

pawnbroker
'ፖ:ንብረ‌ውክ -ስ- ገንዘብ አበ'ዳሪ (መያገ
ተቀ'ብሎ-)

pay
'ፔይ -ግ- መክፈል ፤ [ከ'ፈለ]
salary
-ስ- ደመወዝ

payment
'ፔይመንት -ስ- ክፍ'ያ ፤ መክፈል

pea
'ፒይ -ስ- አተr

peace
'ፒይስ -ስ- ሰላም ፤ እር.ጋታ ፤ ፀ'ጥታ

peaceful
'ፒይስፉል -ቅ- ሰላማዊ ፤ ፀ'ጥ ያለ

peach
'ጲይች -ስ- ኮክ

peak
'ፒይክ -ስ- የተራራ ጫፍ

peal
'ፒይል -ግ- በጣም መደ'ወል [ደ'ወለ]
-ስ- ከፍተ'ኛ የደወል ድምፅ

peanut
'ጲነት -ስ- ለውዝ

pearl
'ፐ:ል -ስ- ሉል

peasant
'ፔዘንት -ስ- ገበሬ ፤ ባላገር

pebble
'ፔበል -ስ- ጠጠr

peck
'ፔክ -ግ- መጠቅጠቅ [ጠቀ'ጠቀ] (ለዶሮ ፤
ለወፍ)

peculiar
ፐክ'ዩሊየr -ቅ- ያልተለ'መደ ፤ እንግዳ (ለሁ-
ኔቴ) ፤ የተለ'የ (ጠባይ)

peculiarity
ፐክዩሊ'ያሪቲ -ስ- ል'ዩ ጠባይ

pecuniary
ፐክ'ዩኒየሪ -ቅ- የገንዘብ

pedal
'ፔዳል -ስ- በእግር እንዲሠ'ራ የ'ሚ'ደ'ረግ
(መወስወሻ ፤ ፍሪሲየን ወዘተ)

pedantic
ፐ'ዳንቲክ -ቅ- ዐዋቂ ነ'ኝ ባይ ፤ ለጥቃ'ቅን
ነገር ል'ጠንቀቅ ባይ ፤ ለ'ዛ የሌ'ለው (ዐዋቂ) ፤
ጥራዝ ነ'ጠቅ

pedestal
'ፔደስተል -ስ- ዐምድ ፤ ሐውልት ወዘተ የ'ሚ
ቆም'በት መሠረት

540

pedestrian

ፒ'ዴስትሪየን -ስ- እግረ'ኛ
-ቅ- አሰልቺ

pedigree

'ፔዲግሪይ -ስ- ትውል'ድ ፣ የትውል'ድ ሐረግ

pedlar

'ፔድለ -ስ- ሱቅ በደረቴ ፣ ከቦታ ወደ ቦታ
የ'ሚ'ዘዋ'ወር'ና ዕቃ የ'ሚ'ሸጥ ነ'ጋዴ

peel

'ፒይል -ስ- ል'ጣጭ (የፍራፍሬ)

peep

'ፒየፕ -ግ- በቀዳዳ ውስጥ መ'መልከት [ተመ
ለ'ከተ] ፣ ማን'ለቅ [አን'ለቀ]

peer

'ፒየ -ግ- ቀረብ ብሎ ማየት [አ'የ]
noble
-ስ- ከ'ፍ ያለ ማዕረግ ያ'ለው ሰው

peevish

'ፔይቪሽ -ቅ- በቀ'ላሉ የ'ሚ'ቆ'ጣ ፣ በት'ንሹ
የ'ሚ'ና'ደድ

peg

'ፔግ -ስ- ማንጠልጠያ (በግድግ'ዳ ላይ የተ
ሰ'ካ)

pelican

'ፔሊከን -ስ- ይብራ

pellet

'ፔለት -ስ- ት'ንሽ ፣ ክ'ብ ቁ'ራጭ
shotgun
-ስ- የረሽ ፍን'ጣቂ

pelt

'ፔልት -ስ- አንጋ'ራ ፣ ቆዳ

pen

'ፔን -ስ- ብዕር
enclosure
-ስ- ጋጥ ፣ ጉረ'ና

penal

'ፒይነል -ቅ- የወንጀል

penalize

'ፒይነላይዝ -ግ- መቅጣት [ቀ'ጣ] (መ'ቀጮ
በመጣል)

penalty

'ፔነልቲ -ስ- መ'ቀጫ ፣ መ'ቀጮ

penance

'ፔነንስ -ስ- የን'ሥሐ ቅጣት

pencil

'ፔንሰል -ስ- እርሳስ (መጻፊያ)

pendant

'ፔንደንት -ስ- ያንገት ጌጥ (በድሪ ላይ የተን
ጠለ'ጠለ)

pending

'ፔንዲንግ -ቅ- የተንጠለ'ጠለ (ው'ሳኔ ያላገ'ኘ)

pendulum

'ፔንድዩለም -ስ- ወዲያ'ና ወዲህ የ'ሚ'መዛ
'ወዝ መ'ወዛወሪያ (የሰዓት)

penetrate

'ፔነትሬይት -ግ- መግባት [ገ'ባ] ፣ መ'ጎስጎስ
[ተጎስ'ጎሰ]

peninsular

ፒ'ኒንስዩለ -ስ- ል'ሳነ ምድር (ከብዙ ወገን
በውሃ የተከ'በበ የብስ)

penis

ፒይ'ኒስ -ስ- የወንድ አባል ፣ የወንድ ሐፍረተ
ሥጋ (ቁላ)

penitence

'ፔኒተንስ -ስ- ን'ሥሐ

penitent

'ፔኒተንት -ቅ- ተነ'ሣሒ

penitentiary

ፔኒ'ቴንሸሪ -ስ- እሥር ቤት (በተለ'ይ እሥረ
'ኛው ወደ በ'ጎ ተግባር እንዲ'መ'ለስ የ'ሚ'ደ
'ከም'በት)

pen-knife

'ፔንናይፍ -ስ- ለንጢ

pennant

'ፔነንት -ስ- ጠ'ባብ'ና ረ'ጅም ሦስት ማዕዘን
ያ'ለው ሰን'ደቅ ዓላማ

penniless

'ፔኒለስ -ቅ- በጣም ደሀ ፣ መንዳ'ካ ደሀ

pension

'ፔንሽን -ስ- የጡረታ አበ'ል ፣ ኪራይ ተከ
ፍሎ የ'ሚ'ታ'ደር'በት ቤት

pensive

'ፔንሲቭ -ቅ- ያዘነ ፣ ሐሳብ የገ'ባው

pentagon

'ፔንተጎን -ስ- አ'ምስት ማዕዘን ያ'ለው ቅርዕ

pentecost

'ፔንተኮስት -ስ- በዓለ ኀምሳ ፣ ጰንጠቆስጤ

penultimate
ፔ'ኖልቲመት -ቅ- ከመጨ'ረሻ በፊት ያለ
(ነገር)

penury
'ፔንዩሪ -ስ- ከል'ክ ያ'ለፈ ችግር፣ 'ችነት

people
'ፒይፕል -ስ- ሕዝብ

pepper
'ፔፕ -ስ- በርበ'ሬ ፣ ቁንዶ በርበ'ሬ

peppermint
'ፔፐሚንት -ስ- ፔፐርሚንት

perambulator
ፕ'ራምብዩሌይተ -ስ- የሕፃናት ጋሪ (ሕፃና
ት ማንሸራሸሪያ)

perceive
ፕ'ሲይቭ -ግ- ማስተዋል [አስተዋለ] ፣ ማየት
[አ'የ] ፣ መ'ረዳት [ተረ'ዳ]

perch
'ፐ፡ች -ስ- የወፍ'ች መሥፈሪያ አግድም ብረት፣
እንጨት
roost
-ግ- ማረፍ [ዐ'ረፈ] (ለወፍ)

cent
ፕ'ሰንት -ተግ- ከመቶ ፣ በመቶ

perdition
ፕ'ዲሸን -ስ- ጥፋት (በሰው ላይ ሊ'ሚመጣ) ፣
ዘለዓለማዊ ኩነኔ

peremptory
'ፔሬምትሪ -ቅ- እም'በታ የ'ማይ ቀ'በል ፣
በመወ'ኛ

perennial
ፕ'ሬኒያል -ቅ- ካመት ዓመት የ'ሚቆ'ይ ፣
ብዙ ዓመታት የ'ሚቆ'ይ (እትክልት)

perfect
'ፐ፡ፌክት -ቅ- ፍ'ጹም ፣ እንከን የሌ'ለው

perfection
ፕ'ፌክሽን -ስ- ፍ'ጹም'ነት ፣ እንከን የ'ለሽ
'ነት

perfidious
ፕ'ፈዲየስ -ቅ- እምነተቢስ ፣ ከሓዲ (እም'ነት
አጉዳይ)

perfidy
'ፐ፡ፈዲ -ስ- ክሕደት

perforate
'ፐ፡ፈሬይት -ግ- መሸንቆር [ሸነ'ቆረ] (በተራ
ብዙ ሽቀቦር'ች

perform
ፕ'ፎ፡ም -ግ- መሥራት [ሠ'ራ] ፣ ማድረግ [አደ
'ረገ]

perfume
'ፐ፡ፍዩም -ስ- ጥሩ ሽ'ታ
liquid
-ስ- ሽ'ቶ

perfunctory
ፕ'ፈንክተሪ -ቅ- ጥን'ቃቄ ያ'ነሰው ፣ ለግብር
ይውጣ የተሠ'ራ

perhaps
ፕ'ሀፕስ -ተግ- ምናልባት

peril
'ፔሪል -ስ- ክ'ባድ አደጋ ፣ ክ'ባድ መከራ

period
'ፒሪየድ -ስ- ጊዜ ፤ ነጥብ (በሩቅት ነገር ማቆ
ሚያ)
menstruation
-ስ- የአደፍ ጊዜ

periodical
ፒሪ'ዮዲከል -ስ- መጽሔት
-ቅ- በተወ'ሰነ ጊዜ የ'ሚሆን

periodically
ፒሪ'ዮዲከሊ -ተግ- በ'የጊዜው

periphery
ፕ'ሪፈሪ -ስ- ዳር ፣ ዳር'ች

perish
'ፔሪሽ -ግ- መጥፋት [ጠ'ፋ] ፣ መሞት [ሞተ]

perjury
'ፐ፡ጀሪ -ስ- የሐ'ሰት ፣ የመዋሸት ወንጀል (በ
ምስ'ክር'ነት)

perky
'ፐ፡ኪ -ቅ- ንቁ ፣ እምነቱን'ና በጉ'ዳ'ዩ አ'ሳቢ
መሆኑን የ'ሚያሳ'ይ ፣ በሪሱ የ'ሚ'ተማ'መን

permanent
'ፐ፡መነንት -ቅ- ቀዋሚ ፣ ነዋሪ ፣ የ'ማይ'ለ
'ወጥ

permeate
'ፐ፡ሚዮይት -ግ- መስፋፋት [ተስፋ'ፋ] ፣ መግ
ባት [ገ'ባ] (ለውሃ)

542

permission

ፐ'ሚሽን -ስ- ፈቃድ

permit

ፐ'ሚት -ግ- ፈቃድ መስጠት [ሰ'ጠ]

permit

'ፐ:ሚት -ስ- ፈቃድ

pernicious

ፐ'ኒሸስ -ቅ- በጣም የ'ሚጎዳ ፡ አደገ'ኛ ፡ ክፉ

perpendicular

ፐ:ፐን'ዲክዩለ -ቅ- ቀ'ጥ ያለ (መሥመር ወዘተ)

perpetual

ፐ'ፔቹውል -ቅ- ዘለዓለማዊ ፡ ነዋሪ ፡ መጨ
'ረሻ የሌ'ለው ፤ ተደጋጋሚ

perplex

ፐፐ'ሌክስ -ግ- ማ'ደናገር [አ'ደና'ገረ] ፡ የ'ሚ
ያደናግጥን ማሳ'ጣት [አሳ'ጣ]

persecute

'ፐ:ሲክዩ:ት -ግ- ማ'ሳደድ [አ'ሳ'ደደ] (ለሃይ
ማኖት ወዘተ)

persevere

ፐሲ'ቪየ -ግ- መቀ'ጠል [ቀ'ጠለ] (ተስፋ ባለ
መቁረጥ)

Persian

'ፐ:ሺን -ቅ- የፋርስ ፡ የኢራን ፡ ኢራናዊ

persist

ፐ'ሲስት -ግ- በሐ'ሳብ መጽናት [ጸ'ና]

person

'ፐ:ሰን -ስ- ሰው

personal

'ፐ:ሰነል -ቅ- የግል

personnel

ፐሰ'ኔል -ስ- ሠ'ራተ'ኞ'ች (የመሥሪያ ቤት)

perspiration

ፐስፐ'ሬይሽን -ስ- ማላብ ፡ ላብ

persuade

ፐስ'ዌይድ -ግ- ማላ'መን [አላ'መነ] ፡ በመ'ወ
ያየት ወደን'ም በኃር'ክር ሐ'ሳብ እንዲ'ቀብ
ሉ ማድረግ [አደ'ረገ]

pert

'ፐ:ት -ቅ- ደ'ፋር ፡ አክብሮት የ'ማያሳ'ይ

pertinent

'ፐ:ቲነንት -ቅ- ከጉ'ዳዩ ጋር የተያያዘ ፡ ጉ'ዳ
ዩን የ'ሚነካ

perturbed

ፐ'ተ:ብድ -ቅ- የታ'ወከ ፡ የተጨ'ነቀ

peruse

ፐ'ሩ:ዝ -ግ- በጥን'ቃቄ ማንበብ [አነ'በበ]

pervade

ፐ'ቬይድ -ግ- መስፋፋት [ተስፋ'ፋ] (አደጋ ፡
ሥል'ጣኔ ወዘተ)

pervert

ፐ'ቨ:ት -ግ- ማ'ጣመም [አ'ጣመመ] (ይ'ጉን
ነገር) ፤ የሰው አእምሮ ከትክ'ክለ'ኛ መንገዲ
ማውጣት [አወ'ጣ] ፡ ማዛባት [አ'ዛ'ባ] ፡ ለክፉ
ማዋል (አዋለ)

pervert

'ፐ:ቨ:ት -ስ- ከሰው የተለ'የ ጠባይ ያ'ለው ፡
ሴስ'ኛ ፡ ከተፈጥሮ ው'ጭ የሆነ ሥራ የ'ሚሠራ
(ለግብረ ሥጋ)

pessimist

'ፔሲሚስት -ቅ- ሁልጊዜ ክፉ ነገር ይሠ
ጣል ብሎ የ'ሚያምን

pest

'ፔስት -ስ- አ'ዋኪ ነገር

animals

-ስ- የ'ሚጎዳ ነፍሳት ፡ ትን'ንሽ እንስ
ሳት ፤ መቅሠፍት ፡ ባጥባጭ ፡ ሁከት'ኛ ሰው
ወይ'ም ነገር

pet

'ፔት -ስ- ለ'ማዳ ት'ን'ንሽ እንስሳ

person

-ስ- በተለ'ይ የ'ሚ'ወ'ደድ (ተማሪ ወ
ዘተ)

caress

-ግ- ማሻሸት [አሻ'ሸ] (ሴት)

petal

'ፔተል -ስ- ያበባ ቅጠል (ከአበባው ጎንደ
ቅጠል)

petition

ፐ'ቲሽን -ስ- ይግባ'ኝ ፡ አቤቱታ

petrol

'ፔትረል -ስ- ቤንዚን

petticoat

'ፔቲከውት -ስ- ቡ'ፍ ያለ የሴት የውስጥ
ልብስ ፡ ቡ'ፋንት

petty

'ፔቲ -ቅ- ጥቃ'ቅን (ዋጋ የሌ'ለው)

543

antasy
'ፋንታሲ -ስ- እውነት'ነት የሌ'ለው ታሪክ ፣ ሕልም የ'ሚመስል ሐ'ሳብ ፣ እንደሕልም ያ'ለ ነገር

,hantom
'ፋንተም -ስ- ረቂቅ ፍጡር ፣ የማይ'ዳ'ሰስ ቅርፅ ፣ እውነት'ነት የሌ'ለው

pharmaceutical
ፋ፡መስ'ዩቲከል -ቅ- የመድኃኒት ቅ'መማ

pharmacy
'ፋ፡መሲ -ስ- መድኃኒት ቅ'መማ

phase
'ፌይዝ -ስ- ባንድ ተመላልሶ በ'ሚ'ደ'ረግ ሁናቴ ውስጥ የእድገት ወይን'ም የለውጥ ጊዜ

philanthropist
ፊ'ላንስረፒስት -ቅ- የሰውን ልጅ ወ'ዳድ ፣ በጎ እድራጊ ፣ ሰብአዊ ፍቅር ያ'ደረ'በት

philology
ፊ'ሎለጂ -ስ- የቋንቋዎ'ች ትምህርት

philosophy
ፊ'ሎሰፊ -ስ- ፍልስፍ'ና

phlegmatic
ፊ.ላግ'ማቲክ -ቅ- በቀ'ላሉ የ'ማይ'ሸ'በር

phonetic
ፊ'ኔቲክ -ቅ- እንዳ'ነባበቡ የተጻፈ ፣ የድምፅ

photograph
'ፌውተግራ፡ፍ -ስ- ፎቶግራፍ

phrase
ፍ'ሬይዝ -ስ- ሐረግ (ሰዋሰው)

physician
ፊ'ዚሽን -ስ- ሐኪም

physics
'ፊዚክስ -ስ- ፊዚክስ (የኃይል'ና የጥንት ነገ ሮ'ች ጠባይ ጥናት)

physiognomy
ፊዚ'ዮነሚ ,-ስ- መልክ ፣ የመልክ ቅርፅ'ና ጠቅላ'ላ ሁኔታው

physique
ፊ'ዚይክ -ስ- የሰው'ነት ቅርፅ

piano
ፒ'ያነው -ስ- ፒያኖ

pick
'ፒክ -ግ- መልቀም [ለ'ቀመ]
choose
-ግ- መምረጥ [መ'ረጠ]
tool
-ስ- መቆ'ፈሪያ ፣ ዶማ

pickaxe
'ፒካክስ -ስ- ዶማ

picnic
'ፒክኒክ -ስ- የሽር'ሽር ቦታ (ምግብ ተይዞ የ'ሚ'ኬድ'በት)

picture
'ፒከቸ -ስ- ሥዕል

picturesque
ፒከቸ'ሬስክ -ቅ- ያማረ (ትእ'ይንት ፣ ለመሣል የ'ሚስማ'ማ)

pie
'ፓይ -ስ- ከሥጋ ወይን'ም ከፍራ፦ፊ'ና ከሊጥ የተሰና'ዳ ምግብ (የተጋ'ገረ)

piece
'ፒይስ -ስ- ቁራ'ጭ ነገር

piecemeal
'ፒይስሚይል -ተግ- ት'ን፦ በት'ን፦ ፣ በተበ ታ'ተነ ሁናቴ

pierce
'ፒየስ -ግ- መውጋት [ወ'ጋ] (በመ'ሣሪያ)

piety
'ፓየቲ -ስ- ሃይማኖተ'ኛ'ነት

pig
'ፒግ -ስ- ዐሣማ

pigeon
'ፒጀን -ስ- እርግብ

pigtail
'ፒግቴይል -ስ- በስተኋላ የወ'ረደ የጠጉር ጉ'ን ጉን

pike
'ፓይክ -ስ- ዶማ

pile
'ፓይል -ስ- ዐሣ የ'ሚበላ ዐሣ
-ግ- መክ'መር [ከ'መረ] ፣ መቆ'ለል [ቆ'ለለ]

pilfer
'ፒልፈ -ግ- መስረቅ [ሰ'ረቀ] (ለጥቃ'ቅን ነገር)

544

pilgrim

'ፒልግሪም -ስ- የተቀ'ደሱ ቦታዎ'ች ለመ
· 'ሳለም የ'ሚ'ጓዝ ሰው ፣ ተሳላሚ (ም'ሳሌ ፣
ኢ'የሩሳሌም ፣ መ'ካ)

pilgrimage

'ፒልግሪሚጅ -ስ- ወደተቀ'ደሱ ቦታዎ'ች የ
'ሚ'ደ'ረግ ጉዞ

pill

'ፒል -ስ- ክኒን ፣ እንክብ'ል (መድኃኒት)

pillage

'ፒለጅ -ግ- መዝረፍ [ዘ'ረፈ]

pillar

'ፒለ -ስ- ዐምድ

pillar-box

'ፒለቦክስ -ስ- ዐምድ መ'ሰል የፖስታ ማስገ
'ቢያ ሣጥን (በመንገድ ዳ'ር የቆመ)

pillion

'ፒለየን -ስ- መ'ፈናጠጫ ወምበር (በሞቶር
ቢስክሌት ኋላ)

pillow

'ፒለው -ስ- ትራስ

pillow-case

'ፒለውኬይስ -ስ- የትራስ ልብስ

pilot

'ፓይለት -ስ- መርከብ ነጃ ፣ አውር'ፕላን
ነጃ

pimp

'ፒምፕ -ግ- ማ'ቃጠር [አ'ቃ'ጠረ] (ሴት
ለወንድ)

pimple

'ፒምፕል -ስ- ብጉር

pin

'ፒን -ግ- በስፒል ማ'ያያዝ [አ'ያያዘ] (ወረ
ቀት)

straight
-ስ- ስፒል\
safety-
-ስ- መርፌ ቁልፍ

pinafore

'ፒነፎ: -ስ- ሽ'ርት (የሕፃናት ፣ ልብሳ'ቸው
እንዳይቆ'ሸሽ)

pincers

'ፒንሰዝ -ስ- ጉጠት

pinch

'ፒንች -ግ- መቆንጠጥ [ቆነ'ጠጠ]

pine

'ፓይን -ግ- መድከም [ደ'ከመ] (ከበ'ሽታ፣ከሐ
ዘን የተነ'ሣ) ፤ የጋል ፍ'ላጎት መፍር [ፍረ]
(አንድ ነገር ለማድረግ)

pineapple

'ፓይናፑል -ስ- አናናስ

pinion

'ፒንየን -ግ- እ'ጅ ማሰር [አ'ሰረ] (ከሰው
'ውነት ጋር)
-ስ- የወፍ ክንፍ

pink

'ፒንክ -ቅ- ክፍት ቀ'ይ

pinnacle

'ፒንክል -ስ- ጫፍ (የቤት፣የተራራ ወዘተ) ፣
ቁንጮ

pioneer

ፓየ'ኒየ -ስ- አንዱን ያ'ለ'ማ እገር ለማልማት
ከሄዱ ሰዎ'ች እንዱ ፤ ያንድ ዕ'ቅድ መሪ፣ያን
ድ ሥራ ጀ'ማሪ

pious

'ፓየስ -ቅ- ሃይማኖታዊ ፣ ጊዜውን ለሃይማ
ኖት ተግባር የሰ'ጠ

pip

'ፒፕ -ስ- ፍሬ (የፍራፍሬ)

pipe

'ፓይፕ -ስ- ቧንቧ
smoking
-ስ- ቲ'ፓ (የትምባሆ ማጤሻ)
flute
-ስ- ዋሽ'ንት

pirate

'ፓይሬት -ስ- የባሕር ወንበዴዎ'ች ፣ መርከብ
ዘራፊዎ'ች

pistol

'ፒስተል -ስ- ሽ'ጉጥ

piston

'ፒስተን -ስ- ፒስቶን

pit

'ፒት -ስ- ጉድጓድ

545

pitch

'ፒች -ስ- የድምፅ ከ'ፍተ'ኛ'ነት 'ና ዝ'ቅተ'ኛ 'ነት
tar

-ስ- ሬንጅ
throw

-ግ- መወርወር [ወረ'ወረ]
sport

-ስ- የስፖርት ሜዳ
a tent

-ግ- ድንኳን መትከል [ተ'ከለ]

pitcher

'ፒቸ -ስ- እንሥራ

piteous

'ፒትየስ -ቅ- አሳ'ዛኝ

pitfall

'ፒትፎ:ል -ስ- የአውራ ማጥመጃ ጉድ'ጓድ ፤
የተደ'በቀ አደጋ

pith

'ፒስ -ስ- ከል'ጣጭ በታች ያ'ለው ሥሥ
ሻፉን (የፍራፍሬ ወዘተ)
importance

-ስ- ቁም ነገር (የንግ'ግር)
vigour

-ስ- ጥን'ካሬ ፤ ጎይል

pity

'ፒቲ -ስ- ሐዘን ፤ ርኅራኄ

pivot

'ፒቨት -ስ- መሽከርከሪያ ሹል መ'ማሪያ

placard

ፕ'ላካ:ድ -ስ- ሕዝብን ለማስታወቅ የተጻፈ
ጽሑፍ

placate

ፕለ'ኬይት -ግ- ማ'ረጋጋት [አ'ረጋጋ] ፤ ቁ'ጣ
ማብረድ [አብ'ረደ]

place

ፕ'ሌይስ -ስ- ቦታ

placenta

ፕለ'ሴንተ -ስ- የእንግዴ ልጅ

placid

ፕ'ላስ ድ -ቅ- ጸ'ጥ ያለ

plague

ፕ'ሌግ -ስ- ጎደለ'ኛ ተላላፊ በ'ሽታ ፤ ቸ
ፈር
disturb

-ግ- ማ'ወክ [አ'ወከ] ፤ መበጥበጥ [በጠ
'በጠ]

plain

ፕ'ሌይን -ስ- ለ'ጥ ያለ ቦታ ፤ ሜዳ
undecorated

-ቅ- ጌጣጌጥ የሌ'ለ'በት
understandable

-ቅ- ግልጽ

plaintiff

ፕ'ሌይንቲፍ -ስ- ከሳሽ

plaintive

ፕ'ሌይንቲቭ -ቅ- የ'ሚያሳ'ዝን (ድምፅ)

plan

ፕ'ላን -ግ- ማ'ቀድ [ዐ'ቀደ]
-ስ- ዕ'ቅድ

plane

ፕ'ሌይን -ቅ- ጠፍጣ'ፋ
aero-

-ስ- አውሮ'ፕላን
tool

-ስ- መላጊያ

planet

ፕ'ላነት -ስ- ፈለክ (ከፀሐይ ጭፍሮ'ች እንዱ)

plank

ፕ'ላንክ -ስ- ጠርብ

plant

ፕ'ላ:ንት -ስ- ተክል

plantation

ፕላን'ቴይሽን -ስ- አትክልት

plaque

ፕ'ላክ -ስ- የደንጊያ ፤ የሸክላ ጽ'ላት (በግድ
ግ'ዳ ላይ እንደገarm የ'ሚንጠለ'ጠል)

plaster

ፕ'ላ:ስተ -ስ- ፕ'ላስተር ፤ እቁስል ላይ የ'ሚ'ለ
'ጠፍ መድኃኒት'ነት ያ'ለው መለ'ጠፊያ
of Paris

-ስ- ጅፕስ
a wall etc

-ግ- መምረግ [መ'ረገ] (በቂጮታ)

plastic

ፕላስቲክ -ስ- ፕላስቲክ

-ቅ- በቀላሉ የሚላመጥ ፣ ቅርጹ የሚ

ለወጥ

plate

ፕሌይት -ስ- ዝርግ ሳሕን ፣ ሥሥና ዝርግ

የብረት ፣ የብ'ር ወዘተ ዕቃ

plateau

ፕላተው -ስ- በደጋ አገር ላይ ሜዳማ ቦታ

platform

ፕላትፎ፡ም -ስ- ከፍ ያለ የተናገሪ መቆሚያ

ቦታ

plausible

ፕሎዝበል -ቅ- እውነት የሚመስል ፣ የሚ

ያሳምን ፣ ሊታመን የሚችል

play

ፕሌይ -ግ- መጫወት [ተጫወተ]

theatrical

-ስ- ቴያትር (ጽሑፍ)

plea

ፕሊይ -ስ- ልመና ፣ ማመልከቻ

plead

ፕሊያይድ -ግ- ምክንያት ለዳኛ ማቅረብ [አቀ

ረብ] (ከስ ሲያቀርብ)

beseech

-ግ- መለማመን [ተለማመን]

pleasant

ፕሌዘንት -ቅ- አስደሳች

pleasantry

ፕሌዘንትሪ -ስ- አስደሳች ጭውውት

please

ፕሊይዝ -ግ- ማደሰት [ተደሰተ]

-ተግ ፡ ቃአ- እባክዎን ፣ እባክህን

pleasure

ፕሌዠ -ስ- ደስታ

pleat

ፕሊይት -ስ- ሽንሽን (የልብስ)

pledge

ፕሌጅ -ግ- ቃል መግባት [ገባ]

-ስ- ውለታ መግባት (አንዳ ዕቃ እሰው

ዘንድ በማስቀመጥ የገባውን ውለታ ሊፈ'ጽም

ዕቃውን ለመውሰድ)

plenty

ፕሌንቲ -ስ- ብዛት ፣ መትረፍረፍ

pliable

ፕላየበል -ቅ- በቀላሉ የሚታጠፍ፤

mind

-ቅ- በቀላሉ የሰውን ሐሳብ የሚቀ

በል

pliers

ፕላየዝ -ስ- የጉጠት ጓይነት መጥበሪያ

plight

ፕላይት -ስ- አዋኪ ፣ አሳዛዥ ሁናቴ

promise

-ግ- ተስፋ መስጠት [ሰጠ] (ለጋብቻ)

plimsolls

ፕሊምሶልዝ -ስ- የላስቲክ ሶል ያለው የሸራ

ጫማ (የስፖርት)

plinth

ፕሊንስ -ስ- ዓንድ ሐውልት መቆሚያ ድንጋይ

plod

ፕሎድ -ግ- እየተንገታገቱ መ'ራመድ [ተ.. መ

ደ] ፣ መሥራት [ወ'ራ] (ለዕረፍት)

plot

ፕሎት -ግ- መሸመ ቀ [ሸ'መ ቀ]

-ስ- ሸ'መቃ

story

-ስ- ያንድ መጽሐፍ ታሪ ፍሬ ነገር

land

-ስ- ትንሽ ቆ'ራጭ መሬት

plough

ፕላው -ግ- ማረስ [አ'ረስ]

-ስ- ማረሻ

pluck

ፕላክ -ግ- መልቀም [ለ'ቀመ] (ፍራፍሬ ከዛፍ)፣

መ'ቅጠፍ [ቀጠ'ፈ] (አበባ) ፣ መንቀል [ነ'ቀለ]

[ላባ]

plug

ፕለግ -ስ- ውታፍ ፣ የኤሌክትሪክ መሰካ ያ

plumage

ፕሉሜጅ -ስ- የወፍ ላባ

plumber

ፕለመ -ስ- ቧምቧ ው'ራተኛ

plumbing

ፕለሚንግ -ስ- በቤት ውስጥ ያ'ለ ውሃ ቧ'ም

ቧ'ና የውሃ ጉ'ዳ

plume
ፕ'ሉ:ም -ስ- ላባ ፤ ከላባ የተሠ'ራ ጌጥ

plump
ፕ'ለምፕ -ስ- ወፍራም ፣ ወደል (ለሰው ፣ ለእ
ንስሳ) ፤ ድምቡ'ጭ ያለ

plunder
ፕ'ለንደ -ግ- መዝረፍ [ዘ'ረፈ] ፣ መበዝበዝ
[በዘ'በዘ]
-ስ- የተዘ'ረፈ ዕቃ

plunge
ፕ'ለንጅ -ግ- መጥለቅ [ጠ'ለቀ] ፣ ማጥለቅ
[አጠ'ለቀ] (እውሃ ውስጥ)

plural
ፕ'ሉረል -ስ- የብዙ ቁጥር (ሰዋሰው)

plus
ፕ'ለስ -ስ- የድ'ምር ምል'ክት
-ቅ- ተጨ'ማሪ

plush
ፕ'ለሽ -ስ- ከፈይ
-ቅ- የተቀማ'ጠለ

ply
ፕ'ላይ -ግ- የንግድ ሥራ ማ'ካሄድ [አ'ካሄደ]
-ስ- ቃ'ጫ (እንዱ ክ'ር)

pneumatic
ንዩ'ማቲክ -ቅ- በአ'የር የ'ሚ'ሠ'ራ ፣ በአ'የር
የተሞ'ላ

pneumonia
ንዩ'መውኒየ -ስ- የሳም'ባ እብጠት በ'ሽታ

poach
'ፐውች -ግ- መስረቅ [ሰ'ረቀ] (ለከብት ፣ ለአ
ደን ወዘተ)

pocket
'ፓከት -ስ- ኪስ

pod
'ፖድ -ስ- የእሸት ል'ጣጭ (የአተር የባቄላ
ወዘተ)

podgy
'ፖጂ -ቅ- አጭር'ና ወፍራም ፣ ዱፍዲ'ፉ

poem
'ፐወም -ስ- ግጥም ፣ ቅኔ

poet
'ፐወት -ስ- ግጥም ገጣሚ ፣ ባለቅኔ ፣ ባለግጥም

poetry
'ፐወትሪ -ስ- ቅኔ ፣ ግጥም ፣ ሥነ ግጥም

point
'ፖይንት -ስ- ነጥብ ፣ ነቁጥ
place, spot
-ስ- ቦታ
indicate
-ግ- ማመልከት [አመለ'ከተ]

pointed
'ፖይንተድ -ቅ- ሹል
of remarks
-ቅ- የተለ'የ ሰውን የ'ሚነካ (አ'ነጋገር)

pointer
'ፖይንተ -ስ- ማመልከቻ (ዘንግ)

poise
'ፖይዝ -ስ- በራስ መ'ተማመን ፣ ኩሩ'ነት ፣
የተመ'ዘነ አ'ቋቋም

poison
'ፖይዘን -ስ- መርዝ
-ግ- በመርዝ መግደል [ገ'ደለ]

poisonous
'ፖይዝነስ -ቅ- መርዛም ፣ መርዘ'ኛ

poke
'ፐውክ -ግ- መቆስቆስ [ቆስ'ቆሰ] (በጣት
በበ'ትር ወዘተ)

poker
'ፐውክ -ስ- የእሳት መቆስቆሻ (ብረት)

pole
'ፐውል -ስ- አጣና ፣ ዘንግ ፣ ምሰ'ሶ
geographical
-ስ- ዋል፡ታ (የሰሜን ፣ የደቡብ)

police
ፐ'ሊስ -ስ- ፖሊስ (ድር'ጅት)

policeman
ፐ'ሊስመን -ስ- ፖሊስ (ሰው)

policy
'ፖሊሲ -ስ- አቅዋም ፣ ዐቅድ (የመንግሥት)
insurance
-ስ- ስምም'ነት (የኢንሹራንስ)

polish
'ፖሊሽ -ግ- መጥረግ [ጠ'ረገ] (እንዲያበራ
አድርጎ) ፤ መቦላት [ቦ'ላ]
-ስ- የጫ'ማ ቀለም
refinement
-ስ- መልካም አስተዳደግ

polite
ፐ'ላይት -ቅ- የታ'ረመ ፣ የተቀ'ጣ

politics
'ፖሊቲክስ -ስ- ፖለቲካ

poll
'ፖውል -ስ- የምርጫ መዝገብ ፣ ቦታ ፣ ድምፅ መስጠት ወዘተ (ለሕዝብ እንደራሴዎ'ች)

pollen
'ፖለን -ስ- በአበባ ውስጥ ያለ ብ'ጫ ዱቄት (ሌሎ'ች አበቦ'ች እንዲ'ራ'ቡ የ'ሚያደርግ)

pollute
ፐ'ሉ:ት -ግ- ማሳ'ደፍ [አሳ'ደፈ] ፣ ማጉደፍ [አጉ'ደፈ]

pollution
ፐ'ሉሽን -ስ- እድፍ'ነት ፣ ጉድፍ'ነት

polygamy
ፐ'ሊገሚ -ስ- ከአንድ የበ'ለጠ ሚስት ማግ ባት

polyglot
'ፖሊግሎት -ስ- አ'ያሌ ቋንቋዎ'ች የ'ሚያ ውቅ ሰው
-ቅ- በብዙ ቋንቋዎ'ች የተጻፈ

polytheism
ፖሊ'ሲይዝም -ስ- በብዙ አማልክት አምልኮ

pomegranate
'ፖሚግራኔት -ስ- ሮማን (የፍሬ ዓይነት)

pomp
'ፖምፕ -ስ- ግሩም የሆነ ሰልፍ

pompous
'ፖምፐስ -ቅ- ል'ታይ ል'ታይ ባይ ፣ ባለግ ርማ

pond
'ፖንድ -ስ- ኩሬ

ponder
'ፖንደ -ግ- አጥልቆ ማ'ሰብ [አ'ሰበ] ፣ አተ ኩ'ሮ ማ'ሰብ [አ'ሰበ]

ponderous
'ፖንደረስ -ቅ- በጣም ከ'ባድ ፣ በቀ'ላሉ የ'ማ ይንቀሳ'ቀስ

ontoon
ፖን'ቱ:ን -ስ- በውሃ ላይ የ'ሚንሳ'ፈፍ የድል ድይ ድጋፍ (በጀልባ ላይ የቆመ)

ony
'ፐውኒ -ስ- ድንክ ፈረስ

pool
'ፑ:ል -ስ- ኩሬ
resources
-ግ- መደባለቅ [ደባ'ለቀ] (ሀብትን ፣ ትር ፍን ለመ'ካፈል)

poor
'ፖ: -ቅ- ድሀ ፣ ች'ግረ'ኛ
weak
-ቅ- ደካማ (በትምህርት ወዘተ)
pitiful
-ቅ- አሳ'ዛኝ

popular
'ፖፐዩለ -ቅ- የታ'ወቀ ፣ ዝ'ነ'ኛ

population
ፖፐዩ'ሌይሽን -ስ- ሕዝብ

porch
'ፖ:ች -ስ- መግቢያ (ጣራ መሳይ ያ'ለው በ'ር)

porcupine
ፖ:ክዩፓይን -ስ- ጃርት

pore
'ፖ: -ስ- ት'ንሽ ቀዳዳ (በሰው'ነት ቆዳ)
concentrate on
-ግ- አተ'ኩሮ ማ'ሰብ [አ'ሰበ]

pork
'ፖ:ክ -ስ- ያሣማ ሥጋ

porous
'ፖ:ረስ -ቅ- ውሃ የ'ሚያፈ'ስ ፣ ቀዳዳ ያ'ለው ፣ ውሃ የ'ማይቋ'ጥር

porridge
'ፖሪጅ -ስ- አጥሚት ፣ ሙቅ (ከአ'ጃ፣ከውሃ'ና ከወተት የተሠ'ራ)

port
'ፖ:ት -ስ- መስኮት (በመርከብ ውስጥ)
harbour
-ስ- የመርከብ ወደብ

portable
'ፖ:ተበል -ቅ- በእ'ጅ ሊ'ያዝ የ'ሚችል (ለማ 'ጓጓዝ)

portal
'ፖ:ተል -ስ- ት'ልቅ በ'ር

portent
'ፖ:ቴንት -ስ- ምል'ክት (ወደፊት የ'ሚሆን ውን የ'ሚያመለ'ክት)

porter
ፖ‘ተ -ስ- ተሸ‘ካሚ ፤ ኩሊ ፣ በ‘ረ‘ኛ (በሆ‘ቴል እንግዳ ከው‘ጭ የ‘ሚ‘ቀ‘በል)

portion
ፖ‘ሸን -ስ- ድርሻ ፣ ክፍ‘ይ ፣ ቁ‘ራሽ

portly
ፖ‘ትሊ -ቅ- ወፍራም ፤ ግዙፍ (በተለ‘ይ ለሽማግ‘ሌ‘ች)

portrait
ፖ‘ትሬይት -ስ- የሰው ፣ የእንስሳ ሥዕል

pose
'ፖውዝ -ግ- ስ‘ው‘ነት ማስተካከል [አስተ ካ‘ከለ] (ለፎቶግራፍ አንሺ)
pretend
-ግ- መምሰል [መ‘ሰለ] (ሌላ ሰው)
set (question)
-ግ- ጥ‘ያቄ ማቅረብ [አቀ‘ረበ]

position
ፖ‘ዚሸን -ስ- ቦታ ፤ ሁኔታ

ositive
ፖ‘ዚቲቭ -ቅ- እርግጠ‘ኛ ፤ የ‘ማያ‘ጠራ‘ጥር

possess
ፖ‘ዜስ -ግ- መ‘ንናዘብ [ተ‘ንና‘ዘበ]

possessive
ፖ‘ዜሲቭ -ቅ- ሰው‘ን ፤ ማ‘ና‘ቸውን‘ም ነገር የራሱ ለማድረግ የ‘ሚፈ‘ልግ ፤ አ‘ንናዛቢ (ሰዋ ሰው)

possible
ፖሲበል -ቅ- የ‘ሚ‘ቻል ፣ ለሀ ን የ‘ሚ‘ችል

post
‘ፖውስት -ስ- እመሬት ላይ የተተ‘ከለ እንጨት
mail
-ስ- ፖስታ ፣ ደብዳ‘ቤ
appointment
-ስ- ሹመት (የሥራ)
despatch
-ግ- ደብዳ‘ቤ በፖስታ መላክ [ላከ]

ostcard
‘ፖውስትካ‘ድ -ስ- ፖስትካርድ

oster
‘ፖውስተ -ስ- የተለ‘ጠፈ ማስታወቂያ

550

posterior
ፖስ‘ቲሪየ -ስ- ኋላ ፣ ዳ‘ሌ ፤ ቂጥ
-ቅ- በተራ ፣ በጊዜ የኋላ‘ኛ የሆነ
after in time
-ቅ- በኋላ ይ‘ለ ፤ ይ‘ለፈ

posterity
ፖስ‘ቴሪቲ -ስ- መጪ ትውል‘ድ ፤ የልጅ ልጅ

posthumous
‘ፖስትዩመስ -ቅ- ከሞት በኋላ ፤ ከፈራሲው ሞት በኋላ የታ‘ተመ

postman
‘ፖውስትመን -ስ- ፖስታ አ‘ዳይ

postmaster
‘ፖውስትግ‘ስተ -ስ- የፖስ‘ታ ቤት ሹም

postmortem
ፖውስት‘ም‘ተም -ስ- በበድን ላይ የ‘ሚ‘ደ‘ረግ የሕ‘ክም‘ና ምርመራ (የ‘ሚ‘ሞ‘ተን ሁኔታ ለ‘ማ ‘ረጋገጥ)

post-office
‘ፖውስት‘ኦፈስ -ስ- የፖስታ ቤት

postpone
ፖስ‘ተውን -ግ- ማስ‘ተላለፍ [አስተላ ለ ፤ ጊዜ ፤ ተ‘ዳደ)

postscript
‘ፖውስክሪፕት -ስ- ደብዳ‘ቤ ከተጻፈ ‘ና ከተ ፈ‘ረመ በኋላ የ‘ሚ‘ጻፍ ተጨ‘ማሪ ጽሑፍ ፤ ጥ‘ያቄ

postulate
‘ፖስትዩሌይት -ግ- ሐ‘ሳብ ማቅረብ [አቀ‘ረበ] (ለክ‘ክር ፤ ለውይ‘ይት)

posture
‘ፖስቸ -ስ- የሰው‘ነት አ‘ደዳ‘ም (ቆ‘ተ ያለ ፤ ያዘ‘በለ ወዘተ)

posy
‘ፖውዚ -ስ- ያበባ እ‘ቅፍ

pot
‘ፖት -ስ- ማሰሮ

potato
ፖ‘ቴይተው -ስ- ድ‘ን‘ች

potent
‘ፖውተንት -ቅ- ችሎ‘ታ ያለው ፤ ኀይለ‘ኛ

potential
ፖ‘ቴንሸል -ስ- ወደፊት ሲሆን ፤ ሲ‘ፈ ‘ረ የ‘ሚ‘ችል ነገር ወይን‘ም ቁ‘ናቱ

potion
'ፖውሽን -ስ- መድኃኒት'ነት ያለው ፣ መር
ዝ'ነት ያለው ወይን'ም አስካሪ መጠ'ጥ

potter
'ፖተ -ስ- ሸክላ ሥሪ

pottery
'ፖተሪ -ስ- የሸክላ ዕቃ

pouch
'ፖውች -ስ- የቆዳ ከረጢት ፣ ቦርሳ

poultice
'ፖልቲስ -ስ- በቆ'ሰለ ወይን'ም ባ'በጠ ሰው
'ነት ላይ የ'ሚ.ደ.'ረግ በሙቅ ወሃ ፣ በተቀ'ቀለ
ተልባ ፣ በሰናፍ'ጭ የተዘፈ'ዘፈ ጨርቅ

poultry
'ፖልትሪ -ስ- ክንፍ ያላቸው የቤት እንስሳት
(ዶሮ ፣ ዳ'ክዬ ወዘተ)

pounce
'ፖውንስ -ግ- ዘ'ሎ መ'ከመር [ተከ'መረ] (እ
ደን ላይ)

pound
'ፖውንድ -ግ- መውቀጥ [ወ'ቀጠ] ፣ ማደ
ቀቅ [አደ'ቀቀ]
-ስ- የእንግሊዝ ገንዘብ (ፖውንድ)

pour
'ፖ: -ግ- መፍሰስ [ፈ'ሰሰ] ፣ ማፍሰስ [አፈ
'ሰሰ]

pout
'ፖውት -ግ- ከንፈር በማውጣት አለመ'ደ
ሰት'ን መግለጽ [ገ'ለጸ]

poverty
'ፖቨቲ -ስ- ድህ'ነት

powder
'ፖውደ -ስ- ዱቄት
cosmetic
-ስ- ፖውደር (መልክ ማሳ'መሪያ ዱ
ቄት)

power
'ፖወ -ስ- ችሎታ ፣ ኃይል
authority
-ስ- ሥልጣን

practical
'ፕራክቲከል -ቅ- ብልኅነት'ኛ (ለእ'ጅ ሥራ):
ብቁ ፣ ጠቃሚ.

practically
'ፕራክቲከሊ. -ተግ- ገደማ ፣ አቅራ'ቢ.ያ ፣ በሙ
ነቱ ፣ በግብር

practice
'ፕራክቲስ -ስ- ልም'ምድ (ለመ'ማር)
·· habitual action
-ስ- ልምድ

practise
'ፕራክቲስ -ግ- መ'ለማመድ [ተለማ'መደ] ፣
መሡልጠን [ሠለ'ጠነ]
carry out profession
-ግ- ሞያን እሥራ ላይ ማዋል [አዋለ]

pragmatic
ፕራግ'ማቲክ -ቅ- ሁናቴን እንዳ'ለ አይቶ የ'
ሚፈርድ ፣ የ'ሚሠራ (በተወ'ሰነ እምነት ላይ
ሆኖ)

praise
ፕ'ሬይዝ -ግ- ማመስገን [አመሰ'ገነ]
-ስ- ምስጋና

prance
ፕ'ራ:ንስ -ግ- መዝለል [ዘ'ለለ] (ለፈረስ)

prank
ፕ'ራንክ -ስ- ቢልት ፣ ቀልድ (ጉዳት የ'ሚያስ
ከ'ትል)

prate
ፕ'ሬይት -ግ- መቀባጠር [ቀባ'ጠረ]

prattle
ፕ'ራተል -ግ- መንተባተብ [ተንተባ'ተብ] (እ
ንደ ሕፃን)

pray
ፕ'ሬይ -ግ- መጸ'ለይ [ጸ'ለየ]

prayer
ፕ'ሬየ -ስ- ጸሎት

preach
ፕ'ሪይች -ግ- መስበክ [ሰ'በከ] (ሃይማኖት)

preacher
ፕ'ሪቸ -ስ- ሰባኪ.

precarious
ፕረ'ኬሪየስ -ቅ- እርግጠ'ኛ ያልሆነ ፣ ድንገት
ሊሆን በ'ሚችል ሁኔታ ላይ የተመሠ'ረተ ፣
አ'ጠራጣሪ

precaution
ፕሪ'ኮ:ሽን -ስ- ጥን'ቃቄ

precede
ፕሪ'ሲይድ -ግ- መቅደም [ቀ'ደመ] (በጊዜ ፣
በቦታ ፤ በቅደም ተከ'ተል)

precedent
ፕ'ሪሲደንት -ስ- ያ'ለፈ ነገር (ለወደፊት እን
ደ ም'ሳሌ የ'ሚ'ወ'ሰድ ፣ በፍርድ ወዘተ)

precept
ፕ'ሪሴፕት -ስ- የግብረ ገ'ብ'ነት ሕ'ግ

precinct
ፕ'ሪሲንክት -ስ- ቅጥር ግ'ቢ. (በቤተ ክርስቲ
ያን ፣ በገዳም ዙሪያ)

precious
ፕ'ሬሸሰ -ቅ- ዋጋው የላቀ ፣ ው'ድ

precipice
ፕ'ሪሲፒስ -ስ- ሽር'ው ያለ ገደል ፣ ታ'ላቅ
አደጋ

precis
ፕ'ሬይሲ -ስ- አሕጽሮተ ጽሑፍ

precise
ፕሪ'ሳይስ -ቅ- በትክ'ክል የተነ'ገረ ፣ ግልጥ ፣
ል'ክ

preclude
ፕሪክ'ሉ:ድ -ግ- መከልከል [ከለ'ከለ] ፣ ማ'ገድ
[አ'ገደ]

precocious
ፕሪ'ከውሸስ -ቅ- ብልጥ (ያለ ዕድሜው)

predatory
ፕ'ሬደትሪ -ቅ- በዘረፋ የ'ሚኖር ፣ እየነ'ጠቀ
የ'ሚኖር

predecessor
ፕ'ሪይዲሰስ -ስ- በሥራ ቀዳሚ'ነት ያ'ለው ፣
በሥራው ላይ የቆ'የ'ና በቦታው ሌላ ሰው የተተ
'ካ'በት

predicament
ፕሪ'ዲከመንት -ስ- አሥጊ ሁናቴ ፣ የ'ማያስ
ደ'ስት ሁናቴ (ማማለት የ'ማይ'ቻል)

predominate
ፕሪ'ዶሚኔይት -ግ- መብለጥ [በ'ለጠ] ፣ በቁ
ጥር መላቅ [ላቀ]

preface
ፕ'ሬፈስ -ስ- መቅድም

prefer
ፕሪ'ፈ: -ግ- መምረጥ [መ'ረጠ]

prefix
ፕ'ሪፊክስ -ስ- ባዕድ መነ'ሻ (ስዋስው)

pregnant
ፕ'ሬግነንት -ቅ- ያረ'ገዘ ፣ የፀ'ነሰ

prejudice
ፕ'ሬጁዲስ -ስ- ማስረ'ጃ የሌ'ለው መጥፎ አስ
ተያየት ፣ ያለ ማስረጃ ፍርድ መስጠት

preliminary
ፕሪ'ሊሚነሪ -ቅ- መቅድማዊ ፣ የመጀ'መሪያ

prelude
ፕ'ሬልዩድ -ስ- መቅድም

premature
ፕ'ሬመቸ -ቅ- ያለዕድሜው ፣ ጊዜው የደ'ረሰ

premier
.ፕ'ሬሚየ -ቅ- በእስፈ'ላጊ'ነቱ የመ'ጀ'መሪያ
'ነትን የያዘ
-ስ- ጠቅላይ ሚኒስትር

premonition
ፕሪመ'ኒሸን -ስ- ክፉ ነገር እንደ'ሚመጣ ማ
መን

preoccupation
ፕሪዮክዩ'ፔይሸን -ስ- ስለአንድ ነገር ጥልቅ
ሐሳብ መ'ያዝ

preparation
ፕሬፕ'ሬይሸን -ስ- ዝግ'ጅት

prepare
ፕሪ'ፔየ -ግ- ማ'ዘጋጀት [አ'ዘጋ'ጀ]

preponderance
ፕሪ'ፖንደረንስ -ስ- የቁጥር ፣ የክብደት ፣ የጎ
ይል ወዘተ ብልጫ

preposition
ፕሬፖ'ዚሸን -ስ- መስተዋድድ (ስዋስው)

prerogative
ፕሪ'ሮጋቲቭ -ስ- የተለ'የ መብት

presage
ፕሪ'ሴይጅ -ግ- መ'ነበይ [ተነ'በየ] (ክፉ ነገር
መምጣቱን)

prescribe
ፕሪስክ'ራይብ -ግ- ማዘዝ [አ'ዘዘ] (ለመድኃ
ኒት) ፣ ሕ'ግ ማውጣት [አወ'ጣ]

prescription
ፕሪስክ'ሪፕሸን -ስ- ትእዛዝ (የሐኪም)

presence
ፕ'ሬዘንስ -ስ- መ'ገኘት (ባንድ ቦታ)

present
ፕ'ሬዘንት -ቅ- ያለ ፣ በ፡ ፣ በ ቦታ ያለ ፣ ያሁ
ን ጊዜ

present
ፕ'ሬዘንት -ስ- ስጦታ ፣ ሽ'ልማት

present
ፕሪ'ዜንት -ግ- ማቅረብ [አቀ'ረበ]
offer gift
-ግ- ስጦታ መስጠት [ሰ'ጠ]
exhibit, show
-ግ- ማሳ'የት [አሳ'የ]

presently
ፕ'ሬዘንትሊ -ተግ- ከጥቂት ጊዜ በኋላ ፣ በቅ
ርቡ
american
-ተግ- በአሁኑ ጊዜ

preserve
ፕሪ'ዘ፡ቭ -ግ- መጠ'በቅ [ጠ'በቀ] ፣ ማኖር
[አ'ኖረ] ፣ ማቆ'የት [አቆ'የ]

preside
ፕሪ'ዛይድ -ግ- ሊቀ መንበር መሆን [ሆነ] ፣
ስብሰባ በሊቀ መንበር'ነት መምራት [መ'ራ]

president
ፕ'ሬዚደንት -ስ- ፕሬዚዴንት ፣ አፈ ጉባኤ ፣
ሊቀ መንበር

press
ፕ'ሬስ -ግ- መጭፍ'መቅ [ጨፈ'መቀ] ፣ መ'ጨን
[ተጨነ]
printing
-ስ- ማ'ተሚያ መኪና
journalism
-ስ- ጋዜጦ'ች
urge
-ግ- መወትወት [ወተ'ወተ]

pressure
ፕ'ሬሽ -ስ- መ'ጨን ፣ ክብደት

prestige
ፕሬስ'ቲይጅ -ስ- ክብር

presume
ፕሪ'ዥዩም -ግ- መገ'መት [ገ'መተ]
impudently
-ግ- ከመጠን በላይ ማለፍ፣ [አ'ለፈ]

pretend
ፕሪ'ቴንድ -ግ- ማስመ'ሰል [አስመ'ሰለ]

pretext
ፕ'ሪይቴክስት -ስ- ትክ'ክል'ኛ ያልሆነ ምክን
ያት

pretty
ፕ'ሪቲ -ቅ- ያማረ ፣ ቆንጆ ፣ ውብ

prevail
ፕሪ'ቬይል -ግ- ድል መንሳት [ነ'ሳ] ፣ መስ
ናከል ማስወ'ገድ [አስወ'ገደ] ፣ መስፋፋት
[ተስፋ'ፋ]
persuade
-ግ- ማሳ'መን [አሳ'መነ]

prevalent
ፕ'ሬቫለንት -ቅ- የተስፋ'ፋ

prevaricate
ፕሪ'ቫሪኬይት -ግ- መዋሸት [ዋ'ሸ] ፣ ጠማማ
መልስ መስጠት [ሰ'ጠ]

prevent
ፕሪ'ቬንት -ግ- መከልከል [ከለ'ከለ]

previous
ፕ'ሪይቪየስ -ቅ- የቀደም ፣ ያለፈ

prey
ፕ'ሬይ -ስ- ታ'ድኖ የ'ሚበ'ላ እንስሳ ፣ አደን

price
ፕ'ራይስ -ስ- ዋጋ

priceless
ፕ'ራይስለስ -ቅ- ባለ ብዙ ዋጋ ፣ ዋጋው ሊ'ገ
'መት የ'ማይ'ቻል

prick
ፕ'ሪክ -ግ- መውጋት [ወ'ጋ] (በሹል ነገር)

prickle
ፕ'ሪክል -ስ- እሾህ (ጎ'ንሽ)

pride
ፕ'ራይድ -ስ- ኩራት ፣ ክብር

priest
ፕ'ሪይስት -ስ- ቄስ ፣ ካህን

prig
ፕ'ሪግ -ስ- ግ'ብዝ ፣ ተመጻዳቂ

prim
ፕ'ሪም -ቅ- በቀ'ላሉ የ'ሚደነ'ግጥ

primary
ፕ'ራይመሪ -ቅ- መጀ'መሪያ ፣ ዋ'ና ፣ የበ'ለጠ
አስተያየት የ'ሚ'ሰ'ጠው

553

prime

ፕ'ራይም -ቅ- አካላ መጠን ፤ ጢና'ግ
most important
-ቅ- በጣም አስፈ'ላጊ.

primer

ፕ'ራይም -ስ- ያንደ'ኛ ደረጃ ት/ቤት መ'ግ
ሪያ መጽሐፍ

primitive

ፕ'ሪመቲቭ -ቅ- በሥል'ጣኔ ወደኋላ የቀ'ረ

prince

ፕ'ሪነስ -ስ- ልዑል

princess

ፕ'ሪን'ሴስ -ስ- ልዕልት

principal

ፕ'ሪንሲፐል -ቅ- ዋ'ና ፤ የበ'ለጠ ዋ.ጋ ያ'ለው፤
ባለት'ልቅ ግዕረግ
capital sum
-ስ- ወ'ለድ የ'ሚ'ገ'ኝ'በት ዋ'ና ገንዘብ

principle

ፕ'ሪንሲፐል -ስ- ጠቅላ'ላ እምነት ፤ መሠረ
ታውያን የግብረ ገ'ብ'ነት ሕ'ገ'ች

print

ፕ'ሪንት -ግ- ማ'ተም [አ'ተመ]
type
-ስ- እ'ትም

printer

ፕ'ሪንተ -ስ- አ'ታሚ

printing-press

'ሪንቲንግፕሬስ -ስ- ማ'ተሚያ ቤት

prior

ፕ'ራየ -ስ- አበምኔት ፤ አለቃ
-ቅ- ያ'ለፈ ፤ የቀ'ደመ

priority

ፕ'ራዮሪቲ -ስ- ቅድሚያ

priory

ፕ'ራየሪ -ስ- ያበምኔት መኖሪያ ቤት

prison

ፕ'ሪዘን -ስ- እሥር ቤት ፤ ወህኒ ቤት

prisoner

ፕ'ሪዘነ -ስ- እሥረ'ኛ

privacy

ፕ'ሪቨሲ -ስ- ግ'ለ'ኛ'ነት

private

ፕ'ራይቨት -ቅ- የግ'ል

privation

ፕ'ራይ'ቪደሽን -ስ- የምግብ እጦት ፤ ድህ'ነት፤
ለሕይወት የ'ሚያስፈ'ልጉትን ነገር'ች ማጣት

privilege

ፕ'ሪቪሊጅ -ስ- ል'ዩ መብት

privy

ፕ'ሪቪ -ቅ- ምስጢር በዋቂ
-ስ- የሽንት ቤት

prize

ፕ'ራይዝ -ስ- ሽ'ልማት

pro

ፕ'ረው -ስ- አንድ ሰው ለመደ'ገፍ የ'ሚ'ደ
'ረግ ክር'ክር ፤ የ'ሚደ'ገፍ

probable

ፕ'ሮበበል -ቅ- ሊሆን የ'ሚችል

probe

ፕ'ረውብ -ግ- መመርመር [መረ'መረ]
-ስ- መመርመሪያ መ'ሣሪያ (ሐኪም
ቁስል የ'ሚመረ'ምር'በት)

probity

ፕ'ረውቢቲ -ስ- ታ'ማኝ'ነት (በተለ'ይ ላን
ገዶ)

problem

ፕ'ሮብለም -ስ- እ'ክል ፤ አስቸ'ጋሪ ጉ'ዳይ ፤
የ'ሚ'ታ'ሰብ'በት ጉ'ዳይ.

procedure

ፕረ'ሲጀር -ስ- መንገድ (ሥራ የመሥራት)

proceed

ፕረ'ሲይድ -ግ- ወደፊት ማምራት [አመ'ራ]
መቀ'ጠል [ቀ'ጠለ]

proceeds

ፕ'ረውሲይድዝ -ስ- ትርፍ፤ ገንዘብ (የሽ'ያጭ)

process

ፕ'ረውሴስ -ስ- ተከታ'ትሎ የተደ'ረገ ድር'ጊ'ት፤

procession

ፕረ'ሴሽን -ስ- ሥርዓት ጉዞ ፤ ሰላማዊ ሰልፍ ፤
ሰልፍ

proclaim

ፕረክ'ላይም -ግ- ማ'ወጅ [ዐ'ወጀ]

proclamation

ፕሮክለ'ሜይሽን -ስ- ዐዋጅ

procrastinate

ፕረክ'ራስቲኔይት -ግ- ሥራን ለሌላ ጊዜ ደጋ
ግሞ ማስተላለፍ [አስተላ'ለፈ] ፤ በ'የጊዜው
ማዘግየት [አዘገ'የ]

554

procure

ፕሮከ'ዩወ -ግ- ማግኘት [አገ'ኘ] (በድካም
ወዘተ) ፤ ማ'ቃጠር [አቃ'ጠረ] [ሴት ለወንድ]

prod

ፕ'ሮድ -ግ- እንዲሠሩ መጉትጉት [ጐተ
'ጐተ] ፤ መጎንተል [ጎነ'ተለ]

prodigal

ፕ'ሮዲጋል -ቅ- ገንዘብ አባካኝ ፡ ሀብቱን ነዥ

prodigious

ፕሮዲ'ጂስ -ቅ- የ'ሚያስገ'ርም ፡ ታ'ላቅ ፡
አስደ'ናቂ

prodigy

ፕ'ሮዲጂ -ስ- ልጅ ስጦታ ያለው ሕፃን ፡
በጣም አስደ'ናቂ (ከሥነ ፍጥረት ሥርዓት
ው'ጭ በመሆኑ)

produce

ፕረድ'ዩ:ስ -ግ- ማስገ'ኘት [አስገ'ኘ] ፤ መው
ለድ [ወ'ለ ደ]

produce

ፕ'ሮድዩስ -ስ- ምርት ፡ ው'ጤት (የሥራ)

producer

ፕረ'ድዩስ -ስ- ባለፋብሪካ
theatrical
 -ስ- የቴያትር ዝግ'ጅት መሪ

product

ፕ ሮደክት -ኅ- ውጤት (የፋብሪካ)

profane

ፕረ'ፌይን -ቅ- የተቀ'ደሰ ነገር የ'ሚጠላ ፡
የሃይማኖት ያልሆነ (ጽሑፍ)

profess

ፕረ'ፌስ -ግ- ማ'ረጋገጥ [አ'ረጋ'ገጠ] (እም
ነትን) ፤ ማ'ታለል [አ'ታ'ለለ] ፤ በውሸት ሆነ
ማለት [አለ]

profession

ፕረ'ፌሽን -ስ- ሞያ

professor

ፕረ'ፌስ -ስ- የዩኒቨርስቲ መምህር

profile

ፕ'ረውፋይል -ስ- መልክ (በአንድ በ'ኩል) ፤
ያንድ ሰው አ'ጭር የሕይወት ታሪክ (በመጽ
ሐፍ ፡ በጋዜጣ)

profit

ፕ'ሮፊት -ግ- ማትረፍ፡ [አተ'ረፈ]
 -ስ- ትርፍ

profitable

ፕ'ሮፊተብል -ቅ- ጠቃሚ ፡ ትርፍ ያለው

profiteer

ፕሮፊ'ቲየ -ስ- ከ'ሚገ'ባው በላይ ትርፍ የ'ሚ
ያገኝ (የንግድ ዕቃ በገበያ በጣ'ፉ ጊዜ)

profligate

ፕ'ሮፍሊጋት -ቅ- ገንዘብ አባካኝ ፤ ግብረ ገ'ብ
'ነት የሌ'ለው ፡ አ'ቃ'ት

profound

ፕረ'ፋውንድ -ቅ- በጣም ጥልቅ (ሐ'ሳብ)

profuse

ፕረፍ'ዩስ -ቅ- ገንዘብ አባካኝ ፤ ቀምጣ'ላ ፡
የተትረፈ'ረፈ ፡ በጣም ቸር

profusion

ፕረፍ'ዩገን -ስ- መትረፍረፍ ፡ ቀምጣ'ላ'ነት

progeny

ፕ'ሮጀኒ -ስ- ልጆ'ች ፡ ዘር ፡ የልጅ ልጅ

prognostication

ፕሮግኖስቲ'ኬይሽን -ስ- ትንቢት ፡ ምል'ክት
(ወደፊት ለ'ሚሆነው)

programme

ፕ'ረውግራም -ስ- የሥራ ዕ'ቅድ ቅደም ተከ
'ተል

progress

ፕ'ረውግሬስ -ስ- እርም'ጃ ፡ መ'ሻሻል

progress

ፕረግ'ሬስ -ግ- መ'ራመድ [ተራ'መደ] (በሥራ
ወዘተ)

prohibit

ፕረ'ሂቢ:ት -ግ- መከልከል [ከል'ከለ]

project

ፕረ'ጀክት -ግ- ዕ'ቅድ ማውጣት [አወ'ጣ] ፡
ብርሃን ፡ ፊልም ፡ ጥላ በአንድ ነገር ላይ አርፎ
እንዲ'ታ'ይ ማድረግ [አደ'ረገ] ፤ የአንድን ነገር
ሁኔቱ ፡ ጠባይ ደጋፎ አደርጎ ማሳ'የት [አሳ'የ] ፡
ተርፎ መውጣት [ወ'ጣ]

project

ፕ'ሮጀክት -ስ- የሥራ ዕ'ቅድ

projector

ፕሮ'ጀክት -ስ- የሲኒማ ማሳ'ያ መኪና

proletariat

ፕሮለ'ቴሪየት -ስ- በጉልበታ'ቸው ትርፍ የ'
ሚኖሩ'ና የግ'ል ንብረት የሌ'ላ'ቸው ወያተ
'ኞ'ች

555

prolong

ፕረ'ሎንግ -ግ- ማስረ'ዘም [አስረ'ዘመ] (ለጊ
ዜ)

prominent

ፕ'ሮሚነንት -ቅ- የተመ'ረጠ ፣ የተከ'በረ ፣
ከ'ፍ ያለ

promiscuous

ፕረ'ሚስከዩወስ -ቅ- ሴስ'ኛ ፣ ከብዙ ሰው ጋር
ፈቃደ ሥጋ የ'ሚፈ'ጽም

promise

ፕ'ሮሚስ -ግ- ተስፋ መስጠት [ሰ'ጠ]
-ስ- ተስፋ

promote

ፕረ'መውት -ግ- ከ'ፍ ማድረግ [አደ'ረገ] (በደ
ረጃ)

initiate

-ግ- መጀ'መር [ጀ'መረ] (ለዕ'ቅድ)

promotion

ፕረ'መውሽን -ስ- የማዕረግ እደገት

prompt

ፕ'ሮምት -ግ- ማ'ነሣሣት [አ'ነሣ'ሣ] (አንድ
ሰው አንድ ሥራ እንዲሠራ)

quick

-ቅ- ፈልጣ'ፋ

theatrical

-ግ- የተረ'ሳ ቃል ፣ ሐረግ ማስታወስ
[አስታ'ወሰ] (ለተናጋሪ ፣ ለቴአትር ሠ'ራተ'ኛ)

promulgate

ፕ'ሮሙልጌይት -ግ- ማ'ወጅ [ዐ'ወጀ] (አ'ዲስ
ሕ'ግ ፣ ደንብ)

prone

ፕ'ረውን -ቅ- የተጋ'ደመ (ራስ ደፍቶ ፣ በግ
ምባር)

disposed

-ቅ- ዝን ባለ ያ'ለው

prong

ፕ'ሮንግ -ስ- ጣት (የሹ'ካ ጠ‖ተ)

pronoun

ፕ'ረውናውን -ስ- ተውላጠ ስም

pronounce

ፕረ'ናውንስ -ግ- መ'ናገር [ተና'ገረ] ፣ አንድ
ቃል መጥራት [ጠ'ራ]

pronunciation

ፕረነንሲ'ዬይሽን -ስ- አ'ጠራር ፣ አ'ባባል ፣
አ'ነጋገር

---

proof

ፕ'ሩፍ -ስ- ማስረ'ጃ

printing

-ስ- የ'ሚ'ታ'ረም የማንተም ጽሑፍ

impervious to

-ቅ- የተፈ'ተነ ፣ ፍቱን (ውሃ ባለማስ
ገ'ባት)

prop

ፕ'ሮፕ -ስ- ድጋፍ (የእንጨት)

propagate

ፕ'ሮፐጌይት -ግ- እንዲስፋ'ፋ ማድረግ [አደ
'ረገ] (ዕውቀት ፣ ወሬ ወዘተ)

multiply

-ግ- እንዲ'ባ'ዛ ማድረግ [አደ'ረገ] (ተ
ክል ፣ እንስሳት)

propel

ፕረ'ፐል -ግ- መግፋት [ገ'ፋ] (ወደፊት)

propeller

ፕረ'ፐለ -ስ- መዘ'ውር (የአውሮ'ፕላን ፣ የመ
ርከብ) ፣ ቢ.ል.ቢ.'ላ

propensity

ፕረ'ፔንሲቲ -ስ- የተፈጥሮ ዝን'ባሌ

proper

ፕ'ሮፐ -ቅ- ተገቢ ፣ ደምበ'ኛ

properly

ፕ'ሮፐሊ -ተግ- በ'ሚ'ገ'ባ ፣ በደምብ

property

ፕ'ሮፐቲ -ስ- ንብረት ፣ ሀብት

land

-ስ- መሬት ፣ ርስት

prophecy

ፕ'ሮፈሲ -ስ- ትንቢት

prophesy

ፕ'ሮፈሳይ -ግ- መ'ናበይ [ተነ'በየ]

prophet

ፕ'ሮፈት -ስ- ነቢ'ይ

propitiate

ፕረ'ፒሺዬይት -ግ- መ'ለማመን [ተለማ'መነ]
(ቁ'ጣ ለማብረድ ፣ ድጋፍ ለማግኘት)

propitious

ፕረ'ፒሽስ -ቅ- ተስማሚ ፣ የሥራ መ'ቃናት
ሊያመጣ የ'ሚችል

proportion

ፐሮፖ፡ሽን -ስ- መጠን ፤ አንድ ነገር ከሌላው ጋር በመጠን ፣ በብዛት ወዘተ ያለው ግን'ኙ 'ነት

proposal

ፐሮፖውዘል -ስ- ሐ'ሳብ (የ'ሚቀርብ) *marriage*

-ስ- የጋብ'ቻ ጥ'ያቄ ፣ ማጨት

propose

ፐሮፖውዝ -ግ- ሐ'ሳብ ማቅረብ [አቀ'ረበ] *marriage*

-ግ- ለጋብ'ቻ መጠ'የቅ [ጠ'የቀ] ፣ ማጨት [አ'ጨ]

proposition

ፐሮፖዚሽን -ስ- ለስምም'ነት ሐ'ሳብ ማቅረብ

propound

ፐሮፖውንድ -ግ- ሐ'ሳብ ማቅረብ [አቀ'ረበ] (ለው'ሳኔ ለስምም'ነት)

proprietor

ፐሮፕ'ራየተ -ስ- ባለንብረት ፣ ባለቤት

propriety

ፐሮፕ'ራየቲ -ስ- የተመስ'ገነ አመል ፣ ተስማ 'ሚ'ነት

prosaic

ፐረውዜይክ -ቅ- ተራ ፣ አሰልቺ ፣ ብሁ የ'ማያሳ'ስብ

prose

ፐ'ረውዝ -ስ- ስ'ድ ንባብ

prosecute

ፐሮሲክዩ፡ት -ግ- መክሰስ [ከ'ሰሰ]

prospect

ፐሮስፔክት -ግ- መቦ'ደን መፈ'ለግ [ፈ'ለገ] -ስ- ወደፊት የ'ሚሆነው ው'ጤት *view*

-ስ- ትዕ'ይንት

prosper

ፐ'ሮስፐ -ግ- መበልጸግ [በለ'ጸገ]

prosperity

ፐሮስ'ፔረቲ -ስ- ብልጽግ'ና

prosperous

ፐ'ሮስፐረስ -ቅ- ባለጸ'ጋ

prostitute

ፐ'ሮስቲትዩ፡ት -ስ- ሴተ'ኛ አዳሪ

prostitution

ፐሮስቲት'ዩ፡ሽን -ስ- ሴተ'ኛ አዳሪ'ነት

prostrate

ፐ'ሮስትሬይት -ቅ- የተዘ'ረረ ፣ የተዘረ'ጋ (ፊ ቱን ደፍቶ)

protect

ፐረ'ቴክት -ግ- መከላከል [ተከላ'ከለ] ፣ መ ከታ መሆን [ሆነ]

protest

ፐረ'ቴስት -ግ- በነገሩ አለመስማማትን መግ ለጽ [ገ'ለጸ] ፤ አቤቱታ ማ'ሰ'ማት [አ'ሰ'ማ]

Protestant

ፐ'ሮቴስተንት -ስ- ፐሮቴስታንት ፣ የሉተር ተከ'ታይ

protestation

ፐሮቴስ'ቴይሽን -ስ- አቤቱታ

protracted

ፐረት'ራክቲድ -ቅ- ጊዜ የፈ'ጀ ፣ የቆ'የ

protrude

ፐረት'ሩ፡ድ -ግ- ወደ ው'ጭ መውጣት [ወ'ጣ] (ማጎንጠጥ)

protuberance

ፐረት'ዩ፡በረንስ -ስ- አፈንግጦ የወ'ጣ ነገር ፣ አፈንግጦ መውጣት

proud

ፐ'ራውድ -ቅ- ኩሩ

prove

ፐ'ሩ፡ቭ -ግ- ማስረ'ጃ መስጠት [ሰ'ጠ]

proverb

ፐ'ሮቨ፡ብ -ስ- ም'ሳሌ

provide

ፐረ'ቫይድ -ግ- ማቅረብ [አቀ'ረበ] ፣ ማ'ዘጋ ጀት [አ'ዘጋ'ጀ]

providence

ፐ'ሮቪደንስ -ስ- የእግዚአብሔር ፈቃድ ፣ የእ ግዚአብሔር ጥ'በቃ

province

ፐ'ሮቪንስ -ስ- አውራ'ጃ

provision

ፐረ'ቪዝን -ስ- መ'ሰናዶ ፣ መ'ሰናዳት

provisions

ፐረ'ቪዠንዝ -ስ- ሥንቅ

provisional

ፐረ'ቪዠነል -ቅ- ጊዜያዊ ፣ የ'ማይቆ'ይ

557

provoke
ፕረ'ቨውክ -ግ- ማ'ነሣሣት [አ'ነሣ'ሣ] ፣ ማስ
ቆ'ጣት [አስቆ'ጣ] ፣ ጠብ ማሜር [አሜረ]

prowess
ፕ'ራዌስ -ስ- ብል'ነት ፣ ችሎታ (የመ'ዋ,ጋት)፣
ጉብዝ'ና

prowl
ፕ'ራውል -ግ- ለማ'ደን በገ'ግታ ወዲያ'ና ወዲ
ህ ማለት [አለ] (ለአውሬ) ፣ ማድባት [አደ'ባ]

proximity
ፕሮክ'ሲሚቲ -ስ- ቅርብ'ነት

proxy
ፕ'ሮክሲ -ቅ- ወ'ኪል'ነት ፣ ወ'ኪል

prudence
ፕ'ሩ:ደንስ -ስ- ጥን'ቃቄ

prudish
ፕ'ሩ:ዲሽ -ቅ- አስመ'ሳይ ፣ የ'ማይፈ'ልግ መ
ሳይ (ግብረ ሥጋ)

prune
ፕ'ሩ:ን -ግ- በመቁረጥ ማስተካከል [አስተካ
ከለ] (ዛፍ ቁጥቋጦ ወዘተ) ፣ ማ'ረም [አ'ረመ]
(ጽሑፍ ወዘተ)

pry
ፕ'ራይ -ግ- የሰው ምስጢር ለማወቅ መሻት
[ሻ] ፣ መሰ'ለል [ሰ'ለለ]

psalm
'ሳ:ም -ስ- መዝሙረ ዳዊት

pseudonym
ስ'ዩደነም -ስ- የውሸት ስም (አንድ ደራሲ
የ'ሚሠራ'በት)

psychology
ሳይ'ኮለጂ -ስ- የሰውን አእምሮ ፣ አስተሳሰብ
የ'ሚያጠና ትምህርት ፣ ሥነ ልቡና

puberty
ፕ'ዩ:በቲ -ስ- የተርምስ'ና ወቅት ፣ አንድ ሰው
ለመውለድ የ'ሚችል'በት ዕድሜ ፣ መባለቅ

public
'ፐብሊክ -ስ- ሕዝብ
-ቅ- ሕዝባዊ

publish
'ፐብሊሽ -ግ- ማሳ'ተም [አሳ'ተመ] (መጽ
ሐፍ)

pucker
'ፐክ -ግ- ማ'ኩሳተር [አ'ኩሳ'ተረ] (ለገምባር)

puddle
'ፐደል -ስ- ኩሬ (የዝናም ውሃ የተጠራ'ቀመ
'በት)

puerile
ፕ'ዩ:ራይል -ቅ- የሕፃን ሥራ ፣ ቂላቂል ፣ እንቶ
ፈንቶ

puff
'ፐፍ -ግ- እ'ፍ ማለት [አለ] ፣ ቡ'ል'ቅ ቡ'ል
'ቅ ማድረግ [አደ'ረገ] ፣ ማለክለክ [አለከ'ለከ]

puffy
'ፐፊ -ቅ- ያ'በጠ ፣ የተነ'ፋ

pugnacious
ፐግ'ኔሽስ -ቅ- አምባጓር ወ'ጻድ ፣ ጠብ አጪ
(ልማደ'ኛ)

pull
'ፑል -ግ- መጎ'ተት [ጎ'ተተ]

pullet
'ፑሌት -ስ- ቄጨጨ'ት

pulley
'ፑሊ -ስ- መዘ'ውር (የወሃ መቅጃ ወዘተ)

pullover
'ፑለውቨ -ስ- ሹ'ራብ (ከሽሚዝ በላይ የ'ሚ'ለ
'በስ) ፣ የገላ ሹ'ራብ

pulp
'ፐልፕ -ስ- የደ'ቀቀ የተፈ'ጨ እርጥብ ነገር
(ፍራፍሬ ወዘተ)

pulpit
'ፑልፒት -ስ- ሰባኪ የ'ሚቆም'በት ከ'ፍ ያለ
ቦታ ፣ ምስባክ

pulsate
ፐል'ሴይት -ግ- ት'ር ት'ር ማለት [አለ]

pulse
'ፐልስ -ስ- ት'ርታ (የደም ሥር)

pummel
'ፐመል -ግ- መደብደብ [ደበ'ደበ] (መምታት፣
በእ'ጅ)

pump
'ፐምፕ -ግ- መንፋት [ነ'ፋ] (አ'የር ወዘተ)
-ስ- መንፈያ

pumpkin
'ፐምኪን -ስ- ዱ'ባ

pun
'ፐን -ስ- ጉብር አ'ነጋገር ፣ ሁለ'ት ትርጉም
ያ'ለው አ'ነጋገር

558

punch

’ፐንች -ግ- በቡ'ጢ መምታት [መ'ታ]

punctilious

ፐንክ’ቲሊየስ -ቅ- ለጥቃ'ቅን ነገር የ'ሚ'ጠ ን'ቀቅ (ሥራን በመፈ'ጸም)

punctual

’ፐንክቹውል -ቅ- ጊዜ ጠ'ባቂ ፡ በቀጠሮ ሰዓት የ'ሚ'ገ'ኝ ፡ ቀጠሮ አክባሪ

punctuation

ፐንክቹ’ዌይሽን -ስ- ሥርዐተ ነጥብ (በጽሑፍ)

puncture

’ፐንክቸ -ስ- ቀዳዳ (የጐ'ማ ወዘተ)

pungent

’ፐንጀንት -ስ- ኀይለ'ኛ ሽ'ታ ፡ ጣዕም

punish

’ፐኒሽ -ግ- መቅጣት [ቀ'ጣ]

punishment

’ፐኒሽመንት -ስ- ቅጣት ፡ መ'ቀጫ

puny

ፕ’ዩ:ኒ -ቅ- ት'ንሽ'ና ደካማ

pup

’ፐፕ -ስ- ቡ'ች'ላ

pupil

ፕ’ዩ:ፐል -ስ- ተማሪ

of eye

-ስ- የዓይን ብሌን

puppet

’ፐፐት -ስ- የንጨት አሻንጉ'ሊት (በክ'ር የ'ሚንቀሳ'ቀስ)

purchase

’ፐ:ቸስ -ግ- መግዛት [ገ'ዛ] (ዕቃ)

thing bought

-ስ- የተገ'ዛ ዕቃ

pure

ፕ’ዩወ -ቅ- ንጹሕ ፡ ምን'ም ነገር ያልተደባ'ለቀ'በት

purgative

’ፐ:ገቲቭ -ስ- የ'ሚያስቀ'ምጥ መድኃኒት

purgatory

’ፐ:ገትሪ -ስ- ኀጢያት የ'ሚያነጹ'በት ቦታ (ከሞት በኋላ) ፡ መካነ ን'ስሐ

purge

’ፐ:ጅ -ግ- ማ'ጣራት [አ'ጣ'ራ] ፡ ማጽዳት [አጸ'ዳ] ፡ ክሶ መጠ'ጣት [ጠ'ጣ]

political

-ግ- ከፖ'ለቲካ ማኅበር የ'ማያ'ስፈ'ልጉ አባሎ'ች ማስወ'ጣት [አስወ'ጣ]

purify

ፕ’ዩ:ሪፋይ -ግ- ማ'ጣራት [አ'ጣ'ራ] ፡ ንጹሕ ማድረግ [አደ'ረገ]

purity

ፕ’ዩ:ሪቲ -ስ- ንጽሕ'ና ፡ ጥራት

purple

’ፐ:ፐል -ቅ- ሐምራዊ

purport

ፐ’ፖ:ት -ግ- ማስመ'ሰል [አስመ'ሰለ] (ያልሆ ነውን)

-ስ- ፍ'ች ፡ ዋ'ና ሐ'ሳብ

purpose

’ፐ:ፐስ -ስ- ምክንያት ፡ ዓላማ ፡ ዕ'ቅድ ፡ ግብ

on-

-ተግ- በማወቅ ፡ ዐውቆ

purposely

’ፐ:ፐስሊ -ተግ- በማወቅ ፡ ዐውቆ

purr

’ፐ: -ግ- ማንኳረፍ [አንኳ'ረፈ] (ለድ'መት በተደ'ሰተ ጊዜ)

purse

’ፐ:ስ -ስ- የገንዘብ ቦርሳ (የሴት)

pursue

ፐስ’ዩ: -ግ- መ'ከተል [ተከ'ተለ]

purulent

ፕ’ዩሩለንት -ቅ- መግላም ፡ የ'ሚመግል

purvey

ፐ’ቬይ -ግ- የምግብ ሸቀጥ ለሺ'ያጭ ማቅ ረብ [አቀ'ረበ]

pus

’ፐስ -ስ- መግል

push

’ፑሽ -ግ- መግፋት [ገ'ፋ]

put

’ፑት -ግ- ማስቀ'መጥ [አስቀ'መጠ]

-aside

አ’ሳይድ -ግ- ወደጐ'ን ማስቀ'መጥ [አስቀ'መጠ]

-on

’ኦን -ግ- መልበስ [ለ'በሰ] ፡ ማድረግ [አደ'ረገ] (ጫ'ማ ፡ መነ'ጽር)

-up
'እ1 -ግ- ማ'ዜ,ጋኝት [እ'ዜ,ኀ'ጀ] (ለእንግጸ)
-up with
'እጕ'ዊ ዘ -ግ- መ';ታ,ኀ,ም [ታ'ኀሙ]
putrid
'ፕ'ዩትሪ₹ -ት- የተ'ላ : የሸ'ተተ (ለሥ,ኀ)
putty
'ፕኑ -ስ- በዘይት የተደባ'ለቀ ስሚ,ንቶ (ለመ
ስተዋት ማገበ'ቲ,ያ) : ስቴ'ኮ
puzzle
'ፐዝል -ስ- በቀ'ላሉ ሊ,'ረ'ዱት የ'ማይ'ቻል
ነገር : ውናቴ : እንቆቅ'ልሽ
-ግ- መ'ጨነቅ [ተ.ጨ,'ነቀ]

pyjamas
ፒ'ጀ:መዘ -ስ- የመኘ'ታ ልብስ : ፒጀማ
pyramid
'ፒረሚ₹ -ስ- ሀረም
pyre
'ፓየ -ስ- አስከሬን የ'ሚ,ታ'ጠል'በት የእን
ጨት እ'ምር
pyx
'ፒክስ -ስ- ሥኀ መደመ. የ'ሚ,ተመ₮'በት
ማጠን

Q

quack
ክ'ዋክ -ስ- የዳ'ክ'የ ጩኸት
doctor
-ስ- ውሸተ'ኛ ሐኪ,ም : አጭበርባሪ
ሐኪ,ም (ሐኪ,ም ሳይሆን ነ'ኝ ባይ)
quadrangle
ክ'ዎድሬ-ንጉል -ስ- አራ'ት ማዕዘን የሆነ ለም
ለም አፀር ግ'በ. : አራት ማዕዘን ያለው ቅርፅ
quagmire
ክ'ዋግማየ -ስ- ረግረግ
quadruped
ክ'ዎድሩ-ፔድ -ስ- አራ'ት እግር ያ'ለመ₮እንስሳ
quail
ክ'ዊይል -ግ- በፍርሀት መንቀጥቀጥ [ተንቀ
ጠ'ቀጠ]
quaint
ክ'ዊይንት -ት- እንግዳ : ያልተለ'መደ (ነገር
ግን አስተያየትን ማራኪ,)
quake
ክ'ዌይክ -ግ- መንቀጥቀጥ [ተንቀጠ'ቀጠ] :
መንዘፍዘፍ [ተንዘፈ'ዘፈ] (ከፍርሀት የተነ'ሣ)
qualify
ክ'ዎሊ,ፋ,ይ -ግ- ለአንድ ተግባር ተስማሚ መ
መሆን [ሆነ]
become trained
ለአንድ ተግባር ማሠልጠን [አሠለ'ጠነ]

quality
ክ'ዎሊ,ቴ -ስ- ዓይነት
qualm
ክ'ዋ:ም -ስ- ት'ንሽ ጥር'ጣሬ (አንድ ሰው ስለ
ሠ'ራው ወይን'ም ስለ'ሚሠራው ሥራ) : ቅል
ሽ'ልሽታ
quandary
ክ'ዎንደሪ -ስ- ግራ የ'ሚ,ያ,ጋ'ባ ች'ግር :
እ'ክል
quantity
ክ'ዎንቲ,ቴ -ስ- ብዛት
quarrel
ክ'ዎረል -ግ- መ'ጣላት [ተጣ'ላ]
-ስ- ጥል
quarrelsome
ክ'ዎረልሰም -ት- አምባጋር'ኛ : ተጣይ
quarry
ክ'ዎረ -ስ- ደንጊይ : አሽዋ የ'ሚ,ገ'ኝበት
ጉድጓ'ዳ ቦታ
prey
-ስ- የ'ሚ,ታ'ደን እንስሳ : አደን
quarter
ክ'ዎ:ተ -ስ- ሩብ : አንድ አ'ራተ'ኛ
area
-ስ- መኖሪያ ሠፈር

quash
ክዎሽ -ግ- ውድቅ ማድረግ [አደ'ረገ] (በፍ፡
ርድ ቤት)

quavering
ክ'ዌይቨሪንግ -ቅ- ቀጥቃ'ጣ (ለድምፅ)

quay
'ኪይ -ስ- የመርከብ መቆሚያ ቦታ

queen
ክ'ዊይን -ስ- ንግሥት ፣ እቴጌ ፡ የንጉሥ ባለ
ቤት (ሚስት)

queer
ክ'ዊየ -ቅ- እንግዳ (ለጠባይ)

quell
ክ'ዌል -ግ- ጸ'ጥ ማድረግ [አደ'ረገ] (ብጥ'ብ
ጥ)

quench
ክ'ዌንች -ግ- ማጥፋት [አጠ'ፋ] (ለእሳት)
thirst
-ግ- መቁረጥ [ቆ'ረጠ] (ለጥም)

querulous
ክ'ፍሩለስ -ቅ- አጉረምራሚ ፣ ደ'ስ ያላለው፡
የከ'ፋው

query
ክ'ዊየሪ -ግ- መጠ'የቅ [ጠ'የቀ] ፣ መ'ጠራ
ጠር [ተጠራ'ጠረ]

quest
ክ'ዌስት -ስ- ፍ'ለጋ

question
ክ'ዌስቸን -ስ- ጥ'ያቄ

queue
ክ'ዩ፡ -ስ- የወረፋ መሥመር

quibble
ክ'ዊበል -ግ- መሸሻ መፈ'ለግ [ፈ'ለገ] (በከ
ር'ክር)
play on words
-ግ- ጋለ'ት ትርጉም በያዘ አነጋገር
መ'ናገር [ተና'ገረ] ፣ በነብር መ'ናገር [ተና'ገረ]

quick
ክ'ዊክ -ቅ- ፈ'ጣን

quickly
ክ'ዊክሊ -ተግ- በፍጥነት

quiet
ክ'ዋየት -ቅ- ፀ'ጥ ያለ ፣ ሰላማዊ

quill
ክ'ዊል -ስ- ላባ (ረ'ጅም)

quilt
ክ'ዊልት -ስ- ለሐፍ (ወፍራም የብርድ ልብስ)

quit
ክ'ዊት -ግ- እርግ'ፍ አድርጎ መተው [ተወ]

quite
ክ'ዋይት -ተግ- በፍ'ጹም ፣ በጣም
-ተግ- በመጠኑ
almost
-ቃአ- በውነት ፣ በርግጥ

quiver
ክ'ዊቨ -ግ- መንቀጥቀጥ [ተንቀጠ'ቀጠ]
-ስ- የፍላ'ፃ ማሕደር

quixotic
ክዊክ'ሶቲክ -ቅ- ለጥቃ'ቅን ነገር ታ'ላቅ ዋጋ
የ'ሚሰጥ ፣ ሌሎ'ችን ለመርዳት እራሱን የ'ሚ
ጐዳ

quiz
ክ'ዊዝ -ስ- የጥ'ያቄና የመልስ ውድ'ድር ፡
የዕውቀት መፈተኛ ጥ'ያቄ

quota
ክ'ዎተ -ስ- ድርሻ ፣ ላንዱ የተወ'ሰነ'ለት
ድርሻ (በተለ'ይ ወደ አንዱ አገር ለመግባት
የተፈ'ቀደ የሰው ብዛት ፡ የንግድ ዕቃ መጠን)

quotation
ከወ'ቴይሽን -ስ- ጥቅስ

quotation-mark
ከወ'ቴይሽን'ማ፡ክ -ስ- የጥቅስ ምል'ክት ፡
ትእምርተ ጥቅስ ("   ")

quote
ክ'ወውት -ግ- መጥቀስ [ጠ'ቀሰ] (የሰው ንግ
'ግር ፡ ጽሑፍ)

quotient
ክ'ወውሽንት -ስ- አንድ ቁጥር ከተከ'ፈለ በኋ
ላ የ'ሚ'ገ'ኘው ውጤት

R

rabbit
ˈራቢት -ስ- ጥንቸል

rabble
ˈራብል -ስ- ልˈቃሚ ሕዝብ ፤ ሥርዓት የሌˈለ
ለው የተሰበˈሰበ ሕዝብ ፤ ጀሌ

rabid
ˈራቢድ -ቅ- ያˈበደ ውˈሻ ፤ ‘ነያለˈኛ ፤ ቁˈጡ

rabies
ˈሬይቢይዝ -ስ- የውˈሻ እብዱት በˈሽታ

race
ˈሬይስ -ስ- እሽቅድˈድም
human
-ስ- ዘር (የሰው)
compete
-ግ- መሽቀዳደም [ተሽቀዳˈደመ]

rack
ˈራክ -ስ- የዕቃ መደርደሪያ (የስሕን መደቀት)

racket
ˈራኬት -ስ- የቴኒስ መምቻ

racy
ˈሬይሲ -ቅ- የˈማይሰለˈች ፤ አስደˈሳች ፤ ሕያ
ው (መጽሐፍ ፡ ቴያትር ፡ ፊልም ወዘተ)

radiant
ˈሬዲየንት -ቅ- ይስትˈኝ ፤ ያማˈረ በት ፤ ፊኪ
ረር የˈሚያ ስራˈዬ ፤ የˈሚያበራ

radiate
ˈሬዲዬይት -ግ- ማˈስራጨት [አˈስራˈጨ]
(ለጨለረር ፡ ለሙቀት)

radiator
ˈሬዲዬይተር -ስ- የቤት ማሞቂያ ፤ የመኪና
ስሲንደር ማቀዝቀዣ መግሪያ ፤ ራዲያተር

radical
ˈራዲከል -ቅ- መሠረታዊ ፤ ፍጹም
political
-ቅ- ተቃዋሚ ፤ ፍጹም ለውጥ ፈˈላጊ
(በፖለቲካ)

radio
ˈሬይዲየው -ስ- ራዲዮ

radish
ˈራዲሽ -ስ- ፍጅል ፤ ሥሩ ነˈጭ የሆነ እንደ
ሰላˈጣ የˈሚˈበˈላ የካሮት ቅርዕ ያˈለው ተክል

radius
ˈሬይዲየስ -ስ- ራዲየስ ፤ በአንድ ክብብ ከመሀ
ˈክሉ እስከ ዳሩ ያˈለው ርቀት

raffle
ˈራፉል -ስ- ሎተሪ (የዕቃ)

raft
ˈራፍት -ስ- ታንካ (ከአንድ ግንድ ወይንˈም
ከአንድ እሥር የተውˈራ)

rafter
ˈራፍተ -ስ- ከንች (የቤት)

rag
ˈራግ -ስ- ብትˈቶ

ragamuffin
ˈራገመፊን -ስ- ልብሱ ያለቀˈበት ፤ ሰው
(በተለˈይ ልጅ)

rage
ˈሬይጅ -ስ- ቁˈጣ
-ግ- መˈጮጣት [ተቆˈጣ]

ragged
ˈራጊድ -ቅ- የተበጣˈጠሰ ፤ ብትˈቶ የሆነ
የተተለˈተለ (ልብስ) ፤ ኩስˈሳ

raid
ˈሬይድ -ግ- መግጠም [ገˈጠመ] (ጦርˈነት)
አደጋ መጣል [ጣለ] ፤ መውረር [ወˈረረ]
-ስ- ግጥሚያ ፤ አደጋ ፤ ወረራ

rail
ˈሬይል -ስ- ሐዲድ (የባቡር) ፤ የቤት ደረጃ
መˈያዣም਼žŭ ብረት
abuse
-ግ- መˈሳደብ [ተሳˈደበ]

railway
ˈሬይልዌይ -ስ- የባቡር ሐዲድ

rain
ˈሬይን -ስ- ዝናም ፤ ዝናብ

rainbow
ˈሬይንቦው -ስ- ቀስተ ደˈመና

raincoat
ˈሬይንከውት -ስ- የዝናም ልብስ

rainy season
ˈሬይኒ ˈሲይዝን -ስ- የዝናም ወራት ፤ ጠረˈን
ዝናማት ፤ ክረምት

562

raise

'ሬይዝ -ግ- ማንሣት [አነ'ሣ]

-ስ- እድገት (የደመወዝ)

raisin

'ሬይዝን -ስ- ዘቢብ

rake

'ሬይክ -ስ- ባለጣት አፈር ማስተካከያ
waster

-ስ- ገንዘብ አባካኝ

rally

'ራሊ -ስ- የስፖርተ'ኞ'ች ፡ የፖለ.ቲካ ደ'ጋፊ.
ዎ'ች ስብሰባ
support

-ግ- ማ'ጃገን [አ'ጃ'ገነ]

ram

'ራም -ግ- መግጨት [ገ'ጨ] (ባንድ ነገር)
male sheep

-ስ- ወጠጡ (በግ)

ramble

'ራምብል -ግ- ወዲያ'ና ወዲህ መሄድ [ሄደ]
(ለሽ'ርሽ'ር)

ramp

'ራምፕ -ስ- መንሸራተቻ ፡ ሽተት'ያ

rampart

'ራምፓት -ስ- የም'ሽግ ግድግ'ዳ

ramshackle

'ራምሻክል -ቅ- ያረ'ጀ'ና የተሰባ'በረ

ranch

'ራ፡ንች -ስ- ት'ልቅ የርሻ'ና የከብት ማርቢያ
ቦታ

rancid

'ራንሲድ -ስ- የቆ'የ ፡ የ'ሚሽ'ት (ቅቤ ፡
ዘይት)

rancour

'ራንክ -ስ- መጥፎ ስ'ሜት ፡ መ'መመረር ፡ ጥላ
'ቻ (የቆ'የ'ና ት'ልቅ)

random

'ራንደም -ቅ- ያለብል'ነት ፡ ያለማ'ሰብ የተ
ም'ራ
at

-ተግ- እ'ዚህ'ና እ'ዚያ ፡ መላ በማጣት

range

'ሬይንጅ -ስ- ሰ'ፊ ግልፕ መሬት
distance

-ስ- ርቀት (የጦር መ'ሣሪያ የ'ሚመ
ታው)
of mountains

-ስ- የተራራ'ች ሰንሰለት
array

-ስ- የዕቃ ዓይነት'ና ብዛት
wander

-ግ- ረ'ጅም ጉዞ መሄድ [ሄደ]
put in order

-ግ- መደርደር [ደረ'ደረ]

rank

'ራንክ -ስ- ማዕረግ
rotting

-ቅ- የበሰ'በሰ አትክልት

rankle

'ራንክል -ግ- በእእምሮ መ'መላለስ [ተመላ
'ለሰ] (መጥፎ ስ'ሜት)

ransack

'ራንሳክ -ግ- መዝረፍ [ዘ'ረፈ] ፡ አንድ ነገር
አጥብቆ መፈ'ለግ [ፈ'ለገ]

ransom

'ራንሰም -ግ- መዋጀት (ዋ'ጀ) ፡ ገንዘብ በመ
ክፈል ከግዞት ማስለ'ቀቅ [አስለ'ቀቀ]-
-ስ- ለቲያዘ ሰው ማስለ'ቀቂያ የ'ሚከ
'ፈል ገንዘብ ፡ ቤዛ

rant

'ራንት -ግ- መጮኽ [ጮኸ] (ባን'ዴት) ፡ እ'የ
ጮኸ መዘለፍ [ዘለ'ፈ]

rap

'ራፕ -ግ- መቆርቆር [ቆረ'ቆረ] (መምታት)

rapacious

ረ'ፔይሸስ -ቅ- ዘራፊ. ፡ አውዳሚ ፡ ቆንዳ'ና ፡
ፕ'ፕታም (በተለ'ይ አገናዘብ)

rape

'ሬይፕ -ግ- አስገ'ድዶ መ'ገናኘት [ተገና'ኘ] ፡
መድፈት [ደ'ፈ] (ሴት)

rapid

'ራፒድ -ቅ- ፈ'ጣን

rapt

'ራፕት -ስ- በሐ'ሳብ የተመ'ጠጠ

563

rapture
'ራፕቸ -ስ- ታላቅ ደ'ስታ ፡ ሐ'ሤት

rare
'ሬየ -ቅ- በብዛት የ'ማይ'ገ'ኝ ፡ ያልተለ'መደ፣
ሁልጊዜ የ'ማይ'ይ'ረግ ፡ ከል'ክ ያ'ለፈ ጥሩ

rascal
'ራ፡ስከል -ስ- የ'ማይረባ ፡ ተንኮለ'ኛ ፡ አ'ታ
ላይ

rash
'ራሽ -ስ- የሰው'ነት መንደብደብ
hasty
-ቅ- በጣም ች'ኩል

rasher
'ራሸ -ስ- ቀ'ጭን ያሣማ ሥጋ ቁ'ራጭ

rasp
'ራ፡ስፕ -ስ- የንጨት መሞ'ረጃ ሞረድ

rat
'ራት -ስ- አይጥ (ት'ልቅ)

rate
'ሬይት -ስ- የተወ'ሰነ ዋጋ ፡ ፍጥነት

rather
'ራ፡ዘ -ተግ- ይልቅ
to a great extent
-ተግ- ... መላይ

ratify
'ራ፡ቲፋይ -ግ- ማጽደቅ [አጸ'ደቀ] (ሕ'ግ)

ration
'ራሽን -ስ- መቁነን

rational
'ራሽነል -ቅ- ማስተዋል ያ'ለ'በት ፡ አስተ
ዋይ ፡ ብልኅነተ'ኛ

rattle
'ራተል -ግ- መንኳኳት (ተንኳ'ኳ)

raucous
'ሮ፡ከስ -ቅ- ሻካራ (ለድምፅ)

ravage
'ራቪጅ -ስ- ማፈራረስ ፡ መደምሰስ ፡ በጣም
መጉዳት

rave
'ሬይቭ -ግ- በቁ'ጣ መቀብ'ዠ [ቀበ'ዠ] ፡ በቁ'ጣ
መ'ናገር [ተና'ገረ]

raven
'ሬይቨን -ስ- ቁራ

ravenous
'ራሽነስ -ቅ- በጣም የራበው

ravine
ረ'ቪይን -ስ- በሁለ'ት ገደል መካ'ከል ያ'ለ
ክፍተት ቦታ ፡ ጥልቀት ያ'ለው ሸለቆ

ravish
'ራቪሽ -ግ- በጉይል መቀ'ማት [ቀ'ማ] ፡ መን
ጠቅ [ነ'ጠቀ] ፡ መድፈት [ደ'ፈ] (ለሴት) ፡ በደ
'ስታ መሙላት [ሞ'ላ]

ravishing
'ራቪሺንግ -ቅ- በጣም ቆንጆ ፡ ውብ ፡ ያማረ

raw
'ሮ፡ -ቅ- ጥሬ (ያልበ'ሰለ)
inexperienced
-ቅ- ልምድ የሌ'ለው ፡ ጀ'ማሪ

ray
'ሬይ -ስ- ጨ'ራ

raze
'ሬይዝ -ግ- ሕንፃ ፡ ከተማ ማፈራረስ [አፈራ
'ረሰ] ፡ መደምሰስ [ደመ'ሰሰ]

razor
'ሬይዘ -ስ- ምላ'ጭ

reach
'ሪይች -ግ- መድረስ [ደ'ረሰ]

react
ሪ'ያክት -ግ- አጸፋ መመ'ለስ [መ'ለሰ] (ከአ
ንድ ሁናቴ ፡ ድርጊ'ት ስ'ሜት በኋላ)

reaction
ሪ'ያክሽን -ስ- ከአንድ ሁናቴ ፡ ድር'ጊት ፡
ስ'ሜት በኋላ የ'ሚ'ታ'ይ የሰው ጠባይ ፡ አጸፋ

read
'ሪይድ -ግ- ማንበብ [አነ'በበ]

ready
'ሬዲ -ቅ- የተዘጋ'ጀ ፡ ዝግ'ጁ

ready-made
ሬዲ'ሜይድ -ቅ- የተዘጋ'ጀ ፡ ወዲያው እሥ'ራ
ሊ. የሙ-ሉ'ት የ'ሚ.ቻል (ለልብስ መዘተ)

real
'ሪየል -ቅ- እውነት

realistic
ሪየ'ሊ.ስቲክ -ቅ- አስተዋይ ፡ ከእውነት ያ
'ራቀ

realize
ʾሪየላይዝ -ግ- መ'ገንዘብ [ተገነ'ዘበ]
accomplish
        -ግ- እሥራ ላይ ማዋል [አዋለ] ፡ መፈ
'ጸም [ፈ'ጸመ]
realm
ʾሬልም -ስ- መንግሥት ፡ እገር ግዛት
reap
ʾሪይፕ -ግ- ማጨድ [አ'ጨደ] (ለሰብል)
rear
ʾሪየ -ግ- ግርባት [አረ'ባ] (ለከብት)
behind part
        -ስ- ጀርባ ፡ ጓላ
raise
        -ግ- ማሳደግ [አሳ'ደገ]
reason
ʾሪይዘን -ግ- ማስተዋል [አስተዋለ]
cause
        -ስ- ምክንያት
intellect
        -ስ- አእምሮ
reasonable
ʾሪይዘነበል -ቅ- ምክንያት ያ'ለው ፡ ተገቢ ፡
ል'ክ ፡ ተመጣጣኝ ፡ ከል'ክ ያላለፈ ፡ ተገቢ
(ዋጋ)
reassure
ሪየ'ሾ፡ -ግ- ማጽናናት [አጸና'ና] ፡ እንደገና
ማ'ረጋገጥ [አ'ረጋ'ገጠ] ፡ ፍርሀትና ጥር'ጣሬ
ማራቅ [አራ·ቀ]
rebate
ʾሪይቤይት -ስ- እንደገና የተከ'ፈለ ገንዘብ
(የተስተካ'ከለ) ፤ የዋጋ ቅ'ናሽ
        -ግ- መቀ'ነስ [ቀ'ነሰ] (ዋጋ)
rebel
ሪ'ቤል -ግ- መሽ'ፈት [ሽ'ፈተ]
rebel
ʾሪበል -ስ- ሽፍታ
rebellion
ሪ'ቤልየን -ስ- ሽ'ፈታ ፡ መሽ'ፈት
rebound
ሪ'ባውንድ -ግ- ነገር መ'መለስ [ተመ'ለሰ]
(ለኳስ)
        -ስ- መንጠር (ለኳስ)

rebuff
ሪ'በፍ -ግ- ማሳ'ፈር [አሳ'ፈረ] (በደ'ግ የመ
'ጣን ሰው)
rebuke
ሪብ'ዩ፡ክ -ግ- መገ'ሠፅ [ገ'ሠፀ]
recalcitrant
ሪ'ካልሲትሪንት -ቅ- እምቢተ'ኛ ፡ ች'ኩ
recall
ሪ'ኮ፡ል -ግ- ማስታወስ [አስታ'ወሰ]
memory
        -ስ- ት'ዝታ
call back
        -ግ- መመ'ለስ [መ'ለሰ] (እው'ዱ አገር
የተሾመን ሰው)
recant
ሪ'ካንት -ግ- ቀደ'ም ብሎ የተና'ገሩት ትክ'ክ
ል እለመሆኑን መግለጽ [ገ'ለጸ]
recede
ሪ'ሲይድ -ግ- ወደኋላ ማለት [አለ] ፡ ወደኋላ
ማፈግፈግ [አፈገ'ፈገ]
receipt
ሪ'ሲይት -ስ- ደ'ረሰ'ኝ ፡ ፋክቱር
receive
ሪ'ሲይቭ -ግ- መ'ቀበል [ተቀ'በለ] ፤ ማስተ
ናገድ [አስተና'ገደ]
receiver
ሪ'ሲይቨ -ስ- ተቀ'ባይ
telephone
        -ስ- የቴሌፎን መስሚያ'ና መ'ናገሪያ
መ'ሣሪያ
dealer in stolen property
        -ስ- የተሰ'ረቀ ዕቃ የ'ሚሸጥ ነ'ጋዴ
recent
ʾሪይሰንት -ቅ- ከጥቂት ጊዜ በፊት የሆነ
receptacle
ሪ'ሰፕቲክል -ስ- ዕቃ ፡ መያዣ
reception
ሪ'ሴፕሽን -ስ- እ'ቀባበል
party
        -ስ- የመስተንግዶ ግብዣ
receptive
ሪ'ሴፕቲቭ -ቅ- ተቀ'ባይ (ለትምሀርት ፡ ለሐ
'ሳብ)

565

recess

ሪ'ሴስ -ስ- ሰር'ጓዳ ቦታ (በቤት ውስጥ ወዘተ)
break for rest
-ስ- ት'ንሽ ዕረፍት

recession

ሪ'ሴሸን -ስ- የኢኮኖሚ ድቀት (ጊዜ)

recipe

'ሬሰፒ -ስ- የምግብ አ'ሠራር ዘዴ ፣ የምግብ
አ'ቀማመም ፤ በአንድ ዓይነት ምግብ አ'ሠራር
የ'ሚገቡ ል'ዩ ል'ዩ ነገሮ'ች

recipient

ሪ'ሲፒየንት -ስ- ተቀ'ባይ

reciprocal

ሪ'ሲፕሪከል -ቅ- ከሁለ'ት ወገን የሆነ (ስም
ም'ነት ፣ ስ'ሜት ፣ መስጠት'ና መ'ቀበል)

reciprocate

ሪ'ሲፕሪኬይት -ግ- አጸፋውን መመ'ለስ [መ
'ለሰ]

recital

ሪ'ሳይተል -ስ- ለሕዝብ የ'ሚቀርብ (የሙዚቃ ፣
የቅኔ በዐል)

recite

ሪ'ሳይት -ግ- ግጥም ማንበብ [አነ'በበ] (በቃል)

reckless

'ሬክሌስ -ቅ- የ'ማይ'ጠነ'ቀቅ ፣ ንዝህላል

reckon

'ሬክን -ግ- ማወቅ [ዐ'ወቀ]
guess
-ግ- ማ'ሰብ [አ'ሰበ] (ለሒሳብ)
add up
-ግ- መደ'መር [ደ'መረ]

reclaim

ሪክ'ሌይም -ግ- መብትን መጠ'የቅ [ጠ'የቀ]
(የተሰ'ረቀን ፣ የተዘ'ረፈን)
recultivate
-ግ- ጠፍ መሬት እንደገና ማረስ [አ'ረ
ሰ]

recline

ሪክ'ላይን -ግ- ጋደ'ም ብሎ መ'ቀመጥ [ተቀ
'መጠ] ፣ ደ'ገ'ፍ ብሎ መ'ቀመጥ [ተቀ'መጠ]

recluse

ሪክ'ሉ፡ስ -ስ- ባሕታዊ ፣ በተባሕተዎ የ'ሚ
ኖር ፣ መ'ናኒ

recognize

'ሬክግናይዝ -ግ- ማወቅ [ዐ'ወቀ] ፣ መለ'የት
[ለ'የ]

recoil

ሪኮይል -ግ- መርገጥ [ረ'ገጠ] (ጠመንጃ ሲ'ተ
'ኮስ)

recollect

ሬክ'ሌክት -ግ- ማስታወስ [አስታ'ወሰ]

recommend

ሬክ'ሜንድ -ግ- አጀራ ማለት [አለ] ፣ አንድ
ነገር ጠቃ'ሚ'ነቱን፣ጥሩ'ነቱን መ'ናገር [ተና
'ገረ]

recompense

'ሬክምፔንስ -ግ- መካሥ [ካሠ]

reconcile

'ሬክንሳይል -ግ- ማስታረቅ [አስታ'ረቀ]

recondition

ሪክን'ዲሸን -ግ- መጠ'ገን [ጠ'ገነ] ፣ ግ'ዴስ
[አ'ደሰ] (የተበ'ላ'ሸ ነገር)

reconnaissance

ሪ'ኮነሰንስ -ስ- ስ'ለላ (አንድን አገር ከመር
'ነት በፊት) ፣ ቀድሞ ሁናቴን ማጥናት

reconnoitre

ሬክ'ኖይተ -ግ- አገር መስ'ለላ [ሰ'ለለ] (ከመ
ውረር በፊት)

reconstruct

ሪክንስት'ራክት -ግ- እንደገና ማቆም [አቆመ] ፣
መሥራት [ሠ'ራ] (ለቤት ፣ ለሕንፃ)

record

'ሬኮ፡ድ -ግ- መመዝገብ [መዘ'ገበ] (ጉ'ዳይ ፣
ድምፅ)

record

'ሬኮ፡ድ -ስ- ሽክላ (የሙዚቃ)
account
-ስ- መዝገብ

recount

ሪ'ካውንት -ግ- ወሬ ማውራት [አወ'ራ]

recoup

ሪ'ኩፕ -ግ- የከ'ሰሩትን ፣ የተሸ'ነፉትን ገን
ዘብ መመ'ለስ [መ'ለሰ]

recourse

ሪ'ኮ፡ስ -ስ- እርዳታ መጠ'የቅ

- 566

recover

ሪከቨ -ግ- እንደገና ማግኘት [አገˈኘ] (የጠ
ˈፋ ነገር)

from illness

-ግ- መዳን [ዳነ]

recreation

ሬክሪˈዬይሽን -ስ- መዝናናት ፡ መˈደሰት (ከ
ሥራ በኋላ)

recrimination

ሪክሪሚˈኔሽን -ስ- እርስበርስ መˈካሰስ ፡
መˈዛለፍ ፡ መˈወቃቀስ

-ግ- እርስበርስ መˈካሰስ [ተካˈሰስ] ፡
መˈዛለፍ [ተዛˈለፈ]፣ መወˈቃቀስ [ተወቃˈቀስ]

recruit

ሪክˈሩት -ግ- መመልመል [መለˈመለ] (ወˈታ
ˈደር ወዘተ)

-ስ- በመሡልጠን ላይ ያˈለ ወˈታˈደር

rectangular

ሬክˈታንጉለ -ቅ- ባለ አራˈት ማዕዘን (ባንጻር
ያˈሉ ሁለˈት ጎˈናˈቸ የˈሚˈመሳˈሰሉ)

rectify

ˈሬክቲፋይ -ግ- ማስተካከል [አስተካˈከለ] (ስ
ሕተትን)

recumbent

ሪˈከምበንት -ቅ- የተጋˈደመ

recuperate

ሪˈኩፐሬይት -ግ- ማገˈገም [አገˈገመ] (ከሕ
መም)

recur

ሪˈከ: -ግ- እንደገና መሆን [ሆነ] ፡ ብዙ ጊዜ
ተመላልሶ መሆን [ሆነ] ፤ ማጋጨት [አጋˈጨ]
(ሐሳብ)

red

ˈሬድ -ቅ- ቀˈይ

redden

ˈሬደን -ግ- መቅላት [ቀˈላ]

redeem

ሪˈዲይም -ግ- ማዳን [አዳነ] (እዳ ከፍሎ)

religious

-ግ- መዋጀት [ዋˈጀ]

redhanded

ሬድˈሃንዳድ -ቅ- ወንጀል በˈሚፈˈጽምˈበት
ጊዜ የተያዘ ፡ እˈጅ ከፍንጅ የተያዘ (ወንጀለˈኛ)

redistribute

ሪዲስትˈሪብዩት -ግ- መደልደል [ደለˈደለ] ፡
ማˈከፋፈል [አˈከፋˈፈለ] (እንደገና)

redolent

ˈሬዶለንት -ቅ- ጥሩ መዓዛ ያˈለው ፡ ጥሩ ጥሩ
የˈሚሽˈት

-of

-ቅ- የˈሚያስታˈውስ

redress

ሪድˈሬስ -ግ- መካሥ [ካሠ]

-ስ- ካሣ

reduce

ሪድˈዩስ -ግ- ማሳˈነስ [አሳˈነሰ] ፡ መቀˈነስ
ˌ[ቀˈነሰ]

reduction

ሪˈደክሽን -ስ- መቀˈነስ

of price

-ስ- ቅˈናሽ (የዋጋ)

redundant

ሪˈደንደንት -ቅ- ካስፈˈላጊ በላይ ፡ ትርፍ(ለሡ
ˈራተˈኞˈች ወዘተ) ፤ ከˈሚያስፈˈልገው በላይ
ቃላት የˈሚያስገባ ፡ ሳያስፈˈልግ የተደጋˈገመ
መ (ቃላት)

reed

ˈሪይድ -ስ- ሽምብˈቆ ፡ መቃ

reedy

ˈሪይዲ -ቅ- ቀˈጭንˈና ከፍ ያለ (ለድምፅ)

reef

ˈሪይፍ -ስ- በባሕር መካˈከል የˈሚˈገˈኝ ቋጥ
ˈኞˈች *

-ግ- ጠቅልሎ ማሠር [አˈሠረ] (ለመርˈ
ከብ ሸራ)

reek

ˈሪይክ -ግ- መክርፋት [ከረˈፋ]

reel

ˈሪይል -ግ- መንገዳገድ [ተንገዳˈገደ] (በስካር
ወዘተ)

dance

-ስ- ዒˈፈራ (ስምˈንት ሰዎˈች ያˈሉˈበት)

bobbin

-ስ- መጠቅለያ ፡ ማጠንጠኛ ፡ ማቅለ
ሚያ

reimburse

ሪይምˈበስ -ግ- ያወˈጡትን ገንዘብ መˈከፈል
[ተከˈፈለ]

567

refer
ዐ'ፈ፡ -ግ- ማ'መባከር [አ'መነ ከረ] (ለጸ'ሐጊ)
to
-ግ- መጥቀስ [ጠ'ቀስ] (ለንግ'ግር)
referee
ሬፈ'ሪይ -ስ- ዳ'ኛ (ለማወጋ፡) ፡ ያሬራ ወረ
ቶት የላከ ሰው
reference
'ሬፈረንስ -ስ- የተጠ ኮ፡ መጻሕፍት (ብደር
ስት መዘተ)
recommendation
-ስ- ያዴራ ወረቀት
refill
ሬ'ፊል -ግ- እንደገና መሙላት [ም ላ]
refine
ሬ'ፋይን -ግ- ማ'ጥራት [አ'ጠረ] (ሰዘይት
ወዘተ)
refined
ሬ'ፋይንድ -ቅ- የተጣ'ራ
refinement
ሬ'ፋይንመንት -ስ- የማ'ጥራት ተግባር (ን
ጾ.ሱ ለማደረግ) ፡ ጥሩ አስተዳደግ
refinery
ሬ'ፋይነሪ -ስ- ማ'ጣሪያ መኪና ወይን'ም ቦታ
reflect
ሬፍ'ሌክት -ግ- ማስተንባት [አስተነ'ባ] (ለብ
ርሃን)
meditate
-ግ- በነገሩ ማ'ሰብ [አ'ሰበ]
reflection
ሬፍ'ሌክሽን -ስ- ማስተንባት
thought
-ስ- ሐ'ሳብ
reform
ሬ'ፎ፡ም -ግ- ማ'ሻሻል [አ'ሻሻለ] ፡ መ'ሻሻል
[ተሻሻለ]
reformatory
ሬ'ፎ፡መትሪ -ስ- ማ'ሻሻያ (አ'ዴስ ሕ'ግ) ፡
አመል ማ'ረሚያ (ለሕጻናት'ና ለወ'ጣቶች)
refractory
ሬፍ'ራክተሪ -ቅ- የማይ'ታዘዝ ፡ እምቢተ'ኛ
refrain
ሬፍ'ሬይን -ግ- ወደኋላ ማለት [አለ] (ከመ'ና
ገር) ፡ ማ'ቀም [አ'ቀመ] (አንድ ነገር ከመስራት)

refreshing
ሬፍ'ሬሺንግ -ቅ- የ'ሚያ'በረታ'ታ ፡ የ'ሚያዝ
ና'ና (ሰው'ነት)
refreshment
ሬፍ'ሬሽመንት -ስ- ቀለ'ል ያለ ምግብ'ና መ
ጠ'ጥ ፡ ቁርስ ፡ መቅሰስ
refrigerator
ሬፍ'ሪጀሬይተ -ስ- ማቀዝቀዣ መኪና ፡ የበ
ረዶ ቤት
refuge
'ሬፊዩ፡ጅ -ስ- መ'ሸሸጊያ ቦታ ፡ ካደጋ የ'ሚያ
መልጡ'በት ቦታ ፡ ተገን
refugee
ሬፊዩ'ጂይ -ስ- ስ'ደተ'ኛ
refund
'ሪፈንድ -ስ- ተመላሽ ገንዘብ (ከተከ'ፈለ በ
ኋላ)
refuse
ሬፍ'ዩ፡ዝ -ግ- እም'በ. ማለት [አለ] ፡ አለመ'ቀ
በል [-ተቀ'በለ]
refuse
'ሬፍዩስ -ስ- እድፍ ፡ ጉድፍ
refute
ሬፍ'ዩ፡ት -ግ- ትክ'ክል አለመሆኑን ማስረ'ዳት
[አስረ'ዳ]
regain
ሬ'ጌይን -ግ- እንደገና ማግኘት [አገ'ኘ] ፡
ማስመ'ሰል [አስመ'ሰለ]
regal
'ሪጋል -ቅ- ንጉሣዊ ፡ ለንጉሥ የ'ሚሰማ'ማ
regale
ሬ'ጌል -ግ- በምግብ'ና በመጠ'ጥ ሰው'ን ፡
ሬስን ማስደ'ሰት [አስደ'ሰተ]
regard
ሬ'ጋ፡ድ -ግ- መ'መልከት [ተመ'ለከተ] (አጥ
ብቶ)
esteem
-ስ- ክብር
regardless
ሬ'ጋ፡ድለስ -ተግ- ዋጋ ሳይሰጡ ፡ ሳይ'መለ
'ከቱ ፡ ች'ላ በማለት
regent
'ሪጀንት -ስ- ባለሙሉ ሥልጣን እን'ደራሲ
(የንጉሥ ሥራ የ'ሚሰራ)

regime
ሬዥይም -ስ- የመንግሥት ዓይነት (ለመጥፎ)፤ የኑሮ ዓይነት

regiment
'ሬጀመንት -ስ- ክፍለ ጦር (በኮሎኔል የሚ'ታ'ዘዝ)

region
'ሪይጀን -ስ- ክፍለ ሀገር ፡ ወረጃ ፡ አ'ካባቢ

register
'ሬጅስት -ግ- መመዝገብ [መዘ'ገበ]
official list
-ስ- መዝገብ
give one's name
-ግ- ስምን ማስመዝገብ [አስመዘ'ገበ]

registration
ሬጂስት'ሬይሽን -ስ- ምዝገባ

regret
ሪግ'ሬት -ስ- መ'ፀፀት [ተፀ'ፀተ]

regrettable
ሪግ'ሬተብል -ቅ- አሳ'ዛኝ ፡ የ'ሚያሳ'ዝን

regular
'ሬግዩለ -ቅ- የተለ'መደ ፡ ተመሳሳይ የሆነ ፡ እ'የተደጋ'ገመ የ'ሚሆን

regulate
'ሬግዩሌይት -ግ- ማስተካከል [አስተካ'ከለ]

regulation
ሬግዩ'ሌይሽን -ስ- ደንብ ፡ ሕ'ግ ፡ ሥርዓት

rehabilitate
ሪሃ'ቢሊቴይት -ግ- ድኩማንን ማሠልጠን [አ ሠለ'ጠነ] ፡ ሪሳ'ቸውን እንዲችሉ ወንጀለ'ኞ 'ችን በትምህርት ማ'ሻሻል [አ'ሻሻል]

rehearse
ሪ'ኸስ -ግ- መ'ለማመድ [ተለማ'መደ] (ቴያ ትር ወዘተ)

reign
'ሬይን -ግ- መንገሥ [ነ'ገሠ]
-ስ- ዘመነ መንግሥት

rein
'ሬይን -ስ- ዛብ ፡ መገጃ

reinforce
ሪይን'ፎ፡ስ -ግ- ማጠንከር [አጠነ'ከረ]

reinstate
ሪይንስ'ቴይት -ግ- እሹመት ላይ መመ'ለስ [መ'ለስ]፤ወደቀደሞው ቦታ መመ'ለስ [መ'ለስ]

reiterate
ሪ'ይተሬይት -ግ- ደጋግሞ መና'ገር [ተና'ገረ]፡ መሥራት [ሥ'ራ]

reject
ሪ'ጀክት -ግ- አለመ'ቀበል [--ተቀ'በለ]

reject
'ሪጀክት -ስ- የ'ሚ'ጣል ዕቃ (ስብርባሪ ወዘተ)

rejoice
ሪ'ጀይስ -ግ- መ'ደሰት [ተደ'ሰተ]

rejoin
ሪ'ጀይን -ግ- እንደገና መ'ገናኘት [ተገና'ኘ]

rejoinder
ሪ'ጀይንደ -ስ- መልስ ፡ ም'ላሽ (የጥ'ያቄ ፡ የክር'ክር)

rejuvenate
ሪ'ጁቨኔይት -ግ- እንደገና ወ'ጣት ማድረግ [አደ'ረገ]

relapse
ሪ'ላፕስ -ግ- ወደ ቀድሞው መጥፎ ሁናቴ መ'መለስ [ተመ'ለሰ] ፡ ማገርሸት [አገረ'ሸ]

relate
ሪ'ሌይት -ግ- ማውራት [አወ'ራ] ፡ ሙተ'ራት [ተ'ራተ]

relation
ሪ'ሌይሽን -ስ- ግን'ኙ'ነት
kinsman
-ስ- ዘመ ድ

relative
'ሬለቲቭ -ቅ- አ'ጻማ (እንዳ'ነጋገሩ ሊ'ተረ 'ጎም የ'ሚ'ችል ቃል)
kinsman
-ስ- ዘመድ

relax
ሪ'ላክስ -ግ- መዝናናት [ተዝና'ና]

relaxation
ሪላክ'ሴይሽን -ስ- መዝናናት

relay
'ሪሌይ -ግ- እምነትን መጣል [ጣለ]

release
ሪ'ሊይስ -ግ- መፍታት [ፈ'ታ] ፡ መልቀቅ [ለ'ቀቀ]

569

relegate
'ሬለጌይት -ግ- ከሹመት ዝቅ ማድረግ [አደ
'ረገ] ፤ አንድ ጉዳይ ለውሳኔ ማስተላለፍ
[አስተላ'ለፈ] (ለሌላ ሰው)

relent
ረ'ሴንት -ግ- መሓሪ መሆን [ሆነ]

relentless
ረ'ሴንትለስ -ቅ- ምሕረት የሴ'ለው ፤ ጨካኝ

relevant
'ሬለቨንት -ቅ- ተገቢ'ነት ያለው ፤ ከጉ'ዳዩ
ጋር የተያያዘ

reliable
ረ'ላየበል -ቅ- ታ'ማኝ ፤ እምነት የ'ሚ'ጣል
'በት

relic
'ሬሊክ -ስ- ታሪካዊ ዕቃ ፤ ያንድ የሞተ ቅ'ዱስ
ሰው የማስታወሻ ዕቃ (ዐፅም ወዘተ)

relief
ረ'ሊይፍ -ስ- ዕረፍት (ከሕ'ሳብ ፤ ከበ'ሽታ)
replacement
-ስ- ተተኪ ሰው (በሥራ ላይ)
sculpture
-ስ- ከደንጊያ የተፈለ'ፈለ የምስል'ነት
ቅርፅ ያ'ለው

relieve
ረ'ሊይቭ -ግ-መ'ገላገል [ተገላ'ገለ] (ከሕ'ሳብ ፤
ከበ'ሽታ)
replace
-ግ- መ'ተካት [ተተ'ካ] (በሥራ)

religion
ረ'ሊጀን -ስ- ሃይማኖት

religious
ረ'ሊጀስ -ቅ- ሃይማኖተ'ኛ

relinquish
ረ'ሊንክዊሽ -ግ- መተው [ተወ] ፤ መ'ስናበት
[ተሰና'በተ] (ከሥራ) ፤ መልቀቅ [ለ'ቀቀ] (የያ
ዘውን ነገር)

relish
'ሬሊሽ -ስ- ቅመማቅመም ፤ የ'ሚጣ'ፍጥ ፤
እ'ጅ የ'ሚያስቆረ'ጥም
enthusiasm
-ስ- ጉይለ'ኛ ፍ'ላጎት

reluctant
ረ'ለክተንት -ቅ- ለማድረግ የ'ማይወ'ድ ፤ ወደ
ኋላ የ'ሚል ፤ አንገራጋሪ

rely
ረ'ላይ -ግ- መ'መካት [ተመ'ካ] ፤ እምነት
መጣል [ጣለ] (በሰው ላይ)

remain
ረ'ሜይን -ግ- መቅረት [ቀ'ረ]

remainder
ረ'ሜይንደ -ስ- ቀሪ

remains
ረ'ሜይንዝ -ስ- ቀሪ ፤ ትርፍ ፤ የቤት ፍ'ራሽ ፤
አስከሬን

remark
ረ'ማክ -ግ- መ'ናገር [ተና'ገረ] ፤ አስተያየት
መስጠት [ሰ'ጠ]
-ስ- ንግ'ግር ፤ አስተያየት (የተነ'ገረ
ወይን'ም የተጻፈ)

remarkable
ረ'ማክበል -ቅ- በጣም ጥሩ ፤ ጉሩም ፤ ያልተ
ለ'መደ

remedy
'ሬመዲ -ግ- ማዳን [አዳነ] ፤ ማ'ቃናት [አ'ቃ
'ና] ፤ መፍትሔ ማግኘት [አገ'ኘ]
-ስ- መድኃኒት (ለበ'ሽታ ፤ ለመከራ)

remember
ረ'ሜምባ -ስ- ማስታወስ [አስታ'ወሰ] ፤ ት'ዝ
ማለት [አለ]

remembrance
ረ'ሜምብረንስ -ስ- ማስታወስ

remind
ረ'ማይንድ -ግ- ማስታወስ [አስታ'ወሰ]

remission
ረ'ሚሽን -ስ- የእስር ጊዜ ቅ'ነሳ

remnant
'ሬምነንት -ስ- ቀሪ ፤ ትርፍ

remonstrate
'ሬመንስትሬይት -ግ- ስሕተት መንገር [ነ'ገረ] ፤
አለመስማማትን መግለጽ [ገ'ለጸ]

remorse
ረ'ሞስ -ስ- ፀፀት ፤ ሓዘን (ላ'ለፈ ነገር)

remorseless
ረ'ሞስሴስ -ቅ- ምሕረት የሴ'ለው ፤ ርኅራኄ
የሴ'ለው

remote
ረ'መውት -ቅ- ሩቅ ፤ ዳር (ለአገር)

570

remove
ሪ'ሙ፥ቭ -ግ- መውሰድ [ወ'ሰደ] ፣ ወደሌላ ቦታ
ማ'ዛወር [አ'ዛ'ወረ] ፣ ማስወ'ገድ [አስወ'ገደ]

remunerate
ሪም'ዩ፡ነሬይት -ግ- መክፈል [ከ'ፈለ] ፣ ገንዘብ
መስጠት [ሰ'ጠ] (ለአንድ አገልግሎት)

remuneration
ሪምዩነ'ሬይሸን -ስ- ለአገልግሎት የ'ሚ'ከ'ፈ
ል ገንዘብ

rend
'ሬንድ -ግ- መሸርከት [ሸረ'ከተ] ፣ መሥን
ጠቅ [ሠነ'ጠቀ]

render
'ሬንደ -ግ- መልስ መስጠት [ሰ'ጠ]፤ መ'ልሶ
መክፈል [ከ'ፈለ] ፣ መተርጐም [ተረ'ጐመ]
(ቋንቋን)

rendezvous
'ሮንዴቩ፡ -ስ- ቀጠሮ (የን'ደ'ኞ'ች ፣ የወዳ
ጆ'ች)

renegade
'ሬነጌይድ -ስ- ከሓዲ ፣ መናፍቅ

renew
ሪን'ዩ፡ -ግ- ማ'ደስ [አ'ደሰ]

renounce
ሪ'ናውንስ -ግ- መካድ [ካደ]

renovate
'ሬነቬይት -ግ- እንደገና ማ'ደስ [አ'ደሰ]፣ ወደ
ቀድሞው ሁናቴ አ'ድሶ መመ'ለስ [መ'ለሰ]

renown
ሪ'ናውን -ስ- ዝ'ና ፣ ስም ጥር'ነት

rent
'ሬንት -ስ- ኪራይ (የቤት)
tear in cloth
-ስ- ቀዳዳ (የልብስ)
occupy house etc.
-ግ- መ'ከራየት [ተከራ'የ] (ለቤት ወዘተ)

reorganize
ሪ'የገናይዝ -ግ- እንደገና ማ'ደራጀት [አ'ደ
ራ'ጀ]፣ መልክ መስጠት [ሰ'ጠ]

repair
ሪ'ፔየ -ግ- መጠ'ገን [ጠ'ገነ]

repartee
ሬፓ'ቲይ -ስ- ፈ'ጣን፣ ቢልጥ ያለ'በት አ'ሥ
ቺ'ኝ መልስ (በንግ'ግር)

repay
ሪ'ፔይ -ግ- መክፈል [ከ'ፈለ] (ብ'ድር)

repeal
ሪ'ፒይል -ግ- የወ'ጣ ሕ'ግ መሻር [ሻረ]

repeat
ሪ'ፒይት -ግ- መደ.ጋገም [ደ.ጋ'ገመ] ፣ መድ
ገም [ደ'ገመ]

repel
ሪ'ፔል -ግ- ማ'ባረር [አ'ባ'ረረ] ፣ አለመ'ቀ
በል [-ተቀ'በለ]

repent
ሪ'ፔንት -ግ- ን'ሥሐ መግባት [ገ'ባ]

repercussion
ሪፐ'ከሸን -ስ- ካንድ ሁናቴ በኋላ የ'ሚ'ከ'ተ
ለው ው'ጤት ፤ የ'ሚያስተጋ'ባ ድምፅ

repetition
ሬፒ'ቲሸን -ስ- መድገም ፣ መ'ልሶ ማድረግ

replace
ሪፕ'ሌይስ -ግ- መተ'ካት [ተ'ካ]

replenish
ሪፕ'ሌኒሽ -ግ- እንደገና መሙላት [ሞ'ላ]

replica
'ሬፕሊካ -ስ- አምሳ'ያ ፤ አስመ'ስሎ የተሥ'ራ
ሥዕል

reply
ሪፕ'ላይ -ግ- መልስ መስጠት [ሰ'ጠ]

report
ሪ'ፖ፡ት -ግ- ስላ'ዩት ፣ ስለሰ'ሙት ፣ ስለሠ'ራ'ት
ጉ'ጻይ መ'ናገር [ተና'ገረ]
rumour
-ስ- ወሬ ፣ ፍምፍም.ታ
sound of explosion
-ስ- ተኩስ

reporter
ሪ'ፖ፡ተ -ስ- ጋዜጠ'ኛ

repose
ሪ'ፐውዝ -ግ- ማረፍ [ዐ'ረፈ]
-ስ- ዕረፍት

represent
ሬፕሪ'ዜንት -ግ- መ'ወ'ከል [ተወ'ከለ]

representative
ሬፕሪ'ዜንተቲቭ -ስ- ወ'ኪል
-ቅ- የ'ሚመ'ስል ፤ የተወ'ከለ

571

repress

ሪፕ'ሬስ -ግ- መጨ'ቆን [ጨ'ቆነ]፣መግታት[ገ'ታ]

reprieve

ሪፕ'ሪይብ -ግ- ምሕረት መስጠት [ሰ'ጠ] (ከ
ስ'ቅላት ፣ ከሞት ቅጣት፣)፣ለጊዜው ፍርድ እንዳ
ይ'ፈ'ጸም ማ'ገድ [አ'ገደ]

reprimand

'ሬፕሪማንድ -ግ- መገ'ሠፅ [ገ'ሠፀ]
-ስ- ተግሣፅ

reprint

ሪፕ'ሪንት -ግ- ደግሞ ማ'ተም [አ'ተመ]

reprisal

ሪፕ'ሪዛል -ስ- ለመ'በቀል ማጥቃት (በጠ
ር'ነት) ፣ ከፋት፣ በክፋት መመ'ለስ

reproach

ሪፕ'ረውች -ግ- መዝለፍ [ዘ'ለፈ] ፣ መውቀስ
[ወ'ቀሰ]

reproduce

ሪፕረድ'ዩ:ስ -ግ- መ'ባዛት [ተባ'ዛ] ፣ መ'ዋ
ለድ [ተዋ'ለደ]

reproduction

ሪፕረ'ደክሽን -ስ- መ'ባዛት ፣ መ'ዋለድ
facsimile
-ስ- ትክ'ክለ'ኛ ግል'ባጭ

reproof

ሪፕ'ሩ:ፍ -ስ- ዘለፋ

reptile

'ሬፕታይል -ስ- በደረት የ'ሚ'ሳብ ፍጡር (እ
ባብ ወዘተ)

republic

ሪፐብሊ.ክ -ስ- ሪፐብሊክ ፣ የመንግሥቱ ሥ
ልጣን በሕዝብ እንደራሴዎች እ'ጅ ያ'ለ
የመንግሥት አስተዳደር

repudiate

ሪፕ'ዩዲየይት -ግ- አለመ'ቀበል [-ተቀ'በለ]፣
መካድ [ካደ] (ሙ'ዋርጎን ልጅ ወዘተ)

repugnant

ሪፐግነንት -ቅ- ማስጠ'ለ ፣ እ'ጸ'ያፈ

repulse

ሪፐ'ልስ -ግ- ወደኋላ መመ'ለስ [መ'ለስ] (ጠ
ላት) ፣ መመ'ከት [መ'ከተ]

repulsive

ሪፐ'ልስ.ብ -ቅ- አስቀ'ያሚ ፣ የ'ሚያስጠ'ላ

reputation

ሪፕዩ'ቴይሽን -ስ- ዝ'ና ፣ ስም

request

ሪክ'ዌስት -ግ- መጠ'የቅ [ጠ'የቀ] (ፈቃድ)

require

ሪክ'ዋየ -ግ- ማስፈ'ለግ [አስፈ'ለገ] ፣ ማዘዝ
[አ'ዘዘ] ፣ መጠ'የቅ [ጠ'የቀ] (እንደ መብት ፣
በሥልጣን)

requisite

'ሬክዊዚት -ቅ- አስፈ'ላጊ ፣ ሊተውት የ'ማ
ይ'ቻል

requisition

ሪክዊ'ዚሽን -ግ- በመር'ነት ጊዜ ከሕዝብ ሥ
ንቅ ወዘተ መውሰድ [ወ'ሰደ]
-ስ- ለግ� በጽሑፍ ዕቃ መጠ'የቅ

rescind

ሪ'ሲንድ -ግ- መፋቅ [ፋቀ] (ሕ'ግን ፣ ደንብን)

rescue

'ሬስክዩ: -ግ- ማዳን [አዳነ] (ከአደ.ጋ) ፣ ከጠ
ላት ፣ ከእሥር ቤት ነጻ ማድረግ [አደ'ረገ]

research

ሪ'ሰ:ች -ግ- ምር'ምር ማድረግ [አደ'ረገ]
-ስ- ምር'ምር ፣ ጥናት (ለትምህርት ወ
ዘተ)

resemble

ሪ'ዜምብል -ግ- መምሰል [መ'ሰለ]

resent

ሪ'ዜንት -ግ- መ'ቃወም [ተቃ'ወመ]፣ አለመ
ስማማት [-ተስማ'ማ]፣እንደ ውርደት መቁጠር
[ቆ'ጠረ]

reservation

ሪዘ'ቪይሽን -ስ- ጥር'ጣሬ (ይ'ንገተ'ኛ) ፣ ከመ
'ናገ ከመሥራት መ'ቆጠብ
special area
-ስ- የተከ'ለለ ቦታ
pre-booking
-ስ- ቦታ መያዝ (በባቡር ፣ አውሮ'ፕላን
ወዘተ)

reserve

ሪ'ዘ:ብ -ስ- ዝ'ም'ታ
reticence
-ስ- መ'ቆጠብ (ከንግ'ግር)
store
-ስ- የተቀ'መጠ ገንዘብ ፣ በቂ (ለሰው)
book seat etc.
-ግ- አስቀ'ድሞ ቦታ መያዝ [ያዘ] (በባ
ቡር ፣ በአውሮ'ፕላን ወዘተ)

572

reservoir
’ሬዘቭዋ: -ስ- የውሃ ማ'ከማቻ ጋን

reside
ሪ'ዛይድ -ግ- መኖር [ኖሬ] (ባንድ ቦታ)

residence
’ሬዚደንስ -ስ- መኖርያ ቤት ፤ መኖርያ ጊዜ

resident
’ሬዚደንት -ስ- ነዋሪ (ባንድ ቦታ)
-ቅ- ነዋሪ

residue
’ሬዚድዩ -ስ- ጥ'ላጥ ፤ ዝ'ቃጭ

resign
ሪ'ዛይን -ግ- ሥራ መልቀቅ [ለ'ቀቀ] (በራስ
ፈቃድ)

resignation
ሬዚግ'ኔይሸን -ስ- ሥራ መልቀቅ (በራስ
ፈቃድ)

resigned
ሪ'ዛይንድ -ቅ- ታ'ጋሽ ፤ ያ'ጋጠመውን በት
ዕግሥት የ'ሚ'ቀ'በል ፤ የ'ማያጉረመ'ርም

resilient
ሪ'ዚሊየንት -ቅ- ወደቀድሞው ሁኔቴ መ'መ
ለስ የ'ሚችል (ከደ'ቀቀ ፤ ከተጨ'መቀ ወዘተ
በኋላ)

resin
’ሬዚን -ስ- መ'ሬጫ

resist
ሪ'ዚስት -ግ- መመከት [መ'ከተ] ፤ አለመ'ስ
ገር [-ተብ'ገረ] ፤ መ'ቃወም [ተቃ'ወመ]

resolute
’ሬዘሉት -ቅ- የጸ'ና ፤ የ'ማያ'ወላ'ውል ፤ ደ'ፋር

resolution
ሬዘ ሉ'ሸን -ስ- ጽናት ፤ አለማ'ወላወል
motion
-ስ- ው'ሳኔ

resolve
ሪ'ዞልቭ -ግ- መወ'ሰን [ወ'ሰነ] ፤ መበተን [በ
'ተነ] (ጉባኤ ፤ ስብስባ)

resonant
’ሬዘነንት -ቅ- የ'ሚያስተጋ'ባ ፤ የ'ሚነ'ብ
(ለድምፅ)

resort
ሪ'ዞ፡ት -ስ- የመ'ደሰቻ ቦታ ፤ ለዕረፍት የ'ሚ
'ኬድ'በት ሥፍራ ፤ አገር
means of help
-ስ- መ'ረጃ
go for help to
-ግ- እርዳታ መጠ'የቅ [ጠ'የቀ]

resource
ሪ'ሶ:ስ -ስ- ምንጭ (የገንዘብ ፤ የሀብት ወዘተ)
expedient
-ስ- ዘዴ ፤ ብልሃት

resources
ሪ'ሶ:ሲዝ -ስ- የተፈጥሮ ሀብት (ማዕ'ድን ወዘተ) ፤
የገንዘብ ምንጭ

respect
ሪስ'ፔክት -ግ- ማክበር [አከ'በረ]
-ስ- ክብር

respectable
ሪስ'ፔክተብል -ቅ- ጨዋ ፤ ታ'ማኝ ፤ የ'ሚ
'ከ'በር

respiration
ሬስፐ'ሬይሸን -ስ- ትንፋሽ ፤ መተንፈስ

respite
’ሬስፓት -ስ- ት'ንሽ ዕረፍት (ከሥራ ፤ ከድ
ካም ፤ ከ'ማያስደ'ስት ነገር)

resplendent
ሪስፕ'ሌንደንት -ቅ- ያሸበ'ረቀ ፤ ያጌጠ ፤ ያማ
ረ'በት (በኣ'ለባበስ)

respond
ሪስ'ፖንድ -ግ- መመ'ለስ [መ'ለሰ] (ንግ'ግር ፤
ሐሳብ)
react favourably
-ግ- ሐ'ሳብ ተቀብሎ አንድ ነገር ማድ
ረግ [አደ'ረገ]

response
ሪስ'ፖንስ -ስ- መልስ

responsibility
ሪስፖን'ሲቢሊቲ -ስ- ጎላፊ'ነት ፤ የጎላፊ'ነት
ስ'ሜት
level-headedness
-ስ- ታ'ማኝ'ነት

responsible
ሪስ'ፖንሰብል -ቅ- ጎላፊ ፤ ታ'ማኝ ፤ እምነት
የ'ሚ'ጣል'በት

573

rest

'ሬስት -ግ- ማረፍ [ዐ'ረፈ]
instrument
-ስ- ድ፡ጋፍ ፣ መደ'ገፊያ
remainder
-ስ- ቀሪ

restaurant

'ሬስትሮንት -ስ- ሆቴል ፣ ሬስቶራንት

restitution

ሬስቲት'ዩ፡ሽን -ስ- ካሣ

restore

ሪስ'ቶ፡ -ግ- መመ'ለስ [መ'ለሰ] (የወ'ሰዱትን
ነገር) ፣ መጠ'ገን [ጠ'ገነ]

restrain

ሪስት'ሬይን -ግ- ወደኋላ መግፋት [ገ'ፋ] ፣
ወደኋላ መያዝ [ይ'ዘ] ፣ ማ'ገድ [አ'ገደ] ፣ መግ
ታት [ገ'ታ]

restrict

ሪስት'ሪክት -ግ- መወ'ሰን [ወ'ሰነ] (እንቅስ
'ቃሴን)

result

፥'ዘልት -ስ- ው'ጤት

resume

ረዝ'ዩ፡ም -ግ- መቀ'ጠል [ቀ'ጠለ] (ሥራ)

resurrection

.ዘ'ሬክሽን -ስ- ትንሣኤ

retail

'ሪይቴይል -ግ- መቸርቸር [ቸረ'ቸረ]
by-
-ተግ- በችርቻሮ (የተሸጠ)

retailer

'ሪይቴይለ -ስ- ቸርቻሪ

retain

ሪ'ቴይን -ግ- ማቆየት [አቆ'የ] ፣ ማስቀ'ረት
[አስቀ'ረ]

retaliate

ሪ'ታሊዬይት -ግ- ክፋትን በክፋት መመ'ለስ
[መ'ለሰ] ፣ መበቀል [ተበ'ቀለ]

retard

ሪ'ታ፡ድ -ግ- ማዘግየት [አዘገ'የ]

retire

ሪ'ታየ -ግ- በእርጅና ምክንያት ሥራን ማ
ቆም [አቆመ]
withdraw
-ግ- ገሸ'ል ማለት [አለ] ፣ ለሙ'ኝታ
መሄድ [ሄደ]

retort

ሪ'ቶ፡ት -ግ- በቁ'ጣ መልስ መስጠት [ሰ'ጠ]
container
-ስ- የውሃ ማፍያ ብርጭ'ቆ በላቦራቶሪ
ውስጥ

retract

ሪት'ራክት -ግ- ቃል ማንሣት [አነ'ሣ] (የተ
ና'ገሩትን)

retreat

ሪት'ሪይት -ግ- ወደኋላ ማለት [አለ] ፣ ማፈግ
ፈግ [አፈገ'ፈገ]

retribution

ሬትሪብ'ዩ፡ሽን -ስ- ቅጣት (የኃጢአት ፣ የጥ
ፋት)

retrieve

ሪት'ሪይቭ -ግ- ማስመ'ለስ [አስመ'ለሰ] (የጠ
'ፋ የተሰ'ረቀ ዕቃ) ፣ የሰው ሀብት መመ
'ለስ [መ'ለሰ]

retrospect

'ሬትሮስፔክት -ስ- ያ'ለፈውን ጊዜ ፣ ያ'ለፉ
ትን ሁኔታዎ'ች ማስታወስ

return

ሪ'ተ፡ን -ግ- መመለስ [መ'ለሰ] ፣ መ'መለስ
[ተመ'ለሰ]
profit
-ስ- ትርፍ

reunion

ሪ'ዩኒየን -ግ- እንደገና መ'ገናኘት [ተገና'ኘ]
(የጓደ'ኞ'ች ፣ የባልንጀሮ'ች)

reveal

ሪ'ቪየል -ግ- መግለጽ [ገ'ለጸ]

revel

'ሬቨል -ግ- መ'ደሰት [ተደ'ሰተ] ፣ መጨ'ፈር
[ጨ'ፈረ] ፣ በዐል ማድረግ [አደ'ረገ]

revelation

ሬቭ'ሌይሽን -ስ- ራእይ ፣ የተገ'ለጸ ነገር

revenge

ሪ'ቨንጅ -ግ- መ'በቀል [ተበ'ቀለ]
-ስ- በቀል

574

revenue
'ሬቨኘዩ፡ -ስ- የመንግሥት ያመት ገቢ (ከቀ
ረጥ) ፤ ያገር ውስጥ ገቢ. መሥሪያ ቤት

reverberate
ሪ'ቨ፡ቨረይት -ግ- ማስተጋባት [አስተጋ'ባ] (ለ
ድምፅ)

revere
ሪ'ቪየ -ግ- ማክበር [አከ'በረ] (በተለ'ይ ለተ
ቀ'ደሱ ነገሮ'ች)

reverence
'ሬቨረንስ -ስ- ክብር (ለተቀ'ደሱ ነገሮ'ች)

reverse
ሪ'ቨ፡ስ -ግ- መገልበጥ [ገለ'በጠ]
a car
-ግ- ወደኋላ መሄድ [ሄደ] (ለመኪ.ና)

revert
ሪ'ቨ፡ት -ግ- ወደ ቀድሞ ሁናቴ መ'መለስ
[ተመ'ለሰ]

review
ሪቨ'ዩ: -ግ- እንደገና መ'መልከት [ተመለ'ከተ]
መከ'ለስ [ከ'ለሰ] (ለትምህርት)
theatrical
-ስ- ል'ዩ ል'ዩ የመ'ደሰቻ ትርኢቶ'ች

revile
ሪ'ቫይል -ግ- አጥብቆ መንቀፍ [ነ'ቀፈ]
አም'ሮ መውቀስ [ወ'ቀሰ]

revise
ሪ'ቫይዝ -ግ- እንደገና መ'መልከት [ተመለ
'ከተ] ፤ ማጥናት [አጠ'ና]

revive
ሪ'ቫይቭ -ግ- ሕይወት መስጠት [ሰ'ጠ] ፤ ሕይ
ወት ማግኘት [አገ'ኘ] ፤ እንደገና እሥራ ላይ
ማዋል [አዋለ]

revoke
ሪ'ቨውክ -ግ- ሕ'ግ መሻር [ሻረ] ፤ የተና'ገ
ሩትን ማንሣት [አነ'ሣ] ፤ የፈ'ቀዱትን እንደገና
መከልከል [ከለ'ከለ]

revolt
ሪ'ቮልት -ግ- መሽፈት [ሸ'ፈተ] ፤ ማ'መፅ
[ዐ'መፀ]
-ስ- ሽ'ፈታ ፤ ዐመፅ

revolting
ሪ'ቮልቲንግ -ቅ- የ'ሚያስጠ'ላ ፤ የ'ሚያ'ሠ
'ቅቅ

revolution
ሪቨ'ሉ፡ሽን -ስ- መዞር ፤ መሽከርከር 'አን'ደ
ገ.ዜ)
political
-ስ- ብጥ'ብጥ ፤ ሁከት (የፖለቲካ)

revolutionary
ሪቨ'ሉ፡ሽነሪ -ቅ- መሠረታዊ ለውጥ እንዲሆን
የ'ሚደ'ግፍ ፤ የ'ሚያደርግ ፤ ሁከተ'ኛ (የፖ.ለ.
ቲካ) ፤ የሰውን የኑሮ ሁናቴ የ'ሚለ'ውጥ

revolve
ሪ'ቮልቭ -ግ- መዞር [ዞረ]

revolver
ሪ'ቮልቨ -ስ- ሽ'ጉጥ (ፍ'ሻሌ)

revulsion
ሪ'ቨልሽን -ስ- መ'ጸየፍ (የመጥላት መንፈስ)

reward
ሪ'ዎ፡ድ -ግ- መሽ'ለም [ሸ'ለመ]
-ስ- ሽ'ልማት

rhapsody
'ራፕሰዲ -ስ- የፍ'ጹም ደ'ስታን ስ'ሜት መግ
ለጽ (በንግ'ግር ፤ በግጥም ፤ በሙዚቃ)

rhetoric
'ሬተሪክ -ስ- በቃላት ያሸበ'ረቀ አ'ነጋገር (ው
ስጡ ፍሬ ቢስ የሆነ)

rheumatism
'ሩ፡መቲዝም -ስ- ቁርጥማት

rhinoceros
ራይ'ኖሰረስ -ስ- አውራሪስ

rhyme
'ራይም -ስ- ቤት (በግጥም)

rhythm
'ሪዘም -ስ- የዜማ አ'ጣጣል ፤ ስን'ኝ

rib
'ሪብ -ስ- የጎድን አጥንት

ribald
'ሪበልድ -ቅ- ንግ'ግሩ ብልግ'ና የተሞ'ላ(ሰው)፤
ፌዘ'ኛ ፤ ያ'ለ'ዘበ (አ'ነጋገር ፤ ግቅ)

ribbon
'ሪብን -ስ- ቀ'ጭን መቀ'ነት ፤ ጥብጣብ

rice
'ራይስ -ስ- ሩዝ

575

rich
'ሪች -ቅ- ሀብታም
sweet
-ቅ- ጣፋጭ ፤ ቅብት የበ'ዛ'በት (ምግብ)

rickety
'ሪከቲ -ቅ- የተነቃ'ነቀ ፤ የወላ'ለቀ ፤ የ'ሚ'ሰ
'በር (በተለ'ይ ለመ'ጋጠሚያ)

riddle
'ሪደል -ስ- እንቆቅ'ልሽ

ride
'ራይድ -ግ- መጋለብ [ጋ'ለበ]

ridge
'ሪጅ -ስ- ጉ'ብታ (የተራራ ወዘተ)

ridicule
'ሪዲከዩ:ል -ግ- ማ'ቂያቂል [አ'ቂያቀለ]

ridiculous
ሪ'ዲክዩለስ -ቅ- የ'ሚያ'ሥቅ ፤ የሚ'ፈዝ'በት

rife
'ራይፍ -ቅ- የተስፋ'ፋ (በ'ሽታ ወዘተ)

riff-raff
'ሪፍ'ራፍ -ስ- ል'ቃሚ ፤ ዱር'ዬ

rifle
'ራይፈል -ስ- ጠመንጃ (ጠብንጃ)

rift
'ሪፍት -ስ- ሥን'ጥቅ

rig
'ሪግ -ግ- ግጭበርበር [አጭበረ'በረ] (ለም
ር'ጫ)
clothes
-ስ- ልብስ

right
'ራይት -ቅ- ል'ክ
direction
-ስ- ቀ'ኝ (አቅጣ'ጫ)
justice
-ስ- መብት
-ግ- ግስተካከል [አስተካ'ከለ]

righteous
'ራይቸስ -ቅ- ጻድቅ

rigid
'ሪጂድ -ቅ- ቀጥ ያለ ፤ በቀ'ላሉ የ'ጓይ'ታ
'ጠፍ ፤ ደረት (ለጠባይ)

rigorous
'ሪገረስ -ቅ- ድካም ያ'ለ'በት ፤ አድካሚ (ለጉ
ር) ፤ ደረቅ (ለጠባይ)

rim
'ሪም -ስ- ወፈ'ር ያለ ጠርዝ (በተለ'ይ የክ'ብ
ነገር)

rind
'ራንድ -ስ- ቅርፊ'ት ፤ ቆዳ ፤ ል'ጣጭ (የፍ
ራፍሬ ወዘተ)

ring
'ሪንግ -ስ- ቀለበት
sound
-ግ- መደ'ወል [ደ'ወለ]
encircle
-ግ- መክበብ [ከ'በበ]

ringleader
'ሪንግሊያደ -ስ- የወ'ርበ'ሎ'ች አለቃ ፤ የሹፋ
ቶ'ች ሹም

ringlet
'ሪንግሌት -ስ- የጸ'ጉ. ቁ'ጥራት ፤ ት'ንሽ
ቀለበት ወይን'ም ክ'ብ ነገር

rinse
'ሪንስ -ግ- ማለቅለቅ [አለቀ'ለቀ]

riot
'ራየት -ስ- ታ'ላቅ ብጥ'ብጥ (ስም'ች የ'ሚያ
ነሡት) ፤ ዓኪታ ፤ ጨቅዥት

rip
'ሪፕ -ግ- መሽርቀት [ሸረ'ከተ]

ripe
'ራይፕ -ቅ- የበ'ሰለ (ለፍራፍሬ) ፤ የደ'ረሰ
(ለፍርድ ወዘተ)

ripple
'ሪፐል -ስ- ቀለበት (በውሃ ውስጥ ድንጋይ
ሲ'ጣል የ'ሚ'ታ'ይ)

rise
'ራይዝ -ግ- መነሣት [ተነ'ሣ]
growth
-ስ- እድገት
sun-
-ስ- መውጣት (የፀሐይ)
of sun
-ግ- መውጣት [ወ'ጣ] (ለፀሐይ)

576

risk
'ሪስክ -ግ- ራስን አደጋ ላይ መጣል [ጣለ]
(እንድ ነገር ለማጻን)
-ስ- አደጋ ሊያመጣ የሚችል ነገር

rite
'ራይት -ስ- ሥርዓተ ቅ'ዳሴ ፤ ሥርዓተ ማሕ
ሌት

ritual
'ሪቸዋል -ስ- ሥርዓተ ቅ'ዳሴ ፤ ሥርዓተ ማሕ
ሌት

rival
'ራይቨል -ስ- ባላንጣ ፤ ተፎካካሪ ፤ ተቀናቃኝ
-ቅ- ባላንጣ ፤ ተፎካካሪ ፤ ተቀናቃኝ

rivalry
'ራይቨልሪ -ስ- ባላንጣ'ነት ፤ ተፎካካሪ'ነት ፤
ተቀናቃኝ'ነት

river
'ሪቨ -ስ- ወንዝ

rivet
'ሪቨት -ስ- በረት'ና ብረት ማ'ያያዣ ሚስ
ማር (ሊ'ነ'ቀል የ'ማይ'ቻል)

rivulet
'ሪቭዩሌት -ስ- ቀ'ጭን ጅረት

road
'ረውድ -ስ- መንገድ

roam
'ረውም -ግ- መንከራተት [ተንከራ'ተተ]

roar
'ሮ፡ -ግ- ማግሳት [አገ'ሳ] (ለአንበሳ)

roast
'ረውስት -ግ- መጥበስ [ጠ'በሰ]

rob
'ሮብ -ግ- መዝረፍ [ዘ'ረፈ]

robber
'ሮበ -ስ- ዘራፊ ፤ ወንበዴ (ወምበዴ)

robe
'ረውብ -ስ- መ'ጐናጸፊያ

robust
ረው'በስት -ቅ- ጠንካ'ራ ፤ ወፍራም ፤ ደንዳ'ና ፤
ጤና'ማ

rock
'ሮክ -ስ- ቋጥ'ኝ
oscillate
-ግ- መ'ወዛወዝ [ተ.ወዛ'ወዘ] (ወደኋ
ላ'ና ወደፊት)
-a baby
-ግ- እ'ሽ'ሩሩ ማለት [አለ]

rocket
'ሮኬት -ስ- ሮኬት ፤ ተስፈንጣሪ መ'ሣሪያ
(በራሱ 'ኃይል)

rod
'ሮድ -ስ- ረ'ጅም በ'ትር ፤ ሽመል

rogue
'ረውግ -ስ- በጥባጭ ፤ ሁከተ'ኛ ፤ ወ'ሮበ'ላ ፤
ዶሮ'ዬ ፤ የ'ማይ'ታ'መን ፤ ወንጀለ'ኛ

role
'ረውል -ስ- በቴአትር አንድ ተዋናይ የ'ሚሠ
ራው ክፍል ፤ በአንድ ሥራ የአንድ ሰው ል'ዩ
ተግባር

roll
'ረውል -ግ- መንከባለል [ተንከባ'ለለ]
-up
-ግ- መጠቅለል [ጠቀ'ለለ]
of bread
-ስ- ት'ንሽ ዳ'ቦ
of paper etc.
-ስ- ጥቅ'ል (የወረቀት ወዘተ)

romance
ረው'ማንስ -ስ- ፍቅር
book
-ስ- ል'ብ ወ'ለድ የፍቅር ታሪክ መጽ
ሐፍ

romantic
ረው'ማንቲክ -ቅ- የፍቅር ስ'ሜት የ'ሚሰጥ

romp
'ሮምፕ -ግ- መ'ፍረጥረጥ [ተፍረጠ'ረጠ] (ለ)

roof
'ሩ፡ፍ -ስ- ጣራ

rook
'ሩክ -ስ- እን'ስ ያለ የቁራ ዓይነት ወፍ

room
'ሩ፡ም -ስ- ክፍል (የቤት)
space
-ስ- ቦታ

577

roomy
'ሩ፡ሚ -ቅ- ሰፊ (ለቦታ)

rooster
'ሩ፡ስተ -ስ- አውራ ዶሮ

root
'ሩ፡ት -ስ- ሥር
source
-ስ- ምንጭ ፣ መሠረት

rope
'ረውፕ -ስ- ገመድ

rose
'ረውዝ -ስ- ጽጌሬዳ

roster
'ሮስተ -ስ- የስም ዝርዝር (የሥራ ተረኞች)

rostrum
'ሮስትረም -ስ- ተናጋሪ የሚቆምበት ከፍ ያለ ቦታ

rot
'ሮት -ግ- መበስበስ [በሰ'በሰ] ፣ መሸተት
[ሸ'ተተ] (ለሥጋ ወዘተ)

rota
'ረውተ -ስ- የተረኞች መዝገብ ፣ ዝርዝር
(የሥራ ፣ በተራ የሚ'ሠ'ራ)

rotation
ረው'ቴይሸን -ስ- መዞር

rotten
'ሮተን -ቅ- የበሰ'በሰ

rotund
ረው'ተንድ -ቅ- የተድበለ'በለ (ለሰው) ፣ ጉል
ህ'ና ጥልቅ (ለድምፅ)

rouge
'ሩ፡ጅ -ስ- የከንፈር ፣ የጉንጭ ቀ'ይ ቀለም
(የሴቶች)

rough
'ረፍ -ቅ- ሻካራ
crude, harsh
-ቅ- ጨ'ካኝ ፣ ርኅራኄ የሌ'ለው
stormy, of weather
-ቅ- መጥፎ አ'የር (ነፋስ)
in unfinished state
-ቅ- ሥራው ንጹሕ ያልሆነ (ዕቃ) ፣ እን
ደነገሩ የተሠ'ራ ፣ የተጀራ'ረገ

round
'ራውንድ -ተ- ክብ

rouse
'ራውዝ -ግ- መቀስቀስ [ቀሰ'ቀሰ] ፣ ማስነ'ሣት
[አስነ'ሣ]

rout
'ራውት -ግ- መደምሰስ [ደመ'ሰሰ] ፣ ፈጽሞ
ማሸ'ነፍ [አ'ሸነፈ] (ጠላትን)

route
'ሩ፡ት -ስ- መንገድ (የመ'ንገር)

routine
ሩ'ቲይን -ስ- የተለ'መደ ሥራ (ተመላልሶ የ
'ሚ'ሠ'ራ)

rove
'ረውሽ -ግ- መዞር [ዞረ] (አገር ላገር)

row
'ረው -ግ- መቅዘፍ [ቀ'ዘፈ]

row
'ራው -ስ- ጥል ፣ ዋካታ ፣ ጭቅጭቅ (በከር'ከር)

rowdy
'ራውዲ -ቅ- የ'ሚያ'ውክ ፣የ'ሚበጠ'ብጥ፣የ'ሚ
ጮኽ (ሰው)

royal
'ሮየል -ቅ- ንጉሣዊ

rub
'ረብ -ግ- መፈ'ተግ [ፈ'ተገ] ፣ መፈግፈግ
[ፈገ'ፈገ]
-out
-ግ- መፋቅ [ፋቀ] (ጽሑፍ)
-off
-ግ- ማጥፋት [አጠ'ፋ] (ከጥቁር ሰሌዳ)

rubber
'ረበ -ስ- ላስቲክ
eraser
-ስ- ላ'ጲስ

rubbish
'ረቢሽ -ስ- ጉድፍ ፣ ቆሻሻ
nonsense
-ስ- ትርኪ ምርኪ ፣ እንቶ ፈንቶ

rubble
'ረበል -ስ- የተከሰ'ከሰ ደንጊያ ፣ ሸክላ

rubicund
'ሩ፡ቢከንድ -ቅ- ደም የመ'ሰለ ቀ'ይ መልክ
ያ'ለው

578

ruby

’ሩ፡ቢ. -ስ- ሩቢ.

in watch

-ስ- ደንጊያ (የሰዓት)

rude

’ሩ፡ድ -ቅ- በደምብ ያልተሠ'ራ.

impolite

-ቅ- ባለጌ ፡ ነውረ'ኛ

rudimentary

ሩ፡ዲ’ሜንትሪ -ቅ- ጥልቅ ያልሆነ ፡ (ሕ'ሳብ፡ ለጥናት መዘተ)፤ ለጥናት ቀ'ላል ፡ ፍ'ጸሜ ያላገ'ኘ

rue

’ሩ፡ -ግ- መ'ፀፀት [ተፀ'ፀተ] ፡ ማዘን [አ'ዘነ]

ruffian

’ረፊየን -ስ- ወንበዴ ፡ ወንጀል የመፈ'ጸም ዝን'ባሌ ያ'ለው ሰው

ruffle

’ረፈል -ግ- ማ'ጨማተር [አ'ጨማ'ተረ] (ለል ብስ) ፡ ማ'በላሸት [አ'በላ'ሸ] (ለፀጉር መዘተ)

annoy

-ግ- ማስቆ'ጣት [አስቆ'ጣ] ፡ ፀ'ጥታ መንሣት [ነ'ሣ]

rug

’ረግ -ስ- ት'ንሽ ምንጣፍ (የወለል) ፡ ት'ንሽ ወፍራም የብርድ ልብስ ለእግር ማሞቂያ የ'ሚ ሆን

rugged

’ረጊድ -ቅ- ኅይለ'ኛ ፡ ብርቱ ፡ ወ'ጣ ገ'ባ ፡ ያለተስተካ'ከለ (ለመሬት) ፡ የተኮማ'ተረ (ለፊት)

ruin

’ሩዊን -ስ- ፍርስራሽ ፡ ፍ'ራሽ

rule

’ሩ፡ል -ግ- መግዛት [ገ'ዛ] (አስተዳደር)

law

-ስ- ሕ'ግ ፡ ደምብ

measure

-ስ- ማሥመሪያ

draw lines

-ግ- ማሥመር [አሠ'መረ]

ruler

’ሩ፡ለ -ስ- አገረ ገዥ ፡ ንጉሥ

for drawing lines

-ስ- ማሥመሪያ

rum

’ረም -ስ- ሩም (መጠ'ጥ)

strange

-ቅ- እንግዳ ፡ ያልተለ'መዶ (ሁኔቴ ፡ ነገር)

rumble

’ረምበል -ግ- መንጓጓት [ተንጓ'ጓ] ፡ መንጓ ዳት [ተንጓ'ዳ]

ruminate

’ሩ፡ሚኔይት -ግ- ማ'ሰላሰል [አ'ሰላ'ሰለ]፡ ማመ ስኳት [አመሰ'ኳ]

rumour

’ሩ፡መ -ስ- ጭምጭምታ ፡ ወሬ

rump

’ረምፕ -ስ- ቂጥ (የእንስሳ) ፡ የወፍ የጅራት ሥጋፍ

rumple

’ረምፕል -ግ- ማ'ጨማተር [አ'ጨማ'ተረ] ፡ ማቆ'ሸሽ [አቆ'ሸሸ]

run

’ረን -ግ- መሮጥ [ሮጠ]

operate a machine, business etc.

-ግ- እንዲሠራ ማድረግ [አደ'ረገ] (መኪና መዘተ)፤ ማ'ካሄድ [አ'ካሄደ] (የንግድ ሥራ)

rung

’ረንግ -ስ- መ'ወጣጫ (የመሰላል)

runner

’ረነ -ስ- ሯጭ

messenger

-ስ- ተላላኪ.

rupture

’ረፕቸ -ግ- መስበር [ሰ'በረ]

strain

-ግ- ሥ'ጋ መ'ቆረጥ [ተቆ'ረጠ] (ሽክም በማንሣት)

breach

-ስ- መ'ቀያየም [ተቀያ'የመ]

rural

’ሩ፡ረል -ቅ- ያገር ቤት ፡ የሀላገር

ruse

’ሩ፡ገ -ስ- ማ'ታለል ፡ ማጭበርበር

579

rush

'ረሽ -ግ- መፍጠን [ፈ'ጠነ] ፣ በፍ'ሉዊ መሄድ [ሄደ] ፣ መምጣት [መ'ጣ]

rust

'ረስት -ግ- መዛግ [ዛግ]
-ስ- ዝገት

rustic

'ረስቲክ -ቅ- የባላገር ፣ ያገር ቤት

rustle

'ረሰል -ግ- መንኮሻኮሽ [ተንኮሻ'ኮሽ]

rut

'ረት -ስ- የመኪና ጎማ የሄደ'በት ምል'ክት
መዘተ)

ruthless

'ሩዕለስ -ቅ- ምሕረት የሌ'ለው ፣ ጨ'ካኝ

S

sabbath

ሳበስ -ስ- ሰንበት ፣ ቅዳሜ (ለአይሁ-ድ) ፣ እሑ
ድ (ለክርስቲያን)

sable

ሴይበል -ቅ- ጥቁር

sabotage

ሳቦታ፡ዥ -ስ- ዐውቆ ማጥፋት ፣ በእ'ሥራ ላይ
አድማ ማድረግ ፤ ያንድ አገር የመ'ከላከያ
ድር'ጅት ለማ'ሰናከል ማ'ደም

sabre

'ሰይብ -ስ- ጎራዴ

sack

'ሳክ -ስ- ኬሻ ፣ ጀን'ያ
dismissal
-ስ- ከሥራ ማስወ'ገድ ፣ ማስወ'ጣት
plunder
-ግ- መዝረፍ [ዘ'ረፈ]

sackcloth

'ሳክ ክሎስ -ስ- የማቅ ልብስ

sacrament

'ሳክረመንት -ስ- ምስጢር (የቤተ ክርስቲያን፡
ም'ሳሌ ፣ ቁርባን ፣ ተክሊል መዘተ)

sacred

'ሴይክሪድ -ቅ- የተቀ'ደስ ፣ ቅ'ዱስ

sacrifice

'ሳክረፋይስ -ግ- መሥዋዕት [ሥ'ዋ]
-ስ- መሥዋዕት

sacrilege

'ሳክረሊጅ -ስ- ማርከስ (ለሃይማኖት)

sad

'ሳድ -ግ- ማዘን [አ'ዘነ]
-ቅ- ያ'ዘነ

saddle

'ሳደል -ስ- ኮር'ቻ

sadism

'ሳዲዝም -ስ- ሰውን በማ'ሠቃየት መ'ደሰት

safe

'ሴይፍ -ቅ- ምን'ም የ'ማያስፈ'ራ (ለቦታ) ፣
አማን የሆነ
money
-ስ- የብረት ሣጥን (ለገንዘብ)

safeguard

'ሴይፍጋ፡ድ -ግ- መ'ጠንቀቅ [ተጠነ'ቀቀ] (ለ
ሰው ፣ ለአንድ ነገር) ፣ ደኅና አድርጎ መጠ'በቅ [ጠ'በቀ]

safety

'ሴይፍቲ -ስ- ጸ'ጥታ ፣ ደኅን'ነት

safety-pin

'ሴይፍቲፒን -ስ- መርፌ ቁልፍ

sag

'ሳግ -ግ- መንከርፈፍ [ተንከረ'ፈፈ] ፣ መር
ገብ [ረ'ገበ] (ለገመድ)

sagacious

ሰ'ጌይሸስ -ቅ- ጥበብ'ኛ ፣ ብልኅ-ነት'ኛ ፣ ብልኅ
(ለአንስሳ)

sage

'ሴይጅ -ቅ- ነጣ ያለ አረንጓዴ ፣ ብልኅ-ነት'ኛ ፣
ጥበብ'ኛ ፣ ዘዬ'ኛ
-ስ- ብልኅ-ነተ'ኛ ሰው

580

sail
'ሴይል -ስ- ሸራ (የመርChቢ)
-ግ- በባሕር መ'ጓዝ [ተጓዘ]

sailor
'ሴይለ -ስ- መርከበ'ኛ

saint
'ሴይንት -ቅ- ጻድቅ ፣ ቅ'ዱስ

sake (for the-of)
'ሴይክ -መዋ- ስለ . . . ፣ ለ . . . ሲል

salad
'ሳለድ -ስ- ሰላጣ

salary
'ሳለሪ -ስ- ደሞወዝ

sale
'ሴይል -ግ- መሸጥ [ሸጠ]
-ስ- በቅ'ናሽ የመሸጫ ጊዜ

salesman
'ሴይልዝመን -ስ- የነ'ጋዴ ወ'ኪል ፣ እ'የዞረ እንዲሸጥ የተቀ'ጠረ ሰው

saliva
ስ'ላይቫ -ስ- ምራቅ

sallow
'ሳለው -ቅ- የደፈ'ረሰ (መልክ)

sally
'ሳሊ -ስ- ድንገተ'ኛ ግጥሚያ (በጠላት የተከ 'በቡ ወ'ታ'ደሮ'ች የ'ሚያደርጉት)፣ ድንገተ'ኛ ፈዝ ያ'ለ'በት መልስ

salmon
'ሳመን -ስ- ሳልሞን (ት'ልቅ ዐሣ ፣ ሥጋው የ'ሚ'በላ)

salon
'ሳሎን -ስ- አ'ዳራሽ ፣ የቁንጅ'ና ቤት

salt
'ሶልት -ስ- ጨው

salutation
ሳልዩ'ቴይሸን -ስ- ሰላምታ

salute
ስ'ሉ፡ት -ግ- ሰላምታ መስጠት [ሰ'ጠ]
-ስ- ሰላምታ

salvage
'ሳልቪጅ -ግ- ማዳን [አዳነ] (ከአደጋ)

salvation
ሳል'ቬይሸን -ስ- ድነነት

salve
'ሳልቭ -ስ- የቁስል ፣ የተቃ'ጠለ ሰው'ነት ፣ የአበጥ ቅባት

salver
'ሳልቨ -ስ- የብ'ር ትሪ (ይብዳ'ቤ. ፣ ካርድ የ'ሚ ቀርብ'በት)

salvo
'ሳልቨው -ስ- የመድፍ ሰላምታ (ለበዐል፣ለታ 'ላቅ የመንግሥት እንግዳ ወዘተ የ'ሚ'ተኮስ)

same
'ሴይም -ቅ- ያው ፣ የታ'ወቀው

sample
'ሳ፡ምፕል -ስ- ለዓይነት የ'ሚ'ተርብ ዕቃ ወዘተ

sanctify
'ሳንክቲፋይ -ግ- መቀ'ደስ [ቀ'ደሰ] ፣ መ'ባ ረክ [ባ'ረክ]

sanctimonious
ሳንክቲ'መውኒየስ -ቅ- ጻድቅ መሳይ

sanction
'ሳንክሸን -ግ- ሥልጣን መስጠት [ሰ'ጠ] ፣ ማጽደቅ [አጸ'ደቀ]
political
-ስ- ንግድ ማ'ገድ ፣ ሕ'ግ በመጣስ የ'ሚወይቅ ቅጣት

sanctity
'ሳንክቲቲ -ስ- ቅ'ድስ'ና

sanctuary
'ሳንክቸሪ -ስ- መቅደስ

sand
'ሳንድ -ስ- አሸዋ

sandal
'ሳንደል -ስ- ነጠላ 'ጫ'ማ

sandwich
'ሳንድዊጅ -ስ- በመካ'ከሉ ሥጋ ፣ እንቁላል ወዘተ ያ'ለበት ሁለ'ት የዳቦ ቁራ'ጭ

sane
'ሴይን -ቅ- አእምሮው ያልተና'ወጠ ፣ የተደ ላ'ደለ አእምሮ ያ'ለው

sanguine
'ሳንግዊን -ቅ- ባለተስፋ ፣ የተማ'መነ ፣ እንደ ደም ቀ'ላ

sanitary
'ሳንትሪ -ቅ- ጽዳት ያ'ለው

581

sanity
'ሳኒተ -ስ- የአእምሮ ጤን'ነት
sap
'ሳፕ -ስ- በእትክልት ግንድ ውስጥ የ'ሚ'ተ
ላ'ለፍ፣ ፈሳሽ (እትክልት የ'ሚ'መ'ገቡ-ትን
ምግብ የ'ሚያስተላ'ልፍ)
drain
-ግ- ማድከም [አደ'ከመ]
sapling
'ሳፕሊ.ንግ -ስ- ለ.ጋ ዛፍ
sarcasm
'ሳ:ካዝም -ስ- ፌዝ ፣ ልግጫ
sardonic
ሳ:ዶኒክ -ቅ- ፌዘ'ኛ ፣ እ'ላጋጭ ፣ አፏፊ
sash
'ሳሽ -ስ- መቀ'ነት
Satan
'ሴይተን -ስ- ሰይጣን
satchel
'ሳቸል -ስ- ት'ንሽ የመጻሕፍት መያዣ ፣ የ'ጅ
ቦርሳ
satiate
'ሴሺዬይት -ግ- ማጥገብ [አጠ'ገበ] (ለምግብ)
satire
'ሳታየ -ስ- ፌዝ ፣ ቂልት (የማንበራዊ ኑሮን
ሁኔቴ የ'ሚ'መለ'ከት)
satisfy
'ሳቲስፋይ -ግ- መጥገብ [ጠ'ገበ] ፤ መስማማት
[ተስማ'ማ]
saturate
'ሳቹሬይት -ግ- መርጠብ [ረ'ጠበ] ፣ መበስ
በስ [በስ'በሰ] (በውሃ)
Saturday
'ሳተዬይ -ስ- ቅዳሜ
sauce
'ሶ:ስ -ስ- መረቅ
saucepan
'ሶ:ስፐን -ስ- እ'ጀታ ያለው ብረት ድስት
(ብረ'ድስት)
saucer
'ሶ:ስ -ስ- የስኒ ማስቀ'መጫ
saunter
'ሶ:ንተ -ግ- መንሽራሽር [ተንሸራ'ሸረ] (ለሽ
'ርሽ'ር)

sausage
'ሶሲጅ -ስ- ቋሊ.ማ
savage
'ሳቪጅ -ስ- አውሬ
-ቅ- ያልሠለ'ጠነ ፣ ጨ'ካኝ
save
'ሴይቭ -ግ- መቆ'ጠብ [ቆ'ጠበ]
rescue
-ግ- ማዳን [አዳነ]
saviour
'ሴይቭየ -ግ- አዳኝ ፣ መድኃኒት
savour
'ሴይቭ -ግ- ማ'ጣጣም [አ'ጣጣመ] ፣ እ'ያ'ጣ
ጠሙ መብላት [በ'ላ]
-ስ- ጣዕም (በጣም ጥሩ)
saw
'ሶ: -ስ- መጋዝ
sawdust
'ሶ:ደስት -ስ- ሰ.ጋቱራ
say
'ሴይ -ግ- ማለት [አለ]
saying
'ሴይንግ -ስ- ም'ሳሌ
scab
ስ'ካብ -ስ- የቁስል ቅርፈ'ት ፣ ሽንኮፍ
scabbard
ስ'ካበድ -ስ- አፎት ፣ ሰገባ
scaffold
ስ'ካፈውልድ -ስ- የሰው መስቀያ እንጨት ፤
ቤት ሲ.'ሠ'ራ መ'ጠጣፊጫ የ'ሚ.ሆን እንጨት
scaffolding
ስ'ካፈውልዲንግ -ስ- ቤት ሲ.'ሠ'ራ የ'ሚ.ቆም
እንጨት (መ'ወጣፊጫ'ና መቆሚያ)
scald
ስ'ኮ:ልድ -ግ- በጦ'ቃት ውሃ መ'ቃጠል [ተቃ
'ጠለ] ፣ በውሃ መንፈር [ነ'ፈረ]
scale
ስ'ኬይል -ግ- መውጣት [ወ'ጣ] (ተራራ
ወዘተ)
balance
-ስ- ሚዛን
of fish
-ስ- ቅር'ፈት (የዐሣ)

scalp
ስ'ካልፕ -ስ- የራስ ቆዳ

scamper
ስ'ካምፐ -ግ- መ'ፈትለክ [ተፈተ'ለክ]

scan
ስ'ካን -ግ- መ'መልከት [ተመለ'ከተ] ፣ በጥን
'ቃቄ መመርመር [መረ'መረ]

scandal
ስ'ካንደል -ስ- የሐሜት ወሬ ፣ አሳ'ፋሪ ድር
'ጊ'ት ፣ ስምን የ'ሚያጠፋ ወሬ

scant
ስ'ካንት -ቅ- በጣም ጥቂት ፣ የ'ማይበቃ

scanty
ስ'ካንቲ -ቅ- ሥሥ (ለልብስ) ፤ በቂ ያልሆነ ፣
በጣም ጥቂት ወይን'ም ት'ንሽ

scapegoat
ስ'ኬይፐገውት -ስ- ሌሎች ባጠፉት ጥፋት
የ'ሚ'ወ'ቀስ ፣ የ'ሚ'ቀ'ጣ

scar
ስ'ካ፡ -ስ- ጠባሳ ፣ ጎዳ'ሳ

scarce
ስ'ኬየስ -ቅ- በብዛት የ'ማይ'ገ'ኝ

scarcely
ስ'ኬስሊ -ተግ- ምን'ም ያህል

scare
ስ'ኬየ -ግ- ማስፈ'ራት [አስፈ'ራ]

scarecrow
ስ'ኬክረው -ስ- በርሻ ላይ ወፍ ለመ'ከላከል
የ'ሚቆም ምስል

scarf
ስ'ካ፡ፍ -ስ- ሻል ፣ ያንገት ጥምጥም

scarlet
ስ'ካ፡ለት -ቅ- ጕፍን ቀ'ይ ፣ ቅርምዝ

scathing
ስ'ኬይዚንገ -ቅ- መራር (ለንግ'ግር)

scatter
ስ'ካተ -ግ- መበተን [በ'ተነ]

scavenger
ስ'ካሽንጀ -ስ- መንገድ ጠራጊ ፤ ጥምብ አንሣ
(አሞራ ፣ ጅብ)

scene
'ሲይን -ስ- የ'ሚ'ታ'ይ ነገር ፣ አንድ ድር'ጊ'
ት የተፈ'ጸመ 'በት ቦታ ፣ ትዕይንት
embarrassing incident
-ስ- አሳ'ፋሪ ድር'ጊ'ት

scenery
'ሲይነሪ -ስ- የአገር ቤት ትዕ'ይንት
theatrical
-ስ- የቴያትር መድረክ ግድግ'ዳዎ'ች
ሥዕል

scent
'ሴንት -ስ- ሽ'ታ

sceptical
ስ'ኬፕ፡ቲከል -ቅ- አሳማኝ ፣ ተጠራጣሪ (ይበ
ልጡን ለሃይማኖት)

schedule
'ሼጀዩል -ስ- የ'ሚ'ፈ'ጸሙ ጉዳዮ'ች ዝርዝር
'ና ?የ'ሚ'ፈ'ጸም'በት ጊዜ መግለጫ ፣ የሥራ
ፕሮግራም

scheme
ስ'ኪይም -ስ- የሥራ ዐቅድ፣ ሥርዓት የያዘ
የሥራ ዕ'ቅድ

schism
'ሲዝም -ስ- መ'ከፋፈል ፣ መ'ለያየት (በሐ'ሳብ)

scholar
ስ'ኮላ -ስ- ተማሪ
learned person
-ስ- የተማረ ሰው ፣ ምሁር

scholarship
ስ'ኮላሺፕ -ስ- የመ'ማርያ ገንዘብ (ከድር'ጅት ፣
ከመንግሥት ወዘተ የ'ሚ'ሰ'ጥ)
learning
-ስ- ትምህርት

school
ስ'ኩ፡ል -ስ- ትምህርት ቤት ፣ ተማሪ ቤት

schoolmaster
ስ'ኩ፡ልማ፡ስተ -ስ- አስተማሪ (ተባዕት)

science
'ሳየንስ -ስ- ሣነ ጥበብ ፣ ሳይንስ

scientific
ሳየን'ቲፈክ -ቅ- ሣነ ጥበባዊ ፣ ሳይንሳዊ

scissors
'ሲዘዝ -ስ- መቀስ ፣ መቁረጫት

583

scoff
ስ'ኮፍ -ግ- ማፈዝ [አፈዘ]
scold
ስ'ከውልድ -ግ- መ'ሳደብ [ተሳ'ደበ] ፣ መገ
ለፍ [ዘ'ለፈ]
scope
ስ'ከውፐ -ስ- ዐላማ ፣ ሐ'ሳብ (የሥራ) ፣ መጠን
(የሥራ ፣ ያስተያየት)
scorch
ስ'ኮፕች -ግ- መለብለብ [ለበ'ለበ] (ለእሳት)
score
ስ'ኮ፡ -ግ- ግብ ማስገ'ባት [አስገ'ባ] (ለስፖ
ርት)
-ስ- ግብ
twenty
-ቁ- ሃያ
musical
-ስ- የሙዚቃ ድርሰት የተጻፈ'በት መጽ
ሐፍ ፣ የሙዚቃ ድርሰት
scorn
ስ'ኮ፡ን -ግ- ማፈዝ [አፈዘ]
scorpion
ስ'ኮ፡ፒየን -ስ- ጊንጥ
scoundrel
ስ'ካውንድረል -ስ- ጠማማ ሰው ፣ የ'ማይ'ታ
'መን ሰው ፣ ወንጀለ'ኛ
scour
ስ'ካወ -ግ- እያ'ሹ እ'የፈ'ተጉ ማጠብ [አ'ጠበ]
scourge
ስ'ከ፡ጅ -ስ- ጉማ'ሬ ፣ አለንጋ
scout
ስ'ካውት -ስ- ቃፈር (የወ'ታ'ደር)
scowl
ስ'ካውል -ግ- ፊት ማጨፍገግ [አ'ጨፈ'ገግ]
scramble
ስከ'ራምበል -ግ- መፍጨርጨር [ተፍጨረ
'ጨረ] (ተራራ ለመውጣት) ፤ እንቁላል በቄ
'ለጠ ቅባት መ'ቶ መጥበስ [ጠ'በሰ]
scrap
ስከ'ራፕ -ስ- ፍር'ፋሪ ፣ ልቅምቃሚ ነገር ፣
ትርፍራፊ (ለማ'ን'ኛውም ነገር)
scrape
ስከ'ሬይፕ -ግ- መ'ቧጠጥ [ቧ'ጠጠ] ፣ መፋቅ
[ፋቀ]

scratch
ስከ'ራች -ግ- ማከክ [አ'ከከ] ፣ መ'ቧጨር [ቧ'ጨረ]
(በ'ጅ)
-ስ- ጭረት
scrawl
ስከ'ሮ፡ል -ግ- መቧጨርጨር [በ'ቧ'ጨረ] (ለጽ
ሕፈት)
scream
ስከ'ሪይም -ግ- መጮኽ [ጮ'ኸ]
-ስ- ጩኸት
screen
ስከ'ሪይን -ግ- መጋረድ [ጋ'ረደ] ፣ መከ'ለል
[ከ'ለለ]
protection
-ስ- መ'ጋረጃ ፣ መከ'ለያ
cinema
-ስ- የሲኒማ መ'ጋረጃ ፣ የሲኒማ ማሳ'ያ
የጨርቅ ቅ'ስት
screw
ስከ'ሩ፡ -ግ- መጠምጠም [ጠመ'ጠመ]
-ስ- ጥርስ ያለው ሚስማር
screwdriver
ስከ'ሩ፡ድራይቨ -ስ- ጠመንጃ መፍቻ
scribble
ስከ'ሪበል -ግ- መቧጨርጨር [በ'ቧ'ጨረ] (ለጽ
ሕፈት)
scripture
ስከ'ሪፕቸ -ስ- መጽሐፍ ቀ'ዱስ ፣ የመጽሐፍ
ቅ'ዱስ ጥናት
scroll
ስከ'ሮል -ስ- ጥቅ'ል ጽሕፍ
scrub
ስከ'ረብ -ግ- መፍገድገድ [ፈገ'ደገ] (ለማጽዳት)
scruple
ስከ'ሩፐል -ስ- ትክ'ክለ'ኛውን ፍርድ ለመስ
ጠት ያለመቻል ጥር'ጣሬ
scrupulous
ስከ'ሩፐዩለስ -ቅ- አንድ ነገር በትክ'ክል ለመ
ሥራት የ'ሚ'ጠነ'ቀቅ ፣ ጥንቁቅ
scrutinize
ስከ'ሩፒቲናይዝ -ግ- አተብቆ መመርመር [መረ
'መረ]
scuffle
ስከፈል -ስ- ት'ንሽ አምባጓሮ (ፈ'ላ ያ'ለ'በት)

sculpture

ስ ከአፈጣ -ስ- ምስል (ከደንጊያ ፣ ከእንጨት፣ ከብረት ተፈልፍሎ የተሠ'ራ)

scum

ስ'ከም -ስ- ውሃ ወይ'ም ሌላ ፈሳሽ ሲፈላ ባናቱ ላይ የ'ሚ'ታይ እሰር ፣ እረፉ
worthless people
-ስ- ወ'ራ'ዳ ሰዎ'ች

scurry

ስ'ከሪ -ግ- በፍጥነት መሮጥ [ሮጠ] ፣ ብ'ር ብሎ መሄድ [ሄደ] (በተለ'ይ በአጫ'ጭር እር ም'ጃ)

scuttle

ስ'ከተል -ግ- መርከብ ማስጠም [አስ'ጠመ] (በውፉ ፣ ቀዳዳ በመብሳት)
run away
-ግ- መሸሽ [ሸ'ሸ]

scythe

'ሳይዝ -ስ- ማጭድ (ት'ልቅ)

sea

'ሲይ -ስ- ባሕር

seal

'ሲይል -ግ- ማ'ተም [አ'ተመ]
-ስ- ማኅተም
stick down
-ግ- ማ'ሸግ [አ'ሸገ]
-ስ- ማ'ሸጊያ ሰም

seam

'ሲይም -ስ- ስፌት (የልብስ)

search

'ሰ፡ች -ግ- መፈ'ለግ [ፈ'ለገ]
by police
መበርበር [በረ'በረ]

seashore

'ሲ፡ሾ፡ -ስ- የባሕር ዳር

seaside

'ሲሳይድ -ስ- የባሕር ዳር (ቦታ ፣ ከተማ)

season

'ሲዘን -ስ- ጊዜ ፣ ወቅት ፣ ያመት ክፍል (ለም 'ሳሌ ፣ ክረምት በጋ ወዘተ)

seasonable

'ሲነነበል -ቅ- ከጊዜው ጋር የተስማ'ማ (እ 'የር) ፣ በራ'ለጉት ጊዜ የተገ'ኘ (እርዳታ ፣ ምክር ፣ ስጦታ ወዘተ)

585

_'ሲዘኒንግ -ስ- ቅመማቅመም

seat

'ሲይት -ስ- ወምበር ፣ መ'ቀመጫ ፤ ቺፕ

secede

ስ'ሲይድ -ግ- መ'ነጠል [ተነ'ጠለ] (ላገር ፣ ለማኅበር ወዘተ)

secluded

ሴክ'ሉ:ዲድ -ቅ- የተለ'የ ፣ ል'ዩ (ለቦታ)

second

'ሴከንድ -ስ- ረ'ዳት ፣ መከታ ፣ እ'ጋ'ዥ
in number
-ቅ- ሁለተ'ኛ
of rulers
-ቅ- ዳግማዊ
time unit
-ስ- ሴኮንድ

secondary

'ሴከንደሪ -ቅ- ሁለ'ተ'ኛ ፣ ዋጋ የሌ'ለው (በአስፈ'ላጊ'ነት)

secondhand

ሴከንድ'ሐንድ -ቅ- የተሠ'ራ'በት ፣ አ'ዲስ ያልሆነ

secret

'ሴክረት -ስ- ምስጢር
-ቅ- ምስጢራዊ

secretary

'ሴክረቴሪ -ስ- ጸሐፊ

sect

'ሴክት -ስ- ሀራጥቃ ፣ ያንድ ሃይማኖት ል'ዩ ክፍል

section

'ሴክሽን -ስ- ክፍል

sector

'ሴክተ -ስ- የከተማ ፣ የቦታ ፣ የኤኮኖሚ ወዘተ ክፍል

secular

'ሴክዩለ -ቅ- ዓለማዊ (መንግሥት) ፣ ሥጋዊ (መንፈሳዊ ያልሆነ)

secularism

'ሴክዩለሪዝም -ስ- ሃይማኖትን'ና መንግሥትን የ'ሚለ'ይ የመንግሥት' እ'ነዛ።

secure
ሰክ'ዩወ ‑ግ‑ እንዲ'ጠ'በቅ ማድረግ [አደ'ረገ]
(ከአደጋ) ፤ ሥራ ማግኘት [አገ'ኝ]
‑ቅ‑ ጸ'ጥ ያለ ፣ የ'ማያ'ሥ'ጋ

security
ሰክ'ዩሪቲ ‑ስ‑ ጸ'ጥታ ፣ ሰላም ፣ መ'ረጋጋት
person
‑ስ‑ ዋስ
guarantee
‑ስ‑ መያዣ

sedate
ስ'ዴይት ‑ቅ‑ ረጋ ያለ ፣ ጭ'ምት ፣ ኩስታ'ራ
(ለሰው ጠባይ)

sedative
'ሴደቲቭ ‑ቅ‑ የ'ሚያ'ረጋ'ጋ ፣ የ'ሚያደነ'ዝዝ
(መድኃኒት)

sediment
'ሴዲመንት ‑ስ‑ ዝ'ቃጭ ፣ አተላ

sedition
ስ'ዲሸን ‑ስ‑ ብጥ'ብጥ or 'ነውጽ ንግ'ገር ፤
ተግባር (በመንግሥት ላይ)

seduce
ስድ'ዩ:ስ ‑ግ‑ መ'ጸራት [ተጸ'ራ] ፣ ከፉ ሥራ
ለመሬ'ጸም ማባበል [አባ'በለ]

see
'ሲይ ‑ግ‑ ማየት [አ'የ] ፤ መ'ረዳት [ተረ'ዳ]

seed
'ሲይድ ‑ስ‑ ዘር (የተከለ)

seedling
'ሲይድሊንግ ‑ስ‑ ች'ግ'ኝ

seedy
'ሲይዲ ‑ቅ‑ ጎስቋላ ፤ ፍሬያ'ማ

seek
'ሲይክ ‑ግ‑ መፈለግ [ፈ'ለገ] ፤ መሻት [ሻ]

seem
'ሲይም ‑ግ‑ መምሰል [መ'ሰለ]

seemly
'ሲይምሊ ‑ቅ‑ \ጥሩ አመል ፤ የተስማ'ማ (ለጊ
ዜው)

seer
'ሲየ: ‑ስ‑ ወደፊት የ'ሚሆነውን ዐውቃ'ለሁ
የ'ሚል ነቢ'ይ

seethe
'ሲይዝ ‑ግ‑ መ'ናደድ [ተና'ደደ] ፤ በጣም መፍ
ላት [ፈ'ላ]

segment
'ሴግመንት ‑ስ‑ ቁ'ራጭ ፣ ብ'ጣሽ ፣ ክፍል
(ካንድ ነገር የተከ'ፈለ)

segregate
'ሴግሪጌይት ‑ግ‑ መለ'የት [ለ'የ] ፣ ከሌላው
ለ'ይቶ ማስቀ'መጥ [አስቀ'መጠ]

seize
'ሲይዝ ‑ግ‑ መያዝ [ያዘ] ፤ ለቀ'ም ማድረግ
[አደ'ረገ]

seldom
'ሴልደም ‑ተግ‑ አንዳንድ ጊዜ ፣ አልፎ አልፎ

select
ሲ'ሌክት ‑ግ‑ መምረጥ [መ'ረጠ]

self
'ሴልፍ ‑ጸተስ‑ ራስ
my‑
‑ጸተስ‑ ራሴ

self-centred
ሴልፍ'ሴንተድ ‑ቅ‑ ራሱን ብ'ቻ ወ'ዳድ

self-conscious
ሴልፍ'ኮንሸስ ‑ቅ‑ ይሉኝተ'ኛ ፣ ዓይነ አ'ፋር

selfish
'ሴልፊሽ ‑ቅ‑ ራስን ወ'ዳድ

sell
'ሴል ‑ግ‑ መሸጥ [ሸጠ]

semester
ሲ'ሜስተ ‑ስ‑ የትምህርት ክፍለ ዓመት (ለሁ
ለ'ት የተከ'ፈለ)

semicolon
ሴሚ'ኮውለን ‑ስ‑ ድር'ብ ሠረዝ (;)

semitic
ሴ'ሚቲክ ‑ቅ‑ ሴማዊ

senate
'ሴነት ‑ስ‑ የሕ'ግ መወ'ሰኛ ምክር ቤት

send
'ሴንድ ‑ግ‑ መላክ [ላከ]

senile
'ሲይናይል ‑ቅ‑ የጃ'ጀ ፣ የገረ'ጀፈ

senior
'ሲይንየ ‑ቅ‑ የ'ሚበልጥ ፣ ሹም ፤ በዕድሜ
የ'ሚበልጥ

586

sensation
ሴን'ሴይሸን -ስ- ግሩም ፣ ድንቅ ነገር
feeling
    -ስ- የስ'ሜት ችሎታ (ለስላሳ'ነት ፣
መደብዘዝ ወዘተ)

sense
'ሴንስ -ግ- መ'ለማት [ተሰ'ማ] (መስማት ፣
ማሸተት ፣ ጣዕም ፣ ስ'ሜት ፣ ማየት)
common-
    -ስ- ዕውቀት (ልማዳዊ)
physical, touch e.g.
    -ስ- ስ'ሜት ፣ ሕዋስ

sensible
'ሴንሲበል -ቅ- ዐዋቂ ፣ የ'ሚ'ቀ'በሉት ፣ የ'
ሚ'ረ'ዱት ፣ አስተዋይ

sensitive
'ሴንሰቲቭ -ቅ- ስ'ሜት ያ'ለው
irritable
    -ቅ- በቀ'ላሉ ተናዳጅ ፣ የ'ሚ'ቆ'ጣ
painful
    -ቅ- የ'ሚያ'ም

sensual
'ሴንስዩወል -ቅ- ዓለማዊ ፣ ለምግብ ፣ ለመጠ
'ጥ'ና ለፈቃደ ሥጋው የ'ሚኖር ፣ ፍትወተ'ኛ

sentence
'ሴንተንስ -ስ- ዐረፍተ ነገር
legal
    -ግ- መፍረድ [ፈ'ረደ] (ለመቅጣት)
judgement
    -ስ- ፍርድ

sentiment
'ሴንቲመንት -ስ- ስ'ሜት

sentimental
ሴንቲ'ሜንተል -ቅ- አዛኝ ፣ ርኅሩኅ ፣ ስ'ሜቱ
የ'ሚማ'ርከው

sentinel
'ሴንቲነል -ስ- ዘብ ፣ ተረ'ኛ ወ'ታ'ደር (የ'ሚ
ጠ'ብቅ)

sentry
'ሴንትሪ -ስ- ዘብ ፣ ተረ'ኛ ወ'ታ'ደር (የ'ሚ
ጠ'ብቅ)

separate
'ሴፐሬይት -ግ- መለ'የት [ለ'የ]

separate
'ሴፐረት -ቅ- የተለ'የ ፣ ል'ዩ ፣ ሌላ

September
ሴፕ'ቴምበ -ስ- መስከረም

septic
'ሴፕቲክ -ቅ- የተመ'ረዘ ፣ መግል የ'ቋ'ጠረ
(ለቁስል)

sepulchre
'ሴፖልከ -ስ- መቃብር

sequel
'ሲይክወል -ቅ- የ'ሚ'ከ'ተል ፣ ተከ'ታይ (ታ
ሪክ ፣ ወሬ)

sequence
'ሲይክወንስ -ስ- ተከታ'ታይ'ነት

serenade
ሴሬ'ነይድ -ስ- በም'ሽት በገላጣ ቦታ የ'ሚ'ዘ
'ፈን ዘፈን ወይን'ም የ'ሚ'ጫ'ወቱት ሙዚቃ
(በተለ'ይ የፍቅር)

serene
ስ'ሪይን -ቅ- ሰላማዊ ፣ ፍ'ጹም ፀ'ጥታ ያ'ለ
'በት ፣ የረ'ጋ (ሁውከት የሌ'ለ'በት)

sergeant
'ሳ:ጀንት -ስ- ያምሳ አለቃ

serial
'ሲሪየል -ስ- ተከታታይ (ታሪክ ፣ ቁጥር ወዘተ)

series
'ሲሪዝ -ስ- ተመሳሳይ'ና ተከታታይ ነገር

serious
'ሲሪየስ -ቅ- ቁም ነገረ'ኛ ፣ ቁም ነገራ'ም ፣
ኮስታ'ራ
grave
    -ቅ- ከ'ባድ

sermon
'ሰ:መን -ስ- ስብከት

serpent
'ሰ:ፐንት -ስ- እባብ

servant
'ሰ:ቨንት -ስ- አገልጋይ ፣ ሎሌ ፣ አሽከር

serve
'ሰ:ቭ -ግ- ማገልገል [አገለ'ገለ]

service
'ሰ:ቪስ -ስ- አገልግሎት

servile
'ሰ:ቫይል -ቅ- ተለማማጭ

587

ɔrvitude

'ሰ:ቪትዩ:ድ -ስ- ባር'ነት

ɔssion

'ሴሸን -ስ- ጉባኤ ፣ ስብሰባ ፣ ችሎት

et

'ሴት -ግ- ሥራ መደልደል [ደለ'ደለ]
solidify
-down
   -ግ- ማስቀ'መጥ [አስቀ'መጠ]
   -ግ- መርጋት [ረ'ጋ] (ዕቃ)
-aside
   -ግ- ማቆ'የት [አቆ'የ]
-on fire
   -ግ- ማ'ቃጠል [አ'ታ'ጠለ] ፣ መለ'ኮስ
[ለ'ኮስ] ፣ ማ'ያያዝ [አ'ያያዘ] (ለእሳት)
-free
   -ግ- ነጻ ማውጣት [አወ'ጣ]
-ስ- ዓይነታቸው አንድ የሆኑ ዕቃዎ'ች፤አንዱ
የሌላው ክፍል የሆኑ ዕቃዎ'ች

setback

'ሴትባክ -ስ- እንቅፋት

setting

'ሴቲንግ -ስ- አ'ካባቢ (ለቦታ) ፣ አንድ ነገር
የ'ሚ'ገ'ጠም'በት ቦታ (ጌጣጌጥ)

settle

'ሴተል -ግ- መ'ቀመጥ [ተቀ'መጠ] ፣ ማረፍ
[ዐ'ረፈ] ፣ ዕዳ መክፈል [ከ'ፈለ]
colonize
   -ግ- መ'ሠራት [ተሠ'ራ] (ባገር ላይ)

settlement

'ሴተልመንት -ስ- ሠፈር ፣ መሠፈሪያ (ቦታ)

seven

'ሴቨን -ቅ- ሰባ'ት

seventeen

ሴቨን'ቲይን -ቅ- ዐሥራ ሰባ'ት

seventh

'ሴቨንስ -ቅ- ሰባ'ተ'ኛ

seventieth

'ሴቨንቲየስ -ስ- ሰባ'ኛ

seventy

'ሴቨንቲ -ቅ- ሰባ

sever

'ሴሸ -ግ- መቁረጥ [ቆ'ረጠ] (ገመድ ለሁለ'ት)፤
ማ'ጽረጥ [አ'ጸ'ረጠ] (ወዳጅ'ነት)

several

'ሴቭረል -ቅ- ብዙ ፣ አ'ያሌ

severe

ሰ'ቪየ -ቅ- ከ'ባድ (ለነገር)

sew

'ሰው -ግ- መስፋት [ሰ'ፋ] (ልብስ)

sewage

'ሱዊጅ -ስ- ሠገራ ፣ እስር ፣ ዓይነ ምድር
(በ'ቧምቧ ውስጥ የ'ሚ'ፈ'ስ)

sewer

'ሱወ -ስ- የሠገራ ቧምቧ (ከምድር በታ'ች)

sex

'ሴክስ -ስ- ግብረ ሥጋ
gender
   -ስ- ጾታ

sexual

'ሴክስዬወል -ቅ- ፈቃደ ሥጋዊ ፣ ከፈቃደ ሥጋ
ጋር ግን'ኙ'ነት ያ'ለው

shabby

'ሻቢ -ቅ- አርጌ (ልብስ) ፣ ብት'ቱ

shackle

'ሻከል -ስ- እግር ብረት

shade

'ሼይድ -ስ- ጥላ
   -ግ- ማጥላት [አጠ'ላ] ፣ መከ'ለል [ከ'ለ
ለ] ፤ መጋረድ [ጋ'ረደ]

shadow

'ሻደው -ስ- ጥላ (የሰው ፣ ያንድ ነገር)

shady

'ሼይዲ -ቅ- ጥላ'ማ
of reputation
   -ቅ- የ'ማይ'ታመን ፣ መጥፎ ስም ያ'ለው

shaft

'ሻ:ፍት -ስ- ቀ'ጭኗ ረ'ጅም ብረት ፤ አገዳ ፤
የመተረቢያ ረ'ጅም እ'ጀታ ፤ የጋሪ መኳ'ተቾ
ጋድሚያ እንጨት (ከሁለ'ት አንዱ)

shaggy

'ሻጊ -ቅ- ጠጉሩ ከርዳ'ዳ ፤ ረ'ጅም'ና ያልተ
በ'ጠረ ጠጉር ያ'ለው

shake

'ሼይክ -ግ- መወዝወዝ [ወዘ'ወዘ]
tremble
   -ግ- መንቀጥቀጥ [ተንቀጠ'ቀጠ]

588

shall
ʾ ሻል -ግ- (ትንቢት መግለጫ ረ'ዳት ግሥ)

shallow
ʾ ሻለው -ቅ- ጥልቀት የሌ'ለው (ለውሃ) ፤ ጥራ
ዝ ነ'ጠቅ

sham
ʾ ሻም -ቅ- አ'ታላይ ፤ እውነት'ነት የሌ'ለው

shamble
ʾ ሻምበል -ግ- መ'ወዛወዝ [ተወዛ'ወዘ]፤ እየተ
ጕ'ተቴ መሄድ [ጕደ] (ለሰው)

shambles
ʾ ሻምበልዝ -ስ- ሥርዓት'ና ወግ የሌ'ለው ቦታ
ወይን'ም ሁናቴ ፤ የደም መፍሰሻ ቦታ ፤ ብዙ
ሰዎ'ች የ'ሚ'ገ'ደሉ'በት ቦታ ፤ ቄራ

shame
ʾ ሼይም -ስ- ሐፍረት

shape
ʾ ሼይፕ -ግ- ቅርፅ መስጠት [ሰ'ጠ] ፤ መቅረፅ
[ቀ'ረፀ]
-ስ- ቅርፅ

share
ʾ ሼየ -ግ- ማ'ካፈል [አ'ካ'ፈለ]
portion
-ስ- ድርሻ ፤ ክፍ'ያ ፤ እጣ
of plough
-ስ- ስለት (የማረሻ)

shareholder
ʾ ሼሆልደ -ስ- ባለእጣ (ባለአክስዮን)

sharp
ʾ ሻ፦ጥ -ቅ- ስለታም

sharpen
ʾ ሻፐን -ግ- መቅረፅ [ቀረፀ] ፤ መሳል [ሳለ]
(ስለት)

shatter
ʾ ሻተ -ግ- መሰባበር [ሰባ'በረ]

shave
ʾ ሼይቭ -ግ- መላጨት [ላ'ጨ] (ጢምን)

shawl
ʾ ሾ፡ል -ስ- ሸ'ማ

she
ʾ ሺይ -ተስ- እርሷ ፤ እ'ሷ

sheaf
ʾ ሺይፍ -ስ- ነዶ

shear
ʾ ሺየ -ግ- መሸ'ለት [ሸ'ለተ]

sheath
ʾ ሺይስ -ስ- አፎት ፤ ሰገባ

shed
ʾ ሼድ -ግ- መጣል [ጣለ] ፤ ማፍሰስ [አፈ'ሰሰ]
(ውሃ ፤ ደም ወዘተ)

sheen
ʾ ሺይን -ስ- ብሩህ'ነት

sheep
ʾ ሺይፕ -ስ- በግ

sheer
ʾ ሺየ -ቅ- ፍ'ፁም ፤ ገደላ'ማ ፤ ሽ'ው ያለ
(ገደል)
-ግ- አቅጣ'ጫን መለ'ወጥ [ለ'ወጠ]
(ለመርከብ)

sheet
ʾ ሺይት -ስ- ያልጋ ምንጣፍ (አንሶላ) ፤ ሉህ.
(ወረቀት)

shelf
ʾ ሼልፍ -ስ- ዕቃ መደርደሪያ ፤ ጨነጎት

shell
ʾ ሼል -ግ- መፈልፈል [ፈለ'ፈለ] (አተር ወዘተ)
casing
-ስ- ቀለህ
hard cover
-ስ- ቅርፊ'ት (የዕንቁላል ፤ የለውዝ
ወዘተ) ፤ ዛጎል
of cannon
-ስ- የመድፍ ጥ'ይት

shelter
ʾ ሼልተ -ግ- መ'ጠጋት [ተጠ'ጋ] (ራስን ከአ
ደጋ ለማዳን) ፤ መ'ጠለል [ተጠ'ለለ]
protection
-ስ- መ'ጠጊያ (ከአደጋ) ፤ መ'ጠለያ
(ከዝናም)
cover
-ስ- የዘበኛ ቤት

shelve
ʾ ሼልቭ -ግ- ማዘግየት [አዘገ'የ] (ለጉ'ዳይ) ፤
እመደርደሪያ ውስጥ ማስቀ'መጥ [አስቀ'መጠ]

shepherd
ʾ ሼፐድ -ስ- እ'ረኛ ፤ በግ ጠ'ባቂ

589

shield

’ሺይልድ -ግ- መከታ መሆን [ሆነ]
    -ስ- ጋ'ｉ (መ'ከላከያ)

shift

’ሺፍት -ግ- ወደ ጐ'ን ግድረገ [አደ'ረገ] ፣
    ካንድ ቦታ ወደ ሌላው መውሰድ [ወ'ሰደ]

shin

’ሺን -ስ- መሀል እገጻ

shine

’ሻይን -ግ- ማብራት [አበ'ራ]

ship

’ሺፕ -ስ- መርከብ

ship

’ሺፕ -ግ- መጫን (ካንድ አገር ወደ ሌላው
    ለመውሰድ)

shirk

’ሸ፡ክ -ግ- ሥራ በ'ሚ'ገ'ባ አለመሥራት [-ሡ
    'ራ] ፣ ማልኩስኩስ [አልኩስ'ኩስ] ፣ ተገባር
    አለመፈ'ጸም [-ፈ'ጸመ] ፣ መስነፍ ፡ [ሰ'ነፈ]

shirt

’ሸ፡ት -ስ- ሸሚዝ

shiver

’ሺቭ -ግ- መንቀጥቀጥ [ተንቀጠ'ቀጠ]

shock

’ሾክ -ስ- ድን'ጋጤ ፣ ንዝረት

shoe

’ሹ፡ -ስ- ጫ'ማ

shoemaker

’ሹ፡ሜይክ -ስ- ጫ'ማ ሰፊ

shoot

’ሹ፡ት ኑ-ግ- መተ'ኩስ [ተ'ኩስ] (ጠር መ'ሣሪያ)፤
    ካስ ወደ ግብ አስተካክሎ መምታት [መ'ታ]

shop

’ሾፕ -ስ- ሱቅ

shopkeeper

’ሾፕኪይፕ -ስ- ባለሱቅ

shore

’ሾ፡ -ስ- የባሕር ጻር

short

’ሾ፡ት -ቅ- አ'ጭር

shorten

’ሾ፡ተን -ግ- ማሳ'ጠር [አሳ'ጠረ]

shortly

’ሾ፡ትሊ -ተግ- ከጥቂት ጊዜ በጓላ

shot

’ሾት ሳ- ተኩስ ፣ አ'ተኳኮስ

shoulder

’ሾውልደ -ስ- ትከ'ሻ

shout

’ሻውት -ግ- መርጨክ [ጮኸ]
    -ስ- ጨኸት

shovel

’ሸቭል -ስ- አካፉ
    -ግ- በአካፉ መዛቅ [ዛቀ]

show

’ሾው -ግ- ማሳ'የት [አሳ'የ]
    appearance
    -ስ- ለይምሰል
    theatrical
    -ስ- ትርኢት (የቴያትር)

shower

’ሻወ -ስ- መ'ጠመቂያ (ለመ'ታጠብ)
    of rain
    -ስ- ካ'ፍያ

shred

ሽ'ሬድ -ግ- መተልተል [ተለ'ተለ]
    -ስ- የተተለ'ተለ ነገር

shrew

ሽ'ሩ፡ -ስ- ፍልፈል አፈር ፤ ጨቅጫ'ቃ ሴት

shrewd

ሽ'ሩ፡ውድ -ቅ- ጮኸ'ሌ ፣ ብልጥ ፣ ተንኮለ'ኛ

shriek

ሽ'ሪይክ -ግ- መጮኸ [ጮኸ] ፣ መንጐ-ር [ን
    'ጐረ]

shrill

ሽ'ሪል -ስ- ተ'ጭን ከ'ፍ ያለ ድምፅ ፡ መነጫ
    ጨር

shrine

ሽ'ራይን -ስ- የተቀ'ደስ ቦታ ፡ መ'ሳለሚያ
    ቦታ

shrink

ሽ'ሪንክ -ግ- መ'ኰማተር [ተኰማ'ተረ]

shrivel

ሽ'ሪቭል -ግ- መ'ጨማደድ [ተጨማ'ደደ]

shroud

ሽ'ራውድ -ስ- ከፈን ፣ መከፈኛ ጨርቅ

shrub

ሽ'ረብ -ግ- ቁጥቋጦ (ት'ንሽ)

shrug
ሽ'ረግ ╶ግ╴ ትከ'ሻ መነጥነት [ነቀ'ነቀ] (ግ'
ድ የ'ለ'ኝም ለማለት)

shudder
'ሽደ ╶ግ╴ በድንጋት መንዘፍዘፍ [ተንዘፈ'ዘፈ] ፣
መንቀጥቀጥ [ተንቀጠ'ቀጠ]

shuffle
'ሽፈል ╶ግ╴ መ'ጉተት [ተጉ'ተተ] (ሲሄዱ) ፤
ካርታ መበ'ወዝ [በ'ወዘ]

shun
'ሽን ╶ግ╴ መራት [ራተ] (ከነገር)

shut
'ሽት ╶ግ╴ መዝጋት [ዘ'ጋ]
-up
╶ግ╴ ዝምበል ፣ አፍከን ዝጋ

shutter
'ሽተ ╶ስ╴ ተጠቅላይ'ና ተዘርጊ የመስኮት መዝ
ጊያ (ከእንጨት ፣ ከብረት የተሠ'ራ)

shy
'ሻይ ╶ቅ╴ ዓይን አ'ፋር

sick
'ሲከ ╶ቅ╴ ሕሙም ፣ ሕመምተ'ኛ

sickle
'ሲከል ╶ስ╴ ማጭድ

sickness
'ሲክኔስ ╶ስ╴ ሕመም

side
'ሳይድ ╶ስ╴ ጎ'ን (የሰው'ነት ከፍል)
direction
╶ስ╴ ጎ'ን (አቅጣ'ጫ)

sideways
'ሳይድዌይዝ ╶ተግ╴ አግድም ፣ ወደ ጎ'ን

seige
'ሲይጅ ╶ስ╴ የመውረሪያ ጊዜ (በጦር'ነት ከተ
ግ ፣ ም'ሽግ)

seive
'ሲቭ ╶ስ╴ ወንፊት

sift
'ሲፍት ╶ግ╴ መንፋት [ነ'ፋ] (በወንፊት)

sigh
'ሳይ ╶ግ╴ እህ ማለት [አለ] (ከድካም ፣ ከሐዘን ፣
ከመንሰራራት የተነ'ሣ)

sight
'ሳይት ╶ግ╴ ማየት [አ'የ] (ተ'ረብ በማለት)
╶ስ╴ ማየት ፣ የማየት ችሎታ
spectacle
╶ስ╴ ትርኢት

sign
'ሳይን ╶ግ╴ መፈ'ረም [ፈ'ረመ]
╶ስ╴ ም'ልክት

signal
'ሲግነል ╶ስ╴ ም'ልክት (የተራፊክ ወዘተ)

signify
'ሲግኒፋይ ╶ግ╴ ማለት [አለ] (ለቃል) ፤ ግመ
ልከት [አመለ'ከተ] (ለቃል)

signature
'ሲግነቸ ╶ስ╴ ፊርማ

signboard
'ሳይንቦ፡ድ ╶ስ╴ የሱቅ ፣ የሆቴል ፣ ወዘተ ስም
ተጽፎ የ'ሚ'ታ'ይ በት ሰሌዳ

significant
ሲግ'ኒፊከንት ╶ቅ╴ አስፈ'ላጊ ፣ ዐቢ'ይ ፣ በማም
አስፈ'ላጊ'ነትን የ'ሚያመለ'ከት

silence
'ሳይለንስ ╶ስ╴ ጸ'ጥታ ፣ ዝ'ምታ

silent
'ሳይለንት ╶ቅ╴ ጸ'ጥ ያለ

silk
'ሲልከ ╶ስ╴ ሐ'ር

silly
'ሲሊ ╶ቅ╴ ቂል ፣ ሞ'ኝ ፣ ጅል

silver
'ሲልቨ ╶ስ╴ ብ'ር (ማዕ'ድን)

similar
'ሲሚለ ╶ቅ╴ ተመሳሳይ ፣ የ'ሚመስል

simmer
'ሲመ ╶ግ╴ መንተከተክ [ተንተከ'ተከ] (ወጥ
ወዘተ) ፤ በን'ዴት መትከን [ተ'ከነ]

simple
'ሲምፐል ╶ቅ╴ ቀ'ላል ፣ የ'ማያስቸ'ግር

simplicity
ሲም'ፕ'ሊሲ'ቲ ╶ስ╴ ቀ'ላል'ነት (አለማ ስቸ'ገር)

simulate
'ሲምዩሌይት ╶ግ╴ መቅዳት [ቀ'ዳ] (ሌላው
የ'ሚያደርገውን) ፣ ማስመ'ሰል [አስመ'ሰለ]
(ያልሆነውን)

591

simultaneously

ሲመል'ተይኒያስሊ. -ተግ- ባንድ ጊዜ (የሆነ ፣ የተደ'ረገ)

sin

'ሲን -ግ- ኃጢአት መሥራት [ሠ'ራ]

since

'ሲንስ -ተግ- ከ . . . ጀምሮ

sincere

ሲን'ሲየ -ቅ- ታ'ማኝ ፣ እውነተ'ኛ ፣ ልባዊ

sinew

'ሲንዩ -ስ- ጅ'ማት (የሰው'ነት)

sing

'ሲንግ -ግ- መዝፈን [ዘ'ፈነ] ፣ መዘ'መር [ዘ'መረ]

singe

'ሲንጅ -ግ- መ'ለብለብ [ተለበ'ለበ] (የጠጉ ር ጫፍ ወዘተ)

single

'ሲንገል -ቅ- ነጠላ ፣ ብ'ቻ

unmarried

-ቅ- ያላገ'ባ

singular

'ሲንጉዩለ -ቅ- ነጠላ (እጥፍ ያልሆነ)

unusual

-ቅ- እንግዳ ፣ ያልተለ'መደ

sinister

'ሲኒስተ -ቅ- አደገ'ኛ ፣ አሥጊ ፣ በ'ጎ ፈቃድ የ'ማያሳ'ይ

sink

'ሲንክ -ግ- መስጠም [ሰ'ጠመ]

-ስ- ሲሐን (መ'ታጠቢያ)

sip

'ሲፕ -ግ- ፉት ማለት [አለ]

sir

'ሰ: -ስ- ጌታዬ

sirloin

'ሰ:ሎይን -ስ- ጥ'ቅ'ና

sister

'ሲስተ -ስ- እህት

sister-in-law

'ሲስተሪንሎ: -ስ- የወንድ'ም ሚስት

sistrum

'ሲስትረም -ስ- ጸናጽል

sit

'ሲት -ግ- መ'ቀመጥ [ተቀ'መጠ]

site

'ሳይት -ስ- ቦታ (እንድ ነገር የተፈ'ጸመ'በት ፣ የ'ሚ'ፈ'ጸም'በት)

situated

'ሲትዩዌይተድ -ቅ- የ'ሚ'ገ'ኘው ፣ ያለ'በት (ቦታ)

situation

ሲትዩ'ዌይሸን -ስ- ሁኔታ ፣ ሁኔታ

six

'ሲክስ -ቅ- ስ'ድስት

sixteen

ሲክስ'ቲይን -ቅ- ዐሥራ ስ'ድስት

sixteenth

ሲክስ'ቲይንስ -ቅ- ዐሥራ ስ'ድስተ'ኛ

sixth

'ሲክስ -ቅ- ስ'ድስተ'ኛ

sixty

'ሲክስቲ -ቅ- ስድሳ (ስልሳ)

size

'ሳይዝ -ስ- መጠን ፣ ል'ክ

sizzle

'ሲዘል -ግ- ች'ስ ማለት [አለ] (ውሃ በእሳት ላይ ሲፈ'ስ)

skate

ስ'ኬይት -ግ- በበረዶ ላይ መንሸራተት [ተን ሸራ'ተተ] (ለመ'ጫጫት)

skein

ስ'ኬይን -ስ- ል'ታቂት (የጥጥ ፣ የሱፍ ወዘተ)

skeleton

ስ'ኬሌተን -ስ- ዐፅም (ሳይ'ለያ'ይ)

sketch

ስ'ኬች -ግ- መንደፍ [ነ'ደፈ] (ሥዕል)

-ስ- ንድፍ ፣ ሥዕል

skewer

ስከ'የወ -ስ- ሥጋ እየተሰ'ካ የ'ሚ'ጠ'በስ'በት ተ'ጥን ረ'ጅም ሹል ብረት

skid

ስ'ኪድ -ግ- መንሸራተት [ተንሸራ'ተተ] ፣ ማዳለጥ [አዳ'ለጠ]

skill

ስ'ኪል -ስ- ከ'ፍተ'ኛ ችሎታ ፣ ብልጎት ፣ ጥበብ (እንድ ነገር የመሥራት)

592

skilful
ስ'ኪልፉል -ቅ- ብልኅነተ'ኛ ፣ ጥበበ'ኛ

skim
'ስኪም -ግ- መገረፍ [ገ'ፈፈ] (ለስልባቦት)

skimp
ስ'ኪምፕ -ግ- የ'ማይበቃውን እሥራ ላይ ማዋል [አዋለ] ፣ የ'ሚበቃ አለመስጠት [-ሰ'ጠ]

skin
ስ'ኪን -ስ- ቆዳ

skinny
ስ'ኪኒ -ቅ- በጣም ከ'ሲ'ታ ፣ ቆዳው ከአጥንቱ ጋር የተጣ'በቀ

skip
ስ'ኪፕ -ግ- እንጣ'ጥ እንጣ'ጥ ማለት [አለ] ፣ ቻ'ላ ማለት [አለ] ፣ ማለፍ [አ'ለፈ]

skirmish
ስ'ከ:ሚሽ -ስ- ግ'ጭት (ቀ'ላል ፣ በወ'ታ'ደር መካ'ከል)

skirt
ስ'ክ:ት -ስ- ሽ'ርጥ

skulk
ስ'ከልክ -ግ- ማድባት [አደ'ባ] ፣ ቀ'ስ ብሎ ማምለጥ [አመ'ለጠ] (ከሥራ ላይ)

skull
'ስከል -ስ- ጭንቅ'ላት ፣ የራስ ቅል

sky
ስ'ካይ -ስ- ሰማይ

slack
ስ'ላክ -ቅ- ልል ፣ ቸ'ልተ'ኛ ፣ ሰነፍ

slam
ስ'ላም -ግ- በ'ር በጎይል መዝጋት [ዘ'ጋ] ፣ መደርገም [ደረ'ገመ]

slander
ስ'ላ:ንደ -ግ- ማማት [አ'ማ] ፣ ስም ማጥፋት [አጠ'ፋ]
-ስ- ሐሜት ፣ ስም ማጥፋት

slang
ስ'ላንግ -ስ- ተራ ቋንቋ (ለጽሑፍ የ'ማይበ'ጅ)

slant
ስ'ላ:ንት -ግ- መ'ዘቅዘቅ [ተዘቀ'ዘቀ] (ለመን ገድ ፣ ወዘተ)

slap
ስ'ላፕ -ግ- በጥ'ፊ መምታት [መ'ታ]

slash
ስ'ላሽ -ግ- መቦ'ደስ [በ'ደሰ] ፣ መብጣት [በ'ጣ] (በተለይ በምላ'ጭ) ፣ መገረፍ [ገ'ረፈ] (በአለንጋ)

slat
ስ'ላት -ስ- ቀ'ጭን እንጨት ፣ ብረት

slate
ስ'ሌት -ስ- ጽ'ላት (ለመጻፊያ)

slaughter
ስ'ሎ:ተ -ግ- ማረድ [አ'ረደ] ፣ መባረክ [ባ'ረከ]

slaughterhouse
ስ'ሎ:ተርሀውስ -ስ- ቤራ

slave
ስ'ሌቭ -ስ- ባሪያ

slavery
ስ'ሌቨሪ -ስ- ባር'ነት

slay
ስ'ሌይ -ግ- ማረድ [አ'ረደ] ፣ መግደል [ገ'ደለ]

sleek
ስ'ሊይክ -ቅ- ለስሳ'ሳ'ና ያማረ (ጥ'ሳሌ ፣ ለጠጉC)

sleep
ስ'ሊይፕ -ግ- ተኛ [መተ'ኛት] ፣ ማሳለፍ [አሳ'ለፈ] ጊዜን ፣ ሕመም ወዘተ

sleepy
ስ'ሊይፒ -ቅ- የደ'ከመው ፣ እንቅልፋም ፣ የፈ'ዘዘ

sleet
ስ'ሊይት -ስ- በረዶ (ከዝናም ጋር የተደባ'ለቀ)

sleeve
ስ'ሊይቭ -ስ- እ'ጅጌ

sleight
ስ'ላይት -ስ- የማ'ታለል ጨዋታ (በእ'ጅ ቅል ጥፍ'ና የ'ሚ'ሠ'ራ ወዘተ)

slender
ስ'ሌንደ -ቅ- ቀ'ጭን

slice
ስ'ላይስ -ግ- መቁረጥ [ቆ'ረጠ] (ሥሥ አድ ርጎ)

slide
ስ'ላይድ -ግ- መንሸራተት [ተንሸራ'ተተ]

slight
ስ'ላይት -ቅ- ት'ንሽ ፡ ጥቂት
   insult
   -ስ- ጽርፈት ፡ ማንጓጠጥ

slim
ስ'ሊም -ቅ- ቀ'ጭን (ለሰው)

slime
ስ'ላይም -ስ- ጭቃ (ቀ'ጭን)

sling
ስ'ሊንግ -ግ- መወርወር (ወረ'ወረ) ፡ መሲን
ጨፍ [ወነ'ጨፈ]
   -ስ- ወንጭፍ

slink
ስ'ሊንክ -ግ- ሹክ'ክ ብሎ መሄድ [ሄደ]

slip
ስ'ሊፕ -ግ- ማዳለጥ [አዳ'ለጠ]
   mistake
   -ስ- ስሕተት
   underclothes
   -ስ- የውስጥ ልብስ (የሴት)
   pillow-
   -ስ- የትራስ ልብስ

slippers
ስ'ሊፐርዝ -ስ- የቤት ጫ'ማ

slippery
ስ'ሊፐሪ -ቅ- አዳላጭ

slipshod
ስ'ሊፕሾድ -ቅ- ደንታ ቢስ (ለሥራ ፡ ለአ'ለባ
 በስ)

slit
ስ'ሊት -ግ- መብጣት [በ'ጣ]
   -ስ- ብጥ ፡ ብጣት

slogan
ስ'ለውገን -ስ- ዐረፍተ ነገር ፡ በቀ'ላሉ የ'ሚ
ጠና ሐረግ (የፖለቲካ ፡ ሕዝብ ለማ'ነሣሣት ፡
አንድ ነገር ለማሳ'ወቅ ፡ ያንድን ማኅበር
ዓላማ ለመግለጽ)

slop
ስ'ሎፕ -ግ- መ'ፈንጠቅ [ተፈነ'ጠቀ] ፡ ተርፎ
መፍሰስ [ፈ'ሰስ]
   -s
   -ስ- ቆሻሻ ውሃ (የወተ ቤት እ'ጣቢ)

slope
ስ'ለውፕ -ስ- ዳገት ፡ ዐቀበት ፡ ቁልቁለት

slot
ስ'ሎት -ስ- ቀዳዳ (የፖስታ ሣጥን ፡ መዘተ)

slothful
ስ'ለውስፉል -ቅ- ሰነፍ ፡ ሀኬተ'ኛ

slouch
ስ'ላውች -ግ- መ'ጐተት [ተጐ'ተተ] ፡ ተዝለ
ፍልፎ መ'ቀመጥ [ተቀ'መጠ]

slovenly
ስ'ለቭንሊይ -ቅ- ጠ'ፍ ያላለ ፡ ስለ ሥራው
የ'ማይ'ጠነ'ተቅ ፡ ያ'ደፈ ልብስ የለ'በሰ

slow
ስ'ለው -ቅ- ዝ'ግ ያለ ፡ ቀርፋ'ፋ

sludge
ስ'ለጅ -ስ- አተላ ፡ ዝ'ቃጭ ፡ ወፍራም ጭቃ ፡
ቁሻሻ ፡ ዝቆት ፡ ቅባት

slug
ስ'ለግ -ስ- የቅጠል ትል

sluggish
ስ'ለጊሽ -ቅ- ሰነፍ ፡ በፍጥነት የ'ማይሥራ ፡
ቀርፋ'ፋ

sluice
ስ'ሉ፡ስ -ስ- የ'ሚ'ከ'ፈት'ና የ'ሚ'ዘ'ጋ የውሃ
ማ'ገጃ (ለቦይ ውሃ መዘተ)

slum
ስ'ለም -ስ- ቁሻ'ሻ ያለ ሠፈር ፡ ንጽሕ'ና የሌ
'ለው ሠፈር ፡ መንደር

slumber
ስ'ለምበ -ግ- ማንቀላፋት [አንቀላ'ፋ]

slump
ስ'ለምፕ -ግ- መ'ደገፍ [ተደ'ገፈ] (ከድካም
የተነ'ሣ) ፡ ተዝለፍልፎ መ'ቀመጥ [ተቀ'መጠ]
   -ስ- የንግድ ዕቃ የ'ማይ'ነ'ሣ'ባት ጊዜ

slur
ስ'ለ፡ -ግ- መንተባተብ [ተነተባ'ተብ]
   -ስ- ማ'ዋረድ ፡ ነቀፌታ

slush
ስ'ለሽ -ስ- ማጥ (ለጭቃ) ፡ በከፊል የቀ'ለጠ
በረዶ

slut
ስ'ለት -ስ- አመንዝራ ፡ መጥፎ ስም ያ'ላት
ሴት

sly
ስ'ላይ -ቅ- አ'ታላይ ፡ ብልጣብልጥ ፡ በሥ
'ውር የ'ሚሠራ

594

smack

ስማክ -ግ- በጥ'ፊ መምታት [መ'ታ]
blow

    -ስ- ጥ'ፊ
taste

    -ስ- ጣዕም

small

ስ'ሞ:ል -ቅ- ት'ንሽ

smallpox

ስ'ሞ:ል፥ክስ -ስ- ፈንጣጣ

smart

ስማ:ት -ግ- ማ'ቃጠል [አ'ቃ'ጠለ] ፣ መለብ
ለብ [ለበ'ለበ] (ለቁስል)
well-dressed

    -ቅ- ጥሩ አድርጎ የለ'በሰ
clever

    -ቅ- ጮ'ሌ

smash

ስ'ማሽ -ግ- በጎይል መስበር [ሰ'በረ] ፣ መሰ
ባበር [ሰባ'በረ]

smattering

ስ'ማተሪንግ -ስ- ት'ንሽ ፣ ጥቂት ዕውቀት

smear

ስ'ሚየ -ግ- መቀ'ባት [ቀ'ባ] (በቅባት ነገር) ፣
መበ'ከል [በ'ከለ] (በቁሻሻ) ፣ ማ'በስ [አ'በሰ]
(ያ'ደፈ እጅ)

smell

ስ'ሜል -ግ- ማሽተት [አሽ'ተተ]

    -ስ- ሽ'ታ ፣ ክርፋት ፣ ግማት

smelt

ስ'ሜልት -ግ- ማቅለጥ [አቀ'ለጠ] (ብረት
ወዘተ)

smile

ስ'ማይል -ግ- ፈገ'ግ ማለት [አለ]

smite

ስ'ማይት -ግ- በጎይል መምታት [መ'ታ]

smith

ስ'ሚስ -ስ- ብረት ቀጥቃጭ ፣ ባላ'ጅ

smoke

ስ'መውክ -ግ- ጢስ [አጢስ] (ሲጃራ) ፣ መ
ጢስ [ጤስ]
of fire etc.

    -ስ- ጢስ

smoker

ስ'መውክ -ስ- ሲጃራ ጠ'ጪ ፣ ሲጃራ አጢያሽ

smoky

ስ'መውኪ -ቅ- ጭጋጋም (ለአ'የር) ፣ ጢሳሳም

smooth

ስ'ሙ:ዝ -ቅ- ለስላ'ሳ ፣ ያለ እንቅፋት የ'ሚንቀ
ሳ'ቀስ

smother

ስ'መዠ -ግ- በጭቅ አ'ፍኖ መግደል [ገ'ደለ]፣
አንቆ መግደል [ኮ'ደለ]

smoulder

ስ'መውልደ -ግ- ነበልባል ሳይኖረው ቀስ በ
ቀ'ስ መ'ቃጠል [ተ'ቃጠለ]

smudge

ስ'መጅ -ግ- መበ'ከል [በ'ከለ] (በቁሻሻ)

smug

ስ'መግ -ቅ- ግ'ብዝ ፣ በራሱ ታ'ላቅ'ነት ወይ
ን'ም ደጋን'ነት የ'ሚ'ደ'ሰት

smuggle

ስ'መገል -ግ- ቀረጥ ያልተከ'ፈለ'በት ዕቃ
አገር ውስጥ ማስገ'ባት [አስገ'ባ] ፣ ወይን'ም
ካገር ማውጣት [አወ'ጣ] ፣ የኮንትሮባንድ ሥራ
መሥራት [ሠ'ራ]

smut

ስ'መት -ስ- ጉድፍ
obscenity

    -ስ- ብልግ'ና

snack

ስ'ናክ -ስ- ቀ'ላል ምግብ ፣ ቁርስ ፣ መቅሰሰ

snag

ስ'ናግ -ስ- እንቅፋት ፣ ች'ግር (ድንገተ'ኛ)

snail

ስ'ኔይል -ስ- ቀንድ አውጣ

snake

ስ'ኔይክ -ስ- እባብ

snap

ስ'ናፕ -ስ- ቀ'ጭ ማለት
of dog

    -ግ- መንከስ [ነ'ከስ] ፣ ለቀ'ም ማድረግ
[አደ'ረገ] (ለው'ሻ በጥርስ)
answer rudely

    -ግ- በቁ'ጣ መመ'ለስ [መ'ለስ]

snare

ስ'ኔየ -ስ- ወጥመድ

595

snarl
ስ'ናːል -ግ- ጥርስ አውጥቶ መጮኽ [ጮ'ኸ] (ለውሻ በተቆ'ጣ ጊዜ) ፣ እም'ሮ መ'ናገር [ተና'ገረ]

snatch
ስ'ናች -ግ- መቀ'ማት [ቀ'ማ] ፣ መንጠቅ [ነ'ጠቀ] ፣ መመንጨቅ [መነ'ጨቀ]

sneak
ስ'ኒይክ -ግ- ማድባት [አደ'ባ]
-ስ- ስብቅያ ፣ ስብቀት

sneer
ስ'ኒየ -ግ- በፈገግታ በሰው ላይ ማፌዝ [አፌዘ] ፣ መዘ'በት [ዘ'በተ]

sneeze
ስ'ኒይዝ -ግ- ማንጠስ [አነ'ጠሰ]

sniff
ስ'ኒፍ -ግ- ባፍንጫ መሳብ [ሳበ]

snip
ስ'ኒፕ -ግ- መቁረጥ [ቆ'ረጠ] (በመቀስ)

sniper
ስ'ናይፐ -ስ- የመ'ሽገ ነፍጠ'ኛ ፣ ያደ'ፈጠ ነፍጠ'ኛ

snivel
ስ'ኒቨል -ግ- መ'ነባረር [ተነባ'ረረ] ፣ ማል ቀስ [አለ'ቀሰ] (ለሕፃን)

snob
ስ'ኖብ -ስ- ኩራተ'ኛ ፣ ሰው የ'ሚንቅ ፣ ያላ ቅሙ የ'ሚንጠራ'ራ ፣ ውʼጥር

snore
ስ'ኖː -ግ- ማንኮራፋት [አንኮራ'ፋ] ፣ ማኩ ረፍ [አኩ'ረፈ] (በእንቅልፍ)

snort
ስ'ኖːት -ግ- ፉ'ር ማለት [አለ] (ለፈረስ)

snout
ስ'ናውት -ስ- የእንስሳት አፍንጫ (እንደ ዐሣ ማ አፍንጫ ያለ)

snow
ስ'ነው -ግ- ጥጥ የ'ሚመስል በረዶ (አመዳይ)

snub
ስ'ነብ -ግ- ማሳ'ፈር [አሳ'ፈረ]
-nosed
-ቅ- ት'ንሽ ደፍጣ'ጣ ከወደጫፉ ቀና ያለ አፍንጫ ያ'ለው

snuff
ስ'ነፍ -ስ- ሱ'ረት ፣ ስንቆ

snug
ስ'ነግ -ቅ- ሙቀት ያ'ለው'ና ም'ቹ (ለቤት)

snuggle
ስ'ነገል -ግ- መ'ታከክ [ታ'ከከ] (ለም'ቾት ፣ ለሙቀት)

so
'ሰው -ተግ- እንደ'ዚህ
very
-ተግ- በጣም
that
-ተግ- እንዲህ (ነው)

soak
'ሰውክ -ግ- በውሃ መዘፍዘፍ [ዘፈ'ዘፈ] ፣ መን ከር [ነ'ከረ]

soap
'ሰውፕ -ስ- ሳሙና

soapsuds
'ሰውፕሰድዝ -ስ- የሳሙና አረፋ

soar
'ሶː -ግ- መምጠቅ [መ'ጠቀ] ፣ ርቆ ወደላይ መብረር [በ'ረረ]

sob
'ሶብ -ግ- እየተንሰቀ'ሰቁ ማልቀስ [አለ'ቀሰ]

sober
'ሰውበ -ቅ- ያልሰ'ከረ ፣ እራሱን የ'ሚ'ቆ'ጣ 'ጠር

sociable
'ሰውሸበል -ቅ- ተግባቢ ፣ ትብ'ብር ፣ ወዳ ጅ'ነት የ'ሚያሳ'ይ

social
'ሰውሸል -ቅ- ማኅበራዊ ፣ ከሌሎ'ች ጋር አብ ሮ የ'ሚኖር

society
ሶ'ሳየቲ -ስ- ማኅበር

sock
'ሶክ -ስ- የግር ሹ'ራብ (አ'ጭር)

socket
'ሶከት -ስ- መሰ'ኪያ (የኤሌክትሪክ ወዘተ) ፣ ያይን ጉድጓድ

sofa
'ሰውፈ -ስ- ሶፋ ፣ ረ'ጅም ም'ቾት ያ'ለው ባለ መ'ደገፊያ ወንበር (ል'ብም ወንበር)

soft
’ሶፍት -ቅ- ለስላ'ሳ
soil
’ሶይል -ግ- ማፉ'ሸሸ [አፉ'ሸሸ]
earth
-ስ- ዐፈር
solace
’ሰወለስ -ግ- ማጽናናት [አጽና'ና]
-ስ- የ'ሚያጽና'ና ፣ ጥንቅ የ'ሚቀ'ንስ
solar
’ሰውለ -ቅ- የፀሐይ
solder
’ሶልደ -ግ- መበ'የድ [በ'የደ]
soldier
’ሶልጀ -ስ- ወ'ታ'ደር
sole
’ሶውል -ቅ- ብ'ቻ
exclusive
-ቅ- የተለ'የ
solemn
’ሶለም -ቅ- የተከ'በረ'ና ጸጥ ያለ ፣ ተከ'ባሪ ፣
ክብረ በዓላዊ
solicitous
ሰ'ሊሲተስ -ቅ- ደ'ግ አ'ሳቢ (ለሌሎች) ፤
አንድ ነገር ለመሥራት የ'ሚጓጓ ፤ በጣም
ጥንቁቅ (ለጥቃ'ቅን ነገር'ች)
solid
’ሶሊድ -ቅ- ጠንካ'ራ ፣ ብርቱ ፣ ጥኑ
solidarity
ሶሊ'ዳሪቲ -ስ- ጓብረት ፣ አንድ'ነት (ለጋራ
ጥቅም)
solitary
’ሶለትሪ -ቅ- ብ'ቸ'ኛ
solitude
’ሶሊትዩ፡ድ -ስ- ብ'ቸ'ኝ'ነት
solution
ሰ'ሉሽን -ስ- መፍትሔ
answer
-ስ- መልስ (ለሒ.ሳብ)
chemical
-ስ- የተቀ'መሠ
solve
’ሶልቭ -ግ- መፍትሔ ማግኘት [አገ'ኘ] ፣ ማው
ጣት [አወ'ጣ] (ለሒ.ሳብ)

sombre
’ሶምበ -ስ- ጥቁግ'ግ ያለው ፣ የጠ'ቆረ
some
’ሰም -ቅ ፣ ተስ- ጥቂት ፣ አንዳንድ
somewhat
’ሰምዋት -ተግ- በመጠኑ
somebody
’ሰምበዲ -ስ- አንድ ሰው
somehow
’ሰምሀው -ተግ- እንደ ምን'ም
someone
’ሰምወን -ስ- አንድ ሰው
something
’ሰምቴ'ንግ -ስ- አንድ ነገር ፣ ነገር
sometime
’ሰምታይም -ተግ- አንድ ጊዜ
somewhere
’ሰምዌየ -ተግ- አንድ ቦታ ፣ የት'ም
son
’ሰን -ስ- ልጅ (ተባዕት)
song
’ሶንግ -ስ- ዘፈን ፣ መዝሙር
son-in-law
’ሰንኢሎ፡ -ስ- አማች ፣ የልጅ ባል
soon
’ሱ፡ን -ተግ- በፍጥነት ፣ አሁኑን
soot
’ሱ፡ት -ስ- ጥቀርሻ ፣ ጥላሸት
soothe
’ሱ፡ዝ -ግ- ን'ዶት ፣ ቁ'ጣ ማ'በረድ [አ'በ'ረ
ደ] ፣ ሕመም ፣ ውጋት ማብረድ [አበ'ረደ]
sop
’ሶፕ -ስ- ማባበያ ፣ ዝ'ም ማ'ሰ'ኛ ፤ ፍትፍት
sophisticated
ሰፈስቴ'ኬይተድ -ቅ- የሠለ'ጠነ ፣ ከተሜ ፣
ዘበናይ
sordid
’ሶ፡ዲድ -ቅ- ቆሻሻ ፣ ወ'ራ'ዳ (አመል) ፣
ም'ቸ ያልሆነ ፣ አሳ'ዛኝ (ለሁኔታ)
sorcerer
’ሶ፡ሰረ -ስ- አስማተ'ኛ ፣ ጠንቋይ
sore
’ሶ፡ -ስ- ቁስል
-ቅ- የቆ'ሰለ

597

sorghum
'ሱ፣ገም -ስ- ማሸ'ላ
sorrow
'ሶረው -ስ- ሐዘን
sorry(to be)
'ሶሪ -ግ- ማዘን [አ'ዘነ] ፣ መፀ'ፀት [ተፀ'ፀተ]
sort
'ሶ፡ት -ግ- መለ'የት [ለ'የ] (በወገን በወገኑ)
soul
'ሰውል -ስ- ነፍስ
sound
'ሳውንድ -ስ- ድምፅ
   in health
   -ቅ- ጤና'ማ
   structurally firm
   -ቅ- ጠንካ'ራ
soup
'ሱፕ -ስ- ሾርባ
sour
'ሳወ -ቅ- የኮመ'ጠጠ ፣ ኮምጣ'ጣ
source
'ሶ፡ስ -ስ- ምንጭ ፣ አንድ ነገር የ'ሚ'ገ'ኝ'በት
ሥር
south
'ሳውስ -ስ- ደቡብ
southern
'ሰጠን -ቅ- ደቡባዊ
southward
'ሰውስወደ -ተግ- ወደ ደቡብ
sovereign
'ሶቭሪን -ስ- ንጉሥ ፣ ነጻ መንግሥት ፣ ጠቅ
ላይ መሪ (አ'መራር)
   -ቅ- ራሱን የቻለ የመንግሥት ግዛት፣
ነጻ (ንጉሥ ፣ መንግሥት)
sow
'ሰው -ግ- መዝራት [ዘ'ራ]
sow
'ሳው -ስ- እንስት ዐሣማ
space
ስ'ፔይስ -ስ- ቦታ
   outer-
   -ስ- ጠፈር
   seating
   -ስ- መ'ቀመጫ ፣ ማረፊያ (ለቦታ)

spacious
ስ'ፔይሸስ -ቅ- ሰ'ፊ ቦታ
spade
ስ'ፔይድ -ስ- አካፋ
span
ስ'ፓን -ቅ- ስፋት (የቦታ ወይን'ም የጊዜ)
   -ስ- ስንዝር
spank
ስ'ፓንክ -ግ- መምታት [መ'ታ] (ለሕፃናት
በተለ'ይ እመ'ቀመጫ ላይ)
spanner
ስ'ፓነ -ስ- መፍቻ (ኪያቬ)
spare
ስ'ፔየ -ግ- መተው [ተወ] ፣ ማዳን [አዳነ]
   extra
   -ስ- መለወ'ጫ (ዕቃ)
   not wanted
   -ቅ- ሌላ ፣ ትርፍ
spark
ስ'ፓ፡ክ -ስ- የሳት ፍን'ጣቂ
sparkle
ስ'ፓ፡ክል -ግ- ማብለጥለጥ [አብለጨ'ለጨ]
sparse
ስ'ፓ፡ስ -ቅ- ች'ፍግ ያላለ ፣ የሣ'ሣ (ለጠጉር ፣
ለሣር ወዘተ)
spasm
ስ'ፓዝም -ስ- ድንገተ'ኛ እንቅስ'ቃሴ (የሰው
'ነት)
spasmodic
ስፓዝ'ሞዲክ -ቅ- አልፎ አልፎ የ'ሚሆን ፣
ጊዜ እ'ያሳ'ለፈ ደጋገም የ'ሚሆን
spatter
ስ'ፓተ -ግ- መ'ረጨት [ተረ'ጨ] ፣ መርጨት
[ረ'ጨ]
spawn
ስ'ፓ፡ን -ስ- የንቁራሪት ፣የዐሣ ወዘተ እንቁ
ላል
   -ግ- እንቁላል መጣል [ጣለ] (ለእንቁራ
ሪት ፣ ለዐሣ)
speak
ስ'ፒየክ -ግ- መ'ናገር [ተና'ገረ]
spear
ስ'ፒየ -ግ- መውጋት [ወ'ጋ] (በጦር)
   -ስ- ጦር

598

special
ስ'ፔሻል -ቅ- ል'ዩ ፣ የተለ'የ
specific
ስፒ'ሲፊክ -ቅ- የተወ'ሰነ ፣ የተለ'የ
specimen
ስ'ፔሲመን -ስ- ለዓይነት ያህል የ'ሚቀርብ
ነገር
specious
ስ'ፒይሽስ -ቅ- ጥሩ መሳይ ፣ እውነት መሳይ
speck
ስ'ፔክ -ስ- ነቁጥ ፣ ጉድፍ
speckled
ስ'ፔክልድ -ቅ- ነቁጣም ፣ ባለነቁጥ ፣ ዝንጉር
ጉር
spectacle
ስ'ፔክተክል -ስ- ትርኢት
spectacles
ስ'ፔክተክልዝ -ስ- መነ'ጥር ፣ መነ'ጽር
spectator
ስፔክ'ቴይተ -ስ- ተመልካች (አንድ ትርኢት)
spectre
ስ'ፔክተ -ስ- መንፈስ (የ'ሚ'ታይ) ፤ ወደፊት
ስለ'ሚመጣው ች'ግር ወዘተ የ'ሚያስጨ'ነቅ
ፍርሃት
speculate
ስ'ፔክዩሌይት -ግ- ግ'መዛ [አ'መዛ] ፣
በአእምሮ ወደፊት የ'ሚሆነውን ግወቅ [ወ'ወቅ]
in business
-ግ- ወደፊት ያተርፈ'ኛል ብሎ መግ
ዛት [ገ'ዛ] ፣ መሸጥ [ሸጠ]
speech
ስ'ፒይች -ስ- ንግ'ግር
speed
ስ'ፒይድ -ስ- ፍጥነት
spell
ስ'ፔል -ግ- አ'ጸጸፍ
of time
-ስ- ጊዜ (አ'ጭር)
magic
-ስ- ድግምት (የጥንቆላ)
spend
ስ'ፔንድ -ግ- ግጥፋት [አጠ'ፋ] (ለገንዘብ)
time
-ግ- ግሳ'ለፍ [አሳ'ለፈ] (ለጊዜ)

sperm
ስ'ፐ፡ም -ስ- ዘር (ጎጢአት)
sphere
ስ'ፊየ -ስ- ክበብ
spherical
ስ'ፌሪከል -ቅ- ክ'ብ
spice
ስ'ፓይስ -ግ- መቀ'መም [ቀ'መመ]
-ስ- ቅመም
spicy
ስ'ፓይሲ -ቅ- የተቀ'መመ ፣ የተመ'ጠነ
ቅመም ያለ'በት
spider
ስ'ፓይደ -ስ- ሸረሪት
spike
ስ'ፓይክ -ስ- የሾለ ብረት ወይን'ም እንጨት ፤
የእሀል እሸት
spill
ስ'ፒል -ግ- ግፍሰስ [አፈ'ሰሰ]
-ስ- ግ'ቀጣጠያ (ለእሳት)
spin
ስ'ፒን -ግ- መፍተል [ፈ'ተለ] ፣ ግሾር [አሾረ]
(በግዞር)
spinach
ስ'ፒነች -ስ- ጎ'መን (ስፒናች)
spindle
ስ'ፒንደል -ስ- ቀለም ፣ ግቅለሚያ ፣ ግጠን
ጠ'ኛ
spine
ስ'ፓይን -ስ- አ'ከርካሪ ፤ የሾለ ነገር (ም'ሳሌ ፣
የጃርት ወስፈንጠር ፣ እሾሀ)
spinster
ስ'ፒንስተ -ስ- ሳዱ'ላ ፣ ያላገ'ባች ሴት
spiny
ስ'ፓይኒ -ቅ- እሾኽ'ማ ፣ ሹል ነገር የበ'ዛ'በት ፣
ያለ'በት
spiral
ስ'ፓይረል -ቅ- ጠምዛ'ዛ ፣ ካንድ ነጥብ እ'የ
ዞረ'ና እ'የሰ'ፋ የ'ሚሄድ
spire
ስ'ፓየ -ስ- ረ'ጅም'ና ሾጣጣ የሆነ (የቤተ
ክርስቲያን ወዘተ) ጫፍ

599

spirit
ስ'ፒረት -ሱ- መንፈስ
zeal
-ሱ- ወ'ኔ
alcohol
-ሱ- አልኮል (መጠ'ጥ)
mood
-ሱ- ሁናቴ

spirit-lamp
ስ'ፒረት'ላምፕ -ሱ- ላምባ ፣ ኩ'ራዝ

spiritual
ስ'ፒረቸዌል -ቅ- መንፈሳዊ

spit
ስ'ፒ፡ት -ግ- እንት'ፍ ማለት [አለ] ፣ መትፋት
[ተፋ]
for roasting
-ሱ- ረ'ጅም ብረት (ለሥጋ መጥበሻ)

spite
ስ'ፓይት -ሱ- ጥላ'ቻ
in-of
-ተግ- ምን'ም እንኳ(ን)

spiteful
ስ'ፓይትፉል -ቅ- ተንኳሽ (ለጥል)

splash
ስፕ'ላሽ -ግ- መርጨት [ረ'ጨ]

splendid
ስፕ'ሌንጺድ -ቅ- ድንቅ
-ተግ- ባገፍ ፣ በብዛት

splice
ስፕ'ላይስ -ግ- መቀ'ጠል [ቀ'ጠለ] (ገመድ
በመፍተል ፣ እንጨት አንዱን ካንዱ ውስጥ
በመሰ'ካት)

splint
ስፕ'ሊንት -ሱ- መጠ'ገኛ (እንጨት ፣ ለተሰ
'በረ ዐጥንት)

splinter
ስፕ'ሊንተ -ሱ- ሹል ስን'ጣሪ ፣ ስ'ባሪ (የን
ጨት ፣ የደንጊያ ፣ የመስተዋት ወዘተ)

split
ስፕ'ሊት -ግ- መሠንጠቅ [ሠነ'ጠቀ]

splutter
ስፕ'ለተ -ግ- መንተባተብ [ተንተባ'ተብ] (ከድ
ን'ጋጤ የተነ'ሣ) ፣ መርጨት [ረ'ጨ] (ቀለም
ከብእር)

spoil
ስ'ፖይል -ግ- ማጥፋት [አጠ'ፋ] ፣ ማ'በላሸት
[አ'በላ'ሸ]

spokesman
ስ'ፐውክስመን -ሱ- ቃል አቀ'ባይ ፣ በአንድ
ማኅበር ስም ተናጋሪ

sponge
ስ'ፐንጅ -ሱ- ሰፍነግ

sponsor
ስ'ፖንስ -ሱ- ጓላፊ ፤ የክርስት'ና አ'ባት ፤ ተጠ
'ያቂ

spontaneous
ስፖን'ቴይኒየስ -ቅ- ያለመ'ዘጋጀት ፣ ድንገ
ተ'ኛ ፣ በስ'ሜት የተሠ'ራ

spool
ስ'ፑ፡ል -ሱ- ማጠንጠኛ ፣ በከራ

spoon
ስ'ፑ፡ን -ሱ- ማንካ ፣ ማንኪያ

sporadic
ስፐ'ራዲክ -ቅ- አልፎ አልፎ የ'ሚሆን ፣ የ'ሚ
'ደ'ረግ ፣ የ'ሚ'ታ'ይ

sport
ስ'ፖ፡ት -ሱ- ስፖርት

spout
ስ'ፓውት -ሱ- አፍ ፣ ጡት (የጀበና ፣ የማንቄ
ርቆሪያ ወዘተ)

sprain
ስፕ'ሬይን -ግ- ወለ'ም ማለት [አለ]
-ሱ- ወለምታ

sprawl
ስፕ'ሮ፡ል -ግ- መ'ጋደም [ተጋ'ደመ] ፣ መ'ዘ
ረር [ተዘ'ረረ]

spray
ስፕ'ሬይ -ግ- መርጨት [ረ'ጨ] (መድኃኒት ፣
ፈሳሽ)
-ሱ- የ'ሚ'ረ'ጭ ነገር

spread
ስፕ'ሬድ -ግ- መስፋፋት [ተስፋ'ፋ] ፣ መ'ዘ
ርጋት [ተዘረ'ጋ] ፤ መቀ'ባት [ቀ'ባ] (ቅቤ)

spree
ስፕ'ሪይ -ሱ- የደ'መቀ ት'ንሽ በዐል ፤ ድንገ
ተ'ኛ የጣባይ መ'ለወጥ (በመጠ'ጥ'ና በዝ'ሙት
ወዘተ)

sprightly
ስፕ'ራይትሊ -ቅ- ቀልጣ'ፋ ፣ ንቁ

600

spring ስፕ'ሪንግ -ስ- ም'ላ ፣ የተወ'ጠረ'ና የ'ሚያረ ገ'ርግ ሽቦ
season
-ስ- ጸደይ
jump
-ግ- መዝለል [ዘ'ለለ]
a jump
-ስ- ዝ'ላይ
water
-ስ- ምንጭ

springy ስፕ'ሪንጊ -ቅ- አረገራጊ ፣ የ'ሚያነጥር

sprinkle ስፕ'ሪንክል -ግ- መርጨት [ረ'ጨ] ፣ ግርከፍ ከፍ [አርከፈ'ከፈ]

sprint ስፕ'ሪንት -ግ- መርጥ [ርጠ] ፣ መሽቀዳደም [ተሽቀዳ'ደመ] (አ'ጭር ርቀት)

sprout ስፕ'ራውት -ግ- ማቆንጐል [አቆነ'ጐለ]

spruce ስፕ'ሩ፡ስ -ቅ- ልብስ ያማረ'በት ፣ የተሽቀረ 'ቀረ

spry ስፕ'ራይ -ቅ- ቀልጣ'ፋ ፣ ንቁ

spur ስ'ፐ፡ -ግ- ማ'ጃገን [አ'ጃ'ገነ] ፤ መኰልኰል [ኰለ'ኰለ] (ለፈረስ ፣ ለበቅሎ)
-ስ- በፈረስ'ኛ ጫ'ማ ላይ ያለ የፈረስ መኰልኰያ ብረት

spurn ስ'ፐ፡ን -ግ- ማ'ባረር [አ'ባ'ረረ] (በጥላ'ቻ)

spurt ስ'ፐ፡ት -ግ- ፍትል'ክ ማለት [አለ] (ለሰው) ፣ ፈ'ን ማለት [አለ] (ለፈሳሽ)

spy ስ'ፓይ -ግ- መሰ'ለል [ሰ'ለለ]
-ስ- ሰ'ላይ

squabble ስክ'ዋበል -ግ- እ'የሮጬኩ መ'ከራከር [ተከራ 'ከረ] (በ'ማይረባ ነገር)

squalid ስክ'ዋሊድ -ቅ- ቁሻሻ ፣ እድፋም ፣ አ'ፀ'ያፊ፤ ድህ'ነት ያ*ጦ'ቃ*ው

squall ስክ'ዎ፡ል -ስ- ድንገተ'ኛ ነፋስ (ይበልጡን ከቦ ረዶ'ና ከዝናም ጋር የተደባ'ለቀ)

squander ስክ'ዎንደ -ግ- ማባከን [አባ'ከነ] ፣ መንዛት [ነ'ዛ] (ለገንዘብ ወዘተ)

square ስክ'ዌየ -ቅ- አራት ማዕዘን
piazza
-ስ- አ'ደባባይ

squash ስክ'ዎሽ -ግ- መጭመቅ [ጨ'መቀ]
-ቅ- ጭ'ማቂ (የሎ'ሚ የብርቱካን ወዘተ)፤ ት'ንሽ ዱ'ባ ፣ ዙ'ኪኒ

squat ስክ'ዎት -ግ- ያለፈቃድ በሰው ቦታ ፣ ሕንፃ ውስጥ መ'ቀመጥ [ተቀ'መጠ]

squeak ስክ'ዊይክ -ግ- ሲ'ጥ ማለት [አለ]

squeal ስክ'ዊይል -ግ- መጮኽ [ጮኸ] (ለትን'ንሽ እንስሳት ፣ ከፍርሃት'ና ከሥቃይ የተነ'ሣ)

squeeze ስኪ'ዊይዝ -ግ- መጭመቅ [ጨ'መቀ] ፣ ማፍ ረጥረጥ [አፍረጠ'ረጠ]

squint ስክ'ዊንት -ግ- መንሽዋረር [ተንሽዋ'ረረ]
-ስ- መንሽዋረር

squirt ስክ'ወ፡ት -ግ- ፈ'ን ማለት [አለ] ፣ ፍጭ'ጭ ማለት [አለ]

stab ስ'ታብ -ግ- መወጋት [ወ'ጋ] (በስለት)

stable ስ'ቴይበል -ስ- ጋጣ (የፈረስ)
firm
-ቅ- ጽኑ ፣ የተደላ'ደለ

stack ስ'ታክ -ስ- ክ'ምር (የድርቆሽ ፣ የ*ጠ*ር) ፤ በደ ምብ የተደረ'ደሩ መጽሐፍት ፣ እንጨት ወዘተ)

stadium ስ'ቴይዲየም -ስ- የስፖርት ክ'ብ ሜዳ ፣ ስታ ዲየም

staff

ስ'ታ:ፍ -ስ- ሠ'ራተ'ኞ'ች (ከአንድ አለቃ ሥር ያ'ሉ)
stick

-ስ- ምርኩዝ ፣ ዘንግ

stage

ስ'ቴይጅ -ስ- ከ'ፍተ'ኛ ቦታ (በቴአትር) ፣ መድረክ
of journey

-ስ- መናኽሪያ

stagger

ስ'ታገ -ግ- መንገዳገድ [ተንገዳ'ገደ]

stagnant

ስ'ታገነንት -ቅ- የ'ማይንቀሳ'ቀስ ፣ የታ'ገደ (ው'ሃ)
inactive

-ቅ- እርም'ጃ የ'ማያሳ'ይ ፣ መ'ሻሻል የ'ማያሳ'ይ

staid

ስ'ቴይድ -ቅ- እርም'ጃ የ'ማይወ'ድ

stain

ስ'ቴይን -ግ- መበ'ከል [በ'ከለ]
-ስ- እድፍ

stair

ስ'ቴየ -ስ- ደረጃ (የቤት) ፣ ዕርከን

staircase

ስ'ቴየኬይስ -ስ- ደረጃዎ'ች (የቤት)

stake

ስ'ቴይክ -ስ- ችካል ፤ ለውር'ርድ የተተ'መጠ ገንዘብ

stale

ስ'ቴይል -ቅ- ደረቅ ፣ ያረ'ጀ (ዳ'ቦ ፣ ወዘተ)

stalk

ስ'ቶ:ክ -ግ- ግድባት [አደ'ባ] (ወደ አደን ለመድረስ)
of plant

-ስ- አገዳ

stall

ስ'ቶ:ል -ስ- ጋጣ ፤ የከብት ማ'ጐሪያ (ለአንድ ከብት)

-ግ- ወደ ጓላ ግለት [አለ]

stallion

ስ'ታሊየን -ስ- ያልተኰላ'ሸ ፈረስ (ተባዕት)

stamina

ስ'ታመነ -ስ- አለመድከም ፣ ንቃት

stammer

ስ'ታመ -ግ- መንተጥተጥ [ተንተጠ'ጠጠ] (ለን ግ'ግር ቃል በመደጋገም)

stamp

ስ'ታምፕ -ግ- ግ'ተም [አ'ተመ]
with foot

-ግ- መርገጥ [ረ'ገጠ]
official mark

-ስ- ግንተም
postage

-ስ- ቴምብር

stand

ስ'ታንድ -ግ- መቆም [ቆመ] ፣ አለመ'ለወጥ [-ተለ'ወጠ] ፤ መ'ታገሥ [ታ'ገሠ]

standard

ስ'ታንደርድ -ስ- መለ'ኪያ (ለሌሎ'ች ነገ ር'ች)
flag

-ስ- የቤተ መንግሥት ሰንደቅ ዓላማ
normal

-ቅ- የተለ'መደ

star

ስ'ታ: -ስ- ኮከብ

starch

ስ'ታ:ች -ስ- የልብስ ግድረቂያ ዱቄት ፤ በዱ ቄት ውስጥ የ'ሚ'ገ'ኝ የምግብ ዓይነት

stare

ስ'ቴየ -ግ- አፍ'ጦ ግየት [አ'የ] ፣ ት'ኩር ብሎ ግየት [አ'የ]

stark

ስ'ታ:ክ -ቅ- የተራ'ቆተ ፣ ባዶ (ለመሬት) ፤ ደረቅ ፣ ራቁት (ለሰውነ'ት)

start

ስ'ታ:ት -ግ- መጀ'መር [ጀ'መረ] ፤ መወ'ጠን [ወ'ጠነ]

startling

ስ'ታ:ትሊንግ -ቅ- አስጠ'ራሚ ፣ አስፈ'ሪ

starve

ስ'ታ:ቭ -ግ- መ'ራብ [ተራ'ብ]፤ በራብ መ'ሠ ቃየት [ተሠቃ'የ]

state

ስ'ቴይት -ስ- አገር'ና ሕዝብ (በመንግሥት የ'ሚ'ተዳ'ደር)

602

condition

  -ስ- ሁኔቴ

say

  -ግ- መ'ናገር [ተና'ገረ] (እንድ ነገር)

governmental

  -ት- መንግሥታዊ

stately

ስ'ቴይትሊ. -ት- የተከ'በረ ፣ ባላገርግ

statement

ስ'ቴይትመንት -ስ- ንግ'ግር ፣ መግለጫ

statesman

ስ'ቴይትስመን -ስ- ታ'ላቅ የመንግሥት ባለ ሥልጣን

station

ስ'ቴይሸን -ስ- ጣቢያ ፣ ግቆሚያ

  position

    -ስ- ደረጃ (ግዕረግ)

  railway

    -ስ- ለጓዝ ፣ ባቡር ጣቢያ

  place

    -ግ- ዘብ ግቆም [አቆም]

stationery

ስ'ቴይሸነሪ -ስ- የጽሕፈት መ'ሣሪያ

statistics

ስታ'ቲስቲክስ -ስ- የል'ዩ ል'ዩ ነገር'ች ዝር ዝር ሒሳብ

statue

ስ'ታቹ -ስ- ሐውልት

stature

ስ'ታቸ -ስ- ቁመት ፣ እርዝግኔ

  standing

    -ስ- ግዕረግ

status

ስ'ቴይተስ -ስ- ሁኔቴ ፣ ግዕረግ

statute

ስ'ታቹት -ስ- ሕግ (ሕግ አውጭዎ'ች ያወ ጡት)

staunch

ስ'ቶንች -ት- ታ'ማኝ ፣ እምነት የሚ'ጣል 'በት ፣ ቀ'ጥተ'ኛ (ለጓ'ደ'ኛና፣በሐ'ሳብ ለ'ሚ

ደ'ግፉ)

  -ግ- ከቁስል ደም እንዳይፈ'ስ ግቆም [አቆም]

stave

ስ'ቴይቭ -ስ- ፉ'ላ ፣ በ'ትር

  off-

    -ግ- ለጊዜው መከልከል [ከለ'ከለ] ፣ ለጊዜው ግራት [አራቀ] (አደጋ ፣ መዐት ወዘተ)

stay

ስ'ቴይ -ግ- መቆ'የት [ቆ'የ] ፣ መኖር [ኖረ]

stead

ስ'ቴድ -ስ- ቦታ ፣ ፋንታ (በሌላ)

steadfast

ስ'ቴድፋስት -ት- ታ'ማ'ኝ ፣ የ'ማይ'ለ'ወጥ

steady

ስ'ቴዲ -ት- ታ'ማኝ ፣ የ'ማያ'ወላ'ውል የ'ማይ'ና'ወጥ ፣ የጸ'ና

steal

ስ'ቲይል -ግ- መስረቅ [ሰ'ረቀ]

stealthy

ስ'ቴልሲ -ት- በጥን'ቃቄ'ና በስ'ውር የተደ 'ረገ

steam

ስ'ቲይም -ስ- እንፋሎት

steamer

ስ'ቲይም -ስ- መርከብ (በሞቶር የ'ሚ'ነ'ዳ)

steel

ስ'ቲይል -ስ- ብረት

steep

ስ'ቲይፕ -ት- ኅር'ው ያለ ፣ ቀ'ጥ ያለ (ገደል)

steeple

ስ'ቲይፕል -ስ- ቁንጮ ፣ ጫፍ (የቤተ ክርስ ቲያን)

steer

ስ'ቲየ -ግ- መንዳት [ነ'ዳ] (ለመኪና ወዘተ)

stem

ስ'ቴም -ስ- ግንድ

stench

ስ'ቴንች -ስ- መጥፎ ሽ'ታ ፣ ክርፋት ፣ ግማት

step

ስ'ቴፕ -ግ- መ'ራመድ [ተራ'መደ]

603

grade, stair

-ሰ- ደረጃ (የቤት)

pace

-ሰ- እርም'ጃ

measure

-ሰ- ው'ሳኔ

stepbrother

ስ'ቴፕብረዘ -ሰ- የሚስት ወይን'ም የባል ወን
ድ'ም

stepchild

ስ'ቴፕቻይድ -ሰ- የንጀራ ልጅ

stepdaughter

ስ'ቴፕዶ:ተ -ሰ- የንጀራ ልጅ (እንስት)

stepfather

ስ'ቴፕፋ:ዘ -ሰ- የንጀራ አ'ባት

stepmother

ስ'ቴፕመዘ -ሰ- የንጀራ እ'ናት

stepsister

ስ'ቴፕሲስተ -ሰ- የንጀራ እ'ናት ወይን'ም የእ
ንጀራ አ'ባት ሴት ልጅ

stepson

ስ'ቴፕሰን -ሰ- የንጀራ ልጅ (ወንድ)

stereotyped

ስ'ቲሪየታይፕት -ቅ- ገልባጭ ፣ እራሱ ሐ'ሳብ
ማፍለቅ የ'ማይችል

sterile

ስ'ቴራይል -ቅ- መ'ካን ፣ የተከላ'ሽ ፣ የተቀ
ጠ'ቀጠ (እንስሳ)

clean

-ቅ- ንጹሕ ፣ ከተውሳክ የነጻ

stew

ስት'የዉ: -ግ- ወጥ መሥራት [ሠ'ራ]

-ሰ- ወጥ

steward

ስት'ዩወድ -ሰ- የመሬት ወ'ኪል ፣ የመሬት
ሹም ፣ አ'ዛዥ ፣ አ'ጋፋሪ (የቤት)

cabin attendant

-ሰ- በመርከብ ፣ በአውሮ'ፕላን ላይ
አስተናጋጅ

stick

ስ'ቲክ -ግ- ማ'ጣበቅ [አ'ጣ'በቀ]

| |

jam

-ግ- ማስገ'ባት [አስገ'ባ] ፣ መደል
[ዶለ] ፣ መሳግ [ሳገ]

-to

-ግ- አለመ'ለ'የት [-ተለ'የ]፣ አለመተው
[-ተወ] ፣ የሙ'ጥ'ኝ ማለት [አለ]

staff

-ሰ- ምርኩዝ ፣ ዱ'ላ ፣ በ'ትር

stiff

ስ'ቲፍ -ቅ- ደረቅ ፣ ግ'ትር

stifle

ስ'ታይፈል -ግ- ማ'ፈን [አ'ፈነ] (እንዳይተነፍስ)

stifling

ስ'ታይፍሊንግ -ቅ- አፋ'ኝ ፣ የ'ሚያንቅ

still

ስ'ቲል -ተግ- ገና

quiet

-ቅ- ጸ'ጥተ'ኛ ፣ የ'ማይንቀሳ'ቀስ

quieten

-ግ- ዝም ማ'ሰ'ኘት [አ'ሰ'ኘ]

still-born

ስ'ቲልቦ:ን -ሰ- ሞቶ የተወ'ለደ

stimulate

ስ'ቲምዩሌይት -ግ- ማ'ነሣሣት [አ'ነሣ'ሣ]

sting

ስ'ቲንግ -ግ- መንደፍ [ነ'ደፈ] (ለንብ ወዘተ)

stingy

ስ'ቲንጂ -ቅ- ሥ'ሥታም ፣ ገብጋ'ባ

stink

ስ'ቲንክ -ግ- መሽተት [ሽ'ተተ] ፣ መከርፋት
[ከረ'ፈ]

-ሰ- ግማት ፣ መጥፎ ሽ'ታ ፣ ክርፋት

stipend

ስ'ታይፔንድ -ሰ- ደመወዝ (የትምህርት ወዘተ)

stipulate

ስ'ቲፕዩሌት -ግ- አጥብቆ መጠ'የቅ [ጠ'የቀ]
(ለአንድ ስምም'ነት አስፈ'ላጊ የሆነውን)

stir

ስ'ተ: -ግ- ማ'ማሰል [አ'ማ'ሰለ] ፣ ማ'ወክ ፣
[አ'ወከ] ፣ መበጥበጥ [በጠ'በጠ]

-up

-ግ- ብጥ'ብጥ ማንሣት [አነ'ሣ]

stirrup

ስ'ቲረፕ -ሰ- እርካብ

604

stitch
ስ'ቲች -ግ- መጣፍ [ጣፈ] ፣ መጥቀም [ጠ'ቀ
መ] (ለልብስ)
   -ስ- ስፌት (የጨርቅ)

stock
ስ'ቶክ -ግ- የሸቀጥ ዕቃ ገዝቶ መደርደር
[ደረ'ደረ]
goods
   -ስ- ሸቀጥ
of rifle
   -ስ- ሰደፍ

stocking
ስ'ቶኪንግ -ስ- ረ'ጅም የእግር ሹ'ራብ

stocky
ስ'ቶኪ. -ቅ- አ'ጭር ፣ ወፍራም'ና ጠንካ'ራ

stoke
ስ'ተውክ -ግ- መማገድ [ማ'ገደ]

stolid
ስ'ቶሊድ -ቅ- ግ'ድ /የሌ'ለው ፣ ስለአንድ
ሁኔቴ ስ'ሜቱን የ'ማይገልጽ

stomach
ስ'ተመክ -ስ- ሆድ (ለሰው)

stone
ስ'ተውን -ግ- መወገር [ወ'ገረ]
   -ስ- ደንጊያ

stony
ስ'ተውኒ -ቅ- ደንጊያ'ማ

stool
ስ'ቱ፡ል -ስ- ወምበር ፣ በርጩ'ማ
faeces
   -ስ- ዓይነ ምድር

stoop
ስ'ቱ፡ፕ -ግ- ማጉንበስ [አጉን'በሰ]

stop
ስ'ቶፕ -ግ- መቆም [ቆመ] ፣ ቆ'ጥ ማለት [አለ]
   -ስ- መቆሚያ

stopper
ስ'ቶፐ -ስ- ቆርኪ ፣ ውታፍ

store
ስ'ቶ: -ስ- ሱቅ ፣ መደ'ብር ፣ ዕቃ ቤት
   -ግ- ማስቀ'መጥ [አስቀ'መጠ] (ማከ
ብት)

storey
ስ'ቶ:ሪ -ስ- ፎቅ ቤት ፣ ደርብ

storm
ስ'ቶ:ም -ስ- አውሎ ነፋስ፣ ማዕበል ፣ መውጅ

story
ስ'ቶ:ሪ -ስ- ተረት ፣ ታሪክ

story-teller
ስ'ቶ:ሪቴለ -ስ- ተ'ራች

stout
ስ'ታውት -ቅ- ወፍራም ፣ ዘጥ'ጣ

stove
ስ'ተውቭ -ስ- ምድ'ጃ

stow
ስ'ተው -ግ- መደርደር [ደረ'ደረ] ፣ ማስቀ
'መጥ [አስቀ'መጠ] (በዕቃ ቤት) ፣ ማ'ሸግ
[አ'ሸገ] (በማሠር)

straddle
ስት'ራደል -ግ- አንፈራ'ጦ መቆም [ቆመ]
ወይ'ም መ'ቀመጥ [ተቀ'መጠ]

straggle
ስት'ራገል -ግ- መ'በታተን [ተበታ'ተነ]

straight
ስት'ሬይት -ቅ- ቀ'ጥ ያለ ፣ ቀጥተ'ኛ
honest
   -ቅ- ታ'ማኝ ፣ ቅን

straighten
ስት'ሬይተን -ግ- ማ'ቃናት [አ'ቃና] ፣ ቀ'ጥ
ማድረግ [አደ'ረገ]

straightforward
ስትሬይት'ፎ:ወድ -ቅ- የ'ማያ'ውክ (ሥራ)
honest
   -ቅ- ታ'ማኝ ፣ ግልጽ (ለጠባይ)

strain
ስት'ሬይን -ግ- ማጥለል [አጠ'ለለ]
tire out
   -ግ- በሥራ ማድከም [አደ'ከመ]
fatigue
   -ስ- ድካም

strait
ስት'ሬይት -ስ- የባሕር ወሽመጥ

stranded
ስት'ራንዲድ -ቅ- ያለርዳታ የቀ'ረ (መ'ጓጓዣ
በማጣት)

605

strange
ስት'ሬይንጅ -ቅ- እንግዳ (ነገር)
unusual
-ቅ- ያልተለ'መደ
unexplained
-ቅ- ግሩም ፣ ድንት
stranger
ስት'ሬይንጅ -ስ- እንግዳ (ለሰው)
strangle
ስት'ራንገል -ግ- አንቆ መግደል [ገ'ደለ]
strap
ስት'ራፕ -ስ- ጠፍር
strategem
ስት'ራተጀም -ስ- ብልጎት (ጠላትን በጦር
'ነት የ'ሚያ'ሸ'ንፉ'በት)
strategy
ስት'ራተጂ -ስ- የጦር ዐቅድ
straw
ስት'ሮ: -ስ- ገለባ
for drinking
-ስ- መጠ'ጥ መምጠጫ ብር
stray
ስት'ራይ -ግ- መጥፋት [ጠ'ፉ] (መንገድ በመ
ሳት)
stream
ስ'ትሪይም -ስ- ድረት ፣ ባለማ'ጽሪጥ የ'ሚጉ
ርፍ ፣ ፈሳሽ ፣ ጋዝ ፣ ሰው ፣ ዕቃ ወዘተ
street
ስት'ሪይት -ስ- ጎዳና ፣ መንገድ
strenuous
ስት'ሬንየወስ -ቅ- ጎይለ'ኛ ፣ ከ'ባድ (ለሥራ)
stress
ስት'ሬስ -ግ- ማጥበቅ [አጠ'በቀ] (ለቃላት)
-ስ- ድካም
stretch
ስት'ሬች -ግ- መዘርጋት [ዘ'ረጋ]
stretcher
ስት'ሬቸ -ስ- ታ'ማሪ አልጋ ፤ የበ'ሽተ'ኛ ማ
'መላለሻ አልጋ
strew
ስት'ሩ፡ -ግ- መበ'ተን [በ'ተነ] ፣ መርጨት
[ረ'ጨ] ፣ መነስነስ [ነሰ'ነሰ]

stricken
ስት'ሪከን -ቅ- የተጉ'ዳ ፣ መከራ ያጠ'ቃው
-in years
-ቅ- በጣም ያረ'ጀ ፣ የሸመ'ገለ
strict
ስት'ሪከት -ቅ- ጥብቅ ፣ የ'ማያ'ወላ'ውል
stride
ስት'ራይድ -ግ- በረ'ጅሙ መ'ራመድ [ተራ
'መደ] ፣ እንጣ'ጥ ብሎ መ'ሄገር [ተሄ'ገረ]
strife
ስት'ራይፍ -ስ- ጥል ፣ ሁከት
strike
ስት'ራይክ -ግ- መምታት [መ'ታ] ፣ ለደሞ
ወዝ ጥ'ማሪ ማ'ደም [አ'ደመ]
-ስ- አድማ
string
ስት'ሪንግ -ስ- ክ'ር ፣ ሲባጎ
strip
ስት'ሪፕ -ግ- መላጥ [ላጠ] (ዛፍ ወዘተ) ፤ ማው
ለቅ [አወ'ለቀ] (ልብስ)
-ስ- ረ'ጅም ቁ'ራጭ (ጨርቅ ፣ መሬት
ወዘተ)
stripe
ስት'ራይፕ -ስ- ሰንበር (በሰው'ነት ላይ የ'ሚ
'ታ'ይ)
coloured line
-ስ- ዝንጉርጉር መሥመር
military
-ስ- ምልክት (የወ'ታ'ደር ሹመት ፣
የ'ህ' ቅስ ያ'ለው)
stripling
ስት'ሪፕሊንግ -ስ- ጎልማ'ሳ
strive
ስት'ራይቭ -ግ- ት'ልቅ ጥረት ማድረግ [አደ'ረገ]
stroke
ስት'ረውክ -ግ- ማዳሽት [አሻ'ሸ] ፣ መደባበስ
[ደባ'በሰ]
blow
-ስ- በ'ትር (የተመ'ቱት)
stroll
ስት'ሮ:ል -ግ- መንሸራሸር [ተንሸረ'ሸረ] (ለሽ
'ርሽ'ር)
strong
ስት'ሮንግ -ቅ- ጎይለ'ኛ

606

stronghold

ስትሮ'ንግሆልድ -ስ- ም'ሽግ

strop

ስት'ሮፕ -ስ- መሳያ ጠፍር

structure

ስት'ረከቸ -ስ- አቋም ፣ አንድ ነገር የተሥ'ራ 'በት ፣ የተገጣ'ጠመ'በት ፣ የተደራ'ጀ'በት መን ገድ
building
-ስ- ታ'ላቅ ሕንፃ

struggle

ስት'ረገል -ግ- መታገል [ታ'ገለ]
-ስ- ትግል

strut

ስት'ረት -ግ- በኩራት መ'ራመድ [ተራ'መደ]፣ መ'ወጠር [ተወ'ጠረ] (ለኩራት)
-ስ- ወጋግራ ፣ የድጋፍ እንጨት

stub

ስ'ተብ -ስ- ቁ'ራጭ ፣ ብ'ጣሽ (የሲጃራ የእርሳስ ወዘተ)
-out
-ግ- መተርከስ [ተረ'ኮሰ] (ለሲጃራ)

stubble

ስ'ተበል -ስ- ቀምቀ'ሞ (የጢም ጠጉር)
grain
-ስ- ቆረን (የእህል)

stubborn

ስ'ተበን -ቅ- ች'ከ ፣ ገ'ታ'ራ ፣ መንጭ'ካ

stud

ስ'ተድ -ስ- ከልብስ ጋር ያልተሰ'ፋ ያንገትጌ ቁልፍ

student

ስት'ዩ፡ደንት -ስ- ተማሪ ፣ ደ'ቀ መዝሙር

study

ስ'ተዲ -ግ- ማጥናት [አጠ'ና]
room
-ስ- ቢሮ (እመ'ናሪያ ቤት ውስጥ)

stuff

ስ'ተፍ -ስ- ጨርቃጨርቅ
nonsense
-ስ- ፍሬ ቢስ
push in
-ግ- ማ'ጨቅ [አ'ጨቀ]

stuffy

ስ'ተፈ -ቅ- አ'የር ያ'ነሰው ቦታ

stumble

ስ'ተምበል -ግ- መ'ደናቀፍ [ተደና'ፈ]

stump

ስ'ተምፕ -ስ- ሥር (ግንዱ የተቆ'ረጠ ነት)
of limb etc.
-ስ- ጉምድ (ተቆርጦ የቀ'ረ) ፣ ጻሽ

stun

ስ'ተን -ግ- በመምታት ነፍስ ገ' ዲስት ማድረግ [አደ'ረገ]

stupid

ስት'ዩ፡ፒድ -ቅ- ደንቆሮ ፣ የ'ማይገባው ፣ ሞ'ኝ

stupor

ስት'ዩ፡ፐ -ስ- አእምሮን የመሳት ሁናቴ (ከመ ድንነት ፣ ከመጠ'ጥ ወዘተ የተነ'ሳ)

sturdy

ስ'ተ፡ዲ -ቅ- ጠንካ'ራ

stutter

ስ'ተተ -ግ- መንተባተብ [ተንተባ'ተበ ፣ መን ገግገም [ተንገገ'ገመ]

sty

ስ'ታይ -ስ- ያሣማ ጋጣ

style

ስ'ታይል -ስ- መንገድ ፣ ዘዴ (ያ'ጸጻፍ ወዘተ)

suave

ስ'ዋ፡ቭ -ቅ- የታ'ረመ ፣ ጠ'ፍ ያለ፣ ጥሩ ጠባይ ያ'ለው

subdue

ሰብድ'ዩ፡ -ግ- ማ'ሸ'ነፍ [አ'ሸ'ነፈ] ፣ ጸ'ጥተ 'ኛ'ና ለስላ'ሳ ማድረግ [አደ'ረገ]

subhuman

ሰብ'ህ'ዩ፡መን -ቅ- ከሰው ተፈጥሮ በታ'ች የሆነ

subject

'ሰብጀክት -ስ- ተገዥ
grammar
-ስ- ባለቤት (ሰዋሰው)
academic
-ስ- ትምህርት (የተለ'የ)

subject

ሰብ'ጀክት -ግ- መ'ገዛድ [ተገ'ዛደ] ፣ መ'ገ ዛት [ተገ'ዛ] ፣ መግበር [ገ'በረ]

607

sublime
ሰብ'ላይም -ቅ- ፍ'ጹም የተከ'በረ ፣ ባለግርማ፣
እ'ጅግ የላቀ
holy
-ቅ- ቅ'ዱስ

submarine
ሰብመ'ሪይን -ስ- በባሕር ውስጥ የ'ሚሄድ
መርከብ

submerge
ሰብ'መ:ጅ -ግ- መጥለቅ [ጠ'ለቀ]፣ መስጠም
[ሰ'ጠመ] ፣ መ'ዘፈቅ [ተዘ'ፈቀ]

submission
ሰብ'ሚሽን -ስ- መ'ማረክ ፣ መ'ሽነፍ፡
legal
-ስ- ማስረ'ጃ ማቅረብ (ለዳ'ኛ)

submit
ሰብ'ሚት -ግ- ማቅረብ [አቀ'ረብ]
surrender
-ግ- ፣መ'ሽነፍ [ተሸ'ነፈ]

subordinate
ሰ'ቦ:ዲነት -ቅ- የበታ'ች (ለማዕረግ)

subscribe
ሰብስክ'ራይብ -ግ- አስተዋፅኦ ማድረግ [አዶ
'ረገ] (የገንዘብ ወዘተ)

subsequent
'ሰብሰክዌንት -ቅ- ተከ'ታይ

subservient
ሰብ'ሰ:ቪየንት -ቅ- ትሕት'ና አብዝ ፣ ተቅላ
ስላሽ ፣ ሽቁጥቁጥ

subside
ሰብ'ሳይድ -ግ- ጸ'ጥ ማለት (አለ) ፣ (ለነፋስ) ፣
እ'ያነሰ መሄድ [ሄደ] (ለጎርፍ)

subsidiary
ሰብ'ሲዲየሪ -ስ- ቅርንጫፍ (የድር'ጅት)

subsidy
'ሰብሲዲ -ስ- መንግሥት የ'ሚሰጠው የርዳታ
ገንዘብ (ላንድ ድር'ጅት)

substance
'ሰብስተንስ -ስ- ነገር (ለዕቃ)

substantial
ሰብስ'ታንሸል -ቅ- ት'ልቅ ፣ ብዙ ፣ ጠንካ'ራ

substitute
'ሰብስቲትዩ:ት -ግ- መተ'ካት [ተ'ካ]
-ስ- ም'ትክ ፣ ተለ'ዋጭ

subterfuge
'ሰብተፍዩ:ጅ -ስ- ማ'ታለል ፣ ተንኮል ፣ የ'ሚ
ፈ'ልጉትን ነገር በተንኮል ማግኘት

subterranean
ሰብተ'ሬይኒየን -ስ- ከመሬት በታ'ች

subtle
'ስተል -ቅ- ረቀ'ሌ ፣ ብልጥ

subtract
ሰብት'ራክት -ግ- መቀ'ነስ [ቀነ'ሰ]

suburb
'ሰበ:ብ -ስ- በከተማ ዳር ያ'ለ መንደር

subversive
ሰብ'ሽ:ሲቨ -ቅ- መንግሥት ፣ ሃይማኖት ወዘተ
ተቃዋሚ

subway
'ሰብዌይ -ስ- ከመሬት በታ'ች የ'ሚሄድ መ'መ
ላለሻ ባቡር

succeed
ሰክ'ሲይድ -ግ- መጎ'በዝ [ጎ'በዘ] ፣ እፈ'ለጉ-ት
ግብ መድረስ [ደ'ረሰ]
prosper
-ግ- መ'ክናወን [ተከና'ወነ] ፣ ጥሩ
ው'ጤት ማግኘት [አገ'ኘ]

success
ሰክ'ሴስ -ስ- ጉብዝ'ና ፣ ክን'ውን

successor
ሰክ'ሴሰ -ስ- ወራሽ ፣ ምት'ክ

succour
'ሰከ -ስ- እርዳታ (በች'ግር ፣ በሕዘን ጊዜ)
-ግ- ማጽናናት (አጽና'ና) ፣ መርዳት
[ረ'ዳ]

succulent
'ሰክዩለንት -ቅ- ጣፋጭ ፣ እ'ጅ የ'ሚያስቆረ
'ጥም ፣ ውሃ የሞ'ላው (ለፍራፍሬ)

succumb
ስ'ከም -ግ- መ'ሽነፍ [ተሽ'ነፈ] ፣ መሞት
[ሞተ]

such
'ሰች -ቅ- እንደ'ዚህ

suck
'ሰክ -ግ- መምጠጥ [መ'ጠጠ] ፣ መጥባት
[ጠ'ባ]

sudden
'ሰደን -ቅ- ድንገተ'ኛ

608

suds
'ሰድዝ -ስ- አረፋ (የሳሙና)

sue
'ሱ: -ግ- መክሰስ [ከ'ሰሰ] (በሕ'ግ ፣ ቀጣሪን
ስላልከ'ፈለው ደመወዝ) ፤ መ'ለማመጥ [ተለማ
'መጠ] (ለዕርቅ ፣ ለምሕረት)

suet
'ሱዊት -ስ- ሞራ

suffer
'ሰፈ -ግ- ሥ'ታመም [ታ'መመ] ፣ መ'ጨነቅ
[ተጨ'ነቀ] ፣ መ'ሠቃየት [ተሠቃ'የ]

suffice
ሰ'ፋይስ -ግ- መብቃት [በ'ቃ]

sufficient
ሰ'ፊሸንት -ቅ- በቂ

suffix
'ሰፊክስ -ስ- ባዕድ መ'ነሻ [ስዋስው]

suffocate
'ሰፈኬይት -ግ- መ'ታነቅ [ታ'ነቀ] ፣ መ'ታ
ፈን [ታ'ፈነ] (ከአ'የር እጦት የተነ'ሣ)

suffrage
'ሰፍረጅ -ስ- የምርጫ መብት (የሕዝብ እንደ
ራሴን)

sugar
'ሹጋ -ስ- ሱ'ካር

sugar-cane
'ሹጋ ኬይን -ስ- ሽንኮራ አገዳ

suggest
ሰ'ጀስት -ግ- ሐ'ሳብ ማቅረብ [አቀ'ረበ]

suggestion
ሰ'ጀስትየን -ስ- የ'ሚቀርብ ሐ'ሳብ

suicide
'ሱዊሳይድ -ስ- ራስን መግደል ፣ የራስን ሕይ
ወት ማጥፋት

suit
ስ'ዩት -ስ- ሙሉ ልብስ (ከአንድ ዓይነት ጨ
ርቅ)
petition
-ስ- አቤቱታ ፣ ክ'ስ (ለፍርድ ቤት)
fit
-ግ- መስማማት [ተስማ'ማ] ፣ መ'መ
ቶት [ተመ'ቶ]

suitable
ስ'ዩተብል -ቅ- ተስማሚ ፣ ምቹ

suitcase
ስ'ዩትኬይስ -ስ- የልብስ ሻንጣ

suitor
'ስዩተ -ስ- ሊያጭ የ'ሚመጣ ፣ ጋብቻ ጠ'ያቂ
ወንድ

sulk
'ሰልክ -ግ- የፈ'ለጉትን ባለማግኘት ማኮረፍ
[አኮ'ረፈ] (ለሕፃን)

sulky
'ሰልኪ -ቅ- አኩራፊ

sullen
'ሰለን -ቅ- አኩራፊ ፣ የ'ማይጠዳው ፣ የጨፈ
'ገገ (ስሜይ)

sulphur
'ሰልፈ -ስ- ድ'ኝ

sultry
'ሰልትሪ -ስ- ከ'ባድ ፤ ሞ'ቃት አ'የር

sum
'ሰም -ስ- ድ'ምር
mathematical
-ስ- ጠቅላላ ድ'ምር

summary
'ሰመሪ -ስ- ማ'ጠቃለያ (ለጽሑፍ) ፣ አ'ጭር
መግለጫ

summer
'ሰመ -ስ- በጋ

summit
'ሰሚት -ስ- ጫፍ (የተራራ) ፤ ከ'ፍተ'ኛ
(ጉባኤ ስብሰባ)

summon
'ሰመን -ግ- መስብሰብ [ሰብ'ሰበ] ፣ መጥራት
[ጠ'ራ] (ለጥ'ር)

summons
'ሰመንዝ -ስ- መጥሪያ (የክ'ስ)

sumptuous
'ሰምችወስ -ቅ- በጣም ም'ቹ ፣ ድሎት ያ'ለ
ው ፣ ዋጋው ከ'ፍ ያለ

sun
'ሰን -ስ- ፀሐይ

sunbeam
'ሰንቢይም -ስ- የፀሐይ ጮ'ራ ፣ ጨረር

sunburn
'ሰንበ፡ን -ስ- ፀሐይ ያ'ቃ'ጠለው ሰው'ነት

609

Sunday
'ሰንደይ -ስ- እሑድ
sunflower
'ሰንፍላወ -ስ- የሱፍ አበባ
sunken
'ሰንከን -ቅ- ዝ'ቅተ'ኛ ፣ ረ'ባ'ዳ (ቦታ) ፤ የጕ
ደ'ጕደ (ለመልክ)
sunlight
'ሰንላይት -ስ- የፀሐይ ብርሃን
sunny
'ሰኒ -ቅ- ፀሐይ'ሙ
sunrise
'ሰንራይዝ -ስ- የፀሐይ መውጣት ፣ የጀምበር
መውጣት
sunset
'ሰንሴት -ስ- የፀሐይ መጥለቅ ፣ የጀምበር
መጥለቅ
sunshade
'ሰንሼይድ -ስ- ጥላ (በ'ጀ የ'ሚ'ያዝ)
sunshine
'ሰንሻይን -ስ- የፀሐይ ብርሃን (ፈገ'ግ ያለ)
sunstroke
'ሰንስትረውክ -ስ- የፀሐይ ም'ት
superannuation
ሱፐራንዩ'ዌይሽን -ስ- የጡረታ አበ'ል ፤ ከሥ
ራ በጡረታ መውጣት
superb
ሱ'ፐ፡ብ -ቅ- ግለፈያ ፣ ግሩም ፣ ድንቅ ፣ እን
ከን የሌ'ለው
supercilious
ሱፐ'ሲሊየስ -ቅ- ፌዘ'ኛ ፣ አልጋጭ ፣ እ'ቡይ
superficial
ሱፐ'ፈሸል -ቅ- ጥራዝ ነ'ጠቅ ፣ ጥልቅ'ነት
የሌ'ለው ፣ ዐዋቂ መሳይ
superfluous
ሱ'ፐ፡ፍሉወስ -ቅ- ከ'ሚ'ፈ'ለገው ባላይ፣ከመ
ጠን በላይ
superhuman
ሱፐህ'ዩ፡መን -ቅ- ከሰው ዐቅም በላይ ፣ ከሰው
ተፈጥሮ በላይ የሆነ
superimpose
ሱፐሪም'ፐውዝ -ግ- መደ'ረብ [ደ'ረበ] ፣ በ
ላይ ማስቀ'መጥ [አስቀ'መጠ]

superintendent
ሱፐሪን'ቴንደንት -ስ- ተቆጣጣሪ ፣ ያንድ ድር
'ጅት ሹም
superior
/ ሱ'ፐሪየ -ቅ- የበላይ
superiority
ሱፐሪ'ዮሪቲ -ስ- የበላይ'ነት
superlative
ሱ'ፐ፡ለቲቭ -ቅ- እ'ጅግ በጣም ጥሩ
-ስ- አ'በላላጭ ደረጃ (ሰዋስው)
supermarket
'ሱፐማ፡ከት -ስ- በ'ያይነቱ ሸቀጣሸጥ የ'ሚ
'ሸጥ'በት የተሟ'ላ ት'ልቅ መደ'ብር
supernatural
ሱፐ'ናቸረል -ቅ- መለኮታዊ ፣ ከሰው ዐቅም
በላይ
supersede
ሱፐ'ሲይድ -ግ- መ'ተካት [ተተ'ካ]
superstition
ሱፐስ'ቲሽን -ስ- በጥንቆላ ፣ በአስማት'ና
በለ'ዩ ል'ዩ ምል'ክቶ'ች ማመን
superstitious
ሱፐስ'ቲሸስ -ቅ- በጣኦት አምልኮ አማኝ
superstructure
'ሱፐስትረክቸ -ስ- የቤት ዋ'ና አካል (ከመሠ
ረት በላይ ያ'ለው)
supervise
'ሱፐቫይዝ -ግ- መ'ቆጣጠር [ተቆጣ'ጠረ]
supervision
ሱፐ'ቪጀን -ስ- ቁጥ'ጥር
supervisor
'ሱፐቫይዘ -ስ- ተቆጣጣሪ
supine
'ሱፓይን -ቅ- የተንጋ'ለለ ፤ ጎይል የጕ'ደ
ለው ፤ የ'ማይንቀሳ'ቀስ
supper
'ሰፐ -ስ- ራት
supple
'ሰፕል -ቅ- ልል ፣ በቀ'ላሉ የ'ሚ'ታ'ጠፍ
supplement
'ሰፕሊመንት -ስ- ተጨ'ማሪ ነገር ፣ ች'ግርን
ለማ'ሟላት የተጨ'መረ ነገር
supplication
ሰፕሊ'ኬሽን -ስ- የል'ብ ጸሎት ፣ አቤቱታ

610

supply
ሰፕ'ላይ -ግ- ማቅረብ [አቀ'ረበ] ፣ መስጠት
[ሰ'ጠ]
-ስ- ሥንቅ ፣ ምግብ

support
ሰ'ፖ፡ት -ግ- መርዳት [ረ'ዳ]
-ስ- እርዳታ

supporter
ሰ'ፖ፡ተ -ስ- ረ'ዳት

suppose
ሰ'ፖውዝ -ግ- ማ'ሰብ [አ'ሰበ] ፣ ሊሆን ይች
ላ'ል ብሎ ማ'ሰብ [አ'ሰበ]

suppress
ሰፕ'ሬስ -ግ- መጨ'ቆን [ጨ'ቆነ]

supremacy
ሱፕ'ሬመሲ -ስ- ታ'ላቅ'ነት ፣ መላቅ ፣ የበላ
ይ'ነት

supreme
ሱፕሪይም -ቅ- የላቅ ፣ ታ'ላቅ፣ብልጫ ያ'ለው፣
ከ'ፍተ'ኛ

sure
'ሽ፡ -ቅ- እርግጥ

surely
'ሽ፡ሊ -ተግ- በርግጥ ፣ በውነት

surf
'ሰ፡ፍ -ስ- የማዕበል አረፋ

surface
'ሰ፡ፈስ -ስ- ፊት (ያንድ ነገር የላይ'ኛው መል
ክ)

surfeit
'ሰ፡ፈት -ግ- ከመጠን በላይ መመ'ገብ [መ'ገበ]
-ስ- ከመጠን በላይ መብላት ፣ መጠ'ጣት
ወዘተ

surge
'ሰ፡ጅ -ግ- መስገግ [ሰ'ገገ] (ለብዙ ሰዎች
ወዘተ)

surgeon
'ሰ፡ጀን -ስ- ቀዳጅ ሐኪም

surly
'ሰ፡ሊ -ቅ- በጥቁቱ የ'ሚ'ቀ'የም ፣ አኩራራ

surmise
ሰ'ማይዝ -ግ- ማ'ሰብ [አ'ሰበ] (ሊሆን የ'ሚ
ችለውን)

surmount
ሰ'ማውንት -ግ- ማ'ሸ'ነፍ [አ'ሸ'ነፈ] ፣ መ'ወ
ጣት [ተወ'ጣ] (ች'ግርን)

surname
'ሰኔይም -ስ- ያ'ባት ስም (ባ'ባት በ'ኩል
የመ'ጣ የቤተሰብ ስም)

surpass
ሰ'ፖ፡ስ -ግ- መላቅ [ላቀ] ፣ መብለጥ [በ'ለጠ]

surplus
'ሰ፡ፕለስ -ስ- ትርፍ ፣ ካስፈ'ላጊ በላይ ያ'ለ
ነገር

surprise
ሰፕ'ራይዝ -ግ- ማስደንገጥ [አስደነ'ገጠ]
-ስ- አስገ'ራሚ ፣ ድልጊ'በቂት ነገር

surrender
ሰ'ሬንደ -ግ- እ'ጅን መስጠት [ሰ'ጠ]
-ስ- እ'ጅን መስጠት

surreptitious
ሰሬፕ'ቲሸስ -ቅ- በድ'ብቅ ፣ በምስጢር የተ
ሠ'ራ ፣ የተገ'ኘ (እምነትን በማጉደል)

surroundings
ሰ'ራውንዲንግዝ -ስ- አ'ካባቢ

survey
ሳ'ቬይ -ግ- መሬትን መለ'ካት [ለ'ካ] ፣ መቀ
'የስ [ቀ'የሰ] ፣ ጠቅላ'ላ ጥናት ማድረግ [አደ
'ረገ]

survey
'ሰ፡ቬይ -ስ- ጠቅላ'ላ ምር'ምር ፣ ጥናት

surveyor
ሰ'ቬየ -ስ- መሬት ቀ'ያሽ (ጅኦሜትሪ)

survive
ሰ'ቫይቭ -ግ- መዳን [ዳነ] ፣ ማለፍ [አ'ለፈ]
(መከራን) ፣ መትረፍ [ተ'ረፈ] (ከመከራ)

susceptible
ስ'ሴፕቲበል -ቅ- ደካማ ፣ በስ'ሜት በቀ'ላሉ
የ'ሚ'ማ'ረክ ፣ በቀ'ላሉ ሊ'ለ'ወጥ የ'ሚችል

suspect
ሰስ'ፔክት -ግ- መ'ጠራጠር [ተጠራ'ጠረ]

suspend
ሰስ'ፔንድ -ግ- ማንጠልጠል [አንጠለ'ጠለ] ፣
መስቀል [ሰ'ቀለ] ፣ መ'ሰቀል [ተሰ'ቀለ]
dismiss temporarily
-ግ- መ'ታገድ [ታ'ገደ] (ከሥራ)

611

suspenders
ሰስ'ፔንደዝ -ስ- የግር ሹ'ራብ መያዣ (ላስ ቲክ'ነት ያ'ለው)
American
-ስ- የሱ'ሪ መያዣ (ላስቲክ'ነት ያ'ለው)

suspense
ሰስ'ፔንስ -ስ- እርግጠ'ኛ ያልሆነ ጉ'ጉት (ስለ ወሬ ፣ ው'ሳኔ ወዘተ)

suspension
ሰስ'ፔንሽን -ስ- የመኪና ሞ'ላ
dismissal
-ስ- ማ'ገድ (ከሥ'ራ)

suspicion
ሰስ'ፒሽን -ስ- ጥር'ጣሬ

sustained
ሰስ'ቴይንድ -ቅ- ቀ'ጣይ ፣ የ'ማያ'ቋ'ርጥ (ለ ሥራ) ፤ የተደ'ገፈ (ለኑሮ)

swagger
ስ'ዋገ -ግ- መንጐራደድ [ተንጐራ'ደደ] ፤ እየ ደነ'ፋ መ'ናገር [ተና'ገረ]

swallow
ስ'ዎለው -ግ- መዋጥ [ዋጠ] (ለመብል)

swamp
ስ'ዎምፕ -ስ- አሮንቃ ፣ ጨቀጨቅ

swan
ስ'ዎን -ስ- ዝ'ይ ፣ የውሃ ዶሮ

swarm
ስ'ዎ:ም -ስ- የንብ መንጋ

swathe
ስ'ዌይዝ -ግ- በጨርቅ መጠቅለል [ጠቀ'ለለ]

sway
ስ'ዌይ -ግ- መ'ወዝወዝ [ተወዘ'ወዘ]

swear
ስ'ዌየ -ግ- መማል [ማለ]
use bad language
-ግ- መስደብ [ሰ'ደበ]

sweat
ስ'ዌት -ግ- ማላብ [አላበ]
-ስ- ላብ

sweep
ስ'ዊይፕ -ግ- መጥረግ [ጠ'ረገ] (ቤት)

sweet
ስ'ዊይት -ቅ- ጣፋጭ
-ስ- ከረሜ'ላ

sweetheart
ስ'ዊይትሃ:ት -ስ- ወዳጅ ፣ ፍቅር

swell
ስ'ዌል -ግ- ማበጥ [አ'በጠ]

swelling
ስ'ዌሊንግ -ስ- እበጥ ፣ እብጠት

sweltering
ስ'ዌልተሪንግ -ቅ- ከሙቀት የተነ'ሣ የተዝ ለፈ'ለፈ ፣ ሐሩር ያ'ደ'ከመው

swerve
ስ'ወ:ቭ -ግ- ማግለል [አገ'ለለ] ፣ መንገድ መለ'ወጥ [ለ'ወጠ]

swift
ስ'ዊፍት -ቅ- ፈ'ጣን

swill
ስ'ዊል -ስ- ፍር'ፋሪ ፣ ት'ራፊ (ለምግብ) ፤ ያሣማ ምግብ (የተበጠ'በጠ)
gulp down
-ግ- መገ'ጠም [ገ'ጠመ] (ወሃ)

swim
ስ'ዊም -ግ- መዋ'ኘት [ዋ'ኘ]

swindle
ስ'ዊንደል -ግ- ማ'ታለል [አ'ታ'ለለ] ፣ ማጭ በርበር [አጭበረ'በረ]
-ስ- ማ'ታለል ፣ ማጭበርበር

swindler
ስ'ዊንደለ -ቅ- አ'ታላይ ፣ አጭበርባሪ

swine
ስ'ዋይን -ስ- ዐሣማ

swing
ስ'ዊንግ -ግ- መ'ወዛወዝ [ተወዛ'ወዘ] ፤ ሲ'ሎ ሽ መ'ጫወት [ተጫ'ወተ]፣ዥ'ው'ዥ'ው መ'ጫ ወት [ተ'ጫ'ወተ]
-ስ- ሲ'ሎሽ ፣ ዥ'ው'ዥ'ው
play apparatus
-ስ- የሲ'ሎሽ ወንበር ፣ የዥ'ው'ዥ'ው ወንበር

swipe
ስ'ዋይፕ -ግ- መለ'ተም [ለ'ተመ] (መምታት)

swirl
ስ'ወ:ል -ግ- መዞር [ዞረ] (አዝዋሪት)

switch
ስ'ዊች -ስ- ግብሪያ (ለኤሌክትሪክ)
-on
-ግ- ግብራት [አበ'ራ] (ለመብራት)
-off
-ግ- ግጥፋት [አጠ'ፋ] (ለመብራት)
transfer
-ግ- መለዋወጥ [ለዋ'ወጠ] (ሐ'ሳብን በንግ'ግር)

swivel
ስ'ዊቨል -ግ- በአንድ ነገር ላይ መዞር [ዞረ]

swoon
ስ'ውን -ግ- መዝለፍለፍ [ተዝለፈ'ለፈ]፤ አእ ምር መሳት [ሳተ]

swoop
ስ'ውፕ -ግ- ሽ'ው ብሎ መውረድ [ወ'ረደ]፤ ድንገት አደጋ መጣል [ጣለ]

sword
'ሶ:ድ -ስ- ጎራዴ ፣ ሠይፍ

sycamore
'ሲከሞ: -ስ- ዋርካ (ወርካ)

syce
'ሳይስ -ስ- ለ'ጓሚ (የፈረስ ፣ የበቅሎ)

syllable
'ሲለበል -ስ- ክፍለ ቃል

syllabus
'ሲለበስ -ስ- መርሐ ትምህርት

symbol
'ሲምበል -ስ- ምል'ክት

symmetrical
ሲ'ሜትሪከል -ቅ- ተመሳሳይ (ቅርፅ ፣ መጠን)፣ ሁለ'ቱም ጎ'ን የ'ሚ'መሳ'ሰል

sympathy
'ሲምፐሺ -ስ- ርኅራኄ ፣ እርስበርስ መስማ ማት ፣ አንዱ ለሌላው ማ'ሰብ

symptom
'ሲምተም -ስ- የበ'ሽታ ምል'ክት ፣ አንድ ነገር መኖሩን የ'ሚያመለ'ክት ምል'ክት

synagogue
'ሲነጎግ -ስ- የአይሁድ ቤተ መቅደስ ፣ ምኩ ራብ አይሁድ

synchronize
'ሲንክረናይዝ -ግ- ግስተካከል [አስተካ'ከለ] (ሰዓት አንድ ዓይነት ጊዜ እንዲነጋር)፣ ባንድ ጊዜ እንዲሄድ ግድረግ [አደ'ረገ]

syndicate
'ሲንዲከት -ስ- ግጎበር (የል'ዩ ል'ዩ ሞያ)

synonym
'ሲነኒም -ስ- ተመሳሳይ ትርጉም ያ'ለው ቃል

synopsis
ሲ'ኖፕሲስ -ስ- አሕጽሮተ ጽሑፍ ፣ ዋ'ና ሐ'ሳብ፣ ፍሬ ነገር (የመጽሐፍ ፣ የቲአትር ፣ የፊ ልም ወዘተ)

syntax
'ሲንታክስ -ስ- አ'ገባብ (የዐሩፍ ነገር)

synthetic
ሲን'ቴቲክ -ቅ- ሰው ሠ'ራሽ

syphilis
'ሲፈሊስ -ስ- ቂጥ'ኝ

syringe
ስ'ሪንጅ -ስ- መርፌ (የሕኪም) ፣ ፈሳሽ መም ጠጫ'ና ግፍሰሻ መ'ሣሪያ

syrup
'ሲረፕ -ስ- ጣፋጭ መጠ'ጥ (ከሱ'ካር'ና ከው ሃ ወይን'ም ከሱ'ካር'ና ከፍራፍሬ ጭ'ማቂ የተ ሠ'ራ)

system
'ሲስተም -ስ- ሕ'ግ ፣ ደምብ

systematic
ሲስ'ተማቲክ -ቅ- ደምበ'ኛ ፣ በደምብ የ'ሚ ሠራ

systematically
ሲስተ'ማቲከሊ -ተግ- በሕ'ግ ፣ በደምብ ፣ በተራ

613

T

tab
’ታብ -ስ- የጨርቅ ምል'ክት (ለግዕረግ)

tabernacle
’ታበናክል -ስ- ደብተራ አሪት

table
’ቴይብል -ስ- ጠረ'ጴዛ

tablecloth
’ቴይቡልክሎ፤ -ስ- የጠረ'ጴዛ ልብስ

tablespoon
’ቴይቡልስፑ:ን -ስ- የሾርባ ማንካ

tablet
’ታብሌት -ስ- ክኒን (መድኃኒት)

taboo
ታ’ቡ: -ስ- ሃይማኖት ወይን'ም ሥነ ምግባር
እንዳይ'ነ'ካ ፣ እንዳይ'ደ'ረግ ፣ በይፉ እንዳ'
ይ'ነ'ገር የ'ሚከለ'ከለው ነገር

tabulate
’ታብዩሌይት -ግ- በወገ መመ'ደብ [መ'ደበ]

tacit
’ታሲት -ቅ- ሳይ'ና'ገር (ሪስ በመነትነት
መስማማት'ና አለመስማማትን) የ'ሚገልጽ

tack
’ታክ -ስ- ት'ንሽ ሚስማር (ሪሱ ሰፉ ያለ)
-ስ- ስፈት (እንዱ)
stitch
-ግ- መወስወስ [ወስ'ወስ]

tackle
’ታክል -ስ- መ'ሣሪያ
approach
-ግ- መፍትሔ መፈ'ለግ [ፈ'ለገ]
football
-ግ- መያዝ [ያዘ] (ተጫዋች'ችን)

tacky
’ታኪ -ቅ- መጣብቅ'ነት ያ'ለው ፣ የ'ሚያ'ጣ
'ብት

tact
’ታክት -ስ- ብልኃነት (ሰውን ሳይነኩ የ'ሚ'ወ
'ጡ'በት)

tactics
’ታክቲክስ -ስ- ዐቅድ ፣ ብልኃት (የወ'ታ'ደር)

tag
’ታግ -ስ- ምል'ክት ፣ የዋጋ መግለጫ ወረቀት
stock phrase
-ስ- በ'የጊዜው የ'ሚ'ነ'ገር ፣ የተለ
'መደ የ'ሚ'ጠ'ቀስ ሐረግ ፣ ዐረፍት ነገር

tail
’ቴይል -ስ- ጅራት

tailor
’ቴይለ -ስ- ልብስ ሰፊ ፣ መኪና ሰፊ

tainted
’ቴይንቲድ -ቅ- እ'ጅ እ'ጅ የ'ሚል (ምግብ)

take
’ቴይክ -ግ- መውሰድ [ወ'ሰደ]

tale
’ቴይል -ግ- ታሪክ ፣ ስለአንድ ሁናቴ የ'ሚ'ነ
'ገር ወሬ

talent
’ታለንት -ግ- ስጦታ ፣ ችሎታ ፣ ተውህቦ

talisman
’ታሊዝመን -ስ- አሽከክታብ ፣ ጠልሰም

talk
’ቶክ -ግ- መ'ናገር [ተና'ገረ]
-ስ- ንግ'ግር
lecture
-ስ- ንግ'ግር

talkative
’ቶክቲቭ -ቅ- ለፍላፊ ፣ ቀባጣሪ ፣ ምላሱ'ኛ

tall
’ቶ:ል -ቅ- ረ'ጅም

tame
’ቴይም -ቅ- ለ'ማዳ (ለአውሬ)
-ግ- ግልመድ [አለ'መደ]

tamper
’ታምፐ -ግ- ጥ'ልቅ ማለት [አለ]

tan
’ታን -ግ- ቆዳ ማልፋት [አለ'ፉ]
sun-
-ስ- በፀሐይ የመቃ'ረ ሰው'ነት
become sunburned
-ግ- በፀሐይ መ'ቃጠል [ተቃ'ጠለ] (ለ
መልክ)

614

tandem

’ታንደም -ስ- ሁለ'ት ሰዎ'ች የ'ሚ ጋ'ልቡት
ቢሲክሌት (ባለሁ'ለት መወስወሻ)

tang

’ታንግ -ስ- መጣጣ ጣዕም ፣ የተለ'የ ጣዕም ፣
ሽ'ታ ያ'ለው ነገር

tangible

’ታንጅበል -ቅ- ግዑዝ ፣ በእጅ የ'ሚ'ዳ'ሰስ ፣
ግልጽ ፣ ደብዛ'ዛ ያልሆነ

tangle

’ታንገል -ግ- መ'ወታተብ [ተወታ'ተብ] (ለ
ክ'ር ፣ ለጠጉር መዘተ)
-ስ- ውትብትብ ክ'ር ፣ ጠጉር (መዘተ)

tank

’ታንክ -ስ- የወሃ ግ'ጠራቀሚያ ፣ የመኪና
ቤንዚን መያዣ
military
-ስ- ታንክ (ብረት ለ'በስ መኪና)

tantalize

’ታንተላይዝ -ግ- ማጓጓት [አጓ'ጓ] ፣ ተስፋ
እ'የሰ'ጡ አለመፈ'ጸም [-ፈ'ጸመ]

tap

’ታፕ -ስ- የቧምቧዋ ውሃ መክፈቻ
-ግ- ማንኳኳት [አንኳ'ኳ] (በ'ር መዘተ)

tape

’ቴይፕ -ስ- ቀ'ጭን ፣ ረ'ጅም ከጨርቅ ፣ ከወ
ረቀት የተሠ'ራ የዕቃ ማሠሪያ
-ስ- የቴ'ፕ ክ'ር

taper

’ቴይፐር -ግ- እ'የቀ'ጠነ መሄድ [ሄደ] (ከአ
ንድ ወገን)
-ስ- ጧፍ

tapestry

’ታፔስትሪ -ስ- ጉብረ ምንጣፍ (የግድግ'ዳ ፣
የወለል)

tapeworm

’ቴፕወ:ም -ስ- የኮሶ ትል

tar

’ታ: -ስ- ሬንጅ

target

’ታ:ጌት -ስ- ዓላማ (የተኩስ) ፣ በቦምብ የ'ሚ
'ደበ'ደበብ ቦታ ፣ ግብ (የሥራ)

tariff

’ታሪፍ -ስ- ቀርጥ ዋጋ (በተለ'ይ ፣ ለሆቴል
ምግብ ፣ ለመ'ኝታ መዘተ) ፣ አገር ውስጥ በ'ሚ
ገቡ ዕቃዎ'ች ላይ የ'ሚ'ጣል የቀረጥ ዝርዝር

tarnish

’ታ:ኒሽ -ግ- መደብዘዝ [ደብ'ዘዘ] ፣ ማደብዘዝ
[አደብ'ዘዘ] (ከመቆ'የት የተነ'ሣ)

tarpaulin

ታ'ፓ:ሊን -ስ- ውሃ የ'ማያስገ'ባ ልብስ
በሬንጅ የተነ'ከረ ሽራ

tart

’ታ:ት -ስ- ኬክ (መርመላታ'ና ፍሬ ያ'ለ'በት)
taste
-ቅ- ኮምጣ'ጣ ጣዕም ያ'ለው

task

’ታ:ስክ -ስ- ሥራ ፣ ተግባር

tassel

’ታሰል -ስ- ባለጌጥ ዘርፍ ፣ መርገፍ

taste

’ቴይስት -ግ- መቅመስ [ቀ'መሰ]
-ስ- ቅምሻ ፣ ጣዕም ፤ አ'መራረጥ

tasty

’ቴይስቲ -ቅ- የ'ሚጥም ፣ የ'ሚጣ'ፍጥ

tattered

’ታተድ -ቅ- የተበጣ'ጨቀ ፣ የተተለ'ተለ (ለ
ልብስ)

tattoo

ታ'ቱ: -ስ- ው'ቅራት ፣ ንቅሳት

taunt

’ቶ:ንት -ግ- መ'ተናኮል [ተተና'ኮለ] ፣ ነገር
መቆስቆስ [ቆስ'ቆሰ] (በንግ'ግር)

taut

’ቶ:ት -ቅ- የተወ'ጠረ (ገመድ ፣ የደም ሥር
መዘተ)

tavern

’ታቨን -ስ- መጠ'ጥ ቤት ፣ መሸታ ቤት

tawny

’ቶ:ኒ -ቅ- ጠየ'ም ያለ ብ'ሩ

tax

’ታክስ -ስ- ቀረጥ
-ግ- መቅረጥ [ቀ'ረጠ]

taxi

’ታክሲ -ስ- ታክሲ

tea

’ቲይ -ስ- ሻይ

teach

’ቲይች -ግ- ማስተማር [አስተማረ]

615

teacher
'ቲቸር -ስ- አስተማሪ

team
'ቲይም -ስ- ቡድን ፤ ጋሪ የ'ሚጎ'ትቱ ሁለ'ት
ወይን'ም የብ'ለጡ ፈረሶ'ች ፤ በሬዎ'ች ወዘተ

tear
'ቴየ -ስ- ቅ'ድ (የጨርቅ) ፡ መቅደድ [ቀ'ደደ]

tear
'ቲየ -ስ- ዕንባ

tease
'ቲይዝ -ግ- ማናደድ [አ'ናደደ] ፡ መ'ቃ
ለድ [ተቃ'ለደ] (ለጨዋታ ወይ'ም ለመጉዳት)

teaspoon
'ቲይስፑ፡ን -ስ- የሻይ ፤ የቡ'ና ማንካ

teat
'ቲይት -ስ- የጡት ጫፍ (የእንስት) ፤ የጡ'ጦ
አፍ

technique
ቴክ'ኒይክ -ስ- አንድ ነገር የመሥራት ብል
ጎት (በተለ'ይ ሜካኒካዊ)

tedious
'ቲይድዮስ -ቅ- ረ'ጅም'ና አሰልቺ ፡ አድካሚ፤
ዝ'ግ ያለ'ና አስተያየትን የ'ማይማ'ርክ

teem
'ቲይም -ግ- መ'ሞላት [ተሞ'ላ] ፡ በብዛት
መ'ገኘት [ተገ'ኘ]

teenager
'ቲይኔይጀ -ስ- ዕድሜው በዐሥራ ሦስት'ና
በዛያ ዓመት መካ'ከል ያ'ለ ወ'ጣት

teetotal
ቲ'ቶተል -ቅ- የ'ሚያሰክር መጠ'ጥ የ'ማይ
ጠ'ጣ ፡ የ'ሚያስክር መጠ'ጥ እንዳይ'ጠ'ጣ
የ'ሚደ'ገፍ

telegram
'ቴለግራም -ስ- ቴሌግራም

telephone
'ቴለፈውን -ስ- ቴሌፎን

telescope
'ቴለስከውፕ -ስ- ቴሌስኮ'ፕ (የሩቁን አቅርቦ
የ'ሚያሳ'ይ መነ'ጥር)

television
'ቴለቪዠን -ስ- ቴሌቪዥን

tell
'ቴል -ግ- መንገር [ነ'ገረ]

temerity
ተ'ሜሪቲ -ስ- የማይ'ገ'ባ ድፍረት ፤ ች'ኩ
ል'ነት ፡ አለመ'ጠንቀቅ

temper
'ቴምፐ -ስ- አመል (ቁ'ጡ'ነት ፡ ገ'ራም'ነት)
-ስ- ጠንካ'ራ'ነት (ለብረት)
steel
-ግ- ማጠንከር [አጠነ'ከረ] (ለብረት
ለመስተዋት ፡ በሙቀት)

temperament
ቴምፐረመንት -ስ- አመል (ቁ'ጡ'ነት ፡ ን'ዴ
ተ'ኛነት ፡ ፀ'ጥተ'ኛ'ነት ወዘተ)

temperance
'ቴምፐረንስ -ስ- አለማብዛት ፡ መጠነ'ኛ'ነት
ራስን ከአስካሪ መጠ'ጥ መከልከል

temperate
'ቴምፐረት -ቅ- መካ'ከለ'ኛ (ለአ'የር ሙቀት)

temperature
'ቴምፐረቸ -ስ- ያ'የር ሁናቴ (ሙቀት ወይን'ም
ቅዝ'ቃዜ) ፤ ሙቀት (የሰው'ነት ከት'ኩሳት
የተነ'ሣ)

tempest
'ቴምፐስት -ስ- ጎይለ'ኛ ነፋስ ፡ ዝናም ወዘተ

temple
'ቴምፕል -ስ- ቤተ መቅደስ

temporal
'ቴምፐረል -ቅ- ጎላፊ ፡ የ'ማይቆ'ይ ፡ ጊዜ
ያዊ ፤ ምድራዊ ፡ ዓለማዊ

temporary
'ቴምፐረ -ቅ- ጊዜያዊ ፡ ጥቂት ጊዜ ብ'ቻ
የ'ሚቆ'ይ

tempt
'ቴምት -ግ- መፈታተን [ተፈታ'ተነ] ፡ ክፉ
ሥራ እንዲሠራ ማባባል [አባ'በለ]

temptation
ቴም'ቴይሽን -ስ- ፈተና (የሥይጣን)

ten
'ቴን -ቅ- ዐ'ሥር

tenable
'ቴነብል -ቅ- የ'ሚ'ደ'ገፍ ፡ የ'ሚ'ቀ'በሉት
(ሐ'ሳብ)

tenacious
ተ'ኔይሸስ -ቅ- ተስፋ የ'ማይቆርጥ ፡ የያዘ
ውን የ'ማይለ'ቅ ፤ አ'ሳብ ጥብቅ ።

616

tenacity

ተ'ናሲቲ -ስ- ተስፋ አለመቁረጥ ፣ በሐ'ሳብ
መጥበቅ

tenant

'ቴነንት -ስ- ኪራየተ'ኛ (የመሬት ፣ የቤት
መዘተ) ፣ ጢሰ'ኛ

tend

'ቴንድ -ግ- ማዘንበል [አዘነ'በለ] ፣ መጠ
በቅ [ጠ'በቀ] (ለእንስሳ)

tendency

'ቴንደንሲ -ስ- ዝን'ባሌ

tender

'ቴንደ -ቅ- ርኅሩኅ ፣ ገር ፤ ለስላ'ሳ
offer

-ግ- ማ'ጫረት [አ'ጫ'ረተ]

tendon

'ቴንደን -ስ- ጅ'ማት

tendril

'ቴንድሪል -ስ- ቀምበጥ (የ'ሚ'ሳቡ አትክልት)

tense

'ቴንስ -ስ- ድርጊ'ቱ የ'ሚ'ፈ'ጸም'በትን ፣
የተፈ'ጸመ'በትን ጊዜ የ'ሚያሳ'ይ የግ'ሥ
ዓይነት ፣ ጊዜ (ሰዋስው)
unrelaxed

-ቅ- ግ'ትር ፣ ያልተዝና'ና (ለሰው'ነት
መዘተ)

tension

'ቴንሽን -ስ- አለመግባባት ፣ ግ'ጥት (የሐ
'ሳብ)

tent

'ቴንት -ስ- ድንኳን

tentative

'ቴንተቲቭ -ቅ- ለሙ'ከራ ያህል የተደ'ረገ ፣
ጊዜያዊ

tenth

'ቴንስ -ቅ- 0'ሥረ'ኛ

tent-peg

'ቴንት'ፔግ -ስ- ካስማ

tenure

'ቴንየ -ስ- ይዞታ (የመሬት ፣ የፖለቲካ ሥራ)

tepid

'ቴፒድ -ቅ- ለ'ብ ያለ (ለውሃ)

term

'ተ:ም -ስ- የትምህርት ክፍለ ዓመት (ለሁለ'ት
መዘተ የተከ'ፈለ)፤ፍርድ ቤቶ'ች ችሎት'የ'ሚያ
ስችሉ'በት ወራት
expression

-ስ- ቃል
of bargain

-ስ- ስምም'ነት (ለገበያ)

terminal

'ተ:ሚነል -ቅ- መጨ'ረሻ (የባቡር መጨ'ረሻ
ጣቢያ)

terminate

'ተ:ሚኔይት -ግ- መጨ'ረስ [ጨ'ረሰ] ፣ መፈ
'ጸም [ፈ'ጸመ]

terminus

'ተ:ሚነስ -ስ- የእውቶቡስ መጨ'ረሻ ጣቢያ

termite

'ተ:ማይት -ስ- ምስጥ

terrace

'ቴረስ -ስ- ደልዳ'ላ ቦታ

terrain

ቴ'ሬይን -ስ- የመሬት አ'ቀማመጥ

terrible

'ቴሪበል -ቅ- በጣም አስደንጋጭ ፣ አስፈ'ሪ
እሳ'ዛኝ

terrify

'ቴሪፋይ -ግ- ማስፈራራት [አስፈራ'ራ]፣ ማስ
ደንገጥ [አስደነ'ገጠ]

territory

'ቴሪትሪ -ስ- ግዛት ፣ በግዛት ውስጥ ያ'ለ
አገር

terror

'ቴረ -ስ- ፍርሃት ፣ ድን'ጋጤ

terse

'ተ:ስ -ቅ- አ'ጭር'ና መሥመሩን ያ'ለ'ቀቀ
(ለንግ'ግር)

test

'ቴስት -ግ- መፈ'ተን [ፈ'ተነ] ፣ መሞ'ከር
(ሞ'ከረ]

testament

'ቴስተመንት -ስ- ኑዛዜ
biblical

-ስ- ኪዳን

testicle
'ቴስቲክል -ስ- ቆለጥ
testify
'ቴስቲፋይ -ግ- መመስከር [መስ'ከረ]
testimonial
ቴስት'ምውኒየል -ስ- የምስ'ክር ወረቀት (የሥ
'ራተኛ ጠባይ)
testimony
'ቴስተመኒ -ስ- ምስ'ክር
text
'ቴክስት -ስ- ጽሑፍ (መጽሐፍ) ፤ የመጽሐፍ
ቅ'ዱስ ጥቅስ
textbook
'ቴክስትቡክ -ስ- የመ'ማሪያ መጽሐፍ
textiles
'ቴክስታየልዝ -ስ- ጨርቃጨርቅ
texture
'ቴክስቸ -ስ- ያንድ ነገር የለስላ'ሳ'ነቱ ፤ የሻ
ካራ'ነቱ ወዘተ ሁናቴ ፤ የጅር'ና የማግ አ'ተግ
መጥ (በጨርቃጨርቅ ፋብሪካ)
than
'ዛን -መዋ- ከ . . . ይልቅ
thank
'ሳንክ -ስ- ማመስገን [አመስ'ገነ]
thank you
'ሳንክዩ አመስ'ግና'ለሁ ፤ እግዚአብሔር
ይስጥ'ል'ኝ
that
'ዛት -አተስ ያ ፤ ያ'ች
-አቅ- ያ ፤ ያ'ች
-መዋ- እንደ
thatch
'ሳች -ስ- የሣር ክዳን ፤ ከፈ፤ክፋ፤
-ግ- በሣር መክደን [ከ'ደነ] ፤ መከፈ፤ክፋ፤
[ከፈ'ከፈ]
thaw
'ሶ: -ግ- መሟሟት [ሟ'ሟ] (ለበረዶ)
the
'ዜ'ዡ -ተመ- -ው : -ዋ
-ዩቱ : -ዩቷ
theatre
'ሲየተር -ስ- ቴአትር ፤ በህ ስፒታል በ'ሽተ
'ኞ'ች የ'ሚ'ቀ'ደዱ'በት ክፍል
theft
ሴፍት -ስ- ስርቆት

thin
ˈθɪn -ቅ- ቀ'ጭን

thing
ˈθɪŋg -ስ- ነገር ፣ ዕቃ

think
ˈθɪŋk -ግ- ማ'ሰብ [አ'ሰበ]

third
ˈθəːd -ቅ- ሢሶ ፣ አን'ድ ሦስተ'ኛ ፣ ሦስት'ያ

thirst
ˈθəːst -ስ- ጥም

thirsty
ˈθəːstɪ -ቅ- የጠ'ማው ፣ የተጠ'ማ

thirteen
ˈθəːˈtiːn -ቅ- ዐሥራ ሦስት

thirteenth
ˈθəːˈtiːnθ -ቅ- ዐሥራ ሦስተ'ኛ

thirtieth
ˈθəːtɪəθ -ቅ- ሠላሳ'ኛ

thirty
ˈθəːtɪ -ቅ- ሠላሳ

this
ˈðɪs -አተሰ- ይህ ፣ ይህ'ች

thong
ˈθɔŋg -ስ- ጠፍር (መ'ጫ'ኛ ፣ ጅራፍ ወዘተ)

thorn
ˈθɔːn -ስ- እሾህ

thorough
ˈθʌrə -ቅ- ጥንቁቅ ፣ ለጥቃ'ቅን ነገር የ'ሚጠ ነ'ቀቅ

thoroughfare
ˈθʌrəfɛə -ስ- ሹር'ው ያለ ጎዳና

though
ˈðəu -መዋ- ቢሆን'ም ፣ ሆኖ'ም

thought
ˈθɔːt -ስ- ሐ'ሳብ

thoughtful
ˈθɔːtful -ቅ- ል'ባም ፣ አ'ስቢ

thoughtless
ˈθɔːtlɪs -ቅ- ሐ'ሳብ ቢስ ፣ ል'ብ ቢስ

thousand
ˈθauzənd -ቅ- ሺህ ፣ ሺ.

thrash
ˈθræʃ -ግ- መደብደብ [ደበ'ደበ] ፣ ደንጋ አድርጎ መግረፍ [ገ'ረፈ] ፤ መውቃት [ወ'ቃ] (እህል)

thread
ˈθrɛd -ስ- ክ'ር
of screw
ጥርስ (የሚስማር)

threadbare
ˈθrɛdbɛə -ቅ- እ'ላቂ (ጨርቅ)

threat
ˈθrɛt -ስ- ዛ'ቻ

threaten
ˈθrɛtn -ግ- መዛት [ዛተ]

three
ˈθriː -ቅ- ሦስት

thresh
ˈθrɛʃ -ግ- መውቃት [ወ'ቃ]

threshold
ˈθrɛʃhəuld -ስ- ምድራክ ፣ መድረክ

thrifty
ˈθrɪftɪ -ቅ- ገንዘብ ቆ'ጣቢ

thrill
ˈθrɪl -ስ- ጥልቅ ስ'ሜት ፣ ጥልቅ የደ'ስታ ስ'ሜት

thrive
ˈθraɪv -ግ- መፋፋት [ፋ'ፋ] ፣ ማደግ [አ'ደገ] ፣ መበልጸግ (በለ'ጸገ)

throat
ˈθrəut -ስ- ጉሮ'ሮ

throb
ˈθrɔb -ግ- መጠዝጠዝ [ጠዘ'ጠዘ] (ለቁስል) ፣ በፍጥነት መምታታ [መ'ታ] (ለል'ብ ፣ ለት'ር'ታ)

throne
ˈθrəun -ስ- ዙፋን

throng
ˈθrɔŋg -ግ- መ'ታፈግ [ታ'ፈገ] ፣ መ'ጋፋት [ተጋ'ፋ]
-ስ- የተሰበ'ሰበ ሕዝብ

throttle
ˈθrɔtl -ግ- ማነቅ [አ'ነቀ]

619

through
ስ'ሩ፡ -መዋ- በ . . . ውስጥ
  by means of
  -መዋ- በ . . . አማካኝ'ነት
throw
ስ'ሩው -ግ- መወርወር [ወረ'ወሪ]
thrust
ስ'ረስት -ግ- መውጋት [ወ'ጋ] ፣ መሻጥ
[ሻጠ]
  push
  -ግ- መጠቅጠቅ [ጠቀ'ጠቀ]
thud
'ሰድ -ግ- እንዝ'ፍ ማለት [አለ]
thumb
ሰም -ስ- አውራ ጣት
thump
'ሰምፕ -ስ- ጎይሊ'ኛ በ'ትር (በጡ'ሪ)
  -ግ- መምታት [መ'ታ] (በጡ'ሪ)
thunder
'ሰንደ -ስ- ነጎድጓድ
Thursday
'ሰ:ዝዴይ -ስ- ሐሙስ
thus
'ዘስ -ተግ- እንዲህ ፣ ስለ'ዚህ ፣ በ'ዚህ ሁኔቱ
thwart
'ስዎ:ት -ግ- ማ'ገድ [አ'ገደ] ፣ ማ'ሰናከል
[አ'ሰና'ከለ] (ሐ'ሳብ ፣ ም'ኞት)
tick
'ቲክ -ስ- ጥሩት (ል'ክ'ነትን የ'ሚያመለ'ክት
'ሥ')
  insect
  -ስ- ደም መጣ1ጭ ተባይ (መ'ኸገር
ወዘተ)
ticket
'ቲከት -ስ- የመግቢያ ወረቀት (ቲኬት)
tickle
'ቲከል -ግ- መኮርኮር [ኮረ'ኮረ] (እንዲ
ሥቅ ለማድረግ)
ticklish
'ቲክሊሽ -ቅ- ሲኮሩ'ኩራት የ'ሚሽኮሩ'መም
  difficult
  -ቅ- ለመሥራት አ'ዋኪ
tide
'ታይድ -ስ- ማዕበል ፣ ሞገድ (የባሕር)

tidings
'ታይዲንግዝ--ስ- ወሬ
tidy
'ታይዲ -ቅ- ንጹሕ ፣ የተሰ'ተረ ፣ ጠ'ፍ ያለ
tie
'ታይ -ግ- ማሠር [አ'ሠረ]
  -ስ- ክራ'ባት
tier
'ቲየ -ስ- ደረጃ'ነት ያ'ለው በመሥመር የተደ
ረ'ደረ መ'ቀመጫ ፣ መደርደሪያ ወዘተ
tiff
'ቲፍ -ስ- ጥቅ'ጥቅ ፣ አለመግባባት (ቀ'ላል)
tiger
'ታይገ -ስ- ነብር ፣ ነምር
tight
'ታይት -ቅ- ጥብቅ ፣ ጠ'ባብ
tighten
'ታይተን -ግ- ማጥበቅ [አጠ'በቀ] ፣ ማጥበብ
[አጠ'በበ] ፣ በውል ማሥር [አ'ሠረ]
till (until)
'ቲል -ተግ- እስከ . . . ድረስ
till
'ቲል -ግ- ማረስ [አ'ረሰ]
  cash
  -ስ- መሳቢያ (የገንዘብ ማስቀ'መጫ)
tilt
'ቲልት -ግ- ማዘንበል [አዘነ'በለ]
timber
'ቲምበ -ስ- ሳንቃ
time
'ታይም -ስ- ሰዓት ፣ ጊዜ ፣ ዘመን
timely
'ታይምሊ -ተግ- በደኅና ጊዜ ፣ በሰዓቱ ፣ በተ
ስማሚ ጊዜ
timetable
'ታይምቴይብል -ስ- የጊዜ ሥሌዳ
timid
'ቲሚድ -ቅ- ንዬን አ'ፋር ፣ ፈሪ
timorous
'ቲመረስ -ቅ- ንዬን አ'ፋር ፣ ፈሪ
tin
'ቲን -ስ- ቆርቆ'ር
  container
  -ስ- ታኒካ

620

tincture 'ቲንክቸ -ስ- ቀለም (መንከሪያ) ፣ በአልኮል ውስጥ የ'ሚሚ'ሚ መድኃኒት

tinder 'ቲንደ -ስ- እሳት ማ'ቀጣጠያ ፣ መለ'ኮሻ

tinged 'ቲንጅድ -ቅ- በቀ'ላሉ የቀ'ለመ

tingle 'ቲንገል -ግ- መውረር [ወ'ረረ] (ስ'ሜት)

tinker 'ቲንከ -ስ- እ'የዞሩ የብረት ድስት'ና መጥበሻ ወዘተ የ'ሚያበ'ጅ ሰው
-ግ- መጉራ-ጉር [ጉራ'ጉረ] (ላያውቁ ለግበ'ጀት መሞ'ከር)

tinkle 'ቲንክል -ግ- መክለል [ክ'ለለ]

tinted 'ቲንቲድ -ቅ- የቀ'ለመ

tiny 'ታይኒ -ቅ- በጣም ት'ንሽ

tip 'ቲፕ -ስ- ጫፍ
gratuity
-ስ- ጉርሻ (የገንዘብ)
advice
-ስ- ጠቃሚ ምክር
-ግ- መገልበጥ [ገለ'በጠ] ፣ ማፍሰስ [አፈ'ሰሰ]

tipsy 'ቲፕሲ -ቅ- ጥ'ቅ ያለው (በመጠ'ጥ)

tiptoe 'ቲፕተው -ግ- በእግር ጣት መሄድ [ሄደ] (ከ'ቴ እንዳይ'ሰ'ማ)

tiptop 'ቲፕ'ቶፕ -ቅ- ዋ'ና ፣ ላ'ቂያ ወይን'ም ብልጫ ያ'ለው

tirade ተ'ሬይድ -ስ- ቁ'ጣ የተመ'ላ ረ'ጅም ንግ'ግር

tire 'ታየ -ግ- መድከም`[ደ'ከመ]

tiresome 'ታየሰም -ቅ- አስቆ'ጪ ፣ አሰልቺ ፣ አድካሚ

tissue 'ቲሹ: -ስ- ቀ'ጭን'ና በውስጡ የ'ሚያሳ'ይ ጨ ርቅ ፣ ወረቀት ፣ የሥጋ ልባስ ወዘተ ፣ ሥጋ (የሰ ው'ነት)

titbit 'ቲትቢት -ስ- የ'ሚጣ'ፍጥ ምግብ ት'ንሽ ጉር ሻ ፣ የ'ሚያስ'ን ወሬ ፣ ጥምጥምታ

tithe 'ታይዝ -ስ- ዐሥራት
-ግ- ዐሥራት ማውጣት [አወ'ጣ]

title 'ታይተል -ስ- አርእስ-
rank
-ስ- ግዕርግ

titter 'ቲተ -ግ- እየተሸኮረ'መመ መሣቅ [ሣቀ] ፣ በዝ'ቅተ'ኛ ድምፅ መሣቅ [ሣቀ]

to 'ቱ: -መዋ- ወደ ፣ ለ ፣ እስከ

toad 'ተውድ -ስ- ጉርጥ (የእንቁራሪት ዓይነት ፍ ጡር)

toast 'ተውስት -ስ- የተጠ'በሰ ዳ'ቦ (ቶስት)

tobacco ተ'ባከው -ስ- ትምባሆ

today ቱ'ዴይ -ተግ- ዛሬ ፣ ባሁኑ ጊዜ

toddle 'ቶደል -ግ- መውተርተር [ተውተረ'ተረ] (እ ንደ ሕፃን እርም'ጃ)

toe 'ተው -ስ- የእግር ጣት

toenail 'ተውኔይል -ስ- የገር ጣት ጥፍር

toffee 'ቶፊ -ስ- ከወተት የተሠ'ራ ከረሜ'ላ

together ቱ'ጌዝ -ተግ- አንድ'ነት ፣ አንድላይ ፣ አብሮ

toil 'ቶይል -ግ- መሥራት [ሠ'ራ] ፣ መጣር [ጣረ]
-ስ- ከ'ባድ ሥራ

621

toilet

'ቶይለት -ስ- ሠገራ ቤት ፣ ሽንት ቤት ፣ ልብ
ስ መለባበስ'ና ጠጉር ማበጣጠር

token

'ተውከን -ስ- መ'ታወቂያ ፣ ምል'ክት ፣ ለመ
ዳ'ጅነት ምል'ክት እንዲሆን የተሰ'ጠ ስጦታ

tolerance

'ቶለረንስ -ስ- ትዕግሥት ፣ ቻይ'ነት

toll

'ቶል -ግ- መረ'ዋ መምታት [መ'ታ].
-ስ- የይለፍ ቀረጥ (በአንድ መንገድ
ወይን'ም ድልድይ ላይ ለማለፍ)

tomato

ተ'ማ:ተው -ስ- ቲማቲም

tomb

'ቱ:ም -ስ- መቃብር

tomboy

'ተምቦይ -ት- ወንዳወንድ (ለሴት)

tomorrow

ተ'ሞረው -ተግ- ነገ

tone

'ተውን -ስ- የሙዚቃ ድምፅ

tongs

'ቶንግዝ -ስ- ወረንጦ

tongue

'ተንግ -ስ- መላስ ፣ ምላስ

tonic

'ቶኒክ -ስ- ማ'ነቃቂያ መድኃኒት

tonight

ቱ'ናይት -ተግ- ዛሬ ማታ

too

'ቱ: -ተግ- ደግሞ ፣ እ'ጅግ ፤ - ም

tool

'ቱ:ል -ስ- መ'ሣሪያ (የሥ'ራተ'ኞ'ች)

tooth

'ቱ:ስ -ስ- ጥርስ

toothache

'ቱ:ሴይክ -ስ- የጥርስ በ'ሽታ፣የጥርስ ሕመም

toothpick

'ቱ:ፒክ -ስ- የጥርስ መጎርጎሪያ (እንጨት)

top

'ቶፕ -ስ- ራስ ፣ ጫፍ ፣ አፋፍ፣
cover
-ስ- መክደኛ

topaz

'ተውፓዝ -ስ- ዕንቁ'ጸዕዮን

topic

'ቶፒክ -ስ- አርእስት

topple

'ቶፐል -ግ- ተንገዳግዶ መውደቅ [መ'ደቀ]

torch

'ቶ:ች -ስ- ፋና ፣ ች'በ

torment

'ቶ:ሜንት -ግ- ማስጨ'ነቅ [አስጨ'ነቀ] ፣
ማ'ሠቃየት [አ'ሠቃ'የ]
-ስ- ጭንቀት ፣ ሥቃይ

tornado

ቶ:'ኔደው -ስ- ኃይለ'ኛ ዐውሎ ነፋስ

torpid

'ቶ:ፒድ -ቅ- ደካማ ፣ የደነ'ዘዘ ፣ ጎታታ

torrent

'ቶረንት -ስ- ጎርፍ ፤ በቁ'ጣ መነጉፈል

torso

'ቶ:ሰው -ስ- እ'ጅ ፣ እግር'ና ራስ የሌ'ለው
ምስል

tortoise

'ቶ:ተስ -ስ- ኤሊ.

torture

'ቶ:ቸ -ግ- ማ'ሠቃየት [አ'ሠቃ'የ]
-ስ- ሥቃይ ፣ ሕማም

toss

'ቶስ -ግ- ማንጣ [አነ'ሳ] ፣ ወደ ላይ ማስፈን
'ጠር [አስፈን'ጠረ] (ም'ሳሌ መሐ'ለቅ ወዘተ) ፣
መ'ገላበጥ [ተገላ'በጠ] (በመ'ኝታ)

total

'ተውተል -ስ- ሙሉ ፣ ፍ'ጹም
-ቅ- ድምር

totter

'ቶተ -ግ- መንገዳገድ [ተንገዳ'ገደ] (ሲ.ሂ.ዱ.)

touch

'ተች -ግ- መንካት [ነ'ካ]

touchy

'ተቺ -ቅ- ፈጥኖ ተቆጪ ፣ ቁ'ጡ ፣ አኩራራ.

tough

'ተፍ -ቅ- ጠንካ'ራ ፣ ኃይለ'ኛ ፣ የ'ማይ.በ'ጠር

tour

'ቱ: -ግ- መዞር [ዞረ] (አገር)

tourist
’ቱሪስት -ስ- አገር ጉብኚ

tournament
’ቱነመንት -ስ- ግጥሚያ (የስፖርት)

tow
’ተው -ግ- መጎተት [ጐ'ተተ] ፣ መሳብ[ሳብ]
(መርከብ ፣ መኪና ወዘተ በገመድ)

towards
ተ’ዎ:ድዝ -መዋ- ወደ ፣ በ . . . አቅጣ’ጫ

towel
’ታወል -ስ- ፎጣ

tower
’ታዋ -ስ- ጥቅም ፣ ክ'ፍተ'ኛ ግምብ

town
’ታውን -ስ- ከተማ
-hall
    -ስ- የማ'ዘጋጃ ቤት አ'ዳራሽ ፣ ማ'ዘጋጃ
ቤት

toxic
’ቶክሲክ -ቅ- የመርዝ ፣ መርዛም

toy
’ቶይ -ስ- መ'ጫወቻ ፣ አሻንጉ'ሊት

trace
ት’ሬይስ -ግ- ፈ'ልጎ ማግኘት [አገ'ኘ]
    -ስ- ምል'ክ)ት ፣ ፋና

trachoma
ትረ'ከውመ -ስ- ዓይን መያዝ (ተላላፊ የዓ
ይን በ'ሽታ)

track
ት’ራክ -ግ- መከታተል [ተከታ'ተለ] (ፈ፡
ንስላ)
    -ስ- ስር፡ መንገድ ፣ የባቡር ሐዲዶች

tractor
ት’ራክተ -ስ- ማረሻ መኪና

trade
ት’ሬይድ -ግ- መነ'ገድ [ነ ገደ] ፣ መሸ'ቀጥ
[ሸ'ቀጠ]
    -ስ- መገዛት ፣ መሸጥ ፣ መነ'ገድ ፣ ጥያ
(ሥራ)

trader
ት’ሬይደ -ስ- ነ'ጋዴ ፣ ሽ'ቀጭ

tradeunion
ትሬይድ'ዩኒየን -ስ- የሞያተ'ኞች ማኅበር

tradition
ትረ’ዲሽን -ስ- ልምድ ፣ ባሀል ፣ ወግ

traffic
ት’ራፊክ -ስ- ተሽከርካሪ መኪናዎ'ች (በመን
ገድ ላይ)

tragedy
ት’ራጀዲ -ስ- የሰውን ድቀት ፣ ሐዘን የ'ሚያ
ሳ'ይ ታሪክ ወይ'ም ቴአትር ፣ አሳ'ዛኝ ውናቱ
(በሰው ሕይወት)

tragic
ት’ራጂክ -ቅ- በጣም አሳ'ዛኝ

trail
ት’ሬይል -ግ- በመሬት ላይ መጎ'ተተ [ጎ'ተተ] ፣
እንላ መቅረት [ቀ'ረ] (በጉዞ)
    -ስ- ኩረኮንች መንገድ ፣ ዱካ

train
ት’ሬይን -ግ- ማሠልጠን [አሠለ'ጠነ] (ለእን
ስሳት)
learn
    -ግ- መ'ማር [ተማረ] ፣ መ'ለማመድ
(ተለማ'መደ]
sport
    -ግ- መ'ለማመድ [ተለማ'መደ] (ለስ
ፖርት)
railway
    -ስ- የምድር ባቡር

trainer
ት’ሬይነ -ስ- አሠልጣኝ ፣ ገራ

trait
ት’ሬት -ስ- የጠባይ ዓይነት ፣ መ'ለያ ጠባይ

traitor
ት’ሬተ -ስ- ከ'ዳተ'ኛ

tram
ት’ራም -ስ- ትራም (በከተማ ውስጥ የ'ሚሄድ
የምድር ባቡር)

tramp
ት’ራምፕ -ግ- መርገጥ [ረ'ገጠ] (ለመ'ታ'ደር)
    -ስ- ዘዋሪ ፣ ቤት የሌ'ለው ፣ ከርተ'ታ

trample
ት’ራምፕል -ግ- መ'ረማረም [ረመ'ረም] ፣ ጣ
በራ' [አበራ' የ]

trance
ት’ራ:ንስ -ስ- ራስን አለማወቅ ፣ ነፍስን መሳ'ለ

tranquil
ት’ራንክዊል -ቅ- ጸ'ተተ'ኛ ፣ ሰማዊ

transact
ት’ራን'ሳክት -ግ- መ'ገበያየት [ተገበያ'የ]

transaction
ትራን'ሳክሽን -ስ- መ'ገበያየት
transcribe
ትራንስክ'ራይብ -ግ- በሌላ ፊደል መጻፍ [ጻፈ]፣ በሙሉ መጻፍ [ጻፈ] ፣ መገልበጥ [ገለ'በጠ] (ጽሑፍ)
transfer
ትራንስፈ፡ -ግ- ማዛወር [አ'ዛ'ወረ]
-ስ- ዝው'ውር
transferable
ትራንስ'ፈ፡ረበል -ቅ- የ'ሚ'ዛ'ወር ፣ ሊ'ዛ'ወር የ'ሚችል
transform
ትራንስ'ፎ፡ም -ግ- መለ'ወጥ [ለ'ወጠ] (ካንድ ሁናቴ ወደ ሌላ)
transgress
ትራንዝግ'ሬስ -ግ- መጣስ [ጣሰ] ፣ መ'ተላለፍ [ተላ'ለፈ] (ሕ'ግን)
transit
ትራንሲት -ስ- አላፊ (መንገደ'ኛ ፣ ሳያርፍ)
transition
ትራን'ዚሽን -ስ- መ'ሽጋገሪያ (ጊዜ)
transitive
ትራንዚቲቭ -ቅ- ተሻጋሪ (ለሰዋስው ፣ ግ'ሥ)
translate
ትራንስ'ሌይት -ግ- መተርጎም [ተረ'ጐመ] (ካንድ ቋንቋ ወደ ሌላው)
transparent
ትራንስ'ፓረንት -ቅ- በውስጡ የ'ሚያሳ'ይ
transport
ትራንስ[ፖ]ት -ግ- ማ'መላለስ [አ'መላ'ለሰ] ፣ ማጓዝ [አጓዘ]
-ስ- ማ'መላለሻ (መኪና፣በቅሎ፣ወዘተ)
trap
ትራ፡ፕ -ግ- ማጥመድ [አጠ'መደ]
-ሴ- ወጥመድ
trash
ትራሽ -ስ- ቄሻሻ ፣ ወ'ራ'ዳ ነገር ፣ ምናምን
travel
ትራቨል -ግ- መ'ጓዝ [ተ'ጓዘ]
-ስ- ጉዞ ፣ መንገድ
traverse
ትራ'ቨ፡ስ -ግ- መ'ሻገር [ተሻ'ገረ]፣ ማ'ጻረጥ [አ'ጻ'ረጠ] (ለነገር)

tray
ት'ሬይ -ስ- ትሪ
treacherous
ት'ሬቸረስ -ቅ- ከ'ዳተ'ኛ
tread
ት'ሬድ -ግ- መርገጥ [ረ'ገጠ] ፣ መ'ራመድ [ተራ'መደ]
treadle
ት'ሬደል -ስ- መወስወሻ (የስፌት መኪና ወዘተ)
treason
ት'ሪይዘን -ስ- ዐመጽ ፣ በሀገር ላይ ማ'መጽ ፣ እምነት ማጉደል
treasure
ት'ሬገ -ስ- መዝገብ (ዋጋ ያ'ለው ዕቃ)
-ግ- በጥን'ቃቴ ማስቀ'መጥ [አስቀ'መ ጠ]
treat
ት'ሪይት -ግ- ማ'ከም [አ'ከመ]
handle
-ግ- በተለ'የ ሁናቴ መያዝ [ያዘ] (ለክፉ፣ ለደ'ግ)
invite
-ግ- መጋበዝ [ጋ'በዘ]
invitation
-ስ- ጋብዞ ማብላት ፣ ግጠ'ጣት ማስ ተናገድ
treaty
ት'ሪይቲ -ስ- ውል ፣ ስምም'ነት (በመንግ ሥ'ታት መካ'ከል)
treble
ት'ሬበል -ቅ- ሦስት እጥፍ ፣ ሦስት እ'ጅ
-ግ- ሦስት ማድረግ [አደ'ረገ]
musical
-ስ- ከ'ፍተ'ኛ ድምፅ (በሙ-ዚቃ)
tree
ት'ሪይ -ስ- ዛፍ
trellis
ት'ሬሊስ -ስ- የእንጨት አጥር (እንደ መረብ የተሠ'ራ) ፣ ፍርግርግ የንጨት አጥር
tremble
ት'ሬምበል -ግ- መንቀጥቀጥ [ተንቀጠ'ቀጠ]
with fear
-ግ- መብረከረክ [ተብረከ'ረከ]

624

tremendous
ትሪ'ሜንደስ -ቅ- አስገ'ራሚ ፣ አስደ'ናቂ ፣
ታ'ላቅ ፣ ጓ'ያል

tremor
ት'ሬመ -ስ- ቀ'ላል የሙራት መንቀጥቀጥ ፣
የፍርሀት ስ'ሜት

trench
ትሬንች -ስ- ቦይ ፣ በረ'ጅሙ የተቆ'ፈረ ቦይ
(ለወ'ታ'ደር ም'ሽግ)

trend
ትሬንድ -ስ- ዝን'ባሌ

trespass
ትሬስፐስ -ግ- ጓጢአት መሥራት [ሠ'ራ] ፣
መ'ተላለፍ [ተላ'ለፈ]
on land
        -ግ- የሰውን ድንበር መጣስ [ጣስ]፣
መግፋት [ገ'ፋ]

tress
ትሬስ -ስ- ኩልኩ'ሉ (የጠጉር)

trestle
ትሬሰል -ስ- የጠረ'ጴዛ መቆሚያ

trial
ትራየል -ስ- ምርመራ (ለዳ'ኛ'ነት) ፣ ሙ'ከራ

triangle
ትራያንገል -ስ- ሦስት ማዕዘን

triangular
ትራ'ያንግዩለ -ቅ- ባለሦስት ማዕዘን

tribe
ት'ራይብ -ስ- ነገድ ፣ ጎሳ

tribunal
ትራይብ'ዩነል -ስ- ል'ዩ ፍርድ ቤት (ለአንድ
ለተለ'የ ጉ'ዳይ)

tribute
ትሪበዩት -ስ- ምስጋና (የውለታ) ፣ ግብር
(አንድ መንግሥት ከሌላው የ'ሚ'ቀ'በለው)፣
ግብር (የገንዘብ ወዘተ)

trick
ትሪክ -ግ- ማ'ታለል [አ'ታ'ለለ] ፣ ማሞ'ኘት
[አሞ'ኘ]

trickle
ትሪከለ -ግ- በትንሹ መፍሰስ [ፈ'ሰስ]
በት'ንሹ ማፍሰስ [አፈ'ሰስ] (ለውሃ)

tricky
ትሪኪ -ቅ- አስቸ'ጋሪ (ለመ'ረዳት ፣ ለመmግ
ባባት)

trifle
ት'ራይፋል -ስ- ተራ ነገር ፣ ት'ንሽ ጣፋጭ
ኬክ ፣ መርመላታ ወዘተ
        -ግ- ማሞ'ኘት [አሞ'ኘ] ፣ የቂል ሥራ
መሥራት [ሠ'ራ]

trigger
ትሪገ -ስ- ምላ'ጭ (የሙንጃ)

trim
ትሪም -ቅ- የተስተካ'ከለ
        -ግ- ማስተካከል [አስተካ'ከለ]

trinity
ትሪኒቲ -ስ- ሥ'ላሴ

trinket
ትሪንከት -ስ- መና'ኛ ጌጥ

trio
ትሪየው -ስ- አንድ ሥራ የ'ሚሠሩ ሦስት
ሰዎ'ች (ሙዚቀ'ኞ'ች ፣ ዘፋኞ'ች ወዘተ)

trip
ትሪፕ -ስ- አ'ጭር ጉዞ
stumble
        -ግ- መ'ደናቀፍ [ተደና'ቀፈ]

tripe
ትራይፕ -ስ- ጨ'ን'ራ (የከብት)
nonsense
        -ስ- ዋጋ የሌ'ለው ንግ'ግር

triple
ትሪፕል -ቅ- ሦስት እጥፍ

tripod
ትራይፖድ -ስ- ባለሦስት እግር ማስቀ'መጫ
(ጠረ'ጴዛ ፣ ወንበር ወዘተ)

trite
ትራይት -ቅ- ተራ (ለንግ'ግር ፣ ብዙ ጊዜ የተ
መላ'ለሰ)

triumph
ትራየምፍ -ግ- ድል በመንሣት መደ'ሰት [ተደ'ሰተ]

trivial
ትሪቪየል -ቅ- ተራ ፣ ዋጋ ቢስ

troop
ት'ሩ፡ፕ -ስ- ሠራዊት ፣ የጦር ሠራዊት

trophy
ት'ረውፊ -ስ- ዋንጫ (ለስፖ'ርት)

trot
ት'ሮት -ግ- መስገር [ሰ'ገረ] ፣ ኩ'ስ ኩ'ስ
ማለት [አለ] (ለሰው)

625

trouble
ት'ረበል -ግ- ማስቸ'ገር [አስቸ'ገረ] ፣ ማ'ወክ [አ'ወከ]
-ስ- ች'ግር
troublesome
ት'ረበልሰም -ቅ- አውከተ'ኛ ፣ አስቸ'ጋሪ
trough
ት'ሮፍ -ስ- ገርግም (የእንስሳት መ'መገቢያ ዕቃ)
trousers
ት'ራውዘዝ -ስ- ሱ'ሪ
trowel
ት'ራወል -ስ- የሲሚንቶ መለ'ጠፊያ ማንካ
truant
ት'ሩወንት -ስ- ከትምህርት ቤት የ'ሚቀር ሕፃን (ለጨዋታ ሲል)
truce
ት'ሩ:ስ -ስ- ጦር'ነት ለጥቂት ጊዜ ለማቆም መስማማት
truck
ት'ረክ -ስ- ጋሪ ፣ መንኩራኩር (ለዕቃ መጫኛ)
trudge
ት'ረጅ -ስ- መ'ጐተት [ተጐ'ተተ] (ሲሄዱ)
true
ት'ሩ: -ስ- እውነት
trumpet
ት'ረምፐት -ስ- ጡሩምባ ፣ መለከት
truncheon
ት'ረንቸን -ስ- ቆመጥ ፣ አ'ጭር ዱ'ላ ፣ (የፖሊስ)
trunk
ት'ረንክ -ስ- ግንድ
of elephant
-ስ- ኩምቢ
of body
-ስ- ዛላ ፣ አካል
container
-ስ- ት'ልቅ ሣጥን (የብረት)
truss
ት'ረስ -ግ- ማሰር [አ'ሰረ]
trust
ት'ረስት -ግ- መ'ተማመን [ተማ'መነ] ፣ ማመን [አ'መነ] ፣ አደራ መስጠት [ሰ'ጠ]
-ስ- እምነት

trustee
ትረስ'ቲይ -ስ- ባላደራ (ዎ'ች)
trustworthy
ት'ረስትወዚ -ቅ- ታ'ማኝ ፣ እሙን ፣ እምነት የ'ሚ'ጣል'በት
truth
ት'ሩ:ስ -ስ- እውነት
try
ት'ራይ -ግ- መሞ'ከር [ሞ'ከረ] ፣ መፈ'ተን [ፈ'ተነ]
trying
ት'ራይንግ -ስ- አ'ዋኪ ፣ አስቸ'ጋሪ ፣ አ'ናዳጅ
tub
'ተብ -ስ- የንጨት በርሚል
tube
ት'ዩ:ብ -ስ- ቧምቧ (ቱ'ቦ)
tuberculosis
ቱበከዩ'ለውሲስ -ስ- የሳምባ ነቀርሳ
tuck
'ተክ -ግ- አጥፎ ማስገ'ባት [አስገ'ባ] (ያልጋ ልብስ ሲያነ'ጥፉ እፍራሽ ውስጥ)
Tuesday
ት'ዩዝደይ -ስ- ማክሰ'ኞ
tuft
'ተፍት -ስ- ቁንጮ ፣ ተ'ሬ (የጠጉር) ፣ አንድ'ነት ች'ፍ'ግ ያለ (ሣር ፣ ጠጉር ወዘተ)
tug
'ተግ -ግ- በኀይል መጎተት [ጎ'ተተ]
tuition
ትዩ'ዊሽን -ስ- ማስተማር
tumble
'ተምበል -ግ- መውደቅ [ወ'ደቀ] (በተለ'ይ በኀይል'ና በፍጥነት)
tumour
ቱ'ዩመ -ስ- የጠ'ጠረ እበጥ ፣ ያህ'ያ ክንታሮት
tumult
ት'ዩ:መልት -ስ- ጩኸት ፣ ዋካታ ፣ ረብሻ ፣ የአእምሮ መ'ታወክ
tune
ት'ዩ:ን -ስ- ጣዕመ ዜማ
tunic
ት'ዩ:ኒክ -ስ- እ'ጀጠ'ባብ

tunnel
'ተነል -ስ- በመሬት ፣ በተራራ ውስጥ የተፈ
ለ'ፈለ የዋ'ሻ መንገድ

turbulent
'ተ፡ብዮለነት -ቅ- የተጨ'ነቀ ፣ የተቸ'ገረ ፣
የተቆ'ጣ (ሕዝብ)

turf
'ተ፡ፍ -ስ- ለምለም ሣር ፣ ሰርዶ

turkey
'ተ፡ኪ -ስ- የፈረንጅ ዶሮ

turmoil
'ተ፡ሞይል -ስ- ብጥ'ብጥ ፣ ሁከት

turn
'ተ፡ን -ግ- መዞር [ዞረ]
-round
-ግ- ወደኋላ መዞር [ዞረ]

turquoise
'ተ፡ክዎይዝ -ስ- አረንጓዴ ፈርጥ ፣ አረንጓዴ'ና
ሰማያዊ ቀለም

turret
'ተሪት -ስ- ት'ንሽ ጥቅም ፣ በጦር መርከብ ፣
በታንክ ፣ በአውሮ'ፕላን ላይ የ'ሚዞር የጦር
መ'ሣሪያ ቤት

turtle
'ተ፡ተል -ስ- የባሕር ኤሊ።

turtle-dove
'ተ፡ተል'ደቭ -ስ- ዋኔ

tusk
'ተስክ -ስ- የዝሆን ፣ የኮርኮር ረ'ጅም ጥርስ

tussle
'ተሰል -ስ- ጎይለ'ኛ ትግል

tutor
ት'ዩተ -ስ- አስተማሪ ፣ አሠልጣኝ

twang
ት'ዋንግ -ስ- የተወ'ጠረ ክ'ር ፣ ሽቦ ተነስቶ
ሲ'ለ'ቀቅ የ'ሚያ'ሰ'ማው ድምፅ

tweezers
ት'ዊይዘዝ -ስ- ወረንጦ

twelfth
ት'ዌልፍስ -ቅ- ዐሥራ ሁለ'ተ'ኛ

twelve
ት'ዌልቭ -ቅ- ዐሥራ ሁለ'ት

twentieth
ት'ዌንቲየስ -ቅ- ሃያ'ኛ

twenty
ት'ዌንቲ -ቅ- ሃያ (ሃያ)

twice
ት'ዋይስ -ተግ- ሁለ'ት ጊዜ

twig
ት'ዊግ -ስ- ቀም'በጥ (የዛፍ ፣ የተክል)

twilight
ት'ዋይላይት -ስ- የፀሐይ ጥልቀት ብርሃን

twin
ት'ዊን -ስ- መንት'ያ ፣ መንታ (ልጆ'ች)

twine
ት'ዋይን -ስ- ሲባጎ
-ግ- መ'ጠምጠም [ተጠመ'ጠመ]

twinge
ት'ዊንጅ -ስ- ውጋት (ድንገተ'ኛ)

twinkle
ት'ዊንከል -ግ- ማብለጥለጥ [አብለጨ'ለጨ]

twirl
ት'ወ፡ል -ግ- መ'ዟዟር [ተዟዟረ] (ብዙ ጊዜ) ፣
መ'ጠምዘዝ [ተጠም'ዘዘ]

twist
ት'ዊስት -ግ- መጠምዘዝ [ጠመ'ዘዘ]
-ስ- ጥም'ዝ ፣ ጥምዘዛ

twitch
ት'ዊች -ግ- መንቀጥቀጥ [ተንቀጠ'ቀጠ] (ድን
ገተ'ኛ የጡንቻ)

twitter
ት'ዊተ -ስ- የወፍ ጫጫታ

two
ቱ: -ቅ- ሁለ'ት

type
'ታይፕ -ስ- ዓይነት
-ግ- በጽሕፈት መኪና መጻፍ [ጻፈ]

typewriter
'ታይፕራይተ -ስ- የጽሕፈት መኪና

typhoon
ታይ'ፉን -ስ- ከ'ባድ አውሎ ነፋስ

typhus
'ታይፈስ -ስ- ተስቦ በ'ሽታ

typical
'ቲፒከል -ቅ- የተለ'መደ ፣ ደምበ'ኛ

tyrant
'ታረንት -ስ- ጨ'ካኝ'ና ፍትሕ የ'ማያውቅ
ገ'ዥ ፣ የበታ'ቹን የ'ሚያጠቃ

627

udder
ኣደ -ስ- ጡት (የእንስሳት)

ugly
ኣግሊ. -ቅ- ፉንጋ ፣ መልከ ጥፉ

ulcer
ኣልስ -ስ- የሚመግል ቁስል

ulterior
ኣል'ቲሪየ -ቅ- የተደ'በቀ (ለሰው ሐ'ሳብ)

ultimate
ኣልተመት -ቅ- የመጨ'ረሻ

ultimatum
ኣልተ'ሚይተም -ስ- ማስጠንቀቂያ ፣ ዛቻ

umbilical cord
ኣም'ቢልከል'ኮ:ድ -ስ- እትብት

umbrage
ኣምብ'ሪጅ -ስ- መ'ከፋት ፣ መ'ቀየም (ከመ 'በደል ስ'ሜት የተነ'ሣ)

umbrella
ኣምብ'ሬለ -ስ- ጥላ ፣ ጃንጥላ

umpire
ኣምፓየ -ስ- ዳኛ (ለስፖርት

unable
ኣ'ኔይበል -ቅ- የ'ማይችል

unaccustomed
ኣነ'ከስተምድ -ቅ- ልምድ የሌ'ለው

unanimous
ዩ'ናነመስ -ቅ- ሁ'ሉም አንድ ሐ'ሳብ ያ'ላ'ቸ ው (በስምም'ነት) ፣ አንድ ል'ብ አንድ ቃል የሆኑ (በስምም'ነት)

unarmed
ኣ'ና:ምድ -ቅ- የጦር መ'ሣሪያ ያልያዘ ፣ መ'ከ ላከያ የሌ'ለው

unassuming
ኣነስ'ዩ:ሚንግ -ቅ- ትሑት ፣ አ'ለሁ አ'ለሁ የ'ማይል

unavoidable
ኣነ'ቮይደበል -ቅ- ቻል የ'ማይሉት ፣ ሊ.ር ቱት የ'ማይ'ቻል ፣ የ'ማይቀር

unaware
ኣነ'ዌየ -ቅ- ያላ'ወቀ ፣ ያላስተዋለ

unbecoming
ኣነቢ'ከሚንግ -ቅ- የ'ማይስማ'ማ ፣ የ'ማይ 'ገ'ባ
of dress
-ቅ- የ'ማያያምር

unbearable
ኣን'ቤረበል -ቅ- የ'ማይ'ቻል ፣ የ'ማይ'ታ'ገ ሡት

unbiased
ኣን'ባየስት -ቅ- የ'ማያ'ዳ'ላ ፣ አድልዎ የ'ሌ 'ለ'በት

uncertain
ኣን'ሰ:ተን -ቅ- እርግጠ'ኛ ያልሆነ ፣ ያልተረ ጋ'ገጠ

uncle
ኣንከል -ስ- አ'ጎት ፣ ያክስት ባል

uncomfortable
ኣን'ከምፈተበል -ስ- ም'ቹ'ነት የሌ'ለው ፣ ም'ቹ ያልሆነ ፣ የ'ማይ'መ'ች

unconscious
ኣን'ኮንሸስ -ቅ- አእምሮውን የሳተ ፣ የ'ማያ ውቅ ፣ ሳያ'ስቡት የተደ'ረገ

uncouth
ኣን'ኩዕ -ቅ- ያልታ'ረመ ፣ ባለጌ ፣ ስ'ድ ፣ አስከ'ፈ ጠባይ ያ'ለው

under
ኣንደ -መዋ- ታ'ች ፣ በ ... ታ'ች ፣ ከ ... ታ'ች

underclothes
ኣንደክለውዝዝ -ስ- የውስጥ ልብስ ፣ ገላ ን'ክ

underdog
ኣንደዶግ -ስ- የሰው ዝ'ቅት'ኛ ፣ የሰው መቀ'ለ ጃ'ና መ'ሣለቂያ ፣ የ'ማይ'ቃ'ና'ለት (አሳዛኝ ሰው)

underestimate
ኣንደ'ሬስቲሜይት -ስ- ዝ'ቅ አርጎ መገ'መት [ገ'መተ]

undergo
ኣንደ'ገው -ግ- መከራን ታ'ገሰ ማሳ'ለፍ [አሳ 'ለፈ] ፣ አንድ ነገር ማለፍ [አ'ለፈ]

628

underhand

አንደ'ሃንድ -ቅ- የ'ማይ'ታ'መነ ፡ ድብቅብቁ፣
(ነገር)

underline

አንደ'ላይነ -ግ- ከበታ'ች ማሥመር [አሥ'መ
ረ] (ለጻሐፍ) ፤ አንድ ነገር ማጥበቅ [አጠ'በቀ]
የበ'ለጠ አስተያየት መስጠት [ሰ'ጠ]

underneath

አንደ'ኒይስ -መዋ- በ . . . ታ'ች ፣ ከ . . . ታ'ች

understand

አንደስ'ታንድ -ግ- መግባት [ገ'ባ] ፣ መ'ረዳት
[ተረ'ዳ]

undertake

አንደ'ቴይክ -ግ- አንድ ሥራ ለመሥራት መስ
ማማት [ተስማ'ማ]

undertaker

'አንደቴይክ -ስ- ገ'ናዥ ፣ ሥራ ተቋራጭ

underwear

'አንደዌየ -ስ- የውስጥ ልብስ ፣ ገላ ነ'ካ

underworld

'አንደወ፡ልድ -ስ- የወንበዴዎ'ች ማኅበር
ወ'ርበ'ሉች
hell

-ስ- ገሀ'ነም እሳት

undesirable

አንደ'ዛረበል -ቅ- ዋዮ'ማይ'ፈ'ለግ ፣ የተጠ'ላ ፣
ያልተወ'ደደ

undo

አን'ዱ፡ -ግ- መፍታት [ፈ'ታ] (እሥር ፣ ቁልፍ
ወዘተ)

undress

አንደ'ሬስ -ግ- ማውለቅ [አወ'ለቀ] (ለልብስ)

undulating

'አንድዩሌይቲንግ -ቅ- ወ'ጣ ገ'ባ (የመሬት
ወዘተ)

uneasy

አ'ኒይዚ -ቅ- የተጨ'ነቀ ፣ የ'ማይ'መ'ች

uneven

አ'ኒይቨነ -ቅ- ያልተስተካ'ከለ ፣ ወ'ጣ ገ'ባ

unexpected

አንኤክስ'ፔክተድ -ቅ- ያልጠ'በቁት ፣ ያልተ
ጠ'በቀ ፣ ድንገተ'ኛ

unfair

አን'ፌየ -ቅ- ግፍ ፣ በደል ፣ ትክ'ክል ያልሆነ
(አድራጎት)

unfit

አን'ፊት -ቅ- የማይስማ'ማ ፣ ጤናው በመጥፎ
ሁናቴ ላይ ያ'ለ

unfortunate

አን'ፎ፡ቸነት -ቅ- ዕ'ድለ ቢስ ፣ የሚያሳ'ዝነ

unhappy

አን'ሀፒ -ቅ- ያ'ዘነ ፣ የከ'ፋው

unhealthy

አን'ሄልሲ -ቅ- የታ'መመ ፣ ጤና የሌ'ለው ፣
እንዲ፡ም ወይን'ም ሰው'ነት የ'ሚጎዳ

unification

ዩኒፊ'ኬይሽን -ስ- መ'ዋሐድ ፣ አንድ'ነት

uniform

'ዩኒፎ፡ም -ስ- መ'ለዩ ልብስ (ዩኒፎርም)
same

-ስ- አንድ ዓይነት

unify

'ዩኒፋይ -ግ- ማ'ዋሐድ [አ'ዋሐደ] ፣ አንድ
ማድረግ [አደ'ረገ]

unilateral

ዩኒ'ላተረል -ቅ- ያንድ ወገን (በስም'ነት ፣
በጥል)

union

'ዩኒየን -ስ- አንድ'ነት ፣ ኅብረት

unique

ዩ'ኒይክ -ቅ- የተለ'የ ፣ ል'ዩ ጠባይ ያ'ለው

unit

'ዩኒት -ስ- ራሱን የቻለ አንድ ክፍል

unite

ዩ'ናይት -ግ- ማ'ዋሐድ [አ'ዋሐደ] ፣ አንድ
ማድረግ [አደ'ረገ]

unity

'ዩኒቲ -ስ- አንድ'ነት ፣ ኅብረት

universal

ዩኒ'ቨ፡ሰል -ስ- ጠቅላ'ላ ፣ የወል ፣ የሁ'ሉ ፣
ለሁ'ሉ የ'ሚሆነ

universe

'ዩኒቨስ -ስ- ዓለም'ና በሥነ ፍጥረት ውስጥ
ያ'ለው ነገር ሁ'ሉ

university

ዩኒ'ቨ፡ሰቲ -ስ- ከ'ፍተ'ኛ ትምህርት ቤት ፣
ዩኒቨርሲቲ

unkempt

አን'ኬምት -ቅ- ጠ'ፍ ያላለ ፣ ጠጉሩ ያልተበ
'ጠረ

629

unless
አን'ለስ -ተገ- ከ . . . በስተቀ'ር

unload
አን'ለውድ -ገ- ጭነት ማ'ራገፍ [አ'ራ'ገፈ]

unlucky
አን'ለኪ -ቅ- ዕ'ድለ ቢስ

unmoved
አን'ሙ-ቭድ -ቅ- ስ'ሜት የሌ'ለው ፣ የ'ማያ
ዝን

unnatural
አ'ንናቸራል -ቅ- ያለተለ'መደ ፣ ጉድ ፤ ግሩም

unnecessary
አ'ኔሰስሪ -ቅ- የ'ማያስፈ'ልግ ፣ ሊቀር የ'ሚ
ቸA

unpleasant
አንፕ'ሌዘንት -ቅ- የ'ማያስደ'ስት ፣ አሳ'ዛኝ

unqualified
አንክ'ዎለፋይድ -ቅ- ያልተግረ፣ያልሠለ'ጠነ
የተለ'የ ሞያ የሌ'ለው

unravel
አን'ራቭል -ገ- መተርተር [ተረ'ተረ] ፣ መለ
ያየት [ለያ'የ] (ለክ'ር)

unreasonable
አን'ሪይዘነብል -ቅ- ምክንያት የሌ'ለው ፣ የ'ማ
ይመስል
excessive
-ቅ- ከ'ሚ'ገ'ባ በላይ

unreliable
አንሪ'ላየበል -ቅ- እምነት የ'ማይ'ጣል'በት

unruly
አን'ሩ-ሊ -ቅ- የ'ማይ'ታ'዗዗ ፣ ስ'ድ

unsatisfactory
አንሳተስ'ፋክትሪ -ቅ- የ'ማያጠግብ (ምክንያ
ት) ፣ በቂ ያልሆነ

unscrew
አንስክ'ሩ: -ገ- መንቀል [ነ'ቀለ] (ለሚስማር ፣
ለቡ'ሽ)

unscrupulous
አንስ'ክሩ:ፕዩለስ -ቅ- ጨ'ካኝ፣ራሱን ወ'ዳድ፣
ይሉኝታ ቢስ

unseemly
አን'ሲይምሊ -ቅ- የ'ማይ'ገ'ባ ፣ ነውር ፣ ከጊ
ዜው ጋር የ'ማይስማ'ማ

unselfish
አን'ሴልፊሽ -ቅ- ራሱን የ'ማይወ'ድ ፣ ለኋ
ብ'ቾ የ'ማይA

unsettled
አን'ሴተልድ -ቅ- የተጨነ'ተ ፣ የሕ'ሳብ ዕረ
ፍት የሌ'ለው ፤ ያልተከ'ፈለ ዕዳ ፣ የመጨ'ረሻ
ው'ሳኔ ያላ'ገኘ

unsightly
አን'ሳይትሊ -ቅ- የ'ማያምር ፣ የ'ሚያስጠ'ላ ፣
አስቀ'ያሚ ፣ ግስጠ'ሉ

unskilled
አንስ'ኪልድ -ቅ- ያልሠለ'ጠነ ፣ ሞያ ቢስ

unsteady
አንስ'ቴዲ -ቅ- ቀ'ጥ ያላለ ፣ የተዘለፈ'ለፈ
(በመ'ራመድ) ፤ እምነት የ'ማይ'ጣል'በት

untie
አን'ታይ -ገ- መፍታት [ፈ'ታ] (እስር)

until
አን'ቲል -መዋ- እስከ . . . ድረስ

untimely
አን'ታይምሊ -ቅ- ያለ ጊዜው ፣ በ'ማይ'መ'ች
ጊዜ የመ'ጣ

untrue
አንት'ሩ: -ቅ- ውሸት ፣ ከውነት የራቀ

unusual
አን'ዩዡወል -ቅ- ያልተለ'መደ ፣ እንግዳ (ለነ
ገር)

unwell
አን'ዌል -ቅ- የታ'መመ ፣ ጤና ያ'ጣ

unwilling
አን'ዊሊንግ -ቅ- ፈቃደ'ኝነት የሌ'ለው ፣ የ
'ማይፈ'ልግ (አንድ ነገር ዘግ዗ድረ዗ ስምም'ነት
የሌለ'ው)

unwise
አን'ዋይዝ -ቅ- ብልጎ ያልሆነ ፣ ሞ'ኝ ፣ ቂል

unworthy
አን'ወ:ዘ -ቅ- የ'ማይረባ ፣ መ'ናኛ ፣ ክብር
የ'ማይ'ገ'ባው

up
'አፕ -ተገ- ላይ ፣ . . . ላይ ፣ ወደ . . . ላይ ፣
እስከ . . .
-to
እስከ . . . ድረስ

upbraid

አፕብ'ሬይድ   መዝለፍ [ዘ'ለፈ]

upheaval

አፕ'ሂይቫል -ስ- ብጥ'ብጥ (ት'ልቅ) ፤ ድንገ
ተ'ኛ'ና በ'የቦታው የተሰራ'ጨ ለውጥ

uphill

'አፕ'ሂል -ተጋ- ወደ ላይ

uphold

'አፕ'ሆልድ -ግ- መደ'ገፍ [ደ'ገፈ]

upholstery

አፕ'ሆልስትሪ -ስ- ሥጋ'ጃ ፤ መ'ጋረጃ ፤ የሶፋ
ወንበር ፤ ፍራሽ'ና የመ'ሰሉት ዕቃዎ'ች

upkeep

'አፕኪይፕ -ስ- የመ'ከባከቢያ ዋጋ
financial
  -ስ- የገንዘብ እርዳታ (ላንድ ሰው ኑር)

upon

እ'ፖን -መዋ- በ . . . ላይ

upper

'አፐ -ቅ- የላይ

upright

'አፕራይት -ቅ- ቀ'ጥ ያለ ፤ የ'ሚ'ከ'በር ፤
ቅን

uprising

'አፕራይዚንግ -ቅ- ብጥ'ብጥ

uproar

'አፕሮ: -ስ- ጫኸት ፤ ሁከት

uproot

አፕ'ሩ፡ት -ግ- መንቀል [ነ'ቀለ] ፤ መመንገል
[መነ'ገለ]

upset

አፕ'ሴት -ቅ- ያ'ዘነ ፤ የተጨ'ነቀ
overturn
  -ግ- መገላበጥ [ገለ'በጠ]
perturb
  -ግ- ማ'ናደድ [አ'ና'ደደ] ፤ ማስቀ'የም
[አስቀ'የመ]

upside-down

አፕሳይድ'ዳውን -ቅ- የተገለ'በጠ ፤ ሥርዓት
ያ'ጣ ፤ የተመሰቃ'ቀለ

upstart

'አፕስታ፡ት -ስ- አምባ ገ'ነን

up-to-date

እፕቱ'ዴይት -ቅ- ዘመናዊ ፤ ስለመጨ'ረሻው
የመ'ሻሻል እርም'ጃ የ'ሚያውቅ

upward

'አፕወድ -ተግ- ወደላይ

urban

'ኸበን -ቅ- የከተማ

urchin

'ኧቺን -ስ- ዘዋሪ ት'ንሽ ልጅ

urge

'ኧጅ -ግ- ማ'ጻፈር [አ'ጻ'ፈረ] ፤ ከል'ብ መለ
'መን [ለ'መነ] (አንድ ነገር እንዲያደርግ)

urgent

'ኧጀንት -ቅ- አስቸ'ኳይ

urine

'ዩሪን -ስ- ሽንት

us

'አስ -ተስ- ለእ'ኛ ፤ እ'ኛን

usage

'ዩዚጅ -ስ- በልምድ የተወ'ሰነ ሕ'ግ (ለቋ
ንቋ ወዘተ) ፤ የተለ'መደ ሥርዓት

use

'ዩዝ -ግ- እሥራ ላይ ማዋል [አዋለ] ፤ ባንድ
ነገር መሥራት [ሠ'ራ]

use

'ዩስ -ስ- ጥቅg ' አገልግሎት ፤ እርባን

useful

'ዩስፉል -ቅ- ጠቃሚ ፤ ለተግባር የ'ሚውል

useless

'ዩስለስ -ቅ- ጥቅም የሌ'ለው ፤ የ'ማይረባ

usher

'አሸ -ስ- አስተናባሪ ፤ አስተናጋጅ

usual

'ዩዡወል -ቅ- የተለ'መደ

usurer

'ዩጀረ -ስ- ገንዘብ በከ'ፍተ'ኛ አራጣ የ'ሚ
ያበ'ድር ሰው

usurp

ዩ'ዘ፡ፕ -ግ- ያለአግባብ መንጠቅ [ነ'ጠቀ]
(የመንግሥት ሥልጣን ወዘተ)

utensil

ዩ'ቴንሰል -ስ- የወጥ ቤት ቆሳቁስ

utilize

'ዩቲላይዝ -ግ- እተቅም ላይ ማዋል [አዋለ]

631

utmost

’እትመውስት -ቅ- የ'ሚበልጠው ፣ ብልጫ
ያ'ለው ፣ የመጨ'ረሻ (በርቀት)

utter

’አተ -ግ- መ'ናገር [ተና'ገረ]
complete
-ቅ- ፍ'ጹም

vacancy

’ቬይከንሲ -ስ- ባዶ ቦታ (ለሥራ) ፣ ክፍት
ቦታ (ለሥራ)

vacant

’ቬይከንት -ቅ- ባዶ
absent-minded
-ቅ- ተላላ ፣ ዝንጉ

vacate

ቫ'ኬይት -ግ- መልቀቅ [ለ'ቀቀ] (ቦታን)

vacation

’ቨኬይሽን -ስ- የዕረፍት ጊዜ

vaccination

’ቫክሲ'ኔይሽን -ስ- ክ'ትባት

vacillate

’ቫሲሌይት ፣ግ- ሐ'ሳብ አለመቁረጥ [-ቆ'
ረጠ] ፣ ማ'ወላወል [አ'ወ ላ'ወለ]

vacuum

’ቫክዩም -ስ- ባዶ ቦታ ፤ ምን'ም ነገር የሌ'ለ
'በት ቦታ
vacuumcleaner
-ስ- የኤሌክትሪክ ቤት መጥረጊያ

vagabond

’ቫገቦንድ -ስ- ወ'ሮበ'ላ ፣ አውደልዳይ ፣ ወ
'መቴ ፣ ኣባ'ጎ'ዮ ፣ ወመኔ

vagina

ቨ'ጃይና -ስ- የሴት አባል ዘር ፣ ብልት (እምስ)

vagrant

’ቬይገረንት -ስ- በ'የቦታው እየተዘዋ'ወረ የ
'ሚለምን ሰው የተወ'ሰነ መኖሪያ የሌ'ለው

vague

’ቬይግ -ቅ- ግልጽ ያልሆነ ፣ ደብዛ'ዛ

utterance

’አተረንስ -ስ- ንግ'ገር ፣ ያ'ነጋገር ሁናቴ

uvula

’ኡቭዩላ -ስ- እንጥል

vain

’ቬይን -ቅ- ከንቱ ፣ ዋጋ ቢስ ፣ በከንቱ የ'ሙ
'ኩራ
-in
-ተግ- በከንቱ

vale

’ቬይል -ስ- ሸለቆ

valet

’ቫሌ -ስ- አልባሽ (ወንድ)

valiant

’ቫሊየንት -ቅ- ደ'ፋር ፣ ጎበዝ

valid

’ቫሊድ -ቅ- ሕ'ጋዊ
of argument
-ቅ- ትክ'ክለ'ኛ (ለክርክር)

valise

ቫ'ሊይስ -ስ- ት'ንሽ ሻንጣ (የመንገድ)

valley

’ቫሊ -ስ- ሸለቆ

valour

’ቫለ -ስ- ድፍረት ፣ ጉብዝ'ና (በጦር ሜዳ)

value

’ቫልዩ -ስ- ዋጋ

valve

’ቫልቭ -ስ- ቫልቮላ ፣ የ'ሚፈ'ስ ነገር ማ'ገጃ
ወይን'ም መለቀቂያ መ'ሣሪያ

van

’ቫን -ስ- የጭነት መኪና (የተሸ'ፈነ) ፣ የተሸ
'ፈነ ፉርጎ
military
-ስ- ገምባር ቀ'ደም ፣ የፈታውራሪ ጦር

632

vanguard
ˈቫንጋድ -ስ- ግምባር ቀ'ደም ፣ የፊታውራሪ ጦር

vanish
ˈቫኒሽ -ግ- መጥፋት [ጠ'ፋ] ፣ እ'ልም ማለት [አለ]

vanity
ˈቫኒቲ -ስ- ከንቱ'ነት

vanquish
ˈቫንክዊሽ -ግ- ድል መንሣት [ነ'ሣ] ፣ ማስ ገ'በር [አስገ'በረ] (በጦር'ነት)

vapour
ˈቬይፐ -ስ- እንፋሎት

variable
ˈቬሪየበል -ቅ- ተለዋዋጭ ፣ የ'ሚ'ለ'ወጥ እምነት የ'ማይ'ጣል'በት

varnish
ˈቫኒሽ -ግ- ቀለም መቀ'ባት [ቀ'ባ]

variety
ቨˈራየቲ -ስ- ል'ዩ ል'ዩ ዓይነት

vary
ˈቬሪ -ግ- መ'ለየት [ተለ'የ] ፣ ል'ዩ'ነት ማሳ 'የት [አሳ'የ] ፣ መ'ለዋወጥ [ተለዋ'ወጠ]

vase
ˈቫ፡ዝ -ስ- ያበባ ማስቀ'መጫ

vassal
ˈቫሰል -ስ- ተወ'ራጅ ፣ አገልጋይ ፣ ሎሌ

vast
ˈቫ፡ስት -ቅ- ሰ'ፊ

vat
ˈቫት -ስ- ት'ልቅ ጋን

vault
ˈቮ፡ልት -ስ- ምድር ቤት
-ግ- እ'መር ማለት [አለ] (አንድ ነገር ተደግ'ግፎ)
-ስ- ቅ'ሥት'ነት ያለው ጣሪ

veal
ˈቪይል -ስ- የጥ'ጃ ሥጋ

veer
ˈቪየ -ግ- አቅጣ'ጫ መለ'ወጥ [ለ'ወጠ] (በተለ'ይ ለነፋስ ፣ ለሐ'ሳብ)

vegetable
ˈቬጅተበል -ስ- አትክልት (የምግብ)

vegetation
ˈቬጀ'ቴይሽን -ስ- ተክላተክል ፣ ልምላሜ

vehemence
ˈቪየመንስ -ስ- ጉይለ ቃል ፣ መራራ ውስጣዊ ስ'ሜት

vehicle
ˈቪይከል -ስ- ተሽከርካሪ

veil
ˈቬይል -ስ- ዓይነ ርግብ

vein
ˈቬይን -ስ- የደም ሥር ፣ በቅጠል ላይ የ'ሚ ታይ መሥመሮ'ች

velocity
ቨˈሎሰቲ -ስ- ፍጥነት

velvet
ˈቬልቨት -ስ- ከፈይ

vendor
ˈቬንደ -ቅ- ሻጭ

veneer
ቨˈኒየ -ስ- ቀ'ጭን ሸፉን ፣ ልባጥ (በጠረ'ጴዛ በወምበር ወዘተ)

venerable
ˈቬነረበል -ቅ- ሊ'ከ'በር የ'ሚ'ገ'ባው (በዕ ድሜው በጠባዩ ምክንያት)

vengeance
ˈቬንጀንስ -ስ- በቀል

venison
ˈቬነዝን -ስ- የሚዳ'ቋ ሥጋ ፣ የአጋዘን ሥጋ

venom
ˈቬነም -ስ- የእባብ መርዝ ፣ ጥላ'ቻ

vent
ˈቬንት -ስ- ያ'የር ፣ የውሃ ማስገ'ቢያ ቀዳዳ

ventilation
ˈቬንቲ'ሌይሽን -ስ- ነፋስ መስጫ

venture
ˈቬንቸ -ግ- መሞ'ከር [ሞ'ከረ]
-ስ- ወደፊት ሲሆን የ'ሚ'ችለውን መ 'መት (ለንግድ)

veracity
ቨˈራሲቲ -ስ- እውነት ፣ ል'ክ'ነት

verb
ˈቨ፡ብ -ስ- ግ'ሥ ፣ አንቀጽ (ስዋስው)

verbal
ˈቨ፡በል -ቅ- የቃል ፣ የንግ'ግሩ ፣ የግሥ

verbose
ቨˈበውስ -ቅ- ለፍላፊ ፣ ብዙ ተናጋሪ

633

verdant
ʼቨ፡ዷንት -ቅ- ለምለም

verdict
ʼቨ፡ዲክት -ስ- ፍርድ ፡ ውሳኔ (የዳኞች)

verge
ʼቨ፡ጅ -ስ- ዳር ፡ ጫፍ

verify
ʼቬረፋይ -ግ- መመርመር [መረ'መረ] ፣ ግስ ረ'ጀ መፈ'ለግ [ፈ'ለገ] (ለተና'ገሩት ነገር እው ነት'ነት)

veritable
ʼቬሪተብለ -ቅ- እውነተ'ኛ ፣ በትክ'ክል የተሰ 'የመ

vermicide
ʼቨ፡ሚሳይድ -ስ- በሆድ ውስጥ ያ'ሉ ትሎ'ችን መግደያ መድኃኒት

vermilion
ቨ'ሚልየን -ቅ- ብሩህ ቀ'ይ (ቀለም)

vermin
ʼቨ፡ሚን -ስ- ትል ፡ አይጥ ወዘተ

vernacular
ቨ'ናክዩለ -ስ- ተራ ቋን'ቋ (የጽሑፍ ያልሆነ)

versatile
ʼቨ፡ሰታይል -ቅ- ባለ ብዙ ሞያ ፣ ብዙ ሥራ ሊሠራ የ'ሚችል ፣ ለብዙ አገልግሎት የ'ሚ ውል

verse
ʼቨ፡ስ -ስ- ቁጥር (የመጽሐፍ ቅ'ዱስ)
poetry
-ስ- የግጥም ክፍል

version
ʼቨ፡ሽን -ስ- እ'ትም ፣ በሌላ ቋንቋ ትርጉም (ያንድ መጽሐፍ)
story
-ስ- ታሪክ (አንድ ሰው ስለ አንድ ሁናቴ የ'ሚያወራው የራሱ አስተያየት)

vertical
ʼቨ፡ቲከል -ቅ- ቀጥ ያለ

very
ʼቬሪ -ተግ- በጣም

vessel
ʼቬሰል -ስ- ዕቃ (መያዣ)
ship
-ስ- መርከብ

vest
ʼቬስት -ስ- የውስጥ ልብስ

vestige
ʼቬስቲጅ -ስ- ያለፈ ነገር ምልክት

vestments
ʼቬስትመንትስ -ስ- ልብስ ተክህኖ ፣ አልባ ሳት ፣ የክብረ በዓል ልብስ

veteran
ʼቬተረን -ስ- የጦንት ወ'ታ'ደር ፣ የተረፈተ ወ'ታ'ደር

veterinary surgeon
ʼቬትሪነሪʼስ፡ጀን -ስ- የከብት ሐኪም

vex
ʼቬክስ -ግ- ማ'ናደድ [አ'ና'ደደ] ፣ ማስቆ'ጣት [አስቆ'ጣ]

viaduct
ʼቫየዳክት -ስ- በጣም ረ'ጅም ድልድይ (ባቡር መኪና ወዘተ የ'ሚያልፍ'በት)

vibrate
ʼቫይብ'ሬይት -ግ- መንዘር [ነ'ዘረ]

vice
ʼቫይስ -ስ- መጥፎ ልምድ (ከግብረ ገብ'ነት የወ'ጣ) ፣ ደካማ ሥጋዊ ጠባይ
assistant
-ስ- ምክ'ትል
wickedness
-ስ- ክፋት

vicinity
ቪ'ሲነቲ -ስ- አቅራ'ቢያ ፡ አ'ካባቢ

vicious
ʼቪሸስ -ቅ- ጨ'ካኝ ፣ አረሜኔ (ለጠባይ) ፣ ክፉ ፣ አመለ'ኛ (ለፈረስ)

vicissitude
ቨ'ሲሲትዩድ -ስ- መ'ለዋወጥ (በተለ'ያ ለዕ ድል)

victim
ʼቪክቲም -ስ- ያለጥፋቱ የ'ሚ'ሠቃይ ሰው ወይን'ም እንስሳ

victor
ʼቪክተ -ቅ- አ'ሸ'ናፊ ፣ ድል ነሽ ፡ ባለ ድል ፣ ድል አድራጊ

victory
ʼቪክተሪ -ስ- ድል ፡ ማ'ሸ'ነፍ

victuals
ʼቪተልዝ -ስ- ምግብ ፡ ቀ'ለብ

vie
'ቫይ -ግ- መ'ፎካከር [ተፎካ'ከሪ] ፣ መ'ወዳ
ደር [ተወዳ'ደሪ]

view .
ቭ'ዩ: -ግ- ማየት [አ'የ]
-ስ- ትዕ'ይንት

viewpoint
ቭ'ዩ:ፖይንት -ስ- አስተያየት ፣ ግ'ምት (አስ
ተያየት)

vigil
'ቪጀል -ስ- ነቅቶ ማደር (ለጸሎት ፣ ለጥ'በቃ)

vigilance
'ቪጂለንስ -ስ- ጥንቁቅ ጥ'በቃ፣ንቃት (ለጥበቃ)

vigour
'ቪገ -ስ- ኃይል ፣ ጥን'ካሬ ፣ ብርታት

vile
'ቫይል -ቅ- አ'ሥቃቂ ፣ እ'ጅግ መጥፎ ፣ አሳ
'ፋሪ

villa
'ቪለ -ስ- ቪ'ላ ፣ በአንድ አገር ግ'ቢ ውስጥ
ያ'ለ ቤት

village
'ቪላጅ -ስ- ያገር ቤት መንደር

villain
'ቪለን -ስ- መጥፎ ሰው ፣ ክፉ፡ ሰውን የ'ሚ
ነዳ ሰው

vindicate
'ቪንዲኬይት -ግ- እውነተ'ኛነትን ማስረ'ዳ
ት [አስረ'ዳ]

vindictive
'ቪን'ዲክቲቭ -ቅ- በቀለ'ኛ ፣ ጨ'ካኝ

vine
'ቫይን -ስ- የወይን ተክል

vinegar
'ቪነገ -ስ- ኮምጣ'ጤ ፣ መጣጣ

violate
'ቫየሌይት -ግ- መጣስ [ጣስ] \
law
-ግ- መድፈት [ደ'ፈ] (ሴት ያለፈቃዷ)

violent
'ቫየለንት -ቅ- ብርቱ ፣ ኃይለ'ኛ ፣ ቁ'ጡ

violet
'ቫየለት -ቅ- ወደሰማያዊነት የ'ሚያደላ ሐም
ራዊ

violin
ቫየ'ሊን -ስ- ቫየሊን ፣ (መሰንቆ ባለአራት
ጭራ)

viper
'ቫየፐ -ስ- እ'ፉኛት (መርዛም እባብ)

virgin
'ቨ:ጂን -ስ- ድንግል
soil
-ቅ- ድንግል (ለመሬት)

virile
'ቪራይል -ቅ- ወንድ (ጠንካ'ራ)

virtue
'ቨ:ቹ -ስ- ምግባር (ጥሩ)

virtuous
'ቨ:ቹወስ -ቅ- ባለ ጥሩ ምግባር ፣ ደ'ግ

visa
'ቪይዛ -ስ- ቪዛ (የይለፍ ወረቀት ፣ ይብዷኒ)

visage
'ቪዚጅ -ስ- የሰው ፊት ፣ መልክ

viscous
'ቪስከስ -ቅ- መጣብቅ'ነት ያ'ለው

visible
'ቪዘበል -ቅ- የ'ሚ'ታ'ይ ፣ ያልተሸ'ሸገ

vision
'ቪዠን -ስ- ራእይ
power of sight
-ስ- የማየት ኃይል

visit
'ቪዚት -ግ- መጎብኘት [ጎበ'ኘ]
-ስ- ጉብ'ኝት

visitor
'ቪዚተ -ስ- ጎብኚ ፣ ጠ'ያቂ (የታ'መመ
መጠት)

visual
'ቪዡየወል -ቅ- ለማየት የ'ሚ'ቾል
-aids -ስ- ለትምህርት መማለኛ የ
ሥዕል ሥዕሎች

vital
'ቫይተል -ቅ- ዋ'ና (ነገር) ፣ በጣም አስ
(ለነር መዘት)

vitality
ቪ'ታሊቲ -ስ- ሕያው'ነት ፣ ንቁ'ነት

vivacity

ቪ'ቫሰቲ -ስ- ንቁ'ነት

vivid

'ቪ ቪ ድ -ቅ- ጠንካ'ራ ፣ ጎደለ'ኛ ፤ ሕያው
(የአ'ገላለጽ)

vocabulary

ቨ'ካብዩለሪ -ስ- አንድ ሰው የ'ሚያውቃ'ቸ
ው'ና በንግ'ግሩ የ'ሚያስገ'ባቸው የቃላት
ብዛት ፣ የቃላት ዝርዝር መጽሐፍ

vocal

'ቨውከል -ቅ- የድምፅ ፣ ድምፃዊ

vocation

ቨ'ኬይሸን -ስ- የተለ'የ ሞያ

vociferous

ቨ'ሲፈረስ -ቅ- በጣም የ'ሚጮኸ

vogue

'ቨውግ -ስ- የጊዜው ሞድ

voice

'ቨይስ -ስ- ድምፅ

void

'ቨይድ -ስ- ባዶነት

    not valid

        -ቅ- ዋጋ ቢስ

volatile

'ቨለታይል -ቅ- በቀ'ላሉ የ'ሚተን ፣ ጠባዩ
በ'የጊዜው የ'ሚ'ለዋ'ወጥ፤ደ'ስተ'ኛ፤ፈገግተ'ኛ

volcano

ቨል'ኬይነው -ስ- እሳተ ገሞራ

volley

'ቨሊ -ስ- እ'ርምታ (ለተከሰ)

volley-ball

'ቨሊቦ:ል -ስ- የመረብ ኳስ ፣ ቨሊ ቦል

volt

'ቨልት -ስ- የኤሌክትሪክ ኃይል መጠን

voluble

'ቨልዩበል -ቅ- የ'ሚ'ና'ገር ፣ በፍጥነት'ና
በ'ቀ'ላሉ መ'ናገር የ'ሚችል

volume

'ቨልዩም -ስ- ጥራዝ

    measure

        -ስ- ይዞታ

    radio

        -ስ- ድምፅ (ለራዲዮ ፣ ክ'ፍተ'ኛ'ነቱ'ና
ዝ'ቅተ'ኛ'ነቱ)

voluminous

ቨል'ዩሚነስ -ቅ- ት'ልቅ ፣ ሰ'ፊ

voluntary

'ቨለንትሪ -ቅ- ፈቃደ'ኛ

volunteer

ቨለን'ቲየ -ስ- በፈቃዱ የ'ሚሠራ ሰው ፣ ላይ
'ገ'ደድ የ'ሚሠራ ሰው

    -ግ- በፈቃዱ መሥራት [ሠ'ራ]

voluptuous

ቨ'ለፕቸወስ -ቅ- በግብረ ሥጋ መ'ደሰት የ'ሚ
ያበዛ'ና በተትረፈ'ረፈ ኑሮ የ'ሚኖር

vomit

'ቨሚት -ግ- ማስታወክ [አስታ'ወከ] ፣ ማስ
መ'ለስ [አስመ'ለሰ]

voracious

ቨ'ራይሸስ -ቅ- ሆዳም

vote

'ቨውት -ግ- መምረጥ [መ'ረጠ] ፣ (ያገር መሪ
ዎ'ችን ፣ የሕዝብ እንደራሴዎ'ችን)

voter

'ቨውተ -ስ- መራጭ

vouch (for)

'ቫውች -ግ- መ'ዋስ [ተዋሰ] ፣ ለአሥነቱ፥ መመ
ስከር [መስ'ከረ]

voucher

'ቫውቸ -ስ- ቫውቸር ፣ ባለሥልጣን የፈ'ረመ
'በት የገንዘብ ማዘዣ ወረቀት

vow

'ቫው -ግ- ስለት መ'ሳል [ተሳለ]

vowel

'ቫወል -ስ- አ'ናባቢ ፊደል ፣ ድምፅ ሰጪ
ፊደል

voyage

'ቨየጅ -ስ- ጉዞ

vulgar

'ቨለገ -ቅ- ስ'ድ ፣ ባለጌ

vulgarity

ቨል'ጋሪቲ -ስ- ስ'ድነት ፣ ባለጌነት

vulnerable

'ቨልነረበል -ቅ- በቀ'ላሉ የ'ሚ'ጎ'ዳ ፣ በቀ
'ላሉ የ'ሚቆስል

vulture

'ቨልቸ -ስ- ጥምብ አንሣ (የሞራ ዓይነት)

vulva

'ቨልቨ -ስ- የሴት ብ'ልት ቀዳዳ

wad

’ዋድ -ስ- ወፍራም ለስላሳ ቁራጭ ጨርቅ (ዕቃ ወይን'ም ቁስል ለማሠር የ'ሚያገለ 'ግል)

wadding

’ዋዲንግ -ስ- ዕቃ ማ'ሸጊያ (ጥጥ ወዘተ)

wade

’ዌይድ -ግ- ጥልቀት የሌ'ለውን ወንዝ በእ ግር መ'ሻገር [ተሻ'ገረ]

wafer

’ዌፈሬ -ስ- ቀ'ጭን ጠፍጣ'ፋ ብስኩት (ም'ሳ ሌ ፡ ከጀላ'ቲ ጋር የ'ሚ'በ'ላ) *communion* -ስ- እ'ኮቴት (ቁርባን)

waft

’ዋፍት -ግ- ማርበብ [አረ'በበ] ፡ በቀ'ስታ እንዲሰ'ፍ ማድረግ [አደ'ረገ]

wag

’ዋግ -ግ- መነቅነቅ [ነቀ'ነቀ] *joker* -ስ- ቀልደ'ኛ ሰው

wage

’ዌይጅ -ግ- ጦር ማንሣት [አነ'ሣ] -ስ- ዋጋ (የቀን ሞያተ'ኛ)

wager

’ዌይጀ -ግ- መ'ወራረድ [ተወራ'ረደ] -ስ- ውር'ር'ድ

waggon

’ዋገን -ስ- የጭነት ፉርጎ ፡ ባለአ'ራት እግር የጭ'ነት ተሽከርካሪ

waif

’ዌይፍ -ስ- የጠ'ፋ ሰው ወይን'ም እንስሳ ፡ አሳ'ዳጊ የሌ'ለው ልጅ

vail

’ቬይል -ግ- መጐናጸፊያ [ጐ'ጉሪ] ፡ ወ'ዮታ ማ'ሰ 'ማት [አ'ሰ'ማ]

vaist

’ዌይስት -ስ- ወገብ

vaistcoat

’ዌይስትከውት -ስ- ሰደር'ያ

wait

’ዌይት -ግ- መጠ'በቅ [ጠ'በቀ] *at table* -ግ- ማሳ'ለፍ [አሳ'ለፈ] (በገበታ)

waiter

’ዌይተ -ስ- አሳ'ላፊ (ቦይ)

wake

’ዌይክ -ግ- መንቃት [ነ'ቃ] -*up* -ግ- መቀስቀስ [ቀስ'ቀሰ] ፡ መ'ቀስቀስ [ተቀስ'ቀሰ]

walk

’ዎክ -ግ- መሄድ [ሄደ]፡መ'ራመድ [ተራ'መደ]

walking-stick

’ዎኪንግስ'ቲክ -ስ- ከዘራ

wall

’ዎል -ስ- ግድግ'ዳ

wallet

’ዋለት -ስ- የገንዘብ ቦርሳ

wallpaper

’ዎልፔፐ -ስ- የግድግ'ዳ ወረቀት

waltz

’ዎልስ -ስ- ወልስ (የዳንስ ዓይነት)

wan

’ዋን -ቅ- የገረ'ጣ (በሕመም) ፡ የሃላ (ከደ ካም የተነ'ሣ)

wand

’ዋንድ -ስ- ቀ'ጭን በ'ትር (በተለ'ይ ምትሃተ 'ኛ'ች የ'ሚይዙት)

wander

’ዋንደ -ግ- መንገድን መሳት [ሳተ] ፡ መንከ ራተት [ተንከራ'ተተ]

wane

’ዌይን -ግ- ማነስ [አ'ነሰ] (ለጨረቃ ወዘተ)

want

’ዋንት -ግ- መፈ'ለግ [ፈ'ለገ] ፡ ማከ'ጀል [ከ'ጀለ] -ስ- ፍ'ላጎት ፡ ክ'ጀላ ፡ አምሮት

wanton

’ዋንተን -ቅ- ግብረ ገ'ብ'ነት የሌ'ለው -ስ- መርን የወ'ጣች ሴት

637

war

'ዎ: -ስ- ጦር'ነት

warble

'ዎ:ብል -ስ- የወፍ ፉጨት ፣ የወፍ ጫጫታ

ward

'ዎ:ድ -ስ- የ'ሚያሳ'ድጉት ልጅ ፣ ነጅ ማሳ
'ደግ

city district

-ስ- የከተማ ክፍል (ለአስተዳደር የተከ
'ፈለ) ፣ በእስር ቤት ፣ በሆስፒታል ያንድ ሕንጻ
ል'ዩ ል'ዩ ክፍሎ'ች

wardrobe

'ዎ:ድረውብ -ስ- የልብስ መስቀያ

warehouse

'ዌየሃውስ -ስ- የሽቀጣሽቀጥ ፣ የዕቃ መጋዘን

wares

'ዌየዝ -ስ- የ'ሚ'ሽጥ ዕቃ (በሱቅ)

warfare

'ዎ:ፌየ -ስ- ጦር'ነት

warm

'ዎ:ም -ቅ- ሙ-ቅ

warmth

'ዎ:ምስ -ስ- ሙቀት ፣ ግለት

warn

'ዎ:ን -ግ- ማስጠንቀቅ [አስጠን'ቀቀ]

warning

'ዎ:ኒንግ -ስ- ማስጠንቀቂያ

warp

'ዎ:ፕ -ግ- መ'ጣመም [ተ'ጠ'መመ] (ለእንጨት)

warrant

'ዎረነት -ስ- መጥሪያ (ለከ'ስ) ፣ በቂ ምክን
ያት

-ግ- ሕ'ጋዊ ፈቃድ ማግኘት [አገ'ኘ]

warren

'ዎረን -ስ- ጉድጓድ (የጥንቸል መዘተ)

warrior

'ዎሪየ -ስ- ተዋጊ ፣ ጦረ'ኛ

warship

'ዎ:ሺፕ -ስ- የጦር መርከብ

wart

'ዎ:ት -ስ- ኪንታሮት

wary

'ዌሪ -ቅ- ጥንቁቅ ፣ አደጋ ለደርስ ይችላል
ብሎ የ'ሚ'ጠነ'ቀቅ

wash

'ዎሽ -ግ- ማጠብ [አ'ጠበ]

-one's self

-ግ- መ'ታጠብ [ታ'ጠበ]

washer

'ዎሽ -ስ- አጣቢ.

washing

'ዎሺንግ -ስ- የ'ሚ'ታ'ጠብ ልብስ

wasp

'ዎስፕ -ስ- የው'ሽ ንብ

waste

'ዌይስት -ግ- ማባከን [አባ'ከነ] ፣ ማጥፋት
[አጠ'ፋ]

wastrel

'ዌይስትረል -ስ- ገንዘብ አባካኝ

watch

'ዎች -ግ- መ'መልከት [ተመለ'ከተ]

guard

-ግ- መጠ'በቅ [ጠ'በቀ]

wrist-

-ስ- የእ'ጅ ሰዓት

watchman

'ዎችመን -ስ- ዘበ'ኛ ፣ ጢ'ባቂ

water

'ዎ:ተ -ስ- ውሃ

water-closet

'ዎ:ተክሎዚት -ስ- ሰገራ ቤት ፣ ሽንት ቤት

watercress

'ዎ:ተክሬስ -ስ- ጉ'ን ብሌ

waterfall

'ዎ:ተፎ:ል -ስ- ፏፏቴ

watering-can

'ዎ:ተሪንግካን -ስ- የአትክልት ማጠ'ሚ ዕቃ
(ባለ ጡ-ት) ፣ ማረጨረጫያ

waterlogged

'ዎ:ተሎግድ -ቅ- በውሃ የረሰ (ጀልባ ፣ አን
ጨት መዘተ) ፣ ውሃ ያጥለቀ'ለቀው

water-melon

'ዎ:ተሜለን -ስ- ኪርቡሽ ፣ በ'ጢኪ

waterproof

'ዎ:ተፕሩ:ፍ -ቅ- ውሃ የ'ማይገባው

waterworks

'ዎ:ተወክስ -ስ- ውሃ ማ'ጣሪያ ሕንጻ ፣ የውሃ
ማ'ደያ መሥሪያ ቤት

638

watery
'ዋ፥ተሪ -ቅ- ውሃ ውሃ የ'ሚል ፤ ወሃ'ማ ፤ ጣዕም
የሌ'ለው

wave
'ዌይቭ -ግ- እ'ጅ ማ'ወዛወዝ [አ'ወዛ'ወዘ]
-ስ- ማዕበል

waver
'ዌይቭ -ግ- ማመንታት [አመነ'ታ] ፤ ማ'ወላ
ወል [አ'ወላ'ወለ]

wavy
'ዌይቪ -ቅ- የማዕበል ቅርፅ ያ'ለው ፤ በማዕ
በል የተመ'ላ

wax
'ዋክስ -ስ- ሰም

way
'ዌይ -ስ- መንገድ ፤ አ'ኳኳን ፤ አቅጣ'ጫ

wayfarer
'ዌይፌረ -ስ- የእግር መንገደ'ኛ

waylay
ዌ'ይሌይ -ግ- ማድፈጥ [አደ'ፈጠ] (አደጋ ለመ
ጣል ፤ ለመዝረፍ ወዘተ)

wayward
'ዌይወድ -ቅ- በመፃ'ኛ ፤ የ'ማይ'ታ'ዘዝ (ደብ
ልቁን ለሕፃናት)

we
'ዊይ --ተስ- እ'ኛ

weak
'ዊይክ -ቅ- ደካማ

weaken
'ዊይከን -ግ- ማድከም [አደ'ከመ]

weakling
'ዊይክሊንግ -ስ- ደካማ ሰው ፤ እንስሳ

weakness
'ዊይክነስ -ስ- ድካም ፤ ደካማ'ነት

weal
'ዊይል -ስ- ስንበር (ከተመ'ቱ በኋላ በሰው
'ነት ላይ የ'ሚ'ታይ) ፤ ጥፉ ዕ'ድል ፤ ደ'ስታ
(የመ'ላው ሕዝብ)

wealth
'ዌልስ -ስ- ሀብት

wealthy
'ዌልሲ -ቅ- ሀብታም

wean
'ዊይን -ግ- ጡት ማስጣል [አስጣለ] ፤ ከመ
ጥፎ ጓደ'ኛ ጋር መ'ገናኘት ፤ መጥፎ ልም
ድ ማስተው [አስተው]

weapon
'ዌፐን -ስ- የጦር መ'ሣሪያ

wear
'ዌየ -ግ- መልበስ [ለ'በሰ]
-out
-ግ- ማለቅ [አ'ለቀ] (ለልብስ)

weariness
'ዊሪነስ -ስ- ድካም ፤ መታከት

weary
'ዊሪ -ግ- ማድከም [አደ'ከመ] ፤ ማታከት
[አታ'ከተ]
-ቅ- ታካች ፤ የደ'ከመ

weather
'ዌዘ -ስ- አ'የር ፤ ነፋስ

weave
'ዊይቭ -ግ- ሽ'ማ መሥራት [ሠ'ራ]

weaver
'ዊይቭ -ስ- ሽ'ማኔ

web
'ዌብ -ስ- የሸረሪት ድር

wed
'ዌድ -ግ- ማገባት [አገ'ባ] (ለሚስት ፤ ለባል)

wedding
'ዌዲንግ -ስ- ሠርግ

wedge
'ዌጅ -ስ- ሽብ'ልቅ (እንጨት መፍለ'ጫ) ፤
ቅርቀር ፤ ውሻ (ሦስት ማዕዘን ያ'ለው መደ
'ገፊያ እንጨት)

Wednesday
'ዌንዝዴይ -ስ- ረቡዕ

weed
'ዊይድ -ግ- ማ'ረም [አ'ረመ] (ለአ'ረሙ'ን)
-ስ- አ'ረሙ'ን

week
'ዊይክ -ስ- ሳ'ምንት

weekend
ዊ'ኬንድ -ስ- የሳ'ምንት መጨ'ረሻ (ቅዳሜ ፤
እሁድ)

weekly
'ዊይክሊ --ተግ- በ'የሳ'ምንቱ

639

weep
'ዊይፕ -ግ- ማልቀስ [አለ'ቀሰ]

weigh
'ዌይ -ግ- መመ'ዘን [መ'ዘነ]

weight
'ዌይት -ስ- ክብደት
balance
-ስ- ሚዛን ፣ መመ'ዘኛ

weird
'ዊየድ -ቅ- ያልተለ'መደ ፣ እንገዳ ፣ በዓላም
ውስጥ የሌ'ለ

welcome
'ዌልከም -ግ- በደኅና መ'ቀበል [ተቀ'በለ] ፣
እንኳን ደኅና ገ'ቡ ማለት [አለ]

weld
'ዌልድ -ግ- መብየድ [በ'የደ] ፣ ብረት ከብ
ረት ጋር ማ'ጣበቅ [አ'ጣበቀ]

welfare
'ዌልፌየ -ስ- ደኅን'ነት

well
'ዌል -ቅ- ጥሩ ፣ ደኅና
fit
-ቅ- ጤና'ማ
water
-ስ- የውሃ ጉድጓድ

well-behaved
ዌልቢ'ሄይቭድ -ቅ- ባለ ጥሩ ጠባይ ፣ የታ'ረመ

well-being
ዌል'ቢይንግ -ስ- ደኅን'ነት

well-off
ዌል'ኦፍ -ቅ- የተደላ'ደለ ሀብት ያ'ለው

well-to-do
ዌል ቱ'ዱ: -ቅ- ሀብታም ፣ የተመቻ'ቸ ፣ የተደ
ላ'ደለ (በሀብት)

welter
'ዌልተ -ስ- መዓት (የዱ'ላ) ፣ ሥርዓት የሌ
'ለው የሕዝብ ብዛት

west
'ዌስት -ስ- ምዕራብ

westward
'ዌስትወድ -ተግ- ወደ ምዕራብ

wet
'ዌት -ግ- መንከር [ነ'ከረ] ፣ ግርጣዝ [አረ
'ጠበ]
-ቅ- እርጥብ

whale
'ዌይል -ስ- ዐሣ አንበሪ ፣ ዐሣነባሪ

what
'ዋት -መተስ- ምንድ'ን ፣ ምን

wheat
'ዊይት -ስ- ስንዴ

wheedle
'ዊይዶል -ግ- መ'ለማመጥ [ተለማ'መጠ]

wheel
'ዊይል -ስ- የተሽከርካሪ እግር
steering-
-ስ- መዘ'ውር ፣ መሪ (የመኪና)

wheelbarrow
'ዊይል ባረው -ስ- የ'ጁ ጋሪ (በ'ጅ የ'ሚ'ገ'ፋ)

wheeze
'ዊይዝ -ግ- በችግር መተንፈስ [ተነ'ፈሰ] (ተ
'ጭን ድምፅ እ'ያ'ሰ'መ)

whelp
'ዌልፕ -ስ- የውሻ ቡ'ች'ላ ፣ ስ'ድ አደግ
ልጅ ፣ ሰው

when
'ዌን -መተግ- መ'ቼ
-ተግ- በ . . . ጊዜ
-መግ- ስ . . .

whence
'ዌንስ -ተግ- ከየት ፣ ከወዴት

whenever
ዌ'ኔቭ -ተግ- በ . . . ጊዜ

where
'ዌየ -መተግ- ወዴት ፣ የት
-ዘተስ- የም . . . . .
-መግ- . . . በት . . .

wherever
'ዌሬቭ -ተግ- በ . . . በታ

whet
'ዌት -ግ- መሳል [ሳለ] (ለስለት) ፣ ማጎምጀት
[አጎመ'ጀ]

whether
'ዌዘ -መግ- የ . . . እንደሆነ

whetstone
 ’ዌትስተውን -ስ- መሳያ ደንጊያ ፣ መሳል ፣ ለሆቴ

whey
 ’ዌይ -ስ- አሬራ

which
 ’ዊች -መቅ- የት'ኛው-
 -ዘተስ- የም . . .

whiff
 ’ዊፍ -ስ- ሽ'ታ ፣ ትንፋሽ ፣ ት'ንሽ የአ'የር እ'ፍታ

while
 ’ዋይል -ተጕ- በ . . . ጊዜ
 short time
 -ስ- አንድ አፍታ

whim
 ’ዊም -ስ- አምሮት (ም'ሳሌ ፣ የእርጉዝ ሴት)

whimper
 ’ዊምፕ -ጕ- መጮኸ [ጩኸ] (ለትና'ንሽ እን ስሳት ፣ ለሕፃን ከሥቃይ ፣ ከፍርሀት የተነ'ሣ)

whimsical
 ’ዊምዚከል -ቅ- አምሮት ያ'ለው ፣ አምሮት የያዘው

whine
 ’ዋይን -ጕ- ማልቀስ [አለ'ቀሰ] (ለው'ሻ)

whip
 ’ዊፕ -ጕ- መግረፍ [ገ'ረፈ]
 -ስ- ጅራፍ ፣ መገረፊያ ፣ አለንጋ

whirl
 ’ወ፥ል -ጕ- እንደእዘዋሪት ፣ እንደዐውሎ ነፋስ መዞር [ዞረ]

whirlpool
 ’ወ፥ልፑ፥ል -ስ- ፡ዘዋሪት

whirlwind
 ’ወ፥ልዊንድ -ስ- አውሎ ነፋስ

whisk
 ’ዊስክ -ጕ- መምታት [መ'ታ] (ላእንቁላል ፣ ለሊጥ ወዘተ)
 -ስ- ማምታት
 fly-
 -ስ- የዝንብ ጭራ (የዝምብ መ'ከላከያ)

whiskers
 ’ዊስከዝ -ስ- ሪዝ (ያንበ'ሳ ፣ የድ'መት ወዘተ)

whisper
 ’ዊስፐ -ጕ- ማሾክሾክ [አሾክ'ሾከ] (በለሆስታ መ'ናገር)
 -ስ- ሹክሹክታ ፣ የለሆስታ ንግ'ገር

whistle
 ’ዊስል -ጕ- ማፏጨት [አፏ'ጨ]
 -ስ- ፉጨት
 instrument
 -ስ- ፊሽኪያ (ፊሽካ)

white
 ’ዋይት -ቅ- ነ'ጭ

whiten
 ’ዋይተን -ጕ- ማንጣት [አነ'ጣ] ፣ ነ'ጭ ግድ ረግ [አደ'ረገ]

whiteness
 ’ዋይትነስ -ስ- ንጣት

white-wash
 ’ዋይትዋሽ -ስ- ኖራ (የቤት መለቀለቂያ)

whittle
 ’ዊተል -ጕ- መተፍተፍ [ተፈ'ተፈ] ፣ መቅ ረፍ [ቀ'ረፈ] (ለእንጨት ወዘተ)

who
 ’ሑ: -መተስ- ማ'ን
 -ዘተ፥ የም . . . ፣ የ . . .

whoever
 ሑ'ዌቨ -ተ፥ስ- ማ'ንም

whole
 ’ሆውል -ቅ- ሙሉ ፣ ጠቅላ'ላ

wholesale
 ’ሆውልሴይል -ስ- ጅምላ

wholesome
 ’ሆውልሰም -ቅ- ደኅና ፣ ጤና'ማ ፣

wholly
 ’ሆውሊ -ተጕ- በሙሉ

whom
 ’ሑ:ም -መተስ- ማ'ንን

whooping-cough
 ’ሁፒንግከፍ -ስ- ት ክታ ፣ ት'ክቱ'ክ (ሳል

whose
 ’ሑ:ዝ -መተስ- የማ'ን

why
 ’ዋይ -መተጕ- ለምን

wick
 ’ዊክ -ስ- ፊትል (የኩ'ራዝ ፣ የሻማ)

641

wicked
’ዊከድ -ቅ- ክፉ ፡ ጠማማ (ለጠባይ)

wicker
’ዊከ -ስ- የሸምበ'ቆ እንጨት (ቅርጫት ወዘተ የ'ሚ'ሠ'ራ'በት)

wicket
’ዊከት -ስ- ት'ንሽ በ'ር (በት'ልቅ በ'ር መካ 'ከል ያ'ለ)

wide
’ዋይድ -ቅ- ሰ'ፊ

widen
’ዋይደን -ቅ- ማስፋት [አሰ'ፋ]

widespread
’ዋይድስፕሬድ -ቅ- የተሰራ'ጨ

widow
’ዊደው -ስ- ጋለሞታ (ባ'ሏ የሞተ'ባት)

widower
’ዊደወ -ስ- ሚስቱ የሞተ'ች'በት ወንድ

width
’ዊድስ -ስ- ስፋት

wife
’ዋይፍ -ስ- ሚስት

wig
’ዊግ -ስ- የተፈጥሮ ያልሆነ ሰው ሥ'ራሽ ጠጉር (እራስ ላይ የ'ሚ'ደ'ረፉ)

wild
’ዋይልድ -ቅ- አውሬ

wilderness
’ዊልደኔስ -ስ- ምድረ በዳ

wildness
’ዋይልደኔስ -ስ- አውሬ'ነት

wile
’ዋይል -ስ- ማ'ታለል ፡ ተንኮል (የሡይጣን ወዘተ)

wilful
’ዊልፉል -ቅ- የ'ማይ'ታ'ዘዝ ፡ የራሱን መን ገድ ብ'ቻ የ'ሚ'ከታ'ተል

will
’ዊል -ስ- ፍ'ላጎት
legal
  -ስ- የኑዛዜ ቃል (ለሀብት)

willing
’ዊሊንግ -ቅ- ፈቃደ'ኛ

wilt
’ዊልት -ግ- ማጠውለግ [አጠወ'ለገ] (ለአት ክልት)

wily
’ዋይሊ -ቅ- አ'ታላይ ፡ ተንኮለ'ኛ

win
’ዊን -ግ- ማ'ሸ'ነፍ [አ'ሸ'ነፈ] ፡ መርታት [ረ'ታ]

wince
’ዊንስ -ግ- ወደ ኋላ ማለት [አለ] (ሰው ሲ'መ 'ታ ሲ'ቃ'ጣ)

winch
’ዊንች -ስ- ማጠንጠኛ ፡ መጠቅለያ

wind
’ዊንድ -ስ- ነፋስ

wind
’ዋይንድ -ግ- መጠምዘዝ [ጠመ'ዘዘ] ፡ ማዞር [አዞረ] ፡ መሙላት [ሞ'ላ] (ሰዓት)

windfall
’ዊንድፎ፡ል -ስ- ነፋስ የጣለው ፍሬ
luck
  -ስ- ድንገተ'ኛ ዕ'ድል

windlass
’ዊንድለስ -ስ- ማጠንጠኛ ፡ መጠቅለያ

windmill
’ዊንድሚል -ስ- የነፋስ ወፍጮ

window
’ዊንደው -ስ- መስኮት

windy
’ዊንዲ -ቅ- ነፋሳም

wine
’ዋይን -ስ- የወይን ጠ'ጅ

wing
’ዊንግ -ስ- ክንፍ

wink
’ዊንክ -ግ- ባይን መጥቀስ [ጠቀ'ሰ] ፡ ዓይን ዘግቶ መክፈት [ከ'ፈተ]

winnow
’ዊነው -ግ- ማበራት [አበ'ራ] (ፍሬውን ከእ 'ብቅ ለመለ'የት)

winter
’ዊንተ -ስ- ክረምት

wipe

’ዋይፕ -ግ- መጥረግ [ጠ'ረገ] ፣ መወልወል [ወለ'ወለ]

wire

’ዋየ -ስ- ሽቦ

telegram

-ስ- ቴሌግራም

wireless

’ዋየለስ -ስ- ራዲዮ

telegraphy

-ስ- የነፋስ ስልክ

wiry

’ዋሪ -ቅ- ቀጭኝ'ና ጠንካ'ራ ፣ ጠምዛዛ (ለሰው)

wisdom

’ዊዝደም -ስ- ጥበብ ፣ ብልኅነት

wise

’ዋይዝ -ቅ- ብልኅ

wish

’ዊሽ -ግ- መ'መኘት [ተመ'ኘ]

-ስ- ምኞት

wishful

’ዊሽፉል -ቅ- የ'ሚ'መ'ኝ (እንደፍ'ላጎቱ እን ዲሆን'ለት)

wistful

’ዊስትፉል -ቅ- አዘ'ነ ያለ ፣ ያልጠ'ዳው

wit

’ዊት -ስ- ቀልድ

person

ቀልደ'ኛ ሰው

witch

’ዊች -ስ- ጠንቋይ (ለሴት)

with

’ዊዝ -መዋ- ከ . . . ጋር

withdraw

ዊዝድ'ሮ: -ግ- ወደ ኋላ ማለት [አለ]

accusation

ከ'ስ ማንሣት [አነ'ሣ]

wither

’ዊዘ -ግ- መድረቅ [ደ'ረቀ] (ለአትክልት)

withhold

ዊዝ'ሆልድ -ግ- ይዞ አለመስጠት [-ሰ'ጠ] ፣ ወደኋላ ማስቀ'ረት [አስቀ'ረ]

within

ዊ'ዚን -ተግ- በ . . . ውስጥ

without

ዊ'ዛውት -ተግ- ያለ

withstand

ዊዝስ'ታንድ -ግ- መቋቋም [ተ'ቋቋመ] ፣ መ ቃወም [ተቃ'ወመ]

witness

’ዊትነስ -ግ- መ'መልከት [ተመለ'ከተ] ፣ መ መስከር [መስ'ከረ]

-ስ- ምስ'ክር

witty

’ዊቲ -ቅ- ቀልደ'ኛ ፣ ጨዋተ'ኛ ፣ ሣቂታ በዋቂ (በንግ'ግር)

wizard

’ዊዛድ -ስ- አስማተ'ኛ ፣ ጠንቋይ (ለወንድ)

wobble

’ዎበል -ግ- መ'ነቃነቅ [ተነቃ'ነቀ] ፣ መ'ወ ዛወዝ [ተወዛ'ወዘ] ፣ ማ'ወላወል [አ'ወላ'ወለ]

woe

’ወው -ስ- ወዮታ ፣ ሐዘን ፣ ች'ግር

wolf

’ውልፍ -ስ- ተኩላ

woman

’ውመን -ስ- ሴት

womb

’ውም -ስ- ማሕፀን

wonder

’ወንደ -ግ- መ'ደነቅ [ተደ'ነቀ] ፣ መ'ገረም [ተገ'ረመ]

wonderful

’ወንደፉል -ቅ- አስደ'ናቂ ፣ ግሩም

woo

’ው: -ግ- ሴት ማባበል [አባ'በለ] ፣ ማግባባት [አግባ'ባ] (ለማፍቀር ፣ ለማግባት)

wood

’ውድ -ስ- እንጨት

forest

-ስ- ደ'ን

wooden

’ውደን -ቅ- ከእንጨት የተሠ'ራ ፣ የእንጨት

woodpecker

’ውድፔከ -ስ- ግንደ ቆርቋር

643

woodwork
'ው-ድ•ዉ:ክ -ስ- እናጢ'ነት
    wooden part
        -ስ- ከንጨት በሙሉ ወይን'ም በከፊል የተሠ'ራ

wool
'ው•ል -ስ- ሱፍ

woollen
'ውለን -ቅ- የሱፍ ፣ ከሱፍ የተሠ'ራ

woolly
'ው•ሊ -ቅ- በሱፍ የተሸ'ፈነ ፣ ከሱፍ የተሠ'ራ ፣ ሱፍ የ'ሚመስል
    vague
        -ቅ- ግልጽ ያልሆነ (ለሰው)

word
'ወ:ድ -ስ- ቃል

work
'ወ:ክ -ግ- መሥራት [ሠ'ራ]
    -ስ- ሥራ

worker
'ወ:ክ -ስ- ሠራተ'ኛ

workman
'ወክ:መን -ስ- የእ'ጅ ሠራተ'ኛ

works
'ወ:ክስ -ስ- ጽሑፍ ፣ ድርስት
    musical
        የሙዚቃ ድርስት
    factory
        ፋብሪካ

workshop
'ወ:ክሾፕ -ስ- ቀለል ያሉ የእ'ጅ ሙ•ያዎ'ች የ'ሚ'ሠ'ሩ•በት ቤት
    garage
        -ስ- ጋራጅ

world
'ወ:ልድ -ስ- ዓለም

worm
'ወ:ም -ስ- ትል

worn-out
ዎ:ን'አውት -ቅ- ያረ'ጀ ፣ ያለቀ (ለልብስ ወዘተ)

worry
'ወሪ -ግ- መ'ጨነቅ [ተጨ'ነቀ] ፣ ማስጨ'ነቅ [አስጨ'ነቀ]

worse
'ወ:ስ -ቅ- የከ'ፋ

worsen
'ወ:ሰን -ግ- ማክፋት [አከ'ፋ]

worship
'ወ:ሺፕ -ግ- ማምለክ [አመ'ለከ]
    -ስ- አምልኮ

worshipper
'ወ:ሺፕ -ስ- አምላኪ

worst
'ወ:ስት -ቅ- እ'ጅግ የከ'ፋ

worth
'ወ:ስ̱ -ስ- ዋጋ
    -ቅ- የ'ሚያወጣ ፣ የ'ሚ'ገ'መት

worthy
'ወ:ዚ̱ -ቅ- የ'ሚ'ገ'ባው ፣ ተገቢ ፣ ጥሩ ግ'ም'ት ያለው

wound
'ውንድ -ግ- ማቁሰል [አቆ'ሰለ]
    -ስ- ቁስል

wrangle
'ራንገ -ግ- መ'ጨቃጨቅ [ተጨቃ'ጨቀ] ፣ መ'ነታረክ [ተነታ'ረክ]

wrap
'ራፕ -ግ- መጠቅለል [ጠቀ'ለለ]

wrapper
'ራፕ -ስ- መጠቅለያ (ወረቀት ፣ ዕቃ ለመ•ላክ)

wrath
'ራ:ስ̱ -ስ- ቁ'ጣ ፣ መዐት

wreath
'ሪይስ̱ -ስ- የአበባ ዕ'ቅፍ (በቀብዛ ላይ የ'ሚ'ቀ'መጥ)

wreck
'ሬክ -ግ- መስጠም [ሰ'ጠመ] ፣ ማስጠም [አሰ'ጠመ] (ለመርከብ)፣መ'ሰባበር [ተሰባ'በር]

wreckage
'ሬኪጅ -ስ- ስብርባሪ (በተለ'ይ የመርከብ)

wrench
'ሬንች -ግ- መገንጠል [ገነ'ጠለ] ፣ በኃይል መጠምዘዝ [ጠመ'ዘዘ]
    spanner
        -ስ- የእንግሊዝ መፍቻ

wrest

’ሬስት -ግ- መንጠቅ [ነ'ጠቀ]

wrestle

’ሬሰል -ግ- መ'ታገል [ታ'ገለ]

wretch

’ሬች -ስ- መንዳ'ካ ፡ ዕ'ድለ ቢስ ፡ ች'ግረ'ኛ

wriggle

’ሪጎል -ግ- መሰለክለክ [ተስለክ'ለክ] (እባብ ወዘተ)

wring

’ሪንግ -ግ- መጠምዘዝ [ጠመ'ዘዘ] (ለልብስ)

wrinkle

’ሪንክል -ስ- የገንባር እ'ጥፋት

wrist

’ሪስት -ስ- የእ'ጅ አንጓ ፡ አምባር ሙያ

wrist-watch

’ሪስት ዋች -ስ- የእ'ጅ ሰዓት

writ

’ሪት -ስ- አንድ ነገር ለማድረግ ወይን>ም
ላለማድረግ የ'ሚያ'ዝ የጉቱሥ ደብዳ'ቤ
written accusation
-ስ- የክ'ስ ማመልከቻ

write

’ራይት -ግ- መጻፍ [ጸፈ]

writer

’ራይተ -ስ- ጸሐፊ ፡ ደራሲ

writhe

’ራይዝ -ግ- መንፈራገጥ [ተንፈራ'ገጠ] (ከሕ
መም የተነ'ሣ)

writing

’ራይቲንግ -ስ- ጽሐፍ ፡ ድርሰት

wrong

’ሮንግ -ስ- ስሕተት
-ቅ- ስሕተት
-ግ- መጉዳት [ጎ'ዳ] ፡ መበደል [በ'ደለ]

wry

’ራይ -ቅ- መራራ (ለንግ'ግር) ፡ የተኮሳ'ተረ
(ለመልክ)

X-rays

’ኤክስሬይዝ -ስ- ራጂ ፡ ኤክስሬይ

X-rayed

’ኤክስሬይድ -ግ- ራ'ጂ መ'ነሣት [ተነ'ሣ]

yacht

’ዮት -ስ- አነስተ'ኛ መርከብ (መንሸራሸሪያ)

yap

’ያፕ -ስ- የቡ'ች'ላ ጨኸት

yard

’ያ፡ድ -ስ- ያጥር ግ'ቢ አትክልት ቦታ
measure
-ስ- ያርድ (መለ'ኪያ ፡ የርዝመት)

yarn

’ያ፡ን -ስ- ማግ (የጥጥ ፡ የሱፍ ወዘተ)
story
-ስ- ወሬ (አንድ ሰው ስላ'የው ሁናቴ
የ'ሚያወራው)

yawn

’ዮ፡ውን -ግ- ማፋሸግ [አፋ'ሸገ] ፡ ማ'ዛጋት
[አ'ዛ'ጋ]

year

’ዪኻ -ስ- ዓመት

645

yearly
'ዪእሊ -ቅ- ዓመታዊ
-ተግ- በ'ያመቱ

yearn
'የ፡ን -ግ- መናፈት [ና'ፈቀ]

yeast
'ይስት -ስ- እርሾ

yell
'የል -ግ- መጮኸ [ጮኸ] ፣ መ'ቆጣት [ተ'ቆ
ጣ]

yellow
'ዬለው -ቅ- ብጫጫ ፣ ወይባ

yelp
'ዬልፕ -ስ- የው'ሻ ጬኸት (ከተመ'ታ በኋላ)

yes
'ዬስ -ተግ- አዎን ፣ አዎ

vesterday
'ዬስተደይ -ስ- ትናንት ፣ ትናንት'ና

yet
'ዬት -ተግ- እስካሁን ድረስ ፣ ገና

yield
'ዪልድ -ግ- መ'ማረክ [ተማ'ረከ] ፣ መ'ሸነፍ
[ተሸ'ነፈ]
agriculture
-ግ- መ'መረት [ተመ'ረተ]

yoke
'የውክ -ስ- ቀንበር

yolk
'የውክ -ስ- አስኳል

yonder
'ዮንደ -ቅ- ግዮ
-ተግ- በግዮ

you
'ዩ፡ -ተስ- አንተ ፣ አንቺ ፣ እርስዎ ፣ እ'ናንተ

young
'የንግ -ቅ- ወ'ጣት ፣ ለጋ

your
'ዮ፡ -ገቅ- ያንተ ፣ ያንቺ ፣ የርስዎ ፣ የ'ናንተ

yours
'ዮ፡ዝ -ገተስቅ- ያንተ ፣ ያንቺ ፣ የርስዎ ፣ የ'ናን

yourself
ዮ፡'ሴልፍ -ጻተስ- እራስህ ፣ እራስሽ ፣ እራስ

youth
'ዩፅ -ስ- ወ'ጣት ፣ ወ'ጣት'ነት

yuletide
'ዩወልታይድ -ስ- የገ'ና በዓል ሰሞን

zeal
'ዚይል -ስ- የጋለ ፍ'ላጎት

zealot
'ዜለት -ስ- ለሃይማኖቱ የ'ሚቀና ፣ ለእምነቱ
የ'ሚ'ቆረ'ቆር

zealous
'ዜለስ -ቅ- የጋለ ፍ'ላጎት ያለው

zebra
'ዜብረ -ስ- የሜዳ አህ'ያ

zenith
'ዜኒፅ -ስ- ጫፍ ፣ ቁንጮ ፣ ፀሐይ በተሰያት
የ'ም'ት'ታ'ይ'ብት ቦታ

zephyr
'ዜፈ -ስ- አስደ'ሳች ነፋስ

zero
'ዚይረው -ስ- ዜሮ ፣ ምን'ም ፣ ባዶ

zest
'ዜስት -ስ- ታ'ላቅ ፍ'ላጎት ፣ በታ'ላቅ ደ'ስታ
ያንድ ነገር ተካፋይ መሆን

zigzag
'ዚግዛግ -ግ- መ'ጠማዘዝ [ተጠማ'ዘዘ]
-ቅ- ጠምዛዛ (መንገድ ወዘተ)

zinc
'ዚንክ -ስ- ዚንክ ፣ ቆርቆር

646